"The Czar of Twickenham"

The History of Julius Hagen and the Film Empire he created at Twickenham Film Studios, from 1927 to 1938.

BOOK 3. ILLUSTRATED.

John V. Watson

In 1978 renowned film director Michael Powell dubbed Julius
Hagen the "Czar of Twickenham", as quoted in Ian Christie's

'The Czar of Twickenham'. The History of Julius Hagen and the Film Empire he created at Twickenham Film Studios, from 1927 to 1938.

book, *"Powell, Pressburger and Others"*, (British Film Institute, 1978, London, on page 18). Powell's soubriquet for Hagen perfectly sums up the career and the style of this British film producer of over a hundred films.

As we shall see, he was in charge of every aspect of his growing film empire, and thus he appeared to be of sufficient stature to allow him to be compared to Britain's one film mogul of the 1930s and 1940s, Alexander Korda.

This definitive book provides a complete record of Julius Hagen's career in the British film industry from 1913, and his subsequent Rise and Fall at Twickenham Film Studios, from 1927 to 1938.

This book contains a complete and extensively detailed filmography of the 115 films Hagen made mostly at Twickenham Film Studios between 1927 and 1938, plus the one film he co-produced in 1937, including contemporary reviews of these films as published at the time by trade journals and movie fan magazines. Details, recently rediscovered, of the British, American and Continental films that Hagen's Twickenham Film Distributors released in the United Kingdom, are also included.

Uniquely, most of this detailed information has never been published in book form.

By

John V. Watson

A WELCOME ACCOLADE FROM A NOTED ACADEMIC AND FILM HISTORIAN:

"I admire this study in many ways. It uses Kinematograph Weekly as a productive and authoritative principal source and the author has assembled the best history of Hagen that's available. The comprehensive filmography is very valuable."
Professor Andrew Spicer, University of the West of England, Bristol..
2019.

CONTENTS

ABBREVIATIONS:

IMDb:	*Internet Movie Data Base.*
M.F.B.:	*Monthly Film Bulletin.*
K.W. :	*Kinematograph Weekly.*
P.L.M.:	P. L. Mannock, the studio correspondent of the *Kinematograph Weekly*.

'The Czar of Twickenham'. The History of Julius Hagen and the Film Empire he created at Twickenham Film Studios, from 1927 to 1938.

ACKNOWLEDGEMENT - PROOF READING:

JOHN ZIPSER:

I am very grateful to my friend, John Zipser, for taking the considerable trouble to proof read the 300-odd pages that make up this book.

It is quite extraordinary just how many (often silly) typographical errors I have managed to conjure up during the process of composing this book on the career of Julius Hagen, particularly his tenure of Twickenham Film Studios. Most of these errors, often called "typos", consist of misspellings, or where words are misused because of spellings that are wrong in the particular contexts that they should have been employed, or stray and unwanted letters, and, in some cases, repeated phrases. But John has managed to take so much time to plough through the entire text of the book to identify these blunders.

His thorough effort in proofreading is so much appreciated.

1. THE STRUCTURE OF THE BOOK:

This book consists of seven sections:

First: The Introduction.

Second: A Short Account of the state of the British Film Industry before and at the start of the Great War (1914-1918), its subsequent collapse after that War, and its continued struggle for survival throughout the 1920s, principally due to the ever-growing global domination of the American film industry. This is offered in order to help the reader understand the background, structure and status of the British film industry into which Julius Hagen was to enter in 1913.

Third: The History of Julius Hagen, his entry into the British Film Industry in 1913, and his eventual tenure of Twickenham Film Studios in 1929 up until 1938.

In order to piece together this section, most of the information and minutiae has been taken from the Kinematograph Weekly supported by some additional data contained in the Kinematograph Year Books from 1927 to 1939. The style employed to construct this book is one that makes extensive use of information published in the Kinematograph Weekly itself, and to present this in the manner of building up a picture of each event as it unfolds through time over the course of the development of each activity. In other words, this style of the presentation of the facts is rather like a diary; a month-by-month, year-by-year account of the Hagen years at Twickenham Studios.

Primarily, the purpose of this book is the preservation of important knowledge about a significant part of British film history of the 1930s, and, therefore, to provide a permanent record, very well researched and documented, about who Julius Hagen was, what he achieved, and a very detailed account of his extensive film empire.

Fourth: Conclusion: Analysis and Comment.

Fifth: A   Biographical   Section   outlining   the participation of the several stars, actors, actresses, directors, story and   script   writers,   cinematographers   and   other   film-making personnel who worked at Twickenham Studios during the time that Julius Hagen reigned there.

Sixth: Bibliography and 'About the Author'.

Seventh: An extensive and comprehensive Filmography which is divided into four distinct parts, as follows:

1.   A complete Filmography of all of the 115 films which were produced by Julius Hagen, from 1927 to 1938. Such an all-embracing documentation about the total Hagen film output has never been published before in any publication, learned or otherwise.

Previous published accounts about Julius Hagen and his films have tended to repeat certain errors and misinterpretations. A critical example of such a fundamental mistake concerns that excellent railway thriller directed by Bernard Vorhaus, *The Last Journey* (1935).   It has been claimed in previous published accounts about Julius Hagen that the film was merely a 'Quota Quickie'; this book provides conclusive evidence that this was never the case, that it was never designed as a stringently budgeted film with a very tight shooting schedule.   Other anomalies have been corrected.

The majority of the information and minutiae has been taken

from the *Kinematograph Weekly* and the *Kinematograph Year Books*. Where possible, further details have been taken from several contemporary film fan magazines, particularly *Picturegoer Weekly* and *Picture Show* and also from the *Monthly Film Bulletin*. Some American trade journals, fan magazines and newspapers have been used as well.

2. This second part of the filmography covers the one co-production which Julius Hagen made in conjunction with Franco-London Films, *A Romance in Flanders* (1937); two versions of the film were made, one in English (released by British Lion), the other in French. Note that, out of the many books published on British film history over the years by respected authors, all covering, always briefly, the career of Julius Hagen, none have ever mentioned this co-production. Thus, the inclusion of this film here in this detailed Filmography will now put the record straight.

3. The third part of this Filmography deals with those films made by the two American companies (Chesterfield and Invincible), by another British film production company, and by two Continental production companies, all of which were released by Twickenham Film Distributors, following the incorporation of this Hagen company in May 1935. Included is *Her Last Affaire* (1935), the society drama directed by Michael Powell for New Ideal Pictures, Ltd.

4. The fourth and final part of this Filmography deals with those seven films - one silent and six sound - produced by Julius Hagen that were released in Great Britain on the 9.5mm amateur gauge by Pathéscope, Ltd. in the 1930s, 1940s and 1950s - in shortened versions.

John V. Watson

INTRODUCTION:

Julius Hagen was born Julius Jacob Kleimenhagen, 1884, in Hamburg, Germany.

He died on the 31st January 1940, in London, of a stroke.

Reading various books about the fascinating subject of the British Film Industry from the late-1920s silent period to the first 10-years-or-so of sound film production to 1939, the name of Julius Hagen so often appears. But modern readers are frequently given the distinct impression, even by certain serious research authors, that Julius Hagen was somewhat a "fly-by-night" operator, producing only 'Quota Quickie' films, many of them bad, that were made solely for the "quick buck" profit available to any "Pound-per-Foot" operator supplying the renting and exhibition sections of the British film industry, in order for these to comply with their legal obligations under the Cinematograph Films Act, 1927.

Thus, the picture given about so much of the British film output in general, and of Julius Hagen in particular, over the whole decade of the 1930s tends to become negative, distorted, indeed sometimes somewhat denigrated, and finally often merely "written off"!

Whilst it is certainly true that many of the films made by Julius Hagen, along with so many other film producers of that period of the 1930s, were not that good, some, in fact, were poor indeed, even frankly awful, but many of the other films he produced were that much better; they were quality productions which certainly offered at least good to very good entertainment value, all contrary to the distinct impression given by some of the academic world in recent books, whereby all his film output is generally disparaged, some even reviled.

'The Czar of Twickenham'. The History of Julius Hagen and the Film Empire he created at Twickenham Film Studios, from 1927 to 1938.

Thus it is this author's underlying aspiration for this book to redress the oft misleading and skewed impression of an early sound-film-era entrepreneur who achieved so much within the limitations of British film legislation over its ten-year life from 1928 to 1937.

The writer finds the career of Julius Hagen of such absolute fascination that his achievements are certainly worth the pleasurable endeavour of putting "the record straight", for the sake of posterity; that is, to illustrate to you, the reader, what Julius Hagen actually accomplished with the quality (or otherwise) of each of his productions at Twickenham, and to record the way in which he expanded his empire – placing stress on the financial implications and, yes, the machinations – before disaster befell upon him in 1938, when his whole "kingdom" collapsed in what turned out to be a financial "house-of-cards".

Consequently, it is hoped that the author's enthusiasm for this absorbing subject will spill over to you, the reader, as you read through this book.

In a fundamental sense, and this is vital for the reader to appreciate about Julius Hagen, he was truly a mini-Alexander Korda, in other words, a movie mogul in his own right. Korda, of course, was the driving force behind London Films, whilst Hagen was equally the driving force behind Twickenham Studios, over his 10-year reign there. However, Korda, as we know, made several expensive British film spectaculars during the 1930s, whereas Hagen did not make any film that could claim to be anywhere near to an expensive spectacular.

Another key difference between Korda and Hagen is: whereas Korda produced almost 40 films in the 1930s, Hagen produced nearly three times this number, namely 115 films in total, plus one co-production.

Therefore, the underlying purpose of this book essentially is four-fold:

1. To provide as complete a chronology, as far as is possible from surviving records, of Hagen's career, from its beginnings in 1913 right up to 1940, with an especial and very extensive focus on his ten-year dominion at Twickenham Studios, from 1927-28 to 1937-38.

2. To provide a complete and extensive filmography of the films he produced at Twickenham Studios, under the banners of The Strand Film Co. Ltd., Real Art Productions, Ltd., Twickenham Film Studios, Ltd., and J. H. Productions, Ltd. Although there have been more than one survey of Julius Hagen's career recently published, these are usually somewhat brief, and none has attempted to provide a comprehensive and complete filmography, and, thus, the prime purpose of this book is to deliver precisely this.

3. To evaluate and record the value of each of the films he made in his ten-year tenure at Twickenham. To do this, the author has taken the decision to use, and thus rely on, only contemporary reviews from the film trade and fan magazines, rather than set them for evaluation within a modern perspective.

This decision is essential for the reader to appreciate, for two reasons:

i. Quite a number of the films are now lost; that is, no prints are known to have survived in the intervening years (approximately 80) since they were first made, including *The Missing Rembrandt* (1932), the second film in which Arthur Wontner appeared as "Sherlock Holmes", and Walter Forde's *Lord Richard in the Pantry* (1930), starring Richard Cooper, and which, at the time of writing this book, is on the British Film Institute's "*75 Most Wanted*" list of missing British feature films. Therefore, it is impossible for them to be viewed now and consequently to be able to evaluate them for their production values and entertainment worth. Also, the author is well aware that some prints have survived in the hands of private collectors, and, given the customary hoarding nature of the collecting

6

instinct, access is once again difficult, if not impossible. Indeed,
the author had many prints of Hagen's films on 16mm in his own
collection thirty or so years ago, long since disposed of to like-
minded enthusiasts, including *The Black Abbot* (1933), with a
soundtrack suffering from significant, intermittent water damage;
and a pristine 16mm print of Whispering Tongues (1934). The
reader needs to remember that this was in an era when collecting
films was not as easy as it is now; in those days, a serious collector
could only rely on buying ex-library prints on 16mm or, as the
1980s progressed, record films off-air onto VHS, or buy pre-
recorded VHS cassettes from suppliers whose catalogue range
was somewhat limited, albeit growing. DVDs and the Internet
were unheard of then!

ii.   Tastes and attitudes change as the years and then as
the decades pass, and thus viewing many of these films today may
well be influenced, and probably unfairly so, by the mores and
values we now have today. Thus, many films can become to look
very dated as time passes and as standards change: many films do
not stand "the test of time"; they can well show their age and as a
result their original freshness and vitality (or otherwise) is lost to
the present-day viewer who will inevitably judge them using a
completely different range of criteria. Accordingly, it is much
safer and consequently that much more reliable to use
contemporary evaluations of all these films – obviously these
were all written in the context of their own time, not of ours
today, in that of our own time, at the end of the second decade of
the Twenty-First Century.

Thus, the author is of the absolute opinion that any film, no
matter how awful, should nonetheless be taken account of and its
existence recorded; after all, someone decided to make them for a
reason (usually for profit, rarely for the sake of art, regularly, in
the days of the British "Quota", for legal obligations), but that
intention was not achieved.

4.   Julius Hagen employed an extraordinary array of talent

during his years at Twickenham in the 1930s, both in front of the camera and behind it:

- ◆ **Top stars:**
    - ▪ Gracie Fields, for one film: *This Week of Grace* (1931, her third picture).
    - ▪ Conrad Veidt, for two: *The Wandering Jew* (1933) and *Bella Donna* (1934).
    - ▪ Ivor Novello, again for two: *The Lodger* (1932) and the screen adaptation of his stage success, *I Lived with You* (1933).
    - ▪ Seymour Hicks, for three: *Vintage Wine* (1935), and the excellent first sound version of *Scrooge* (1935), and *Eliza Comes to Stay* (1936, co-starring Betty Balfour), amongst many other artistes.
    - ▪ The very popular music hall team, Bud Flanagan and Chesney Allen, for two films, *A Fire Has Been Arranged* (1935) and *Underneath the Arches* (1937).
    - ▪ And, it should be noted, none of these particular films were "quota quickies".

- ◆ **Top directors, such as:**
    - ▪ Walter Forde, the former very popular British silent film comedian, for *Splinters in the Navy* (1931, starring the comedian, Sydney Howard).
    - ▪ Maurice Elvey for several films including *The Man in the Mirror* (1936, starring the American character actor, Edward Everett Horton).
    - ▪ And, again, it should be noted, these particular films were not "quota quickies".

- ◆ **Behind the camera, such as:**
    - ▪ The German cinematographer, Curt Courant, filmed five films at Twickenham in the mid 1930s, including the sound remake of *Broken Blossoms* (1936, starring Dolly Haas and Emlyn Williams) before going on to photograph two of the renowned classics of 1930s

'The Czar of Twickenham'. The History of Julius Hagen and the Film Empire he created at Twickenham Film Studios, from 1927 to 1938.

> French cinema, *La Bête Humaine* (1938) and *Le Jour Se Lève* (1939).

♦ **Fledgling acting talent, such as:**
- John Mills, Ida Lupino and Jack Hawkins, in front of the camera, and behind it, directors such as Bernard Vorhaus and John Baxter, along with many more talents.
- Several since famous acting talent were under contract to Hagen, including Alastair Sim and Margaret Rutherford.

In conclusion, the aim of the book is provide as complete a record as possible, for the benefit of posterity, (a) of the business achievements (and failures) of Julius Hagen, and (b) a full account of all the films that were made under his auspices. As it is intended to be an historical testimony, this book does not attempt to discover any possible subliminal drives, or thus analyse any hidden meanings or urges, behind the reasons for the concept and production of each of these films, other than to set their creation and presentation into the context of the social and cinema trade circumstances as existed during that period of the late 1920s and the 1930s decade.

Thus this author will now take the reader on a journey – and it is certainly quite a voyage, full of drama, sheer determination and total ambition – to illustrate the way that Julius Hagen took to accomplish his objective of running a film studio.

2. THE GREAT WAR AND THE COLLAPSE OF THE BRITISH FILM INDUSTRY. ITS STRUGGLE FOR SURVIVAL FROM 1914:

It is essential for the reader to appreciate what the state of the British Film Industry was in at the start of The Great War (the First World War), and at that very time when Julius Hagen had first entered it.

The history of the British cinema has always been a story of an uphill struggle for the survival of its industry in an autonomous state ever since the mid-1910s.

Before the war, London had been a world-clearing house for the huge volume of films offered in the open market. Many of these were imported in negative form and then printed here for foreign buyers. London was a distributor of entire foreign film outputs, imported for a round sum and then sold over a period of months.

F. Maurice Speed (in his *Movie Cavalcade*, published in 1944 by Raven) succinctly describes the situation:

"By the outbreak of the First World War the motion picture was already established as one of the foremost industries in the world. In America alone there were about 15,000 cinemas; as one writer has put it — Europe went to war and America went to the movies."

Before 1914, Britain had been the leading film production centre for many years. Not only had it had exported hundreds of films to the United States, its pictures had regularly been shown in all the cities of Europe for some ten years.

But when Britain became involved in war, its film industry was allowed to drift, and to such a degree that, for long periods during the conflict, not one film was being produced in this country!

In complete contrast, the number of movies being produced in Hollywood increased considerably. Thus, for British cinemas, this upsurge was hugely significant for it; from 1914 to 1919 an increasing stream of American films arrived here and, coupled with the depressing fact that a continually declining number of new British films were trickling out from English studios (such as Gaumont, Hepworth and Stoll), British audiences then had a continually-falling opportunity to see a home-made film!

The situation was made even worse; early in the war, the government imposed an import duty to increase finance necessary for "the war effort", and this measure combined with the other negative factors to destroy London's position as a world market for films. In any case, the war situation itself made it impossible for London to continue being the printing and clearing house for the Continental market. The big American producers began to set up their own distribution outlets, not only in England but also in other European countries.

And, it must be recognised and thus remembered; by its sheer geographical magnitude and its economic size, America's film industry generally was able to secure a profit from the release of its product to its own market. Thus, gaining additional revenues and resultant profits from releasing and distributing their own pictures abroad to other film markets was really and simply just "the icing on the cake"!

Therefore, by the pure force of sheer number, the American film industry was always in a position to dominate foreign film markets – and, here in the second decade of the 21st century, this economic fact still remains – American films still do dominate world markets!

Thus, during the First World War, America had acquired an unassailable supremacy in the world market for films.

When the First World War ended, the British film industry, like those of other European countries, sought to re-establish itself, but it found that the great American stranglehold was far too strong to break. The industry was optimistic and thought that the pre-war situation would be restored. A number of companies set out to break into foreign markets, but many of the films sent were second-rate. Gaining distribution in America became difficult indeed, if not virtually impossible as the prestige of British films there declined rapidly – in 1919, an American correspondent for *The Bioscope* magazine stated sadly that the latest British offerings were of "a school of production which was considered very good in this country (USA) about nine or ten years ago".

At home, the number of British pictures exhibited in Britain was estimated to be 25 per cent in 1914. But this percentage fell sharply over the rest of the decade. By 1923, it had fallen further, to 10 per cent; and in 1925 it fell even further, to a most meagre 2 per cent.

The British films that were made were generally slow and their staging too obvious. By comparison, they fell far short of the superiority of American technical standards. Consequently, the flood of American films entering Britain continued unabated. This ever-deepening foreign deluge, coupled with the economic weakness and consequent technical limitations of British film producers, was a vicious circle, seemingly impossible to break -

two insuperable handicaps that soon were to threaten the possible
commercial extinction of British film production.

Its struggle for survival appeared hopeless; the film
production slump of 1918-19, which caused many bankruptcies,
seemed to confirm this.

Julius Hagen was one of these casualties, as we shall see
below.

---

3. JULIUS HAGEN:

3.1. His Beginnings:

Very little is known about the earlier years of Julian Hagen,
and what is known has already been published in several other
film histories and critiques, and is repeated here for the sake of
good reporting, as follows:

He was born Julius Jacob Kleimenhagen, in 1884, in
Hamburg, Germany.

He came to Great Britain as a child, and began his working
career in his father's cigar business.

At the age of eighteen, Hagen went into partnership with
Leon M. Lion in various plays. Afterwards he joined the London-
based Fred Terry and Julia Neilson theatrical company. (*The
Kinematograph Year Book, 1929*). Terry and Neilson had entered
into theatre management in 1900, producing and starring in
popular, lightweight plays together for the next 30 years, most
notably in *The Scarlet Pimpernel*, 1905, at London's New Theatre,
adapted for the stage from Baroness Orczy's manuscript.

John V. Watson

3.2. 1913-1916:
Hagen's Early Film Career:

Hagen left the stage to enter the film industry in 1913 joining Ruffells' Pictures, the film rental company, as a film salesman. (*The Kinematograph Year Book, 1929*).

Now a long-forgotten British film distributor, Ruffells' commenced trading the same year when Hagen joined it. The company went on to release a total of 15 films from 1913 up until 1920. One of the films that Ruffells' released was the first version of ***A Little Bit of Fluff***, made in 1919; a five-reeler produced by Kew Films, with Dorothy Minto as 'Mamie Scott', a role which would give Betty Balfour one of her biggest successes in the remake of the film nine years later (trade shown in May 1928).

From Ruffells', Hagen was engaged by Essanay Company to break down the boycott which existed all over the United Kingdom on the Chaplin films. (*The Kinematograph Year Book*, 1929).

The 'Essanay' logo.

14

3.3. 1917-1919:
Hagen continues in the Film Trade:

At the beginning of 1917, Hagen and H. F. (Harold) Double (like Hagen, Double was also a film renter) formed their own distribution company.

Later that year, they branched out into film production. Their first was *All the World's a Stage*, directed by Harold Weston, from Herbert Everett's novel, with Eve Balfour, which they also distributed.

Then, in 1918, they started making a series of short comedies at the old Phoenix Studio (a converted boat builder's shed) on Eel Pie Island, Twickenham, again distributing them. Called *Kinekature Komedies*, these were made specifically to exploit a patented gimmick (a special lens) which distorted the film image for comic effect, with the transformation often triggered by a device such as a magic ring in the same style as other such pantomime devices, including *Alf's Button* and *Ali Baba's Magic Lantern*.

Nine one-reeler and mostly two-reeler Kinekature Komedies were made by the Hagen/Double partnership, all during 1918, five of which starred the top music-hall artist Lupino Lane as his "Mr. Butterbun" character, as follows:
1. *A Case of Comfort* (with Will Asher). Length: 1,190 feet.
2. *Diamonds and Dimples* (with Will Asher). Length: 1,000 feet.
3. *His Busy Day* (with Lupino Lane as 'Mr. Butterbun'). Length: 1,630 feet.
4. *His Salad Days* (with Lupino Lane as 'Mr. Butterbun'). Length: 2,130 feet.
5. *Love and Lobster* (with Lupino Lane as 'Mr.

Butterbun'). Length: 1,950 feet.

6. ***Paint and Passion*** (with Will Asher). Length: 1,190 feet.

7. ***The Blunders of Mr. Butterbun: Trips and Tribunals*** (with Lupino Lane as 'Mr. Butterbun', with Judd Green as 'Stopson'). Length: 2,070 feet.

8. ***The Blunders of Mr. Butterbun: Unexpected Treasure*** (with Lupino Lane as 'Mr. Butterbun', with Wallace Lupino). Length: 2,000 feet.

9. ***The Haunted Hotel*** (with Will Asher as 'Buttons' and Marion Peake as 'Miss Falloffski'). Length: 1,000 feet.

Amazingly, two of these nine one- and two-reel comedies still survive and are now preserved in the British National Film Archive.

Fred Rains directed all nine films. Rains was also an actor, appearing in British films up until 1936. He entered the film industry as an actor and director in 1910. Born in 1860, Rains died in December 1945, at the age of 84 or 85.

By the middle of 1919, like many other companies around this time, the "Hagen & Double" company went bankrupt.

There are then conflicting reports which confuse the matter as to what happened to Hagen next. One eminent account of British film history published in 1971, *The History of the British Film: 1918-1929* by Rachael Low (published by George Allen & Unwin), states on page 72 that:

"In February 1919, J (Julius) Hagen co-founded the distributors W. & F. Film Service with S. Freedman, D. Tebbitt, and C. M. Woolf, a company formed with a capital of £10,000, and named using the surname initials of C. M. Woolf and S. Freedman."

However, that author does not then state how long Hagen remained with W. & F. for, but it is a well-documented fact that the company continued to trade primarily as a distributor right up until 1933. It started out as a renting company to handle mostly American productions including the popular American films of

Harold Lloyd. W. & F. Film Service was soon to become important in providing financial backing to British film productions.

The first British-made film it distributed was **Damaged Goods** (1919), produced by Samuelson Film Manufacturing Company. This company was formed by G. B. Samuelson in 1913 and ceased trading in 1920 when it was bought by General Film Renters in November that year. In February 1922, that company was taken over by British Super Films. From then until 1924, Samuelson products were known as "Napoleon" and "Reciprocity" films.

For Julius Hagen, there followed a couple of difficult years when he and his wife lived in just one room in Clapham. He survived the hard way by travelling throughout Britain to peddle films that nobody else wanted to handle. The actual years of this period are not nominated but we can safely conclude they were probably from 1919-20 to 1922-23.

Hilda Hagen later would recall (in an interview with A. Jympson Harmon of *The Star*, published on 2 December 1935) that cinema-owners would tell her: 'He's a nice man but I wish you would try to keep him away. He is always selling me films I don't want.'

But, his persistence clearly demonstrates that Hagen was a natural salesman, and that, full of flamboyance and gregariousness, and willing to take chances, he had all the exceptional qualities that encompass the essential "wheeler-dealer" instincts to make a successful film producer, with the potential to become an enormous success, or a spectacular failure.

3.4. The Early 1920s: Hagen at Stoll Studios and at Universal:

The exterior of the Stoll Studios building; date of the picture is unknown, but it looks to have been taken in the 1920s.

In the early 1920s, Hagen was taken on as a production manager at Stoll Studios, a big new production outfit operating from a converted aircraft hangar in Cricklewood. This was Hagen's first experience of large-scale film production run on factory lines and it was here that he really learned his trade as a film producer.

Hagen then moved to the London office of Universal as their British manager – but the dates of his tenure with that company are now not known. (*The Kinematograph Year Book, 1929*).

As is well known, Universal was founded in 1912 by Carl Laemmle, in an area of Los Angeles which has since become known as Universal City.

3.5. 1923-1924:
Hagen at British and Colonial Studios:

Then, in 1923, Hagen became manager of the British and

'The Czar of Twickenham'. The History of Julius Hagen and the Film Empire he created at Twickenham Film Studios, from 1927 to 1938.

Colonial Studios.

B. & C. was the old British and Colonial Kinematograph Company, which had studios in Walthamstow, East London. Soon after the Great War, their new managing director Edward Godal made plans for expansion. The basic idea was to try to gain access to the American market with the strategy of using American directors and stars. Whilst their first film *12.10* (1919), a thriller directed by Herbert Brenon and starring Marie Doro, was a considerable success, other films followed during 1919 and 1920 but their output was small and the company did not prosper, probably because of the chronic shortage of capital. Thus, by late 1920, the studio was being rented briefly by Granger-Binger and then in 1921 by H. W. Thompson.

But, in 1923, under Julius Hagen's new management, serious efforts were made to revive film production. Initially several series of shorts were made including *The Romance of History*, *Wonder Women of the World* and *Gems of Literature*; the later series offered audiences two-reel truncations of classic texts, including Shakespeare's *The Taming of the Shrew* with Dacia Deane (Katharina), Lauderdale Maitland (Petruchio), M. Gray Murray (Baptista), Cynthia Murtagh (Bianca), Roy Beard (Lucentio). All these shorts were made in 1922 and 1923, and were directed by either Edwin J. Collins or Edwin Greenwood.

Then, feature films were produced; the first was *The Audacious Mr Squire* (1923), with Jack Buchanan, directed by Edwin Greenwood, which was quickly followed by *The Heart Strings* (1923), with Gertrude McCoy and Victor McLaglen.

Several other productions followed, all produced by Edward Godal, including some José Collins dramas, but the total production output of 29 films (including the two-reelers) were generally not successful.

The British and Colonial company, like many others at that time, was to be placed in the hands of the receivers by June 1924.

However, Godal, seemingly undeterred by this financial difficulty, set up another company - Godal International Films - later that year, in December 1924, and which continued to trade for another year.

What happened to Hagen from the middle of 1924 to his 1926 appointment at Astra-National (see below) is not known. Possibly – or even probably - he returned to what he was already good at, selling unwanted films to independent exhibitors who did not really want to rent and show them. But it is possible that this period was the two years to which his wife, Hilda, referred to in her interview with A. Jympson Harmon of *The Star* newspaper, on 2 December 1935.

3.6. 1926:
Julius Hagen at Astra-National: Part 1:

Hagen's luck held when he was taken on as general manager by Astra-National in 1926.

Astra-National had started trading in 1922, following a merger with Astra Films, a British film production and distribution company, which was set up in Leeds after the First World War by the film director Herbert Wilcox, his younger brother Charles Wilcox and H. W. Thompson, a leading figure in film distribution in the North of England.

Between 1923 and 1925, (before Hagen joined it) the merged company produced and released six films, all of some importance and quality, as follows:
1. *The Woman Who Obeyed* (1923) with Stewart Rome (trade shown September).
2. *The Beloved Vagabond* (1923) with Carlyle Blackwell (trade shown October).
3. *Miriam Rozella* (1924) with Moyna MacGill in the title role, and Owen Nares (trade shown March).
4. *Shadow of Egypt* (1924) with Carlyle Blackwell (trade shown December).
5. *Trainer and Temptress* (1925) with Juliette Compton

(trade shown August).

6.*Bulldog Drummond's Third Round* (1925) with Jack Buchanan (trade shown December).

The company had also distributed **Bulldog Drummond** (1922), with Carlyle Blackwell as 'Capt. Hugh "Bulldog" Drummond', produced by Hollandia Film Corporation.

Significantly for Julius Hagen, all the Astra-National films were made at Twickenham Studios at St. Margaret's, Twickenham, which was to become his centre of operations for the next decade, the most significant period of his professional life and of his career in films.

At Astra-National, Hagen co-produced with Henry Edwards, *The Flag Lieutenant* (1926). Because of Hagen's skilful exploitation, this film, which starred Edwards, then Britain's most popular screen star, was one of the box-office hits of the year.

But the success of *The Flag Lieutenant* was even more significant because it occurred at a time when British screens were saturated with American films whilst British film production was verging on the point of extinction.

The following chapter describes in detail the ominous situation and the eventual solution by legislation.

3.7. 1925-1927:
The British Film Industry continues to struggle for survival, and then Legislation is enacted.

So serious was the dire state of British film production, it was felt that drastic action had to be taken in order to save the entire industry.

Films continued to pour in from Hollywood flooding the British market. Prices fell. Exhibitors booked ahead for longer and longer periods, which were no hardship to the Americans, when their main revenue was already secured in their home market and thus they could afford to wait for the British receipts to be realised. But this presented a very serious problem to British producers not so fortunately placed.

By 1925 it was estimated that 95 per cent of screen time was given over to American films. Furthermore American distributors were entrenching themselves even more firmly in an already impregnable position by the practices of mass salesmanship known as blind booking and block booking.

"**Blind booking**" occurred when, say, a series of perhaps six, ten or more films would be announced by renters, with exhibitors then being required (forced!) to book the whole block or series when only the first one or two had been made and shown to the trade.

"**Block booking**" was a stipulation imposed by renters on exhibitors giving them no real choice at all; if exhibitors wanted to show a "super" film (or a group of such films), then the renters also "obliged" them to accept a certain number of much inferior films.

It was at this point, around 1925, that there began a movement agitating for some form of protective legislation for the British film industry; it was at last generally realised that the problem was one which must be attacked in the first instance on purely economic grounds.

Then, in 1926, another film industry depression led to major cutbacks in film production. That year proved to be the very nadir of British production, a situation so gloomy that it spurred an even further and more fervent drive for legislation to be introduced to combat this apparent irreversible problem.

Thus, in response to those vociferous demands from production interests and, more importantly, the powerful Empire

lobby, in 1927 the government passed the Cinematograph Films
Act (1927) which made it compulsory for cinemas to show a
proportion of British films. The theory was that finance would
follow once a market had been guaranteed for British films. If
distributors were going to continue to earn the very substantial
profits previously made largely from handling American films,
then they had to establish a supply of British films.

The passing of the Cinematograph Films Act in 1927 was
described as 'an act to restrict blind booking and advance booking
of cinematograph films, and to secure the renting and exhibition
of a certain proportion of British films, and for purposes
connected therewith'. Firstly, it was designed to regulate the
trading methods between renters and exhibitors by making blind
booking impossible, and by rigidly curtailing the practice of
advance (or block) booking. Secondly, it imposed on both renter
and exhibitor the obligation to acquire and show respectively, a
minimum proportion, or quota, of British films in respect of the
foreign films acquired and exhibited.

Hence the Act became popularly known as the "Quota" Act.

The Act was due to become effective as from the 1st January,
1928.

The renters' quota was to rise from 7.5 per cent in 1928-29 to
20 per cent, in 1934-35; and the exhibitors' quota from 5 per cent
in 1928-29 to 20 per cent in 1935-36.

NOTE: The Act was modified by the Cinematograph Films
Act 1938 and by further acts, and it was eventually repealed by the
Films Act 1960.

But even before the Quota Act came into effect, the tremors
of upheaval were suddenly felt throughout the whole of the film
industry. The arrival of sound in the cinema! *The Jazz Singer*
premiered in New York on 6th October 1927 and it caused a
box-office sensation. The film was actual only a part-"talkie"; it
has dialogue and musical sequences, but begins as a silent picture

with background music. The first spoken dialogue occurs in the "Coffee Dan's" sequence, in which "Jakie Rabinowitz" (Al Jolson) sings the song "Dirty Hands, Dirty Face", after which the café's patrons show their appreciation by striking little gavels on their tables. The first words of spoken dialogue in the film are uttered by Jolson, who says, "Wait a minute, wait a minute. You ain't heard nothin' yet. Wait a minute I tell ya, you ain't heard nothin'. You want to hear 'Toot, Toot, Tootsie'?"

Thus into a world of cinematic silent shadows a voice had suddenly burst, and within a few months there was a wild scramble to wire studios and cinemas for sound, to make every film all-talking or all-singing.

The American stampede towards sound gave British producers a fierce jolt as they were preparing to settle down under the protective shield of the Quota Act. They met the new challenge at the very outset of their new effort to achieve a significant recovery of making films, and ultimately found in sound itself an ally.

In 1926, the number of British feature films was 26. In 1929 it had risen to 128, as against the minimum quota of 50 required by law. After a temporary setback in 1930, the number rose to 122 in 1931, 153 in 1932, 159 in 1933 and 190 in 1934, when exhibitors were actually screening twice the minimum amount of British films required by law.

Moreover, this increase in British production came opportunely at a time when there was a decline in the supply of foreign (principally American) films caused by the economic depression, which was heralded in by the Wall Street Crash of October 1929, together with the limitations on foreign-language markets imposed by the dialogue film. In 1934 the number of foreign films imported had fallen to 484, as against 550 in 1929 or 556 in 1931.

3.8. 1926:
Julius Hagen at Astra-National:

'The Czar of Twickenham'. The History of Julius Hagen and the Film Empire he created at Twickenham Film Studios, from 1927 to 1938.

Part 2:

Julius Hagen was always quick to recognise an opportunity when one presented itself; he had the right experience behind him to capitalise on the new legislation imposed by the "Quota" Act.

Hagen was still looking for a means to get in to first-class film production. His ambition was soon to be realised, when, as we have seen above, he was taken on as Astra-National's general manager in 1926.

Whilst at Astra, he had met the film star, and director/producer, Henry Edwards. Edwards was Britain's first major male film star. Previously, Edwards had been a principal actor in the Hepworth Picture Players at the Walton Studios following his earlier career as a stage actor.

An original still of *The Flag Lieutenant* showing Lilian Oldland and Henry Edwards in a scene from the film.

In 1926, Henry Edwards played the lead (as the manly and jovial 'Lt. Dicky Lascelles') in Maurice Elvey's forceful and lively naval drama The Flag Lieutenant for Astra-National; released in

October that year, it was a very popular and an immense success at the box office.

The box office success of **The Flag Lieutenant** was achieved mainly by the sheer drive of Hagen's promotional and sales expertise, and this greatly impressed Edwards. Combined with the sudden upheaval given by the new opportunities presented by (a) the forthcoming government legislation (the 1927 'Quota' Act) and (b) the impending new sound film revolution, encouraged Edwards to join Hagen in independent film production.

3.9.   1927: Julius Hagen at W. P. and 'Neo-Art':

Thus, in April 1927, together with W. B. Williams, Hagen and Edwards broke away from Astra-National to form the W. P. (Williams and Pritchard) Film Company to both produce and rent films. The production company was registered as 'Neo-Art' in June 1927 with a capital of £1,000. Hagen was general manager of the company.

Hiring the very same Twickenham studios as had previously been used by Astra-National, the new company, 'Neo-Art', soon commenced production on two films:

1. **The Fake** (trade shown on 9 September 1927). Directed by the German Georg Jacoby, it was a dramatic story, adapted from the Frederick Lonsdale play, about a girl married to a degenerate aristocrat in order to satisfy her father's ambition. Henry Edwards himself took the leading role with German actress Elga Brink, British actor Miles Mander, and American actress Juliette Compton heading the excellent cast.

The Fake was the very first film produced by Julius Hagen.

Kinematograph Weekly remarked: "Brilliant direction and acting make this film version of Frederick Lonsdale's play better and more gripping than the stage version. ... As W. P.'s first

26

production it is indeed a happy augury of the future." (*K.W.*, 15 September 1928, page 65).

2. *The Further Adventures of the Flag Lieutenant* (trade shown on 4 November 1927). Clearly, to both Hagen and Edwards, it was obvious what one of their very first films for their new company would be; they quickly came up with a film that blatantly capitalised on their previous hit which they made for Astra-National the previous year, *The Flag Lieutenant*. It was directed by W. P. Kellino and was a naval spy thriller written by the same author of *The Flag Lieutenant*, W. P. Drury, and using the same cast, with Henry Edwards playing the lead as 'Lt. Dicky Lascelles'; but the second film was not based on a successful play (this time, Drury had specially-written the story). It was a competently made film and it had a reasonably successful release.

The Further Adventures of the Flag Lieutenant was Julius Hagen's second film as a producer.

Kinematograph Weekly remarked: "A safe showman's proposition, largely on account of its tremendously successful predecessor. Melodramatic treatment is certainly much cruder; but action is lively, with first-rate atmosphere of battleships and Shanghai mob episodes, and some humour. Production values are admirable." (*K.W.*, 10 November 1927, page 64).

But, the blatant capitalising backfired; as *Further Adventures* was so obviously "close" to the original *Flag Lieutenant* film, its producer (Astra-National) was forced to bring an action for infringement of copyright in the summer of 1928, which was settled out of court with damages.

Both films were adapted by George A. Cooper, and photographed by Horace Wheddon and William Shenton.

That 'Neo-Art' was quickly making a name for itself in the industry is illustrated in the *Kinematograph Weekly* article in which P. L. Mannock remarked:
"HAGEN BUSY"

"It is extremely refreshing when a new and enterprising production house completes two elaborate films in three months, when one considers the fact that they were not made concurrently. W. P. Films have an energetic chief in J. Hagen ...". (K.W., 8 September 1927, page 66).

To illustrate that Hagen was determined to take the new company onto further important film production, some five weeks later *Kinematograph Weekly* reported: "HAGEN'S SCOOP — Julius Hagen has acquired the film rights of The Joker, and it will be directed by Georg Jacoby, partly in Monte Carlo, partly in Denmark, with possibly some British scenes. The production is a joint one of W. P. and Nordisk, and the leading parts will be played by the successful protagonists of *The Fake* – Henry Edwards, Elga Brink and Miles Mander." ..... "W. P. is understood to have secured the rights of a tremendously famous New York and London stage success." However, the film announced, The Joker, was never made, and the second, the filming of "a tremendously famous New York and London stage success", does not appear to have been made either. (*K.W.*, 13 October 1927, page 44).

However, both Julius Hagen and Henry Edwards were soon to leave W. P., for reasons not now known, recorded, or (apparently) reported.

At this stage, the most significant thing for Julius Hagen was that the production of the first two 'Neo-Art' productions, *The Fake* and *The Further Adventures of the Flag Lieutenant*, were to take him to Alliance Studios, Twickenham, soon to become his permanent film production home for ten years.

1927: The Year before the introduction of the 'Quota' Act:

100 British films were first shown during the year 1927.

This number is arrived at by using the data contained in The British Film Catalogue: 1895-1970 by Denis Gifford, as follows:

'The Czar of Twickenham'. The History of Julius Hagen and the Film Empire he created at Twickenham Film Studios, from 1927 to 1938.

08297: Closing Gifford Catalogue Number.
08197: Opening Gifford Catalogue Number.
  100: Total.

The majority of these films made were short subjects; the actual number of these shorts has not been determined, but it is estimated there were about 60 made. Therefore, the British features produced in 1927 were approximately a mere 40 films.

3.10. 1928: Julius Hagen and the Strand Film Company:

At the beginning of 1928, Julius Hagen and Henry Edwards left W. P.

W. P. continued to make two further films without either Hagen or Edwards: *The Rising Generation* (trade shown September 1928) directed by Harley Knoles and George Dewhurst, and *White Cargo* (trade shown May 1929), directed by J. B. Williams, with Gypsy Rhouma as 'Tondelayo' (the role which Hedy Lamarr was to make her own eleven years later at M-G-M). Both were made at Twickenham and the latter, made at the turn of the year, was later fitted with a sound track at the Whitehall studios at Elstree and a sound version was trade shown in October 1929.

In January 1928, Hagen announced in the trade press that he was the prime mover in the formation of a '£250,000 company', as yet to be named, which in the near future would make a public share issue.

P. L. Mannock in *Kinematograph Weekly* reported Hagen's announcement in some detail:
"NEW PRODUCTION COMPANY".

"Henry Edwards with J. Hagen in £250,000 Concern".

"Details will shortly be available of a new British producing company, for which a public appeal for capital is to be made. It will probably be called Anglo-European Films. A reciprocal contract for producing films in England and in Central Europe has just been fixed up." "The board will include the popular actor-producer, Henry Edwards, who will alternately direct and star, besides being in charge of production arrangements, also a very prominent exhibitor. By the proposed arrangement, pictures are planned for making here on a basis which will save one third of the production cost."

"It is also interesting to note that Julius Hagen, who has just terminated his association with W. P. Films, joins the new company as general manager. Mr. Hagen's long experience in many sides of the Industry, especially latterly on the studio side, is allied to a first-class salesmanship angle, and his identification with the new organisation gives it additional stability."

"The capital is fixed at £250,000." (K.W., 5 January 1928, page 45).

Over the next several months, Julius Hagen was involved in a series of complex deals while he struggled to establish himself as a major participant in the British film industry. During this time he issued a series of press releases which tended to be vague about what he had definitely agreed, and which gave a false impression of the progress of various negotiations, all probably deliberately.

It would appear that at this point he was negotiating for the acquisition of Twickenham Studios, realising that if he was to be anything more than one of an overabundance of new independent production companies all scrambling for contracts on the strength of the new quota legislation, then he had to gain control of a studio.

Indeed, put into the context of this period of the development of the British film industry, many early motion picture entrepreneurs had more-or-less the same experience – rapid commercial development earlier (1927-1932) and, for some, subsequent severe financial decline in the latter 1930s.

'The Czar of Twickenham'. The History of Julius Hagen and the Film Empire he created at Twickenham Film Studios, from 1927 to 1938.

And, so, Julius Hagen was not alone in his drive to create a British film production and later distribution empire. Other leading industry names such as C. M. Woolf, Michael Balcon, John Maxwell, Herbert Wilcox, and the Ostrer brothers were already on their way to becoming British "movie moguls" (or would soon be so) at that period of the later 1920s when Hagen made his own push for industry prominence.

In the meantime, Henry Edwards had gone his separate way to Hagen - but only temporarily; during 1928, he went on to star in two films: *Fear* (German: *Angst - Die schwache Stunde einer Frau*, released September 1928) and *The Three Kings* (German: *Ein Mädel und drei Clowns*, based on the 1925 novella by Stefan Zweig, released January 1929), both directed by Hans Steinhoff under an Anglo-German production arrangement.

In June 1928, Hagen formed the Strand Film Company with Cecil Cattermoul, a film agent, and the director Leslie Hiscott. Hiscott, who had worked for Famous Players in Britain and later for George Pearson, had recently made a series of two-reel comedies based on the Mrs. May stories with Sydney Fairbrother, and was considered to be a director of some promise.

Strand soon started to produce two films:
1. *The Passing of Mr Quin* (1928), adapted from a thriller by Agatha Christie, starring Stewart Rome and Trilby Clark.

Kinematograph Weekly reported that agreements had been reached between Argosy Film Co., Ltd, and Cecil Cattermoul, Ltd., whereby Cattermoul would produce the film for Argosy, its first quota picture. Julius Hagen (as joint managing director with Cattermoul of the Strand Film Company) was in charge of the production as business manager. Filming started on Monday, 7 May 1928 at the Alliance Studios, Twickenham, under the direction of Leslie Hiscott, for release by Argosy. (*K.W.*, 15 March 1928, page 51).

The Passing of Mr Quin was Trade shown on 31 July 1928; *Kinematograph Weekly* reviewed the film stating: "Murder story interestingly produced and well acted. Adaptation of a murder story by Agatha Christie, capably directed and well acted. Treatment is a little on the slow side, but this can be remedied by a little cutting, when the picture should appeal to most audiences." (*K.W.*, 2 August 1928, page 43).

2.*S.O.S.* (1928), adapted from Walter Ellis's St. James's Theatre then current success, it starred the successful London and Broadway stage actor, actor-manager and former soldier, Robert Loraine; the new London and Broadway stage star, Bramwell Fletcher, in his film début; and British stage actress, Ursula Jeans, in her sixth film role.

Filming started on 1 August 1928 at the Gaumont Lime Grove Studios. Leslie Hiscott directed. In early August, it was announced that the film would be released by The Allied Artists Corporation Ltd., the British renting subsidiary of the American parent company, United Artists.

NOTE: For the record, the company directors of The Allied Artists Corporation Ltd. (the British film renter or distributor), were listed at the bottom of a trade advertisement in early 1929 as: the stars, Mary Pickford, Norma Talmadge, Gloria Swanson, Charles Chaplin, Douglas Fairbanks; the director, D. W. Griffith; the producer, Samuel Goldwyn; and the entrepreneur, Joseph M. Schenck, as Chairman, Board of Directors. In March 1929, the name of the company was changed to United Artists, now the same as its American parent.

S.O.S. was Trade shown on 4 December 1928; *Kinematograph Weekly* reviewed the film stating: "Average popular booking. A mystery drama, freely adapted from Walter Ellis's St. James's Theatre success, which represents average popular entertainment." "Acting: Robert Loraine gives a sound performance as Owen Heriot in the circumstances, but it is obvious that he is handicapped by being unable to exploit his fine speaking voice" (the film was a silent). "Production: Leslie Hiscott never seems to get to grips with the story, with the result that the action is too slow for this type of fare." (K.W., 6 December 1928, page 57).

Kinematograph Weekly announced that Leslie Hiscott had been added to the board of directors, and that Captain Marshall O. Roberts, the author and playwright, had also been added to the board of directors. (*K.W.*, 14 June 1928, page 35).

A tribute was paid to Julius Hagen in the *Kinematograph Weekly*: "Unlike some who transfer their energies from renting to production, the managing director of Strand is a success – but then he has studied picture-making as a business." (*K.W.*, 27 September 1928, page 24).

Two further films were then announced for production by Strand:

* **Ringing the Changes** - *Kinematograph Weekly* stated: "goes into production on 12 November 1928 at the Alliance Studios – distribution throughout the U.K. by Argosy." (*K.W.*, 18 October 1928). The film was set to star Henry Edwards.
* **The Feather** - *Kinematograph Weekly* stated: "for production early in January 1929, and will be made at the British International Studios at Elstree– negotiations are at present pending for two big stars – Allied Artists Corporation will distribute in the U.K. and Australia." (*K.W.*, 18 October 1928). Filming did not actually commence until late March 1929.

Both films were to be directed by Leslie S. Hiscott.

A further tribute was paid to the Strand Company by P. L. Mannock in the *Kinematograph Weekly*: "To me, the Strand organisation is an excellent example of steady efficiency and output, and for a six month's old company, it is certainly healthy. The reason is sound business management and economy without niggardliness." (K.W., 18 October 1928, page 60).

Kinematograph Weekly reported: "***Ringing the Changes*** – Julius Hagen has just returned from Berlin where he has sold the German rights. Ralph Scotoni is handling all foreign rights outside the British Colonies, and will be present at the Strand Film Company, 177, Regent Street, W. Shooting begins at St. Margaret's next week." (*K.W.*, 8 November 1928).

Kinematograph Weekly reported: "Hagen scoop – **To What Red**

Hell – secured the screen rights." (K.W., 29 November 1928, page 34). It was to be Strand's final production.

1928:
The First Year of the Cinematograph Films Act (1927):

204 British films were first shown during the year 1928.

This number is arrived at by using the data contained in The British Film Catalogue: 1895-1970 by Denis Gifford, as follows:

08502: Closing Gifford Catalogue Number.

08298: Opening Gifford Catalogue Number.

204: Total. A huge increase of 104 films over the previous year's total of 100.

Counting through the actual listings in Gifford's Catalogue, however, reveals that 125 of these films were short subjects. Therefore, 79 British feature films were Trade shown during 1928.

4. HAGEN'S CAREER: FROM 1929 TO 1935.

1. 1929: Julius Hagen and Henry Edwards start Twickenham Film Studios, Ltd.:

1929 was to be the year in which Julius Hagen would achieve his ambition of running his own film studios; to become a film producer of prestige; and to be a business impresario in his own right. It was in that year that Hagen took over St. Margaret's Studios.

St. Margaret's Studios was originally established in 1913 by Dr. Ralph Jupp, on the site of a former ice-rink. At the time of its construction, St. Margaret's became the largest film studio in the United Kingdom. The first film to be made there was *The House of Temperley* (1913), a British silent drama running 4,800 feet, directed by Harold M. Shaw; it was based on the novel *Rodney Stone* by Arthur Conan Doyle, with a cast headed by Charles Maude, Ben Webster and Lillian Logan, and released by Jury Films.

Twickenham Film Studios Ltd. formed:

Once again, Henry Edwards joined forces with Julius Hagen, this time to form Twickenham Film Studios Ltd. on 29 January 1929, in order to take over the assets of Alliance Studios at St. Margaret's, Twickenham.

Kinematograph Weekly, in their issue dated 7 February 1929, gave a detailed account of the formation of the new company and the deal it had struck:

"ALLIANCE'S FUTURE"
"Hagen's Studio Deal; Completed".
"As I announced some weeks ago, the Alliance Studios, associated with the history of native production for over fifteen years, have changed hands."

"A new company, Twickenham Film Studios, Ltd., which has taken over the studios, has been formed by Julius Hagen, the energetic business impresario. It is only ten months since he was the prime mover in the formation of the Strand Film Company, which is now on its fourth British picture, and has a fifth in active preparation for Allied Artists. Leslie Hiscott, who has been closely associated with Hagen in the Strand Film Company, is also on the board of the new company."

"Henry Edwards, the popular star, who has made several of his successful pictures under the auspices of Julius Hagen, is financially interested, and is chairman of the studio company. He proposes to produce and act in two pictures in this studio during the year. His partner, E. G. Norman, is also on the board of directors. Ralph and Edwin Scotoni, of Munich, are on the board, and have big film interests on the Continent, both in production and distribution."

"Hagen is devoting his energy and interest in making this studio company a financial success. He hopes to keep the studios at work continuously throughout the year."

"Mr. Hagen wishes it to be known that in becoming managing director of the studio company, he is in no way limiting the scope of his activities on behalf of the Strand Film Company. It is expected that he will shortly announce an ambitious programme for Twickenham Film Studios, Ltd., and also for the Strand. Under his auspices, films will be directed by Leslie Hiscott and Edwin Greenwood."

In that same issue, *Kinematograph Weekly* went on to note the legal details of the company:

'The Czar of Twickenham'. The History of Julius Hagen and the Film Empire he created at Twickenham Film Studios, from 1927 to 1938.

"Twickenham Film Studios, Limited. Private company.
Registered January 29, 1929.

£15,000 in 12,000 7.5 per cent cumulative participating preference shares of £1 each, and 60,000 deferred shares of £1 each.

Objects: To acquire from Neo-Art Productions. Ltd., the freehold studios and buildings standing on a site of approximately two acres, known as the Alliance Studios, St. Margaret's, and to carry on the business of producers of motion picture films, etc.

The first directors are: Henry Edwards, J. Hagen, L. S. Hiscott, E. G. Norman, R. Scotini, and E. Scotini.

Qualification: £100 shares.

Solicitors: Denton, Hall and Burgin, 3 Gray's Inn Place, London E.C.1.

Registered office: Alliance Street, St. Margaret's, Middlesex."

Film Production continues at Twickenham with two films:

As Hagen's new company was being formed and launched, film production was already well under way at the studios.

On 3 January 1929, *Kinematograph Weekly* reported:

♦ Tiffany Productions Ltd. announced their first British production *To What Red Hell* in a double-page advertisement. The film was due to start production at the Alliance Studios (Twickenham) the following week. It was to be a Strand Film production.

A silent film, *To What Red Hell* was scripted by Leslie Hiscott but Edwin Greenwood directed it instead, with a large cast headed by Sybil Thorndike, John Hamilton and Bramwell Fletcher, and photographed by Basil Emmott.

♦ *White Cargo* was to start at Twickenham; it was a Neo-Art (W. P.) production, directed by J. B. Williams and starring Leslie Faber, John F. Hamilton and Maurice Evans. Hagen had nothing to do with the actual production of this film; Twickenham was used as a studio facility by its producers.

The Winds of Change: Sound arrives in Britain:

And, at that very same time, the winds of change were battering the British film industry - the rush of sound!

The Singing Fool (1928) had just been released in Great Britain, and had opened to sensational business at British cinema box-offices. Al Jolson starred in this part-talking musical drama from Warner Bros.; a follow-up to his previous hit part-sound film, *The Jazz Singer* (1927).

An advertisement in *Kinematograph Weekly* on 10 January announced:

"Al Jolson, The Greatest Entertainer in *The Singing Fool* plays to phenomenal figures!"

"The number of people who have paid to see *The Singing Fool* - London, Regal: 8.5 weeks to 276,630; Glasgow, Coliseum: 3 weeks to 253,762; Manchester, New Oxford: 3 weeks to 58,655 – Total: 589,047".

The new novelty of sound was apparently here to stay - and, as we shall shortly see, this new phenomenon was soon to have an enormous effect - and upheaval - on Julius Hagen, Henry Edwards, and Twickenham Studios.

More Film Production at Twickenham:

In late March 1929, production of Strand's fifth film commenced:

+ ***The Feather*** (1929).
  Starring Jameson Thomas (his first film since the expiration of his B.I.P. contract).

  Véra Flory – "the pretty Franco-Russian blond" – headed the supporting cast which included Randle Ayrton, John Hamilton, James Reardon, Charles Paton, Irene Tripod (her come-back after an eighteen month's absence from films owing to illness), Grace Lane (the famous stage actress), Mary Clare, and, in the heavy lead, W. Cronin Wilson.

  Leslie Hiscott directed; Basil Emmott, the cameraman; and the art director, James Carter.

  Filming commenced in late March and was completed in late April.

Ringing the Changes: Strand's third film is Trade Shown:

On the same day, 25 March, Strand's third film was Trade shown:

+ ***Ringing the Changes*** (1929).
  Comedy, adapted from the novel *JIX* by Raleigh King. Written and directed by Leslie Hiscott, it starred Henry Edwards, with the German actress, Margot Landa.

  Ringing the Changes was Trade shown on Monday,

March 25, at the New Gallery Kinema, London W.1. *Kinematograph Weekly* reviewed the film stating: "Quite a good comedy idea which has been lost in the making. There is a good comedy theme in this picture, but neither direction nor production help to bring it out. Henry Edwards is fair as Lord Bemerton, but he is made to behave so absurdly that he hardly wins sympathy. There is a lack of polish about Leslie Hiscott's production, which appears too hurried and sometimes haphazard. Some laughs are undoubtedly gained, but the general effect strikes a weak note. Box Office Angle: Booking on star." (*K.W.*, 28 March 1929).

The film was the second British release by Argosy Film Co., Ltd.

Twickenham Studios Convert to Sound:

In April, production was halted on *To What Red Hell* as the shock of the new novelty of the sound film had just arrived in Britain. There was no alternative; Twickenham studios **had** to switch to sound!

Henry Edwards was largely responsible for the decision in April 1929 to install R.C.A. sound equipment at Twickenham (although Hagen himself later claimed that it he who determined the conversion to sound at the studio).

In May, *Kinematograph Weekly* reported:

"IN NEW YORK"

"Hiscott and Emmott on Intensive R.C.A. Study"

"Just over a week ago, Julius Hagen and Henry Edwards gave

a send-off to director Leslie Hiscott and cameraman Basil Emmott at Waterloo. Hiscott and cameraman Basil Emmott sailed by the Olympic and are now in New York, where, representing Twickenham Film Studios, Ltd., they are studying at first hand the R.C.A. talkie method. Expected back in time to begin the first Twickenham talkie under that system before the end of June. Without posing as an expert, ---- mastered the art of making talkies in the space of three to four weeks, Hiscott and Emmott will be entitled to emphatic congratulations." (*K.W.*, 16 May 1929).

The following week, *Kinematograph Weekly* reported that Twickenham Studios were equipping for sound. (*K.W.*, 23 May 1929).

In June, *Kinematograph Weekly* reported further:

"SCRAPPED - TIFFANY CHANGE PLANS"

"Sound Version of Famous Play".

"Tiffany Productions Ltd., have signed contracts for the talking-film rights of the successful West End play by Percy Robinson, *To What Red Hell?* Their recent silent production is to be scrapped, and production on the sound version will commence immediately."

"The sum of £50,000 is to be spent on the new 100% talking production, and Sybil Thorndike will make her first appearance as a talkie star in the leading rôle."

"The studios at Twickenham are being equipped by R. C. A., and this will be the first talking production to be made there."

"C. F. Bernhard, managing director of Tiffany, is leaving at the end of the week for New York to confer with R. C. A.

directors concerning the production, which will be Tiffany's first super film to be made in the country."

"It is estimated that three months will be required for the production, and Edwin Greenwood is to be in charge as director."

"An imposing array of film and theatrical stars are being secured for the supporting rôles."

"Percy Robinson, author of the play, will be in constant attendance at the studio during the production in order to give every possible assistance to the producers."

"Those who saw the play when it was produced at Wyndham's Theatre will realise what an enormous opportunity has in making *To What Red Hell?* The greatest talking drama yet to be shown on screen." (*K.W.*, 20 June 1929).

In the same June edition, *Kinematograph Weekly* also reported:

"Twickenham busy - RCA".

"Leslie Hiscott and Basil Emmott, of Twickenham Film Studios, Ltd., who went to New York six weeks ago to study at first hand American talkie methods, returned to England last Friday, 14th June 1929."

"Spirit of renewed optimism."

"Hiscott spent 2 days with Hagen, the managing director."

"No reason why this country should not now becomes leaders of the Film Industry rather than follow the American precedent as before."

"Alliance Studios are about to emerge as the biggest sound

studios in England, as already building work has begun on a smaller studio for projecting rushes and for musical synchronisation – both for Twickenham F S Ltd and any other films that are made in this studio."

"While in New York, Hiscott visited all the film studios and inspected the various kinds of talkie apparatus. He is convinced that by installing the R.C.A. Photophone process, Twickenham Film Studios will have the advantage of the best possible system."

"Hagen – new script-writing and box office values."

"*To What Red Hell* scheduled to start shooting in July."

"Expected to startle the industry by reason of the knowledge and apparatus now at hand." (*K.W.*, 20 June 1929).

Thus, the silent film footage of *To What Red Hell* was scrapped in June and it was re-made during the next two months as a sound film. Tiffany was taking it for release as their first British quota film.

The Warner Bros. Contract: More Films for Twickenham:

The Warner Bros. contract:

During the middle of 1929, Julius Hagen won his first big contract with the British renting subsidiary of a major American company to make films. Warner Bros. needed to fulfil their 'Quota' liabilities as a British distributor under the requirements of the new legislation

Hagen was to make to six pictures for Warner Bros. at Twickenham Studios under his contract with them.

John V. Watson

This deal marked a defining moment for Julius Hagen; it enabled him to put the future of Twickenham Film Studios on a much more secure financial footing by having a contract to supply a regular number of films.

This was the first of many such contracts was able to secure over the next few years to make films mostly for the British renting subsidiaries of American film companies, such as Radio, Fox and United Artists.

In August 1929, the first film to be made for Warner Bros. was *At the Villa Rose* was announced; it was also the first production to be made by Twickenham Film Studios:

♦ *At the Villa Rose.*
Kinematograph Weekly reported in August:

"Hagen has secured *At the Villa Rose*, the fine detective story which gave the late Arthur Bourchier a capital stage role, and was filmed some years ago, very differently, by Stoll. Leslie Hiscott will direct a new talkie version in English; and a French talkie version is to be directed by Louis Mercanton. This subject is due to begin in September." (*K.W.*, 1 August 1929).

Adapted from a novel by A.E.W. Mason, the English version starred Northern Irish actor, Austin Trevor, in his screen début, as Mason's detective character, 'Inspector Hanaud'.

At the Villa Rose was the first of six films which Julius Hagen was to make for Warner Bros. to help fill their British 'Quota' requirements as a British film distributor.

The French language version was titled: *The Mystery of the Villa Rose* (French: *Le mystère de la villa rose*); it

44

was made by Les Établissements Jacques Haïk, and directed by Louis Mercanton and René Hervil. Léon Mathot starred as the detective called 'Langeac' instead of 'Hanaud'. The Twickenham Studios' personnel used to make this French version were: Camera - Basil Emmott, Set Designer - James A. Carter, Sound - Rex Haworth.

Both versions started filming in October, and finished in later November, were in the editing stages in the two languages. (*K.W.*, 5 December 1929)

Another Tenant Film Producer for Twickenham:

In September 1929, New Era started to make a film at St. Margaret's, Twickenham, a production made independent of Hagen, but using personnel from Twickenham Studios:

- ◆ *The Co-Optimists.*
On Monday 9 September 1929, Edwin Greenwood started work for New Era on the talking version of the famous "*Co-optimists*" entertainment.

The principals were Davy Burnaby, Laddie Cliff, Melville Gideon, Gilbert Childs, Stanley Holloway, Phyllis Monkman, Betty Chester and Elsa MacFarlane.

Twickenham personnel were used: Photography by Sydney Blythe and Basil Emmott, and Art Direction by James Carter.

The Co-Optimists was Britain's first talkie revue (and it was slated by the critics when it was first released).

French Sound Films made at Twickenham

Studios:

♦ The French language version of *At the Villa Rose* was titled *The Mystery of the Villa Rose* (French: *Le mystère de la villa rose*).

A French poster for *Le mystère de la villa rose*, the French film version of *At the Villa Rose*.

The film was made by **Les Établissements Jacques Haïk,** and directed by Louis Mercanton and René Hervil. Léon Mathot starred as the detective called 'Langeac' instead of 'Hanaud'.

Twickenham Studios' personnel were used to make

this French version were: Camera, Basil Emmott; Set Designer, James A. Carter; and Sound, Rex Haworth.

Jacques Haïk:

Back in February 1929, *Kinematograph Weekly* carried an item about him, stating:

"**Jacques Haïk**, who has been in the French Industry since 1910, has been made a Chevalier of the Legion of Honour by the President of the Republic. At that time he was in the Paris office of M. P. Sales. Since 1913 he has represented Western Import, which then imported the Keystone, Kay-Bee and Broncho films."

"He then successfully handled Universal, Selznick, and Warner outputs and produced several pictures, which have proved successful over here. His latest production, and (to the writer's mind) his best is ***The Soul of France*** which was Trade shown some time ago, and will probably have a West End run." (*K.W.*, 14 February 1929).

In July 1929, *Kinematograph Weekly* reported about another French film production arrangement at Twickenham:
"Another French tie-up is a contract with **M. Hugon**, of Paris, for two French talkies to be made at St. Margarets – one to be ***The Three Masks***. The Hugon units will occupy the studio for six weeks from August 19." (*K.W.*, 25 July 1929).

André Hugon (17 December 1886 – 22 August 1960) was a French film director, screenwriter and film producer. He was born in Algiers in 1886 which at that time was part of France. He directed some 90 films between 1913 and 1952.

The Three Masks (French title: *Les trois masques*) was released in France in November. Directed by Hugon, it starred Renée Héribel, Jean Toulout and François Rozet. It was France's first talking picture, and was made in Britain to take advantage of the better sound equipment at Twickenham Studios.

The *Kinematograph Weekly* report on 29 August 1929 confirmed that *The Three Masks* was the first French talkie.

To What Red Hell restarts with Sound:

By the end of July 1929, according to various issues of *Kinematograph Weekly* published in late July and early August, work on the talkie version of *To What Red Hell* was in "full swing", under the direction of Edwin Greenwood. (During the previous May, *Kinematograph Weekly* reported: Greenwood had signed a long-term contract with Julius Hagen to direct talking pictures for Twickenham Film Studios.)

By the beginning of August, Gillian Sande and Bramwell Fletcher had already "completed their sequences" and "Sybil Thorndike and Bramwell Fletcher had completed their speech sequences."

Filming was completed during the earlier part of August.

To What Red Hell: American rights sold:

Kinematograph Weekly reported on 22 August 1929:

" " *To What Red Hell* " - America Purchase for Record

'The Czar of Twickenham'. The History of Julius Hagen and the Film Empire he created at Twickenham Film Studios, from 1927 to 1938.

Sum".

"FRED BERNHARD (of Tiffany), who returned recently from America, announces the success of his journey. He has received from Tiffany-Stahl Productions of America a cable offering the sum of £75,000 for the American rights of Sybil Thorndike's first talkie production: *To What Red Hell*. This picture, it will be remembered, was made some time back as a silent picture, but, unfortunately, its completion coincided with the advent of talking films, and Mr. Bernhard was commended for his courage in deciding to scrap the picture. Production was commenced immediately on the new version, and so successful was the recording of Miss Thorndike and Bramwell Fletcher that Mr. Bernhard made a special visit to America in connection with its distribution."

"This is Miss Thorndike's first venture as a talkie star, and the results of the RCA recording of her voice have exceeded all expectations, and this actress, rightly described as England's greatest tragedienne, will doubtless draw many more thousands to the kinema than she has even been able to draw to the legitimate theatre."

"Bramwell Fletcher, who plays the leading supporting rôle in the picture, left last week for America to complete a contract recently signed with Al Woods, America's foremost theatrical producer, and there is little doubt that when his success in Tiffany's *To What Red Hell* is seen in America he will become a star of some magnitude in American film-producing studios."

Kinematograph Weekly further reported in the same issue, on 22 August 1929:

"St. Margaret's First".

"This is the first talking picture that has been made in the recently equipped Alliance Studios at St. Margaret's-on-Thames, and the results are a great tribute to the RCA method of recording, and the complete sound proofing of the studios."

"Edwin Greenwood produced both the silent and talking version at the studios of the Strand Film Co. at St. Margaret's, and this 100 per cent talkie is claimed to be the greatest drama ever produced in a British studio."

"The film is now completed and arrangements are being made for a West End premiere and season about the middle of September."

"It should be clearly understood that Tiffany-Stahl Productions of America is a separate organisation from Tiffany Productions of England. Although allied as regards to distribution of Tiffany-Stahl Productions, the controlling interest of Tiffany Productions is British."

To What Red Hell: London Premier and Trade Show:

Kinematograph Weekly, in their issue dated 12 September 1929, covered the London Premier of *To What Red Hell*, with several pictures published on page 56, and reported:
"Mr. Hagen produced the film for Mr. Bernhard (Tiffany)"
"John Greenwood wrote the entirely original music score. Greenwood was for some time stage conductor for Sir Thomas Beecham at Drury Lane."
"Greenwood's orchestra for *To What Red Hell* consists of fifty hand picked musicians from the Queen's hall orchestra."

To What Red Hell was Trade shown at midnight on 13 September 1929 at the Plaza, Piccadilly Circus, London West End. *Kinematograph Weekly*, on 24 October 1929, reviewed the

'The Czar of Twickenham'. The History of Julius Hagen and the Film
Empire he created at Twickenham Film Studios, from 1927 to 1938.

film stating:

> "RCA, full talking; synchronised, 90 minutes, "A"
> certificate".

> "Remarks: Story of a man falsely accused of murder and
> saved by the real murderer's, an epileptic's, confession.
> Average production."

> "Box Office Angle: Moderate booking on star and stage
> play's success."

> "Percy Robinson's play has been adapted in a straightforward
> manner, with some introductory scenes, and Edwin
> Greenwood's direction combines sound and silent
> techniques without titling. The story is a sordid one and
> fails to point any definite moral, while the action is slow
> and the general effect rather depressing. Its mere
> sensationalism will attract some audiences."

> "Acting: The construction of the film brings out the part of
> the mother in less sharp relief than in the play, so Sybil
> Thorndike has few opportunities. She is good when given a
> chance. John Hamilton as Harold and Bramwell Fletcher
> as Tim are both good, the former especially, considering the
> difficult nature of the portrayal and the theatricality of the
> part."

> "Production: The story develops very slowly, and the attempt
> to put over heart-rending scenes fails through over-
> emphasis and lack of balance. Edwin Greenwood has
> handled the difficult scenes attending the trial and the
> problems confronting the epileptic murderer fairly well."

> "In a prologue Sybil Thorndike hopes the audience will
> appreciate the picture, and points out that it is directed

against capital punishment. It cannot be said, however, to contribute much to that question."

"Sound Technique: There are no sub-titles, but minor scenes are mimed, while the others contain dialogue. The alternation is an irritating one, and occasionally gives one the impression that the apparatus has broken down. Speech comes over well. In a number of scenes the actors are rather too near the camera for sound and sight to maintain the illusion of reality. John Greenwood has composed a musical accompaniment which is used occasionally at places where silence would have been much more effective."

"Points of Appeal: The success of the play, the title, stars, and situations in a sensational melodrama."

To What Red Hell: The Silent Version was Trade shown in London on Monday, 6 January 1930 (11.15 a.m.) at a Private Viewing Theatre.

The Feather: Strand's fifth and final film is Trade Shown:

The Feather (1929), a synchronised sound version of C. M. Matheson's well-known novel, directed by Leslie S. Hiscott, it starred Jameson Thomas and the French actress, Véra Flory, in her only British film.

The Feather was Trade shown on Tuesday, 12 November 1929; *Kinematograph Weekly* reviewed the film stating:

"RCA synchronised, songs."

"Remarks: Unconvincing story with good atmosphere and minor characterisations."

'The Czar of Twickenham'. The History of Julius Hagen and the Film Empire he created at Twickenham Film Studios, from 1927 to 1938.

"Box Office Angle: Average quota booking."

"Good supporting characterisation, adequate production, a tuneful love theme, well plugged, and a fairly emotional appeal represent the best features of this unconvincing drama, which points no particular moral."

"Acting: Jameson Thomas interprets the part of Roger with a fair measure of success, but is not too happy during the unconvincing, emotional moments. Vera Flory makes a languid heroine, and is usually equal to the modest histrionic demands afforded by the rôle. Whether she actually sings it is difficult to say, but the lack of synchrony suggests that she is doubled."

"Production: Leslie Hiscott has certainly shown distinct improvement in this, his latest effort, and considering how difficult it is to unfold a story clearly when it is told in retrospect, he has certainly kept the continuity smooth."

"Sound Technique: The synchronised music is tuneful and appropriate, but the songs are occasionally out of synchrony."

"Settings and Photography: Technically, the picture is good..."

"Points of Appeal: The star, the music, and unsophisticated emotional appeal." (*K.W.*, 21 November 1929).

Fewer British Films being made:

In *Kinematograph Weekly*, 21 November 1929, P. L. Mannock reported:

"Fewer Films on the Floor:"

"British picture-making has undergone, during the past year, the difficult and uneasy transition from silent to talkies. This time 12 months ago, 19 features were in actual course of production on our studio floors."

"Every one of them was silent. At that time, not a single talkie had started, and very few of our executives foresaw the need for making them to the practical extent of getting good sound equipment."

"The Great Transition:"

"Today there is not a silent picture in production. The number of films in the making is fewer. But one or two projected subjects are hung up for floor space equipment; and at least two active studios will shortly be added to the list."

"Pictures Long Awaited:"

"The exhibitor, especially outside the big cities, still requires silent Quota pictures. .... But there still remain one or two films completed many months ago which I should like to see – without speech; and I imagine some showmen would also be interested."

Mannock added that currently in production were *Balaclava* ("– the famous charge wonderfully done at Aldershot on 31 October, 1928", *Young Woodley*, *Red Aces*, *Lady of the Lake*, *Warned Off* and *The Warning*. but he asked: "Where is *High Seas*, Denison Clift's B.I.P. melodrama?"

He closed, pointing out: "Talkies are already being made in considerably less time than silent films."

'The Czar of Twickenham'. The History of Julius Hagen and the Film Empire he created at Twickenham Film Studios, from 1927 to 1938.

No Julius Hagen/Twickenham films were mentioned as being made currently in Mannock's report. (*K.W.*, 21 November 1929).

The Second Film for Warner Bros.:

Kinematograph Weekly, 5 December 1929, reported: "Twickenham Sound Studios are now empty but I (the magazine's writer) would not be surprised if Julius Hagen finds a tenant for the next few weeks."

Kinematograph Weekly announced in the same issue:

"*The House of the Arrow* (to start) in January – A. E. W. Mason's further thriller of the detective Hanaud. Austin Trevor will again be seen in the rôle." A week later *Kinematograph Weekly* was announced: "Denis Neilson-Terry will be the leading man" instead of Trevor.

"Leading lady, Benita Hume whose talkie début in *High Treason* was so successful, has another good chance in *The House of the Arrow*."

"*The House of the Arrow* was dramatised for Dennis Eadie, whose lamentable death occurred during its West End run."

"Warner Bros. will distribute *The House of the Arrow*, as was the case with *At the Villa Rose*."

"Cyril Twyford is again adapting the dialogue for *The House of the Arrow*; informed that the picture will be made "in several languages"."

- *The House of the Arrow* was the second film to be made for Warner Bros. by Twickenham Film Studios.

- *The House of the Arrow*: a French language version was also made at Twickenham Film Studios, entitled *La Maison de la Flèche* (1930), once again produced by Les Établissements Jacques Haïk, directed by Henri Fescourt, with a script by Pierre Maudru, from A. E. W. Mason's novel, and, once again, starring Léon Mathot as the detective called 'Langeac' (instead of using the name of Mason's original character, 'Hanaud').

1929: The Second Year of the 'Quota' Act (1927):

258 British films were first shown during the year 1929.

This number is arrived at by using the data contained in *The British Film Catalogue: 1895-1970* by Denis Gifford, as follows:

08761: Closing Gifford Catalogue Number.
08503: Opening Gifford Catalogue Number.
  258: Total. An increase of 54 over the previous year's total of 204.

Some of these films were short subjects; the actual number of these shorts has not been determined.

1. 1930:
The Expectations of British

'The Czar of Twickenham'. The History of Julius Hagen and the Film Empire he created at Twickenham Film Studios, from 1927 to 1938.

Cinema Audiences in the 1930s:

As the 1930s opened, British cinema audiences had already come to expect to see two feature films when they made their regular visits to the cinema in those days.

A typical programme presented at the cinemas of Great Britain in those days would have consisted of:

- The main feature - a top feature film, usually with big box-office stars, typically running anywhere between 75 minutes (maybe less) and often much longer;
- A co-feature film, typically running anywhere between 60 minutes and over, **or** a second feature film, typically running 40 to 60 minutes;
- PLUS a newsreel (usually running 10 minutes);
- PLUS a short film (often a one-reel comedy, typically running 10 minutes or so, and/or a cartoon, with cartoons usually running 7 to 8 minutes;
- AND there would have been the advertisements and the trailers for the forthcoming feature film attractions.
- Consequently, a typical British film programme at the cinema could run some three hours, possibly more.

Note that the composition of the typical 1930s cinema programme and the running times of each of its component films as outlined above are not mandatory; they are simply examples.

With such a demand for film product to make up any cinema programme throughout the country, the reader can now appreciate the underlying reason why so many British films had to be made following the implementation of the 1927 'Quota' Act in

1928.

This practice of presenting a double-feature film programme in British cinemas continued to dominate the Industry up until the 1960s, but it did not really start to die out until the 1970s.

In the meantime, the production of the cheap second-feature film ('the programme filler') virtually came to a halt from the mid 1950s onwards; most significantly the American 60-minute series 'B-western' which did cease completely in 1953-54.

A final point: the double-feature film programme was NOT a British phenomenon at all; it was equally important to the American film industry, as well as to so many other countries, for example, to Australia.

2. 1930:
Sound Film Production Increases at Twickenham:
The Expansion of Sound in British Studios and Cinemas in 1930:

The production of sound ("talkie") films increased significantly in British studios throughout 1930; hardly surprising as the new technique was clearly "here to stay". Indeed, *Kinematograph Weekly* declared in late January that "**Talkies still booming**"!

Indeed, as a direct consequence of this boom, P. L. Mannock reported in *Kinematograph Weekly* on 6 February 1930, the

premiums demanded and achieved by studio owners for the rental
of floor space had grown substantially as the pace of British film
production increased under the overall necessity to meet the legal
requirements of the 'Quota' Act.

"Staggering Studio Rentals – Talkie Floor Space at a Premium".

"The rentals quoted for British talkie floor space are rather
staggering. £1,000 and £1,200 per week are figures asked several
times, and last week I heard of £1,400 per week being asked for a
single floor. It is certain that until fresh installations are made
these studio prices will be raised to even higher figures. Britain
must have more installations. The higher rates now current will
otherwise become prohibitive, and as our legal Quota of 1931
pictures will be about 100 subjects, it seems to me that whoever
buys and installs half a dozen recording units between now and
July is becoming a benefactor as well as making a sound business
move. (*K.W.*, 6 February 1930, page 34).

After all, sound film production **had** to keep pace with the
fast growing number of cinemas (or 'kinemas' as they were then
known) converting to sound. As *Kinematograph Weekly* confirmed
later that February, the installation of sound into cinemas was
increasing at a hectic rate:

"Progress of the Talkies".

"Western Electric installations in the British Isles now
number 552. Fifteen installations were opened last week." (*K.W.*,
20 February 1930).

The cost for the installation of sound equipment into
cinemas was certainly not a cheap capital investment, as is
illustrated by these three advertisements appearing in

Kinematograph Weekly during March 1930:

> "**An RCA Photophone for $1,475 will put your theatre in the front rank**". (*K.W.*, 13 March 1930, page 79).

> " **'Picturetone' Sound on Film and Sound on Disc £725**". (*K.W.*, 20 March 1930, page 20).

> "**RCA Photophone – Type F: £1,475 – Type C: £2,750 – Type B £3,350**" (*K.W.*, 20 March 1930, page 57).

1930:
Twickenham's In-House Film Productions:

Right from the very start of the year, Twickenham Studios was a major beneficiary of the quickening expansion of sound film production.

Twickenham announce they were to make eight of their own films in-house, and, as we shall see in the next section to follow, the studio was also to be host to another fifteen films to be made by various independent producers.

The following narrative now details all of the films Twickenham Film Studios that were announced to be made, and those that were actually made during 1930, as each of the events unfolded chronologically throughout the year as reported and described by *Kinematograph Weekly*:

January 1930:

On 2 January 1930, *Kinematograph Weekly* reported that an ambitious all-taking production was being prepared at Twickenham Studios:

'The Czar of Twickenham'. The History of Julius Hagen and the Film Empire he created at Twickenham Film Studios, from 1927 to 1938.

"Talkies from Twickenham:"

"Likely to be particularly busy during 1930 – ambitious programme is being prepared. Every film made by this company will be an all-talking production recorded on RCA Photophone."

"*At the Villa Rose* has just been completed – undoubtedly the most elaborate production that has ever been made at the Alliance Studios, and James Carter, Julius Hagen's clever art director has staged some really beautiful backgrounds ... Directed by Leslie S. Hiscott, photographed by Sidney Blythe and William Luff, and recorded by Leslie Murray on RCA Photophone. The cast is composed of well-known stage artistes, with the exception of Norah Baring who makes her debut in a "talkie"."

"A French version of *At the Villa Rose* was also made in conjunction with Etablissements Jacques Haik, and directed by MM (*sic* - meaning 'Messieurs') Mercanton and Hervil. Shooting continued day and night for several weeks, and thanks to a veritable triumph of studio organisation, both units achieved a successful and simultaneous conclusion."

"Immediately after the New Year, Twickenham Film Studios will commence on all-talking version of *The House of the Arrow*. Hiscott directing, James Carter, Basil Emmott with William Luff, and Leslie Murray recording. Dennis Neilson Terry will talk on the screen for the first time."

"Another film to be made in 1930 is *Lord Richard in the Pantry* – important negotiations now in hand with regard to the casting – Julius Hagen tells us to be ready for a big surprise."

The same issue of *Kinematograph Weekly* also reported that, for the renter United Artists (the British subsidiary of the American company), "... British sound productions are" (being)

61

"represented in *The Feather*, produced by the Strand Film Company, directed by Hiscott, and, for the sound synchronised accompaniment to the film W. T. Trytel (*sic*), is responsible." (William Trytel (1894-1964), frequently credited as W. L. Trytel, was a Dutch-born composer. He became the director of music at Twickenham Studios (circa 1929); Trytel later became a director on that company's board.)

Later in January, P. L. Mannock reported in *Kinematograph Weekly*:

"On Monday afternoon, I paid a visit Julius Hagen at Twickenham studios where A. E. W. Mason's *The House of the Arrow* is being made into a talkie for Warner Brothers. Leslie Hiscott was directing a scene between Dennis Neilson-Terry (as Hanaud) and Wilfred Fletcher. His make up was artistic, Benita Hume the leading lady, handsome library set designed by James Carter, Sydney Blythe photographing, and Cyril Stanborough, in charge of "stills". (*Kinematograph Weekly*, 23 January 1930).

In the following issue, P. L. Mannock reported further:

"Hagen's "*Hello Europe*"

"Hagen, now managing director of Twickenham Film Studios, hinted an indication to embark upon a £50,000 production, which is so novel that I must give him the fullest credit. Realising that the British home market cannot, at present, yield returns that justify the expenditure, Julius Hagen has cast his eyes further afield – across Europe. Pictures are already being made with French and German versions. "*Hello Europe*" will be the first multi-lingual super film revue; it will contain at least six languages: English, French, German, Italian, Swedish and Spanish. Not six separate versions but *one* film. Large portion to be made Twickenham, but would use foreign studios and settings, when it is not practical to bring Continental artistes to England. Vast production will occupy four months. Once his plans are fully made, Julius Hagen will leave himself free to trade with the biggest renting houses in all countries. *"Hello, Europe"* will neither be a Quota nor a Continental film, but it will be, nevertheless, a British picture, conceived by British brains and having its headquarters in a British studio." (*K.W.*, 30 January 1930, page 27).

February 1930:

During February, *Kinematograph Weekly* reported:

"Julius Hagen: Three Warner Talkies - Edward's first."

"Twickenham Film Studios are going to be very busy during 1930 on all-talking productions recorded on RCA." (*K.W.*, 20 February 1930).

"At the Villa Rose was excellently received lately. A French version was also made at the same time in conjunction with Jacques Haïk, directed by Mercanton and Hervil, starred Leon Mathot and Simon (e) Vaudry." (*K.W.*, 20 February 1930).

"The House of the Arrow has just been completed – the 2nd for Warner." (*K.W.*, 20 February 1930).

"A third big Twickenham all-talking feature scheduled for production in the near future is **Lord Richard in the Pantry**, the farcical comedy in which Cyril Maude made such a great success on stage. Richard Cooper, who made a successful talkie début in **At the Villa Rose**, has been assigned the lead role of Lord Richard, in which he should be immense. He has played the part all over the British Isles and Canada." (*K.W.*, 20 February 1930).

"All three Twickenham Film Studios' all-talking productions will be distributed throughout the British Isles by Warner Bros." (*K.W.*, 20 February 1930).

""Tedwards" New Subject:"

"Henry Edwards and Chrissie White are shortly to make a joint appearance on the sound floor at Twickenham. Edwards has a wonderful story entitled *The Man with a Million Pounds* which he himself has written and will direct."

<u>Note</u>: Henry Edwards was nicknamed "Tedwards" and Chrissie White was his wife. Their joint appearance on the sound floor at Twickenham was to be for the film *Call of the Sea*. As to the announcement of Edward's "wonderful story, *The Man with a Million Pounds*", it is unclear whether this story was ever made into a film, or, if it was made under a different title. (*K.W.*, 20 February 1930).

In the same issue, *Kinematograph Weekly* reported further news about the production of *Hello, Europe*:

"As already announced, there is also Julius Hagen's ambitious international revue, *Hello, Europe*, to be made in six languages – English, French, German, Italian, Swedish and Spanish – and will include song, dance, opera, ballet, drama, farce, circus, and some great spectacular scenes. Each of these six countries will express itself under local conditions and its own tongue, and although six languages will be employed, a clever device will link these tongues together so that *Hello, Europe* will appeal to every nation. (*K.W.*, 20 February 1930).

A week later that February, *Kinematograph Weekly* reported further news about the production of *Hello, Europe*:

'The Czar of Twickenham'. The History of Julius Hagen and the Film Empire he created at Twickenham Film Studios, from 1927 to 1938.

"*Hello, Europe* – announced a few weeks ago – has aroused the greatest interest and enthusiasm abroad. A scenario has been completed and Julius Hagen leaves almost immediately for the Continent, where he will confer with prominent showmen abroad ...". (*K.W.*, 27 February 1930, page 29).

March 1930:

During March, *Kinematograph Weekly* reported:

"Walter Forde to direct Twickenham production for Hagen – Julius Hagen has secured, by arrangement with Mr. W. Lott of Archibald Nettlefold Productions, the services of Walter Forde as director of *Lord Richard of the Pantry*, the all-talking version of the famous farce which he is producing for Warner Bros. First time Forde directs a farce. Richard Cooper has been cast and Barbara Gott is the only artiste engaged so far, as the amorous cook. The script is in the capable hands of H. Fowler Mear, who has been associated with Walter Forde in the script writing of all his successes." (*K.W.*, 27 March 1930, page 24, *British production*).

"Forde has just completed *The Last Hour*" (see below) "for Nettlefold Productions with Stewart Rome and Richard Cooper." (*K.W.*, 27 March 1930, page 24, *British production*).

"A French version of *Lord Richard of the Pantry* will also be shot at Twickenham simultaneously with the English version in conjunction with Établissements Jacques Haïk, whose *Mystère de la Villa Rose*, also made at Twickenham, has now been playing to capacity in Paris." (*K.W.*, 27 March 1930, page 24, *British production*).

"*Lord Richard of the Pantry* is scheduled for production during the second week of April." "Forde has influenza but is already convalescent." (*K.W.*, 27 March 1930, page 24, *British production*).

April 1930:

During April, *Kinematograph Weekly* reported:

"Shooting has begun on **Lord Richard in the Pantry** – the third successive all-talking production of Twickenham Film Studios for Warner Bros." (*K.W.*, 10 April 1930, page 29).

"In French, by Night."
"A **French version** is also being shot at Twickenham in conjunction with Établissements Jacques Haïk, under the direction of Grantham Hayes, Basil Emmott is chief cameraman, M. Rose sound engineer, and the cast is headed by Andree Lafayette, Henri Garat, and Baron-fils." (*K.W.*, 10 April 1930, page 29).

"**Call of the Sea** announced – Henry Edwards and Chrissie White talkie debuts - based on a story by Captain Frank Shaw." (*K.W.*, 17 April 1930, page 51).

"**Call of the Sea** – work on the story now in hand".
"**Hello Europe** – further progress towards the planning of Julius Hagen's big spectacular international revue". (*K.W.*, 24 April 1930, page 24).

May 1930:

During May, *Kinematograph Weekly* reported:

"Walter Forde completing **Lord Richard in the Pantry**."
"**Richard Cooper** in two recent products has given performances of outstanding merit; as a result he was signed up to a long term contract by Julius Hagen. **Lord Richard in the Pantry**, the well-known play, was purchased by J.H. for Richard Cooper." (*K.W.*, 1 May 1930, page 31).

"Julius Hagen announces **The Fires of Fate**, the fifth successive Twickenham Film Studios all-talking production for Warner Bros. Author of this play is Sir Arthur Conan Doyle, and

is based on his famous book, *The Tragedy of the Korosko*. Scheduled
for production in September, to be directed by Leslie Hiscott.
Negotiations in progress with a famous actor for the star role. "
(*K.W.*, 29 May 1930, page 35).

June 1930:

During June, *Kinematograph Weekly* reported:

"**Call of the Sea** – production begins on Monday (9 June
1930) – with Bernard Nedell, American actor – Leslie Hiscott
directs – for Warner distribution." (*K.W.*, 5 June 1930, pages 30-
31, *British production*).

"Richard Cooper, by arrangement with Julius Hagen, replaces
Billy Leonard in the Gaumont-British talkie comedy, **Bed and
Breakfast**, directed by Walter Forde." (*K.W.*, 5 June 1930, pages
30-31, *British production*).

"**Call of the Sea** - after a week of rehearsals, the first interior
episodes were begun on Tuesday, 10 June 1930." (*K.W.*, 12 June
1930, page 31, *British production*).

"Twickenham - **Call of the Sea** – Leslie Hiscott directing –
cameraman: J. Rogers – second week." (*K.W.*, 26 June 1930, page
51, *Pulse of the Studios*).

"**Call of the Sea** – tropical night-club set – Bernard Nedell,
Billy Milton, and Chili Bouchier." (*K.W.*, 26 June 1930, pages 53-
54, *British production*).

On 10 July 1930, *Kinematograph Weekly* reported:

"**The Call of the Sea** has just been completed." (*K.W.*, 10
July 1930, page 31).

July 1930:

During July, *Kinematograph Weekly* reported:

"*Lord Richard of the Pantry* – new star: Richard Cooper – Julius Hagen and Henry Edwards are rapidly establishing a reputation for turning out excellent British talking pictures." (*K.W.*, 17 July 1930, page 51).

August 1930:

During August, *Kinematograph Weekly* reported:

"Twickenham – confirmation that M. **Jacques Haik** had made French versions of *At the Villa Rose* and *The House of the Arrow* at Twickenham – F. Philip, publicity department, Twickenham Film Studios, Ltd." (*K.W.*, 28 August 1930).

September 1930:

During September, *Kinematograph Weekly* reported:

"*Brown Sugar* is to be modernised and made into a talkie by Julius Hagen, Warner's will handle it as a Quota film. Leslie Hiscott to direct the new version this month and Cyril Twyford is at work on the dialogue. Francis Lister is to have the leading male role." (*K.W.*, 4 September 1930, page 26).

"**Chili Bouchier** has just been signed up on a long term contract to the Twickenham Studios by Julius Hagen." (*K.W.*, 11 September 1930, page 26).

"Next Monday, 15 September 1930, *Brown Sugar* starts production, Leslie Hiscott directing, photography by Sydney Blythe, with Francis Lister, Celia Johnson, Helen Haye and Cecily Byrne. *Fires of Fate* will be the next production." (*K.W.*, 11

'The Czar of Twickenham'. The History of Julius Hagen and the Film Empire he created at Twickenham Film Studios, from 1927 to 1938.

September 1930, page 27).

"Twickenham – *Brown Sugar* – first week – Allan Aynesworth – talkie debut." (*K.W.*, 18 September 1930, page 57, *Pulse of the Studios*).

October 1930:

During October, *Kinematograph Weekly* reported:

"*Brown Sugar* cutting – Leslie Hiscott is in the throes of editing." (*Kinematograph Weekly*, 16 October 1930, page 57).

November 1930:

During November, *Kinematograph Weekly* reported:

"British talkies mean big business – Australia - *At the Villa Rose* premiere in Melbourne and Sydney." (*Kinematograph Weekly*, 6 November 1930, page 52).

"Twickenham: completed *Call of the Sea* and *Brown Sugar* – starting *Fires of Fate*." (*Kinematograph Weekly*, 6 November 1930, page 60).

A double-page advertisement published: "Julius Hagen and Henry Edwards present Henry Edwards and Chrissie White in their first talking picture, *The Call of the Sea* – from an original story by Capt. Frank Shaw, R.N. Trade Show: 19 November 1930, Wednesday, 11.00 a.m. - New Gallery Kinema." (*Kinematograph Weekly*, 13 November 1930).

December 1930:

During December, *Kinematograph Weekly* reported:

"Concurrent with *The Speckled Band* (with Raymond Massey), a new Sherlock Holmes story is being filmed at Twickenham, *The Sleeping Cardinal*. Hiscott plans to complete the film by Christmas." (*K.W.*, 11 December 1930, page 30, *British production*).

"Twickenham - *The Sleeping Cardinal* - Leslie Hiscott – Arthur Wontner – Sydney Blythe – second week." (*K.W.*, 18 December 1930, page 35, *Pulse of the Studios*).

Summary 1930: In-house Film Production at Twickenham Studios:

To summarise, throughout 1930 Twickenham Studios announced eight film titles for production:

1. *At the Villa Rose.*
2. *The House of the Arrow.*
3. *Lord Richard in the Pantry.*
4. *Hello, Europe.*
5. *Call of the Sea.*
6. *Brown Sugar.*
7. *The Fires of Fate.*
8. *The Sleeping Cardinal.*

Four films were filmed, completed and Trade shown:

* *At the Villa Rose.*
* *The House of the Arrow.*
* *Lord Richard in the Pantry.*
* *Call of the Sea.*

One film was in the editing stage as the year ended:

* *Brown Sugar.*

'The Czar of Twickenham'. The History of Julius Hagen and the Film Empire he created at Twickenham Film Studios, from 1927 to 1938.

Two films were in production as the year was ending:
- *The Fires of Fate.*
- *The Sleeping Cardinal.*

And:

- *Hello, Europe.*
  As can been seen above, several announcements were published during the first half of 1930, that preparations for the production of **Hello, Europe** were being made. But, this film never did get made. No reason appears to have been given, or announced, or published, as to why plans for its production never materialised. Thus, it is a Hagen "mystery".

Tenant Sound Film Producers at Twickenham: 1930:

The following fifteen films were made by independent film producers using rented floor space at Twickenham Studios during late 1929 and throughout 1930:

1. *Comets* was Trade shown that day, Friday, 31 January 1930, and a *K.W.* article stated that the film was produced at Twickenham Studios later the previous year. It was Alpha's first British talkie, directed by Sascha Geneen; a variety review featuring sketches from Heather Thatcher, Jack Raine, Randle Ayrton, Billy Merson, etc., and early film appearances by Charles Laughton and Elsa Lanchester. (*Kinematograph Weekly*, 31 January 1930).

- *Cockney War Stories* - February 1930 - "Twickenham – *Cockney War Stories*, directed by Castleton Knight, with Alf Goddard, John Hamilton and Johnny Butt; on second subject." (*Kinematograph Weekly*, 20 February 1930, page 49, item: '*The Pulse of the Studios*').

The film title announced by *Kinematograph Weekly* as then in production was actually the second of three stories made as a series of shorts produced by F. W. Baker for Butcher's Film Service at Twickenham Studios; they were based on war stories by readers of the *Evening News*.

The third of this series of three shorts was in production the following month - *Kinematograph Weekly* reported: "Twickenham – the third Cockney war story directed by Castleton Knight, with Donald Calthrop, Ambrose Thorne, Alexander Field, George Turner, and a talented mule." (*Kinematograph Weekly*, 13 March 1930).

Inspection of *The British Film Catalogue: 1895-1970* by Denis Gifford (David & Charles, 1973) that the series title was changed to *The Cockney Spirit in the War* (1930), and that the titles of the three episodes were:

2.   Episode 1: ***All Riot on the Western Front*** (22 minutes), with Donald Calthrop, Gordon Harker, Ambrose Thorne, Alexander Field, Melville Cooper.

3.   Episode 2: ***The Cockney Spirit in the War, No. 2*** (30 minutes), with John Hamilton, Donald Calthrop, Alf Goddard, Ambrose Thorne, Alexander Field.

4.   Episode 3: ***The Cockney Spirit in the War, No. 3*** (21 minutes), with Donald Calthrop, John Hamilton, Alexander Field, Hal Gordon, Ambrose Thorne.

Episodes 1 and 2 were combined as a 43-minute feature in July 1930.

Kinematograph Weekly reported the release date for **Cockney Spirit in the War** was to be 21 April 1930: "Talking - Butcher – (U) 1,990 feet – Donald Calthrop, Gordon Harker, Ambrose Thorne". (*K.W.*, 3 April 1930). This film would appear to be **All Riot on the Western Front** (22 minutes) as recorded by Denis Gifford.

5.   *The Last Hour:*
"At Twickenham: Lott Transfers Unit: Production of **The Last Hour** began on Monday, and Walter Forde is directing it, not at Walton, but at the St. Margaret's Studios, Twickenham, as an all-talkie, by RCA process. W. A. Lott, General Manager of Nettlefold Productions, has shifted the unit, after rehearsals, to its temporary home." (*Kinematograph Weekly*, 27 February 1930, page 29).

The Last Hour (1930) was first shown in June that year, running 85 minutes. Adapted from a play by Charles Bennett, the film was produced by Archibald Nettlefold, directed by Walter Forde, and starred Stewart Rome (as the villain), with Richard Cooper and Kathleen Vaughan.

The playwright, Charles Bennett, was also a successful screenwriter who wrote the screenplays for many of the famous films directed by Alfred Hitchcock, including **The Man Who Knew Too Much** (1934), **The 39 Steps** (1935), **Secret Agent** (1936), **Sabotage** (1936), **Young and Innocent** (1937), and Hitchcock's second American film, **Foreign Correspondent** (1940).

6.   *Spanish Eyes (The Spanish Rose):*
"Twickenham -   **The Spanish Rose** – director: G. B.

Samuelson – stars: Edna Davies, Donald Calthrop – first week." (*Kinematograph Weekly*, 20 March 1930, page 47: *The Pulse of the Studios*).

"Anglo-Spanish talkie – **The Spanish Rose** – G. B. Samuelson, sponsored by M. Carreras. (*Kinematograph Weekly*, 20 March 1930, page 49: *British Production*).

According to Denis Gifford in *The British Film Catalogue: 1895-1970*, this film was first shown in September 1930 under the title: **Spanish Eyes** (1930). Gifford states it was a bilingual musical feature film (at 71 minutes), made by Julian Wylie-Ulargui for MGM to release as a 'Quota' film to help fulfil its legal obligation as a British renter. Directed by G. B. Samuelson, it featured Edna Davies, Denis Noble, Donald Calthrop and Anthony Ireland.

7. ***Bedrock (Finding a Friend):***
"Twickenham - **Finding a Friend** – director: Carlyle Blackwell – Carlyle." (*Kinematograph Weekly*, 20 March 1930, page 47: *The Pulse of the Studios*).

According to Denis Gifford, *The British Film Catalogue: 1895-1970*, **Finding a Friend** was first shown in June 1930 under the title: **Bedrock** (1930). Gifford states it was a short feature film drama (running at 39 minutes), produced by Carlyle Blackwell for Piccadilly Films, which the company made for Paramount British to release as a 'Quota' film to help fulfil their legal obligation as a British renter. Directed by Blackwell, it featured Carlyle Blackwell, Jane Baxter and Sunday Wilshin.

It is most likely that **Bedrock** was filmed at night at

Twickenham Studios whilst *Spanish Eyes* was filmed at the same time during the day. Twickenham, at that time, had only one floor space. As we shall see, doubling up the use of the one sound stage to film two films concurrently - one by day; the other at night - was soon to become a common feature of film production methods at St. Margaret's, Twickenham.

8. *Beyond the Cities (Reparation):*
    "Twickenham - *Reparation* – director: Carlyle Blackwell – stars Carlyle Blackwell, Edna Best – Scenarist: Noel Shammon – first week." (*Kinematograph Weekly*, 22 May 1930, page 56: *The Pulse of the Studios*).

    By July, the title had changed from *Reparation* to *Beyond the Cities*:

    "Twickenham Studios – ... – *Beyond the Cities* (directed by Carlyle Blackwell) ... at present being produced at Twickenham, being made for Paramount." (*Kinematograph Weekly*, 17 July 1930, page 34).

    According to Denis Gifford, *The British Film Catalogue: 1895-1970*, *Beyond the Cities* (1930) was first shown in September that year. Gifford states it was a feature-length drama (at 70 minutes) set in Canada, produced by Carlyle Blackwell for Piccadilly Films (as was his *Bedrock*, *q.v.*), which the company made (once again) for Paramount British to release as one of their 'Quota' film commitments. Directed by Blackwell, it also starred Blackwell, and Edna Best and Alexander Field.

    Carlyle Blackwell (1884—1955) was an American silent film actor who made his film debut in the 1910 Vitagraph Studios production of *Uncle Tom's Cabin*,

75

directed by J. Stuart Blackton. He came to England in 1921 where he starred in **Bulldog Drummond** (1922), the first film adaptation of the fictional character created by H. C. McNeile under his pen name "Sapper". **Bedrock** and **Beyond the Cities** were Blackwell's only two sound films.

9. *The Eternal Feminine:*

"Twickenham Studios – ... – *The Eternal Feminine* (directed by Arthur Varney) ... at present being produced at Twickenham, being made for Paramount." (*Kinematograph Weekly*, 17 July 1930, page 34).

According to Denis Gifford, *The British Film Catalogue: 1895-1970*, *The Eternal Feminine* (1931) was first shown in February that year. Gifford states it was a feature-length romance (at 82 minutes), starring Guy Newall, Doria March and Jill Esmond. Produced, directed and story by Arthur Varney, the film was made by Starcraft for Paramount British to release as one of their 'Quota' film commitments. The screenplay was written by Hugh Broadbridge and Brock Williams.

Arthur Varney: Born Amerigo Serrao in Italy, he immigrated to the United States and became a naturalized citizen. In 1927, Varney directed the American silent drama, *Winds of the Pampas*, produced and starring Ralph Cloninger. Between 1930 and 1931, he directed six British films, all 'Quota Quickies', including the three short features with Herbert Mundin. Then, in 1933, he directed the American comedy, *Get That Venus*, starring Ernest Truex, Jean Arthur and Harry Davenport, for a very small independent company.

Arthur Varney Serrao was generally a mediocre film director, although his pocket-sized British comedy, *Almost a Divorce* (1931), running 58 minutes, produced by Herbert Wilcox, and starring Nelson Keys, Sydney Howard and Margery Binner, was, according to David Quinlan in *British Sound Films: The Studio Years 1928-1959* (Batsford, 1984), "highly regarded in some quarters (although not all)".

10. *Too Many Crooks:*

"George King gets Quota contract – the first quota picture to be made expressly for the Fox Film Company will be produced by George King." (*Kinematograph Weekly*, 5 June 1930, pages 30-31).

"Twickenham - George King – first talkie – starts at St. Margaret's Studios early next week." (*Kinematograph Weekly*, 12 June 1930, page 31).

"George King completes *Too Many Cooks* (*sic*) with Laurence Olivier and Dorothy Boyd. (*Kinematograph Weekly*, 26 June 1930, pages 53-54, *British Production*).

According to Denis Gifford, *The British Film Catalogue: 1895-1970*, *Too Many Crooks* (1930) was first shown in August that year; it was a comedy short feature (at 38 minutes), with Laurence Olivier (in his second film), Dorothy Boyd, A. Bromley Davenport and Arthur Stratton; and produced and directed by George King for Fox Film Company to release as one of their 'Quota' film commitments.

As at the time of writing, *Too Many Crooks* is listed as one of the "*75 Most Wanted*" lost films sought by the British Film Institute.

George King: *Too Many Crooks* was the first film directed by George King, who went on to direct several films up until 1949. King is probably best remembered today for the many films he made starring Tod Slaughter, that most famous theatrical "barnstormer": *Sweeney Todd: The Demon Barber of Fleet Street* (1936), *The Crimes of Stephen Hawke* (1936), *The Ticket of Leave Man* (1938), *The Face at the Window* (1939), and *Crimes at the Dark House* (1940). King also produced the other two Slaughter melodramas: *Maria Marten* or *Murder in the Red Barn* (1935), directed by Milton Rosmer; and *It's Never Too Late to Mend* (1937), directed by David MacDonald.

11. *Big Business*:

"Twickenham – *Big Business* – Fox – director: Oscar Sheridan – Frances Day, Jimmy Godden – first week." (*Kinematograph Weekly*, 28 August 1930, page 47, *Pulse of the Studios*).

According to Denis Gifford, *The British Film Catalogue: 1895-1970*, *Big Business* (1930) was first shown in September that year. A feature-length musical (at 75 minutes), starring Frances Day, Barrie Oliver and Virginia Vaughan, it was produced and directed by Oscar M. Sheridan for Fox Film Company to release as one of their 'Quota' film commitments.

12. *Leave It to Me*:

"George King busy at Twickenham making *Leave It to Me*, with Robin Irvine is the leading role." (*Kinematograph Weekly*, 11 September 1930, page 27, *British production*).

According to Denis Gifford, *The British Film Catalogue: 1895-1970*, **Leave It to Me** (1930) was first shown in October that year. A comedy short feature (at 40 minutes), starring Robin Irvine, Dorothy Seacombe and A. Bromley Davenport, it was produced and directed by George King for Fox Film Company to release as one of their 'Quota' film commitments. It was George King's second film.

13. *Who Killed Doc Robin?*:

"W. P. Kellino, "the experienced comedy director" will make several comedy burlesques, of about 4,000 feet length as part of Gainsborough Pictures' immediate programme – at Twickenham. The first begins next Monday and is **Doc Robin** with **Bull Rushes** and **Aroma of the South Seas** to follow." (*Kinematograph Weekly*, 9 October 1930, page 27).

"Kellino busy at Twickenham – **Who Killed Doc Robin?**" (*Kinematograph Weekly*, 23 October 1930, page 25).

According to Denis Gifford, *The British Film Catalogue: 1895-1970*, **Who Killed Doc Robin?** (1931) was first shown in February that year. A comedy short feature (at 36 minutes), starring Clifford Heatherley, Dorrie Deane and Dennis Wyndham, it was directed by W. P. Kellino, and produced by Gainsborough Pictures, which Ideal Films released as a 'Quota' film.

Ideal Films was a British film production and distribution company which started operations in 1911. In 1917, the company acquired the first of the Elstree Studios in Borehamwood from the Neptune Film

Company. However, the company was badly hit by the British Film Slump of 1924, which consequently led to it stopping the production of films altogether, but the film distribution arm continued. In 1927, Ideal Films was merged into the Gaumont British empire, and within which it continued to distribute films under its own banner until 1934. During its 23 years of operation, the company distributed almost 400 films and produced more than 80. Most of the films made by the company are now lost, but a few still survive.

14. *The Wrong Mr. Perkins*:
"Arthur Varney busy at Twickenham on his new film ***The Wrong Mr. Perkins*** with Herbert Mundin". (*Kinematograph Weekly*, 27 November 1930, pages 28-29, *British production*).

According to Denis Gifford, *The British Film Catalogue: 1895-1970*, ***The Wrong Mr. Perkins*** (1931) was first shown in January that year. A comedy short feature (at 38 minutes), starring Herbert Mundin, it was directed by Arthur Varney and produced by Harry Cohen for Starcraft; Fox Film Company released the film as one of its 'Quota' commitments.

15. *Immediate Possession*:
"Twickenham — ***Immediate Possession*** – Arthur Varney – Herbert Mundin – started." (*Kinematograph Weekly*, 18 December 1930, page 35, *Pulse of the Studios*).

"***Immediate Possession*** – Arthur Varney – Herbert Mundin – cutting." (*Kinematograph Weekly*, 8 January 1931, page 91, *Pulse of the Studios*).

"Arthur Varney has just finished shooting ***Immediate***

Possession at Twickenham, his third production for Fox Films." (*Kinematograph Weekly*, 29 January 1931, page 41).

According to Denis Gifford, *The British Film Catalogue: 1895-1970*, *Immediate Possession* (1931) was first shown in February that year. A comedy short feature (at 42 minutes), starring Herbert Mundin, it was directed by Arthur Varney, script written by Brock Williams and produced by Harry Cohen for Starcraft; Fox Film Company released the film as one of its 'Quota' commitments.

Herbert Mundin was an English character actor and comedian who was always immediately recognisable to cinemagoers of the 1930s by his distinctive jowled features and cheerful disposition. In *Picturegoer Weekly*, 12 November 1932, page 15, W. H. Mooring described Mundin as having "a front elevation like a query mark and a face like a cod-fish". *The Wrong Mr. Perkins* (1931) was one of a short series of British comedy featurettes (*Immediate Possession* was another) which were made by Harry Cohen's Starcraft company for Fox Film Company, the British film rental subsidiary (of the American, Fox Film Corporation), as a 'Quota' film to help Fox fulfil its legal obligation as a British renter. In late 1931, Herbert Mundin immigrated to America; he had just been given a long-term contract by Fox Film Corporation in Hollywood. He then appeared in a several distinguished American films, including *David Copperfield* (1935), *Mutiny on the Bounty* (1935, starring Charles Laughton and Clark Gable), Under Two Flags (1936, starring Ronald Colman, Claudette Colbert and Victor McLaglen), and *The Adventures of Robin Hood* (1938, starring Errol Flynn in the title role), in which Mundin played 'Much'; a part for which he is perhaps best remembered for today. Sadly, Mundin was killed instantly in a car crash at a street intersection in Van Nuys, California. He was just 40 years old.

Twickenham's Four Films Trade Shown during 1930:

The quality of the next four of Twickenham's film productions improved significantly; the first two were described as "excellent", and other two as "well acted" and "robust". The overall competence of the direction by Leslie Hiscott (of the first two films) had uniformly improved significantly. And, the sound recording and performance of all four films was also that much better; the dialogue was now "free from the usual mechanical accent", with the sound having "well-varied tonal qualities", and it was deemed "... doubtful, indeed, if recording and reproduction could have been much better."

February:

1. At the Villa Rose (1930)

A full-talking screen version of A. E. W. Mason's mystery thriller novel, directed by Leslie S. Hiscott, it starred Austin Trevor as 'Inspector Hanaud' and Norah Baring (now best remembered for portraying the female lead, in the Alfred Hitchcock thriller *Murder!* (1930).

It was the first film made for Warner Bros. under Hagen's contract to produce six 'Quota' pictures for the renter.

The film was Trade shown on Wednesday, 5 February 1930 at the New Gallery Kinema, Regent Street, London, W.1; *Kinematograph Weekly* reviewed the film stating:

'The Czar of Twickenham'. The History of Julius Hagen and the Film Empire he created at Twickenham Film Studios, from 1927 to 1938.

"Full-talking, RCA Photophone, 100 minutes, "U" certificate."

"Remarks: Excellent version of A. E. W. Mason's novel, well acted."

"Box Office Angle: Excellent general booking."

"Despite the fact that treatment is a trifle too detailed, this adaptation of A. E. W. Mason's novel is as good a picture of its kind as any other sent out from British or American studios for a long time ....."

"Acting: Norah Baring's tense acting as Celia gives life to the character without diminishing the mysterious effect of the plot, while Austin Trevor as Hanaud, whose detached calm rises suddenly at the end to anger when he denounces" the villain.

"Production: The story has been particularly well adapted, the problems arising from the murder being set out without undue mystification, and the final solution coming as a cleverly staged surprise." ... "Leslie Hiscott's direction is straightforward and sound throughout. It subordinates dialogue and camera work to the story, balances drama with light relief, and is marked by no neglect of opportunity. His achievement is one which he deserves congratulations."

"Sound Technique: Very occasionally indistinct, the dialogue comes for the most part very well indeed and is free from the usual mechanical accent. It is doubtful, indeed, if recording and reproduction could have been much better, except as regards volume.

"Settings and Photography: ... photography and lighting

are excellent."

"Points of Appeal: The excellent production will attract readers of the novel while appealing to others on the strength of the story and acting."

(*Kinematograph Weekly*, 13 February 1930, page 40).

March:

2. *The House of the Arrow (1930)*

A full-talking screen version of A. E. W. Mason's detective story, directed by Leslie S. Hiscott, it starred Dennis Neilson Terry, this time, as 'Inspector Hanaud' and Benita Hume, the British actress who later married the then major film star, Ronald Colman, in 1938.

It was the second film made for Warner Bros. under Hagen's contract to produce six 'Quota' pictures for the renter.

The film was Trade shown on Thursday, 20 March 1930 at the New Gallery Kinema, Regent Street, London, W.1; *Kinematograph Weekly* reviewed the film (on page 33) stating:

"Full-talking, RCA Photophone, 76 minutes, "A" certificate."

"Remarks: Excellent picturisation of A. E. W. Mason's detective story. Very well acted and produced."

"Box Office Angle: Very good general booking."

"Another success for Leslie Hiscott. An excellent and holding picturisation of A. E. W. Mason's story, showing a further adventure in the career of Hanaud, the French detective, of *At the Villa Rose* fame. Very good acting and production generally.

"Acting: Dennis Neilson-Terry is admirable as Hanaud, and suggests his French origin convincingly."

"Production: The story is too complicated to put in short synopsis form, but Leslie Hiscott handles it admirably, without trying to confuse the issues. There is sensible deduction here, and not just haphazard discoveries. The tension is held and the dénouement well concealed, until the final scene, without any "red herring trails". Characterisation, too, is good, as well as the personal direction of the artistes. Hiscott has made a sequence where no talking is required, and this is put over with telling effect."

"Sound Technique: Recording is excellent with practically no background, and well-varied tonal qualities.

"Settings and Photography: Most of the action takes place in the house, which is very well set and photographed."

"Points of Appeal: The excellence of the story and its origin. The strong cast, acting and character force of the production."

(*Kinematograph Weekly*, 27 March 1930, page 33).

Kinematograph Weekly reported that a French version of *The House of the Arrow* was also made at Twickenham in conjunction with Établissements Jacques Haïk; entitled *Mystère de la Villa Rose*, that film "has now been playing to capacity in Paris". (*K.W.*, 27 March 1930, page 24).

July:

3. *Lord Richard of the Pantry (1930)*

A full-talking screen version of the play by Sydney Blow and Douglas Hoare (1919, which was based on a novel by Martin Swayne), directed by former British silent film comedian, Walter Forde. It starred Richard Cooper, a British comedy actor who first appeared on the stage in 1913, and who started appearing in films in 1930; this was the third - or fourth - of the seven he made in his film début year.

It was the third film made for Warner Bros. by Julius Hagen.

The film was Trade shown on Thursday, 24 July 1930 at the New Gallery Kinema, Regent Street, London, W.1; *Kinematograph Weekly* reviewed the film stating:

A scene from **Lord Richard of the Pantry** showing Richard Cooper (as 'Lord Richard Sandridge') in bed with Barbara Gott (as 'the Cook').

"Full-talking, RCA Photophone, 89 minutes, "U" certificate."

"Remarks: A well acted farce of good quality adapted from the stage success."

"Box Office Angle: Good popular booking."

"A well-acted farce of good quality, adapted from the stage success, which takes some time to warm up, but once it gets going it is crisp and even, and leads to a succession of laughable *?final word missing?*". Richard Cooper is excellent in the leading rôle and is one of the main contributors to the picture's success. This is one of the few Quota pictures which deserves inclusion in any programme on its merits alone.

"Acting: Richard Cooper is a little stilted and screen-conscious during the opening stages, but he soon settles down and gives a performance which is a sheer delight."

"Production: Walter Forde, the producer, has been a bit laboured in his treatment of the opening scenes, and it is some time before the plot's really clear, but once the introductory episodes are over, the farce unfolds with an easy sweep. The characters are extraordinarily well drawn, there are many original touches of humour, and an appealing, yet unobtrusive, love interest."

"Sound Technique: The quality of the speaking voices are well above average, and nothing is lost in the

87

process of reproduction."

"Settings and Photography: There is an extraordinarily fine range of settings, interiors as well as exteriors, all of which are of fine quality. Sydney Blythe's camera work is excellent."

"Points of Appeal: Title, amusing story, good individual acting of a strong popular cast, and fine technique."

(*Kinematograph Weekly*, 31 July 1930, page 30).

The French Version: *Kinematograph Weekly* reported that a French version of **Lord Richard of the Pantry** would also be shot at Twickenham simultaneously with the English version in conjunction with Établissements Jacques Haïk. (*K.W.*, 27 March 1930, page 24). *Kinematograph Weekly* further reported that the French version would be directed by Grantham Hayes; Basil Emmott, the chief cameraman; M. Rose, the sound engineer; and the cast was to be headed by Andree Lafayette, Henri Garat, and Baron-fils. (*K.W.*, 10 April 1930, page 29).

November:

4. *The Call of the Sea (1930)*

A full-talking naval melodrama, directed by Leslie Hiscott, which returned to the screen two popular English favourites, Henry Edwards and Chrissie White (Edward's wife), of which this film was to become her last-but-one screen appearance.

It was the fourth film made for Warner Bros. by Julius Hagen.

'The Czar of Twickenham'. The History of Julius Hagen and the Film Empire he created at Twickenham Film Studios, from 1927 to 1938.

The film was Trade shown on Wednesday, 19 November 1930 at the New Gallery Kinema, Regent Street, London, W.1; *Kinematograph Weekly* reviewed the film stating:

"Full-talking, RCA Photophone, 66 minutes, "A" certificate."

"Remarks: Robust naval melodrama, which brings back to the screen two popular English favourites."

"Box Office Angle: Good average booking."

"Good old-fashioned robust naval melodrama which, although unpretentious, is well mounted and excellently recorded. The picture welcomes back two old favourites, Henry Edwards and Chrissie White, both of whom do well and strengthen the appeal."

"Acting: Henry Edwards gives an easy, breezy performance as the hero, and delivers his lines perfectly. Chrissie White is perhaps a little mature to play the rôle of the heroine, but nevertheless is quite charming, while Bernard Nedell makes a first-class villain."

"Production: The fact that this drama unfolds according to formula does not detract in any way from the quality of the entertainment, which is essentially popular in its appeal. There is plenty of action, a pleasing love interest, and a quiet vein of humour. Altogether a clean, refreshing feature."

"Settings and Photography: The scenes, mostly interior, are a little cramped, but they are appropriate, and quite a good atmosphere prevails."

John V. Watson

"Points of Appeal: Popular story, popular English co-stars, and robust atmosphere."

(*Kinematograph Weekly*, 27 November 1930, page 42).

To What Red Hell: Silent Version Trade Shown and Release:

In addition to the four new Twickenham's film productions, outline above, that were Trade shown during 1930, the silent film version of their 1929 film was also Trade shown in early January 1930:

* *To What Red Hell – The Silent Version* (1929); *Kinematograph Weekly* reviewed the silent version of the film stating:
"Tiffany. British. ('A' BBFC Certificate). Silent. 8,300 feet. 80 minutes. To be released April 1930."

"Remarks: Adaptation of Percy Robinson's sordid stage play, which was previewed as an all-talking film in our issue of 24 October 1929. The drama does not grip nor convince, and depends mainly on the success of the play and the strength of its cast for its pull."

"Production: The points which we criticised in our review of the talking version, the morbid and agonising nature of the theme, the absence of any definite moral, and the slowness of the unfolding, are just as apparent in the silent version, and will undoubtedly militate against the chances of the picture proving a safe, popular booking. The acting is quite good in the circumstances; Bramwell Fletcher is easily the best of the strong, popular cast, while a good atmosphere prevails."

"Points of Appeal: Sensational character of the drama, success of the stage play, the strong British cast, and

90

the fact that it fulfils quota requirements."

"<u>Box Office Angle</u>: Possible quota booking."

(*Kinematograph Weekly*, 9 January 1930, page 39).

On 7 April 1930, both the sound and the silent versions of *To What Red Hell* was going into release; *Kinematograph Weekly* commented:

"*To What Red Hell* – Release Monday, 7 April 1930 - Tiffany - "A" Certificate".

"Silent 8,300 feet: 80 minutes - Sound 8,256 feet: 90 minutes - Quota Registration No.: Br. 3,305".

"Adaptation of a play having a rather depressing theme, but possessing interest by its sensationalism and interplay of character."

"<u>Exploitation Suggestions</u>: It is difficult to suggest exploitation of the popular kind with this film, which demands subtle treatment even in the matter of putting it over. Lay stress upon arrest of innocent man, and the mother's anxiety for him, and, where possible, introduce the pros and cons of capital punishment, now being discussed by Police Commission."

"<u>Star Appeal</u>: No effort should be lost in making Sybil Thorndike's acting a big point, especially in the sound version. Bramwell Fletcher and John Hamilton are other important names.

(*Kinematograph Weekly*, 6 March 1930, *Putting over Coming Releases*).

To What Red Hell: Litigation:

John V. Watson

"Tiffany Productions Ltd (£5 nominal penalty) and British Exhibitor Films Ltd fined £75 and 25 guineas costs for failure to produce or acquire the required quota of British films during the year 1 April 1928 to 31 March 1929."

"*To What Red Hell* delay:

"The management expected to use this film as being sufficient to fill the quota for both companies."

"The company had spent about £14,000 upon the production. It had been delayed for a fortnight at a very vital time owing to an actor's illness, and at that time there was very great uncertainty owing to the talkie films boom. In fact, when the film was made nobody would take it for a period, and later in the year it had to be made into a talkie."

"Two versions made:

"Both a long and a short version of each were then made – the long silent 10,929 feet; the short silent 9,247 feet; the long talkie 11,722 feet, and the short talkie 8,256 feet. Tiffany's version was 5,500 feet. A. E. Davis, secretary to the company, said to the court that everything was to speed up *To What Red Hell* before March 31. They were going to use it for 1929-30.

(*Kinematograph Weekly*, 9 January 1930).

"*To What Red Hell* – synchronised silent version – King's Bench Division on 25 July 1930 Twickenham Film Studios, Ltd. sued Tiffany Productions, Ltd. of Wardour Street, London, W., the owners of the silent film, for the sum of £824, which was alleged to be due under the terms of a contact dated 13 June 1929, whereby the plaintiff undertook the synchronisation of the film."

'The Czar of Twickenham'. The History of Julius Hagen and the Film Empire he created at Twickenham Film Studios, from 1927 to 1938.

"It was agreed that RCA Photophone apparatus should be used. The work was duly carried out and the plaintiffs became indebted to the amount of £824 to the RCA Photophone Incorporated for certain royalties."

"Tiffany Productions, Ltd., maintained that this expense fell within the clause of their agreement with the plaintiffs whereby it was set out that Twickenham Film Studios, Ltd., were to receive remuneration amounting to £2,150 in respect of:

a)   The services of the producer, Mr. Greenwood.
b)   All rental and other payments for (1) the use of the studios; (2) the use of the sound recording and reproducing apparatus, and all equipment, no matter how long the work would take.
c)   All services rendered to the plaintiffs, for example, the cutting and editing of the film.
d)   Cost of the scenario and treatment."

"His Lordship, giving judgement, said that in his view the payment of £824 to the Photophone Company, though it has been as described as a royalty, was a payment for the use of the Photophone apparatus. It fell within the clause of the agreement between the parties as to the remuneration of the plaintiffs."

"The defendants were not liable to pay this sum and there would be judgment in their favour, with costs."

(*Kinematograph Weekly*, 31 July 1930, page 26).

Other Events at Twickenham Studios during 1930:

"Twickenham Fire".

"Fire originated in a dressing-room connected with the studio, which was not subject to inspection under the Factory Acts."

(*Kinematograph Weekly*, 17 April 1930, page 25).

"Twickenham Annual Outing".

A photograph of the event "shows Mr. and Mrs. Hagen, Leslie Hiscott, Basil Emmott, Sydney Blythe, Richard Cooper, Jack Harris, Jimmy Carter, Billy Luff and Baynham Honri. Outing to be annual event."

This was the first annual outing of the Twickenham Film Studios staff, held at Marlow, Buckinghamshire, on the 6th July 1930.

(*Kinematograph Weekly*, 10 July 1930, page 31).

"Twickenham Studios - A big extension is proposed".

"Julius Hagen's plans will result in doubling the present production capacity."

(*Kinematograph Weekly*, 17 July 1930, page 34).

"Twickenham – Impending Changes".

"The board of Twickenham Film Studios, Ltd., is likely to be reconstructed in the immediate future. JH not in a position to make any announcement on the matter ..."

Leaves "JH as managing director of the most important independent British production concern."

(*Kinematograph Weekly*, 20 November 1930, page 31).

1930: The British Film Industry: Trends and Other Events throughout the Year:

The generally poor standard of 'Quota' films was a continual complaint made by various British film industry bodies throughout the year:

"Low Quality Quota Films Denounced".

(*Kinematograph Weekly*, 16 January 1930, page 59).

"C. E. A. – those terrible quota pictures".

Note: C. E. A. stands for the Circuit Exhibitors' Association.

(*Kinematograph Weekly*, 23 January 1930).

**"Breakdown of the Quota – C. E. A. demands revision
of the Act."**
(*Kinematograph Weekly*, 13 March 1930, page ii).

**"British production – unfulfilled boom prophecies –
"dud" Quota films."**

(*Kinematograph Weekly*, 16 October 1930, page 56).

In other words, the 1927 'Quota' Act was seen to have
created an economic incentive for cheap British second features.
This view was indeed true.

How British films were created was also seen as an obstacle
to any semblance of quality of film production:

**"British production: contempt for the scenario – script
neglect still rife – the stage-play complex."**

The last comment in the quote referred to the fact that so
many British 'Quota' films were adaptations of stage plays, which
tended to be stilted, to say the least.

(*Kinematograph Weekly*, 20 November 1930, page 30).

John V. Watson

Nevertheless, there was a view, at least in some quarters, that British film production should be increased further:

"Increasing the Quota".

(*Kinematograph Weekly*, 24 July 1930, page 55).

However, the charge of lack of quality could not be levelled at the four films which Twickenham Films Studios had completed production in 1930.

1930: The Third Year of the 'Quota' Act (1927):

153 British films were first shown during the year 1930.

This number is arrived at by using the data contained in *The British Film Catalogue: 1895-1970* by Denis Gifford, as follows:

08915: Closing Gifford Catalogue Number.

08762: Opening Gifford Catalogue Number.

153: Total. A decrease of 105 films against the previous year's total of 258.

Some of these films were short subjects; the actual number of these shorts has not been determined.

Thus, there was certainly a setback of the number of British films made overall in 1930, compared to the previous year, but, as we shall see, this was temporary.

3. 1931:
A Major Year for Hagen at Twickenham Studios:

The year of 1931 started off well for Julius Hagen and for Twickenham Studios.

Julius Hagen's new Contract at Twickenham Film Studios:

Julius Hagen was appointed managing director of Twickenham Film Studios for two years from 1 January 1931, at a salary of £140 a week, plus expenses.

Leaving aside the additional payment of his expenses, the level of the salary paid to Julius Hagen per annum, at £7,280, was enormous by the standard of what the average wage was paid in 1931. In contrast, it would be reasonably safe to assume that the average salary paid to "the man in the street" that year would have been around £200 per annum, i.e. £4 per week, if indeed it was as high as that. (And note that, for once, this author makes an assumption!)

The reader should also consider the global economic situation of the early 1930s, and how this may well have affected the level of wages in Great Britain then. "The stock market crash of 1929 precipitated a global recession. The United States was particularly badly affected by the stock market crash because of the growth in credit in the years leading up to it. The United Kingdom was more insulated because it had experienced no real credit boom in the 1920s. In fact, the United Kingdom was already in a prolonged economic stagnation of low growth. Because the UK economy relied heavily on trade, the decline in global demand, hit the UK economy, and with lower exports, the UK economy went into recession. 1931 was particularly damaging, with real GDP falling 5%." (GDP means Gross Domestic Product).

(Internet source quoted: http://www.economicshelp.org/blog/7483/economics/the-uk-economy-in-the-1930s/).

As the reader will see later, the high level of salaries paid to Julius Hagen and to his fellow directors of Twickenham Film Studios would come home to haunt them in a few years time.

January 1931:
Production Expands at Twickenham Studios:

Twickenham Studios applauded itself in its advertisement published in *Kinematograph Weekly* in early January, and, at the same time, announced it had a new major contract to make a programme of six films for another renting (or distribution) company (Woolf & Freedman Film Service):

"**Twickenham advertisement**: Twickenham have achieved 6 great pictures for Warner Bros. – will achieve 6 super features for W. & F. – first *Alibi*. Julius Hagen, Managing Director, Twickenham Film Studios."

(*Kinematograph Weekly*, 8 January 1931, pages 38-39).

Later in the same issue of *Kinematograph Weekly*, details of the contract that Hagen had gained from W. & F. were outlined:

"W. & F.'s new programme – three studios producing for distribution – C. M. Woolf, managing director has entered into contracts with Gainsborough Pictures, British and Dominions

Film Corporation, Ltd., Leslie Henson and Firth Shephard (Leslie Henson's partner), and the Twickenham Film Studios to produce a large number of pictures, the majority of which will be handled by the W. and F. organisation. ....."

(*Kinematograph Weekly*, 8 January 1931, page 118).

Woolf & Freedman Film Service: a British film distributor founded by the film producer C. M. Woolf, and which operated from 1919 to 1934. The company distributed more than 140 films over this 15-year period. In 1935, Woolf formed a new company, General Film Distributors. Some of Alfred Hitchcock's were produced by Gainsborough Pictures and distributed by Woolf & Freedman, including *Downhill* (1927, with Ivor Novello) and *Easy Virtue* (1928, with Isabel Jeans).

In the same issue of *Kinematograph Weekly*, progress of Twickenham's production programme was reported:

"*Sleeping Cardinal* - filming completed, film is being assembled".

"*Alibi* is scheduled to go into production on Monday, 19 January 1931".

(*Kinematograph Weekly*, 8 January 1931, page 100).

The Sleeping Cardinal was the last of the six films that were made by Twickenham for distribution by Warner Bros.

Alibi was the first of the six 'super features' to be made by Twickenham for distribution by W. and F.

The following week, *Kinematograph Weekly* reported:

"Julius Hagen has persuaded Sir John Martin Harvey to

99

appear in *The Lyons Mail*."

(*Kinematograph Weekly*, 15 January 1931, page 30).

Sir John Martin-Harvey (1863–1944) was one of last great romantic actors of the English theatre. He joined Sir Henry Irving's famous Lyceum Theatre company in 1882. Martin Harvey did appear in a few British silent films; *The Lyons Mail* (1931) was to be his first and only British sound film. He had appeared in the stage version from 1927 to 1930.

The Lyons Mail was to be the second of the six films Twickenham was contracted to make for W. & F.

Later that January, *Kinematograph Weekly* reported an Australian success for Twickenham:

"*The House of the Arrow* – handled in Australia by B.D.F. was billed as a "b" feature for its Melbourne premier at the State Theatre, with Paramount's musical-comedy – *Let's Go Native* – at the head of the programme. In the majority of cases it was given Press prominence in the laudatory critiques."

(*Kinematograph Weekly*, 22 January 1931, page 40).

Note: *Let's Go Native* (1930) was an American musical comedy made by Paramount, starring Jack Oakie and Jeanette MacDonald, and directed by Leo McCarey.

In the last issue of *Kinematograph Weekly* in January, P. L. Mannock reported about the filming of the next production at Twickenham:

"Shooting on *The Lyons Mail* (for W. and F. Distribution) is progressing well. 'Sir John Martin Harvey wears the same tattered, faded cloak that Sir Henry Irving wore in the same rôle some forty years ago, and the knife he uses was also brandished by Irving on many occasions on the stage. Thus is the property of the greatest actor of one generation handed down to the greatest actor of the next, to be used in the most modern of artistic mediums' ".

"*The Lyons Mail* - alteration to the cast: Michael Hogan will play the rôle originally assigned to Henry Mollison."

"*The Lyons Mail* - The 'tramp' turned out to be none other than George Moore Marriott – Choppard, the villainous innkeeper."

Note: **George Moore Marriott** is of course Moore Marriott, one of the three members of the Will Hay/Graham Moffatt/Moore Marriott famous partnership, who appeared in several successful British comedies in the 1930s, including *Oh, Mr Porter!* (1937) and *Ask a Policeman* (1939).

(*Kinematograph Weekly*, 29 January 1931, page 41).

February 1931:

Alibi, with Austin Trevor was in its third week of filming; Leslie Hiscott directing, Sydney Blythe photographing.

(*Kinematograph Weekly*, 19 February 1931).

The Sleeping Cardinal was Trade shown in London on Friday, 27 February 1931 at the Leicester Square Theatre.

(*Kinematograph Weekly*, 26 February 1931).

March 1931:

An advertisement in *Kinematograph Weekly* stated: *"The Sleeping Cardinal* played to phenomenal business at the Leicester Square Theatre" in London's West End.

(*Kinematograph Weekly*, 12 March 1931).

"Alibi is now completed at Twickenham. One of the biggest sets ever was constructed at Twickenham for the lounge hall of an English country mansion. Two additions to the cast: Mary Jerrold and Ronald Ward, who replaces Leslie Perrins."

(*Kinematograph Weekly*, 12 March 1931, page 59).

April 1931:

An advertisement in *Kinematograph Weekly* stated:

"Julius Hagen presents Constance Carpenter in *Brown Sugar*, with Helen Haye, Cecily Byrne, Eva Moore, Chili Bouchier, Francis Lister, Allan Aynesworth, Gerald Rawlinson, Wallace Geoffrey, and Alfred Drayton."

"London Trade Show: Friday, 17 April 1931 at the New Gallery Kinema."

"A Twickenham Film Studios Production."

(*Kinematograph Weekly*, 9 April 1931).

P. L. Mannock, *Kinematograph Weekly* reported:

"Sydney Blythe signed long-term contract with Julius Hagen to become a member of the permanent staff at Twickenham Film Studios. It will be remembered that Sydney Blythe has, by courtesy of New Era, been responsible for the camera work on all the recent Twickenham successes – including *At The Villa Rose*,

The House of the Arrow, Lord Richard in the Pantry, The Call of the Sea and *The Sleeping Cardinal*. He has also shot three more films which have yet to be Trade shown – viz. *Brown Sugar, The Lyons Mail* and *Alibi*".

(*Kinematograph Weekly*, 9 April 1931, page 43).

P. L. Mannock in *Kinematograph Weekly* reported:

"Julius Hagen has just concluded negotiations for *Splinters in the Navy* to be one of the six 1931 Twickenham subjects for distribution by W. and F."

"Practically the entire cast of the original *Splinters*. 'Hagen has the good fortune to secure Walter Forde by arrangement with Gainsborough Pictures, Ltd., to direct this picture'. Shooting on *Splinters in the Navy* is scheduled for July."

(*Kinematograph Weekly*, 16 April 1931, page 55).

Splinters (1929) was a British musical comedy based on the stage revue, *Splinters*. This revue told the story of the founding of the concert party, *Splinters*, which was formed by a group of British soldiers in France in 1915, during the Great War.

"*Black Coffee* – Henry Edwards has promptly acquired the talkie rights, which opened at the St. Martin's last Thursday. 'Mr. Edwards will make the film version at the Teddington studios, lately acquired by his new syndicate. Work on the reconstruction is going well ahead, and the floors will be ready during the summer'."

(*Kinematograph Weekly*, 16 April 1931).

As events turned out, *Black Coffee* was not to be made at

Teddington studios; it was actually filmed at Twickenham instead.

P. L. Mannock, *Kinematograph Weekly*, reported:

"W. P. Films, Ltd. have chosen as their next subject an entirely original story by Guy Newall and John McNady, entitled *The Rosary*."

"Goes into production at Twickenham studios this week, during the week commencing Monday, 27 April 1931."

"Directed by Guy Newall; it will be his first talkie direction since the George Clark days."

"The cast were booked through Sidney Jay."

"James Carter: art direction; Basil Emmott: camera; and Cyril Stanborough: stills."

"Tune of a well-known song will be introduced and will be adapted by Noel Gay."

(*K. W.*, 23 April 1931, page 61).

George Clark (1888-1946) was a British film actor and film producer of the silent era. For many years, Clark worked with the British star Guy Newall, who he had met during the First World War. They founded Lucky Cat Films and later George Clark Productions, securing a distribution arrangement with the larger Stoll Pictures. After first working at a studio in Ebury Street, in

Central London, they raised finance to construct Beaconsfield Studios; work began in 1921. The new studio opened the following year, but after being hit by the Slump of 1924, it remained mostly inactive for the rest of the decade. Clark sold the studios to the British Lion Film Corporation in 1929.

P. L. Mannock, *Kinematograph Weekly*, reported:

"Harry J. Revier directs Leslie Fuller in **Bill's Legacy** at Twickenham. Work began last Saturday, 25 April 1931."

(*K. W.*, 30 April 1931, page 56).

May 1931:

Kinematograph Weekly reported throughout the month:

"Shooting of **The Rosary** is up to schedule and will be completed within the next week."

(*K. W.*, 7 May 1931, page 35, P. L. Mannock).

"**Rodney Steps In** – Arthur Varney to direct at Twickenham – he began the first scenes yesterday, Wednesday, 13 May 1931 – Richard Cooper, Elizabeth Allan, Leo Sheffield, Melville Cooper, Walter Piers and John R. Turnbull."

(*K. W.*, 14 May 1931).

"Julius Hagen has signed up Elizabeth Allan on a long-term contract with Twickenham Film Studios at the end of the run of *Mr. Faintheart*, the Shaftesbury Theatre success, in which she is now appearing. She began her talkie career at Twickenham, under Leslie Hiscott, who cast her in a small part in **Alibi**. She has recently played opposite Frank Lawton in **Michael and**

Mary, and she will probably play the ingénue role in the forthcoming Twickenham W. and F. production of *Black Coffee*".

(*K. W.*, 14 May 1931).

"Adrianne Allen (not so busy recently) cast as the leading lady in *Black Coffee* – starts immediately after Whitsun".

(*K. W.*, 21 May 1931, P. L. Mannock).

"Guy Newall has been signed up to a long-term contract by Julius Hagen to direct films at Twickenham – he has recently finished directing his first talkie *The Rosary* at Twickenham for W.P. and is now at work on *Rodney Steps In* for Fox at Twickenham."

(*K. W.*, 21 May 1931).

"Harry Cohen, Fox production manager in this country, is now busy supervising two new pictures *Rodney Steps In* at Twickenham and *The Professional Guest* at Walton-on-Thames."

(*K. W.*, 21 May 1931).

"Twickenham – *Rodney Steps In* (Fox) – Guy Newall: director – second week".

(*K. W.*, 21 May 1931, page 55, *Pulse at the Studios*).

"*Black Coffee* - Leslie Hiscott has begun footage – Sydney Blythe: camera; Baynham Honri: recording; and Jack Harris: film editor."

(*K. W.*, 28 May 1931, pages 47 and 48, P. L. Mannock).

June 1931:

Kinematograph Weekly reported throughout the month:

"Julius Hagen announces that he has purchased the rights of
W. J. Makin's successful novel, *Murder at Covent Garden*, to
be the fourth of the six 1931 Twickenham supers for W. and F.
Murder at Covent Garden will go into production shortly after
completion of *Splinters in the Navy*, which is scheduled for
next month (July 1931). Meanwhile, *Black Coffee* is shooting."

(*K. W.*, 18 June 1931, page 41, P. L. Mannock).

"Twickenham – *Black Coffee* – Leslie Hiscott (director) –
Austin Trevor, Adrienne Allen (cast) – Sydney Blythe (camera) –
third week."

(*K. W.*, 25 June 1931, pages 49, *Pulse of the Studios*).

Advertisement published in *Kinematograph Weekly*:

"Twickenham Film Studios Ltd., St. Margaret's,
Twickenham."

"Last week's record: (in 4 London cinemas):
    Capitol – *Alibi*
    Marble Arch – *The Lyons Mail*
    New Gallery – *Brown Sugar*

    Stoll, Kingsway – *The Sleeping Cardinal*".

"Will shortly present – *Black Coffee*."

"In preparation:
    Splinters in the Navy – directed by Walter Forde.
    Murder in Covent Garden – W. J. Makin's

successful novel.
Will be distributed by W. & F. Film Service Ltd.

(*K. W.*, 25 June 1931, pages 52 and 53, *Advertisement*).

"Twickenham Films - Increase in Output - Julius Hagen's success."

Alibi – 1ˢᵗ W. & F. release.

Black Coffee – great success at the Capitol for its pre-release – 2ⁿᵈ W. & F. release.

Splinters in the Navy – 3ʳᵈ W. & F. release.

Murder in Covent Garden – 4ᵗʰ W. & F. release.

The Lyons Mail was pre-released at the Marble Arch Pavilion".

"Critics were unanimous in acclaiming Sir John Martin Harvey's performance in the famous dual rôle" (in *The Lyons Mail*).

"Worth noting that recently Twickenham Film Studios, Ltd., created a record for an independent company by having four of their productions running concurrently in the West End. In the same week, *The Lyons Mail* headed the bill at the Marble Arch Pavilion, *Alibi* was featured at the Capitol, *The Sleeping Cardinal* was given a second pre-release at the Stoll, and *Brown Sugar* at the New Gallery."

"Twickenham's Technical Staff headed by James Carter (art director), Sydney Blythe (camera), Basil Emmott (camera), Cyril Stanborough (stills department), Baynham Honri (sound) and Jack Harris (film editor)."

'The Czar of Twickenham'. The History of Julius Hagen and the Film Empire he created at Twickenham Film Studios, from 1927 to 1938.

"Guy Newall was recently handed a contract to direct films at Twickenham."

"Richard Cooper (already one of the best-known names in British films), and Elizabeth Allan, a promising ingénue, are also under contract" at Twickenham Film Studios.

(*K. W.*, 25 June 1931, page 55).

July 1931:

Kinematograph Weekly reported throughout the month:

"Leon M. Lion is to make his talkie debut this week in ***Chin Chin Chinaman***, a short subject which Guy Newall is to direct next week at Twickenham. It is from a one-act play by Percy Walsh, which played to great success at the Coliseum a short while ago. Elizabeth Allan in the feminine lead."

(*K. W.*, 2 July 1931).

"***Splinters in the Navy*** – the third of the Twickenham-W. and F. six, is scheduled to commence on 13 July. Walter Forde to direct."

(*K. W.*, 9 July 1931, pages 52 and 53, P. L. Mannock).

"Twickenham:

Splinters in the Navy – Walter Forde – Sydney Howard – starting; interiors.

Chin, Chin, Chinaman – Guy Newall – Leon M. Lion – Basil Emmott - completing.

(*K. W.*, 16 July 1931, *Pulse of the Studios*).

John V. Watson

"Walter Forde is making rapid progress with **Splinters *in the Navy*** – weather permitting, the later half of this week will be devoted to exteriors at Grays, in Essex, where special naval facilities are being afforded. Chief worry – the Twickenham unit containing their mirth on the sound stage while Sydney Howard does his stuff."

(*K. W.*, 23 July 1931, page 57, P. L. Mannock).

"Arthur Wontner is likely to go to Hollywood towards the end of the year."

(*K. W.*, 30 July 1931, page 39, P. L. Mannock).

"Arthur Wontner has been signed up by Julius Hagen to make at least one more picture before he departs. He will star in ***Jack o'Lantern***, the successful novel by George Goodchild."

(*K. W.*, 30 July 1931, page 39, P. L. Mannock).

"Leon M. Lion: the last of the six Twickenham-W. and F. supers will be a film version of **The Chinese Puzzle**, the famous play by Leon M. Lion and Marian Bower. Guy Newall will direct."

(*K. W.*, 30 July 1931, page 39, P. L. Mannock).

"Dennis Neilson Terry has been assigned the lead role in **Murder at Covent Garden**, directed by Leslie Hiscott. H. Fowler Mear is now busy on the script.

(*K. W.*, 30 July 1931, page 39, P. L. Mannock).

August 1931:

Kinematograph Weekly reported throughout the month:

'The Czar of Twickenham'. The History of Julius Hagen and the Film Empire he created at Twickenham Film Studios, from 1927 to 1938.

"Anne Grey, now completing her fifth star part since the beginning of the year, has been signed by Julius Hagen to co-star with Dennis Neilson Terry in *Murder at Covent Garden*."

(*K. W.*, 13 August 1931, pages 49 and 51, P. L. Mannock).

"*Splinters in the Navy* has now been completed. Wilfred Temple and Alexander Field were recent additions to the cast."

(*K. W.*, 13 August 1931, pages 49 and 51, P. L. Mannock).

"*Chin Chin Chinaman,* a short subject, has recently been completed at Twickenham. As a result of his clever performance in it, George Curzon has been placed under contract at Twickenham Film Studios. Curzon has a big reputation on the stage, and was particularly successful as Captain Hook in last year's *Peter Pan*. He will play a leading part in *Murder at Covent Garden*, the next Twickenham film."

(*K. W.*, 13 August 1931, pages 49 and 51, P. L. Mannock).

"*Splinters in the Navy* – Walter Forde's weather luck - his schedule for making scenes on a battleship coincided with the only three "brilliant sunshine" days the country has enjoyed in the last month."

(*K. W.*, 20 August 1931, page 53, P. L. Mannock).

September 1931:

Kinematograph Weekly reported throughout the month:

"Next Monday (14 September 1931) shooting starts on *Jack O'Lantern*. Script by Harry F. Mear. Play lately had a brief run in the West End."

111

John V. Watson

(*K. W.*, 10 September 1931, pages 44 and 45, P. L. Mannock).

"This week the final footage of ***Murder in Covent Garden*** will be completed. Tonight (Thursday, 10 September 1931), by special permission, a number of scenes will be made inside Covent Garden Opera House itself, under Leslie Hiscott's direction. Early this week an entire street was erected and burned down in the studio for the picture."

(*K. W.*, 10 September 1931, pages 44 and 45, P. L. Mannock).

(Walter) "Forde's two heroines – Gillian Lind and Jane Welsh, two popular West End actresses to appear in ***Jack o'Lantern***."

(*K. W.*, 17 September 1931, pages 55-56, P. L. Mannock).

"Walter Forde's seven – creating a record in the number of talkies directed by one person - ***Third Time Lucky***, ***The Ringer***, ***The Ghost Train***, ***Splinters in the Navy***, ***Jack o'Lantern***, and ***Lord Babs***."

(*K. W.*, 24 September 1931, pages 56-57, P. L. Mannock).

Note that the writer, P. L. Mannock, states "seven" as the number of films Forde made as the "record number of talkies" but he names only six titles.

Walter Forde's six films; listed by the company Forde made each of these films for:

1. Gainsborough: ***Third Time Lucky*** (1931, starring Gordon Harker).
2. Gainsborough-British Lion: ***The Ringer*** (1931, starring Gordon Harker).
3. Gainsborough: ***The Ghost Train*** (1931, starring Jack Hulbert).

112

'The Czar of Twickenham'. The History of Julius Hagen and the Film Empire he created at Twickenham Film Studios, from 1927 to 1938.

4. Twickenham: *Splinters in the Navy* (1931, starring Sydney Howard).
5. Twickenham: *Condemned to Death* (1931; renamed from *Jack o'Lantern*, starring Arthur Wontner).
6. Gainsborough: *Lord Babs* (1932, starring Bobby Howes).

October 1931:

Kinematograph Weekly reported throughout the month:

"*Jack o'Lantern* – the usual Sunday calm of the Temple was broken last week when exterior scenes were shot there by the courtesy of the Treasurers and Benchers. Crowds watched Arthur Wontner, Edmund Gwenn and Gordon Harker at work under the direction of Walter Forde. The scenes included the porch of the Temple Church, Lamb's Building, the Cloisters, the passage between Fig Tree Court and Pump Court, and Middle Temple Lane."

(*K. W.*, 8 October 1931).

"Boom for British films in Australia".

"*Lord Richard of the Pantry* was regarded as a poor film there, while *Alibi* was appreciated.

(*K. W.*, 15 October 1931, page 26).

"**Maurice Elvey** has severed his connection with A.R.P. and will shortly be associated with Twickenham productions and Julius Hagen."

(*K. W.*, 15 October 1931, page 55, P. L. Mannock).

NOTE that A.R.P. stands for Associated Radio Pictures.

Maurice Elvey's new association with Julius Hagen at Twickenham was an important move for both men; Elvey went on to direct several films for Hagen over the next few years; many of these were big productions, such as the sound remake of Hitchcock's 1927 silent, *The Lodger* (1932, starring Ivor Novello), *This Week of Grace* (1933, Gracie Field's third film) and *The Wandering Jew* (1933, starring Conrad Veidt). In a 1963 recorded interview, Maurice Elvey spoke of his "writing his own ticket" when he contracted, in 1931, to make films for Twickenham, thus implying that he was that important to Julius Hagen and could therefore come to Twickenham Studios on his own terms.

"*Jack o'Lantern* – footage has been completed."

(*K. W.*, 15 October 1931, page 55, P. L. Mannock).

"*Frail Woman* – Mary Newcomb – American actress – talkie debut – Maurice Elvey's first for Julius Hagen. Hagen and Elvey were jointly responsible for *The Flag Lieutenant*, one of the most successful silent pictures ever made.

(*K. W.*, 22 October 1931, page 51, P. L. Mannock).

November 1931:

Kinematograph Weekly reported throughout the month:

"P.D.C. British productions – an agreement has just been completed between Reginald Smith of P.D.C., Ltd., and Julius Hagen, of Twickenham Film Studios, Ltd., the latter company is to produce three pictures for P.D.C."

"The first will go into production almost immediately. These productions will be produced on an ambitious scale. Stories and casts will be chosen with the care which has always marked Mr. Hagen's Twickenham enterprise, and his pictures for P.D.C. will be of the same super quality as *The Sleeping Cardinal* (one of the few British pictures to make a real hit in the United States.)

(*K. W.*, 5 November 1931, page 20).

"Mary Newcomb, the American stage star, has signed a contract with Mr. Hagen to appear in three further films next year (1932). Hagen declares that he has discovered the greatest emotional screen actress since the advent of the talkies. 'Her performance in *Frail Woman* will create a sensation. In my opinion there is no one of her type to touch her, either in England or Hollywood. Although she has never faced a camera before, she has either studied film technique or she is a born screen actress. Her playing is forceful and vigorous; her slight husky voice is excellent for recording purposes and has a wide range of inflexions; she photographs well; and she possesses the most expressive pair of hands I have yet seen on a screen actress. She has a great mind for detail, and is the exact opposite of those flaccid-faced stars who fear that a display of emotion may bring a wrinkle to their marble brows'."

"Her stories, Mr. Hagen states, will be chosen with the utmost care, and will probably be written specially for her."

"Miss Newcomb, who is married to Henry Higginson, the Boston sportsman, has made her home in England since she came over in 1929, after years of success on Broadway, to star in the stage version of *Jealousy*. She created an equally good impression in *The Infinite Shoeblack* and *Emma Hamilton*."

(*K. W.*, 12 November 1931, page 55).

"Hagen's P.D.C. first: Julius Hagen announces that the first three of the Twickenham supers for distribution by P.D.C. will be a Sherlock Holmes adventure, adapted from the story by the late Sir Arthur Conan Doyle, *"The Adventure of Charles Augustus Milverton"*, by H. Fowler Mear and Cyril Twyford.

(*K. W.*, 12 November 1931, page 55).

"The Missing Rembrandt – casting concluded – production will take the floor this week, as the final shots of *Frail Woman* are disposed of – Leslie Hiscott, Basil Emmott, Baynham Honri, recording, Cyril Stanborough stills."

(*K. W.*, 19 November 1931, page 59, P. L. Mannock).

December 1931:

"The Other Mrs. Phipps, an original comedy by Brock Williams, is being directed by Guy Newall. Shooting is taking place at night owing to the floor being occupied during the day by *The Missing Rembrandt* unit, which is well up to schedule, with the most lavish sets ever used in a British talkie, designed by James Carter."

(*K. W.*, 3 December 1931, page 47, P. L. Mannock).

"Julius Hagen, whose latest production, *The Missing Rembrandt*, is now nearing completion for P.D.C., announces his next production will be *In a Monastery Garden*. This will be presented by Fred White and Gilbert Church for the Associated Producing and Distribution Company. Original story by H. Fowler Mear and Michael Barringer, who are also collaborating on the scenario. Scenes in London and Italy, the story serves as a vehicle for the introduction of one of the world's most popular tunes, Ketelby's *In a Monastery Garden*."

116

'The Czar of Twickenham'. The History of Julius Hagen and the Film Empire he created at Twickenham Film Studios, from 1927 to 1938.

(*K. W.*, 10 December 1931, page 50, P. L. Mannock).

"Julius Hagen has signed Maurice Elvey to direct *In a Monastery Garden* – a strong cast has been lined up, headed by John Stuart and Joan Maude, supported by Hugh Williams, Alan Napier, Humberstone Wright, Frank Pettingell, and Dino Galvani. Joan Maude will be remembered as Salome in the recently revived stage play, and she was one of the featured players in the talkie version of *Hobson's Choice*."

(*K. W.*, 17 December 1931, page 36, P. L. Mannock).

"*Frail Woman* – Julius Hagen states that the world rights will be controlled by Radio Pictures, Ltd. He then claims that 'I have no hesitation in saying that *Frail Woman* is the most interesting production that I ever sponsored'."

(*K. W.*, 31 December 1931).

Tenant Film Producers at Twickenham: 1931:

Twickenham Film Studios continued their policy of leasing out their studio floor space to independent film producers. Doing such of course increased revenue into the company's coffers.

Three independent productions were filmed at Twickenham between January and April 1931, as follows:

1. *We Dine at Seven:*
    "George Smith making *We Dine at Seven* – the first of a series of 4-reelers for Fox. Filming began at the beginning of this week at Twickenham. James Carter, art director and Basil Emmott, camera, and stills Lewis

117

John V. Watson

G. Jonas. F. Attwood Richardson is the director of the series." (*Kinematograph Weekly*, 29 January 1931, page 41).

A '**four-reeler**' refers to a film that is assembled onto four metal reels (or spools), with each reel containing a maximum of 1,000 feet of 35mm film. A 1,000 feet of sound film, when projected, will run for approximately 11 minutes, on the mechanical basis of a speed of 90 feet per minute; thus a '4-reeler' will screen at a running time of a maximum of about 44 minutes.

Several of the production personnel who were employed on the making of *We Dine at Seven* were employees of Twickenham Film Studios, including James Carter, the art director, and Basil Emmott, the cameraman.

According to Denis Gifford, *The British Film Catalogue: 1895-1970*, *We Dine at Seven* (1931) was first shown in April that year, and it ran 44 minutes. A comedy with Herbert Mundin, Dorothy Bartlam and Leslie Perrins, directed by Frank Richardson, from a story by Brock Williams, and produced by George Smith and Harry Cohen for G. S. Enterprises; it was made for Fox Film Company to release as one of their 'Quota' film commitments. Note: The director of this film, Frank Richardson, was also a director of the company, G. S. Enterprises, as can be seen in the following item.

2. *Peace and Quiet:*
"G. S. Enterprises, Ltd. – George Smith embarks on the second of his comedy series for Fox at Twickenham – farcical thriller, *Peace and Quiet*, with Herbert Mundin – F. Attwood Richardson, a director of G.S. is the director – James Carter, art director, recording Carlisle Mounteney, Basil Emmott camera, Lewis Jones stills."

'The Czar of Twickenham'. The History of Julius Hagen and the Film Empire he created at Twickenham Film Studios, from 1927 to 1938.

(*Kinematograph Weekly*, 26 February 1931).

"G.S. Enterprises now completed *Peace and Quiet* at Twickenham." (*Kinematograph Weekly*, 12 March 1931, page 60).

Again, several of the production personnel who were employed on the making of *Peace and Quiet* were employees of Twickenham Film Studios, including James Carter, the art director, Carlisle Mounteney, the sound recording engineer, and Basil Emmott, the cameraman.

According to Denis Gifford, *Peace and Quiet* (1931) was first shown in July that year, and it ran 42 minutes. A comedy with Herbert Mundin, Iris Darbyshire and D. A. Clarke-Smith, directed by Frank Richardson, from a story by Brock Williams, and produced by George Smith and Harry Cohen for G. S. Enterprises; it was made for Fox Film Company to release as another one of their 'Quota' film commitments.

♦   *Kinematograph Weekly* noted the success at the box-office of the short feature film made by Fox, including the two titles the company had made at Twickenham Studios mentioned above: *The Wrong Mr. Perkins* and *Immediate Possession*:
   "Fox Production – 14 films scheduled".

"W. J. Hutchinson, managing director of Fox plans to produce 14 films during the year ending 31 March 1932. These will be 4-reelers of the type of *Enter the Queen*, *The Wrong Mr. Perkins*, *Midnight* and *Immediate Possession* have all proved exceedingly popular in this country. (*K. W.*, 28 May 1931, pages 47-48).

John V. Watson

3. *A Night in Montmartre:*

"Hiscott directs the first scenes of *A Night in Montmartre* at Twickenham for Gainsborough." (*Kinematograph Weekly*, 12 March 1931, page 60).

"Twickenham – *A Night in Montmartre* – Leslie Hiscott (director) – Franklin Dyall (star) – Sydney Blythe (camera) – J. Orton, Scenarist – second week" of filming. (*Kinematograph Weekly*, 19 March 1931, page 68).

"Twickenham – *A Night in Montmartre* – Leslie Hiscott – Franklin Dyall – Sydney Blythe – J. Orton, scenarist – final stages – made for Gaumont." (*Kinematograph Weekly*, 23 April 1931, page 59).

Once again, several of the production personnel employed on the making of *A Night in Montmartre* were employees of Twickenham Film Studios, including James Carter, the art director, and Sydney Blythe, the cameraman.

According to Denis Gifford, *A Night in Montmartre* (1931) was first shown in July that year, and it ran 70 minutes. A mystery feature film based on a play by Miles Malleson and Walter Peacock, with a cast headed by Horace Hodges, Franklin Dyall, Hugh Williams, Reginald Purdell, Heather Angel and Austin Trevor. Directed by Leslie S. Hiscott, and produced by Michael Balcon who made the film for Gainsborough Pictures for release as one of their 'Quota' film commitments.

According to David Quinlan, *British Sound Films: The Studio Years 1928-1959* (Batsford, 1984), *A Night in Montmartre* was a "feeble romantic thriller which kills off its villain half-way through", and he accordingly gave the film a score of just "1" out of a possible maximum of "6".

After the last of these three independent productions were completed by the end of April that year, Twickenham ceased leasing out their studio floor space to independent film producers altogether (but with one exception to come).

That month, 'Real Art Productions' was formed primarily to make what have become to be known as 'Quota Quickies'; i.e. films which were made cheaply for client film renters (or distributors):

APRIL 1931:
THE FORMATION OF REAL ART PRODUCTIONS:

Kinematograph Weekly reported the formation of a new production company by Julius Hagen:

+ **"Real Art Productions, Ltd.**
+ Private company, registered 15 April 1931.
+ Capital £100 in £1 shares.
+ Objects: to produce motion picture films.
+ Secretary: (pro tem.) G. O. Mitchell.
+ Solicitors: Norman Hart and Mitchell, 21 Panton Street, London, S.W.1.
+ Registered Office: Broadmead House, 21 Panton Street, London, S.W.1."

(*K. W.*, 23 April 1931, page 38).

The establishment of a new production company at Twickenham to operate there was a very important corporate move on the part of Hagen and company.

Clearly, as we shall see over the coming years, as the events are unfolded in this narrative, 'Real Art' was formed to make films under supply contracts to various renting companies, the majority of them American-owned British subsidiaries. Most of the films 'Real Art' were to make were 'Quota Quickies', probably often supplied on the 'Pound-per-Foot' contract basis. Some of the films made under this banner, however, were not necessarily cheaply made. But, as no financial records now appear to exist, it is impossible to find out what the cost of making each of these films actually was.

In total, 'Real Art' was to make no less than 52 films between 1931 and 1935, the first of which, **Rodney Steps In**, was to go into production in May, the month after the new company was formed.

Of the 52 films produced by 'Real Art', 35 of these we made for Radio Pictures, the American-owned British renting (or film distribution) subsidiary, in other words, just over 66% of their total production output over their four years of operation.

The British **Radio Pictures** was itself formed by its American parent the year before, as *Kinematograph Weekly* reported:

"RKO in England – Radio Pictures, Ltd., - S. G. Newman, managing director."

"Radio Pictures, Ltd. registered on 18 June 1930 with a nominal capital of £10,000 in £1 shares."

(*K. W.*, 26 June 1930, pages 21 and 24).

New Capitalisation for Twickenham Film Studios:

A debenture for £15,000 was issued on 1 April 1931, to Westminster Bank, Limited.

'The Czar of Twickenham'. The History of Julius Hagen and the Film Empire he created at Twickenham Film Studios, from 1927 to 1938.

In corporate finance, a debenture is a medium to long-term debt instrument used by large companies to borrow money, at a fixed rate of interest. A debenture is thus like a certificate of loan or a loan bond evidencing the fact that the company is liable to pay a specified amount with interest and, although the money raised by the debenture becomes a part of the company's capital structure, it does not become part of the company's share capital. A debenture is thus a debt to the company, not an asset for it.

Again, as the reader will discover later, this and other later debentures (or loans) raised by Twickenham Film Studios would come home to haunt the company, as well as several other British film production organisations, in a few years time.

It is significant to note that the raising of finance for Twickenham Studios via the issue of this debenture for £15,000, on the 1st April 1931, coincided with the formation of Real Art Productions, Ltd., Hagen's new production company, just two weeks later, on the 15th April 1931.

Twickenham's Eleven Films Trade Shown
during 1931:

Twickenham completed eleven films during 1931.

The quality of this group was very good overall, in particular the first release, *The Sleeping Cardinal*, which proved to be a big success at the box-office. It was directed by Twickenham's in-house director, Leslie Hiscott, who was praised by *Kinematograph Weekly* for making "an excellent detective drama" ... because "Hiscott's direction is capable and allows movement and change of scenes to punctuate the good dialogue ...".

Hiscott made three other films at Twickenham that year, but, as usual, his competence as a director was varied, with the poorest of his four films being **Brown Sugar**, described by *Kinematograph Weekly* as "... concentrated too much on the stage version ... long sequences with very little camera movement ... a cramped air about the production, and the grouping of characters is unimaginative and crude."

Julius Hagen expanded significantly his production capacity at Twickenham Studios by acquiring three new clients, making four big or 'super' films for W. and F. Film Service (**The Lyons Mail, Alibi, Black Coffee, Splinters in the Navy**); one film for W. P. Film Company (**The Rosary**), and a smaller shorter film for Ideal Films (**Bill's Legacy**).

A further three new clients were acquired for Julius Hagen's new production company, Real Art, which produced one film each for three American-owned renting companies: Fox (**Rodney Steps In**), M-G-M (**Chin Chin Chinaman**) and First National Film Distributors (**The Other Mrs. Phipps**). All were cheaply made (apparently), and all of them ran for about 40 to 45 minutes each.

The other two films, the first two of the eleven completed that year, were made for Warner Bros. (**The Sleeping Cardinal** and **Brown Sugar**). These were the final two projects made for that American-owned renter under Hagen's contract to produce six films for them, which was struck in the middle of 1929.

The eleven films are listed in order of the date of each Trade show:

March:

1. The Sleeping Cardinal (1931)
An adaptation of two Conan Doyle stories, *The Final*

Problem and *The Empty House*, starring Arthur Wontner as Sherlock Holmes, directed by Leslie Hiscott.

It was the fifth film made for Warner Bros. by Julius Hagen.

A lobby card for the American release of ***The Sleeping Cardinal***. The card shows Jane Welsh (as 'Kathleen Adair' and Arthur Wontner (as 'Sherlock Holmes') in a scene from the retitled ***Sherlock Holmes' Fatal Hour***. The film was made in black-and-white but the card itself suggests that the film was made in colour! This was a standard marketing ploy used by American film distributors for decades, suggesting films actually made in black-and-white were filmed in colour.

The film was Trade shown on Friday, 27 February 1931 at the Leicester Square Theatre in the West End of London. It was preceded by the screening of a *Pathétone Variety* production, ***The Lost Policeman***, a comedy short running nine minutes, with Sandy Powell, the famous theatre and radio comedian, repeating his very successful 78 r.p.m.

record release of this skit.

The Sleeping Cardinal was reviewed by *Kinematograph Weekly*:

"RCA Photophone, full talking, 85 minutes, "U" certificate."

"<u>Remarks</u>: Great performance by Arthur Wontner in excellent adaptation of Conan Doyle's Sherlock Holmes' story."

"<u>Box Office Angle</u>: First rate booking with strong publicity."

"An excellent detective drama, British all through, which is adapted from two well-known stories by Conan Doyle. The play is cleverly constructed, and succeeds in keeping the interest maintained until the very end."

"Hiscott's direction is capable and allows movement and change of scenes to punctuate the good dialogue, while Arthur Wontner is admirable as Sherlock Holmes and brings life to the immortal character."

"A first-rate booking with obvious publicity angles."

"<u>Acting</u>: Arthur Wontner is brilliant as Sherlock Holmes, every gesture, intonation and mannerism is perfect. It is his characterisation that is mainly responsible for the picture's success. Ian Fleming is a little stagey as Watson, and not always at ease, but Norman McKinnel, Minnie Rayner and Jane Welsh contribute sterling support."

"<u>Production</u>: Conan Doyle's stories, on which the play is based, have been slightly modernised, but only in detail,

126

and all the clever construction and art of telling remains. Interest is cleverly worked up, and the situations appear quite plausible, and there is always an unexpected twist. The individual characterisation is amazingly good, and although there is a good deal of talk, the dialogue is interesting and entertaining, and is never allowed to restrict movement or change of scene. There is little unconscious humour, and there is always a laugh for the familiar expression "elementary, my dear Watson", which crops up with glorious frequency. Not only is the picture excellent entertainment, but it goes to prove that despite the passing of years Conan Doyle has no peer as a creator of crime fiction."

"Settings and Photography: There is a good variety of interior settings which, of course, include the famous detective's well-known rooms in Baker Street. The lighting and photography are very good."

"Points of Appeal: Good story, popular thrills, excellent characterisation, and fine atmosphere."

(*Kinematograph Weekly*, 5 March 1931, page 47).

The Sleeping Cardinal had two London key-cinema pre-release runs:

- An advertisement in *Kinematograph Weekly*, 12 March 1931, stated *The Sleeping Cardinal* played to phenomenal business at the Leicester Square Theatre.
- *Kinematograph Weekly*, 25 June 1931, reported: *The Sleeping Cardinal* was given a second pre-release at the Stoll, Kingsway. In those days, the Stoll in Kingsway, London was a major, and most important, suburban cinema.

127

The Sleeping Cardinal went into General Release on Monday, 27 July 1931.

The Sleeping Cardinal was also very successful in the United States.

April:

2. *Brown Sugar (1931)*

A drawing-room drama about a chorus girl who marries into aristocracy, adapted from Lady Arthur Lever's stage play, starring Constance Carpenter, directed by Leslie Hiscott.

It was the sixth and final film made for Warner Bros. by Julius Hagen.

The film was Trade shown on Friday, 17 April 1931 at the New Gallery Kinema, in Regent Street, London. It was preceded by the screening of two *Vitaphone* Shorts: **Yodeling Yokels**, a Looney Tunes cartoon, and **One Good Turn**.

Brown Sugar was reviewed by *Kinematograph Weekly*:

"RCA Photophone, full talking, 70 minutes, "A" certificate."

"Remarks: A photographed version of the stage play. Stinted in production and rather thin in humour and plot."

"Box Office Angle: Moderate booking."

"Story of a chorus girl who marries into aristocracy, and meets with "refaned" opposition. It is all very superficial, and is not helped by the direction. There are some bright moments, and the picture's title carries weight."

"Acting: Whether it be on account of direction or not, the fact remains that there is an air of crudeness about the acting in general. Constance Carpenter is artificial, and neither Cecile Byrne as Honoria, nor Francis Lister appear to advantage. The older artistes, Allan Aynesworth as Lord Knightsbridge, Helen Haye as his wife, and Eva Moore as a friend of the family's, stand out, but are unable to bring much conviction to the story."

"Production: Leslie S. Hiscott has done much better than this. His fault seems to be that he has concentrated too much on the stage version, and gives long sequences with very little camera movement. There is a cramped air about the production, and the grouping of characters is unimaginative and crude."

"Settings and Photography: Wealthy home interiors, with too infrequent changes of angle and locale. Quite good photography."

"Points of Appeal: The strong cast and title."

(*Kinematograph Weekly*, 23 April 1931, page 45).

Brown Sugar went into General Release on Monday, 14 September 1931.

3. *The Lyons Mail (1931)*

Adapted from the famous stage play, starring Sir John Martin Harvey, who had appeared in the stage version from 1927 to 1930, directed by Arthur Maude.

It was the first film made for W. and F. Film Service by Julius Hagen.

The film was Trade shown in London on Wednesday, 22 April 1931, at the Phoenix Theatre.

The Lyons Mail was reviewed by *Kinematograph Weekly*:

"RCA Photophone, full talking, 75 minutes, "A" certificate."

"Remarks: Unimaginative picturisation of Irving's old melodrama, with possible title pull."

"Box Office Angle: Title and star booking for unsophisticated audiences."

"Slow, old-fashioned melodrama, adapted from the famous stage play, which never convinces, and occasionally excites laughter. Good settings and excellent photography represent the best features of the picture. This type of entertainment is outmoded, and is unlikely to appeal to the modern, sophisticated film fan."

"Acting: Martin Harvey is so steeped in the traditions of the stage that he fails to adapt his histrionics to the screen. His dual characterisation as Lesurques and Dubosc lacks power and conviction. Norah Baring is not too happy in the rôle of heroine, and the principal supporting players, Moore Marriott, Michael Hogan, and Ben Webster, are screen conscious and stagy."

"Production: Arthur Maude, the producer (the old theatrical term for 'the director'), has used little imagination in the handling of this picture, which is nothing more than a photographed version of the stage play.   The action is slow, and, as a result, the artificialities and weaknesses in the story are magnified. There are times when the highly dramatic situations completely misfire, and cause a smile. The dialogue, too, belongs to another decade. The staging, however, is artistic, and the quality of the photography is very good."

"Settings and Photography: The period interiors are well furnished and dressed, the inn scenes are effectively lighted, and a fair atmosphere prevails. Sydney Blythe's camera work is efficient."

"Points of Appeal: Title and star."

(*Kinematograph Weekly*, 30 April 1931, page 43).

THE LYONS MAIL
The actor-manager Sir John Martin-Harvey appeared for Julius Hagen in a mini-spectacular film of his favourite stage part, made at the tiny Twickenham studio in 1930.

A dramatic scene from *The Lyons Mail* (1931) showing Sir John Martin-Harvey in silhouette.

The Lyons Mail went into General Release on Monday,

131

12 October 1931.

4. *Alibi (1931)*

Adapted from the 1928 play, *Alibi*, by Michael Morton which in turn was based on the Agatha Christie novel, *The Murder of Roger Ackroyd*, featuring her famous Belgian detective, Hercule Poirot, with Austin Trevor as the sleuth, directed by Leslie Hiscott.

It was the second film made for W. and F. Film Service by Julius Hagen.

The film was Trade shown in London on Tuesday, 28 April 1931, at the Phoenix Theatre.

Alibi was reviewed by *Kinematograph Weekly*:

"RCA Photophone, full talking, 75 minutes, "A" certificate".

"Remarks: A holding murder mystery drama, which succeeds in creating suspense and keeping the end in doubt. Popular entertainment."

"Box Office Angle: Good programme booking."

"A holding murder mystery drama, which makes a magnificent recovery after a slow start, and succeeds in keeping the ending a secret. The characterisation is not entirely flawless, but the acting as a whole reaches a high standard, Austin Trevor being particularly good in the leading role. Production qualities are satisfactory, and there is plenty of movement. Good popular entertainment."

"Acting: Austin Trevor gives a carefully studied portrayal

of Poirot, and speaks with a convincing accent, while all the time appearing delightfully natural. Franklin Dyall gives a strong portrayal as Sir Roger, and J. H. Roberts' delivery is exceptionally good, as is his accent, as Dr. Shepherd. John Deverell is good in a "silly ass" part, as an amateur criminologist, but Harvey Brabin is poor as a Scotland Yard detective. The women in the cast, Mercia Swinburne, Mary Jerrold, and Clare Greet, are adequate."

"Production: Once the introductory stage is past, the story gathers momentum, and builds up suspense stage by stage to a most unexpected climax. Leslie Hiscott has taken full advantage of the wider scope offered by the screen - the picture was adapted from a stage play by Michael Morton – and does not allow the dialogue to restrict camera movement."

"Settings and Photography: The scenes, mostly interiors, are convincing, and the lighting and photography are very good."

"Points of Appeal: Holding story, suspense values, good work by star, and efficient treatment."

(*Kinematograph Weekly*, 30 April 1931, page 45).

July:

5. *Rodney Steps In (1931)*

A 'Quota Quickie' comedy drama, with Richard Cooper, directed by Guy Newall.

It was the first film made for Fox Film Co., Ltd. by Julius Hagen; it was co-produced by Harry Cohen, Fox' production manager in England.

It was also the first film made by Hagen's new production company, Real Art Productions, Ltd.

The film was Trade shown in London on Tuesday, 30 June 1931 at the Palace Theatre. It was Trade shown together with two other Fox releases: *Peace and Quiet* (1931, made by G. S. Enterprises at Twickenham Studios, with Herbert Mundin - see above), and *Number Please* (1931, produced by Harry Cohen, with former silent film star, Mabel Poulton).

Rodney Steps In was reviewed by *Kinematograph Weekly*:

"RCA Photophone, full talking, 43 minutes, "U" certificate".

"Remarks: Comedy crook drama; good production and unexpected climax."

"Box Office Angle: Average light booking."

"A polished comedy crook drama, which has a slight but amusing story and one which furnishes an unexpected climax. The individual characterisation is good and the picture is well mounted. Average light booking for the majority of halls" (i.e. cinemas).

"Acting: Richard Cooper plays Rodney, a silly ass part, with the necessary lightness and conviction, and is mainly responsible for the comedy element. Elizabeth Allan is mysterious and intriguing as the girl, and there is a good cast in support."

"Production: Guy Newall has made quite a good job of

this comedy crook drama and sees that the picture moves at a steady gait. Humour, sentiment and thrills are agreeably blended, while the finish furnishes a pleasant surprise."

"Settings and Photography: A realistic atmosphere prevails. There are a few exterior shots as well as interiors, and lighting and photography are good."

"Points of Appeal: Good characterisation, amusing story and good presentation."

(*Kinematograph Weekly*, 2 July 1931, page 51).

6. *The Rosary (1931)*

A melodrama, directed by Guy Newall, starring Elizabeth Allan and Margot Grahame. Guy Newall and John McNally wrote the original story. The tune of a well-known song was introduced in the film, adapted by Noel Gay.

It was the first film made for W. P. Film Company, Ltd. by Julius Hagen.

The film was Trade shown in London on Friday, 3 July 1931 at the Phoenix Theatre.

The Rosary was reviewed by *Kinematograph Weekly*:

"RCA Photophone, full talking, 70 minutes, "A" certificate".

"Remarks: Sentimental story of a woman's sacrifices for her sister, but popular in conception. Very good direction and production values."

"Box Office Angle: Very good popular hall booking."

"Popular sentiment concerning a woman who gives up her lover and stands a murder trial on her sister's behalf, is the mainstay of this picture. It should go down very well with popular audiences, especially as the direction is good and the technical qualities of excellent quality."

"Acting: Elizabeth Allan is excellent as Vera. She is natural and convincing, even in artificial circumstances, and acts Margot Grahame right off the stage. Margot Grahame is, unfortunately, very stagey in both voice production and gesture. It is a difficult part which needs a lot to make it convincing. Leslie Perrins is very natural and quite effective as Ronald, and Robert Holmes makes a good villain. Excellent character studies come from Walter Piers as Major Mannering, and Charles Groves as a confidential butler; in fact, the latter is one of the real successes of the picture."

"Production: Guy Newall has written a story which is evidently intended to appeal to the masses, and has succeeded. Frankly it is conventional stuff, but he has directed it very well. He has not attempted a conventional continuity, but has dealt in episodic scenes connected by their pictorial suggestions, and it is most effective. If fact, so far as technique and polish goes, it is equal to anything America can give us. The court scene is particularly good."

"Settings and Photography: No praise can be too high for Basil Emmott's camera work, which shows imagination and technical efficiency. Settings, too, are very well composed."

"Points of Appeal: The story of the woman's sacrifice is one which has a definite and well-proven popular appeal. This is augmented by the acting of Elizabeth Allan and the male cast, as well as by the "finish" of the production generally."

(*Kinematograph Weekly*, 9 July 1931, page 41).

The Rosary went into General Release on Monday, 8 February 1932.

August:

7. *Black Coffee (1931)*

Mystery thriller adapted from the play by Agatha Christie, directed by Leslie Hiscott, with Austin Trevor starring as Hercule Poirot for the second time on screen.

It was the third film made for W. and F. Film Service by Julius Hagen.

The film was Trade shown in London on Monday, 24 August 1931 at the New Gallery Kinema.

Black Coffee was reviewed by *Kinematograph Weekly*:

"RCA Photophone, full talking, 80 minutes, "U" certificate"

"Remarks: Mystery thriller adapted from Agatha Christie's stage success. Treatment rather dilatory, but humour and suspense furnish satisfactory entertainment."

"Box Office Angle: Average programme booking."

"A popular, workmanlike mystery drama, an adaptation of Agatha Christie's stage success. The treatment is a little dilatory for this type of entertainment, but the

John V. Watson

picture nevertheless contains a few surprises and is
embellished with diverting bi-play. The individual
acting is good, and the production qualities satisfactory.
Average programme booking."

"Acting: Austin Trevor gives another of his clever
studies as Poirot, and convinces and cleverly maintains
an intriguing accent. His performance is the high-light
of the picture. Richard Cooper plays a Doctor Watson
type of role, and is amusingly dull in his own inimitable
way, while Adrianne Allen is good as Lucia, and
satisfactory support comes from C. V. France, Philip
Strange and Dino Galvani."

"Production: This "spot the murderer" type of mystery
play is now getting hackneyed, but it compels a certain
amount of concentration by leading one up the garden
path until the climax is reached. In this case the
denouement is not exactly a first-class surprise, but it is
quite a good imitation. Leslie Hiscott's direction is
sound, but it rather lacks speed and imagination, for it
gives one time to think out the plot and furnish its
solution, and this rather minimises the dramatic effect."

"Settings and Photography: The picture is staged with
ingenious economy, the scenes are restricted to a few
adequate interiors, while lighting and photography are
good."

"Points of Appeal: Title, cast, popular mystery, element,
humour and suspense."

(*Kinematograph Weekly*, 27 August 1931, page 31).

Black Coffee went into General Release on Monday, 14
December 1931.

September:

8. *Chin Chin Chinaman (1931)*

A crime drama, directed by Guy Newall, starring British stage character supremo, Leon M. Lion, well-known for his use of extravagant disguise, making his talkie debut, with Elizabeth Allan. Adapted from a one-act play by Percy Walsh, which played to great success at the Coliseum Theatre in London a short while before the production of the film.

It was the first film made for M-G-M by Julius Hagen.

Chin Chin Chinaman was the second film made by Hagen's new production company, Real Art.

The film was Trade shown in London in either late-August or early-September 1931; exact date and location undetermined.

Chin Chin Chinaman was reviewed by *Kinematograph Weekly*:

"RCA Photophone, full talking, 48 minutes, "U" certificate."

"Remarks: Light, diverting crook drama, with an Oriental flavour."

"Box Office Angle: Useful supporting offering."

"A light, diverting crook drama, which is occasionally reminiscent of the popular "Charlie Chan" series. The plot is unoriginal, but it works out satisfactorily, and has a novel twist. Useful supporting offering."

"Acting: Leon M. Lion makes up quite well as the Chinaman. Elizabeth Allen is sufficiently alluring and

139

mystifying as the Countess, while George Curzon is good as the polished crook."

"Production: There is nothing remarkable about Guy Newall's direction, but he keeps things on the move, and succeeds in condensing pleasant dramatic diversion into a small compass. Taking all in all, the picture is attractive enough to make a useful supporting offering for most halls."

"Settings and Photography: The scenes on board the boat are realistic, while the apartment scenes are tastefully devised. Lighting and photography are good."

"Points of Appeal: Interesting story, good cast, and adequate presentation."

(*Kinematograph Weekly*, 3 September 1931, pages 41 and 42).

Chin Chin Chinaman was released in the United States under the title, **The Boat from Shanghai**.

November:

9. *Bill's Legacy (1931)*

A Cockney comedy, directed by Harry J. Revier, starring British comedian, Leslie Fuller.

It was the first film made for Ideal Films by Julius Hagen.

The film was Trade shown in London on Tuesday, 3 November 1931 at the Astoria.

Bill's Legacy was reviewed by *Kinematograph Weekly*:

"RCA Photophone, full talking, 55 minutes, "A" certificate."

"*Remarks*: Cockney comedy presented on musical-hall lines. A few laughs are scored by Leslie Fuller."

"Box Office Angle: Moderate supporting offering for industrial halls."

"Conventional Cockney comedy presented on musical-hall lines. Leslie Fuller's robust humour is the backbone of the entertainment, the appeal of which is definitely directed towards the masses. Moderate supporting offering for industrial halls."

"Acting: Leslie Fuller's methods are a little crude, but he succeeds in extracting a few laughs from the hackneyed material. Mary Clare, who is worthy of something better, is Nellie, while the supporting cast is moderate."

"Production: Construction of this comedy is old, as are the jokes and gags, and its success as entertainment depends on the strength of Leslie Fuller, whose humour, judging by his past efforts, apparently satisfies the masses."

"Settings and Photography: The picture is staged on rather a meagre scale, but the slapstick sequences are well timed. Lighting and photography are satisfactory."

"Points of Appeal: Popularity of Leslie Fuller.

(*Kinematograph Weekly*, 5 November 1931, page 37).

10. *Splinters in the Navy (1931)*

Nautical comedy introducing the well known *Splinters* wartime concert party, directed by Walter Forde, starring British comedian, Sydney Howard.

It was the fourth film made for W. and F. Film Service by Julius Hagen.

The film was Trade shown in London on Monday, 9 November 1931 at the New Victoria.

Splinters of the Navy was reviewed by *Kinematograph Weekly*:

> "RCA Photophone, full talking, 77 minutes, "U" certificate"

> "Remarks: Nautical extravaganza introducing the well known wartime concert party. Excellent production qualities and amusing performance by star."

> "Box Office Angle: Good booking for the masses."

> "A nautical hotchpotch, a popular collation of broad comedy, music and songs, which is rather lacking in cohesion and action, but, nevertheless, scores the laughs, and should appeal to the masses. Although Walter Forde has dovetailed the Splinters Concert Party fairly successfully into the main theme, the humour gained at the expense of the female impersonation is not only rather old-fashioned, but it may be a little pleasing to some. It is the original comedy methods of Sydney Howard and the excellent presentation that get the picture over."

> "Acting: Sydney Howard is in first-rate form as Joe, and makes the most of every gag and situation. He is

certainly the backbone of the entertainment. Frederic Bentley makes a good foil as Bill, Alf Goddard is well cast as the heavyweight champion, and some interesting supporting types are drawn by Helena Pickard, Paddy Browne, Rupert Lister and Harold Heath."

"<u>Production</u>: The picture opens well, but the journey up to the culminating fight scene is rather slow, and the quality of the by-play, particularly that furnished by the Splinters Concert Party, is apt to fluctuate. The fight scene, however, is well worth waiting for, for it is excruciatingly funny, and allows the picture to end on a riotous and satisfying note. Sydney Howard is exploited to the full, and his performance is infinitely more enjoyable than the entertainment provided by the female impersonators, who are the main plank of the concert party. Taking all in all, this extravaganza contains most of the ingredients that can be depended upon to delight the masses, all of which are presented with a good sense of popular showmanship."

"<u>Settings and Photography</u>: The nautical atmosphere is realistic, and the comedy situations, music and songs, are slipped in with such skill that the incongruities are avoided."

"<u>Points of Appeal</u>: Title, star, popular broad comedy, and good presentation."

(*Kinematograph Weekly*, 12 November 1931, page 43).

Splinters of the Navy had a London key-theatre run at the Astoria, week commencing Monday, 28 December 1931; the supporting feature film has not been determined.

John V. Watson

Splinters of the Navy went into General Release on Monday, 15 February 1932.

December:

11. The Other Mrs. Phipps (1931)

A 'Quota Quickie' comedy about female impersonation, directed by Guy Newall, starring Richard Cooper.

It was the first film made for First National Film Distributors by Julius Hagen.

The Other Mrs. Phipps was the third film made by Hagen's new production company, Real Art.

The film was Trade shown in London on Wednesday, 6 January 1932 at the Carlton.

The Other Mrs. Phipps was reviewed by *Kinematograph Weekly*:

"RCA Photophone, full talking, 40 minutes, "A" certificate."

"Remarks: Amusing trifle dealing with a female impersonation, brightly put over."

"Box Office Angle: Very useful popular supporting feature."

"Amusing trifle in which we are introduced to the somewhat familiar situation of a man posing as a woman and finding himself in familiar company. It is quite well put over and should find popular favour in most programmes."

"Acting: Richard Cooper is quite good in his usual "silly

ass" part, and is also amusing in disguise. Sydney Fairbrother makes the most of her part as Mrs. Phipps, with more that a reminder of her "*A Sister to Assist 'Er*" rôle. Jane Welsh makes a most attractive heroine, who should go far in films if given the opportunity."

"Production: Guy Newall has crowded his plot with too much dialogue and not enough action, but it is generally quite neat and workmanlike in direction. The dialogue is not remarkably subtle, but it is nevertheless bright, and is good for a number of laughs."

"Settings and Photography: The interior house settings, which comprise the background, are good, and the camera work good."

"Points of Appeal: The light farcical situations involved in the female impersonation, and the stars."

(*Kinematograph Weekly*, 31 December 1931, page 21).

The Other Mrs. Phipps had a London key-theatre pre-release run at the Carlton, week commencing Monday, 4 January 1932; it supported *Five Star Final* (1931) starring Edward G. Robinson, which was also released by First National Film Distributors.

The Other Mrs. Phipps went into General Release on Monday, 2 May 1932.

Other Events at Twickenham during 1931:

"Twickenham – when the studio makes "Whoopee" – staff dance at the Cole Court Hotel, Twickenham. Mrs. Hagen was presented with a beautiful big bouquet with a card bearing New Year wishes from the studio staff."

John V. Watson

(*Kinematograph Weekly*, 8 January 1931, page 127).

"Twickenham Studios outing".

"The second annual outing of the Twickenham Film Studios staff took place on Sunday, 28 June 1931, when the company made a river trip from Staines to Cookham, where an excellent lunch was waiting in a specially constructed marquee on the lawn of the Ferry Hotel".

"After lunch Julius Hagen expressed the pleasure it gave him and his co-directors to entertain once more 'this most loyal and efficient of studio staffs'".

(*Kinematograph Weekly*, 2 July 1931, page 45).

"Hagen's Endowment Scheme".

"To show his confidence in them, and to prove that he hoped and expected them all to be with him for many years to come, he proposed to inaugurate an endowment scheme for the benefit of all the members of the staff in their old age or disability, and this appeared to him to be a suitable occasion on which to outline the scheme".

"A certain percentage of every salary would be deducted weekly, to which sum the company would add one-half as much again. Thus the general fund would accumulate and at the end of their term of service each member of the staff would be in possession of a lump sum proportionate to their age. In case of total disability the sum already accrued would be immediately handed over. In the case of death the money would form part of their estate. He felt that a scheme such as this would be looked upon with favour by the staff".

"Sydney Blythe replied on behalf of the staff and, after

thanking Mr. Hagen and his co-directors for the wonderful consideration always shown to their staff, said that such a scheme as had been outlined to them not only would be of enormous benefit to all the staff, but was helping to place the Film trade on a solid basis side by side with England's greatest industries".

"Ted Eyres, the oldest member of the Twickenham staff, both in years and in length of service, then made presentations to Mr. Hagen and his two co-directors, Leslie Hiscott and James Carter, who both made short speeches".

Among the guests present were Max Berman, Mr. and Mrs. Alec Saville, Brock Williams, H. Fowler Mear, W. J. O'Bryen, George Humphries, Austin Trevor, Richard Cooper, and Elizabeth Allan".

(*Kinematograph Weekly*, 2 July 1931, page 45).

1931: The British Film Industry: Trends and Other Events throughout the Year — in England and Hollywood:

"**Laurence Olivier** has been signed up to a contract by R.K.O. and starts work this month in Hollywood. He joins his wife, Jill Esmond, who has already been secured a talkie contract by the same company."

(*Kinematograph Weekly*, 7 May 1931, page 35).

"**Walt Disney Productions, Ltd.**, registered on 15 May 1931 as a private company. Capital: £100 in 1 shilling shares."

(*Kinematograph Weekly*, 21 May 1931, page 21).

John V. Watson

"The Picturegoer, Britain's most popular film magazine, will be launched as a weekly on Friday, 29 May 1931 – printed throughout in art photogravure – backed by a big advertising campaign, with a guaranteed net sale of 100,000 copies a week, and an advertisement rate of £40 per page."

(*Kinematograph Weekly*, 21 May 1931, page 45).

<u>Note</u>: There were three other British weekly film fan magazines at that time: *Picture Show*, *Film Pictorial* and *Film Weekly*, of which the later was, in the author's opinion, by far and away the best.

P. L. Mannock raised the question:

"Ready-made Stage Comedy. Will the supply dry up?"

(*Kinematograph Weekly*, 16 July 1931, page 38).

P. L. Mannock further raised the problem of British screen writing in general:

"The neglected British scenario".

(*Kinematograph Weekly*, 23 July 1931, page 56).

Entertainment Tax was increased.

A table compared the old and new charges.

(*Kinematograph Weekly*, 17 September 1931, page 32).

P. L. Mannock again raised the issue of the overall quality of British films in general:

"Our films too padded – an American cutter's verdict."

(*Kinematograph Weekly*, 8 October 1931, page 48).

'The Czar of Twickenham'. The History of Julius Hagen and the Film Empire he created at Twickenham Film Studios, from 1927 to 1938.

"The passing of the sound-on-disc recording".

An item quoting Max Milder, the managing director of Warner Bros. in the United Kingdom.

(*Kinematograph Weekly*, 10 December 1931, page 20).

Note: Almost from the start of the phenomenon of sound in the cinema in the late 1920s, films were supplied to cinemas in one of two formats, according to the equipment each individual house had installed, either sound-on-film or sound-on-disc. Sound-on-disc used a phonograph or other disc to play back the sound in synchronisation with the motion picture film itself. Early sound-on-disc systems used a mechanical interlock with the film projector. However, problems arose when there was a break in the film itself, usually caused by some damage, whereby the broken film frames **had** to be removed, or spliced out, otherwise that part of the film would not be able to pass through the projector's mechanism easily, or more likely, not at all. This then caused a major problem immediately with the synchronisation of the image with the sound; obviously it would be physically impossible to remove that same amount of sound time from the disc. The only way out of the problem was to replace the damaged frames with exactly the same amount of black film. But this would look blatantly obvious, and thus jarring, to the audience. Max Milder was thus heralding in the withdrawal of sound-on-disc film availability. Thus, during 1932, this process was phased out, whereby sound-on-film became the only method to show sound films.

1931: The Fourth Year of the 'Quota' Act:

164 British films were first shown during the year 1931.

This number is arrived at by using the data contained in *The*

British Film Catalogue: 1895-1970 by Denis Gifford, as follows:

09080: Closing Gifford Catalogue Number.

08916: Opening Gifford Catalogue Number.

    164: Total. An increase of 9 films over the previous year's total of 153.

Some of these films were short subjects; the actual number of these shorts has not been determined.

---

5.   1932: Production expands further at Twickenham:

January 1932:

The *Kinematograph Weekly*, 7 January 1932, carried a major advertisement (on pages 92 and 93) about the significant success made by Twickenham Film Studios. Ltd., which claimed "the second largest output of films from any British studio!"

In the same issue of the *Kine*, a full page editorial was carried on page 100, headed **"An Independent's Record – Many Twickenham Successes in 1931 – Julius Hagen's Busy New Year."**

The journal reported:

Four Supers Ready – practically completed.
Mary Newcomb's success in the Twickenham- made film *"Frail Woman"* (1931).

'The Czar of Twickenham'. The History of Julius Hagen and the Film Empire he created at Twickenham Film Studios, from 1927 to 1938.

Stars Under Contract: Mary Newcomb, Elizabeth Allan, and Richard Cooper.
Maurice Elvey has signed to make six pictures exclusively for Twickenham.
P. L. Mannock of the *Kinematograph Weekly*, 21 January 1932, reported, on page 43:

Maurice Elvey's next *The Marriage Bond* with Mary Newcomb and Guy Newall, starts shortly with Hagen discovery, Elizabeth Allan.

The *Kinematograph Weekly*, 28 January 1932, reported, on page 24, that Reginald Smith, managing director of P.D.C. is arranging an early trade show for *The Missing Rembrandt*.

On page 43 of that issue, P. L. Mannock reported that:

"Cyril Stanborough, the well-known still cameraman, has just been signed up for his third year with Julius Hagen at Twickenham."

February 1932:

Kinematograph Weekly reported throughout the month:

FILM PRODUCTION AT TWICKENHAM STUDIOS:

"*The Crooked Lady* is being made so mysteriously at night at Twickenham. Ursula Jeans, as heroine, starts work at 8 p.m. and has lunch at 4 a.m."

"*The Marriage Bond* – the current super for Radio – Maurice Elvey has recently secured fine English countryside exteriors, including very realistic hunting scenes at Gattistock, in Dorsetshire, where Mary Newcomb's husband, Mr. Henry Higginson, who is M.F.H., has arranged special facilities for Elvey to film his pack at the local meets.

151

An elaborate hunt-ball sequence is to be filmed this week, for which James Carter is building a spectacular set."

"*Once Bitten*, a short feature farce, is to go into production at nights this week at Twickenham, for distribution by Fox. Starring Richard Cooper, Ursula Jeans, Jeanne Stuart and Frank Pettingell. From an original story by John Barrow, of which the scenario has been written by H. Fowler Mear. Director: Leslie Hiscott. Camera: Sydney Blythe."

(*K. W.*, 8 February 1932, pages 44 and 45, P. L. Mannock).

"*Once Bitten* – Fox's next British four-reeler – has now started at Twickenham. John Barrow, the author of *Once Bitten*, recently published a travel book, "*Digression*", which won him favourable recognition. He joined the Fox publicity department some 18 months ago and is now attached to the Fox production department."

"*The Marriage Bond* – Hagen's new super for Radio release – is now nearing completion. Maurice Elvey has been occupied during most of the week on the hunt ball sequence, of which he has obtained some extremely spectacular effects."

(*K. W.*, 25 February 1932, page 51, P. L. Mannock).

March 1932:

Kinematograph Weekly reported throughout the month:

FILM DISTRIBUTION ARRANGEMENTS IN AUSTRALIA:

"Julius Hagen announced that the British Dominion Films, Limited (of Australia) will be the sole distributors throughout Australia of the entire Twickenham product for the present year."

"The new deal is an encouraging testimony to the popularity of Twickenham films in the Dominions", says Mr. Hagen, "and the terms of the contract provide a striking example of the good will and liberality by British Dominion Films towards the release of good British pictures in Australia".

'The Czar of Twickenham'. The History of Julius Hagen and the Film Empire he created at Twickenham Film Studios, from 1927 to 1938.

(*K. W.*, 3 March 1932, page 23).

FILM PRODUCTION AT TWICKENHAM STUDIOS:

"Leslie Hiscott has now completed *Once Bitten* for Fox."

"Work has now started on another Fox 4-reeler at Twickenham – *Stormy Weather*, Frank Richardson directing." NOTE: This film is not recorded in Denis Gifford's *The British Film Catalogue: 1895-1970*. This suggests that the title was changed for a reason not yet identified, but see the further notes below.

(*K. W.*, 10 March 1932, page 69, P. L. Mannock).

"Twickenham – double-shifts at top pressure have been the rule all this year." This is another reference to the fact that the small Twickenham Film Studios had just one sound stage, of which they were still able to produce two films at the same time, using a day and night filming rotation; manic, hectic, but the system worked.

"Julius Hagen has acquired *When London Sleeps* by Charles Darrell."

"Twickenham shorts – Hagen will begin a series of short *"Masters of Music"*, based on the lives of the greatest composers, similar to the series made by James Fitzpatrick a few years ago – first week of production."

(*K. W.*, 17 March 1932, page 64, P. L. Mannock).

"*Double Dealing* – night work begins. The director is Leslie Hiscott."

(*K. W.*, 31 March 1932, pages 48 and 49, P. L. Mannock).

TWICKENHAM'S AMAZING 1932 RECORD:

A feature article in the *Kinematograph Weekly* asked:

"What is the secret that enables Julius Hagen and the Twickenham unit to produce with but one sound-stage at their disposal so many films of quality?"

John V. Watson

"During 1931, Twickenham had the second largest output of any British studio. This year, within three months, considerably more films have been shown than any other British producing centre. In fact, nine Twickenham productions have been Trade shown since the beginning of this year, and there is still a further one to come out before the end of the month. Without exception these productions have received very fine notices from both Trade and lay Press critics, and Julius Hagen may well be proud of this fine achievement. Of the nine productions two, *Frail Woman* and *The Marriage Bond*, are being distributed by Radio; three, *Condemned to Death*, *Murder at Covent Garden* and *The Chinese Puzzle*, by W. & F.; *The Missing Rembrandt* by P.D.C.; *The Crooked Lady* by M-G-M; *In a Monastery Garden* by A.P.D. Film Co.; and *Once Bitten* by Fox. All but one has been a full-length feature".

(*K. W.*, 31 March 1932, pages 48 and 49, P. L. Mannock).

April 1932:

Kinematograph Weekly reported throughout the month:

FILM PRODUCTION AT TWICKENHAM STUDIOS:

"*When London Sleeps* – the plans for production have been altered. Leslie Hiscott will probably direct instead of Maurice Elvey, who is likely to take charge of the musical *Old Masters* series."

(*K. W.*, 14 April 1932, page 59, P. L. Mannock).

"*When London Sleeps* – for A.P.D. Film Co., Ltd. is an up-to-date version of the famous old melodrama by Charles Darrell (who died this month) – scenario by H. Fowler Mear and Bernard Merivale – camera Basil Emmott."

'The Czar of Twickenham'. The History of Julius Hagen and the Film Empire he created at Twickenham Film Studios, from 1927 to 1938.

"Julius Hagen stated "I have also agreed to make two further films for this company – *The Lost Chord* and *Darby and Joan*." (The latter film was later retitled.)
(*K. W.*, 21 April 1932, pages 50 and 51, P. L. Mannock).

"*When London Sleeps* – busy in a circus tent, Hiscott directing in the grounds outside the studio floor."

(*K. W.*, 28 April 1932, page 53, P. L. Mannock).

May 1932:

Kinematograph Weekly reported throughout the month:

"Ten since 1931! – Julius (Box-Office) Hagen":

An article in the *Kinematograph Weekly* reported under the above heading:

"Although only one sound stage has been available at Twickenham Studios, Julius Hagen has been responsible for the completion of ten talkie productions since January of this year."

"Mr. Hagen, who firmly believes that a popular title is a great factor in the initial box-office appeal of a picture, and comparable with the drawing power of a star artist, says that, judging by present heavy bookings, *The Rosary* and *In a Monastery Garden* are likely to prove two of his greatest financial successes."

(*K. W.*, 5 May 1932, page 54, P. L. Mannock).

FILM PRODUCTION AT TWICKENHAM STUDIOS:

"*When London Sleeps* – big scenes include a sinister gambling den; the kidnapping of the heroine by crooks; and exciting fire sequences. Twickenham Studios are now presenting a very gay appearance, with the studio grounds packed with sets representing a section of the Country Fair which figures in the film. Roundabouts, boxing booths, side-shows, caravans, and tents have all been commandeered and erected for these sequences, and Leslie Hiscott, the director, has taken full advantage of the opportunity of presenting in the film a medley of those striking character types with which our country fairs abound. Ben Field is arrayed in check suits loud enough to be heard in the White City. Renee Ray is an enchantress in the hooded robes of a professional palmist – Hiscott is convinced that her performance in *When London Sleeps* will justify her present promotion to stellar ranks."

(*K. W.*, 5 May 1932, page 54, P. L. Mannock).

"Within a few hours of completing *When London Sleeps*, Hiscott was at work on a new four-reel comedy *A Tight Corner* with Frank Pettingell and Harold French. Gina Malo is taking the feminine lead, from *The Cat and the Fiddle*, at the Palace Theatre."

(*K. W.*, 19 May 1932).

FILM SALES LIMITED - OVERSEAS AGENT FOR TWICKENHAM STUDIOS FILM PRODUCT:

The *Kinematograph Weekly*, 19 May 1932, printed an advertisement on page 33:

"Film Sales Limited – controlling overseas rights of Twickenham Film Studios Ltd., Butcher's Film Service Ltd., Archibald Nettlefold Productions and George King Productions, Ltd., plus Nero Films Berlin.

"The four Twickenham films are *Splinters in the Navy, The Rosary, In a Monastery Garden*, and *When London Sleeps*."

'The Czar of Twickenham'. The History of Julius Hagen and the Film Empire he created at Twickenham Film Studios, from 1927 to 1938.

"A. Fried, Managing Director, Films Sales Limited, 185 a Wardour Street, London, W.1."

(*K. W.*, 19 May 1932, an advertisement on page 33).

June 1932:

Kinematograph Weekly reported throughout the month:

NEW TWICKENHAM FILM STUDIOS SPORTS CLUB:

"Twickenham Film Studios Sports Club – the staff of TFS have just founded a sports club and have some vacant dates for Sunday cricket matches. The honorary secretary is Lister Laurence, who would be pleased to hear from other clubs with a view to arranging fixtures."

NOTE that Lister Laurence was a film editor who was regularly employed at Twickenham Film Studios.

(*K. W.*, 9 June 1932, page 24).

NATIONAL DISTRIBUTORS, LTD: NEW PRIVATE COMPANY FORMED WITH JULIUS HAGEN:

"**National Distributors, Ltd**. – private company – registered 9 June 1932 – capital: £5,000 in £1 shares – to manufacture, distribute and deal in motion or other picture films, etc.

The subscribers are:-

Julius Hagen, 1 William Street House, Knightsbridge, managing director, film producing company;
E. Mollinson, 225 Oxford Street, W.1., managing director;
Qualification: £10 shares."

(*K. W.*, 16 June 1932, report on page 30).

FILM PRODUCTION AT TWICKENHAM STUDIOS:

"Elizabeth Allan is announced to play the leading feminine rôle opposite Ivor Novello in the forthcoming production of *The Lodger*. *The Lodger* will be the first British picture to be controlled by **National Distributors, Ltd.**"

(*K. W.*, 16 June 1932, page 44, P. L. Mannock).

"*The Lodger* starts production on Friday, 24 June 1932 – the director is Maurice Elvey."

(*K. W.*, 23 June 1932, P. L. Mannock).

July 1932:

Kinematograph Weekly reported throughout the month:

FILM PRODUCTION AT TWICKENHAM STUDIOS:

"*The Lodger* is now in production. A. W. Baskcomb joins the cast in a leading character part. The film will be controlled by National Distributors, Ltd."

(*K. W.*, 7 July 1932, page 45, P. L. Mannock).

NATIONAL DISTRIBUTORS, LTD: JULIUS HAGEN DEPARTS:

Julius Hagen terminates his connection with the recently established National Distributors, Ltd.

"As a result of a mutual arrangement between Julius Hagen and Eric Hakim, the former has terminated his connection with National Distributors, Ltd., and has recently retired from the directorate."

'The Czar of Twickenham'. The History of Julius Hagen and the Film Empire he created at Twickenham Film Studios, from 1927 to 1938.

"The change will necessitate a few alterations to programme, but National Distributors will still forge ahead. Twickenham Film Studios, Limited, will shortly announce their arrangements in respect of their production of *The Lodger* with Ivor Novello".

(*K. W.*, 14 July 1932, page 21).

SUCCESSFUL GENERAL RELEASE OF '*IN A MONASTERY GARDEN*':

"*In a Monastery Garden*, being distributed by the A.P.D. film company, is having a remarkably successful general release, and is, in fact, showing at fifty-two London kinemas this week. The original melodrama was specially written by H. Fowler Mear to incorporate W. J. Ketelbey's world-famous musical suite. Features John Stuart and Joan Maude, with Gina Malo and Hugh Williams."

(*K. W.*, 14 July 1932, page 28).

FILM PRODUCTION AT TWICKENHAM STUDIOS:

"*The Lodger* – Twickenham is transformed into a telephone exchange; by courtesy of the G.P.O., several genuine "hello" girls have been busy giving wrong numbers to Elizabeth Allan and Molly Fisher."

(*K. W.*, 21 July 1932, page 47, P. L. Mannock).

"*The Lodger* directed by Maurice Elvey now in its fifth week."

(*K. W.*, 28 July 1932, page 33).

"*The Lodger* is now nearing completion."

John V. Watson

(*K. W.*, 28 July 1932, page 34).

August 1932:

Kinematograph Weekly apparently did not contain any reports about any activities at Twickenham Film Studios throughout this month:

September 1932:

Kinematograph Weekly reported throughout the month:

JULIUS HAGEN EXTENDS HIS ACTIVITIES TO STAGE PRODUCTION:

"Julius Hagen is extending his activities in many directions. He has decided to send one of his film stars on a provincial tour of all the important theatres, with a London season to follow, and has commissioned the well-known theatrical manager, Robert Jorgensen, to prepare a completely revised version of **Lord Richard of the Pantry** to exploit Richard Cooper, who made such a decided hit in Mr. Hagen's film version of Sydney Blow and Douglas Hoare's play. It will be brought up to date, and known as *She Couldn't Say No*".

(*K. W.*, 15 September 1932, page 21, "*Long Shots*" column).

FILM PRODUCTION AT TWICKENHAM STUDIOS:

"**The Face at the Window** is to be made into a talkie at Twickenham, the modern version written by H. Fowler Mear. Leslie Hiscott to direct. Claude Hulbert is the only member of the cast already fixed."

(*K. W.*, 15 September 1932, page 43, P. L. Mannock).

'The Czar of Twickenham'. The History of Julius Hagen and the Film Empire he created at Twickenham Film Studios, from 1927 to 1938.

"*The Lodger* – Julius Hagen states that the credit for the dialogue should be divided equally between Miles Mander, Ivor Novello and H. Fowler Mear, "each of whom has his own share in the feature of the picture".

(*K. W.*, 22 September 1932, page 25).

"Twickenham Studios: *The Face at the Window*, Leslie Hiscott directing Raymond Massey, is in its second week."

(*K. W.*, 29 September 1932, page 46, *"Pulse at the Studios"* column).

October 1932:

Kinematograph Weekly reported throughout the month:

FILM PRODUCTION AT TWICKENHAM STUDIOS:

"*The Face at the Window* last week of production. Scenes filmed: rescue of the heroine (Isla Bevan) from one of the most notorious haunts of the Parisian apache, whither she had been lured under false pretext by the dastardly Count (Eric Maturin). The cast includes the sensational dancers, Berenott and Charlot."

(*K. W.*, 6 October 1932, page 45, P. L. Mannock).

"*The World, The Flesh and The Devil*. George Cooper directing Harold Huth in the leading rôle. A melodrama written by Laurence Cowan, adapted by H. Fowler Mear. George Cooper's returned welcomed by the correspondent, PLM."

(*K. W.*, 13 October 1932, page 53, P. L. Mannock).

"*The World, The Flesh and The Devil*. Shooting will be completed this week by George A. Cooper. "For the exciting flood finale in which the villain meets his richly deserved doom, hundreds of gallons of water will, at a given moment, be released in a gigantic tank and completely swamp an inn, which James Carter has constructed in the grounds of the studio".

(*K. W.*, 20 October 1932, page 51, P. L. Mannock).

"Twickenham Studios: *The World, The Flesh and The Devil*. Geo. Cooper directs Harold Huth, Isla Bevan. In its third week."

(*K. W.*, 27 October 1932, page 45, *"Pulse at the Studios"* column).

November 1932:

Kinematograph Weekly reported throughout the month:

FILM PRODUCTION AT TWICKENHAM STUDIOS:

"*Puppets of Fate* – the first of two Julius Hagen productions for United Artists – is now in production at Twickenham – adapted for the screen by H. Fowler Mear, directed by George Cooper – the highlight, a big train smash, was successfully staged and shot in the grounds of the studio last week. The star is Godfrey Tearle, with Russell Thorndike, that distinguished actor of Grand Guignol, is aptly cast in his first talkie."

(*K. W.*, 17 November 1932, page 43, P. L. Mannock).

"*The Iron Stair* – a screen adaptation of the well-known story by "Rita" has been made by H. Fowler Mear and will go into production this week. Provides dual rôle for Henry Kendall. Leslie Hiscott is directing. Ernest Palmer is chief cameraman. A silent version was made by Stoll ten years ago."

'The Czar of Twickenham'. The History of Julius Hagen and the Film Empire he created at Twickenham Film Studios, from 1927 to 1938.

(*K. W.*, 24 November 1932, page 41, P. L. Mannock).

"Hagen's current film *Puppets of Fate* has been completed."

(*K. W.*, 24 November 1932, page 41, P. L. Mannock).

December 1932:

Kinematograph Weekly reported throughout the month:

FILM PRODUCTION AT TWICKENHAM STUDIOS:

"George Cooper began directing *The Shadow* at Twickenham last week with Henry Kendall, Elizabeth Allan, Cyril Raymond, etc."

(*K. W.*, 8 December 1932, page 26, P. L. Mannock).

ELIZABETH ALLAN – HOLLYWOOD MGM CONTRACT:

"The eventual departure of Elizabeth Allan has been fairly obvious for some months, and the **Julius Hagen contract** having been bought out, this delightful young actress has been able to accept one from MGM."

"Before sailing in the New Year, Miss Allan (Mrs. W. J. O'Bryen) is to complete two Twickenham subjects".

"The willingness of our studios to neglect the obvious contract value of this young star is a puzzle to me."

(*K. W.*, 15 December 1932, page 28).

1932: Independent Films made at Twickenham: 1932:

The facilities of Twickenham Film Studios was used for just

one independent production in the year 1932, and that one film was made very early that year, as the following entry reveals:

Stormy Weather: Working Title.
> "Work has now started on another Fox 4-reeler at Twickenham – **Stormy Weather**, Frank Richardson directing."

> (*Kinematograph Weekly*, 29 January 1931, page 41).

The film is probably **Flat No. 9**, a 42-minute comedy, made by V. E. Deucher, directed by Frank Richardson, featuring Jane Baxter and Reginald Gardiner, and released by Fox Films, which was trade shown in late May 1932.

It should be noted that there was a British film entitled **Stormy Weather**. Released in 1935, it starred farceurs Tom Walls and Ralph Lynn, with Robertson Hare and Yvonne Arnaud in support, and it was one of the several popular of film adaptations of Ben Traver's Aldwych Farces of the 1930s.

The making of this one independent production at Twickenham was in direct contrast to how the Studio was previously made available to outside producers, whereby three independent films were made at Twickenham in 1931, and, in the previous year of 1930, a five-fold number — 15 — were made that year!

Twickenham's 16 Films Trade Shown during 1932:

Twickenham completed sixteen films during 1932. This number made gave an increase of five more films over the eleven films that the studio completed during the previous year, 1931.

'The Czar of Twickenham'. The History of Julius Hagen and the Film Empire he created at Twickenham Film Studios, from 1927 to 1938.

Six of these sixteen films were all "Quota Quickies"; all six were made by Julius Hagen's 'Real Art Productions' (formed in April 1931), and all ran for under an hour. Three of these six films were made for Fox-British, two for Radio Pictures, and one for M-G-M, as follows:

> *Once Bitten* was the second of the five short-length 'Quota Quickie' features which 'Real Art Productions' made for Fox-British from 1931 to 1933. It ran 47 minutes.
>
> *Double Dealing* was the third of the five short-length 'Quota Quickie' films which 'Real Art Productions' made for Fox-British from 1931 to 1933. It ran 48 minutes.
>
> *A Safe Proposition* was the fourth of the five short-length 'Quota Quickie' films which 'Real Art Productions' made for Fox-British from 1931 to 1933. It ran 45 minutes.
>
> *A Tight Corner* was the third Real Art 'Quota Quickie' film made for Metro-Goldwyn-Mayer Pictures, Ltd., M-G-M's British renting subsidiary. It ran 49 minutes.
>
> *The Face at the Window* was the first 'Quota Quickie' film made by Hagen's Twickenham subsidiary film production company, Real Art Productions Ltd, for the British distribution subsidiary of the American Radio Pictures. It ran 52 minutes.
>
> *The World, the Flesh, and the Devil* was the second 'Quota Quickie' film made by Hagen's Twickenham subsidiary film production company, Real Art Productions Ltd, for the British distribution subsidiary of the American Radio Pictures. It ran 54 minutes.

January:

Frail Woman (1931)

Heavy social drama with a poignant theme with Mary Newcomb, Owen Nares and Edmund Gwenn.

It was the first film that Maurice Elvey directed for Julius Hagen.

Frail Woman was Trade shown in London on Friday, 15 January 1932 at the Leicester Square Theatre.

Frail Woman was reviewed by *Kinematograph Weekly* on 21 January 1932:

RCA Photophone, 72.5 minutes, although 75 minutes was stated in the review in '*Kine Weekly*', "A" certificate.

"Remarks: Heavy social drama with a poignant theme. Good individual acting, particularly by star, and competent direction.

"Box Office Angle: Proposition for the more serious minded,

"Heavy, social drama, which takes for its subject the unhappy plight of the illegitimate child. The problem is treated with dramatic skill by Maurice Elvey and his experienced cast, and, although it is impossible to avoid the obvious, there remains much to interest and provide food for thought. This picture, which is provocative rather than entertaining, should appeal to all who can appreciate good acting.

"Story: An aristocrat learns that a girl, barred from marriage into a wealthy family because of her illegitimacy, is his own daughter. He does the right thing and marries her mother, who through force of circumstances had been the mistress of a bookmaker, but the woman, realising the hopelessness of her lot, takes her own life following the ceremony, rather than jeopardise the future of her husband and her daughter.

"Acting: Mary Newcomb plays the part of a woman who has fallen through a wartime indiscretion, with subtlety and understanding, and it is her interesting performance which gives the picture poignancy and feminine appeal. Owen Nares is rather given to sentimentality as the man, but Margaret Vines is very charming and sympathetic as the daughter. Edmund Gwenn gives a perfect characterisation as the bookmaker, and Athole Stewart, Herbert Lomas and Miles Malleson furnish clever support in minor rôles.

"Production: The story is transparent, and it is left to the characters, most of which are competently portrayed, to extract humanity and poignancy from the theme. Mary Newcomb's performance if the highlight of the picture, and her experienced histrionics compel concentration. Maurice Elvey has handled his subject with a sound sense of the dramatic, introduces clever and diverting cameos, assures adequate movement, and, by illustrating the strictness of the social code, establishes feminine appeal.

"Settings and Photography: The staging is unpretentious but adequate, while lighting and photography good.

"Points of Appeal: Interesting and human story, excellent performance by star, and feminine appeal.

The World Premier of *Frail Woman* was held at the RKO Theatre, Leicester Square, London on Friday, 15 January 1932 at 9 p.m., the same date and time as the London Trade show of the film.

London: Key theatre first-run for the week commencing Monday, 18 January 1932, held at the Leicester Square

Theatre, *Frail Woman* was double-billed with the Columbia Pictures drama, *The Pagan Lady*, with Evelyn Brent, Conrad Nagel and Charles Bickford, released by United Artists in the United Kingdom.

Frail Woman went out on General Release on Monday, 30 May 1932.

Condemned to Death (1931)

Murder mystery drama with an unusual twist.

Starring Arthur Wontner, Edmund Gwenn and Gordon Harker. Arthur Wontner played 'Sherlock Holmes' in five British films of the 1930s, of which four were made by Julius Hagen.

Directed by Walter Forde, the third of the three films this former British silent film comedian made for Julius Hagen.

Adapted from the play *'Jack O'Lantern'* by George Goodchild.

Condemned to Death was Trade shown on Thursday, 21 January 1932, at the Palace Theatre.

Condemned to Death was reviewed by *Kinematograph Weekly* on 28 January 1932:

RCA Photophone, 70 minutes, "A" certificate.

"Remarks: Fantastic but fascinating crime play with good thrills. Good individual characterisation, competent direction and realistic atmosphere.

"Box Office Angle: Good general booking.

'The Czar of Twickenham'. The History of Julius Hagen and the Film Empire he created at Twickenham Film Studios, from 1927 to 1938.

> "This arresting murder mystery drama is, when you get down to the fundamentals, an extravagant study in posthumous hypnotism, but its fantastic theme is presented with such conviction that tension is always held. Walter Forde has handled the plot cleverly, and it is this, together with sterling characterisations by a strong cast, that results in a convincing atmosphere.

> "Although the identity of the killer is quickly established, this does not lessen interest or destroy the effect of the thrilling ending, which is both highly dramatic and logical. Good programme booking.

> "Story: A series of cruel murders have been committed, all of which are attributed to a maniac. Jim Wrench, of Scotland Yard, sets to work to bring the culprit to justice and is helped in his investigations by Sir Charles Wallington, a retired judge.

> "Sir Charles, who had sentenced Tobias Lantern to death some years before, observes that all the victims so far had testified against Lantern at his trial. He imparts this information to Wrench, and solicits the aid Professor Mich(a)els, who is confident that the killer is working under hypnotic influence.

> "Sir Charles' observations and Mich(a)els' theory lead to the solution, and it is ultimately proved that Sir Charles is the killer, and that he has been acting on the posthumous influence of Lantern, who had forced him to develop a dual personality so that he could have vengeance on the man who had brought about his conviction.

> "Acting: Arthur Wontner plays the dual personality rôle

169

John V. Watson

with skill and understanding, and always retains a cultivated sense of dignity. Cyril Raymond is well cast as Wrench, Edmund Gwenn and Gordon Harker are excellent as two hardened criminals, Griffiths Humphreys convinces as the professor, and Jane Welsh and Gillian Lind are both good in the only feminine rôles.

"Production: The hypnotic theme may appear a trifle advanced, but it nevertheless furnishes an excellent pivot for the thrilling mystery plot. Walter Forde has taken the picture seriously, particularly in his characterisation and detail work, and his convincing atmosphere allows the thrills to register with telling effect and the suspense to be well held.

"One has little difficulty in establishing the identity of the killer, but the side issues are so cleverly woven into the main theme that the ending, although obvious, has all the kick of the unexpected. The picture represents good entertainment of its type, and this being a popular type, success can be predicted.

"Settings and Photography: Many phases of London life figure prominently in the development, and each is presented with commendable realism. Lighting and photography are particularly good.

"Points of Appeal: Arresting story, clever acting by star and support, popular thrills and suspense, and painstaking development.

London key-theatre pre-release run at the Astoria, week commencing Monday, 16 May 1932, *Condemned to Death* supported *A Night Like This*, with Ralph Lynn and Tom Walls, also released by W. & F.

170

Condemned to Death went out on General Release on Monday, 30 May 1932.

The Missing Rembrandt (1932)
'Sherlock Holmes' detective drama.

The Missing Rembrandt was the second appearance by Arthur Wontner as 'Sherlock Holmes' for Julius Hagen. Wontner was to make three more film appearances as the famous detective, including two more for Hagen.

The Missing Rembrandt was the only film Julius Hagen made for the British distribution company: P.D.C. (Producers Distributing Corporation).

The Missing Rembrandt was Trade shown on Friday, 12 February 1932, at the Phoenix Theatre, Charing Cross Road, London.

Trade Press comments about *The Missing Rembrandt* as printed in an advertisement on the front page of *Kinematograph Weekly*, 18 February 1932:

Daily Film Renter: "Should readily find big appeal".

To-day's Cinema: "Excellent popular entertainment".

The Missing Rembrandt was reviewed by *Kinematograph Weekly* on 18 February 1932:

RCA Photophone, 84 minutes (although 80 minutes was listed as the running time in the '*Kine Weekly*' review). "A" certificate.

"Remarks: Clean, popular and entertaining adaptation of

one of the Sherlock Holmes series. Good work by star, and efficient production qualities.

"Box Office Angle: Good general booking with box office pull.

"Clean, entertaining detective drama, based on one of the well-known Conan Doyle Sherlock Holmes stories, which gives life to the exploits of the famous character of fiction and retains all those qualities which have made the author's detective fiction so eminently popular.

"Arthur Wontner is Holmes personified, and the quality of the entertainment lies principally in his intriguing performance. The directorial work is efficient, a good atmosphere prevails, and the team work of the supporting players is commendable. Attractive booking proposition with obvious box-office pull.

"Story: Sherlock Holmes interests himself in the strange case of a stolen Rembrandt. The planning of the theft points to the work of a master criminal, and this narrows Holmes' field down to Baron von Guntermann, who carries out his nefarious schemes beneath the cloak of a respectable art dealer. Holmes' deductions prove to be correct, and the clumsy blackmailing of a lady by one of Guntermann's assistants, enables him to establish Guntermann's guilt beyond all question of doubt.

"Acting: Arthur Wontner not only has the facial and physical characteristics of Holmes, but gets beneath the skin of the character. His performance is flawless in every detail, and holds the picture together. Ian Fleming and Philip Newland are a little too lacking in understanding as Dr. Watson and Inspector Lestrade respectively, but Francis L. Sullivan is excellent as Guntermann. Dino Galvani, Miles Mander, Minnie Rayner and Jane Welsh all give interesting supporting studies.

"Production: Although Leslie Hiscott has hardly succeeded in establishing adequate movement, he has retained the quality and freshness of Conan Doyle's story. By allowing Arthur Wontner to dominate the screen he gives full play to the intriguing characteristics of the famous detective, whose nonchalant deductions and sly humour, gained at the expense of Dr. Watson, afford endless amusement and entertainment. All admirers of the famous Sherlock Holmes stories, and these are legion, are certain to enjoy this engaging effort.

"Settings and Photography: Limehouse sequences, the famous Baker Street consulting rooms, and other adequate interiors, contribute a good atmosphere, while lighting and photography are very good.

"Points of Appeal: Title, star, popularity of the Holmes stories, competent portrayals and workmanlike direction.

Condemned to Death went out on General Release on Monday, 22 August 1932.

Murder at Covent Garden (1932)

Mystery drama starring stage actor, Dennis Neilson-Terry.

Murder at Covent Garden was the thirteenth film

173

directed by Leslie Hiscott for Julius Hagen; it was also the only one he co-directed. The reason why there were two directors (instead of the customary one) has not been determined.

Murder at Covent Garden was produced for W. & F. Film Service, Ltd.

Murder at Covent Garden was Trade shown on Thursday, 18 February 1932, at the Capitol Theatre in London; the film commenced its West End run at that cinema on the following Monday.

Murder at Covent Garden was reviewed by *Kinematograph Weekly* on 25 February 1932 (page 22):

RCA Photophone, 66 minutes, "A" certificate.

"Remarks: Refreshing, ingenious mystery drama, with good London atmosphere. Strong cast and adequate production qualities.

"Box Office Angle: Useful programme booking.

"This murder mystery drama has a very good atmosphere and a strong cast, but as the story is pieced together with rather slow deliberation momentum is occasionally lost and its development becomes apparent. However, despite its transparency, it carries a full complement of ingenious thrills, and it is sufficiently diverting to make a satisfactory offering for the majority of halls.

"Story: Donald Walpace is employed by the South African Diamond Syndicate to track down crooks who are smuggling stones into England. With the help of his sister, Helen, Donald discovers the identity of the receiver, a night-club proprietor, but he is tricked by a crook who poses as Belmont, one of the company's other detectives who has been sent over to assist him. The real Belmont, however, side-tracks the crook, who had killed the receiver, sees that Walpace gets the glory and the reward; and wins the love of Helen, after rescuing her from a fire in the cabaret.

"Acting: Dennis Neilson Terry gives a cool and engaging performance as the real Belmont, and tempers his portrayal with sly humour and popular romantic qualities. Anne Grey is a charming and natural heroine, and useful support comes from Walter Fitzgerald, Henry de Vries and George Curzon.

"Production: Although this drama moves at an even pace, the fact that it rather on the slow side accentuates the light texture of the story. This, however, should not seriously militate against its success as popular diversion, for suspense is fairly well held and the characters themselves are interesting. The joint producers, Michael Barringer and Leslie S. Hiscott, have established a good atmosphere, and there is a spectacular fire thrill to put the necessary kick into the climax.

"Settings and Photography: Scenes in Covent Garden market are good in detail, the cabaret sequences are suitably embellished with music and dancing, while the culminating fire thrill is effectively executed. Lighting and photography are good.

"Points of Appeal: Popularity of mystery drama, refreshing English atmosphere, good cast, and painstaking detail.

Murder at Covent Garden went out on General Release on Monday, 2 May 1932.

In a Monastery Garden (1932)

Drama set in Italy. Two brothers (John Stuart and Hugh Williams) study music in Rome and fall in love with the same woman (Joan Maude), the fiancée of a prince..

In a Monastery Garden was the first of the Julius Hagen/Twickenham Studios productions to be made for A. P. & D. (Associated Producing and Distribution).

"Frederick White and Gilbert Church present a Julius Hagen Production." Associated Producing & Distribution Co. were the Sole Distributors throughout the United Kingdom and Irish Free State.

In a Monastery Garden was Trade shown on Friday, 11 March 1932 at the Phoenix Theatre, Charing Cross Road.

In a Monastery Garden was reviewed by *Kinematograph Weekly* on 17 March 1932:

> RCA Photophone, 80.67 minutes exactly according to the registered length when it is divided by the 90 feet per minute sound film speed (but 77 minutes was stated with the '*Kine Weekly*' review), "A" certificate.

> "Remarks: Pleasing and colourful drama with simple but appealing theme. Good acting, direction and box-office title.

> "Box Office Angle: Excellent booking for masses.

"A pleasing drama which, apart from a certain slowness in the development, represents excellent entertainment for all but the most sophisticated audience. Very little action takes place within the precincts of a monastery, which is all to the good, but there is sufficient to justify the picture's box-office title. Both the atmosphere and the acting are good, and plenty of local colour, as well as appropriate music, is introduced into the presentation.

"Story: Michael and Paul Ferrier, both studying music in Italy, fall in love with Roma, who is already engaged to Prince Bonelli, a rakish officer. Bonelli is shot dead in such circumstances as to incriminate Michael, the more brilliant of the brothers, and he is tried for murder and sentenced to life imprisonment.

"During his absence, Paul steals his compositions and claims the glory. Just as Paul and Roma are about to be married, the late Bonelli's mistress confesses to the murder: Michael is released and goes into a monastery. Paul, whose conscience is uneasy, goes to Michael and tells him the truth. Michael, however, realises that Roma is in love with Paul, and he keeps his secret and remains in the monastery.

"Acting: John Stuart and Hugh Williams play Michael and Paul respectively, and their finished portrayals result in good dramatic contrast. Joan Maude is a refined and charming Roma, and Dino Galvani and Gina Malo are very good as the rakish officer and his volatile and jealous mistress.

"Production: Whatever the picture may lack in evenness is offset by its engaging sincerity. Maurice Elvey has

177

told his story with colour and good showmanship, and picks up the threads with a competence born of an experienced study of popular box-office values.

"Music plays an integral part of the development, and it gives full expression to the appealing sentiments. The slowness of action is apparent during the early stages, but once the story gets a grip on its audience this fault is relegated to the background and fails to disturb quality as a whole.

"Settings and Photography: The story is told in retrospective, and the monastic opening and closing scenes are most effective. The Italian atmosphere has colour, while ballet sequences result in exquisite light relief. Lighting and photography are good.

"Points of Appeal: Title, popular story, good acting, sentimental appeal, and good staging and direction.

In a Monastery Garden went out on General Release on Monday, 11 July 1932.

The Crooked Lady (1932)

Crime drama. A down-and-out ex-army officer, Captain James Kent (Austin Trevor) is forced to resort to a life of crime.

The Crooked Lady was the fourteenth film Leslie Hiscott directed for Julius Hagen at their Twickenham Film Studios; it was his first 'Real Art' picture.

The Crooked Lady was the second Real Art 'Quota Quickie' film made for Metro-Goldwyn-Mayer Pictures, Ltd., M-G-M's British renting subsidiary.

'The Czar of Twickenham'. The History of Julius Hagen and the Film
Empire he created at Twickenham Film Studios, from 1927 to 1938.

The Crooked Lady supported *Mata Hari*, the Greta
Garbo 'showcase' drama made by M.G.M. at the London
key-theatre run held at the Metropole Cinema, week
commencing Monday, 8 August 1932. *Mata Hari* and *The
Crooked Lady* were both released in the United Kingdom
by Metro-Goldwyn-Mayer Pictures, Ltd.

The Crooked Lady was Trade shown on Wednesday,
16 March 1932 at the Phoenix Theatre, Charing Cross Road.

The Crooked Lady was reviewed by *Kinematograph
Weekly* on 17 March 1932:

RCA Photophone, 77 minutes, "U" certificate.

"Remarks: Live melodrama with Cockney element. Well
put over. Good acting.

"Box Office Angle: Very good general attraction.

"A thoroughly sound British melodrama livened with
Cockney humour and very well acted and produced. It
should go down with practically any audience, the
stars' performances, though of the thumbnail variety,
afford an additional box-office pull

"Story: Slim Barrett's and Captain Kent's lives are saved
in the war by a Major Barton. Later, Kent, down and
out, is introduced by Slim to a gangster, Garstin, who
sends him to rob a famous actress of her pearls, and,
incidentally, to score off a woman detective, Joan
Collinson.

"Finding the pearls belong to Major Barton's widow,
Kent returns them and starts a new life, writing novels

179

under an assumed name. Joan is employed by Scotland
Yard to trace Kent. Garstin wants him to claim a share
of the reward for the pearls, which Kent in reality has
refused. Garstin surprises Joan at Kent's cottage, but
after a tussle is overmastered by Kent and arrested by a
Scotland Yard man. Joan and Kent become engaged.

"Acting: George Graves as an elderly fop is at once a
success and a delight during his short-lived rôle. Isobel
Elsom is a most dignified recipient of the hero's
confession of the theft of her pearls.

"The main burden of the acting, however, rests with
Austin Trevor, who plays Kent with sincerity, if at
times slowly. Ursula Jeans is a charming lady detective
and uses her voice to advantage. From Alexander
Field comes a very good study of a Cockney, in which
he is ably supported by Moore Marriott as a fellow-
crook, and Edmund Willard, a truly melodramatic
gangster.

"Production: Leslie Hiscott knows how to seize on the
salient points of a story and make them effective. He
also has the art of interesting us in the minor
characters, and rôles like the private detective or book
publisher are real.

"He opens with a short war scene and a long, but
amusing and convincing, sequence at a coffee-stall,
where Slim and the ex-captain meet. The country
house party, where the hero perpetrates the robbery, is
skilfully visualised and introduces George Graves.
There is a spate of dialogue, which, however, is
generally amusing.

"Settings and Photography: Exteriors introduce a

coffee-stall and one or two countryside scenes. Interiors of a country house and cottage are tasteful. Photography is quite up to standard.

"Points of Appeal: Good plot, well-known actors and actresses, and, above all, English atmosphere and production at its best.

The Crooked Lady: the date of the General Release of this film has not been determined.

Once Bitten (1932)

Comedy: Short-length feature. Rich Sir Timothy Blott (Frank Pettingell) vanishes thinking he has killed his son-in-law's blackmailer.

Once Bitten was the second of the five short-length 'Quota Quickie' features which 'Real Art Productions' made for Fox-British from 1931 to 1933. That this film is a 'Quota Quickie' there is no question, because the film runs for just over three-quarters of an hour; at that length it was clearly made for Fox-British so that the renter could fulfil its distribution quota obligations by supplying exhibitors with British-made programme fillers. Its actual running time is 47 minutes.

Once Bitten was the fifteenth film Leslie Hiscott directed for Julius Hagen at their Twickenham Film Studios; and his second 'Real Art' picture.

Once Bitten supported *Forbidden* (1932), starring Barbara Stanwyck, with Adolphe Menjou and Ralph Bellamy, for the London key-theatre pre-release run at the Shepherd's Bush Pavilion, week commencing Monday, 13 June 1932.

Forbidden was directed by Frank Capra for Columbia Pictures, and was released in the United Kingdom by United Artists.

Once Bitten was Trade shown on Wednesday, 16 March 1932 at the Cambridge Theatre.

Once Bitten was reviewed by *Kinematograph Weekly* on 24 March 1932 (page 25):

RCA Photophone, 47 minutes, "A" certificate.

"<u>Remarks</u>: Humorous portrayal by Frank Pettingell in a breezy British comedy.

"<u>Box Office Angle</u>: Attractive light booking.

"A breezy British comedy, a trifle blue perhaps in its humour, which, thanks to the robust comicalities of the North Country comedian, Frank Pettingell, provides good fun for the majority of audiences. The staging is modern, while the team work is adequate.

"<u>Story</u>: Sir Timothy Blott, a gay knight from the North Country, falls into the clutches of Alicia and Mario Fideli while celebrating in the West End, and believes that he has killed Mario in a fight. He goes to Toby, his god-daughter's young husband, for help, and Toby, who is estranged from his wife, Clare, tells Timothy to hide in a country hotel. Following this, Toby loses his memory in a car smash, and is taken to the hotel, where Timothy has been mistaken for a waiter. The manner in which extricates himself from his difficulties and Toby's memory provides the fun.

"<u>Acting</u>: Frank Pettingell proves himself to be a first-rate comedian, and his North Country accent and quaint mannerisms, together with his sense of character, are responsible for most of the laughs. Richard Cooper is a useful foil as Toby, and Ursula Jeans, Dino Galvani and Jeanne Stuart are all satisfactory in support.

"Production: The story, built round the star, is quite good, and it leads to a riotous mix-up, the disentanglement of which gives play to hearty, irresponsible fooling. There is always plenty of movement.

"Settings and Photography: Cocktail bar, hotel reception, restaurant and apartment interiors contribute to a good atmosphere.

"Points of Appeal: Bright story, robust and popular humour of star, good support, presentation and treatment.

Once Bitten went out on General Release on Monday, 4 July 1932.

The Marriage Bond (1932)
Romantic drama, starring Mary Newcombe, Guy Newall and Stewart Rome.

The Marriage Bond was the second film produced by Julius Hagen, again under the 'Twickenham Film Studios' banner for Radio Pictures, Ltd., the British distribution subsidiary of the American Radio Pictures, in order to supply it with British film product, so that it could fulfil its legal quota obligations..

The Marriage Bond was the third film Maurice Elvey

directed for Julius Hagen.

The Marriage Bond was Trade shown on Tuesday, 22 March 1932 at the Cambridge Theatre.

The Marriage Bond was reviewed by *Kinematograph Weekly* on 24 March 1932:

> RCA Photophone, 75 minutes (but the running time was actually 82 minutes), "A" certificate.

> "<u>Remarks</u>: Elaborately produced triangle drama beautifully acted, but too long.

> "<u>Box Office Angle</u>: A good booking on stars' names.

> "Charming English scenery and first-class acting are features of this long-drawn-out triangle drama, in which a drunken husband is the all-important base. Audiences, particularly feminine ones, will probably appreciate the considerable emotional pull.

> "<u>Story</u>: Arriving drunk in the middle of the hunt ball, Toby Heron so disgusts his very modern daughter that he feels obliged to leave home for the seclusion of a remote cottage. Jacqueline, his wife, loves him, but when she visits the cottage and finds Toby in the company of the local barmaid she is ready to turn to her admirer, Paul Swaythling.

> "Meanwhile the daughter has married, and Toby returns home. Unable to leave him, Jacqueline returns to mother him for always.

> "<u>Acting</u>: Mary Newcomb brings brains and beauty to the emotional rôle of the sorely tried wife. Guy Newall puts up an amazingly good show as the drunkard,

whilst Ann Casson provides a clean-cut portrait of an offensively modern damsel.

"Florence Desmond is extremely good as the barmaid; in fact, not a member of the cast but maintains the high standard of performances.

"Production: Maurice Elvey has adhered to a stage technique, and except for some opening shots of a hunt relies very much on the dialogue. He has worked in some good emotional scenes, however. There is a tendency to slowness, although a very intelligent terrier prevents many scenes concerning the drunken husband from being boring.

"Settings and Photography: Delightful exteriors of the hunt, with interiors of mansion and cottage, are well photographed. Close-ups rather overdone at times.

"Points of Appeal: The stars, English scenery, and, last, the theme, which exacts sympathy chiefly on account of the acting.

The Marriage Bond went out on General Release on Monday, 29 August 1932.

The Chinese Puzzle (1932)

Crime drama. Repeating his role in the 1919 silent film version, Leon M. Lion appears as a Chinese mandarin who discovers that information about a treaty is being leaked from the British foreign office.

After the first six 'super feature' films were made by Twickenham Film Studios, Ltd during 1931 for W. & F. Film Service, Ltd., two further pictures were then made for this

185

renter; *The Chinese Puzzle* was the first. The second film was *The Lodger* (1932 - see below).

The Chinese Puzzle was the fifth of the six films Guy Newall directed for Julius Hagen.

The Chinese Puzzle was Trade shown on Wednesday, 23 March 1932; the Trade show was first announced to be held at the Prince Edward Theatre, but it was then actually shown at a Private Theatre for reasons not determined. Whilst the *Kinematograph Weekly* stated that the Trade show was held on 23 March 1932, the *Kinematograph Year Book* maintains it was held two days earlier, on 21 March.

London key-theatre first-run of *The Chinese Puzzle* was held at the Olympic, week commencing Monday, 11 April 1932. *The Chinese Puzzle* was booked into a double-bill with *Suicide Fleet* (1931) with Bill Boyd, Robert Armstrong, James Gleason and Ginger Rogers; a Charles R. Rogers Production for RKO Pathé Pictures, it was released in the United Kingdom by P.D.C.

The Chinese Puzzle was reviewed by *Kinematograph Weekly* on 24 March 1932:

RCA Photophone, 80 minutes, "A" certificate.

"Remarks: Drama of the diplomatic service with strong Oriental flavour. Well acted.

"Box Office Angle: Good general booking.

"The performance of Leon M. Lion as a Chinese dignitary gives distinction to this story of a Chinese debt of honour. The plot is artificial, but the characterisation is good and the production attractive.

'The Czar of Twickenham'. The History of Julius Hagen and the Film Empire he created at Twickenham Film Studios, from 1927 to 1938.

An intriguing booking for the general audience.

"Story: Chi-Lung, by receiving a valuable casket from a member of the De la Haye family, acknowledges a life-long debt. Later, Roger De la Haye, of the Diplomatic Service, is ordered to arrange a secret loan with Chi-Lung. The document ratifying it is stolen, and as a result Roger is suspected and dismissed.

"Chi-Lung knows that Naomi, now Roger's wife, stole the document for an agent of the British Government in order to save her mother from going to gaol for forgery, and, realising that Roger adores his wife, makes out that he stole the document himself. He kills the agent, sears Naomi to secrecy, and finally commits suicide.

"Acting: Leon M. Lion gives a practised study of the faithful Chinaman, with his thorough-going contempt for all things Western. Elizabeth Allan rises to the emotional demands made by her part as the guilty wife.

"Lilian Braithwaite is always charming and is delightful as the aristocratic mother of the hero, while from Mabel Sealby comes an amusing thumb-nail sketch of an adventuress.

"James Raglan, as Roger, and Austin Trevor are good examples of young Englishmen and speak well.

"Production: Guy Newall has provided graceful as well as strong situations, and groups his characters well, but his story is rather spun out, especially after Chi-Lung has decided to take the onus of betrayal on his shoulders. He opens thrillingly, however, and ends

187

dramatically. Dialogue rather swamps action, but is in keeping and provides some humour.

"Settings and Photography: Charming and well-photographed settings comprise English country-house interiors and those of Chi-Lung's abode. Oriental splendour is suggested, but is not overdone.

"Points of Appeal: The stars – Leon M. Lion's performance in particular – unusual plot, and Oriental element.

    Other contemporary reviews for *The Chinese Puzzle* as printed in the advertisement on page 4, Kine Weekly, 31 March 1932:

> *Daily Film Renter*: "Splendid booking. Leon M. Lion gives a masterly impersonation of the subtle enigmatic Oriental, full of flowery Chinese epigrams and woman-hating cynicisms. His acting has moments of gripping suspense. The story grips consistently, and is amply seasoned with humour. Here is a first-class booking for any house".

> *Cinema*: "There is some good atmosphere in the tale of a mandarin's gratitude, and popular patrons will doubtless respond to its appealing sentiment. The important part of the Chinaman is played by Leon M. Lion, who has few equals in this type of role, and who gives a memorable performance in his artistic revelation of a noble soul. A word should go to the resourceful settings, not only of a Chinese garden in the earlier scenes, but of the palatial apartments in which the major part of the development is enacted. Recording, too, is first-rate, and does not permit us to lose a word, even of the Chinaman's throaty English".

> *Bioscope*: "Good popular booking. The touch of
> the Oriental has a certain fascination for most
> people, and to these the picture cannot fail to
> appeal. Acting is good all round, with, of
> course, the limelight focussed on the colourful
> role of Chi Lung, ably played by Leon M.
> Lion".

The Chinese Puzzle went out on General Release on Monday, 8 August 1932.

Double Dealing (1932)

Broad Yorkshire comedy featuring character star Frank Pettingell as Rufus Moon, a pious and prudish politician who disapproves of his nephew Toby Traill (Richard Cooper) marrying an actress.

Double Dealing was the third of the five short-length 'Quota Quickie' features which 'Real Art Productions' made for Fox-British from 1931 to 1933. The film ran 48 minutes.

Double Dealing was the sixteenth film Leslie Hiscott directed for Julius Hagen at their Twickenham Film Studios; it was his third 'Real Art' production.

Double Dealing was Trade shown on Wednesday, 27 April 1932, at the Phoenix Theatre, Charing Cross Road, London.

Double Dealing was reviewed by *Kinematograph Weekly* on 5 May 1932, (page 40):

RCA Photophone, 50 minutes, "A" certificate.

"Remarks: A raw but amusing comedy burlesque, which makes riotous sport of killjoys and other hypocritical humbugs. Bright performance by star.

"<u>Box Office Angle</u>: Good quota second feature for popular audiences.

"A raw but amusing comedy which makes sport of killjoys and other hypocritical humbugs. The humour is certainly topical, and is put over with good effect by Frank Pettingell, who is in first-rate form as the two-faced chairman of a Watch Committee. Some of the lines are a bit near the mark, but they nevertheless score the laughs. Good quota second feature for popular audiences.

"<u>Story</u>: Toby Trail, a young reporter, wishes to get married to Dolly Simms, an actress, but cannot get the consent of his uncle, Rufus Moon, who is the pious chairman of a North Country Watch Committee.

"Dolly, however, recognises Rufus as the backer of a show in which she is playing, and informs Toby, who has no difficulty in unmasking the old hypocrite and forcing him to consent to their marriage.

"<u>Acting</u>: Frank Pettingell gives a bright study as the old hypocrite, Rufus, and his North Country accent softens the raw lines and adds to their unblushing humour. Sydney Fairbrother is as usual good as the straight-laced wife, while Richard Cooper and Zoe Palmer furnish the love interest.

"<u>Production</u>: The unwarrantable interference of local busybodies has undoubtedly inspired this broad burlesque and satire, which makes sport of their activities with great gusto and enthusiasm. The central character is played with such good-hearted but scathing truth by Frank Pettingell, who has been well primed with fruity and ambiguous lines, of which nobody can miss the point. The humour, however, never rises above the level of the man in the street, and its broadness and obviousness can be relied upon to score the laughs.

"Settings and Photography: Amusing light is shed on the meeting of a local Watch Committee, and the leading character's domestic life is amusingly depicted, while the night club sequences result in brightness and colour. Lighting and photography are good.

"Points of Appeal: Broad, but popular humour, hilarious portrayal by star, and bright treatment.

Double Dealing went out on General Release on Monday, 8 August 1932.

A Safe Proposition (1932)

Short-length feature film. Comedy. A man (A. W. Baskcomb) retrieves a woman's pearls from a bogus Count (Austin Trevor).

A Safe Proposition was the fourth of the five short-length 'Quota Quickie' films which 'Real Art Productions' made for Fox-British from 1931 to 1933.

A Safe Proposition was the talkie début of A. W. Baskcomb, the star of the film.

A Safe Proposition was the seventeenth film Leslie Hiscott directed for Julius Hagen at their Twickenham Film Studios; it was also his fourth 'Real Art' picture.

John V. Watson

A Safe Proposition was Trade shown on Tuesday, 28 June 1932, at the Palace Theatre, London; the screening of which preceded the trade showing of **Society Girl** with James Dunn, Peggy Shannon and Spencer Tracy, another Fox release.

A Safe Proposition was reviewed by *Kinematograph Weekly* on 30 June 1932 (page 35):

RCA Photophone, "U" certificate.

"<u>Remarks</u>: Crook comedy. Good performances by stars. Moderate direction.

"<u>Box Office Angle</u>: Usable supporting feature.

"An amusing little crook comedy, enlivened by the performances of the stars as nouveaux riches. Of average merit in every way, it should prove an acceptable second feature in the general programme.

"<u>Story</u>: Mrs. Woodford, to cover her bridge losses, has sold a valuable necklace given her by her husband, and purchased a fake. She entreats Reggie, who is attached to her daughter Margaret, to steal the fake, not knowing that her husband has seen through her deception and repurchased the real necklace.

"Reggie surprises Ginger, a cat burglar, at the safe, and helps him to get away with the necklace, which Reggie believes to be the fake. He later exposes a Count Tonelli, a rival for Margaret's affections, as a would-be thief, and wins the lady and the necklace.

"<u>Acting</u>: A. W. Baskcomb gives a very finished performance as the husband, Barbara Gott being also

most effective as the agitated and homely wife.
Younger members of the cast are not so successful in
their portrayals, though they work hard to give good
support.

"<u>Production</u>: Leslie Hiscott, though rather inclined to let
his characters talk too much, easily handles his plot.
The personalities of the parvenus and the
complications between real and fake necklace keep up
the interest. The Cockney Ginger's behaviour at a
police station supplies a humorous interlude. Dialogue
is sometimes rather drawn-out, but contains a few
good sallies.

"<u>Settings and Photography</u>: Lavish house interiors are
well lighted, the few exteriors are also attractive.
Lighting satisfactory. A police station interior is
included.

"<u>Points of Appeal</u>: The acting, the plot and light
atmosphere.

A Safe Proposition went out on General Release on
Monday, 17 October 1932.

When London Sleeps (1932)
Crime drama.

When London Sleeps was the second of the Julius
Hagen/Twickenham Film Studios productions to be made
for A. P. & D. (Associated Producing and Distribution Co.,
Ltd.) The opening on-screen credits on the British release
print state: "Frederick White & Gilbert Church present a
Julius Hagen production."

John V. Watson

A. P. & D were Sole Distributors of *When London Sleeps* throughout the United Kingdom and Irish Free State

When London Sleeps was the eighteenth film Leslie Hiscott directed for Julius Hagen.

When London Sleeps was Trade shown on Friday, 22 July 1932, at the Prince Edward Theatre, Old Compton Street, London, W.1.

When London Sleeps was reviewed by *Kinematograph Weekly* on 28 July 1932 (page 27):

RCA Photophone, 75 minutes, "A" certificate.

"Remarks: Rousing melodrama; film version of a well-known stage success; naïve but exciting story well put over.

"Box Office Angle: Good stuff for the masses.

"Rousing melodrama, a hectic panorama of London life, adapted from Charles Darrell's famous stage play. The story has been modernised, and it is put over with sufficient elaboration and gusto to conceal much of its artlessness.

"There is, too, a strong cast of accomplished stage and screen players, which helps to establish box-office pull. Outside of the few high-class halls which cater for a discriminating public, this picture stands a capital chance of meeting with success.

"Story: Tommy Blythe, a reckless young gambler, visits a fair ground to forget his unfortunate turf speculations, and falls in love with Mary, an attractive palmist, the

194

adopted daughter of Lamberti, the impecunious owner
of the fair. Tommy promises to help Lamberti and
goes to a night club, a rendezvous of Society gamblers,
where he wins a useful sum.

"By a strange coincidence, Mary turns out to be the
long-lost cousin of Rodney Haines, the unscrupulous
proprietor of the club, and he tries to get rid of her so
that he can gain her dead father's fortune. He abducts
her, but Tommy comes to her rescue, saves her from a
fire on the club premises, where she is imprisoned, and
sees that Haines gets his just deserts.

"Acting: Harold French is good as Tommy and behaves
as a hero should. Rene Ray is adequate as Mary;
Francis L. Sullivan gives a clever performance as the
unscrupulous Haines; while Alexander Field and Ben
Field are responsible for two excellent character
studies.

"Production: Virtue triumphs over vice in this picture in
the accepted manner, and the working out of the plot
certainly leads to variety, if not to the unexpected. The
elaborate night-club scenes are symbolical of the seamy
side of London life, while the fair-ground sequences,
the heroine's world, form an effective contrast.

"There are times when the action is on the slow side, but
once the stage is set for the fire things warm up
considerably, and the proceedings end on a hectic,
thrilling and satisfying note.

"Settings and Photography: The night club, complete
with gambling saloon, is staged on a lavish scale, and
all the paraphernalia of the fair-ground is given in

195

detail, while the culminating fire scene carries a good thrill. Lighting and photography are good.

"Points of Appeal: Naïve, but popular and exciting story, good staging, competent cast, and title.

When London Sleeps: the date this film went out on General Release has not been determined.

A Tight Corner (1932)

Short-length feature film. Knockabout comedy: Two luckless detectives (Harold French and Frank Pettingell) are hired to recover a baron's incriminating letters from a blackmailer.

A Tight Corner was the third Real Art 'Quota Quickie' film made for Metro-Goldwyn-Mayer Pictures, Ltd., M-G-M's British renting subsidiary.

A Tight Corner was the nineteenth film Leslie Hiscott directed for Julius Hagen at their Twickenham Film Studios; his fifth 'Real Art' picture.

A Tight Corner was Trade shown on Thursday, 18 August 1932 at MGM's own private theatre in London.

A Tight Corner was reviewed by *Kinematograph Weekly* on 25 August 1932 (page 23):

RCA Photophone, 49 minutes, "A" certificate.

"Remarks: Commonplace farcical comedy, a leg show with broad and risqué lines.

"Box Office Angle: Light booking for industrial halls only.

'The Czar of Twickenham'. The History of Julius Hagen and the Film Empire he created at Twickenham Film Studios, from 1927 to 1938.

"A thin British comedy which falls back on old situations and ripe innuendos for its laughs, which are conspicuously few. The leading players do their best to enliven the proceedings, and the technical qualities are good, but the film still remains a very indifferent effort and can only be employed as a supporting feature for small halls.

"Story: Oswald Blenkinsop and Tony Titmouse, private inquiry agents, are commissioned by Baron Yodel to retrieve incriminating letters which he had written to Madame Ginkenstein, proprietress of a physical culture school. They gain an entrance by posing as instructors, and get involved in a network of love and intrigue before they satisfactorily fulfil their tasks.

"Acting: Frank Pettingell, the ample North-county comedian, cuts an amusing figure as Blenkinsop and gets away with some suggestive lines. Harold French, a useful light comedian, is entrusted with the love interest, and the feminine appeal is in the hands of Gina Malo, Madeleine Gibson and Betty Astell.

"Production: This comedy, part leg show and part farce, is dispensed from a very old formula, and the gags and situations are too threadbare to raise a laugh except from the unsophisticated, who may appreciate the ripe lines. The market value of this effort is definitely restricted to the small industrial hall.

"Settings and Photography: The beauty parlour and gymnasium sequences are well staged and are decorated with shapely feminine limbs, while lighting and photography are satisfactory.

197

"Points of Appeal: Stars, good staging, and broad humour.

A Tight Corner: the date this film went out on General Release has not been determined.

The Lodger (1932)

The Lodger was a major film production in 1932. It starred Ivor Novello, a huge matinee idol in those days, primarily in the theatre, and who had been so since the Great War (World War One).

Adaptation of Mrs. Belloc Lowndes' novel about the baffling murders of helpless women, the suspicious behaviour of the Buntings' lodger, his love for their daughter, and the final grim reckoning. It was a remake of *The Lodger: A Story of the London Fog* (1926), a silent film directed by Alfred Hitchcock, which also starred Ivor Novello.

After the first six 'super feature' films were made by Twickenham Film Studios during 1931 for W. & F. Film Service, two further pictures were then made by Twickenham for this renter (distributor); *The Lodger* was the second film.

A British Front-of-House Card showing Ivor Novello and Elizabeth Allan in a dramatic scene from *The Lodger*.

The Lodger was the fourth film Maurice Elvey directed for Julius Hagen. Elvey was a major film director then and had been so since the later silent period.

The Lodger was made by Julius Hagen's film production company, Twickenham Film Studios, Ltd., for W. & F. Film Service, Ltd. Woolf & Freedman Film Service had become a major force in the British film industry in the later silent era. C. M. Woolf of W. & F. Film Service became part of the Rank Organisation in the later 1930s.

Julius Hagen announced a correction in the *Kinematograph Weekly* issue of 22 September 1932, (page 25), that the credit for the dialogue for *The Lodger* should be divided equally between Miles Mander, Ivor Novello and H. Fowler Mear, adding "each of whom has his own share in the feature of the picture".

The Lodger was Trade shown on Thursday, 8 September 1932, at the London Hippodrome.

John V. Watson

The Lodger was reviewed by *Kinematograph Weekly* on 15 September 1932, (page 33):

RCA Photophone, 85 minutes, "A" certificate.

"Remarks: Mystery drama; a skilful adaptation of the famous novel. Good atmosphere, intelligent direction, and sound characterisation, all contribute to the high quality of the eminently popular entertainment.

"Box Office Angle: Very good general booking with star and title pull.

"A very good mystery thriller, a smooth adaptation of Mrs. Belloc Lowndes's famous story, which escapes from the conventional, yet furnishes first-class popular entertainment. The action is not exactly fierce, but exceedingly good characterisation and intelligent treatment build up interest and suspense with logical precision, while the ending, although slightly incredible, has a real element of surprise, which gets it over.

"Very good general booking, with definite box-office potentialities in the title and star.

"Story: Mr. and Mrs. Bunting, a homely married couple, let one of their rooms to Angeloff, a foreigner, at a time when the police are devoting all their energy to arrest the perpetrator of a number of cruel murders.

"The murderer, obviously a sex maniac, is believed to be a foreigner, and the description tallies with that of Angeloff. Angeloff and Daisy, the Bunting's daughter, fall in love, and Daisy remains loyal to him when he is arrested on suspicion. He escapes, however, and arranges to meet her in the park, and he arrives in time to save her from the real murderer, who is his own brother.

"Acting: Ivor Novello plays the part of Angeloff, an aesthete, with conviction, but is not quite equal to the acting demands of the ending. Elizabeth Allan is quite good as Daisy, and A. W. Baskcomb gives a great comedy study as Mr. Bunting.

"Barbara Everest, Jack Hawkins, Peter Gawthorne and Shayle Gardner are the most prominent of the supporting cast.

"Production: Maurice Elvey has handled his subject very well, and has cleverly avoided cheap sensationalism. The story unfolds logically, and the characterisation and atmosphere are most convincing. There is perhaps a little too much detail, which tends to retard the action – the newspaper sequences are weak – but this is merely by the way, and does not lessen the tension.

"Having built up so much evidence against the lodger, the fact that he turns out to be innocent rather stretches one's credulity, but the surprise is a good one, and is all the better for paving the way for a happy ending.

"The dialogue, for which Miles Mander was responsible, is natural and fits well into the characterisation.

"Settings and Photography: A London wrapped up in November fog furnishes a true atmosphere, while detail of newspaper life, police activity, and domesticity vary the interest and enhance the dramatic effect.

Lighting and photography are good.

"Points of Appeal: Star and title, good story, suspense and thrills, love interest, good characterisation and treatment.

The Lodger went out on General Release on Monday, 12 December 1932.

The Face at the Window (1932)

Crime detective thriller. Paris is stunned by a series of bank robberies in which the night watchmen or security guards are always fatally poisoned. The celebrated Parisian detective, Paul Le Gros (Raymond Massey), is called in to investigate.

The Face at the Window was the first 'Quota Quickie' film made by Hagen's Twickenham subsidiary film production company, Real Art Productions Ltd, for the British distribution subsidiary of the American Radio Pictures.

The film ran for 52 minutes, according to the registered length, of 4,717 feet.

The Face at the Window was the twentieth film which Leslie Hiscott directed for Julius Hagen at their Twickenham Film Studios; his sixth 'Real Art' picture.

The Face at the Window was the only film appearance by Raymond Massey for Julius Hagen. It was his second leading screen rôle in British films, his first was as 'Sherlock Holmes' in Herbert Wilcox's production of *The Speckled Band* (1931), directed by Jack Raymond.

The Face at the Window was Trade shown on Tuesday, 18 October 1932, at the Prince Edward Theatre, Old Compton Street, London, W.1.; *The Face at the Window* was screened before the Trade Showing of **Hold 'Em Jail** (1932), the American feature film, starring the then very popular Wheeler and Woolsey comedy team, made by RKO Radio Pictures, Inc.

The Face at the Window was reviewed by *Kinematograph Weekly* on 20 October 1932, (page 43):

RCA Photophone, 52 minutes, "A" certificate.

"Remarks: Lyceum type of melodrama adequately put over and acted.

"Box Office Angle: Moderate popular hall booking.

"The well-known old drama does not wear too well, and for these sophisticated days strikes rather too disingenuous a note. As a support in a two-feature programme in popular halls it should, however, prove useful.

"Story: A series of bank robberies is being committed in Paris, and Paul le Gros, a detective, in called in to elucidate them. De Brisson's bank is burgled, and a cashier, Lucien Cortier, who loves De Brisson's niece, Marie, is suspected. As Paul continues his investigations with the help of a doctor and a "silly ass" friend, Peter Pomeroy, another suspicion is cast on Count Fournal, a friend of Brisson. Fournal accuses Cortier of being the mysterious robber, and shoots him in a duel. A false message lures Marie to his underworld haunt. She is rescued, however, by

Paul and Peter. Finally Paul, by a ruse, traps the real criminal, who turns out to be Brisson himself. Fournal follows him to prison.

"Acting: Raymond Massey is the most natural actor in the cast, and makes the most of the part of Paul. Both Eric Maturin as Fournal and Henry Mollison as Cortier are very theatrical. Bromley Davenport is quite good as Brisson, and Isla Bevan an attractive-looking heroine.

"Production: Played in broad melodramatic vein with equally broad comedy relief in the presentation of Peter, the picture fails to register a real thrill or really to interest one very deeply. The plot is otherwise quite adequately unfolded, though the "surprise" ending has little genuine suspense in it.

"Settings and Photography: Quite well set with good average camera work.

"Points of Appeal: Title of well-known melodrama forms the best angle of appeal.

The Face at the Window went out on General Release on Monday, 20 February 1933.

The World, The Flesh, and The Devil (1932)

Crime drama. The impressive and intriguing title of this drama is actually the name of a London dockland public house where the story is set. A dishonest criminal lawyer (the illegitimate son of a baronet) plans to deprive the lawful son and heir to the baronetcy of his inheritance, but he fails to get rid of him.

The World, the Flesh, and the Devil was the second 'Quota Quickie' film made by Hagen's Twickenham subsidiary film production company, Real Art Productions Ltd, for the British distribution subsidiary of the American Radio Pictures.

The World, the Flesh, and the Devil was made at Beaconsfield Studios; it was the first Hagen film to be made away from his "home" Twickenham Studios. The reason why this film was not made at Twickenham Studios has not been determined, but this was probably due to production overcrowding there at that time when *The World, the Flesh, and the Devil* was scheduled to be filmed.

The World, the Flesh, and the Devil gave Harold Huth his third leading film rôle, but this was his only film for Julius Hagen.

The World, the Flesh, and the Devil was the first film George A. Cooper directed for Julius Hagen. George A. Cooper directed fifteen British sound films from 1932 to 1939; this film was the first of the eleven pictures he made for Julius Hagen between 1932 and 1934.

The World, the Flesh, and the Devil was Trade shown in London on Wednesday, 23 November 1932, at the Cambridge Theatre. *The World, the Flesh, and the Devil* preceded the Trade showing of the American psychological thriller *Thirteen Women* (1932), made by RKO Radio Pictures, starring Irene Dunne and Ricardo Cortez; it was released throughout the United Kingdom by Radio Pictures.

The World, the Flesh, and the Devil was reviewed by *Kinematograph Weekly* on 1 December 1932 (page 20):

John V. Watson

RCA Photophone, 54 minutes, "A" certificate.

"Remarks: Crime melodrama with a good story, clear cut characterisation, popular thrills and good atmosphere.

"Box Office Angle: Good supporting feature.

"Story, Acting and Production: Microfiche entries all unreadable.

"Settings and Photography: The Thames waterfront atmosphere has a grim picturesqueness, a dockside inn is true in detail, and the rest of the interiors are appropriate. Lighting and photography are very good.

"Points of Appeal: Popular and holding story, good thrills, pleasing love interest, sound characterisation, and effective and painstaking treatment.

The World, the Flesh, and the Devil probably went out on General Release on Monday, 27 March 1933.

1932: The British Film Industry: Trends and Other Events throughout the Year — in England, the United States, Germany and France:

In the *Kinematograph Weekly* of 7 January 1932, P. L. Mannock reported (on pages 81 and 84) in an article, entitled "**Where our Producers score – and where they miss**", that "Out of 40 new British films to be made in 1932, I observe 27 are based on plays."

The *Kinematograph Weekly* of 28 January 1932 reported (on Page 27) two company registrations:

'The Czar of Twickenham'. The History of Julius Hagen and the Film Empire he created at Twickenham Film Studios, from 1927 to 1938.

Eric Rhodes Theatres (Gillingham) Ltd, a private company was registered on 22 January 1932. Eric Rhodes would eventually head the Classic chain of repertory Cinemas operating throughout the country. I actually worked for Classic starting in the autumn of 1968 and would soon become their very first Cinema Clubs Controller.

Westminster Films, Ltd., a private company registered 18 January 1932. Share capital: £2,000 in £1 shares. The directors were J. Nadler; J. J. Jackson; and **Michael Powell** of Roseleaf Cottage, Chalfont St. Peter, Bucks. This was the second film production company which was set up by famed director, Michael Powell, and his partner, Jerome Jackson to make cheap "Quota Quickie" films. Westminster Films made three films: *C.O.D.* (1932, trade shown in March), a crime-thriller, starring Garry Marsh, also made for United Artists; *His Lordship* (1932, trade shown in June), a musical-comedy, starring Jerry Verno, made for United Artists; and *Born Lucky* (1932, trade shown in December), a musical, starring Talbot O'Farrell and Renee Ray (Rene Ray), made for M-G-M.

British International opened a new exchange in New Orleans, its eleventh to operate in the United States. British International Pictures was formed in 1927 and soon became a major force in the British film industry, a vertical integrated corporation combining production, distribution and exhibition. In 1933, the name of the parent company was changed to Associated British Picture Corporation (ABPC).

(*K. W.*, 18 February 1932, page 22).

The unexpected death of **Edgar Wallace**. An appreciation written by P. L. Mannock.

(*K. W.*, 18 February 1932, page 24).

London Film Productions, Ltd., a private company was

registered on 13 February 1932. Capital structure: nominal £100 in $1 shares. The secretary: E. H. George.

London Film Productions was the famous company formed by the Hungarian film producer/director, **Alexander Korda**, who was soon to become a major force in the British film production industry, making such important films as *The Private Life of Henry VIII* (1933), which established Korda internationally and made a star of Charles Laughton; *The Rise of Catherine the Great* (1934); *The Scarlet Pimpernel* (1934); *Things to Come* (1936); *Elephant Boy* (1937); *Knight Without Armour* (1937); *The Four Feathers* (1939); *The Spy in Black* (1939); amongst many other memorable films.

(*K. W.*, 18 February 1932, page 31).

Herbert Wilcox signs **Victor McLaglen** at £1,000 per week for the talkie version of Jeffrey Farnol's famous novel, *The Broad Highway*. The 1924 slump (in British film production) left McLaglen penniless and his exit to Hollywood.

NOTE that it appears that a film version of the Jeffrey Farnol novel was not actually made. Nor has any evidence been found that Victor McLaglen actually made any film for Herbert Wilcox.

(*K. W.*, 25 February 1932, page 51, P. L. Mannock).

Cinematograph Exhibitors' Association of Great Britain Report: "Although the Statutory Quota of British films to be shown during last year was 7.5 per cent, the figure actually shown by numberless kinemas during the greater part of that period was in the neighbourhood of 20 per cent." 145 British films, it is stated, were trade shown, and 502 foreign.

(*K. W.*, 10 March 1932, back page advertisement).

'The Czar of Twickenham'. The History of Julius Hagen and the Film Empire he created at Twickenham Film Studios, from 1927 to 1938.

Cecil Cattermoul is the British Empire representative of Svensk Filmindustri of Stockholm, better known here as Swedish Biograph.

NOTE that the reader is reminded that **Cecil Cattermoul** was a former business associate of Julius Hagen. Their first business relationship occurred in June 1928, when Julius Hagen formed the Strand Film Company with Cecil Cattermoul, a film agent, and the director Leslie Hiscott.

(*K. W.*, 17 March 1932, page 32).

50 of the **Compton Organ** had been installed in cinemas in Greater London alone.

(*K. W.*, 17 March 1932, page 22, The Technical Section).

The actress, **Heather Angel**, under contract with British International is called "the British Janet Gaynor".

(*K. W.*, 24 March 1932, page 45, P. L. Mannock).

M.G.M. has signed the British actress **Diana Wynyard** to a long term contract.

(*K. W.*, 31 March 1932, page 26).

Wardour Street history. Example: **Mozart**, as a child of eight, lodging with his mother and father in Cecil Court. As featured in *The Romance of Soho*, by E. Beresford Chancellor, published by Country Life, Ltd. 12s. 6d.

NOTE that **Wardour Street** was one of the streets in Soho that then housed so many companies that made up the British film history in those days. This residential status continued well into the 1970s and beyond; indeed, this author worked in several addresses in Soho in the late 1960s and 1970s when he was in the film industry, in either film distribution or exhibition. One of these addresses was 84 Wardour Street, the business "home" of E. J. Fancey and Olive Negus-Fancey.

(*K. W.*, 31 March 1932, page 28).

Madeleine Carroll sues Regina Films, Ltd. for payment of her fee of £500 for starring in *Fascination*, which was filmed in April 1931.

(*K. W.*, 7 April 1932).

M-G-M British film production contract. Statement from British International Pictures, Ltd., authorised by John Maxwell on Tuesday, 5 April 1932, stated:

"B.I.P. have contracted to supply Metro-Goldwyn-Mayer Pictures, Ltd., with feature pictures to meet M-G-M's British requirements for the year to March 1933".

"The terms of the contract ensure pictures of a quality that will compare favourably with the films supplied on the market at the present time".

"The number of pictures covered by the contract will probably be ten".

(*K. W.*, 7 April 1932, page 22).

The British actress, **Adrianne Allen**, had been placed on a long-term contract by Paramount, and was due to make her California debut with Fredric March and Sylvia Sidney in *Merrily We Go to Hell*.

(*K. W.*, 7 April 1932).

'The Czar of Twickenham'. The History of Julius Hagen and the Film Empire he created at Twickenham Film Studios, from 1927 to 1938.

Alfred Hitchcock was appointed as B.I.P.'s new production supervisor at Elstree.

(*K. W.*, 7 April 1932, page 44, P. L. Mannock).

P.D.C., Ltd. (the British film distributor) acquires the output of **Monogram Pictures** Corporation (the American film production company).

(*K. W.*, 14 April 1932, page 32).

B.I.P. (**British International Pictures**) announced an important deal with Pat Powers (of Pat Powers, Inc.) to distribute about two dozen of its features a year in the United States.

(*K. W.*, 14 April 1932, page 38).

John Stuart is back in London from Berlin, where he has had the leading rôle in *Atlantide*, directed by G. W. Pabst.

NOTE that *L'Atlantide* (1932) was a German-French co-production which was made in three different languages: English, French and German. The German actress, Brigitte Helm, starred in all three versions.

(*K. W.*, 14 April 1932, page 59, P. L. Mannock).

Herbert Marshall (the British actor) has been signed up by Paramount.

(*K. W.*, 21 April 1932, page 26).

Clark Gable has been signed to a new long-term contract with MGM.

(*K. W.*, 21 April 1932, page 28).

Gaumont-British is to produce (films) in Germany with **UFA** (Universum-Film AG).

(*K. W.*, 5 May 1932, page 29).

Alexander Korda is directing *Wedding Rehearsal*, the first vehicle of London Film Productions, Ltd. Heading the cast are Roland Young, George Grossmith, Jr., John Loder. Wendy Barrie, Joan Gardner (her film debut), and Merle Oberon.

(*K. W.*, 5 May 1932, page 55, P. L. Mannock).

Louis Mercanton, the French-Swiss producer; sudden death at the age of 55.

(*K. W.*, 5 May 1932, page 55, P. L. Mannock).

James Cagney, who "walked out" on the Warner Bros., announces a forthcoming vaudeville tour in Great Britain. He hints that he would be open to a film engagement.

(*K. W.*, 12 May 1932, page 22).

On the petition of Edith **Madeleine** Astley (formerly **Carroll**), who was stated to be a judgment creditor, Mr. Justice Eve of the Chancery Division, on 30 June made an order for the compulsory winding up of Regina Films, Ltd. Madeleine Carroll was not paid her fee for starring in *Fascination*, which was filmed in April 1931.

(*K. W.*, 23 June 1932, page 42).

Wedding Rehearsal – **Alexander Korda** has completed the film at the Wembley Studios, the first but ambitious effort of London Film Productions.

(*K. W.*, 30 June 1932, page 45, P. L. Mannock).

'The Czar of Twickenham'. The History of Julius Hagen and the Film Empire he created at Twickenham Film Studios, from 1927 to 1938.

Joinville Studios, Paris: French productions of *Shanghai Express* (already released in Paris with French text), *Dr. Jekyll and Mr. Hyde* and Harold Lloyd's *R.U.R.* being produced. NOTE that in the early 1930s, the American company Paramount Pictures took over the studios and made French-language versions of their hit films.

(*K. W.*, 30 June 1932, page 53).

Advertisement: *Picturegoer Weekly* – all photogravure printing – has certified net sales exceed 228,000; statement by Philip Emanuel, Advertising Director.

NOTE that in the 1930s there were four leading weekly film fan magazines; the other three were *Film Weekly*, *Picture Show* and *Film Pictorial*. By far and away, the best of the four was *Film Weekly*; it usually contained well written and researched articles and its film reviews tended to be far better than those written for the other three weekly magazines.

(*K. W.*, 7 July 1932, page 2, advertisement).

P.D.C. have agreed that its British productions will have their American release through **Monogram Pictures** Corporation.

(*K. W.*, 7 July 1932, page 27).

"**British Lion Film Corporation**, Ltd., announces a big expansion of its renting activities whereby twenty-four feature productions from **Mascot Pictures** Corporation will be distributed in 1932-1933, constituting the whole output of this important American company".

(*K. W.*, 14 July 1932, page 26).

213

Salary cuts of 35 per cent have been announced by **MGM**, for those earning $1,500 a week or upwards. NOTE that the American Depression was biting deep following the Wall Street Crash of October 1929.

(*K. W.*, 28 July 1932, page 15).

Welsh-Pearson Films, Ltd. propose to go into voluntary liquidation in order to reconstruct.

(*K. W.*, 28 July 1932, page 21).

United Cinemas, Ltd., a public company, is registered in Edinburgh on 20 July 1932.

(*K. W.*, 4 August 1932, page 20).

In the Courts: the proprietors of the **Plaza, Great Yarmouth sued by Warner Bros**. for £10 and 7 shillings rent of the films, *Brown Sugar* and *Lord Richard of the Pantry*. A counter-claim was entered of non-fulfilment of contract. The films were supplied with sound-on-disc. These two films were made by Julius Hagen for Warner Bros. (full details above.

(*K. W.*, 4 August 1932, page 20).

Fox British Pictures, Ltd., was registered as a private company on 26 July 1932 with a nominal capital of £100 in £1 shares. The objects are to produce and generally deal in motion or other pictures by means of records, films and other devices. The permanent directors are: E. Gartside, company secretary; and G. J. Maidment, incorporated accountant.

(*K. W.*, 11 August 1932, page 20).

Welsh-Pearson Films (1932), Ltd. is registered as a public company on 22 August 1932.

'The Czar of Twickenham'. The History of Julius Hagen and the Film Empire he created at Twickenham Film Studios, from 1927 to 1938.

(*K. W.*, 1 September 1932, page 27).

Edward G. Robinson re-signs with First National.

(*K. W.*, 1 September 1932, page 38).

Her First Affaire – Sterling Film Co., Ltd. - designation: "St. George-Sterling Productions" – goes into immediate production. This film gave **Ida Lupino** her first starring rôle, at the age of 14! It was her second film though; she already had a minor, uncredited part in *The Love Race* (1931), a British comedy film directed by her father, Stanley Lupino. Ida Lupino was cast in October 1932.

(*K. W.*, 8 September 1932, page 41, P. L. Mannock).

Welsh-Pearson Productions, Ltd. is incorporated on 24 September 1932. The subscribers: T. A. Welsh, film producer, and L. C. Lawson, associated accountant. The objects: to adopt an agreement with Welsh-Pearson Films, Ltd., and A. Laban, the liquidator thereof, and to carry on the business of film producers, proprietors of film-producing studios, etc.

(*K. W.*, 29 September 1932, page 32).

Madeleine Carroll signs Gaumont contract for two pictures per annum, and her salary, when working, will be at the rate of £1,000 per week

(*K. W.*, 27 October 1932, page 45).

Jack Buchanan signs new four-year contract with Herbert Wilcox, expiring in 1936.

(*K. W.*, 27 October 1932, page 45).

John V. Watson

Edward Everett Horton, one of the world's highest-paid freelance film actors, cast in Maurice Elvey's *Soldiers of the King*. Cicely Courtneidge stars.

(*K. W.*, 3 November 1932, page 45, P. L. Mannock).

London's licences reported for 329 kinema shows (cinemas).

(*K. W.*, 10 November 1932, page 22).

London Film Productions, Ltd., has increased in nominal capital by an addition of £20,000 beyond the registered capital of £100.

(*K. W.*, 24 November 1932, page 28).

Karma is the first talkie made by Indians in a British studio, at Stoll Cricklewood.

(*K. W.*, 27 October 1932, page 26, P. L. Mannock).

Article: "**The Exchange and Foreign Markets**" by Simon Rowson.

The amount of British remittances to America for films can be taken roughly at £6 million per annum. Before Britain went off the gold standard this represented in American currency about twenty-nine million dollars; at the present time, this represents only about nineteen and a half million dollars

(*K. W.*, 15 December 1932, page 4).

1932: The Fifth Year of the 'Quota' Act:

181 British films were first shown during the year 1932.

This number is arrived at by using the data contained in *The*

'The Czar of Twickenham'. The History of Julius Hagen and the Film Empire he created at Twickenham Film Studios, from 1927 to 1938.

British Film Catalogue: 1895-1970 by Denis Gifford, as follows:

09261: Closing Gifford Catalogue Number for 1932.

09080: Opening Gifford Catalogue Number for 1932.

181: Total. An increase of 17 films over the previous year's total of 164.

Some of these films were short subjects; the actual number of these shorts has not been determined.

6. 1933:
The British Film Production Boom Continues:

1933 saw the continuation of the great British film production boom gaining further momentum with total production reaching over 200 films per year for the first time ever. And we should consider this fine record of British film production against the disastrous years of the results from British film producers in the mid 1920s during which time so few British features films were being produced.

1933: Film Production explodes at Twickenham:

Even Julius Hagen at Twickenham Film Studios excelled upon his production output in 1933, from the 16 films he made in 1932 to the 20 he produced in 1933. Indeed, in 1933, Hagen surpassed his output of films he produced in 1931 by almost 100 per cent, from 11 films made in 1931 to the 20 he produced in 1933.

As we shall see below, many of these films made at Twickenham were 'Quota Quickies' which, by definition, were obviously filmed speedily.

January 1933:

Kinematograph Weekly reported throughout the month:

FILM PRODUCTION AT TWICKENHAM STUDIOS:

The Medicine Man, a farcical comedy by Michael Barringer, is in production this week. Redd Davis is directing; Ernest Palmer on camera.

The Lost Chord is forthcoming "super" for P.D.C. The director will be Maurice Elvey.

(*K. W.*, 5 January 1933).

Article: **Looking Ahead in the Year 1933.** "Congratulations" by Julius Hagen.

(*K. W.*, 12 January 1933. page 51).

Twickenham Studios working both day and night.

Reginald Denham and Jack Harris directing *Called Back*.

The Lost Chord goes into production this week. The scenes with Elizabeth Allan will be shot first, in order that she may leave for Hollywood.

(*K. W.*, 12 January 1933, page 128, P. L. Mannock).

'The Czar of Twickenham'. The History of Julius Hagen and the Film Empire he created at Twickenham Film Studios, from 1927 to 1938.

The Lost Chord. The director, Maurice Elvey, laid low with flu. The "high spot": big first-night party which takes place on the stage of a London theatre shot last week. A song has been written by W. L. Trytel and Tudor Davies, the operatic tenor, will sing it. Billy Mayerl, the well-known pianist, also appears.

(*K. W.*, 26 January 1933, page 42B, P. L. Mannock).

FOUR CONTRACT ARTISTES AT TWICKENHAM STUDIOS:

Elizabeth Allan; Isla Bevan; Frank Pettingell; and S. Victor Stanley. Elizabeth Allan, who has been with Julius Hagen for two years, will be released next month in order that she may go to Hollywood under long-term contract.

(*K. W.*, 12 January 1933, page 117).

VISATONE MOBILE VAN AT TWICKENHAM STUDIOS:

"The curious will naturally wonder what is the secret of the popularity of the Twickenham Film Studio, in face of which it is amusing to recall that carpers foretold the doom of the outfit when sound came, owing to its proximity to the railway line! That it was able to overcome a difficulty of that nature with ready ease is proof of the efficiency of the organisation."

"Last year Hagen made another surprise move, when he took delivery of a Visatone mobile van, and so converted his studio into the first one in the country to operate a dual recording system. When not on location, the van is housed alongside the sound stage, so that the occupant is given the choice of two systems."

"Outside the Studio is an extensive lot, covering a large part of the three-acre site of which the studio stands, and this is frequently used for built-up exteriors, which can be very

219

realistically faked."

(*K. W.*, 12 January 1933, page 117).

CONTRACT RENEWAL AT TWICKENHAM STUDIOS:

"**Cyril Stanborough**, the studio's stills cameraman: his contract has been renewed by Julius Hagen."

(*K. W.*, 12 January 1933, page 128, P. L. Mannock).

TWICKENHAM FILM STUDIOS, LTD.: NOMINAL CAPITAL INCREASE:

"Twickenham Film Studios, Ltd.: the nominal capital has been increased by the addition of £15,000 beyond the registered capital of £15,000. The additional capital is divided into 6,000 irredeemable preference shares of £1 each and 180,000 deferred shares of 1 shilling each."

(*K. W.*, 19 January 1933, page 35, The City Editor).

February 1933:

Kinematograph Weekly reported throughout the month:

FILM PRODUCTION AT TWICKENHAM STUDIOS:

The Lost Chord. **Maurice Elvey recovered from the 'flu. All the scenes with Elizabeth Allan have now been completed, she leaves for Hollywood on Saturday under MGM contract. At the end of the week, the entire floor space at Twickenham will be transformed into the banqueting hall of a mediaeval castle in Italy, where John Stuart and Leslie Perrins will fight a duel.**

'The Czar of Twickenham'. The History of Julius Hagen and the Film Empire he created at Twickenham Film Studios, from 1927 to 1938.

(*K. W.*, 2 February 1933, page E1, P. L. Mannock).

Excess Baggage – Redd Davis is now directing. The comic novel by Capt. H. M. Raleigh; Harry Fowler Mear has evolved a "crazy" scenario. To be released by Radio.

(*K. W.*, 23 February 1933, page 25, P. L. Mannock).

Excess Baggage: Redd Davis has almost completed.

March 1933:

Kinematograph Weekly reported throughout the month:

FILM PRODUCTION AT TWICKENHAM STUDIOS:

The Man Outside: George Cooper to direct immediately after *Excess Baggage* is completed. It is a new mystery drama by Donald Stuart.

(*K. W.*, 2 March 1933, page 31, P. L. Mannock).

Four "Supers" and many features (a number of programme pictures) scheduled:
I Lived With You, with Ivor Novello.
This Week of Grace, with Gracie Fields.
The Wandering Jew, with Conrad Veidt.
Fourth super-film will be a world-wide story by an English author.
(*K. W.*, 9 March 1933).

Julius Hagen announced: "I have made arrangements with Maurice Elvey to direct three of these films - *I Lived With You*, *This Week of Grace* and *The Wandering Jew*. Elvey has been turning out very fine pictures for my company, and his latest, *The Lost Chord*, which will be shown very shortly, is a grand film,

221

and will certainly rank among the British successes in 1933."

(*K. W.*, 9 March 1933).

"*The Wandering Jew*: Julius Hagen concluded negotiations with Conrad Veidt to star as Matathias, the Wandering Jew. E. Temple Thurston is now at work on the scenario of his famous play. He proclaims himself delighted with the choice of Conrad Veidt as Matathias. James Carter, brilliant art director, is looking forward to constructing some marvellous interior settings; exteriors will be shot either in Egypt or the South of France. Four leading ladies are required for this picture, and interesting negotiations with regard to casting are already in progress."

(*K. W.*, 9 March 1933).

I Lived With You: Ivor Novello has himself collaborated with George Cooper and H. Fowler Mear on the scenario of his play; it goes into production immediately. Ursula Jeans is coming back from America to play opposite to Novello. Will be distributed by W. and F.

(*K. W.*, 9 March 1933).

This Week of Grace is an original story by Maurice Braddell and Mrs. Nell Emerald Beatty, specially written for Gracie Fields. The film will be made at A.T.P. studios at Ealing under the supervision of Julius Hagen and by Twickenham technicians. Release by Radio.

(*K. W.*, 9 March 1933).

Another unit will be working at Twickenham studios on two other features for Radio, one of which will most likely be another hilarious comedy co-starring Claud Allister and Frank Pettingell.

'The Czar of Twickenham'. The History of Julius Hagen and the Film Empire he created at Twickenham Film Studios, from 1927 to 1938.

(*K. W.*, 9 March 1933).

The Man Outside: George A. Cooper now directing. Joan Gardner appears by courtesy of London Film Productions. Louis Hayward also cast.

(*K. W.*, 9 March 1933, page 28, P. L. Mannock).

I Lived With You: Julius Hagen announces that A. W. Baskcomb and Ida Lupino have been assigned leading parts in *I Lived With You*, Ivor Novello's second Twickenham talkie goes into production at the end of this week. Maurice Elvey directing for W. and F. release.

(*K. W.*, 16 March 1933, page 45, P. L. Mannock).

"Two more for Hagen. The rights of two big film subjects, *In Old Madrid* and *The Ghost Camera*, have been purchased by Julius Hagen, and will be put into production at Twickenham as soon as the existing contracts on which this company is employed for the next few months are completed."

In Old Madrid - written by Adrian Brunel – exteriors will most probably be shot in Madrid and the Spanish Pyrenees.

(NOTE that *In Old Madrid* was not actually produced; the reason for this has not been determined.)

I Lived With You is now on the floor.

(*K. W.*, 23 March 1933, page 25).

I Lived With You now in production. The rôle of Mr. Wallis is being played by Eliot Makeham, who created this part in the play. A. W. Baskcomb had to relinquish the rôle owing to sudden illness which seized him on his first day's work on the

223

picture last Friday, (17 March 1933). There are now eleven members of the original stage cast taking part in the film version: they are Ivor Novello, Ursula Jeans, Minnie Rayner, Eliot Makeham, Cicely Oates, Beryl Harrison, Hannah Jones, Gwen Floyd, Maud Buchanan, Douglas Beaumont, and Davina Craig. Ida Lupino and Jack Hawkins are also important members of the cast."

(*K. W.*, 23 March 1933, page 34, P. L. Mannock).

I Lived With You: Maurice Elvey spent last Saturday afternoon at Selfridge's directing Ursula Jeans, Mollie Fisher and some extras in scenes. Elvey at the moment is having a certain amount of difficulty in obtaining the requisite permission to shoot at Hampton Court, but he hopes to be able to complete these exteriors before the present spell of fine weather breaks. Ursula Jeans plays the part of Gladys Wallis, who works with her friend in the "fancy goods" department, and they decide to spend the afternoon at Hampton Court where they meet the attractive Prince Felix Lenieff (Ivor Novello) in the Maze.

(*K. W.*, 30 March 1933, page 31, P. L. Mannock).

April 1933:

Kinematograph Weekly reported throughout the month:

FILM PRODUCTION AT TWICKENHAM STUDIOS:

I Lived with You: A small section of the celebrated maze at Hampton Court has been reconstructed at the back of Twickenham studios "when I (P. L. Mannock) arrived on Monday to watch" filming. The blazing sunshine was reinforced by a sun arc or two, and a violet muslin screen was filtering the rays on Ivor Novello and Ursula Jeans, busy on the introductory sequences of the film version of Novello's successful play.

'The Czar of Twickenham'. The History of Julius Hagen and the Film Empire he created at Twickenham Film Studios, from 1927 to 1938.

"Maurice Elvey's progress was extraordinary, in spite of the periodic and frequent passing of Southern Railway electric train traffic not 20 yards away. In fact, before I left I witnessed some scenes shot inside on the floor – which is certainly a record for any studio visit of mine, on the same picture."

"There is no doubt that Elvey is one of Britain's most energetic directors. That is why he is most in demand: for he tells me he is fully engaged for seven films ahead!"

The Twickenham crew will shortly begin Gracie Field's new comedy (*This Week of Grace*) under his charge, emigrating to the Ealing studios for the purpose.

Elvey is completing *I Lived With You* this week, having secured some fine early morning scenes at Hampton Court Palace.

P.L.M. then stated: "I always meet many old friends at St. Margaret's, where Julius Hagen fosters the friendliest family atmosphere – production's most valuable asset. Sydney Blythe, Cyril Stanborough, Gerald Malvern, Harry Mear, Redd Davis, Lester Gard, George A. Cooper, Baynham Honri and Frank Philip were some of them."

(*K. W.*, 13 April 1933, page 43, P. L. Mannock).

This Week of Grace is scheduled to start production next week at the A.T.P. Studios at Ealing. The story is written by Maurice Braddell and Neil Emerald. Scenario: H. Fowler Mear. Sydney Blythe, chief cameraman. Baynham Honri: sound recording.

(*K. W.*, 27 April 1933, page 23, P. L. Mannock).

His Grace Gives Notice by Lady Trowbridge. George A.

225

John V. Watson

Cooper is busy directing at Twickenham; Ernest Palmer is chief cameraman. Cast: Arthur Margetson, with S. Victor Stanley and Viola Keats.

(*K. W.*, 27 April 1933, page 23, P. L. Mannock).

May 1933:

Kinematograph Weekly reported throughout the month:

FILM PRODUCTION AT TWICKENHAM STUDIOS:

Maurice Elvey starts directing *This Week of Grace* at Ealing Studios.

(*K. W.*, 4 May 1933, page 23, P. L. Mannock).

This Week of Grace: first week of shooting. Nina Boucicault (famous as the original 'Peter Pan') will play the part of the Duchess, and Vivian Foster, the irrepressible "Vicar of Mirth", makes his début.

(*K. W.*, 11 May 1933, page 58, P. L. Mannock).

His Grace Gives Notice: Owing to a car smash in which Arthur Margetson was injured, shooting has been temporarily suspended.

(*K. W.*, 11 May 1933, page 58, P. L. Mannock).

Redd Davis took the floor this week with a comedy by Laurence Meynell, entitled *The Umbrella*; Ernest Palmer is cameraman.

(*K. W.*, 11 May 1933, page 58, P. L. Mannock).

This Week of Grace: big scene in a large mansion – Maurice

226

'The Czar of Twickenham'. The History of Julius Hagen and the Film Empire he created at Twickenham Film Studios, from 1927 to 1938.

Elvey has now completed the interior shooting, apart from a theatrical sequence. Next ten days: location shooting, including Eridge Castle, Kent; Great Fosters at Egham; and Stoke Poges (on a golf round with Frank Pettingell, Minnie Rayner and Douglas Wakefield).

(K. W., 25 May 1933, page 38, P. L. Mannock).

The Ghost Camera: Julius Hagen has entrusted direction to Bernard Vorhaus (by courtesy of Hall Mark Films). The film goes into production next week. Harry Fowler Mear has written to scenario in collaboration with Vorhaus. Ida Lupino only cast so far.

(NOTE that Hall Mark Films was the production company owned by Bernard Vorhaus).

(K. W., 25 May 1933, page 38, P. L. Mannock).

The Umbrella: Shooting now completed by Redd Davis.

(K. W., 25 May 1933, page 38, P. L. Mannock).

June 1933:

Kinematograph Weekly reported throughout the month:

Film production at Twickenham Studios:

George Cooper resumes production of *His Grace Gives Notice*, now that Arthur Margetson has recovered from the effects of the motor smash in which he was involved. Cooper will complete the picture this week.

(K. W., 1 June 1933, page 25, P. L. Mannock).

John V. Watson

The Ghost Camera was postponed as a result of the delay in the production of His Grace Gives Notice, due to Arthur Margetson was involved in a motor smash. Henry Kendall has been chosen to play the lead. Shooting starts on Monday (5 June 1933).

(*K. W.*, 1 June 1933, page 25, P. L. Mannock).

The Ghost Camera: Bernard Vorhaus is due to complete interior shooting this week. Bernard Vorhaus first started with Harry Cohn in Hollywood for Columbia Pictures, as script-writer, afterwards becoming assistant.

(*K. W.*, 15 June 1933, page 27, P. L. Mannock).

"*The Wandering Jew*: Shooting starts next week. Busy now casting; four big feminine rôles, two of which will be played by well-know film stars, while the other two will in all likelihood be sustained by famous actresses who have not yet been seen on the screen. The costumes are being designed by Lady Queensberry."

(*K. W.*, 15 June 1933, page 27, P. L. Mannock).

RECORD FILM PRODUCTION LINE-UP AT TWICKENHAM STUDIOS:

"Record line-up planned by Hagen. Twickenham busy on ambitious programme."

"The present year looks like breaking all records as far as Twickenham Film Studios, Ltd. are concerned. Under the energetic leadership of Julius Hagen, this independent concern has gone from strength to strength since the inception of the company in 1928...."

'The Czar of Twickenham'. The History of Julius Hagen and the Film Empire he created at Twickenham Film Studios, from 1927 to 1938.

"Hagen is now embarking on what is certainly the most ambitious and spectacular subject yet attempted – E. Temple Thurston's world famous story, *The Wandering Jew*."

(*K. W.*, 22 June 1933, page 43, P. L. Mannock).

"Anne Grey – our busiest star – since January 1931, she has played heroine in eighteen subjects. Now in *The Wandering Jew*."

(*K. W.*, 22 June 1933, page 43, P. L. Mannock).

FILM PRODUCTION AT TWICKENHAM STUDIOS:

"One of the biggest and finest British studio sets ever constructed has been erected at Twickenham Studios for The Wandering Jew – the grounds have been transformed into a portion of the Holy City by the ingenuity of Jim Carter, Twickenham's art director."

"An exact replica of the famous Damascus gate, the great Praetorium where Christ was brought for trial before Pontius Pilate, the home of Matathias the Jew, and an entire street of native shops, are among the more important features included in this remarkable structure."

"Two large marquees have been erected for the crowd of more than 200. A humorous touch was provided when some Jewish members of the crowd found themselves supplied with ham sandwiches for lunch."

(*K. W.*, 29 June 1933, page 33, P. L. Mannock).

July 1933:

Kinematograph Weekly reported throughout the month:

John V. Watson

FILM PRODUCTION AT TWICKENHAM STUDIOS:

"*The Wandering Jew*: Julius Hagen has arranged for the big exterior sequence of the Knights' Tournament in the Second Phase to be shot in the grounds of Sound City, Shepperton. Given good weather, Maurice Elvey will complete this phase by the end of the week."

"A vast arena has been constructed for the tourney, and a crowd of several hundred will watch and yell their encouragement to the participants of the jousting. Maurice Elvey has been fortunate enough to obtain the services of experts from the Military Tattoo."

"Chief parts in the Second Phase: Veidt, Anne Grey, Bertram Wallis, Dennis Hoey and Victor Abbas."

(*K. W.*, 13 July 1933, page 45, P. L. Mannock).

"*The Wandering Jew*: Final shots now being done. The film is easily the most ambitious and most expensive picture Julius Hagen has yet made. Some Spanish sets which the studio correspondent was agreeably surprised; Jimmy Carter can take it as a compliment."

"Joan Maude signed to play opposite Veidt in the Third Phase, on which Maurice Elvey is now on the last week of production. Joan Maude is the daughter of Nancy Price."

(*K. W.*, 27 July 1933, page 39, The Studio Correspondent).

August 1933:

Kinematograph Weekly reported throughout the month:

'The Czar of Twickenham'. The History of Julius Hagen and the Film Empire he created at Twickenham Film Studios, from 1927 to 1938.

MAJOR FILM PRESENTATION TO EXHIBITORS BY JULIUS HAGEN:

This Week of Grace: Julius Hagen entertained a large party of exhibitors at the May Fair. Hagen said: "the Gracie Fields film I consider the best thing the Lancastrian comedienne has done"

(*K. W.*, 3 August 1933, page 4).

FILM PRODUCTION AT TWICKENHAM STUDIOS:

"*The Wandering Jew* – the final scenes were shot last weekend."

(*K. W.*, 3 August 1933, page 24, P. L. Mannock).

"*Home, Sweet Home* – George A. Cooper starts directing this week."

(*K. W.*, 3 August 1933, page 24, P. L. Mannock).

"*Home, Sweet Home*: The interior shooting is likely to be completed at the end of this week, after which George A. Cooper will concentrate on exteriors, including scenes aboard a liner, and for this purpose John Stuart, Cooper and the camera staff will board the R.M.S.P. liner Atlantis at Tilbury on Friday night and journey up to Leith, returning home on Sunday. An interesting addition to the cast is little Joan Carter (aged 10), the daughter of Jim Carter, art director and studio manager at Twickenham. Joan made her début three years ago in *The Rosary*."

(*K. W.*, 17 August 1933, page 25, P. L. Mannock).

"*Lily of Killarney* will be the next production at Twickenham, a spectacular melodrama written by H. Fowler Mear, in which many popular Irish songs will be interpolated.

231

Fred White, of A.P.D. Films, who will distribute this production, is now in Ireland with George Dewhurst and a technical unit, obtaining the requisite exteriors at Lake Killarney. Maurice Elvey to direct."

(*K. W.*, 17 August 1933, page 25, P. L. Mannock).

"Julius Hagen plans to make a version of Robert Hichens' famous novel and play, ***Bella Donna***, in January next. Conrad Veidt will have the leading rôle of Dr. Isaacson, originally created on the stage by the late Sir George Alexander."

(*K. W.*, 24 August 1933, page 25, P. L. Mannock).

September 1933:

Kinematograph Weekly reported throughout the month:

FILM PRODUCTION AT TWICKENHAM STUDIOS:

George Pearson directing *A Shot in the Dark* at Twickenham.

(*K. W.*, 14 September 1933, page 55, P. L. Mannock).

Lily of Killarney: Concluding shots are now in hand; the unit is working alternatively between location and a large studio set which has been built by James Carter as a photographic replica of a lake-side cavern. The musical production contains many of the best tunes from the opera by Sir Julius Benedict and favourites from Moore's Irish Melodies.

(*K. W.*, 14 September 1933, page 55, P. L. Mannock).

The Roof – George Pearson now directing with George Zucco, Michael Hogan and D. J. Williams.

'The Czar of Twickenham'. The History of Julius Hagen and the Film Empire he created at Twickenham Film Studios, from 1927 to 1938.

(*K. W.*, 28 September 1933, page 29, P. L. Mannock).

George Pearson's next will be *The Pointing Finger*.

(*K. W.*, 28 September 1933, page 29, P. L. Mannock).

October 1933:

Kinematograph Weekly reported throughout the month:

FILM PRODUCTION AT TWICKENHAM STUDIOS:

The Pointing Finger: George Pearson has begun shooting Rita's well-known novel; John Stuart in a dual rôle, and Viola Keats in the feminine lead.

(*K. W.*, 5 October 1933, page 33, P. L. Mannock).

George Pearson entered films in 1913 as a scenario writer, he has just finished production on *The Pointing Finger*, which H. Fowler Mear adapted from Rita's well-known novel. During the week he has been busy on scenes on the old Abbey of Edensore, which was reconstructed inside the studio at Twickenham by James Carter, art director. The set was erected in record time – one night the whole of the floor was occupied with a jungle scene, and by the morning the baronial hall of the Edensore family had been substituted, complete with massive oak staircase and wall tapestries. A. Bromley Davenport has replaced Arthur Metcalf as Lord Edensore.

(*K. W.*, 19 October 1933, page 33, P. L. Mannock).

Mannequin – George Cooper has started production on Monday (16 October 1933). The story has been written by Charles Bennett.

John V. Watson

(*K. W.*, 19 October 1933, page 33, P. L. Mannock).

Mannequin directed by George Cooper is in its second week. "James and Frank Carter have excelled themselves in the designing of artistic modern settings, including a large salon, where a brilliant mannequin parade is held, a Mayfair drawing-room, a reproduction of a famous boxing ring, and a West End restaurant. Over fifty model gowns and lingerie are shown during the mannequin parades, which play an important part in the development of the story."

(*K. W.*, 26 October 1933, page 43, P. L. Mannock).

SUCCESSFUL FILM BOOKING FOR TWICKENHAM STUDIOS:

The Lost Chord: up to date, 1,465 theatres in the United Kingdom have booked the film, and on October 16, 56 theatres in London and suburbs will screen this film for one week.

(*K. W.*, 26 October 1933, page 5).

November 1933:

Kinematograph Weekly reported throughout the month:

FILM SALES DISTRIBUTION ERROR AT TWICKENHAM STUDIOS:

"A. Fried, managing director of Film Sales, Ltd., writes us with reference to an inadvertent mistake which occurred in last week's paper. *Bella Donna*, he says, is not going to be distributed by "Films Hakim", as this does not constitute a part of the Gaumont-British output, but is a "Julius Hagen Twickenham production", for which other arrangements have been made previously."

234

'The Czar of Twickenham'. The History of Julius Hagen and the Film Empire he created at Twickenham Film Studios, from 1927 to 1938.

(*K. W.*, 2 November 1933, page 40).

FILM PRODUCTION AT TWICKENHAM STUDIOS:

Mannequin: "For the final scenes, George Cooper directing, the floor was turned into a boxing club over the week-end, and many famous world champion boxers took prominent parts in the scene as fighters and time-keepers. Jack Bloomfield, undefeated cruiser-weight champion, refereed the film fight between Whitmore Humphreys, the hero of the story, and Charles Christie, who was an Army champion some years ago. A second fight between Humphreys and another professional boxer was refereed by Alf Maneini, well-known champion welter-weight. Patrick Regan and Mr. Nichols, of the British Boxing Board of Control, acted as M.C. and time-keeper, respectively, and Eddie McGuire, the South African middle-weight, Ben Foord and Johnny Sullivan also appeared in the ring."

(*K. W.*, 2 November 1933, page 48, P. L. Mannock).

Say It With Flowers: "A striking cast has been assembled, which took the floor on Monday (30 October 1933), under the direction of John Baxter of Doss House and Reunion fame. Mary Clare was the "Jane Marryot of the stage version of Cavalcade. George Carney is the brother of Kate Carney, the musical-hall artiste. An elaborate set representing Berwick Market has been constructed in the studio, and the picturesque atmosphere of London's market life has been recaptured by James Carter, who designed the set."

(*K. W.*, 2 November 1933, page 48, P. L. Mannock).

Say It with Flowers – "On Sunday, costers in their pearly suits, fishwives in their best clothes and befeathered, hawkers, and all the other colourful types of market dwellers assembled in a

235

concert hall at Twickenham studios, where John Baxter reached the final stages. Florrie Forde, large and queenly, Marie Kendall, wistful and still beautiful, Tom Costello and Charles Coborn (now 82 years old) took the audience back to the Victorian variety days. Well remembered songs such as *The Lassie from Lancashire*, *Kelly*, *Antonio* and *Comrades* followed in turn, and the old music-hall artistes in the crowd, assistant directors, electricians and carpenters alike joined lustily in the choruses. Marie Lloyd's old success, *Won't You Buy My Pretty Flowers*, is the theme song for the film."

(*K. W.*, 16 November 1933, page 32, P. L. Mannock).

The Black Abbot – "George A. Cooper took over the space left by *Say It with Flowers* this week. Adapted from Philip Godfrey's novel, *The Grange Mystery*. Richard Cooper is the necessary comic relief, and as a result of her excellent work in *Mannequin* just completed at Twickenham, Judy Kelly has been rewarded with the leading feminine part in *The Black Abbot*. John Stuart, Edgar Norfolk, Ben Welden, Drusilla Wells and John Turnbull are also in the picture."

(*K. W.*, 16 November 1933, page 32, P. L. Mannock).

AT TWICKENHAM – GREAT PRODUCTION ACTIVITY:

"From now until January, when ***Bella Donna***, Julius Hagen's next super-production takes the floor, two units are to work night and day to fill the demand for films from Twickenham Studios."

"During the week George Pearson will start production, working at night, on ***The Lion and the Lamb*** for Radio release. The story has been written by Edward Dignon and Geoffrey Swaffer, and is a comedy of a sea-faring man. Michael Hogan in the lead, with Margaret Vines, Helga Moray, Mark Daly and D. J. Williams."

"Helga Moray is Julius Hagen's new discovery, of whom great things are expected. Mr. Hagen feels confident that she will follow Elizabeth Allan and Ida Lupino, who were both given their first big parts at Twickenham."

(NOTE that *The Lion and the Lamb* was later called *The River Wolves*.)

(*K. W.*, 23 November 1933, page 45, P. L. Mannock).

The Lion and the Lamb – "George Pearson is at work during the night. Margaret Vines, on the sick list, has given up her part to Hope Davey. Ben Welden and John Mills are additions to the cast."

(*K. W.*, 30 November 1933, page 41, P. L. Mannock).

The Broken Melody - "Joan Wyndham was taken ill on Friday night and by Sunday morning Merle Oberon was tested and was on the floor playing her part. John Garrick, the stage star now playing in *Give Me a Ring* at the London Hippodrome, has been chosen to play the part of the young composer. Bernard Vorhaus directing."

(*K. W.*, 30 November 1933, page 41, P. L. Mannock).

December 1933:

Kinematograph Weekly reported throughout the month:

FILM PRODUCTION SPACE PLANNED TO DOUBLE AT TWICKENHAM STUDIOS:

"Important developments are proposed at Alliance Studios, St. Margaret's, Twickenham, early in the New Year. Julius Hagen, the managing director, intends to have plans prepared for the erection of a new studio similar in size to the existing buildings, and hopes to be able to submit them to the local Council shortly. It is also proposed to carry out certain improvements in the existing studio".

(*K. W.*, 7 December 1933, page 5).

FILM PRODUCTION AT TWICKENHAM STUDIOS:

"Merle Oberon makes her singing début in *The Broken Melody*. W. L. Trytel is at present working on the composition of one act of an original opera, which will be performed in part during the story; also several love songs and a convict's march for the Devil's island scenes. Scenes have been shot last week showing John Garrick's desertion of Merle Oberon, who loves him, and his life with Margot Grahame in Paris. The sophisticated sets designed by James Carter including a modern Parisian boudoir."

(*K. W.*, 7 December 1933, page 39, P. L. Mannock).

Lion and Lamb – "Pearson's last scenes; will complete work this. Visitors were surprised to fall over chains and barrels standing outside the public-house where most of the action of the film takes place. An odd fishing boat leans tipsily on one side, and fishing nets and other tackle make it almost impossible to cross the floor."

(*K. W.*, 7 December 1933, page 39, P. L. Mannock).

The Broken Melody – "Scenes have been made showing the murder of Pierre (Austin Trevor), who is Margot Grahame's lover in the film, by her husband (John Garrick). This week, Vorhaus will be occupied with scenes on Devil's Island."

(*K. W.*, 14 December 1933, page 37, P. L. Mannock).

'The Czar of Twickenham'. The History of Julius Hagen and the Film Empire he created at Twickenham Film Studios, from 1927 to 1938.

The Broken Melody - "Last week, convicts of all nationalities – Frenchmen, Englishmen, Chinamen and Negroes – aligned the studios and herded together, irrespective of colour, in the narrow cells on the set built to represent a convict ship *en route* for Devil's Island. In these cells, shots were taken to show every phase of the prisoners' life on board one of these "hell ships". Onlookers saw the coarse mush which the guards called food, saw the prisoners flogged for imaginary breaches of discipline, and, above all, they saw the steam being turned on the prisoners in their cages when they attempted mutiny. This scene promises to be the most realistic ever taken in a "chain gang" picture. A long pipe running the length of the cages contained the steam, and at a given signal it was turned on the unfortunate prisoners who could not escape and fell screaming in their tracks."

"It was a relief to find oneself in another part of the Twickenham studios, in the French Café Chantant, where Germaine (Merle Oberon) sings for a living, and where she finds a job for Paul Verlaine (John Garrick)."

"The final shots on *The Broken Melody* to be done this week, will include scenes from the opera in which Merle Oberon and John Garrick sing."

(*K. W.*, 21 December 1933, page 22, P. L. Mannock).

NEW FILM CONTRACTS SIGNED AT TWICKENHAM STUDIOS:

"As a result of her good work in *Mannequin* and *The Black Abbot*, and following Julius Hagen's policy of signing up promising new players, **Judy Kelly** has been given a year's contract with Twickenham Studios. Although she has only been in England just over a year, Miss Kelly has already established herself as a young star of considerable promise."

239

John V. Watson

(*K. W.*, 14 December 1933, page 37, P. L. Mannock).

"**Davina Craig**, lately in *I Lived with You*, *Mannequin* and *The Black Abbot* at Twickenham, has also been given a contract with Julius Hagen for the coming year."

(*K. W.*, 14 December 1933, page 37, P. L. Mannock).

Twickenham's 20 Films Trade Shown during 1933:

Twickenham completed twenty films during 1933. This number produced gave an increase of four more films over the sixteen films that the studio completed during the previous year, 1932.

Julius Hagen produced three very important British films during 1933, namely *I Lived with You*, starring matinee idol, Ivor Novello; *This Week of Grace*, Gracie Fields' third starring vehicle; and *The Wandering Jew*, starring the distinguished German actor, Conrad Veidt. *The Lost Chord*, starring John Stuart and Elizabeth Allan, which was made for Associated Producing and Distribution Co., Ltd., was also a big film production from Julius Hagen.

Of those twenty films made by Julius Hagen in 1933, sixteen were "Quota Quickies", fifteen of which were made Hagen's Real Art Productions, Ltd, and the other one was made by Twickenham Film Studios.

Puppets of Fate (1933)

Crime thriller. A notorious forger escapes from Dartmoor and sets up a gang in London's Whitechapel.

Puppets of Fate was the first full-length feature film

240

made by Julius Hagen's Real Art Productions for the British renting subsidiary of United Artists. At a running time of just under one-hour-and-a-quarter, this feature film was clearly designed as a co-feature, or even as a "top-of-the-bill" attraction for certain British cinemas.

Puppets of Fate was the second film George A. Cooper directed for Julius Hagen.

Puppets of Fate: British Registration Details:
  Quota Registration No.: Br. 8296.   Registration Date: 10 January 1933.
  Registered Length: 6,541 feet.   Registered by: United Artists.
  Maker's name: Real Art Productions, Ltd. Certificate: "A".

Puppets of Fate was reviewed by *Kinematograph Weekly* on 12 January 1933 on page 9:

> RCA Photophone, 70 minutes, "A" certificate.
>
> "Remarks: Naïve but rousing crime melodrama, with plenty of thrills, strong love interest, and attractive cast.
>
> "Box Office Angle: Safe entertainment for the masses.
>
> "A hectic study in revenge, crime and punishment, a British drama which leaves nothing out in its effort to thrill, and covers places as far as New York, London and Dartmoor. The involved story works out with a clear directness, and spectacular sequences, romance and rough stuff play their allotted part in the comprehensiveness of the

241

artless but gripping entertainment. Safe fare for the masses.

"Story: Richard Sabine, an amateur detective, comes to the aid of Joan, whose Uncle, Dr. Munroe, is in the power of Arthur Brandon, an undesirable gentleman. He discovers that Brandon is an escaped convict, who knows that Munroe, a secret crook, is responsible for the murder of a man whose death was supposed to have resulted from a train accident. He succeeds in bringing both Munroe and Brandon to book after a desperate struggle, and, of course, wins Joan.

"Acting: Godfrey Tearle is a little stilted as Sabine, but, nevertheless, makes a handsome and cultured hero. Russell Thorndike is effectively sinister as Munroe, Fred Groves is good as Brandon, and Isla Bevan is an attractive Joan.

"Production: There are so many strings to the plot that it is only possible to give the story in the barest outline, but they are skilfully gathered up by the producer who makes the exciting story easy to follow.

"Settings and Photography: The escape from Dartmoor is well handled, and the train smash is a good piece of realism, while the rest of the settings are in no way skimped.

"Points of Appeal: Hearty melodramatic story, good atmosphere, useful cast, spectacular thrills.

Puppets of Fate went out on General Release on Monday, 3 July 1933.

Hundred to One (1933)

Racing drama. Irish publican (Arthur Sinclair) risks all of his savings to buy a horse to fulfil an ambition to own one that will win the Derby.

Hundred to One was the last of the five short-length 'Quota Quickie' features which Julius Hagen made for Fox-British in 1931 and 1932.

Hundred to One was the only film Walter West directed for Julius Hagen.

Hundred to One was the second Hagen picture to be made away from his "home" Twickenham Studios; it was the only occasion he used Wembley, and it was probably done so because of his association with Harry Cohen and Fox-British, who were based at Wembley. From 1932, Wembley Studios were hired by independent producers to make films, usually Quota Quickies, particularly for Fox-British.

Hundred To One: British Registration Details:
Quota Registration No.: Br. 8301. Registration Date: 11 January 1933.
Registered Length: 4,018 feet. Registered by: Fox Film Company, Ltd.
Maker's name: Twickenham Film Studios, Ltd. Certificate: "U".

Hundred to One was reviewed by *Kinematograph Weekly*, 12 January 1933 (page 9):

RCA Photophone, 55 minutes, "U" certificate.

"<u>Remarks</u>: Mildly entertaining story of the turf, featuring the Derby. Treatment and characterisation fair. Good camera work.

243

"Box Office Angle: Useful quota inclusion in popular programmes.

"A quite story of the turf, culminating in topical shots of the Derby. Plot is frankly weak, but the character of the jovial Irish landlord and the horse interest, with the English countryside atmosphere, should make the short feature a useful quota proposition in the average programme.

"Story: Landlord Flynn is bent on winning the Derby with his specially bred horse Mavourneen. His daughter Molly is in love with Bob, who leaves home to run a riding school, but returns in time to ride Mavourneen to win.

"Acting: Arthur Sinclair gives a sincere study of the Irish innkeeper, his daughter being attractively played by Dodo Watts. Remainder of the cast fair.

"Production: Walter West has very little story to develop, and the tempo at first is inclined to drag.

"Settings and Photography: Charming scenes of rural England with interiors of an inn are efficiently photographed.

"Points of Appeal: The horses, English background, and the personalities of Flynn and Molly.

Hundred to One went out on General Release on Monday, 6 March 1933.

The Iron Stair (1933)

Crime thriller with a very complex plot. In order to

forge cheques, George (Henry Kendall), needs to impersonate his twin brother, Geoffrey (Kendall again), and then letting Geoffrey to go to prison for the crime.

The Iron Stair was the first of the seven film appearances made by Henry Kendall for Julius Hagen, five of which were made in the same year.

The Iron Stair was the twenty-first film Leslie Hiscott directed for Julius Hagen at their Twickenham Film Studios; his seventh 'Real Art' picture.

The Iron Stair was Trade shown on Tuesday, 10 January 1933 at the Cambridge Theatre, London. *The Iron Stair* preceded the Trade Showing of the American sports drama, *The Sport Parade* (1932), starring Joel McCrea, Marian Marsh and William Gargan, made by RKO Radio Pictures, and released throughout the United Kingdom by Radio Pictures.

> *The Iron Stair*: British Registration Details:
> Quota Registration No.: Br. 8302. Registration Date: 11 January 1933.
> Registered Length: 4,575 feet. Registered by: Radio Pictures, Ltd.
> Maker's name: Real Art Productions, Ltd. Certificate: "A".

The Iron Stair was reviewed by *Kinematograph Weekly* on 12 January 1933 (page 9):

> RCA Photophone, 51 minutes, "A" certificate.

> "Remarks: Popular melodrama, put over with holding interest and realism by a good cast. Competent direction and convincing atmosphere.

John V. Watson

"Box Office Angle: Good stuff for the majority.

"Melodrama, a lively story of treachery and deception, put over with vigour which disarms criticism and makes for safe popular entertainment. The casting is sound, the treatment is straightforward, and realistic atmosphere prevails. Good stuff for the majority.

"Story: George and Geoffrey Gale are twins, but George is a waster, while Geoffrey is the apple of his father's eye. George, engaged to his wealthy cousin, Eve Marshall, is heavily involved financially, and, with the help of his mistress, Elsa, forges a cheque on his father's account for a thousand pounds, and plants the blame on Geoffrey. Geoffrey is unable to furnish an alibi, and goes to prison for five years. Patrick Deringham, Eve's lawyer, is in love with her, and is dismayed at the thoughts of her marrying George. Benjamin Marks, a moneylender, informs Patrick that he believes that George had framed Geoffrey, and the two plot to prove Geoffrey's innocence, and Geoffrey's spectacular escape from prison helps them to prove his case. Coincident with this, George is killed in an accident. Eve's freedom, of course, allows her to marry Patrick.

"Acting: Henry Kendall plays the dual rôle, and clever photography enables him to draw good contrast. Dorothy Boyd is charming as Eve, and Michael Hogan, Michael Sherbrook are excellent as Patrick and Marks respectively.

"Production: The spirit of true, popular melodrama

246

finds its way into this workmanlike Twickenham production, which contains all the situations which make for popular success.

"<u>Settings and Photography</u>: Lavish interiors, smart apartment scenes, rural sequences and prison episodes furnish the backgrounds and build up a good atmosphere.

"<u>Points of Appeal</u>: Holding story, good characterisation, popular appeal, and sound treatment.

The Iron Stair went out on British General Release on Monday, 8 May 1933.

Called Back (1933)

Modernized adaptation of a once-famous book by Hugh Conway, first published in 1883. A rich young Englishman, Geoffrey (Lester Matthews; [but his character was actually named 'Gilbert' in the film]), recuperating in Spain after being temporarily blinded, falls in love with a girl (Dorothy Boyd), whose evil uncle (Anthony Ireland) has spent money left in trust and murdered his nephew.

Called Back was directed by Reginald Denham and Jack Harris. Why a 'Quota Quickie' needed two directors to make has not been established; Jack Harris was a film editor.

Called Back: British Registration Details:
Quota Registration No.: Br. 8433. Registration Date: 15 February 1933.
Registered Length: 4,527 feet. Registered by: Radio Pictures, Ltd.
Maker's name: Real Art Productions, Ltd.

John V. Watson

British Board of Film Censor's Certificate: "A".
British distributor: Radio. Running Time: 50 minutes.
Called Back was the fourth 'Quota Quickie' film made by Real Art Productions for the British distribution subsidiary of the American Radio Pictures.

Called Back was Trade shown on Tuesday, 14 February 1933 at the Prince Edward Theatre, Old Compton Street, London, W.1. The screening of *Called Back* preceded the Trade showing of the American comedy, *The Half-Naked Truth* (1932), which was made by RKO Radio Pictures, directed by Gregory La Cava and starred Lupe Vélez and Lee Tracy; it was released throughout the United Kingdom by Radio Pictures.

Called Back was reviewed in *Kinematograph Weekly*, 16 February 1933, page 25:
RCA Photophone, 50 minutes, "A" certificate.

"Remarks: Crime drama, with a fantastic but interesting theme. Atmosphere occasionally unreal, but characterisation and direction sound.

"Box Office Angle: Useful supporting feature.

"Crime drama, a trifle fantastic in theme, competently portrayed by a cast of established stage favourites. The story is told partly in retrospect, and the device secures adequate suspense which in turn stimulates interest and leads to holding situations. Useful supporting attraction for most halls.

"Story: Gilbert Vaughan, a wealthy young man suffering from blindness, leaves his house one night intent upon visiting friends. He is

248

misdirected and enters a strange house, where he
hears a woman scream and a strange thud. He is
immediately seized and given a potent draught.
On recovering consciousness, he finds himself in
his own home, where his story is attributed to
delirium. His sight is restored following an
operation, and he goes to Spain to recuperate and
there he meets and marries Pauline March. Later
he discovers that she is suffering from loss of
memory and has no recollection of her past. He
determines to probe the mystery, and his
adventures carry him back to his early adventure
before the solution is found.

"Acting: Lester Matthews is quietly effective as
Vaughan, Dorothy Boyd is convincing as Pauline,
Franklin Dyall is clever in a sinister rôle, and Ian
Fleming, Anthony Ireland and Alexander Sarner
are adequate in prominent supporting parts.

"Production: The story, which leads us to Spain and
Russia, is not always convincing in atmosphere,
but the intricacies of the plot pave the way to
good drama and strong suspense, which atone for
the technical deficiencies. Easy anticipation is
avoided by competent direction, while sound
characterisation secures some human interest.
The entertainment is certainly comprehensive and
has most of the considered essentials of the safe
supporting offering.

"Settings and Photography: The London interiors
and exteriors are quite good, and the Spanish
sequences have colour if not conviction, but the
Russian interludes are definitely theatrical.

249

John V. Watson

"Points of Appeal: Unusual story, quiet drama, good suspense, popular love interest, sound acting by strong cast.

Called Back went out on British General Release on Monday, 26 June 1933; the release was originally planned for 5 June 1933.

The Medicine Man (1933)

Comedy. Inveigled into swapping identities with a doctor friend, 'silly ass' Freddie (Claud Allister) finds himself in demand by a criminal gang: they want him to perform surgery on one of the wounded on a "job".

The Medicine Man: leading players: Frank Pettingell, Claude Allister and Ben Weldon.

The Medicine Man was the fifth 'Quota Quickie' film made by Real Art for the British distribution subsidiary of the American Radio Pictures.

The Medicine Man was the first of the four films Redd Davis directed for Julius Hagen. The biggest of these four, in terms of budget and length, was the Flanagan and Allen musical comedy, *Underneath the Arches* (1937– see below); it was the last film he directed for Hagen.

The Medicine Man: British Registration Details:
Quota Registration No.: Br. 8448. Registration Date: 17 February 1933.
Registered Length: 4,704 feet. Registered by: Radio Pictures, Ltd.
Maker's name: Real Art Productions, Ltd. Certificate: "A".

The Medicine Man was Trade shown on Thursday, 16

February 1933 at the Prince Edward Theatre, Old Compton Street, London, W.1. The screening of *The Medicine Man* preceded the Trade showing of the American romantic melodrama, *No Other Woman* (1933), which was made by RKO Radio Pictures, directed by J. Walter Ruben, and starred Irene Dunne, with Charles Bickford, Gwili Andre and Eric Linden; it was released throughout the United Kingdom by Radio Pictures.

The Medicine Man was reviewed in *Kinematograph Weekly* on 23 February 1933, page 15:
RCA Photophone, 50 minutes, "A" certificate.

"Remarks: A hectic fruity comedy extravaganza, with lively team work and good presentation.

"Box Office Angle: Good supporting fare for the masses.

"Farcical entertainment, a pot-pourri of comedy, crime and romance, splashed with fruity quips. The development is not too even, but the robust comedy of Frank Pettingell and good team work keep the lively spirit of the fooling at an even length. Technically, the film is first class. Good light stuff for the masses.

"Story: Freddie Wiltshire, an impecunious asinine youth, agrees for a monetary consideration to impersonate his friend, Dr. Primus, who wishes to establish an alibi. His excursion into medicine leads him to the police court, to certify a drunken reveller who turns out to be his would-be father-in-law, Amos Wells, a hypocritical temperance advocate. Following this, Freddie is captured by

251

gunmen, and excitement mingles with the humour before he extricates himself from his difficulties.

"Acting: Frank Pettingell is in capital form as the hypocritical Amos, Claude Allister is bright as the asinine Freddie, Ben Weldon is a first-class gunman, and many other prominent players lend their support.

"Production: Every conceivable device is employed to keep the entertainment bright, and the hectic melange is staged on quite an extravagant scale. Many of the gags border on the suggestive, and the dialogue is fruity, but the broadness of the humour is seasoned to the taste of the masses. Used with discretion, the film has the makings of a good, popular supporting feature.

"Settings and Photography: The consulting-room and police station sequences are really bright, while the rounding-up of the gunmen is staged with a good sense of burlesque.

"Points of Appeal: Hectic story, breezy situations, boisterous humour, good staging and team work.

The Medicine Man went out on General Release on Monday, 3 July 1933.

The Shadow (1933)

Comedy-thriller. Scotland Yard are mystified by the activities of a murderous blackmailer, known only as '*The Shadow*', who terrorises the rich of England; his victims are threatened with ruin or even worse if he is not paid.

London Trade Show: Thursday, 2 March 1933 (3.00 p.m.) at the Cambridge Theatre. The screening of *The Shadow* preceded the Trade showing of the American crime melodrama, *State Trooper*, which was made by Columbia Pictures, directed by D. Ross Lederman, and starred Regis Toomey and Evalyn Knapp; it was released throughout the United Kingdom by United Artists.

British Registration Details:
Quota Registration No.: Br. 8497. Registration Date: 4 March 1933.
Registered Length: 6,752 feet. Registered by: United Artists.
Maker's name: Real Art Productions, Ltd. Certificate: "A".

The Shadow was reviewed in *Kinematograph Weekly*, 9 March 1933, page 18:
RCA Photophone, 75 minutes, "A" certificate.

"<u>Remarks</u>: Mystery drama, with a strong comedy element. Situation well held, characterisations sound, and presentation, but slow in tempo.

"<u>Box Office Angle</u>: Acceptable two-feature programme offering.

"Mystery drama, with a strong comedy element, which has the merit of concealing the identity of the central character until the end, thereby keeping the entertainment maintained at an even level.

"The action is a trifle leisurely, but the abundant humour, eminently popular in character, is deftly employed to prevent monotony and give contrast. Acceptable two-feature programme offering, with an additional advantage, eligibility for quota purposes.

"Story: The murder of a detective gives the police a clue to the whereabouts of a mysterious blackmailer, known as "The Shadow", and they trick the gentleman to the home of Sir Richard Bryant. They arrive in the midst of a small house-party which includes fogbound travellers, crooks, members of the family, and a facetious novelist. Murder follows the arrival of the police, and their investigations lead to a surprise denouement.

"Acting: Henry Kendall is in good form as the facetious novelist and cleverly cloaks the identity of *"The Shadow"*. Elizabeth Allan is quite good in the feminine lead. Sam Livesey acts with quiet dignity as Sir Richard, and the rest of the cast is drawn from experienced players.

"Production: The story will not withstand serious analysis, but it has ingenuity on its side and succeeds in leading the audience right up the garden until the last. Unnecessary talk impairs the action, but the slowness of the tempo is offset by the bright, disarming comedy. The picture is a good example of its type, a popular one, and it should meet with approval in the majority of halls.

"Settings and Photography: The interiors are spacious, the atmosphere is good, and the photography and lighting efficient.

"Points of Appeal: Thrilling and amusing story, good element of surprise, capable characterisation and effective presentation.

'The Czar of Twickenham'. The History of Julius Hagen and the Film Empire he created at Twickenham Film Studios, from 1927 to 1938.

The Shadow went into British General Release on Monday, 28 August 1933.

Excess Baggage (1933)

Comedy.   Colonel   Murgatroyd   (Claud   Allister) mistakenly thinks he has shot dead his superior officer, General Booster (Frank Pettingell), while hunting a ghost.

London Trade Show: Thursday, 23 March 1933 at the Prince Edward Theatre. The screening of *Excess Baggage* which preceded the Trade showing of the American comedy thriller, *The Penguin Pool Mystery* (1932), which was made by RKO Radio Pictures, and starred Edna May Oliver as the amateur sleuth, 'Hildegarde Withers', with James Gleason and Robert Armstrong; it was released throughout the United Kingdom by Radio Pictures.

British Registration Details:
Quota Registration No.: Br. 8549.   Registration Date: 24 March 1933.
Registered Length: 5,358 feet. Registered by: Radio Pictures, Ltd.
Maker's name: Real Art Productions, Ltd. Certificate: "U".

Excess Baggage was reviewed in *Kinematograph Weekly*, 30 March 1933, page 17:
RCA Photophone, 55 minutes, "U" certificate.

"Remarks: A laughable absurdity, treated in the right vein by a popular comedy cast.

"Box Office Angle: Sound supporting fare for the masses.

"A comedy absurdity, so preposterous that it defies

255

serious criticism, but nevertheless scores laughs with its artless, irresponsible fooling. The principal players get down to their work with a seriousness that exaggerates the genial craziness of the entertainment, and good team work thrusts the picture into the supporting feature category.

"Story: Col. Murgatroyd has a heated altercation with his C.O., General Booster, and strikes him over the head with a bottle. Believing the General to be dead, he sets out with the aid of his wife, Martha, to dispose of the body. It is put in a trunk, but by mistake the trunk is exchanged for one owned by the Duchess of Dillwater, and is carried into a house supposed to be haunted by a ghost. From thence on things become very involved and lead to lively fooling before the General and Murgatroyd meet and bury the hatchet.

"Acting: Frank Pettingell's ample form and spacious humour make him a good General, Claude Allister contrasts well as the harassed Murgatroyd, while Viola Compton, Sydney Fairbrother and Finlay Currie enter the spirit of the fooling in support.

"Production: The picture is indescribable nonsense, but its craziness is not without popular humour. The cast takes matters with a mock seriousness and draws character which is in itself entertaining and spirited presentation rounds off the entertainment.

"Settings and Photography: The settings follow the action, and the backgrounds fit effectively into the varying moods. Lighting and photography are good.

"<u>Points of Appeal</u>: Absurdly laughable theme, good cast, and suitable treatment.

Excess Baggage went out on General Release on Monday, 7 August 1933.

The Lost Chord (1933)

Romantic drama with music. Music composer, David Graham (John Stuart), kills Count Zara (Leslie Perrins) for his wife, the countess (Mary Glynne). As a result of the duel, David loses the strength in his hands to play the piano; later the countess dies in his arms. Twenty years pass; he falls in love with her daughter, Joan (Elizabeth Allan), but his nephew, Jim Selby (Jack Hawkins), a surgeon who wants to operate on David's hands so he can play again, also loves Joan, thus complicating matters.

The Lost Chord was the third Hagen/Twickenham film which was made for the distributor, A.P.D. (Associated Producers and Distributors).

London Trade Show: Tuesday, 4 April 1933 at the Cambridge Theatre.

British Registration Details:
Quota Registration No.: Br. 8626. Registration Date: 7 April 1933.
Registered Length: 8,274 feet.
Registered by: A.P.D. (Associated Producing and Distribution Co., Ltd).
Maker's name: Twickenham Film Studios, Ltd.
British Board of Film Censor's Certificate: "A".
British distributor: A.P.D. Running Time: 90 minutes.

John V. Watson

The Lost Chord: Successful bookings for its General Release:

Kinematograph Weekly, 26 October 1933, reported that:

"1,465 theatres in the United Kingdom had booked '*The Lost Chord*' so far, and 56 theatres in London and suburbs screened this film for one week, the week commencing Monday, 16 October" (1933).

The Lost Chord was reviewed in *Kinematograph Weekly*, 13 March 1933, page 14:

> RCA Photophone, 85 minutes (as reported in *Kinematograph Weekly*, but 8274 feet divided by 90 feet per minute gives a running time of almost 92 minutes), "A" certificate.

> "Remarks: Sentimental melodrama, inspired by the famous song. Good story, clever treatment, strong feminine appeal, bright humour, tender emotionalism, and picturesque presentation.

> "Box Office Angle: Excellent popular booking.

> "Sentimental melodrama, inspired by Arthur Sullivan's famous song, the theme of which is truly engaging and appeals to all tastes. The narrative is constructed with experienced dramatic skill, and it is carried pleasantly through the essential paths, building up good, honest entertainment cunningly attuned to the requirements of the masses. Excellent popular booking.

> "Story: David Graham, a brilliant composer, returns after a lengthy stay abroad, to find that Madeline,

258

the woman he loves, is now married to Count Carol Zara. She is unhappy, and turns to David for solace, and Zara uses their innocent friendship to secure a divorce and the custody of his child. David looses the use of his right hand in a duel with Zara, and Madeline, heartbroken, dies. Twenty years later David's nephew, Jim Selby, a doctor, falls in love with Joan Elton, a chorus girl, but a tiff separates them. David then takes an interest in Joan, and writes the score for a musical play in which she stars. He decides to marry her, and allows Jim to operate on his hand. The use is restored, but David learns that Joan is Madeline's daughter. This intelligence, coupled with the knowledge that it is Jim whom she really loves, prompts David to step aside.

"Acting: John Stuart gives a carefully graduated study as David, and ages with conviction and dignity, subtly stressing the emotional note. Mary Glynne is sensitive and appealing as Madeline, Elizabeth Allan remains to true to type as Joan, Leslie Perrins is good as Zara, and Jack Hawkins is breezy and likeable as Jim.

"Production: The story has an experienced hardness, and allows strong drama and bright humour to punctuate the emotional theme. Semi-classical and popular music flow logically into the development and enhance the picturesqueness of the atmosphere. The director, Maurice Elvey, has again displayed his unquestionable flair for showmanship in his treatment of the narrative and his handling of the fine cast. The tender romance motif remains in true perspective throughout, and, wide as the entertainment is, it never loses feminine appeal.

"Settings and Photography: The early sequences, staged in England and Italy, have majesty and colour, the modern settings are true in detail, and the backstage atmosphere is gay and mellifluous. The additional song numbers are well scored and rendered.

"Points of Appeal: Popular emotional theme, good and versatile characterisation, undeniable feminine appeal, bright humour, tuneful music, and skilful direction.

The Lost Chord went out on General Release on Monday, 30 October 1933.

The Man Outside (1933)

Crime thriller. Following a major robbery, a criminal gang search for stolen diamonds hidden in a country house, where a murder takes place. A private detective, Harry Wainwright (Henry Kendall), is called in to investigate, but finds that Inspector Jukes, (John Turnbull), has already arrived on the scene to look into the matter.

The Man Outside was the seventh 'Quota Quickie' which was made by Real Art Productions for Radio Pictures.

The Man Outside was the fourth film George A. Cooper directed for Julius Hagen.

London Trade Show: Wednesday, 31 May 1933 at the Cambridge Theatre.

'The Czar of Twickenham'. The History of Julius Hagen and the Film Empire he created at Twickenham Film Studios, from 1927 to 1938.

British Registration Details:
Quota Registration No.: Br. 8815. Registration Date: 1 June 1933.
Registered Length: 4,781 feet. Registered by: Radio Pictures, Ltd.
Maker's name: Real Art Productions, Ltd.
British Board of Film Censor's Certificate: "A".
British distributor: Radio. Running Time: 52 minutes.

The Man Outside was reviewed in *Kinematograph Weekly*, 8 June 1933, page 20:
RCA Photophone, 53 minutes, "A" certificate.

"Remarks: Popular mystery story with a good cast, bright dialogue and capable direction.

"Box Office Angle: Good supporting offering. No juvenile appeal.

"A mystery drama with clever plot put over in good style by a capable cast. The story has plenty of light repartee in its dialogue, and the artistes make the most of their chances. It is entertainment from beginning to end, the mystery being well sustained and the direction keeping the action going strongly. A supporting feature of merit.

"Story: From a little-known uncle, Captain Fordyce inherits Ravensdale, a lonely house which has become the subject of the attentions of a masked stranger. Mysterious rappings inside the house alarm the inhabitants, who include Henry Wainwright, a friend of Fordyce, and when Gore, the chauffeur, is found murdered, Inspector Jukes, of the local police, investigates. A will is found which bequeaths the house and contents to "Shiner Talbot", a crook concerned in diamond robbery, the proceeds of which were never traced. Gore is recognised as Talbot, and later the diamonds are discovered in the house. They are hidden again, and the masked man's attempt to get them is frustrated by Wainwright, who exposes Jukes as the criminal.

"<u>Acting</u>: Henry Kendall enacts the rôle of Wainwright, a private detective, with ease, and disguises his profession with a light and disarming air. Gillian Lind, a maid at Ravensdale and wife of Talbot, with feeling; an amusing study is given by Ethel Warwick as Fordyce's aunt; and John Turnbull makes a capable police inspector. Good support is given by Cyril Raymond, Joan Gardner and Louis Hayward.

"<u>Production</u>: Preliminaries over, the story develops rapidly, with drama and mystery well interspersed with humour. Dramatic situations occur at well-timed intervals and are carried through competently by the cast, and throughout the story the dialogue is bright and pointed. The identity of the mysterious intruder is effectively hidden until the dénouement, and the setting of the story, although restricted in a country mansion, provides good atmosphere.

"<u>Settings and Photography</u>: Well furnished interiors form the majority of settings and are well photographed.

"<u>Points of Appeal</u>: Popular mystery plot well sustained, bright dialogue, and light romance.

Competent playing by the cast.

The Man Outside went out on General Release on Monday, 6 November 1933.

I Lived with You (1933)

Comedy romantic drama. An exiled Russian prince (Ivor Novello), lodging with an English working-class family, falls for his landlady's shop-assistant daughter (Ursula Jeans). Adapted from the play by Ivor Novello (1932).

I Lived with You was the sixth film Maurice Elvey directed for Julius Hagen.

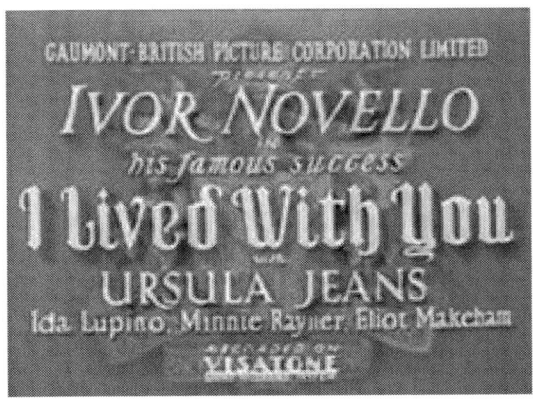

The opening on-screen main title card for *I Lived with You*.

I Lived with You was the second and final leading film rôle Ivor Novello made for Julius Hagen. He was to make one more film, *Autumn Crocus* (1934), in which he starred with Fay Compton; a British romance directed by

John V. Watson

Basil Dean for Associated Talking Pictures, it was based on Dodie Smith's first play Autumn Crocus, which had been a West End theatre hit for its director Basil Dean.

London Trade Show: Wednesday, 14 June 1933 at the Prince Edward Theatre.

British Registration Details:
Quota Registration No.: Br. 8881. Registration Date: 17 June 1933.
Registered Length: 8,800 feet. Registered by: W. & F. Film Service, Ltd.
Maker's name: Twickenham Film Studios, Ltd.
British Board of Film Censor's Certificate: "A".
British distributor: released by Gaumont-British Distributors, Ltd from October 1933, following the merger of Gaumont-Ideal, Ltd. and W. & F. Film Service, Ltd. late the previous month.

Running Time: 98 or 100 minutes.

I Lived with You was reviewed in *Kinematograph Weekly*, 22 June 1933, page 22:
RCA Photophone, 100 minutes (although the registered length of 8,800 feet when divided by 90-feet-per-minutes gives 97.78 minutes), "A" certificate.

The *Kinematograph Weekly* reviewer incorrectly stated that RCA Photophone was the sound recording system used for the film: the system actually used was Visatone Sound Recording.

"Remarks: Domestic comedy drama, the original theme of which finds point and rich popular entertainment through clever individual characterisation. Shrewd treatment and flawless

264

atmosphere.

"Box Office Angle: Excellent popular booking, hardly suitable for juveniles.

"Domestic comedy-drama, adapted from Ivor Novello's stage success, which gives an interesting and thoroughly entertaining study of working-class family life through the brilliance of the individual characterisation. The theme is a trifle fantastic, but it has the merit of originality and paves the way to neatly contrived situations which allow rich humour, popular drama, homely sentiment, and romance to follow in cunning sequence. The star, who acts extremely well, is supported by first-class players, and the atmosphere and direction, which reveals shrewd observation, leaves nothing to be desired. First-class booking for all classes, and the masses in particular.

"Story: Prince Felix Lenieff, a Russian exile, is befriended by Gladys Wallis, a working girl, whose parents give him a home. He lacks the cold English sense of morality, and his easy influence soon undermines the staid respectability of the family. The head of the house takes a mistress, Mrs. Wallis imbibes to freely, Ada, the younger daughter, finds a paramour, and Gladys is prepared to give herself to him. Flossie, Mrs. Wallis's sister, a silent witness to the unhappy transformation, however, slowly convinces Felix of the trouble he has caused, and he, in his remorse, silently departs. Gladys, nevertheless, follows him, and the happy ending, suggested by the reunion of the family, and the end of recrimination, follows.

"Acting: Ivor Novello has no difficulty in acquiring an intriguing accent, and his good looks help him bring conviction to a difficult part. Good as he is, however, the outstanding honours are gained by Minnie Rayner as Mrs. Wallis, and Eliot Makeham as Mr. Wallis. Ursula Jeans, Ida Lupino, Cecily Oates and Jack Hawkins all represent living, amusing and human types.

"Production: The unhealthy influence of the Russian temperament on English family life is the object of the theme, and is exploited in a manner which cleverly introduces comprehensive entertainment to the screen without stopping to be sordid. The lowering of the tone of the family morality is depicted in human and richly humorous colours, and the characterisation is so faithful, vivid and lifelike that it furnishes an entertainment in itself. The action, however, is a trifle leisurely at times, and the ending is not good drama, for its forced happiness tends to destroy the main purpose of the plot, but these trivialities in no way detract from the all-round excellence of the eminently popular product.

"Settings and Photography: Apart from one or two exteriors, the action is restricted to the Wallis home, but atmosphere is, nevertheless, effectively built up. Lighting and photography are satisfactory.

"Points of Appeal: Original theme, excellent situations, biting humour, outstanding characterisation, popular sentiment, title, star, and experienced direction.

I Lived with You went out on General Release on Monday, 29 January 1934; this was previously planned for Monday, 30 October 1933.

The Umbrella (1933)

Comedy. Two pickpockets (S. Victor Stanley and Dick Francis) are released from prison, one of whom has an umbrella with some stolen jewels hidden in the handle.

The Umbrella was the eighth 'Quota Quickie' made by Real Art Productions for Radio Pictures; it was the first of the four 'Real Art' films made for release by Radio that were trade shown throughout July 1933.

The Umbrella was the only film appearance by Kay Hammond for Julius Hagen, having already made several British films before for other film producers, between 1930 and 1932.

London Trade Show: Tuesday, 18 July 1933 at the Cambridge Theatre.

British Registration Details:
Quota Registration No.: Br. 8984. Registration Date: 19 July 1933.
Registered Length: 5,011 feet. Registered by: Radio Pictures, Ltd.
Maker's name: Real Art Productions, Ltd.
British Board of Film Censor's Certificate: "A".
British distributor: Radio Pictures.

John V. Watson

The Umbrella was reviewed in *Kinematograph Weekly*, 30 July 1933, page 19:
RCA Photophone, 56 minutes, "A" certificate.

"Remarks: Simple quota comedy of convenient length, with bright idea and good team work.

"Box Office Angle: Useful supporting offering. Safe for juveniles.

"The quest of two ex-convicts for a valuable lost umbrella provides this simple little comedy with its motive power. The situations are agreeably absurd, and the players make the most of the modest opportunities. A quota film which, by reason of its convenient length and clean fun, can be useful.

"Story: Victor and Mike, ex-convicts, embark on a pocket-picking campaign, but lose their umbrella, employed to hide jewels, while working a lift. The umbrella passes to a young man-about-town, from him to a girl, to whom he offers protection from the rain, and from her to Mabel, another ex-convict. The original owners set out in pursuit, and the tangle, which leads to romance, is straightened out at a masked ball.

"Acting: Kay Hammond is droll as the very Cockney Mabel, S. Victor Stanley and Dick Francis make an amusing pair of crooks, and Harold French and Kathleen Tremaine furnish the essential love interest.

"Production: The story has quite a bright idea behind it, and ingenious economy and lively team work combine to exploit it fairly successfully. Although the fun is not exactly fast and furious, it nevertheless has sufficient tempo to secure satisfactory results.

"Settings and Photography: The street scenes and interiors are adequate, while the masked ball sequence has life.

"Points of Appeal: Simple fun, convenient length, and bright team work.

The Umbrella went out on General Release on Monday, 4 December 1933.

His Grace Gives Notice (1933)

Romantic comedy. A young butler, George Barwick (Arthur Margetson), inherits a title but keeps this quiet while he sets out to gain the affections of Barbara Rannock (Viola Keats), the daughter of his aristocrat employer, Lord Rannock (O. B. Clarence).

His Grace Gives Notice was the fifth film George A. Cooper directed for Julius Hagen.

His Grace Gives Notice was the ninth 'Quota Quickie' made by Real Art Productions for Radio Pictures; it was the second of the four 'Real Art' films made for release by Radio that were trade shown during July 1933.

His Grace Gives Notice was the fifth British film made by Arthur Margetson and the first of his three appearances for Julius Hagen; the other two films were *Juggernaut* and *Broken Blossoms* (both 1936 – see below).

269

London Trade Show: Friday, 21 July 1933 at the Cambridge Theatre.

British Registration Details:
> Quota Registration No.: Br. 9002. Registration Date: 22 July 1933.
> Registered Length: 5,131 feet. Registered by: Radio Pictures, Ltd.
> Maker's name: Real Art Productions, Ltd.
> British Board of Film Censor's Certificate: "A".
> British distributor: Radio Pictures. Running Time: 57 minutes.

His Grace Gives Notice was reviewed in the *Kinematograph Weekly*, 27 July 1933, page 17:
> RCA Photophone, 57 minutes, "A" certificate.

> "Remarks: Simple, refreshing romantic comedy drama, with good cast and competent direction.

> "Box Office Angle: Useful supporting feature. Safe entertainment for children.

> "An obvious romantic comedy which draws simple, refreshing entertainment from its contrast of life above and below stairs. The evergreen ingredients are mixed with disarming naiveté, the characterisation is sound, and the production qualities are sufficiently good to accentuate the point of the play. Useful supporting feature for popular halls.

> "Story: George Berwick, young footman to Lord Rannock, is informed that he has inherited a dukedom shortly after being reprimanded by Barbara, the attractive but haughty daughter of the house, with whom he is secretly in love. Some

time after taking over his estate George learns that Barbara is about to elope with a man who, unknown to her, is a Chicago gangster. He then poses as the man's valet in order to protect her, and, after giving the outsider a severe hiding, convinces her of her folly and wins her for himself.

"Acting: Arthur Margetson plays his part well as George, Viola Keats is a dignified yet attractive Barbara, S. Victor Stanley is effective as a very cockney valet, and Dick Francis, Ben Welden, O. B. Clarence and Barry Livesey make a useful supporting team.

"Production: The character of this comedy is a trifle old-fashioned, but its theme has stood the test of time and can always be depended upon to amuse and please the masses. A good cast brings fresh humour to the comedy situations, and the stars take good care of the simple romantic interest. Clean in sentiment and convenient in length, the film has the makings of an acceptable second feature.

"Settings and Photography: Interiors are convincing, and by revealing life below and above stairs, result in amusing contrast as well as good atmosphere.

"Points of Appeal: Light, amusing story, good characterisation, popular romance, and adequate presentation and direction.

His Grace Gives Notice went out on General

271

John V. Watson

Release on Monday, 1 January 1934.

The Ghost Camera (1933)

Crime thriller. When a photograph is taken at the scene of a murder, the camera is tossed out of a castle window to destroy the evidence but it falls into the back of a passing car belonging to chemist John Gray (Henry Kendall). He becomes an amateur sleuth after developing the film and goes in search of the woman (Ida Lupino) who is shown in the photograph. When the camera is then stolen from his laboratory, Gray's suspicions are further aroused.....

The Ghost Camera was the tenth 'Quota Quickie' made by Real Art Productions for Radio Pictures; it was the third of the four 'Real Art' films which was made for release by Radio that were trade shown during July 1933.

The Ghost Camera was the first of several films which Bernard Vorhaus directed for Julius Hagen.

Henry Kendall and (a very young) Ida Lupino in a scene from *The Ghost Camera*.

272

The Ghost Camera was the sixth film appearance made by Ida Lupino and her second film for Julius Hagen; this time in the leading feminine rôle.

Twickenham's resident film editor, Jack Harris, was otherwise busy and so director Bernard Vorhaus was able to get David Lean to edit *The Ghost Camera*. Lean's editorial participation certainly shows.

London Trade Show: Thursday, 20 July 1933 (8.45 p.m.) at the Prince Edward Theatre.

British Registration Details:
Quota Registration No.: Br. 9003. Registration Date: 22 July 1933.
Registered Length: 6,139 feet. Alteration to the Registered Length: 6,061 feet, as reported in the *Kinematograph Weekly*, 21 December 1933. The reduction of 68 feet of film would shorten the running time of *The Ghost Camera* by just over four-fifths of one minute; this calculation is arrived at by using 90 feet per minute rule, which is the speed required to photograph and project sound films.
Registered by: Radio Pictures, Ltd. Maker's name: Real Art Productions, Ltd.
British Board of Film Censor's Certificate: "A".
British distributor: Radio Pictures. Running Time: 68 minutes.

The Ghost Camera was reviewed in the *Kinematograph Weekly*, 27 July 1933, on page 17:
RCA Photophone, 68 minutes, "A" certificate.

"Remarks: Quiet, unhurried British crime drama with an ingenious story, pleasing characterisation and refreshing atmosphere. Development

273

leisurely, but culminating episodes slick and satisfactory.

"Box Office Angle: Good general booking. Should prove harmless for children.

"A quiet, unhurried British crime drama with an ingenious story, natural and amusing characterisation, and picturesque outdoor backgrounds. Although the development is on the leisurely side, the producer has employed his camera and cast to advantage, and soon allows the tranquillity of the opening to be swiftly overtaken by good suspense, ending in a lively thrill and pleasing romance. Good general booking.

"Story: John Gray, a young chemist, discovers on returning from his holiday a camera amongst his luggage. In order to trace its owner he develops the films, and on one of the snaps discovers evidence of murder. The others lead him to May Elton, pretty sister of the owner, Ernest, and when she tells him that Ernest is missing they set out together to solve the mystery. Ernest, who is implicated in the murder, is eventually arrested, but luck and deduction enable John to prove his innocence and win May.

"Acting: Henry Kendall displays a quiet sense of humour as the serious and studious John Gray, Ida Lupino has charm and freshness as May, John Mills is good as Ernest, and George Merritt, Felix Aylmer and S. Victor Stanley more than pull their weight in support.

"Production: Although essentially a mystery drama,

'The Czar of Twickenham'. The History of Julius Hagen and the Film Empire he created at Twickenham Film Studios, from 1927 to 1938.

this film has charm and freshness which is usually denied this type of entertainment. The gathering up of the threads takes some time, but the process is accompanied by engaging detail, some of it romantic and some amusing. Once the picture takes firm dramatic shape the interests are more exciting, but still pleasantly and agreeably light. The appeal is addressed to all classes and all ages, and its universal interests make the picture a British attraction of commendable quality.

"Settings and Photography: The interiors are particularly good, a coroner's court sequence is extremely well handled, while the exteriors are carefully chosen and delightfully photographed. The culminating fight, resulting in the unmasking of the real murderer, is brisk and paves the way to a good and happy ending.

"Points of Appeal: Amusing, ingenious and holding story, happy and convincing characterisation, pleasing sentiment, quiet humour, thrills, popular romance, and refreshing atmosphere.

The Ghost Camera went out on General Release on Monday, 18 December 1933.

This Week of Grace (1933)

Comedy with music. Factory girl, Grace Milroy (Gracie Fields), sorts out the home of the eccentric Duchess of Swinford (Nina Boucicault), with the help of her family (Frank Pettingell, Minnie Rayner, Douglas Wakefield), who stir things up by using lots of working-class common sense. She falls in love with the Duchess'

275

son, Viscount Swinford (Henry Kendall), and eventually marries him.

This Week of Grace was the eleventh film made by Real Art Productions for Radio Pictures, Ltd.

This Week of Grace was certainly not a 'Quota Quickie'; it was Gracie Field's third film, and, by then, she had become a huge box-office star.

Gracie Fields received the then enormous sum of £20,000 from Radio to appear in *This Week of Grace*; indeed, her fee alone would have been enough to finance the entire production costs to make four 'Quota Quickie' films of one hour's length.

'The Czar of Twickenham'. The History of Julius Hagen and the Film Empire he created at Twickenham Film Studios, from 1927 to 1938.

An advertisement for *This Week of Grace* (1933) printed on the front of the programme for the Paramount Theatre in Leeds.

This Week of Grace was the first major picture made by Real Art Productions, but, as we shall see, it would be the company's only major, non-'Quota Quickie' film.

277

This Week of Grace was also the last of the four Real Art films made for release by Radio that were trade shown during July; the other three were all 'Quota Quickies'.

This Week of Grace was the seventh film Maurice Elvey directed for Julius Hagen. He had already directed Gracie Fields in her first film, *Sally in our Alley* (1931), which was made by Associated Talking Pictures; and he would direct her once again the following year in *Love, Life and Laughter* (1934), which again was made by Associated Talking Pictures.

London Trade Show: Thursday, 27 July 1933 at the Prince Edward Theatre.

British Registration Details:
Quota Registration No.: Br. 9025.
Registration Date: 28 July 1933.
Registered Length: 8,245 feet.
Registered by: Radio Pictures, Ltd.
Maker's name: Real Art Productions, Ltd.
British Board of Film Censor's Certificate: "U".
British distributor: Radio Pictures.

Running Time: 92 minutes.

This Week of Grace was reviewed in the *Kinematograph Weekly*, 3 August 1933, on page 14:
RCA Photophone, 92 minutes, "U" certificate.

"Remarks: Broad romantic comedy with music, which rings the changes successfully on an evergreen theme. Great performance by star, first-class support, and excellent staging.

"Box Office Angle: Outstanding box office

278

attraction. Great stuff for the youngsters.

"Broad romantic comedy with music, a picture bringing the obvious but popular humour of the music-hall to the screen, and putting over the evergreen comedy situations with an elaboration, skill and enthusiasm that calls for the highest commendation. Gracie Fields, who has never looked more attractive, nor worked with greater effect, draws liberally from her repertoire, and contributes a versatile performance which is in itself a great entertainment. She is, however, backed up by a sound team of experienced players, and has in Maurice Elvey a director who knows his job backwards, and it is the first-class combination of talent, experience and ambitious staging that makes the film a star and general attraction of the first box-office magnitude.

"Story: The eccentric Duchess of Swinford is dissatisfied with the way in which her step-sister, Lady Warmington, is running her estate, and supplants her by Gracie Milroy, a factory girl. Gracie, her father and mother, and brother Joe, take possession of the ancestral castle and soon give Lady Warmington, her son Clive, and the aristocratic neighbours something to think about. Gracie and Clive eventually fall in love, but a slight misunderstanding, fostered by Clive's ex-fiancée, causes her to leave after the marriage ceremony. However, they are eventually reconciled, and the story ends on a happy note.

"Acting: Gracie Fields puts up a versatile and tireless performance as Gracie, and whether

279

singing, gagging, miming, or romancing, shows herself to be a master of every department, and consolidates her position as England's premier entertainer. Frank Pettingell as Gracie's father, Douglas Wakefield as the half-wit brother, Joe, and Vivian Foster as a comedy curate, furnish the capital supporting team, while Henry Kendall, John Stuart, Minnie Rayner and Nina Boucicault bring their experience to bear and are resourceful in minor rôles.

"Production: The story, which relies on the never-failing device of contrasting high and low life for its entertainment, is pitted with conventional jokes and situations, but such is the resourcefulness and versatility of the star, the soundness of the team work, the experience displayed by the producer, and the ambitiousness of the production, that the gags, situations, and touches of burlesque register with a newness that compels laughter and makes for clean, honest, popular entertainment. Once the theme is firmly established, the film is perhaps a trifle long in reaching a climax, but the star, ever at hand, slips quickly into the breach when the entertainment is in danger of flagging, with a fresh card up her sleeve, and successfully staves off possibility of dull patches.

"Settings and Photography: No expense has been spared to establish essential contrast; delightful exteriors give scope to the development, with the song numbers, every one a certain winner, are rendered in the star's own inimitable way and fit logically into the action. Lighting and photography are particularly good.

'The Czar of Twickenham'. The History of Julius Hagen and the Film Empire he created at Twickenham Film Studios, from 1927 to 1938.

> "Points of Appeal: Brilliance, assurance, versatility, and popularity of star. Artless but amusing story, homely humour, excellent supporting cast, resourceful direction and excellent presentation.

This Week of Grace went out on the London Release on Monday, 16 October 1933.

Home Sweet Home (1933)

Melodrama. Dicky Pelham (John Stuart), a mining engineer, learns on the day of his departure, on leave to England, that his wife, Constance (Marie Ney), is about to go off with John Falkirk (Cyril Raymond).

Home Sweet Home was the twelfth film made by Real Art Productions for Radio Pictures.

Primarily a stage actress, *Home Sweet Home* marked the British sound film début of Marie Ney; it was her only film in which she had the feminine leading rôle. It was the first of her three film appearances for Julius Hagen; in the other two films, she had a major supporting rôle in *The Wandering Jew* (1933 - see below), and had a small but still important part as 'the Spirit of Christmas Past' (she appeared only in silhouette) in *Scrooge* (1935 - see below).

Home Sweet Home was the sixth film George A. Cooper directed for Julius Hagen.

London Trade Show: Thursday, 14 September 1933 at the Prince Edward Theatre.

British Registration Details:
Quota Registration No.: Br. 9201. Registration Date: 15 September 1933.

John V. Watson

Registered Length: 6,502 feet. Alteration to the
Registered Length: 6,465 feet (as reported in the
Kinematograph Weekly, 21 December 1933).
Registered by: Radio Pictures, Ltd. Maker's
name: Real Art Productions, Ltd.
British Board of Film Censor's Certificate: "A".
British distributor: Radio Pictures. Running
Time: 72 minutes.

Home Sweet Home was reviewed in the
Kinematograph Weekly, 21 September 1933, on page 15:
RCA Photophone, 72 minutes, "A" certificate.

John Stuart, Marie Ney, Richard Cooper.
"Remarks: Emotional drama, the artificial story of
which is given some popular appeal through the
sincerity of the acting and breadth of treatment.
Strong cast, and box office title.

"Box Office Angle: Moderate dramatic booking for
the masses, with obvious exploitation angles.
Unsuitable for children.

"Emotional drama, a practical tale of human frailty,
accompanied by generous by-play, which covers
the whole gamut in its leisurely journey to the
inevitable happy climax. The sentiments are
rather forced, and unnecessary directorial
acrobatics tend to prolong the development
without emphasising the purpose and moral of the
plot. Moderate dramatic booking for the masses,
the strong selling angles of which are the box-
office title and strong cast.

"Story: Dicky Pelham, a mining engineer, learns on
the day of his departure, on leave to England, that
his wife, Constance, is about to go off with John

282

Falkirk. By the time he reaches home Constance has changed her mind and has set off to inform Falkirk, who is waiting for her in an hotel in Dover. She is involved in a motor smash and taken to the hotel unconscious. Dickie pursues her, knocks Falkirk down, and accidentally kills him. On her recovery, Constance realises that she can only save Dickie from a heavy sentence for manslaughter by admitting to misconduct, and makes the sacrifice. By chance Pelham learns the truth shortly after his release, and the story ends happily.

"Acting: John Stuart acts with sincerity and strength as the unhappy Pelham and helps to bring human interest to the artificial theme. Marie Ney, too, has her moments as Constance and wins a little sympathy, but is poorly served by the camera. Richard Cooper and Sidney Fairbrother contribute two effective comedy studies, and Cyril Raymond, Felix Aylmer and Barbara Everest complete the strong cast.

"Production: The director, George A. Cooper, employs every known modern device, such as spoken thoughts, montage and symbolism to heighten the emotional appeal of the story, but its transparent artifice makes his task difficult. Still, if the credibility of the theme is open to doubt, there remains much to entertain, interest and move the masses in the sincerity of the acting and the breadth of the treatment. It is these fundamentals that compensate for naïveté of the drama and, together with its title and cast, make it worthy of the attention of the industrial showman.

"Settings and Photography: South American sequences, dignified English interiors, an interesting court scene, and good exteriors promote adequate atmosphere and give scope to the play, while lighting and photography are excellent.

"Points of Appeal: Title, feminine appeal, human interest, moving sentiment, good cast, and wide treatment.

Home Sweet Home went out on General Release on Monday, 19 February 1934. (Monday, 22 January 1934 was the original date planned for the general release).

The Roof (1933)

Crime drama. Inspector Darrow (Leslie Perrins) investigates the death of wealthy James Renton (George Zucco) who has jewels entrusted to his lawyer, Rutherford (Eliot Makeham).

The Roof was the thirteenth film made by Real Art Productions for Radio Pictures; another 'Quota Quickie'.

The Roof was the seventh film George A. Cooper directed for Julius Hagen.

The Roof was the fourth film appearance by Leslie Perrins for Julius Hagen, and his first leading film rôle.

London Trade Show: Wednesday, 1 November 1933 at the Cambridge Theatre.

British Registration Details:

Quota Registration No.: Br. 9375. Registration Date: 2 November 1933.
Registered Length: 5,223 feet.
Registered by: Radio Pictures, Ltd.
Maker's name: Real Art Productions, Ltd.
British Board of Film Censor's Certificate: "A".
British distributor: Radio Pictures.
Running Time: 58 minutes.

The Roof was reviewed in the *Kinematograph Weekly*, 9 November 1933, page 15:

RCA Photophone, 58 minutes, "A" certificate.

"Remarks: Popular crime story, with a surprising climax. Competent direction and good work by cast.

"Box Office Angle: Acceptable two-feature booking for the masses. Juvenile appeal slight.

"A popular crime story, put over by a competent cast, which develops to a dramatic and exciting climax. The pre-war opening atmosphere is well caught and refreshing, and later gives place to a present-day setting. Acceptable two-feature booking for the masses.

"Story: James Renton is handed a box of jewels to be held in trust for the son of his friend, Otto Bemberg, who thus foils the plans of Clive Bristow, a jewel thief. Renton places the jewels, together with an inventory and a list of questions to identify the owner, in the keeping of Rutherford, his lawyer. Many years later, Renton is found murdered, and shortly afterwards a claimant appears. Tony Freyne, Renton's friend, finds that he is an impostor, and this clue leads to Bristow, who admits robbing Renton of the duplicate identification papers, but denies the murder, which is eventually traced to the lawyer who committed the crime to cover defalcations.

"<u>Acting</u>: Competent playing by a lengthy cast contributes largely to the success of the picture, but outstanding work comes from Russell Thorndike as Bristow, George Zucco as Renton, and Eliot Makeham as Rutherford. The slight feminine rôles are capably undertaken by Judy Gunn and Barbara Everest.

"<u>Production</u>: Overlooking the coincidences inseparable from this type of crime plot, competent direction has obtained good entertainment and sent the story along with an easy swing from its pre-war opening to the present-day climax. The unexpected twist is a good feature of the closing stages, but brisker action in some scenes would have effected an improvement, and the Cockney accent of a police inspector strikes a jarring note.

"<u>Settings and Photography</u>: Action is confined to interior settings, but these are varied and cover home, shop, office, and club scenes. They are well lighted and photographed.

"<u>Points of Appeal</u>: Popular crime theme, slight sentiment, dramatic and unexpected climax. Strong and capable cast.

The Roof went out on General Release on Monday, 2

April 1934. The original date planned for the General Release was Monday, 9 April 1934.

(A) *Shot in the Dark* (1933)

Note that modern reference books quote the title as "*A Shot in the Dark*"; however this is certainly incorrect as the opening credits on the original release print clearly show that there is not a capital letter "A" at the start of the actual title.

Crime; murder mystery: Several relatives attempt to murder a hated recluse (A. Bromley Davenport).

A Shot in the Dark was the fourteenth film made by Real Art Productions for Radio Pictures; another 'Quota Quickie'.

A Shot in the Dark was the first of the eight 'Quota Quickies' George Pearson directed for Julius Hagen at Twickenham Studios.

A Shot in the Dark was the third of several film appearances O. B. Clarence made for Julius Hagen, but, in this film, he had a rare leading rôle as the amateur sleuth.

London Trade Show: Tuesday, 31 October 1933 at the Cambridge Theatre.

British Registration Details:
Quota Registration No.: Br. 9376. Registration Date: 2 November 1933.
Registered Length: 4,847 feet.
Registered by: Radio Pictures, Ltd.
Maker's name: Real Art Productions, Ltd.
British Board of Film Censor's Certificate: "A".
British distributor: Radio Pictures.

John V. Watson

Running Time: 53 minutes.

A Shot in the Dark was reviewed in the *Kinematograph Weekly*, 2 November 1933, page 39:

RCA Photophone, 54 minutes, "A" certificate.

"Remarks: Moderate murder mystery set in an eerie atmosphere. Capable cast and popular situations.

"Box Office Angle: Fair supporting offering for industrial halls. Unsuitable for children.

"Murder mystery which opens with a well-captured air of tenseness, but slow development and too many coincidental happenings render it unconvincing. Popular situations and a few light touches, together with a competent cast, may get the picture over in not too critical situations.

"Story: Peter Browne, an aged recluse obsessed with a fear of murder, lives in a closely guarded house attended only by his adopted niece. Browne is found shot, and a verdict of suicide is returned, but the local clergyman, John Malcolm, is not satisfied, and investigates the circumstances of the death. He meets Browne's relatives, who are gathered for the reading of the will, and stages the crime in its original setting. With everyone gathered, he sets a trap for which the murderer, a nephew, falls.

"Acting: A. Bromley Davenport gives a good portrayal of a neurotic type as Browne, and O. B. Clarence as Malcolm is also well cast. Dorothy Boyd, Michael Shepley and Russell Thorndike are

288

adequate support.

"Production: The opening stages are well developed, but the progress of the plot is considerably slowed by the many false clues which hinder the investigator. Credulity is strained by so many people attempting to commit murder on the same stormy evening.

"Settings and Photography: The old mansion setting and stormy atmosphere is well caught by efficient sound and camera work.

"Points of Appeal: Crime story, eerie atmosphere, capable cast and quota.

A Shot in the Dark went out on General Release on Monday, 19 March 1934; the original date planned for the General Release was Monday, 26 March 1934.

The Wandering Jew (1933)

Drama, adapted from the 1920 play by E. Temple Thurston. A Jew, Matathias (Conrad Veidt), spits upon Christ as He carries the cross up to Calvary, and is then doomed to wander the earth through the centuries until Christ comes to him again and grants him death.

The Wandering Jew was the first Julius Hagen production that was made for the British distributor, Gaumont-British Picture Corporation.

A poster designed for the Spanish release of *The Wandering Jew* (1933).

The Wandering Jew was the second Julius Hagen Twickenham Film Studios, Ltd. production made with the financial participation of Gaumont-British. The first of these was the Ivor Novello picture, *I Lived with You*, released earlier that year, 1933, via the distribution company, W. & F. Film Service (Woolf & Freedman Film Service), a Gaumont-British company. See the entry above. With a running time of almost two hours (110 minutes) and with the major star, Conrad Veidt, in the leading role, *The Wandering Jew* was clearly designed as a "top-of-the-bill" attraction, and it was to be a very big box-office draw at that!

The Wandering Jew was the eighth film Maurice Elvey directed for Julius Hagen.

The Wandering Jew was the first of the two starring rôles which Conrad Veidt was to make for Julius Hagen; the other film was *Bella Donna* (1934). Born in Germany, Conrad Veidt had to flee his native land as he was fervently opposed to the Nazi regime; although not Jewish himself, his wife was. Veidt was a huge star in British films in the 1930s.

The Wandering Jew was "Distributed throughout the United Kingdom by Gaumont-British Distributors, Ltd." according to film's onscreen credit titles.

The Wandering Jew: "Overseas Rights handled by Film Sales, Ltd., 185a, Wardour Street, London, W.1.", again according to film's onscreen credit titles.

London Trade Show: Monday, 20 November 1933 at the Tivoli.

British Registration Details:
Quota Registration No.: Br. 9475.
Registration Date: 22 November 1933.
Registered Length: 9,900 feet.

Registered by: Gaumont-British
Distributors, Ltd.
Maker's name: Twickenham Film Studios,
Ltd.
British Board of Film Censor's Certificate:
"A".
British distributor: Gaumont-British.
Running Time: 110 minutes.

The Wandering Jew was reviewed in the
Kinematograph Weekly, 23 November 1933, page 37:

> RCA Photophone, 110 minutes, "A"
> certificate.
>
> "Remarks: Protracted but nevertheless
> arresting and impressively spectacular
> picturisation of Temple Thurston's famous
> stage play. Magnificent performance by
> Conrad Veidt, adequate support and
> intelligent treatment.
>
> "Box Office Angle: Strong title and star
> booking, particularly for high-class halls.
> Unsuitable for children.
>
> "Spectacular melodrama, adapted from Temple
> Thurston's famous play upon the ancient and
> colourful legend of the Jew who spat upon
> the Nazarene and was condemned to
> everlastingly walk this planet. The picture
> takes a tremendous time to get into its stride;
> three of the four phases of the intriguing
> story are dignified but desultory, and not too

clear in their message or particularly powerful
in their emotional appeal. The last phase,
however – that concerned with the
Inquisition – is magnificently handled, and
the force of its drama, the strength of its
acting, more than atone for the leisurely
chapters. There is so much that is uninspired
in this film, and so much that is brilliant, that
it is difficult to access its true box-office value
confidently, but the superb and consistent
acting of Conrad Veidt and the magnetic title
should weigh tremendously in its favour, and
enable it to register yet another British
popular success.

"Story: Matathias, a Jew, scoffs at the
Nazarene, who dares to claim himself King of
the Jews, and spits upon Him as He passes on
His way to the Cross. He is condemned by
Jesus to wander through the ages – "until I
come to thee again". We then follow his
melancholy and unhappy journey until we
finally see him practicing as a doctor in Old
Seville. Here Olalla Quintana, a harlot, brings
him to God, and when he is dragged before a
Court of Inquisitors as a suspected Jew, he
confesses to his faith. He is sentenced to
death, and anxiously hopes that God make
possible their sentence to be carried out. The
faggots around the stake at first refuse to
burn, but there is suddenly a light in the sky

and he dies, Christ having come to him again.

"Acting: Whether he is the mocking Jew in Jerusalem, the wicked knight of the first Crusade, the unhappy merchant and family man in Sicily, or the loved and respected doctor of Old Seville, Conrad Veidt is more than equal to the demands made upon his talents. He strides through the film with tragic confidence, until finally he rises to unexplored emotional heights. His performance is a magnetic one, and does much to hold the film together. Peggy Ashcroft is very good as Olalla Quintana, Joan Maude is tender and understanding as the Sicilian merchant's wife, and Francis L. Sullivan and Felix Aylmer are convincing as the Inquisitors.

"Production: Maurice Elvey, the producer, invests the picture with quiet dignity, but tends to prolong the development of the story. Each incident is of interest, but true emotional appeal does not overtake the proceedings until they are dangerously near their close. The handling of the last phase, however, is a fine imaginative, moving, and highly dramatic piece of screen rhetoric, and gives the film a memorable and unforgettable ending. Whatever faults the film may have, nothing can rob Conrad Veidt's performance of its brilliance, and herein lies its undeniable dramatic strength.

"Settings and Photography: The opening
scenes in Jerusalem are approached with
reverence, the days of the First Crusade are
mirrored in all their spacious glory, the
domestic life of the Jew has tragic tenderness,
while the Inquisition makes an opening for
emotional drama which is brilliant.

"Points of Appeal: Box-office title, magnificent
acting by Conrad Veidt, fine, impressive
story, and spectacular treatment.

**The French Release of 'The Wandering Jew',
Kinematograph Weekly:** The *Kinematograph Weekly*,
11 January 1934, reported that *The Wandering Jew*
was showing at the Theatre de l'Avenue, Paris. The
magazine noted: "The lay Press in particular is
rapturous in their eulogies of Veidt's performance,
and the general polish of this Hagen film. One critic
remarks that this 'is the most staggeringly perfect
film ever seen in Paris', and demands that more of
our" (English) "pictures be seen in Paris and the
provincial cities."

The Wandering Jew went out on General
Release on Monday, 26 February 1934.

Mannequin (1933)

Melodrama. A boxer (Whitmore Humphries)
becomes conceited and leaves his true love, a model (Judy
Kelly), for a society lady (Diana Beaumont). But he finds

out that she is only toying with him and has actually bet on his opponent to win in his next fight. But, not only does he win the match, he gets his girl back as well.

Mannequin was the fifteenth film made by Real Art Productions for Radio Pictures; another 'Quota Quickie'.

Mannequin was the eighth film George A. Cooper directed for Julius Hagen.

Mannequin was the fifth film appearance by star, Harold French, for Julius Hagen.

London Trade Show: Tuesday, 5 December 1933 at the Phoenix Theatre.

British Registration Details:
Quota Registration No.: Br. 9536. Registration Date: 8 December 1933.
Registered Length: 4,855 feet. Registered by: Radio Pictures, Ltd.
Maker's name: Real Art Productions, Ltd.
British Board of Film Censor's Certificate: "A".
British distributor: Radio Pictures. Running Time: 54 minutes.

Mannequin was reviewed in the *Kinematograph Weekly*, 7 December 1933, page 33:

RCA Photophone, 54 minutes, "A" certificate.

"Harold French, Whitmore Humphries, Diana Beaumont, Judy Kelly.

"Remarks: Unconvincing story of a boxer's deterioration due to society vamp. Quite well put over and acted.

"Box Office Angle: Moderate dramatic offer. No

appeal to children.

"Lavish, and in some respects imaginative, production has been extended on a poor story of the ruin of a boxer's career due to a Society vamp. Acting and attractive settings in some measure compensate for an offer that cannot be recommended as a winner, but which might go down in the popular programme. Definitely not for children, though unlikely to be harmful.

"Story: Lady Diana meets Billy, a promising boxer, who yields to her charms sufficiently, in the eyes of his trainer, to spoil his chances of winning a championship. Overhearing Lady Diana backing his opponent over the telephone, Billy breaks with her. In spite of being drunk, he knocks out his protagonist, who is not expected to live. Hearing this, Nancy, who has temporarily deserted Billy, to whom she has been engaged, for a young millionaire, leaves the latter to stand by her first love.

"Acting: Neither Harold French nor Whitmore Humphries, as millionaire and boxer respectively, have enough personality to win entire sympathy for the rather worthless characters they are called upon to play. Diana Beaumont is good, but not quite strong enough for the Society vamp. Judy Kelly does quite well in the easier part of the ingenuous mannequin. Minor rôles are adequately fulfilled.

"Production: George Cooper has dealt interestingly with individual situations, but fails to supply conviction to scenes intended to be dramatic. Boxing sequences are not good enough for the initiated, particularly that in which Billy, half drunk, knocks out his opponent with doubtfully fatal results. It is also difficult to believe in Nancy's, the mannequin's, sudden change of front towards Billy, who has obviously treated her very badly. There are some mildly amusing and well-put-over scenes at the mannequin's establishment, while the dilettante millionaire is not badly drawn. Dialogue is natural and very fairly recorded.

"Settings and Photography: Interiors of a salon and mannequin's dressing-room are limited, but tasteful and well lighted. Ringside shots satisfactory. Exteriors practically nil.

"Points of Appeal: Limited to the performances of the stars, the production, and the humorous interludes.

Mannequin went out on General Release on Monday, 7 May 1934.

The Pointing Finger (1933)

Crime melodrama. The Honourable James Mallory (Leslie Perrins) tries to murder his relative, Lord Rollestone (John Stuart), to inherit an earldom.

The Pointing Finger was the sixteenth film made by Real Art Productions for Radio Pictures; another 'Quota Quickie', but this time with a slightly longer running time than usual.

The Pointing Finger was the second of the eight

'The Czar of Twickenham'. The History of Julius Hagen and the Film Empire he created at Twickenham Film Studios, from 1927 to 1938.

'Quota Quickies' which George Pearson directed for Julius Hagen at Twickenham Studios.

The Pointing Finger was the sixth film appearance which star, John Stuart, made for Julius Hagen.

London Trade Show: Wednesday, 6 December 1933 at the Phoenix Theatre.

British Registration Details:
>   Quota Registration No.: Br. 9544.
>   Registration Date: 8 December 1933.
>   Registered Length: 6,118 feet.
>   Registered by: Radio Pictures, Ltd.
>   Maker's name: Real Art Productions, Ltd.
>   British Board of Film Censor's Certificate: "U".
>   British distributor: Radio Pictures.
>   Running Time: 68 minutes.

The Pointing Finger was reviewed in the *Kinematograph Weekly*, 14 December 1933, page 30:

RCA Photophone, 68 minutes, "U" certificate.

"John Stuart, Viola Keats, Leslie Perrins.

"<u>Remarks</u>: Good honest melodrama, adapted from a novel by Rita. Story played in the right spirit by a good cast, element of mystery well sustained, and production qualities adequate.

"<u>Box Office Angle</u>: Quite a good supporting programme proposition for the majority of halls. Safe stuff for juveniles.

"<u>Story</u>, <u>Acting</u>, <u>Production</u>, <u>Settings and Photography</u> and <u>Points of Appeal</u>: Microfiche copy unreadable for all these categories.

The Pointing Finger went out on General Release on Monday, 23 April 1934.

1933: The British Film Industry: Trends and Other Events throughout the Year — in England, the United States, Germany and France:

The *Kinematograph Weekly*, 26 January 1933 (page 13) that **Alexander Korda**'s first British-made film, *Service for Ladies*, made for Paramount-British, starring Leslie Howard, was a box-office triumph in the United States. *Service for Ladies* was also voted the second best British film of 1932; the film that topped the annual poll conducted in England was *Sunshine Susie*, the musical comedy film directed by Victor Saville for Gainsborough Pictures, which starred Renate Müller and Jack Hulbert.

P. L. Mannock of the *Kinematograph Weekly*, 2 February 1933 (page E1) reported that **John Stuart** had signed for six pictures by Irving Asher at Teddington Studios. The star was a regular in films produced by Julius Hagen at Twickenham Studios.

German film director, E. A. Dupont, was in the U.S. to make *Invisible Man*. For reasons yet to be determined, Universal Pictures assigned James Whale to direct the film instead.

(*K. W.*, 16 February 1933, page 28).

David O'Selznick joins MGM as Associate Producer.

(*K. W.*, 23 February 1933, page 26).

'The Czar of Twickenham'. The History of Julius Hagen and the Film Empire he created at Twickenham Film Studios, from 1927 to 1938.

The passing of **Pat Sullivan**, the creator of the popular cartoon character, *Felix the Cat*, was reported.

(*K. W.*, 23 February 1933, page 26).

Spectacular technological increase: in 1926, 100 theatres in the U.K. used **Automaticket**, whereas, in 1933, 2,000 use Automaticket. Automaticket was an automatic cinema ticket dispenser located in the cash desk at the front of the foyer.

(*K. W.*, 23 February 1933, page 29).

A new British renting unit is established: **Associated British Film Distributors**, Ltd.

(*K. W.*, 2 March 1933, page 5).

America stops film production? Critical film situation – shortage of product likely – the absence of quotations of dollars against pounds, or pounds against dollars has put a temporary stop to financial transactions between this country and America, until the moratorium is declared in America.

(*K. W.*, 9 March 1933, page 3).

British film production quality under the quota is discussed.

(*K. W.*, 9 March 1933, page 4).

British lead as film fans – 24 million attend weekly – the highest known per capita attendance of any country in the world at present.

(*K. W.*, 9 March 1933, page 5).

CEA (Circuits Exhibitors Association) report: **Box Office**

records on British films – outstanding success.

(*K. W.*, 9 March 1933, page 5).

Small halls (cinemas) are crippled by **the Entertainments Tax**.

(*K. W.*, 9 March 1933, page 8).

Owing to casting difficulties, and the short time before the expiration of his contract, **Alfred Hitchcock** last week relinquished the B.I.P. production of *The Return of Bulldog Drummond*.

(*K. W.*, 9 March 1933, page 28).

New long-term contracts with MGM for **Joan Crawford** and **Lionel Barrymore**.

(*K. W.*, 23 March 1933, page 23).

British Film Institute – the film trade adopts the scheme to establish this organization.

(*K. W.*, 30 March 1933, page 5).

Circuit Exhibitors Association: **Quality of quota pictures** discussed.

(*K. W.*, 9 March 1933, page 8).

King Kong creates a sensation.

(*K. W.*, 6 April 1933, page 26).

London Film Productions to increase capital by £80,000.

(*K. W.*, 13 April 1933, page 5).

'The Czar of Twickenham'. The History of Julius Hagen and the Film Empire he created at Twickenham Film Studios, from 1927 to 1938.

Fighting "fifty-fifty"; no higher maximum than 40 per cent for **film rental** by kinemas (cinemas). CEA resolution.

(*K. W.*, 20 April 1933, page 3).

CEA alarm at increasing percentages for **film rental**.

(*K. W.*, 20 April 1933, page 11).

Leslie Hiscott's career – a Beaconsfield contract. L.H. has signed a long-term contract to direct a number of important productions for the British Lion Film Corporation at Beaconsfield. He was once a law student at Cambridge.

NOTE that Leslie Hiscott had been a close associate of Julius Hagen for some years at Twickenham Film Studios, indeed as a fellow director of Hagen companies. Why therefore Hiscott chose to continue his career away from Hagen by joining British Lion is somewhat of a puzzle; in other words, the author has not been able to determine Hiscott's reasoning.

(*K. W.*, 20 April 1933, page 23, P. L. Mannock).

Hollywood in Travail.

(*K. W.*, 27 April 1933, page 4).

Hal Wallis is appointed production manager at the Warner studios. **Darryl Zanuck**, who had hitherto held that position, is organising his own unit to make pictures for United Artists release. That new unit was to become Twentieth Century Pictures.

(*K. W.*, 27 April 1933, page 5).

New **Greta Garbo** contract signed with MGM.

John V. Watson

(*K. W.*, 27 April 1933, page 5).

Quota quality – Government and **unworthy British films**.

(*K. W.*, 27 April 1933, page 3).

Comm. Ludovico Toeplitz, formerly associated with the Pittaluga organisation, is to become chairman of **London Film Productions**.

(*K. W.*, 4 May 1933, page 4).

Columbia Pictures will produce four films in England.

(*K. W.*, 11 May 1933, page 3).

United Artists to handle **London Film Productions** product.

(*K. W.*, 25 May 1933, page 3).

3,187 kinemas in **France**.

(*K. W.*, 25 May 1933, page 5).

British films' success in **Australia**.

(*K. W.*, 1 June 1933, page 3).

The **Nazi** control of the German Film situation is discussed

(*K. W.*, 1 June 1933, page 27).

German films are banned in Manchester, owing to the attitude towards Jews by the Hitler regime.

(*K. W.*, 22 June 1933, page 3).

'The Czar of Twickenham'. The History of Julius Hagen and the Film Empire he created at Twickenham Film Studios, from 1927 to 1938.

London Film Productions, Ltd.: increase in nominal capital by the addition of £70,000 beyond the registered capital of £20,100. The additional capital is divided into 70,000 redeemable 6 per cent first cumulative preference shares of £1 each.

(*K. W.*, 22 June 1933, page 14).

Boris Karloff quits *The Invisible Man*.

(Claude Rains was given the leading role in place of Karloff.)

(*K. W.*, 29 June 1933, page 20).

The first British colour feature – *The Skipper of the Osprey* – in Raycol.

(*K. W.*, 6 July 1933, page 17).

Columbia (British) Productions, Ltd. was registered on 3 July 1933 with a nominal capital of £25,000 in £1 shares.

(*K. W.*, 13 July 1933, page 6).

Columbia's first British production is *The Lady is Willing* and is to star Leslie Howard, Cedric Hardwicke and Binnie Barnes.

(*K. W.*, 13 July 1933, page 45, The Studio Correspondent).

Independent cinemas' quota – shortage of good pictures causes difficulties. C. A. Mathes states: "In London, we find that showing a quota film often gives us one-third our normal takings. My books at one of my theatres could prove this on countless occasions."

305

John V. Watson

(*K. W.*, 20 July 1933, page 8).

Gracie Fields' £22,000 per picture contract – the biggest film salary yet known

(*K. W.*, 10 August 1933, page 47, P. L. Mannock).

Jack Buchanan reopens **Leicester Square Theatre** in London. Korda's "*Henry VIII*" is booked.

(*K. W.*, 31 August 1933, page 3).

The consolidation of the film renting interests of **W. & F. and Gaumont-Ideal** is reviewed by the journal.

(*K. W.*, 28 September 1933, page 5).

British pictures shown in **Canada** represent 25% of programmes.

(*K. W.*, 5 October 1933, page 3).

Italy's new quota law – 25 per cent regulation.

(*K. W.*, 12 October 1933, page 12A).

Gaumont-British Distributors starts to function

(*K. W.*, 26 October 1933).

The formation of **G-B Instructional**, Ltd. for the distribution of educational and industrial propaganda films.

(*K. W.*, 2 November 1933, page 5).

Will Hay is signed by British International Pictures.

(*K. W.*, 2 November 1933).

'The Czar of Twickenham'. The History of Julius Hagen and the Film Empire he created at Twickenham Film Studios, from 1927 to 1938.

G-B Instructional, Ltd. is registered on 6 November 1933

(*K. W.*, 16 November 1933, page 13).

British Film Institute – London offices opened at 4, Great Russell Street, London, W.C.

(*K. W.*, 16 November 1933, page 43).

The provinces favour **the two-and-a-half-hour programme**. The menace of the two-feature programme is also discussed.

(*K. W.*, 14 December 1933, page 12).

Boxing Day was Box Office Day – **record business** for London kinemas.

(*K. W.*, 28 December 1933, page 3).

1933: The Sixth Year of the 'Quota' Act:

205 British films were first shown during the year 1933.

This number is arrived at by using the data contained in *The British Film Catalogue: 1895-1970* by Denis Gifford, as follows:

09467: Closing Gifford Catalogue Number for 1933.

09262: Opening Gifford Catalogue Number for 1933.

205: Total. An increase of 24 films over the previous year's total of 181.

John V. Watson

Some of these films were short subjects; the actual number of these shorts has not been determined.

---

7. 1934:
British Film Production
Continues to Soar:

1934 saw the major British film production boom maintaining strong momentum with total production now reaching over 200 films per year for the second year. British film producers achieved a record 214 films made, an increase of nine films over the previous year.

1934:
Film Production increases at
Twickenham:

Julius Hagen at Twickenham Film Studios slightly increased his output of films he made in 1934 - from 20 pictures in 1933 to 21 titles produced in 1934. As we shall see below, many of these films made at Twickenham were filmed at night.

And, from September 1934, Julian Hagen increased his film-making advantage by doubling his production capacity at Twickenham with the opening of a second floor (sound stage) at the studios.

1934 - COVERAGE ABOUT TWICKENHAM

STUDIOS BY THE BRITISH FAN MAGAZINES AND ANNUALS - *PICTURE SHOW* AND *PICTUREGOER*:

The Personnel at the Twickenham Film Studios:
During the early months of 1934, the British fan magazine, *Picture Show*, ran a series called "Our British Studios". Two issues covered Twickenham Film Studios, shown as Number 8 in the series, as follows:

The issue, dated 10 February 1934, gave descriptions and showed photographs of the following personnel:

- **Julius Hagen**, the managing-director and chairman of the company;
- **Baynham Honri**, chief of the sound department;
- **Jack Harris**, assistant-director and chief (film) editor;
- **Sydney Blythe**, chief cameraman; and
- **Cyril Stanborough**, chief still-cameraman.

The next issue, dated 17 February 1934, continued:

- **Miss Enid Jones**, the publicity manageress;
- **Fred Merrick**, assistant director;
- **Ronald Philip**, casting manager;
- **Harry F. Mear**, scenario chief;
- **James A. Carter**, art director, studio manager and a (company) director.

The following issue of *Picture Show*, dated 24 February 1934, covered the British Lion Studios at Beaconsfield (Number 9 in the series), which showed pictures of and described S. W. Smith (the managing director), Herbert Smith (the production supervisor), and Leslie Hiscott, director.

The essential point to be made and stressed here is the presence of **Leslie Hiscott** at the British Lion Studios and not at Twickenham.

Filming by day and at night:
Picture Show, 14 April 1934, reported that **Whispering Tongues** was filmed at night whilst **The Night Club Queen** was being shot during the day. Studio correspondent, Edith Nepean, commented: "Work is being carried out at such high pressure at Twickenham that it is impossible to leave the studios idle either by day or by night."

"In a Desert Tent": the production of "Bella Donna": Sydney Blythe and Billy Luff:
Edith Nepean, the Studio Correspondent for *Picture Show*, in the issue dated 9 June 1934, was moved to make comment about the quality of set design and construction for the Conrad Veidt film, **Bella Donna**: "Such realistic scenes, with great palm trees towering high above me, whilst I watched daring tracking shots in the making from perilous positions". She asked: "How would you like to be a cameraman perched on a terrifically high platform shooting scenes down a steep wooden chute, with miniature steel lines along which the camera glides?" "**Sydney Blythe** and **Billy Luff**, who are the famous cameramen at Twickenham studios, are never tired of experiments. The famous director of **Bella Donna**, **Robert Milton,** specialises in new camera angles, as he intensely dislikes shooting straight on to the players. Such tricky work is a delight to Sydney Blythe and Billy Luff. They revel in perilous positions, for their dream in life is to obtain unusual shots".

James Carter: the Set Designer and a company director of Twickenham Studios:
Edith Nepean, in that same issue, continued: "**James Carter**, who was with me whilst I was watching these scenes" (of **Bella Donna**), "a director of the Twickenham

'The Czar of Twickenham'. The History of Julius Hagen and the Film Empire he created at Twickenham Film Studios, from 1927 to 1938.

Film Studios, is certainly one of Twickenham's most interesting personalities. He is a strongly built man, with a head which reminds one of the pictures of Beethoven, and it is an interesting fact that he is a very brilliant musician. He is also a very clever artist, and he is responsible for the wonderful sets that were seen in *The Wandering Jew* and for the sets in use in *Bella Donna*. Inside the studio, Mr. Carter has built a replica of an Egyptian dahabiya, the sailing-boat which is in use on the Nile".

Sound-proofing the Studio:
Picturegoer Weekly, December 15, 1934, page 38, E. G. Cousins' "On the British Sets" reported: "… about the trouble they have with the passing railway-trains on the main line to Twickenham; the new studio has vibration-proof foundations, but in the old one they still have signal "train coming" and suspend operations until it's passed".

January 1934:

Kinematograph Weekly reported throughout the month:

NEW STUDIO BUILDING FOR TWICKENHAM STUDIOS:

"Plans have been passed for the erection of a new studio for the Twickenham Film Studios, Ltd., of St. Margaret's, Twickenham. The new building will measure 120 feet long and 82 feet wide, and will also include dressing-room, cutting-rooms and a further projection theatre"

(*K. W.*, 4 January 1934, page 16B).

FILM PRODUCTION AT TWICKENHAM STUDIOS:

"Julius Hagen starts the New Year at Twickenham Studios with a burst of activity with the following productions:

John V. Watson

Behind the Mask (Four Masked Men) – the first feature production for release by Universal Pictures – took the floor on Tuesday (2 January 1934). George Pearson directs an adaptation of Cyril Campion's *The Masqueraders*. John Stuart and Judy Kelly are co-starred, and Richard Cooper, Miles Mander and Athole Stewart are also in the cast.

The Admiral's Secret also started production on Tuesday (2 January 1934) for Radio Pictures. Guy Newall, absent from the screen for some time, occupied with stage work, will direct for Radio. Edmund Gwenn, and Hope Davey, Andreas Malandrinos, James Raglan, Abraham Sofaer, Agnes Imlay, and Aubrey Mather.

"Owing to the large production schedule for the coming year, Twickenham Studios, pending the construction of their own second stage, have been compelled to hire space at Merton Park Studios for *The Admiral's Secret*. The studio, which is owned by Publicity Films, Ltd., has a rock-wool lined stage. It is fully equipped with modern R.C.A. recording equipment, a fine large synchronising theatre, modern cutting rooms, work-shops, dressing rooms and good offices. It is built entirely sound-proof, and has fine lighting equipment and ample power supply. This studio is unknown to the Trade generally, in spite of its very convenient situation. It has in the past been working solely on non-entertainment films".

(*K. W.*, 4 January 1934, page 25, P. L. Mannock).

"John Garrick, who recently played in *Lily of Killarney* and *The Broken Melody* at Twickenham, has been placed under long-term contract by Julius Hagen, who is convinced that Mr. Garrick has all the qualities required to make him a first-class box office bet in 1934. He has a fine singing voice and good looks. His first parts were in Hollywood."

312

'The Czar of Twickenham'. The History of Julius Hagen and the Film Empire he created at Twickenham Film Studios, from 1927 to 1938.

(*K. W.*, 4 January 1934, page 25, P. L. Mannock).

MAKING MERRY AT TWICKENHAM STUDIOS:

Twickenham's big night of fun. Staff and stars make merry – Julius Hagen's hospitality.

(*K. W.*, 18 January 1934, page 14).

FILM PRODUCTION AT TWICKENHAM STUDIOS:

Behind the Mask – George Pearson has just completed. A large and magnificent set was constructed by James Carter for the final shots. "Two-thirds of the floor space available was occupied by a set representing the Presidential Palace in Peruvia on the occasion of a grand ball held by the President. During the festivities masked men invade the ball-room and held up the company, while others robbed them of their jewels. A well-dressed crowd of nearly two hundred extras thronged the dance floor for this scene, which promises to be the most spectacular recently seen in a British production".

(*K. W.*, 25 January 1934, pages 29 and 31, P. L. Mannock).

Henry Edwards and George Pearson are now busy on *The Man Who Changed His Name* (the second Universal feature) and *Tangled Evidence* (for Radio release), respectively. George Cooper's unit is at present at Merton Park Studios.

(*K. W.*, 25 January 1934, pages 29 and 31, P. L. Mannock).

February 1934:

Kinematograph Weekly reported throughout the month:

313

John V. Watson

SENIOR PERSONNEL CONTRACTED AT TWICKENHAM STUDIOS:

W. L. Trytel has been signed by Julius Hagen for three years to supervise and arrange all the music in Twickenham films during that period.

"Mr. Trytel will, however, remain free to undertake other assignments and to continue his own composition work providing it does not interfere with his duties at Twickenham". "Mr. Trytel is well known to the film industry as being one of the pioneers of film music accompaniments in this country. At one time he conducted orchestras and arranged accompaniments for all big Trade shows, including that of *The Queen of Sheba* at the Albert Hall, *Vaudeville*, *The Rat*, etc. He has also written over two hundred original compositions for films, and wrote the entire musical score for *Kitty* in America".

(*K. W.*, 1 February 1934, page 37, P. L. Mannock).

NEW STUDIO FLOOR AT TWICKENHAM STUDIOS:

"On Friday, 2nd February 1934, at 3 p.m., His Worship the Mayor of Twickenham, Alderman G. A. Farrar, will lay the foundation stone of the new floor which is to be erected next to the existing studio at St. Margaret's, Twickenham. The historic studio will thus enter into a new phase of its triumphant career."

"Many celebrities of the stage and screen have already promised to attend, among them some who will return to the scene of their early triumphs on the screen. Sir John Martin Harvey, who made *The Lyons Mail*, his first talkie, at St. Margaret's, Sir Cedric and Lady Hardwicke, Dame Sybil Thorndike are among those who have already accepted Julius Hagen's invitation to be present."

314

'The Czar of Twickenham'. The History of Julius Hagen and the Film Empire he created at Twickenham Film Studios, from 1927 to 1938.

"There is more tradition centred upon the little studio at St. Margaret's than upon any other studio in the country. In January 1929, "Julius Hagen took over the Studio and the founding of the existing company of Twickenham Film Studios, Ltd. These studios became the second studio in England to acquire RCA Phototone equipment for the production of talking films. The studio was sound-proofed and, overcoming the disadvantages bound to exist in studios primarily designed for the making of silent films, Twickenham Studios set out bravely to compete in the new world of talking pictures."

(*K. W.*, 1 February 1934).

FILM PRODUCTION AT TWICKENHAM STUDIOS:

Tangled Evidence – George Cooper is still busy at Merton Park Studios. The cast includes Sam Livesey, Dorothy Boyd, and screen newcomer, Gillian Maude.

(*K. W.*, 1 February 1934).

"Owing to the enormous success of *Say It with Flowers*, by agreement with Julius Hagen of Real Art Productions, Radio Pictures, Ltd. have arranged with John Baxter (author and director of *Say It with Flowers*) to produce another human story, *Say It With Song*, which will go into production immediately and will be released in the early Autumn".

(*K. W.*, 8 February 1934, double-page advertisement).

The Man Who Changed His Mind - final shots have been made by Henry Edwards – with Betty Stockfeld, who has been starring in a series of French films.

The Night Club Queen – the second Julius Hagen-

Universal production begins today, (Thursday, 8 February 1934). The director Bernard Vorhaus; Mary Clare has the title rôle (her character in the film is based on a real life person.) Adaptation of the play by Anthony Kimmins, which had a brief run at the Playhouse.

> (*K. W.*, 8 February 1934, pages 54b and 55, P. L. Mannock).

Tangled Evidence – the unit returned from Merton Park Studios last night (Wednesday, 14 February 1934) "and will be engaged on night work throughout the week. In spite of the set-back received owing to Dorothy Boyd's illness, progress on the film has been rapid, and it is expected that the last shots will be taken this week. Joan Marion, who has recently been playing on the London stage, and has not done any film work for some time, has proved an excellent substitute for Miss Boyd."

Night Club Queen – George Carney, Merle Tottenham, Pat Noonan and Lewis Shaw, the young stage actor, who played in *The Marriage Bond* for Julius Hagen, have now been added to the cast. *Night Club Queen* is in its second week. James Carter is constructing a magnificent night club set, which will come into use this week.

> (*K. W.*, 15 February 1934).

Whispering Tongues took the floor this week, working at night only – from an original story Bernard Mainwaring, adapted for the screen by H. Fowler Mear, directed by George Pearson. Reginald Tate has been awarded the starring rôle opposite Judy Kelly. Charles Carson and Russell Thorndike are also in the cast.

> (*K. W.*, 22 February 1934).

March 1934:

Kinematograph Weekly reported throughout the month:

The Lash, Henry Edward's next, takes the floor next week on the completion of *The Night Club Queen*. It is a screen version of Cyril Campion's successful play which ran at the "Q" and Royalty theatres in 1926. John Mills has already been chosen to play the son. This picture will be the first of a new series to be made for Radio Pictures release.

(*K. W.*, 1 March 1934, page 39, P. L. Mannock).

Judy Kelly, owing to an attack of laryngitis, was unable to take up her part in *Whispering Tongues*. Jane Welsh has been chosen to take her place.

(*K. W.*, 1 March 1934, page 39, P. L. Mannock).

The Lash, the screen adaptation of Cyril Campion's stage success, went into production on Monday (5 March 1934). Henry Edwards is directing..

Meanwhile, at night, George Pearson is directing *Whispering Tongues*.

(*K. W.*, 8 March 1934, page 42, P. L. Mannock).

John Baxter will shortly start production on *Say It With Song*. Baxter wrote the story. Cast headed by George Carney, Mark Daly and Edgar Driver.

The Lash. Peggy Blythe, made her real screen début in *The Constant Nymph* as Paulina, has been given an important part of the deserted young wife. Mary Jerrold also added to the cast.

The Australian sequences were completed last week, and a realistic set of a lumber camp was erected in the studio by James Carter. Henry Edwards has finished shots in the night club owned by Leslie Perrins and John Mills. "Work this week consists of scenes in Lyn Harding's home and in Joan Maude's flat, where a dramatic horse-whipping scene takes place".

(*K. W.*, 15 March 1934, page 43, P. L. Mannock).

Say It with Song: John Baxter took the floor this week with his second production for Julius Hagen.

"For the music-hall sequences which form an integral part of the plot, an imposing band of variety artistes has been assembled, including Debroy Somers and his Band, Macari's Accordion Band, G. H. Elliott, the Parkington Quintette, Billy Danvers, Dan Young and Bertram Dench, Chester's Dogs, Twenty-four Sherman Fisher Girls, and an operatic chorus of eighty singers. The provincial musical-hall round which the story is written will be represented from both sides of the curtain".

(*K. W.*, 22 March 1934, page 55, P. L. Mannock).

The Lash – Henry Edwards' current production is now to be completed at night, while John Baxter *(Say It with Song)* occupies the floor by day.

(*K. W.*, 22 March 1934, page 55, P. L. Mannock).

The Night Club Queen – Realistic train smash; Bernard Vorhaus did not consider built-up sets in the studio sufficiently realistic or vivid when it came to staging a train smash for the film. Southern Railway officials were consulted and heartily agreed to co-operate – squads of technicians and a battery of cameras were hurried to one of the main lines, where some superb shots of expresses hurtling by. Having obtained the real railway background, the next difficulty arose with regard to the train smash itself. An actual railway carriage was obtained, which was treated in the railway workshops so as to resemble a total wreck. This was then taken at night to a deserted track of line, where bonfires were lit which threw into bold relief the twisted steel skeleton of the carriage with telegraph poles in the background and people running wildly about.

"This tragic but exciting sequence provides an unparalleled opportunity for a piece of brilliant emotional acting on the part of Mary Clare and Lewis Casson."

The Night Club Queen – Night club sequences : excitable and irresponsible behaviour of undergraduates on the spree celebrating the boat-race result: they shoot a chef of tremendous girth down the chute that is primarily intended for introducing the dancing girls on the floor – "extras employed in the night club sequences must count themselves very fortunate in being in the stalls, so to speak, while such celebrated artists as the Sherman Fisher Girls, and the famous Eight Black Streaks, not to mention Jane Carr, disported themselves in typical variety acts. Five musical numbers have been specially composed for the film, and three of these are sung by Jane Carr, who is well-known on the radio by the name of Rita Brunstown.

(*K. W.*, 22 March 1934, page 55, P. L. Mannock).

Twickenham Studios: *Bella Donna* directed by Robert Milton, with Mary Ellis, Conrad Veidt, in its fourth week.

(*K. W.*, 26 April 1934, page 52).

Bella Donna now in its fifth week, scheduled to be completed in about three weeks' time.

John V. Watson

(*K. W.*, 3 May 1934, page 36, P. L. Mannock).

May 1934:

Kinematograph Weekly reported throughout the month:

NEW COMPANY AT TWICKENHAM STUDIOS:

Twickenham Films Ltd.

New company with £240,000 capital.

Contract to make seventeen films.

To acquire the business undertakings of Twickenham Film Studios, Ltd., and Real Art Productions, Ltd.

(*K. W.*, 10 May 1934, page 14).

FILM PRODUCTION AT TWICKENHAM STUDIOS:

Lord Edgware Dies. While (John) Baxter is on location, Henry Edwards occupies the floor during the day.

(*K. W.*, 24 May 1934, pages 40 and 41).

June 1934:

Kinematograph Weekly reported throughout the month:

STAGE AND SCREEN ACTOR CONTRACTED AT TWICKENHAM STUDIOS:

Michael Shepley, the stage and screen actor has been placed under contract to Julius Hagen.

(*K. W.*, 14 June 1934, page 52).

'The Czar of Twickenham'. The History of Julius Hagen and the Film Empire he created at Twickenham Film Studios, from 1927 to 1938.

PROGRESS OF NEW STAGE AT TWICKENHAM STUDIOS:

Twickenham Studios. The new floor is nearly ready.

(*K. W.*, 21 June 1934, page 39, P. L. Mannock).

August 1934:

Kinematograph Weekly reported throughout the month:

FILM PRODUCTION AT TWICKENHAM STUDIOS:

The Rocks of Valpre is in its second week of production; the company will depart for Cornwall for exterior scenes in a fortnight.

(*K. W.*, 30 August 1934, page 47).

FOREIGN SALES OF FILMS MADE AT TWICKENHAM STUDIOS:

"The recent visit of A. Fried, of Film Sales, Ltd., to America on Mr Hagen's behalf has borne excellent fruit. Since Mr. Hagen's engagements made it impossible for him to go to America, Mr. Kandel, the president of Olympic Pictures Corporation, came to England to conclude contracts between his company and Twickenham Film Studios, Ltd. Under the terms of the contract, all important Twickenham films will in future be distributed throughout the United States of America by Mr. Kandel's company, a special distribution concern being founded to handle Twickenham output. Among the pictures to be released immediately are *The Wandering Jew*, *The Broken Melody*, *Bella Donna*, etc."

"Other contracts have also been signed securing the distribution of a certain number of Twickenham films in Canada, through Anglo-Canadian Distribution Co., Ltd."

"The final contract, added to those already in existence with Australia, the Federated Malay States, Straits Settlements and Singapore, etc., will ensure that films from Twickenham shall be adequately represented in every English-speaking territory in the world."

"Contract also signed with Gaumont-British Distributors, Ltd., for two more pictures on the scale surpassing *The Wandering Jew* and *Bella Donna*."

"Existing contracts with Radio Pictures, Ltd., Universal Pictures, Ltd., and A.P. and D."

(*K. W.*, 30 August 1934, page 47).

September 1934:

Kinematograph Weekly reported throughout the month:

FOREIGN SALES OF FILMS MADE AT TWICKENHAM STUDIOS:

M. J. Kandel, president of Ideal Pictures Corporation, has announced that his company will distribute 16 Twickenham pictures annually in the United States and Canada.

MGM is to handle *The Wandering Jew*.

(NOTE: As we shall see below, MGM was to withdraw from releasing *The Wandering Jew*.

(*K. W.*, 6 September 1934, page 2).

FILM PRODUCTION AT TWICKENHAM STUDIOS:

"*The Rocks of Valpre* now in the third week of production. Scenes have been taken during the week have given Winifred Shotter the difficult task of ageing gracefully. An impressive court-martial scene, in which John Garrick is sentenced to life imprisonment on Devil's Island, has also been shot this week."

(*K. W.*, 6 September 1934, page 25, P. L. Mannock).

Lewis Shaw, the young contract player at Twickenham Studios, was married on Tuesday (4 September 1934) at St. George's, Hanover Square, London, to Betty Ross-Gore, the Champion girl racquets player of New South Wales. He is in *Rocks of Valpre*."

(*K. W.*, 6 September 1934, page 25, P. L. Mannock).

D'ye Ken John Peel? the title of the famous old hunting song, has finally been chosen for Julius Hagen's next film for Fred White of A.P. and D.

(*K. W.*, 6 September 1934, page 25, P. L. Mannock).

Winifred Shotter has now been signed to star in *D'ye Ken John Peel?* John Garrick, Leslie Perrins and Stanley Holloway have already been cast.

(*K. W.*, 13 September 1934, page 37, P. L. Mannock).

The Rocks of Valpre – James Carter has designed a French village set on the studio grounds, comprising a village square with a café and church in the background. Henry Edwards left this week with John Garrick, Leslie Perrins and Lewis Shaw for Mullion Cove, Cornwall, for exterior sea shore scenes, including a night search along the cliffs.

(*K. W.*, 13 September 1934, page 37, P. L. Mannock).

NEW SOUND STAGE OPENS AT TWICKENHAM STUDIOS:

John V. Watson

Great developments at Twickenham.

New Sound Stage opened.

Six super films planned.

The new floor at Twickenham Studios opened on Monday
(17 September 1934).

Opening ceremony held that evening.

Andrew Soutar, the novelist, compèred the opening
ceremony which was performed by the Mayor of Twickenham,
would recall that six-and-a-half months ago he had laid the
foundation stone of the new building.

Mrs. Hagen, signalling the launch of the Twickenham
"endeavour", broke a bottle of champagne against the studio
doors.

500 guests – primarily designed as a staff get-together. The
guests included Mr. and Mrs. S. G. Newman of Radio; Frederick
White of A.P.D., Universal, etc.

The Mayor of Twickenham, in his address at the opening
ceremony, stressed that team work was the secret of the constant
success of the Twickenham studio organisation.

Julius Hagen, replying, said: "Five and a half years ago when
they had bought these studios they hardly knew how they would
be paid for it." "Practically every renting firm had approached
them with the request to make pictures, and they were going on
from good to better things."

The new sound stage more than doubles the capacity of the
studios. They were designed by James Carter. Formerly the
studio manager of Twickenham, he had recently been appointed a

director of the company.

The *Kine* reporter stated "Few people in the Trade throw a
better party than the Twickenham chief and Monday's
celebrations surpassed even the high standard of hospitality set by
Mr. Hagen."

A feature of the fabric of the studios' construction is its
acoustic insulation by means of wool slag. So effectively has this
been performed that notwithstanding that the Southern Railway
metals are only 20 yards distant, no sound of trains enters the
studio.

24-foot square tank was temporarily converted into a bar for
the celebrations.

Visitors all had the run of the spectacular outdoor set of a
Belgian market place, which was used in the recently completed
production The Rocks of Valpre – where Trytel's orchestra
played during the evening.

(*K. W.*, 20 September 1934, page 1).

FILM PRODUCTION AT TWICKENHAM STUDIOS:

Lazybones is the first film to take the floor after the opening
this week of the new Twickenham sound stage. Michael Powell
directs. Clare Luce, Ian Hunter and Bernard Nedell already
signed. For the time being the two productions will use the old
stage or the new one according to the requirements of the sets
involved.

The Rocks of Valpre returned from location on Friday (14
September 1934).

D'ye Ken John Peel? – Henry Edwards, Winifred Shotter,

John Garrick and Leslie Perrins – no rest between pictures as *D'ye Ken John Peel?* will begin shooting on Wednesday (19 September 1934). Stanley Holloway and Mary Lawson have been signed for important parts. Written by H. Fowler Mear

(*K. W.*, 20 September 1934, page 35, P. L. Mannock).

Lazybones "promises to be one of the best comedies turned out by Twickenham". Michael Shepley, Pamela Carme, Denis Blakelock, Bobbie Comber and Marjorie Gaskell have joined the cast.

(*K. W.*, 27 September 1934, page 35).

D'ye Ken John Peel? – production in its second week. John Stuart added to the cast as Captain Moonlight. W. L. Trytel has written other songs, including *Vivandiere*, sung by Mary Lawson, and a cheerful *Soldiers' Chorus*. Henry Edwards is assisted by Arthur Barnes.

(*K. W.*, 27 September 1934, page 35).

October 1934:

Kinematograph Weekly reported throughout the month:

FILM PRODUCTION AT TWICKENHAM STUDIOS:

The Morals of Marcus – Lupe Velez sailed from New York on the Ile de France last Saturday (29 September 1934) and is due in England at the end of the week – Ian Hunter, now filming *Lazybones*, will play opposite her – Noel Madison, the well-known Hollywood actor, has been cast in an important part – Miles Mander to direct the adaptation of W. J. Locke's novel – production to start in about ten days' time.

'The Czar of Twickenham'. The History of Julius Hagen and the Film Empire he created at Twickenham Film Studios, from 1927 to 1938.

> (*K. W.*, 4 October 1934, pages 25 and 27, P. L. Mannock).

D'ye Ken John Peel? now in its third week. John Stuart makes his first appearance as a screen singer in this film, although he has often sung on the stage. W. L. Trytel, the musical director, has his first talking part in this film, he plays a violinist.

> (*K. W.*, 4 October 1934, pages 25 and 27, P. L. Mannock).

The Morals of Marcus – Miles Mander will start direction on Tuesday (16 October 1934). Scenario prepared by H. Fowler Mear.

> (*K. W.*, 11 October 1934, page 37, P. L. Mannock).

The Ace of Spades – George Pearson starts work this week.

> (*K. W.*, 11 October 1934, page 37, P. L. Mannock).

Lazybones has been on the floor at night. Finished on Tuesday (9 October 1934). Michael Shepley and Ian Hunter found themselves in a curious position in the film in which they play brothers-in-law; the coincidence is that they are related in this way.

> (*K. W.*, 11 October 1934, page 37, P. L. Mannock).

D'ye Ken John Peel? nearing completion. The first spectacular set to be built on the new Twickenham sound stage is being erected this week.

> (*K. W.*, 11 October 1934, page 37, P. L. Mannock).

The Morals of Marcus – first scenes take place aboard a

liner; the corridor outside a cabin and the interior of the cabin, were shot last week.

Ace of Spades occupies Studio No. 1.

(*K. W.*, 25 October 1934, page 42).

November 1934:

Kinematograph Weekly reported throughout the month:

The Valley of Fear which had previously been titled The Private Life of Sherlock Holmes. Leslie Hiscott begins direction of the film version of Conan Doyle's story *The Valley of Fear* has been adapted by H. Fowler Mear. William Luff, who has acted as assistant cameraman to Sydney Blythe at Twickenham for some years, will be in full charge of this production. The film was later retitled *The Triumph of Sherlock Holmes*.

(*K. W.*, 1 November 1934, page 40A, P. L. Mannock).

The Morals of Marcus is now in its third week. Miles Mander is now working on Carlotta's life in London in London in the house of Professor Marcus, and her first meeting with Toni Pasquale, who later becomes her lover and takes her away with him to Paris. James Raglan and H. F. Maltby have joined the cast.

(*K. W.*, 1 November 1934, page 40A, P. L. Mannock).

Ace of Spades – George Pearson has staged a fight between Michael Hogan and Felix Aylmer. Filming now completed.

(*K. W.*, 1 November 1934, page 40A, P. L. Mannock).

The Valley of Fear (Triumph of Sherlock Holmes) – Lyn Harding has signed to play Professor Moriarty – now in its second week of production – shooting last week showed Sherlock Holmes in the unusual rôle of bee-keeper in his Sussex retreat.

(*K. W.*, 8 November 1934, page 49, P. L. Mannock).

The Morals of Marcus – Adrianne Allen took up her part as Judith, the unhappily married woman who acts as secretary to Marcus.

Adrianne Allen is the wife of Raymond Massey. Both are appearing in the St. James' Theatre success, *The Shining Hour.*

(*K. W.*, 8 November 1934, page 49, P. L. Mannock).

Julius Hagen announces that he has bought the play *Spendlove Hall* by Norman Cannon - **Annie, Leave the Room!** This farcical comedy ran in London with Sydney Fairbrother and Ena Grossmith in the cast, toured the provinces as *The Cat's Whiskers*, adopted as the provisional film's title.

(*K. W.*, 15 November 1934, page 35, P. L. Mannock).

Twickenham at full pressure with three productions.

"This is the first time that Twickenham has been able to make three films concurrently inside the studio, but, working the day and night system, it will be possible to make four films at once when the demand for extra output has to be met".

The Morals of Marcus – unit working during the day. Two very different sets occupied the *Morals of Marcus* stage last week – one half of the stage was occupied by a harem scene in which Lupe Velez appears as a timid young girl being forced into marriage with a revolting old Turk – the other half of the stage was occupied by a magnificent modernistic restaurant scene in London. Members of the Amateur Cinematographers'

329

John V. Watson

Association meet Lupe Velez and director Miles Mander.

Squibs - unit working during the day

The Valley of Fear has been transferred to night work until its completion in about ten days' time.

(*K. W.*, 22 November 1934, page 47, P. L. Mannock).

Squibs. Ralph Reader, the stage producer, has been engaged by Julius Hagen to arrange the dances for the film.

"Vocal numbers are now being prepared by the authors of the popular tunes, *Little Man You've Had a Busy Day* and *I Saw Stars*, Maurice Sigler, Al Goodhart and Al Hoffman. Among the songs they have written are Londonola (recently broadcast during a B.B.C. Guest Night), *Have You Ever Had a Feeling You're Flying?*, *One Way Street*, and a *Policeman's Song*. In addition to these songs Stanley Holloway will sing his well-known monologue, *Beefeaters*, by Weston and Lee.".

Sydney Blythe has taken over the camera work with Reg. Cavender assisting. Michael Hogan, who has written several wireless sketches and short stories, is collaborating with H. Fowler Mear in preparing the scenario of ***Squibs***."

(*K. W.*, 29 November 1934, page 59, P. L. Mannock).

"***The Valley of Fear*** – Roy Emerton has been added to the cast in the part of "Boss McGinty". Leslie Hiscott hopes to complete the film this week."

(*K. W.*, 29 November 1934, page 59, P. L. Mannock).

"***The Morals of Marcus*** – Lupe Velez has finished her part last week; she is now on her way back to America. Concluding scenes of the film included a Syrian street scene – a set occupying all the available floor space in the new studio."

(*K. W.*, 29 November 1934, page 59, P. L. Mannock).

Twickenham production in December/January:

The Cats Whiskers (Annie, Leave the Room!) starts next week.

Concurrently, Henry Edwards will work on ***Squibs*** until the end of December.

After which Edwards is to direct the screen version of Edgar Wallace's ***The Lad***. Gerald Fairlie is doing the screen adaptation.

Vintage Wine, also to be directed Henry Edwards, with Seymour Hicks and Clare Luce, with follow ***The Lad*** in January.

(*K. W.*, 29 November 1934, page 59, P. L. Mannock).

December 1934:

Kinematograph Weekly reported throughout the month:

"***Squibs*** – all the bustle and romance of Covent Garden filled the Twickenham Studios last week. The scene was the conflict between market folk, headed by Betty Balfour, and the Law, represented by Stanley Holloway until when Michael Shepley comes along and smoothes things over.

A song and dance number, *One-Way Street*, was supervised by Ralph Reeder. Apart from the principles in this scene, a motley crew of celebrities were present: chief of these was Philip Rome, 16-year old champion of Yo-Yo and Bif-Bat; Du Calion, the Man on the Tottering Ladder – veteran musical-hall artiste, now floor manager at Twickenham; and Mike, the donkey which Gordon Richards rode to victory in last year's Donkey Derby."

(*K. W.*, 6 December 1934, page 30, P. L. Mannock).

"One Crazy Week – Annie, Leave the Room – began production this week. Davina Craig will play the part of Annie. Cast includes Eva Moore, Morton Selten, Richard Cooper and Jane Carr."

(*K. W.*, 6 December 1934, page 30, P. L. Mannock).

Squibs – Piccadilly Circus in studio because bad weather made location work impossible. Twickenham's new sound stage was transformed last week into a set representing part of Piccadilly Circus. A full-size reproduction of the Eros fountain occupied the centre of the floor, and Swan and Edgar's corner was built at one end of the studio. Crowds of people thronged the pavement and a constant stream of traffic entered the studio, circulated round Eros and departed. Gladys Hamer and Vivien Chatterton have joined the cast as flower girls.

Ralph Reader, who is directing the dance numbers, will bring the chorus from the London Hippodrome success *Yes, Madam* to Twickenham next week.

(*K. W.*, 13 December 1934, page 43, P. L. Mannock).

"Street Song – Bernard Vorhaus will begin production on Monday (17 December 1934). John Garrick to star in an original story by Paul Gang(e)lin and Bernard Vorhaus."

(*K. W.*, 13 December 1934, page 43, P. L. Mannock).

Scrooge – "Julius Hagen, managing director of Twickenham Film Studios, announces that he has signed Seymour Hicks to play his greatest success of all time, Scrooge, from the play by

'The Czar of Twickenham'. The History of Julius Hagen and the Film Empire he created at Twickenham Film Studios, from 1927 to 1938.

Seymour Hicks, founded on Charles Dickens' *A Christmas Carol*'. This play, produced several times with Seymour Hicks in the leading rôle, ran for over 2,000 performances.

The film will be produced on a lavish scale, and Mr. Hagen is arranging that the film will be completed and ready for Trade showing and release, Christmas 1935".

(*K. W.*, 20 December 1934, page 31, P. L. Mannock).

Street Song – Bernard Vorhaus has started production. Wally Patch has the biggest part of his screen career as Wally, a kind-hearted crook. Several new songs will be introduced, to be sung by John Garrick in the part of Tom.

The 21 Films Trade Shown by Twickenham during 1934:

Twickenham completed twenty one films during 1934. This number gave an increase of one film over the twenty films that the studio completed during the previous year, 1933.

The breakdown of Twickenham's production record for 1934 was:

Twickenham's biggest film that year, **Bella Donna**, was made for Gaumont-British;

Two big productions, **Lily of Killarney** and **The Broken Melody**, were made for Associated Producing and Distribution Co., Ltd;

Six films were made for Universal Pictures, Ltd, including **The Four Masked Men**;

The remaining 12 films were made by Real Art Productions, Ltd., for the renter, Radio Pictures, Ltd; all 12 pictures were 'quota quickies' which were produced for Radio in order to satisfy its liabilities under the British Quota legislation of 1927.

1. *Lily of Killarney (1934)*

Drama with music, song and dance, set in Ireland, filmed in Killarney. A poor landowner, Sir Patrick Cregeen (John Garrick), is in love with a peasant girl (Gina Malo) who is kidnapped by an infamous smuggler (Dennis Hoey). To raise the ransom, he mortgages his estate to Sir James (Leslie Perrins), but who soon threatens foreclosure.

Lily of Killarney was the fourth Twickenham Film Studios, Ltd. film made for the distributor A. P. & D. (Associated Producing and Distribution Co.)

Lily of Killarney was the ninth film Maurice Elvey directed for Julius Hagen.

London Trade Show: Friday, 5 January 1934 at the Prince Edward Theatre.

British Registration Details:
Quota Registration No.: Br. 9634.
Registration Date: 8 January 1934.
Registered Length: 7,850 feet.
Registered by: Associated Producing and Distribution Co., Ltd.
Maker's name: Twickenham Film Studios, Ltd.
British Board of Film Censor's Certificate: "U".
British distributor: A. P. & D.
Running Time: 87 minutes.

Lily of Killarney was reviewed in the *Kinematograph Weekly*, 11 January 1934, on page 8:

334

'The Czar of Twickenham'. The History of Julius Hagen and the Film Empire he created at Twickenham Film Studios, from 1927 to 1938.

RCA Photophone, 87 minutes, "U" certificate.

"Remarks: Refreshing romantic melodrama, set in an Irish atmosphere, and accompanied by delightful tunes, familiar to all. Good story, straight-forward, resourceful treatment, picturesque atmosphere, excellent team work, and strong feminine appeal.

"Box Office Angle: Excellent box office attraction for the masses. Juvenile appeal particularly strong.

"Refreshing romantic melodrama, set in an Irish atmosphere and accompanied by irresistible national airs. Although the story is ingenious, it not only charms, but provides a welcome excuse for introducing romance and drama of a highly popular order, makes way for clean popular humour, and makes possible the logical introduction of delightful song melodies which will never die. Considering how difficult it is to compress such varied entertainment into a concise whole, Maurice Elvey has tackled his task with his proven flair for showmanship and certainly delivers the goods. The cast is an excellent one from the stars downwards, and the backgrounds are picturesque. Here is a film that recaptures the healthy early spirit of the screen, the spirit upon which the industry is built, and cannot on this account fail to hit the box-office high spots in popular and industrial areas.

"Story: Sir Patrick Creegan, an impoverished Irish landowner, is secretly in love with Eileen O'Connor, a peasant girl, and refuses to marry an

335

heiress, the obvious way out of his difficulties. He wages his all on a race between a horse owned by himself and one owned by Sir James Corrigan, the unscrupulous holder of the mortgage on his estate, but the night before the race one of his servants attempts to kill Eileen in a misguided attempt to throw him into the arms of the heiress, and he is held on suspicion. Corrigan plans to win the wager for forfeit, but Creegan, with the help of the sporting Father O'Flynn, clears away misunderstanding and arrives in time to ride and win.

"Acting: John Garrick, who has a pleasant voice, is exceedingly well cast as Creegan and makes the ideal hero of fiction. Stanley Holloway, past-master in the art of delivering a gay song, is immense as Father O'Flynn, and Leslie Perrins makes a suave villain as Corrigan. Gina Malo hardly suggests the Irish colleen as Eileen, but the rest of the cast work in harmonious accord.

"Production: The idea of presenting romantic melodrama to musical accompaniment is a good one, and although the supplement of action by song tends to hinder the development, the expedient is entirely justifiable, for the musical score – which includes such famous ballads as *The Hunting Song, Father O'Flynn, My Sheepdog and I,* and *My Little Irish Gig* – is one of the film's most fascinating and definitely box-office features. The romantic and dramatic sides of the picture are always held in clear perspective, and are boldly portrayed by players selected for their vocal abilities as well as their histrionic talents. The picture does not come under any particular category, but its new departure in showmanship results in such comprehensive entertainment that it can be viewed not in the light of an experiment, but from the angle of an assured popular success.

"Settings and Photography: The Irish backgrounds, both interiors and exteriors, are effectively approached pictorially, the atmosphere, and the chorus and individual vocal work are in complete co-ordination with the camera.

"Points of Appeal: Cast-iron story values, irresistible romance, undoubted feminine appeal, resourceful direction, good drama, occasional thrills, delightful musical treatment.

Lily of Killarney went out on General Release on Monday, 13 August 1934.

2. Say It With Flowers (1934)

Comedy-drama, with musical numbers. *Say It With Flowers* was more-or-less a celebration of Cockney Victorian music hall, with appearances by celebrated Music Hall artistes of that time. A group of Cockneys give a benefit show to help a sick flower-woman and her husband (Mary Clare and Ben Field) have a long rest at the seaside.

Say It With Flowers was the seventeenth film made by Real Art Productions for Radio Pictures. Whether the film was actually a 'Quota Quickie', or not, is unclear. That it is unlikely to be a 'Quota Quickie' lies in the fact that *Say It With Flowers* runs 70 minutes, rather than the standard hour, or even less, running time, which was so common then for the cheaply-made 'Pound-a-Foot' British pictures.

Say It With Flowers was the first of the four films John Baxter directed for Julius Hagen.

London Trade Show: Monday, 8 January 1934 at the Prince Edward Theatre, Old Compton Street, W.1.

British Registration Details:
    Quota Registration No.: Br. 9635.
    Registration Date: 9 January 1934.
    Registered Length: 6,347 feet.
    Registered by: Radio Pictures, Ltd.
    Maker's name: Real Art Productions, Ltd.
    British Board of Film Censor's Certificate: "U".
    British distributor: Radio Pictures.

Running Time: 70 minutes.

Say It With Flowers was reviewed in the *Kinematograph Weekly*, 11 January 1934, on page 9:

RCA Photophone, 70 minutes, "U" certificate.

"Remarks: Cockney romance, with a simple appealing story, and rich humour. Excellent characterisation, and resourceful treatment. Memorable concert by old-time musical hall favourites.

"Box Office Angle: Very good entertainment for the masses and youngsters; one with strong exploitation angles.

"Cockney romance, with appealing Darby and Joan

theme which unveils a simple human story: one which provides rich entertainment in its amusing and human sketches of Cockney character and finds an excellent excuse for staging a concert of old-time music-hall favourites. The picture makes a firm and confident appeal to both younger and older generations and is presented with workmanlike efficiency and showmanship. There is not a flaw in the casting, the famous old songs fit logically into the development, and the atmosphere is convincing. This is just the stuff to give the masses.

"Story: Kate, a flower seller in a London market, becomes ill, and is advised to take a holiday in a warmer climate. Joe, her husband, decides to sell his donkey, and approaches Bill, an old friend, the owner of the local fried fish shop. Bill, learning of his plight, then rallies all the other stall-holders, and they decide to hold a concert for the benefit of the old couple. Old timers, including Florrie Ford, Charles Coborn, and Marie Kendall volunteer their service, and their efforts are successful.

"Acting: Mary Field and Ben Field are delightful as the old Cockney couple, and succeed in winning a measure of sympathy. George Carney is excellent as Bill, and Florrie Ford, Marie Kendall, and Charles Coborn revive tender memories of their old songs.

"Production: The early scenes, devoted to establishing atmosphere and character, are slightly protracted, but once the story takes tangible shape, it carries real heart interest. The benefit concert gives the picture an excellent ending, and is staged with really good showmanship. The music hall artists of yesterday recapture their past glories for the moment, and hold the audience by the sheer force of their personalities, undimmed by time.

"Settings and Photography: The portrait of Cockney characters is vividly accurate, the market place atmosphere is perfect, and the musical score, which includes such famous song as *The Man Who Broke the Bank at Monte Carlo, Hold Your Hand Out Naughty Boy,* and *The Ivy on the Old Garden Wall,* is excellent.

"Points of Appeal: Good story, effective treatment, excellent characterisation, strong human interest, rich comedy and good tunes.

The British Circuit Exhibitors Report, date of weekly issue unknown:
The C.E.A Report awarded 8-and-a-half marks to ***Say It with Flowers***; it was the top score for all the new films reviewed in that week's issue.

Say It With Flowers went out on General Release on Monday, 28 May 1934; the original general release date planned was for Monday, 21 May 1934.

3. *The Black Abbot (1934)*

Crime thriller. Taking advantage of a legend of a ghost, a gang of crooks headed by Charlie (Ben Welden) enter the home of a rich man, Lord Jerry (Richard Cooper), and hold him to ransom. His friend, Frank

(John Stuart) tries to rescue him and, with the eventual arrival of the police, succeeds.

The onscreen opening main credit title for *The Black Abbot*.

The Black Abbot was the eighteenth film made by Real Art Productions for Radio Pictures; yet another 'Quota Quickie'.

The Black Abbot was the ninth of the eleven films George A. Cooper directed for Julius Hagen.

The Black Abbot was the seventh film appearance by the star, John Stuart, for Julius Hagen.

London Trade Show: Tuesday, 9 January 1934 at the Prince Edward Theatre.

British Registration Details:
Quota Registration No.: Br. 9645.
Registration Date: 10 January 1934.
Registered Length: 5,047 feet.
Registered by: Radio Pictures, Ltd.
Maker's name: Real Art Productions, Ltd.
British Board of Film Censor's Certificate: "A".
British distributor: Radio Pictures.

John V. Watson

Running Time: 56 minutes.

The Black Abbot was reviewed in the *Kinematograph Weekly*, 11 January 1934, on page 9:

RCA Photophone, 56 minutes, "A" certificate.

"Remarks: Conventional crime drama, somewhat mechanical in story values, but sufficiently well acted to produce the necessary quota of thrills.

"Box Office Angle: Useful quota second feature for the masses. Should please the youngsters.

"Unpretentious crime drama, conventional "spot the culprit" stuff, not particularly strong in dramatic values, but sufficiently mystifying in its development to hold the interest and enable the ending to occasion surprise. A second feature of convenient length for popular and industrial audiences.

"Story: John Hillcrist, a wealthy man, purchases a country mansion to which legend attaches a ghost. Shortly after he and his family move in he is kidnapped and held to ransom, and among the many suspects is his prospective son-in-law. The police are called in to investigate and, after the usual preliminaries, nail down the culprits.

"Acting: John Stuart is quite good as the hero, Judy Kelly is an attractive heroine, Richard Cooper is effective in a silly ass rôle, and the others are satisfactory.

"Production: The story, a mechanical one, is a trifle

involved, but its complexities nevertheless pave the way to a few exciting situations which culminate with the customary thrill. The film is unimaginative but efficient, primarily designed to fulfil quota requirements.

"Settings and Photography: The settings are confined to a few interiors, and the photography does not reveal a great deal of originality.

"Points of Appeal: Popular subject, convenient length, good cast and quota angle.

Leslie Halliwell, Halliwell's Film Guide, 1977 stated:

"Dire upper-class thriller with stilted acting and excruciating comic relief supplied by the servants." Halliwell gave **The Black Abbot** no stars at all (meaning "a totally routine production or worse; such films may be watchable but are at least equally missable") out of a possible score of 4. Having suffered one viewing of my (briefly-owned) 16mm print some 40 years ago, this author concurs with Halliwell; the film **is** dire and the comic relief **is** excruciating!

The Black Abbot went out on General Release on Monday, 28 May 1934.

4. *The River Wolves (1934)*

Crime melodrama set in Tilbury. Merchant Captain Guest (Michael Hogan) visits the dockside at Tilbury for material for a novel, where he meets another aspiring writer, Peter (John Mills). They both fall for the same girl,

343

Heather (Hope Davy). But a gang of crooks is blackmailing Peter; later the captain is able to save the day.

The River Wolves was the nineteenth film made by Real Art Productions for Radio Pictures; another 'Quota Quickie'.

The River Wolves was the third of the eight "quota-quickies" George Pearson directed for Julius Hagen at Twickenham Studios.

The River Wolves was also the fourth of the four films made by Julius Hagen that were trade shown during January 1934.

The River Wolves was his second film appearance by John Mills for Julius Hagen.

London Trade Show: Wednesday, 10 January 1934 at the Prince Edward Theatre.

British Registration Details:
Quota Registration No.: Br. 9671.
Registration Date: 12 January 1934.
Registered Length: 5,089 feet.
Registered by: Radio Pictures, Ltd.
Maker's name: Real Art Productions, Ltd.
British Board of Film Censor's Certificate: "A".
British distributor: Radio Pictures.
Running Time: 56 minutes.

The River Wolves was reviewed in the *Kinematograph Weekly*, 18 January 1934, on page 22:

RCA Photophone, 56 minutes, "A" certificate.

"Remarks: Hearty British melodrama with realistic

waterfront background, situations strong, actions smooth, characterisation interesting.

"Box Office Angle: Good supporting entertainment for the masses. Not for juvenile audiences.

"Hearty British melodrama, played against realistic waterfront settings. The story, although good, takes some time to get into its stride, but after the slow opening the picture gets well under way and rides steadily to a hectic climax. The principal players acquit themselves adequately, the situations are competently handled, and the ending is accompanied by popular rough stuff. Quite good supporting entertainment for the masses.

"Story: Captain Guest, a tough skipper, decides to seek colour for a book which he intends to write while his boat is being refitted at Tilbury. While staying at a local hostel he falls in love with the proprietress's niece, Heather, and through her becomes acquainted with Peter Farrel, who is in the coils of "Flash Lawson", a blackmailer. A stern battle of wits and brawn then follows between Guest and Lawson, and Lawson's seductive employer, Moira, but Guest eventually wins and frees Farrel from further trouble. By this time he realises that Farrel is in love with Heather, and he philosophically returns to his old love, the sea.

"Acting: Michael Hogan strides confidently through the picture as Guest, Ben Welden admirably measures up to the conventional villain of fiction as Lawson, John Mills is good as Farrel, and Helga Moray is a most seductive Moira. The supporting cast is particularly good.

"Production: George Pearson, the producer, is rather dilatory in coming to the point, but once he establishes the motive of the theme, the clash between Guest and Lawson, the melodrama takes hectic and popular shape and explores many colourful by-ways. Restrained sentiment softens the rough stuff, while adequate humorous relief is found in the accuracy of the supporting characterisation.

"Settings and Photography: The waterfront scenes are forbidding and give realism to the main action, while sophisticated party scenes furnish good atmospheric contrast. Lighting and photography are good.

"Points of Appeal: Meaty story, popular dramatic punch, pleasing sentiment, good humour, sound characterisation, and neat, straightforward treatment.

The River Wolves went out on General Release on Monday, 18 June 1934 - the original general release date was planned for Monday, 4 June 1934.

5. *The Four Masked Men (1934)*

Crime thriller. After his brother has been shot during a hold-up by masked crooks, barrister Trevor Phillips (John Stuart) swears to avenge his death. He also discovers that the gang are responsible for several other robberies. Then, posing as a thief, he determines to track them down, and, with the help of his friend, Lord Richard Clyde (Richard Cooper), he finally succeeds in bringing them all to book.

The Four Masked Men was the first of the ten films which were made by Twickenham Film Studios, Ltd., for Universal's British renting subsidiary, Universal Pictures, Ltd. The 81-minute running time suggests that *The Four Masked Men* was designed as, at least, a co-feature film, or even as a "top-of-the-bill" attraction for some cinemas. Universal's British-renting subsidiary also commissioned many feature films from several other British 'Quota' film producers.

London Trade Show: Friday, 16 February 1934 at the Prince Edward Theatre.

British Registration Details:
Quota Registration No.: Br. 9833.
Registration Date: 19 February 1934.
Registered Length: 7,317 feet.
Registered by: Universal Pictures, Ltd.
Maker's name: Twickenham Film Studios, Ltd.
British Board of Film Censor's Certificate: "A".
British distributor: Universal Pictures.
Running Time: 81 minutes.

The Four Masked Men was reviewed in the *Kinematograph Weekly*, 22 February 1934, page 21:

RCA Photophone, 81 minutes, "A" certificate.
"Remarks: Popular crime drama, well acted and presented. Story a trifle fantastic, but nevertheless thrilling and entertaining. Technical qualities particularly good.

John V. Watson

"Box Office Angle: Safe popular booking. Should not harm juveniles.

"Crime drama, the story of which is suggestive of an Edgar Wallace thriller, but rather lacks its craftsmanship. There does remain, however, much in the characterisation to sustain interest, and it is the good individual acting, coupled with excellent staging, that enables the film to hold suspense, develop a strong and intriguing hint of romance, and cater for lively thrills. Safe popular booking, particularly for industrial areas.

"Story: Trevor Phillips, a young barrister, determines to bring to justice a mysterious man, head of a secret gang of masked bandits who are responsible for the cruel murder of his brother, Arthur. He discovers that Rodney Fraser, an old friend, is a member of the gang, and by terrorising him and eliciting the aid of Lord Richard Clyde, another friend, he unmasks the killer, who, unknown to his fiancée, Patricia, turns out to be Colonel St. John Clive, her uncle.

"Acting: John Stuart acts with quiet determination and dignity as Trevor, Judy Kelly is a charming Patricia, Athole Stewart gives a polished, disarming portrayal as Clive, Miles Mander is clever as the degenerate Fraser, Richard Cooper is amusing as Lord Richard and S. Victor Stanley contributes a bright Cockney study in support.

"Production: Boiled down the story is wildly fantastic, but the method of its telling and the manner in which it is wrapped up in a variety of backgrounds results in it keeping its secret firmly

348

until the end. It is this quality, together with sound character drawing, that invests the good situations with interest and enables them to follow through with an easy dramatic flow that builds up suspense. The film is not an inspired effort, but it is a workmanlike show safely designed to entertain, thrill and intrigue the masses.

"Settings and Photography: There is an exceedingly wide range of settings, all of which are appropriate and contribute to good atmosphere, while lighting and photography are excellent.

"Points of Appeal: Popular theme, interesting and amusing characterisation, exceptionally good staging, lively thrills, intriguing suspense, and pleasing love interest.

The Four Masked Men went out on General Release on Monday, 13 August 1934.

The Four Masked Men was filmed under the title, *Behind the Mask.*

6. *The Admiral's Secret (1934)*

Comedy-adventure. Spanish thieves pursue retired British Admiral Fitzporter (Edmund Gwenn) to steal his valuable diamond, but they delay doing this by continually trying to outwit each other.

The Admiral's Secret was the twentieth film made by Real Art Productions for Radio Pictures; another 'Quota Quickie'.

John V. Watson

Edmund Gwenn: *The Admiral's Secret* was his third and final film for Julius Hagen; it was the only one of the three in which Gwenn had the leading rôle.

The Admiral's Secret was made at Merton Park Studios instead of Twickenham Film Studios. In his article, P. L. Mannock for the *Kinematograph Weekly*, 4 January 1934, page 25, explained why *The Admiral's Secret* had to be filmed at the Merton Park Studios instead of using Twickenham Studios as was normal for Julius Hagen:

"Twickenham burst of activity."

"Julius Hagen starts the New Year at Twickenham Studios with a burst of activity."

"Owing to the large production schedule for the coming year, Twickenham Studios, pending the construction of their own second stage, have been compelled to hire space at Merton Park Studios for *The Admiral's Secret*. The studio, which is owned by Publicity Films, Ltd., has a rock-wool lined stage. It is fully equipped with modern R.C.A. recording equipment, a fine large synchronising theatre, modern cutting rooms, work-shops, dressing rooms and good offices. It is built entirely sound-proof, and has fine lighting equipment and ample power supply. This studio is unknown to the Trade generally, in spite of its very convenient situation. It has in the past been working solely on non-entertainment films."

London Trade Show: Friday, 23 February 1934 at the Phoenix Theatre.

'The Czar of Twickenham'. The History of Julius Hagen and the Film Empire he created at Twickenham Film Studios, from 1927 to 1938.

British Registration Details:
Quota Registration No.: Br. 9867. Registration Date: 24 February 1934.
Registered Length: 5,753 feet.
Registered by: Radio Pictures, Ltd.
Maker's name: Real Art Productions, Ltd.
British Board of Film Censor's Certificate: "U".
British distributor: Radio Pictures.
Running Time: 64 minutes.

The Admiral's Secret was reviewed in the *Kinematograph Weekly*, 1 March 1934, page 32:

RCA Photophone, 64 minutes, "U" certificate.

"Remarks: Light drama, a naïve incorporation of comedy, crime and romance. Story sketchy, but clever acting of star circumvents narrative and directorial shortcomings.

"Box Office Angle: Average supporting feature for industrial areas. Will not harm juveniles.

"Light drama, a hotch-potch of crime, comedy and romance, woven into harmless light diversion through the resourcefulness and cleverness of Edmund Gwenn, who brings entertainment in the pivotal rôle. The direction is very ordinary, but the situations are fashioned on lines that can be depended upon to amuse and thrill the masses. Average supporting feature for industrial areas.

"Story: Admiral Fitzporter, a peppery gentleman who spends his retirement fishing in Devonshire, has the serenity of his home life disturbed by Don Pablo, Guido d'Elvira and Questa, three Spaniards

John V. Watson

who are eager to gain possession of the Star of
Peru, which he secretly possesses. He is
eventually compelled to confide in his old friend,
Captain Brooke: Frank Bruce (engaged to his
daughter, Pamela); and his batman, Hawkins, to
help him meet the Spaniards' unceremonious
methods of approach. Ultimately it is his own
shrewdness which enables him to hoodwink the
invaders and retain possession of the coveted
prize.

"Acting: Edmund Gwenn gives a crisp performance
as Fitzporter, and such is his experience that he
can bring an artificial rôle to life and make
commonplace dialogue tell. James Raglan and
Hope Davey take safe care of the modest love
interest, Abraham Sofaer, Andreas Malandrinos
and D. J. Williams make good villains, and Edgar
Driver is responsible for the low comedy relief.

"Production: Guy Newall's hands appear to have
lost a little of their cunning, for his direction lacks
decision. Comedy and drama are not too surely
defined, and the overlapping does not reflect too
favourably on the quality of the entertainment. In
fact, it is Edmund Gwenn who holds the show
together and enables the simple situations, with
their obvious humour and naïve thrills, to register.
The film has its weaknesses, but these should not
prevent it from proving a satisfactory supporting
offering for an industrial public.

"Settings and Photography: The settings are
confined to ordinary interiors, but lighting and
photography are good.

"<u>Points of Appeal</u>: Simple humour, modest thrills, and entertaining performance by star.

The Admiral's Secret went out on General Release on Monday, 6 August 1934.

7. *The Man Who Changed His Name (1934)*

Thriller.   Extremely jealous, the husband (Lyn Harding) of an adulterous wife (Betty Stockfeld) leads her to believe that he is a murderer, who had cleverly avoided conviction by the jury.   He continues this deception to stop her from eloping with another man (Leslie Perrins), by carefully building an ever more fearful picture of himself.   Gradually he drives them to the edge of hysteria by making his every innocent move look like the subtle and deadly acts of a madman.   But, all this is really a clever ploy he had planned to show his rival as a weakling unworthy of his wife's love.

The Man Who Changed His Name was the second of the ten films which were made by Twickenham Film Studios, Ltd. for Universal Pictures, Ltd., the British renting subsidiary of Universal Pictures.   The 80-minute running time suggests that *The Man Who Changed His Name* was designed as, at least, a co-feature film, or even as a "top-of-the-bill" attraction for some cinemas.

The Man Who Changed His Name was the first film Henry Edwards was to direct for his partnership with Julius Hagen and Leslie Hiscott, although he already had been a co-director of Twickenham Films Studios and its associated companies for some years.

John V. Watson

The Man Who Changed His Name was the second film appearance by Lyn Harding for Julius Hagen. As we shall see below, the Welsh actor, Lyn Harding, played the part of 'Professor Moriarty', the evil mastermind nemesis of 'Sherlock Holmes', in several film adaptations of Conan Doyle's detective stories in the 1930s.

London Trade Show: Thursday, 1 March 1934 at the Prince Edward Theatre.

British Registration Details:
Quota Registration No.: Br. 9873.
Registration Date: 2 March 1934.
Registered Length: 7,203 feet.
Registered by: Universal Pictures, Ltd.
  Maker's name: Twickenham Film Studios, Ltd. NOTE that several film reference books credit Julius Hagen's other production company, Real Art Productions Ltd., as the maker of *The Man Who Changed His Name* but the registration notification makes absolutely clear that this was not the case.
British Board of Film Censor's Certificate: "A".
British distributor: Universal Pictures.
Running Time: 80 minutes.

The Man Who Changed His Name was reviewed in the *Kinematograph Weekly*, 1 March 1934, page 32:

RCA Photophone, 80 minutes, "A" certificate.

"Remarks: Mystery thriller, with a strong measure of comedy, shrewdly adapted from an Edgar Wallace story. Treatment efficient, situations exciting, and individual acting convincing.

"Box Office Angle: Good popular booking. Cannot harm juveniles.

"Mystery thriller, a sound, straightforward adaptation of one of Edgar Wallace's most successful stories. The shrewd ploy combines suspense and humour in entertaining proportions, and good characterisation and sound direction enable its secrets to be successfully preserved. Surprise punctuates the smooth development, and bright humour deftly turns the more exciting situations. The picture makes a firm appeal to the masses, and with its powerful exploitation angles, represented by the title, author, and strong cast, has all the accompaniments of a sound success. Good popular booking.

"Story: Frank Ryan, an unscrupulous young philanderer, has an intrigue with Nita, young wife of Selby Clyde, a wealthy middle-aged man, in the hope that he will be able to influence her to secure for him the lease of land, owned by her husband, which he knows to be rich in silver. Selby is quite aware of Ryan's intentions, and allows the impression to be circulated that he is a murderer, so that he can test the character of the interloper. His ruse succeeds in revealing the cowardly Ryan in his true colours, and following his departure, Nita generously acknowledges her folly.

"Acting: Lyn Harding gives a firm impressive portrayal as Selby, and carries through his bluff with excellent effect. Betty Stockfeld has charm and dignity as the rather foolish Nita, Leslie Perrins is good as Ryan, and interesting supporting studies come from Ben Welden, Aubrey Mather and Stanley Vine.

"Production: Edgar Wallace knew all there is to know about the art of story writing, and his gifts are quite successfully translated in screen terms. Henry Edwards, who directed, keeps the main plot in clear perspective, all the time taking advantage of its ability to thrill, and, by clearly separating comedy from drama, not only sustains good balance, but maintains the secret of the exciting ending. The character of the entertainment is eminently popular, and the manner of its presentation should guarantee a more than favourable reception from the majority.

"Settings and Photography: The settings are mostly interiors, but they nevertheless succeed in promoting good atmosphere. Lighting and photography, however, are rather dark: in fact, the camerawork throughout reveals little imagination: it is static.

"Points of Appeal: Title, author, good story, lively thrills, bright humour, adequate treatment, and strong cast.

The Man Who Changed His Name went out on General Release on Monday, 10 September 1934.

8. *Night Club Queen (1934)*

Drama with music. To support her son at university (Lewis Shaw) and her paralysed husband (Lewis Casson), Mary Brown (Mary Clare) opens a teashop, but the business fails. Her new partner, Hale (George Carney), persuades her to turn it into a nightclub. The partners quarrel; Hale is killed, and Mary is charged with the crime. But her husband, a former counsel, defends her, relying on his recounting of Mary's unhappy life (in a lengthy flashback) to convince the jury.

Night Club Queen was the third of the ten films which were made by Twickenham Film Studios, Ltd. for Universal Pictures, Ltd., the British renting subsidiary of Universal Pictures. Once again, like the cases of the previous two films made by Hagen for Universal, *The Four Masked Men* and *The Man Who Changed His Name* , the 88-minute running time suggests that *Night Club Queen* was designed as, at least, a co-feature film, or even as a "top-of-the-bill" attraction for some cinemas.

Night Club Queen was the second film Bernard Vorhaus directed for Julius Hagen.

London Trade Show: Thursday, 22 March 1934 at the Prince Edward Theatre.

British Registration Details:
Quota Registration No.: Br. 9946.
Registration Date: 23 March 1934.
Registered Length: 7,970 feet.
Registered by: Universal Pictures, Ltd.
Maker's name: Twickenham Film Studios, Ltd.
British Board of Film Censor's Certificate: "A".
British distributor: Universal Pictures.
Running Time: 88 minutes.

Night Club Queen was reviewed in the *Kinematograph Weekly*, 29 March 1934, on page 24:

RCA Photophone, 88 minutes, "A" certificate.

"Remarks: Human drama of parental love and sacrifice set against scintillating night-club background. Story, strong, acting confident and presentation excellent.

"Box Office Angle: Very good general booking. Unsuitable for children.

"Human drama of parental love and sacrifice set against scintillating night-club backgrounds. The story, told in retrospect, is a trifle theatrical, but the method of its presentation reveals sound craftsmanship and enables it to pave the way to arresting popular entertainment. The acting is in the capable hands of an exceedingly strong cast, while the presentation can compare with the best. Very good general booking.

"Story: Mary, a middle-aged woman, married to Edward Brown, a barrister, who has turned journalist, following an accident which had rendered him paralytic, secretly runs a night club to pay for the education of her son, Peter, at Oxford. Hale, her partner, reveals his unscrupulousness when he attempts to sell her his share just before a police raid, and during a quarrel she accidentally kills him. She is brought for trial, and Edward returns to the bar to defend her, making her sacrificial life story his plea to the jury. Their verdict is left to the imagination.

"Acting: Mary Clare gives an intelligent and thoroughly convincing performance as Mary, Lewis Casson contributes a strong study as Edward, embittered by infirmity, Lewis Shaw is perfectly natural as Peter, and Jane Carr and George Carney are very good in supporting rôles.

'The Czar of Twickenham'. The History of Julius Hagen and the Film Empire he created at Twickenham Film Studios, from 1927 to 1938.

> "Production: Bernard Vorhaus' direction is a little lacking in finish, the continuity is a little ragged, some scenes are clipped and others are unduly prolonged, but his methods show imagination and stagecraft. The human side to the story is always given clear recognition, resulting in strong feminine interest, while the night-club backgrounds, decorated with the inevitable cabaret show, are skilfully employed to amplify the drama by means of contrast.

> "Settings and Photography: The domestic interiors are true in aspect, while the night-club scenes are accompanied by the gayest embellishments. Lighting and photography are very good.

> "Points of Appeal: Good story, capable treatment, lavish presentation, strong dramatic moments, pleasing romantic sentiment, human interest, and excellent staging.

Night Club Queen went out on General Release on Monday, 24 September 1934.

9. *Tangled Evidence (1934)*

Crime thriller: Suspicion falls on Anne (Joan Marion) when her occultist uncle is found murdered. But Inspector Drayton (Sam Livesey) proves she did not kill him, and that instead someone who feared the dead man's contacts with 'the other world' had committed the crime.

Tangled Evidence was the twenty-first film made by Real Art Productions for Radio Pictures; yet another 'Quota Quickie' for that renter.

John V. Watson

Tangled Evidence was the only film appearance by Sam Livesey for Julius Hagen. Born on 14 October 1873, in Flintshire, Wales, Sam Livesey was already a noted stage actor before he made his first British silent film in 1916.

London Trade Show: Tuesday, 27 March 1934 at the Cambridge Theatre.

British Registration Details:
Quota Registration No.: Br. 9970.
Registration Date: 28 March 1934.
Registered Length: 5,136 feet.
Registered by: Radio Pictures, Ltd.
Maker's name: Real Art Productions, Ltd.
British Board of Film Censor's Certificate: "A".
British distributor: Radio Pictures.

Running Time: 57 minutes.

Tangled Evidence was reviewed in the *Kinematograph Weekly*, 29 March 1934, on page 31:

RCA Photophone, 57 minutes, "A" certificate.

"<u>Remarks</u>: Detective story interestingly presented though rather far-fetched in solution. Well produced and acted.

"<u>Box Office Angle</u>: Useful general booking. Reasonably safe for children.

"An ingeniously written detective drama which distributes suspicion fairly evenly among the characters before revealing the murderer. Situations have been very ably handled, suspense is well maintained, and acting and production are of good quality.

"Story: On the eve of the publication of a best-selling novel by Ingram Underhill, his friend, Colonel Wilmot, is found murdered. Suspicion falls upon Wilmot's two nieces, Anne and Paula, the former of whom was in the room after the murder was committed, while the latter was away from the house at the time when she should have been in bed. Inspector Drayton questions also Wilson's librarian, who has evidence against Anne and who is subsequently murdered. Finally a trap is set by the fixing of a battery and bell to Wilmot's safe. Underhill is discovered at the safe. It transpires that the novel was written really by Wilmot and that the librarian, knowing this, had blackmailed Underhill.

"Acting: Sam Livesey plays Inspector Drayton with quiet, sure efficiency, and most of the other parts are equally well cast. Joan Marion's Anne is a dramatic figure, perhaps a little too tense, while Michael Hogan as the murderer gives genuine effect to his part, handling skilfully scenes in which he is supposed to be at ease as well as scenes in which he is moved to desperate action. Davina Craig's comedy relief as a maid is overdone, but helps to soften the dominant air of tragedy.

"Production: The story, having been constructed with sufficient skill to hold attention without the use of irrelevant scenes, too many false clues or the deliberate suppression of necessary evidence, moves smoothly from the statement of the problems surrounding the crime to their solution;

and if the explanation taxes credulity, it is certainly made as reasonable as possible. George Cooper's direction deserves praise. It is crisp, interesting, effective. Its one weakness is shown in the humorous scenes, which fortunately are few and short, but even these are unable to divert or slacken interest.

"Settings and Photography: The country house settings are impressive without being over-elaborate. Lighting is good throughout, and camera work excellent.

"Points of Appeal: The popularity usually enjoyed by detective stories will be extended to this specimen, and the acting will attract.

Tangled Evidence went out on General Release on Monday, 17 September 1934.

10. *Whispering Tongues (1934)*

Thriller. A man (Reginald Tate) and his secretary steal gems from those responsible for his father's death.

Whispering Tongues was the twenty-second film made by Real Art Productions for Radio Pictures; one more 'Quota Quickie' made for that renter.

Whispering Tongues was the fifth of the eight films George Pearson directed for Julius Hagen at Twickenham Studios.

Whispering Tongues was the first leading film rôle by Reginald Tate; it was his second film appearance for Julius Hagen. Reginald Tate is probably best remembered today as the first actor to play the television science-fiction character, 'Professor Bernard Quatermass', in the 1953 BBC Television serial, *The Quatermass Experiment*.

London Trade Show: Wednesday, 28 March 1934 at the Phoenix Theatre.

British Registration Details:
Quota Registration No.: Br. 9976.
Registration Date: 29 March 1934.
Registered Length: 4,951 feet.
Registered by: Radio Pictures, Ltd.
Maker's name: Real Art Productions, Ltd.
British Board of Film Censor's Certificate: "A".
British distributor: Radio Pictures.

Running Time: 55 minutes.

Trade Show advertisement in the *Kine Weekly*: *Whispering Tongues*. Reginald Tate, Jane Walsh (Welsh misspelt), with Russell Thorndike, Malcolm Keen. Produced by Julius Hagen. Directed by George Pearson. Tagline: "A Modern "Raffles" Drama!"
Whispering Tongues was reviewed in the *Kinematograph Weekly*, 5 April 1934, on page 35:

RCA Photophone, 55 minutes, "A" certificate.

"Remarks: Interesting crook story of the Raffles type. Well presented and acted.

"Box Office Angle: Very good general booking. Not really harmful to children.

"Russell Thorndike and a good cast ensure the entertainment value of an original and live crook story. Production and photography are well up to standard, and the whole undoubtedly should be an asset to the general programme. The "A" certificate implies nothing unpleasant, the arch criminal being of the Raffles order.

"Story: In a spirit of revenge for the suicide of a devoted father, Alan Norton, taught by Fenwick, an "old lag", perpetrates robberies on the people who were the elder Norton's ruin. When Alan discovers the chief of these, Roger Mayland, to be the father of Claudia, with whom he is in love, he decides against rifling Mayland's safe of stolen bonds. Furious at the loss of a promised share of this money, Fenwick informs Inspector Dawley, who has been trailing Alan. Alan, who has taken the bonds to satisfy himself of Mayland's fraud against his father, and has incidentally discovered Mayland's wish to make restitution, is returning them when the inspector arrives. Instead of being arrested, Alan acquaints the inspector of his engagement to Claudia.

"Acting: Russell Thorndike is quite and forceful as the butler and thief, rising to dramatic heights when he turns on his employer and pupil. Reginald Tate, a trifle stagey, is nevertheless a personality as Alan, evincing far more character than the average British juvenile lead. Jane Welsh is an attractive Claudia, while Malcolm Kean as the discomfited Inspector Dawley provides a natural rendering of a part only too easy to burlesque.

"Production: George Pearson has unfolded a good story well, if on the leisurely side and with a tendency towards stage technique. Opening scenes are dramatic, relations between Alan and the butler are clearly established, and entertaining sequences follow between the temporary crook and the inspector. Love interest is skilfully developed; the removal of the bonds by Alan from Mayland's safe while a manservant reads the newspaper outside the room provides a genuine thrill. Finally there are some lively sequences in which Alan has the laugh on the inspector, though handcuffed at one point in the drama. Dialogue is sound and well fitted to the action.

"Settings and Photography: Interiors of a millionaire's house, with one or two exteriors of gardens and shots of Alan's rooms, are well photographed and lighted. Close-ups specially vivid.

"Points of Appeal: Good story, interesting cast, technical soundness, and the ever-popular subject of crookery seen through rose-coloured spectacles.

popular subject of crookery seen through rose-coloured spectacles.

Whispering Tongues went out on General Release on Monday, 24 September 1934.

11. The Lash (1934)

Drama. A self-made millionaire (Lyn Harding) has a weakling son (John Mills) who constantly lets him down, even continuing his affair with a married woman (Joan Maude). Finally, his patience exhausted, he horsewhips his son in an attempt to cure him of his drunken and wastrel ways.

The Lash was the twenty-third film made by Real Art Productions for Radio Pictures. *The Lash* was also the first of a new series of films to be made by Julius Hagen for Radio release, as reported in the Kinematograph Weekly, 1 March 1934.

The Lash was the second film Henry Edwards directed for his partnership with Julius Hagen and Leslie Hiscott, as a co-director of Twickenham Films Studios and its associated companies.

The Lash was the third sound film appearance by Lyn Harding for Julius Hagen.

Trade Show advertisement in the *Kinematograph Weekly*: "Lyn Harding in *"The Lash"*, with Joan Maude and John Mills. Adapted from the famous play by Cyril Campion. Produced by Julius Hagen. Directed by Henry Edwards." Tagline: "Powerful drama of a father who dealt with modern youth in his own way."

London Trade Show: Wednesday, 2 May 1934 at the Prince Edward Theatre.

British Registration Details:
Quota Registration No.: Br. 10114.
Registration Date: 3 May 1934.
Registered Length: 5,766 feet.
Registered by: Radio Pictures, Ltd.
Maker's name: Real Art Productions, Ltd.
British Board of Film Censor's Certificate: "A".
British distributor: Radio Pictures.

Running Time: 64 minutes.

The Lash was reviewed in the *Kinematograph Weekly*, 10 May 1934, on page 26:

RCA Photophone, 64 minutes, "A" certificate.

"Remarks: Powerful domestic drama, adapted from the famous stage success. Story a trifle heavy, but treatment sound, situations strong, and moral clear.

"Box Office Angle: Sound dramatic booking for the masses. Hardly suitable for children.

"Powerful domestic drama, adapted from the famous stage success of the same name. The construction of the play is a trifle old-fashioned, but its hearty sentiments wear well and its moral is sound. The principle players interpret their parts in the right spirit, the staging is suitably varied to fit the story's turbulent moods, while the ending has definite punch. Useful dramatic booking for the masses.

"Story: Bronson Haughton, millionaire, who has made his fortune in Australia, is seriously disturbed by the conduct of his son, Arthur. When he discovers that the boy is mixed up with shady night-club habitués, and that he is secretly married to Mary, a girl of respectable middle-class family, he gives him one more chance to make good, but he again lets him down. In desperation he ships him off to Australia, but he jumps ship at the nearest port and returns to town to continue his intrigue with a married woman. This time Bronson's patience is exhausted, and he sets about his son with a whip and beats some sense into him.

"Acting: Lyn Harding gives a strong portrayal as Bronson, John Mills is well cast as the weak Arthur, Peggy Blyth is adequate as his unhappy wife, and sound support comes from Leslie Perrins, Aubrey Mather, Joan Maude, and Mary Jerrold.

"Production: Although the title reveals the secret of the ending, the events that lead up to it are paved with good drama. There is no attempt at subtlety, the story is straight-forwardly told, and its moral is expressed with abundant clarity through the arresting situations which follow in smooth, logical sequence. The sentiments are not designed to appeal to the more sophisticated patron, but they are interpreted in a language which will thrill and appeal to the masses. The film represents sound dramatic entertainment, and with its quota tag should prove a more than useful proposition for popular and industrial halls.

"Settings and Photography: The staging is not expensive, but it is adequate, and lighting and photography are satisfactory.

"Points of Appeal: Strong story, honest sentiment, human interest, sound interpretation, and adequate treatment and presentation.

The Lash went out on General Release on Monday, 22 October 1934.

12. The Broken Melody (1934)

Musical drama set in France. The story is told by one well-dressed gentleman to another between the scenes of an opera in Paris: a struggling young composer, Paul Verlaine (John Garrick), marries a prima donna, Simone (Margot Grahame). But later she casts him off, and he then reciprocates by killing her lover (Austin Trevor) in a jealous rage. He is sent to Devil's Island, the French penal colony, but he escapes some years later, and returns to France and writes an opera about his experience.

The Broken Melody was the fifth Twickenham Film Studios film production which was made for the distribution company, A. P. & D. (Associated Producing & Distribution).

The Broken Melody was the third film Bernard Vorhaus directed for Julius Hagen.

The Broken Melody was the only film appearance by Merle Oberon for Julius Hagen; she was loaned out by Alexander Korda for the film. The actress made this film before she starred as 'Lady Blakeney' with Leslie Howard as 'Sir Percy Blakeney' in Alexander Korda's production of *The Scarlet Pimpernel* (1934). Merle Oberon replaced the actress, Joan Wyndham, who fell ill immediately before filming was due to commence.

London Trade Show: Tuesday, 15 May 1934 at the Prince Edward Theatre.

British Registration Details:
Quota Registration No.: Br. 10155.
Registration Date: 17 May 1934.
Registered Length: 7,500 feet.

John V. Watson

Registered by: Associated Producing and Distribution Co., Ltd.
Maker's name: Twickenham Film Studios, Ltd.
British Board of Film Censor's Certificate: "A".
British distributor: A. P. & D.

Running Time: 83 minutes.

Trade Show advertisement in the *Kinematograph Weekly*: "John Garrick as "Paul Verlaine", Margot Grahame as "Simone St. Cloud", then below the title: Austin Trevor as "Pierre Falaise, Merle Oberon as "Germaine Brisson." Tagline: "Frederick White and Gilbert Church have pleasure in announcing the Trade Show of *"The Broken Melody."* (A Julius Hagen Production)."

The Broken Melody was reviewed in the *Kinematograph Weekly*, 17 May 1934, on page 31:

> Visatone Sound Recording System, 83 minutes, "A" certificate.

> "Remarks: Romantic melodrama with music, presented on popular and colourful lines. Story artless, but strong in sentimental and dramatic appeal. Musical setting appropriate and effective.

> "Box Office Angle: Good entertainment for the masses. Hardly suitable for children.

> "Romantic melodrama with music, presented on lines which have proved their popularity. The story contains no surprises, but the manner of its telling reveals good showmanship, resulting in appealing sentimental interludes, moments of arresting drama, and a useful compliment of thrills. Although the atmosphere is not entirely

‘The Czar of Twickenham’. The History of Julius Hagen and the Film Empire he created at Twickenham Film Studios, from 1927 to 1938.

convincing, it has colour and always provides appropriate settings for the narrative's turbulent and tender moods. The cast is both competent and contains attractive names, while the musical score has well rendered original numbers, vocal and orchestral. Here is a film which, by including all these elements essential to mass appeal and weaving these into attractive entertainment, should have no difficulty in meeting with the approval of the crowd.

"Story: Paul Verlaine, a struggling composer, living in Paris, is secretly loved by Germaine, daughter of the house in which he resides, but allows himself to be swept of his feet by Simone, a tempestuous opera singer, whom he marries. This marriage, however, proves disastrous, and in a fit of rage he kills Pierre, Simone's lover. He is charged with murder and convicted, and sent to Devil's Island, from which he eventually escapes. He renews his friendship with Germaine, who on the death of Simone had adopted her child, and she inspires him to write around his own life story an opera in which she appears with him.

"Acting: John Garrick succeeds in giving a convincing portrayal as the unhappy Paul, and is more than equal for the demands set by the song numbers. Margot Grahame tends a little to overact as Simone, but is good enough to make the turning points in the drama clear, and Merle Oberon, who sings pleasantly, wins a good deal of sympathy as the faithful and understanding Germaine. Austin Trevor and Charles Carson are

371

the most prominent of the supporting players.

"Production: The appeal of the picture is directed towards the masses. There is no attempt at subtlety or finesse; it is just good honest melodrama given additional effect through the aid of music. The romantic interest is transparent but sincere, the poignant moments quietly touch the emotions, while the dramatic interludes are heartily and arrestingly frank. The formula from which the film is made is one that has withstood the acid test at the box office, and, once again it has produced good, all-round entertainment, strong in mass appeal.

"Settings and Photography: The Parisian sequences are decorative, the Devil's Island scenes have essential grimness, while good camera work enables the story to be clearly told through a third person, an effective dramatic device.

"Points of Appeal: Popular story, straightforward treatment, human and emotional interest, pleasant music, good drama, attractive cast, and colourful and spectacular presentation.

The Broken Melody went out on General Release on 3 December 1934.

13. *Music Hall (1934)*

Musical. An old music hall is failing badly because it is being run on old-fashioned ideas and methods. Yet, despite his being old, a retired showman (George Carney) is employed to revitalise it and run it using modern methods of showmanship. Against "all the odds", the wisdom of his age and consequent experience shines through; under his wise guidance, the building takes on a new lease of life. Renovating the hall, he then re-opens it with a mammoth programme, all to great success, thus putting it firmly on its feet once more.

Music Hall was the twenty-fourth film made by Real Art Productions for Radio Pictures.

Music Hall was the second of the four films John Baxter directed for Julius Hagen.

Trade Show advertisement for *Music Hall*: GEORGE CARNEY, Mark Daly, G. H. ELLIOTT, Eve Chapman, Macari's Dutch Serenaders, Jimmie Bryant, Chester's Dogs, Gershom Parkington Quintette, Raymond Newall, Harvard Kendrick & Mortimer, Debroy Somers Band. Produced by Julius Hagen. Directed by John Baxter. Tagline: "The Romance of Variety".

London Trade Show: Tuesday, 26 June 1934 at the Prince Edward Theatre.

British Registration Details:
Quota Registration No.: Br. 10335.
Registration Date: 28 June 1934.
Registered Length: 6,715 feet.
The registered length was altered to 6,568 feet in late-July 1934, thus reducing the running time by one and two-thirds minutes.
Registered by: Radio Pictures, Ltd.
Maker's name: Real Art Productions, Ltd.
British Board of Film Censor's Certificate: "U".

Music Hall was reviewed in the *Kinematograph Weekly*, 28 June 1934, page 21:

RCA Photophone, 75 minutes – later reduced to 73 minutes, "U" certificate.

"Remarks: Slight story introducing series of popular "turns" in straightforward manner.

"Box Office Angle: Popular draw on attraction of well-varied music-hall turns.

"Slight story of a music-hall which has fallen on evil days and is brought back to success forms the introduction of a well-varied music-hall turns presented in a straightforward manner. The names of the artistes carry weight and should prove a draw in themselves.

"Story: The proprietor, since retired, of a provincial music-hall, learning that it has fallen on evil days, is persuaded to take charge again, and by his extensive knowledge of showmanship sets it off on its feet again.

"Acting: George Carney is good as the stage manager, and is supported by sound character sketches from Mark Daly, Ben Field and others. The "turns" include the Sherman Fisher Girls, G. H. Elliott, Macari's Dutch Serenaders, Jimmie Bryant, Eve Chapman, Chester's Dogs, Gershom Parkington Quintette, Raymond Newall, Harvard Kendrick and Mortimer, and Debroy Somers' Band. The last-mentioned put over an exceedingly good act.

"Production: The opening, which shows the stage manager and hands depressed at the failure of the hall, is convincing in atmosphere, but it is very drawn out and over-dialogued. Characterisations are realistic, but the material with which the artistes have to work is distinctly thin. The music-hall proper is staged in a straightforward and, of course, intentionally theatrical manner.

"Settings and Photography: Front and back-stage settings, competently photographed.

"Points of Appeal: The strong programme of music-hall turns should prove a popular draw.

Music Hall went out on General Release on Monday, 3 December 1934.

14. *Lord Edgware Dies (1934)*

Crime whodunit based on a story by Agatha Christie. Belgian detective Hercule Poirot (Austin Trevor) sets out to prove that the attractive American actress wife (Jane Carr) of old Lord Edgware (C. V. France) is innocent of his murder. In the course of his investigation, two other murders are committed and a very ingenious plot is unfolded, which finally results in the arrest of the criminal.

Lord Edgware Dies was the twenty-fifth film made by Real Art Productions for Radio Pictures, Ltd.

Lord Edgware Dies was the third film Henry Edwards directed for his partnership with Julius Hagen and Leslie Hiscott.

Lord Edgware Dies was the eighth film appearance by Austin Trevor for Julius Hagen, and his third and final appearance as 'Hercule Poirot' for this producer; he previously played the detective in *Alibi* and *Black Coffee* for him at Twickenham Film Studios", both released in 1931. (See both entries above).

London Trade Show: Wednesday, 1 August 1934 at the Prince Edward Theatre.

British Registration Details:
Quota Registration No.: Br. 10469.
Registration Date: 2 August 1934.
Registered Length: 7,344 feet.
Registered by: Radio Pictures, Ltd.
Maker's name: Real Art Productions, Ltd.
British Board of Film Censor's Certificate: "A".

Lord Edgware Dies was reviewed in the *Kinematograph Weekly*, 9 August 1934, page 22:

RCA Photophone, 82 minutes, "A" certificate.

"Remarks: Conventional crime drama adapted from a story by Agatha Christie. Development slow and unimaginative, but characterisation sound.

"Box Office Angle: Fair average programme booking. Safe for children.

"Crime drama, adapted from a novel by Agatha Christie, which is ingeniously constructed, but loses a good deal of suspense by being allowed to run to length. Although the acting is competent, tedium is not avoided; too much verbiage and the lateness of the ending rob it of real surprise. Fair average programme picture for the masses.

"Story: Lord Edgware is found murdered, and his American wife, who wishes to divorce him, is suspected. The famous French detective, Hercule

Poirot, takes charge of the case, and soon discovers that Lady Edgware has a watertight alibi. He then turns his attention to other suspects, and two more murders follow in rapid succession. Undaunted, Poirot continues, and his chain of clues eventually lead back to Lord Edgware, whom he proves to be a monomaniac, the author of all three murders.

"Acting: Austin Trevor is convincing as the French sleuth, Poirot; Richard Cooper makes a humorous foil as his asinine "Dr. Watson"; Jane Carr is an attractive and disarming Lady Edgware; and John Turnbull, Michael Shepley and Leslie Perrins earn commendation in support.

"Production: This picture is not just a screen adaptation pf Agatha Christie's novel; it is a literal translation, and it is here where its weakness lies. Had the producer substituted wherever possible action for dialogue, the picture would have been a real hair-raiser; as it is it is just another conventional mystery play.

"Settings and Photography: The interior settings promote adequate atmosphere, while lighting and photography are good.

"Points of Appeal: Popularity of crime dramas, good cast, occasional thrills, pleasant humorous relief, and attractive title.

Lord Edgware Dies was reviewed in the *Monthly Film Bulletin*, August 1934, page 58:

"Lord Edgware Dies. (Great Britain). Censors' Certificate: "A." Distributors: Radio. Production: Julius Hagen. Direction: Henry Edwards. Stars: Austin Trevor and Jane Carr. 82 mins. Based on a story by Agatha Christie of the famous French detective, Hercule Poirot (*Austin Trevor*), and his unravelling of the mystery of the murder of Lord Edgware, the elderly husband of an attractive American actress. In the course of the investigation two other murder are committed mad a very ingenious plot is unfolded resulting in the arrest of the criminal. Quite good entertainment and excellent acting throughout in both principal and minor characters. Suitability: A, B, C. Reviewer: K.L.V.H."

Lord Edgware Dies went out on General Release on Monday, 4 February 1935.

15. *Bella Donna (1934)*

Romantic triangle drama. Widow Mona Chepstow (Mary Ellis), a lady of allure and questionable background, marries an engineer, Nigel Armine (John Stuart), and goes with him to Egypt. There, she becomes infatuated with a suave and fascinating Egyptian, Mahmoud Baroudi (Conrad Veidt), and has an affair with him. Seeking to hasten her widowhood, she administers small doses of poison to her unsuspecting husband. But her husband's friend, Dr. Isaacson (Cedric Hardwicke), discovers the plot and exposes the lady to her husband. Then Baroudi expresses his contempt for her failure when the guilty Mrs. Armine runs to him; he rejects her, turning her away. Creeping back to her husband, she finds his door closed.

Bella Donna was considered a lost film until a print

was recently found at the Czech film archive, with Czech
subtitles; it is now held by the British Film Institute.

Bella Donna was the second Julius Hagen
production made for the British distributor, Gaumont-
British Picture Corporation.

Bella Donna was the only film Robert Milton
directed for Julius Hagen, of the three British pictures he
made in the 1930s. The other two were *Strange
Evidence* (trade shown January 1935) with Carol
Goodner, Leslie Banks, Diana Napier and Frank Vosper,
produced by Alexander Korda for London Film
Productions, released by Paramount; and *Luck of a
Sailor* (trade shown May 1934) with David Manners,
Camilla Horn, Greta Nissen and Clifford Mollison,
produced by Walter Mycroft for B.I.P.

Bella Donna was the second of the two film
appearances Conrad Veidt made for Julius Hagen.

London Trade Show: Tuesday, 31 July 1934 at the
Prince Edward Theatre.

British Registration Details:
Quota Registration No.: Br. 10475.
Registration Date: 2 August 1934.
Registered Length: 8,243 feet.
Registered by: Gaumont-British Distributors, Ltd.
Maker's name: Twickenham Film Studios, Ltd.
British Board of Film Censor's Certificate: "A".

Kinematograph Weekly: Trade Show Advertisement:
"Conrad Veidt, Mary Ellis and Cedric Hardwicke in
"*Bella Donna*." From the book by Robert Hichens and
the play by James Bernard Fagan. A Twickenham Film

John V. Watson

Studios Production. Directed by Robert Milton. Produced by Julius Hagen."

Bella Donna was reviewed in the *Kinematograph Weekly*, 9 August 1934, page 22:

RCA Photophone, 91 minutes, "A" certificate.

"Remarks: Sex drama freely adapted from the successful pre-war play. Story arresting, but development rather leisurely. Characterisation very good, and staging spectacular.

"Box Office Angle: Very good general booking with box-office stars and title. Not for children.

"Sex drama, freely adapted from the pre-war (pre-World War One) play by Robert Hichens. The story is not too direct in its development, but the salient points in its drama nevertheless register with telling effect and colourful atmosphere is promoted. Mary Ellis contributes a vital and convincing performance in the name part, and receives strong support from Cedric Hardwicke and Conrad Veidt, two fine actors, whose methods establish interesting contrast, while the production is presented on a spectacular scale. The appeal of the highly dramatic entertainment is definitely directed to the masses, and this concession, coupled with its undoubted box-office angles represented by the attractive title and cast, makes it a general booking proposition of wide potentiality.

"Story: Mona Chepstow, an unscrupulous Society woman known as *Bella Donna*, so captivates Nigel

Armine, a young engineer, that he marries her against the guarded advice of his friends, and one in particular, Dr. Isaacson, a Harley Street specialist. He takes his bride to Egypt, and there she comes under the spell of Mahmoud Baroudi, a wealthy Egyptian. When she learns that twins born to Nigel's sister-in-law will deprive them of wealth and a title she is willing to give herself completely to Mahmoud Baroudi, but he refuses to invite a scandal. Instead he persuades her slowly to poison Nigel. Just as soon as she is about to complete the evil work, Isaacson arrives on the scene and thwarts her. She then tells Nigel the truth, and goes to Mahmoud Baroudi, but he turns her away when he learns that she has failed him, and so she finds herself completely ostracised.

"Acting: Mary Ellis finds a few of the emotional situations a trifle beyond her range, but apart from this she gives an interesting study as Mona Chepstow, and cleverly suggests the type. John Stuart is adequate as the unhappy Nigel, Sir Cedric Hardwicke cultivates the bedside manner and subtly mirrors shrewdness as the understanding Isaacson, and Conrad Veidt is vital as the Eastern fatalist, Mahmoud Baroudi.

"Production: This psychological drama of an unscrupulous woman who finds an evil outlet for her sex is rather hindered in its development by a pronounced tendency on the part of the director to concentrate on detail. The building up of the plot plays second fiddle to the establishment of atmosphere, and this tends to water down its dramatic consistency. In spite of this fault, however, the players succeed in finding individual freedom, and it is their handling of the story rather than that of the producer that makes its purpose clear and its arresting situations register. The sex interest, approached with restraint, is a popular one, and herein lies the film's appeal and strength.

"Settings and Photography: The London interiors have a dignity compatible with the story, while the Eastern sequences have colour and pronounced glamour. Good atmosphere aids the story considerably. Lighting and photography are very good.

"Points of Appeal: Good story, strong cast, box-office title, sex interest, intelligently planned dramatic situations, mass appeal, and good staging.

Bella Donna was reviewed in the *Monthly Film Bulletin*, August 1934, page 56:

"*Bella Donna*. (Great Britain). Censors' Certificate "A". Distributors: G.-B. Distributors. Direction: Robert Milton. Production: Twickenham Film Studios. Adapted from Robert Hichen's story. Stars: Mary Ellis, Cedric Hardwicke, Conrad Veidt, and John Stuart. 91 minutes. Infatuation, in an Egyptian setting. From the technical point of view, including the acting, it achieves a level of efficiency which gives the film its chief attraction. Cedric Hardwicke, as the solidly reliable friend who saves the hero, stands out from the rest of

the cast with a dominating reality, although his
part is not a major one. Conrad Veidt deserves
something better than his part in this film as a
wealthy, degenerate Egyptian. Only a certain
seriousness in the direction and acting lift this film
out of the common run. Suitability A. Reviewer:
E.H.L."

Bella Donna went out on British General Release on
Monday, 21 January 1935.

16. Are You a Mason? (1934)

Farce, adapted from a stage success. Adapted from
the German play by Leo Dietrichstein (1901), translated
by Emmanuel Lederer.

For many years, Amos Bloodgood (Robertson Hare)
tells his wife (Bertha Belmore) that, as a Mason, he must
regularly attend meetings. But he really uses these
'meetings' as an excuse to escape from his wife once a
week in order to go out on the town (he actually knows
nothing of the fraternal order). However his scheme is
nearly wrecked when his daughter (Gwyneth Lloyd) and
son-in-law Frank (Sonnie Hale) arrive for a visit. Believing
that Frank is a real Mason, Amos tries to impress him with
everything he knows about the order, but Frank is also a
fake Mason; he uses this as a ploy to impress his mother-
in-law to get a loan from her, to clear his gambling debts.
Frantic complications ensue, with Frank having his friend,
Lulu (Joyce Kirby) pose as his father-in-law's illegitimate
daughter.

Are You A Mason? was the fourth of the ten films
made by Twickenham Film Studios, Ltd. for Universal

383

Pictures, Ltd., the British renting subsidiary of the Hollywood studio. Once again, the 84-minute running time suggests that *Are You A Mason?* was designed as a co-feature on a "double-bill", or even as a "top-of-the-bill" attraction at some cinemas.

Are You a Mason? was the fourth film Henry Edwards directed for the Hagen/Edwards partnership.

Sonnie Hale was primarily a musical and revue theatre star. He appeared in fourteen British films from 1932 to 1939, one of which, *Are You a Mason?*, was to be his only film appearance for Julius Hagen.

London Trade Show: Tuesday, 14 August 1934 at the Prince Edward Theatre.

British Registration Details:
Quota Registration No.: Br. 10515.
Registration Date: 15 August 1934.
Registered Length: 7,690 feet.
Registered by: Universal Pictures, Ltd.
Maker's name: Twickenham Film Studios, Ltd.
British Board of Film Censor's Certificate: "U".

Are You a Mason? was reviewed in the *Kinematograph Weekly*, 16 August 1934, page 26:
RCA Photophone, 83 minutes, "U" certificate.

"<u>Remarks</u>: Hilarious farce exploiting sure popular laugh situations with resourceful comedy by stellar cast.

"<u>Box Office Angle</u>: Safe comedy bet on title which has good exploitation angles as well as strong entertainment values of its type. Nothing to harm juveniles.

"Hilarious adaptation of the famous stage farce which finds rich comedy in the amusing complications arising from husbands who masquerade as Masons in order to deceive wives. Resourceful fooling of the cast achieves the maximum out of typical farce situations and help disguise a somewhat wordy script. Safe comedy booking with stellar and title credentials.

"Story: Frank Perry, a young married man, poses as having joined the Freemasonry order to please his wife and formidable mother-in-law, who are obsessed with the idea of masonry for married men. The latter's husband, Amos Bloodgood, who has been under her thumb for the duration of their married life owing to a youthful indiscretion with a lady named Angeline, has by regular attendance at Lodge meetings every Saturday night for 20 years, risen to high rank in the craft (according to his story). The meeting of the bogus brother masons when the Bloodgoods go to stay with their daughter causes complications for both of them, as neither knows that the other is masquerading. The younger man breaks down first and confesses to his father-in-law who, however, takes up a severe and outraged attitude about the deception. The situation is made even more difficult when Ernest Morrison, a genuine mason, and suitor for the hand of Frank's sister-in-law, arrives. In the meanwhile, Perry, by way of revenge, persuades a friend to masquerade as Fareham, the supposed offspring of Bloodgood's association with Angeline. Still further complications, including the real, long-missing

Angeline, turn up before it is all worked out to a happy conclusion.

"<u>Acting</u>: Sonnie Hale's spirited and resourceful comedy is well suited to the rôle of Frank, and he missies few chances. Robertson Hare has seldom been so well served with opportunities, and his Bloodgood is in the best Robertson Hare vein of hen-pecked martyrdom. In the more or less "straight" rôle of the dragon-like mother-in-law, Bertha Belmore turns in a polished and convincing performance that lends point to the comedy situations. No great strain is imposed on the histrionic abilities of Gwyneth Lloyd, as Frank's wife, and Joyce Kirby, as her sister, but they provide adequate feminine decoration and interest.

"<u>Production</u>: The old Shaftesbury farce stands the test of time well enough, and has translated admirably into the talkie medium. Henry Edwards' direction is smooth and straightforward, and if at times it does not escape from the staginess of its inspiration, the film moves at a fair pace throughout.

"<u>Settings and Photography</u>: Action is confined almost exclusively to the house and garden of the hero, which are adequately and convincingly represented.

"<u>Points of Appeal</u>: Valuable title and stage record, first-rate portrayals and stellar comedy cast, and sure-fire farce story.

Are You A Mason? went out on General Release on

Monday, 25 February 1935.

17. Anything Might Happen (1934)

Crime. Framed for a murder, reformed thief, Nicholson (John Garrick) suspects that his double, a crook named Raybourn (John Garrick) is the culprit, but the killer turns out to be the dead man's lawyer.

Anything Might Happen was the twenty-sixth film made by Real Art Productions for Radio Pictures, probably another 'Quota Quickie'.

Anything Might Happen was the eleventh and final film George A. Cooper directed for Julius Hagen.

Anything Might Happen was the third film appearance John Garrick made for Julius Hagen.

London Trade Show: Wednesday, 12 September 1934 at the Cambridge Theatre.

British Registration Details:
Quota Registration No.: Br. 10611.
Registration Date: 13 September 1934.
Registered Length: 5,949 feet.
Registered by: Radio Pictures, Ltd.
Maker's name: Real Art Productions, Ltd.
British Board of Film Censor's Certificate: "A".

Kinematograph Weekly: Trade Show Advertisement: "*Anything Might Happen*. John Garrick and Judy Kelly. Directed by George Cooper. Produced by Julius Hagen." Tagline: "A man who was hired to assassinate himself!"

Anything Might Happen was reviewed in the

John V. Watson

Kinematograph Weekly, 20 September 1934, page 27:

RCA Photophone, 66 minutes, "A" certificate.

"<u>Remarks</u>: Involved crime drama. Dialogue hinders development.

"<u>Box Office Angle</u>: Moderate entertainment for the masses. Nothing to offend juveniles.

"This crime story is never lost for a word; it is talk, talk, talk from beginning to end. The plot, which hinges on the hackneyed mistaken identity theme, is very complicated, and its development is rendered all the more difficult to follow by reason of the fact that the star mainly plays many rôles. John Garrick's performance suggests a histrionic one-man band. A lukewarm thriller this, just passable supporting entertainment for the industrial masses.

"<u>Story</u>: Stephen Nicholson, a reformed crook, is unofficially employed by the police to help them solve a baffling murder mystery. Kit Dundas, secretary to Kenneth Waring, a solicitor, thinks that Nicholson is the murderer, having mistaken him for his double, Raybourn, another crook whom she had seen leave the scene of the crime, but he allays her suspicions. Then follows a ding-dong battle of wits between Nicholson and Raybourn, ending with the former spectacularly unmasking the head of the gang, who is none other than Waring.

"<u>Acting</u>: John Garrick plays with fair conviction the parts of Nicholson and Raybourn, filling in his spare time by masquerading as the man employed to bring about his own murder. Judy Kelly talks her way out of trouble with a certain amount of charm as Kit, and Martin Walker and Aubrey Mather adequately complete the verbal chorus.

"Production: The story of this picture is not acted, it is just told, only pausing to introduce a few scraps of the popular thick-ear variety. The mistaken identity angle is not clearly defined, a directorial defect which robs many of the situations of essential punch.

"Settings and Photography: The settings are restricted to a few meagre interiors, and photography is static.

"Points of Appeal: Popularity of crime plays, convenient length, and quota angle.

Anything Might Happen went out on General Release on Monday, 18 March 1935.

18. Blind Justice (1934)

Crime thriller. When Peggy (Geraldine Fitzgerald) wants to break off her engagement to Dick (Frank Vosper) to marry Gilbert (Roger Livesey), he then blackmails her; he has discovered that her brother Ralph (John Mills) did not die a hero's death during the First World War, but was actually shot as a coward. However her older brother, John (John Stuart) plans to murder Dick, but fate inevitably takes a hand; by sheer accident Fluffy, the housekeeper (Eva Moore) sends the blackmailer to his death.

Blind Justice was the fifth of the ten films made by Twickenham Film Studios for Universal Pictures, the British renting subsidiary of the Hollywood studio.

Blind Justice was the fourth film Bernard Vorhaus directed for Julius Hagen.

Blind Justice was the second film appearance by the English actress, Eva Moore, for Julius Hagen. Eva Moore appeared in more than two dozen films from 1920 until 1946, many of which were made in Hollywood, including *The Old Dark House* (1932), directed by James Whale for Universal; and *Of Human Bondage* (1946), the Warner Bros. version of the W. Somerset Maugham novel, starring Paul Henreid, Eleanor Parker and Alexis Smith.

London Trade Show: Thursday, 18 October 1934 at the Prince Edward Theatre.

British Registration Details:
Quota Registration No.: Br. 10739.
Registration Date: 22 October 1934.
Registered Length: 6,602 feet.
Registered by: Universal Pictures, Ltd.
    Maker's name: Twickenham Film Studios, Ltd.
    Note: Many modern reference sources, including Denis Gifford, state 'Real Art Productions' as the production company, but the Quota Act registration details stated here make it clear that 'Twickenham Film Studios' made *Blind Justice*.
British Board of Film Censor's Certificate: "A".

Blind Justice was reviewed in the *Kinematograph Weekly*, 25 October 1934, on page 31:

RCA Photophone, 73 minutes, "A" certificate.

"Remarks: Perfect crime drama adapted from a play by Arnold Ridley. Story ingenious, but direction weak and hesitant. Clever performance by Eva Moore provides most of the entertainment.

"Box Office Angle: Sound supporting feature for most halls. Hardly suitable for juveniles.

"Adapted from a play by Arnold Ridley, this film presents yet another version of the perfect crime theme. The plot reveals invention and the ending is accompanied by surprise, but the producer's inability to stem the flood of superfluous dialogue prevents the film from completely "making the grade". It is Eva Moore, excellent in the pivotal rôle, who supplies most of the entertainment. Sound supporting feature, one adequately to fill quota requirements, nothing more.

"Story: John Summers is compelled to shoot his own brother, Ralph, for cowardice during the war, and he is blackmailed by Dick Cheriton, the man who knows his secret. When his sister, Peggy, wishes to break her engagement with Cheriton he threatens to tell John's secret to the ailing Mrs. Summers, who cherishes the belief that Ralph died a hero's death. John determines to kill Cheriton and plans the perfect crime, but Fluffy, the old family housekeeper, cheats him out of the pleasure be sending Cheriton "accidentally" to eternity.

"Acting: Eva Moore gives a clever portrayal as Fluffy; it is her flair for character drawing, born of vast stage experience, that causes the story's ingenious twists to register. Frank Vosper is

391

altogether too stagey as Cheriton, but a sound piece of acting comes from John Stuart as John. Geraldine Fitzgerald, Lucy Beaumont, Hay Petrie and Roger Livesey contribute adequate support.

"Production: The story of this film is good; its ingenuity compels concentration, but the treatment is unimaginative. The producer makes no attempt to break from the conventions of the stage; the plot is not only told mainly in dialogue, but unnecessary flashbacks still further hold up essential action. It is the clever, disarming character drawing of Eva Moore alone that reveals the story's invention and allows the ending to carry surprise. Without her the film would have been dull, with her it provides average entertainment for the not too sophisticated.

"Settings and Photography: The war flashbacks are unnecessary, but convincing, and the rural atmosphere is picturesque. Lighting and photography are satisfactory.

"Points of Appeal: Good title, soundly constructed crime story, neat ending, clever performance by Eva Moore, and quota angle.

Blind Justice went out on General Release on Monday, 4 March 1935.

19. *Open All Night (1934)*

Drama. Anton (Frank Vosper), an exiled Grand Duke, forced to flee Russia after the 1917 revolution, is night manager at a hotel. He helps many people in trouble, and eventually sacrifices his life in a gallant gesture, killing himself to save a girl from a murder charge.

Open All Night was the twenty-seventh film made by Real Art Productions for Radio Pictures, yet another 'Quota Quickie'.

Open All Night was the sixth of the eight "quota-quickies" George Pearson directed for Julius Hagen at Twickenham Studios.

Open All Night was the second of the three film appearances Frank Vosper made for Julius Hagen, and his fifth British sound picture.

London Trade Show: Monday, 22 October 1934 at the Prince Edward Theatre.

British Registration Details:
Quota Registration No.: Br. 10748.
Registration Date: 23 October 1934.
Registered Length: 5,560 feet.
Registered by: Radio Pictures, Ltd.
Maker's name: Real Art Productions, Ltd.
British Board of Film Censor's Certificate: "A".

Trade Show Advertisement in the *Kinematograph Weekly*: "*Open All Night*: Frank Vosper. Directed by George Pearson. Produced by Julius Hagen." Tagline: "Behind the scenes in a great hotel. Romance . . . . . Love! Tragedy . . . . Murder!!" [logo] "Radio Pictures".
Open All Hours was partly filmed at night.

Open All Night was reviewed in the *Kinematograph Weekly*, 25 October 1934, on page 33:

RCA Photophone, 62 minutes, "A" certificate.

John V. Watson

"Remarks: Ingenious colourful drama of London's night life, with a good story, and resourceful direction. Presentation realistic and characterisation convincing.

"Box Office Angle: Good popular entertainment. Nothing to offend juveniles.

"Ingenious, colourful drama of London's night life fashioned on similar lines to those successfully exploited in *Grand Hotel*. The many strings to the plot are spun into an intriguing dramatic design and it is presented with commendable smoothness and slickness. The entertainment is refreshingly comprehensive and its appeal is addressed to all classes. Good popular booking.

"Story: Anton, formerly a Russian Grand Duke, spends many years as night manager at Paragon House, cosmopolitan hotel, but is dismissed, because of his years, just when he anticipates promotion. Among the guests in the hotel on his last night of duty are Bill Warren, a youth waiting for the repayment of a loan from a crook so that he can take his ailing wife, Elsie, to Vienna, and Jill, fiancée of one of the waiters, compelled to entertain her dissolute boss, Hilary, because he has found her guilty of theft. The waiter sees Jill and is tempted to cause trouble, and Bill, following an altercation, kills the crook, but Anton first straightens out the love affair and then saves Bill by accepting the blame for the killing. His altruism leaves him with nothing to live for, and he takes the easiest way out – suicide.

"Acting: Frank Vosper plays Anton and invests the character with dignity. The power of his acting holds the film in firm dramatic unity. The supporting honours are equally shared by Gillian Lind, Margaret Vines, Lewis Shaw, Leslie Perrins, Colin Keith Johnston, Geraldine Fitzgerald and Michael Shepley, all of whom aid the story in the clarity of its development by the accuracy of their character drawing.

"Production: Many interests are crowded into the plot, and the hotel settings colour each rich phase of the drama effectively. The opening is a trifle slow, but once the picture begins to take shape the pace is suitably accelerated, and good entertainment accompanies the subsequent development. Although the ending strikes a tragic note, it is dignified and imparts a subtle touch of realism to the praiseworthy production.

"Settings and Photography: The hotel interiors are realistic, good atmosphere being one of the film's happiest and most noteworthy features. Lighting and photography are very good.

"Points of Appeal: Intriguing, arresting story, smart treatment, sound characterisation, excellent atmosphere, varied interests, and popular entertainment.

Open All Night went out on General Release on Monday, 8 April 1935.

20. *Kentucky Minstrels (1934)*

Musical. Now unfashionable, old-style minstrels Mott

and Bayley (Scott and Whaley) struggle to make a living, and are reduced to busking and casual labour. But they finally make a successful comeback in a modern revue.

Kentucky Minstrels was the sixth of the ten films made by Twickenham Film Studios, Ltd. for Universal Pictures, Ltd., the British renting subsidiary of the Hollywood studio. Once again, the 84-minute running time suggests that *Kentucky Minstrels* was designed as a co-feature on a "double-bill", or even as a "top-of-the-bill" attraction at some cinemas.

Kentucky Minstrels was the third of the four films John Baxter directed for Julius Hagen.

Trade Show Advertisement in the *Kinematograph Weekly*: "*Kentucky Minstrels*: Carl Laemmle presents SCOTT AND WHALEY, Nina Mae McKinney, Debroy Somers and His Band, Denier Warren, Harry Pepper's "White Coons", Leo Sheffield, 8 Black Streaks. Directed by John Baxter. Produced at Twickenham Film Studios." Tagline: "The Favourite Radio Show of Millions of British Listeners . . . Now a tremendous Musical Drama from Universal." [Logo]: "Step Out with Universal."

Note the presenter of this film, Carl Laemmle, was the head of Universal Pictures, the American parent company of the British film renting company who sponsored the making of *Kentucky Minstrels* from Julius Hagen's production company, Twickenham Film Studios, Ltd.

London Trade Show: Tuesday, 13 November 1934 at the Prince Edward Theatre.

British Registration Details:

Quota Registration No.: Br. 10872.
Registration Date: 15 November 1934.
Registered Length: 7,671 feet.
Registered by: Universal Pictures, Ltd.
Maker's name: Twickenham Film Studios, Ltd.
Note that many modern reference sources, including *Denis Gifford*, state 'Real Art Productions' as the production company, but the Quota Act registration details stated here make it clear that 'Twickenham Film Studios' actually made ***Kentucky Minstrels***.
British Board of Film Censor's Certificate: "U".

Kentucky Minstrels was reviewed in the *Kinematograph Weekly*, on 22 November 1934, page 30:

RCA Photophone, 85 minutes, "U" certificate.

"<u>Remarks</u>: Slender character comedy with music, the most entertaining features of which are the good team work of Scott and Whaley, and the effective finale. Development rather scrappy.

"<u>Box Office Angle</u>: Average light booking, mainly on obvious exploitation angles. Safe for youngsters.

"Character comedy with music, a picture which sketchily traces the evolution of popular musical entertainment during the last three decades. The story values are definitely thin, and it is left to Scott and Whaley, the popular music hall and wireless comedians, to kill time during the long interval that elapses between the opening of the picture and its spectacular musical grand finale. They do well considering the paucity of material at their command, but good as they are they had fully to atone for the film's excessive footage, and lack of action. Although not entirely devoid of popular entertainment, this department is so neglected that the film's booking angles must be principally in its title, stars, and minor box-office embellishments, represented by Nina Mae McKinney, who figures in one song number, and Debroy Somers and his Band.

"Story: Mott and Bayley, two minstrels, refuse to belief that the minstrel show is dead, and reject an offer to play on the music-hall stage. Their stubbornness leads to poverty; as time goes on they are forced to busk on the sands and outside public houses, but in health and sickness, good times and bad, their friendship stands firm, and their faith in the revival of the old minstrel show never deserts them. Just as things look hopeless, Danny Goodman, a theatrical impresario, decides to incorporate a minstrel show in his big new musical production, and Mott and Bayley's big chance to make a grand comeback at last comes their way.

"Production: This part of the microfiche copy was unreadable.

"Settings and Photography: The opening minstrel show is effective, but the journey through the years is only casually suggested by such economic situations as those represented by a seaside concert party and street singing. The final scenes, however, are staged on quite an extravagant scale, and carry sufficient colour and (unreadable) to help conceal the early moments of approaching boredom. Lighting and photography are good.

"Points of Appeal: Good title, attractive cast, novel theme, simple sentiment, conventional humour, and obvious exploitation angles.

Kentucky Minstrels went out on General Release on Monday, 27 May 1935.

21. Flood Tide (1934)

Romance, filmed-on-location on the Thames Estuary. After doubts all round, Ted, a lock-keeper's officer son (Leslie Hatton) decides he does want to marry the bargee's daughter, Betty (Janice Adair). And the bargee (George Carney) himself goes on to win the cup at the Bargees' Regatta.

Flood Tide was the twenty-eighth film made by Real Art Productions for Radio Pictures, Ltd.; another 'Quota Quickie' supplied to that renter.

Flood Tide was the last of the four films John Baxter directed for Julius Hagen.

Flood Tide was the fourth film appearance by George Carney for Julius Hagen.

London Trade Show: Tuesday, 27 November 1934 at the Prince Edward Theatre.

British Registration Details:
Quota Registration No.: Br. 10914.
Registration Date: 28 November 1934.
Registered Length: 5,768 feet.
Registered by: Radio Pictures, Ltd.

John V. Watson

Maker's name: Real Art Productions, Ltd.
British Board of Film Censor's Certificate: "U".

Trade Show Advertisement in the *Kinematograph Weekly*: "*Flood Tide*: George Carney, Peggy Novak, Leslie Hatton, Janice Adair (misspelt "Adaire"). Directed by John Baxter. Produced by Julius Hagen." Tagline: A vivid story of Life with FATHER THAMES as chief character". [logo] "Radio Pictures."

Flood Tide was reviewed in the *Kinematograph Weekly*, on 29 November 1934, page 26:

RCA Photophone, 64 minutes, "U" certificate.

"Remarks: Unpretentious comedy drama, with an amusing plot. Characterisation adequate, staging satisfactory and action smooth.

"Box Office Angle: Useful supporting feature, a handy quota film for most halls. Safe for children.

"The "saga" of the River Thames is produced on unpretentious lines, but the fact that it succeeds in putting a romantic phase of British life on the screen gives it obvious exploitation values while its pleasing sentiment, attractive characterisations and good quotas of action and river spectacle should make it an attractive proposition on its own merit for popular audiences.

"Story: Ben Salter, a real son of the river, and his wife, about to retire after thirty years as a lock-keeper, are anxious that their son, Ted, should marry Betty, the daughter of their old friend, Bill Buckett, captain of a barge. Ted, who is in the Navy, is temporarily infatuated with a worthless

400

barmaid in a waterside saloon. Buckett secures a public-house for the retiring couple, who are compensated by the fact that in their new occupation they will still be within sight of their beloved river.

In the meanwhile the other girl leaves to marry a wealthier suitor. Ted goes to remonstrate with her and returns, disillusioned at last, but finds that he has missed his ship. Buckett comes to the rescue with his trusty barge, which manages to win the race against time and get him aboard. The happy ending is completed when Buckett achieves his life's ambition by winning the cup at the Bargee's Regatta.

"<u>Acting</u>: George Carney reveals a sure sense of character and succeeds in winning sympathy in the rôle of Captain Buckett. Minnie Rayner and Wilson Colman (misspelt Coleman) give polished performances as the Salters, and the love interest is capably handled by Janice Adair and Leslie Hatton. Mark Daly and Peggy Novak contribute valuable support.

"<u>Production</u>: The plot is obviously on the slender side, and the background and characterisation must be relied on to carry the main interest. After a somewhat traveloguey opening, the atmosphere is established surely, and the film moves smoothly to the climax, helped along by amusing by-play on robust lines and such sentiment and thrills as are provided by the life of the simple river folk.

"<u>Settings and Photography</u>: There are some

impressive shots of the Thames, while a barge trip enables the producers to include a sort of Cook's Tour of the river. Interior sets are realistic enough to help the atmosphere, and the photography and lighting are excellent.

"Points of Appeal: Exploitation possibilities, simple but attractive story, popular humour and sentiment.

Flood Tide went out on General Release on Monday, 17 June 1935; Monday, 10 June 1935 was originally planned as the date of the general release.

1934: The British Film Industry: Trends and Other Events throughout the Year — in England, the United States, Germany and France:

Paramount (in Hollywood) has ambitious plans for **Ida Lupino**, even though she did not secure the title rôle in *Alice in Wonderland*. Ida Lupino and Buster Crabbe made quite an impression in *The Search for Beauty*; Paramount are now reteaming them in *Lovers in Quarantine*, which was made as a silent film some years ago with Bebe Daniels,

(*K. W.*, 4 January 1934, page 12).

"The **Weston Hall Studios** have been taken over by the Interworld Films, Ltd., of 80-82 Wardour Street, London, W.1. We understand that important improvements are contemplated,

'The Czar of Twickenham'. The History of Julius Hagen and the Film Empire he created at Twickenham Film Studios, from 1927 to 1938.

including the construction of a new studio".

(*K. W.*, 4 January 1934, page 16B).

George Formby is in a Butcher's Film – *Boots! Boots!*

(*K. W.*, 18 January 1934, page 6).

A record British contract has been fixed: £100,000 for eighteen films over a period of the next three years to **Jack Hulbert and Cicely Courtneidge**.

(*K. W.*, 25 January 1934, pages 29 and 31, P. L. Mannock).

Charles Laughton is to star as *The Scarlet Pimpernel* announced by London Films.

(As events transpired, Leslie Howard starred as 'Sir Percy Blakeney' instead of Laughton; why Charles Laughton did not appear in this film has not been determined.)

(*K. W.*, 22 February 1934, page 3).

Charles Laughton has been announced by M-G-M to appear as 'Louis XVI' in *Marie Antoinette* with Norma Shearer.

(However, for various reasons, the production was delayed a number of times, and after Irving Thalberg's death in mid-September 1936, it appeared that the film might be shelved. By the time the picture was again back on M-G-M's production schedule in 1937, Charles Laughton was no longer available for the role of 'Louis XVI' and finally English actor Robert Morley had been awarded the part.)

(*K. W.*, 22 February 1934, page 3).

Eros Productions, Ltd. was registered on 12 February 1934 as theatre and kinema managers.

(Eros later went on to become successful independent British film distributors until the late 1950s.)

(*K. W.*, 22 February 1934, page 22.)

Walter J. Hutchinson, managing director of Fox Films, has discovered a new director, **Desmond Hurst**, an adventurous young Irishman who has been a soldier, lumberman, portrait painter, drifting thus by easy stages in the position of art director in Hollywood – with Fox and Warner – and eventually, before he returned to this country, personal assistant to **John Ford**.

Brian Desmond Hurst went on to direct several successful and acclaimed British films, such as the grim thriller, *On the Night of the Fire* (1939), and by the far best film adaptation of the Dickens' classic, *Scrooge* (1951).

(*K. W.*, 1 March 1934, page 5.)

1,200 kinemas are in Poverty Row. Revelations in a K.R.S. report which states that box office takings average between £1 and £8 a day!
(The K.R.S. was the **Kinematograph Renters' Society**, an industry trade body which represented British film distributors.)

(*K. W.*, 12 April 1934, page 17).

Warner's acquire Teddington Studios from Teddington Studios, Ltd., of which Henry Edwards and E. G. Norman are managing directors. A very high price was paid for the premises, which were built by Henry Edwards four years ago, and almost immediately let on lease to Warner-First National Productions.

(*K. W.*, 19 April 1934, page 5).

'The Czar of Twickenham'. The History of Julius Hagen and the Film Empire he created at Twickenham Film Studios, from 1927 to 1938.

Jane Baxter, the British 24-year-old ingénue, has just signed a contract with **Sam Goldwyn** to appear in United Artists' productions.

(*K. W.*, 10 May 1934, page 39, P. L. Mannock).

Walter Wanger is leaving Metro with the idea of starting an independent production unit.

(*K. W.*, 24 May 1934, page 4).

Max Miller signs a contract with Gaumont-British.

(*K. W.*, 14 June 1934, page 52).

Mancunian Film Corporation, Ltd., is registered on 16 June 1934.

(Note that Mancunian was founded by John E. Blakeley. The company produced films in London on extremely low budgets. Blakeley's first studio consisted of a single soundstage in a loft space above a taxi garage. Whenever the filmmakers wanted to shoot a scene, they would first have to signal the mechanics below to stop working, so the noise from below wouldn't register on the soundtracks. Blakeley's first production was *Boots! Boots!* (1934), starring the young variety entertainer **George Formby**. Production values were so low that some scenes were filmed in semi-darkness, to hide the lack of set decorations. Despite these technical flaws, Blakeley's first film was a huge success in the local provinces, recouping Blakeley's investment several times over and launching George Formby as Britain's leading screen comedian.)

(*K. W.*, 21 June 1934, page 19).

South African-born, British actor, **Ian Hunter**, has signed a big contract with Warner Bros. in Hollywood.

John V. Watson

(*K. W.*, 28 June 1934, page 24).

Francis L. Sullivan signs a long-term contract with Universal Pictures.
(*K. W.*, 5 July 1934, page 33, P. L. Mannock).

London Film's capital has been increased by an additional £50,000.
(*K. W.*, 26 July 1934, page 8).

Gaumont-British to distribute its own films in America.
(*K. W.*, 2 August 1934, page 5).

L.F.P. Trust, Ltd is to handle the financial side of **London Film Productions**, Ltd.
(*K. W.*, 16 August 1934).

£5 million is sent abroad for **film hire**. Kinemas have £40,200,000 takings. Simon Rowson's British Association paper.
(*K. W.*, 13 September 1934, page 1).

Leslie Fuller's big contract – Leslie Fuller Pictures, Ltd. – for Gaumont-British distribution.
(Leslie Fuller (1888 —1948) was a British comedian. By the 1930s he had become well known as 'The rubber-faced comedian' and spent his summer seasons in Margate. In the winter he and his Margate 'Ped'lers' toured the Oswald Stoll theatre circuit, including The Coliseum and The Alhambra in London. Between 1930 and 1945, Fuller made 26 British films.)
(*K. W.*, 27 September 1934, page 1).

The **Odeon cinema circuit** is now a hundred strong.
(*K. W.*, 25 October 1934, page 9).

Union Cinemas' £32,000 profit to pay 10% dividend. (Union was soon to become part of Associated British Cinemas.)
(*K. W.*, 25 October 1934, page 25).

Errol Flynn joins Teddington with a seven years' contract.

'The Czar of Twickenham'. The History of Julius Hagen and the Film Empire he created at Twickenham Film Studios, from 1927 to 1938.

Flynn joins Laura La Plante, Ian Hunter, Esmond Knight, Claude Hulbert, and Barry Clifton, the Teddington roster of long-contract players.
(*K. W.*, 25 October 1934, page 42).

Charles Laughton withdraws from *David Copperfield* in which he was to have played Micawber. He is replaced by **W. C. Fields**.
(*K. W.*, 1 November 1934, page 8).

Douglas Fairbanks cancels his contract with **London Films**, Ltd.
(*K. W.*, 8 November 1934, page 3).

Paramount Studios at Saint-Maurice. The **Paris** facilities for independent producers.
(*K. W.*, 8 November 1934, page 49).

Germany's big barrier because a £1,000 tax upon imported films.
(Note that the Nazi's had been in power since early 1933.)
(*K. W.*, 15 November 1934, page 3).

Hammer Productions, Ltd., was registered on 9 November 1934.
(*K. W.*, 15 November 1934, page 14).

Ian Hunter, the Warner Bros.-First National contract star, leaves for Burbank on 1 December 1934, under the long-term contract signed between the Teddington parent company and the artiste some months ago, "and exclusively reported to me."
(*K. W.*, 15 November 1934, page 35, P. L. Mannock).

4,897 kinemas in British Isles as at 1 October 1934 according to **Western Electric**'s latest statistics are wired for sound. There are still 6 silent houses. Western Electric have now wired 1,750 theatres.
(*K. W.*, 15 November 1934, page 35, P. L. Mannock).

John V. Watson

"**Miss Mary Field** has begun to build up a new series of
nature films for **G-B Instructional**."
(*K. W.*, 22 November 1934).

Gainsborough Pictures (1928) Ltd. to pay 9% dividend on
a trading profit of £26,289.
(*K. W.*, 6 December 1934, page 18).

The **quota** is abolished in **France**.
(*K. W.*, 20 December 1934, page 22).

1934: The Seventh Year of the 'Quota' Act:

214 British films were first shown during the year 1934.

This number is arrived at by using the data contained in *The British Film Catalogue: 1895-1970* by Denis Gifford, as follows:

09682: Closing Gifford Catalogue Number for 1934.

09468: Opening Gifford Catalogue Number for 1934.

214: Total. An increase of 9 films over the previous year's total of 205.

Some of these films were short subjects; the actual number of these shorts has not been determined.

5. JULIUS HAGEN IN 1935:

1935: British production consolidates with over 200 films made; a record achievement of 214:

The year 1935 saw the major British film production boom continuing its strong momentum with total production now reaching over 200 films per year for the second year in a row. British film producers achieved a record of 214 films made, an increase of 9 films over the previous year.

1935: Rate of film production remains steady at Twickenham, and Julius Hagen becomes his own film distributor:

Julius Hagen at Twickenham Film Studios slightly increased his output of films he made in 1934 - from the twenty pictures he made in 1933 to the twenty one titles he produced in 1934. Many of these films made at Twickenham were filmed at night.

And, from September 1934, Julian Hagen increased his film-making advantage by doubling his production capacity at Twickenham with the opening of a second floor (sound stage) at the studios.

However, the number of films Hagen made at Twickenham during 1935 — twenty-one — remained exactly the same as were produced during the previous year. But there was a significant reason for this, which came in two parts, interlinked, as follows:

- Hagen stopped making films for other companies sometime before the middle of the year. His last film-making assignment for the American-owned British renter Radio Pictures was **Bargain Basement** after making no less than 35 films for that renter since 1932, and then there were the two further - and final - commissions from Gaumont-British Distributors, Ltd.: **Squibs** and **Vintage Wine**. The total of the films made for clients in 1935 was fifteen.

- Hagen was to start his own distribution company, Twickenham Film Distributors, Ltd., which went into operation in June 1935. The company then released five of Hagen's pictures, namely **Scrooge**, **The Private Secretary**, **The Last Journey**, **A Fire has been Arranged** and **She Shall Have Music**. All five films took much longer to make than those films did make previously for renter clients; those films were usually 'Quota Quickies' as indeed we have already discussed and analysed above.

We shall look at the pros and cons of starting one's own film distribution later, analysing then the economics and the overall strategy that Julius Hagen would have had to consider and grasp in great detail.

January 1935:

Kinematograph Weekly reported throughout the month:

TWICKENHAM STUDIOS PRODUCTION RECORD FOR 1934:

25 films came from Twickenham in 1934:
- 4 for G-B

'The Czar of Twickenham'. The History of Julius Hagen and the Film Empire he created at Twickenham Film Studios, from 1927 to 1938.

- 7 for Universal
- 12 for Radio
- 2 for A. P. & D.
  (*K. W.*, 10 January 1935).

TWICKENHAM STUDIOS STAFF DANCE:

Twickenham Studios staff dance is fixed for Friday, 25 January 1935, at York House, Twickenham. Dancing 9 till 2.
(*K. W.*, 10 January 1935).

The huge staff dance and party held at Cambridge House, hard by Richmond Bridge, was attended by 900 people.

(*K. W.*, 31 January 1935).

FILM PRODUCTION AT TWICKENHAM STUDIOS DURING JANUARY:

The Lad: shooting commenced on Thursday (3 January 1935). The Edgar Wallace story has been adapted for the screen by Gerald Fairlie, Fred Merrick is assistant director; Sydney Blythe cameraman; and Baynham Honri in charge of sound.

Squibs is now completed. Betty Balfour has sailed with her husband, Jimmy Campbell, on a trip to South America.

Death on the Set went on the floor on Monday (7 January 1935). The scenario is by Michael Barringer from the popular mystery novel by Victor McClure.

(*K. W.*, 10 January 1935, P. L. Mannock, pages 133 and 143).

Street Song – Bernard Vorhaus – John Garrick, Rene Ray – Ernest Palmer – third week

411

The Lad – Henry Edwards – Gordon Harker, Betty Stockfeld – Sydney Blythe – first week

Death on the Set – Leslie Hiscott – Henry Kendall, Gillian Lind – first week

> (*K. W.*, 10 January 1935, the *Pulse of the Studios* column).

Twickenham to make thirty films this year.

£200,000 worth of contracts and the subjects selected cover every type of entertainment

Players under contract at Twickenham for several pictures are Betty Balfour, Stanley Holloway, John Garrick, Davina Craig, Michael Shepley, Jane Carr, and, should his American contracts permit, Ian Hunter.

Seymour Hicks and Clare Luce have also been signed for further pictures.

> (*K. W.*, 10 January 1935, page 137).

The Lad – in its third week – this week, Henry Edwards is shooting a prison yard.

Death on the Set – second week – William Luff had begun the camera work but was taken seriously ill; Ernest Palmer has taken over.

Street Song – a realistic Soho street designed by James Carter – among the numbers written by W. L. Trytel, Fred Grundland and Tommy Connor is *Little Noah's Ark*, the music of which is played as an accompaniment to the tricks of the various animals in the pet shop round which much of the action of the picture centres.

(*K. W.*, 17 January 1935, P. L. Mannock, page 35).

Three Witnesses – now casting and will follow *Death on the Set* – adapted from a novel shortly to be published by S. Fowler Wright.

Vintage Wine – Seymour Hicks and Clare Luce play their original stage rôles. A. Bromley Davenport has joined the cast.

Death on the Set – now in its third week of production.

"By a trick of the microphone, Henry Kendall has been talking to himself all week. As this meant that he spoke the part of the director first and then the track was run through again in order that he might speak the lines of the double to synchronise with the previous dialogue".

Elizabeth Arkell has been added to the cast.

Leslie Hiscott expects to complete this week (week ending 26 January 1935).

The Lad – comedy sequences were filmed last week in the palatial home of Lord Fandon (Gerald Barry) with the Lad (Gordon Harker) finding himself in the most extraordinary situation owing to his being mistaken for a private detective.

(*K. W.*, 24 January 1935, P. L. Mannock, page 43).

Vintage Wine – production has started – adapted by H. Fowler Mear from the witty comedy by Ashley Dukes and Seymour Hicks. James Carter has designed three "particularly attractive" sets for the big scenes. The Chateau Popinot is constructed in Louis XIV style with furniture and furnishings in accord. The most striking set will be that representing the garden of a Roman villa, with a large marble bath. Arthur Barnes is assistant director, and Sydney Blythe cameraman.

Louis Brooks, the well-known fashion artist, has designed and executed all the dresses.

(*K. W.*, 31 January 1935, P. L. Mannock, page 45).

February 1935:

K. W. reported throughout the month:

FILM PRODUCTION AT TWICKENHAM STUDIOS DURING FEBRUARY:

"*Vintage Wine* – Henry Edwards is making headway. Charles Hasler, in charge of the property department at Twickenham, has excelled himself in obtaining correct period furniture for the lovely set designed by James Carter."

"*Three Witnesses* – Eve Gray, Geraldine Fitzgerald, Noel Dryden, Ralph Truman and Clifton Boyne have been added to the cast. Noel Dryden is "a promising newcomer to the screen was engaged for the part of Cyril Truscott, the younger brother of Roger, played by Sebastian Shaw, because of the strong resemblance to the latter. Leslie Hiscott has already shot scenes in solicitor Rowton's offices showing the quarrel between the two brothers, which is later to play an important part in the trial of Roger."

(*K. W.*, 7 February 1935, P. L. Mannock, page 44).

Three more for Twickenham:

Johnson's Stores – Department Store – has already gone

into production. The story of the film was written by H. F. Maltby, the well-known actor and dramatist. H. Fowler Mear has supervised the adaptation of the screen story. Garry Marsh and Sebastian Shaw already cast."

The remaining two stories in this group are – both for release by Universal:

The Iron Woman - That's My Uncle – adapted from the play by Frederick Jackson – to be directed by George Pearson

Inside the Room – based on the stage play by Marten Cumberland which had a brief West End run

Also:

Scrooge – Henry Edwards assigned to direct – will follow *Vintage Wine* in a few weeks' time.

Three Witnesses – completed.

(*K. W.*, 14 February 1935, P. L. Mannock, page 37).

Johnson's Stores – Department Store – "Last Friday, I found Leslie Hiscott at work on this film."

Vintage Wine – an imposing Roman villa with an attractive loggia occupied practically the whole of Sound Stage 2 last Friday (15 February 1935).

(*K. W.*, 21 February 1935, P. L. Mannock, page 27).

Vintage Wine – now in its sixth week.

The Iron Woman - That's My Uncle – went into production last week – *Iron Woman* is the provisional title – in production at night while *Johnson's Stores* and *Vintage Wine* occupy the two sound stages during the day.

Inside the Room – towards the end of this week when Leslie Hiscott has completed work on *Johnson's Stores* for release by Radio, the director will begin production on *Inside The Room*.

Johnson's Stores now in its final stages

(*K. W.*, 28 February 1935, P. L. Mannock, page 35).

March 1935:

Kinematograph Weekly reported throughout the month:

FILM PRODUCTION AT TWICKENHAM STUDIOS DURING MARCH:

Inside the Room – production began at the latter end of last week – from the play by Martin Cumberland, adapted for the screen by H. Fowler Mear.

Vintage Wine – final scenes were shot last week; now in the cutting room.

Johnson's Stores – Department Store – a large department store occupied Sound Stage No. 1 last week. Designed by James Carter, "the set was the most realistic representation of any huge department store. Commissioners continuously opened doors to women shoppers who crowded the counters, and kept the saleswomen busy coping with orders." Final shots were completed on Thursday (28 February 1935).

The Iron Woman – George Pearson has made excellent progress at night. Scenes have been shot in a country pub, a modern luxury flat, a dive in the water-front in the East End, a bedroom and library. Richard Cooper, Betty Astell, Hope Davy, Michael Shepley, Mark Daly, Wally Patch, Margaret Yarde and Colin Lesslie.

> (*K. W.*, 7 March 1935, P. L. Mannock, pages 26 and 29).

Temporary lull in film production at Twickenham Studios.

"The Iron Woman – George Pearson completed on Sunday night (10 March 1935) – for Universal. One of the final scenes to be shot was a dramatic reconstruction of the crime by the detective, played by Frederick Burtwell, in which suspicion is cast upon Ah Sing, an Oriental servant."

Although there will be no production units at work during the week at Twickenham, plenty of work is being done in the art and scenario departments.

"Scrooge – Julius Hagen begins production on a large scale towards the end of this week – and before the production actually takes the floor under the direction of Henry Edwards, weeks of hard research work have been done. James Carter, in the art department, has made intensive research into costumes, manners and architecture of the period and is busily constructing beautiful sets to illustrate one of the most loved of Dickens' stories. Seymour Hicks and Donald Calthrop, as already announced, have been cast in leading rôles."

> (*K. W.*, 14 March 1935, P. L. Mannock, page 55).

Scrooge to start on Monday (25 March 1935) – the rest of the cast are being chosen.

> (*K. W.*, 21 March 1935, P. L. Mannock, pages 53 and

54).

Scrooge will be on the floor for at least four weeks. Seymour Hicks is, of course, no stranger to the part of Scrooge. He first played it at the Vaudeville Theatre in 1901, and has repeated it over 2,000 times.

(*K. W.*, 28 March 1935, P. L. Mannock, page 35).

April 1935:

Kinematograph Weekly reported throughout the month:

FILM PRODUCTION AT TWICKENHAM STUDIOS DURING APRIL:

Scrooge now in its second week. Oscar Asche, Mary Glynne, Robert Cochran (under contract to London Film Productions), Maurice Evans, Mary Lawson and Eve Gray have joined the cast. Production in the first week centred round the dismal offices of Scrooge.

The property chief at Twickenham, Charles Hasler, has now perfected a **new system of artificial fog**. It has no smell and does not choke the technicians who have to work in its atmosphere.

(*K. W.*, 4 April 1935, P. L. Mannock, pages 40 and 41).

Scrooge – steady progress – now in its fourth week. Basil Gill has been cast as Marley's Ghost.

(*K. W.*, 18 April 1935, P. L. Mannock, page 41).

Scrooge – The staff at Twickenham worked throughout Easter in order to release Seymour Hicks from his part in the film for his forthcoming production at the Victoria Place Theatre. Oscar Asche, the famous stage actor, took up his part as the Spirit of Christmas Present last week. George Bellamy has took up his part last week as the Spirit of Christmas yet to Come.

(*K. W.*, 25 April 1935, P. L. Mannock, page 34).

INCREASE OF NOMINAL CAPITAL: TWICKENHAM FILM STUDIOS, LTD.:

Twickenham Film Studios, Ltd – increase in capital – the nominal capital has been increased by the addition of £3,500 beyond the registered capital of £30,000. The additional capital is divided into 3,500 preference shares of £1 each.

(*K. W.*, 11 April 1935, page 15).

CONTRACTS FOR STARS AT TWICKENHAM STUDIOS:

Judy Gunn has been signed by Julius Hagen to a three-year contract as a result of her excellent work in *Vintage Wine*.

Jane Carr, another Twickenham contract star, is now having a great personal success in the revue, *Let's Go Gay*.

(*K. W.*, 18 April 1935, P. L. Mannock, page 41).

May 1935:

Kinematograph Weekly reported throughout the month:

JULIUS HAGEN LAUNCHES TWICKENHAM FILM DISTRIBUTORS, LTD.:

Julius Hagen launches Twickenham Film Distributors, Ltd.

The artistes under contract to Julius Hagen:

- Edward Everett Horton, Flanagan and Allen, Stanley Holloway, Betty Balfour, Jane Carr, John Garrick, Michael Shepley, Davina Craig and Judy Gunn.

Three British Directors:

- Bernard Vorhaus, Henry Edwards and Maurice Elvey; the latter will probably renew his association with Julius Hagen.

Twickenham forthcoming releases:

- *Scrooge.*
- *The Last Journey.*
- *The Romance of Beethoven* – adapted from an original story by Michael Barringer – Bernard Vorhaus to direct.
- *The Private Secretary* – Edward Everett Horton has been signed to play in this world-famous farce by the late Sir Charles Hawtrey.
- *A.1. at Lloyds* – a director and cast have yet to be chosen.
- *Oliver Cromwell* – powerful story written for the screen by Richard Fisher.
- *A Fire Has Been Arranged* – Flanagan and Allen will appear in an original extravaganza written by James Carter and H. Fowler Mear. H. Fowler Mear is the chief Scenarist at Twickenham, and also author of a number of popular novels.
- *Madame Sans Gene* – the silent film of this famous operetta proved a great success with Gloria Swanson in the leading rôle – Hagen will sign Lupe Velez.
- In addition, Hagen intends to star Betty Balfour in two big-scale films.
- Stanley Holloway will also be starred in three subjects especially chosen for his fine talents.
- Arthur Wontner will probably appear in another Sherlock Holmes picture.

Note that the following four of the films announced were

never made by Julius Hagen at Twickenham: *The Romance of Beethoven*, *A.1. at Lloyds*, *Oliver Cromwell* and *Madame Sans Gene*.

(*K. W.*, 2 May 1935, pages 3 and 23).

Arthur Clavering is to join Julius Hagen as joint managing director Twickenham Film Distributors, Ltd. This renews their association of early days, when Julius Hagen and Arthur Clavering were working with Ruffell's Exclusives and Essanay.

Clavering also inaugurated Warner Bros. Pictures, Ltd., as a separate renting organisation.

Also manages the twelve kinemas of the Clavering and Rose circuit.

(*K. W.*, 9 May 1935, page 3).

FILM PRODUCTION AT TWICKENHAM STUDIOS DURING MAY:

Scrooge is scheduled to be completed by the end of this week (week ending 11 May 1935). W. L. Trytel, Twickenham's musical director, has complete the score for *Scrooge*.

The Last Journey to be made early next week

(*K. W.*, 9 May 1935, P. L. Mannock, page 37).

The Last Journey will begin production this week. It will be the second film to be produced for Julius Hagen's new company, Twickenham Film Distributors, Ltd.

(*K. W.*, 16 May 1935, P. L. Mannock, page 43).

D. W. Griffith is to direct the talkie version of *Broken*

421

John V. Watson

Blossoms for Julius Hagen

(*K. W.*, 23 May 1935, page 3).

The Last Journey. As there is much exterior material required, Bernard Vorhaus and a cameraman left this week for three weeks' location work.

A.1. at Lloyds. So Hugh Williams and Judy Gunn, whilst waiting for *The Last Journey*, will begin work on this picture this week under the direction of Leslie Hiscott. This film will deal with British shipping in its present state and as it has been throughout the ages.

NOTE that it appears that *A.1. at Lloyds* was never actually made, or, if it was, then it was released under a different title. If that was the case, this author cannot find any reference whatsoever to the retitled film, despite very extensive investigation.

Henry Edwards has been working almost continuously since last summer, and who recently completed **Scrooge**, has been ordered to take a rest cruise. He left England last week on a sea voyage to Morocco.

The Private Secretary. On Henry Edward's return in June, he will start work immediately on this picture.

Jack Hylton, the world famous dance band conductor and organiser, has signed a contract with Julius Hagen. Hylton's famous signature tune *Oh, Listen to the Band* provides the title for the picture. He and his "boys" have been engaged at the largest salary ever paid to a dance-band; they will receive more than £20,000. Jack's current success at the London Palladium, *Life Begins at Oxford Circus*, has lately proved his ability as an actor. Since 1905, when he began as The Singing Mill-boy, in his native

422

village near Bolton, Lancashire, Jack Hylton has taken a leading part in the musical and entertainment worlds.

NOTE that *Oh, Listen to the Band* was retitled *She Shall Have Music*.

(*K. W.*, 23 May 1935, P. L. Mannock, page 57).

June 1935:

Kinematograph Weekly reported throughout the month:

TWICKENHAM FILM DISTRIBUTORS - SALES MANAGEMENT APPOINTMENT:

Twickenham Distributors' Sales Manager. **Monty Morton** take up his duties as and from Monday (17 June 1935).

(*K. W.*, 6 June 1935, page 5).

TWICKENHAM FILM DISTRIBUTORS - 1935-6 RELEASE PROGRAMME:

Twickenham Distributors' 1935-6 Programme. Nine 'supers' are already scheduled – one release a month – including *Broken Blossoms, Nippy* and *Oliver Cromwell*.

NOTE that we have already seen that *Nippy* and *Oliver Cromwell* were never actually made.

(*K. W.*, 6 June 1935, page 36).

FILM PRODUCTION AT TWICKENHAM STUDIOS DURING JUNE:

Betty Balfour is to star in *Nippy* for Julius Hagen.

John V. Watson

NOTE that *Nippy* was never actually made.

The Last Journey.   Exterior work is progressing rapidly.
Towards the end of this week some flying shots will be taken at
Heston Aerodrome, where Air Hire, Ltd., a civil air service, has
placed a number of planes at the disposal of the unit

(*K. W.*, 6 June 1935, P. L. Mannock, page 38).

The Last Journey – returning to the studio at the end of the
week.   The unit had spent the week shooting in and around
Paddington Station and at Slough, where 50 extras were busy for
two days.   Passengers at Slough were astonished to see three
express trains flash through the station one after the other
without stopping.   The scene in question is when the driver of the
train (Julian Mitchell) refuses to stop the express at the proper
station and forces Michael Hogan (as the fireman) to stoke up
until the train reaches danger speed.   Donald Calthrop, who was
to have played the part of a petty crook, has been compelled to
give up his rôle through illness, and Eliot Makeham will replace
him.   Newcomers to the cast are Frank Pettingell, Olga Lindo and
Michael Hogan.

Nippy – Julius Hagen announced last week that he had
purchased the screen rights of the musical comedy, Nippy,
produced in the West End in 1930 with Binnie Hale.   Betty
Balfour, who is under contract to make several pictures at
Twickenham.   Three clever American composers, Al Goodman,
Al Hoffman and Maurice Sigler, who composed the musical
numbers for *Squibs*.   It is hoped to obtain the co-operation of
Messrs. J. Lyons and Co., the famous caterers, for *Nippy*, which
bears the name of their well-known waitresses.

(*K. W.*, 13 June 1935, P. L. Mannock, page 47).

424

'The Czar of Twickenham'. The History of Julius Hagen and the Film Empire he created at Twickenham Film Studios, from 1927 to 1938.

Mary Lawson has been placed under long-term contract by Julius Hagen. She will be given both "straight" and musical parts.

The Last Journey. Tom Lewis, driver of the record-breaking "Cheltenham Flyer" - he was at the centre of attraction last week on the film, now in its fifth week of production. Tom Lewis has been acting as technical adviser for the railway engine sequences. A replica of the G.W.R. locomotive cab has been built inside the studio, and he taught Julien Mitchell and Michael Hogan the tricks of driving the engine. Scenes shot last week (week ending 15 June 1935) included those at the railway station, when Eve Gray, as a petty crook, steals a wallet. Eliot Makeham, Frank Pettingell, Mickey Brantford and Aubrey Fitzgerald have joined the cast.

(*K. W.*, 20 June 1935, P. L. Mannock, page 32).

A Fire Has Been Arranged - started production on Monday (24 June 1935). Mary Lawson plays her first part under her new contract, plus Harold French, Hal Walters, Robb Wilton, Alastair Sim and Denier Warren. Leslie Hiscott is directed assisted by Arthur Barnes. The farcical story was written by H. Fowler Mear and James Carter.

The Last Journey – Godfrey Tearle has now joined the cast in its sixth week of production. Further exterior were taken last week (week ending 22 June 1935) at Bramley, near Reading, when Michael Hogan and Julien Mitchell drove trains up and down the track.

Broken Blossoms – D. W. Griffith seeks a quiet corner where he can test some of the numerous actors and actresses who want to play the parts made famous by Lilian Gish and Richard Barthelmess many years ago.

John V. Watson

(*K. W.*, 27 June 1935, page 63).

July 1935:

Kinematograph Weekly reported throughout the month:

JULIUS HAGEN ARTICLE - THE FORMATION OF TWICKENHAM FILM DISTRIBUTORS:

Julius Hagen's 22 years in the trade:

"Born 1884, Julius Hagen was, at the age of 18, a stage actor. He left the stage to enter the film business in 1913 and one of his first appointments was with Ruffells Exclusives and then the Essanay Company. He then joined Stolls and later became the London manager for Universal. His first experience of producing was with the Astra National Company, and he subsequently founded the W. P. Company and produced for this company several outstanding films. In 1928 he organised Twickenham Film Studios, Ltd., of which he is now chairman and managing director."

"Julius Hagen is now chairman and joint managing director with Arthur Clavering of Twickenham Film Distributors, Ltd."

(Rachael Low states that the company was registered in May 1935 with a capital of £55,000.)

"Arthur Clavering was previously associated with Julius Hagen in the days of Ruffells Exclusives and Essanay. He formed the Film Booking Offices, Ltd., in 1916, of which he was managing director, and subsequently established Warner Bros. Pictures, Ltd., in this country as a renting organisation."

"Since his resignation in 1931 from Warners, Mr. Clavering has been occupied with the management of some 12 kinemas in

'The Czar of Twickenham'. The History of Julius Hagen and the Film Empire he created at Twickenham Film Studios, from 1927 to 1938.

which he has a financial interest and which are controlled by his brother, Sir Albert Clavering."

"Monty Morton, the sales manager, is thoroughly well known and liked in the film Industry. He has wide experience on the renting side and has been connected with the trade since 1919, when joined Ruffells. He was later Cardiff branch manager for Universal and afterwards joined Graham Wilcox for a number of years. He left this company to form his own independent renting company of Morton, Lever and Co. in South Wales.

Mr. Morton has been London branch manager of Radio Pictures since the inauguration of the company five years ago until his recent appointment to the sales staff of Twickenham Film Distributors, Ltd."

(Kinematograph Weekly, 4 July 1935).

FILM PRODUCTION AT TWICKENHAM STUDIOS DURING JULY:

The Private Secretary – Edward Everett Horton arrived in England last week. Henry Edwards to shortly direct.

A Fire Has Been Arranged. Now in its second week of production. While less fortunate technicians and stars worked in intense heat inside the studio last week, Flanagan and Allen enjoyed themselves on location at the Bell Road House in Beaconsfield. The unit spent several days during the heat-wave making exterior scenes adjoining the bathing-pool, and technicians and players found many excuses for a quick bathe between takes!

The Last Journey. Now in its seventh week – Nelson Keys has joined the cast. Scenes were taken last week showing Julien Mitchell and Michael Hogan. Godfrey Tearle also took part in exciting scenes showing his climb from the coaches of the train over the tender into the driver's cab.

(*K. W.*, 4 July 1935, P. L. Mannock, page 39).

Three units at work at Twickenham:

The Private Secretary – Edward Everett Horton started work on Monday (8 July 1935).

A Fire Has Been Arranged – filming on Sound Stage No. 2 and at Brooklands Racing Circuit.

The Last Journey – now working at night on the final scenes – Paddington Station set – swaying coaches and the countryside flashing by, with the aid of "back projection", gave a vivid impression of terrific speed.

Broken Blossoms – D. W. Griffith has spent some weeks testing artistes for the very important rôles.

Cyril Stanborough, Twickenham's chief still cameraman, has been admitted an associate member of the Royal Photographic Society of Great Britain.

(*K. W.*, 11 July 1935, page 43).

The Private Secretary – Henry Edwards director – E. E. Horton – Sydney Blythe cameraman – second week.

A Fire Has Been Arranged - Leslie Hiscott director – Flanagan and Allen – Sydney Blythe cameraman – fourth week.

The Last Journey – Judy Gunn, Godfrey Tearle – William Luff cameraman – nearing completion.

(*K. W.*, 18 July 1935, *Pulse at the Studios* column).

August 1935:

Kinematograph Weekly reported throughout the month:

FILM PRODUCTION AT TWICKENHAM STUDIOS DURING AUGUST:

The Private Secretary - Oscar Asche has been signed by Julius Hagen to play the Colonel's role.

A Fire Has been Arranged – completed last week (week ending Saturday, 27 July 1935).

(*K. W.*, 1 August 1935, P. L. Mannock, page 25).

The Private Secretary – Sydney Fairbrother took up her part this week. Scenes to be shot next week include a hunt. These shots will be taken at Horsham.

(*K. W.*, 8 August 1935, P. L. Mannock, page 25).

Leslie Hiscott is to direct Jack Hylton (*She Shall Have Music*).

(*K. W.*, 15 August 1935, P. L. Mannock, page 36A).

The Private Secretary. After six weeks' of production, Henry Edwards has completed work over the week-end. Concluding scenes to be shot included a night-club sequence.

Edward Everett Horton sailed for America last Wednesday. He entertained the executives and technicians of the studio to a farewell dinner at the Mitre, Hampton Court.

(*K. W.*, 22 August 1935, P. L. Mannock, page 40).

Oh, Listen to the Band (She Shall Have Music) - Leslie Hiscott – Jack Hylton – first week.

The Private Secretary – Henry Edwards directing – E. E. Horton - William Luff camera – final stages.

(*K. W.*, 22 August 1935, *Pulse of the Studios* column).

Oh, Listen to the Band preparing (*She Shall Have Music*) – Claude Dampier and the musical numbers.

Al Hoffman, Al Goodhart and Maurice Sigler, the three Americans responsible for the tuneful music of *Squibs* and other Twickenham films, have written several excellent numbers, including *The Band That Jack Built, My First Thrill, May All Your Troubles be Little Ones, She Shall Have Music, Sailing Along on a Carpet of Clouds*, and *Nothing on Earth Can Make Me Dance*.

The story has been written for the screen by Paul England, in collaboration with H. Fowler Mear.

(*K. W.*, 29 August 1935, P. L. Mannock, page 43).

September 1935:

Kinematograph Weekly reported throughout the month:

FILM PRODUCTION AT TWICKENHAM STUDIOS DURING SEPTEMBER:

She Shall Have Music. The title has been changed to *She Shall Have Music* from the provisional working title, *Oh, Listen to the Band*.

Broken Blossoms. "I hear that the casting of this film has presented some difficulties, and caused an unexpected delay in the

commencement of the production. D. W. Griffith, who it was
intended to direct, is not now able to do so owing to the delay
which has taken place as he has other commitments to fulfil. In
these circumstances, Twickenham has arranged, with Mr.
Griffith's full approval, for the film to be directed by another
director."

(*K. W.*, 12 September 1935, P. L. Mannock, page 35).

Broken Blossoms – "As recently stated, D. W. Griffith, who
directed the famous silent film Broken Blossoms, will not handle
the new talking version at Twickenham studios. Hans Brahm
starts it in a fortnight. Arthur Margetson has been selected to
play the important rôle of Battling Burrows, the brutal prize-
fighter. He joins Dolly Haas and Emlyn Williams, who have
already been announced as playing leading parts in the picture.
Emlyn Williams has also been largely responsible for the
treatment and scenario."

(*K. W.*, 26 September 1935, P. L. Mannock, page 42).

October 1935:

Kinematograph Weekly reported throughout the month:

FILM PRODUCTION AT TWICKENHAM STUDIOS DURING
OCTOBER:

She Shall Have Music. Members of the Woizikosky Ballet
(now appearing at the Coliseum Theatre, London) - Magda
Neeld, the Australian singer; the Dalmora Can-Can Dancers; the
Mackey Twins (coloured syncopated dancers; Mathea Merryfield;
and Sweet Carmona, Spanish dancer.

(*K. W.*, 3 October 1935, P. L. Mannock, page 37).

Broken Blossoms. Curt Courant, camera, assisted by Hal Young and "Skippy" Lewis – Hans Brahm now directing. Production this week will be confined to atmosphere and exterior shots. Actual shooting on the floor will begin in a few days' time, with Emlyn Williams, Dolly Hass, Arthur Margetson, Donald Calthrop, and Gibb McLaughlin.

She Shall Have Music. Twickenham's own contract cameramen, Sydney Blythe and William Luff, are engaged on this film which is now nearing completion. Howard Deighton supervising the girls in the lively number. "The Run-around" composed by Al Good(h)ard, Al Hoffman, and Maurice Sigler.

(*K. W.*, 10 October 1935, P. L. Mannock, page 43).

NEW WIRELESS ROOM AT TWICKENHAM STUDIOS:

A wireless room has been constructed under the supervision of **Baynham Honri**, the Twickenham sound engineer, who worked for many years with the B.B.C.

(*K. W.*, 3 October 1935, P. L. Mannock, page 37).

ACTOR SIGNED TO THREE YEAR CONTRACT - TWICKENHAM STUDIOS:

Alastair Sim has been signed on a three years' contract by Julius Hagen. He has already made his reputation as a Shakespearian actor on the London stage. He played for three years at the Old Vic. Hagen intends to feature Sim in a series of three subjects.

(*K. W.*, 3 October 1935, P. L. Mannock, page 37).

The Twenty-One Films Trade Shown by Twickenham during 1935:

1. D'ye Ken John Peel? (1935)

Costume melodrama.

88 minutes, "A" certificate.

Trade Show advertisement: Billing: Frederick White & Gilbert Church present *D'ye Ken John Peel?*, featuring John Garrick, Winifred Shotter, Stanley Holloway. A Julius Hagen Twickenham Production. Directed by Henry Edwards.

British Registration Details:
Quota Registration No.: Br. 11,108.
Registration Date: 12 January 1935.
Registered Length: 7,950 feet.
Registered by: Associated Producing and Distribution Co., Ltd.
Maker's name: Twickenham Film Studios, Ltd.
Certificate: (A).

British General Release: Monday, 22 July 1935.

D'ye Ken John Peel? was reviewed in the *Kinematograph Weekly*, 17 January 1935, page 21:

88 minutes, "A" certificate.

"<u>Remarks</u>: Costume melodrama, with popular musical embellishments. Story a trifle naïve, but treatment on showmanship lines and by-play entertaining.

"Box Office Angle: Very good industrial booking, with box-office title. Good for children.

"Simple melodrama, with a period setting and popular song embellishment. The story, although a trifle dated, nevertheless paves the way to robust dramatic action, smartly punctuated with good, honest comedy, artless romance, and rousing melody. The strong and versatile cast enters into the spirit of the show with a sincerity that cloaks much of its artifice. The staging is particularly good; it has a spaciousness that is highly commendable.

"The form of entertainment represented here defies the canons of established convention, but its popularity has already been proven in the past. The showmanship employed in its presentation indicates that it will register yet again at the industrial box-office. The title certainly lends itself to exploitation.

"Story: Major John Peel, while celebrating the victory at Waterloo, learns that Toinette, favourite entertainer of the regiment, has been betrayed by Craven, a gambler. He forces Craven to marry her, and following this, Craven makes an unsuccessful attempt on his life. Craven precedes the troops to England, and fleeces Francis Merrall, father of Lucy, the girl whom Peel secretly loves.

"Merrall reluctantly agrees to honour the debt by consenting to Lucy's marriage to Craven, but an accident in the hunting field leads to Peel arriving on the scene immediately after the ceremony. He recognises Craven, and denounces him as a bigamist and cheat. Lucy, unsullied, then forms a happy bond with Peel.

"Acting: John Garrick is well cast as John Peel, his acting is competent, and his singing voice good. Winifred Shotter is adequate as Lucy, and Leslie Perrins is the traditional villain of fiction as Craven.

"Sound as the principal players are, however, the best performance comes from Stanley Holloway in a comedy rôle. He scores a big hit with his famous 'Sam, pick up thy musket' monologue. The support is sound.

"Production: The range of this film is terrific. Nothing is left out; there is good period melodrama, character comedy, rousing fights, spirited songs, old-time romance, and exhilarating fox-hunting sequences. The only serious fault to be found with the picture is that quality has at times been neglected for quantity. The story is barely strong enough to carry the uneven weight of the embellishments, and this leads to obscure development.

"Many phases of the show entertain individually, but they do not merge into too secure and definite a whole. The film does, however, give good money's worth, and by playing unfailingly to the gallery, has definite box-office possibilities.

"Settings and Photography: The ballroom, café, inn,

435

sporting club, and mansion interiors are elaborate, and admirably indicate period, while the exterior scenes, represented by a fox-hunt and a hold-up by a highwayman, are refreshingly invigorating. The recording of the many good songs is clear, and lighting and photography are excellent.

"Points of Appeal: Popular story, good dramatic interludes, outdoor thrills, rousing song scenes, honest sentiment, good team work, shrewd treatment, and box-office title.

2. *The Rocks of Valpré (1935)*
Period romantic melodrama.

London Trade Show: Wednesday, 16 January 1935 at the Cambridge Theatre.

British Registration Details:
Quota Registration No.: Br. 11,135.
Registration Date: 17 January 1935.
Registered Length: 6,446 feet.
Registered by: Radio Pictures, Ltd.
Maker's name: Real Art Productions, Ltd. Certificate: (A).

Trade Show advertisement: "*The Rocks of Valpré*: Winifred Shotter, John Garrick. Produced by Julius Hagen. Directed by Henry Edwards." Tagline: "The ever popular best seller". "Radio Pictures" logo.
British General Release: Monday, 8 July 1935.

The Rocks of Valpré was reviewed in the *Kinematograph Weekly*, 24 January 1935, page 28:

72 minutes, "A" certificate.

'The Czar of Twickenham'. The History of Julius Hagen and the Film Empire he created at Twickenham Film Studios, from 1927 to 1938.

"Remarks: Popular period romantic melodrama, with music, adapted from Ethel M. Dell's novel. Story sound, treatment resourceful, acting good, and staging colourful.

"Box Office Angle: Good booking, particularly for family and industrial audiences. Title values strong.

"Period, sentimental, romantic drama, mixed with music, spectacularly adapted from the novel by Ethel M. Dell. The story is a trifle dated in its drama and romantic appeal, but it is well acted and presented with colourful elaboration. There is unquestionably a wide market for this type of simple entertainment, and with such excellent selling angles as those represented by the title and the wide popularity of the authoress to back it up, the film should readily respond to exploitation in popular family and industrial halls. It has wide potentialities.

"Story: Captain Louis de Monteville, a French cavalry officer is in love with Christine Wyndham, a demure English girl, and she with him, but the smooth course of their romance is irrevocably checked by Captain Rodolphe, an unscrupulous rival for Christine's hand. He has Louis arrested on a false charge of selling an invention to an enemy agent, convicted and sent to Devil's Island. While he is incarcerated, Mary marries, and when he is released on the grounds of ill-health 10 years later, he learns that Rodolphe, having come into possession of letters written by Mary to him before her marriage, is attempting blackmail. He

437

meets him in mortal combat, retrieves the letters before Rodolphe is sent to his death, and then peacefully passes out himself into Christine's arms.

"Acting: John Garrick plays the noble hero with quiet distinction, and makes full use of his vocal accomplishments, Winifred Shotter does not age too convincingly as Christine, but is demure and appealing, and Leslie Perrins is true to tradition as the unscrupulous Rodolphe. Michael Shepley, Lewis Shaw, Athene Seyler and Agnes Imlay are quietly competent in support.

"Production: The producer is content to leave well alone when it comes to handling the story, the treatment is as artless as the plot. This is all to the good, for its appeal must stand or fall on its refreshing, colourful naïveté. The tempo, however, is at times a trifle slow; the error of paving the development with too many unattractive close-ups is the cause of this fault. Apart from this one blemish, drama and sentiment are effectively blended, both being aided in their exploitation by appropriate music and effective theatrical devices. The retrospective presentation lends colour and enchantment to the theme.

"Settings and Photography: The staging is ambitious, the interiors and exteriors are spacious, and lighting and photography are excellent.

"Points of Appeal: Popular story, straightforward treatment, good, honest drama, simple heart interest, sound acting, generous presentation, and attractive title.

3. Lazybones (1935)

Comedy.

London Trade Show: Thursday, 17 January 1935 at the Phoenix Theatre.

British Registration Details:
Quota Registration No.: Br. 11,150.
Registration Date: 18 January 1935.
Registered Length: 5,811 feet.
Registered by: Radio Pictures, Ltd.
Maker's name: Real Art Productions, Ltd. Certificate: (U).

Trade Show advertisement: *"Lazybones*: Ian Hunter, Clare Luce, Sara Allgood."
Tagline: "A comedy of an idler who took a work cure!" "Radio Pictures" logo.
British General Release: Monday, 24 June 1935.

The making of *Lazybones*: It is worth reminding ourselves that Michael Powell had to shoot most of *Lazybones* over thirteen nights: a common practice at Hagen's Twickenham Studios then; it operated 24 hours a day. This filming schedule was also necessitated by the fact that the film's two stars, Ian Hunter and Claire Luce, were appearing in West End plays at the same time.

Lazybones was the first film first film to take to the studio floor after the opening of the new Twickenham sound stage on Monday, 17 September 1934.

Lazybones was reviewed in the *Kinematograph Weekly*, 24 January 1935, page 36:

Recorded on RCA Photophone, 65 minutes, "U"

certificate.

"<u>Remarks</u>: Simple, attractively mounted romantic comedy. Story slight but acting good and treatment effective.

"<u>Box Office Angle</u>: Sound supporting feature for the majority of halls. Good for the family and youngsters.

"Simple, attractively mounted romantic comedy, the entertainment of which is more firmly vested in the individual performances of the popular English players than in the story. Basically the plot is transparent, but sound team work and resourceful direction hide much of its naïveté by decorating its development with pretty sentiment and happy comedy. Sound supporting feature for the majority of halls.

"<u>Story</u>: Reginald Ford, a lazy, impecunious baronet, is persuaded by his parasitical family to propose to Kitty McCarthy, an American heiress, recent purchaser of a picturesque local hostelry. When he pops the question he learns that she is broke, but his love for her impels him to marry her.

"She gets down to business in her new acquisition, but he shows no desire to work. Complications arise when Michael, her cousin, tries to relieve Reginald's brother-in-law, a government agent, of important papers, and she is implicated, but they are soon straightened out, and the film ends with concrete evidence of Reginald's willingness to support his wife.

"<u>Acting</u>: Ian Hunter is too good an actor and pleasing a personality to allow the artificiality of the central rôle to cramp his style. As the reformed Reginald he is most amusing. Clare Luce has glamour as Kitty, and Bernard Nedell is well cast as the unscrupulous Michael. The rest of the supporting players are quite sound, but irritate occasionally with their "ritzy" inflections.

"Production: This comedy is just ingenious make believe, fashioned from material that seldom fails to bring pleasure to the masses. The complexities of the plot brighten the journey to the obvious happy ending, and the principal players see that humour, sentiment and drama alternate in entertaining sequence. In contrast to a good drama, the film has its uses on the average programme.

"Settings and Photography: The inn interiors and exteriors are picturesque, but the baronial manor is a trifle ostentatious; the producer makes the common mistake of thinking that an Englishman's home is a castle. Lighting and photography are very good.

"Points of Appeal: Bright, ingenious story, competent team work, adequate direction, and quota angle.

Lazybones was reviewed in the *Monthly Film Bulletin*: January 1935:

"A comedy of impoverished aristocracy endeavouring to retrieve the family fortune by marrying the lazy eldest son to an American heiress. A very English background of old manors,

retainers, dogs and much talk of beer. The purely
farcical moments were quite entertaining, but such
an incredible story needs more pace and a lighter
touch throughout. 66 minutes. Reviewer: M.A."

4. The Triumph of Sherlock Holmes (1935)

Sherlock Holmes detective mystery thriller.

London Trade Show: Thursday, 31 January 1935 at
the Prince Edward Theatre.
British Registration Details:
Quota Registration No.: Br. 11,225.
Registration Date: 4 February 1935.
Registered Length: 7,544 feet.
Registered by: Gaumont-British Distributors, Ltd.
Maker's name: Real Art Productions, Ltd. Certificate:
(A).

Trade Show advertisement: "Arthur Wontner in '*The
Triumph of Sherlock Holmes*', with Lyn Harding, Leslie
Perrins, Jane Carr. Based on the late Sir Arthur Conan
Doyle's "*The Valley of Fear*". Produced by Julius Hagen for
Real Art Productions, Ltd. Directed by Leslie Hiscott."
Logo: Gaumont-British Distributors."
London key-theatre pre-release run held at the
Capitol, week commencing Monday, 13 May 1935.

British General Release: Monday, 26 August 1935.

The Triumph of Sherlock Holmes was reviewed in
the *Kinematograph Weekly*, 7 February 1935, page 31:

Visatone Sound System, 84 minutes, "A" certificate.

"Remarks: Detective drama, a straightforward
adaptation of Conan Doyle's story, *The Valley of*

'The Czar of Twickenham'. The History of Julius Hagen and the Film Empire he created at Twickenham Film Studios, from 1927 to 1938.

Fear. Story treatment rather unimaginative, but excellent performance by Arthur Wontner, as Sherlock Holmes, supplies adequate need of popular entertainment.

"Box Office Angle: Good general and title booking. Sound family and juvenile appeal.

"Detective drama, a popular adaptation of Conan Doyle's story *The Valley of Fear*, distinguished by an exceedingly fascinating portrayal of Sherlock Holmes by Arthur Wontner. The story treatment is a trifle haphazard, but the drama is so interspersed with thrills and illuminated by the bright deductions of Holmes and his cross-talk with the well-meaning Watson as to provide sound entertainment for the masses. Good general booking with big title pull.

"Story: Sherlock Holmes is prompted to withdraw from retirement by a threat made by his old enemy, Professor Moriarty. He has reason to believe that the arch-fiend is behind the mysterious murder of John Douglas, and he goes to the victim's lonely country house to investigate. The story told of Douglas's early history in America by his wife puts Holmes on the right scent, and it is not long before his deductions lead to the solution of a neat mystery. In the end he crosses swords with Moriarty, whose death closes his career.

"Acting: Arthur Wontner is excellent as Sherlock Holmes, succeeding admirably in bringing the famous character of fiction to life; Ian Fleming is a trifle too stupid as Dr. Watson, but he nevertheless makes a good foil; and Lyn Harding, Leslie Perrins and Jane Carr acquit themselves adequately in support.

"Production: The film is quite good Sherlock Holmes, but it would have been better had a more even feeling of balance been preserved. Too much footage is devoted to the American flashback dealing with the supposed victim's early life in America, and not enough to the solving of the crime. Holmes is the character in whom all interest is centred, and much entertainment is lost during the period the fascinating character is absent from the screen. Nevertheless, as a piece of detective fiction the film is quite well up in its class, and with such a good drawing card as that represented by the title should do well in the majority of halls.

"Settings and Photography: The country house interiors admirably fit the major action, while the flashback is convincingly American in atmosphere. Lighting and photography are satisfactory.

"Points of Appeal: Ingenious story, good treatment, great performance by Arthur Wontner, adequate staging, good suspense, and obvious exploitation angles.

The Cinema:
"Safe, popular booking, with pull on title, star and author".
Daily Film Renter:
"Sound popular booking . . . First-rate performance from Arthur Wontner".

5. *Annie, Leave the Room!* (1935)
Farce.

London Trade Show: Tuesday, 12 February 1935 at the Phoenix Theatre.

British Registration Details:
Quota Registration No.: Br. 11,269.
Registration Date: 14 February 1935.
Registered Length: 6,927 feet.
Registered by: Universal Pictures, Ltd.
Maker's name: Twickenham Film Studios, Ltd.
Certificate: (A).

Trade Show advertisement: *"Annie, Leave the Room!* Starring Eva Moore, Morton Selten, Jane Carr, Davina Craig, with Richard Cooper, Jane Welsh, Ben Welden. From the play, *"Spendlove Hall"*. Directed by Leslie Hiscott. Tagline: "Fast-moving Farce-Comedy." Logo: "Step Out with Universal".
British General Release: Monday, 15 July 1935.

Annie, Leave the Room! was reviewed in the *Kinematograph Weekly*, 14 February 1935, page 27:

77 minutes, "A" certificate.

"Remarks: Broad farce. Somewhat crude and slapdash in production values, but good novelty angle with sound quota of laughs.

"Box Office Angle: Quite good light booking for popular halls. Of little use for juveniles.

"In spite of rather crude production values, this

broad farce dealing with a noble lord who is instrumental in getting a servant on the films, has many amusing situations and a good quota of laughs, and it should go down quite well in popular halls.

"Story: Lord Spendlove suffers from a mother-in-law who holds the purse-strings. He sees a way to escape when a film company offers him a thousand pounds to lend them his baronial mansion. He puts up the leading artistes, Adrienne Ditmar, with whom he flirts, and John Brandon, who later wins his daughter's love.

"The advent of the film company leads to many amusing situations, but the crux of the story is the way in which Lord Spendlove gets a screen test of himself taken with his dumb servant, Annie. By mistake a big film executive sees this, and promptly contracts Annie as the funniest thing he has seen. Lord Spendlove's hopes of getting rid of his mother-in-law are dashed when he discovers that she is a director of the company which has hired his mansion.

"Acting: Morton Selten, in spite of a tendency to overact and over-emphasise the comedy, is nevertheless very amusing, and Davina Craig scores decidedly as the dumb servant. As the American actress, Adrienne, Jane Carr is exceedingly good, and Eva Moore gives a sound and unforced characterisation of the mother-in-law. Arthur Finn shows to advantage as a film director, and Ben Welden is good as a cameraman.

"Production: The whole story is staged in rather a

haphazard and theatrical manner, but there are
really good farcical touches cropping up every
now and again which score the laughs. The
"shooting" sequences in the old mansion are well
done, and even if the continuity is ragged and the
scenery somewhat restricted the action is kept on
the move. Dialogue is good but at times very near
the knuckle. One joke, though bound to be
hilariously received, rather oversteps the bounds.

"Settings and Photography: Adequate ancestral
home settings with up-to-the-standard camera
work.

"Points of Appeal: The novel nature of the broad
farce, the wisecracks, and the humorous
caricatures of characters.

6. *The Ace of Spades (1935)*
Political drama.

London Trade Show: Wednesday, 20 February 1935
at the Cambridge Theatre.

British Registration Details:
Quota Registration No.: Br. 11,291.
Registration Date: 21 February 1935.
Registered Length: 5,934 feet.
Registered by: Radio Pictures, Ltd.
Maker's name: Real Art Productions, Ltd. Certificate:
(U).

Trade Show advertisement: "*The Ace of Spades*:
Michael Hogan, Dorothy Boyd. Produced by Julius
Hagen. Directed by George Pearson. Tagline: "A novel
comedy drama." "Radio Pictures" logo.

447

John V. Watson

British General Release: Monday, 5 August 1935.

The Ace of Spades was reviewed in the *Kinematograph Weekly*, 28 February 1935, page 26:

66 minutes, "U" certificate.

"Remarks: Political drama, quite well acted but weak in story values. Development unnecessarily involved and unproductive of other than very ordinary entertainment.

"Box Office Angle: Quota second feature for the smaller halls. Nothing to offend juveniles.

"Political drama, a tedious rigmarole, too neglectful of popular essentials to offer other than third-rate entertainment. The artificial plot is unnecessarily involved, the treatment patchy, and the acting seldom more than elementary. As for dialogue, it is worse than trite; many of the quips are painful. Just a passable quota second feature for other than first-class halls.

"Story: Nick Trent, candidate in a by-election, receives threats of blackmail after a card, the ace of spades (on which he records his quarrel with Lord Yardleigh, later found dead) is missing. His brother, Harry, guilty of a liaison with Cleo, wife of George Despard, Nick's political opponent, kills Yardleigh accidentally with his car, and the card, by coming into the possession of Evelyn, Nick's prospective sister-in-law, causes her to suspect him. Her jealousy of her sister, Nita, Nick's fiancée, causes her to resort to blackmail, but when Yardleigh's death is eventually satisfactorily explained her hand is stayed, and Nick finds himself elected.

"<u>Acting</u>: Michael Hogan does his best as Nick, but it is difficult to reconcile his brogue with the toney English of his brother, Harry, played by Sebastian Shaw. Dorothy Boyd, Jane Carr and Geraldine Fitzgerald, the three women in the cast, are definitely weak, but Michael Shepley, Richard Cooper, Bobbie Comber and Felix Aylmer put in fairly sound work in support.

"<u>Production</u>: The direction is far from good, but this is partly due to the involved character of the story; nothing short of genius could straighten it out. The political and mystery elements never mix with conviction, and the romance is just an excrescence. It is anticipation, unfortunately never realised, rather than story values, that keeps the interest fairly well held.

"<u>Settings and Photography</u>: The staging puts variety before conviction, but is adequate for the story's needs. Lighting and photography are up to standard.

"<u>Points of Appeal</u>: Good title, naïve blending of comedy, drama and mystery, useful cast, and quota angle.

7. *The Lad (1935)*
Character comedy with Gordon Harker.

London Trade Show: Monday, 25 February 1935 at the Cambridge Theatre.

British Registration Details:
Quota Registration No.: Br. 11,340.
Registration Date: 27 February 1935.
Registered Length: 6,736 feet.
Registered by: Universal Pictures, Ltd.
Maker's name: Twickenham Film Studios, Ltd.
Certificate: (A).

The Lad booked into London key-theatre pre-release runs:

+ At the New Gallery, week commencing Monday, 8 April 1935, in a double-bill supporting *Fighting Stock*, with Tom Walls, Ralph Lynn, and Robertson Hare, directed by Tom Walls, produced and released by Gaumont-British.
+ Programme was held over for a second week at the New Gallery, week commencing Monday, 15 April 1935.
+ Programme was held over for a third week at the New Gallery, week commencing Monday, 22 April 1935.
+ At the Astoria, week commencing Monday, 6 May 1935, in a double-bill supporting *British Agent*, with Leslie Howard and Kay Francis, directed by Michael Curtiz, produced by First National Pictures, and released by Warner Bros.

Trade Show advertisement: Billing: Gordon Harker in *"The Lad"*, with Jane Carr, Betty Stockfeld, and Gerald Barry, Geraldine Fitzgerald, Sebastian Shaw. Directed by Henry Edwards. Tagline: "From the Famous Comedy by Edgar Wallace." Logo: "Step Out with Universal."
British General Release: Monday, 22 July 1935.

The Lad was reviewed in the *Kinematograph Weekly*, 28 February 1935, page 27:

75 minutes, "A" certificate.

"Remarks: Bright character comedy, adapted from

the play by Edgar Wallace. Treatment undistinguished, but great performance by star keeps the humour consistently alive.

"Box Office Angle: Attractive general booking, with strong star values. Safe for juveniles.

"Edgar Wallace's play, from which this comedy is adapted, is not greatly improved by conventional screen embellishment, the original was, in fact, more compact and consistent in its humour. However, the neatness of the plot and the clever inimitable character drawing of Gordon Harker fortunately allow it easily to survive the handicap imposed by undistinguished direction and treatment. Although definitely a one-man show, it provides capital comedy entertainment for the crowd. This and its star and title values make it an attractive general booking.

"Story: The Lad, a convict, by overhearing the conversation of two fellow-inmates, learns that a valuable necklace stolen from Lord Fandon has been hidden in a flowerpot in his lordship's mansion. On his release he makes for the house, and the guilty conscience of Lord Fandon, who has had an intrigue with Pauline, a guest, and Lady Fandon, who has secretly been betting in conjunction with an unscrupulous bookmaker, results in him being mistaken for a private detective. He keeps up this deception, straightens out the domestic tangle, discovers the necklace and returns it, brings happiness to Joan, Lord Fandon's daughter, in love with a man disapproved of by her father, and picks up the threads of an early romance.

"Acting: Gordon Harker is in irresistible form as The Lad, such is his flair for Cockney character-drawing that he is able to bring human interest as well as comedy to the part. Every situation in which he features registers. Jane Carr, Betty Stockfeld and Geraldine Fitzgerald are attractive as Pauline, Lady Fandon, and Joan respectively, but there are times when their affected speaking voices are little short of infuriating. Gerald Barry, Michael Shepley, Sebastian Shaw, and John Turnbull are adequate in prominent supporting rôles.

"Production: Edgar Wallace's ingenious story furnishes an excellent vehicle for Gordon Harker, and he is not slow in seizing the opportunities it provides. The rôle of bogus detective is fraught with funny incidents and they follow, in spite of the hindrance of trifling detail, with smoothness. Devised for popular consumption, the film unquestionably represents cast-iron light, general entertainment.

"Settings and Photography: The settings are a trifle stagey, but adequate, and lighting and photography are satisfactory.

"Points of Appeal: Bright, ingenious story, great performance by Gordon Harker, smart dialogue, adequate support and powerful title and star values.

8. *Death on the Set (1935)*

Ingenious murder mystery.

London Trade Show: Friday, 1 March 1935 at the Cambridge Theatre.

British Registration Details:
Quota Registration No.: Br. 11,352.
Registration Date: 4 March 1935.
Registered Length: 6,502 feet.
Registered by: Universal Pictures, Ltd.
Maker's name: Twickenham Film Studios, Ltd.
Certificate: (A).

Trade Show advertisement: *"Death on the Set*: From Victor McClure's Great Mystery Thriller. With Henry Kendall, Eve Gray, Jeanne Stuart, Lewis Shaw, Rita Helsham, Garry Marsh, and Wally Patch, Elizabeth Arkell. Directed by Leslie Hiscott."

Further Trade Show advertisement: *"Death on the Set*: Starring Henry Kendall, Eve Gray, Jeanne Stuart, Garry Marsh. Tagline: "Another great Universal-Twickenham winner . . . A mystery drama worthy of Sherlock Holmes and Edgar Wallace combined!!" Logo: "Step Out with Universal".

British General Release: Monday, 29 July 1935.

Death on the Set was reviewed in the *Kinematograph Weekly* on 7 March 1935, page 21:

72 minutes, "A" certificate.

"Remarks: Ingenious murder story, well directed but rather lacking in subtlety and occasional somewhat naïve.

"Box Office Angle: Quite useful, popular programme booking. Not for children.

John V. Watson

"There is a good deal of ingenuity in this murder story, based on a novel by Victor McClure, but, as in most cases of plots relying on the perfect double, it lacks full conviction and has some rather naïve sequences.

"The acting of the principals is very good, however, even if it is not too well supported by the entire cast, and there are strongly dramatic moments as well as good comedy.

"Story: Cayley Morden, a film director, hated by the players and studio staff, plans to murder his double, a gangster, Charlie Marsh, and takes his place. He arranges an alibi by persuading one of Marsh's molls to say he spent the night with her, and then shoots Marsh in his office, so arranging it that suspicion falls on his principal actress, Lady Blanche, whom he has attempted to blackmail. Inspector Burford, who has been warned by the American police about Morden's past, takes up the trail, but cannot prove what he believes – that the dead man is Marsh and not Morden.

"Secure in his alibi, Morden laughs at the police, but he changes his tune when he discovers that his woman witness has been strangled. Actually, Marsh had accidentally killed her when she threatened to expose him. Morden is, therefore, faced with the alternative of being accused of killing Marsh – or, if he insisted on his other identity – of having killed the girl.

"Acting: Henry Kendall is very good in the dual rôle of Morden and Marsh, and differentiates well between the two characters. Garry Marsh is

454

convincing as the Inspector, while a very good comedy characterisation comes from Wally Patch as a Cockney sergeant; it is never overdrawn. Jeanne Stuart is quite effective as Lady Blanche, but Eve Gray is weak as another member of the studio players who is suspected of the crime, as is Lewis Shaw as her fiancé.

"Production: The story is well told, although, perhaps, it would have been stronger to have kept the fact that Marsh had murdered his mistress for a curtain climax. Direction is sound, but there is at times rather a lack of polish and subtlety, which arises from poor characterisation of minor rôles and some indifferent dialogue which strikes a distinctly pathetic note.

"Settings and Photography: Settings are quite good and the camera work efficient.

"Points of Appeal: Somewhat novel murder story, and good acting of principals.

9. *Three Witnesses (1935)*
Mystery drama.

London Trade Show: Thursday, 21 March 1935 at the Prince Edward Theatre.

British Registration Details:
Quota Registration No.: Br. 11,406.
Registration Date: 22 March 1935.
Registered Length: 6,130 feet.
Registered by: Universal Pictures, Ltd.
Maker's name: Twickenham Film Studios, Ltd.
Certificate: (A).

John V. Watson

Trade Show advertisement: *"Three Witnesses*: Eve Gray, Henry Kendall, and Sebastian Shaw, Garry Marsh, Richard Cooper, Noel Dryden. Tagline: "An Amazing Murder Mystery Drama – By S. Fowler Wright". Universal Logo: "Step Out with Universal".

British General Release: Monday, 12 August 1935.

Three Witnesses was reviewed in the *Kinematograph Weekly* on 28 March 1935, page 29:

68 minutes, "A" certificate.

Henry Kendall, Eve Gray, Garry Marsh.

"Remarks: Unconvincing mystery drama, lacking in punch and popular appeal. Story thin, and acting with few exceptions, cold.

"Box Office Angle: Very ordinary quota booking for the unsophisticated. Nothing to offend youngsters.

"Non-stop talking mystery play, the plot of which thickens and thickens until it becomes a little too thick. The greatest mystery of all, however, is the object of the entertainment's appeal, for the masses demand action and better-class patrons some measure of intelligence, neither of which are conceded. Very ordinary quota booking.

"Story: The story deals with the mystery surrounding the murder of Cyril Truscott, youngest of three partners in a firm of contractors, his death taking place following a quarrel with Roger Truscott, his elder brother, over money

456

matters. When Roger is arrested on suspicion, Margaret, his sister, seeks the help of her fiancé, Leslie Trent, a solicitor. He turns detective, and, with the aid of Margaret, and Roger's fiancée, Diana, brings the guilt home to the right party, Charles Rowton, the avaricious senior partner.

"Acting: Henry Kendall has an easy way with him as Trent, and Eve Gary is adequate as Margaret, but the rest of the players, with the exception of Geraldine Fitzgerald, who shapes well as Diana, fail to find in the story any outlet.

"Production: It is the mechanical care with which the plot is constructed that robs it of suspense and conviction. Humour, romance and excitement alternate with such slow precision that the audience is allowed to think ahead of the development. There are no surprises, just wordy explanations of the obvious.

"Settings and Photography: The staging, although confined to interiors, is moderately good.

"Points of Appeal: Good title, well-known cast, popularity of thrillers, and quota ticket.

10. Street Song (1935)
Romantic drama.

London Trade Show: Monday, 25 March 1935 at the Cambridge Theatre.

British Registration Details:
Quota Registration No.: Br. 11,425.

John V. Watson

Registration Date: 26 March 1935.
Registered Length: 5,773 feet.
Registered by: Radio Pictures, Ltd.
Maker's name: Real Art Productions, Ltd. British
Board of Film Censor's Certificate: "A".

Trade Show advertisement: *Street Song*. John
Garrick, Rene Ray, Wally Patch. A Twickenham
Production. Directed by Bernard Vorhaus. Tagline:
"Something really new in story and setting – from begging
to broadcasting via a pet shop!"

British General Release: Monday, 16 September 1935.

Street Song was reviewed in the *Kinematograph Weekly*,
28 March 1935, page 29:

> RCA Photophone System, 64 minutes, "A"
> certificate.

> John Garrick, Rene Ray, Wally Patch.

> "Remarks: Romantic drama, slight and ingenious in
> story values, but secure in its heart interest.
> Acting adequate, staging good, and musical
> treatment effective.

> "Box Office Angle: Sound supporting feature for
> the masses, family and juveniles.

> "Romantic drama of London life, the simple story
> of which successfully resorts to artifice to build up
> heart interest and point a moral. The acting,
> sincere rather than distinguished, is always equal
> to the modest demands of the dramatic situations,
> most of which are neatly handled, while music is
> cunningly employed to amplify the firm emotional

structure of the theme. For the masses, to whom its appeal is obviously addressed, it is a sound supporting feature.

"Story: Tom Tucker, a street singer, partner in crime with Wally, a hardened crook, is forced to seek refuge in a pet store owned by Lucy, following a raid on Tuttle's pawn broking establishment. By coincidence Tuttle is threatening to evict Lucy for non-payment of rent, and out of gratitude Tom and Wally finance her. Just as Lucy's happiness is at its height, however, she learns the true source of her benefactors' wealth and refuses to touch it. Thinking that he failed in a B.B.C. audition, Tom reluctantly decides to join Wally in another robbery, and so once again stave off Tuttle, but he repents at the last minute. Wally commits the robbery on his own, and by an unhappy chance "the goods" are found on Tom. He is arrested, but Wally, moved by the hero-worship of Billy, Lucy's brother, injured in a street accident, confesses. Tom, following his release, learns that he has earned a B.B.C. contract, and so success and romantic happiness come.

"Acting: John Garrick's good voice aids his performance as Tom; he does quite well in the part. Wally Patch reveals unsuspected emotional ability as the tough but human Wally, Lawrence Hanray is good as Tuttle, and John Singer gives a bright performance as Billy. Rene Ray, however, is a trifle lacking in experience as Lucy.

"Production: Here is a pleasant, friendly piece of

make-believe, which finds in artifice a sound medium for tender emotional expression. The plot never for a moment holds water, but its healthy sentiment, small-child interest, quiet undercurrent of suspense, moving poignancy and popular romance so intertwine as to fashion into an agreeable and entertaining design. It has mass appeal, and it is this which carries it into the supporting feature category.

"Settings and Photography: The staging is quite good, the musical numbers are appropriately selected, and lighting and photography are satisfactory.

"Points of Appeal: Appealing story, sincere acting, heart interest, juvenile appeal, popular romance, and good title.

11. The Morals of Marcus (1935)

Romantic comedy-drama.
London Trade Show: Tuesday, 26 March 1935 at the Prince Edward Theatre.

British Registration Details:
Quota Registration No.: Br. 11,452.
Registration Date: 28 March 1935.
Registered Length: 6,902 feet.
Registered by: Gaumont-British Distributors, Ltd.
Maker's name: Real Art Productions, Ltd. Certificate: (A).
Trade Show advertisement: Billing: Lupe Velez (large font size), Ian Hunter, Adrianne Allen (the later two names in smaller font size). Directed by Miles Mander. Produced by Julius Hagen for Real Art Productions, Ltd. Recorded on Visatone Sound System." Tagline: "From W. J. Locke's famous play."

London key-theatre pre-release runs of *The Morals of Marcus*:

At the New Gallery, week commencing Monday, 29 April 1935, in a double-bill supported by *The King of Paris* (1934) with Cedric Hardwicke, Marie Glory and Ralph Richardson, a Herbert Wilcox production, distributed by United Artists. The programme held over for a second week at the New Gallery, week commencing Monday, 6 May 1935.

"*The Morals of Marcus*" held over for another two days; Monday and Tuesday, 13 and 14 May 1935. The title of the other feature film was not documented in the '*Kinematograph Weekly*', but it almost certainly was *The King of Paris* as already programmed in the preceding two weeks.

At the Stoll, Kingsway, week commencing Monday, 3 June 1935, in a double-bill with *Masquerade in Vienna*, an Austrian film with Paula Wessely and Anton Walbrook, released in the United Kingdom by Reunion.

London key-theatre run: London General Release of *The Morals of Marcus*:

At the Davis, Croydon: week commencing 19 August 1935, double-billed with *Ruggles of Red Gap* with Charles Laughton, released by Paramount.

British General Release: Monday, 19 August 1935.

The Morals of Marcus was reviewed in the *Kinematograph Weekly*, 4 April 1935, page 31:

461

John V. Watson

Visatone Sound System, 77 minutes, "A" certificate.

Lupe Velez, Ian Hunter, Adrianne Allen.

"Remarks: Clever performances by co-stars in a straightforward adaptation of W. J. Locke's stage play. Comedy, romance and drama adroitly blended, and appropriately presented.

"Box Office Angle: Good general booking. Safe for the family.

"Popular romantic comedy-drama, a straightforward adaptation of W. J. Locke's successful play, which owes its sound entertainment to the happy casting of Lupe Velez and Ian Hunter in the principal rôles. The atmosphere does not always convince, nor is the supporting acting distinguished, but the stars reveal a firm grasp of fundamentals and force the point of the story home. Through them drama, sentiment and humour are adroitly blended. Good general booking, backed by star values.

"Story: Marcus Ordeyne, a middle-aged scientist, finds Carlotta, an attractive girl, half Syrian and half English, hiding in his cabin on embarking at a Syrian port for England. When she tells him that she is hoping to escape from an odious marriage he takes pity on her and brings her to his Mayfair home. She falls in love with him, but he fails to warm to her wild, untamed attractiveness until Judith, a Society divorcee in love with him, tries to get rid of her by persuading Tony Pasquale, a man of loose morals, to entice her to Paris. It is then that he realises his love for her, and he rescues her from a low Parisian dive before harm has come to her and leads her to the altar.

"Acting: Lupe Velez is exceedingly good as the wild Carlotta; her volatility is delightfully feminine and manages to win much sympathy. Ian Hunter, too, is effective as Marcus; his quiet manner procures essential contrast. It is the stars who make the picture. Noel Madison has no difficulty in suggesting the cad, Tony, but Adrienne Allan (*sic*) is very wooden as Judith.

"Production: This romantic comedy-drama, a spirited flight of fantasy, makes a very shaky take-off from Syria, but settles down comfortably on reaching London by providing bright humour and piquant romance at the expense of the snobbishness and unscrupulousness of Society. When it switches to Paris for its climax, however, it again encounters stormy weather, for the ending is as artificial as the opening. It is the middle portion that counts, for it is here that Miles Mander, the producer, comes into its own. The satisfaction he gets from peeling the polished veneer off life in Mayfair through the rough treatment handed out to the heroine is reflected in the bright quality of this phase of the picture. The film is unmistakably patchy, but by playing on safe ground and employing popular and talented stars it nevertheless builds up adequate all-round entertainment.

"Settings and Photography: The Syrian and Parisian sequences are very theatrical, but the Mayfair atmosphere, which fortunately dominates, is accurate.   Lighting   and   photography   are satisfactory.

"Points of Appeal: Good story, adequate treatment, bright humour, appealing romance, and excellent acting by box-office stars.

Review in the *Monthly Film Bulletin*, April 35, page 38:

"*The Morals of Marcus*. (Great Britain). Censors' Certificate: "A". Distributor: G.-B. Distributors. Director: Miles Mander. Stars: Lupe Velez, Ian Hunter, and Adrianne Allen.   75 minutes.   A bachelor archaeologist, holding sex to be the "fundamental blunder of creation" finds in one of the cases of ancient sculpture with which he is returning to England, a very much alive girl stowaway who has fled the harem rather than accept the honour of being the thirty-sixth wife of a gap-toothed but highly placed official. A social success in England, this very vital young woman conquers her rival, eludes her wrathful stepfather, flings off the persecution of the villain, and marries her hero the archaeologist. This screen version of a novel is bright, full of varied incidents, has some very good comic touches, and is technically well-produced; yet notwithstanding the vivacious acting of Lupe Velez the thought rises that success as a novel is no guarantee of success when the same theme is put on the screen. Suitability: A, B, C. Reviewer: A. C. F."

12. That's My Uncle (1935)
Comedy crime drama.

'The Czar of Twickenham'. The History of Julius Hagen and the Film Empire he created at Twickenham Film Studios, from 1927 to 1938.

London Trade Show: Monday, 25 March 1935 at the Prince Edward Theatre.

British Registration Details:
Quota Registration No.: Br. 11,454.
Registration Date: 28 March 1935.
Registered Length: 5,218 feet.
Registered by: Universal Pictures, Ltd.
Maker's name: Twickenham Film Studios, Ltd.
Certificate: (U).
British General Release: Monday, 26 August 1935.

That's My Uncle was reviewed in the *Kinematograph Weekly, 28 March 1935, page 31:*

58 minutes, "U" certificate.

Betty Astell, Mark Daly, Richard Cooper.

"Remarks: Comedy crime drama, with a thin, scrappy story. Acting moderately good, but direction weak, and continuity jerky.

"Box Office Angle: Quota booking for uncritical audiences. No appeal to juveniles.

"Comedy-drama, a purposeless pot-pourri of crime, romance and humour, loosely held together by a slight and far from clear story. The thin plot becomes so unnecessarily involved as it develops that it soon reaches the stage when the straightening-out process becomes impossibility, hence the abrupt and indefinite ending. There is little entertainment here for other than uncritical audiences.

"Story: Walter Frisby, a henpecked married man,

465

comes to town ostensibly to give London's underworld the once over, but in reality to escape from the eagle eye of his wife, Hannah, and have a good time. He becomes the innocent scapegoat of crooks and is forced to masquerade as a butler to escape arrest. The crooks are out to secure a wallet in his possession and rob the household in which he is temporarily employed of a valuable vase, and they, in turn, are pursued by his nephew, Arthur, who hopes to become a crime reporter. To add to the complications, Hannah, having learned of Walter's whereabouts by accident over the telephone, also arrives on the scene. Walter fails completely to extricate himself from his difficulties, but he has in the end the satisfaction of seeing Hannah branded as a confederate.

"Acting: Betty Astell, Mark Daly, Michael Shepley, Richard Cooper, Margaret Yarde and Wally Patch are entrusted with the principle rôles, but it is only the last named who survives the handicap of the scrappy story.

"Production: The weakness of the picture lies in the planning of the story; it is needlessly overcrowded. By attempting to introduce a little of everything, comedy, romance, crime and thrills, it defeats itself, for it is neither one thing nor the other. Outside of a few laughs, it is barren of good entertainment.

"Settings and Photography: The many interior scenes are very stagey, the atmosphere is definitely theatrical, while the camera is employed with little imagination.

"Points of Appeal: Convenient length, good title, and quota angle.

13. *Inside the Room (1935)*
Murder mystery drama.

London Trade Show: Wednesday, 27 March 1935 (3.00 p.m.) at the Prince Edward Theatre.

British Registration Details:
Quota Registration No.: Br. 11,453.
Registration Date: 28 March 1935.
Registered Length: 5,989 feet.
Registered by: Universal Pictures, Ltd.
Maker's name: Twickenham Film Studios, Ltd.
Certificate: (A).

British General Release: Monday, 26 August 1935.

Inside the Room was reviewed in the *Kinematograph Weekly*, 4 April 1935, page 30:

"A" certificate. Austin Trevor, Dorothy Boyd, Garry Marsh.

"Remarks: Workmanlike murder mystery drama of "find-the-killer" type. Staging and acting adequate.

"Box Office Angle: Good second feature proposition of its kind. Not suitable for juveniles.

"Workmanlike murder mystery drama, of the find-the-killer type, set against not unfamiliar background of country-house party. Story is developed on straight-forward lines, with the solution of the mystery reasonably well concealed until the last few hundred feet. In fact, the film has all the merits of its type as a sound second-feature proposition for popular halls.

"Story: A once-famous actress dies in poverty. Just before her death, however, a mysterious visitor had received a packet of papers from her. Shortly afterwards two elderly men are found murdered in similar circumstances, and in each case an extract from the diary of the dead actress mentioning them by name is found pinned to the body. The police, who are convinced that a former lover of the actress is the murderer, ask Pierre Santos, a wealthy amateur criminologist, to help them. At a house party given by Lady Groombridge, Santos meets Sir George Frame, who has received a page from the "death diary". Also in the house party are Henry Otis, an explorer; Geoffrey Luce, an amiable toper; Adam Steel, a well-known singer; Dorothy Ayres, Santos' fiancée; and two oriental servants. Sir George is found murdered next morning in a room locked on the inside. Santos solves the mystery.

"Acting: Austin Trevor brings considerable experience in similar characterisations to the rôle and admirably suggests the shrewd Gallic detective. Garry Marsh fulfils the dual function of providing comedy relief and skilfully insinuating himself into the position of a "red herring" suspect. There is little for Dorothy Boyd to do beyond lightly suggesting a love interest.

"Production: The opening and introduction of the mystery elements is a little confusing, but once it gets into its stride the story moves smoothly to an effective and well-concealed denouement, with the interest maintained to the last.

'The Czar of Twickenham'. The History of Julius Hagen and the Film
Empire he created at Twickenham Film Studios, from 1927 to 1938.

"Settings and Photography: Settings are limited to
interiors, adequately presented, but the camera has
been used effectively to give a sense of movement and
variety.

"Points of Appeal: Good, straightforward example of
mystery thriller type, developed on popular lines.

14. Department Store (1935)
"Bargain Basement" – the original
title, very briefly used.

Comedy crime drama.

London Trade Show: Friday, 10 May 1935 at the
Prince Edward Theatre: the film was trade shown under
the title of *Bargain Basement.*

British Registration Details:
Quota Registration No.: Br. 11,664.
Registration Date: 14 May 1935.
Registered Length: 6,004 feet.
Registered by: Radio Pictures, Ltd.
Maker's name: Real Art Productions, Ltd. Certificate:
(A).

Trade Show advertisement: "Garry Marsh, Eve Gray"
('Grey' was misspelt in the advertisement), "Sebastian
Shaw in **Bargain Basement**. From an original story by H.
B. Maltby. Produced by Julius Hagen. Directed by Leslie
Hiscott." Tagline: "Comedy Drama of too many crooks
in a modern store". "Radio Pictures" logo.

British General Release: Monday, 7 October 1935.

Department Store was reviewed in the *Kinematograph*

Weekly on 16 May 1935, page 35:

RCA Photophone System, 67 minutes, "A" certificate.

"Remarks: Unpretentious comedy crime drama, put over by sound acting, and set in convincing atmosphere. Entertainment artless but popular.

"Box Office Angle: Safe quota booking for the masses and the family.

"Unpretentious comedy crime drama, which turns somewhat creakily on the hackneyed mistaken identity theme. The character-drawing and atmosphere, however, are not too bad, and it is to these attributes that the film owes its ability to provide adequate supporting entertainment for the unsophisticated. Safe quota booking for the masses.

"Story: John Goodman Johnson, nephew of Joshua Johnson, proprietor of a big store, is, in the absence of his uncle, instructed by the family solicitor to take up a small position in the store, the intention being for him to work his way up and so equip himself eventually to take over the management. Rather than he should receive favours from the staff, it is decided that he should work under an assumed name. By coincidence Bob Goodman, and ex-convict, gets a job at the same time, and the crooked manager, Timothy Bradbury, mixes their identity. John, however, decides to keep up the deception, and in the end he is the means of preventing Bradbury from making a big haul. His good work is rewarded, and he finds romance in the shape of the store's lady detective.

"Acting: Sebastian Shaw and Jack Melford are quite good as the real and bogus Goodman, Gary (*sic* - *'Garry' misspelt*) Marsh is convincing as the crooked Bradbury, Geraldine Fitzgerald takes good care of the love interest, and adequate support is forthcoming from Patrick Curwen, Hal Walters and Eve Gray.

"Production: As far as possible the obvious is avoided in the working out of the simple plot. The principal players approach the artless situations with all seriousness, and it is the sincerity of their work that compels the majority to register. There is plenty of comedy, a popular touch of romance, and just enough excitement to round off the story satisfactorily.

"Settings and Photography: The big-store backgrounds, against which most of the action is played, are convincing, and lighting and photography give no cause for complaint.

"Points of Appeal: Ingenuous, popular story, straight-forward treatment, and good team work.

The review in the *Monthly Film Bulletin*, May 1935, page 52:

"Departmental Store. * (Great Britain). Censors' Certificate "A." Distributors: Radio. Director: Leslie Hiscott. Stars: Garry Marsh, Eve Gray, Sebastian Shaw. 65 minutes. This is an amusing

471

film, the story of which centres on the confusion between two young men of the same name, one the rich nephew of the owner of a huge stores, the other the impecunious nephew of a friend of the stores-manager with a penchant for safe-cracking. Both are given a job in the store, the rich one intending to be incognito, which intention is fulfilled owing to the confusion. The dialogue is exceedingly funny, full of ambiguous statements which can be taken in two ways, and which are! The acting is good; the only blemish is that the hero remains faultlessly groomed and shining despite his first day's unaccustomed toil at heaving about enormous packing cases. All ends well with the exposure of the manager (Garry Marsh) who has been cooking the accounts for some years, and with the union of the hero and the lady detective. Good photography and good entertainment. * Original entitled *"Bargain Basement"*. Suitability: A, B. Reviewers: A. R. and F. R."

15. Squibs (1935)

Romantic comedy with music.
London Trade Show: Tuesday, 18 June 1935 (8.45 p.m.) at the Prince Edward Theatre.

British Registration Details:
Quota Registration No.: Br. 11,809.
Registration Date: 21 June 1935.
Registered Length: 6,947 feet.
Registered by: Gaumont-British Distributors, Ltd.
Maker's name: Twickenham Film Studios, Ltd.
Certificate: (U).

Trade Show advertisement: Billing: BETTY BALFOUR (large font size), Gordon Harker and Stanley Holloway (smaller font size). A Twickenham Film Studios Production. Produced by Julius Hagen. Directed by Henry Edwards. Musical Numbers: "The Londonola"; "Did you ever have a feeling you're flying?"; "Squibs"; "One way Street"; Song of the Law". Recorded on Visatone Sound System.

The *Kinematograph Weekly* on 10 January 1934 reported: Julius Hagen bought the world rights of the **Squibs** series.

British General Release: Monday, 30 December 1935.

Squibs was reviewed in the *Kinematograph Weekly*, 27 June 1935, page 34:

Visatone Sound System, 77 minutes, "U" certificate.

"<u>Remarks</u>: Romantic comedy with music woven around the original Squibs theme. Human interest is a trifle weak, but humorous and spectacular embellishment score through excellent teamwork.

"<u>Box Office Angle</u>: Sound, light entertainment for the masses, with star and title pull. Should please the youngsters.

"Romantic comedy with music, which finds in the original "**Squibs**" story a peg on which to hang popular sentiment, humour, and musical spectacle. The plot is not too clearly defined, but its thematic shortcomings are admirably concealed by the versatility of the principal players. Betty Balfour contributes a performance of tireless resource and energy in the lead, Gordon Harker never fails to register with his Cockney humour, and Stanley

Holloway turns his inimitable technique to song and character acting with equal facility. Added to the enthusiastic team work is pleasing spectacle set to music. Although absence of clear-cut story values prevents the entertainment from being uniform in quality, it nevertheless has in its bright embellishments the key to mass appeal, and in its richly endowed title and star values no vain hope of box-office recognition.

"Story: Squibs, a Piccadilly flower girl, and Charlie Lee, a policeman of Yorkshire extraction, meet and fall in love through the improvidence of Sam Hoskins, Squib's ne'er-do-well father, but later the unreliable conduct results in their drifting apart. Eventually Squibs has to call on Charlie's aid when Sam speculates with money that does not belong to him and is faced with imprisonment. Charlie does his best to oblige, but finds himself short of the necessary. At this juncture, however, a winning sweepstake ticket comes into Squibs' possession, and with it the money to end all trouble and misunderstanding.

"Acting: Betty Balfour is in her element as Squibs, and has no difficulty in meeting the entertainment's wide demands. Gordon Harker is immense as Sam; he is the shifty customer to a T; and Stanley Holloway sings and acts with ease as Charlie. No fault can be found with the support.

"Production: Those who can remember the original Squibs comedies may miss the human touch, but the masses no doubt will find in the light-hearted musical treatment and sustained stressing of the artless comedy element plenty to keep them entertained. The principal players certainly do their part, and production values are well up to standard.

"Settings and Photography: The ground covered by the plot is extensive – London slums, Piccadilly, Doncaster racecourse, and a North-country palais-de-danse supply the backgrounds. The songs are tuneful, and lighting and photography are good.

"Points of Appeal: Happy-go-lucky plot, bright comedy intermissions, pleasing touch of sentiment, good team work by well-known stars, and big selling angles.

16. *Vintage Wine (1935)*

Farcical comedy.
London Trade Show: Thursday, 20 June 1935 (8.45 p.m.) at the Prince Edward Theatre.

British Registration Details:
Quota Registration No.: Br. 11,811.
Registration Date: 22 June 1935.
Registered Length: 7,277 feet.
Registered by: Gaumont-British Distributors, Ltd.
Maker's name: Real Art Productions, Ltd.
Certificate: (A).

Trade Show advertisement: "SEYMOUR HICKS & CLAIRE LUCE in *VINTAGE WINE* with Eva Moore. Adapted from Alexander Engle's, *Der Ewige Juengling*. Produced by Julius Hagen for Real Art Productions, Ltd. Directed by Henry Edwards. Recorded on Visatone Sound System. Gaumont-British Distributors, Ltd.": G-B Logo.

475

London key-theatre pre-release run of *Vintage Wine*:

- At the Plaza, week commencing Monday, 8 July 1935, in a double-bill with *The Clock Strikes 8* (1935), starring Arline Judge, Kent Taylor and Wendy Barrie, directed by Elliott Nugent, produced and released by Paramount Pictures.

London key-theatre run of *Vintage Wine*:

- At the Stoll, Kingsway: week commencing Monday, 5 August 1935, supporting *Bright Eyes* (1934), starring Shirley Temple, directed by David Butler, produced and released by Fox.

British General Release: Monday, 4 November 1935.

Vintage Wine was reviewed in the *Kinematograph Weekly*, 27 June 1935, page 34:

> Visatone Sound System, 80 minutes, "A" certificate.
>
> "Remarks: Gay, farcical comedy of French vintage. Story piquant, dialogue smart, staging effective, and star's performance brilliant.
>
> "Box Office Angle: Capital light booking, particularly for good and high-class halls. Nothing to offend the family.
>
> "Gay farcical comedy of French vintage, which finds its sparkle in the brilliant acting of Seymour Hicks. He has a part perfectly suited to his age and active personality, and carries it off with characteristic poise and volatility. Sex gives spice to the entertainment, and the star sees that the snappy situations are flavoured to popular taste. He is aided in his good work by a first-rate supporting team, under the competent direction

of Henry Edwards, and staging which suggests convincing atmosphere. Capital light booking, particularly for good and high-class halls.

"Story: Charles Popinot, a gay widower in his sixties, marries a young girl, Nina, without disclosing to her that he is a grandfather and without telling his mother, sons, and grandchildren that he has taken a wife. His straight-laced family, however, eventually learns of the association with Nina, and, thinking that he has taken a mistress, demands his return to home and respectability.

"He refuses to be browbeaten, and the fracas leads to Nina and his family learning of his deception. He is then roughly jostled from one camp to another until Blanche, his courageous grand-daughter, takes sides with him and sees that he and Nina are reconciled and that she is welcomed into the family fold.

"Acting: Seymour Hicks is excellent as Charles; he gallops through the picture with gay volatility, yet finds in his predicament opportunities to strike the sentimental note. He is the master of all the emotions, and an entertainment in himself. Claire Luce is attractive and makes a good foil as Nina; Eva Moore is clever as Charles's mother; Judy Gunn is refreshing as Blanche; and Miles Malleson and B. Kynaston Reeve head the attractive supporting cast.

"Production: Although this comedy mainly is expressed in conversation, it is never shackled by stage conventions. Once the point is made clear it moves merrily along, and each intriguing situation finds perfect humorous exploitation in the polished antics of the star. The deception upon which the plot hinges permits sex to be introduced without offence, and piquancy gives the play a richness of flavour which should be accepted with relish by all classes. It is snappy diversion with a sparkle that enables it to live up to the title.

"Settings and Photography: The interiors are spacious, artistic, and appropriate, while lighting and photography are excellent.

"Points of Appeal: Piquant story, smart lines, clever team work, irresistible comedy situations, brilliant performance by star, and title values.

1935: Julius Hagen starts his own film rental company, Twickenham Film Distributors:

Having been in the film industry myself, and, in particular, having worked as a film booking executive, I can definitely see the logic that Julius Hagen obviously took in deciding to start and operate his own film distribution company. Basically, greater autonomy is given to any film producer which also has direct control of the distribution of his films. The producer is accorded a greater, or larger, share of the pot of money gained from the sale of cinema tickets.

'The Czar of Twickenham'. The History of Julius Hagen and the Film
Empire he created at Twickenham Film Studios, from 1927 to 1938.

To make it absolutely clear to the reader, cinema
takings, i.e. the income achieved from the sale of tickets,
are firstly split two ways, with a further division occurring
of the second split, as follows:

- Normally, the cinema would retain 'the lion's
  share', or the greater proportion, of his sale of
  tickets. His share thus retained will pay for his
  staffing, management, cleaning, and maintenance
  costs, plus possibly a contribution to his profit.
- The rental company, or film distributor, is paid
  the balance. Out of this, he will have to pay for
  the cost of prints for each film handled, plus his
  own administration costs and other expenditure.
- The distributor will also have to pay the
  producer, or maker, of that film shown. The
  amount, usually a percentage, will be determined
  between the renter and the distributor before the
  distributor starts to sell, i.e. rent, the film to
  exhibitors.

However, operating a film distribution company
inherently comes at a cost - there are always risks. The
new film distributor will now be competing in a large
market full of other film distributors. The majority of
these will already be well established and will usually be
much bigger than the newcomer.

Before Hagen decided to open his own distribution
outfit, he was making, or supplying, films to the 'big boys',
such as the huge British company, Gaumont-British Film
Distributors, and Radio Pictures, Ltd., the British rental
subsidiary of the American parent company, RKO Radio
Pictures.

Any film distributor needs a solid supply of films;
Hagen could not produce that many films even though he
now had two studios to make them. Therefore, he needed
an outside source of supply, and this he did achieve, but
with American film product from the so-called 'Poverty
Row' production companies, Chesterfield Motion Pictures
Corporation and Invincible Pictures Corporation.

Actually, although always made on very tight budgets, some of the Chesterfield/Invincible films weren't that bad. But, most obviously, they could not afford the luxury of employing very expensive, big American stars.

We shall review later all the films made by Chesterfield and Invincible which Twickenham Film Distributors handled in the United Kingdom; there weren't that many of them.

We shall also analyse later where and why Julius Hagen got it so wrong, in that starting his own distribution company was big, and expensive, mistake.

Twickenham Film Distributors: Head Office and Regional Offices:

According to the *Kinematograph Year Book* for 1936, Twickenham Film Distributors had the following offices premises throughout the United Kingdom and the Republic of Ireland, as follows:

1. Head Office, Dean House, 2, 3 and 4, Dean Street, London W.1. Telephone: Gerrard 3421. Telegrams: Hagenfil, Rath.
2. Twickenham Film Distributors, Ltd., 38, John Bright Street, Birmingham. Telephone: Midland 3769.
3. Twickenham Film Distributors, Ltd., Dominions House, Queen Street, Cardiff. Telephone: Cardiff 3414.
4. Twickenham Film Distributors, Ltd., Veritas House, 7-8, Lower Abbey Street, Dublin. Telephone: Dublin 44631.
5. Twickenham Film Distributors, Ltd., 173, Bath Street, Glasgow. Telephone: Douglas 4451.
6. Twickenham Film Distributors, Ltd., 12, Carlton Chambers, 84A, Albion Street, Leeds. Telephone: Leeds 21538.
7. Twickenham Film Distributors, Ltd., 11a, Renshaw Street, Liverpool. Telephone: Royal 3518.

8. Twickenham Film Distributors, Ltd., Parsonage Chambers, 3, The Parsonage, Manchester. Telephone: Blackfriars 5399.
9. Twickenham Film Distributors, Ltd., 11, Bath Lane, Newcastle. Telephone: Central 24601.

Note that Twickenham Film Distributors had eight regional offices, including one in Wales (Cardiff), one in Scotland (Glasgow), and, most important to take note of, one in the Republic of Eire (in Dublin).

The Hagen films that were released by his own new distribution company:

17. Scrooge (1935)

The first sound film version of Charles Dickens' immortal Christmas fantasy.

London Trade Show: Tuesday, 2 July 1935 at the Prince Edward Theatre.

British Registration Details:
Quota Registration No.: Br. 11,837.
Registration Date: 5 July 1935.
Registered Length: 7,006 feet.
Registered by: Twickenham Film Distributors Ltd.
Maker's name: Twickenham Film Studios, Ltd.
Certificate: (U).

Scrooge was the first film distributed by Twickenham Film Distributors. Ltd

John V. Watson

Trade Show advertisement: Billing: Julius Hagen will present the First Trade Show from Twickenham Film Distributors, Ltd. "*SCROOGE*". A Twickenham Studios Production. To be released Christmas 1935. Starring SEYMOUR HICKS, with an amazing array of talent: Donald Calthrop, Oscar Asche, Athene Seyler, Mary Lawson, Eve Gray, Mary Glynne, Barbara Everest, Maurice Evans, Robert Cochran, Charles Carson, Garry Marsh, Hugh E. Wright, Morris Harvey, Philip Frost, Margaret Yarde. Directed by Henry Edwards."

Scrooge was reviewed in the *Kinematograph Weekly*, 11 July 1935, page 22:
Visatone Sound System, 78 minutes, "U" certificate.

"Remarks: Delightful picturisation of Dickens' immortal Christmas fantasy. Acting excellent, atmosphere picturesque, and treatment resourceful.

"Box Office Angle: Great Christmas box-office attraction for all classes, and the family and youngsters in particular.

"Delightful period dramatic fantasy, adapted with great charm and resource from Dickens' immortal Yuletide story, *A Christmas Carol*. The moral of the tale is splendidly interpreted through the brilliance of Seymour Hicks' performance in the name part, and its appeal to the emotions is enhanced by the artistically composed backgrounds filled in with perfectly drawn cameos of famous Dickensian types. The film is not merely a flawlessly photographed version of one of the author's most lovable and popular works; it is splendid screen entertainment designed to captivate all classes. Excellent general booking, a

strongly recommended box-office proposition for
Christmas release.

"Story: Ebenezer Scrooge, miserly surviving partner
in the firm of Scrooge and Marley, has no patience
with those who invest their modest savings in
festivities for Christmas. After grudgingly giving
his browbeaten clerk, Bob Cratchit, a holiday on
Christmas day and refusing an invitation to dinner
from his nephew, Fred, he returns on Christmas
Eve to his lonely chambers, once the home of
Marley. Marley's ghost visits him and warns him
that his miserly ways will bring him terrible
punishment in the next world and implores him to
amend them. Scrooge, genuinely frightened,
repairs to bed and dreams accompany his
slumbers in which he sees the past, the present,
and the future. Each has a message of warning,
but it is the last, in which he sees himself in a
lonely grave, that brings about his regeneration
and with it a desire to help those less fortunate
than himself.

"Acting: Seymour Hicks is superb as **Scrooge**; he
lives the part, and by his tutored genius never
allows the moral of the tale to escape. There is
magnificent drama in his performance. Donald
Calthrop contributes a flawless study as Bob
Cratchit, Robert Cochran is good as Fred, and
Philip Frost is appealing as Tiny Tim, Cratchit's
crippled son, Mary Glynne, Garry Marsh, Oscar
Asche, Barbara Everest and Hugh E. Wright
adequately complete the portrait gallery of
internationally beloved Dickensian types.

"<u>Production</u>: Great credit is due to Henry Edwards, the producer, for the artistic and competent handling of Dickens' story, which contains in its fantasy strong human interest, compelling pathos, and a message which few can afford to neglect. Every phase of the delightful entertainment is composed in perfect perspective against colourful backgrounds of period authenticity, and its grand simplicity is brilliantly illuminated by the genius of Seymour Hicks in the pivotal rôle. By capturing the splendid spirit of the book in all its rich detail, the film has given to the screen splendid Christmas fare, gloriously English in character and unrestricted in its appeal.

"<u>Settings and Photography</u>: Technically the film is excellent, the atmosphere is faithful and colourful, while the dream sequences are worked evenly and smoothly into the development. Lighting and photography are very good.

"<u>Points of Appeal</u>: Human story, artistic treatment, strong human interest, gentle pathos, rich comedy, brilliant character-drawing by star and support, selling title, and obvious exploitation angles.

18. The Private Secretary (1935)
Comedy, starring Edward Everett Horton.

London Trade Show: Thursday, 12 September 1935 at the Adelphi Theatre, Strand.

British Registration Details:
Quota Registration No.: Br. 12,118.

'The Czar of Twickenham'. The History of Julius Hagen and the Film Empire he created at Twickenham Film Studios, from 1927 to 1938.

> Registration Date: 16 September 1935.
> Registered Length: 6,320 feet.
> Registered by: Twickenham Film Distributors, Ltd.
> Registered Maker's Name: Twickenham Film Studios, Ltd.
> British Board of Film Censor's Certificate: "U".

Trade Show advertisement: *"The Private Secretary*: Edward Everett Horton, with Barry MacKay, Judy Gunn & Oscar Asche. Adapted from the famous play by Sir Charles Hawtrey. Produced by Julius Hagen at Twickenham Film Studios. Directed by Henry Edwards." Tagline: "Pray remember this Date dear Mr. Exhibitor. I shall be there – with all my Goods and Chattels! Edward Everett Horton." Twickenham Film Distributors Ltd.

London key-theatre pre-release run of *The Private Secretary*:
   ♦   At the Plaza, week commencing Monday, 30 September 1935, *The Private Secretary* supported the comedy-musical, *Two for To-night*, starring Bing Crosby and Joan Bennett, with Mary Boland, directed by Frank Tuttle, made and released by Paramount.

The Private Secretary went out on General Release on 24 February 1936.

The Private Secretary was reviewed by the *Kinematograph Weekly*, 19 September 1935, page 32:

> "Twickenham. British. (U). Directed by Henry Edwards. Featuring Edward Everett, Oscar Asche and Judy Gunn. 6350 feet. Release date not fixed.
> "COMEDY. Considering that it is of a similar vintage to that of " *Charley's Aunt.*" this farce, adapted from the perennial stage success, carries

its age splendidly. It has not, of course, the daring of its modern counterpart — sex was taboo when it first saw the light of day — but in its refreshingly artless way it gathers a satisfying numbers of laughs. The team work is excellent, there is a fine cast headed by the inimitable Edward Everett Horton. and the production work is comparable with the best. Very good comedy entertainment with a big appeal to the family and youngsters.

"Story: Douglas Cattermole, an improvident, reckless young man, poses as the timid Reverend Robert Spalding, new secretary to Thomas Marsland, uncle of his friend, Harry Marsland, so as to dodge his creditors while awaiting the arrival of his own fruity uncle, Robert Cattermole, expected any moment from India. The Reverend Spalding is installed in Douglas' flat, and when Robert Cattermole arrives he mistakes him for Douglas. Robert Cattermole and Thomas Marsland are old friends, and their relationship brings all the characters under one roof. Further complications follow because Douglas' love for Edith Marsland, Thomas' niece, prevents him from disclosing his identity, but in the end he comes through smiling with his debts cleared and romance awaiting him.

"Acting: Edward Everett Horton is perfectly cast as the timid Reverend Spalding, and Oscar Asche is equally good as the peppery old Robert Cattermole. The next in order of merit are Sydney Fairbrother, O. B. Clarence, Aubrey Dexter and Alastair Sim. Although Judy Gunn, Barry Mackay and Michael Shepley are adequate as Edith,

486

Douglas and Harry respectively, they fall short of the high standard set by the "old stagers."

"<u>Production</u>: Since this play was written it has had many imitators, but so concrete is the foundation of its humour that it can still hold its own with the best. There is no lack of incident, and the comedy has further been strengthened by up-to-date gags, worked into the story without harm to it's original equipoise. The ending, which takes the form of a séance, is a grand piece of fooling. Taking it all in all, the picture can literally be called " nice work," clean fun for the crowd.

"<u>Settings and Photography</u>: The interiors are appropriate, while picturesque exteriors make room for a spacious gag, represented by a burlesque hunting sequence. Lighting and photography are very good.

"<u>Points of Appeal</u>: Laughable story, refreshingly irresponsible treatment, particularly strong cast, general appeal, and box-office title.

19. The Last Journey (1935)

Action-packed thriller set on a steam train.

London Trade Show: Friday, 11 October 1935 (8.45 p.m.) at the Prince Edward Theatre.

British Registration Details:
Quota Registration No.: Br. 12,225.
Registration Date: 16 October 1935.

Registered Length: 6,000 feet.
Registered by: Twickenham Film Distributors, Ltd.
Registered Maker's Name: Twickenham Film Studios, Ltd.
British Board of Film Censor's Certificate: "A".
Running Time: 66 minutes.

Trade Show advertisements: "Hugh Williams & Godfrey Tearle in *The Last Journey*" by J. Jefferson Farjeon. Julien Mitchell as 'The Driver', with Judy Gunn, Nelson Keys, Michael Hogan, Olga Lindo, Sydney Fairbrother, Frank Pettingell.   Directed by Bernard Vorhaus. Produced by Julius Hagen at Twickenham Film Studios." Tagline: "Dramatic!   Different!! A Thrill A Minute!!!" Logo: "Twickenham Film Distributors Ltd."

The Second Trade Show advertisement for "*The Last Journey*", published in the *Kinematograph Weekly* a week later, alters the billing order of the supporting cast as follows: With Julien Mitchell, Michael Hogan, Judy Gunn, Sydney Fairbrother, Frank Pettingell, Nelson Keys. Note: Olga Lindo is omitted from the listing. New Tagline: "Stark Drama and Breath-taking Thrills as The Limited Hurtles Along With A Madman At The Controls!" Logo: "Twickenham Film Distributors Ltd."

British General Release: Monday, 20 April 1936.

The *Kinematograph Weekly*, 10 October 1935, Trade Show Review:

> *The Last Journey* (Twickenham Film Dist.) Prince Edward Theatre, 11 October, at 8.45 p.m."

> "*The Last Journey*," produced by Julius Hagen at Twickenham, is adapted from an original screen story by J. Jefferson Farjeon. and contains all the elements in thrills, drama and comedy that have made this author world famous. Practically the

whole of the action in the film takes place on board an express train."

"We are introduced to a number of people travelling to Mulchester. Amongst the more important are the engine driver, the fireman, an adventurer, his bigamous wife, a couple of crooks, a detective, a member of the Anti-Alcohol Society, a famous brain specialist, and an excitable Frenchman."

"The passengers are unaware that the train is in the hands of a man driven temporarily insane from jealousy, because of his wife's suspected infidelity.

"Various little dramas and comedies are played during the dramatic journey, but the strongest element is fear, as the passengers realise that something is dreadfully wrong with the train that tears through stations, at which it is scheduled to stop, at 80 miles an hour."

"The train hurtles on at increasing speed — ever nearer to the terminus at Mulchester. What will happen? *The Last Journey*," directed by Bernard Vorhaus, is said to be exciting, dramatic and to contain a thrill a minute !

"A brilliant cast includes Hugh Williams, Godfrey Tearle, Julien Mitchell (as the driver), Judy Gunn, Frank Pettingell, Eve Gray, Michael Hogan, Eliot Makeham, Nelson Keys and Sydney Fairbrother."

The Last Journey was reviewed in the *Kinematograph Weekly* on 17 October 1935, page 34:

John V. Watson

66 minutes, "A" certificate.

"<u>Remarks</u>: Railroad thriller, cleverly devised, and executed with actionful directness. Acting and treatment first rate, and staging slick and spectacular.

"<u>Box Office Angle</u>: Capital melodramatic fare for the masses. Will thrill the youngsters.

"<u>Points of Appeal</u>: Rousing story, high pressure development, big thrills, good by-play, and convincing character drawing.

The Last Journey was reviewed in the *Monthly Film Bulletin*, October 1935, Volume 2, No.21, page 147:

"*The Last Journey*. Railway melodrama; a sensational and exciting if improbable story of an engine driver's last journey. As a result of brooding over his impending retirement and doubting his wife's faithfulness to him he goes mad and drives his train at terrific speed, disregarding all signals, and disaster is only averted at the last moment. The action takes place mainly in the train and thanks to the co-operation of the Great Western Railway has satisfactory accuracy of staging. We are first shown nervous people who are about to make a journey by this particular train - a young criminal who has just married (bigamously) a rich girl; two crooks making a get-away; a disguised detective; a brain specialist called to perform an operation in the country. The development is necessarily episodic, but a connecting link between the different groups is found in their common emotion of fear when they realise that the train is running away. Brief sketches of these people allow displays of very varying characteristics including those of the scientist, the criminal, the crank, and the vulgarian.

Suspense is well-maintained and the climax is thrilling. The acting generally is on a high level though opportunities in this type of plot are obviously limited. The direction is skilful and imaginative and the camera work is good."

20. *A Fire Has Been Arranged (1935)*

Comedy featuring the popular singing and comedy double act popular, Flanagan and Allen.

Chesney Allen and Bud Flanagan listen to Hal Walters (left) in a scene from *A Fire Has Been Arranged*.

London Trade Show: Monday, 14 October 1935 at the Prince Edward Theatre.

British Registration Details:
Quota Registration No.: Br. 12,226.
Registration Date: 17 October 1935.
Registered Length: 6,300 feet.
Registered by: Twickenham Film Distributors, Ltd.
Registered Maker's Name: Twickenham Film

Studios, Ltd.

British Board of Censor's Certificate: "U."

British distributor: Twickenham Film Distributors, Ltd.

Running Time: 70 minutes.

Trade Show advertisement: "Flanagan and Allen in *"A Fire Has Been Arranged"*, directed by Leslie Hiscott, produced by Julius Hagen at Twickenham Film Studios." Taglines: "Hello customers, this picture is going to be a real aspic – one long jell (Oi!)". "He's crazy – so is the film and it is the life of a laughtime! (Oi)" Logo: "Twickenham Film Distributors Ltd."

A Fire Has Been Arranged went out on General Release in either late April or early May 1936; the exact date has not been determined.

A Fire Has Been Arranged was reviewed in the *Kinematograph Weekly*, 17 October 1935, page 43:

> "Twickenham. British (U). Directed by Leslie Hiscott.

> "Featuring Flanagan and Allen and Mary Lawson. 6,300 feet. Release date not fixed.

> "ROBUST comedy, a picture which relays fruity music-hall humour to the screen without loss of laughs. Flanagan and Allen, the popular variety team, are given plenty of scope in the absurdly funny story, and with the help of a first-rate supporting cast deliver side-splitting gags with healthy rapidity. Although the production is adequate, the film lacks a little of the polish of the American product, but the cheery, homely nature of the typically English humour more than offsets this. The principal comedians know their public,

and by playing to the gallery with an unfailing
touch they leave no doubt as to the ability of the
crazy entertainment to register. Capital light
booking with exceptional star values

"Story: Bud, Ches and Hal, three crooks, rob a
jeweller's store, bury their ill-gotten gains in waste
ground, and are then led by the Flying Squad to
gaol. A ten years' stretch faces them, and when
they come out they find that an imposing
emporium has been erected on the grave of their
loot. It so happens, however, that Shuffle and
Cutte, managing directors of the store, are in
financial distress, and when they plan to burn
down the building, together with the falsified
books, for the insurance money, they, Bud, Ches
and Hal have no difficulty in getting together.
Needless to say, the plot does not work out
according to plan; in the first place the daughter of
the man whom they had robbed gets hold of the
jewellery first, and then the insurance policy lapses
before Bud and Ches can prevent Hal from
putting a match to the building, but the merry
bunch of   twisters   nevertheless emerge
unscathed

"Acting: Flanagan and Allen easily adapt their broad
technique to the requirements of the screen as
Bud and Ches; they are in great form, and they get
first-rate backing in Hal Walters, Denier Warren
and Alastair Sim. The love interest is next door to
negligible, but what there is is pleasantly dispensed
by Mary Lawson and Harold French, and the
comedy is further strengthened by an additional

amusing cameo contributed by the inimitable Rob Wilton.

"Production: This crazy comedy is no experiment; having proved its success in variety it finds its way to the screen confident of conquering new worlds. The tone of the comedy and the production is a trifle rough and ready, but this is in perfect-accord with the humour. The film is a made-to-measure mirth-maker for the masses.

"Settings and Photography: The odd dance ensembles are a trifle meagre, but apart from this the stagecraft is adequate.

"Points of Appeal: Great team work by established music-hall favourites, bright plot, good gags, excellent title, and big exploitation angles.

21. She Shall Have Music (1935)
Musical featuring Jack Hylton and his Orchestra.

London Trade Show: was held in either late November or early December 1935; the time and venue have not been identified.

British Registration Details:
Quota Registration No.: Br. 12,433.
Registration Date: 2 December 1935.
Registered Length: 8,310 feet.
Registered by: Twickenham Film Distributors, Ltd.
Registered Maker's Name: Twickenham Film Studios, Ltd.
British Board of Censor's Certificate: "U."

'The Czar of Twickenham'. The History of Julius Hagen and the Film Empire he created at Twickenham Film Studios, from 1927 to 1938.

> British distributor: Twickenham Film Distributors, Ltd.
> Running Time: 91-92 minutes.

She Shall Have Music went out on General Release on 23 March 1936.

The issue of *Kinematograph Weekly* which included a review of *She Shall Have Music* is not available.

The review in the *Monthly Film Bulletin*, December 1935, page 200 stated:

> "*She Shall Have Music*. Gt. Britain. Certificate: U. Distributors: Twickenham. Producers: Twickenham. Director: Leslie Hiscott. Leading Players Jack Hylton and his band, June Clyde, Brian Lawrence, Claude Dampier. 91 minutes. Musical romance concerned mainly with performances by Jack Hylton's band and attempts to wreck a special broadcast. The director is, perhaps wisely, content to let the succession of "turns" take each its own way, linked together by a slender story of a romance. The band numbers are the main feature, a "repartee" number being specially noteworthy for its splendid timing. The Leon Woizikowsky Ballet makes an interesting appearance, not too much cut up by any attempt at fancy editing, and Claude Dampier intrudes his eccentric fooling at intervals. A versatile film of many talents. Suitability: A,B,C. Reviewer: D. F. R."

John V. Watson

1935: The British Film Industry: Trends and Other Events throughout the Year:

Worton Hall studios to be leased by London Films.

The former **Blattner Studios** to be leased by Leslie Fuller Productions.

Walter Summers, producer, bankrupt.

(*K. W.*, 3 January 1935).

Article: **The fault of British script writers** – words that must be eliminated for the American market.

Article: **Are we marking time on production?** Quantity should keep pace with Quality.

(*K. W.*, 10 January 1935).

New Ideal Pictures, Ltd. is formed by Simon Rowson.

New George Formby picture – *Off the Dole!* (This was the second and final film Formby made for John E. Blakeley of the Mancunian Film Corporation. It was made in revue format.)

(*K. W.*, 24 January 1935).

The Jazz Singer is reissued with brand new prints with sound-on-film! But the reviewer commented: "Too dated to entertain the majority".

Sterling Film Co., Ltd. went into Receivership.

(*K. W.*, 31 January 1935).

496

'The Czar of Twickenham'. The History of Julius Hagen and the Film Empire he created at Twickenham Film Studios, from 1927 to 1938.

Radio has signed a contract to run **G-B product** in its 45 kinemas in New York City.

Gracie Fields' two-year contract with A.T.P. (Associated Talking Pictures.)

(*K. W.*, 7 February 1935).

Kenneth McLaglen Productions, Ltd. – the company is wound up.

(Kenneth McLaglen was one of the brothers of Victor McLaglen.)

Edward Godal in court to answer three alleged offences under the Companies Act, 1929.

(Edward Godal was a British film producer and director, who became a leading independent producer of British films after the First World War, becoming managing director of the small but ambitious British & Colonial, based at Walthamstow Studios from 1918 to 1924. His producing career virtually ended with the arrival of sound in 1929, after which he made only one further film in 1938.)

Maurice Elvey talks to an audience at the Gaumont Palace, Hammersmith, about his twenty years of film.

(*K. W.*, 14 February 1935).

Ludwig Blattner Picture Corporation, Ltd., goes into receivership.

(Ludwig Blattner [1881–1935] was a German-born inventor, film producer, director and studio owner in the United Kingdom, and developer of one of the earliest magnetic sound recording devices. Months later, Blattner committed suicide by hanging himself.)

(K. W., 21 February 1935).

Gaumont-British pictures are playing in 152 theatres in Greater New York this week.

Rene Clair and **Lothar Mendes** are signed by **Alexander Korda**.

(**Lothar Mendes** was a German-born film director and screenwriter. He is best known for directing the British films *Jew Süss* (1934) and *The Man Who Could Work Miracles* (1936). **Rene Clair** was the famous French director and writer; *The Ghost Goes West* (1935) was one of his best British-made films.

(K. W., 7 March 1935).

The **50ᵗʰ Odeon cinema** opens at Kenton.

(The first Odeon cinema was opened by Oscar Deutsch in 1928, in Brierley Hill, Staffordshire although initially it was called "Picture House". The first cinema to use the Odeon brand name was Deutsch's cinema at Perry Barr, Birmingham in 1930. Ten years later Odeon became part of the Rank Organisation which continued its ownership of the circuit for a further sixty years.)

(K. W., 14 March 1935, page 13).

Provincial Cinematograph Theatres, Ltd., announce that their profits increased to £482,508. A 15% dividend is to be paid again.

Francis L. Sullivan was married on Saturday, 16 March 1934 to Miss Danae Gaylen, talented young stage designer. Signed by Carl Laemmle last July for Universal.

'The Czar of Twickenham'. The History of Julius Hagen and the Film Empire he created at Twickenham Film Studios, from 1927 to 1938.

(Francis Loftus Sullivan [1903–1956] was an English film and stage actor. A heavily built man with a striking double-chin and a deep voice, Sullivan made his acting debut at the Old Vic at age 18 in Shakespeare's Richard III. He had considerable theatrical experience before he appeared in his first film in 1932, *The Missing Rembrandt*, as a German villain opposite Arthur Wontner as 'Sherlock Holmes'. Among his later memorable film roles were Mr. Bumble in *Oliver Twist* (1948) and Phil Nosseross in the British film noir *Night and the City* (1950).

(*K. W.*, 21 March 1935).

Elizabeth Allan's contract has been extended by MGM.

Gaumont-British will release 16 pictures in the United States during the coming season.

(*K. W.*, 28 March 1935, page 8).

Robert Donat is ill in a West End nursing home recovering from a serious operation. His return to Hollywood, where he is due for *Captain Blood*, is indefinitely postponed.

(The asthmatic Donat had to finally turn down the title role for *Captain Blood*, concerned that the action sequences would be too strenuous for him. After testing several unknowns, Warner Bros.-First National finally decided the give the star part to the then unknown Tasmanian actor, Errol Flynn, whom they had placed under contract in London earlier that year. *Captain Blood* (1935) made Errol Flynn a star, thus beginning his successful career as a swashbuckling actor!)

(*K. W.*, 28 March 1935, page 35, P. L. Mannock).

According to **Western Electric**'s latest half-yearly survey of the British Isles, there is now a total of 4,994 kinemas, of which **4,637 are wired for sound reproduction,** 356 closed and one remaining silent house.

(K. W., 11 April 1935, page 3).

Marlene Dietrich signs new Paramount contract.

(K. W., 11 April 1935, page 8).

St. George's Pictures, Ltd. is incorporated on 4 April 1935.

Transoceanic Film Productions, Ltd. is incorporated on 3 April 1935.

Twickenham Film Studios, Ltd. – increase in capital – the nominal capital has been increased by the addition of £3,500 beyond the registered capital of £30,000. The additional capital is divided into 3,500 preference shares of £1 each.

(K. W., 11 April 1935, page 15).

Larry Darmour has been appointed representative on the Coast (i.e. in Southern California) for **Gaumont-British Distributors.**

(K. W., 18 April 1935, page 3).

Ace Distributors, Ltd. is incorporated on 8 April 1935.

(K. W., 18 April 1935, page 18).

Article: **No More Quickies,** says **Irving Asher.** "The day of the Quota quickie is dead", Asher declares.

(Irving Asher (1903–1985) was an American film producer. Born in San Francisco in September 1903, he began his film production career in Hollywood in 1919. After joining the staff of

500

'The Czar of Twickenham'. The History of Julius Hagen and the Film Empire he created at Twickenham Film Studios, from 1927 to 1938.

Warner Brothers he was sent over to England to be the managing director of their British subsidiary based at **Teddington Studios** in Middlesex from the early 1930s.)

(*K. W.*, 18 April 1935, page 43).

Big developments at **Teddington Studios – Jack Warner**'s visit.

(*K. W.*, 2 May 1935, page 30, P. L. Mannock).

C. M. Woolf resigns as joint managing director of **Gaumont-British Picture Corporation.**

(*K. W.*, 16 May 1935, page 3).

Exclusive Films, Ltd. is incorporated on 10 May 1935. The directors are William Hinds and Enrique Carreras.

(Exclusive Films was the forerunner of the famous **Hammer Film Productions** who made so many British horror films from the late 1950s up to 1974.)

(*K. W.*, 16 May 1935, page 21).

Edward Godal is found not guilty of anything fraudulent. (See the first report about Godal's charge in the *K. W.* on 14 February 1935).

(*K. W.*, 16 May 1935, page 27).

Joseph M. Schenck, for nine years president of United Artists, has resigned and has joined Fox Film Corporation as chairman of the board. The merger is also announces of Fox Film and **20th Century Pictures** with Schenck as President.

(*K. W.*, 30 May 1935, page 3).

John V. Watson

C. M. Woolf's distribution unit is formed – **General Film Distributors, Ltd.** – capital £270,000.

(*K. W.*, 6 June 1935, page 14).

Mascot Pictures and **Republic Pictures** have merged.

(*K. W.*, 20 June 1935, page 4).

Al Lichtman is to succeed **Joseph M. Schenck** as president of **United Artists** – he was vice-president in charge of distribution for the last nine and a half years.

(*K. W.*, 20 June 1935, page 5).

Lost Horizon is to be Capra's next picture for Columbia.

(*K. W.*, 20 June 1935, page 29).

Criterion Film Productions, Ltd., is incorporated on 29 June 1935. The objects: to acquire the film production business of **Douglas Fairbanks, Junr.** and/or Douglas Fairbanks, Junr., Productions, Ltd.

(Criterion made several British films including *The Amateur Gentleman* (1936), *Accused* (1936), and *Jump for Glory* (1937).

(*K. W.*, 4 July 1935, page 19).

Sam Goldwyn emphasised the importance of the British market in helping American producers to recoup expensive negative costs.

(*K. W.*, 18 July 1935, page 4).

Technicolor, Ltd. is formed on 22 July 1935; capital: £160,000 in £1 shares.

'The Czar of Twickenham'. The History of Julius Hagen and the Film Empire he created at Twickenham Film Studios, from 1927 to 1938.

Stanley Lupino Productions, Ltd. is formed on 26 July 1935; capital: £1,000 in £1 shares.

(*K. W.*, 1 August 1935, page 12).

Article: **British pictures in Canada** – an ever increasing market.

(*K. W.*, 1 August 1935, page 12).

C. M. Woolf joins British and Dominions as managing director.

(*K. W.*, 15 August 1935, page 3).

British Lion deal with Republic. The British renter with distribute the films made the American studio in Great Britain.

(*K. W.*, 15 August 1935, page 5).

Herbert Wilcox Productions, Ltd. is formed on 15 August 1935.

(*K. W.*, 22 August 1935, page 23).

Paul Soskin's unit starts - Soskin Productions, Ltd.

(Paul Soskin [1905–1975] was a Russian-born British screenwriter and film producer.)

(*K. W.*, 5 September 1935, page 42, P. L. Mannock).

Alexander Korda has been made a member of the Board of **United Artists.**

(United Artists was founded in 1919 by the director D. W. Griffith, and the stars Charlie Chaplin, Mary Pickford, and

Douglas Fairbanks who all wanted to control their own interests, rather than being dependent upon other studios.)

(*K. W.*, 12 September 1935).

British Lion capital is increased to £750,000.

(*K. W.*, 12 September 1935).

Darryl Zanuck has superseded the office of supervisor by appointing groups of associate producers in charge of individual units at **Twentieth Century-Fox.**

(*K. W.*, 10 October 1935, page 4).

1935: The Eighth Year of the 'Quota' Act:

212 British films were first shown during the year 1935.

This number is arrived at by using the data contained in *The British Film Catalogue: 1895-1970* by Denis Gifford, as follows:

09895: Closing Gifford Catalogue Number for 1935.

09683: Opening Gifford Catalogue Number for 1935.

212: Total. A very small decrease of just two films against the previous year's total of 214.

Some of these films were short subjects; the actual number of shorts made has not been determined.

6. 1936: BRITISH FILM PRODUCTION REACHES A NEW

PEAK:

The year saw British film production strengthen again with well over 200 films being made for the third year in a row. British producers made 256 films in 1936, creating another record for British film production. Against the 212 films produced the previous year, this gave a decisive increase of forty two pictures, a new record high.

1936: JULIUS HAGEN CONSOLIDATES HIS FILM PRODUCTION AND NEW FILM DISTRIBUTION VENTURES:

Meanwhile, Julius Hagen produced just seven films in 1936 all of which were handled by his new distribution company, Twickenham Film Distributors, Ltd. All were productions of some quality, and certainly none of them were 'quota quickies'. But, as we shall soon see, it turned out that just seven films were not enough to sustain a new film renting company, no matter the good commercial intent, and the overall quality of the pictures themselves.

1936:

"THE MIGHTY NEW JULIUS HAGEN STUDIOS AT TWICKENHAM":
The *Picture Show Annual* for 1936: Edith Nepean's British Studio Correspondent (for *Picture Show*) reported under the sub-heading **"Keeping Unemployment Down"**: "The seriously-minded know that the making of films in England helps to solve some of the difficulties of unemployment. Thousands of plasterers and joiners are engaged in this great industry to-day. I

am amazed to see the gigantic "beehive" assembled during the making of the mighty new Julius Hagen Studios at Twickenham. Vast sound-proof walls, so that even the rumbling of a train cannot be heard, labyrinths of scaffolding, and beneath the floor an enormous well that can be filled with tons of water to provide a "lake" for romantic shots, or a "swimming-pool" for bathing belles".

The picture shows much intense activity at the newly extended Twickenham film studios.

January 1936:

Kinematograph Weekly reported throughout the month:

FILM PRODUCTION AT TWICKENHAM STUDIOS DURING JANUARY:

Eliza Comes to Stay. Henry Edwards hopes to resume production soon, interrupted before Christmas by Betty Balfour's illness. There still remains a week's work on this picture.

In the Soup will start immediately after *Eliza Comes to Stay* finishes.

Broken Blossoms. Two day's holiday over Christmas, Hans Brahm busy all last week, where intricate model shots of a

Chinese village were taken. Production almost completed; Brahm busy for another week or two.

(*K. W.*, 2 January 1936, page 39, P. L. Mannock).

DEVELOPMENTS AT TWICKENHAM STUDIOS DURING JANUARY:

*   Julius Hagen statement: "Pictures that pay their way." "Quality but not extravagance."
*   Julius Hagen's new company, J. H. Productions, is formed.
*   Julius Hagen's recent purchase of studios at Elstree. (*K. W.*, 9 January 1936, page 39).

Julius Hagen now producing films in two centres, at Twickenham and at Elstree. Hagen is specialising in British stars of proven talent.

(*K. W.*, 9 January 1936, page 117).

J. H. Productions have recently acquired the latest RCA High Fidelity recording equipment fitted on a Reo-Speed truck. The apparatus includes "silent track" moving-coil microphones and High Fidelity recorder and amplifiers

(*K. W.*, 9 January 1936).

Full-page article: Twickenham Distributors makes good in six months.

Release dates are given for *A Fire Has Been Arranged*, *The Last Journey* (pre-release in January at the Plaza) and *She Shall Have Music*.

(*K. W.*, 9 January 1936, page 85).

John V. Watson

Film production at Twickenham Studios during January:

The announcements included Sir Seymour Hicks in *The Pickwick Papers*, and *Underneath the Arches* and *Money Makers*, both to be directed by Monty Banks. (Note that Monty Banks did not finally direct *Underneath the Arches* (Redd Davis eventual did) and *Money Makers* was never made. And *The Pickwick Papers* became *Scrooge*.)

Further announcements: three Conan Doyle stories, *The House of Temperley, The Poison Belt*, and *Silver Blaze*; then *Broken Blossoms* (technical supervisor: Bernard Vorhaus), and *A Spy of Napoleon*; then *The Whirlpool* (working title), a dramatic sea story by John Oxenham, *In the Soup*; then *Eliza Comes to Stay* and *A.1 at Lloyds*; finally *Nippy* and an Edward Everett Horton project.

(Note that *The Whirlpool*, *A.1 at Lloyds* and *Nippy* were never made.)

(*K. W.*, 9 January 1936, coverage over eight pages in total).

Eliza Comes to Stay – Henry Edwards directs – Betty Balfour, Sir Seymour Hicks – Sydney Blythe camera – fifth week.

Broken Blossoms – Hans Brahm directs – Emlyn Williams, Dolly Haas – Curt Courant camera – eleventh week.

(*K. W.*, 9 January 1936, *Pulse at the Studios* column).

Eliza Comes to Stay. Clapham and Dwyer, Billie Worth, American tap-dancer, the Grosvenor House Girls, William Trytel's band. Howard Deighton supervised the cabaret set.

508

'The Czar of Twickenham'. The History of Julius Hagen and the Film Empire he created at Twickenham Film Studios, from 1927 to 1938.

Morton Selten is ill, Nelson Keys replaces him.

(*K. W.*, 16 January 1936, page 36, P. L. Mannock).

Dusty Ermine is the first J. H. Production with Dr. Sokol, Continental film impresario, as producer. It will be made at the new Elstree Studios.

(*K. W.*, 16 January 1936, page 42, P. L. Mannock).

In the Soup begins this week. Sydney Blythe and William Luff cameras; Arthur Barnes and Victor Trytel as assistant directors.

Dusty Ermine – Austrian Tyrol chosen as the locale for the exterior scenes. Paul Cavanagh arrived in London on Tuesday evening (28 January 1936). Interiors to be done at the J. H. Studios at Elstree.

(Note that the British actor, Paul Cavanagh, did not eventually appear in *Dusty Ermine*; as we shall see, he broke his ankle in the very early stages of production.)

(*K. W.*, 30 January 1936, page 32, P. L. Mannock).

CHANGE IN COMPANY DIRECTORSHIP: TWICKENHAM FILM DISTRIBUTORS, LTD.:

"**Arthur Clavering** will shortly relinquish his joint managing directorship of Twickenham Film Distributors, Ltd."

"He is taking the step consequent on the acquisition of additional Kinemas, the operation of which will require most of his time."

"This decision was arrived at after consultation with his co-

509

directors of Twickenham Film Distributors, Ltd."

"Mr Hagen, while regretting Mr. Clavering's retirement, appreciates the considerations which have weighed with him, and has consented to his release."

(*K. W.*, 13 February 1936, page 3).

February 1936:

Kinematograph Weekly reported throughout the month:

FILM PRODUCTION AT TWICKENHAM AND ELSTREE STUDIOS DURING FEBRUARY:

J. H. Productions, Ltd., the newly-formed company, is to operate at the J. H. Studios, Elstree.

(*K. W.*, 6 February 1936, page 51, P. L. Mannock).

Dusty Ermine. Dr. Sokol, technical supervisor, has spent the last week in Kitzbühel, in the Austrian Tyrol, seeking suitable locations. He had previous experience of mountain scenery in films like ***The White Hell of Pitz Palu***. Paul Cavanagh and Bernard Vorhaus left England on Saturday (1 February 1936) for the Austrian Tyrol, where much of the action of the story takes place. A complete technical crew with cameras, sound equipment, continuity writers and assistant directors followed on Monday (3 February 1936). Raymond Elton, the cameraman from Twickenham, will be joined by Otto Martini, Continental camera expert, who will be in charge of photography on location.

Curt Courant, recently working on ***Broken Blossoms,*** will take over from him when the unit returns in about a fortnight's time.

'The Czar of Twickenham'. The History of Julius Hagen and the Film Empire he created at Twickenham Film Studios, from 1927 to 1938.

In the Soup began filming on Monday (3 February 1936).

(*K. W.*, 6 February 1936, page 51, P. L. Mannock).

Dusty Ermine. Paul Cavanagh breaks an ankle. Anthony Bushell has been signed to replace Paul Cavanagh. Julius Hagen left for Austria on Saturday (8 February 1936).

Paul Cavanagh is to make two further pictures for Julius Hagen, the first of which will be *Fall of an Empire*, from Baroness Orczy's *Spy of Napoleon*, to be directed by Maurice Elvey.

(*K. W.*, 13 February 1936, page 35, P. L. Mannock).

Dusty Ermine in progress at Kitzbühel.

(*K. W.*, 20 February 1936, page 37, P. L. Mannock).

Dusty Ermine due back from Austria within 2 weeks.

(*K. W.*, 27 February 1936, page 46, P. L. Mannock).

SOUND IMPROVEMENTS AT TWICKENHAM AND ELSTREE STUDIOS:

Twickenham's "Eel Track". Sound improvements at Hagen's Studios. The newest type of **Visatone recording equipment** – Type 6B – recently installed. This apparatus represents a big step forward in recording technique, including channels for simultaneous recording of film and disc, improved optical system, and, most important of all, the Visatone equivalent of "noiseless" or "silent track" recording.

(*K. W.*, 27 February 1936, page 47).

March 1936:

John V. Watson

Kinematograph Weekly reported throughout the month:

FILM PRODUCTION AT TWICKENHAM AND ELSTREE STUDIOS DURING MARCH:

In the Soup – Henry Edwards expects to complete the film within the next two or three weeks.

Dusty Ermine is still on location, with the unit moving from hotel to hotel.

(*K. W.*, 5 March 1936, page 38, P. L. Mannock).

In the Soup is finishing soon.

Dusty Ermine is still on location in Switzerland.

(*K. W.*, 12 March 1936, page 39, P. L. Mannock).

In the Soup will be completed early this week (week ending Saturday, 21 March 1936).

Dusty Ermine. The unit moved from Kitzbühel to Innsbruck. Before leaving Kitzbühel, Bernard Vorhaus (the director) took many shots in the grounds of their hotel, all the residents and staff were pressed into service for one scene. The unit returns from Austria at the end of this week (week ending Saturday (21 March 1936).

(*K. W.*, 19 March 1936, P. L. Mannock).

Juggernaut. Julius Hagen has signed Boris Karloff to star, goes into production within a fortnight. Henry Edwards to direct – Joan Wyndham to have the feminine lead - from the novel by Alice Campbell.

(*K. W.*, 26 March 1936, page 50, P. L. Mannock).

'The Czar of Twickenham'. The History of Julius Hagen and the Film Empire he created at Twickenham Film Studios, from 1927 to 1938.

Dusty Ermine – first week in the studio – with Jane Baxter and Anthony Bushell.

(*K. W.*, 26 March 1936, *Pulse of the Studios* column).

THE PRODUCTION PERSONNEL AT ELSTREE STUDIOS:

The personnel of the Elstree studio is announced as follows:-

- Curt Courant has been placed under contract as lighting and camera specialist for J. H. Productions.
- Andrew Mazzei is art director.
- John Bourne, who has been working at Twickenham in another capacity, will act as studio manager.
- Cyril Stanborough will be in control of the stills departments at both Twickenham and Elstree.
- Jack Harris, chief film editor, will for the present act in a supervisory capacity for both studios.
- Baynham Honri, sound expert, will for the present act in a supervisory capacity for both studios.
- Ronnie Philip will continue to act as casting director for all Julius Hagen's productions.

Recent improvements at Elstree include a canteen, new still camera-rooms, with a large portrait studio.

Additional sound and camera equipment.

(*K. W.*, 19 March 1936, page 45, P. L. Mannock).

April 1936:

Kinematograph Weekly reported throughout the month:

ACQUISITION OF THE ASSETS OF PRODUCERS' DISTRIBUTING CO., LTD.:

Acquisition of the assets of **Producers' Distributing Co.**,

Ltd., Julius Hagen, already a power in the Industry, strengthen further his interests.

(*K. W.*, 2 April 1936, page 3).

Hagen deal with **P.D.C.** completed. Twickenham Distributors' plan to increase output.

(*K. W.*, 2 April 1936, page 16, The *City* column).

FILM PRODUCTION AT TWICKENHAM AND ELSTREE STUDIOS DURING APRIL:

Dusty Ermine now progressing quickly. The sets are designed by Andrew Mazzei.

Twickenham at a standstill until after Easter. The *Juggernaut* script is in active preparation.

(*K. W.*, 2 April 1936, page 36, P. L. Mannock).

Dusty Ermine. Additions to cast; Athole Stewart, Davina Craig and Katie Johnson (she played the part of Mrs. Kent in the stage version). Hans Lackner and Hans Langer, two Austrian skiing guides, and Dr. Schloss, a village photographer, who took the first stills of the film unit at the little Alpine resort – made their first appearance "in a strange new world" when they arrived at the J. H. Studios, Elstree, to play parts in the film.

(*K. W.*, 9 April 1936, page 27, P. L. Mannock).

Juggernaut started production this week.

Dusty Ermine: Austin Trevor joins the cast, as does Hal Gordon and Margaret Rutherford.

(*K. W.*, 23 April 1936, page 43, P. L. Mannock).

'The Czar of Twickenham'. The History of Julius Hagen and the Film Empire he created at Twickenham Film Studios, from 1927 to 1938.

Juggernaut – Mona Goya, the Continental star, added to the cast.

Dusty Ermine – Vorhaus hopes to complete within the next 10 days.

(*K. W.*, 30 April 1936, page 37, P. L. Mannock).

Juggernaut – Henry Edwards directs – Boris Karloff – Sydney Blythe and William Luff, camera – second week.

Dusty Ermine – Bernard Vorhaus directs – Ronald Squire – Curt Courant, camera – final stages.

(*K. W.*, 30 April 1936, page 37, *Pulse of the Studios* column).

ACQUISITION OF THE ASSETS OF PRODUCERS' DISTRIBUTING CO., LTD.:

P.D.C. - receiver's analysis of P.D.C. and New Ideal. £65,000 sale to Twickenham Film Distributors, Ltd. – agreement on 26 March – completion took place on 23 April – compulsory liquidation on 27 April – secured claims £77,000.

(*K. W.*, 14 May 1936, page 5).

May 1936:

Kinematograph Weekly reported throughout the month:

FILM PRODUCTION AT TWICKENHAM AND ELSTREE STUDIOS DURING MAY:

The Man in the Mirror. Owing to Edward Everett Horton's Hollywood commitments, production has been set back until the middle of July.

Fall of an Empire - Spy of Napoleon – Dolly Haas, Francis L. Sullivan cast – Curt Courant in charge of lighting and photography – Andrew Mazzei art director.

Juggernaut. Nina Boucicault, the famous stage actress, engaged. Arthur Margetson was originally signed to play the "menace" of the picture, has now switched over to the rôle of Roger, the hero, while Anthony Ireland takes the part of Halliday. First scenes shot last week.

Dusty Ermine - Walton Studios hired for back projection, as the installation of this equipment has not yet been completed. The unit left on Wednesday for Walton – a week's work here on back projection and a few extra exteriors will see the completion of this picture.

(*K. W.*, 7 May 1936).

Fall of an Empire (Spy of Napoleon) starts at Elstree Studios next week (week commencing Monday, 18 May 1936) under the direction of Maurice Elvey. Fred Merrick – assistant director – Ronnie Philip, the casting director, is busy.

Juggernaut – James Carter has designed a most attractive interior hall of a villa in Nice.

Dusty Ermine completes this week. Curt Courant and Andrew Mazzei will then be free to start ***Spy of Napoleon.***

(*K. W.*, 14 May 1936, page 40, P. L. Mannock).

Fall of an Empire (Spy of Napoleon). Frank Vosper signed.

'The Czar of Twickenham'. The History of Julius Hagen and the Film Empire he created at Twickenham Film Studios, from 1927 to 1938.

Juggernaut ending.

The Man in the Mirror – Genevieve Tobin signed.

(*K. W.*, 21 May 1936, page 35, P. L. Mannock).

"As a result of the success of **Broken Blossoms**, Julius Hagen announces that he is forming a separate production company with Dolly Haas and Hans Brahm as directors, whereby they will both in future work exclusively for him. Under a new contract Hans Brahm will direct two pictures a year over a number of years with Dolly Haas in leading rôles, to be released by Twickenham Film Distributors."

RCA High Fidelity equipment has been installed by Julius Hagen in TFD's private theatre. The sound-heads are the same type as those installed in Radio City Music Hall, New York – the largest Kinematograph in the world, with a seating capacity of 6,200.

(*K. W.*, 28 May 1936, page 47, P. L. Mannock).

JULIUS HAGEN'S AMBITIOUS PLANS FOR TWICKENHAM:

Hagen's ambitious plans. Twickenham's position "most satisfactory" – important subjects scheduled, including many American productions.

(*K. W.*, 21 May 1936, page 16).

June 1936:

Kinematograph Weekly reported throughout the month:

TWICKENHAM FILM DISTRIBUTORS SALES DRIVE IN THE UNITED STATES:

John V. Watson

Monty Morton to visit America. **Monty Morton, general sales manger of Twickenham Film Distributors**, will be leaving on the *Normandie* for America next Wednesday (17 June, 1935) as Julius Hagen's representative in important business negotiations which are proceeding and which necessitates the presence of an executive from T.F.D. in New York. Julius Hagen was to have made the trip himself, but owing to his many production activities he finds it impossible to be away at the moment. He intends, however, to pay a fairly prolonged visit to America in the autumn. During Mr. Morton's absence his work will be carried out by his assistant, Fred Fletcher.

(*K. W.*, 11 June 1936, page 16).

FILM PRODUCTION AT TWICKENHAM AND ELSTREE STUDIOS DURING JUNE:

Spy of Napoleon – Richard Barthelmess signed.

Juggernaut – completed - almost.

(*K. W.*, 4 June 1936, page 39, P. L. Mannock).

Beauty and the Barge. Twickenham's next, will go into production at Hammersmith Studios in two weeks' time. Gordon Harker signed – adapted from the famous old stage farce by W. W. Jacobs, first produced in the New Theatre in London, with Cyril Maude in Gordon Harker's part. Henry Edwards is to direct. Exteriors to be shot at Southend and up the river.

(*K. W.*, 11 June 1936, page 41).

Fall of an Empire – *Spy of Napoleon* – Maurice Elvey – Richard Barthelmess, Dolly Haas – third week – Curt Courant – Andrew Mazzei – unit moved from Elstree to Twickenham to continue production.

518

'The Czar of Twickenham'. The History of Julius Hagen and the Film Empire he created at Twickenham Film Studios, from 1927 to 1938.

Beauty and the Barge – Henry Edwards – Gordon Harker, Judy Gunn, Jack Hawkins – starting Monday (22 June 1936) – Arthur Barnes and Victor Trytel assistant directors – Hammersmith Studios, with their location on the river's edge, are particularly well suited for this production – shooting to be made at locations – from Southend right up river beyond Maidenhead.

> (*K. W.*, 18 June 1936, page 35, *Pulse of the Studios* column).

July 1936:

Kinematograph Weekly reported throughout the month:

FILM PRODUCTION AT TWICKENHAM AND ELSTREE STUDIOS DURING JULY:

Fall of an Empire - Spy of Napoleon – on location.

Underneath The Arches to be directed by Albert de Courville at Hammersmith Studios.

Beauty and the Barge – ideal location weather favoured production in the first week of shooting.

> (*K. W.*, 2 July 1936, page 35, P. L. Mannock).

Fall of an Empire – title changed to *Spy of Napoleon* – on location in Loch Lomond.

Beauty and the Barge – Gordon Harker ill with throat trouble. Production held up for a week.

Underneath the Arches starting this week at Twickenham Studios.

John V. Watson

(*K. W.*, 9 July 1936, page 33).

Spy of Napoleon – Maurice Elvey completing exteriors at Loch Lomond on Saturday (11 July 1936). The steamer "Princess Patricia' was renamed "La Princesse', needed for lake excursions. The captain and crew played prominent parts in the crowd scenes on the steamer, appeared for the days' work dressed in French costume, period 1870. Sir Kain Colquhoun: beautiful estate at Luss was loaned to the unit, paid several visits to the location which adjoins his house.

Beauty and the Barge – production is still held up – Gordon Harker not yet recovered from the quinsy of the throat.

Underneath the Arches. Redd Davis has taken over direction of the picture which goes into production this week. de Courville delayed on a film he is completing at Gaumont-British studios. Enid Stamp Taylor, Aubrey Mather and Harvey Braban have been given important rôles. James Davidson is assistant director, Sydney Blythe in charge of lighting and photography.

The Man in the Mirror. Genevieve Tobin has been signed to star opposite Edward Everett Horton. To be made at J. H. Studios. Production is scheduled to begin on Wednesday (22 July 1936).

(*K. W.*, 16 July 1936, page 56).

Underneath the Arches – Redd Davis directs – Sydney Blythe camera – third week at J H Studios, Elstree.

The Man in the Mirror is starting. Maurice Elvey, director of productions for Julius Hagen's Elstree Studios – novel by William Garrett - F. McGrew Willis, "one of the foremost American writers – hoped to capture British and American markets".

520

'The Czar of Twickenham'. The History of Julius Hagen and the Film Empire he created at Twickenham Film Studios, from 1927 to 1938.

(*K. W.*, 23 July 1936, page 31, P. L. Mannock).

Spy of Napoleon. The final shots were made last week at Elstree. It is now in the cutting rooms.

(*K. W.*, 30 July 1936, page 29, P. L. Mannock).

August 1936:

Kinematograph Weekly reported throughout the month:

FILM PRODUCTION AT TWICKENHAM AND ELSTREE STUDIOS DURING AUGUST:

Underneath the Arches. Boxing sequence: - Gunner Moir, ex-heavyweight champion of Great Britain; Leo Wax, Australian middle- and welter weight champion; Jan van Houten, Dutch wrestler, who has also boxed under his own name, Ted Zegwaard.

Beauty and the Barge resumed last week (week ending Saturday, 1 August 1936). Location filming on the River Wey near Weybridge.

Man in the Mirror – Andrew L. Mazzei, art direction; Curt Courant, camera; Maurice Elvey, director.

(*K. W.*, 6 August 1936, page 26A, P. L. Mannock).

Man in the Mirror is making excellent progress – concentrating on large station scenes showing Horton on his homeward journey from the office carrying the mirror which is the cause of all the trouble.

(*K. W.*, 13 August 1936, page 28).

John V. Watson

J. H. Studios – *The Man in the Mirror* – third week.

Hammersmith – *Beauty and the Barge* – fifth week.

(*K. W.*, 20 August 1936, *Pulse of the Studios* Column).

Julius Hagen announced that he had come to an agreement with **Franco-London Films** to produce two films in French and English versions. First film, *Widow's Island*, is to co-star Marcelle Chantal. Maurice Elvey to direct. Details of the second production to be announced later.

(Note that *Widow's Island* would later be retitled *A Romance of Flanders*.)

(*K. W.*, 20 August 1936, page 39, P. L. Mannock).

Man in the Mirror. Genevieve Tobin completed her part early this week. 150 extras were used last week to appear in crowd scenes in the evening rush hour in the Tube station. Mazzei supervised the building of complete Tube train and station platforms. *Man in the Mirror* has another two weeks to run on the floor of Elstree.

(*K. W.*, 20 August 1936, page 39, P. L. Mannock).

Beauty and the Barge is scheduled to be completed by 1 September - after completing exteriors at Weybridge and on a beautiful farm at Esher, unit moved into Hammersmith studios for interior sequences. First few days at Hammersmith on a public-house set. Towards the end of the month, Edwards will take the unit with the barge to Southend and Lower Helstow, and afterwards by train to Bournemouth for further sequences.

(*K. W.*, 20 August 1936, page 39, P. L. Mannock).

'The Czar of Twickenham'. The History of Julius Hagen and the Film Empire he created at Twickenham Film Studios, from 1927 to 1938.

Man in the Mirror. Edward Everett Horton caught a severe chill last week – shooting suspended for two days. Joyce Bland has joined the cast, and two Hagen "discoveries", Alastair Sim and Julien Mitchell.

(*K. W.*, 27 August 1936, page 37, P. L. Mannock).

Beauty and the Barge. Set: quiet fishing village on a deserted part of the cost, with local inn, little whitewashed coastguard cottages with fishing nets drying in the sun, tiny village shops, and a few "old salts" sitting dreamily over their clay pipes – out-of-doors scene designed by James Carter.

(*K. W.*, 27 August 1936, page 37, P. L. Mannock).

TWICKENHAM STUDIOS: SOCIAL EVENT:

Picture: During shooting of *Underneath the Arches,* Julius Hagen presented a silver tea set and cheque to Miss Doris Smith, cashier at the studio, and John Orton, commercial supervisor to Hagen's companies, who were married on Saturday (8 August 1936).

(*K. W.*, 13 August 1936).

TWICKENHAM FILM DISTRIBUTORS - ACTIVITIES:

Twickenham Film Distributors branch appointments – Manchester and other branches hard at work selling *Broken Blossoms.*

(*K. W.*, 20 August 1936, page 13).

Monty Morton in Sheffield to make the acquaintance of a number of local exhibitors. (Morton was the head of Twickenham Film Distributors, Ltd.)

523

John V. Watson

(*K. W.*, 27 August 1936, page 28).

September 1936:

Kinematograph Weekly reported throughout the month:

FILM PRODUCTION AT TWICKENHAM AND ELSTREE STUDIOS DURING SEPTEMBER:

Silver Blaze. Director Thomas Bentley to be begin about 23 September.

(*K. W.*, 3 September 1936, page 38).

Man in the Mirror. Horton completes his part at Elstree this week, then leaves for Hollywood almost immediately. Joyce Bland and Julien Mitchell have relinquished their parts and Renee Gadd and Garry Marsh have replaced them. Night club environment with music provided by W. L. Trytel's band. "Bubbles" Stewart, famous American radio entertainer has been added to the cast for these scenes; she plays the part of an attractive siren who tries to lead Jeremy astray.

(*K. W.*, 3 September 1936, page 38).

Beauty and the Barge. With final exteriors taken at Bournemouth over the weekend (of Saturday, 29 August 1936) and a few remaining interior shots at Hammersmith, Henry Edwards winds up production this week. Gordon Harker, Judy Gunn and Jack Hawkins in the leading rôles.

(*K. W.*, 3 September 1936, page 38).

With the completion of *The Man in the Mirror* at the J. H. Studios, Elstree, all three of Julius Hagen's studios will be quiet for a fortnight, when a new burst of production activity will begin with **Widow's Island**, a bilingual production to be made in conjunction with Franco London Films, and **Silver Blaze**.

> (*K. W.*, 10 September 1936, page 53, P. L. Mannock).

Widow's Island (*A Romance in Flanders*) – Hagen's bilingual starts – Julius Hagen is producing in conjunction with Franco-London Films – the story of the film was written by Mario Fort and Ralph Vanio (novel *"The Widow's Island"*) and is being adapted for the screen by Harold Simpson (who was responsible for dialogue and treatment for *"Spy of Napoleon"*. The leading parts in the English version are to be played by Paul Cavanagh, Marcelle Chantal and Garry Marsh with Olga Lindo and Alastair Sim), while Pierre Renoir and Marcelle Chantal (Aimé Clariond and Prieur) will have the leading rôles in the French version, which will be directed by Claude Heymann. Maurice Elvey directs the English version assisted by Fred Merrick – they have been in Belgium for the last fortnight supervising exteriors – goes into production at Hammersmith Studio. Most of the action of the film is laid on the French and Italian battlefields, with occasional flashbacks to action during the (First World) war. The title of the film is taken from a famous landmark on the battlefields.

> (*K. W.*, 24 September 1936, page 37, P. L. Mannock).

Silver Blaze. Thomas Bentley will begin direction early next week at Twickenham Film Studios – adapted by H. Fowler Mear – William Luff: camera – Victor Trytel: assistant director.

> (*K. W.*, 24 September 1936, page 37, P. L. Mannock).

John V. Watson

BRITISH FILMS AT VENICE:

The only British feature films to receive recognition were Twickenham's *Scrooge* and

Concordia's *Robber Symphony*.

(*K. W.*, 10 September 1936, page 3).

HAGEN'S FUTURE DISTRIBUTION PLANS:

Julius Hagen is to distribute the **Joe Rock film output**. 8 a year planned for Hagen.

(*K. W.*, 1 October 1936, page 21).

October 1936:

Kinematograph Weekly reported throughout the month:

FILM PRODUCTION AT TWICKENHAM AND ELSTREE STUDIOS DURING OCTOBER:

Marcelle Chantal arrived in London on Tuesday (6 October 1936) to star in both versions of *Widow's Island* – now being made at Hammersmith Studios. Maurice Elvey and Claude Heymann take it in turns on the floor at Hammersmith to shoot the different versions. The title of the English version has been changed to *No Return*.

(*K. W.*, 8 October 1936, page 39, P. L. Mannock).

Silver Blaze in second week. Arthur Barnes (assistant director) has been placed in charge of exteriors.

(*K. W.*, 8 October 1936, page 39, P. L. Mannock).

'The Czar of Twickenham'. The History of Julius Hagen and the Film Empire he created at Twickenham Film Studios, from 1927 to 1938.

Clothes and the Woman. Julius Hagen announced that he will begin production next Monday at Elstree on a film based on a story by Franz Schultz. Albert de Courville will direct, F. McGrew Willis, dialogue. The film will take to the floor as *She Got What She Wanted.* Tucker McGuire (gained a great personal hit in the recent West End success, *Three Men on a Horse*) will have her first opportunity of film stardom. Constance Collier and Alastair Sim also cast.

(*K. W.*, 15 October 1936, page 45, P. L. Mannock).

Silver Blaze. Production has been held up for the past week as Thomas Bentley (the director) is suffering from acute influenza.

(*K. W.*, 15 October 1936, page 45, P. L. Mannock).

Silver Blaze – after an absence of two week due to illness, Thomas Bentley returned to work on the film on Monday (19 October 1936).

(*K. W.*, 22 October 1936, page 41).

(Clothes and the Woman) She Got What She Wanted originally scheduled to start at Elstree on Thursday (22 October 1936) has been postponed until later in the week owing to casting difficulties. Albert de Courville will direct.

(*K. W.*, 22 October 1936, page 41).

Widow's Island – the Julius Hagen-Franco London production at Hammersmith studios. Marcelle Chantal had a hectic rush to Paris over the weekend to complete the last scene in a French film on which she had been working before her English visit. She left on Friday and returned on Monday (19

527

October) to start work again at Hammersmith.

(*K. W.*, 22 October 1936, page 41).

Silver Blaze – a camera unit left for Newbury on Friday (23 October 1936) where they attended the two days' race meeting in order to obtain shots.

(*K. W.*, 29 October 1936, page 53, P. L. Mannock).

(Clothes and the Woman) She Got What She Wanted begins this week as negotiations still proceeding for a leading actor to play opposite Tucker McGuire, the first shots of the film will centre round Miss McGuire, Constance Collier and Alastair Sim – Curt Courant: camera – Andrew L. Mazzei: art director – Arthur Barnes: assistant director – F. McGrew Willis in charge of dialogue.

(*K. W.*, 29 October 1936, page 53, P. L. Mannock).

Widow's Island. The current Julius Hagen-Franco London production at Hammersmith studios – later in the week scenes were taken inside a French laundry between Olga Lindo and Paul Cavanagh in the English version and Line Noro and Aimé Clariond in the French.

(*K. W.*, 29 October 1936, page 53, P. L. Mannock).

November 1936:

Kinematograph Weekly reported throughout the month:

FILM PRODUCTION AT TWICKENHAM AND J. H. STUDIOS DURING NOVEMBER:

Silver Blaze. Interruptions from rain – stable sequences.

'The Czar of Twickenham'. The History of Julius Hagen and the Film Empire he created at Twickenham Film Studios, from 1927 to 1938.

(*K. W.*, 5 November 1936, page 33).

(Clothes and the Woman) She Got What She Wanted. American actor George E. Stone is cast.

(*K. W.*, 5 November 1936, page 33).

Widow's Island is making good progress.

(*K. W.*, 5 November 1936, page 33).

Silver Blaze. Further exterior sets and Baskerville Hall.

(*K. W.*, 12 November 1936, page 51).

(Clothes and the Woman) She Got What She Wanted – Rod La Rocque signed – now in its second week at J. H. Studios, Elstree.

(*K. W.*, 12 November 1936, page 51).

Widow's Island – both versions completed.

(*K. W.*, 12 November 1936, page 51).

Silver Blaze – **Thomas Bentley hopes to complete production by the end of this week, ending Friday (20 November 1936).**

(*K. W.*, 19 November 1936, page 39).

(Clothes and the Woman) She Got What She Wanted – Rod La Rocque spent last week in 'a girls' school.

(*K. W.*, 19 November 1936, page 39).

The Vicar of Bray. Henry Edwards began direction on

Wednesday (18 November 1936) at Hammersmith Studios, based on the famous character of the same name – Stanley Holloway signed – Fred Merrick and Ted Deason: assistant directors – William Luff: photography – W. L. Trytel: director of music.

(*K. W.*, 19 November 1936, page 39).

December 1936:

Kinematograph Weekly reported throughout the month:

FILM PRODUCTION AT TWICKENHAM AND J. H. STUDIOS DURING DECEMBER:

She Got What She Wanted – French actress, Mona Goya joins the cast.

The Vicar of Bray in third week. Last week Henry Edwards had a difficult time with animal players. A set represented the exterior of Castle Brendon, a stately Irish home.

(*K. W.*, 3 December 1936, page 43, P. L. Mannock).

Hammersmith and Elstree:

The Vicar of Bray – the film will be completed by Christmas 1936.

She Got What She Wanted – Albert de Courville expects to complete within the next ten days.

(*K. W.*, 10 December 1936, page 43, P. L. Mannock).

The Vicar of Bray – Henry Edwards moved from Hammersmith Studios to Twickenham this week for the final ten days' work.

'The Czar of Twickenham'. The History of Julius Hagen and the Film Empire he created at Twickenham Film Studios, from 1927 to 1938.

(*K. W.*, 17 December 1936, page 31).

She Got What She Wanted at J. H. Studios, completes this week.

(*K. W.*, 17 December 1936, page 31).

Twickenham Studios - *The Vicar of Bray* – sixth week.

(*K. W.*, 24 December 1936, page 33, *Pulse at the Studios* column).

The Vicar of Bray. The entire stage at Twickenham was occupied by a reconstruction of the village square of Bray, near Dublin, in the seventeenth century. The old war horse destined for the slaughter house was bought by Henry Edwards, Cyril Stanborough (still cameraman) and Bill Cavender (studio electrician) so that the old horse could end its days at Imber Court, Surrey, at the expense of the three.

(*K. W.*, 31 December 1936, page 39, P. L. Mannock).

J. H. PRODUCTIONS, LTD - NEW APPARATUS INSTALLED:

Rear Projection – new apparatus has been for J. H. Studios.

(*K. W.*, 26 November 1936, page 51).

1936, FROM OCTOBER:
Julius Hagen significantly
increases the debt of two of his

companies, Twickenham Film Distributors and J. H. Productions.

TWICKENHAM FILM DISTRIBUTORS, LTD - MORTGAGES AND CHARGES:

Twickenham Film Distributors, Ltd., 111 Wardour Street, London, W.1. – Debenture, charged on the company's property (supplemental to debenture dated 30 May 1935), dated 1 October 1936, to secure all sums as the mortgagees. C. T. Bowring and Co., (Insurance), Ltd., 52 Leadenhall Street, London, E.C. may be called upon to pay under a guarantee to Lloyds Bank, Ltd., not exceeding £150,000.

(*K. W.*, 22 October 1936, page 26).

J. H. PRODUCTIONS, LTD - MORTGAGES AND CHARGES:

J. H. Productions, Ltd., 111 Wardour Street, London, W.1. – Debenture, charged on the company's property dated 3 November 1936 (supplemental to debenture dated 20 January 1936), to secure all such sums as the mortgagees – C. T. Bowring and Co., (Insurance), Ltd. – may be called upon to pay under a guarantee to Lloyds Bank, Ltd., not exceeding £25,000.

(*K. W.*, 19 November 1936, page 14).

TWICKENHAM FILM DISTRIBUTORS, LTD . - MORTGAGES AND CHARGES:

Twickenham Film Distributors, Ltd., 111 Wardour Street, London, W.1. – Charge, dated 30 October 1936, to secure balance of £35,000 remaining due under heads of agreement dated 26 March 1936, and supplemental agreement dated 29

'The Czar of Twickenham'. The History of Julius Hagen and the Film Empire he created at Twickenham Film Studios, from 1927 to 1938.

October 1936. Holder: H. G. Judd, 8 Fredericks Place, E.C.2.

(*K. W.*, 3 December 1936, page 14).

J. H. PRODUCTIONS, LTD . - MORTGAGES AND CHARGES:

J. H. Productions, Ltd., 111 Wardour Street, London, W.1. – Debenture, dated 16 November 1936, to secure all such sums as the mortgagees may be called upon to pay under a guarantee to Lloyds Bank., Ltd. not exceeding £100,000. Holders: C. T. Bowring and Co., (Insurance), Ltd., 52 Leadenhall Street, London, E.C.3.

(*K. W.*, 3 December 1936, page 14).

TWICKENHAM FILM DISTRIBUTORS, LTD . - MORTGAGES AND CHARGES:

Twickenham Film Distributors, Ltd., 56 Cannon Street, London, E.C. – Charge on company's interest in certain films dated 11 December 1936, to secure £34,500. Holders: C. T. Bowring and Co., (Insurance), Ltd., 52 Leadenhall Street, London, E.C.3.

(*K. W.*, 31 December 1936, page 14).

1936: DECEMBER:
Julius Hagen discontinues Twickenham Film Distributors - new distribution deal arranged with John Maxwell's Wardour Films, Ltd:

John V. Watson

Twickenham/Wardour Distribution Deal:

Maxwell-Hagen deal.

Twickenham film product to be released through **Wardour Films, Ltd**. – twelve pictures a year planned. Six 'supers' now ready: *Beauty and the Barge, Underneath the Arches, Widow's Island, Silver Blaze, She Got What She Wanted* and *The Vicar of Bray*.

12 pictures from Twickenham Film Distributors will now be handled by Wardour, from *Scrooge* to *The Man in the Mirror*.

The world rights of all the films mentioned above will be negotiated by Twickenham Film Distributors, but all future films produced by Mr. Hagen's studios will be controlled throughout the world by Mr. Maxwell's company.

(Note that Wardour Films was the renting arm of the Associated British Picture Corporation, a company run by its founder, John Maxwell.)

(*K. W.*, 17 December 1936, pages 5 and 13).

The Seven films trade shown by Julius Hagen during 1936:

1. In The Soup (1936)
Comedy starring Ralph Lynn.

'The Czar of Twickenham'. The History of Julius Hagen and the Film Empire he created at Twickenham Film Studios, from 1927 to 1938.

Directed by Henry Edwards.

London Trade Show: Tuesday, 7 April 1936 at the Piccadilly Theatre.

British Registration Details:
Quota Registration No.: Br. 12,951
Registration Date: 9 April 1936
Registered Length: 6,600 feet
Registered by: Twickenham Film Distributors, Ltd
Maker's name: Twickenham Film Studios, Ltd.
Certificate: (U)

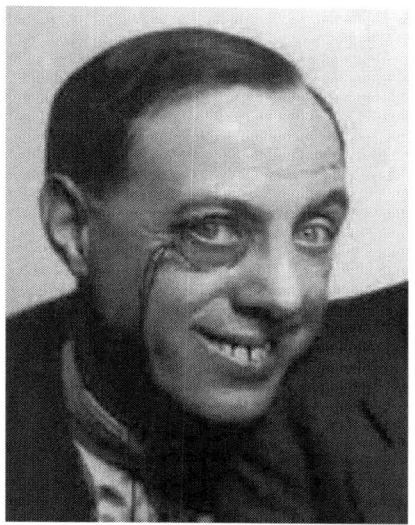

A typical picture of the star, Ralph Lynn, replete with his monocle.

Trade Show advertisement: "Ralph Lynn gets '*In the Soup*'" with Morton Selten, Judy Gunn, Nelson Keys." Tagline: "It's laughter all the way – when Ralph Lynn gets

John V. Watson

'In the Soup'". Logo: "Twickenham Film Distributors Ltd."
London key-theatre pre-release runs:

At the Paramount, week commencing Monday, 1 June 1936. *In the Soup* was presented in a double-bill with the American comedy-thriller, ***Murder on the Bridle Path*** (1936), starring James Gleason and Helen Broderick, made and released by RKO Radio Pictures. It was the fourth film in the 'Hildegarde Withers' series made by RKO Radio in the 1930s; it was the first and only film in which Helen Broderick played 'Hildegarde Withers'.

At the Stoll, Kingsway, week commencing Monday, 8 June 1936. *In the Soup* was top-billed over the American musical, ***The Melody Lingers On*** (1935), starring Josephine Hutchinson, George Houston and John Halliday, an Edward Small production for his Reliance Pictures, released by United Artists.

British General Release: Monday, 2 November 1936.

In the Soup was reviewed in the *Kinematograph Weekly*, 16 April 1936, page 22:

73 minutes, "U" certificate.

"Remarks: Clean, typically English comedy, put over with plenty of pep. Great performance by Ralph Lynn, good support, snappy quips, and slick staging and direction.

"Box Office Angle: Capital light booking for the majority of audiences. Fine stuff for the juvenile element.

'The Czar of Twickenham'. The History of Julius Hagen and the Film Empire he created at Twickenham Film Studios, from 1927 to 1938.

"Clean, wholesome, typically English farcical comedy, a graduate of the time-honoured, but perennially popular, school as *The Private Secretary*. The crazily involved plot is productive of much genuine amusement, and the team work and direction are good, but the real pillar of the entertainment is Ralph Lynn. He is in exceptional form, and scores as many laughs off his own bat as the preposterous situations and supporting cast put together.

"The picture is not pretentious, it makes no overtures to the sophisticated public, but its refreshing, inconsequential wit, together with its star value and equitable balance, mark it down as a capital light booking for the majority of audiences, and family and suburban ones in particular.

"Story: Horace Gillibrand, a briefless barrister, is forced, through lack of funds, to sublet his flat. His friend, Paul Hemming, finds him tenants in his prospective in-laws, while Horace's wife, Kitty, ignorant of the deal, lets the flat to his peppery uncle Abernethy Ruppershaw.

"Complications start when the tenants overlap, and Horace, now acting with Kitty as butler and servant respectively, has to keep his marriage a secret from Uncle Abernethy, trustee of his father's will which states that he must not marry until he is over forty. To smooth temporarily the troubled waters, Kitty puts a sleeping draught in the soup, but the results are unexpected, and lead to Uncle Abernethy being compromised. At this juncture, however, Horace does his stuff, and in

537

getting Uncle Abernethy out of a jam, he has his marriage to Kitty condoned.

"Acting: Ralph Lynn is excellent as the asinine, absent-minded Horace; he combines clowning with a finished flair for character-drawing. Morton Selten is clever as Abernethy, he fits the part perfectly; Judy Gunn is attractive and appealing as the harassed Kitty; and Michael Shepley, Olive Melville, Nelson Keys, Bertha Belmore, Morris Harvey and Margaret Yarde bring all their stage experience to bear in support.

"Production: The complexities of the plot call for more dialogue than action, but such is the pep imparted to the conventional farcical comedy by Ralph Lynn that adequate movement is secured.

"The creating of the tangle is accompanied by good fun, while the straightening out process is productive of even more hilarity. The humour is evergreen, and it has the additional advantage of being smoothly and attractively served. Only the highbrows will cavil at the comedy's artlessness.

"Settings and Photography: The picture opens with an amusing law court scene, and from thence on the interiors are always in keeping with the simple fooling. Lighting and photography are very good.

"Points of Appeal: Bright, cheery, amusing story, clever and resourceful performance by box-office star, good support, competent direction, and first-class production qualities.

2. *Eliza Comes To Stay (1936)*

Farcical comedy starring Sir Seymour Hicks and Betty Balfour.

Directed by Henry Edwards.

London Trade Show: Wednesday, 8 April 1936 at the Piccadilly Theatre.

British Registration Details:
Quota Registration No.: Br. 12,963.
Registration Date: 14 April 1936.
Registered Length: 6,500 feet.
Registered by: Twickenham Film Distributors, Ltd.
Maker's name: Twickenham Film Studios, Ltd.
Certificate: "A".

Trade Show advertisement: *Eliza Comes to Stay*: "Seymour Hicks - Betty Balfour, with Oscar Asche & Ellis Jeffreys. Adapted from the world famous farce by H. V. Esmond. Directed by Henry Edwards. Produced by Julius Hagen." Logo: "Twickenham Film Distributors Ltd."

British General Release: Monday, 19 October 1936.

John V. Watson

A signed portrait of the star, Sir Seymour Hicks.

Eliza Comes To Stay was reviewed in the *Kinematograph Weekly*, 16 April 1936, page 22:

72 minutes, "A" certificate.

"Remarks: Old-fashioned farcical comedy, adapted with little imagination from a pre-war stage success. Team work moderate, dialogue trite and direction lacking in resource.
"Box Office Angle: Second-feature booking on star values for small halls only. Nothing to offend youngsters.

"Old-fashioned, commonplace farcical comedy, too far behind the times in its humour, trite in its dialogue, and colourless in its interpretation to appeal to other than very unsophisticated audiences. The entertainment belongs to a bygone age and crumples at the misguided attempt at resuscitation. Moderate supporting feature, entirely on its star values, for small industrial and family halls.

"Story: The Hon. Sandy Verrall, a gay bachelor, accepts the guardianship of Eliza Vandan, daughter of a man who had saved his life in a motor accident. After proposing to Vera Laurance, an actress, to provide a mother for his adopted offspring (whom he believes to be an infant), she turns out to be an unprepossessing young man.

"However, Eliza knows her way around, and after placing herself in the hands of a fashionable dressmaker she circumvents all attempts on the part of Sandy's upstage aunt, Lady Elizabeth, to marry her off to Monty Jordan, the family solicitor, and catches Sandy on the rebound when Vera jilts him for his wealthy uncle, the susceptible Sir Gregory.

"Acting: Betty Balfour is hopelessly out of her element as the provocative Eliza; in fact, so ineffective is she that she unconsciously reverses the metamorphosis. The fine feathers she adopts in the concluding reels merely accentuate her lack of colour and resource.

"Although Seymour Hicks is not too bad as Sandy, his experience and polished artistry barely compensate for his amiable but obvious maturity.

A. R. Whatmore, Nelson Keys, Vera Bogetti (misspelt "Boggetti"), Ellis Jeffreys and Oscar Asche work hard with the odds against them in support.

"Production: This farcical comedy is pre-war stuff; the treatment is as old as H. V. Esmond's play from which it is adapted, but neither has improved with age. There is dust in the dialogue and cobwebs on the gags and situations. Eliza would have been far wiser to have stayed where she was, honourably buried in the past.

"Settings and Photography: In spite of the introductory superfluous cabaret entertainment, the staging is cramped. Light and photography are satisfactory.

"Points of Appeal: Quota angle, title and star values.

3. Broken Blossoms (1936)
Romantic drama adapted from Thomas Burke's famous short story (1916).

Starring Dolly Haas and Emlyn Williams with Arthur Margetson.

'The Czar of Twickenham'. The History of Julius Hagen and the Film Empire he created at Twickenham Film Studios, from 1927 to 1938.

Directed by Hans Brahm (later John Brahm). D. W. Griffith was originally signed by Julius Hagen to remake his silent classic of 1919, but apparently Griffith's persistent drinking prevented this.

London Trade Show: Wednesday, 20 May 1936 at the Cambridge Theatre. The Trade Show was originally announced to be held on Thursday, 23 April 1936 at the Cambridge Theatre.

British Registration Details:
Quota Registration No.: Br. 13,191.
Registration Date: 28 May 1936.
Registered Length: 7,725 feet.
Registered by: Twickenham Film Distributors, Ltd.
Maker's name: Twickenham Film Studios, Ltd.
Certificate: "A".

British Distributor: Wardour Films from December 1936.

Trade Show advertisement: *Broken Blossoms*: DOLLY HAAS – EMLYN WILLIAMS – Arthur Margetson. Directed by Hans Brahm. Produced by Julius

Hagen at Twickenham Film Studios. Tagline: "The Most
Beautiful Love Story ever Screened" Logo: "Twickenham
Film Distributors Ltd"

London key-theatre pre-release runs:
♦   At the London Pavilion, week commencing
Monday, 22 June 1936; no supporting feature (if any) was
listed in the *Kinematograph London Cinema Guide*.
♦   ***Broken Blossoms*** was held-over for a second
week, commencing Monday, 29 June 1936; again no
supporting feature (if any) was listed in the
Kinematograph London Cinema Guide.
♦   At the Paramount, week commencing Monday,
24 August 1936, ***Broken Blossoms*** was supported by the
American comedy-romance, His Majesty Bunker Bean,
(1936) with Owen Davis Jr., Louise Latimer and Robert
McWade, released by Radio Pictures.
♦
British General Release: Monday, 18 January 1937.

Broken Blossoms was reviewed in the *Kinematograph
Weekly*, 28 May 1936, page 33:

80 minutes, "A" certificate.

"Remarks: An artistic and emotionally satisfying
romantic drama, intelligently adapted from
Thomas Burke's famous short story. Treatment a
little pedestrian but star's performance exquisite.
Technical treatment vivid, dialogue good and
feminine appeal immense.
"Box Office Angle: Outstanding general booking,
one with a box-office title. Hardly suitable for
youngsters.

"Romantic drama of sombre beauty and drab
charm, intelligently and artistically adapted from
Thomas Burke's famous short story. The

atmosphere in which the delicate love interest is
prompted is one of harsh brutality, but arising
from ugly soil is sentiment of exquisite delicacy
and immense appeal, and situations of tremendous
power.

"Stark, vivid, capably characterised, particularly by
Dolly Haas in the lead, and brilliantly mounted,
the film is the equal of its famous silent
predecessor in quality and entertainment.
Outstanding general booking, one with a valuable
box-office heritage in its title.

"Story: Chen, a young Chinaman, comes to
England with joy in his heart intent upon
spreading the lofty teachings of Buddha, but his
reception is hostile and he fails in his mission.
While running a curio shop in Limehouse, he
meets Lucy, a waif bullied and cowed by her brutal
father, Burrows, and their kindred spirit leads to
shy friendship.

"Following a particularly brutal assault on Lucy,
Burrows leaves his drab home to go into training,
and she is found unconscious by Chen and carried
into her house. Their tender idyll, however, is
short lived, for it comes to the notice of Burrows,
and he, outraged at the idea of daughter
associating with a Chinaman, kills her. Chen kills
him, and so the romance ends.

"Acting: Dolly Haas is tremendously appealing as
Lucy, a superb actress with a fine command of
facial expressions she finds her accent no
handicap in her drawing of the tender Cockney

rôle. Arthur Margetson contributes a powerful dramatic caricature as the brutal Burrows, and Emlyn Williams, although the least satisfactory cast of the three, promotes colourful contrast as Chen. Ernest Sefton, Donald Calthrop, and Gibb McLaughlin are clever in support.

"Production: Hans Brahm's direction of this picture reveals imagination, but he has yet to learn to put fundamentals before artistry. The opening scenes, those devoted to the establishment of character, are long drawn out.

"Once it moves, however, perfect co-operation between producer, principal players, art director and photographer, is evinced, and from thence onward the brutal, the pathetic, and the exquisite moods of the tale fashion into stark entertainment of impeccable quality and wide appeal. It is the last hour of the film that puts it in a class of its own.

"Settings and Photography: The opening shots have artistic merit, the Limehouse sequences are sketched with a vividness that catches all the squalor, and the fight scene provides vigorous light relief, while the romantic interludes are shaded with all the exotic colour of the Orient.

"Lighting and photography are excellent.

"Points of Appeal: Poignantly tragic story, vigorous settings, tender romance, flawless and appealing acting by Dolly Haas, and obvious exploitation angles.

4. *Spy of Napoleon (1936)*

Period espionage romantic drama, based on Baroness Orczy's best seller.

Starring Dolly Haas and Richard Barthelmess, with Frank Vosper, Francis L. Sullivan, Joyce Bland and Henry Oscar.

Directed by Maurice Elvey.

London Trade Show: Wednesday, 9 September 1936 at the Piccadilly Theatre.

British Registration Details:
Quota Registration No.: Br. 13,652.
Registration Date: 22 September 1936.
Registered Length: 9,048 feet.
Registered by: Twickenham Film Distributors, Ltd.
Maker's name: J. H. Productions, Ltd.
Certificate: "U".
British Distributor: Wardour Films.

Trade Show advertisement: "*Spy of Napoleon*. Dolly Haas, Richard Barthelmess (billed above the title). Frank Vosper, Francis L. Sullivan, Joyce Bland, Henry Oscar (billed below the title). A J. H. Production. Produced by Julius Hagen. Directed by Maurice Elvey. Tagline: "A lavish and spectacular version of Baroness Orczy's greatest historical romance." Logo: "Twickenham Film Distributors Ltd".

John V. Watson

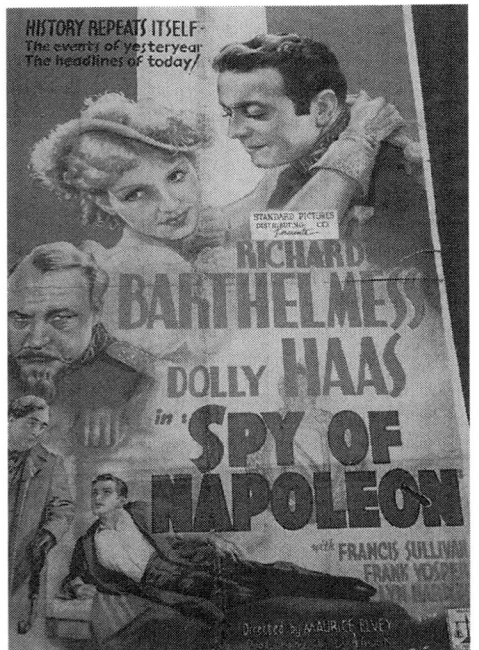

An American poster for the American release of *Spy of Napoleon* by Standard Pictures Distributing Company.

Provincial city key-theatre release run: Leeds: week commencing Monday, 15 March 1937: At the Ritz, *Spy of Napoleon* played in a double-bill programme with ***Charlie Chan at the Racetrack***, with Warner Oland, released by Fox.

British General Release: Monday, 1 March 1937.

Spy of Napoleon was reviewed in the *Kinematograph Weekly*, 17 September 1936, page 25:

101 minutes, "U" certificate.

'The Czar of Twickenham'. The History of Julius Hagen and the Film Empire he created at Twickenham Film Studios, from 1927 to 1938.

"Remarks: Polished period espionage romantic drama, artistically and spectacularly from Baroness Orczy's best seller. Development a little slow, but acting outstanding and stagecraft brilliant.

"Box Office Angle: Prestige picture with star values, one with big box-office potentialities. Excellent for the family.

"Polished period espionage romantic drama, artistically and spectacularly from Baroness Orczy's best seller. The thematic development may lack a little of the briskness so essential to mass appeal, but to counteract occasional loss of action are flawless atmosphere, brilliant character drawing and intelligent direction. The picture creates profound heart interest, and progresses to a memorable emotional climax. Richard Barthelmess and Dolly Haas lend star values to the production as well as acting ability. Francis L. Sullivan and Frank Vosper are magnificent in supporting rôles, while every department of the technical work is superlative. A prestige picture with many popular angles, the film is unquestionably an outstanding booking proposition.

"Story: Toulon, chief of the French police, is troubled by rumours of a plot on the part of the old aristocracy to overthrow Napoleon III. The situation calls for a counter-spy, and to fill the need he has Gerard de Lanoy, a young member of the nobility, arrested for treason, and then forces him to marry Eloise, pretty natural daughter of the Emperor. Once the ceremony is completed,

John V. Watson

Gerard is exiled, while Eloise, now equipped to mix with the élite, becomes the spy of Napoleon.

"Fate decrees, however, that both Eloise and Gerard shall eventually work together in the interests of France, but when they discover what attitude Italy and Austria can be expected to take should war with Germany arise, the authenticity of their message is doubted by Toulon, and the Franco-German conflict sees France crushed by her enemy. The humiliation kills Napoleon, but before he dies he decorates Gerard and sees him and Eloise happy.

"Acting: Richard Barthelmess contributes a sensitive portrayal as Gerard, and Dolly Haas is tender and provocative as Eloise, but it is the acting of Francis L. Sullivan as Toulon, Frank Vosper as Napoleon and Henry Oscar as the aristocratic traitor that give the picture prestige.

"Production: Technically and histrionically this picture is a praiseworthy effort, but the story, although adapted from a novel by Baroness Orczy, falls a little short of full kinematic requirements. There is a compelling love interest and a full measure of intrigue, both of which are firmly wedded to historic fact, but the spice of suspense is too delicately applied for the development to acquire keen momentum. Still, if mass demands are sometimes ignored, there is in the fine acting much that will stimulate intelligent emotional appeal, and it is on this score that the picture can rightfully claim a position close to the best artistic productions of the year.

"Settings and Photography: The interiors and exteriors are beautifully composed, the details conform to fact, and the lighting and photography are brilliant.

"Points of Appeal: Title and author values, box office cast, good story, human interest, artistic spectacle and family appeal.

5. *Dusty Ermine (1936)*

Elaborate drama adapted from a stage success. Much location work in the Alps.

Directed by Bernard Vorhaus. Starring Ronald Squire, Jane Baxter and Anthony Bushell.

On-screen opening main title card for *Dusty Ermine*.

Dusty Ermine was the first picture to be made under the new Hagen film production banner, J. H. Productions, Ltd., the company formed by Julius Hagen in January 1936 specifically to make films at the then newly-acquired Elstree Studios, renamed J. H. Studios.

551

John V. Watson

London Trade Show: Thursday, 10 September 1936 at the Piccadilly Theatre.

British Registration Details:
Quota Registration No.: Br. 13,653.
Registration Date: 22 September 1936.
Registered Length: 7,666 feet.
Registered by: Twickenham Film Distributors, Ltd.
Maker's name: J. H. Productions, Ltd.
British Board of Censor's Certificate: "A".
British Distributor: Wardour Films.

Trade Show advertisement: *Dusty Ermine*: Anthony Bushell, Jane Baxter, Ronald Squire. From the successful play by Neil Grant. A J. H. Production. Produced by Julius Hagen. Directed by Bernard Vorhaus. Tagline: "An exciting crime story set amid the splendour of the Alpine Snows." Logo: "Twickenham Film Distributors Ltd."

London key-theatre pre-release runs: At the Plaza, week commencing Monday, 4 January 1937, *Dusty Ermine* supported the comedy-romance, *Hideaway Girl*, with Shirley Ross, Robert Cummings and Martha Raye, released by Paramount.

Provincial city key-theatre release runs:
- Manchester: week commencing Monday, 8 March 1937: At the Piccadilly, *Dusty Ermine* was supported by the Chesterfield picture, *Ring Around the Moon*, with Donald Cook and Erin O'Brien-Moore, released by Pathé. (Note: *Ring Around the Moon* was one of several American pictures made by Chesterfield and Invincible that were originally being distributed by Twickenham Film Distributors, before that company went into receivership).
- Birmingham: week commencing Monday, 15 March 1937: At the Forum, *Dusty Ermine*

supported the Howard Hawks war-drama, **Road to Glory**, with Fredric March, Warner Baxter and Lionel Barrymore, released by Fox

♦ Liverpool: week commencing Monday, 15 March 1937: At the Forum, **Dusty Ermine** supported the comedy-drama, **Old Hutch**, with Wallace Beery, released by M-G-M.

British General Release: Monday, 22 February 1937

Dusty Ermine was reviewed in the *Kinematograph Weekly*, 17 September 1936, page 25:

85 minutes, "A" certificate.

"Remarks: Elaborate adaptation of stage success. Far-fetched crime plot eked out with shots of ski-ing in the Alps.

"Box Office Angle: Useful where British star names have box-office value. Uninteresting to children.

"This is a case where the tendency to alter the titles of plays adapted for the screen might well have been given its head. The title of this one is likely to prove a bit of a stumbling block to effective exploitation, as its meaning does not leap to the mind, nor is anything said in the film which would immediately explain it.

"Actually it refers to the smirching of an honoured family name associated with a long line of judges. Jim Kent, brother of an eminent K.C., is a forger who has blotted his ancestor's copybook and brought the judicial ermine to the dust. But nothing appears to emphasise this aspect of the affair, and the film resolves itself into a rather complicated melodrama concerned mainly with the tracking down of a gang of counterfeiters in their Austrian stronghold.

"Several incidents are neatly planned, and the theme claims a certain novelty of setting and circumstances. But it lacks the dramatic drive calculated to enchain the attention.

"Story: On finishing a four years' sentence for forgery, Jim Kent is approached by a wily old woman, emissary of a gang of bank-note counterfeiters, from whom he gathers that his nephew, Gilbert, has been roped in by the gang. He journeys to Austria , where he finds Gilbert "forging ahead" in the cellar of a fashionable hotel. Forsyth, a detective, suspecting Jim, gets there ahead of him.

"Linda, his niece, accompanies Gilbert, and when she and the detective meet they fall in love. Jim and Gilbert return to London, but in the train Jim discovers that his nephew is carrying forged notes. He takes the notes and hides them, but they are found and Jim is arrested.

"Later Forsyth becomes aware that the gang use Alpine guides to carry the notes over the frontier. He and Linda follow these men and are trapped in a mountain hut. By a ruse they escape, and a chase on skis ensues. Gilbert learns that his sister is in danger and sets out to the rescue. But in saving Linda and Forsyth he loses his own life. Jim is finally cleared of the charge, and the lovers start on a life partnership.

"Acting: In the character of another "Jim the Penman", Ronald Squire acts with assurance and sangfroid, and Jane Baxter easily sustains the none too onerous part of his sporty niece. But neither Anthony Bushell as the detective nor Arthur Macrae as Gilbert manages to put any kick into the character assigned to him. The best individual contribution is made by Margaret Rutherford as the craft agent of the forgers.

"Production: The lay-out of this film goes far beyond the scope of the original play without adding to its dramatic value. At times the plot appears in danger of being submerged beneath an avalanche of snow. The ski-ing scenes make a picturesque appeal, but there are too many of them.

"Settings and Photography: The main highlight on the spectacular side is the Alpine sequence, but here we suspect the camera of being more ingenious than the ski experts are daring. The lighting good throughout, especially in the close-ups of Jane Baxter.

"Points of Appeal: The prestige attaching to a successful London stage play, the attraction of one or two well-known names, novel plot, and a wonderful display of ski-ing.

6. Juggernaut (1936)

Melodramatic thriller starring Boris Karloff.
Directed by Henry Edwards.

London Trade Show: Tuesday, 8 September 1936 at

John V. Watson

the Piccadilly Theatre.

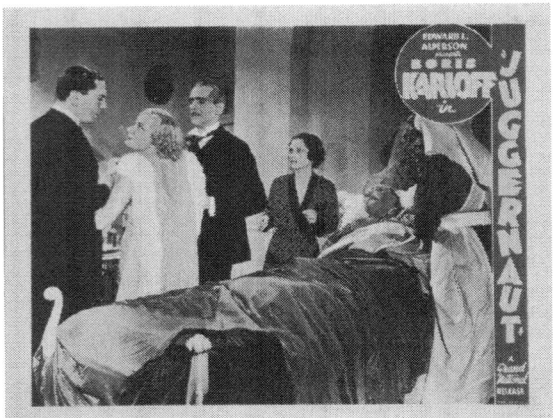

An American lobby card produced for the American release of *Juggernaut*. Boris Karloff is seen third from left. The card is printed in colour to suggest to audiences that the film was made in colour whereas it was actually made in black-and-white. This was common practice in the film business in those days.

British Registration Details:
Quota Registration No.: Br. 13,661.
Registration Date: 23 September 1936.
Registered Length: 6,518 feet.
Registered by: Twickenham Film Distributors, Ltd.
Maker's name: J. H. Productions, Ltd.
British Board of Censor's Certificate: "A".
Running Time: 72 minutes.

British Distributor: Wardour Films.

Trade Show advertisement: "*Juggernaut*: Boris Karloff (above the title). Mona Goya, Arthur Margetson, Joan Wyndham (below the title). A J. H. Production. Produced by Julius Hagen. Directed by Henry Edwards." Tagline: "Karloff at his Most Sensational in a dramatic and unusual film." Logo: "Twickenham Film Distributors Ltd."

London key-theatre pre-release runs: *Juggernaut* must have had various runs in London but details of any of these have not been located.

Provincial city key-theatre pre-release runs:
Week commencing Monday, 8 March 1937:

- Bristol: At the King's, *Juggernaut* supported John Ford's *The Plough and the Stars* (1937), with Barbara Stanwyck, Preston Foster, Una O'Connor and Barry Fitzgerald, produced and released by Radio.
- Bristol: At the Whiteladies, *Juggernaut* supported John Ford's *The Plough and the Stars* (1937).
- Cardiff: At the Olympia, *Juggernaut* supported the American comedy-drama, *The Devil Takes the Count* (1936; U.S. title: *The Devil is a Sissy*), with Freddie Bartholomew, Jackie Cooper and Mickey Rooney, directed by W. S. Van Dyke and Rowland Brown, produced and released by Metro-Goldwyn-Mayer.
- Glasgow: At the Coliseum, *Juggernaut* supported the American musical-comedy, *Pennies from Heaven* (1936), with Bing Crosby and Madge Evans, directed by Norman Z. McLeod, an Emanuel Cohen Production for Major Pictures Corporation (a company co-owned by star, Bing Crosby), and released by Columbia Pictures.
- Glasgow: At the Regal, *Juggernaut* supported *Pennies from Heaven* (1936).
- Liverpool: At the Olympia, *Juggernaut* supported the Hal Roach comedy, *General Spanky* (1936), with 'Spanky' McFarland, Phillips Holmes and Ralph Morgan, directed by Fred Newmeyer and

557

John V. Watson

Gordon Douglas, and released by Metro-Goldwyn-Mayer.

Provincial city key-theatre release run: Week commencing Monday, 7 June 1937:
- Sheffield: At the Electra Palace, *Juggernaut* was supported by the American drama, *Tango* (1936), with Marian Nixon, Chick Chandler and Marie Prevost, directed by Phil Rosen, made by Invincible Pictures.

British General Release: Monday, 15 March 1937.

Juggernaut was reviewed in the *Kinematograph Weekly* on 17 September 1936, page 27:

72 minutes, "A" certificate.

"Remarks: Spectacular, melodramatic thriller. Story far-fetched, and direction unimaginative, but clever performance on the part of Boris Karloff. The star is the picture and its selling angle.

"Box Office Angle: Reliable thriller for industrial and popular audiences. Nothing to harm youngsters.

"Spectacular, melodramatic thriller, presenting in a frame grimly fantastic an extravagant story of a scientist who stoops to murder in the interests of humanity, but finds in Nemesis a ruthless and cunning adversary.

"Neither the context of the story nor its pseudo scientific-cum-high society trimmings is closely related to reality, but transcending the film's unabashed artifice is a holding performance on the part of Boris Karloff, and it is he who turns it into a sound mass and star booking. Reliable proposition, one with good selling angles, for industrial audiences – the serial minded.

"Story: Dr. Sartorius, a brilliant scientist, needs money to perfect his cure for paralysis, and Yvonne, the extravagant, unfaithful wife of Lord Clifford, a doddering millionaire, is tired of waiting for her husband to pass out, so they get together, the arrangement being for Sartorius to bump off Clifford in return for a lump sum.

"Clifford is despatched wit alacrity, but a hitch comes when Eve Rowe, a pretty nurse in love with Clifford's son, Roger, now trustee of his father's estate, accidentally discovers an incriminating syringe charged with poison.

"Sartorius promptly sees a way out in the elimination of Eve and Roger, but again he trips up owing to the astuteness of Eve. By this time he realises that fame is not for him, and he takes his own life, while Yvonne involuntarily migrates to police headquarters.

"Acting: Boris Karloff is not at first at ease without the make-up man's artful aid. He portrays the rôle of Sartorius straight, but he soon gets acclimatised, and finishes up by putting a kick into the manufactured thrills.

"Mona Goya is inclined to be too theatrical and melodramatic as Yvonne, but Joan Wyndham makes a pleasing and appealing Eve, and Arthur Margetson is adequate as Roger. Anthony Ireland,

559

John V. Watson

Morton Selten, Nina Boucicault, Gibb McLaughlin and J. H. Roberts live up to their stage reputations in support.

"Production: The wildly incredible plot gets very little help from the director, Henry Edwards – his timing of the thrills is frequently clumsy – and less from the dialogue, which is incredibly naïve; but fortunately Boris Karloff knows his stuff too well to be severely handicapped by the shortcomings of others. By cloaking himself securely in the sinister he manages to invest the picture with eeriness far in excess of its story values. He is, in fact, the entertainment.

"Settings and Photography: Although the staging is more colourful than convincing, it fits the story's hectic moods, and the lighting and photography are up to standard.

"Points of Appeal: Popularity of thrillers, good performance by Karloff, star values and intriguing title.

7. The Man in the Mirror (1936)

Psychological comedy starring Edward Everett Horton and Genevieve Tobin.

Directed by Maurice Elvey.

London Trade Show: Thursday, 15 October 1936 at the Piccadilly Theatre.

British Registration Details:
Quota Registration No.: Br. 13,811.
Registration Date: 29 October 1936.

'The Czar of Twickenham'. The History of Julius Hagen and the Film
Empire he created at Twickenham Film Studios, from 1927 to 1938.

> Registered Length: 7,362 feet.
> Registered by: Twickenham Film Distributors, Ltd.
> Maker's name: J. H. Productions, Ltd.
> British Board of Censor's Certificate: "A".

> British Distributor: Wardour Films.

> Trade Show advertisement: "*The Man in the
> Mirror*: Edward Everett Horton and Genevieve Tobin.
> Garry Marsh, Ursula Jeans, Alastair Sim (smaller font size).
> A J. H. Production. Produced by Julius Hagen. Directed
> by Maurice Elvey." Tagline: Edward Everett Horton –
> The Inimitable! In the greatest role of his career." Logo:
> "Twickenham Film Distributors Ltd."

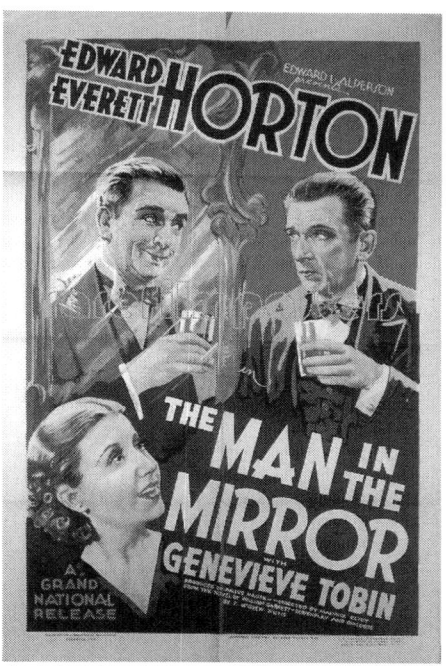

An American One-Sheet poster designed for the

American release of *The Man in the Mirror* by Edward L. Alperson of Grand National Pictures.

London key-theatre pre-release runs:
- At the New Gallery, week commencing Monday, 8 February 1937, *The Man in the Mirror* supported the comedy, *Three Men on a Horse*, with Frank McHugh, Joan Blondell and Guy Kibbee, released by Warner.
- At the Dominion and the New Victoria, week commencing Monday, 22 March 1937, *The Man in the Mirror* supported the comedy-romance, *Theodora Goes Wild*, with Irene Dunne and Melvyn Douglas, released by Columbia.

Provincial city key-theatre pre-release runs:
Sheffield: week commencing Monday, 15 March 1937:
- At the Albert Hall, *The Man in the Mirror* double-billed with *36 Hours to Kill*, with Brian Donlevy and Gloria Stuart, released by Fox.
Leeds: week commencing Monday, 22 March 1937 for 3 days:
- At the Coliseum, *The Man in the Mirror* was supported by *Bengal Tiger*, with Barton MacLane, June Travis and Warren Hull, released by Warner Bros.
Leeds: week commencing Monday, 22 March 1937:
- At the Scala, *The Man in the Mirror* was supported by *Bengal Tiger*, with Barton MacLane, June Travis and Warren Hull, released by Warner Bros.
London key-theatre release run:
- At the Davis, Croydon, week commencing Monday, 19 April 1937, *The Man in the Mirror* supported the romantic comedy, *Libelled Lady*, with Jean Harlow, William Powell, Myrna Loy and Spencer Tracy, released by MGM.

British General Release: Monday, 29 March 1937.

The Man in the Mirror was reviewed in the *Kinematograph Weekly*, 22 October 1936, page 28:

82 minutes, "A" certificate.

"Remarks: Clever psychological comedy approached from a popular angle. Story ingenious, star's acting brilliant, support good, and staging and direction excellent.

"Box Office Angle: Box-office comedy bet for all classes, the family included.

"Psychological in theme, but broadly farcical in interpretation, this comedy of a nit-wit who involuntarily plunges into a Jekyll and Hyde existence and, ultimately finds, in the battle between his two personalities, his real self, is as novel as it is laughable. The grand possibilities presented by the ingenious and piquant plot are firmly grasped by the star, producer and cameraman – Edward Everett Horton is marvellous in the lead, Maurice Elvey's direction combines imagination with a superb sense of humour, and the double-exposure photography is brilliant.

"In their splendid co-ordination is to be found the master key to gay, original entertainment of unqualified success. As good a comedy as any made in England, or America for that matter, the film is generously equipped for box-office success.

John V. Watson

"Story: Jeremy Dilke, a timid man, henpecked by his attractive wife, Helen, and garrulous mother-in-law, Mrs. Massiter, and bullied by Tarkington, his unscrupulous partner in a stock-broking firm, gazes in the mirror after a particularly provoking day and there sees the reflection of his other self. Jeremy the Second has all the cool arrogance, aggressiveness and vices of the real he-man, and he immediately dominates the life of Jeremy the First.

"He proceeds to put Helen and Mrs. Massiter in their place, beat Tarkington hands down in a business deal when he is hoaxed by a couple of bogus Eastern industrialists, and also visits Tarkington's susceptible wife, Veronica, in circumstances that leave no doubt as to the purpose of his mission. During the hectic period of domination Jeremy the First slowly learns the value of self-confidence, and the story ends with the return of his reflection to its proper sphere and the merging of the two mental entities into a perfectly balanced Jeremy.

"Acting: Edward Everett Horton is excellent in the lead; he establishes cleverly two distinct personalities, and out of the clash of mentality brings point to the humour.

"Genevieve Tobin and Ursula Jeans are delightfully provocative as Helen and Veronica respectively; Garry (misspelt "Gary") Marsh is sound as the bullying, unscrupulous Tarkington; and Aubrey Mather and Alastair (misspelt "Alister") Sim are great as the bogus gentlemen from way out East.

'The Czar of Twickenham'. The History of Julius Hagen and the Film Empire he created at Twickenham Film Studios, from 1927 to 1938.

"Production: This farce can boast of a really novel theme and though it is allowed to run to length, it provides at all times clever and laughable light diversion. The task of separating two sides to the central character is made delightfully easy by the star's brilliant acting and the resourceful camerawork, and the good work is followed up by showmanlike direction and enthusiastic supporting team work. The two phases of the mental analysis never fail to contrast effectively, and the net result is comedy that covers the field from sex to whimsicality. There is purpose in every gag, and a moral attached to the pivotal theme, while riotous entertainment marks the whole show.

"Settings and Photography: The staging is wide and comprehensive; it includes office sequences, artistic interiors, and night-club scenes, and the lighting and photography are outstanding.

"Points of Appeal: Clever, laughable story, brilliant performance by Edward Everett Horton, first-class support, good dialogue, piquant situations, touch of popular romance, and title and star values.

1936: The British Film Industry: Trends and Other Events throughout the Year:

A leading article by P. L. Mannock stated that **1936 will be a**

John V. Watson

landmark for British pictures.

(*K. W.*, 9 January 1936, page 93, P. L. Mannock).

United Artists becomes partners in the Odeon cinema chain.

(*K. W.*, 23 January 1936, page 41).

Captain Blood shatters Broadway records.

(Readers will recall that Robert Donat was originally cast in the title role but had to withdraw because of ongoing asthmatic condition. Newcomer Errol Flynn was given the part instead, and accordingly *Captain Blood* made him a huge swashbuckling star.)

(*K. W.*, 30 January 1936, page 29).

Max Schach forms a new production unit – **Capitol Films**.

(Following a career in the German film industry, Max Schacherl, a Jew, emigrated to Britain in 1934 following the rise to power of the Nazis. He then secured financial backing from the City of London who wanted to invest in the growing British film industry. He oversaw a series of independent film companies which made large-budget productions aimed at international markets. Many of his films employed fellow European exiles from the Nazis, including Fritz Kortner, Richard Tauber and Karl Grune. Because of his lavish budgets Schach was able to attract prominent figures away from more established film companies. While some of the films he produced, such as *Abdul the Damned* (1934), were profitable, many struggled to recover their large budgets. By 1937 a production slump hit the British industry which saw several companies go out of business, including the many production companies that Schach created. The failure of Schach's film empire led to a lengthy legal case,

'The Czar of Twickenham'. The History of Julius Hagen and the Film Empire he created at Twickenham Film Studios, from 1927 to 1938.

and, as a result, he never made another film.)

(*K. W.*, 6 February 1936).

O. P. Heggie, the Australian character actor, died in Hollywood on Friday.

(Note that O. P. Heggie is probably best remembered today for portraying the hermit who befriends the Monster [Boris Karloff] in ***Bride of Frankenstein*** (1935).

(*K. W.*, 13 February 1936, page 4).

John V. Watson

The disastrous fire at Elstree. The fire ruined six stages of the British and Dominions and British International studios.

(*The London Illustrated News*, 15 February 1936, front page illustration - as shown above).

Quota Act defaulters – 448 exhibitors and 17 renters (film distributors).

(*K. W.*, 20 February 1936, page 3).

Fox-British expands its film production.

(*K. W.*, 20 February 1936, page 37, P. L. Mannock).

Sam Spiegel (34, Polish) is remanded for a bounced cheque.

(Sam Spiegel was a legendary independent film producer who produced such films as *The Stranger* (1946, directed by Orson Welles); *The African Queen* (1951, directed by John Huston); *On the Waterfront* (1954, directed by Elia Kazan); *The Bridge on the River Kwai* (1957, directed by David Lean); and *Lawrence of Arabia* (1962, directed by Lean).

(*K. W.*, 12 March 1936, page 23).

London Film Studio blaze. The No. 1 Set is only affected.

(*K. W.*, 19 March 1936).

C. M. Woolf group tie-up with **Universal Pictures** of Hollywood.

(*K. W.*, 19 March 1936).

Carl Laemmle retires.

568

'The Czar of Twickenham'. The History of Julius Hagen and the Film Empire he created at Twickenham Film Studios, from 1927 to 1938.

(Carl Laemmle was an early film pioneer in Hollywood who founded what became Universal Pictures in 1912.)

(*K. W.*, 19 March 1936).

James Cagney succeeds in his suit to close his contract with Warner. The studio said they will appeal.

(*K. W.*, 19 March 1936).

Universal-Wainwright Studios, Ltd., is formed on14 March 1936.

(*K. W.*, 26 March 1936, page 22).

Aldgate Trustees, Ltd. Millions of pounds for British film production. The mystery financiers wanting unlimited backing for British pictures.

(*K. W.*, 9 April 1936, page 3, City Editor).

Victor Saville Productions, Ltd., is formed on 2 April 1936.

(*K. W.*, 9 April 1936).

Excelsior Film Productions, Ltd., is formed on 15 April 1936 by the producer, Marcel Hellman.

(**Marcel Hellman** (1898-1986) was a Romanian-born British film producer, who worked closely with Douglas Fairbanks Jr. and Harold French.)

(*K. W.*, 23 April 1936, page 16).

Twentieth Century-Fox announced it would invest £1 million for British films.

John V. Watson

(*K. W.*, 30 April 1936, page 5).

The United States adopts **the 2,000-foot reel**; will be in general use by August.(Note that the 1,000 spool was the industry norm.)

(*K. W.*, 21 May 1936).

The **world's largest Kinema** has been completed in Moscow seating 15,000 people.

(*K. W.*, 21 May 1936).

Decrease in British films according to the Board of Trade footage figures.

(*K. W.*, 28 May 1936).

The Australian market – specialised handling of British films.

"A long-period contract by which Gaumont-British, Twickenham and British Lion product will exclusively be marketed in Australia in an efficient and specialised manner by Dominion Film Distributors, Ltd., was announced by Ernest Turnbull previous to leaving England on Wednesday. Other independent product may also be similarly marketed by the company."

(*K. W.*, 4 June 1936, page 3).

The adoption of the **new 2,000-foot reel** is delayed until September.

(*K. W.*, 18 June 1936, page 4).

Columbia's big British programme is announced.

(*K. W.*, 18 June 1936, page 35, P. L. Mannock).

'The Czar of Twickenham'. The History of Julius Hagen and the Film Empire he created at Twickenham Film Studios, from 1927 to 1938.

£174 million is paid by Kinema-goers.

(*K. W.*, 25 June 1936, page 21, City Editor).

Henry Fonda starts work at Denham on *Wings of the Morning.* (Note that *Wings of the Morning* was the first British film to be made in Technicolor.)

(*K. W.*, 25 June 1936, page 71, P. L. Mannock).

Edward L. Alperson, the president of the newly-formed **Grand National** in the United States, sails to England to form a British distribution unit.

(*K. W.*, 30 July 1936).

Rock Studios, Ltd., is formed with £200,000 capital.

(*K. W.*, 30 July 1936).

4,836 Kinemas are wired for sound in the United Kingdom, according to Western Electric's latest half-yearly survey of the British Isles.

(*K. W.*, 13 August 1936).

Report on the **British Lion meeting** regarding the financial aspect of the **Republic Pictures** contract.

(*K. W.*, 27 August 1936, page 17, the City column).

The **Tudor Films** board is reorganised – Lord Ely and Campbell Black at the helm.

(*K. W.*, 3 September 1936, page 5).

The death of **Irving Thalberg**, MGM's head of production

John V. Watson

in Hollywood, is reported.

(Note that during his twelve years with MGM, until his early death at age 37, Irving Thalberg produced about four hundred films, most of which bore his imprint and innovations, including story conferences with writers, sneak previews to gain early feedback, and extensive re-shooting of scenes to improve the film. In addition, he introduced horror films to audiences and co-authored the "Production Code," the guidelines for morality which was followed by all the Hollywood studios. During the 1920s and 1930s, he synthesized and merged the world of stage drama and literary classics with Hollywood films. Thalberg created numerous new stars and groomed their screen images. Among them were Lon Chaney, Ramon Novarro, John Gilbert, Joan Crawford, Clark Gable, Jean Harlow, Wallace Beery, Luise Rainer, Greta Garbo, Lionel Barrymore, and Norma Shearer, who became his wife. He had the ability to combine quality with commercial success, and was credited with bringing his artistic aspirations in line with the demands of audiences.)

(*K. W.*, 17 September 1936, page 3).

W. Ray Johnston intends to revive **Monogram Pictures** in Hollywood next year

(*K. W.*, 17 September 1936, page 4).

The British **Technicolor** is booked to capacity.

(*K. W.*, 17 September 1936, page 16, The City Column).

Jacey Cinemas, Ltd., Birmingham, increase in capital.

(*K. W.*, 1 October 1936, page 14, The City Column).

Pinewood Studios opened on Wednesday, 30 September 1936.

'The Czar of Twickenham'. The History of Julius Hagen and the Film Empire he created at Twickenham Film Studios, from 1927 to 1938.

(*K. W.*, 1 October 1936).

Samuel Goldwyn and Douglas Fairbanks have joined partnership to produce *The Adventures of Marco Polo*.

(Note that the film was eventually made and released in 1938; it starred Gary Cooper. Fairbanks was no longer involved.)

(*K. W.*, 29 October 1936, page 3).

Metro-Goldwyn-Mayer British Studios, Ltd,, is formed on 10 November 1936 with a nominal capital of £25,000.

(*K. W.*, 19 November 1936).

Accounts for **London Film Productions** during the period to 2 May 1936 show that the company operated at a loss of £330,842.

(*K. W.*, 17 December 1936, page 14, The City Column).

Michael Balcon joins the MGM British film unit.

(Note that **Michael Balcon** produced MGM's first British-made film, *A Yank at Oxford*, starring Robert Taylor; it was a huge box-office hit. Continually falling out with Louis B. Mayer, the studio head of the American parent company, in 1938 Balcon was invited to head Ealing Studios and the rest is history.)

(*K. W.*, 17 December 1936, page 16).

Simon Rowson re-enters film production becoming the joint managing director of Grosvenor Sound Films, Ltd.

(*K. W.*, 24 December 1936, page 33, P. L. Mannock).

Gaumont-British films are only for Fox release in the

John V. Watson

United States.

(*K. W.*, 31 December 1936, page 3).

1936: The Ninth Year of the 'Quota' Act:

256 British films were first shown during the year 1936.

This number is arrived at by using the data contained in *The British Film Catalogue: 1895-1970* by Denis Gifford, as follows:

10152: Closing Gifford Catalogue Number for 1936.

09896: Opening Gifford Catalogue Number for 1936.

256: Total. An increase of 44 films over the previous year's total of 212.

Some of these films were short subjects; the actual number of these shorts has not been determined.

7. 1937:
BRITISH FILM
PRODUCTION SLUMPS:

The year saw British film production fall significantly, and it quickly became clear that the production boom was over. And it was soon to become clear that the huge financial capital invested into British film production over recent years was built on what was really a 'house of cards'. The capital monies invested into the British film industry were virtually all loans, much of it short term credit financing, and, if not, debentures.

For the financially unaware to understand the basic problem here, the reader should understand that serious long-term investment in any business, whether it be in film production or in any other business activity, should always be in the form of capital invested for the long term; that strategy should therefore ensure the financial viability of any business if, of course, everything else is also and equally in place, particularly that essential for financial health - growing and sustainable profitability.

1937:
JULIUS HAGEN FACES
RECEIVERSHIP FORCING THE
CLOSURE OF HIS FILM EMPIRE:

Meanwhile, the output that Julius Hagen achieved in 1937 was static; he produced six films in 1937 instead of seven pictures he produced in 1936. There was also his one and only co-production: *A Romance in Flanders* which Hagen made in conjunction with Franco-London Films. This film brought the total number Hagen made in 1937 to seven films, the same number as for 1936.

But, right from the start of 1937, Julius Hagen was certainly not going to escape the financial onslaught that was now starting to grip the British film production industry that year. Indeed, he was already facing huge financial problems with the placing into receivership of Twickenham Film Distributors, Ltd., Twickenham Film Studios, Ltd., and J. H. Productions, Ltd., as discussed below in detail in the articles published in the *Kinematograph Weekly* of 14 January 1937, as follows:

"Twickenham receiverships – The Twickenham Tragedy."

"The news of receiverships for Julius Hagen's Twickenham studios and other two companies has been received by misgivings which, so far as they apply generally to the Industry, have been unduly magnified in some quarters".

"It is a serious thing when a concern with such a fine steady production record over a long period comes to grief. The irony of it is that Hagen is the very last man who can be accused of that prodigal studio waste which has existed in one or two other enterprises".

"Twickenham has successfully followed a policy of well-organised expenditure on films planned and carried out with the minimum delay. Hagen himself is a big-hearted, hard-working chief of real experience, and on that score I cannot recall any personal failure in the Trade being received in the Trade with more sympathetic regret".

"Hagen's qualities, indeed, are such that I am confident he

will only suffer a temporary eclipse; and that we shall soon find him again active in the saddle. His staff had a team spirit unequalled elsewhere, and its extinction is unthinkable".

(*K. W.*, 14 January 1937, page 4).

"Twickenham distribution arrangements."

"The appointment of a receivership for Twickenham Film Distributors, Twickenham Film Studios, and J. H. Productions will in no way affect the deal, recently concluded, as a result of which John Maxwell's company will handle the Twickenham output".

"Wardour are now taking contracts for '*Man in the Mirror*', '*Spy of Napoleon*', '*Juggernaut*', '*Broken Blossoms*' and '*Dusty Ermine*'".

"The following pictures, formerly handled by Twickenham Distributors, will be released by Pathé: -

'*Tango*', with Marion Nixon, Chick Chandler and Warren Hymer (release Monday, 8 February 1937); '*Ring Around the Moon*', with Donald Cook and Erin O'Brien Moore (release Monday, 15 February 1937); and '*Bridge of Sighs*', with Dorothy Tree and Jack La Rue (release Monday, 8 March 1937).

"A further list for later dates to be handled by Pathé comprises:

'*Beauty and the Barge*', in which Gordon Harker will be supported by Judy Gunn; '*Underneath the Arches*' for Flanagan and Allen; '*Widow's Island*' ('*A Romance of Flanders*'), with

577

Marcelle Chantal and Paul Cavanagh; '*Silver Blaze*', a Sherlock Holmes story, starring Arthur Wontner and Lyn Harding; '*She Got What She Wanted*' ('*Clothes and the Woman*'), with Rod La Rocque and Tucker McGuire; '*The Vicar of Bray*', featuring Stanley Holloway as the vicar; and '*The Lily of Killarney*', directed by Henry Edwards.

"The closing down of the Birmingham Branch of Twickenham Film Distributors, of which Mott Cowan had charge, means that Claude Solomon, Midland manager of Wardour Films, Ltd., 53, John Bright Street, Birmingham, took over the distribution of the new Twickenham products as and from Monday last, 11 January 1937".

(K. W., 14 January 1937, page 19).

"Pound-a-foot film perils", says Jack Prendergast:

"The exhibitors' loss in this one-sided Films Act was far greater than that of the pound-a-foot film maker and distributor".

"Let us take an example: A 6,000-ft. film at £1 per foot cost £6,000. One thousand bookings at an average of £6 per booking and the £6,000 is back, and ready to germinate another Quickie destined to the balance sheets and the reputation of the kinemas compelled to show it."

"Uneconomic Prices."

"This entertainment shortage of British quota created the added hardship on independents, that when a tolerable piece of entertainment was available to him the price was invariably uneconomic. If, on the other hand, the exhibitor had been able to purchase this quota-quickie film at £6 per subject average, and

spread the cost over the foreign films he screened against his
quota, then the Moyne Report would not look like the charter it
does to-day for him. It is impossible for the exhibitor to assess
the cost of his quota apart from the price cost because the unseen
cost – incalculable loss of patronage. The position of a
manufacturer being able to sell to another retailer by Act of
Parliament goods which the public will not buy is an untenable
position for the retailer".

"What is the Exhibitor's View?"

"We are told that the setting up of a committee to implement
the quality clause is madness. . . Yet the public who have not the
privilege of seeing a Trade show before they spend their
sixpences have an unerring gift of knowing the kind of
entertainment they want. We have heard many varied opinions
on the Report, some brogue and some sweet-scented Oxford; but
all put forth as though the spokesman represented the whole film
trade. But we have yet to hear the definite expressions of the
exhibitors".

(*K. W.*, 14 January 1937, page 33, Jack Prendergast was a
correspondent for *K.W*).

"Big Films in Twickenham's 1937 Programme – Wardour to release."

"Recent financial developments in connection with the
Twickenham Films organisation obviously will affect the
production plans originally formulated by Julius Hagen, whose
future activities it is not possible to forecast. Several big pictures
with strong story and title values were made during 1936 at
Twickenham, Elstree and Hammersmith, and the production of
other films on a similarly ambitious scale had been planned".

"Among the properties which were being considered for production by Mr. Hagen were the following:

Rodney Stone, the late Sir Arthur Conan Doyle's' famous and popular novel, which was a tremendous success as a silent picture, when it was called *The House of Temperley*; *The Poison Belt*, also by Sir Arthur Conan Doyle, a sensational story of which the theme is life or death to mankind; *The Duchess of Soho*, a romance with music by Hans May, the famous Continental composer; *This City Was Afraid*, an exciting, original crime story; *The Whirlpool*, a dramatic sea story by John Oxenham; and *The Great Impostor*, adapted for the screen by Jefferson Farjeon and based on the famous Tichborne Trial of 1871."

(Note that, as events turned out, none of these proposed films were ever made.)

"For Early Release."

"Four Twickenham films being released by Wardour Films early in the New Year are:

Dusty Ermine, directed by Bernard Vorhaus; *Spy of Napoleon*, directed by Maurice Elvey; *Juggernaut*, directed by Henry Edwards; and *The Man in the Mirror*, directed by Maurice Elvey."

"Other Offerings for 1937."

"Other Twickenham films practically completed, all of which will be Trade shown early in the New Year and released in 1937, comprise the following: -

Beauty and the Barge, in which Gordon Harker will be supported by Judy Gunn; and *Underneath the Arches*, with Flanagan and Allen; their famous song is featured, and also a new one, entitled 'A Million Tears', directed by Redd Davis.''

"Film with Two Versions."

"*Widow's Island* (*A Romance in Flanders*), made in two versions, English and French, in conjunction with Franco-London Films. A strong drama with a "flashback" to the Great War, and starring Marcelle Chantal, the most beautiful woman in France, in both versions, with Paul Cavanaugh and Garry Marsh in the English version. Directed by Maurice Elvey.''

"These will be followed by...":

"*Silver Blaze*, from the Sherlock Holmes, starring Arthur Wontner and Lyn Harding. *She Got What She Wanted* (*Clothes and the Woman*). Rod La Rocque is starred in his first British film; Tucker McGuire (seen recently in the stage play, '*Three Men on a Horse*'; Constance Collier and George E. Stone are featured, with Alastair Sim, Dorothy Dare, Mary Cole and Jim Gerald. Albert de Courville directing. *The Vicar of Bray*, featuring Stanley Holloway as the vicar. *The Lily of Killarney*, directed by Henry Edwards.''

"All these films will, of course, now be distributed by Wardour Films.''

(*K. W.*, 14 January 1937, page 88).

The *Kinematograph Weekly* of 21 January 1937 reported in its City column:

"Official announcements of the Twickenham receiverships."

581

- **Twickenham Film Distributors**, Ltd., 111 Wardour – Two notices of appointment: receiver appointed on 6 January 1937, under powers contained in (a) debenture dated 30 May 1935, and (b) deed of charge dated 11 December 1936. Both appointments were made by C. T. Bowring (Insurance) Ltd., as nominees.
- **Twickenham Film Studios**, Ltd., 111 Wardour – Roddison C. Brewis was appointed Receiver and Manager by the Westminster Bank, Ltd., on 7 January 1937 under powers contained in two debentures, dated 1 April 1931, and 7 January 1935, for £15,000 and £30,000 respectively.
- **J. H. Productions**, Ltd., 111 Wardour - W. B. Cullen was appointed Receiver on 8 January 1937, under powers contained in debenture dated 18 December 1935.
- (Note that the amounts involved in the three events of receivership illustrate just how deep Julius Hagen's corporate empire was in debt via the debentures and deeds of charge he had committed to since 1931.)

    (*K. W.*, 21 January 1937, page 21).

The same issue of the *Kinematograph Weekly* of 21 January 1937 carried an important, revealing and frank account by Julius Hagen of how he had arrived at the detrimental condition he now had to face, as follows:

"Julius Hagen's Own Story."
"Frank Statement Explains Twickenham Affairs."

"'I got caught – hook, line and sinker'. Julius Hagen, in an outspoken address, of which this sentence is typical, gave first-hand figures of his production activities, their cost and the revenue they earned, as an explanation of the plight in which his companies found themselves. Of even greater importance than his philosophy of struggle was the intimation that he had contracted to make for John Maxwell a series of twelve pictures a year for five years."

'The Czar of Twickenham'. The History of Julius Hagen and the Film Empire he created at Twickenham Film Studios, from 1927 to 1938.

"Mr. Hagen candidly confessed he had been a victim of the optimism engendered among British producers by the American success of '*The Private Lives of Henry VIII*'".

"He pointed out that he was one of the oldest pioneers in the business, in which, through him, over £3 million had been invested. While he was producing solid British programme pictures for British audiences which were profitable for his financial backers, he was happy, and so were his friends. But he was assured that he could reap a rich harvest by following in the footsteps of 'Henry VIII'. Various renters assured him that if he spent more money and looked towards the world market he would show a much greater profit. All that was music to his ears, and he got caught, hook, line and sinker!"

"And parenthetically, Mr. Hagen observed that a number of people of fluent speech, and no financial interests, had forced up during the past few years salaries of artistes, film directors and other personnel, to the tune of probably one thousand per cent, of their true commercial value."

"Although he himself got caught in the net and, judging from certain recent balance-sheets, he was in fairly good company, he was still convinced that, if one can resist the temptations of unnecessary lavishing of fortunes on the screen for the sake of one's own selfish satisfactions, it was possible to place the production side of the British Film Industry on a solid basis and create a great means for commercial investment".

"His future activities, Mr. Hagen announced, would include the formation of a new company with which John Maxwell would be associated which had signed a contract to make twelve pictures a year. They would be first-class films and would be regarded as marvellous value – because they would not cost so much."

John V. Watson

"Frank details of his experience as a renter provided one of the sensations of the occasion. The following figures referred to pictures which he considered were very good films of their kind and each of which booked to an average of about 1,500 theatres: -

	Cost:	Bookings, inc. foreign rights:
"Scrooge" (Seymour Hicks)	£44,000	£33,000
"Private Secretary" (Edward Everett Horton)	£30,000	£25,000
"Last Journey"	£27,000	£26,000
"A Fire Has Been Arranged" (Flanagan and Allen)	£29,000	£18,000
"She Shall Have Music"	£48,000	£60,000
(Jack Hylton took £7,000 and 22 per cent of the gross)		
"In the Soup" (Ralph Lynn)	£32,000	£20,000

"Mr. Hagen added that his later pictures were more expensive. It would be unfair to say what they would gross, but, in his own sorrowful mind, he knew they would not gross the cost, apart from distribution expenses."

"There must be something fundamentally wrong when one heard producers "swanking" as to the amounts received from their pictures and the value of the American market."

"The renting business to-day, Mr. Hagen confessed, is not nearly so good as it was ten or twelve years ago."

"'I do not think', he added, 'that the Trade in general takes nearly sufficient notice of what is discussed in nearly every issue of the Trade papers. I refer to redundancy.'"

"Surely, it was common sense that in a district were for years there was only one kinema and there are now four, it did not matter whether the renter's traveller obtained 50 per cent or $33^{1/3}$

per cent, his returns at the end of the week were going to be very poor compared with what they were years ago."

"The second factor was the terrible nonsense that nearly everybody talked about the American market. They did not try to help the British producer, and had never tried to do so."

"He illustrated his contention by reference to '*Scrooge*'. He was a happy man when he was told the Americans would make 140 prints of this picture, and he felt assured of a reasonable profit. Later, however, he was told it was too near Christmas to make proper arrangements for distribution, and last Christmas – for '*Scrooge*' was essentially a seasonable release – he found that it had yielded from the States the colossal sum of $6,000, as against an estimated $200,000."

"It was no use trying, for the time being, to make pictures for America, Mr. Hagen declared. The only way to get real American release was to get the dollars at the same time as they sign up their artistes – that would be a guarantee of good faith."

"At the same time, he was convinced that first-class British pictures could be produced on a sound commercial basis – if one resisted the temptation of unnecessary overhead costs. For some years to come it was his intention to make very modest pictures for this country and the Colonies."
(*K. W.*, 21 January 1937, page 37).

Financial Analysis - Profit or Loss - from the Detail above:

	Cost:	Bookings, inc. Foreign Rights:	Profit:	Loss:
"*Scrooge*" (Seymour Hicks)	£44,000	£33,000		£ 11,000
"*Private Secretary*" (Edward Everett Horton)				

John V. Watson

£30,000   £25,000   £ 5,000
"Last Journey" £27,000   £26,000   £ 1,000
"A Fire Has Been Arranged" (Flanagan and Allen)
£29,000   £18,000   £ 11.000
"She Shall Have Music"
£48,000   £60,000   **£12,000**
(Jack Hylton took £7,000 and 22 per cent of the gross)
"In the Soup" (Ralph Lynn)
£32,000   £20,000   £ 12,000

TOTALS: **£12,000**   £ 40,000
OVERALL LOSS: £ 28,000

In the first issue of the *Kinematograph Weekly* for 1937, the trade journal reported that there was optimism overall at **Wardour's sales conference**, with the value of Hagen tie-up being particularly valued.

(*K. W.*, 7 January 1937, page 14).

Julius Hagen is to resume at Twickenham. 12 films are scheduled.

(*K. W.*, 4 February 1937, page 3).

February 1937:
Continued legal problems for Julius Hagen:

Kinematograph Weekly reported throughout the month:

A meeting of the creditors of Twickenham Film Studios has been arranged to take place at the Twickenham Studios, St. Margaret's at 10.30 a.m. on Tuesday, 16 February 1937.

(*K. W.*, 11 February 1937, page 3).

High Court decision in Twickenham application.

'The Czar of Twickenham'. The History of Julius Hagen and the Film Empire he created at Twickenham Film Studios, from 1927 to 1938.

(*K. W.*, 18 February 1937, page 3).

Arrangements are being made for the handling by Gaumont-British of a certain number of American films, it was revealed during the hearing of a High Court action on Tuesday, 16 February 1937. The pictures concerned are the Chesterfield and Invincible product formerly handled by Twickenham Film Distributors.

The action was brought by the Chesterfield Motion Picture Corporation against Twickenham Film Distributors, Ltd., and Pathé Pictures, Ltd.

(*K. W.*, 18 February 1937, page 3).

Under the original agreement with Twickenham, T.F.D. could not assign the rights without the consent of the plaintiffs.

(*K. W.*, 18 February 1937, page 3).

The amount advanced by the Twickenham company was £11,250.

(*K. W.*, 18 February 1937, page 43).

A similar action by Invincible Picture Corporation against Twickenham Film Distributors, Ltd., and Pathé Pictures, Ltd.

(*K. W.*, 18 February 1937, page 43).

Twickenham Studios winding-up.

(*K. W.*, 25 February 1937, page 27).

Riverside Studios reopen.

(*K. W.*, 25 February 1937, page 49).

John V. Watson

"Twickenham Studios winding up."

"Hagen reveals week-end drama."

"Property sold for £34,183."

"Some of the drama behind the decision to close Twickenham Film Studios was revealed on Friday by Julius Hagen. It had been announced that the buildings and equipment had been sold by the Receiver for £34,183. It was decided that the voluntary liquidation should be continued, a decision which was subsequently reversed by a High Court order."

"Mr. Hagen revealed that at the time of the crisis his financial backers in the City were prepared to go on, and arrangements were come to with them that, provided he could find first-class distribution for the pictures made up to end of last year, they would back further pictures. They stated that they were also prepared to loan his company sufficient funds to pay the creditors and to pay overheads."

"On Friday, January 1, he signed two contracts and the money was supposed to be forthcoming on the following Monday. On Tuesday evening the financial people put in a Receiver in possession of J. H. Production Co., Ltd's assets and on the Wednesday they entered the Twickenham Film Distributors, Ltd., in Wardour Street. As soon as the Bank knew that they immediately placed a Receiver in possession of Twickenham Film Studios, Ltd."

"He added that his financial backers did give him the opportunity of raising sufficient money. If he had an opportunity of doing so, he was sure he would have been able to find the necessary finance to carry on."

(*K. W.*, 4 March 1937, page 16.)

'The Czar of Twickenham'. The History of Julius Hagen and the Film Empire he created at Twickenham Film Studios, from 1927 to 1938.

The first statutory meetings of creditors and shareholder were held last week at London Bankruptcy Buildings, under the compulsory liquidation of J. H. Productions, Ltd.

Costs of Production: J. H. Productions, Ltd.:
1. *Dusty Ermine*: £39,111
2. *Spy of Napoleon*: £45,449
3. *The Man in the Mirror*: £33,397
4. *The Girl Without Morale* (*Clothes and the Woman*): £30,278
5. *Silver Blaze*: £30,777
6. *The Vicar of Bray*: £ 20,398
7. *The Widow's Island* (*A Romance in Flanders*): £16,306.

The first three pictures, namely *Dusty Ermine*, *Spy of Napoleon*, and *The Man in the Mirror*, had been Trade shown, and the receipts from provincial pre-release bookings had amounted to £235 at the end of 1936.

The remaining four films were not then completed. The costs of production had absorbed the company's liquid capital.

(*K. W.*, 4 March 1937, page 16.)

"Independent Producer Scheme"

"New Company acquires Hagen Studio"

"A company with a capital of £100,000 has been formed to take over the J. H. Studios at Elstree, formerly owned by Julius Hagen."

"The company is to be one of independent producers, who will make and distribute their pictures themselves and undertake their own renting of kinemas."

589

"J. Bamberger, the managing director of the new company, states that the new organisation expected to reduce production costs by as much as 33$^{1/3}$ or 40 per cent, through the reduction of studio charges."

"We have a very strong group behind us financially, and we expect to do big things for British production."

(K. W., 11 March 1937, page 3.)

"New film studio owners"

"Prominent industrialists"

"The person associated with Joseph Bamberger in the acquisition of (exclusively reported in the Kine last week) of the former J. H. Studios at Elstree are a group of industrialists whose intention is to cater for the independent producer."

"Among those concerned in the deal are Lord Grimthorpe; Eustace Watkins, the motor magnate; C. A. O. Berner; A. H. Maxwell, a prominent landowner; W. B. Anderson; and J. Bamberger, who has been appointed managing director."

The studios, originally known as the Whitehall Studios, were taken over by Julius Hagen when he formed J. H. Productions, Ltd., in 1935, but this company was recently wound up."

"It is stated that the new company, the capital of which is £100,000, will, if necessary, create their own renting organisation."

(*K. W.*, 18 March 1937, page 18.)

"Twickenham Film Studios, Ltd"

"Meeting of creditor and shareholders"

'The Czar of Twickenham'. The History of Julius Hagen and the Film Empire he created at Twickenham Film Studios, from 1927 to 1938.

"The statutory first meeting of the creditors and shareholders of Twickenham Film Studios, Limited, 111, Wardour Street, W.1. were held on April 2 at London Bankruptcy Buildings, before George W. Hutcheson, Assistant Official Receiver."

"The winding up order was made on March 1, upon the petition of Mrs. Betty Balfour Campbell-Tyrie, a judgment creditor for £59 and costs £196."

(Note that the lady petitioner was actually the film star, **Betty Balfour**.)

"The chairman reported that a draft statement of affairs had been lodged, but the values placed therein upon the assets must be taken with a considerable amount of reserve. The liabilities amounted to £130,205 and were made of unsecured debts of £89,441. preferential claims £1,206 and debenture bonds and interest £39,556. The assets were valued at £133,220, which would yield a surplus of £3,015 in assets above liabilities. The issued capital was returned at £33,500, and the account with the shareholders disclosed a deficiency of £30,484."

"The company was registered as a private company on January 29, 1929, to acquire from Neo-Art Productions, Limited, the Alliance Studios, St. Margaret's, Twickenham. The directors at the date of the winding-up order were Julius Hagen, J. A. Carter, F. P. Philip and R. P. Philip."

"The purchase consideration for the property which was acquired by Henry Edwards was £32,000 payable in cash by instalments. The property was apparently transferred to the company on January 21, 1929, and on the following day the company created a mortgage for £25,000 over the property in favour of the Neo-Art Productions, Limited. That charge has since been satisfied."

"Mr. Hagen's Salary"

"Julius Hagen was appointed managing director for two years from January 1. 1931, at a salary of £140, plus expenses."

"Another company was registered on May 3, 1935, as Twickenham Film Distributors, Limited, for the exploitation for seven years of each film produced by the company."

"The company was apparently handicapped by cash working capital from its inception, and since 1931 it had carried on with the assistance of bank advances on policies of guarantee from underwriters."

"A debenture was issued for £15,000 on   April 1, 1931, to Westminster Bank, Limited, and January 7, 1935, a further bond for £30,000 was issued to the same bank. On January 7, 1937, the debenture holders appointed R. D. Brewis, chartered accountant, as receiver and manager of the company's property."

"A fire occurred at the studios in October, 1935. The company was insured for £80,000, and it received £50,073 by way of compensation,"

"Lack of Capital"

"The failure of the company was attributed by Julius Hagen to lack of cash working capital; to heavy production and overhead expenses; to the proceeds of film distribution not realising the amount anticipated; and to depreciation in the value in its assets."

"In reply to W. H. Cork, who represented a number of creditors, Julius Hagen stated that he received his remuneration until one week before the appointment of a receiver for the debenture holders."

"W. B. Cullen, C. A., was appointed liquidator. The

following committee of inspection was elected: representatives of the petitioning creditor, Kodak, Limited, J. Rayman, Maple and Company, Limited, C. T. Bowring (Insurance), Limited, George Humphries and Company, Limited, and Gilbert Church."

(K. W., 8 April 1937, page 11.)

"St. Margaret's Film Studio, Ltd."

"Registered 2 April 1937 with a nominal capital of 10,000 shares in 40,000 ordinary shares of 5 shillings each. The subscribers are: Cecil A. Helmore, accountant; S. D. Baum – both of 4 Old Burlington Street, London W.1, the address of the registered office. Acting secretary: B. R. McNaught. The registered office is 4, Old Burlington Street, W.1."

(K. W., 8 April 1937, page 11.)

An anxious time for British film production.

Few British pictures in work. The production slump causes anxiety. 13 films in production on the 58 floors available, including one at Twickenham.

(K. W., 15 April 1937, page 3.)

"Twickenham Film Distributors"

"Order for compulsory winding-up"

" Mr. Justice Bennett, in the Chancery Division, on April 12, on the petition of Twickenham Film Distributors, Limited, made an order for the compulsory winding-up of British Artistic Films, Limited."

"Mr. Thomas appeared for the petitioner, who was a judgment creditor. Mr. Phillips appeared for the opposing

593

creditors for £1,277."

"Mr. Wolf, for the company, opposed the petition."

"Mr. Justice Bennett: Why should you make one man who wants his money wait while you speculate in the production in a film?"

"Mr. Wolf: If you make a winding-up order the petitioners will get nothing."

"Mr. Justice Bennett: I do not know. Perhaps other people will lose money."

"Mr. Wolf: No."

"Mr. Justice Bennett: There will be the usual winding-up order."

(*K. W.*, 15 April 1937, page 13, the City column.)

"Hagen production for Ambassador"

"Under the title of '*The Angelus*', Julius Hagen is making his first film for distribution by Gilbert Church's newly-formed company (registered on 24 December 1936), Ambassador Film Productions, Limited. The picture, based upon the world-famous song, '*The Last Rose of Summer*', has started production at Twickenham by St. Margaret's Film Studio, Limited. Thomas Bentley: director – Michael Barringer: script. The famous Twickenham unit remains practically unchanged for the production of this picture: James A. Carter: set design; Sydney Blythe: lighting expert; William Luff: photographer; William Trytel: special musical score; Jack Harris: editing; Ronnie Philip: in charge of casting. Cast:

Anthony Bushell, Nancy O'Neill, Eve Gray, Garry Marsh, Mary Glynne, Charles Carson, Joyce Evans, and the ever-popular light comedian, Richard Cooper. "It is hoped that '*The Angelus*' will even prove a bigger success than the several "popular" winners for which Gilbert Church and the late Frederick White built up a reputation."

(*K. W.*, 15 April 1937, page 13, P. L. Mannock.)

Production slump is only temporary, according to some current opinion..

(*K. W.*, 22 April 1937, page 37, P. L. Mannock.)

Baynham Honri has relinquished his position at Riverside Studios to join Cricklewood Studios as general manager. From 1931, he was associated with Twickenham Film Studios in charge of sound, and from 1935 he was also responsible for the supervision of sound at J. H. Studios, Elstree, and Riverside Studios.

(*K. W.*, 22 April 1937, page 37, P. L. Mannock.)

The Angelus is nearing completion.

James A. Carter and William Trytel are directors of the recently-formed St. Margaret's Studios, Ltd.

(*K. W.*, 29 April 1937, page 49, P. L. Mannock.)

The Angelus. Thomas Bentley completes, Jack Harris is now editing.

(*K. W.*, 29 April 1937, page 35, P. L. Mannock.)

"New Hagen subject"

John V. Watson

"Preparation is well in advance on a subject (*Death Croons the Blues*) which will be produced at Twickenham for MGM release. David Macdonald is to direct and casting is now in progress."

(*K. W.*, 26 August 1937, page 63, P. L. Mannock.)

"New disclosures on film finance"

"Twickenham Film Studios' Receivers Report"

"Insurance company's support withdrawn"

"The sudden withdrawal of the promised support by an insurance company and the appointment of a Receiver for the debenture holder before the directors could obtain financial assistance from other sources, was a dramatic move which precipitated the crisis of affairs of Twickenham Film Studios, Ltd., earlier this year."

"The report of the Assistant Official Receiver shows an estimated deficiency of assets to meet liabilities, subject to the cost of liquidation, amounting to £12,267 as regards creditors, and including contributors, a total deficiency of £46,767."

"The report states that the company was handicapped by a deficiency of cash working capital from its inception and since 1931 has carried on by means of bank advances. The failure and insolvency of the company, according to Julius Hagen, the managing director, who was appointed at a salary of £140 per week, plus travelling, entertaining and other expenses, were attributed to lack of working capital; to heavy production and overhead expenses; to the proceeds of film distribution not realising the amount anticipated; and to depreciation in the value of assets."

"Receiver's Opinion"

"But in the opinion of the Receiver the failure was primarily attributable to the omission of the directors to make proper provision for the capital necessary to finance the programme on which they embarked, to the excessive optimism of Mr. Hagen regarding the value of film production and to heavy salaries paid to the directors, particularly to Mr. Hagen."

"In the early days the company derived its revenue mainly from letting its studios to various film producing companies, and the accounts to March 1932 showed that £65,000 was received from that source."

"Thereafter, the company produced films on a considerable scale. According to the accounts for the period January 1929 to March 1934, the profit on film production was £168,052, the trading and gross profit £55,898, and the net profit £33,613."

"In March 1934, £27,599 was charged to profit and loss appropriation account as an adjustment in respect of the costs of earlier production. The accounts for the following period showed profit on film production £73,543, trading and gross profits £25,779, and net profit £5,276. But £41,517 was charged to the profit and loss appropriation account in respect of over-valuation of the company's stock of productions."

"A 7.5 per cent dividend on the Preference shares was paid in each of the four years 1931-1934."

"The company's gross liabilities at the time of the Receivership amounted to £138,590, comprising unsecured creditors £97,876, including £60,337 for cash advanced, £26,180 for goods supplied and the work done, £6,284 for artistes' salaries and £2,506 for film directors' fees."

John V. Watson

"Preferential creditors £1,157 and debenture holders £39,556. The assets were estimated to produce £126,322."

(*K. W.*, 2 September 1937, page 13)

"At Twickenham, studio work resumes"

"It is good to record the reopening of Twickenham Studios after several months of inactivity. David Macdonald began direction on Monday, 30 August 1937 of *Death Croons the Blues*, with Sydney Blythe at the camera."

(*K. W.*, 2 September 1937, page 39, P. L. Mannock.)

"Julius Hagen on Production Losses"

"Handicapped by lack of capital.

"Particulars regarding the winding-up of J. H. Productions, Ltd, 11, Wardour Street, London, W.1. have been issued from the offices of the Official Receiver, in the Companies Winding-up Department of the Board of Trade, Carey Street, W.C."

(*K. W.*, 9 September 1937, page 9, The City Column)

"St. Margaret's Film Studios, Ltd., 4 Old Burlington Street, London, W."

"Debenture charged on the company's undertaking and property, present and future, including uncalled capital, dated 2 September 1937, to secure £5,000. Holder: R. Philip, Thames Eyot, Twickenham."

(*K. W.*, 16 September 1937, page 26, The City Column)

The eight films trade shown by Julius Hagen during 1937:

1. Beauty and the Barge (1937)

Nautical comedy, adapted from a play by W. W. Jacobs.
Starring Gordon Harker, with Judy Gunn and Jack Hawkins.
Directed by Henry Edwards.

London Trade Show: Tuesday, 9 February 1937 at the Piccadilly Theatre.

British Registration Details:
Quota Registration No.: Br. 14,302.
Registration Date: 17 February 1937.
Registered Length: 6,493 feet.
Registered by: Wardour Films.
Maker's name: Twickenham Film Studios, Ltd.
Certificate: "U".

Released by: Associated British Film Distributors (following the absorption of its sister company, Wardour Films, in early 1937).

John V. Watson

Gordon Harker and Judy Gunn in a scene from *Beauty and the Barge*.

- Manchester: key-theatre run: week commencing Monday, 5 July 1937, at the Gaiety, *Beauty and the Barge* was double-billed with the American drama, *The Mighty Treve (of Arizona)*, with Noah Beery Jr., released by G.F.D. (General Film Distributors).
- Birmingham: key-theatre run: week commencing Monday, 23 August 1937, at the Forum, *Beauty and the Barge* was double-billed with *Michael Strogoff*, with Anton Walbrook, Elizabeth Allan and Akim Tamiroff, released by Radio Pictures.
- Bristol: two key-theatre runs: week commencing Monday, 18 October 1937:
  - At the Empire, *Beauty and the Barge* supported the crime drama, *Her Husband Lies*, with Gail Patrick and Ricardo Cortez, released by Paramount.
  - At the Triangle, *Beauty and the Barge* supported the crime drama, *Her Husband Lies*, with Gail Patrick and Ricardo Cortez, released by Paramount.

British General Release: Monday, 28 June 1937.

Beauty and the Barge was reviewed in the *Kine Weekly*, 18 February 1937, on page 27:

72 minutes, "U" certificate.

"<u>Remarks</u>: Nautical comedy of ingenuous picturesqueness adapted from a play by W. W. Jacobs. Story a little old-fashioned, but direction good, star's performance clever, and atmosphere delightful.
"<u>Box Office Angle</u>: Useful two-feature programme booking for the family and youngsters included.

"Nautical comedy of ingenuous picturesqueness adapted from a play by W. W. Jacobs. The story as a story is, of course, slightly tinged with age, but its simple fun nevertheless retains much of its pristine freshness; it is preserved by the salty wit of the author and the fruity humour of Gordon Harker. It should have no difficulty in bringing enjoyment to the industrial and family element.

"Added to the picture's kindly pleasantries are indisputable star values. Useful two-feature programme booking.

"<u>Story</u>: Captain Barley, a bargee, and Seton Boyne, a young lieutenant in the Navy, make for peppery Major Smedley's home, the former to court Mrs. Baldwin, the gentleman's housekeeper, and the latter to make the acquaintance of Ethel, daughter of the house. Ethel is in disgrace because of her refusal to marry the man of her father's choice and she pleads with Barley, who, meanwhile, has had a spot of bother with Mrs. Baldwin, to hide her on his barge and take her to London.

"Thinking he has made a conquest, Barley agrees, but Boyne overhears the arrangements, gets a job on the barge, and smuggles Mrs. Baldwin aboard. Once under way, Boyne cooks Barley's goose in such a way as to win Ethel and soothe her irate father.

"Acting: Gordon Harker occasionally finds his style cramped by the gentility of W. W. Jacob's humour, but he is too good a character actor to miss chances. Taken as a whole his performance is well up to standard; it will satisfy his fans. Judy Gunn is quite an attractive Ethel, and Jack Hawkins is good as Boyne. Margaret Rutherford, Ronald Shiner, George Carney, Margaret Yarde and Sebastian Smith are the best of the supporting players.

"Settings and Photography: There are moments when the fun is somewhat laboured, sociologically the humour is a little too exact, but apart from its irritating class distinctions it covers sufficient territory at sufficient speed to conjure up amiable light entertainment.

"The narratal twists are neat, while the character drawing has in its clear definition amusing contrast. Furthermore, the waterfront, seascape and canal sequences are refreshingly picturesque. These, the homely touch, and star values, are the film's not inconsiderable assets.

"Points of Appeal: Clean humour, popular romantic sentiment, artistically composed backgrounds, good performance by Gordon Harker, and title and star values.

2. *Underneath the Arches (1937)*

Comedy extravaganza starring Flanagan and Allen.

Directed by Redd Davis.

London Trade Show: Tuesday, 23 February 1937 at the Piccadilly Theatre.

British Registration Details:
Quota Registration No.: Br. 14,347.
Registration Date: 26 February 1937.
Registered Length: 6,500 feet.
Registered by: Associated British Film Distributors.
Maker's name: Twickenham Film Studios, Ltd.
Certificate: "U".

Bud Flanagan and Chesney Allen in a scene from *Underneath the Arches*.

♦   Cardiff: two key-theatre runs: week commencing Monday, 31 May 1937:
     ♦ At the Pavilion, supported by the Australian-made Zane Grey action-adventure, *Rangle River*, with Victor Jory, released by Columbia.

John V. Watson

♦ At the Queen's, supported by the Australian-made Zane Grey action-adventure, *Rangle River*, with Victor Jory, released by Columbia. British General Release: Monday, 19 July 1937.

Underneath The Arches was reviewed in the *Kine Weekly*, 4 March 1937, page 31:

72 minutes, "U" certificate.

"<u>Remarks</u>: Boisterous comedy extravaganza. Story slight, but fooling of popular co-stars bright and staging adequate.
"<u>Box Office Angle</u>: Sound light booking, one with star pull for the masses and youngsters.

"Boisterous, crazy comedy extravaganza, presenting a fairly popular compromise between raw humour and rough stuff. The gags and situations are not particularly original, nor is the story designed to link them together written with any great regard for continuity or showmanship, but Flanagan and Allen, rough and ready as their methods are, know their public. Their artless, ribald fooling promotes sufficient hearty fun to get the film over with the masses.

"Adequate light booking, particularly for the co-stars' many fans.

"<u>Story</u>: Bud and Ches, a couple of buskers, find the going hard and decide to end it all, but bungle their attempt at suicide and find themselves on a ship bound for South America. The captain puts them to work and, in the course of their duties, they discover a plot on the part of revolutionaries to secure the formula of a gas reputed to have the power to promote international good will. When the boat docks the inventor is kidnapped, but Bud and Ches rescue him and quell a rebellion, only to find that it takes more than gas to establish permanent peace.

"<u>Acting</u>: Flanagan is the biggest noise in the Flanagan and Allen partnership, and it is he who scores most of the laughs. He is at his most amusing as a boxer and champion dice-thrower. Stella Moya, an exotic young lady, Lyn Harding, Enid Stamp-Taylor and Aubrey Mather are in support, but they are no more than necessary stooges.

"<u>Production</u>: The gags, taken individually, are, in spite of their antiquity, quite amusing, and the antics of the co-stars, first as stewards, then as counter-espionage agents, and later as restorers of law and order, lead to much fooling.

"The bright spots outnumber the flat, and, by the time the film ends, it records a goodly number of laughs. It should register with the crowd.

"<u>Points of Appeal</u>: Evergreen laughable gags, good team work by box-office stars, adequate production qualities, and popular vocal relief.

3. *The Vicar of Bray (1937)*

Historical romantic comedy drama starring Stanley Holloway.

Directed by Henry Edwards.

John V. Watson

The onscreen opening main title for *The Vicar of Bray*.

London Trade Show: Monday, 5 April 1937 at the Piccadilly Theatre. The London Trade Show was originally due to be held almost three weeks earlier; on Wednesday, 17 March 1937 at the Piccadilly Theatre.

British Registration Details:
Quota Registration No.: Br. 14,688.
Registration Date: 4 May 1937.
Registered Length: 6,110 feet.
Registered by: Associated British Film Distributors.
Maker's name: J. H. Productions, Ltd.
Certificate: "U".

Trade Show advertisement: Billing: Starring Stanley Holloway as '*The Vicar of Bray*', with Hugh Miller, K. Hamilton Price, Felix Aylmer, Margaret Vines, Garry Marsh, Eve Gray, Esmond Knight, Martin Walker. Directed by Henry Edwards. A Twickenham Production. Distributed by Associated British.
Tagline: "*The Vicar of Bray*" impresses the critics!" (With five trade press quotes.)

- Cardiff: key-theatre pre-release run: week commencing Monday, 16 August 1937, at the Olympia, supporting the Samuel Goldwyn drama, **Beloved Enemy**, with Merle Oberon and Brian Aherne, released by United Artists.

British General Release: Monday, 6 December 1937.

The Vicar of Bray:
The Cost of Production: £ 20,398; '*Kine Weekly*', 4 March 1937, page 16.

The Vicar of Bray was reviewed in the *Kinematograph Weekly*, 8 April 1937, on page 29:

68 minutes, "U" certificate.

"Remarks: Artless, historical, romantic comedy-drama, built to accommodate the humour of Stanley Holloway. Story sketchy and production unpretentious, but team work satisfactory.
"Box Office Angle: Fair average two-feature booking for unsophisticated audiences. Good for youngsters.

"Artless historical romantic comedy drama, built to accommodate the homely humour of Stanley Holloway. The production is not on a grand scale – for instance, subtitles are frequently substituted when the development calls for spectacle – but so wide is the range of the simple story that the handicap of unpretentiousness fails to divert the entertainment from new popular channels.

"Colourful and comely, and endowed with star vales, the film is, on balance, a fair average two-feature programme proposition for other than sophisticated audiences. The Quota ticket is by no means its least important asset.

"Story: On the advice of his trusted friend, the Earl of Brendon, Charles I appoints the Vicar of Bray, a man of wit and human understanding, as tutor to his son, Prince Charles. After successfully completing his tenure of office the Vicar returns to his poor Irish parishioners, but before leaving, the Prince, out of friendship, promises him that he will always grant any subsequent bequest he may make.

"In the years that follow Charles I loses his head, Cromwell becomes Dictator, and, after his death, Charles II comes to the throne, and the swift changes result in Dennis, young friend of the Vicar, being sentenced to death for treason. Dennis is in love with Norah, daughter of the Earl of Brendon, their respective parents being in opposite camps, and to save the situation the Vicar rushes to London and implores the King to redeem his promise by sparing Dennis's life. He does, and so all ends well in Bray.

"Acting: Stanley Holloway is responsible for a sound character comedy cameo as the Vicar, and puts over the many appropriate song numbers with agreeable gusto.

"Hugh Miller acts with quiet histrionic dignity as Charles I; Felix Aylmer, master of elocution, is good as the Earl of Brendon; Garry Marsh and Martin Walker are adequate as leaders of the Roundheads; and Esmond Knight and Margaret

Vines please as the chequered lovers, Dennis and Norah.

"Production: Thematically, the film bites off a little more than its sponsors are prepared to chew. The story, although simple, covers a period that is rich in opportunity for spectacle, but such is the friendly intimacy of the production that in spite of its technical limitations it finds no great difficulty in promoting kindly entertainment of picturesque versatility.

"The star, Stanley Holloway, adapts his inimitable technique to the demands of the period without effort, and his good work is supported by a team of competent stage players. More enlightened audiences will, of course, criticise that which is because it falls far short of that which might have been, but the unsophisticated, particularly family audiences, should nevertheless find the film's naïve prettiness to their liking.

"Points of Appeal: Star values, colourful atmosphere, adequate supporting cast and quota angle.

4. *The Angelus (1937)*

Released under the title of *Who Killed Fen Markham?*

Romantic melodrama with Anthony Bushell and Nancy O'Neil.

Directed by Thomas Bentley.

London Trade Show: Thursday, 3 June 1937 at the Phoenix Theatre.

British Registration Details:
Quota Registration No.: Br. 14,813.
Registration Date: 7 June 1937.
Registered Length: 6,840 feet.
Registered by: Ambassador Film Productions, Limited.
Maker's name: St. Margaret's Film Studios, Limited.
British Board of Censor's Certificate: "A".

Trade Show advertisement: Advertisement Billing:
— Gilbert Church presents (a) Julius Hagen production.
— Directed by Thomas Bentley.
— Anthony Bushell, Nancy O'Neil (in large type font),
— Eve Gray, Mary Glynne, Garry Marsh, Zoe Wynn (in smaller type font),
— Richard Cooper, Joyce Evans, Charles Carson, Amy Veness (in small type font)
— Based on a story by Michael Barringer inspired by the famous song "*The Last Rose of Summer*".
Tagline: "Produced to achieve the same Box-Office success as: *The Last Chord, Lily of Killarney, In a Monastery Garden*". Logo: Ambassador Film Productions Limited.
NOTE: *The Last Chord, Lily of Killarney* and *In a Monastery Garden* were all produced by Julius Hagen for Gilbert Church (and the late Frederick White) for their previous company: Associated Producing and Distribution Co., Ltd.

◆ Glasgow: key-theatre run: week commencing Monday, 6 December 1937, at the Playhouse, *Who Killed Fen Markham?* supported the crime action-thriller, ***Behind the Headlines***, with Lee Tracy, released by RKO-Radio.

♦ Liverpool: key-theatre run: week commencing Monday, 13 December 1937, at the Palais de Luxe, ***Who Killed Fen Markham?*** was double-billed with the comedy, ***Step Lively, Jeeves***, with Arthur Treacher, released by Twentieth Century-Fox.

♦ Bristol: two key-theatre runs: week commencing Monday, 20 December 1937, at the King's and the Whiteladies, ***Who Killed Fen Markham?*** supported the romantic comedy, Ladies in Love, with Janet Gaynor, Loretta Young, Constance Bennett, Simone Simon, Don Ameche, Paul Lukas and Tyrone Power, released by Twentieth Century-Fox.

British General Release: Monday, 6 December 1937.

Who Killed Fen Markham? was reviewed in the *Kinematograph Weekly*, 10 June 1937, page 30:

76 minutes, "A" certificate.

"<u>Remarks</u>: Sentimental, romantic melodrama. Story artless, but treatment showmanlike, staging ambitious and acting adequate. Title values outstanding.

"<u>Box Office Angle</u>: Very good booking for industrial, provincial and family halls.

"Here is an artless emotional potpourri, a sentimental romantic melodrama containing every element of traditional old-time theatre fare, from crime to the convent. The piecing together of the plot does not reveal a great deal of imagination, nor is the acting outstanding, but with all its

611

blushing naiveté, it has undoubted possibilities as a tear jerker for the masses. Moreover, it comes from the same successful stable as In a Monastery Garden, box-office epic of yesterday, and it inherits the same valuable credentials. Very good booking for industrial and provincial halls.

"Story: Jane Rowland, a young actress, is innocently involved in a scandal, with the result that a West End engagement is denied her. Brian Ware, her fiancé, is loyal to her, but his father, Jim Ware, a big financier, is all against the marriage to June, and she, rather than jeopardising her future, leaves him. She finds the going hard and is soon forced to apply to Fenn Markham, a licentious producer, for a job.

"Meanwhile, Maisie, an old friend, learns that June's aunt, formerly the famous actress, Cecili ?? (Cecily) Manners, and now identified as Sister Angelica, was once in love with John Ware, and she pleads with her to intervene on the lovers' behalf. She does, and later she is the means of saving Brian, falsely accused of murdering Markham, and persuading John Ware to give the young couple his blessing.

"Acting: Anthony Bushell and Nancy O'Neil are the lovers, Eve Gray is Maisie, Charles Carson is John Ware, Mary Glynne is Sister Angelica, and Garry (misspelt Gary) Marsh is Markham, but not one of them acts with distinction. They are, however, adequate, but this cannot be said of Alice O'Day, who gets laughs in the wrong place.

"Production: The staging, in spite of its versatility,

has the same touch of theatricality as the story, while the musical accompaniment, which includes *The Last Rose of Summer*, is in a similar key. But although the highly coloured emotionalism is not in tune with high-brow tastes, there is no doubt that it will strike a responsive chord with the masses. Nothing is left out in the fashioning of the melodrama, and it is the picture's scope which amounts to good showmanship that places it well within striking distance of the big money class. It is good sentimental hokum made by people who know their jobs.

"<u>Points of Appeal</u>: Ingenuous but moving story, adequate team work, cunning blend of suspense, drama, romance, comedy and tender pathos, obvious title pull and outstanding exploitation angles.

Other Trade Press Comments: as per the advertisement published by Ambassador Film Productions, Limited, in the *Kinematograph Weekly*, 24 June 1937:

The Era: "Recipe that never fails ..... if they don't eat it, they deserve to die of famine."

The Daily Film Renter: "..... obviously aimed at mass market, for which it makes direct appeal. Will ..... manage to accomplish this with satisfaction."

The Cinema: "Will appeal quite well to the masses, especially in the provinces. The settings ..... are commendable."

5. *Silver Blaze (1937)*

Sherlock Holmes adventure starring Arthur Wontner as the detective.

Directed by Thomas Bentley.

London Trade Show: Wednesday, 30 June 1937 at the Adelphi Theatre, Strand.

British Registration Details:
Quota Registration No.: Br. 14,944.
Registration Date: 13 July 1937.
Registered Length: 6,358 feet.
Registered by: Associated British Picture Corporation, Ltd.
Maker's name: Twickenham Film Studios, Ltd.

> Note: Maker's Name: although Twickenham Film Studios, Ltd. is recorded as the maker of this film in the formal Quota Registration, it is absolutely clear from the *Kinematograph Weekly* report, issue dated 4 March 1937 (page 16) regarding the statutory first meetings of creditors and shareholders under the compulsory liquidation of J. H. Productions, Ltd. held in late February 1937, that **Silver Blaze** was actually made by J. H. Productions, Ltd., as the cost of its production (of £30,777) is clearly stated within the statement regarding the total cost of the seven pictures made by the company during 1936.

British Board of Censor's Certificate: "U".
Running Time: 71 minutes.
Sound System: Visatone Sound System.

Trade Show advertisement: Billing: Arthur Wontner as Sherlock Holmes. A Twickenham Production. Directed by Thomas Bentley. Tagline: "Fiction's Immortal Hero – who enthralled young and old alike – Will again hold his Millions of fans spellbound by his uncanny powers of deduction in solving this punch-packed Mystery".

British General Release: Monday, 25 October 1937.

- ◆ Cardiff: key-theatre run: week commencing Monday, 15 November 1937, at the Olympia, *Silver Blaze* supported the musical, *On the Avenue*, with Dick Powell, Madeleine Carroll and Alice Faye, released by Twentieth Century-Fox.
- ◆ Birmingham: key-theatre run: week commencing Monday, 13 December 1937, at the Forum, *Silver Blaze* supported the Edward Small biographical drama, *The Toast of New York*, with Edward Arnold, Cary Grant and Frances Farmer, released by RKO-Radio.
- ◆ Glasgow: two key-theatre runs: week commencing Monday, 13 December 1937, at the Regal and the Coliseum, *Silver Blaze* supported the Samuel Goldwyn romantic comedy, *Woman Chases Man*, with Miriam Hopkins and Joel McCrea, released by United Artists.

Silver Blaze:
The Cost of Production: £30,777; *'Kine Weekly'*, 4 March 1937, page 16.

Silver Blaze was reviewed in the *Kinematograph Weekly*, 8 July 1937, page 35:

71 minutes, "U" certificate.

"Remarks: Famous Sherlock Holmes adventure, introducing sinister elements from other Conan Doyle stories. Arthur Wontner, as the detective, an unforgettable figure.

"Box Office Angle: Certain popular hit for astute

showmen. Good for all types and ages.

"Detective drama, freely adapted from a Sherlock
Holmes Adventure. All the main essentials of
Conan Doyle's famous racehorse mystery story are
here – and a lot more besides. Although the plot
is, therefore, of a somewhat composite nature, this
will not spoil – and may even add to – the
enjoyment of the ordinary kinema audience in a
production which is packed with excitement and
surprises.

"Story: While on a visit to Sir Henry Baskerville in
Devon Sherlock Holmes is called in by the owner
of "*Silver Blaze*", a racehorse favourite for a big
event, to investigate the disappearance on the eve
of the race.

"Not only is "*Silver Blaze*" missing, but Hunter,
the groom, is found dead from opium poisoning,
and later the trainer, Straker, is also discovered
apparently murdered on the moors. Suspicion
fastens on Jack Trevor, in love with Baskerville's
daughter, Diana, as he has backed the second
favourite to win him £5,000, and was found round
"*Silver Blaze*'s" stable on the night of the crime.
But a more sinister hand has been at work, the
hand of Professor Moriarty who, for a huge bribe
by a bookmaker, has undertaken to see that the
favourite does not go to the post. How he exerts
his influence on Straker to nobble the horse; how
Straker is killed by "*Silver Blaze*" in attempting
to carry out this design; how Holmes finds the
favourite, and ensures its taking part in the race;
how the jockey is shot when nearing the winning

post, and how Moriarty and his minions are finally trapped by the detective form the principle ingredients of a well-told yarn.

"Acting: Arthur Wontner's performance as Sherlock Holmes is easily the best histrionic contribution in this film, and he succeeds triumphantly in convincing us that he would really have deduced the main elements and perpetrator of the crime. As Moriarty, Lyn Harding is unctuously ferocious; Ian Fleming, a prize rabbit as a docile Watson; John Turnbull an appropriately blustering and wooden-headed Lestrade, and Gilbert Davis sufficiently realistic as the bookie who has overlaid the favourite. Judy Gunn is persuasive in the part of Diana, and Eve Gray appealing as Mrs. Straker.

"Production: Scenes of the moors, in the racing stables and in Sir Henry's country mansion have been devised with an expert eye for visual effect. The racehorse sequences are suitably sensational (although there seems to be a technical error in the running of the race), and Holmes' lodgings in Baker Street, present us with the looked-for surroundings and appurtenances of the detective's domestic ménage. Photography and recording throughout are first-rate.

"Points of Appeal: A rattling good mystery thriller. Familiar story embellished by novel kinema effects. Superb performance of the leading character by Arthur Wontner and sensational finale.

John V. Watson

Other Trade Press Comments: per the advertisement published in '*Kine Weekly*', 15 July 1937

"*Faulkner's Bulletin*": "... Arthur Wontner is Sherlock as we always fancied him, and remains the immortal detective ... This picture is well produced and the story is well known."

"*Daily Film Renter*": "Good robust material of popular type ... one of the best of the Conan Doyle stories."

"*The Era*": "Very good popular entertainment".

"*The Cinema*": "Remarkable true-to-character portrayal of great detective by Arthur Wontner ... offering of assured popularity, enhanced by Sherlock Holmes appeal".

6. *Clothes and the Woman (1937)*

Farcical comedy starring Tucker McGuire and Rod La Rocque.

Directed by Albert de Courville.

London Trade Show: Friday, 2 July 1937 at the Phoenix Theatre.

British Registration Details:
Quota Registration No.: Br. 15,097.
Registration Date: 9 August 1937.
Registered Length: 6,294 feet.
Registered by: Associated British Picture Corporation, Ltd.
Maker's name: J. H. Productions, Ltd.
British Board of Censor's Certificate: "A".

'The Czar of Twickenham'. The History of Julius Hagen and the Film
Empire he created at Twickenham Film Studios, from 1927 to 1938.

British General Release: Monday, 14 February 1938.

Clothes and the Woman:
The Cost of Production: *The Girl Without Morale*
(*Clothes and the Woman*): £30,278; '*Kine Weekly*', 4
March 1937, page 16.

The working title was: *The Girl Without Morale*.

A picture of Tucker McGuire, the star of *Clothes
and the Woman*.

Clothes and the Woman was reviewed in the
Kinematograph Weekly, 8 July 1937, page 45:

70 minutes, "A" certificate.

"Remarks: Frivolous farcical comedy. Story weak,
and atmosphere unconvincing. Acting of well-
known supporting players represents the happiest

John V. Watson

feature of the entertainment.

"<u>Box Office Angle</u>: Fair average support for the not too sophisticated. Safe for the family.

"Frivolous romantic comedy fashioned in stereotyped lines. There is some point to the story, but so casual is the treatment that few will grasp it. The only humour frankly exposed is that confined to the amiable and amusing technique and mannerisms of such well-known stage players as Constance Collier and Alastair (misspelt "Alistair") Sim. They, in fact, save the picture. Fair average supporting feature for the not too sophisticated.

"<u>Story</u>: Joan Moore, pupil at a French school, anticipates with delight the prospect of spending a holiday at Cannes, but her hopes are dashed when Count Tommy Bernhardt, her fiancé, arrives on the scene and informs her that it has been arranged for her to spend her vacation in the vicinity. She revolts, however, and, aided by Eric Thrale, airman brother of her friend Marie, flies to Cannes. Conscious of her dowdy dress, she seeks advice of Eugenia, wealthy middle-aged neighbour whom she mistakes for the famous courtesan, Comtesse de Chautemps, and Eugenia, without revealing her identity, takes her under her wing. When next she meets Eric she is over-dressed, and her scheme to acquire sex appeal defeats itself. Still, Eric has understanding, and after persuading Joan to be herself, the path to true love is made easy, thanks to the susceptibility of Tommy, who, meanwhile, has fallen for Marie.

620

"<u>Acting</u>: Tucker McGuire has very little personality as Joan, she makes little of her subterfuge, and Rod La Rocque is not exactly in his element as Eric. The best performances by far come from Constance Collier as Eugenia and Alastair (misspelt "Alistair") Sim as her man servant. The rest of the cast is of little account.

"<u>Production</u>: Both the technical work and the direction are slipshod. The Continental settings never for a moment convince, while the development is hampered by much superfluous by-play. By the time the story does reach conclusions it is too late to recognise humour in its objective. However, one or two players entertain individually, and it is to them that the comedy owes a few laughs.

"<u>Points of Appeal</u>: Good title, attractive cast and quota values.

7. A Romance in Flanders (1937)

Released in the U.S. under the title: *'Lost on the Western Front'*

Melodrama starring Paul Cavanagh and Marcelle Chantal, with Garry Marsh.

The English version was directed by Maurice Elvey. London Trade Show: Wednesday, 18 August 1937 at the Piccadilly Theatre.

John V. Watson

A French postcard showing Marcelle Chantal, the star
of both the English and French versions of *A
Romance in Flanders*.

British Registration Details:
Quota Registration No.: Br. 15,153.
Registration Date: 1 September 1937.
Registered Length: 6,897 feet.
Registered by: British Lion Film Corporation, Ltd.
Maker's name: Franco-London Film. (Franco-
London Films.)
British Board of Censor's Certificate: "A".

Trade Show advertisement: published in the
Kinematograph Weekly, 12 August 1937: "Paul Cavanaugh
(large type font) and Marcelle Chantal (medium type font)
in '*A Romance in Flanders*', with Garry Marsh (smaller
type font), Olga Lindo, Alastair Sim (both small font type
- Alastair was misspelt "Alistair"). A Franco-London
Film. Directed by Maurice Elvey." Tagline: "Two men in

No Man's Land . . . in love with the same girl . . . One returned to become a hero. The other was "among those missing" . . . The years roll on . . . and the three meet again in the little village in Flanders where one was left for dead nineteen years before . . ." Logo: British Lion Film Corp. Ltd.

British General Release: Monday, 7 February 1938.

A Romance in Flanders:

The Cost of Production: *The Widow's Island* (*A Romance in Flanders*): £16,306; '*Kine Weekly*', 4 March 1937, page 16.

Note that the cost of £16,306 seems very low compared to the costs of the other six films made by J. H. Productions (the highest production cost was £45,449 for *Spy of Napoleon*), but it must be remembered that this film was produced in conjunction with Franco-London Films who obviously would have borne the balance of the production cost.

Production Notes:

- Working Title: '*Widow's Island*'.
- *Widow's Island* was made simultaneously in two versions, English and French.
- Made by J. H. Productions in conjunction with Franco-London Films.
- Marcelle Chantal starred as "Yvonne" in both versions.
- The English version was directed by Maurice Elvey.

A Romance in Flanders was reviewed in the *Kinematograph Weekly*, 26 August 1937, page 53:

76 minutes, "A" certificate.

"Remarks: Fictional yet interesting melodrama played against actual war and post-war

623

backgrounds. Story theatrical, but action sound, treatment resourceful and staging realistic.

"Box Office Angle: Sound two-feature programme booking for most halls. Hardly suitable for children.

"Fictional yet interesting triangle melodrama, played against actual war and post-war backgrounds. The development is mainly retrospective, and it is the efficacy of the treatment rather than the depth of the plot that enables the drama to survive the conventional and, at the same time, conjure up serious entertainment of no more little mass and feminine appeal. The cast is a capable one. Sound two-feature programme proposition for most halls.

"Story: While *en route* for Ostend with his with his French wife Yvonne, and small daughter Muriel, ex-Sergeant-Major Rodd Berry meets Captain Stanford, his former C.O., and is persuaded to join a regimental reunion in Flander-Muyden. Berry is the hero of the regiment, he having rescued a detachment of soldiers from an isolated post by a tank, but official records also reveal that John Morley, his best friend and rival for Yvonne, then living with her father, a French farmer, has been left for dead in no-man's land.

"During the celebrations Yvonne recognises Morley, now a courier to visitors to the battlefields, but he claims he is suffering from loss of memory, and refuses to acknowledge her. However, his lie is eventually nailed, and he later proves to Yvonne that Berry not only deliberately deserted him in no-man's land, but had subsequently refused to identify him when he was actually suffering from loss of memory, because of their rivalry for her. Yvonne decides to leave Berry, and Morley plans to kill him, but before long the two realise that is impossible to resurrect the past, and they become reconciled to their respective fates.

"Acting: Paul Cavanagh contributes a smooth, telling portrayal as Morley, and Garry Marsh strikes the correct vigorous note of contrast as Berry, but Marcelle Chantal, although actually French, is somewhat colourless as Yvonne. The best of the supporting players are Olga Lindo, Alastair Sim and Evelyn Roberts.

"Production: The subject matter is inherently sombre, but the director, Maurice Elvey, has relieved the tension adequately by introducing friendly reunion celebrations and carefully planned thrills. In fact, it is the framing of the emotional theme, rather than the theme itself, that constitutes the major portion of the popular entertainment. The film is, in spite of its orthodoxy, not at all bad theatre.

"Points of Appeal: Synthetic human angle, realistic war scenes, sound acting, feminine appeal, popular cast and title values.

8. *Death Croons the Blues (1937)*

Murder mystery drama with Hugh Wakefield.

Directed by David MacDonald.

London Trade Show: Monday, 25 October 1937 at the Cambridge Theatre.

British Registration Details:
Quota Registration No.: Br. 15,395.
Registration Date: 26 October 1937.
Registered Length: 6,636 feet.
Registered by: M-G-M.
Maker's name: St. Margaret's Film Studios, Limited.
British Board of Censor's Certificate: "A".
Running Time: 74 minutes.

A signed portrait of Hugh Wakefield, the star of *Death Croons the Blues*.

Death Croons the Blues was reviewed in the *Kinematograph Weekly*, 28 October 1937, page 35:

74 minutes, "A" certificate

"<u>Remarks</u>: Murder mystery drama. Story sketchy, comedy forced and thrills manufactured. Acting only fair.

"<u>Box Office Angle</u>: Quota booking for the unsophisticated. Hardly suitable for children.

"Murder mystery drama, presenting with unbecoming and incredible facetiousness a new interpretation of the perfect crime theme. The plot, in spite of its inherent seriousness, never gains ascendancy over the comedy trimmings. In comparison with its crisp American counterpart, and comparisons are inevitable, the film is sketchy and colourless. Quota booking for the unsophisticated.

"<u>Story</u>: Jim Morton, a reporter with a weakness for liquor, learns through the indiscretions of Cuffey, an old lag, that Adele Vallee, an entertainer, has been murdered. Viscount Brent, a wayward young aristocrat, is suspected, but before he can be interrogated, he mysteriously disappears. Lady Constance Gaye, Brent's sister, is certain that her brother is innocent, and Morton succeeds in securing her co-operation in his quest for the real story.

"Clues then take them on a tour of Mayfair and the slums, and finally they trap down their quarry, Hugo Branker, a crooked financier, in time to prevent him from disposing of Brent in circumstances that would make his intended victim his perfect alibi. The success of the Morton-Constance partnership is celebrated in matrimony.

"Acting: Hugh Wakefield is amusing at times as the alcoholic Morton, but his performance lacks conviction when seriousness is demanded. Antoinette Cellier is adequate as Constance, but George Groves grossly overacts as the villain Branker. The support is of little account.

"Production: This melodrama is prevented from grappling with reality by the long arm of coincidence. It unfolds with such mechanical precision that intended thrills merely become stillborn heirs of the obvious. There is a fair amount of comedy, but this, too, is too forced to save the fictional face. The film is purely a pot-boiler.

"Points of Appeal: Cast and quota ticket.

1937: The British Film Industry: Trends and Other Events throughout the Year:

Gaumont-British drops Fox as its U.S. distributor.

(*K. W.*, 7 January 1937, page 3)

Ambassador Film Productions, Ltd., was formed on 24 December 1936 with a capital of £100 in £1 shares.

(*K. W.*, 7 January 1937, page 20, The City Column)

Statement published that "**money is not lacking for British pictures**" as British Lion outlines its Denham production plans.

(*K. W.*, 14 January 1937, page 3)

"Production isn't just spending" by P L Mannock.

"Last year we spent **£4 million** on production ..."

(*K. W.*, 14 January 1937, page 85, P. L. Mannock)

The CEA and the **Moyne Report** stated that the 50% Quota proposal was "impracticable".

(*K. W.*, 21 January 1937)

Ten millions for film trade investment. There are **record company flotations**.

John V. Watson

(K. W., 21 January 1937, page 21, the City column)

Union Cinemas announces profits of £270,000.

(K. W., 21 January 1937, page 21, the City column)

Studio Holdings Trust, Ltd., was registered 29 January 1937. Capital £100 in 100 shares of £1 each. **Investment trust company**. Solicitors; Forsyte, Kerman and Phillips, 9 Carlos Place, London W.1

(K. W., 4 February 1937, page 14, the City column)

Gaumont-British film production crisis.

(K. W., 25 February 1937, page 3)

Gainsborough Pictures' £98,000 losses.

(K. W., 4 March 1937, page 16)

Alexander Korda's production of *I, Claudius* is suspended.

(K. W., 18 March 1937, page 39, P. L. Mannock)

The **Kinematograph Renters Society** (K.R.S.) comes of age.

(K. W., 25 March 1937, page 3)

"Riverside Studios' New Manager"

"John Auton's Appointment"

"Following the appointment of Baynham Honri to Cricklewood Studios, John Auton, of Twickenham, succeeds him as studio manager as from March 22 last."

'The Czar of Twickenham'. The History of Julius Hagen and the Film Empire he created at Twickenham Film Studios, from 1927 to 1938.

"John Auton. In 1928, joined New Era Productions as production manager, working with Harold Auten, V. C. He continued with this company after the appointment of a liquidator until his appointment as production manager to Twickenham Films in 1933."

(Note that **Baynham Honri**, from 1931, was associated with Twickenham Film Studios in charge of sound, and from 1935 he was also responsible for the supervision of sound at J. H. Studios, Elstree, and Riverside Studios.)

(*K. W.*, 8 April 1937, page 34)

Few British pictures in work – **production slump causes anxiety** – 13 films in production on the 58 floors available, including one at Twickenham.

(*K. W.*, 15 April 1937, page 3)

Tay Garnett, John Ford and Ronald Colman form Renowned Artists' Corporation to become new producing unit at United Artists.

(*K. W.*, 22 April 1937, page 5)

Production slump is only temporary, reports P. L. Mannock.

(*K. W.*, 22 April 1937, page 37)

Lawrence of Arabia picture is abandoned by **Alexander Korda**.

(*K. W.*, 29 April 1937)

A strike in **Hollywood**.

631

John V. Watson

(*K. W.*, 6 May 1937, page 5)

Another **Max Schach** company is formed – Max Schach Productions, Ltd.

(*K. W.*, 6 May 1937, page 17)

£4 million **Odeon** issue shortly. 5 per cent debentures for public.

(*K. W.*, 13 May 1937)

Alexander Korda insists that British pictures are not treated fairly by large circuits in America.

(*K. W.*, 20 May 1937)

George King schedules 20 films during 1937 to be released by MGM, Sound City and Paramount. The first is *John Halifax, Gentleman*.

(*K. W.*, 27 May 1937, page 49, P. L. Mannock)

Guenther Stapenhorst to co-produce films with Alexander Korda.

(*K. W.*, 27 May 1937, page 49, P. L. Mannock)

Obstacles to the **2,000 ft. reel** revealed.

(*K. W.*, 17 June 1937, page 5)

The official basis of the **new Films Act** – exhibitor 15% Quota – renter 20% Quota - £15,000 minimum cost.

(*K. W.*, 17 June 1937, page 5)

MGM schedules four films to be made in England.

'The Czar of Twickenham'. The History of Julius Hagen and the Film Empire he created at Twickenham Film Studios, from 1927 to 1938.

(Note that the first three films were: *A Yank at Oxford*, *The Citadel* and *Goodbye, Mr. Chips*. All three films were very successful for MGM; each making substantial profits.)

(*K. W.*, 1 July 1937, page 41, P. L. Mannock)

Odeon Theatres Limited – issue of £1.8 million 5% first mortgage debenture stock at £99 per cent.

(*K. W.*, 8 July 1937)

Trade views on **Government White Paper** – death threat to small producers – fewer films for independent cinemas.

(*K. W.*, 5 August 1937, page 3)

Government's **Quota proposals** - £7,500 labour cost qualification.

(*K. W.*, 5 August 1937, page 7)

City – **film loan difficulties** – caution in the City.

(*K. W.*, 12 August 1937, page 28)

British Lion loss of £14,016.

(*K. W.*, 26 August 1937, page 5)

MGM's first film starts at Denham – *A Yank at Oxford*.

(*K. W.*, 26 August 1937, page 63, P. L. Mannock)

MGM's plans for **Greta Garbo** and **Spencer Tracy**; they are scheduled to come to England to film *Shadow of the Wings*.
(Note that neither star came to England then and that the film itself was never made.)

John V. Watson

(*K. W.*, 9 September 1937, page 3)

20 films are scheduled for **Teddington Studios**.

(*K. W.*, 9 September 1937, page 27, P. L. Mannock)

Our **producer shortage** is discussed.

(*K. W.*, 30 September 1937, page 47, P. L. Mannock)

MGM sign stage player **Greer Garson**.
(Note that **Greer Garson** had a very successful career at MGM where she reigned up to 1954.)

(*K. W.*, 30 September 1937)

Lost Horizon makes film history; it had a run for 24 week run in London.

(*K. W.*, 7 October 1937, page 34)

A.B.P.C. takes control of **Union Cinemas**.

(Note that ABPC is the Associated British Pictures Corporation.)

(*K. W.*, 21 October 1937, page 10A)

A.B.P.C.'s new production schedule is announced.

(*K. W.*, 4 November 1937, page 51)

25 more amendments to the **Films Bill**.

(*K. W.*, 11 November 1937, page 3)

The new **Films Bill** is explained.

(*K. W.*, 18 November 1937, page 17)

634

'The Czar of Twickenham'. The History of Julius Hagen and the Film Empire he created at Twickenham Film Studios, from 1927 to 1938.

The effect of the **film production slow down** is highlighted.

(*K. W.*, 9 December 1937, page 19)

The Citadel is to start in January.

(*K. W.*, 9 December 1937, page 41, P. L. Mannock)

1937: The Tenth Year of the 'Quota' Act:

216 British films were first shown during the year 1937.

This number is arrived at by using the data contained in *The British Film Catalogue: 1895-1970* by Denis Gifford, as follows:

10369: Closing Gifford Catalogue Number for 1937.

10153: Opening Gifford Catalogue Number for 1937.

216: Total. A **significant decrease** of 40 fewer films made over the previous year's total of 256.

Some of these films were short subjects; the actual number of shorts made has not been determined.

John V. Watson

1938:
THE LAUNCH OF THE
SECOND "QUOTA"
FILMS ACT:

In order to provide the reader with an informed preamble prior to the actual enactment of the 1938 Films Act, it is certainly worthwhile, and consequently informative, to replicate here the view of S. G. Rayment, the Editor of *The Kinematograph Weekly*, in the 1938 Year Book, to facilitate a meaningful understanding about the concerns of the film industry generally for the intent and content of the new Act. Mr. Rayment stated:

"A YEAR FOR THE STATESMAN."

"ALTHOUGH there are troubles and difficulties and puzzles in nearly every direction, at the time this introduction is written none is so prominent in the minds of kinema men as the measure to take the place of the expiring Act of 1927. The draft of this Bill was issued at the end of October last, but a very few weeks on the floor of the House, and especially in the Committee room so mangled the original that but little resemblance remains either to the original or to the White Paper representing the findings of Lord Moyne's Committee, whose work was intended to be the basis of future action."

"Politicians rather than statesmen have hitherto been taking the leading parts in the very wordy discussions on the Bill, but I am materialistic enough to assert that it is what we put on our screens that matters and everything else is of secondary importance, including the formulation of a code to govern our affairs."

"The object is, of course, to foster the production of British

636

films, but the whole of the laborious efforts to do better what the 1927 Act aimed at have failed to convince the onlooker that any really big effect is likely to be attained. The main flaw in the provisions just about to expire lay in the possibility of complying with the letter of the law, whilst treating with contempt the spirit of it. The "quota quickie" having been recognised as the villain of the piece, our legislators' minds were for months concentrated upon plans to ensure not merely a certain percentage of British films for production, distribution, and exhibition, but a minimum guarantee of entertainment quality."

"UNFORTUNATELY there is a vast difference between the official mind and that of the practical kinema man. Any Government department naturally wishes to see a neatly drawn-up series of demands and definitions, capable of being rigidly enforced. With most businesses something of the sort is practicable ; with the film it is hopeless. A line can be drawn in the specification of most goods which would divide accurately the eligible quality from the rest ; but no set rules have ever been devised which can adequately settle the boundaries dividing good from bad films."

So there we have it — legislation can rule upon and control the physical elements of any commercial enterprise, in the form of its revenue and costs, and the limitations imposed upon the latter, but how do you really quantify the abstractness of quality into any legal framework? Impossible, do I hear your cry?

Well, let us now examine what S. G. Rayment, the Editor of *The Kinematograph Weekly*, wrote the following year, in the 1939 *Kinematograph Year Book*, after the new Act came into being. He said:

"THE aspect of grim earnestness and even anxiety which marks every department of the film business at the dawn of 1939 sits very ill on a branch of enterprise devoted to amusement and entertainment. But although as far as the public is concerned we have been able to supply first-class fare, in ever-growing conditions of luxury, we behind the scenes have serious reason to question the healthy condition of business, and the experience of its first nine months' working makes us less and less confident about the efficacy of the new Films Act."

"Designed as a measure which would ensure the well-being

of British production, the methods and degrees of encouragement were amended and adjusted up to the last possible moment before the Act appeared on the Statute Book, with what success the New Year stocktaking tells only too well."

"HOPE, not achievement, is the best we can register as the early results of the enactment, but he would be an optimist who would expect to see any material advancement in the near future, or at least any harvest at all proportionate to the labour and energy that went to the preparatory stages."

"Enthusiasm and confidence are essentially the spirits that have to animate the efforts in aid of British films, but my own task is to act as a candid friend, to whom a realistic appreciation of things as they are is more important than the presentation of only the bright side of the medal.

"I am far from being a pessimist, but I insist upon the need to face the facts. These prove that in our studios there is the man-power, the equipment and the enterprise to produce pictures ranking in quality with the best the world can make."

"Even more important, they have been proved as attractive to the general public, without which the most expensive or artistic films ever produced are without interest to the present argument."

"AS far as quality is concerned, we have shown that we need fear comparison with nobody, but when one takes stock of the actual numbers of films available or in the making it is clear that the present rate of progress is not nearly good enough. There are in and around London no fewer than twenty-one sound stages which have passed the whole year without producing a single picture. Only 98 have been made here altogether, which is completely inadequate for the needs of the exhibitor ; it compares with 225 in the preceding twelve months."

"When I add that these 98 pictures cost over $2^{3/4}$ million pounds it will perhaps lead to unwarrantable estimates as to the average cost, but before drawing conclusions as to this it would be well to remember that four pictures alone accounted for just under a million pounds between them ; the remaining 94 do not therefore represent a very extravagant expenditure."

"I MUST not pass on without referring more explicitly to the really high grade of our best work, and in this respect honours are easy as between the British side of American organisations and our own native output. One name on each side will indicate my meaning—" *The Citadel* " and " *Pygmalion.*" Yes, if all we had wanted had been proof that we could make a fine film, we might have been satisfied."

"**But it is far more important to stock the shop than to dress the window.** That is where we are experiencing our greatest anxiety, and I must confess there is no consolation in being able to do big things unsupported by the one essential, steady and growing performance."

And so, once again, the Editor expresses so eloquently and at such great length that essential question: How do you legislate for quality and how do you ensure a well stocked organization?

THE FILM PRODUCTION SLUMP.

And it is certainly worth repeating the Editor's comments about the current poor state of British film production:

- ♦ "There are in and around London no fewer than twenty-one sound stages which have passed the whole year without producing a single picture."
- ♦ "Only 98 have been made here altogether, which is completely inadequate for the needs of the exhibitor ; it compares with 225 in the preceding twelve months."

THE FUTURE FOR BRITISH FILM PRODUCTION.

A. L. Carter, a senior correspondent for *The Kinematograph Weekly*, specifically stated in the 1939 *Year Book*, as follows:

"IT cannot be said that the hopes for the establishment of a flourishing British production industry, which were entertained at the passing of the 1938 Films Act, have been fulfilled. True, the purpose of the Act—the elimination of the quota "quickie"—has been accomplished by the raising of the labour qualification to £7,500, and it will be admitted that during the first nine months of the incidence of the Act there has been a general improvement in the quality and technical values of the product."

John V. Watson

"On the whole, however, the production aspect of 1938 was remarkable for its extremes. On the one hand there was the improvement already referred to, which was particularly noticeable in the exceptional quality of films of the class of " *The Drum*," " *Pygmalion*," " *Sixty Glorious Years*," " *The Lady Vanishes*," and the American sponsored subjects : " *A Yank at Oxford*," " *The Citadel* " and " *Keep Smiling*." On the other hand, however, there is reported a huge decline in the quantity of British product which reached the lowest figure recorded for five years."

"THE FILMS ACT AND ITS EFFECTS."

At this early stage it is futile to speculate on the ultimate effect of the Act, particularly as so much divergence exists among well informed opinion. Certain production executives consider that the decrease in the number of films made is more than offset, in the economic sense, by the admitted increase in quality. This, too, is the view taken in official quarters, which declare that even in the first few months of its operation, the new legislation has proved beneficial to the Industry and that the present situation will prove of eventual advantage by the financial rehabilitation of British production and attracting to it fresh finance."

"The main criticism of the Act is that the reduction of the quota requirements on renters from 20 per cent, to 15 per cent, and exhibitors from 20 per cent, to $12^{1/2}$ per cent, calls for fewer British pictures and consequently a more restricted production industry. This opposition is reinforced by exhibitors who experienced a film shortage due to reduced production activities in America. They have been unable to make good the deficiency because of the lack of British feature films. The double and treble quota provisions of the Act are also criticised by American renters, who contend that the more they increase their registered footage by the making of double or treble quota subjects, the greater is the amount of single footage necessary to fulfil the requirements of the clause which insists upon 50 per cent, of quota commitments being taken out in actual footage. It is not improbable that renters will be disinclined to proceed with the bigger films, but will be satisfied by concentrating on single quota pictures. The production of short subjects has also been hardly hit in spite of the introduction of a shorts quota ; the difficulty appears to obtain an economically sound distribution outlet. The low return on short subjects has encouraged the rise of the short "quickie" merchant who can turn out quota subjects from anything up to £100 as compared with £700 or £800, the normal cost of quality product."

Both editorials, now reproduced here, not only highlighted the benefits the new Act produced — particularly the far higher quality of so many of the British films now made — but equally pointed to the fact that the new Act also called for far fewer British films to be made, thus creating a decided disadvantage to exhibitors because of the product shortage it made.

In the meantime, the *Kinematograph Weekly* reported during the first six months of 1938 the following items:

Waiting on Quota decision as 240 employees lay idle at Teddington Studios.

(*K. W.*, 3 February 1938, page 41, P. L. Mannock)

Why this production hold up? Exhibitors' anxiety about future product.

(*K. W.*, 17 February 1938, page 37, P. L. Mannock)

No production at A.T.P., British Lion, Riverside, Sound City, Teddington, and Worton Hall.

(*K. W.*, 17 February 1938, The *Pulse of the Studios* Column)

Treble Quota is a bombshell for exhibitors.

John V. Watson

(*K. W.*, 24 February 1938, page 3)

Production restarts at British studios.

(*K. W.*, 3 March 1938, page 43, P. L. Mannock)

Exhibitors consider return to variety – probable sequel to film shortage.

(*K. W.*, 10 March 1938, page 5)

Provincial Cinematograph Theatres' record year - £492,121 profits.

(*K. W.*, 17 March 1938, page 13, the City Column)

The **Films Bill is now law**. It creates a fear of product shortage.

(*K. W.*, 31 March 1938, page 3)

Prosperity returns to **Pinewood** with 16 films scheduled.

(*K. W.*, 19 May 1938, page 39, P. L. Mannock)

James Carter has joined Highbury Studios as production director.

(Note that, for years, James Carter was central to the Julius Hagen film empire; he served as Hagen's Art Director, and he was also a company director of at least one of Hagen companies.)

(*K. W.*, 19 May 1938, page 41)

"Does Production cost matter?"
"Fabulous figures that mean nothing"
By P. L. Mannock.

'The Czar of Twickenham'. The History of Julius Hagen and the Film Empire he created at Twickenham Film Studios, from 1927 to 1938.

"Why do British production companies still cherish the pathetic delusion that it is a good thing to announce what is going to be spent on a picture?"

"It is, I am glad to say, not a general practice; but why it should be done at all is a mystery. It is especially foolish when such a declaration is sent out as advance publicity. Recent examples have come under my notice, as they have come under the notice of every Fleet Street writer, and in each case, I deplore the policy - if any - behind it."

"I am told £200,000 is going to be spent on " *Nelson*," with Leslie Howard. I am also officially informed that another £200,000 is to be the cost of " *The Mikado*," and that " *The Yeomen of the Guard*," to follow, will cost £100,000."

"Why one Savoy opera film should cost exactly twice as much as another is a puzzle. But as no one with any glimmering of studio knowledge will attach the least of importance to either figure, it is a puzzle that will worry only the credulous."

(Note that only *The Mikado* was actually made, whereas the other two films mentioned, *Nelson* and *The Yeomen of the Guard*, were never made.)

"The new Films Act lays down a quality test based primarily on cost; a test which is so fallacious that the Act itself provides a loophole to avoid its strict enforcement."

"A legal cost test, however, has possibly infected afresh one or two production heads with the old superstition that the more money spent on a picture, the better it is. This is probably the most mischievous half-truth current in the film industry."

"I should have thought that to-day, of all times, was the worst possible time to blazon forth figures of studio expense. Are any showmen deluded into booking a film because of its high cost? If so, they have little claim to be regarded as competent exhibitors."

"Is it serious thought that the public will be any more eager to see a film on similar grounds?"

"The very reverse is true. The public have short memories, but the exposures of waste and prodigal expenditure made early in 1937, when City finance called a halt, are still fairly fresh in the national mind. At present there is a positive public revulsion from all stories of budgeting. Ask any showman what effect

John V. Watson

would be made by screen announcements of big sums of money spent. Such publicity is to-day not only ridiculous, but actually damaging."

(K. W., 26 May 1938, page 39, P. L. Mannock).

£2 million studio capital idle. 5,000 are unemployed. No early resumption of production.

(K. W., 16 June 1938, page 3).

Still awaiting a revival in film production.

(K. W., 23 June 1938, page 27, P. L. Mannock).

So there we have it once again - throughout the first half of 1938, the trade press was repeatedly questioning the wisdom of the formation of the new Films Act to equate quality with the legal cost test. This was a fallacy, as so many authoritative people saw it.

The new Act also reduced the percentage requirement for British films to be made which directly brought about an acute product shortage.

However, in the meantime, several exhibition combines, such Provincial Cinematograph Theatres, report record profits, this indicating that cinema-going not remains extremely popular but that popularity continues to blossom.

---

8. JULIUS HAGEN IN 1938:

But what of Julius Hagen in 1938?

As it transpires, there is now so little to report about him in 1938; his vast film empire had come to an end; it collapsed the previous year with enormous losses recorded.

He managed to return to film production in later 1937 at Twickenham film studios under the new corporate entity called St. Margaret's Film Studios, Limited. But he manages to make just one film at Twickenham under this regime, and it is yet another quota quickie made under the previous Films Act of 1928.

In 1938, Julius Hagen manages to make and trade show just one film, *Make It Three*. It turns out to be the very last film he ever produced, and it is a stinker; as the review of it in the *Kinematograph Weekly* points out "There is no point in holding an inquest; the film is a quota quickie in the worst sense of the term; and Points of Appeal: None.

Julius Hagen trade shows just one film in 1938 — it becomes his very last film:

1. Make It Three (1938)

Comedy with Hugh Wakefield, Edmund Willard and Diana Beaumont.

Directed by David MacDonald.

London Trade Shows: Tuesday, 15 February 1938 at a Private Theatre; it was probably held at MGM's own private theatre.

British Registration Details:
Quota Registration No.: Br. 15,852.
Registration Date: 16 February 1938.
Registered Length: 7,003 feet.
Registered by: M-G-M.
Maker's name: St. Margaret's Film Studios, Limited.
British Board of Censor's Certificate: "U".

Running Time: 78 minutes.

British General Release: 6 June 1938.

Make It Three was reviewed in the *Kinematograph Weekly*, 17 February 1938, page 32:

> 78 minutes, "U" certificate.
>
> "Remarks: Crude prison burlesque, a film without rhyme or reason.
>
> "Box Office Angle: Not recommended.

"An alleged prison burlesque, this British comedy so bores with its childish travesty that to sit through it is to equal a long stretch. Hugh Wakefield, Edmund Willard and Diana Beaumont are the stars, but they merely move one to pity for the waste of their undoubted gifts. Although it has the quota ticket, this does give it leave to pass. Definitely not recommended.

"Story: Percy Higgins, struggling bank clerk, henpecked by his maiden Aunt Aggie, promises under pressure to marry his fiancée, Annie, within a month. Following this he learns that he has inherited eighty thousand pounds from an outcast uncle, the condition being that he takes a leaf out of his uncle's book and goes to prison for three months. It so happens that he is a member of the prisoners' aid society, and contact with Big Ed, an old lag, results in the stage being set for the necessary sentence. His next worry is that he may not get out in time to marry Annie, but the benevolent prison authorities relieve him of the headache by staging the ceremony in goal.

"Acting: Hugh Wakefield, Edmund Willard, Diana Beaumont, Sydney Fairbrother and Jack Hobbs are the principal players, and we'll leave it at that.

"Production: There is no point in holding an inquest; the film is a quota quickie in the worst sense of the term.

"Points of Appeal: None

Note that it is highly likely that *Make It Three* never had a wide release in Great Britain, if indeed it had any semblance of a release at all. This position is pure speculation on the author's part but, as the above review in the *Kinematograph Weekly* tells us, this film is awful; there is absolutely nothing to recommend it.

However, the BFI's *Monthly Film Bulletin* also reviewed *Make It Three* which does suggest that the film did have some form of release to, at least, some cinemas in the country.

1938:
Julius Hagen is declared bankrupt:

Julius Hagen is declared bankrupt in 1938 with half-a-million pounds in debts.
(*K.W.*, date of issue unknown).

1939:
Twickenham Film Studios:

The 'Receivers, Appointments or Releases' section of the *Kinematograph Year Book* for 1940 reported two legal events (on page 191):

'The Czar of Twickenham'. The History of Julius Hagen and the Film Empire he created at Twickenham Film Studios, from 1927 to 1938.

- ♦ **Twickenham Film Studios, Ltd.**, 4, Lloyds Avenue, E.C.—R. D. Brewis, of 56, Cannon Street, E.C, ceased to act as Receiver and Manager on January 6, 1939.
- ♦ **Twickenham Film Studios, Ltd.**, 4, Lloyds Avenue, E.C.—R. D. Brewis, of 56, Cannon Street, E.C, was appointed Receiver and Manager on February 8, 1939, under powers contained in instruments dated April 1, 1931, and January 7, 1935.

The following entry in the 'British Studios' section of the *Kinematograph Year Book* for 1940 (on page 321) confirms that Twickenham Studios was operating during 1939:

"TWICKENHAM STUDIOS."

"St. Margaret's, Twickenham. Telephone: Popesgrove 5511.

"Proprietors: Studio Holdings Trust, Ltd., 44, Brook Street, Mayfair, W.1.

"Lessees : Highbury Studios, Ltd.

"Directorate : J. A. Carter and G. S. Ogg, Joint Managing Directors. F. Kingdom Ward.

"Floors. No. 1, 140 ft. by 80 ft.

"Recording System : RCA and Film Recorders ; three channel re-recording.

"Electrical Equipment : B.T.-H., Mole-Richardson, Kandem.

"Studio Manager : Charles Leeds.

"Chief Sound Engineer : N. Daines.

"Productions, 1939: *'The Stars Look Down'* and *'Law and Disorder.'*

Note that there was no mention of **Julius Hagen** at all. Consequently, it is quite apparent that Hagen had no connection now with either Twickenham Studios, or with its Proprietor, or with its Lessees.

John V. Watson

1940:
Julius Hagen's sudden
death:

The *Kinematograph Weekly* reported in its issue dated 1
February 1940:
"SUDDEN DEATH OF JULIUS HAGEN"

"We regret to announce the death of Julius Hagen, which
took place from pneumonia on Wednesday morning at a nursing
home."

"Mr. Hagen, who was in his fifty-seventh year, was for many
years a prominent figure in British renting and production circles.
He leaves a widow and daughters, the eldest of whom is married
to A. Fried."

"The funeral is on Friday at 2 p.m. at Golders Green
crematorium. Flowers should be sent c/o William Tookey and
Sons, 51, Marylebone High Street."

(*K. W.*, 1 February 1940)

The following week, on 8 February 1940, published a tribute
to Julius Hagen in the *Kinematograph Weekly*:

"A TRIBUTE TO JULIUS HAGEN"
"By P. L. Mannock"

"Julius Hagen, for many years a picturesque figure in British
production, was only 56 when he died suddenly at his London flat
last week following a stroke. He had been in poor health for
some time. A popular, shrewd personality, he will be sadly
missed."

'The Czar of Twickenham'. The History of Julius Hagen and the Film Empire he created at Twickenham Film Studios, from 1927 to 1938.

"In his early days Hagen was an actor and manager, but gravitated to the renting side of films about 1910, becoming general manager at Universal, after periods with Ruffells and Essanay."

"After the war he was associated with Percy Felce and Frank Smith in Astra-National, and it was for them in 1926 that he was first directly connected with production, on *"The Flag Lieutenant"*. Henry Edwards, that film's leading man, soon after joined in Hagen in re-establishing the former Alliance Studios at St. Margarets."

"Twickenham Control"

"In 1929, Twickenham Film Productions began is long series of pictures under Hagen's control, over a period of seven years. So sought after were the floors that it became regular practice to work the clock round; actors would go down after their theatre duties and work all night on subjects that were replaced by others during the daytime."

"For several years Hagen's personal income was enormous, probably unequalled in the studio world. His generosity and hospitality were marked, as his loyal staff and countless friends constantly experienced; but his judgment, until 1936, was invariably shrewd."

"His financial collapse was due not his production expenditure, but to his unlucky attempt to run his own renting company and taking over two other studios as well as Twickenham. But he took his reverses in sporting spirit, actually giving a Press lunch to explain his position. In the last two years he made several courageous attempts to get back, and, assisted by friends, was partially successful."

"Hagen's record, over dozens of pictures, was one of real achievement, and his withdrawal from the field made a serious difference to British output."

"Cremation took place on Friday last. The Trade's sympathy goes to Mrs. Hagen and his four daughters."

(*K. W.*, 8 February 1940, page 5, P. L. Mannock)

HOW JULIUS HAGEN WAS SEEN BY SOME OF HIS PEERS:

The sum of the following quotations drawn from various publications give a sound impression of what the character of Julius Hagen was — about his general likeability, about his generosity, and about his business acumen.

♦ Julius Hagen's wife, **Hilda Hagen**, later would recall that cinema-owners would tell her: 'He's a nice man but I wish you would try to keep him away. He is always selling me films I don't want.'
(Interview with A. Jympson Harmon of *The Star*, 2 December 1935)

♦ The tribute to Julius Hagen which was paid by **P. L. Mannock**, the Studio Correspondent for the *Kinematograph Weekly*, stated:
Julius Hagen was "a popular, shrewd personality, he will be sadly missed."
"His generosity and hospitality were marked, as his loyal staff and countless friends constantly experienced;

but his judgment, until 1936, was invariably shrewd."

"Hagen's record, over dozens of pictures, was one of real achievement, and his withdrawal from the field made a serious difference to British output."

(*K. W.*, 8 February 1940, page 5, P. L. Mannock)

♦ **Rachael Low** described three observations about Julius Hagen which were made by participants from various sections of the British film industry:

♦ The writer **Peter Cotes** later described Hagen as "a philistine and a sharp businessman";

♦ whereas **Michael Balcon**, the head of Ealing Studios, said that Hagen was "rather nice, likeable but somewhat irresponsible and careless about money":

♦ and **Walter Forde**, the British film director and former silent film comedian, has endearingly described Hagen as "a beautiful man, very sweet." [Note that Walter Forde directed three films for Hagen: *Lord Richard in the Pantry* (1930), *Splinters in the Navy* (1931), and *Condemned to Death* (1932).]

(*Film Making in 1930s Britain*, Rachael Low, 1985, page 216)

---

9. CONCLUSION AND TRIBUTE TO HAGEN:

Many academics these days, when reviewing the British film industry in the 1930s, tend to concentrate on key figures such as Alexander Korda in their analyses of the era. This is wrong, short-sighted and, frankly, it smacks of sheer ignorance — they really don't really know (or understand) what they are talking about.

This is such a shame as that era of the nineteen-thirties was rich in so many facets of the British social scene — cinema had long become the entertainment of the masses. It was cheap to go to "the flicks", to "the pictures", and, as the cinema building boom progressed throughout that decade, one could buy a ticket to enter a virtual paradise, to see a favourite star in the lavish and grand comfort offered by the fast growing number of Picture Palaces being opened and operated throughout the country.

But cinemas needed product to show to the masses, and a lot of it. In other words, a continual supply of lots and lots of films. But films had to be made and, consequently, producers were constantly called to make and supply them. And there were lots of British producers on hand to make them — from the 'quota quickie' merchants, such as Donovan Pedelty (whose films really were awful) and George King (whose films made in the 1930s were somewhat better, but whose quality improved considerably in the 1940s) — to the purveyors of quality, not only Alexander Korda but equally Victor Saville, Michael Balcon and other notables.

And then we come to Julius Hagen. What of him and his film output? Well, Hagen made very many 'quota quickies' but he equally made films of absolute quality and entertainment value.

Of the former type of film, one has only to think of the sheer agony of watching the sheer inanity of *The Black Abbot* (1934), but, by the same token, *The Ghost Camera* (1933) was an excellent example of the usually maligned 'Quickie'. Of the later type of film, that of a quality production, Hagen made several, particularly in his earlier years as a producer, of which excellent examples are *The Wandering Jew* (1933), *Scrooge* (1935), and *The Last Journey* (also 1935).

And, of course, we have already reviewed in great detail above all of his contributions to British film production in the late 1920s and throughout most of the 1930s.

Personally, I would have loved to have met and got to know him. As an industry veteran myself, but of much later decades, I would certainly understand the problems and the opportunities he would have faced, in his earlier decades.

To me, he was a man of great courage, of great determination, and, as we have seen, he was generally very popular - and also very generous.

And, yes, he had his faults - over-optimism seems to be a prime flaw of his - but you certainly need optimism to succeed in the film business. He over extended himself in 1936, as we have seen and in such detail, and he certainly paid for this huge error; his film empire collapsed.

But the contribution that Julius Hagen made to the British film industry in the 1930s was enormous, and this should never ever be forgotten. Hence the underlying purpose of this book, and the very detailed filmography book that accompany it.

ABOUT THE AUTHOR:

♦ *Honorary Research Fellow in Film Studies at the University of Kent:*
From 2010 to 2012. In late 2010, I was given this appointment via the good and kind support of Professor Elizabeth Cowie and Dr. (now Professor) Peter Stanfield of the Faculty of Film at the University.

♦ *Working in the British film industry:*
I have considerable experience of the film industry gained over more than twenty years in a variety of positions: starting briefly in 1968 as a cinema manager in Nottingham with the Classic Cinemas chain, I was soon promoted to become its first cinema clubs controller. An executive appointment soon followed as a film booking executive for a large cinema circuit which no longer exists, The Star Group of Companies based in Leeds (1969-1973). Later, I became a film distributor based at 84 Wardour Street in Soho, London; and subsequently a film sales promoter.

In the later rôle, I spent almost six months in Hollywood during 1977, where I was promoting an original film script treatment to interested producers, eventually obtaining a sale (but the actual film was never produced).

During my time in Los Angeles, I had the pleasure of meeting many film stars, directors and producers, including Kirk Douglas, William Castle, George Cukor, Tony Curtis, Jane Greer, John Cromwell and his wife Ruth Nelson, and John Wayne (almost! I was in his 'Batjac' office suite twice but missed actually meeting him on both occasions as he was currently away on his boat on Balboa Island), and even one of the cast members of the 1930s Hal Roach 'Our Gang' series of comedy shorts (but regrettably I have forgotten his name!) I had a great time in the fabulously glamorous, but yet very shallow, "Tinsel Town", and I had the privilege of having my photograph taken holding the Oscar for Best Picture (1974), *The Sting*, at the home of the producers, Michael and Julia Phillips! See the actual picture below.

I was offered (I think) three jobs in Hollywood — in the movies, of course, but, because of the stringent American "Green Card" immigration rules, none of them came to fruition, unfortunately.

When I was working as a Film Booking Executive at The Star Group in Leeds, I was given a further appointment (in 1972) as the film booking manager for the Saturday Children's Film Clubs held at fifty-five of the company's cinemas around the country. It was quite an experience; most of the films shown were supplied by the now defunct Children's Film Foundation. Henry Geddes was the chief executive of this fine organisation which was founded in 1951; he was a dedicated manager and (as I now remember) a fine man!

I was directly involved with the promotion of one of the first films that was marketed on a region-by-region television area, namely *Flame* (1975), starring the then hugely popular "Glam-rock" group, Slade. This trend of saturation cinema bookings on a TV-area basis started in the early 1970s with the release of the Bruce Lee mega-hit, *Enter the Dragon* (1973). It was a very costly strategy but one which had the potential of giving a spectacular pay-off by producing some great box-office grosses. I remember that we spent around a quarter of a million pounds on advertising *Flame*, i.e. on local radio stations, newspapers and regional television stations, with the later representing the largest percentage of the cost.

Later (in either late 1980-or early 1981), at Poseidon Films in Shaftesbury Avenue, London, I met and got to know the

657

renowned director, Michael Powell, enjoying several talks with him about his long career and some of the people he had worked with over the years. Fascinating to sit 'at the feet' of "The Master"! I wish I had much more time to talk to him (so many questions), but I was paid to do a job by Poseidon, selling ('booking') its films to circuit and independent cinemas. Michael was being hosted by the managing director of Poseidon which was co-producing *Anna Pavlova* (1983) with the Soviet film production company, Mosfilm. Michael was 'Supervisor of the Western version'.

In 1963, I started my career in the leisure industries in the Tenpin Bowling Centres division operated by The Rank Organisation, within which I soon become the youngest General Manager in the division, operating in several situations throughout England. That part of my working biography has since been published on the Internet.

♦ *Film historian and researcher:*
I am always committed to the use of hard facts, supported by impeccable references, usually from contemporary source materials. The methodology I employ is both crucial and essential to establish the absolute truth from the evidence available. Conjecture, naturally, is often inevitable but I always temper the use of this with the character of the point under investigation, and thus I always avoid the temptation to impose my own personal agenda upon that particular theme, genre or specific point.

Thus the use of unauthenticated fact or speculation is NOT the method I ever employ, nor is it my underlying guiding principle! Notwithstanding the above, that of having a firm commitment to factual veracity and historical accuracy, I equally welcome the opportunity, as and when this arises, to explore themes within, say, a group of films from a studio, producer, actor or even a country, and thus to draw out inferences and some conclusions about their underlying premise, which at first might not be noticed by the casual observer or average cinema-goer.

* *An authority on films and their history:*

I most confidently consider myself an expert on British and American films made from the early 1920s until the late 1980s with very extensive knowledge. The classical French and German cinemas are also my specialities. I enjoy a superb memory, very able to retain an abundant amount of detailed facts about films and their history. Indeed, I am able to reiterate hundreds, if not thousands, of pieces of data already committed to memory.

* *A collector of film ephemera*:

I am an ardent collector, and have been so for well over 40 years now, accumulating hundreds of film posters (mostly British and American), stills, lobby cards, magazines, annuals, books, etc., including many rare items particularly from the silent era.

* *A collector of films on celluloid*:

I am, or now rather was, a fervent collector of many of the films themselves on most gauges, mostly on 16mm, but also on 9.5mm, 8mm, and even 35mm, including a couple of prints on that very dangerous and unstable celluloid base — nitrate! In the days of the 1970s, before the advent of VHS, and then much later DVD, it was much harder for collectors to obtain copies of vintage films than it is today.

However, moving home twice in the 1990s to smaller premises each time, turned out to be a logistical nightmare for my huge film collection, as the space required to store literally dozens upon dozens of film prints was extremely inadequate, and finally proved impossible to continue. Consequently, I sold on my prints to other private film collectors.

659

John V. Watson

In the early 1990s, I also supplied dozens of films (all vintage titles on 16mm, mostly features) to the National Film Archive, under the auspices of David Meeker.

+ *A movie memorabilia dealer*:
I have been a dealer in movie memorabilia for more than 40 years, originally trading through specialist magazines and at film fairs.

Since 1998, when the Internet was then growing rapidly, I joined eBay on their American site which gave me considerable success for some years, but the economic downturn in recent years, combined with the effect of a most noticeable change in buyer attitude and behaviour generally, has certainly seen an adverse effect on sales. Many wonderful items, some quite rare, have passed through my hands over the years!

+ *Other biographical information: CinemaScope and the spread of commercial television:*
I 'fell in love' with 'the movies' in 1951-52 when I was a boy of just 10 (or 11) years of age. I decided even then that I wanted to go into the film industry when I grew up - and eventually I did just that.

I still remember most vividly how the arrival of CinemaScope in 1953-54 revolutionised the cinema, giving it such a fresh impetus. And it also struck me then - and it still does now - that 1955 was very much a pivotal year for the cinema. The ambience and the social environment of the early 1950s, up to 1955, were so very different to that of the second half of the decade, starting in 1956.

From 1959, I also witnessed how commercial television continually and increasingly encroached on the power of the film industry in Great Britain during the later 1950s and well into the 1960s.

'The Czar of Twickenham'. The History of Julius Hagen and the Film Empire he created at Twickenham Film Studios, from 1927 to 1938.

♦ The author is also an *accountant*, a former *business consultant*, a former *business executive* and a former *hotelier/restaurateur*.

♦ *Film history projects: in preparation, completed or published*:

The author is currently working on several projects about various aspects of British and American film history. These include the following books and articles which are now complete ready for publication, nearing completion, or in preparation:

♦ *'PARADISE LOST' - The history of a rural picture house long since vanished - THE REGAL CINEMA, SWAFFHAM: 1919-1960.* A tribute from a young teenage patron of this wonderful local Picture House from the Golden Age of Cinema-going. A serious endeavour to piece together the history of this small town cinema that served a market town and rural community in Norfolk for over 40 years, from the sporadic information currently available. This History of the Regal Cinema provides an exceptional opportunity to describe how the operation of the film distribution and exhibition sectors of the British industry worked, particularly in the 1950s, and how this small rural cinema fitted into the overall national system. This book also includes an explanation of how the "Barring System" operated then, and why it was so central to the operation of this huge British industry. (Published as an Amazon Paperback.)

♦ *JULIUS HAGEN: "THE CZAR OF TWICKENHAM" FILM STUDIOS. The Complete Filmography of all the films he produced from 1927 to 1938. BOOK ONE.* Illustrated. The first part of the very detailed analysis of the 115 films Hagen made plus the one co-production. (Published as an Amazon Paperback.)

♦ *JULIUS HAGEN: "THE CZAR OF TWICKENHAM" FILM STUDIOS. The Complete Filmography of all the films he produced from 1927 to 1938. BOOK TWO.* Illustrated. The second part of the very detailed analysis of the 115 films Hagen made plus the one co-production. (Published as an Amazon Paperback.)

♦ *FROM POLYVISION TO CINEMASCOPE: 1927 TO 1953.* The Definitive History of Widescreen in the Cinema: Part 1. Illustrated. This history includes an analysis of the Abel Gance 'Polyvision', 65mm 'VitaScope', 70mm 'Grandeur', 70mm 'Realife', and the 3-projector 'Cinerama' systems. (Published as an Amazon Paperback.)

♦ *'THE MODERN MIRACLE YOU SEE WITHOUT GLASSES': 'TWENTIETH CENTURY-FOX PRESENTS A CINEMASCOPE PRODUCTION': 1953.* The Definitive History of Widescreen in the Cinema: Part 2. Illustrated. (Published as an Amazon Paperback.)

♦ *1954: THE YEAR OF THE REMARKABLE SUCCESS OF CINEMASCOPE.* The Definitive History of Widescreen in the Cinema: Part 3. Illustrated. This history includes an analysis of 'VistaVision' and 'SuperScope', the other two new anamorphic systems in use then. (Published as an Amazon Paperback.)

♦ *1955: THE YEAR OF THE CONSOLIDATION OF CINEMASCOPE.* The Definitive History of Widescreen in the Cinema: Part 4. Illustrated. Eighty-two films were released in CinemaScope that year: seventy-one were American made, seven were made in England, and the other four were foreign productions. This book also includes a further complete filmography of the other thirty-six films which were presented in all the other wide-film/wide-screen systems during 1955. 32 of these 36 films were made or presented in the two main rival

662

widescreen systems, namely 'VistaVision' and 'SuperScope', with 20 and 12 productions respectively. Two other wide-film/wide-screen systems were used for just one roadshow-limited engagement film presentation each, namely 'Todd-AO' for *Oklahoma!* and 'Cinerama' for *Cinerama Holiday*. The final anamorphic system used in 1955 was the British 'CameraScope' process employed by the tiny, family-own company, Adelphi Films, to make two comedy films: *You Lucky People!* and *Fun at St. Fanny's*. (Published as an Amazon Paperback.)

♦ In preparation: *1956: THE YEAR OF THE CONTINUED SUCCESS OF CINEMASCOPE AND THE RISE OF COMPETING PROCESSES.* The Definitive History of Widescreen in the Cinema: Part 5. Illustrated. This book will also include an analysis of the new Continental anamorphic processes that appeared that year, including 'Cinepanoramic', 'Franscope' and 'Totalscope'. (For publication as an Amazon Paperback.)

♦ *FILM NOIR: THE CLASSIC ERA, 1941 to 1959: A Concise Introduction.* (Published on Amazon Kindle.)

♦ *FILM NOIR: 1941 to 1959: A Treasure Trove of 60 Film Titles from the Classic Era.* (Published on Amazon Kindle.)

♦ *1971: A YEAR OF VIOLENCE IN THE CINEMA.* (Published in *Cinema Retro* magazine, Number 43, Volume 15, Winter 2018-2019.)

♦ *MADIGAN (1968): An appreciation of Don Siegel's magnificent 'Neo-Noir' film of the late 1960s, now possibly in danger of becoming forgotten.* (Published in the Christmas 2019 issue (No. 46) of *Cinema Retro* magazine.)

John V. Watson

♦ *CLASSIC CINEMA CLUBS: 1969:* A short article based on the author's own experience as the very first Cinema Clubs Controller for the Classic Cinema Circuit, when the company started two club operations: Sunday Cinema Clubs and the Tatler 'art house' cinema clubs. (To be published in a future issue of *Cinema Retro* magazine.)

♦ In preparation: a definitive account of the *HISTORY OF WARNER BROTHERS FIRST NATIONAL PRODUCTIONS LTD AT THE TEDDINGTON FILM STUDIOS IN THE 1930S*, including a complete filmography. Unlike all the other American companies in the 1930s, who farmed out the production of their British-made film requirements, to satisfy their liabilities under the British Quota legislation of 1927, two associated American production companies, Warner Bros. Pictures and First National Productions, decided in 1931 to make their own British films at their own studios, Teddington.

♦ *FILM NOIR: THE CLASSIC ERA, 1941 to 1959: A Concise Introduction.* (Published as an Amazon Paperback.)

♦ *FILM NOIR: 1941 to 1959: A Treasure Trove of 60 Film Titles from the Classic Era.* (Published as an Amazon Paperback.)

♦ Some years ago, Professor Andrew Spicer asked me to assist him with a particular part of his research into the career of the British film producer, Michael Klinger, which eventually became the book: *THE MAN WHO GOT CARTER: MICHAEL KLINGER, Independent Production and the British Film Industry, 1960-1980* (2013). The section I helped him with dealt with Klinger's involvement with the Eckart brothers of The Star Group of Companies, based in Leeds, from the late 1960s to the

'The Czar of Twickenham'. The History of Julius Hagen and the Film Empire he created at Twickenham Film Studios, from 1927 to 1938.

early 1970s, culminating with Star's aborted reverse takeover of British Lion. I was a film booking executive at Star at that time and I was thus able to describe and explain several details about the Eckarts for Professor Spicer.

The author holding the Oscar for Best Picture (1974), *The Sting*, taken in 1977 at the fabulous home of the producers, Michael and Julia Phillips, in Coldwater Canyon.

Printed in Great Britain
by Amazon

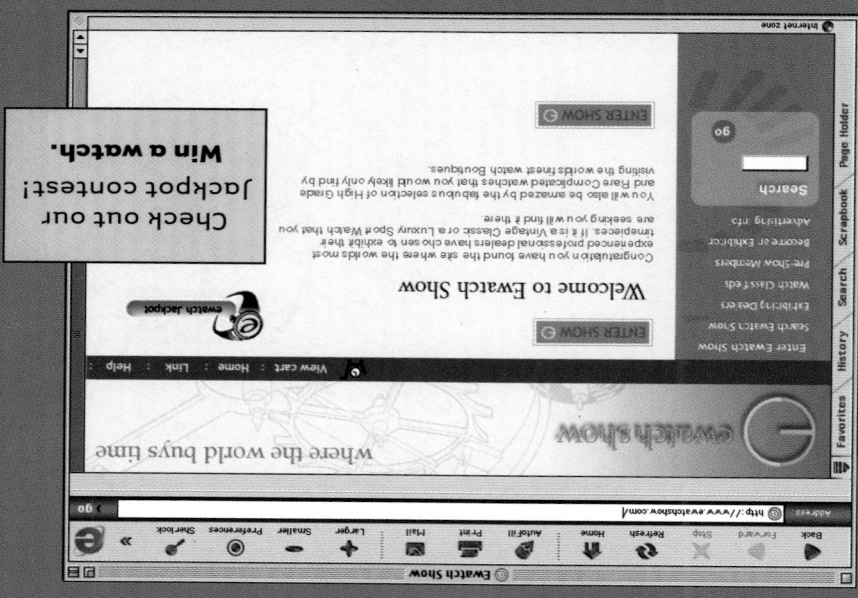

Catch A New Wave!

WatchParadise.com is an exciting new online destination that provides a meeting place, market place and educational resource center for watch collectors, manufacturers, watch dealers and jewelers worldwide.

WatchParadise.com's unique format is for everyone! The combination of state-of-the-art site design, ease of use and intuitive content make it *the* site to visit for watch-related information.

From vintage to new watches, repairs to accessories, WatchParadise.com has it all!

Log On and Experience the Premier Watch Resource Center of the World:

www.WatchParadise.com

COMPLETE
PRICE   GUIDE   TO
WATCHES

COOKSEY SHUGART
TOM ENGLE • RICHARD E. GILBERT

EDITED BY MARTHA SHUGART

Important Notice. All of the information, including valuations, in this book has been compiled from the most reliable sources, and every effort has been made to eliminate errors and questionable data. Nevertheless, the possibility of error, in a work of such immense scope, always exists. The publisher or authors will not be held responsible for losses which may occur in the purchase, sale, statements of its advertisers or other transaction of items, because of information contained herein. Readers who feel they have discovered errors are invited to write and inform us, so they may be corrected in subsequent editions.

The Complete Price Guide To Watches is published independently and is not associated with any watch manufacturer.

This book endeavors to be a **Guide** or helpful manual and offers a wealth of material and information to be used as a tool not as a absolute document. The Complete Price Guide To Watches is like some *watches*, the worst may be better than none at all, but at best cannot be expected to be 100% accurate.

The Complete Price Guide to Watches goal is to stimulate the orderly exchange of Watches between *"buyers"* and *"sellers"*.

Copyright 2002 by Cooksey G. Shugart

Published by: **COOKSEY SHUGART PUBLICATIONS**
P. O. BOX 3147
CLEVELAND, TN. 37320-3147
TEL. OR FAX (423) 479 – 4813

Distributed by: **COLLECTOR BOOKS**
P. O. BOX 3009
5801 KENTUCKY DAM ROAD
PADUCAH, KY.   42001

ISBN 1 – 57432 – 291 – 5
TWENTY SECOND EDITION: JAN., 2002

Manufactured in the United States of America

COOKSEY SHUGART

TOM ENGLE

RICHARD E. GILBERT

The *Complete Price Guide To Watches*, published by Shugart Publications, authored by Cooksey Shugart with co-authors Tom Engle and Richard E. Gilbert. All three have been active horologists since the early 1960's and members of the National Association of Watch and Clock Collectors since the early 1970's. They have searched for fine timepieces all over the world and are the foremost experts in the field of antique horology.

They each have traveled extensively to auctions throughout the United States and Europe, to regional and national conventions, meets and shows, and keep an up-to-date pulse of the watch market. They continually expand their horological reference library and their extensive selection of watch photographs. Because of the unique knowledge of the market these co-authors possess, this volume should be considered one of the most authoritative watch references on the market today. Each edition contains updated and revised information and prices, and has become the accepted standard reference work of the watch market. ''We see this book as an extension of the information we have been gathering for years and take great pride in sharing it with other collectors who have a deep and abiding interest in watches,'' the authors stated.

Mr. Shugart resides in Cleveland, Tenn., Mr. Engle resides in Louisville, KY. and Mr. Gilbert resides in Sarasota, FL.

TABLE OF CONTENTS

4

ACKNOWLEDGMENTS

I am especially appreciative of **Bob Overstreet,** author of The Overstreet Comic Book Price Guide, for his encouragement and without his assistance this book would have been impossible.

To my wife **Martha,** for her complete understanding and assistance in compiling this book.

To best friend **TOM ENGLE** whose help is invaluable a very special thanks.

A special thanks to Henry B. Fried, Dr. Adolphe Chapiro, Derek Pratt, Joe Cerullo, Philippe Dufour, and Dan Crawley.

To the NAWCC Museum, Hamilton Watch Co., and Bowman Technical School, for allowing us to photograph their watches.

To Christie's, Osvaldo Patrizzi, Dr. H. Crott, J. Wachsmann of Pieces of Time and Gisbert A. Joseph of Joseph Auctions for photographs of watches.

And to the following people whose help was invaluable and will be long remembered: Frank Irick, John Cubbins, Harold Harris, Paul Gibson, Robert L. Ravel, M.D., William C. Heilman Jr., M.D., Thomas McEntyre, Paul Morgan, Bill Selover, Oscar Laube, Ed Kieft, Charles Wallace, Bob Walters, Jack Warren, Howard Schroeder, Edward M. McGinnis, James Gardner, Paul Zuercher, Irving E. Roth, Don Bass, Stephen Polednak, Dick Stacy, Ernest J. Lewis, Herbert McDonald, David Steger, Fred Favour, Ralph Warner, Estus Harris, Norman Howard, Charles Cleves, Tom McIntyre, Ralph Ferone, Arnold C. Varey, Jeffrey Ollswang, Tom Rohr, Leon Beard, Glenn Smith, Kenneth Vergin, Thomas Rumpf, Frank Diggs, Tom Thacker, Bob Lavoie, Constantin Tanasecu, Rod Minter, Ernest Luffman, John Amneus, Lawrence D. Harnden, Mike Kirkpatrick, Clint B. Geller, Art W. Rontree, and a special thanks to Peter Kushnir, Dr. J. Mauss, Robert D. Gruen, Jeff Hess, Col. R. A. Mulholland, Dick Ziebell, Jack Warren, Dick Flaute, Ralph Vinge, Edward Fletcher, Richard Walker, Alex Wolanguk, Carl Goetz, Miles Sandler, Dave Mycko, Martin & Patrick Cullen, Benjy Rook, Phillip Welsh, Paul Craft, Fred Fox, Fred Andrus, Ellis Gifford, Steve Berger, Bruce Ellison, Lawrence D. Harnden, Geoff White, Bob & Pat Wingate, David Searles, Ray R. Tyulty Jr., Don Levison, Robert M. Toborowsky M.D., Dr. John R. Dimar, Jonathan Snellenburg, Kent L. Singer, Tom Reindl, Paul A. Duggan, Gregory A. Hill, Don & Sandy Robbins, Bernie Kraus, Veron Willams, Fred Hansen, Drew Schmidt, Norman M. Tallan, Harry Blair, Jack Kurdzionak, Robert Schussel, Douglas L. Conner, Ira P. Mish, Dan Anderson, Seth Finkelstein, R.H.(Dick) Hanewald, Bill Campbell, Ted Hake, Don Barret, Darold Hanson, John Grass, Lyle & Donna Stratton, Joe Demesy.

Special Consultant & Advisors

JIM WOLF

JACK KURDZIONAK

PAUL DUGGAN

MILES SANDLER
Associate Editor

Send only corrections, additions, deletions and comments to
COOKSEY SHUGART, P. O. BOX 3147, CLEVELAND, TN. 37320-3147.
When *corresponding, please send a* ✉ *self-addressed, stamped envelope.*

INTRODUCTION

This book is dedicated to all watch collectors who we hope will find it an enjoyable and valuable reference to carry on buying trips or to trace the lost history of that priceless family heirloom.

The origin of this book began when I was given a pocket watch that had been in our family for many years. After receiving the prized heirloom I wanted to know its complete history, and thus the search began. Because of the lack of a comprehensive reference on American pocket watches the venture took me through volume after volume. Over the course of ten years many hours were accumulated in running down the history of this one watch. The research sparked my interest in the pocket watch field and pointed to the need for a book such as this one. We hope it will provide the information that you are looking for.

— The Authors

Watches are unique collectibles and since the beginning of civilization man has held a fascination for time. When man scooped up a handful of sand and created the hourglass, portable timepieces have been in demand for the wealthy and poor alike. Man has sought constantly to improve his time-measuring instruments and has made them with the finest metals and jewels. The pocket watch, in particular, became an ornamentation and a source of pride, and this accounts for its value among families for generation after generation.

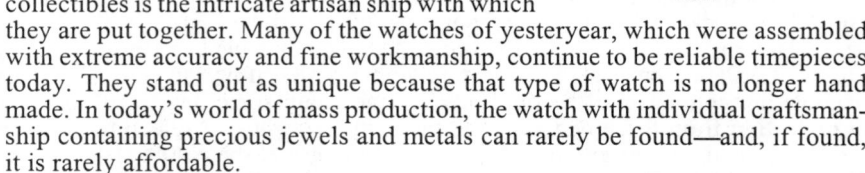

The watch has become precious and senti-mental to so many because it is one of the true personal companions of the individual night and day. Mahatma Gandhi, the father of India and one of the rare people in history who was able to renounce worldly possessions, was obsessed with the proper use of his time. Each minute, he held, was to be used in the service of his fellow man. His own days were ordered by one of his few personal possessions, a sixteen-year-old, eight-shilling Ingersoll pocket watch that was always tied to his waist with a piece of string.

Another factor that has made watches unique collectibles is the intricate artisan ship with which they are put together. Many of the watches of yesteryear, which were assembled with extreme accuracy and fine workmanship, continue to be reliable timepieces today. They stand out as unique because that type of watch is no longer hand made. In today's world of mass production, the watch with individual craftsman-ship containing precious jewels and metals can rarely be found—and, if found, it is rarely affordable.

The well-made watch is a tribute to man's skills, artisanship and craftsman-ship at their finest level. That is why the watch holds a special place in the collectible field.

In America, there are more than 240,000 avid watch collectors and millions own several watches, also an untold number possess at least one or more of these precious heirlooms.

🕐 **The Complete Price Guide to Watches goal is to stimulate the orderly exchange of <u>Watches</u> between** *"buyers"* **and** *"sellers"*.

The Complete Price Guide to Watches does not attempt to establish or fix values or selling prices in the watch trade market.

It does, however, reflect the trends of buying and selling in the collector market. Prices listed in this volume are based on data collected and analyzed from dealers and shops all over the country. These prices should serve the collector as a guide only. The price you pay for any watch will be determined by the value it has to you. The intrinsic value of any particular watch can be measured only by you, the collector, and a fair price can be derived only after mutual agreement between both the buyer and the seller.

Keep in mind the fair market values at the **Trade Show** level (as outlined in this price guide) and buying wisely, but don't hesitate, as the better and scarce pieces are quickly sold.

It is our hope that this volume can help make your watch collecting venture both pleasurable and profitable. Hopefully, everyone interested in horology will research the watch and add to his library on the subject.

Information contained herein may not necessarily apply to every situation. Data is still being found, which may alter statements made in this book. These changes, however, will be reflected in future editions.

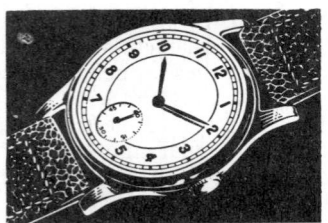

COLLECTAMANIA
Hobby — Business — Pastime — Entertainment

Just name it. More than likely someone will want to buy or sell it: books, coins, stamps, bottles, beer cans, gold, glassware, baseball cards, guns, clocks, watches, comics, art, cars, and the list goes on and on.

Most Americans seem to be caught up in collectamania . More and more Americans are spending hour after hour searching through antique shops, auctions, flea markets and yard sales for those rare treasures of delight that have been lying tucked away for generations just waiting to be found.

This sudden boom in the field of collecting may have been influenced by fears of inflation or disenchantment with other types of investments. But more people are coming into the field because they gain some degree of nostalgic satisfaction from these new tangible ties with yesteryear. Collecting provides great fun and excitement. The tales of collecting and the resultant "fabulous finds" could fill volumes and inspire even the non-collector to embark upon a treasure hunt.

Collecting for the primary purpose of investment may prove to have many pitfalls for the amateur. The lack of sufficient knowledge is the main cause of disappointment. The inability to spot fakes or flawed merchandise can turn excitement into disappointment. And, in many fields, high-class forgers are at work, doing good and faithful reproductions in large quantities that can sometimes fool even the experts the first time they see them.

Collecting for fun and profit can be just that if you observe a fair amount of caution. Always remember, amidst your enthusiasm, that an object may not be what it would first appear. Next are a few guidelines that may be helpful.

LEARN - FOCUS - CONDITION - TRUST

" LOOK UNDER THE HOOD "

1. **Gain all the knowledge you can** and **LEARN** all about the objects you collect. The more knowledge you have the more successful you will be in finding valuable, quality pieces. The best way to predict the future is to study the past. Amassing the knowledge required to be a good collector is easier if you have narrowed your scope of interest. Otherwise, it may take years to become an ''expert.'' Don't try to learn everything there is to know about a variety of fields. This will end in frustration and disappointment. Specialize and **learn** NAWCC trade show fair market **values** (Used in this BOOK).

2. **Make up your mind** and **FOCUS** on what you want to collect and concentrate in this area. Your field of collecting should be one that you have a genuine liking for, and it helps if you can use the objects. It may also help to narrow your field even further, for instance, in collecting watches, to choose only one company or one type or style and have a method of collecting.

3. **Buy the best CONDITION you can afford**, assuming the prices are fair. The advanced collector may want only mint articles; but the novice collector may be willing to accept something far less than mint condition due to caution and economics. Collectible items in better condition continue to rise in value at a steady rate.

4. **Deal with reputable dealers** whom you can **TRUST**. Talk with the dealer; get to know the seller; get a business card; know where you can contact the dealer if you have problems, or if you want the dealer to help you find something else you may be looking for.

FAIR MARKET PRICE: Fair price may be defined as a fair **reasonable** range of prices usually paid for a watch or a watch of **good value** as used in this book (*at the* Trade Show LEVEL). This market level includes a particular time frame, desirability, condition and quality. A guide to fair purchase prices is subject to sales and transaction between a large number of buyers and sellers who are informed, up to date on all normal market influences (while keeping in mind the difference between compulsiveness and acceptable buying), and buy and sell on a large scale from coast to coast. A willing buyer and a willing seller acting carefully and judiciously in their own best interest while, doing business in a normal and fair manner and preferable with payment immediately.

The Complete Price Guide to Watches goal is to stimulate the orderly exchange of WATCHES between buyers and sellers.

Keep in mind the **Trade Show fair market values** as outlined in this price guide and buying wisely, but don't *hesitate*, as the better and scarce watches are *quickly* sold. *The best way to predict the future is study the past.*

⊕ Pricing in this Guide are fair market price for **COMPLETE** watches which are reflected from the "**NAWCC**" National and regional shows.

HOW TO USE THIS BOOK

The Complete Price Guide to Watches is a simple reference, with clear and carefully selected information. The first part of the book is devoted to history, general information, and a how-to section. The second part of the guide consists mainly of a listing of watch manufacturers, identification guides, and prices. This is a unique book because it is designed to be taken along as a handy pocket reference for identifying and pricing watches. With the aid of this book, the collector should be able to make on-the-spot judgments as to identification, age, quality, and value. This complete guide and a pocket magnifying glass will be all you need to take on your buying trips.

Watch collecting is fast growing as a hobby and business. Many people collect for the enjoyment and profit. The popularity of watches continues to rise because watches are a part of history. The American railroad brought about the greatest watch of that time, the railroad pocket watch. Since that time America has produced some of the best quality pocket watches that money could buy. The gold-filled cases made in America have never been surpassed in quality or price in the foreign market. With the quality of movement and cases being made with guaranteed high standards as well as beauty, the American pocket watch became very desirable. Because they are no longer being made in the U. S. A., pocket watches continue to rise in value.

The watch is collected for its beauty, quality in movement and case, and the value of metal content. Solid gold and platinum are the top of the line; silver is also very desirable. (Consider that some watches in the early 1900's sold between $700 and $1,000. This is equal to or greater than the price of a good car of the same period.)

As with limited edition prints, a watch of supreme excellence is also limited and will increase in value. There is universal appeal and excitement in owning a piece of history, and your heirloom is just that. At one time pocket watches were a status symbol. Everyone competed for beauty and quality in the movement and case. Solid gold cases were adorned with elaborate engraving's, diamonds, and other precious jewels. The movements were beautiful and of high quality. Manufacturers went to great lengths to provide movements that were both accurate and lovely. Fancy damaskeening on the back plates of nickel with gold lettering, 26 jewels in gold settings, and a solid gold train (gears) were features of some of the more elaborate timepieces. The jewels were red rubies, or diamond-end stones, or sapphires for the pallet stones. There were gold timing screws, and more. The faces were made by the best artisans of the day. Hand-painted, jewel-studded, with fancy hands and double-sunk dials made of enamel and precious metals.

HOW TO DETERMINE MANUFACTURER

When identifying a watch, look on the face or dial for the name of the company and then refer to the alphabetical list of watch companies in this book. If the face or dial does not reveal the company name you will have to seek information from the movement's back plate. **First** determine from what **country** the watch originated. The company name or the town where it was manufactured will likely be inscribed there. The name engraved on the back plate is referred to as the "signature." After locating the place of manufacture, see what companies manufactured in that town. This may require reading the histories of several companies to find the exact one. Use the process of elimination to narrow the list. Note: Some of the hard-to-identify watches are extremely collectible and valuable. Therefore, it is important to learn to identify them.

In order to establish the true manufacturer of the movement, one must **study** the construction, taking note of the **SIZE**, number of jewels, shape, location of parts, plate layout (is it full or 3/4), shape of the balance cock and the regulator, location of jewels, location of screws, etc. Compare and match your watch movement with every photograph or drawing from each watch company in this volume until the manufacturer is located.

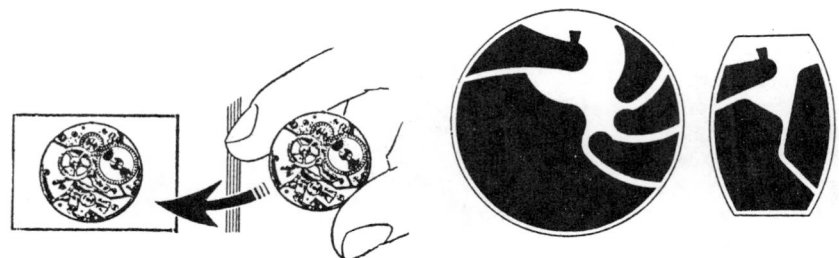

Compare & match your watch to a illustration in this book.

HOW TO DETERMINE AGE

After establishing the name of the manufacturer, you may be interested in the age of the watch (where production tables are listed). This information can be obtained by using the serial number inscribed on the back movement plate and referring to the production table. It is often difficult to establish the exact age, but this method will put you within a two or three-year period of the date of the manufacture.

To establish the age of a pre-1850 watch there are many points to be considered. The dial, hands, pillars, balance cock and pendant, for example, contain important clues in determining the age of your watch. However, no one part alone should be considered sufficient evidence to draw a definite conclusion as to age. The watch as a whole must be considered. First determine from what country the case originated and from what country did the movement originate for example, an English-made silver-cased watch will have a hallmark inside the case. It is quite simple to refer to the London Hallmark Table for hallmarks after 1697. The hallmark will reveal the age of the case only. This does not fix the age of the movement. Many movements are housed in cases made years before or after the movement was produced.

The **case** that houses the movement is **not** necessarily a good clue to the origin of the movement and the case serial number is of **no** help. It was a common practice for manufacturers to ship the movements to the jewelers and watchmakers uncased. The customer then married the movement and case. That explains why an expensive movement can be found in a cheaper case or vice versa.

If the "manufacturer's" name and location are no help, the inscription could possibly be that of a jeweler and his location. Then it becomes obvious there is no quick and easy way to identify some American made watches. However, the following steps may be helpful. Some watches can be identified by comparing the models of each company until the correct model is found. Start by sizing the watch and then comparing the varied plate shapes and styles. The cock or bridge for the balance may also be a clue. The general arrangement of the movement as to jeweling, whether it is an open face or hunting case, and style of regulators may help to find the correct identification of the manufacturer of the movement.

Numbers on a watch case should not be considered as clues to the age of the movement because cases were both American and foreign made, and many of the good watches were re-cased through the years.

APPRAISING WATCHES

Watch collecting is still young when compared to fields of the standard collectibles: coins and stamps. The watch collecting field is growing but information is still scarce, fragmented, and sometimes unreliable. To be knowledgeable in any field, one must spend the time required to study it.

The value of any collectible is determined first by demand. Without demand there is no market. In the watch trade, the law of supply and demand is also true. The supply of the American watches has stopped and the demand among collectors continues to rise. There are many factors that make a watch desired or in demand. Only time and study will tell a collector just which pieces are most collectible. After the collector or investor finds out what is desirable, then a value must be placed on it before it is sold. If it is priced too high, the watch will not sell; but, on the other hand, if it is priced too low, it will be hard to replace at the selling price. The dealer must arrive at a fair market price that will move the watch. As with limited edition prints, a watch of supreme excellence is also limited and will increase in value. There is universal appeal and excitement in owning a piece of history, and your heirloom is just that. At one time pocket watches were a status symbol. Everyone competed for beauty and quality in the movement and case. Solid gold cases were adorned with elaborate engraving's, diamonds, and other precious jewels.

Note: The value of a watch may be $5,000.00 today, $1,000.00 or $50,000.00 five years from now.

The movements were beautiful and of high quality. Manufacturers went to great lengths to provide movements that were both accurate and lovely. Fancy damaskeening on the back plates of nickel with gold lettering, 26 jewels in gold settings, and a solid gold train (gears) were features of some of the more elaborate timepieces. The jewels were red rubies, or diamond-end stones, or sapphires for the pallet stones. There were gold timing screws, and more. The faces were made by the best artisans of the day. Hand-painted, jewel-studded, with fancy hands and double-sunk dials made of enamel and precious metals.

There are no two watches alike. This makes the appraising more difficult and often-times arbitrary. But there are certain guidelines one can follow to arrive at a fair market price. When watches were manufactured, most companies sold the movements to a jeweler, and the buyer had a choice of dials and cases. Some high-grade movements were placed in a low-grade case and vice versa. Some had hand-painted multi-colored dials; some were plain. The list of contrasts goes on. Conditions of watches will vary greatly, and this is a big factor in the value. The best movement in the best original case will bring the top price for any type of watch.

Prices are constantly changing in the watch field. Gold and silver markets affect the price of the cases. Scarcity and age also affect the value. These prices will fluctuate regularly.

APPRAISING GUIDELINES

Demand, supply, **desirability**, <u>condition</u>, and value must be the prime factors in appraising a watch. Demand maybe the most important element. Demand can be determined by the **number** of buyers for the particular item. The watch may be rare (one or a few) but the *number* of collectors may be even more rare & the collector just as hard to find. A simple but true axiom is that value is determined by the price someone is willing to pay. (*What is it worth to you?*)

In order to obtain a better knowledge in appraising and judging watches, the following guidelines are most useful. Consider all these factors before placing a value on the watch. (There is no rank or priority to the considerations listed.)

1. Demand: **Interest** high or low? (**very important desirability**)
   How many collectors **want** your **rare** watch.
2. Supply & Availability: How *rare* or *scarce* is the watch?
   How many of the total production remain? (Survival rate)
3. **Condition** of both the case and movement (very important) .
4. Low serial numbers: The first one made would be more
   valuable than later models.
5. Historical value.   6. Age, how old is the Watch.
7. Value of metal content, style or type of case, beauty and eye appeal.

8. Is it in its **original** case? (very important).
9. Is it an early handmade watch?
10. Complications: Repeaters, for example.
11. Type of **escapement also technical design of movement. (Unique)**
12. Size, number of jewels, type of plates (3/4, full and bridge), type of balance, type of winding (key-wind, lever-set, etc.), number of adjustments, gold jeweled settings, damaskeening, gold train.
13. What grade of **condition** is it? Pristine, Mint, Extra Fine, Average, Fair, or Scrap?
14. Identification ability.
15. Future potential as an **investment**.
16. Quality (high or low grade), or low cost production watches (dollar watch).
17. How much will this watch scrap for?

GRADING WATCHES

Pricing in this book is based on the following grading system:

100% **PRISTINE MINT (G-10):** *NEW OLD STOCK.* Absolutely factory new; sealed in factory box with wax paper still intact & all tags & papers etc. The pristine mint grade is not listed in this book & command significant **premiums**. (A select group of watches maybe assigned to a "rarity grade" which are historical or technically important also, early horological examples.)

MINT PLUS (G-9): 99% Still in factory box. (**Exceptional**)

MINT (G-8): 97% Same as factory new but with very little use; **no** faint scratches & **no** trace of a screwdriver mark; is original in every way crystal, hands, dial, case, movement; used briefly & stored away, may still be in box. (**Dealers "Trade Show" price after OVERHAUL**)

NEAR MINT (G-7): 93% Completely original in every way; faint marks may be seen with a loop only; expertly repaired; movement may have been cleaned and oiled. (Excellent)

EXTRA FINE (G-6): 87% May or may not be in factory box; looks as though watch was used very little; original case, hands, dial, and movement. If watch has been repaired, all original replacement parts have been used. Faint case scratches are evident but hard to detect with the eye. No dents & no hairline on dial are detectable.

FINE (G-5): 80% May have new hands and new crystal, but original case, dial and movement; **faint** hairline & no chips on dial; no large scratches & no brass seen on case; slight stain on movement; movement must be sharp with only **minor** scratches.

AVERAGE- GOOD (G-4): 75% Original case, dial & movement; movement may have had a part replaced, but part was near to original; no brass showing through on gold-filled case; no rust or chips in dial; may have hairlines in dial that are hard to see. Marks are hard to detect, but may be seen without a loop. (What some dealer "MAY" pay - **Wholesale** price.)

FAIR (G-3): 60% Hairlines in dial and small chips; slight amount of brass can be seen through worn spots on gold-filled case; rust marks in movement; a small dent in case; wear in case, dial, and movement; well used; may not have original dial or case.

POOR (G-2): 30% Watch not working; needs new dial; case well worn, many dents; hands may be gone; replacement crystal may be needed.

SCRAP (G-1): 15% Movement not working; bad dial; rusty movement; brass showing badly; may not have case; some parts not original; no crystal or hands. Good for parts only.

☺ Pricing in this Guide are fair market price for **COMPLETE** watches which are reflected from the "**NAWCC**" National and regional shows.
☺ **The Complete Price Guide to Watches goal is to stimulate the orderly exchange of Watches between "*buyers*" and "*sellers*".**

Hamilton 992B

100%	G-10	$675
99%	G-9	$575
97%	**G-8**	**$500**
93%	G-7	$395
87%	**G-6**	**$325**
80%	G-5	$285
75%	**G-4**	**$265**
60%	G-3	$175
30%	G-2	$95
15%	G-1	$65

MINT
G-8 = (Retail)

AVERAGE
G-4 = (Wholesale)

Above is an example of how the price is affected by the different grades of the same watch:

Note: The value of a watch may be $5,000.00 today, $1,000.00 or $50,000.00 five years from now.

The value of a watch can only be assessed after the watch has been carefully inspected and graded. It may be difficult to evaluate a watch honestly and objectively, especially in the rare or scarce models.

If the watch has any defects, such as a small scratch on it, it can not be Pristine. It is important to realize that older watches in grades of Extra Fine or above are extremely rare and may never be found.

Watches listed in this book are priced at the collectable **Trade Show level,** as **COMPLETE** watches having an original 14k gold-filled case and Key Wind with silver, an original white enamel single sunk dial, and with the entire original movement in good working order with no repairs needed.

Keep in mind the fair market values at **Trade Show level,** as outlined in this price guide and buying wisely, but don't *"hesitate"*, as the better and scarce watches are *quickly* sold.

☺ **The value of a watch may be $5,000.00 today, $1,000.00 or $50,000.00 five years from now.**

COLLECTING ON A LIMITED BUDGET

Most collectors are always looking for that sleeper, which is out there waiting to be found. One story goes that the collector went into a pawn shop and asked the owner if he had any gold pocket watches for sale. The pawn broker replied, ''No, but I have a 23J silver cased pocket watch at a good price.'' Even though the pocket watch was in a cheaper case, the collector decided to further explore the movement. When he opened the back to look at the movement, there he saw engraved on the plates 24J Bunn Special and knew immediately he wanted to buy the pocket watch. The movement was running, and looked to be in first grade shape. The collector asked the price. The broker said he has been trying to get rid of the pocket watch, but had no luck and if he wanted it, he would sell it for $35. The collector took the pocket watch and replaced the bent-up silver case for a gold-filled J. Boss case, and sold it a month later for $400. He had a total of $100 invested when he sold it, netting a cool $300 profit.

Most collectors want a pocket watch that is in mint or near-mint condition and original in every way. But consider the railroad pocket watches such as the Bunn Special in a cheaper case. The railroad man was compelled to buy a watch with a quality movement, even though he may have only been able to afford a cheap case. The railroad man had to have a pocket watch that met certain standards set by the railroad company. A watch should always be judged on quality and performance and not just on its appearance. The American railroad pocket watch was unsurpassed in reliability. It was durable and accurate for its time, and that accounts for its continuing value today.

If you are a limited-budget collector, you would be well advised not to go beyond your means. But watch collecting can still be an interesting, adventurous, and profitable hobby. If you are to be successful in quadrupling your purchases that you believe to be sleepers, you must first be a hard worker, have perseverance and let shrewdness and skill of knowledge take the place of money. A good starting place is to get a working knowledge of how a pocket watch works. Learn the basic skills such as cleaning, mainspring and staff replacement. One does not have to be a watchmaker, but should learn the names of parts and what they do. If a watch that you are considering buying does not work, you should know how and what it takes to get it in good running order or pass it by. Stay away from pocket watches that do not wind and set. Also avoid ''odd'' movements that you hope to be able to find a case for.

Old watches with broken or missing parts are expensive and all but impossible to have repaired. Some parts must be made by hand. The odd and low-cost production watches are fun to get but hard to repair. Start out on the more common basic-jeweled lever pocket watches. The older the watch, the harder it is to get parts. Buy an inexpensive pocket watch movement that runs and play with it. Get the one that is newer and for which parts can be bought; and get a book on watch repairing.

You will need to know the ***pricing history*** and **demand** of a watch. Know what collectors are looking for in your area. If you cannot find a buyer, then, of course, someone else's stock has become yours.

JOIN THE NAWCC®

The authors of this book Mr. Shugart, Mr. Richard Gilbert & Mr. Tom Engle recommend you join the NAWCC ® today and share a fascination for watches with other members.

The National Association of Watch and Clock Collectors (NAWCC ®) is a non-profit, scientific and educational corporation founded in 1943 and now serving the horological needs and interests of about 34,000 members (professional horologists and **amateurs**) in the United States and 40 others countries. Help to its members is only a telephone call away.

Participation in National & Regional ***Conventions*** also Local ***Activities*** and ***Seminars.***

A **PUBLICATION** sent to you each month.

The **NAWCC ® Mart Sent to you every odd - month**

The **NAWCC ® Bulletin Sent to you every even - month**

The **Bulletin** sent to you every even - month is an absorbing, abundantly illustrated articles on historic, artistic and technical aspects of time keeping, answers by experts to your questions in the "Answer Box" , concise reviews of horological books, members' opinions and comments in "VOX TEMPORIS", research findings and request, slide programs available to Chapters, news and announcements of local Chapters, Regional and National activities.

The **Mart** sent to you every odd - month. An informal medium of exchange in which, for a nominal fee, you can list any horological item you may wish to **buy, sell or trade**... an absorbing and entertaining way to find items to fill out your collection or dispose of pieces you no-longer want. Announcements of Regional and National **Conventions & Seminars**.

TO JOIN THE NAWCC ® Call or Send for a FREE copy of their brochure with additional information on the NAWCC ®, membership and benefits.

NAWCC, INC.
514 Poplar Street
Columbia, PA   17512
(717) 684-8261

Recommended by member COOKSEY SHUGART membership number - **23,843.**
Also see AD in the ADVERTISING SECTION of this book.

THAT GREAT AMERICAN
RAILROAD POCKET WATCH

It was the late nineteenth century in America. The automobile had not yet been discovered. The personal Kodak camera was still not on the market. Women wore long dresses, and the rub board was still the most common way to wash clothes. Few homes had electricity, and certainly the radio had not yet invaded their lives. Benjamin Harrison was president. To be sure, those days of yesteryear were not quite as nostalgically simple as most reminiscing would have them be. They were slower, yes, because it took longer to get things done and longer to get from one place to another. The U.S. mail was the chief form of communication linking this country together, as America was inching toward the Twentieth Century.

Above: **Allen A. Shugart** (my father) was photographed in the summer of 1981 at the Chattanooga Tenn. train station also called Chattanooga **Choo-Choo** Station.

The tremendous impact of the railroad on the country during this era should not be under estimated. Most of the progress since the 1830s had chugged along on the back of the black giant locomotives that belched steam and fire, up and down the countryside. In fact, the trains brought much life and hope to the people all across the country, delivering their goods and food, bringing people from one city to another, carrying the U.S. mail, and bringing the democratic process to the people by enabling candidates for the U.S. Presidency to meet and talk with people in every state.

Truly the train station held memories for most everyone and had a link with every family.

In 1891, the country had just eased into the period that historians would later term the "Gay Nineties." It was on April 19 of that year that events occurred near Cleveland, Ohio, that clearly pointed out that the nation's chief form of transportation was running on timepieces that were not reliable. The time had come for strict standards and guide lines for accurate pocket watches to be used by the railroad men and the railroad industry with precision in time keeping.

The micrometric regulator or the patent regulator is a device used on all railroad grade and higher grade watches for the purpose of assisting in the finer manipulation of the regulator. It is arranged so that the regulator can be moved the shortest possible distance without fear of moving it too far. There is always a fine graduated index attached which makes it possible to determine just how much the regulator has been moved.

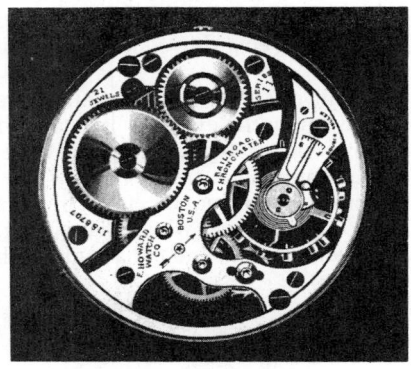

E. Howard Watch Co. Railroad Chronometer, Series 11, 16 size, 21 jewels, expressly designed for the railroad trade.

The hairspring used on the so-called ordinary and medium-grade watches is known as the flat hairspring. The Breguet hairspring was an improvement over the flat hairspring and was used on railroad and high-grade watches. The inside coil of any hairspring is attached to a collet on the balance staff and the end of the outside coil of the hairspring is attached to a stud which is held firmly by a screw in the balance wheel bridge. Two small regulator pins are fastened to the regulator. These pins clasp the outer side of the hairspring a short distance from the hairspring stud. If the regulator index is moved toward the "S," the regulator pins will move, allowing the hairspring to lengthen and the balance wheel to make a longer arc of rotation. This causes the watch to run slower because it requires a longer time for the wheel to perform the longer arc.

𝔅unn 𝔖pecial

1924 AD
Jewelers listed cost for movement only = **$24.00**
&
Jewelers selling price for movement only = **$45.00**

18 Size, 21 Jewels, Adjusted 6 Positions

21 ruby and sapphire jewels; gold settings; adjusted to temperature, SIX positions and isochronism; compensating balance; gold screws including timing screws; double roller; steel escape wheel; Breguet hairspring, patent micrometric screw regulator, safety screw center pinion, beautifully damaskeened with black enamel lettering, double sunk dial.

When the regulator is moved toward the "F" these regulator pins are moved from the stud which shortens the hairspring and makes shorter arcs of the balance wheel, thus causing the movement to run faster. Sometimes, after a heavy jolt, the coil next to the outside one will catch between these regulator pins and this will shorten the length of the hairspring just one round, causing a gaining rate of one hour per day. When this occurs, the hairspring can be easily released and will resume its former rate.

The Breguet <u>overcoil</u> hairspring, which is used on railroad grade movements, prevented the hairspring from catching on the regulator pins and protected against any lateral or side motion of the balance wheel ensuring equal expansion of the outside coil.

Railroad grade watches also used the patent or safety pinion which was developed to protect the train of gears from damage in the event of breakage of the mainspring. These pinions unscrewed in event of mainspring breakage, allowing the force to be harmlessly spent by the spinning barrel.

Some earlier railroad grade watches had non-magnetic movements. This was achieved by the use of non-magnetic metals for the balance wheel, hairspring, roller table and pallet. Two of the metals used were iridium and palladium, both very expensive.

Waltham, 18 size, unusual Railroad double sunk white porcelain dial is marked with uniquely placed minute numbers on the outer chapter and the hour chapter is in the center, the dial is also marked "Waltham Pat. Appl'd. For". This watch is a 1892 model & Appleton Tracy & Co. grade.

Ball Watch Co. Motto: "Carry a Ball and Time Them All." This **(20th Century Model)** case is made of base metal with a Ball's patented Stirrup Bow. With the simple easy to read dial, this watch was a favorite among railroad men. The **20th Century Model,** first appeared in early 1900s.

RAILROAD WATCH DIALS

Railroad watch dials are distinguished by their simplicity. A true railroad watch dial contained no fancy lettering or beautiful backgrounds. The watches were designed to be functional and in order to achieve that, the dials contained bold black Arabic numbers against a white background. This facilitated ease of reading the time under even the most adverse conditions.

True railroad watches had the winding stem at the 12 o'clock position. The so-called *side winder*, that winds at the 3 o'clock position, was not approved for railroad use. (The **side winder** is a watch movement designed for a hunter case but one that has been placed in an open-faced case.)

One railroad watch dial design was patented by a Mr. Ferguson. On this dial, the five minute numbers were much larger than the hour numbers which were on the inside. This dial never became very popular.

About 1904 the Montgomery dials began to appear on some RR watches. The distinguishing feature of the Montgomery dial is that each minute is numbered around the hour chapter. The five-minute divisions were in red, and the true Montgomery dial has the number "6" inside the minute register. These dials were favored by the railroad men.

The so-called Canadian dial had a 24-hour division inside the hour chapter.

The double time hands are also found on some railroad grade watches. One hour hand was in blue or black and the other was in red or gold, one hour apart, to compensate for passing from one time zone to another. About 1900 **"Double Time Hands"** began to appear on 18 & 16 size watches.

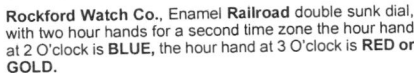

Rockford Watch Co., Enamel **Railroad** double sunk dial, with two hour hands for a second time zone the hour hand at 2 O'clock is **BLUE**, the hour hand at 3 O'clock is **RED or GOLD**.

This style **Illinois** railroad watch cases were fitted with movements, re-rated and timed in their specially designed case at the factory as complete watches in a gold filled case with a hinged bezel . Note: This Illinois 60 hour single sunk dial, 17 size & referred to as a 16 size by the trade.

RAILROAD WATCH CASES

Open face cases were the only ones approved for railroad use. Railroad men sought a case that was tough and durable; one that would provide a dust-free environment for the movement.

The swing-out case offered the best protection against dust, but the screw-on back and bezel were the most popular open-face cases.

The lever-set was a must for railroad-approved watches and some of the case manufacturers patented their own styles of cases, most with a heavy bow. One example is the Stirrup Bow by the Ball Watch Co. Hamilton used a bar above the crown to prevent the stem from being pulled out. Glass was most commonly used for the crystal because it was not as likely to scratch.

RAILROAD GRADE OR
RAILROAD SERVICE

Note: Not all railroad GRADE watches were railroad **APPROVED**, to be approved each railroad line or company made a list of watch grades that they would approve for example, Southern Railway, Lake Shore Railroad & Santa Fe Railway System etc. Not all watches listed here are railroad approved, even though all are railroad grade.
(This list changed from year to year.)

BALL
All official R.R. standard with 19, 21, & 23J, Adj.5p, 18 &16S, open face.

COLUMBUS WATCH CO.
Columbus King, 21, 23, 25J; Railway King, 17-25J; Time King, 21-25J, 18S; Ruby Model, 16S.

ELGIN
1. "Pennsylvania Railroad Co." on dial, 18S, 15J & 17J, KW-KS, first model "B. W. Raymond."
2. "No. 349," 18S, seventh model, 17-21J.
3. Veritas, B. W. Raymond, or Father Time, 18S, 21-23J.
4. Grades 162, 270, 280, or 342 marked on back plate, 16S, 17-21J.
5. Veritas, Father Time, or Paillard Non-Magnetic, 16S, 19-23J.
6. 571, 21J or 572, 16S, 19J., also All wind indicator models.

HAMILTON
1. 18S= Grade 946= 23J, & 940, 942= 21J, & 944= 19J, & 924, 926, 934, 936, 938, 948 = 17J.
2. 16S = Grades 950, 950B, 950E= 23J, & 992, 992B, 992E, 954, 960, 970, 994, 990= 21J.
3. 16S = Grade 996= 19J & 972, 968, 964= 17J.

HAMPDEN
1. Special Railway, 17J, 21J, 23J; New Railway, 23J & 17J; North Am. Railroad, 21J; Wm. McKinley, 21J; John Hancock, 21J & 23J; John C. Duber, 21J, 18S.
2. 105, 21J; 104, 23J; John C. Duber, 21J; Wm. McKinley, 17, 21, & 23J; New Railway, 21J; Railway, 19J; Special Railway, 23J, 16S.

E. HOWARD & CO.
1. All Howard models marked "Adjusted" or deer symbol.
2. Split plate models, 18S or N size; 16S or L size.

HOWARD WATCH CO.
All 16S with 19, 21, & 23J.

Above: Double Hour Time Zone Hands,
available in, RED & BLUE or GOLD & BLACK.

ILLINOIS
1. Bunn 15J "Adjusted," & Stuart, 15J "Adjusted," 18S; Burlington,19J.DR.Adj. 16S;
2. Benjamin Franklin,17-26J; Bunn 17- 24J; Bunn Special,21-26J; Chesapeake & Ohio Sp.,21-24J; Interstate Chronometer, 23J;Lafayette, 24J; A. Lincoln, 21J; Paillard W. Co., 17-24J; Trainsmen, 23J; Pennsylvania Special 17-26J; The Railroader & Railroad King, 18S.
3. Benjamin Franklin,17-25J; Bunn,17-19J; Bunn Special,21-23J; Diamond Ruby Sapphire,21-23J; Interstate Chronometer,23J; Lafayette,23J; A.Lincoln,21J; Paillard Non-MagneticW.Co.,17-21J; Pennsylvania Special, 17, 21, & 23J; Santa Fe Special, 21J; Sangamo, 21-26J; Sangamo Special, 19-23J; grades 161, 161A=21J;163, 163A=23J & 187, and 189, 17J, 16S.

PEORIA WATCH CO.
15 & 17J with a patented regulator, 18S.

ROCKFORD
1. All 21 or more jewels, 16-18S, All and wind indicators.
2. Grades 900, 905, 910, 912, 918, 945, 200, 205, 18S.
3. Winnebago, 17-21J, 505, 515, 525, 535, 545, 555, 16S.

SETH THOMAS
Maiden Lane, 21-28J; Henry Molineux, 20J; 260 Model, 18S.

SOUTH BEND
1. Studebaker 329, Grade Nos. 323, and 327, 17-21J, 18S.
2. Studebaker 229, Grade Nos. 223, 227, 293, 295, 299, 17-21J, Polaris,21J; 16S.

UNITED STATES WATCH CO., MARION
United States, 18 size, 17-19J, gold train.

U. S. WATCH CO., WALTHAM
The President, 17-21J, 18 size, double roller.

WALTHAM
1. 1857 KW with Pennsylvania R.R. on dial, Appleton Tracy & Co. on movement.
2. Crescent Street, 17-23J; 1883 & 1892 Models; Appleton Tracy & Co., 1892 Model; Railroader, 1892 Model; Pennsylvania Railroad; Special RR, Special RR King, Vanguard, 17 -23J, 1892 Model; Grade 845, All wind indicators 18S.
3. American Watch Co., 17-21J, 1872 Models; American Watch Co., All wind indicators, ALL 17-23J Bridge Models; Crescent Street, 17-21J, 1899 & 1908 Models; Premier Maximus; Railroader; Riverside Maximus, 21-23J; Vanguard, 19-23J; 645 16S.

RAILROAD
MODEL
NO. 2

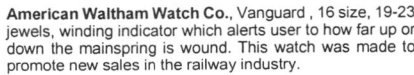

American Waltham Watch Co., Vanguard , 16 size, 19-23 jewels, winding indicator which alerts user to how far up or down the mainspring is wound. This watch was made to promote new sales in the railway industry.

Hamilton Watch Co., This was a favorite railroad style case by Hamilton model NO. 2 supplied in 10K or 14K gold filled. Note the Railroad style dial with red marginal figures as well as the bar-over-crown with "Hamilton Railroad" on crown.

CANADIAN PACIFIC SERVICE
RAILROAD APPROVED WATCHES 1899 to 1910

WALTHAM
Vanguard, 18-16S, 19-21-23 jewels
Crescent St., 18S, 19J; 18-16S, 21J
Appleton-Tracy 17J; also No. 845, 21J
Riverside 16S, 19J; Riverside Maximus, 16S, 23J;
No. 645, 16S, 21J, C. P. R. 18-16S, 17J; C.T. S. 18-16S, 17J
ELGIN
Veritas, 18-16S, 21-23J
B. W. R. 18-16S, 17-19-21J
Father Time 18-16S, 21J
Grade 349, 18S, 21J
HAMILTON
18S, 946, 23J; 940-942, 21J; 944, 19J; 936-938, 17J
16S, 950, 23J; 960-990-992, 21J; 952, 19J; 972, 17J
SOUTH BEND
18S, 327-329, 21J; 323, 17J
16S, 227-229, 21J; 223, 17J
BALL
All Balls 18S, 16S, 17-19-21-23J
ILLINOIS
Bunn Special, 18-16S, 21-23J; also Bunn 18-16S, 17-19J
A. Lincoln, 18-16S, 21J; Sangamo Special, 16S, 19-21-23J
SETH THOMAS
Maiden Lane, 18S, 25J; No. 260, 21J; No. 382, 17J
E. HOWARD WATCH CO.
16S Series, 0-23J, 5-19J, 2-17J, 10-21J; also No. 1, 21J
ROCKFORD
18S, Grade 918-905, 21J; Winnebago, 17J; also Grade 900, 24J
16S, Grades 545, 525, 515, 505, 21J; 655 W.I., 21J; and Grade 405, 17J
LONGINES
18S, Express Monarch, 17-19-21-23J
16S, Express Monarch, 17-19-21-23J
BRANDT-OMEGA
18S& 16S, D.D.R., 23J = very best, 18 gold settings; D.R., 19J = extra fine, 15 gold settings;
        C.C.C.R., 23J = fine quality; 15 gold settings; C.C.R., 19J = quality, 10 gold settings.
(This list changed from year to year.)

AMERICAN RAILROAD APPROVED WATCHES 1930

The following requirements for **NEW** railroad approved watches are outlined by Mr. R. D. Montgomery, General Watch Inspector of the Santa Fe Railway System:

"Regulation for **new** watches designated as of 1930 to be standard is described as follows:"

"16 size, American, lever-setting, 19 jewels or more, open face, winding at "12", double-roller escapement, steel escape wheel, adjusted to 5 positions, temperature and isochronism, which will rate within a variation not exceeding 6 seconds in 72 hour tests, pendant up, dial up and dial down, and be regulated to run within a variation not exceeding 30 seconds per week."

"The following listed makes and grades meet the requirements and comprise a complete list of watches acceptable. Watches bearing the name of jewelers or other names not standard trade marks or trade numbers will not be accepted:" (**This list changed from year to year.**)

AMERICAN WALTHAM W. CO.
(16 Size)
23J Premier Maximus
23J Riverside Maximus
23J Vanguard
   6 position
   winding indicator
23J Vanguard
   6 position
21J Crescent Street
21J No. 645
19J Vanguard
19J Riverside

BALL WATCH CO.
(16 Size)
23J Official R.R. Standard
21J Official R.R. Standard
19J Official R.R. Standard

ELGIN WATCH CO.
(16 Size)
23J Veritas
21J Veritas
21J B. W. Raymond
21J Father Time
21J No. 270

HAMILTON WATCH CO.
(16 Size)
23J No. 950
21J No. 990
21J No. 992
19J No. 952
19J No. 996

HAMPDEN WATCH CO.
(16 Size)
23J Special Railway
21J New Railway
19J Railway

HOWARD WATCH CO.
(16 Size)
All 23J
All 21J
All 19J

ILLINOIS WATCH CO.
(16 Size)
23J Sangamo Special
23J Sangamo
23J Bunn Special
21J Bunn Special
21J Sangamo
21J A. Lincoln
19J Bunn

SOUTH BEND WATCH CO.
(16 Size)
21J No. 227
21J No. 229
21J No. 295
19J No. 293

Union Pacific Railroad Time Inspectors , June, 1936

All new WATCHES must be **16 size with double roller** adjust to 5 positions & so stamped on plates, lever set, plain Arabic numbers , open-faced & wind at 12, maintain a rate of 30 seconds. The following will govern the NEW RAILROAD STANDARDS. **BALL**=21&23 jeweled "Official Railroad Standard"; **ELGIN**=21&23 jeweled "B.W. Raymond"; **HAMILTON**="950 & 992"; **ILLINOIS**=21&23 jeweled "Bunn Special"; **WALTHAM**=23 jeweled "Vanguard".

CP RAIL SERVICE AS OF FEBRUARY 1, 1957

WALTHAM (16 SIZE)
23J Vanguard S. # 29, 634, 001 and up

ELGIN (16 Size)
21J B.W.R.
21J No. 571

HAMILTON (16 SIZE)
23J No. 950B
21J No. 992B

BALL W. Co.(16 Size)
21J (Hamilton) No. 992B
21J No. 435C

ZENITH (16 Size)
21J Extra RR 56

APPROVED WRIST WATCHES IN
CP RAIL SERVICE

CYMA
17J RR 2852 M
25J RR 2872 A

GIRARD PERREGAUX
17J CP 307H.F.

LONGINES
17J RR 280

UNIVERSAL
19J RR 1205

ZENITH
18J RR 120 T

FERGUSON Patented Railroad Dial : Patent number on back. Valued at ; BALL = **$350 to $550** and A.W.W.Co., Elgin, Hamilton, Illinois, etc. = **$200 to $350** for MINT dials.

ELGIN WATCH CO., Classic Montgomery RR Dial (note 6 inside seconds bit) with red marginal numbers at 5, 10, 15, 20, 25, 30, 35, 40, 45, 50, 55, & 60. Valued at **$75 to $135**. **Montgomery RR Dials first used about 1904.**

APPROVED WRIST WATCHES IN
CP RAIL SERVICE 1965
BATTERY POWERED

BULOVA ACCUTRON
17J 214
17J 218 Calendar

RODANIA
13J RR 2780 Calendar

WITTNAUER
13J RR 12 WT Calendar

APPROVED WRIST WATCHES SEMI-MECHANICAL
QUARTZ ANALOG BATTERY POWERED
IN CP RAIL SERVICE AS OF 1978

CYMA
7J Calendar RR 9361 Q
6J Calendar RR 960 Q
BULOVA
7J Calendar RR 9362 Q
6J Calendar RR 960.111Q

RODANIA
6J Calendar 9952.111RR
7J Calendar RR 9361 Q
ROTARY
7J Calendar RR 9366 Q

WYLER
7J Calendar RR 9361 Q

WITTNAUER
7J Calendar RR 2 Q 115 C

ADJUSTMENTS

There are **nine** basic adjustments for watch movements. They are:

heat 1
cold 1
isochronism 1
positions 6
TOTAL 9

THE SIX POSITION ADJUSTMENTS ARE:

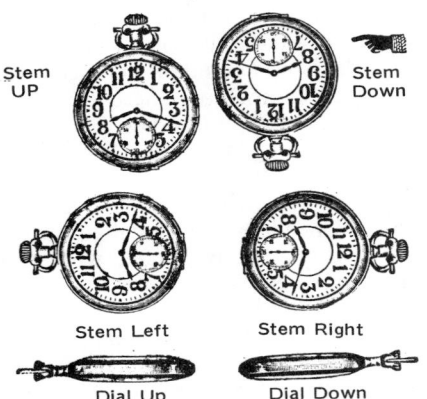

Stem UP — Stem Down

This position adjustment not required on railroad watches.

Stem Left — Stem Right

Dial Up — Dial Down

A watch marked as **5 positions** is equivalent to one marked *eight adjustments* (the most common found on RR watches) and will be listed in this book as: **"Adj.5P"** (adjusted to heat,cold, isochronism and 5 positions). A watch marked as **nine adjustments** is equivalent to one marked *6 positions* & listed as **"Adj.6P"** (adjusted to heat,cold, isochronism and 6 positions). A watch that is marked as *ADJUSTED* only is adjusted to isochronism & in poise in all temperatures & is listed as **"Adj."**.
* Later some manufactures used a variations of **8 adjustments, six to position, 1-isochronism, 1-temperature**, (*temperature* of heat & cold was combined to.= one adjustment not two).

Not all railroad GRADE watches were railroad **APPROVED**, to be approved each railroad line or company made a **list** of watch grades that they would **approve** for example, Southern Railway, Lake Shore Railroad, CP Rail Service & Santa Fe Railway System etc.

WRIST WATCHES POSITION ADJUSTMENTS

CROWN UP - CROWN DOWN- CROWN LEFT - CROWN RIGHT - DIAL DOWN - DIAL UP
Main vertical position: Wrist Watches = CROWN DOWN & Pocket Watches = PENDANT UP.

The total number of pocket watches made for the railroad industry was small in comparison to the total pocket watches produced. Generally, watches defined as "Railroad Watches" fall into five categories:

1. **Railroad Approved-** A list of Grades and Models approved by the railway companies.
2. **Railroad Grade-**Those advertised as being able to pass or exceed railroad inspection.
3. **Pre-Commission Watches-**Those used by the railroads before 1893.
4. **Company Watches-**Those with a railroad logo or company name on the dial.
5. **Train Watches-**Those with a locomotive painted on the dial or inscribed on the case.

1.Not all railroad employees were required to purchase or use approved watches, just the employees that were responsible for schedules. But many employees did buy the approved watches because they were the standard in reliability.
2. These were used primarily by those railroaders who were not required to submit their watches for inspection.
3. There were many watches made for railroad use prior to 1893. **Some of the key wind ones, especially, are good quality and highly collectible.**
4 & 5. Some manufacturers inscribed logos & terms such as railroader, special railroad, dispatcher, etc. on the dials & back plates of the movements.

NOTE: Railroad Standards, Railroad Approved & Railroad Grade **terminology,** as defined and used in this **_BOOK_**. **RAILROAD STANDARDS** = A commission or board appointed by the railroad companies outlined a set of **guidelines** or requirements to be approved by each railroad line. **RAILROAD APPROVED** = After 1875-80 a RR employee had to buy his own watch. A **_LIST_** of watches each railroad line would approve if purchased by their employee's. **This list changed through the year. RAILROAD GRADE** = A watch made by manufactures to meet or exceed the railroad **standards.** Grades such as 992, Vanguard and B.W. Raymond, etc.
* Some GRADES **exceeded** the R.R. standards requirements such as 23 jewels, diamond end stone, gold train, raised gold jewel settings, double sunk dial and the list goes on. Examples: such as Veritas, Sangamo, 950 & Riverside Maximus and many others.

COLONIAL WATCHMAKERS
(PRE—1850)

Early American watchmakers came from Europe; little is known about them, and few of their watches exist today. Their hand-fabricated watches were made largely from imported parts. It was common practice for a watchmaker to use rough castings made by several craftsmen. These were referred to as or "movements in the gray." The watchmaker finished the Ebauche movements and parts and assembled them to make a complete watch. He would then engrave his name on the finished timepiece.

Some of the early American watchmakers designed the cases or other parts, but most imported what they needed. The so called early **COLONIAL** watchmakers showed little originality as designers and we can only guess how many watches were really made in America.

These early hand-made watches are almost non-existent; therefore, only the name of the watchmaker will be listed. This compilation comes from old ads in newspapers and journals and other sources. It is not considered to be complete. Because of the rarity and condition of these early watches, prices may vary widely from **$400, $800 to $12,000.**

As early as 1775 the first Swiss made watches came into the U.S.A. and made in the London style. In 1830, Vacheron & Constantin established a connection in New York through Jean Magnin. Later in mid 1830's extending their trade to Philadelphia and New Orleans and by 1838 Agassiz and later Jurgensen.

Early in the 1860's Swiss watches were sent to America. The Swiss Firms of Cortebert, E. Borel and Courvoisier made and **designed** watches to closely resemble the style of American watch case and movement. Examples the Ohio Watch Co. was distributed by Leon Lesquereaux and son (Junior) of Columbus, Ohio. E. Borel & Co. produced American style watches and shipped them to Lucien Morel & Ed. Droz at New York. These were followed later by the entire original designs of Omega, Tissot, Movado and Zenith.

Sibley, O. E. (New York, NY, 1820)
Simpson, Saml. (Clarksville,Tenn - 1855)
Smith, J. L. (Middletown, CT, 1830)
Smith & Goodrich (Bristol, CT, 1827-1840)
Soloman, Henry (Boston, MA, 1820)
Souza, Sammuel (Phila., PA, 1820)
Sprogell, John (Phila., PA, 1791)
Spurck, Peter (Phila., PA, 1795-1799)
Stanton, Job (New York, NY, 1810)
Stein, Abraham (Phila., PA, 1799)
Stever & Bryant (Wigville, CT, 1830)
Stillas, John (Phila., PA, 1785-1793)
Stinnett, John (Phila., PA, 1769)
Stokel, John (New York, NY, 1820-1840)
Store, Marmaduke (Phila., PA, 1742)
Strech, Thomas (Phila., PA, 1782)
Syderman, Philip (Phila., PA, 1785)
Taf, John James (Phila., PA, 1794)
Taylor, Samuel (Phila, PA, 1799)
Tonchure, Francis (Baltimore, MD, 1805)

Townsend, Charles (Phila., PA, 1799)
Townsend, David (Boston, MA, 1800)
Trott, Andrew (Boston, MA, 1800-1810)
Turrell, Samuel (Boston, MA, 1790)
Voight, Henry (Phila., PA, 1775-1793)
Voight, Sebastian (Phila., PA, 1775-1799)
Voight, Thomas (Henry's son) (Phila., PA, 1811-1835)
Vuille, Alexander (Baltimore, MD, 1766)
Warner, George T. (New York, NY, 1795)
Watson, Davis (Boston, 1840-50)
Weller, Francis (Phila., PA, 1780)
Wells, George & Co. (Boston, MA, 1825)
Wells, J.S. (Boston, MA, 1800)
Wetherell, Nathan (Phila., PA, 1830-1840)
Wheaton, Caleb (Providence, RI, 1800)
White, Sebastian (Phila., PA, 1795)
Whittaker, William (NY, NY, 1731-1755)
Wood, John (Phila., PA, 1770-1793)
Wright, John (New York, NY, 1712-1735)
Zahm, G.M. (Lancaster, PA, 1865)

Watch made by Andrew, Dunheim of New York in about 1775. Note the hand pierced case.

Louis Mathey, Philadelphia engraved on movement, about 18 size, very thin movement, Virgule escapement, key wind & set from back, Ca.1795-1805.

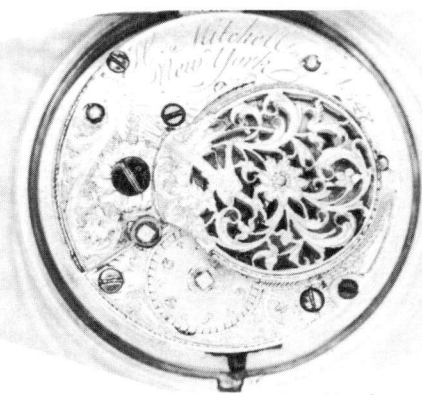

H. Mitchell, New York, 18 size, verge chain driven fusee; note the regulator below hand-pierced cock, Ca. 1790.

MILLIMETERS

(ruler: 10 20 30 40 50 60 70 80 90 100 110)

HOW TO DETERMINE SIZE

AMERICAN MOVEMENT SIZES
LANCASHIRE GAUGE

NOTE: There are many movements styles with many different sizes in thickness and diameter, making it very difficult trying to find a case to fit a movement. This it true in ALL sizes.

Size	Inches	Inches	mm	Lignes	Size	Inches	Inches	mm	Lignes
18/0	18/30	.600	15.24	6 3/4	2	1 7/30	1.233	31.32	13 7/8
17/0	19/30	.633	16.08	7 1/8	3	1 8/30	1.266	32.16	14 1/4
16/0	20/30	.666	16.92	7 1/2	4	1 9/30	1.300	33.02	14 7/8
15/0	21/30	.700	17.78	7 7/8	5	1 10/30	1.333	33.86	15 1/8
14/0	22/30	.733	18.62	8 1/4	6	1 11/30	1.366	34.70	15 3/8
13/0	23/30	.766	19.46	8 5/8	7	1 12/30	1.400	35.56	15 3/4
12/0	24/30	.800	20.32	9 1/8	8	1 13/30	1.433	36.40	16 1/8
11/0	25/30	.833	21.16	9 3/8	9	1 14/30	1.466	37.24	16 1/2
10/0	26/30	.866	22.00	9 3/4	10	1 15/30	1.500	38.10	16 7/8
9/0	27/30	.900	22.86	10 1/8	11	1 16/30	1.533	38.94	17 1/4
8/0	28/30	.933	23.70	10 1/2	12	1 17/30	1.566	39.78	17 5/8
7/0	29/30	.966	24.54	10 7/8	13	1 18/30	1.600	40.64	18 1/8
6/0	1	1.000	25.40	11 1/4	14	1 19/30	1.633	41.48	18 3/8
5/0	1 1/30	1.033	26.24	11 5/8	15	1 20/30	1.666	42.32	18 3/4
4/0	1 2/30	1.066	27.08	12 1/8	16	1 21/30	1.700	43.18	19 1/8
3/0	1 3/30	1.100	27.94	12 3/8	17	1 22/30	1.733	44.02	19 1/2
2/0	1 4/30	1.133	28.78	12 3/4	18	1 23/30	1.766	44.86	19 7/8
0	1 5/30	1.166	29.62	13 1/8	19	1 24/30	1.800	45.72	20 1/4
1	1 6/30	1.200	30.48	13 1/2	20	1 25/30	1.833	46.56	20 3/4

SWISS MOVEMENT SIZES
Lignes With Their Equivalents in Millimeters and Decimal Parts of an Inch

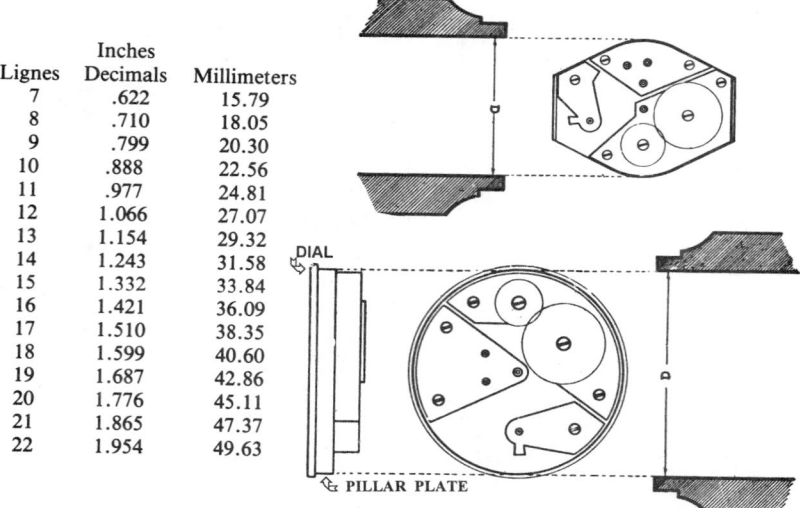

Lignes	Inches Decimals	Millimeters
7	.622	15.79
8	.710	18.05
9	.799	20.30
10	.888	22.56
11	.977	24.81
12	1.066	27.07
13	1.154	29.32
14	1.243	31.58
15	1.332	33.84
16	1.421	36.09
17	1.510	38.35
18	1.599	40.60
19	1.687	42.86
20	1.776	45.11
21	1.865	47.37
22	1.954	49.63

DIAL

PILLAR PLATE

GAUGES FOR MEASURING YOUR WATCH SIZE

The size of a watch is determined by measuring the outside diameter of the dial side of the lower pillar plate. The gauges below may be placed across the face of your watch to calculate its approximate size.

AMER. MOVEMENT SIZES

SWISS MOVEMENT SIZES
LIGNES

IMPORTANT NOTE: Have your watch case **TESTED** to make sure of gold quality or Karat.

SOLID GOLD MARKS

IMPORTANT NOTE: Have your watch case TESTED to make sure of gold quality or Karat.

The term **KARAT** is a word of definition in regards to the quality of gold, one 24th part (of pure gold). For example: Pure or fine gold is 24 karats; 18 Karat (abbreviated 18 K)consist of 18 parts of pure gold and mixed with 6 parts of other metal. The term **CARAT** is a unit of weight for gemstones, 200 milligrams equal 1 Carat. Karat = gold content & Carat = weight of GEMS.

GOLD-FILLED CASES

The first patent for gold-filled cases was given to J. Boss on **May 3, 1859.** Gold-filled cases are far more common than solid gold cases. Only about 5 percent of the cases were solid gold. In making the gold-filled case, the following process was used: two bars of gold, 12'' long, 2'' wide, and 1/2 '' thick were placed on either side of a bar of base metal. The bar of base metal was 3/4'' thick and the same length and width as the gold bars. These three bars were soldered together under pressure at high temperature. The bars were sent through rolling mills under tremendous pressure; this rolling was repeated until the desired thickness was reached. The new sandwich-type gold was now in a sheet. Discs were punched out of the sheet and pressed in a die to form a dish-shaped cover. Finally the lip, or ridge, was added. The bezel, snap, and dust caps were added in the finishing room. Gold-filled cases are usually 10k or 14k gold. The cases were marked ten-year, fifteen-year, twenty-year, twenty-five-year, or thirty-year. The number of years indicated the duration of guarantee that the gold on the case would not wear through to the base metal. The higher the number of years indicates that more gold used and that a higher original price was paid.

In 1924 the government prohibited any further use of the guarantee terms of 5, 10, 15, 20, 25, or 30 years. After that, manufacturers marked their cases 10k or 14k Gold-Filled and 10k Rolled Gold Plate. Anytime you see the terms ''5, 10, 15, 20, 25 and 30-year,'' this immediately identifies the case as being gold-filled. The word ''guaranteed'' on the case also denotes gold-filled.

Rolled Gold

Rolled gold involved rolling gold into a micro thinness and, under extreme pressure, bonding it to each sheet of base metal. Rolled gold carried a five-year guarantee. The thickness of the gold sheet varied and had a direct bearing on value, as did the richness of the engraving.

Gold Gilding

Brass plates, wheels and cases are often gilded with gold. To do this, the parts are hung by a copper wire in a vessel or porous cell of a galvanic battery filled with a solution of ferro-cyanide of potassium, carbonate of soda, chloride of gold, and distilled water. An electric current deposits the gold evenly over the surface in about a six-minute period. One ounce of gold is enough for heavy gilding of six hundred watches. After gilding, the plates are polished with a soft buff using powdered rouge mixed with water and alcohol. The older method is fire-gilt which uses a gold and mercury solution. The metal is subjected to a high temperature so the mercury will evaporate and leave the gold plating. This is a very dangerous method, however, due to the harmful mercury vapor.

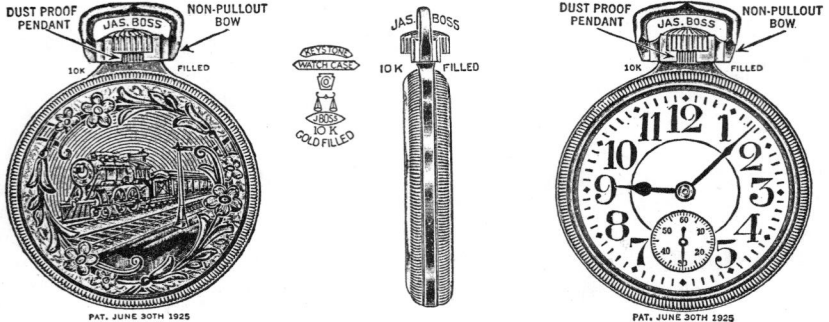

JAS. BOSS **Railroad Model** 10K Gold Filled cases sold for $14.00 in 1927

SILVER CASE MARKS

(Sterling Silver.)

STERLING
SILVER
UNITED STATES
ASSAY
925/1000
FINE.

ILLINOIS
W.C.CO,
ELGIN
STERLING

HUNTING CASES

A hunting case is identified by a cover over the face (concealed dial) of the watch. The case is opened by pressing the stem or the crown of the watch. The hunter style watch was used for protection of the watch and carried by men of status and used as a dress watch.

HOW TO HANDLE A HUNTING CASE WATCH

Hold the watch in your right hand with the bow or swing ring between the index finger and thumb. Press on the pendant-crown with the right thumb to release the cover exposing the face.

When closing, do not **SNAP** the cover. Press the crown to move the catch in, close the cover, then release the crown. This will prevent wear to the soft gold on the rim and catch.

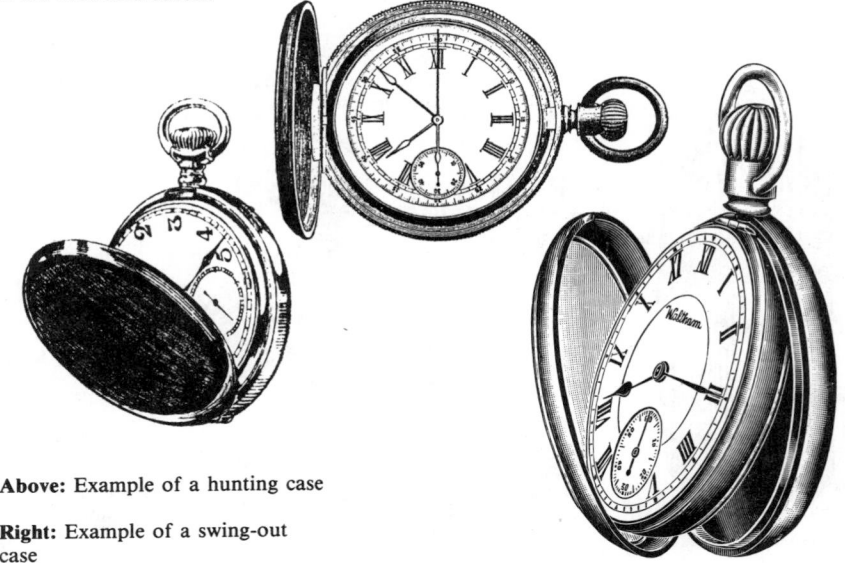

Above: Example of a hunting case

Right: Example of a swing-out case

SWING-OUT MOVEMENT

On some pocket watches the movement swings out from the front. On these type watches the movement can be swung out by unscrewing the bezel and pulling the stem out to **release** the movement. **SEE EXAMPLE ABOVE.**

40

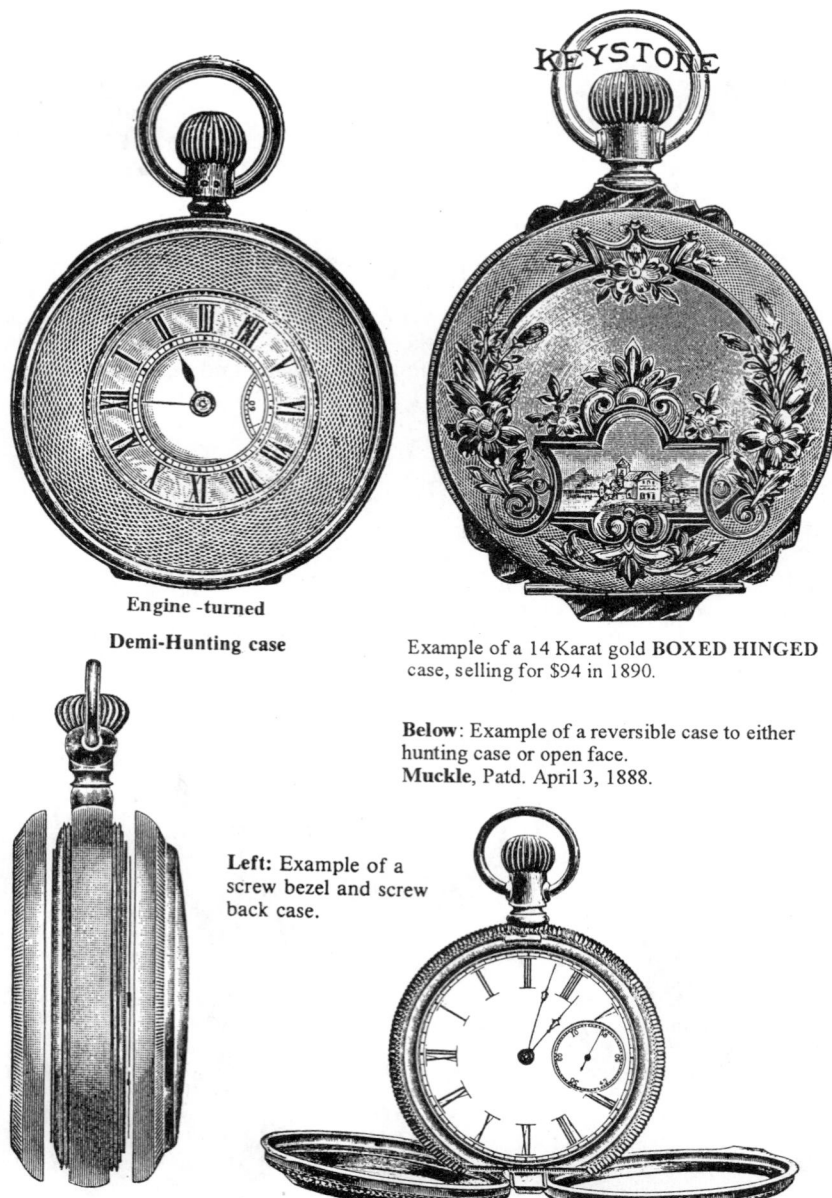

Engine -turned

Demi-Hunting case

Example of a 14 Karat gold **BOXED HINGED** case, selling for $94 in 1890.

Below: Example of a reversible case to either hunting case or open face.
Muckle, Patd. April 3, 1888.

Left: Example of a screw bezel and screw back case.

Note: The screw on bezel was invented by E. C. Fitch in 1886.

51

TRAIN OF A ELGIN VERITAS (18 size 23 jewel) MOVEMENT & EACH PART NAMED

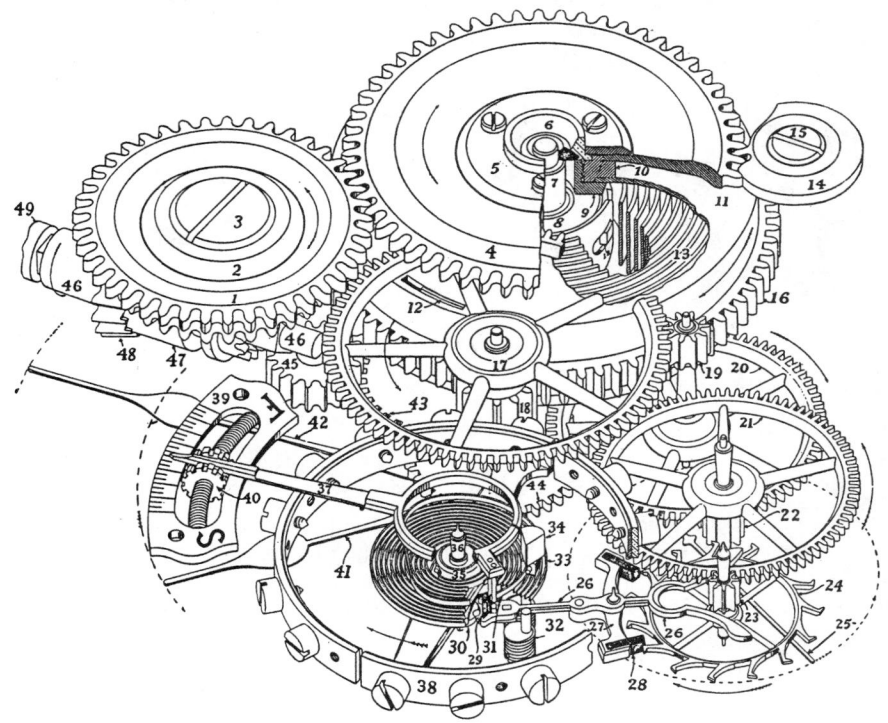

1 Main Wheel.	26 Fork or (Counter-poised lever)	
2 Main Wheel Washer.	27 Pallet.	
3 Main Screw.	28 Pallet Stones.	
4 Ratchet Wheel.	29 Roller Jewel Pin.	First Wheel 78 Teeth, 1 Rev. in 6 Hours, 30 Minutes.
5 Ratchet Wheel Washer.	30 Safety Roller.	Center Pinion 12 Teeth, 1 Rev. in 1 Hour.
6 Jewel Setting.	31 Table Roller.	Center Wheel 80 Teeth, 1 Rev. in 1 Hour.
7 Barrel Arbor.	32 Banking Screws.	3rd Pinion 10 Teeth, 1 Rev. in 7½ Minutes.
8 Barrel Arbor Hub.	33 Breg. Hair Spring.	3rd Wheel 75 Teeth, 1 Rev. in 7½ Minutes.
9 Barrel Hub Screw.	34 Hair Spring Stud.	4th Pinion 10 Teeth, 1 Rev. in 1 Minute.
10 Barrel Hub.	35 Hair Spring Collet.	4th Wheel 80 Teeth, 1 Rev. in 1 Minute.
11 Barrel.	36 Balance Staff.	Escape Pinion 8 Teeth, 1 Rev. in 6 Seconds.
12 Main Spring Hooked.	37 Regulator.	Escape Wheel 15 Teeth, 1 Rev. in 6 Seconds.
13 Main Spring.	38 Balance.	Balance Vibrates 30 times in 6 Seconds.
14 Recoiling Click.	39 Index.	300 times in 1 Minute.
15 Click Screw.	40 Reg. Adj. Nut.	18,000 times in 1 Hour.
16 First Wheel.	41 Hour Hand.	432,000 times in 1 Day.
17 Center Wheel.	42 Minute Hand.	157,680,000 times in 1 Year.
18 Center Pinion.	43 Minute Wheel.	
19 Third Pinion.	44 Hour Wheel.	
20 Third Wheel.	45 Setting Wheel.	
21 Fourth Wheel.	46 Winding Arbor.	
22 Fourth Pinion.	47 Wind. & Set. Clutch.	
23 Escape Pinion.	48 Bevel Pinion.	
24 Escape Wheel.	49 Pendant Bar.	
25 Second Hand.		

52

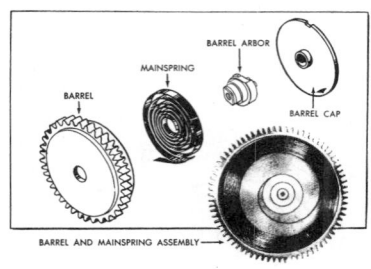

Power unit for modern watch showing the various parts.

Early style watch with a stackfreed (tear shaped cam). Note the balance is dumbbell shaped.

THE MAINSPRING

Watches were developed from the early portable clocks. The coiled spring or mainspring provided the drive power. The first coiled springs were applied to clocks about 1450. For the small portable watch, coiled springs were first used about 1470. The power from a mainspring is not consistent and this irregular power was disastrous to the first watches.

The Germans' answer to irregular power was a device called a stackfreed. Another apparatus employed was the fusee. The fusee proved to be the best choice. At first catgut was used between the spring barrel and fusee. By around 1660 the catgut was replaced by a chain. Today, the fusee is still used in naval chronometers. One drawback to the fusee is the amount of space it takes up in the watch. Generally, the simplest devices are best.

The mainspring is made of a piece of hardened and tempered steel about 20 inches long and coiled in a closed barrel between the upper and lower plates of the movement. It is matched in degree of strength, width, and thickness most suitable for the watch's need or design. It is subject to differing conditions of temperature and tensions (the wound-up position having the greatest tension). The lack of uniformity in the mainspring affects the time keeping qualities of a watch.

The power assembly in a watch consists of the mainspring, mainspring barrel, arbor, and cap. The mainspring furnishes the power to run the watch. It is coiled around the arbor and is contained in the mainspring barrel, which is cylindrical and has a gear on it which serves as the first wheel of the train. The arbor is a cylindrical shaft with a hook for the mainspring in the center of the body. The cap is a flat disk which snaps into a recess in the barrel. A hook on the inside of the mainspring barrel is for attaching the mainspring to the barrel.

The mainspring is made of a long thin strip of steel, hardened to give the desired resiliency. Mainsprings vary in size but are similar in design; they have a hook on the outer end to attach to the mainspring barrel, and a hole in the inner end to fasten to the mainspring barrel arbor.

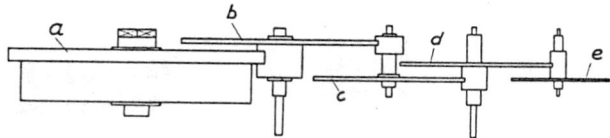

57

Elevation of a **GEAR-TRAIN**
(a.) mainspring barrel, (b.) center wheel (carries minute hand), (c.) third wheel, (d.) fourth wheel (carries seconds hand),
(e.) escape wheel, 8 day watches use a intermediate (8 day wheel) placed between the barrel and the center wheel.

THE TRAIN

The gear-train which, transmits mainspring-barrel torque to the escape-wheel consists of a four-wheel multiplying train. The time train consists of the mainspring barrel, center wheel and pinion, third wheel and pinion, fourth wheel and pinion, and escape wheel which is part of the escapement. The function of the time train is to reduce the power of the mainspring and extend its time to 36 hours or more. The mainspring supplies energy in small units to the escapement, and the escapement delays the power from being spent too quickly. The Escapement is the turnstile of the watch, metering out a tiny unit of power for each tick and tock.

The long center wheel arbor projects through the pillar plate and above the dial to receive the cannon pinion and hour wheel. The cannon pinion receives the minute hand and the hour wheel the hour hand. As the mainspring drives the barrel, the center wheel is rotated once each hour.

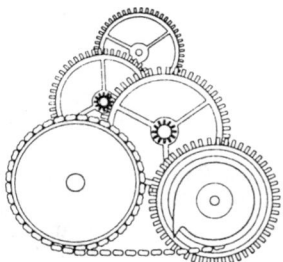

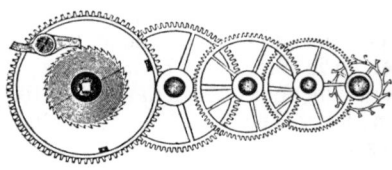

Alignment of chain driven fusee with train. **Fusee** at right and main-spring barrel at left. Note chain between fusee and main-spring barrel.

The gear-train which "transmits" mainspring-barrel torque to the escape wheel consists of a four-wheel multiplying train.

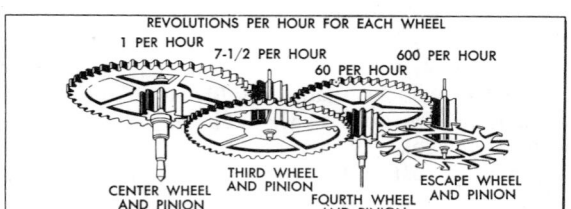

REVOLUTIONS PER HOUR FOR EACH WHEEL
1 PER HOUR
7-1/2 PER HOUR   600 PER HOUR
60 PER HOUR

CENTER WHEEL AND PINION
THIRD WHEEL AND PINION
FOURTH WHEEL AND PINION
ESCAPE WHEEL AND PINION

Actual alignment of **Train Unit**

58

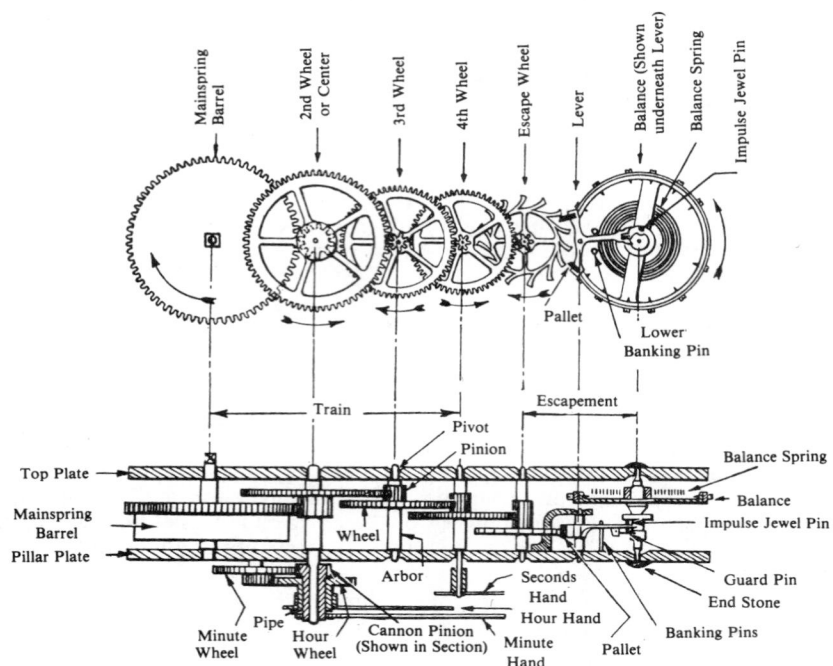

The second or center wheel of the watch turns once every hour. It is the second largest wheel in the watch, and the arbor or post of the center wheel carries the minute hand. The center wheel pinion is in mesh with the mainspring barrel (pinions follow and the wheel supplies the power). The center wheel is in mesh with the third wheel pinion (the third wheel makes eight turns to each turn of the center wheel). The third wheel is in mesh with the fourth wheel pinion, and the fourth wheel pinion is in mesh with the escape wheel pinion. The fourth wheel post carries the second hand and is in a 1:60 ratio to the center wheel (the center wheel turns once every hour and the fourth wheel turns 60 turns every hour). The escape wheel has 15 teeth (shaped like a flat foot) and works with two pallets on the lever. The two pallet jewels lock and unlock the escape wheel at intervals (1/5 sec.) allowing the train of gears to move in one direction under the influence of the mainspring. The lever (quick train) vibrates 18,000 times to one turn of the center wheel (every hour). The hour hand works from a motion train. The mainspring barrel generally makes about five turns every 36 hours.

SOLID GOLD TRAIN

Some watches have a gold train instead of brass wheels. These watches are more desirable. To identify gold wheels within the train, look at a Hamilton 992; in most of these watches, the **center** wheel is made of gold and the other wheels are made of brass. Why a gold train? Pure gold is soft, but it has a smooth surface and it molds easily. Therefore, the wheels have less friction and properly alloyed it is sturdy. These wheels do not move fast, and a smooth action is more important than a hard metal. Gold does not tarnish or rust and is non-magnetic. The arbors and pinions in these watches will be steel. Many watches have some gold in them, and the collector should learn to distinguish it.

The escape wheel is in most cases made of steel and is staked on a pinion and arbor. It is the last wheel of the train and connects the train with the escapement. It is constructed so that the pallet jewels move in and out between its teeth, allowing but one tooth to escape at a time, turnstile fashion. The teeth are club-foot-shaped for additional impulse.

The pallet jewels are set at an angle to make their inside corners reach over three teeth and two spaces of the escape wheel. The outside corners of the jewels will reach over two teeth and three spaces of the escape wheel with a small amount of clearance. At the opposite end of the pallet, directly under the center of the fork slot, is a steel or brass pin called the guard pin. The fork is the connecting link to the balance assembly.

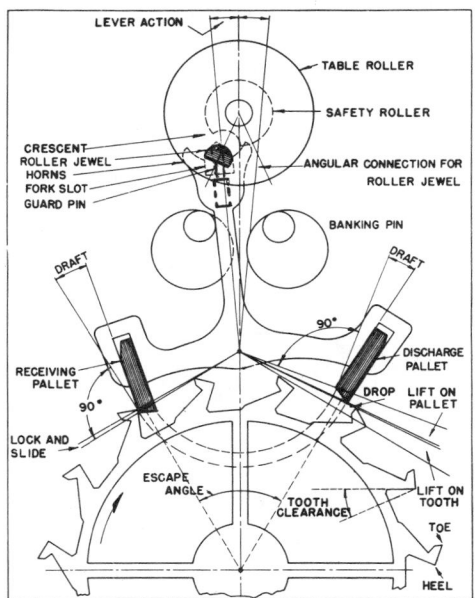

BALANCE AND HAIRSPRING

In earlier watches the hairspring was just that. Bristles from a wild boar was used to control the balance wheel. The rotation of the balance wheel is controlled by the hairspring. The inner end of the hairspring is pinned to the collet, and the collet is held friction-tight on the staff above the balance wheel.

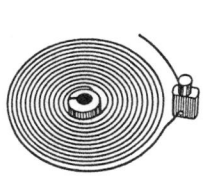
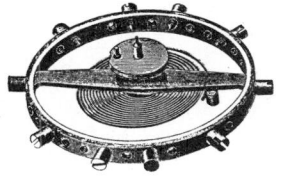

Left: example of **flat hairspring**.   Center: Balance & Hairspring.   Right: example of Breguet or **overcoil hairspring**.

The outer end of the hairspring is pinned to a stud which is held stationary on the balance cock by the stud screw. The roller jewel is cemented in the large roller assembly, which is mounted on the staff directly under the balance wheel. Under the first roller is a smaller one which acts as a safety roller. This is necessary because of the crescent cut out in the roller table which allows the guard pin of the escapement assembly to pass through.

The balance wheel rotates clockwise and counterclockwise on its axis by means of the impulse it receives from the escapement. The motion of the balance wheel is constant due to the coiling and uncoiling of the hairspring. The impulse, transmitted to the roller jewel by the swinging of the pallet fork to the left, causes the balance to rotate in a counterclockwise direction. The position of the fork allows the roller jewel to move out of the slot of the fork freely and in the same direction. The fork continues on until it reaches the banking pin. Meanwhile the balance continues in the same direction until the tension of the hairspring overcomes the momentum of the balance wheel. When this occurs the balance returns to its original position, which causes the roller jewel to again enter the slot of the fork.

Modern or Swiss Lever Escapement

A. Lever
B. Entrance pallet
C. Exit pallet
D. Fork
E. Banking pins
F. Fork slot
G. Horns
H. Impulse roller jewel
K. Safety finger
L. Notch of small plate M
M. Safety roller
N. Roller table
P. Impulse plane of the teeth of the wheel
R. Escape wheel

Pallet and Escape Tooth Action. The momentum that has been built up during the return of the balance, causes the roller pin to impart an impulse on the inside of the fork slot. This impulse is great enough to push the fork away from its position against the banking pin. As the fork is pushed away, it causes the pallet stone to slide on the toe of the escape wheel tooth. When the pallet stone has slid down to its edge, it frees the escape wheel tooth, thereby unlocking the escape wheel. The escape wheel, being impelled by the force of the mainspring, starts to rotate. As the escape wheel turns, the tooth glides along the impulse face of the pallet jewel, forcing it to move out of the way. The moving pallet carries the fork with it and imparts the impulse to the roller jewel. The right pallet stone intercepts a tooth of the escape wheel to lock it, as the fork moves toward the banking pin. Having a short "run" left to the banking pin, the pressure of the escape wheel tooth against the locking face of the pallet jewel draws the stone deeper into the escape wheel and, therefore, causes the fork to complete its run and holds it against the banking pin. Meanwhile the balance continues in a clockwise direction until the tension of the hairspring overcomes the momentum of the balance and returns it to its original position.

Rate of Escape Tooth Release. Through the motion of the escapement, the mainspring keeps the balance vibrating, and the balance regulates the train. The escape wheel has 15 teeth and is allowed to revolve 10 turns per minute. Thus, 150 teeth glide over each pallet stone in 1 minute. The gliding of the escape wheel teeth over the impulse faces of the pallet stones will cause the balance to vibrate 300 vibrations or beats per minute. These vibrations will continue until the force of the mainspring is spent.

SCREWS

Screws used in watches are very small and precise. These screws measure 254 threads to the inch and 47,000 of them can be put into a thimble. The screws were hardened and tempered and polished to a cold hard brilliance. By looking at these screws through a magnifying glass one can see the uniformity.

EQUIDISTANT ESCAPEMENT

The term Equidistant Escapement is a form of lever escapement. The locking of each pallet takes place at the same distance from the pallet arbor. A similar form of escapement is the circular pallet with the circular form of escapement. The impulses are given at equal distance from the center line. The Swiss preferred the equidistant while the Americans preferred the circular. There is little difference in performance between these two types of escapement.

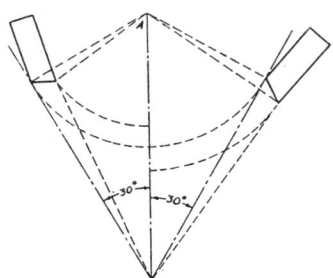

Equidistant form of Escapement

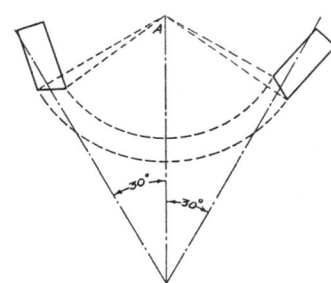

Circular form of Escapement

66

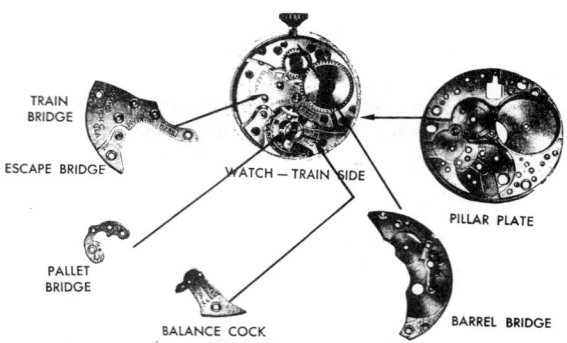

TRAIN BRIDGE

ESCAPE BRIDGE

WATCH — TRAIN SIDE

PILLAR PLATE

PALLET BRIDGE

BALANCE COCK

BARREL BRIDGE

The plates and bridges which hold all the parts in proper relation to each other.

THE PLATES

The movement of a watch has two plates and the works are sandwiched in between. The plates are called the top plate and the pillar plate. The top plate fully covers the movement. The 3/4 plate watch and the balance cock are flush and about 1/4 of a full plate is cut out to allow for the balance, thus the 3/4 plate. The bridge style watch has two or three fingers to hold the wheels in place and together are called a bridge. The term bridge (horologically) is one that is anchored at both ends. A cock is a wheel support that is attached at one end only. English balance cock for verge watches and lever watches have but one screw. French and Dutch verge watches have their balance bridges secured at both ends. The metal is generally brass, but on better grade watches, nickel is used. The full plate is held apart by four pillars. In older watches the pillars were very fancy, and the plates were pinned, not screwed, together. The plates can be gilded or engraved when using brass. Some of the nickel plates have damaskeening. There are a few watches with plates made of gold. The plates are also used to hold the jewels, settings, etc. Over 30 holes are drilled in each plate for pillars, pivots, and screws.

The pinion is the smaller of the two wheels that exist on the shaft or arbor. They are small steel gears and usually have six teeth called leaves. Steel is used wherever there is great strain, but where there is much friction, steel and brass are used together; one gear of brass, and a pinion of steel. After the leaves have been cut, the pinions are hardened, tempered, and polished.

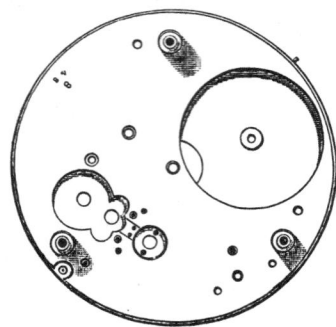

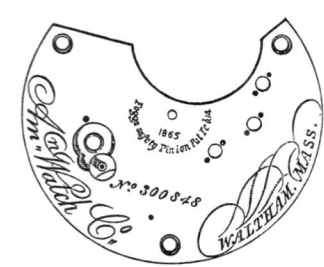

LEFT = PILLAR PLATE

RIGHT = TOP PLATE -(3/4 plate)

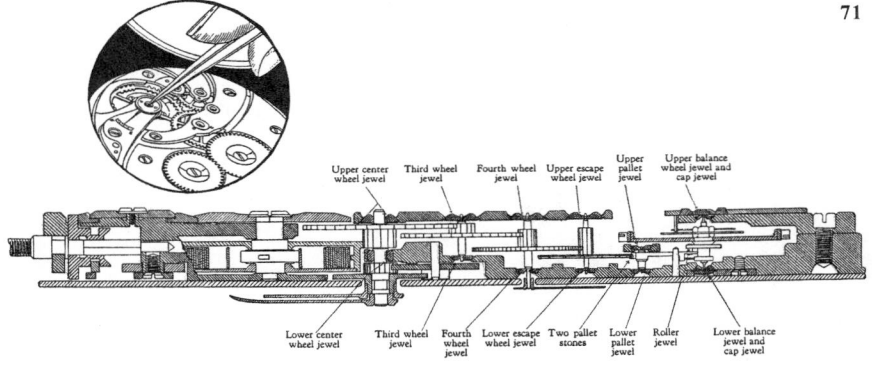

Above: Cross section of a 17 jewel pocket watch showing upper and lower jewel location.

19-JEWEL WATCHES. In these watches, the jewels are distributed as in the 17-jewel watch, with the addition of one for each pivot of the **barrel & mainspring.**

21-JEWEL WATCHES. The jewels in these are distributed as in the 17-jeweled grade, with the addition of two cap jewels (**USUALLY** placed on the pallet arbor and escape wheel) or 2 jewels for the barrel & mainspring.

Center Wheel — 2	Center Wheel— 2	Center Wheel— 2	Center Wheel— 2
Third Wheel — 2	Third Wheel — 2	Third Wheel — 2	Third Wheel — 2
Fourth Wheel — 2	Fourth Wheel— 2	Fourth Wheel— 2	Fourth Wheel— 2
Escape Wheel— 2	Escape Wheel—2	Escape Wheel—2+2	Escape Wheel— 2+2
Pallet & Arbor— 4	**Barrel Arbor** — 2	Pallet & Arbor— 4+2	**Barrel Arbor** — 2
Balance Staff — 4	Pallet & Arbor— 4	Balance Staff — 4	Pallet & Arbor— 4+2
Roller jewel — <u>1</u>	Balance Staff — 4	Roller jewel — <u>1</u>	Balance Staff — 4
TOTAL — 17J	Roller jewel — <u>1</u>	TOTAL—21J	Roller jewel — <u>1</u>
	TOTAL — 19J		TOTAL— 23J

23-JEWEL WATCHES. The jewels are distributed as in the 21-jewel watch, with the addition of one for each pivot of the **barrel & mainspring**.

24J., 25J., and 26 JEWEL WATCHES. In all of these watches, the additional jewels were distributed as cap jewels. These were not very functional but were offered as **prestige** movements for the person who wanted more. **In many cases, these jewel arrangements varied according to manufacturer. All jeweled watches may <u>NOT</u> fit these descriptions.**

Collectable watches with a higher jewel count usually demand a greater price, *when watches were produced the higher the jewel count the higher the cost*, however, lower production of some models this <u>collectable</u> **rule** does not apply. Example 7, 11 and 15 jewel Hamiltons will bring higher prices than a 17 jewel Hamilton, also a 19 jeweled "Sangamo Special" will bring a higher price than 21 jeweled "Sangamo Special". Most American made watches with 15 jewels and up are marked. (**Generally speaking it is accepted that good to medium quality watches have 15 to 17 jewels and are said to be "fully jeweled".**)

When counting **VISIBLE** jewels beware that some manufactures added <u>non-functional</u> jewels for eye appeal, disassembling the watch is the only way to get a true accurate count. Note: When counting jewels from the movement back plate (with dial on) at the visible jewels a 11J. could appear to be a 15J. watch. A jewel which has a scribed circle around it plus two screws is a **mock** setting and usually have one jewel for top jewel only & no lower jewel.

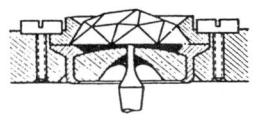

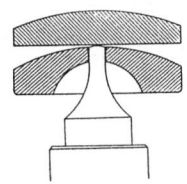

Left: Diamond faceted end stone.   **Center**: Cylindrical pivot.   **Right**: Conical pivot & end stone.

WINDING AND SETTING

The simplest, but not the most practical method for winding up the main-spring of a pocket watch was to wind the barrel staff by means of a key, but then it is necessary to open up the watch case. The key method of winding proved unpopular, as oftentimes the key became lost.

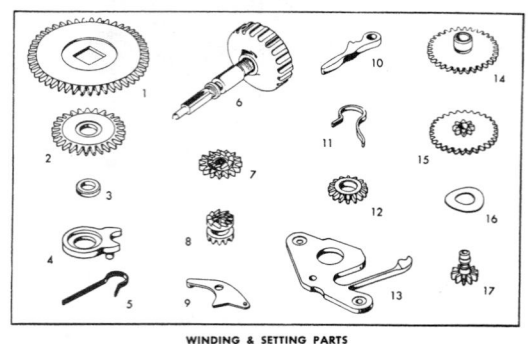

WINDING & SETTING PARTS

1. Ratchet Wheel	6. Stem and Crown	10. Clutch Lever	14. Hour Wheel
2. Crown Wheel	7. Winding Pinion	11. Clutch Lever Spring	15. Minute Wheel
3. Crown Wheel Center	8. Clutch Wheel	12. Setting Wheel	16. Dial Washer
4. Click	9. Setting Lever	13. Yoke	17. Cannon Pinion
5. Click Spring			

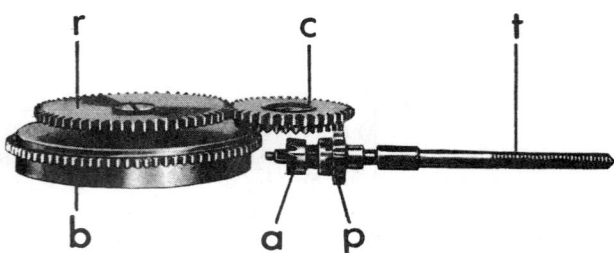

WINDING MECHANISM. a-Winding and setting clutch. p-Winding pinion. b-Barrel. r-Ratchet wheel. c-Crown or main wheel. t- Winding arbor.

The modern principle of the winding of the mainspring and hand setting by pulling on the crown, dates back to 1842. We owe this combination to Adrian Philippe, associate of Patek, of Geneva.

The winding and setting mechanism consists of the stem, crown, winding pinion, clutch wheel, setting wheel, setting lever, clutch lever, clutch spring, crown wheel, and ratchet wheel. When the stem is pushed in, the clutch lever throws the clutch wheel to winding position. Then, when the stem is turned clockwise, it causes the winding pinion to turn the crown and ratchet wheels. The ratchet wheel is fitted on the square of the mainspring arbor and is held in place with a screw. When the stem and crown are turned, the ratchet wheel turns and revolves the arbor which winds the mainspring, thereby giving motive power to the train. Pulling the stem and crown outward pushes the setting lever against the clutch lever, engaging the clutch wheel with the setting wheel. The setting wheel is in constant mesh with the minute wheel; therefore, turning the stem and crown permits setting the hands to any desired time.

SETTING MECHANISM. Clutch a. meshes with m. and the minute works wheel b. The minute works wheel meshes with the cannon pinion h. The hour cannon d. bears the hour hand H. C. center wheel M. Minute hand.

The dial train consists of the cannon pinion, minute, and hour wheels. The cannon pinion is a hollow steel pinion which is mounted on the center wheel arbor. A stud which is secured in the pillar plate holds the minute wheel in mesh with the cannon pinion. A small pinion is attached to the minute wheel which is meshed with the hour wheel.

The center arbor revolves once per hour. A hand affixed to the cannon pinion on the center arbor would travel around the dial once per hour. This hand is used to denote minutes. The hour wheel has a pipe that allows the hour wheel to telescope over the cannon pinion. The hour wheel meshes with the minute wheel pinion. This completes the train of the cannon pinion, minute wheel, and hour wheel. The ratio between the cannon pinion and the hour wheel is 12 to 1; therefore, the hand affixed to the hour wheel is to denote the hours. With this arrangement, time is recorded and read.

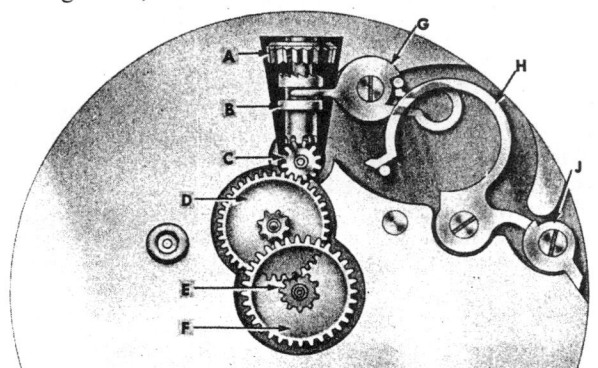

A—PINION
B—CLUTCH WHEEL
C—SETTING WHEEL
D—MINUTE WHEEL
E—CANNON PINION
F—HOUR WHEEL
G—CLUTCH LEVER
H—SETTING SPRING
J—SETTING SPRING CAM

KENDRICK & DAVIS, WATCH KEY FACTORY was founded in 1876. They produced a dust-proof key which was looked upon as quite a wonderful patented watch key & sold world wide & also found with different foreign trade marks.

AUTOMATIC WINDING.

The self-winding watch uses the movements of the body in order to wind up the mainspring slowly and nearly continuously. The first pocket self-winding watches were executed by a watchmaker from Le Locle, Abraham-Louis Perrelet, around 1770. They were improved soon after by Abraham-Louis Breguet. In the case of the pocket watch, the movements causing the winding of the watch were essentially the result of walking. This system of winding was never widely adopted. The watch was a fancy model and not a really useful one. Herman von der Heydt was the only maker in America to work with the self-winding pocket watch. However, inventors always kept the idea of the self-winding watch in mind.

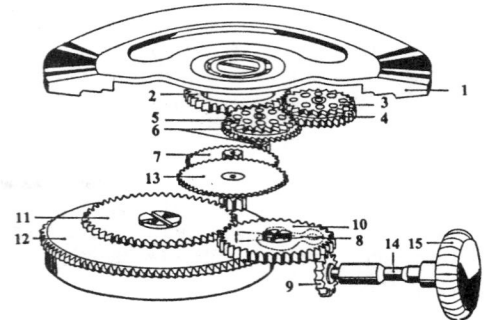

Early self wind pocket watch by Breguet.

ETERNA-MATIC AUTOMATIC WINDING MECHANISM. 1–Oscillating Weight. 2–Oscillating gear. 3–Upper wheel of auxiliary pawl-wheel. 4–Lower wheel of auxiliary pawl-wheel. 5–Pawl-wheel with pinion. 6–Lower wheel of pawl-wheel with pinion. 7–Transmission-wheel with pinion. 8–Crown-wheel yoke. 9–Winding pinion. 10–Crown-wheel. 11–Ratchet-wheel. 12–Barrel. 13–Driving runner for ratchet-wheel. 14–Winding stem. 15–Winding button.

In 1923, the British firm Harwood took up once again the solution of the problem of automatic winding, for wrist watches. This was the spark which rapidly resulted in research to improve and simplify this type of mechanism. A company was formed in London to manufacture Harwood's watch, and before long over 500 jewelers in the United Kingdom were selling his automatic watch. A second company was formed in France, and a third in the United States. The business flourished about two and one-half years. Then, in 1931, these companies were liquidated.

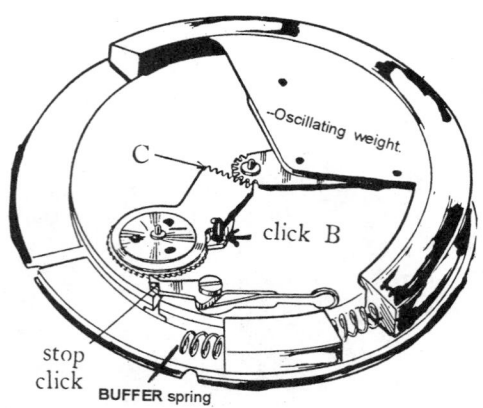

Illustration of Self Winding mechanism used by Harwood
NOTE: The 2 BUFFER springs used on earlier movements.

This 1931 wrist watch made by Perpetual Self-Winding Watch Co. of America originally sold for $29.75.

COTTAGE INDUSTRY WATCHMAKING IN COLONIAL AMERICA

The cottage industry (pre-1700s to 1800s) consisted of organized, skilled craftsmen having separate divisions for the purpose of producing watches. The movements were handmade using manpowered tools. The parts generally were not given a final finish. The cottage industries were in most countries including France, England, Switzerland, Germany, and others, but not in America. Each skilled parts maker specialized in a specific part of the watch. There were fusee makers, wheel makers, plate and cock makers, spring makers, case makers and enamelers, to name a few. In the cottage industry each maker became an expert in his field. Expenses and overhead were less because fewer tools and less labor were required. Because all components were produced separately, a larger volume of watches resulted.

The enterprising colonial watchmaker in America would order all the parts and assemble them to complete a finished movement. This finisher, or watchmaker, would detail the parts, such as filing them to fit, polishing and gilding the parts, fitting the movement to a case, installing a dial, and adjusting the movement to perform. The finisher would then engrave his name and town of manufacture to the movement or dial. The finisher determined the time keeping quality of the completed watch, thus gaining a good reputation for some watchmakers.

Most watchmakers used this system during this period; even, to some extent, Abraham L. Breguet. A colonial watchmaker or finisher could produce about 50 watches a year. There were few colonial watchmakers because only the wealthy could afford such a prized possession as a watch. Most colonial watchmakers struggled financially, and supplemented their businesses with repair work on European-made watches. Since most of them understood the verge escapement, and imported this type of part from England to produce watches, many colonial watches have the verge escapement. Few colonial watches survive today.

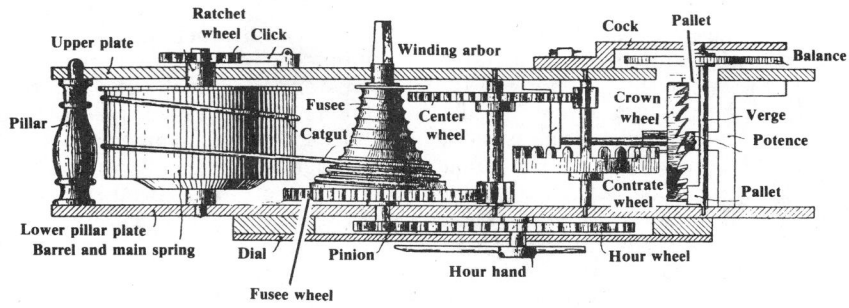

Side-view of 17th Century single-hand movement with fusee and catgut line to barrel. This three-wheel movement normally ran from 15 to 16 hours between windings. Also note the balance has no hairspring.

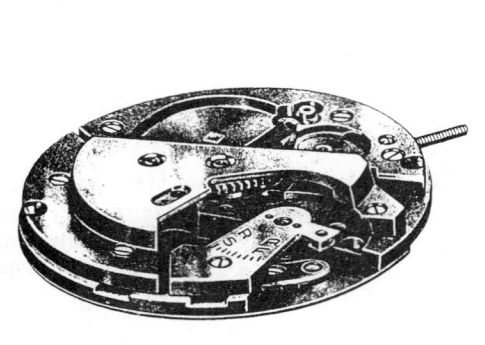

EBAUCHES

The stamping out of plates and bridges began with Frederic Japy of Beaucourt, France, around 1770. At first, ebauches consisted of two plates with barrel and train bridges, the cock and fusee, pillars, and the clicks and assembly screws. The ebauches were stamped-out or rough movements. Japy invented machinery a common laborer could operate, including a circular saw to cut brass sheets into strips, a machine for cutting teeth in a wheel, a machine for making pillars, a press for the balance, and more. These machines were semi-automatic and hard to keep in alignment or register. But, with the aid of these new machines the principal parts of the movement could be produced in a short period of time with some precision. However, the parts of watches at this time were not interchangeable. These movements in the rough or ''gray'' were purchased by finishers. The finisher was responsible for fitting and polishing all parts and seeing to the freedom and depth of these wheels and working parts. He had to drill the holes to fit the dial and hands. The plates, cock and wheel, after being fitted and polished, were gilded. After the parts were gilded, the movement would be reassembled, regulated for good time keeping, and placed in a case. The finisher had to be a master watchmaker.

In England, during the 1800s, Lancashire became the center of the movement trade. One of the better known English ebauche makers was Joseph Preston & Sons of Prescot. The movements were stamped J. P. Some Swiss ebauches would imitate or stylize the movement for the country in which they were to be sold, making it even harder to identify the origin.

As the watch industry progressed, the transformation of the ebauche to a more completed movement occurred. Automation eventually made possible the watch with interchangeable parts, standard sizing, and precision movements that did not need retouching. This automation began about 1850 (in America) with such talented mechanics as Pierre Fredric Ingold, the Pitkins Brothers, A. L. Dennison, G. A. Leschot with Vacheron and Constantin, Patek, Philippe, and Frederic Japy of Beaucourt. The pioneers in the 1850s who set the standards for modern watchmaking included the American Pitkin Brothers, Dennison, Howard, and Jacob Custer. By 1880 most other countries had begun to follow the lead of America in the manufacture of the complete pocket watch with interchangeable parts.

In Switzerland there are **four** major categories of watch producers :
1. Complete 2. Ebauche 3. Parts or **Specialized 4. Finishers.** *Complete* watch producers manufacture 75% to 100% on their own premises as Le Coultre. *Ebauche* produce rough movements or movements in the gray called ebauche or blank movements such as ETA in Grenchen. These are made in the valley of Joux and Val-de-Ruz regions, in and around the towns of Granges, Grenchen, La Chaux-de-Fonds, Le Locle and Solothurn, in the Bernese Jura, the valley of St. Imier, Val-de-Travers, at Preseux, in the Ticino, and elsewhere. *Specialized or Parts* are made more or less all over the Swiss regions. Balances more so in Valley of Sagne and at Les Ponts. Lever assortments as the escape wheel, fork, & roller in Jour Valley, at Bienne, in Bernese Jura and especially, at Le Locle. Hairsprings as *"Nivarox"* are made near La Chaux-de-Fonds, Geneva, Bienne and St. Imier. Mainspring, dial, hands, cases, jewels, pendant, bow, crowns, crystals, screws, pins, generally speaking are made throughout Switzerland. *Finishers* buy blank movements, parts, cases, etc. and finish the watch as a complete watch with their own name engraved on the watch as *Tiffany & Co., Ball W. Co.* and many more.

By mid 1950s' the high quality watches made under **"one roof"** by Am.Waltham, Elgin, Hamilton and Illinois could not compete with the Swiss division of manufacturing. This Swiss system of manufacturing encourages improvement within its own field. Each **specialist** company has experience and can improve quality while speeding up large production at a competitive price. This specialized system is still used today with most Swiss Watch Companies.

Five typical Ebauches. Three with bar movements, one with a three -quarter plate, one with a half plate. Four with lever escapements, one with a cylinder escapement. The age ranges from 1860 to 1890.

Ebauches   S.A.

Ebauches S.A. with its main office in Neuchatel, Switzerland, at one time the following 17 affiliated firms were part of Ebauche S.A. and in the year of 1968 they had produced ABOUT- 40,000,000 WATCHES. In 1932 Eterna divided into 2 companies Eterna and ETA.

A. Schild S.A., Grenchen

Fabrique d'Horlogerie de Fontainemelon, fontainemelon

Eta S.A., Fabrique d'Ebauches, Grenchen

Fabrique d'Horlogerie de Fontainemelon, Succursale du Landeron, Le Landeron

A. Michel S.A., Grenchen

Felsa S.A., Grenchen

Fabriques d'Ebauches Bernoises S.A., Etablissement Aurore, Villeret

Fabrique d'Ebauches Venus S.A., Moutier

Fabrique d'Ebauches Unitas S.A., Tramelan

Fabrique d'Ebauches de Fleurier S.A., Fleurier

Fabrique d' Ebauches de Peseux S.A., Peseux

Fabriques d'Ebauches Reunies Arogno S.A., Arogno

Fabriques d'Ebauches de bettlach, Bettlach

Fabrique d'Ebauches de Chezard S.A., Chezard

Derby S.A., La Chaux-de-Fonds

Nouvelle Fabrique S.A., Tavannes

Valjoux S.A., Les Bioux

FRENCH EBAUCHE

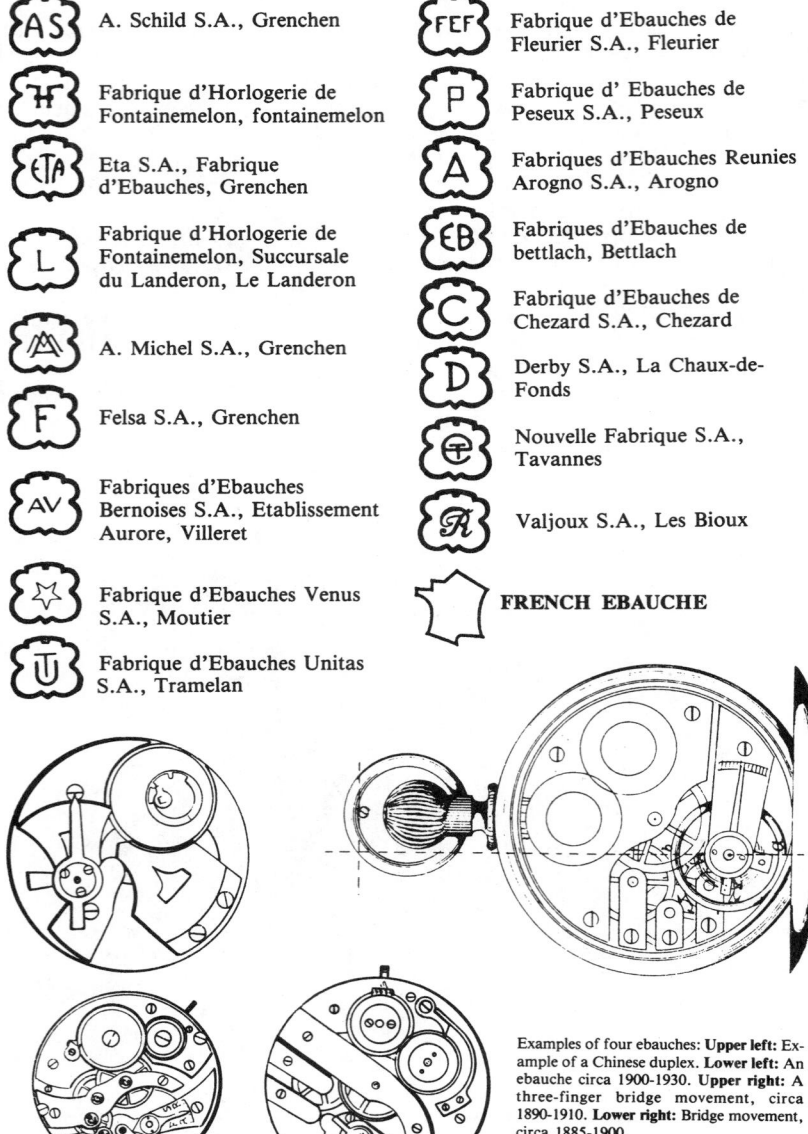

Examples of four ebauches: **Upper left:** Example of a Chinese duplex. **Lower left:** An ebauche circa 1900-1930. **Upper right:** A three-finger bridge movement, circa 1890-1910. **Lower right:** Bridge movement, circa 1885-1900.

WORM GEAR ESCAPEMENT

This oddity was advertised as,"The Watch With a Worm in It," Robert J. Clay of Jersey City was given a patent on October 16, 1886. Mr. Clay said, "The principal object of my invention is to provide a watch movement that is very simple and has but few parts." The worm gear or continuous screw was by no means simple. Mr. Clay and William Hanson of Brooklyn revamped the original worm gear and obtained another patent on January 18, 1887.

The first watch containing a worm gear escapement reached the market in 1887. However, the New York Standard Watch Co. soon converted to a more conventional lever escapement. About 12,000 watches with the worm gear were made, but few survived.

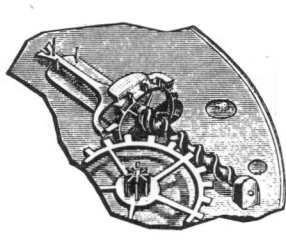

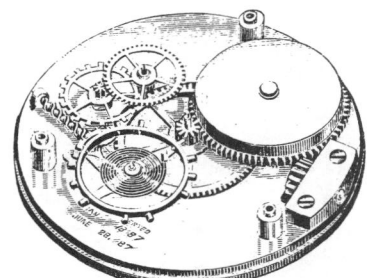

Enlarged **worm gear escapement.** Note endless screw was referred to by the New York Watch Co. as "A watch with a worm in it.."

Movement with top plate removed.

DIAL MAKING

Enamel is a glass substance that may be transparent or colored. It acts as a protective surface on the metals and is resistant to acid, corrosion, and weather. Enamel is made of feldspar, quartz, silica, borax, lead, and mineral oxides for coloring. Enamel watch dials are basically hand produced. The base for enamel dials is a disc stamped out of copper, next an impression is made for the dial feet. Enamel is ground to a very fine powder and sifted upon the copper disc. It is then fired in a furnace at a high heat (about 1500 degrees fahrenheit) which fuses the enamel and causes it to flow evenly over the copper disc. This process may be repeated 2 or 3 times. Next a steel plate with numbers engraved in it, the depressions are filled with a black enamel. A rubber pad then comes in contact with the steel plate, the black enamel adhering to the rubber, is then transferred to the enameled dial. This operation is repeated in order to insure a good impression of the transfer.

Next the dial with the new applied numbers is placed in a furnace at a lower heat than the original process. Double-sunk dials are formed by stamping these parts out separately, treating them the same as the main part of the dial already described and then soldering these dial pieces carefully together. So that a double sunk dial is really a combination of three separate dials.

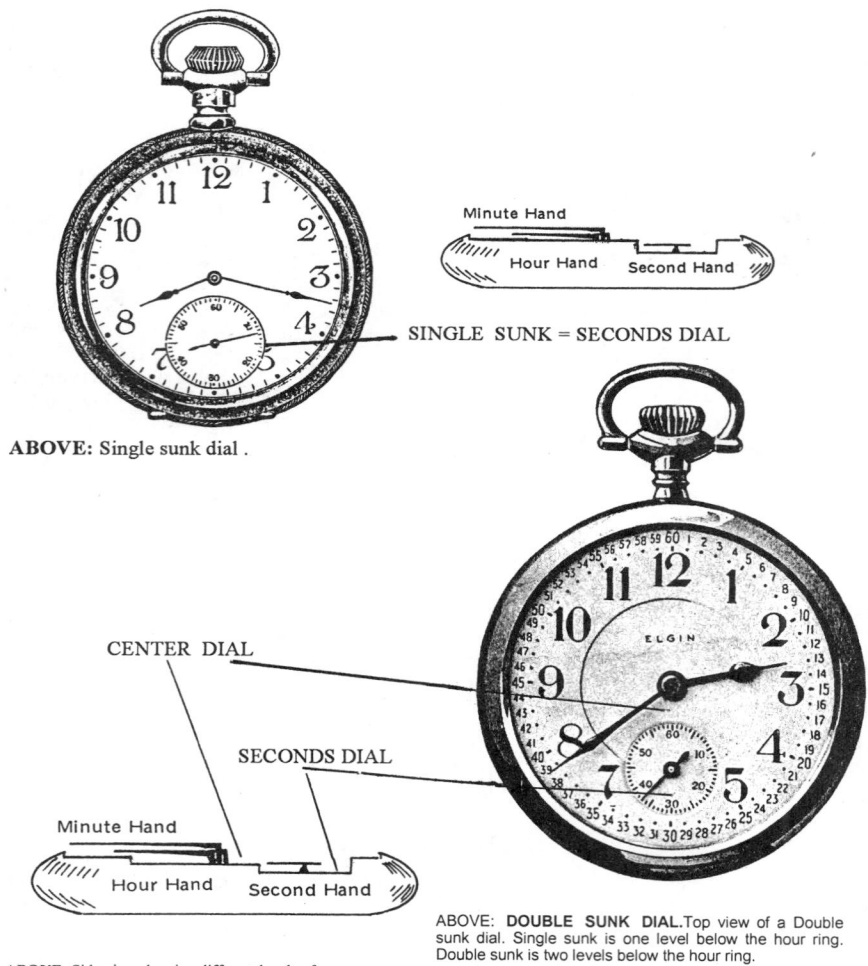

SINGLE SUNK = SECONDS DIAL

Minute Hand
Hour Hand   Second Hand

ABOVE: Single sunk dial .

CENTER DIAL

SECONDS DIAL

Minute Hand
Hour Hand   Second Hand

ELGIN

ABOVE: **DOUBLE SUNK DIAL.**Top view of a Double sunk dial. Single sunk is one level below the hour ring. Double sunk is two levels below the hour ring.

ABOVE: Side view showing different levels of a **double sunk dial.**

Note: Some single sunk dial have inner marked circle made to look like double sunk dial.

Note: Due to numbers being fired at a lower heat a enamel dial can not be fired again at a higher heat (such as for repair purposes).

CRAZING

The word "craze" means a minute crack in the glaze of the enamel. This is not a **crack** in the dial because the dial has a backing of copper. Crazing does little damage to the structure of the enamel, even though it may go all the way through to the copper.

FIRST DIALS

Thomas Gold was the first to make enamel dials in America in about 1838 in New York City. Thomas had a partner from 1846-51 named Thomas Reeves of Brooklyn. American Watch Co. (Waltham) made their own dial from the beginning by dial-makers John Todd & John T. Gold. Henry Foucy found employment in 1856 with the American Watch Co. he was from Geneva.

PIN LEVER ESCAPEMENT (DOLLAR WATCHES)

The pin lever escapement is sometimes erroneously referred to as "Roskopf escapement" and watches with pin lever escapements are sometimes referred to as "Roskopf watches."

The original Roskopf watch, which was publicly exhibited at the Paris Exposition in 1867, was a rugged "poor man's watch." The chief Roskopf patent, decreases the number of wheels by creating a large barrel whose diameter encroached upon the center of the watch. The loose cannon pinion and hour wheel were driven by a friction-clutch minute wheel mounted to the barrel cover and enmeshing with the loose cannon pinion and hour wheel. The cannon pinion rode loosely on a steel pin threaded to the center of the main plate. The true term, "Roskopf" applies to the barrel with its clutch fitted minute wheel driving the dial train. The Roskopf ebauches watch was made by **Cortebert** factory in La Chaux-de-Fonds, Switzerland. The first Roskopf watch was sold for 25 franks in January of 1870.

⊕NOTE: Some fakes use the name **"Rosskopf."**

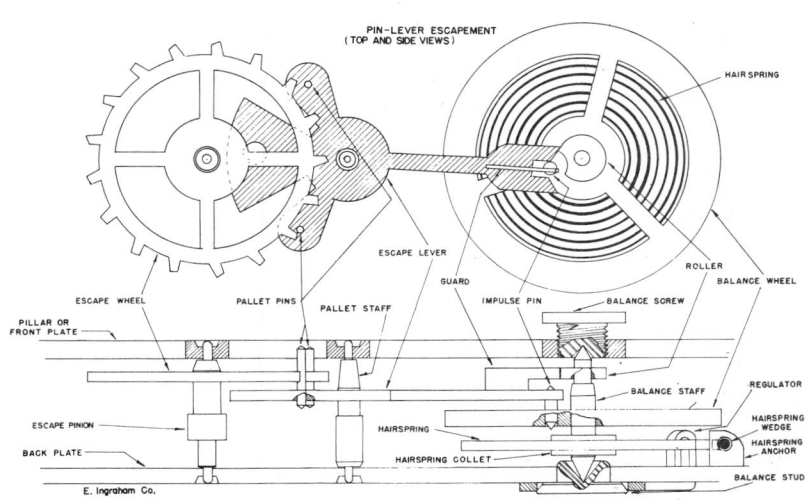

PIN-LEVER ESCAPEMENT
(TOP AND SIDE VIEWS)

HAIR SPRING

ESCAPE LEVER

GUARD

ROLLER

BALANCE WHEEL

ESCAPE WHEEL

PALLET PINS

PALLET STAFF

IMPULSE PIN

BALANCE SCREW

PILLAR OR
FRONT PLATE

BALANCE STAFF

REGULATOR

ESCAPE PINION

HAIRSPRING

HAIRSPRING
WEDGE

HAIRSPRING
ANCHOR

BACK PLATE

HAIRSPRING COLLET

BALANCE STUD

E. Ingraham Co.

LOW COST PRODUCTION WATCHES
(DOLLAR WATCHES)

Jason R. Hopkins hoped to produce a watch that would sell for no more than 50 cents as early as the 1870s. He had a plan for which he received a patent (No. 161513) on July 20, 1875. It was a noble idea even though it was never fully realized. In 1876, Mr. Hopkins met a Mr. Fowle who bought an interest in the Hopkins watch. The movement was developed by the Auburndale Watch Co., and the Auburndale Rotary Watch was marketed in 1877. It cost $10, and 1,000 were made. The 20 size had two jewels and was open-face, pendant wind, lever set, and detent escapement. The 18 size had no jewels and was open-face.

In December, 1878, D. A. A. Buck introduced a new watch, at a record low price of $3.50, under the name of Benedict and Burnham Manufacturing Co. It was a rotary watch, open-face, with a skeleton dial which was covered with paper and celluloid. The movement turned around in the case, once every hour, and carried the minute hand with it. There were 58 parts and all of them were interchangeable. They had no jewels but did have a duplex style escapement. The teeth on the brass escape wheel were alternately long and short, and the short teeth were bent down to give the impulse. The Long main spring is laid on a plate on the bed of the case. The click was also fastened to the case. The extremely long mainspring took 120 to 140 full turns of the stem to be fully wound. It came to be known as the "long wind" Waterbury and was the source of many jokes, *Here, wind my Waterbury for awhile; when you get tired, I'll finish winding it.*

"Trail Blazer" by E. Ingraham Co. TOP view is the original Box, bottom. LEFT is Fob "Wings Over The Pole". RIGHT: Watch has original green crystal. Note: engraving on the back of watch is same scene as depicted on box.

MARKET REPORT
2,001
A $20,000 INVESTMENT IN 1975 NOW WORTH $125,250!

	1975	2001
Patek Philippe minute repeater pocket watch	$2,000	$10,000
Rockford multi-color box hinge hunters case 18 size	$500	$3,750
Bovet gold and enamel Chinese duplex	$4,000	$20,000
Sun and Moon verge c. 1700	$1,200	$7,500
Waltham Premier Maximus 18k	$2,000	$8,000
Patek Philippe 18k chronograph wrist watch c. 1948	$2,500	$25,000
Patek Philippe 18k calatrava wrist watch c.1950	$800	$4,500
Rolex 18k gold bubble back c.1940	$800	$4,500
Rolex 18k duo dial rectangle c.1930	$1,200	$12,000
Rolex 18k oyster moon phase and calendar star dial c.1945	$5,000	$30,000
Totals	**$20,000**	**$125,250**

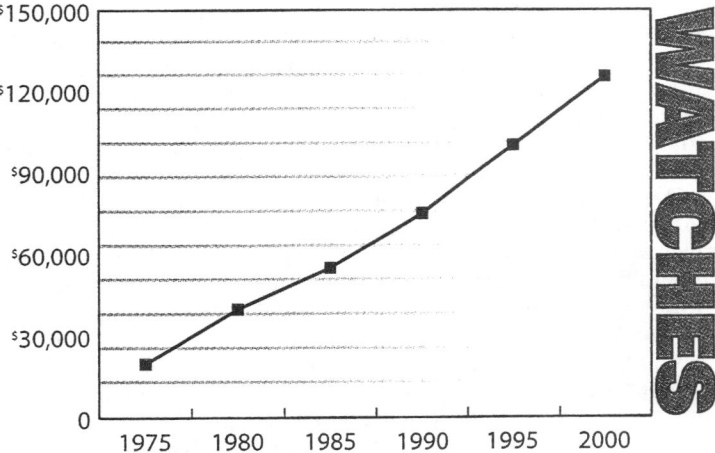

Above prices are based on actual sales of watches. The watches used in this graph analysis are listed above with the 1975 selling price and the current price. Major watch firms such as Breguet, Patek Philippe, Swatch and many others are investing in rare watches for their Museums they fully realize the importance of these horological treasures. Watches have enjoyed an upward trend in value and collectors will always be collectors. Once there is a rebound economically the watch market will see new record levels in the watch market. Keep in mind as SUPPLY DWINDLES and DEMAND in the Collectors Marketplace Expands buy at the fair market values, as outlined in this price guide and buying wisely, but don't *hesitate*, as the better and scarce watches are *quickly* sold.

Join your fellow pocket watch collectors for a seminar "Boston: Cradle of Industrial Watchmaking", October 17-19, 2002. Tour historic Waltham, speakers will trace the origins of early American watchmaking, with scholarly presentations as "Revolution in Time", "Pitkins and Goddard", "Automatic Watchmaking Machinery at Waltham", "First Mass-Produced American Watches", "Inventions and Legacy of Charles Woerd" and much more. For more information, contact Clint Geller, 412-521-8092 or Ron Price at: rprice@pricelessads.com. See ad **"2002 NAWCC Seminar"** in this book in the advertising section (back of book).

AMERICAN LISTINGS

Pricing At Collectable Fair Market Value At Trade Show Level
(As Complete Watches With Case & Movement)

Watches listed in this book are priced at the collectable fair market value at the **Trade Show** level (A collector should expect to pay modestly higher prices at **local shops**) and as *complete watches*, having an original 14k gold-filled case with an original white enamel single sunk dial. The entire original movement is in good working order with no repairs needed, unless otherwise noted. Watches listed as 14k and 18k are solid gold cases. Coin or silveroid-type and stainless steel cases will be listed as such. Keywind and keyset watches are listed as having original coin silver cases. Dollar-type watches or low cost production watches are listed as having a base metal type case and a composition dial. Wrist watches are priced as having original gold-filled case with the movement being all original and in good working order, and the wrist watch band being made of leather except where bracelet is described.

Many of the watch manufacturers were commissioned to put jewelers' or jobbers' names on their movements in place of their own. Due to this practice, the true manufacturers of these movements are difficult to identify. These watch models are listed under the original manufacturer and can be identified by comparison with the model sections under each manufacturer. See ''Personalized & CustomWatches'' for more detailed information.

The watch manufacturers who personalized & custom made watches for jobbers or jewelry firms, with exclusive private signed or marked movements must first be found by using a illustration & matched to the manufacture shown in this book. After you identify the movement now the value can be determined. The valuable collectable watches are listed under the signed or marked movement. Other exclusive private signed or marked movements will have equivalent value are only slightly higher value & should be compared to Generic or Nameless movements. Railroad signed or marked (dials & movements) are usually more collectable & higher in value .

The prices shown were averaged from dealers' lists just prior to publication and are an indication of the collectable trade show level or what collectors will pay. Prices are provided in three categories: average condition, extra fine, and mint condition, and are shown in whole dollar amounts only. The values listed are a guide for the collectable trade show level and are provided for your information only. Dealers will not necessarily pay **full trade show price**. Prices listed are for watches with original cases and dials.

Important Notice. All of the information, including valuations, in this book has been compiled from the most reliable sources, and every effort has been made to eliminate errors and questionable data. Nevertheless, the possibility of error, in a work of such immense scope, always exists. The publisher or authors will not be held responsible for losses which may occur in the purchase, sale, statements of its advertisers, or other transaction of items, because of information contained herein. Readers who feel they have discovered errors are invited to write and inform us, so they may be corrected in subsequent editions.

🕑 Descriptions and serial number ranges listed for early watches cannot be considered 100 percent accurate due to the manner in which records were kept by these companies.

🕑 Watch terminology or communication in this book has evolved over the years, in search of better and more precise language with a effort to improve, purify, adjust itself and make it easier to understand.

ABBREVIATIONS USED IN
THE COMPLETE PRICE GUIDE TO WATCHES

🕐— IMPORTANT NOTE.
below: ★ (Star Rating) & **5 Stars = Rarest**
★ ★ ★ ★ ★ — **RARE**
★ ★ ★ ★ — **SCARCE**
★ ★ ★ — **VERY FEW**
★ ★ — **SPARCE**
★ — **UNCOMMON**
☑ — In Demand, technical or historical interest.
ADJ —Adjusted (to temperature or heat & cold, also isochronism). Adj.5P = Adjusted to 5 positions, 3 positions or 4 positions etc
aux. sec.—auxiliary seconds
BASE—Base metal used in cases; e.g., silveroid
BB —Bubble Back (Rolex style case)
BRG—Bridge plate design movement
Ca. — Circa (about or approximate date)
Cal. —Calendar also Calibre (model)
C&B — Case and Band
Chrono.—Chronograph
Co.—Company
COIN—Coin silver
DES—Diamond end stones
DMK—Damaskeened
DSD—Double sunk dial
DR—Double roller
DWT—Penny weight: 1/20 Troy ounce
ETP—Estimated total production
ESC.—Escapement
EX—Extra nice; far above average
FULL—Full plate design movement
3/4—3/4 plate design movement
1F brg—One finger bridge design and a 3/4 plate (see Illinois 16s M#5)
2F brg—Two finger bridge design
3F brg—Three finger bridge design
GF—Gold filled
GJS—Gold jewel settings
G#—Grade number
GT—Gold train (gold gears)
GCW—Gold center wheel
GRO—Good running order
HC—Hunter case
id. — identification
(illo.) —Illustration of watches etc.
J—jewel (as 21J)
K—Karat (14k solid gold—not gold filled)

K(w) —WHITE GOLD as in 14k(w)
K(y) —YELLOW GOLD as in 14k(y)
KS—Key set
KW—Key wind
KW/SW— transition (Key wind/stem wind)
LS—Lever set
MCC—Multi-color case
MCD—Multi-color dial
M#—Model number
mm —Millemeter (over all case size)
Mvt.— Only Dial and movement; no case
NI—Nickel plates or frames
OF—Open face
P—as Adj.5P = Adjusted to 5 positions, 3 positions or 4 positions etc.
PORC—Porcelain (porc. dial)
PS—Pendant set
PW — Pocket Watch
RF#—Reference Factory number
Reg.—Register on a chronograph
REP.—Repeater
RGJS—Raised gold jewel setting
RGP—Rolled gold plate
RR—Railroad
S—Size as 16S = 16 size
SBB—Screw back and bezel
SR—Single Roller
SRC—Swing ring case
SS—Stainless steel
SSD—Single Sunk Dial
SW—Stem wind
S#—Serial number
TEMP—Temperature
TP—Total production
2T—Two-tone (damaskeened in 2 colors)
WGF—White gold filled
W.I. also W. Ind. —Wind indicator or (up and down indicator)
/ = **WITH** as KW/SW or SW/LS
/ = **Also** as OF/HC
WW—Wrist watch
YGF—Yellow gold filled
@ = AT or About

MODEL = Size, open face or hunter, full or 3/4 plate, key or stem wind, design & layout of parts.
GRADE= 1st., 2nd., & 3rd., Quality etc. some manufactures used names or numbers (**Bunn , 992**).
1. **Ebauche** = Manufacture movements in the rough.
2. **Manufacture** = 75% to 100% of movements Manufacture on premises.
3. **Watchmaker** & **Finisher** = Finished movement in the rough or used <u>Special named</u> movement.
4. **Jobber**, Distributor, Firms, <u>Special named</u>, Customized or Personalized movement = Retail only.

🕐 **The Complete Price Guide to Watches goal is to stimulate the orderly exchange of <u>Watches</u> between "*buyers*" and "*sellers*".**

INFORMATION NEEDED: We are interested in any facts and information you might have that should possibly be considered for future editions. Documented facts are needed, so please send photo or sources of information. Send to: Cooksey Shugart, P. O. BOX 3147, Cleveland, Tennessee 37320-3147.

(When *Corresponding*, Please Include A 🖃 *Self-addressed, Stamped Envelope.*)

NOTE: Railroad Standards, Railroad Approved & Railroad Grade **terminology,** as defined and used in this ***BOOK***.

1. **RAILROAD STANDARDS** = A commission or board appointed by the railroad companies outlined a set of **guidelines** to be accepted or approved by each railroad line.

2. **RAILROAD APPROVED** = A ***LIST*** of watches each railroad line would approve if purchased by their employee's. (this list changed through the years).

3. **RAILROAD GRADE** = A watch made by manufactures to meet or exceed the guidelines set by the railroad **standards**. Grades such as 992, Vanguard and B.W. Raymond, etc.

🕐 Some GRADES **exceeded** the R.R. standards such as 23 jewels, diamond end stone, gold train, raised gold jewel settings, double sunk dial and the list goes on. Examples: such as Veritas, Sangamo, 950 & Riverside Maximus and many others.

ABOVE: **GENERIC, NAMELESS OR UNMARKED MOVEMENTS**

Generic, Nameless or Unmarked grades for watch movements are listed under the Company name or initials of the Company, etc. by size, jewel count and description. Such as American Watch Co. or Amn Watch Co. or A.W.W.Co., Elgin W. Co. or Elgin National W. Co., Hampden W.Co. or Duber W.Co., Illinois W. Co.or I.W.Co., Rockford or R.W.Co., South Bend. **Example** name on movement Illinois Watch Co. and the watch is 18 size, 17 jewels, stem wind, adjusted, nickel, and damaskeened this watch can be found and will be listed under Illinois Watch Co. next look under the correct size (18 size) unmarked grade section as **Illinois Watch Co. or I.W.C., 15J, SW, ADJ, NI, DMK** these are Generic or unmarked grades. Movements with a grade **name** such as Bunn can be found and listed under **SIZE** then the name **Bunn** & jewels & etc..

MODEL = Size, open face or hunter, full or 3/4 plate, key or stem wind, design & layout of parts.
GRADE= 1st., 2nd., & 3rd., Quality etc. some manufactures used names or numbers (**Bunn , 992**).

🕐 **The Complete Price Guide to Watches goal is to stimulate the orderly exchange of Watches between "buyers" and "sellers".**

🕐 Watch terminology or communication in this book has evolved over the years, in search of better and more precise language with a effort to improve, purify, adjust itself and make it easier to understand.

ABBOTT'S STEM WIND

Henry Abbott first patented his stem wind attachment on June 30, 1876. The complete Abbott's stem wind mechanism is arranged in such a way as to convert key wind to stem wind. He also made a repeater-type slide mechanism for winding. On January 18, 1881, he received a patent for an improved stem wind attachment. Abbott sold over 50,000 wind attachments, and were fitted to Cornell, Elgin, Hampden, Illinois, N.Y. W. Co., Rockford, Tremont, U.S. Marion, Waltham 16-18-20 size and Howard above S# 30,000.

 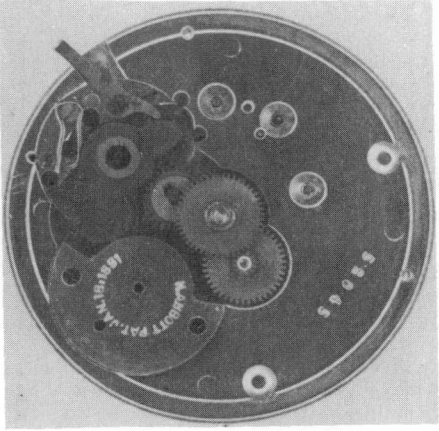

Abbott Stem Wind Attachment. LEFT: normal view of an Illinois watch movement with 'hidden' Abbott Stem Wind Attachment (pat. Jan., 18th, 1881). **RIGHT:** Same watch with dial removed exposing the Abbott Stem Wind Attachment. NOTE: Most Abbott's stem wind levers move up and down, while most standard levers move up & out.

ABBOTT WATCH CO.
(MADE BY **HOWARD WATCH CO.**) 1908 - 1912

Abbott Sure Time Watches were made by the E. Howard Watch Co.(Keystone), and are similar to Howard Watch Co. 1905 model. These watches sold for $8.75 and had 17 jewels. Some of the open face watches are actually hunting case models without the second bits register.

Description	Avg	Ex-Fn	Mint
Abbott Sure Time, 16S, 17J, OF, GF Case .... ★	$80	$125	$300
Abbott Sure Time, 16S, 17J, HC, GF Case	100	150	400
Abbott Sure Time, 16S, 17J, **14K Abbott HC** .... ⬧	300	400	700

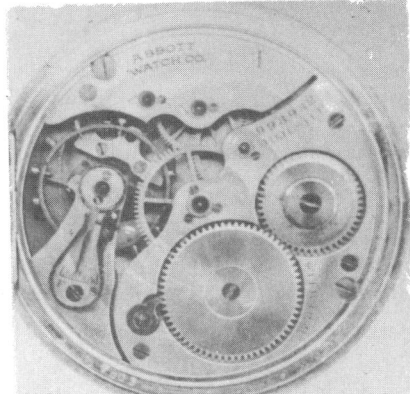 

Abbott Watch Co., 16 size, 17 jewels, gold jeweled settings, hunting case. Note similarity to the Howard Watch Co. model 1905. Serial number 993932.

Abbott Watch Co., 16 size, 17 jewels, gold jeweled settings, open face. Note similarity to the Howard Watch Co. series 9.

ADAMS AND PERRY WATCH MANUFACTURING CO.

Lancaster, Pennsylvania
1874 - 1877

This company, like so many others, did not have sufficient capital to stay in business for long. The first year was spent in setting up and becoming incorporated. The building was completed in mid-1875, and watches were being produced by September. The first watches were limited to three grades, and the escapement and balance were bought from other sources. By December 1875, the company was short of money and,by the spring of 1876, they had standardized their movements to 18 size. The first movement went on sale (**very few watches were sold from this factory name**) April 7, 1876. The next year the company remained idle. In August 1877, the company was sold to the Lancaster Watch Company. In 1892 Hamilton acquired the assets.

Description		Avg	Ex-Fn	Mint
19S, 20J, GJS, PS, KW, 18K original	★ ★ ★	$2,000	$2,500	$5,000
19S, 20J, GJS, PS	★ ★	900	1,500	3,000

Lancaster Watch Penna. movement. This basic model consists of 20 jewels, gold jeweled settings, key wind and pendant set, serial number 1681.

J. H. ALLISON movement 16 jewels,gold train and escape wheel with a pivoted detent, key wind and key set, serial number 19.

J. H. ALLISON

Detroit, Michigan
1853 - 1890

The first watch J. H. Allison made was in 1853; it was a chronometer with full plate and a fusee with chain drive. The balance had time screws and sliding weights. In 1864, he made a 3/4 plate chronometer with gold wheels. He also damaskeened the nickel movement. He produced only about 25 watches, of which 20 were chronometers. By 1883 he was making 3/4 plate movements with a stem wind of his own design.Allison made most of his own parts and designed his own tools. He also altered some key wind watches to stem wind. Allison died in 1890.

Description		Avg	Ex-Fn	Mint
Full Plate & 3\4 Plate, GT, NI, DMK	★ ★ ★ ★	$5,000	$7,000	$18,000
Detent Chronometer Escapement, 16J, KW/KS, GT	★ ★ ★ ★	9,000	$12,000	20,000

⊕ **The Complete Price Guide to Watches goal is to stimulate the orderly exchange of <u>Watches</u> between "*buyers*" and "*sellers*".**

AMERICAN REPEATING WATCH CO.

Elizabeth, New Jersey

1885 - 1892

Around 1675, a repeating mechanism was attached to a clock for the first time. The first repeating watch was made about 1687 by Thomas Tompion or Daniel Quare. Five-minute, quarter-hour and half-hour repeaters were popular by 1730. The minute repeater became common about 1830.

Fred Terstegen applied for a patent on August 21, 1882, for a repeating attachment that would work with any American key-wind or stem-wind watch. He was granted three patents: No. 311,270 on January 27, 1885; No. 421,844 on February 18, 1890; and No. 436,162 in September 1890. It is not known how many repeaters were made, but it is estimated to be about **500** to **1,000**. This repeating attachment fits most American **18 & 16** size movements. The Terstegen repeating attachments were made and sold as a **KIT** to fit different models of American watches.

18 SIZE, with REPEATER ATTACHMENT

Name — Description		Avg	Ex-Fn	Mint
HOWARD, w/ 5 min. repeater attachment, COIN	★★	$3,500	$4,500	$6,500
GOLD CASE	★★	6,000	7,000	10,000
Keystone,or Lancaster, w/ 5 min. rep. attachment, COIN	★★	3,000	3,500	5,700
GOLD CASE	★★	3,300	4,500	6,600
SETH THOMAS,w/ 5 min. repeater attachment, COIN	★★	3,000	3,500	4,900
GOLD CASE	★★	3,500	4,500	7,000

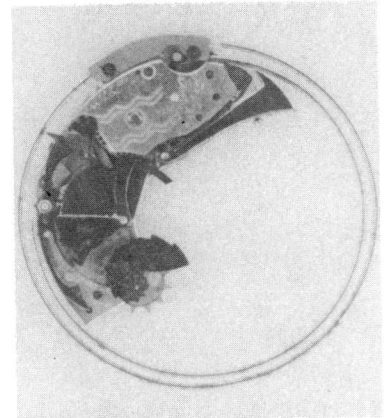 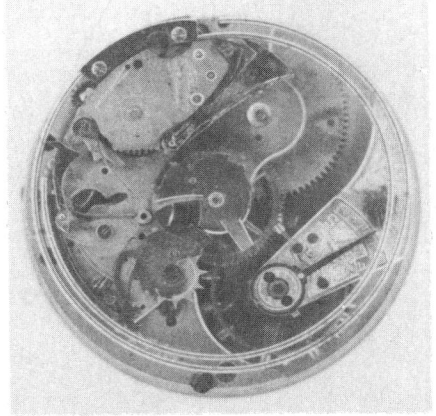

ABOVE: **American Repeating Attachment**. illustration at **LEFT** shows Terstegen's patented repeating attachment only. Illustration at **RIGHT** shows attachment as normally found on movement. The two outside circles on left illustration are wire gongs. The hammer can be seen at upper **LEFT** Illustration in the shape of a boot.

🕐 Watches listed in this book are priced at the collectable fair market value at the **Trade Show** level, as complete watches having an original 14k gold filled case, KEY WIND with silver, an original white enamel single sunk dial, and with the entire original movement in good working order with no repairs needed, unless otherwise noted.

🕐 Some grades are not included. Their values can be determined by comparing with **similar** age, size, metal content, style, models and grades listed.

16 SIZE, with REPEATER ATTACHMENT

Name — Description	Avg	Ex-Fn	Mint
COLUMBUS, w/ 5 min. rep. attachment, GF or COIN .... ★★	$3,000	$3,500	$5,500
GOLD CASE .... ★★	4,000	4,500	6,500
ELGIN, w/ 5 min. rep. attachment, GF or COIN .... ★★	3,000	3,500	5,500
GOLD CASE .... ★★	4,000	4,500	6,500
HAMPDEN, w/ 5 min. rep. attachment, GF or COIN .... ★★	2,500	3,000	4,500
GOLD CASE .... ★★	3,000	4,000	6,000
HOWARD, w/ 5 min. rep. attachment, GF or COIN .... ★★	3,500	4,500	6,500
GOLD CASE .... ★★	6,000	7,000	10,000
ILLINOIS, w/ 5 min. rep. attachment, GF or COIN .... ★★	3,000	4,000	6,000
GOLD CASE .... ★★	4,500	5,500	8,500
Non-magnetic (Paillard),w/ 5 min. rep. attachment, gold-filled ★★	2,000	3,000	4,500
GOLD CASE .... ★★	3,000	4,000	6,000

NOVEL STRIKING ATTACHMENTS

Five-Minute Repeaters.

(Manufactured under Terstegen's Patents.)

They are made to fit the following American Watch Movements :

16 SIZE

ILLINOIS
COLUMBUS
HOWARD
HAMPDEN
NON-MAGNETIC
   PAILLARD
WALTHAM and
ELGIN

18 SIZE

ONLY TO

LANCASTER
or
KEYSTONE
SETH THOMAS
and
HOWARD

HUNTING OR OPEN-FACE.

Handsome, Simple and Durable.

American Repeating Watch Factory

of Elizabeth, N. J.

🕐 A collector should expect to pay modestly higher prices at local shops.

🕐 Watches listed in this book are priced at the **collectable fair market value** at the Trade Show level, as complete watches having an original 14k gold filled case, KEY WIND with silver, an original white enamel single sunk dial, and with the entire original movement in good working order with no repairs needed, unless otherwise noted.

🕐 Some grades are not included. Their values can be determined by comparing with **similar** age, size, metal content, style, models and grades listed.

🕐 **The Complete Price Guide to Watches goal is to stimulate the orderly exchange of <u>Watches</u> between "***buyers***" and "***sellers***".**

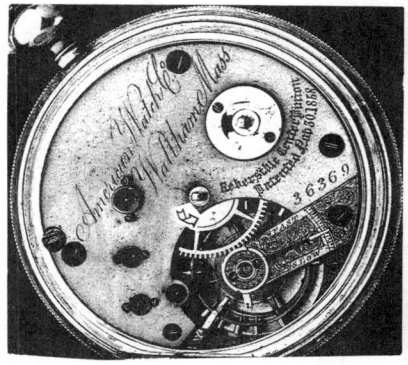

American Watch Co., Model 18KW, 18 size, 15 jewels, serial number 36369. Reversible clutch center pinion, patented Nov. 30th, 1858. Note: Thin disk at the center of the center wheel.

Model 1857, 18 size, 15-16 jewels, "**Chronodrometer**" on dial, "Appleton Tracy & Co." or "P.S. Bartlett, key wind & set, 1/4 jump seconds, S.# 14,752 . Listed under "**Appleton Tracy & Co. Chronodrometer**", lst serial # 13,701. Note: Stop - start botton at 4 o'clock.

18 SIZE
MODELS 1857, (18 KW =1859), 1870, 1877, 1879, 1883, 1892

Grade or Name – Description		Avg	Ex-Fn	Mint
American Watch Co., 17J,3/4, M#1859 or M#**18KW**	★ ★ ★ ★	$3,000	$4,000	$8,000
American Watch Co., 19J, 3/4, M#1859	★ ★ ★ ★	5,500	7,500	12,500
American Watch Co., 15J, M#1859,3/4, Pat. Nov. 30, 1858,				
Reversible center pinion, original silver case	★ ★ ★	4,200	5,200	8,900
American Watch Co., 17J, M#1859,3/4, KW, Fitts Pat.				
Reversible center pinion, Originial **18K case**	★ ★ ★ ★	5,000	6,000	10,000
American Watch Co., 21J, M#1883, Special, ADJ, GJS	★ ★ ★ ★	850	1,100	2,200
☉ Generic, nameless or unmarked grades for watch movements are listed under the Company name or initials of the Company, etc. by size, jewel count and description.				
AM'n. Watch Co., 15J, M#1857, (*Waltham W. Co.*), KW, KS		$165	$210	$395
AM'n. Watch Co., 15J, M#1857, (*Waltham W. Co.*), SW / KS	★	195	300	500
AM'n. Watch Co., 15J, M#1857, (*Waltham W. Co.*), SW / KW	★	195	300	500
AM'n. Watch Co., 15-17J, M#1857, (*Waltham W. Co.)*, SW / LS		165	200	400
AM'n. Watch Co., 17J, M#1857, KW, KS	★	165	200	400
AM'n. Watch Co., **14K, HC, heavy box hinged, multi - 4 colors**		2,500	3,500	5,500
AM'n. Watch Co., 11J, thin model, KW, 3/4 plate	★	125	195	500
AM'n Watch Co., 15J, M#1870, KW		125	195	500
AM'n. Watch Co., 17J, M#1870, KW, ADJ		150	250	550
AM'n. Watch Co., 17J, M#1892		125	150	350
AM'n. Watch Co., 21J, M#1892		195	295	500
AM'n. Watch Co., 7J, M#1877		90	125	250
AM'n. Watch Co., 11J, M#1877		90	125	250
AM'n. Watch Co., 7J, M#1883, SW/ KW		90	125	250
AM'n. Watch Co., 11-13J, M#1883, SW/ KW		90	125	250
AM'n. Watch Co., 15J, M#1883, SW/ KW		100	150	295
AM'n Watch Co., 16-17J, M#1883		100	150	300
Appleton, Tracy & Co., 15J, M#1857, SW / LS		150	200	400
Appleton, Tracy & Co., 7-11J, M#1857		150	200	400
Appleton, Tracy & Co., 11J, thin model, KW,3/4	★	225	325	600
Appleton, Tracy & Co., 15J, M#1857, KW		125	195	400
Appleton, Tracy & Co., 15-16J, M#1857, KW,				
serial # below 10,000	★	800	1,000	2,000

☉ Some watch manufacturers personalize watches for jobbers or jewelry firms, with exclusive private signed or marked movements. The valuable collectable watches are listed under the signed or marked movement. Other exclusive private signed or marked movements will have equivalent value are only slightly higher value and should be compared to Generic or Nameless movements. Railroad signed or marked (dials & movements) are usually more collectable & higher in value.

Grade or Name–Description	Avg	Ex-Fn	Mint
Appleton, Tracy & Co., 15J, M#1859, 3/4, reverse pinion,			
Pat. Nov. 30, 1858, orig. silver case .... ★ ★ ★	$1,500	$1,800	$3,800
Appleton, Tracy & Co., 11-15-16-17J, KW, 3/4, M# 1859 .... ★	195	295	600
Appleton, Tracy & Co., 16J, M#1857, **Ist run** (5,001-5,100)			
Am.W. Co. (Eagle) silver HC .... ★ ★ ★ ★	1,300	1,700	3,500
Appleton, Tracy & Co., 15J, M#1857, KW, **18K HC**..............	1,000	1,500	3,200
Appleton, Tracy & Co., 15J, M#1857, KW	225	300	600
Appleton, Tracy & Co., 15J, 3/4, KW, with vibrating hairspring stud,			
Stratton's Pat., coin case .... ★ ★ ★	1,600	2,400	4,000
Appleton, Tracy & Co., 15J, 3/4, KW, with vibrating hairspring stud,			
orig. **18K case** .... ★ ★ ★	2,500	3,500	5,500
Appleton, Tracy & Co., **Sporting, (Chronodrometer)**,M#1857,			
15-16J, KW,KS, orig. case, with stop feature............ ★ ★	2,500	3,500	5,500
Appleton, Tracy & Co., 15J, 3/4, M# 1859, KW........................ ★	195	295	500
Appleton, Tracy & Co., 11-15J, M#s 1877, 1879, SW	65	120	300
Appleton, Tracy & Co., 15J, M#1877, KW	65	120	300
Appleton, Tracy & Co., 15J, M#s 1877-1879, SW, OF	65	120	300
Appleton, Tracy & Co., 15J, M#s 1877-1879, SW, HC	95	195	350
Appleton, Tracy & Co., 15J, M#1883, SW, OF	65	120	300
Appleton, Tracy & Co., 15J, M#1883, SW, **non- magnet,** OF	125	195	350
Appleton, Tracy & Co., 15-17J, M#1883, **gold plate** -Mvt.	150	225	400
Appleton, Tracy & Co., 15J, M#1883, SW, HC	95	150	300
Appleton, Tracy & Co., 15J, M#1892, SW, OF .... ★ ★	225	325	650
Appleton, Tracy & Co., 17J, M#1883, SW, HC	65	120	300
Appleton, Tracy & Co., 17J, M#1892, SW, Premiere	65	120	300
Appleton, Tracy & Co., 17J, M#1892, NI, SW, OF	65	120	300
Appleton, Tracy & Co., 17J, M#1883, OF	65	120	300
Appleton, Tracy & Co., 17J, M#1892, SW, HC	120	150	295
Appleton, Tracy & Co., 19J, M#1892, SW, OF	195	275	450
Appleton, Tracy & Co., 19J, M#1892, SW, HC	250	350	500
Appleton, Tracy & Co., 21J, M#1892, SW, OF	200	275	450
Appleton, Tracy & Co., 21J, M#1892, SW, HC	250	350	500

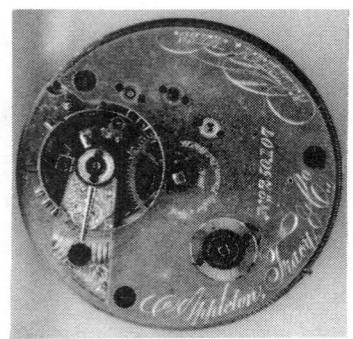

Appleton, Tracy & Co. (20 size), 15-17 jewels, Fogg's safety pinion pat. Feb. 14, 1865, key wind & set from back, serial number 250107.

P. S. Bartlett, Model 18KW or 1859, 18 size, 11 jewels, key wind & set from back, serial number 41597.

🕐 A collector should expect to pay modestly higher prices at local shops.

🕐 **The Complete Price Guide to Watches goal is to stimulate the orderly exchange of <u>Watches</u> between "*buyers*" and "*sellers*".**

🕐 Generic, nameless or unmarked grades for watch movements are listed under the Company name or initials of the Company, etc. by size, jewel count and description.

Grade or Name – Description	Avg	Ex-Fn	Mint
A. W. W. Co., 7-9J, M#1883, **KW,** ....★	$200	$275	$550
A. W. W. Co., 7-9J, M#1883, SW	70	95	200
A. W. W. Co., 11-13J, LS, HC............................	70	95	200
A. W. W. Co., 11-13J, M#1879, OF............................	70	95	200
A. W. W. Co., 11-13J, M#1883, SW, OF............................	70	95	200
A. W. W. Co., 15J, OF	70	95	200
A. W. W. Co., 15J, HC............................	70	95	200
A. W. W. Co., 15J, **14K multi-color boxcase HC**	2,400	3,000	5,000
A. W. W. Co., 15J, M#1879, OF............................	70	95	200
A. W. W. Co., 15J, M#1883............................	70	95	200
A. W. W. Co., 16 or 18J, OF or HC............................	100	125	200
A. W. W. Co., 17J, M#1857, gold bal. wheel, GJS, ...★	300	400	650
A. W. W. Co., 17J, "for R.R. Service" on dial ....★★	550	750	1,100
A. W. W. Co., 17J, M#1883, OF............................	90	125	250
A. W. W. Co., 17J, M#1883, HC............................	100	150	300
A. W. W. Co., 17J, M#1892, LS, OF............................	75	100	200
A. W. W. Co., 17J, M#1892, PS, OF............................	75	100	200
A. W. W. Co., 17J, M#1892, HC............................	100	150	275
A. W. W. Co., 19J, M#1892............................	150	200	450
A. W. W. Co., 21J, M#1892............................	250	300	650
A. W. W. Co., 23J, M#1892............................	300	450	800

P.S. Bartlett, 18 size, 15 jewels, Model 1857, Engraved on back "4 PR. Jewels." Serial number 13446.

Marked Canadian Railway Time Service, Model 1892, 18 size, 17 jewels, serial number 22,017,534.

Grade or Name – Description	Avg	Ex-Fn	Mint
P. S. Bartlett, 7J, M#1857, KW, **1st Run** (1,401-1,500)			
Am.W. Co. (Eagle) silver HC ....★★★★	$2,000	$3,000	$6,500
P. S. Bartlett, 15J, M#1857, KW, **2nd Run** (1,551-1,650)			
Am.W. Co. (Eagle) silver HC ....★★★	1,500	2,000	4,000
P. S. Bartlett, 11J, M#1857, KW, **3rd Run** ....★	700	800	1,800
P. S. Bartlett, 15J, M#1857, KW, **3rd Run** ....★	750	850	1,900
P. S. Bartlett, 7J, M#1857, KW............................	150	175	300
P. S. Bartlett, 11J, M#1857, KW............................	175	200	350
P. S. Bartlett, 15J, M#1857, KW............................	150	175	300
P. S. Bartlett, 15J, M#1857, KW , S# below 250,000 (Pre Civil War)	350	450	800
P. S. Bartlett, 11-15J, M#1857, KW, Eagle inside case lid	350	450	800
P. S. Bartlett, 15J, M#1857, SW / LS **(note let down screw)**	250	300	600
P. S. Bartlett, 7-11J, M#1859, KW/KS............................	175	200	400
P. S. Bartlett, 11-15J, M#1877, KW	100	150	300

Grade or Name – Description	Avg	Ex-Fn	Mint
P. S. Bartlett, 11J, M#1879, KW	$85	$100	$200
P. S. Bartlett, 15J, M#1879, KW	95	125	250
P. S. Bartlett, 11J, M#1883, SW	70	95	200
P. S. Bartlett, 15J, M#1883, **KW** ★	195	295	500
P. S. Bartlett, 15J, M#1883, SW	70	95	200
P. S. Bartlett, 17J, M#1883, SW	70	95	200
P. S. Bartlett, 11J, M#1859, 3/4, thin model, KS from back	400	500	1,000
P. S. Bartlett, 15J, M#1859, 3/4, thin model, KS from back	500	600	1,100
P. S. Bartlett, 15J, **pinned plates**, M#1857, KW ★ ★	700	900	1,600
P. S. Bartlett, 15J, M#1892, SW ★	100	200	350
P. S. Bartlett, 17J, M#1892, SW, OF, LS	95	125	300
P. S. Bartlett, 17J, M#1892, SW, HC	125	200	375
P. S. Bartlett, 17J, M#1892, SW, OF, PS	95	125	300
P. S. Bartlett, 17J, M#1892, SW, **2-Tone**	150	250	400
P. S. Bartlett, 19J, M#1892, SW	150	250	400
P. S. Bartlett, 21J, M#1892, SW	225	275	450
P. S. Bartlett, 21J, M#1892, SW, **2-Tone**	250	350	600
Broadway, 7J, M#1857, KW, HC	100	150	400
Broadway, 11J, M#1857, KW, HC	125	175	400
Broadway, 7-11J, M#1877, KW, SW, NI, HC	100	150	400
Broadway, 7J, M#1883, KW, HC	100	150	400
Broadway, 11J, M#1883, KW, HC	100	150	400
Broadway, 11J, M#1883, SW, HC	100	150	250
Canadian Pacific R.R., 17J, M#1883 ★ ★	550	750	1,400
Canadian Pacific R.R., 17J, M#1892 ★ ★	700	900	1,800
Canadian Pacific R.R., 21J, M#1892 ★ ★	850	1,100	2,250
Canadian Railway Time Service, 17J, M#1883-1892, Adj.5P.. ★ ★	500	700	1,000
Central Park, 15J, M#1857, KW	200	250	400
Champion, 15J, M#1877, OF	60	80	175
Conklins Railroad Special, 21J, G#1892 ★ ★	550	650	950

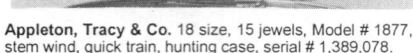

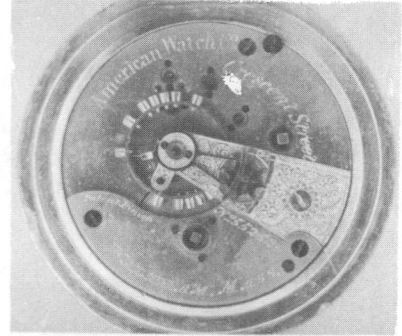

Appleton, Tracy & Co. 18 size, 15 jewels, Model # 1877, stem wind, quick train, hunting case, serial # 1,389,078.

Crescent Street, Model 1870, 18 size, 15 J., Key wind & set from back, serial number 552,526. This grade was the **first** American watch to be advertised as a railroad watch.

IMPORTANT NOTE: Railroad Standards, Railroad Approved & Railroad Grade **terminology**, as defined and used in this **_BOOK_**.
1. **RAILROAD STANDARDS** = A commission or board appointed by the railroad companies outlined a set of **guidelines** to be accepted or approved by each railroad line.
2. **RAILROAD APPROVED** = A **_LIST_** of watches each railroad line would approve if purchased by their employee's. (this list changed through the years).
3. **RAILROAD GRADE** = A watch made by manufactures to meet or exceed the guidelines set by the railroad **standards**. Grades such as 992, Vanguard and B.W. Raymond, etc.
Some GRADES **exceeded** the R.R. standards such as 23 jewels, diamond end stone, gold train, raised gold jewel settings, double sunk dial and the list goes on. Examples: such as Veritas, Sangamo, 950 & Riverside Maximus and many others.

Grade or Name–Description	Avg	Ex-Fn	Mint
Crescent Street, 15J, M#1870, KW...	$150	$225	$450
Crescent Street, 15J, M#1870, **pin or nail set**................................	175	250	500
Crescent Street, 17J, M#1870, KW/SW ....★	175	250	500
Crescent Street, 15J, M#1870, SW	85	125	295
Crescent Street, 15J, M#1883, SW, non-magnetic, OF	85	125	295
Crescent Street, 15J, M#1883, SW, non-magnetic, HC	125	175	395
Crescent Street, 15J, M#1883, SW, 2-Tone	125	175	395
Crescent Street, 17J, M#1883, SW, OF	75	100	275
Crescent Street, 17J, M#1883, SW, HC	95	150	300
Crescent Street, 19J, M#1883 ....★	195	295	550
Crescent Street, 17J, M#1892, SW, **GJS**	100	165	275
Crescent Street, 17J, M#1892, SW, OF	95	150	250
Crescent Street, 17J, M#1892, SW, HC	125	195	300
Crescent Street, 19J, M#1892, SW, Adj.5P, GJS ,OF.....................	150	225	350
Crescent Street, 19J, M#1892, SW, Adj.5P, GJS ,HC	185	250	450
Crescent Street, 21J, M#1892, SW, Adj.5P, GJS, OF	200	295	500
Crescent Street, 21J, M#1892, SW, Adj.5P, GJS, HC	250	325	550
Crescent Street, 21J, M#1892, **Wind Indicator** ....★	1,100	1,400	2,200
Cronometro Supremo, 21J, M#1892, Adj., GJS, OF............. ★★★	500	600	900
Cronometro Victoria, 17J, dial & mvt. marked Adjusted...... ★★★	500	600	900
Samuel Curtis, 11-15J, M#1857, KW, S# less than **200**,			
original 17S silver case ....★★	2,800	3,300	6,000
Samuel Curtis, 11-15J, M#1857, KW, S# less than **400**,			
original 17S silver case ....★★	2,200	2,800	5,000
Samuel Curtis, 11-15J, M#1857, KW, S# less than **600**,			
original 17S silver case ....★★	2,000	2,300	4,000
Samuel Curtis, 11-15J, M#1857, KW, S# less than **1,000**,			
original 17S silver case ....★★	1,800	2,100	3,500
(Samuel Curtis **"not"** in original silver case, deduct $800 to $1,000 from value)			
Dennison, Howard, Davis, 7J, M#1857, KW, W/**original case**	1,000	1,800	3,000
Dennison, Howard, Davis, 11-13J, M#1857, KW, W/**original case**	1,200	1,900	3,200
Dennison, Howard, Davis, 15J, M#1857, KW, W/**original case** ...	1,400	2,000	3,500
Dennison, Howard, Davis, 15J, M#1857, KW, 1st. run (**1,002-1,100**)			
W/**original** case Am.W. Co. (**Eagle**)silver HC .... ★★★	1,600	2,500	3,800
Dennison, Howard, Davis, 15J, M#1857, KW, S# less than **2,000**			
W/**original** case Am.W. Co. (**Eagle**)silver HC .... ★	1,200	1,900	3,200

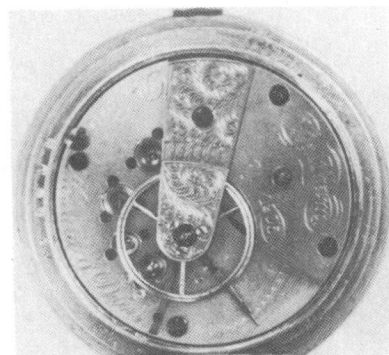

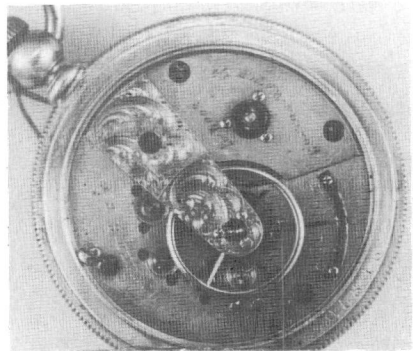

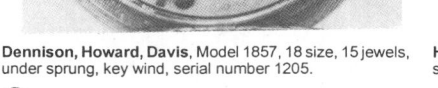

Dennison, Howard, Davis, Model 1857, 18 size, 15 jewels, under sprung, key wind, serial number 1205.

Howard & Rice, Model 1857, 18 size, 15 jewels, under sprung, serial number 6003.

🕐 Watches listed in this book are priced at the collectable Trade Show level, as **complete** watches having an original 14k gold-filled case and Key Wind with silver, an original white enamel single sunk dial, and with the entire original movement in good working order with no repairs needed.

Grade or Name –Description		Avg	Ex-Fn	Mint
D.& R.G. Special (Denver & Rio Grande), 17J, M#1892, GJS, Adj.5P	★★★	$2,500	$3,000	$6,000
D.& R.G. Special (Denver & Rio Grande), 21J, M#1892, GJS, Adj.5P	★★★	3,000	3,500	6,500
Dominion Railways, 15-17J, M#1883, OF, SW, train on dial	★★★	2,500	3,000	6,000
Wm. Ellery, 7-11J, M#1857, Boston, Mass. all original silver HC case with Am. Watch Co.& eagle, serial # below **46,600**	★★	395	550	900
Wm. Ellery, 7-11J, M#1857, Boston, Mass.		95	150	350
Wm. Ellery, 7-11J, M#KW, 3/4		95	150	350
Wm. Ellery, 15J, KW, 3/4	★	200	250	500
Wm. Ellery, 7-11J, M#18KW, KW-KS from back, **18K, HC**		1,400	1,800	3,500
Wm. Ellery, 7J, M#1857, KW, KS from back		195	275	550
Wm. Ellery, 15J, M#1857, **SW / LS**, (note let down screw)	★	200	300	600
Wm. Ellery, 7-15J, M#1877, M#1879, KW		95	150	300
Wm. Ellery, 11-15J, M#1877 & 1879, SW		95	150	300
Wm. Ellery, 7-13J, M#1883		95	150	300
Excelsior, M#1877, KW		95	150	300
Export, 7-11J, M#1877		95	150	300
Export, 7-11J, M#1883, KW		95	150	300
Express Train, 15-17J, M# 1883, LS, OF	★★	400	500	800
Favorite, 15J, M#1877		95	150	300
Fellows & Schell, 15J, KW, KS, 1857 model	★★★	2,500	3,400	7,000
Franklin, 7J, M#1877, SW		125	175	400
Home Watch Co., 7-15J, M#1857-1883, KW		80	125	250
Home Watch Co., 7J, M#1877, KW		80	125	250
Home Watch Co., 7-11J, M#1879, SW		80	125	250
Howard & Rice, 15J, M#1857, KW, KS, **mvt. by Waltham,** (serial numbers range from 6,000 to 6,500)	★★★	2,400	2,800	5,000
E. Howard & Co., Boston (on dial & mvt.), English style escape wheel, upright pallets, 15J, M#1857, KW, KS, mvt. by Waltham, S#s about 6,400 to 6,500	★★★★	3,000	4,000	8,000
Lehigh Valley Railroad 17J, M#1883, SW, Appleton, Tracy & Co. grade	★★	1,000	1,500	2,200
Lehigh Valley Railroad 17J, M#1883, SW, **2 tone mvt.** Appleton, Tracy & Co. grade	★★	1,500	2,000	3,000
Martyn Square, 7-15J, M#1857-77-79, KW, SW (exported)	★	200	250	500
Mermod, Jaccard & King Paragon Timekeeper, **23J,** M#1892, Vanguard, LS, GJS, HC	★★	500	650	900

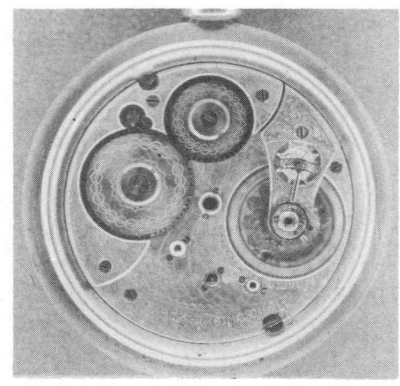

Pennsylvania Special, Model 1892, 18 size, 21 jewels, serial number 14,000,015.

American Waltham Watch Co., Model 1883, 18 size, 15 jewels, serial number 3,093,425.

Grade or Name –Description	Avg	Ex-Fn	Mint
Non-Magnetic, 15J, SW, LS, NI	$100	$150	$300
Non-Magnetic, 17J, M#1892, SW, LS	125	175	375
Paragon, 15J, M#1883, HC ★	295	350	600
"Chas. T. Parker" marked, 11-15J, M#1857, KW, HC ★★	1,500	1,900	3,200
C. T. Parker, 7-11J, M#1857, KW, Am.W. Co. (Eagle) silver HC serial # below 1,200 ★★	1,800	2,400	4,000
C. T. Parker, 7-11J, M#1857, KW, Am.W. Co. 18K, HC serial # below 1,200 ★★	2,000	3,000	5,000
Pennsylvania R.R. on dial, Appleton, Tracy & Co. on Mvt., KW, KS, M# 1857 ★★★★★	4,000	5,000	10,000
Pennsylvania Special, 21J, M#1892, HC ★★★	2,500	3,200	4,500
Pennsylvania Special, 21J, M#1892, OF ★★★	3,000	3,800	5,000
Pennsylvania Special, 21J, M#1892, HC GOLD DAMASKEENED, gold train ★★★★★	9,000	12,000	18,000
Pennsylvania Special, 23J, M#1892, OF ★★★★	4,000	5,000	7,000
Pioneer, 7J, M#1883	65	75	150
Premier, 17J, M#1892, LS, OF	80	100	175
Railroader, 17J, M#1892, LS ★★★	2,000	2,400	3,500
Railroader, 21J, M#1892, LS, ★★★	2,500	3,000	4,500
Railroad inspector, 21J, M#1892, LS, (loaner with # on case) ★★	600	750	1,500
Railroad King, 15J, M#1883, LS ★★	350	450	850
Railroad King, 15J, M#1883, 2-Tone ★★	375	550	900
Railroad King, 17J, Special, M#1883, LS ★★	425	600	950
Railroad Standard, 19J, G#1892, OF ★★★	1,200	1,800	2,800
Railwaw TimeKeeper 15J, Gilded ★★	200	250	500
Riverside, 17J, M#1892 ★	150	225	450
Roadmaster, 17J, M#1892, LS ★★	600	700	1,200
R. E. Robbins, 11-15J, M#1857, KW S# (25,101-25,200) ★★	1,400	1,600	3,000
R. E. Robbins, 13-15J, M#1877, KW	225	300	600
R. E. Robbins, 13J, M#1883	125	150	300
Royal, 17J, M#1892, OF	100	125	250
Royal, 17J, M#1892, HC	150	175	300

Sidereal, model #1892, 17j, 24 hour dial used by astrono-mers. (marked Sidereal on dial)

Vanguard, model 1892, 18S, 23J, diamond end stone, gold jewel settings, exposed winding gears, S# 10,533,465.

🕐 A collector should expect to pay modestly higher prices at local shops.

🕐 **The Complete Price Guide to Watches goal is to stimulate the orderly exchange of** <u>Watches</u> **between** *"buyers"* **and** *"sellers"*.

Grade or Name – Description	Avg	Ex-Fn	Mint
Santa Fe Route, 17J, M#1883-92, HC-OF ★★	$500	$650	$1,200
Santa Fe Route, 21J, M#1892, OF ★★	750	900	1,400
Santa Fe Route, 21J, M#1892, HC ★★★	850	1,000	2,000
Sidereal, M#1892, 19J, (marked **Sidereal** on dial) OF ★★★	1,500	2,000	3,600
M#1892, 17J, Astronomical (marked **Sidereal** on dial) OF.. ★★★	1,500	2,000	3,600
Sol, 7-11J, M#1883, (with sun on dial), OF ★	150	250	500
Sol, 17J, OF	80	125	200
Special Railroad, 17J, M#1883, LS, OF ★★	400	500	900
Special R. R. King, 15-17J, M#1883 ★★	450	550	1,000
Special R. R. King, 15-17J, M#1883, HC ★★	500	650	1,200
Sterling, 7J, M#1857, KW, **Silver** case	125	150	300
Sterling, 7-11J, M#1877, M#1879	65	110	195
Sterling, 7-11J, M#1883, **KW** ★	100	125	250
Sterling, 11-15J, M#1883, SW	65	110	195
Tourist, 11J, M#1877	65	110	195
Tourist, 7J, M#1877	65	110	195
Tracy, Baker & Co., 15J, **18K original A.W.W. Co.** case ★★★★★	9,000	15,000	30,000
Vanguard, 17J, M#1892, GJS, HC ★★	450	600	1,000
Vanguard, 17J, M#1892, LS, Adj.5P, DR, GJS, OF ★★	400	500	900
Vanguard, 17J, M#1892, **Wind Indicator**, Adj.5P, DR, GJS . ★★	1,500	2,000	3,000
Vanguard, 19J, M#1892, LS, Adj.5P, Diamond end stones	195	300	550
Vanguard, 19J, M#1892, LS, Adj.5P, DR, GJS, OF	195	300	550
Vanguard, 19J, M#1892, **Wind Ind.**, LS, Adj.5P, DR, GJS ★	1,500	2,000	3,000
Vanguard, 19J, M#1892, Adj.5P, GJS, HC ★	325	400	700
Vanguard, 21J, M#1892, Adj.5P, PS	250	300	500
Vanguard, 21J, M#1892, GJS, Adj.5P, HC	325	400	600
Vanguard, 21J, M#1892, LS, Adj.5P, DR, GJS, OF	250	300	500
Vanguard, 21J, M#1892, LS, Adj.5P, Diamond end stone	250	300	500
Vanguard, 21J, M#1892, **Wind Indicator**, Adj.5P, GJS, OF ★	1,800	2,200	3,000
Vanguard, 23J, M#1892, LS, Adj.5P, DR, GJS, OF	295	350	550
Vanguard, 23J, M#1892, LS, Adj.5P, DR, GJS, HC ★	400	500	800
Vanguard, 23J, M#1892, LS, Adj.5P, DR, GJS, Diamond end stone	295	400	600
Vanguard, 23J, M#1892, PS, Adj.5P, DR, GJS, OF	300	400	600
Vanguard, 23J, M#1892, **Wind Indicator**, Adj.5P, OF. ★	2,500	3,000	4,200
Vanguard, 23J, M#1892, **Wind Indicator**, Adj.5P, HC .... ★★★★	3,500	4,500	6,500
Waltham,17J, Adj., G#1892, (**non magnetic**), OF	195	250	400
Waltham Standard,17J, Adj., G#1892, (locomotive)OF ★★★	850	1,000	2,000
Waltham Standard,19J, Adj., G#1892, (locomotive), OF ★★★	1,500	2,000	3,000
Waltham Watch Co., 15J, **M#1857**, SW / LS, (let down screw)	225	300	500

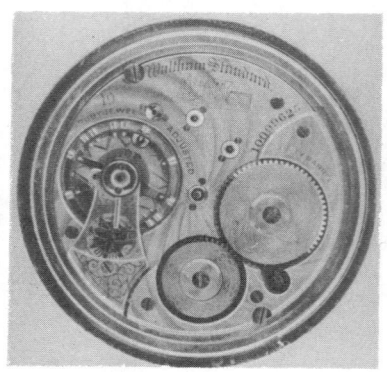

Waltham Standard, Grade 1892, 18 size, 19 jewels, Adj5P, open face, note engine & coal car (locomotive) engraved on movement, serial number 10,099,625.

Grade 845, Model 1892, 18 size, 21 jewels, railroad grade, Adj.5P, serial number 15,097,475

Waltham Watch Co., 1857 model with factory stem wind, 18S, 15J, S# 778763, Fogg's Patent. This is not a Abbott's stem wind conversion. NOTE **let down screw.** Most Abbott's stem wind with lever set, the levers move up and down, while most stem winds the levers move up & out.

J. WATSON, Boston Mass engraved on movement, 18 size, 11 jewels, hunting case, key wind key set, serial number 28,635, Ca. April 1863.

Grade or Name – Description		Avg	Ex-Fn	Mint
Warren, 15J, M#1857, KW, KS, **S#18-29**, original 17S silver case	★★★★★	$25,000	$35,000	$70,000
Warren, 15J, M#1857, KW, KS, **S#30-60**, original 17S silver case	★★★★	20,000	25,000	50,000
Warren, 15J, M#1857, KW, KS, **S#61-90**, original 17S silver case	★★★★	18,000	22,000	45,000
Warren, 15J, M#1857, KW, KS, **S#91-110**, original 17S silver case	★★★★	15,000	18,000	40,000
(Warren not in original silver case, deduct $5,000 to $10,000)				
George Washington, M#1857, KW	★★	600	750	1,600
George Washington, M#1879, SW		200	250	400
J. Watson, 7J, M#1857, KW, marked"Boston" ★ **S# (28,201-28,270)**	★★★	1,100	1,400	3,200
J. Watson, 7-11J, M#1857, KW, marked"London" **S# (23,700-23,800)**	★★★	1,100	1,400	3,200
454, 21J, GT, 3/4,	★	195	250	500
820, 15j, OF		65	95	150
845, 21J, M#1892, OF		195	250	500
845, 21J, M#1892, HC		295	350	600
836, 17J, DR, Adj.4P, LS, OF		75	100	195

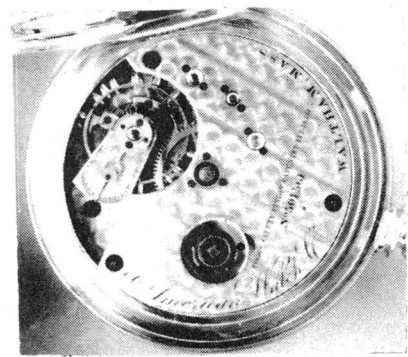

American Watch Co., Model 16KW or Model 1868, 16 size, key wind and set from back, Gold Train, serial number 501,561.

American Watch Co., Model 1888, 16 size, 19 jewels, gold jewel settings, gold train, high grade movement, serial number 5,000,297.

16 SIZE

MODELS 16KW =1860, 1868, 1872, 1888,

1899, 1908, BRIDGE MODEL

Grade or Name – Description	Avg	Ex-Fn	Mint
AM'n. Watch Co., 7-15J, M#1872, KW KS,			
sweep sec. with a **slide stop** button............................ ★ ★	$700	$800	$1,600
AM'n. Watch Co., 7-11J, M#1888, 3/4, SW	85	100	200
AM'n. Watch Co., 7-11J, M#1888-1899	85	100	195
AM'n. Watch Co., 11J, M#16KW or 1868, KW & KS from back,			
original silver case .... ★ ★	1,000	1,200	2,400
AM'n. Watch Co., 11J, M#1868, 3/4, KW	700	800	1,600
AM'n. Watch Co., 13J, M#1888-1899................................	100	125	250
AM'n. Watch Co., 15-17J, M#1868, 3/4, KW............................... ★	700	900	1,700
AM'n. Watch Co., 15J, M#1868-1872, 3/4, SW	300	500	1,000
AM'n. Watch Co., 15J, M#16KW, KW & KS from back .... ★ ★	500	700	1,500
AM'n. Watch Co., 15-16J, M#1888-1899, HC	80	120	350
AM'n. Watch Co., 15J, M#1888-1899, SW, HC............................	80	120	350
AM'n. Watch Co., 15J, M#1888-1899, SW, ...	60	95	225
AM'n. Watch Co., 16-17J, M#1872, 3/4, SW	195	250	650
AM'n. Watch Co., 17J, M#1888-1899................................	90	110	275
AM'n. Watch Co., 19J, M#1872, 3/4, SW........................... ★ ★ ★	1,200	1,600	2,800
AM'n. Watch Co., 19J, M#1899..	125	195	350

🕐 Generic, nameless or unmarked grades for watch movements are listed under the Company name or initials of the Company, etc. by size, jewel count and description.

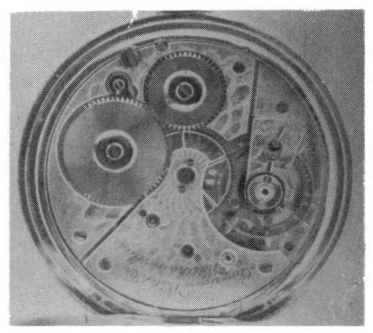

American Watch Co., Model 1888, 16 size, 21 jewels, gold train, note tadpole regulator.

American Watch Co., Bridge Model, 16size, 23 jewels gold train, Adj.5P.

Grade or Name –Description	Avg	Ex-Fn	Mint
American Watch Co., 19J Maltese cross stopwork, gilt mvt.			
all original 1860 Model, **18K**case .... ★ ★	$1,900	$3,000	$4,500
American Watch Co., 17-19J, 3/4, KW & KS from back,			
vibrating hairspring stud, 1860 Model, **18K**case .... ★ ★ ★	1,900	3,500	4,500
American Watch Co., 19J, 3/4 , KW & KS from back, **nickel mvt**.			
1860 Model, original case, **18K** case .... ★ ★ ★ ★	5,500	6,500	10,500
American Watch Co., 15J, M#1868, 3/4, KW, Silver .... ★ ★ ★	1,000	1,500	2,800
American Watch Co., 17-18J, M#1872,3/4,SW,**HC,14K** .... ★	1,400	1,800	3,300
American Watch Co., 17J, M#1868, 3/4, KW, ADJ, Silver ..... ★ ★	1,000	1,400	2,200
American Watch Co., 17J, M#1899, Adj.5P, ... ★	400	500	700
American Watch Co., 18J, M#1868, SW, nickel mvt. .... ★	450	550	900
American Watch Co., 19J, M#1868, SW, nickel mvt.			
Silver case .... ★ ★ ★	5,000	6,000	8,000
American Watch Co., 19J, M#1888, SW, nickel mvt. .... ★ ★ ★	1,000	1,800	3,000
American Watch Co., 19J, M#1899, SW, nickel mvt. .... ★ ★	550	700	1,000

🕐 Pricing in this Guide are fair market price for COMPLETE watches which are reflected from the **"NAWCC"** National and regional shows.

Grade or Name — Description	Avg	Ex-Fn	Mint
American Watch Co., 19-21J, M#**1872**, 3/4, SW .... ★★★	$3,500	$4,500	$7,000
American Watch Co., 19-21J, M# **1872**, GJS, all original"Woerd's pat.- (**see illo. below**)			
compensating bal.", **With** sawtooth bal.,.................... ★★★★	5,000	6,500	9,000
American Watch Co., 19-21J, M#1868-1872, 3/4, GJS,			
"Woerd's pat." on movt. **"NO"** sawtooth bal. .... ★★	1,500	2,000	3,800
American Watch Co., 19-21J, M#1872, 3/4, SW, **18k**......... ★★★	2,000	2,500	5,000
American Watch Co., 19J, M#1888, **14K** .... ★★★	1,600	2,000	3,600
American Watch Co., 19J, M#1888 .... ★★★	800	1,000	2,100
American Watch Co., 21J, M#1888, NI, 3/4 .... ★★★	900	1,100	2,400
American Watch Co., 23J, M# 1899, Adj.5P, GT, GJS .... ★★	600	800	1,800
American Watch Co., 23J, BRG, Adj.5P, GT, GJS, **14K**			
original case .... ★★	1,200	1,600	2,400
American Watch Co., 23J, BRG, Adj.5P, GT, GJS, **18K**			
original case .... ★★	1,400	1,800	3,000
American Watch Co., 23J, BRG, Adj.5P, GT, GJS .... ★★	850	1,000	1,800
American Watch Co., 21J, BRG, Adj.5P, GT, GJS .... ★	450	600	1,000
American Watch Co., 19J, BRG, Adj.5P, GT, GJS .... ★	350	400	700
American Watch Co., 17J, BRG, Adj.5P, GT, GJS	250	300	600
Appleton, Tracy & Co., 15J, M#1860, 3/4, KW & KS from			
back, all original silver case	600	700	1,500
Appleton, Tracy & Co., 15-19J, M#1868, 3/4, KW	600	700	1,500
Appleton, Tracy & Co., 15-19J, 3/4, KW, with vibrating			
hairspring stud, all original, silver case .... ★★	1,000	1,400	2,400
Appleton, Tracy & Co., 15-19J, 3/4, KW, with vibrating			
hairspring stud, **18K**, original case .... ★★★	1,600	2,000	3,800

🕐 Generic, nameless or unmarked grades for watch movements are listed under the Company name or initials of the Company, etc. by size, jewel count and description.

	Avg	Ex-Fn	Mint
A. W. Co., 7J, M#1872, SW, HC..	$100	$125	$300
A. W. Co., 7J, SW, M#1888..	65	90	195
A. W. Co., 7J, SW, DMK...	65	90	195
A. W. Co., 9J, SW, ...	65	90	195
A. W. W. Co., 11-13J, SW	65	90	195
A. W. Co., 11J, M#1899, SW..	65	90	195
A. W. W. Co., 11-15J, M#1872, SW, HC......................................	125	195	350
A. W. W. Co., 13J, M#1888-99, OF	65	90	195

RIGHT: **Woerd's pat. compensating balance,**
this is a illustration copied from a blue print of
Mr. Woerd's patented <u>**Saw Tooth Balance.**</u>
This balance **must** be in watch for **top prices.**

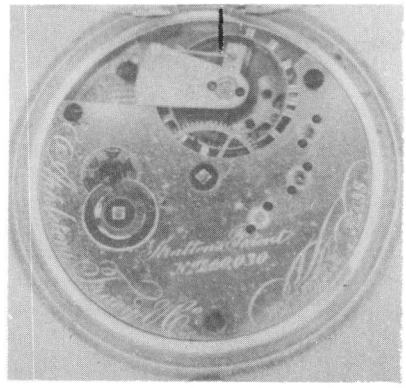

Appleton, Tracy & Co. (16 size), 15J, with vibrating hairspring stud, key wind & set from back, S# 140030.

Crescent Street, Model 16–S (CENTER SECONDS), 16 size, movement, 22J, Adj6p, lever set, Wind indicator.

☉ Generic, nameless or unmarked grades for watch movements are listed under the Company name or initials of the Company, etc. by size, jewel count and description.

Grade or Name—Descripion	Avg	Ex-Fn	Mint
A. W. W. Co., 15J, M#1899, OF	$85	$100	$250
A. W. W. Co., 15J, M#1888, SW, HC	85	100	275
A. W. W. Co., 16-17J, M#1888, SW, OF	85	100	250
A. W. W. Co., 16J, M#1899, SW, DMK, HC	95	125	275
A. W.W. Co., 17J, M#1872, SW, DMK, GJS, DES, HC ★	295	400	800
A. W. W. Co., 17J, SW, OF	85	95	250
A.W.W.Co., 19J, Adj.5P, LS, OF	95	125	295
A.W.W.Co., 19J, Adj.5P, LS, HC	125	150	400
A.W.W.Co., 21J, Adj.5P, PS, OF	195	225	500
A.W.W.Co., 21J, Adj.5P, PS, HC	225	250	600
A.W.W.Co., 23J, Adj.5P, PS, OF	225	250	600
A.W.W.Co., 23J, Adj.5P, PS, HC	250	275	650
P. S. Bartlett, 17J, M#1899, OF	65	90	195
P. S. Bartlett, 17J, M#1899, HC	100	125	250
P. S. Bartlett, 17J, M#1908, OF	65	90	195
Bond St., 7J, M#1888	65	90	195
Bond St., 11J, M#1888	65	90	195
Bond St., 15J, M#1888	65	90	195
Bond St., 7J, M#1899	65	90	195
Canadian Pacific RR, M#s 1888, 1899, 1908 ★★★	650	900	1,800
Canadian Railway Time Service, M#1908 ★★	500	600	1,200
CHRONOGRAPH are listed as 14 SIZE SEE Chronograph under 14 size			
Crescent St., 19J, M#1899, Adj.5P, LS, OF	95	150	295
Crescent St., 19J, M#1899, Adj.5P, PS, OF	95	150	295
Crescent St., 19J, M#1899, Adj.5P,LS, HC	125	175	350
Crescent St., 21J, M#1899, Adj.5P, LS, OF	95	150	295
Crescent St., 21J, M#1899, Adj.5P, LS, OF	95	150	295
Crescent St., 21J, M#1899, Adj.5P, PS, HC	150	250	400
Crescent St., 19J, M#1908, Adj.5P, LS, OF	95	150	295
Crescent St., 19J, M#1908, Adj.5P, PS, OF	95	150	295
Crescent St., 21J, M#1908, Adj.5P, LS, OF	150	175	400
Crescent St., 21J, M#1908, Adj.5P, PS, OF	150	175	400
Crescent St., 21J, M#1908, Adj.6P, LS, OF	150	175	400
Crescent St., 21J, M#1908, Adj.5P, PS, HC	195	250	500
Crescent St., 21J, M#1908, Adj.5P, LS, **Wind Indicator** ★	700	850	1,300
Crescent St., 21J, M#1912, Adj.5P, LS, **Wind Indicator** ★	700	850	1,300
Crescent St., 22J, M#16–S, Adj.6P, **DECK WATCH**			
LS, center sec., **Wind Indicator.** ★★★	800	1,000	1,600
Cronometro Supremo &Victoria, may have a **Sun logo**, ("EXPORT") to Spanish Countries.			
Cronometro Victoria, 15J, M#1899, OF ★★	250	350	600
Cronometro Victoria, 15J, M#1899, HC ★★	295	400	650
Cronometro Supremo, 21J, M#1899, LS, OF ★★	350	500	900
Cronometro Victoria, 21J, M#1899, HC ★★	350	450	900
Diamond Express, 17J, M#1888, PS, OF,			
Diamond End Stones ★★	700	1,000	2,000
Electric Railway, 17J, OF, LS, Adj.3P	150	195	500
Equity, 7-11J, PS, OF, 16 1/2 Size	50	70	150
Equity, 7-11J, PS, HC, 16 1/2 Size	50	70	150
Equity, 15-17J, PS, OF, 16 1/2 Size	50	70	150
Equity, 15-17J, PS, HC, 16 1/2 Size	50	70	150
Giant, 7-11J, PS, OF, 16 1/2 Size	50	70	150
Giant, 7-11J, PS, HC, 16 1/2 Size	50	70	150
Hillside, 7J, M#1868, ADJ	95	125	295
Hillside, 7J, M#1868-1872, **sweep sec. & STOP** ★★★	1,000	1,600	3,600
Marquis, 15J, M#1899, LS	65	85	195
Marquis, 15J, M#1908, LS	65	85	195
Non-Magnetic, 15J, NI, HC	95	150	295
Park Road, 11-13-15J, M#1872, PS	175	195	400
Park Road, 16J, M#1872, PS	175	195	400

Note: A true O'Hara dial is signed O'Hara Dial Company in a logo on back of the dial.

Premier Maximus, "Premier" on movement. "Maximus" on dial, 16 size, 23 jewels (two diamond end stones), open face, pendant set, serial number 17,000,014.

American Waltham Watch Co., 5 minute repeater, 16 size, 16 jewels, 3/4 plate, grade 1888, adj, 2 gongs, ca. 1900.

Grade or Name — Description	Avg	Ex-Fn	Mint
Premier, 9J, M#1908, PS, OF...	$45	$60	$150
Premier, 11J, M#1908..	65	90	195
Premier, 15J, M#1908, LS, OF..	65	90	195
Premier, 17J, M#1908, PS, OF..	65	90	195
Premier, 17J, M#1908, PS, OF, Silveroid.........................	65	90	195
Premier, 21J, M#1908, ...	125	150	350
Premier, 22J, M#1908, LS, Adj.6P, **Stainless steel case,** OF.........	150	175	400
Premier, 23J, M#1908, LS, OF..	195	250	450
Premier Maximus, 23J, GT, gold case, LS,GJS, Adj.6P, original WI, DR, **18K** Maximus case, **box & papers**................. ★★	9,500	10,500	15,500
Premier Maximus, 23J, GT, gold case, LS, GJS,Adj.6P, WI, DR, **original 14K or 18K** Maximus case, **NO** box .. ★★	7,000	7,500	11,000
Premier Maximus, 23J, GT, **RECASED**	1,800	2,200	3,500
Railroader, 17J, M#1888, LS, NI ★★★	600	800	1,600
Railroad Time, 15-17J, ADJ, OF ....★	195	250	650
REPEATER, 16J, M#1872, original **gold filled** case, 5 min. ... ★★	2,000	2,500	4,500
REPEATER, 16J, M#1872, original **coin** case, 5 min. .... ★★	2,200	2,700	5,000
REPEATER, 16J, M#1872, 5 Min., original **14K** case ... ★★	3,000	3,500	6,000
REPEATER, 16J, M#1872, 5 min., original **18K** case .... ★★★	4,000	4,500	7,000
REPEATER, 16J, M#1872, 5 min., chronograph with register, 18K case, all original... ★★★	6,500	7,500	12,000
REPEATER, **1 minute**, moon phase, M#1872, Perpetual Calendar, **18K** case, all original .... ★★★★	40,000	50,000	80,000

🕐 Watches listed in this book are priced at the collectable trade show level, as **complete** watches having an original 14k gold-filled case and *Key Wind* with silver, an original white enamel single sunk dial, and with the entire original movement in good working order with no repairs needed.

🕐 Some watch manufacturers personalize watches for jobbers or jewelry firms, with exclusive private signed or marked movements. The valuable collectable watches are listed under the signed or marked movement. Other exclusive private signed or marked movements will have equivalent value are only slightly higher value and should be compared to Generic or Nameless movements. Railroad signed or marked (dials & movements) are usually more collectable & higher in value.

🕐 **The Complete Price Guide to Watches goal is to stimulate the orderly exchange of <u>Watches</u> between *"buyers"* and *"sellers"*.**

🕐 A collector should expect to pay modestly higher prices at local shops.

Grade or Name — Description	Avg	Ex-Fn	Mint
Riverside, 15-16J, M#1872, NI, OF	$95	$150	$295
Riverside, 15-16J, M#1872, **gilded**, OF	95	150	295
Riverside, 16-17J, M#1888, NI, OF, **14K**	500	600	1,000
Riverside, 16-17J, M#1888, NI, OF	95	150	295
Riverside, 17J, M#1888, gilded, OF	95	150	295
Riverside, 15J, M#1888, gilded, OF	95	150	295
Riverside, 17J, M#1888, checker goldtone DMK, raised gold jewel settings, OF	95	150	295
Riverside, 17J, M#1899, LS, DR, OF	95	150	295
Riverside, 17J, M#1899, LS, DR, HC	95	150	295
Riverside, 19J, M#1899, LS, DR, OF	95	150	295
Riverside, 19J, M#1908, Adj.5P, LS, DR	95	150	295
Riverside, 19J, M#1908, Adj.5P, PS, DR, HC ★	125	175	350
Riverside, 21J, M#1888-1899-1908, LS, DR, OF	195	225	400
Riverside, 21J, M#1888-1899-1908, LS, DR, HC	250	275	550

Note: **Riverside Maximus have Raised gold jewel settings, gold train, Diamond end stones, Adj. to positions**

	Avg	Ex-Fn	Mint
Riverside Maximus, 21J, M#1888, Adj., GJS, GT, DR, OF ..... ★ ★	675	800	1,500
Riverside Maximus, 21J, M#1888, Adj., GJS, GT, DR, HC ... ★ ★	750	900	1,600
Riverside Maximus, 21J, M#1888, Adj., GJS, GT, DR, HC, **14K** ★ ★	1,100	1,300	2,000
Riverside Maximus, 21J, M#1899, Adj., GJS, GT, DR, OF .... ★	400	500	900
Riverside Maximus, 21J, M#1899, Adj., GJS, GT, DR, HC ... ★ ★	600	700	1,200
Riverside Maximus, 23J, M#1899, Adj., GJS, GT, DR, OF	400	500	900
Riverside Maximus, 23J, M#1899, Adj., GJS, GT, DR, HC	500	800	1,300
Riverside Maximus, 23J, M#1899 Adj., GJS, GT, DR, **Wind Ind., OF** ★ ★ ★ ★	3,000	4,000	6,000
Riverside Maximus, 23J, M#1908, Adj., GJS, DR, OF	450	550	950
Riverside Maximus, 23J, M#1908, Adj., GJS, DR, HC ★ ★ ★	600	750	1,300
Riverside Maximus, 23J, M#1908, Adj., GJS, GT, DR, **14K HC** ★ ★ ★	800	900	1,600
Riverside Maximus, 23J, M#1908, Adj., GJS, GT, DR, **Wind Ind. OF** ★ ★ ★	3,000	4,000	6,000

American Watch Co., model 1872, 16 size, 16-17-21 jewels, gold train, serial number 871199.

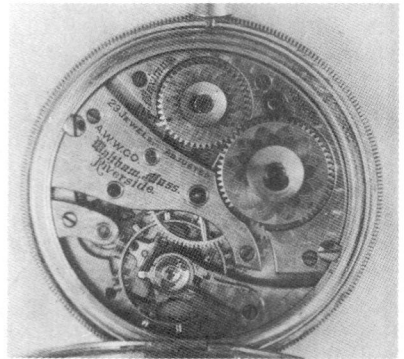

Riverside Maximus, Model 1899, 16 size, 23 jewels, gold train, raised gold jewel settings, **4** diamond end stones, adjusted to 5 positions, hunting case, serial # 12,509,200.

🕐 Some grades are not included. Their values can be determined by comparing with similar age, size, metal content, style, models and grades listed.

🕐 A collector should expect to pay modestly higher prices at local shops.

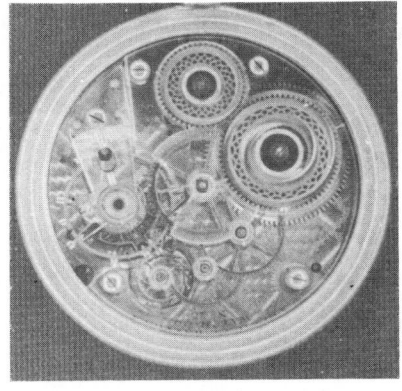

Stone Movement, 16 size, 16 jewels, crystal plates, Model 1872, gold train, gold jeweled settings, Adj5p, serial # 20.

Vanguard, 16 size, 23 jewels, Adj6p, note pressed-in jewels rather than gold jewel settings. c. 1945.

Grade or Name — Description	Avg	Ex-Fn	Mint
Roadmaster, 17J, M#1899, LS, OF GJS .... ★★	$450	$550	$950
Royal, 13-15J, M#1872	65	85	175
Royal, 17J, M#1888, PS, OF	65	85	175
Royal, 17J, M#1888, PS, HC	95	120	250
Royal, 17J, M#1899, Adj.3P, OF	65	85	175
Royal, 17J, M#1899-1908, Adj.5P, OF	65	85	175
Royal, 17J, M#1899-1908, Adj.5P,HC	85	100	250
Royal Special, 17J, M#1888	95	125	295
Santa Fe Route, M#s 1888, 1899, 1908 .... ★★★	750	950	1,600
Sol, 7J, M#1888	50	65	150
Sol, 7J, M#1908	50	65	150
Stone Movement, 16J, M#1872, GT, Crystal plates .... ★★★★	10,000	15,000	25,000
Supremo, 17J, M#1899..	65	85	175
SWISS made, 17-25J, ...	50	65	150
Traveler, 7J, M#1888, 1899, 1908 & 16 1/2 size(Equity)..............	50	65	150
Tennyson,15J, M#1888, OF .... ★	150	200	400
Vanguard, 19J, M#1899, PS, LS, Adj.5P, GJS, DR, OF	175	200	400
Vanguard, 19J, M#1899, PS, LS, Adj.5P, GJS, DR, HC	225	250	450
Vanguard, 21J, M#1899, Adj.5P, OF .... ★★	250	300	550
Vanguard, 21J, M#1899, Adj.5P, **HC** .... ★★	300	350	600
Vanguard, 23J, M#1899, LS, Adj.5P, GJS, DR, OF	250	300	500
Vanguard, 23J, M#1899, PS, Adj.5P, GJS, DR, OF	250	300	500
Vanguard, 23J, M#1899, Adj.6P, OF..	250	300	500
Vanguard, 23J, M#1899, Adj.5P, **HC**	275	325	650
Vanguard, 23J, M#1899, PS, **Wind Indicator**, Adj.5P, GJS, DR ★	600	700	1,000

🕐 Watches listed in this book are priced at the collectable trade show level, as **complete** watches having an original 14k gold-filled case and *Key Wind* with silver, an original white enamel single sunk dial, and with the entire original movement in good working order with no repairs needed.

🕐 Some grades are not included. Their values can be determined by comparing with similar age, size, metal content, style, models and grades listed.

🕐 Watch **terminology or communication** in this book has evolved over the years, in search of better and more precise language with a effort to improve, purify, adjust itself and make it easier to understand.

🕐 The Complete Price Guide to Watches goal is to stimulate the orderly exchange of <u>Watches</u> between *"buyers"* and *"sellers"*.

Grade or Name — Description	Avg	Ex-Fn	Mint
Vanguard, 19J, M#1908, LS & PS, Adj.5P, GJS, DR	$195	$225	$400
Vanguard, 21J, M#1908, Adj.5P, GJS, DR, PS, LS, OF .... ★★	275	325	550
Vanguard, 21J, M#1908, Adj.5P, GJS, DR, PS, LS, HC .... ★★	325	400	600
Vanguard, 23J, M#1908, LS, Adj.5P, GJS, DR, OF	275	325	550
Vanguard, 23J, M#1908, LS, Adj.5P, GJS, DR, HC	325	400	600
Vanguard, 23J, M#1908, PS, Adj.5P, GJS, DR	275	325	550
Vanguard, 23J, M#1908, Adj.5P, **Wind Indicator**, GJS, DR	650	850	1,200
Vanguard, 23J, M#1908, Adj.5P, GJS, Diamond end stone	250	300	500
Vanguard, 23J, M#1908, Adj.5P, GJS, HC .... ★	325	350	650
Vanguard, 23J, M#1908, OF, **14K**	650	850	1,200
Vanguard, 23J, M#1908, Adj.6P, **Wind Indicator**, GJS, DR	650	850	1,200
Vanguard, 23J, M#1908, Adj.5-6P, **Wind Ind.**, **Lossier**, GJS,DR	600	700	1,000
Vanguard, 23J, M#1912, **Press Jewels**	175	225	375
Vanguard, 23J, M#1912, PS, military (case), **Wind Indicator** ★	800	900	1,300
Vanguard, **24J**, & marked 9J., center sec. .... ★★★	700	800	1,400
Weems, 21J, Navigation watch, **Wind Indicator** .... ★★★	900	1,200	1,800
Weems, 23J, Navigation watch, **Wind Indicator** .... ★★★	1,000	1,400	2,400
M#1888, G #s 650, 640	50	60	150
M#1899, G #s 615, 618, 620, 625, 628, ...	50	60	150
M#1908, G #s 611, 613, 614, 618, 621, 623,			
628, 630, 641, 642	50	60	150
G#637-640=3 pos., G#636=4pos., G#1617=2 pos., ALL=17J.	50	60	150
G#610=7-11J., **unadjusted** & 620=15J.................................	50	60	150
G#620-625-630-635=17J., Adj., OF	50	60	150
G#645, 21J, GCW, OF, LS	175	200	395
G#645, 21J, GCW, OF, LS, **wind indicator** .... ★★★	1,300	1,700	3,000
G#645, 19J, OF, LS	175	225	395
G#665, 19J, GJS, BRG, HC	600	700	1,000
G#16-A, 22J, Adj.3P, 24 hr. dial	200	250	400
G#16-A, & G#1024, 17J, Adj.5P	80	90	195
G#1617, 17J, adj.	80	90	195
G#1621, 21J, Adj.5P	150	175	350
G#1622, 22J, Adj.5P	175	200	400
G#1623, 23J, Adj.5P	250	300	550

Weems Navigation watch, 21j, Weems pat. seconds dial, pusher for seconds scale setting, ca. 1942.

Vanguard, Model 1908, 16 size, 23 jewels, diamond end stone, gold jewel settings, exposed winding gears, serial number 11,012,533.

14 SIZE
MODELS 14KW FULL PLATE, 1874,
1884, 1895, 1897, COLONIAL-A

Grade or Name — Description	Avg	Ex-Fn	Mint
Adams Street, 7J, M#14KW, full plate, KW, Coin	$60	$125	$250
Adams Street, 11J, M#14KW, full plate, KW, Coin	80	150	350
Adams Street, 15J, M#14KW, full plate, KW	100	150	400

☉ Generic, nameless or unmarked grades for watch movements are listed under the Company name or initials of the Company, etc. by size, jewel count and description.

A. W. Co., 7-11J, M#14KW, full plate, KW	45	65	175
A. W. W. Co., 7-11J, M#1874, SW, LS, HC	60	85	225
A. W. Co., 7-11J, M#s FP, 1884, & 1895	45	65	175
A. W. Co., 13J, M#1884	45	65	175
A. W. Co., 15-16J, M#1874, SW	45	65	175
A. W. Co., 17J, SW, OF	60	75	200
A.W.Co., 19J, GJS, GCW	75	90	250
Am. Watch Co., 7-11J	45	65	175
Am. Watch Co., 13J, M#1874-84, SW	45	65	175
Am. Watch Co., 15J, M#1874-84,	45	65	175
Am. Watch Co., 16J, M#1874, SW	60	85	225
Am. Watch Co., 7-11J, M#14KW, **Full Plate**, KW	75	125	275
Am. Watch Co., 16J, M#1884, SW	75	125	275
Am. Watch Co., 15J, M#1897, SW	45	65	175
Bond St., 7-11J, M#1895, SW	45	65	175
Bond St., 9-11J, M#1884, KW	45	65	175
Bond St., 7J, M#1884, SW, PS	45	65	175
Beacon, 15J, M#1897, SW	45	65	175
Chronograph, 13J, 1874, **14K**, OF, **Am. W. Co. case**	950	1,200	2,000
Chronograph, 13J, 1874, **14K**, OF, W/ register, Am. W. Co. case ★	1,200	1,400	2,400
Chronograph, 13J, 1874, **14K, HC**, W/ register, Am. W. Co. case ★	1,500	1,900	3,600
Chronograph, 13J, 1874, **18K**, HC, W/ register, Am. W. Co. case ★	1,800	2,400	3,800
Chronograph, 13J, 1874, **SILVER HC, *Am. W. Co. case***	400	500	1,000
Chronograph, 16J, 1874, **double dial, "coin"**, Am. W. Co. case	2,200	3,000	5,000
Chronograph, 16J, 1874, **double dial, 18K,** Am. W. Co. case	3,500	4,000	7,000

Chronograph, Model 1874, split-second, 14 size. Note two split second hands on dial and two pushers at 2 & 4.

Hillside, 14 size, 13 jewels, M#1874, stem wind, hunting case, Woerds Pat., serial number 1,696,188, 18K.

☉ This book endeavours to be a GUIDE or helpful manual and offers a wealth of material to be used as a tool not as a absolute document. Price Guides are like watches the worst may be better than none at all, but at best cannot be expected to be 100% accurate.

Grade or Name — Description	Avg	Ex-Fn	Mint
Chronograph, 13J, M# 1884 , OF	$195	$250	$600
Chronograph, 13J, M# 1884, HC	295	400	700
Chronograph, 13J, 1884, **14K**, HC, **Am. W. Co. case**	900	1,000	2,400
Chronograph, 13J, 1884, **18K**, HC, **Am. W. Co. case** ★	1,000	1,400	2,600
Chronograph, 15J, M# 1874-1884 , OF	195	250	500
Chronograph, 15J, M#1874-1884, HC	250	300	600
Chronograph, 17J, M#1874-1884 , OF	195	250	500
Chronograph, 17J, M#1874-1884, HC	250	300	600
Chronograph, 17J, split second, Am. W. Co. case ★★★	700	800	1,500
Chronograph, 15J, split sec., **14K**, HC ★★★	1,800	2,000	4,000
Chronograph, 15J, split second, **min. register, 14K** Am. W. Co. HC ★★★	2,000	2,500	5,000
Church St., 7J, M#1884,	75	90	250
Crescent Garden, 7-11J, M#14KW	45	65	175
Crescent Garden, 7J, Full Plate, KW	45	65	175
Cronometro Victoria, 15J, M#1897, OF (may have sun logo) . ★★	400	500	750
Wm. Ellery, 7J, M#1874, SW	45	65	175
Gentleman, 7J, M#1884, SW	45	65	175
Hillside, 7-15J, M#1874, SW	45	65	175
Hillside, 7-11J, M#FP, SW	45	65	175
Hillside, 7-13J, M#1884, KW	45	65	175
Hillside, 9-11J, M#1884, KW	45	65	175
Hillside, 15J, M#1884, SW	45	65	175
Hillside, 16J, M#1874, (calendar date only on outside chapter) SW, GJS, OF,(calendar sets from back with lever) ★★★	650	850	1,500
Hillside, 7-13J, M#1895	45	65	175
Maximus, 21J, Colonial A, Adj.5P, GT, model 1912, OF ★	125	175	400
Maximus, 21J, Colonial A, Adj.5P, GT, model 1912, **14K OF** ★	295	400	675
Night Clock, 7J, M#1884, KW	95	125	225
Perfection, 15J, M#1897, OF ★	65	95	200
Perfection, 15J, M#1897, HC ★★	95	150	250

Chronograph, M# 1884-double dial, 14 size, 15 jewels, hunting case.

Chronograph, Model 1884-Split Second, 14 size, 15 jewels, open face, gold escape wheel, gold train, serial number 303,094.

🕐 Some watch manufacturers personalize watches for jobbers or jewelry firms, with exclusive private signed or marked movements. The valuable collectable watches are listed under the signed or marked movement. Other exclusive private signed or marked movements will have equivalent value are only slightly higher value and should be compared to Generic or Nameless movements. Railroad signed or marked (dials & movements) are usually more collectable & higher in value.

🕐 A collector should expect to pay modestly higher prices at local shops.

Five Minute Repeater, Model 1884, 14 size, 13-15 jewels, hunting case, slide activated, serial number 2,605,848. Note: estimated Total about 1,250 to 1,300.

Chronograph, 14 size, Model # 1874, Lugrin Pat., Sept. 28, 1880, serial # 3,162,800. Also Pat. date (Oct. 3,1876).

Grade or Name — Description	Avg	Ex-Fn	Mint
Repeater (5 min.), 16J, M#1884, SW, LS, **14K** ....★	$3,500	$4,200	$6,500
Repeater (5 min.), 16J, M#1884, SW, LS, **18K** ....★	3,800	4,400	7,000
Repeater (5 min.), 16J, M#1884, split second chronograph, 18K case ....★★	5,000	6,500	10,000
Repeater (5 min.), 16J, M#1884, SW, LS, chronograph , with register, **14K** Am. W. Co. case	4,000	4,500	7,000
Repeater (5 min.), 16J, M#1884, SW, LS, chronograph , with register, **18K** Am. W. Co. case	4,500	5,000	8,500
Repeater (5 min.), 16J, M#1884, SW, LS, original **Coin** case.........	2,800	3,500	5,000
Repeater (5 min.), 16J, M#1884, SW, LS, original **gold filled** case	2,200	2,600	3,500
Repeater (5 Min.), **18K**, HC ....★★	4,000	5,000	8,000
Repeater **(1 Min.), perpetual calendar, moon ph., 18K**..★★★★	30,000	50,000	90,000
Riverside, 11-15J, M#s 1874	95	125	275
Riverside, 15J, M#1884	45	65	175
Riverside, 19J, Colonial A, Adj.5P, OF	95	165	250
Riverside, 21J, Colonial A, Adj.5P, OF ....★★	150	200	400
Royal, 11-13-15J, M#s 1874, 1884	45	65	175
Seaside, 7-11J, M#1884, SW	45	65	175
Sol, 7J, M#1897..	45	65	175
Special, 7J, M#1895, HC	45	65	175
Sterling, 7J, M#1884	45	65	175
Waltham, Mass., 7J, Full Plate, KW	95	125	250

12 SIZE
MODELS KW, 1894, BRIDGE, COLONIAL SERIES

Grade or Name — Description	Avg	Ex-Fn	Mint
A. W. W. Co., 7J, M#1894, **14K**, OF	$150	$200	$500
A. W. W. Co., 11J, M#1894, also Colonial model	45	65	175
A. W. W. Co., 15J, M#1894, also Colonial model	45	65	175
A. W. W. Co., 15J, M#1894, Colonial, **14K**, HC	250	300	550
A. W. W. Co., 17J, M#1894, also Colonial model	45	65	175
A. W. W. Co., 17J, M#1894, also Colonial, **14K** OF....................	200	275	400
A. W. W. Co., 19J, OF	45	65	175
A. W. W. Co., 21J, OF	65	85	200
A. W. W. Co., 23J, OF	150	200	350
P. S. Bartlett, 19J, M#1894, **14K**, HC	250	300	600
P. S. Bartlett, 19J, M#1894	45	65	175
Bond St., 7-13J, M#1894	45	65	175
Bridge Model, 21J, GJS, Adj.5P, GT, OF ....★★	200	275	400
Bridge Model, 21J, GJS, Adj.5P, GT, **14K**, HC ....★★	400	475	800
Bridge Model, 23J, GJS, Adj.5P, GT ....★★	250	300	600

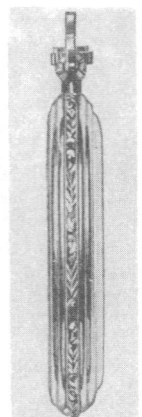

Actual size illustration of a cushion style shaped watch depicting thinness with emphasis on style and beauty. This watch was popular in the 1930s.

Grade or Name — Description	Avg	Ex-Fn	Mint
Duke, 7-15J, M#1894	$50	$65	$150
Digital Hour & Second Window, 17J	75	100	250
Elite, 17J, OF	45	65	175
Ensign, 7J, OF	45	65	175
Equity, 7J,adj.	45	65	175
Martyn Square, 7-11J, M#KW	95	125	250
Maximus, 21J, GJS, GT	150	200	350
Premier, 17-19J, M#1894	45	65	175
Premier, 21J, M#1894	125	175	300
Premier, 23J, M#1894, OF **14K**	200	300	550
Riverside, 17-19J, M#1894, Colonial	45	65	175
Riverside, 21J, M#1894, Colonial	150	200	350

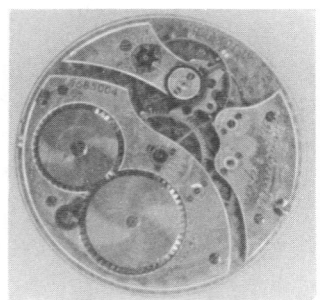
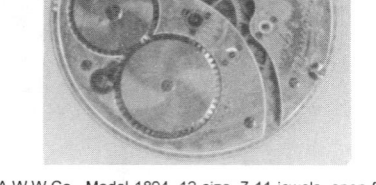

A.W.W.Co., Model 1894, 12 size, 7-11 jewels, open face, serial number 7,565,004.

Riverside, Colonial series, 12 size, 19 jewels, open face or hunting, Adj5p, double roller.

Grade or Name – Description	Avg	Ex-Fn	Mint
Riverside, 19-21J, M#1894, also Colonial, **14K**, HC	$275	$400	$700
Riverside Maximus, 21J, M#1894, also Colonial, GT, GJS, **14K** ..	350	450	650
Riverside Maximus, 21J, M#1894, also Colonial, GT, GJS	200	250	500
Riverside Maximus, 23J, M#1894, also Colonial, GT, GJS .... ★	250	300	550
Riverside Maximus, 23J, M#1894, also Colonial, GT, GJS,14K ★	350	450	700
Royal, 17J, OF, PS, Adj, or Adj.3P	30	40	150
Royal, 19J, OF, PS, Adj.3P	30	40	150
Secometer, 17J, (revolving seconds dial only) OF	85	95	300
G# 210, 7J, G# 220, 15J	30	40	150
G# 225, 17J	40	50	175

THE OPERA WATCH
10-12 size case & a 6/0 size Jewel Series movement

Grade or Name – Description	Avg	Ex-Fn	Mint
12-6/0 size, 17-19J, Adj, **18K gold case**..	$400	$475	$700
12-6/0 size, 17-19J, Adj, **14K gold case**..	250	300	500
12-6/0 size, 17-19J, Adj, **Platinum case**	450	600	900
12-6/0 size, 17-19J, Adj, **gold filled case**	95	125	250

A unique designed Gents dress watch about 10-12 size case with a fancy framed 6/0 movement (Jewel Series).

10 SIZE
MODEL KW, 1861, 1865, 1874

Grade or Name – Description	Avg	Ex-Fn	Mint
Am. W. Co., 7-15J, M#1874-1878, KW, **14K**	$195	$295	$600
A. W. Co., 7-11J, SW , OF..	45	65	175
A. W. Co.,15-17J, SW , OF...	45	65	175
A. W. Co., 19-21J, SW , OF..	75	100	250
American Watch Co., 11-15J, M#1874, **14K, HC**	225	275	500
Appleton, Tracy & Co., 7-11-15J, M#1861 or 1874, **14K**, KW	225	275	500
Appleton, Tracy & Co., 7-11-15J, M#1861, **KW** multi-color box case, **18K**..	700	900	1,800
P. S. Bartlett, 7-11J, M#1861, KW, **14K**	300	400	700
P. S. Bartlett, 13J, M#KW, gold balance, 1st S# 45,801, last 46,200, Pat. Nov. 3, 1858, **14K,**............................. ★★★	500	600	900
P. S. Bartlett, 13J, M#KW, gold balance, 1st S#45,801, last 46,200, Pat. Nov. 3, 1858, **18K** .... ★★★	600	700	1,000
P. S. Bartlett, 13J, M#1861 or 1865, KW, **14K**	275	375	575

Appleton Tracy & Co., Model 10KW, 10 size, 7-15 jewels,   P. S. Bartlett, 10 size, 7-15 jewels, serial # 181,602.
key wind and set from back, serial number 370,411.

NOTE: These watches (excluding Colonial) are usually found with solid gold cases, and are therefore priced accordingly. Without cases, these watches have very little value due to the fact that the cases are difficult to find. Many of the cases came in octagon, decagon, hexagon, cushion and triad shapes.

Grade or Name – Description	Avg	Ex-Fn	Mint
Crescent Garden, 7J, M#1861, KW, **14K**	$150	$250	$400
Colonial R, 9J, model 1945	45	65	175
Colonial R, 17J, Adj.5P, model 1945..	45	65	175
Colonial R, 21J, Adj.5P, model 1945..	65	95	195
Colonial R, 23J, Adj.5P, model 1945.. ★★	100	150	300
Wm. Ellery, 7,11,15J, M#1861, KW, **14K**	150	250	400
Home W. Co., 7J, M#1874, KW, **14K**	150	250	400
Martyn Square, 7-11J, M#1861, **14K**	150	250	400
Maximus "A", 21J, model 1918, **14K** .... ★★★	200	275	500
Maximus "A", 23J, model 1918, **14K** ....★	200	275	500
Riverside A, 19J, Adj.5P, model 1918, GF	65	95	195

8 SIZE
MODEL 1873

NOTE: Collectors usually want solid gold cases in small watches.

Grade or Name – Description	Avg	Ex-Fn	Mint
Am. W. Co., 15-17J, M#1873, **14K, Multi-Color Box Hinged case**	$400	$500	$1,000
Am. W. Co., 15-16J, M#1873	35	50	150
P. S. Bartlett, 15-16J, M#1873	35	50	150
Wm. Ellery, 7-11J, M#1873	35	50	150
Wm. Ellery, 7J, **14K, HC**	195	250	450
Riverside, 7-11J, M#1873, **18K, HC**	250	300	600
Riverside, 7-16J, M#1873	35	50	150
Royal, 7-16J, M#1873	35	50	150
Victoria, 11-15J, tu-tone movement, **18k HC** ....★	195	250	550

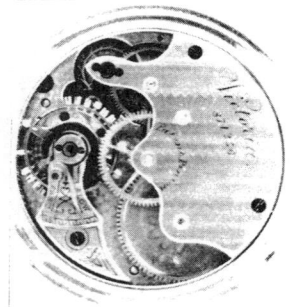

VICTORIA, 8 size 1873 model, 11-15 jewels, tu-tone high grade movement, HC, S# 871256

6 size Ladies movement this basic model came in the following grades: J=7 jewels, gilt; Y=7 jewels, nickel; N=15 jewels,gilded or nickel; X=15 jewels, nickel, gold jewel settings; K=16 jewels nickel, raised gold settings; RIVERSIDE=17 jewels, nickel, raised gold settings.

6 SIZE
MODEL 1873, 1889 , 1890

Grade or Name – Description	Avg	Ex-Fn	Mint
A,B,C,D,E,F,G,H,J,K	$25	$45	$150
A,B,C,D,E,F,G,H,J,K, **14K, HC**	150	200	400
A. W. W. Co., 19J, **18K, HC**	225	300	550
A. W. W. Co., 19J, **14K, Multi-Color gold case**	400	450	900
A. W. W. Co., 7J, M#1873	25	45	150

Grade or Name – Description	Avg	Ex-Fn	Mint
A. W. W. Co., 15J, multi-color GF, HC	$150	$225	$475
A. W. W. Co., 15J, 2 tone mvt., HC	60	80	250
A. W. W. Co., 11J, HC	25	45	150
Am. W. Co., 7-11J, M#1889 -1890	25	45	150
American W. Co., 7J, KW & KS from back, **10K, HC**	150	200	400
Wm. Ellery, 7J, M#1873	25	45	150
Lady Waltham, 16J, M#1873, Demi, HC, **14K**	175	225	500
Lady Waltham, 16J, M#1873, **18K**	225	250	600
Riverside Maximus, 19J, GT, Adj., DR, HC ★★★	225	250	600
Riverside, 15-17J, PS	25	45	150
Seaside, 7-15J, M#1873	25	45	150
Royal, 16J, HC	45	60	175

American Watch Co., Model 1889, 6 size 7 jewels, serial number 4,700,246.

Stone Movement or Crystal clear see through Plates, size 4, 16 jewels, gold train, open face, serial number 28.

4 SIZE

Grade or Name – Description	Avg	Ex-Fn	Mint
Stone Movement or crystal movement, 4 size, 16 ruby jewels in gold settings, gold train, exposed pallets, compensation balance adjusted to temperature, isochronism & positions, Breguet hairspring, and crystal top plate, 14K case ★★★★	$3,500	$4,500	$7,500

☺ Watches listed in this book are priced at the collectable Trade Show level, as **complete** watches having an original 14k gold-filled case and *Key Wind* with silver, an original white enamel single sunk dial, and with the entire original movement in good working order with no repairs needed.

1 SIZE & 0 SIZE
MODELS 1882, 1891, 1900, 1907

Grade or Name – Description	Avg	Ex-Fn	Mint
A.W.Co., 7-16J, OF	$25	$45	$150
A.W.Co., 7-16J, HC	50	60	225
A.W.Co., 7-15J, multi-color **14K HC**	300	400	675
A. W. Co., 7J, **14K, HC**	175	275	500
American Watch Co., 15J, SW, OF &HC	50	60	250

🕑 Generic, nameless or unmarked grades for watch movements are listed under the Company name or initials of the Company, etc. by size, jewel count and description.

🕑 Watch terminology or communication in this book has evolved over the years, in search of better and more precise language with a effort to improve, purify, adjust itself and make it easier to understand.

Lady Waltham, Model 1900, 0 size, 16 jewels, open face or hunting, adjusted, stem wind, pendant set.

American Watch Co., Model 1891, 0 size, 7 jewels, stem wind, originally sold for $13.00.

Grade or Name – Description	Avg	Ex-Fn	Mint
American Watch Co., 15J, S.W., **14K, HC**	$175	$275	$475
P. S. Bartlett, 11J, M#1891, OF, **14K**	150	175	295
P. S. Bartlett, 16J, **14K, HC**	195	275	450
Cronometro Victoria, 15J ★★	195	275	450
Lady Waltham, 15J, SW, **14K, HC**	195	275	450
Lady Waltham, 15-16J, SW, HC	65	95	250
Maximus, 19J, SW, HC ★	195	250	350
Riverside, 15J,16J,17J, SW, HC	95	150	250
Riverside, 15J,16J,17J, SW, **14K, HC**	195	275	400
Riverside Maximus, 19J, SW, HC	175	250	400
Riverside Maximus, 19J, **14K, HC** ★	295	400	650
Royal, 16J, SW, HC	40	60	175
Seaside, 15J, SW, **14K, HC**	125	175	350
Seaside, 11J, SW, OF, **multi-color dial, no chips**	150	200	400
Seaside, 11J, SW, HC	50	85	195
Seaside, 7J, HC	45	75	175
Seaside, 7J, **14K, HC**	150	225	450
Special, 11J, M#1891, **14K, OF**	150	200	400
G# 61, 7J, HC	35	45	150
G# 115, 15J, HC	40	50	175

Riverside, Jewel Series, 6/0 size, 17 ruby jewels, raised gold settings, gold center wheel.

Ruby, Jewel Series, 6/0 size, 15 jewels, adjusted to temperature, open face or hunting.

JEWEL SERIES or 6/0 SIZE

Grade or Name – Description	Avg	Ex-Fn	Mint
Diamond, 15J, Jewel Series, **14K, HC** ★	$150	$200	$400
Patrician, 15J, pin set, GJS, **18K, OF** ★	200	250	500
Riverside, 17J, Jewel Series, **14K, HC** ★	200	250	400
Ruby, 15J-17, Jewel Series, **14K, OF** ★	150	200	350
Sapphire, 15J, Jewel Series, **14K, OF** ★	150	200	350

RF # 1A
gold filled : $60 - $80 - $250
dial: $40 - $80 - $180

RF # 2B
gold filled : $60- $80 - $250
dial: $20 - $40 - $100

RF # 3C
gold plate: $50 - $70 - $165
dial: $10 - $20 - $50

RF # 4D
gold filled : $60 - $80 - $225
dial: $40 - $80 - $150

RF # 5E
gold filled : $80 - $125 - $350
dial: $40 - $80 - $160

RF # 6F
gold filled : $70 - $100 - $250
dial: $20 - $40 - $100

MONTGOMERY DIAL

RF # 7G
LOCOMOTIVE model
gold filled : $70 - $90 - $240
dial: $40 - $60 - $120

RF # 8H
Hevi-Duty
gold filled : $80 - $100 - $285
dial: $20 - $40 - $80

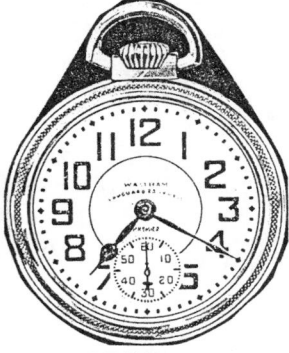

RF # 9L
gold filled : $50 - $75 - $200
dial: $20 - $40 - $80

🕐 NOTE: Factory Advertised as a **complete** watch and was fitted with a certain matched, timed and rated movement and sold in the factory designed case style as a **complete** watch. The factory also sold _uncased_ movements to **JOBBERS** such as Jewelry stores & they cased the movement in a case styles the **CUSTOMER requested.** All the factory advertised **complete** watches came with a enamel dial **SHOWN or CHOICE** of other **Railroad** dials.

AMERICAN WALTHAM WATCH CO.
IDENTIFICATION OF MOVEMENTS
BY MODEL NUMBER

How to Identify Your Watch Size & Model: Compare the movement of your watch with the illustrations in this section. While comparing, note the location of the balance, jewels, screws, gears, and type of back plate (Full, 3/4, Bridge) these will be clues in identifying the movement you have.

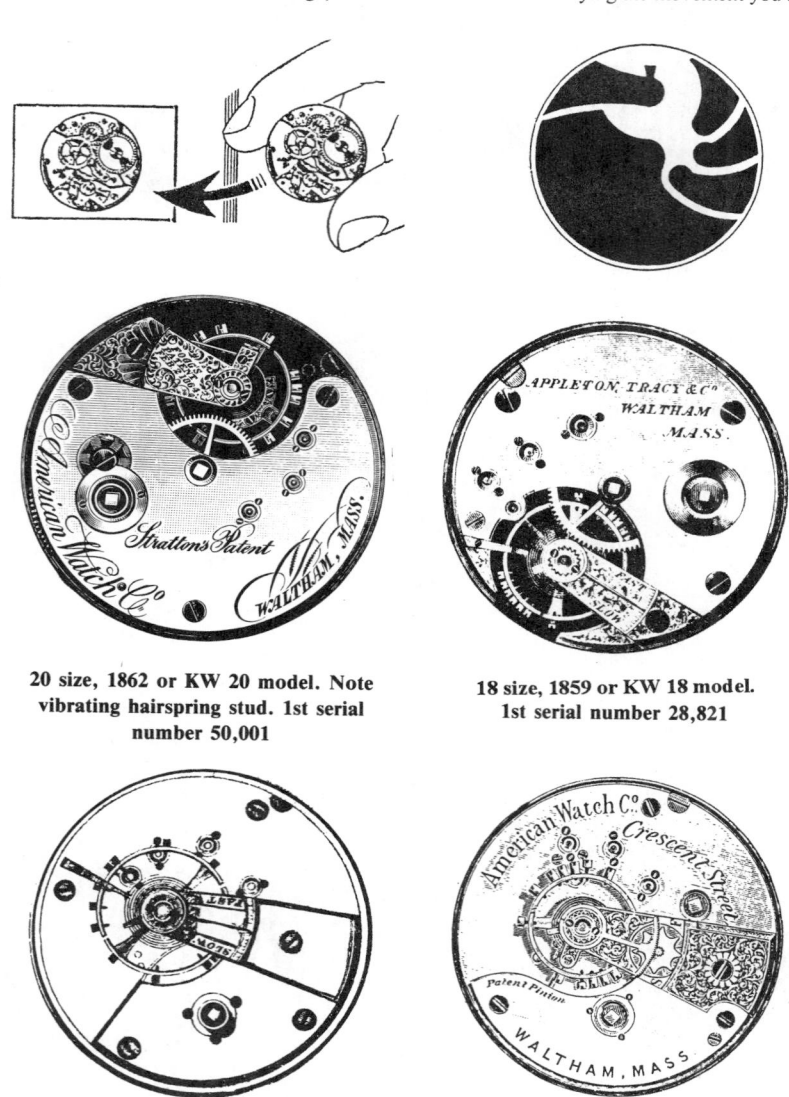

20 size, 1862 or KW 20 model. Note vibrating hairspring stud. 1st serial number 50,001

18 size, 1859 or KW 18 model. 1st serial number 28,821

Model 1857, KW, KS. 1st serial number 1,001

Model 1870, KW, KS from back 1st serial number 500,001

Model 1877, 18 size

Model 1879, 18 size

Model 1883, hunting
1st serial number 2,354,001

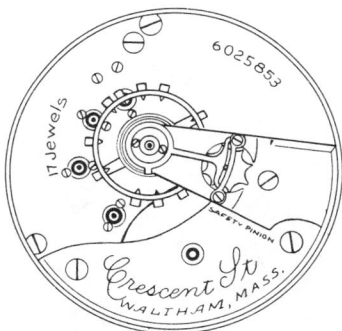

Model 1883, open face

Model 1892, open face

Model 1892, hunting.
1st serial number 6,026,001

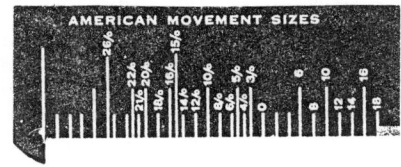

16½ size, Equity open face

Model 1860=16KW or 1868
16 size

Model 1872, 16 size open face

Model 1872, 16 size hunting case

Model 1888, 16 size, hunting

Bridge Model, 16 size

**Model 1895, 14 size,
open face**

Model 1897, 14 size

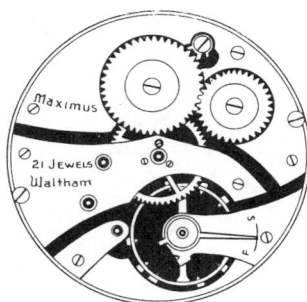

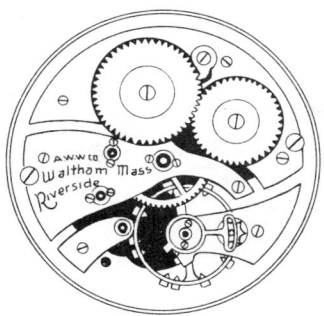

Colonial A Model, 14 size

Colonial Series, 14 size

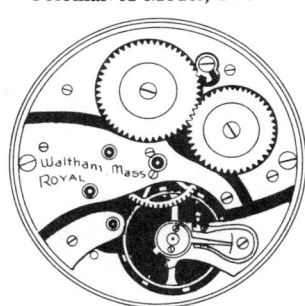

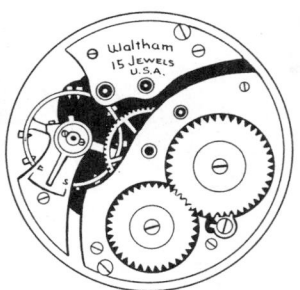

Model 1924, The Colonial

Model 1894, 12 size

Model 1924, The Colonial

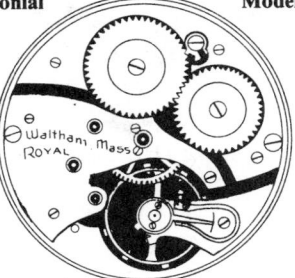

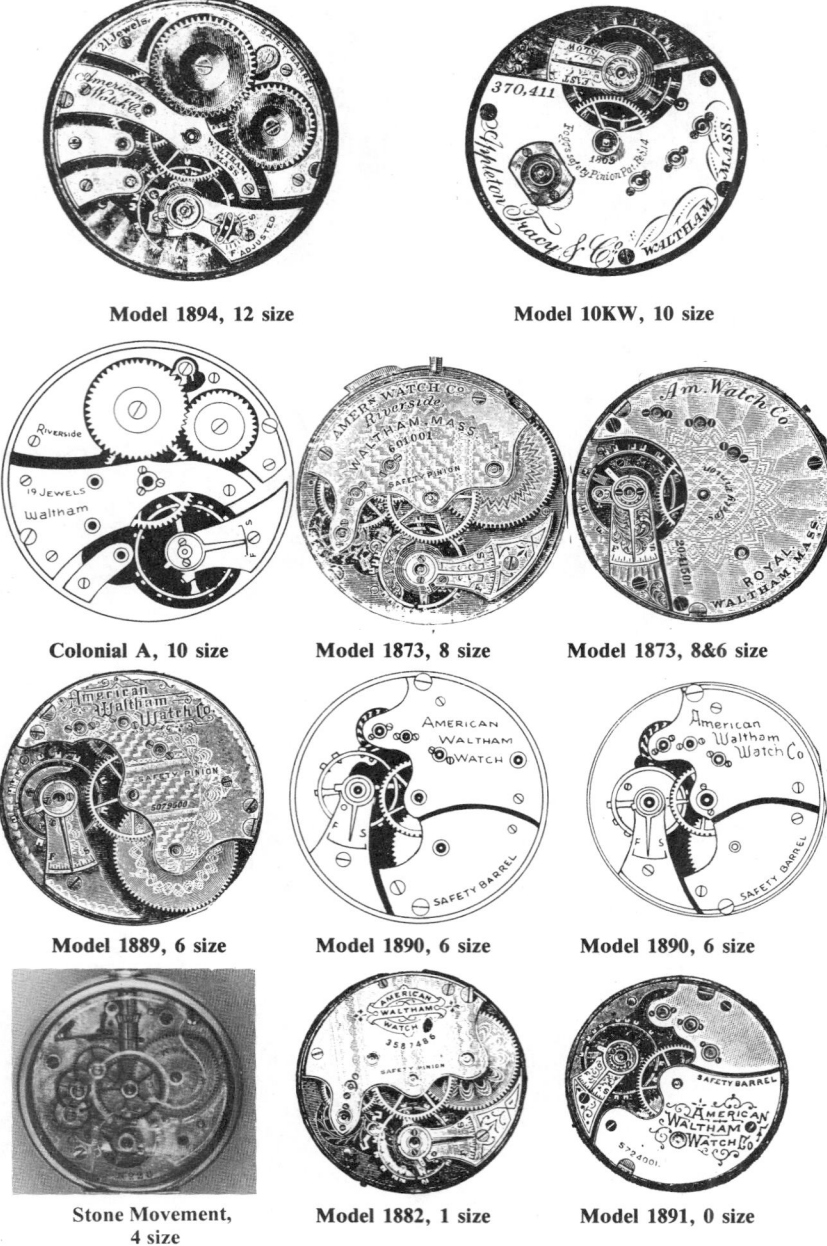

Model 1894, 12 size

Model 10KW, 10 size

Colonial A, 10 size

Model 1873, 8 size

Model 1873, 8&6 size

Model 1889, 6 size

Model 1890, 6 size

Model 1890, 6 size

Stone Movement, 4 size

Model 1882, 1 size

Model 1891, 0 size

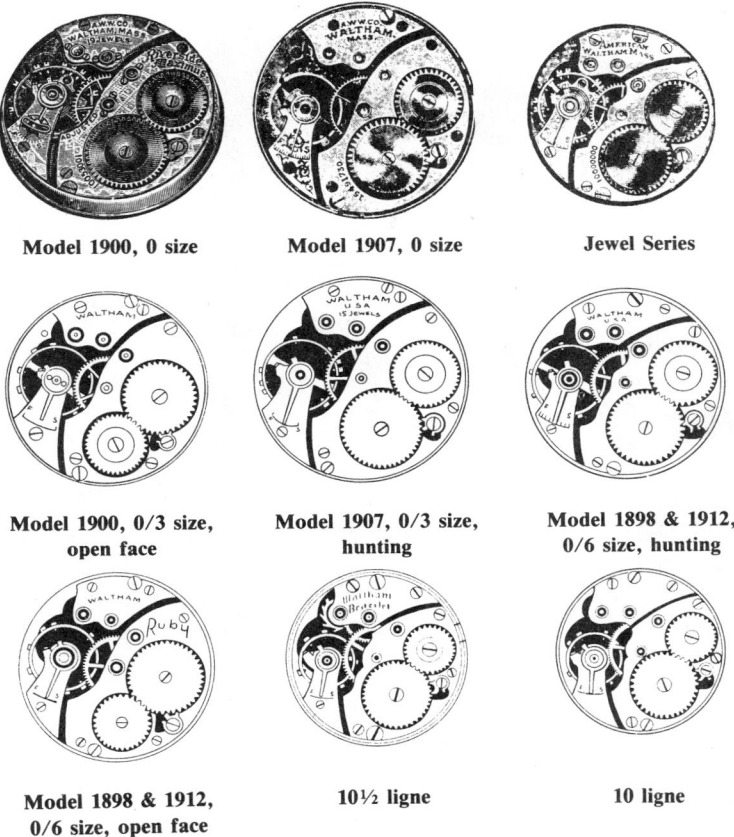

Model 1900, 0 size   Model 1907, 0 size   Jewel Series

Model 1900, 0/3 size,   Model 1907, 0/3 size,   Model 1898 & 1912,
open face   hunting   0/6 size, hunting

Model 1898 & 1912,   10½ ligne   10 ligne
0/6 size, open face

⊕ Generic, nameless or unmarked grades for watch movements are listed under the Company name or initials of the Company, etc. by size, jewel count and description.

⊕ Some grades are not included. Their values can be determined by comparing with similar age, size, metal content, style, models and grades listed.

⊕ Watches listed in this book are priced at the collectable Trade Show level, as complete watches having an original 14k gold-filled case and Key Wind with silver, an original white enamel single sunk dial, and with the entire original movement in good working order with no repairs needed.

⊕ This book endeavours to be a GUIDE or helpful manual and offers a wealth of material to be used as a tool not as a absolute document. Price Guides are like watches the worst may be better than none at all, but at best cannot be expected to be 100% accurate.

⊕ Characteristics of watches differ for the same age of both case and movement, because these features vary it may not be accurate to date a watch by one single influence. Example: the second hand was not commonly found on watches before 1750, but common about 1800. The first second hand appeared in 1665 and another in 1690. Therefore statements are broad rather than accurate.

140

ANSONIA CLOCK CO.

Brooklyn, New York
1896 - 1929

The Ansonia Watch Co. was owned by the Ansonia Clock Company in Ansonia, Connecticut. Ansonia started making clocks in about 1850 and began manufacturing watches in 1896. They produced about 10,000,000 dollar- type watches. The company was sold to a Russian investor in 1930. ''Patented April 17, 1888,'' is on the back plate of some Ansonia watches.

Ansonia Watch Company. Example of a basic movement, 16 size, stem wind.

Ansonia Watch Co., Sesqui-Centennial model.

Grade or Name–Description	Avg	Ex-Fn	Mint
Ansonia watch with a White Dial in Nickel case	$25	$35	$85
Ansonia watch with a Radium Dial in Nickel case	30	40	90
Ansonia watch with a Black Dial in Nickel case	35	45	100
Ascot	30	40	90
Bonnie Laddie Shoes	60	95	225
Dispatch	30	40	90
Faultless	35	45	100
Guide	35	45	100
Lenox	35	40	85
Mentor	35	45	95
Piccadilly	45	60	120
Rural	35	45	100
Sesqui-Centennial	250	275	450
Superior	45	60	100
Tutor	45	60	100

⊕ Some grades are not included. Their values can be determined by comparing with similar age, size, metal content, style, models and grades listed.

⊕ A collector should expect to pay modestly higher prices at local shops.

APPLETON WATCH CO.
(REMINGTON WATCH CO.)
Appleton, Wisconsin
1901 - 1903

In 1901, O. E. Bell bought the machinery of the defunct Cheshire Watch Company and moved it to Appleton, Wisconsin, where he had organized the Remington Watch Company. The first watches were shipped from the factory in February 1902; production ceased in mid-1903 and the contents were sold off before the end of that year. Most movements made by this firm were modified Cheshire movements and were marked "Appleton Watch Company." Advertisements for the firm in 1903 stated that they made 16 and 18 size movements with 11, 15, or 17 jewels. Serial numbers range from 89,000 to 104,950. During the two years they were in business, the company produced about 2,000 to 3,000 watches.

 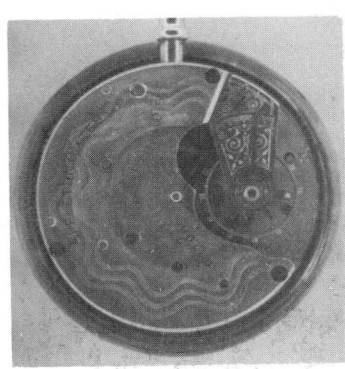

Appleton Watch Co., 18 size, 7 jewels, "The Appleton Watch Co." on dial. Engraved on movement "Appleton Watch Co., Appleton, Wis." Note that the stem is attached to movement. Serial number 93,106.

Description		Avg	Ex-Fn	Mint
18S, 7J, OF, NI, 3/4, DMK, SW, PS, stem attached .... ★★		$400	$500	$1,000
18S, 7J, OF, NI, 3/4, DMK, SW, PS, Coin, OF .... ★★		400	500	1,000
18S, 15J, NI, LS, SW, 3/4, M#2 .... ★★		500	600	1,200
16S, 7-11J, 3/4, stem attached .... ★★★		550	650	1,300

Note:With **ORIGINAL** APPLETON cases add **$300 to $400** more. This case is **difficult** to find.

AUBURNDALE WATCH CO.
Auburndale, Massachusetts
1876 - 1883

This company was the first to attempt an inexpensive watch. Jason Hopkins was issued two patents in 1875 covering the "rotary design." The rotary design eliminated the need of adjusting to various positions, resulting in a less expensive watch. The company was formed about 1876, and the first watches were known as the "Auburndale Rotary." In 1876, equipment was purchased from the Marion Watch Co., and the first rotary designed watches were placed on the market for $10 in 1877. Auburndale produced about 6,000 watches before closing in 1883. **Rotary** design as few as **500** made and **very few** known to exist.

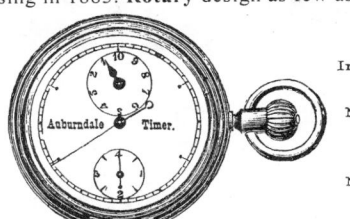

HORSE TIMERS—(only.)

In Nickel Cases.　　　　　　　　Stem Wind.

No. 633.　Auburndale Timer.　Sweep Second Hand, Beats ¼ Seconds, Stop and Fly Back.　(3 hands.)....$17 25

No. 634.　Auburndale Timer.　Split Sweep Seconds, Beats ¼ Seconds, Stop and Fly Back..........　31 50

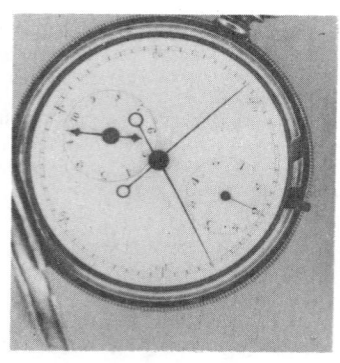

Auburndale Timer, 18 size, 7 jewels, stem wind, 10 minute, split seconds, fly back, 1/4 second jump timer.

Auburndale 10 min. Timer, 1/4 beat jump seconds, sweep second hand, stop & fly back, back wind.

Grade or Name – Description		Avg	Ex-Fn	Mint
Auburndale Rotary, 20S, 2-5J, SW, NI case, detent ...... ★★★★★		$1,800	$3,000	$5,000
Auburndale Rotary, 18S, 2-5J, SW, NI case, lever .... ★★★★		1,300	2,000	3,500
Bentley, 18S, 7J, LS, NI case, SW, 3/4................................ ★★★		800	1,000	2,000
Lincoln, 18S, 7J, LS, NI case, KW, 3/4 .... ★★★		800	1,000	2,000
Auburndale Timer, 18S, 5-7J, SW, NI case, 10 min. timer, 1/4 sec. jump second...		350	400	700
Auburndale Timer, 18S, 5-7J, SW, NI case, 10 min. timer, 1/4 sec. jump seconds, with a 24 hour dial .... ★		400	450	800
Auburndale Timer, 18S, 5-7J, KW, NI case, 10 min. timer, 1/4 sec. jump seconds, with split seconds .... ★★		600	650	1,100
Auburndale Timer, 18S, marked "207", gold balance, OF		325	400	700

Bentley, 18 size, 7 jewels, 3/4 plate, stem wind, serial number 2.

Auburndale Rotary Mass, 16 size, 2-5 jewels, rotating once in about 2.5 hours, stem wind, lever set, "Patents, Mar. 30 1875, July 20 1875, June 20 1876, Jan. 30 1877", S# 319. Note: Extremely RARE.

Auburndale Rotary, Serial # list: 3 - 46 - 116 - 124 - 176 - 224 - 241 - 161 - 250 - 319 - 361 - 370 - 387 - 403 - 423 - 447 - 448 - 507.

🕐 The Complete Price Guide to Watches goal is to stimulate the orderly exchange of <u>Watches</u> between "buyers" and "sellers".

AURORA WATCH CO.

Aurora, Illinois
1883 - 1892

Aurora Watch Co. was organized in mid-1883 with the goal of getting one jeweler in every town to handle Aurora watches. The first movements were 18S, full plate, and were first sold in the fall of 1884. There were several watches marked No. 1. About 95% were 18 size & 5% 6 size. For the most part Aurora produced medium to low grade; and at one time made about 100 movements per day. The Hamilton Watch Co. purchased the company on June 19, 1890.

AURORA WATCH CO.
Estimated Serial Nos. and Production Dates

1884 –	10,001	1888 – 200,000
1885 –	60,000	1889 – 215,000
1886 – 101,000		1891 – 230,901
1887 – 160,000		

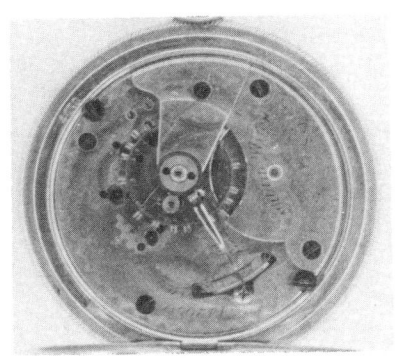

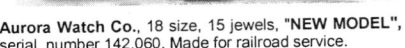

Aurora Watch Co., 18 size, 15 jewels, "NEW MODEL", serial number 142,060. Made for railroad service.

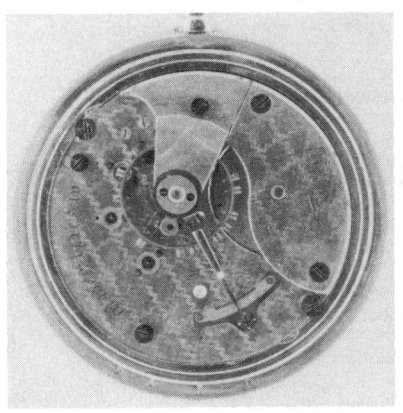

Aurora Watch Co., 18 size, 15 jewels, Adj, engraved on movement "Made expressly R.J.A.," **5th pinion** serial number 73,529.

Description	Avg	Ex-Fn	Mint
18S, 7J, KW, KS, Gilded, OF	$90	$150	$300
18S, 7J, KW, KS, Gilded, HC	150	175	450
18S, 7J, 5th pinion, Gilded, LS, SW, OF	90	150	300
18S, 7J, LS, SW, Gilded, new model, HC	150	175	450
18S, 11J, KW, KS, Gilded, HC	125	150	400
18S, 11J, KW, KS, Gilded, OF	125	150	400
18S, 11J, 5th pinion, LS, SW, Gilded, new model, OF	90	150	300
18S, 11J, 5th pinion, LS, SW, NI, GJS, OF	125	150	400
18S, 11J, 5th pinion, LS, SW, NI, GJS, new model, OF	125	150	400
18S, 11J, LS, SW, Gilded, **made expressly for the guild**, HC ....★	200	300	550
18S, 11J, 5th pinion, LS, SW, NI, OF			
made expressly for the guild............★	250	350	600
18S, 15J, KW, KS, NI, GJS, DMK, OF or HC............★	175	250	450
18S, 15J, 5th pinion, LS, SW, Gilded, OF	125	150	400
18S, 15J, 5th pinion, LS, SW, NI, GJS, DMK, ADT, OF	125	150	400
18S, 15J, 5th pinion, LS, SW, NI, GJS, DMK, ADJ, new model, OF	150	175	450
18S, 15J, LS, SW, NI, GJS, DMK, ADJ, new model, HC	150	175	450
18S, 15J, LS, SW, NI, GJS, ADJ, marked **Ruby Jewels** ....★★	450	500	1,000
18S, 15J, LS, SW, NI, GJS, ADJ, 2 Tone DMK, checker-			
board or snowflake, **Ruby Jewels**, HC............★★	500	600	1,200
18S, 15J, LS, SW, NI, GJS, ADJ, 2 Tone DMK, checker-			
board or snowflake, 5th pinion, **Ruby Jewels**, OF.......★★★	600	700	1,400

MARKED **"RUBY JEWELS"**, = Aurora's highest grade.

Size and Description	Avg	Ex-Fn	Mint
18S, marked **15 Ruby Jewels** but has 17J, 5th pinion, LS, SW, NI, GJS, 2 Tone, ADJ, OF .... ★★★	$700	$850	$1,400
18S, marked **15 Ruby Jewels**, only 15J, LS, SW, NI, GJS, 2 Tone DMK, ADJ, HC .... ★★★	650	800	1,300
18S, marked **15 Ruby Jewels**, only 15J, LS, SW, NI, GJS, ADJ, 2 Tone DMK, OF .... ★★★	650	800	1,300
18S, 15J, LS, SW, NI, GJS, DMK, ADJ, Railroad Time Service or Caufield Watch, new model, HC .... ★★	650	800	1,300
18S, 15J, Chronometer, LS, SW, NI, DMK, ADJ, new model HC .... ★★	600	700	1,200
18S, 15J, Chronometer, LS, SW, NI, GJS, DMK, ADJ, HC .... ★★	600	700	1,200
18S, 15J, LS, Gilded, "Eclipse, Chicago", new model, HC	300	450	700
18S, 15J, LS, SW, NI, DMK, made expressly for the guild, HC .. ★	275	375	625
18S, 15J, 5th pinion, LS, SW, Gilded, made expressly for the guild, OF .... ★	300	450	750
18S, 15J, LS, SW, Gilded, made expressly for the "RJA" (Retail Jeweler's Assoc.), HC .... ★	300	450	750

6 SIZE

Size and Description	Avg	Ex-Fn	Mint
6S, 11-15J, LS, SW, Gilded, 3/4, HC	$65	$95	$250
6S, 11-15J, LS, SW, NI, GJS, DMK, 3/4, HC..............................	70	100	295
6S, 11-15J, LS, SW, 3/4 plate, **14K, HC**..................................	250	300	600

BALL WATCH CO.

Cleveland, Ohio
1879 - 1969

The Ball Watch Company did not manufacture watches but did help formulate the specifications of watches used for railroad service. Webb C. Ball of Cleveland, Ohio, was the general time inspector for over 125,000 miles of railroad in the U. S., Mexico, and Canada. In 1891 there was a collision between the Lake Shore and Michigan Southern Railways at Kipton, Ohio. The collision was reported to have occurred because an engineer's watch had stopped, for about four minutes, then started running again. The railroad officials commissioned Ball to establish the timepiece inspection system. Ball knew that the key to safe operations of the railroad was the manufacturing of sturdy, precision timepieces. He also knew they must be able to withstand hard use and still be accurate. Before this time, each railroad company had its own rules and standards. After Ball presented his guidelines, most American manufacturers set out to meet these standards and soon a list was made of the manufacturers that produced watches of the grade that would pass inspection. Each railroad employee had a card that he carried showing the record of how his watch performed on inspection. Ball was also instrumental in the formation of the Horological Institute of America. By 1908 Ball furnished over **100 different railroad** companies with watches.

🕐 NOTE: BALL WATCHES ARE PRICED AS HAVING A ORIGINAL BALL DIAL & CASE.

ESTIMATED SERIAL NUMBERS AND PRODUCTION DATES
FOR RAILROAD GRADE WATCHES

(Hamilton)	(Waltham)	(Elgin)
Date – Serial #	Date – Serial #	**1904-1906**
1895 - 13,000	1900 - 060,700	S # range:
1897 - 20,500	1905 - 202,000	11,853,000 - 12,282,000
1900 - 42,000	1910 - 216,000	
1902 - 170,000	1915 - 250,000	
1905 - 462,000	1920 - 260,000	**(E. Howard & C0.)**
1910 - 600,000	1925 - 270,000	**1893-1895**
1915 - 603,000		S # range:
1920 - 610,000		226,000 - 308,000
1925 - 620,000		
1930 - 637,000	**(Illinois)**	**(Hampden)**
1935 - 641,000	Date – Serial #	**1890-1892**
1938 - 647,000	1929 - 800,000	S # range:
1939 - 650,000	1930 - 801,000	626,750 - 657,960
1940 - 651,000	1931 - 803,000	759,720
1941 - 652,000	1932 - 804,000	
1942 - 654,000		

The above list is provided for determining the **APPROXIMATE** age of your watch. Match serial number with date. Watches were not necessarily sold in the exact order of manufactured date.

BALL — AURORA
18 SIZE

Description		Avg	Ex-Fn	Mint
15-17J, marked Webb C. Ball, OF .... ★★★		$3,000	$3,500	$5,000
15-17J, marked Ball, HC .... ★★★		4,500	6,000	9,000

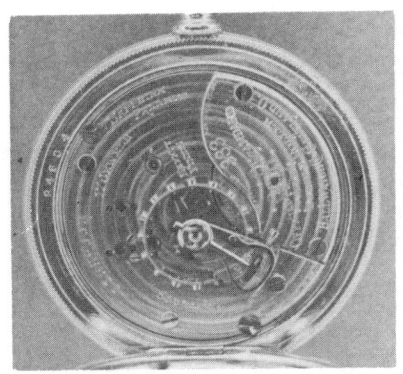
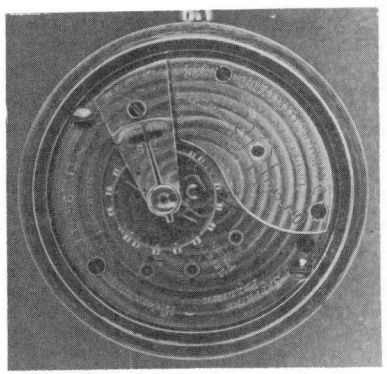

Ball-Elgin, Grade 333, 18 size, 17 jewels, rare hunting case model, serial number 11,958,002.

Ball-Elgin, Grade 333, 18 size, 17 jewels, open face model, serial number 11,856,801.

BALL — ELGIN
18 SIZE G. F. CASES

Description		Avg	Ex-Fn	Mint
16J, G#327, Commercial Standard, LS, OF .... ★		$300	$400	$700
17J, G#328, Commercial Standard, LS, HC .... ★		450	550	900

🕐 **The Complete Price Guide to Watches goal is to stimulate the orderly exchange of** <u>Watches</u> **between** *"buyers"* **and** *"sellers"*.

Description		Avg	Ex-Fn	Mint
17J, G#328, Coin, LS, HC	★	$350	$425	$800
17J, G#329, NI, Adj.5P, LS, HC	★ ★	1,200	1,400	2,400
16J, G#331, NI, Adj.5P, PS, Commercial Std, OF.	★ ★	375	425	800
16J, G#331, NI, Adj.5P, PS, Commercial Std, HC	★ ★ ★	400	450	900
17J, G#331, NI, Adj.5P, PS, OF		250	300	500
17J, G#332, Commercial Std, OF	★	250	300	500
17J, G#333, NI, Adj.5P, LS, OF		250	300	500
17J, G#333, NI, Adj.5P, LS, HC	★ ★ ★	1,500	2,000	3,000
21J, G#333, NI, Adj.5P, LS, OF		650	800	1,200
21J, G#333, NI, Adj.5P, LS, HC		700	900	1,400
21J, G#330, LS, Official RR std., HC	★ ★ ★ ★	2,000	2,500	5,000
21J, G#334, NI, Adj.5P, LS, OF		700	900	1,400

🕐 Note: 18 Size Ball watches in **hunting cases** are scarce.

BALL — HAMILTON
18 SIZE G. F. CASES

Description		Avg	Ex-Fn	Mint
17J, M#936, **first trial run S# 601 to 625** single roller	★ ★ ★	$2,500	$3,200	$6,500
17J, M#936, single roller or double roller		1,000	1,200	2,000
17J, M#936, marked Superior, Adj.		1,200	1,500	2,800
17J, M#-937-939, Official RR std, LS, Adj., **HC**	★ ★	2,000	2,500	4,200
17J, M#938, NI, DR, OF	★ ★	700	850	1,200
17J, M#999, Commercial Standard		300	400	800
17J, Off. Ball marked jewelers name on dial & mvt., OF	★	600	800	1,400
17J, M#999, NI, Official RR std, Adj.5P, LS, OF, Coin		300	400	800
17J, M#999, Official RR std, NI, Adj.5P, LS, OF		300	400	800
17J, M#999, "A" model adj. OF	★	350	400	800
17J, M#999, NI, Adj.5P, marked **"Loaner"** on case	★	500	600	1,000
19J, M#999, Official RR std, NI, Adj.5P, LS, OF		500	600	1,000
21J, M#999, Official RR std, NI, Adj.5P, LS, OF		500	600	1,000
23J, M#999, NI, Adj.5P, LS, Gold Filled OF Case	★ ★	4,000	4,500	7,000
23J, M#999, NI, Adj.5P, LS , OF, **14K case**	★ ★ ★	6,000	7,000	11,000
23J, M#999, NI, Adj.5P, LS, HC,**14K case**	★ ★ ★ ★	7,000	9,000	13,000
Early Ball & Co., 16-17J, (low serial # 13,001 to 13,400), OF marked dial & mvt. *Railroad Watch Co.* (second run)	★ ★ ★	1,400	1,800	3,200
Early Ball & Co., 16-17J, (low serial # 14,001 to 15,000), OF marked dial & mvt. *Railroad Watch Co.* (third run)	★ ★	1,200	1,500	3,000
Ball & Co., 16-17J, marked dial & mvt. *Railroad Watch Co*	★ ★	1,100	1,400	2,800
Brotherhood of Locomotive Engineers, 17J, OF	★ ★	3,000	3,600	5,000
Brotherhood of Locomotive Engineers, 19J, OF	★ ★	3,200	4,300	6,000

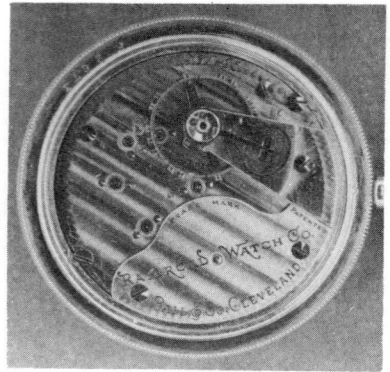

BALL-HAMILTON, 17J, **Webb C. Ball** marked on dial, marked on movement Ball standard superior grade, also marked adjusted and serial # **601.**

BALL-HAMILTON, Grade 999, 18 size, 17 jewels, marked *"Railroad Watch Co."* Ca. 1896, serial number 20,793.

Ball Watch Co., Brotherhood of RR trainmen, 18 size, 17J, movement made by Hamilton, serial number 13,020.

Ball Watch Co. (Hamilton). Grade 999, 18 size, 21-23 J., sun ray damaskeening, serial number 548,157, c.1906.

Description	Avg	Ex-Fn	Mint
Brotherhood of Locomotive Engineers, 21J, OF ★★	$3,500	$4,500	$6,500
Brotherhood of Locomotive Firemen, 17J, OF ★★	3,000	3,400	5,500
Brotherhood of Locomotive Firemen, 19J, OF ★★	3,200	4,300	6,000
Brotherhood of Locomotive Firemen, 21J, OF ★★	3,500	4,500	6,500
Brotherhood of Railroad Trainsmen, 17J, OF ★★	3,000	3,400	5,500
Brotherhood of Railroad Trainsmen, 19J, OF ★★	3,200	3,800	6,000
Brotherhood of Railroad Trainsmen, 21J, OF ★★	3,500	4,500	6,500
Order of Railroad Conductors, 17J, OF ★★	3,000	3,400	5,500
Order of Railroad Conductors, 19J, OF ★★	3,200	4,300	6,000
Order of Railroad Conductors, 21J, OF ★★★★	4,500	5,500	7,500
Order of Railroad Telegraphers, 17J, OF ★★★★	4,000	5,000	7,500
Order of Railroad Telegraphers, 19J, OF ★★★★	4,200	5,200	7,300
Order of Railroad Telegraphers, 21J, OF ★★★★	5,000	6,000	8,000
Private Label or Jewelers name, 17J, Adj., OF ★★	900	1,200	2,000

BALL WATCH Co. (OFFICIAL R.R. STANDARD) Dial, NOTE: 20th Century bow with snap back.

BALL WATCH Co. DIAL (Order of Railroad Conductors), 18 size.

BALL– DeLONG ESCAPEMENT
16 SIZE

Description		Avg	Ex-Fn	Mint
21-23J, **14K OF Case**	★★★★	$2,000	$3,000	$5,500

Ball-Hamilton, Model 998 Elinvar, 16 size, 23 jewels, with center bridge.

BALL W. CO. (HAMILTON),16 size, 21jewels, official RR standard, ADJ.5p, serial no.611429

BALL — HAMILTON
16 SIZE G. F. CASES

Description		Avg	Ex-Fn	Mint
16J, M#976, 977, 999-HC, NI, OF, LS	★	$350	$450	$850
17J, M#974, NI, OF, LS		200	250	550
17J, Official RR Standard, OF		250	300	600
19J, Official RR Standard, OF		250	300	600
19J, M#999, NI, Off. RR Stan., OF, LS		250	300	600
21J, M#999, NI, Off. RR Stan., OF, LS		400	500	800
21J, M#**999B-marked**, Off. RR Stan., OF, **marked-Adj.6P**		500	650	1,200
21J, M#999, Off. RR Stan., Coin case		400	500	800
21J, M#999 , Off. RR Stan., marked Loaner, coin case	★★	600	700	1,200
21J, M#992B, NI, marked **992B** & Off RR Stan. **Adj.6P**	★★★	1,000	1,400	3,000
23J, M#999B, Off. RR Stan., NI, OF, LS, Adj.6P		800	1,000	2,200
23J, M#998 **marked-Elinvar,** Off. RR Stan., Adj.5P		1,600	2,200	3,000
23J, M#999, NI, Off. RR Stan., OF, LS	★★	800	1,000	2,200
Brotherhood of Locomotive **Engineers**, OF	★★	2,500	3,200	4,000
Brotherhood of Locomotive Firemen, OF	★★	2,500	3,200	4,000
Brotherhood of Railroad Trainmen, OF	★★	2,500	3,200	4,000
Order of Railroad Conductors, OF	★★	2,500	3,200	4,000
17-19J, Brotherhood or Order, HUNTING CASE	★★★	2,000	2,500	5,000
Private Label or Jewelers name, 21J, Adj., OF	★	600	700	1,400

BALL — HAMPDEN
18 SIZE

Description		Avg	Ex-Fn	Mint
15-17J, LS, SW, HC, marked Superior Grade	★★★	$2,500	$3,000	$4,500
15-17J, LS, SW, OF, marked **Superior Grade**	★★	1,800	2,200	3,000
15-17J, LS, SW, OF	★	400	550	1,000
15-17J, LS, SW, HC	★★★	600	800	1,600

BALL- NEW YORK WATCH CO.

Description		Avg	Ex-Fn	Mint
Whitcomb & Ball, E.W. Bond Style 3/4 plate, 17-19J, NI,	★★★	$2,500	$3,500	$7,000

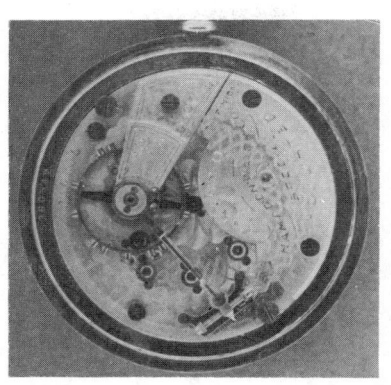

Ball-Hampden, 18 size, 17 jewels, serial number 759,728.

BALL & CO. (E. HOWARD & CO.), Series VIII, 18 size, 17 jewels. (Order of Railway Conductors), serial number 307,488. c.1900.

BALL — E. HOWARD & CO.
18 SIZE

Description		Avg	Ex-Fn	Mint
VII, Ball, 17J, nickel, SW, GF, HC	★ ★ ★	$3,500	$4,800	$7,500
VII, Ball, 17J, nickel, SW, **14K** orig. HC	★ ★ ★	4,000	5,000	9,500
VII, Ball ,17J, nickel, SW, **18K** orig. HC	★ ★ ★	7,000	9,000	13,500
VIII, Ball, 17J, nickel, SW, GF, OF	★ ★ ★	2,000	2,500	4,000
VIII, Ball, 17J, nickel, SW, **14K** orig. OF	★ ★ ★	3,000	3,500	5,600
VIII, Ball, 17J, 3/4, PS, GJS, *Brotherhood of Locomotive Engineers,* *or Order of Railroad Conductors*, **14K** orig.OF,	★ ★ ★	6,000	8,000	14,000

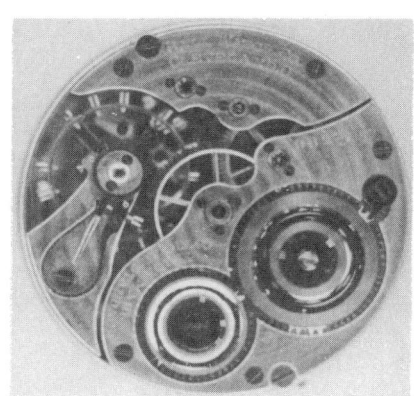

BALL W. Co. (E. HOWARD WATCH CO.), 16 size, 21J. (KEYSTONE). This watch believed to be one-of-a-kind prototype, serial number 982,201.

Ball Watch Co., Illinois Model, 16 size, 23 jewels. Note: The CORRECT HANDS FOR BALL ILLINOIS WATCH.

🕐 Some grades are not included. Their values can be determined by comparing with similar age, size, metal content, style, models and grades listed.

🕐 BALL Watches are priced as having a **ORIGINAL BALL DIAL & CASE.**

BALL — E. HOWARD WATCH CO. (Keystone)
16 SIZE

Description	Avg	Ex-Fn	Mint
17J, Keystone Howard, GJS, OF..	$2,000	$2,500	$4,000
21J, Keystone Howard, Adj, GJS, OF .... ★ ★ ★ ★ ★	6,000	7,000	10,000

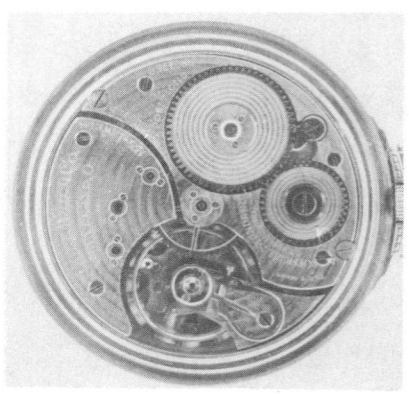

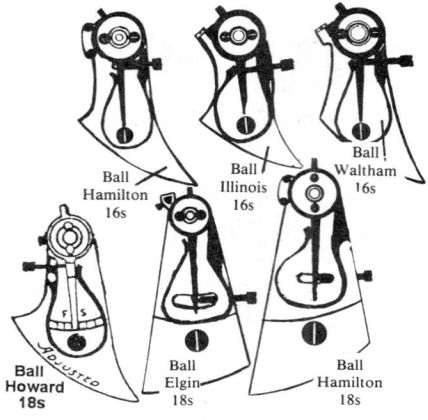

Ball Watch Co., Illinois Model # 11, 16 size, 23 jewels. To identify, note back plates that circle around balance wheel, serial number B801,758.

BALL regulator identification, note: styles and location of hairspring stud.

BALL — ILLINOIS
18 & 16 SIZE

Description	Avg	Ex-Fn	Mint
18 size, 11-15J. or (Garland model), OF...	$200	$250	$500
16 size, 23J, 3/4, LS, Off. RR Stan., Adj. 5P, GJS, OF............ ★ ★	1,500	1,900	3,600

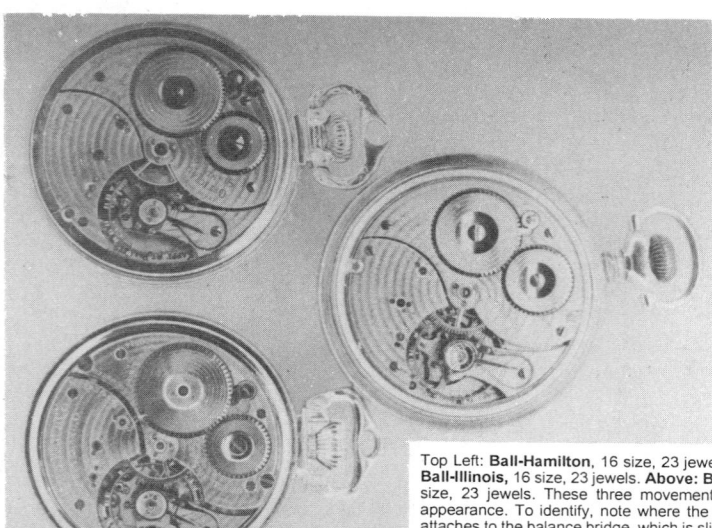

Top Left: Ball-Hamilton, 16 size, 23 jewels. Bottom left: Ball-Illinois, 16 size, 23 jewels. Above: Ball Waltham, 16 size, 23 jewels. These three movements are similar in appearance. To identify, note where the hair spring stud attaches to the balance bridge, which is slightly different on each movement.

BALL — SETH THOMAS
18 SIZE

Description	Avg	Ex-Fn	Mint
17J, M#3, LS, OF,3/4, GJS .... ★★★★	$6,000	$8,000	$14,000

BALL — WALTHAM
18 SIZE

Description	Avg	Ex-Fn	Mint
1892, 17J, OF, LS, SW, marked Webb C. Ball, Cleveland .... ★★★	$3,000	$4,000	$6,500

BALL — WALTHAM
16 SIZE

Description	Avg	Ex-Fn	Mint
15J, Commercial Std.,3/4, **HC**, GCW .... ★★	$300	$400	$800
15-16J, Commercial std., OF	150	200	400
16J, Commercial std., HC	225	300	600
17-19J, Commercial std., OF	150	200	400
17-19J, Commercial std., HC	225	300	600
17J, LS, 3/4, Adj.5P, Multi-color case, GF, OF	300	400	800
17J, LS, 3/4, Adj.5P, Off. RR Stan., OF	225	300	600
17J,Official RR std., HC .... ★★	800	900	1,600

Ball-Waltham, 16 size, 19 jewels, ORC (Order of Railroad Conductors), serial number B204,475.

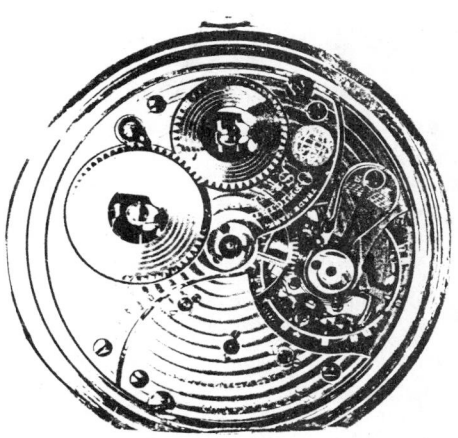

BALL–WALTHAM, 23 jewels, Official Railroad Standard, lever set, Adjusted to 5 positions, serial# B060,915.

Description	Avg	Ex-Fn	Mint
19J, Official RR std., LS, GCW,GJS, OF	$275	$350	$700
19J, LS, Off. RR Stan., stirrup style case, OF	275	350	700
19J, LS, Off. RR Stan., OF, Coin	275	350	700
19J, LS, Off. RR Stan., **OF 14K** .... ★★	1,200	1,600	3,200
19J, Official RR std., LS, GCW,GJS, **HC** .... ★★	800	1,000	2,000
19J, LS, 3/4, Adj.5P, Off. RR Stan., OF, Wind Indicator .... ★★★	5,500	6,500	10,000
21J, Commercial std., LS, OF	200	250	500
21J, Official RR std., LS, GCW,GJS, OF	400	500	800
21J, LS, 3/4, Adj.5P, Off. RR Stan., OF	400	500	800
21J, LS, OF, Adj.5P, Off. RR Stan., marked **Loaner,** OF .... ★	450	600	1,000
23J, LS, Adj.5P, NI, GJS, Off. RR Stand., OF, very rare .... ★★★★★	6,000	7,500	12,000

Watches MARKED "BALL & Co." are more difficult to find than BALL WATCH Co.

Description		Avg	Ex-Fn	Mint
17J, Brotherhood, marked ORC, BoFLE & *other etc. dials*, OF.	★★	$2,500	$3,000	$4,000
19J, Brotherhood, marked ORC, BoFLE & *other etc. dials*, OF.	★★	2,800	3,300	4,300
17-19J, Brotherhood, marked ORC, BoFLE & *other etc. dials*, HC	★★	4,000	5,000	7,000
21J, Brotherhood, marked ORC, BoFLE & *other etc. dials*, OF.	★★	3,000	3,500	4,500
21J, Brotherhood, marked ORC, BoFLE & *other etc. dials*, HC.	★★★	3,500	4,500	7,500

Ball Watch Co. by Illinois, **Secometer**, rotating digital sec, open face, 12 size, 19 jewels,

Record Watch Co. (BXC), 16 size, 21jewels, M#477-B, Adj.6P, Swiss made Ca.1961.

12 SIZE (Not Railroad Grade)

Description	Avg	Ex-Fn	Mint
17J, Garland, OF	$95	$125	$225
19J, Illinois, OF, PS	150	200	350
19J, Illinois, **14 K** OF	250	350	600
19J, Illinois, Secometer, rotating digital sec, OF ★	250	350	600
17J, Waltham, Commercial Standard, OF, PS, ★	150	200	350

0 SIZE (Not Railroad Grade)

Description	Avg	Ex-Fn	Mint
17-19J, Waltham, OF, PS	$200	$275	$450
19J, HC, PS, ''Queen'' in Ball case	250	350	500

NO. 333
NO. 999

999 STANDARD.

OFFICIAL RR STANDARD

OFFICIAL TIME SERVICE STANDARD

STANDARD

B OF RT STANDARD

B OF LE STANDARD

Railway Queen

O OF RC STANDARD

B OF LF STANDARD

SAFETY FIRST

The B. of L. E. Standard Watch.
The B. of L. F. Standard Watch.
The B. of R. T. Standard Watch.
The O. of R. C. Standard Watch.
The Official R. R. Standard Watch.
The O. of R. T. Standard Watch.

TRADE MARKS REGISTERED IN U. S. PATENT OFFICE

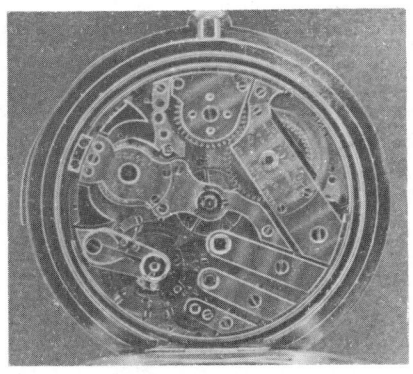

Ball-Audemars Piguet & Co., 14 size, 31 jewels, minute repeater, open face, serial number 4,220.

Ball-Vacheron & Constantin, 43mm, 18 jewels, hunting; note wolf-teeth winding.

BALL — SWISS
12-16 SIZE

Description	Avg	Ex-Fn	Mint
17J, "Garland"	$100	$125	$250
18-21J, Longines, OF	100	125	250
21J, Time Ball Special,OF	75	100	200
21J, M#435-B, LS, Adj.6P, Ball case, stirrup bow, OF	100	150	250
21J, M#435-C, LS, Adj.6P, Ball case, stirrup bow, OF	100	150	250
21J, M#477-B, Adj.6P (BXC-Record Watch Co.)	100	150	250
40mm Audemar Piguet, min. repeater, jeweled thru hammers, triple signed Webb C. Ball, **18K, OF** ★★	4,500	5,500	9,500
43-44mm Vacheron & Constantin, 18J, **HC, 18K** ★★	1,600	2,200	3,800
12 size, 17J, by Longines, marked "Made expressly for Webb C. Ball" AdJ. temperature 2 pos. Ca. 1922	125	150	200

20 th CENTURY CASE

18 size: 14K=$500 - $600 - $1,100
18 size: gold filled= $175 - $250 - $500
16 size: 14K = $400 -$500 - $950
16 size: gold filled= $125 - $195 - $400
16-18 size: silveroid=$100 - $175 - $350
  Ball RR Dials
18 size: $40 - $80 - $150
16 size: $35 - $60 - $100

ANTIQUE BOW

18 size: 14K=$550 - $650 - $1,200
18 size: gold filled= $175 - $250 - $500
16 size: 14K= $450 -$550 - $1,000
16 size: gold filled= $125 - $195 - $400
BLE (Brotherhood dials)
18size: $250 - $300 - $600
16 size: $200 - $250 - $400

CATALOG CASE # 106
gold filled case $100 - $175 - $375

CATALOG CASE # 110
gold filled case $150 - $175 - $425

"BOX CAR" Dial;
found on Hamilton & Illinois made Ball

"CONVENTIONAL" Dial;
found on Waltham made Ball

CATALOG CASE # 114
gold filled case $150 - $175- $425

CATALOG CASE # 118
gold filled case $175 - $200 - $425

🕐 NOTE: A 1902 advertisement for Ball Watch Company read, "We do not sell movements or cases separately". BALL Advertised as a **COMPLETE** watch with a choice of BALL dials and was fitted with a certain matched, timed and rated movement and sold in the BALL designed case style as a **COMPLETE** watch. <u>**ALL THE ABOVE CASES ARE GOLD FILLED.**</u>

Serial numbers range from 201 to 89,650. All Cheshire watches were sold through L. W. Sweet, general selling agent, in New York City. The factory closed in 1890, going into receivership. The receiver had 3,000 movements finished in 1892. In 1901 O. E. Bell bought the machinery and had it shipped to Appleton, Wisconsin, where he had formed the Remington Watch Company. The watches produced by Remington are marked ''Appleton Watch Co.'' on the movements.

Cheshire Watch Co., 20 size, 4 jewels, **model** number 1. Note stem attached and will not fit standard size case, serial number **201**. NOTE: Closed top plate near balance. The Cheshire Watch Co. may have started with S# **201**.

Cheshire Watch Co., 20 size, 4 jewels, **model** number 1.

Description	Avg	Ex-Fn	Mint
20S, 4-7J, FULL, OF, SW, NI case, stem attached, low serial #			
1st **model**, closed top plate (S # **201 to 300**) .... ★ ★ ★	$500	$650	$1,200
20S, 4-7J, FULL, OF, SW, NI case, stem attached,			
1st **model**, closed top plate .... ★ ★	400	550	800
18S, 4-7J, 3/4, SW, OF, NI case, stem attached, 2nd model .... ★	295	350	550
18S, 4-7J, HC/ OF fits standard case, 3rd model.......................... ★	250	300	500
18S, 11J, HC/ OF, standard case, 3rd model .... ★	275	325	525
18S, 15J, HC/ OF, NI, ADJ, standard case, 3rd model .... ★	295	350	550
18S, 21J, HC / OF, SW, Coin, standard case, 3rd model .... ★ ★	400	500	650
6S, 3/4, HC/ OF, SW, NI case.. ★	195	250	450

Cheshire Watch Co., 18 size, 4-7 jewels. This model number 2 was manufactured with the stem attached and requires a special case. NOTE: open top plate at Balance.

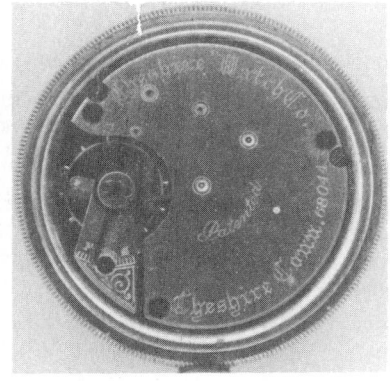

Cheshire Watch Co., 18 size, 4-7 jewels. This model fits **standard 18 size cases.** Model number 3.

🕐 1st & 2nd model Cheshire movements will not fit standard 18 size cases.
Model # 1, S# 201 to15,000 - Model # 2, S # 30,001 to 40,000 - Model # 3, S # 50,001 to 89,650.

CHICAGO WATCH CO.

Chicago, Illinois
1895 - 1903

The Chicago Watch Company's ALL watches in ALL sizes were made by **other manufacturing companies** and sold by Chicago Watch Co.

Description	Avg	Ex-Fn	Mint
18S, 7J, OF	$95	$145	$295
18S, 7-11J, HC or OF, Swiss	35	45	75
18S, 11J, KW	150	195	350
18S, 15J, OF, SW	125	195	350
Columbus, 18S, 15J, SW, NI, OF ★	150	185	375
Columbus, 18S, 15J, SW, NI, HC ★	195	250	400
Illinois, 18S, 11J, SW, NI ★	195	250	400
Waltham, 18S, 15J ★	195	250	400
12S, 15J, OF	40	60	150
12S, 15J, YGF, HC	85	125	195

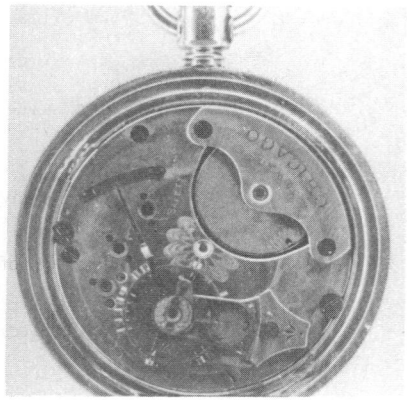

Chicago Watch Co., 18 size, 15 jewels, Hunting case, made by COLUMBUS Watch Co., nickel movement, lever set, serial # 209,145.

Columbia Watch Co., 0 size, 4 jewels, stem wind, open face and hunting, duplex escapement, the escape wheel teeth were milled to give better quality than the Waterbury movements.

COLUMBIA WATCH CO.

Waltham, Massachusetts
1896 - 1899

The Columbia Watch Company was organized in 1896 by Edward A. Locke, formerly General Manager of the Waterbury Watch Company. The firm began manufacturing an 0-size, 4-jewel gilt movement with duplex escapement in 1897. These movements were marked "Columbia Watch Co., Waltham, Mass." The firm also made movements marked "Hollers Watch Co., Brooklyn, NY," as well as nickeled movements marked "Cambridge Watch Co., New York."

Locke turned the business over to his son-in-law, Renton Whidden, in 1898, and the firm changed to an 0-size, 7-jewel nickel movement with lever escapement called the Suffolk. The firm name was not changed until early 1901.

Description	Avg	Ex-Fn	Mint
0S, 4J, SW, Duplex, gilded, HC	$40	$65	$150
0S, 4J, SW, Duplex, gilded, OF	35	50	135
0S, 7J, SW, lever escapement, OF	40	65	150

COLUMBUS WATCH CO.

Columbus, Ohio
1874 - 1903

Dietrich Gruen, born in Osthofen, Germany in 1847, started a business as the Columbus Watch Co. on Dec. 22, 1874 in Columbus, Ohio. At the age of 27, he received a U.S. patent for an improved safety pinion. The new company finished movements made from **Madretsch**, Switzerland, a suburb of Beil. The imported movements were made in a variety of sizes and were in nickel or gilt. The early watches usually had the initials C.W.CO. intertwined in script on the dial. The serial numbers generally ran up to around 20,000's a few examples are in the 70,000's.

D. Gruen and W.J. Savage decided in late 1882 to manufacture watches locally. By August of 1883 the first movements were being produced with a train consisting of 72 teeth on the barrel, 72 on the center wheel, 11 on the center pinion, 60 on the third wheel with a pinion of 9, 70 on the fourth wheel with a pinion of 9 with a 7 leaf escape pinion. The new manufacture primarily made 18 size movements but also pioneered the 16 size watch while reducing the size and thickness. Several new innovations were used into the design including a completely covered main spring barrel, a new micrometric regulator and the ability to change the main spring without removing the balance cock. By 1884 they were making their own dials, but no cases were ever manufactured.

The company went into receivership in 1894 with new management. That same year Frederick Gruen started again as D. Gruen & Son. They had PAUL ASSMANN to produce 18 size & 16 size movements with 18 & 21 jewels with the escapement designed by Moritz Grossman of Glasshute. Soon after this time movements were obtained from Switzerland and the new Gruen veri-thin movement was developed. In 1898 this company moved to Cincinnati, Ohio.

From 1894 through February 14, 1903 the Columbus Watch Co. produced watches both under the Columbus Watch Co. and the New Columbus Watch Co. name. The re-organized company produced the same models, but switched primarily to named grades such as Time King, Columbus King, etc. The higher grade watches were assigned a special block of serial numbers from 500,000 to 506,000 . In keeping with the industry several models with 25 jewels were produced in this block of serial numbers.

In 1903 the Columbus Watch Co. was sold to the Studebakers and the South Bend Watch Co. started. The machinery, unfinished movements, parts and approximately 3/4 of the 150 employees moved to South Bend, Indiana. Some marked Columbus Watch Co. movements were finished by the South Bend W. Co. Examples exist of dials made in the South Bend style and movements marked Columbus Watch Co.

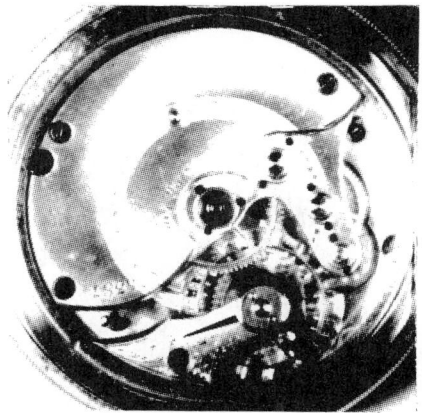

1874

COLUMBUS WATCH CO., 19 Lignes or about 14-16 size, 16 jewels, gold jewel settings, marked Gruen's Pat. pinion, OPEN FACE model, serial # 5,387. (Swiss contract)

COLUMBUS WATCH CO., 19 Lignes or about 14-16 size, 15 jewels, hunting case, engraved on movement *"1874"* .

COLUMBUS
ESTIMATED SERIAL NUMBERS AND PRODUCTION DATES

DATE - SERIAL NO.	DATE— SERIAL NO.	21 jewels or more
1874—- 1	1888 – 97,000	Columbus King or
1875– 1,000	1889 – 119,000	Railway King
1876– 3,000	1890 – 141,000	
1877– 6,000	1891 – 163,000	SPECIAL BLOCK
1878– 9,000	1892 – 185,000	OF SERIAL NOS.
1879– 12,000	1893 – 207,000	DATE— SERIAL NO.
1880– 15,000	1894 – 229,000	1894 – 500,001
1881– 18,000	1895 – 251,000	1896 – 501,500
1882– 21,000	1896 – 273,000	1898 – 503,000
1883– 25,000	1897 – 295,000	1900 – 504,500
1884 – 30,000	1898 – 317,000	1902 – 506,000
1885 – 40,000	1899 – 339,000	
1886 – 53,000	1900 – 361,000	
1887 – 75,000	1901 – 383,000	

The above list is provided for determining the **APPROXIMATE** age of your watch. Match serial number with date. Watches were not necessarily **SOLD** and **DELIVERED** in the exact order of manufactured or production dates.

SWISS, 3/4 PLATE, & MADE FROM 1874–1883
Most marked COL. WATCH CO. with single sunk dials and may be SW/KW Transitional, serial # up to 20,000.

Grade or Name — Description	Avg	Ex-Fn	Mint
18S, 7J, pressed J., nickel or gilded, OF/HC	$80	$95	$250
18S, 11J, pressed J., nickel or gilded, OF/HC	95	150	295
18S, 15J, GJS or pressed J., nickel, Adj., OF/HC	150	195	350
18S, 16J, raised GJS, 2 tone or nickel, Adj., OF/HC......................	195	300	450
Grade or Name — Description	**Avg**	**Ex-Fn**	**Mint**
16S, 11J, pressed J., nickel, OF/HC......................................	$150	$195	$400
16S, 15J, pressed J. or GJS, Adj., nickel, OF/HC	150	195	400
16S, 16J, raised GJS, Adj., nickel, OF/HC	175	225	450
Grade or Name — Description	**Avg**	**Ex-Fn**	**Mint**
14S, 16J, GJS, nickel, Adj., OF/HC..	$150	$195	$400
Grade or Name — Description	**Avg**	**Ex-Fn**	**Mint**
9S, 15J, GJS or pressed J., nickel, Adj., OF/HC	$95	$150	$300
Grade or Name — Description	**Avg**	**Ex-Fn**	**Mint**
8S, 11J, pressed J., nickel, OF/HC..	$95	$150	$300
8S, 15J, pressed J., nickel, OF/HC..	95	150	300

FOR ABOVE HUNTING CASED MODEL ADD $35.00 to $65.00
NOTE: These Odd size movements are difficult to case.

COLUMBUS WATCH CO., 19 Lignes or about 16 size, 15 jewels, exposed winding wheels, marked Gruen Patent, OPEN FACE model, serial # 1,661. (Swiss contract)

COLUMBUS WATCH CO., about 14 size, 16 jewels, gold jewel settings, nickel plates, marked Gruen's pat. pinion, HUNTING CASE model. (Swiss contract)

18 SIZE-KW, FULL PLATE, MODEL # 1 & TRANSITIONAL
Serial # up to 100,000, balance cock set flush to barrel bridge and may have pinned dial.
Marked Col. Watch Co., Ohio Columbus Watch Co.

Grade or Name — Description	Avg	Ex-Fn	Mint
11-13J, KW / KS, gilded, OF/HC	$250	$375	$650
13J, KW / KS, nickel,(marked 13 jewels), OF/HC.................... ★ ★	350	450	700
15J, KW / KS, gilded, Adj., OF/HC...	300	400	600
16J, KW / KS, gilded, OF/HC.. ★	325	425	700
Grade or Name — Description	**Avg**	**Ex-Fn**	**Mint**
11-13J, SW/ KW, gilded or nickel, OF/HC	$135	$160	$400
15J, SW/ KW, gilded or nickel, GJS, OF/HC...................................	150	200	450
16J, SW/ KW, gilded or nickel, GJS, OF/HC..................................	175	250	475

FOR ABOVE HUNTING CASED MODEL ADD **$25.00 to $50.00**

COLUMBUS WATCH CO., 18 size, marked 13 jewels, pressed jewels, key wind key set, nickel plates, marked on movement Col. Watch Co. Columbus Ohio Pat. pinion, on dial "OHIO COLUMBUS WATCH CO.", serial #40,198.

COLUMBUS WATCH CO., 18 size, 15 jewels, key wind key set, hunting case, on movement "Columbus Watch Co. Columbus, Ohio Pat. Pinion", serial # 66,577.

18 SIZE, FULL PLATE, PRE-1894
Marked "Columbus Watch Co. Columbus, Ohio", all marked Safety Pinion

Grade or Name — Description	Avg	Ex-Fn	Mint
7J, G#90, pressed J., OF...	$65	$100	$195
7J, G#20, pressed J., HC..	90	125	250
11J, G#92, pressed J., nickel, OF...	65	100	195
11J, G#22, pressed J., nickel, HC...	95	150	250
15J, G#64 / G#93, gilded, OF...	65	100	195
15J, G#24 / G#32, gilded, HC...	95	150	250
15J, G#63 / G#94, nickel, Adj., OF..	80	120	195
15J, G#23 / G#33, nickel, Adj., HC	95	150	250
15J, G#95, nickel, Adj., D.S. dial, OF	75	110	250
15J, G#34, nickel, Adj., D.S. dial, HC	95	150	350
16J, G#97, GJS, nickel, Adj., D.S. dial, OF	95	150	250
16J, G#27, GJS, nickel, Adj., D.S. dial, HC	110	200	350
16J, G#98, raised GJS, 2 tone nickel, Adj., D.S. dial, OF...............	110	200	350
16J, G#28, raised GJS, 2 tone nickel, Adj., D.S. dial, HC...............	150	225	400
16J, G#99, raised GJS, 2 tone nickel, Adj., D.S. dial, OF...............	125	250	450
16J, G#18, raised GJS, 2 tone nickel, Adj., D.S. dial, HC	150	275	500

18 SIZE-FULL PLATE, POST-1894

Some Marked "New Columbus Watch Co. Columbus Ohio"

Grade or Name — Description	Avg	Ex-Fn	Mint
7J, G#10, pressed J., gilded, OF	$60	$100	$195
7J, G#9, pressed J., gilded, HC	80	125	275
11J, G#8, nickel, OF	65	100	195
11J, G#7, nickel, HC	90	150	295
16J, G#6, nickel, OF	80	100	195
16J, G#5, nickel, HC	95	150	295
16J, G#4, GJS, 2 tone nickel, Adj., D.S. dial, OF	100	175	350
16J, G#3, GJS, 2 tone nickel, Adj., D.S. dial, HC	150	195	400
17J, G#204, GJS, 2 tone nickel, Adj., D.S. dial, OF	150	195	400
17J, G#203, GJS, 2 tone nickel, Adj., D.S. dial, HC	165	250	450
17J, G#2, raised GJS, 2 tone nickel, Adj., D.S. dial, OF	175	275	450
17J, G#1, raised GJS, 2 tone nickel, Adj., D.S. dial, HC	195	300	475

COLUMBUS WATCH CO., with a "Choo Choo" Railway King double sunk dial.

COLUMBUS WATCH CO., Railway King, 18 size, 17 jewels, 2 tone, serial # 313,005.

18 SIZE FULL PLATE, NAMED GRADES

Marked Names, Double Sunk Dials

Grade or Name — Description	Avg	Ex-Fn	Mint
Am. Watch Club, 15J, 2 tone, Adj., D.S. dial, OF/HC ★	$300	$450	$600
Burlington Route C.B. & QR.R., 15J, nickel, Adj., D.S. dial, OF ★★★★★	2,500	3,500	5,000
Champion, 15J, gilded, Adj., D.S.dial, OF	65	110	250
Champion, 15J, gilded, Adj., D.S.dial, HC	85	150	300
Champion, 15J, Nickel, Adj., D.S.dial, OF	65	110	250
Champion, 15J, Nickel, Adj., D.S.dial, HC	85	150	300
Champion, 16J, nickel, Adj., D.S.dial, OF	85	150	300
Champion, 16J, Nickel, Adj., D.S.dial, HC	125	295	350

* Chicago W. Co. made by Columbus W. Co. (see listing under Chicago W. Co. HEADING)

🕐 Watches listed in this book are priced at the collectable trade show level, as **complete** watches having an original 14k gold-filled case & *KEY W IND* with silver case, an original white enamel single sunk dial, and with the entire original movement in good working order with no repairs needed.

Grade or Name — Description	Avg	Ex-Fn	Mint
Columbus King, 17J, raised GJS, nickel, Adj., D.S. dial, OF	$195	$275	$500
Columbus King, 17J, raised GJS, nickel, Adj., D.S. dial, HC	250	350	600
Columbus King, 17J, raised GJS, nickel, Adj., choo choo D.S. dial, OF	500	600	1,100
Columbus King, 17J, raised GJS, nickel, Adj., Angled choo choo D.S. dial, OF	500	600	1,100
Columbus King, 21J, raised GJS, nickel, Adj., D.S. dial, OF	450	550	900
Columbus King, 21J, raised GJS, nickel, Adj., D.S. dial, HC	400	500	850
Columbus King, 23J, raised GJS, nickel, Adj., D.S. dial, OF ......★	1,000	1,300	2,300
Columbus King, 23J, raised GJS, nickel, Adj., D.S. dial, HC .....★	1,000	1,300	2,300
Columbus King, 25J, raised GJS, nickel, Adj., D.S. dial, OF .... ★★★	3,200	3,500	5,500
Columbus King, 25J, raised GJS, nickel, Adj., D.S. dial, HC... ★★★	2,800	3,300	5,000
F.C. & P.R.R., 17J, GJS, nickel, Adj., D.S. dial, OF .... ★★★	900	1,200	2,000
Jackson Park, 15J, 2 tone, Adj., D.S. dial, OF.............................★	450	550	900
Jay Gould, Railroad King, 15J, nickel,Adj., D.S. dial, OF .. ★★★	1,000	1,300	2,200
New York Susquehanna &Western R.R.,16J, GJS, SW/KW, gold flash, D.S. dial, OF .... ★★★★	2,500	3,000	4,500
Non-magnetic, 16J, raised GJS, 2 tone, Adj., OF/HC	295	400	700
North Star, 11J, gilded, OF..	95	125	295
North Star, 11J, gilded, HC	125	150	350
North Star, 11J, nickel, OF..	95	125	295
North Star, 11J, nickel, HC	125	150	350
North Star, 15J, nickel, OF..	125	150	350
North Star, 15J, nickel, HC	150	175	400
The President, 17J, GJS, Adj, 2 tone, D.S. dial, OF.....................★	400	500	800
Railroad Regulator, 15J, GJS, nickel, Adj., D.S. dial, OF ....★	450	550	900
Railroad Regulator, 16J, GJS, nickel, Adj., D.S. dial, OF ....★	450	500	900
Railway, 17J, GJS, 2 tone, Adj., D.S. dial, OF............................★	295	350	650

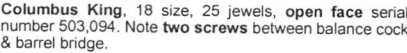

Columbus King, 18 size, 25 jewels, **open face** serial number 503,094. Note **two screws** between balance cock & barrel bridge.

Railway King, 18 size, 23 jewels, adjusted, stem wind, **hunting case**, serial number 503,315. Note **one screw** between balance cock & barrel bridge.

⊕ Watches listed in this book are priced at the collectable Trade Show level, as **complete** watches having an original 14k gold-filled case & *KEY W IND* with silver case, an original white enamel single sunk dial, and with the entire original movement in good working order with no repairs needed.

⊕ **The Complete Price Guide to Watches goal is to stimulate the orderly exchange of Watches between "*buyers*" and "*sellers*".**

Grade or Name — Description	Avg	Ex-Fn	Mint
Railway King, 16J, GJS, 2 tone nickel, Adj., D.S. dial, OF	$275	$300	$550
Railway King, 16J, GJS, 2 tone nickel, Adj., D.S. dial, HC	350	450	650
Railway King, 16J, GJS, 2 tone nickel, Adj., (black red blue) **choo choo** D.S. dial, OF	400	550	1,000
Railway King, 16J, GJS, 2 tone nickel, Adj., (black red blue) **choo choo** D.S. dial, HC	400	550	1,000
Railway King, 16J, GJS, 2 tone nickel, Adj., Angled **choo choo** dial, OF	550	650	1,100
Railway King, 16J, GJS, 2 tone nickel, Adj., Angled **choo choo** dial, HC	550	650	1,100
Railway King, 17J, raised GJS, nickel, Adj., D.S. dial, OF	275	325	550
Railway King, 17J, raised GJS, nickel, Adj., D.S. dial, HC	300	400	600
Railway King, 21J, raised GJS, nickel, Adj., D.S. dial, OF	450	500	750
Railway King, 21J, raised GJS, nickel, Adj., D.S. dial, HC	450	500	800
Railway King, 23J, raised GJS, nickel, Adj., Railway King D.S. dial, OF ★★★	1,000	1,200	2,000
Railway King, 23J, raised GJS, nickel, Adj., Railway King D.S. dial, HC ★★★	1,000	1,200	2,000
Railway King, 25J, raised GJS, nickel, Adj., Railway King D.S. dial, OF ★★★★	2,500	3,000	4,200
Railway King, 25J, raised GJS, nickel, Adj., Railway King D.S. dial, HC ★★★★	3,000	4,000	5,500
Railway King Special, 17J, GJS, nickel, Adj., D.S. dial, OF	295	400	600
Railway Monarch, 17J, GJS, nickel, Adj., D.S. dial, OF ★	295	400	600
Railway Monarch, 17J, GJS, nickel, Adj., D.S. dial, HC ★	295	400	600
Railway Time Service, 17J, GJS, nickel, Adj., D.S. dial, OF ★	375	450	800
The Regent, 15J, D.S. dial, OF	150	195	400
R.W.K. Special, 15J, GJS, Adj., 2 tone, D.S. dial, OF	250	295	500
R.W.K. Special, 15J, GJS, Adj., 2 tone, D.S. dial, HC	250	295	500
R.W.K. Special, 16J, GJS, Adj., 2 tone, D.S. dial, OF	250	295	500
R.W.K. Special, 16J, GJS, Adj., 2 tone, D.S. dial, HC	295	350	550
Springfield Mo.W. Club, 16J, GJS, nickel, Adj., D.S. dial, HC ★	350	450	650
Special, 17J, GJS, nickel, D.S. dial, OF	200	250	450
J.P. Stevens & Co. (see listing under J.P. Stevens & Co. **HEADING**)			
The New Menlo Park, 15J, HC ★★	195	295	500
The Star, 11J, nickel, OF/HC	175	200	400
Time King, 21J, raised GJS, 2 tone nickel, Adj., D.S. dial, OF	300	400	600
Time King, 21J, raised GJS, 2 tone nickel, Adj., D.S. dial, HC	325	425	625
U.S. Army, 15J, nickel, HC ★	400	500	700

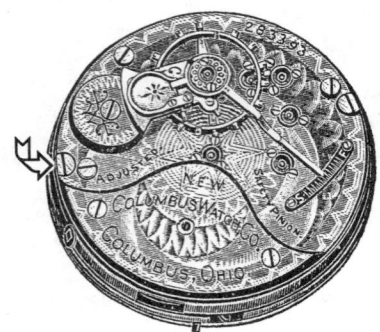

18 size **OPEN FACE** Model
NOTE: (2) SCREWS

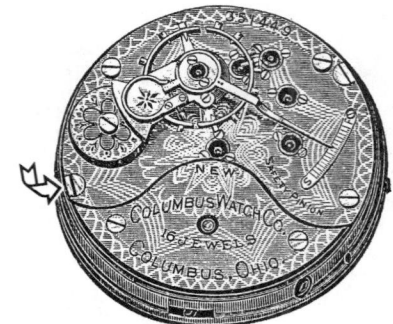

18 size **HUNTING CASE** Model
NOTE: (1) SCREW

NOTE: May not be true for KEY WIND or TRANSITIONAL MODELS

16 SIZE, 3/4 Plate

Marked "New Columbus Watch Co. Columbus Ohio"

Grade or Name — Description	Avg	Ex-Fn	Mint
7J, G#80 / G#20, gilded, OF	$60	$95	$195
7J, G#40 / G#19, gilded, HC	75	125	225
11J, G#81, gilded, OF	60	95	195
11J, G#41, gilded, HC	75	125	225
11J, G#83 / G#18, nickel, OF	60	95	195
11J, G#43 / G#17, nickel, HC	75	125	225
15J, G#84, Adj., gilded, OF	60	95	195
15J, G#44, Adj., gilded, HC	80	100	250
15J, G#86, GJS, Adj., nickel, D.S. dial, OF	70	95	225
15J, G#46, GJS, Adj., nickel, D.S. dial, HC	80	100	250
16J, G#87 / G#316, GJS, Adj., nickel, D.S. dial, OF	80	100	250
16J, G#47 / G#315, GJS, Adj., nickel, D.S. dial, HC	85	110	275
16J, G#14, GJS, Adj., 2 tone nickel, D.S. dial, OF	125	150	300
16J, G#13, GJS, Adj., 2 tone nickel, D.S. dial, HC	150	175	400
16J, G#88, raised GJS, Adj., 2 tone nickel, D.S. dial, OF	125	150	300
16J, G#48, raised GJS, Adj., 2 tone nickel, D.S. dial, HC	150	175	400
17J, G#12, raised GJS, Adj., 2 tone nickel, D.S. dial, OF	125	150	300
17J, G#11, raised GJS, Adj., 2 tone nickel, D.S. dial, HC	150	175	400
Ruby, 21J, raised GJS, Adj., 2 tone nickel, D.S. dial, OF ★★	350	450	900
Ruby, 21J, raised GJS, Adj., 2 tone nickel, D.S. dial, HC ★★	400	500	1,100

NEW Columbus Watch Co., 16 size, 16 jewels, gold train, 2-tone, serial number 341,339.

Columbus Watch Co., Ruby Model, 16 size, 21 jewels, three quarter plate, gold jewel settings, gold train, Adj.6p.

🕐 Some grades are not included. Their values can be determined by comparing with similar age, size, metal content, style, models and grades listed.

🕐 This book endeavours to be a GUIDE or helpful manual and offers a wealth of material to be used as a tool not as a absolute document. Price Guides are like watches the worst may be better than none at all, but at best cannot be expected to be 100% accurate.

🕐 Characteristics of watches differ for the same age of both case and movement, because these features vary it may not be accurate to date a watch by one single influence. Example: the second hand was not commonly found on watches before 1750, but common about 1800. The first second hand appeared in 1665 and another in 1690. Therefore statements are broad rather than accurate.

🕐 Pricing in this Guide are fair market price for COMPLETE watches which are reflected from the **"NAWCC"** National and regional shows.

6 SIZE

Grade or Name — Description	Avg	Ex-Fn	Mint
7J, G#102, gilded, OF	$40	$65	$195
7J, G#102, gilded, HC	60	85	225
11J, G#101 / G#51 / G#53, nickel or gilded, HC	60	85	225
13J, G#103, nickel, HC	60	85	225
15J, G#104 / G#55, GJS, nickel, D.S. dial, HC	75	125	250
16J, G#57, raised GJS, nickel, D.S. dial, OF/HC	75	125	250
16J, G#100, raised GJS, 2 tone, D.S. dial, (marked 16J.), OF	95	175	325
16J, G#100, raised GJS, 2 tone, D.S. dial, (marked 16J.), HC	95	175	325

Columbus Watch Co., 8-10 size, 13 jewels, 3/4 plate, stem wind, serial number 13,372. For price see 2nd page of Columbus W. Co. under Swiss, 3/4 plate (1874-1883).

New Columbus Watch Co. Example of a basic model for 6 size, 3/4 plate, 7-16 jewels, gilded and nickel.

4 SIZE

Grade or Name — Description		Avg	Ex-Fn	Mint
11J, nickel or gilded, OF/HC	★	$80	$125	$300
15J, nickel or gilded, OF/HC	★	95	175	325

🕐 Watches listed in this book are priced at the collectable Trade Show level, as **complete** watches having an original 14k gold-filled case & **KEY W IND** with silver case, an original white enamel single sunk dial, and with the entire original movement in good working order with no repairs needed.

🕐 **The Complete Price Guide to Watches goal is to stimulate the orderly exchange of <u>Watches</u> between "*buyers*" and "*sellers*".**

🕐 Pricing in this Guide are fair market price for COMPLETE watches which are reflected from the **"NAWCC"** National and regional shows.

CORNELL WATCH CO.
Chicago, Illinois
1870 - 1874
San Francisco, California
1875 - 1876

The Cornell Watch Co. bought the Newark Watch Co. and greatly improved the movements being produced. In the fall of 1874, the company moved to San Francisco, Calif., with about 60 of its employees. The movements made in California were virtually the same as those made in Chicago. The company wanted to employ Chinese who would work cheaper, but the skilled employees refused to go along and went on strike. The company stayed alive until 1875 and was sold to the California Watch Co. in January 1876. But death came a few months later.

C.L. Kidder from 1869 to 1872 worked with F.A. Jones in Switzerland to form the *International Watch Co.*. Mr. Kidder returned to U.S.A. and took on a position with Cornell.

The Chronology of the Development of Cornell Watch Co.
Newark Watch Co. 1864-1870; S#s 6901 to about 12,000.
Cornell Watch Co., Chicago, Ill. 1870-1874; S#s 12,001 to about 23,000-25,000.
Cornell Watch Co., San Francisco, Calif. 1874-Jan. 1876; S# s 23,001 to about 35,000.
California Watch Co., Jan. 1876-mid 1876.

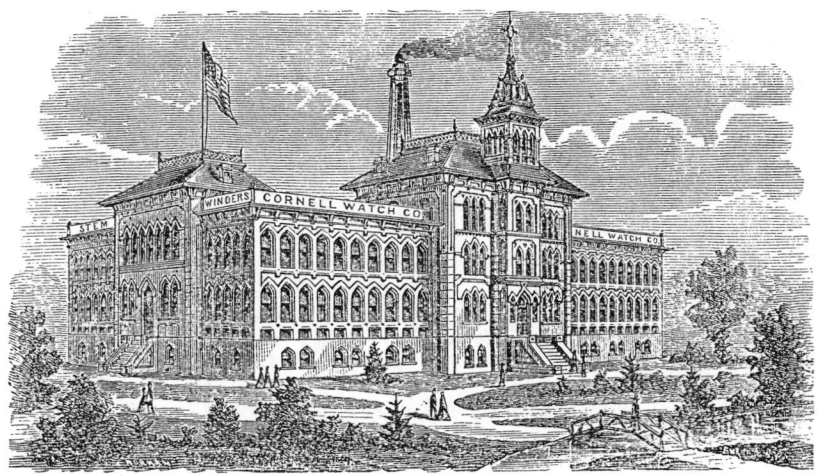

1871 AD for the Cornell Watch Co. Factory

18 SIZE

Grade or Name — Description		Avg	Ex-Fn	Mint
J. C. Adams, 11J, KW	★	$250	$300	$650
C. T. Bowen, FULL, KW	★	300	350	800
C. M. Cady, 15J, SW	★	400	450	850
Cornell W. Co., 7J, San Francisco on mvt., KW	★	700	900	1,800
Cornell W. Co., 11J, KW	★	200	250	600
Cornell W. Co., 11J, San Francisco on mvt., KW	★ ★	900	1,200	1,900
Cornell W. Co., 15J, KW	★	300	400	800
Cornell W. Co., 15J, San Francisco on mvt., KW	★	900	1,300	2,100
Cornell W. Co., 15J, San Francisco on mvt., SW	★ ★	950	1,300	2,200
Cornell W. Co., 19-20J, San Francisco on mvt., GJS, ADJ., SW	★ ★ ★	2,200	2,600	4,000
Paul Cornell, 19-20J, GJS, ADJ, SW	★ ★ ★	2,200	2,600	4,000
John Evans, 15J, KW		250	350	675
Excelsior, 15J, FULL, KW, KS	★	275	375	700

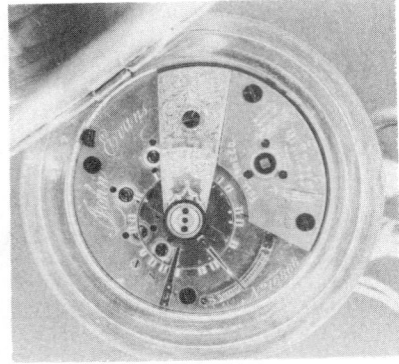

Cornell Watch Co., J.C. Adams, 18 size, 11 jewels, key wind & set, made in Chicago, Ill, serial number 13,647.

Cornell Watch Co., 18 size, 15 jewels, key wind & set, marked "John Evans," serial number 16,868.

Grade or Name — Description		Avg	Ex-Fn	Mint
H. N. Hibbard, 11J, KW, ADJ	★	$350	$450	$800
C.L. Kidder, 7J, KW,KS, OF	★	350	450	800
George F. Root, 15J, KW	★	400	500	900
George Waite, 7J, (Hyde Park), KW	★★	350	450	800
E. S. Williams, 7J, KW	★	250	350	700
Eugene Smith, 17J	★	450	550	900
Ladies Stemwind	★	200	275	500

JACOB D. CUSTER

Norristown, Pennsylvania

1840 - 1845

At the age of 19, Jacob Custer repaired his father's watch. He was then asked to repair all the watches within his community. Custer was basically self-taught and had very little formal education and little training in clocks and watches. He made all the parts except the hairspring and fusee chains. The watches were about 14 size, and only 12 to 15 watches were made. The 14S fusee watches had lever escapement, 3/4 plate and were sold in his own gold cases. He made a few chronometers, one with a helical spring.

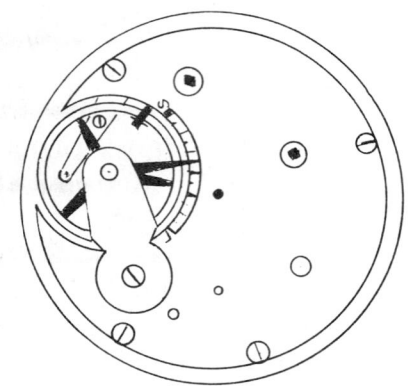

J.D. Custer, 14-16 size, engraved on movement is J.D. Custer, Norristown, Pa. Patented Feb. 4, 1843.

Description		Avg	Ex-Fn	Mint
14S, OF, engraved on mvt. (*J. D. Custer, Patented Feb. 4, 1843*)				
very RARE watch	★★★★	$16,000	$23,000	$50,000

DUDLEY WATCH CO.

Lancaster, Pennsylvania
1920 - 1925

William Wallace Dudley became interested in watches and horology at the age of 13 and became an apprentice making ship chronometers in Canada. When he moved to America, he worked for the South Bend and Illinois Watch companies and the Trenton Watch Co. before going to Hamilton Watch Co. in Lancaster. He left Hamilton at age 69 to start his own watch company. In 1922 his first watches were produced; they were 14S, 19J, and used many Waltham Model 1894 – 1897, 14 size parts, including the train and escapement. The plates and winding mechanism were made at the Dudley plant. Dials and hands were made to Dudley's specifications in Switzerland. At first jewels were obtained from a manufacturer in Lancaster, but by 1925 they were Swiss supplied. The cases came from Wadsworth Keystone and the Star Watch Case Co. Dudley also made a 12S, 19J watch. By 1924, the company was heavily in debt, and on February 20, 1925, a petition for bankruptcy was filed. The Masonic Watch was his most unusual watch.

DUDLEY WATCHES			ESTAMATED TOTAL PRODUCTION
Dudley Watch Co.	1920-1925	Model No.1	= S# 500—1,900 = 1,400
P. W. Baker Co.	1925-1935	Model No.2	= S# 2,001—4,800 = 2,800
XL Watch Co., N.Y.	1935-1976	Model No.3	= S# 4,801—6,500 = 1,700
			TOTAL = 5,900

NOTE: Not all movements were finished and sold as complete watches.

Model No. 1, 14S, 19J, OF, can be distinguished by the "Holy Bible" engraved on the winding arbor plate, and a gilded pallet bridge matching the plates.

Model No. 2, 12S, 19J, used the 910 and 912 Hamilton wheels and escapement, has a flat silver-colored Bible.

Model No. 3, 12S, can be distinguished by the silver Bible which was riveted in place and was more three-dimensional. The 3rd wheel bridge was rounded off at one end.

Dudley Watch Co., Model 1, 14 size, 19J., open face, Masonic form plates, flip back, serial # 1232, Ca. 1924.

Dudley Watch Co., Model 2, 14 size, 19J., open face, with original paper. The watch also came with a keystone shaped box, Ca 1927.

12 SIZE - 14 SIZE
"MASONS" MODEL

Grade or Name — Description	Avg	Ex-Fn	Mint
14S, Dudley, 19J, 14K, flip open back, Serial #1 (made 5 experimental models with Serial #1) .... ★	$5,500	$8,000	$14,000
14S, M#1, 19J, OF, **14K** flip open back .... ★	2,800	3,200	4,500
14S, M#1, 19J, OF, **14K** flip open back, w/box & papers .... ★	3,100	3,600	4,800
12S, M#2, 19J, OF, flip open back, GF .... ★	1,800	2,300	3,000
12S, M#2, 19J, OF, **14K,** flip open back case .... ★	2,200	2,600	3,600
12S, M#2, 19J, OF, **14K** display case .... ★	1,900	2,400	3,300
12S, M#3, 19J, OF, display case, GF .... ★	1,500	2,000	3,000
12S, M#3, 19J, OF, **14K** flip open case .... ★	2,100	2,400	3,500

Dudley Watch Co., Model 2, 12 size, 19 jewels, open face, serial number 2,420.

Dudley Watch Co., Model 3, 12 size, 19 jewels, open face. NOTE: 3rd wheel bridge is rounded off at one end.

ELGIN WATCH CO.
(NATIONAL WATCH CO.)
Elgin, Illinois   1864 - 1964

Above: *B. W. Raymond*

First wooden building in Jan. 1865.(30X60)

This was the largest watch company in terms of production; in fact, Elgin produced half of the total number of pocket watches (dollar-type not included). Some of the organizers came from Waltham Watch Co., including P. S. Bartlett, D. G. Currier, Otis Hoyt, Charles H. Mason and others. The idea of beginning a large watch company for the mid-West was discussed by J. C. Adams, Bartlett and Blake. After a trip to Waltham, Adams went back to Chicago and approached Benjamin W. Raymond, a former mayor of Chicago, to put up the necessary capital to get the company started. Adams and Raymond succeeded in getting others to pledge their financial support. The National Watch Co. (Elgin) was formed in August 1864. The factory was completed in 1866, & the 1st. movement was a B. W. Raymond, 18 size.

Elgin 1st Movements

Movements	1st App.	1st S#	Movements	1st. App.	1st. S#
18S B. W. Raymond	April 1867	101	10S Lady Elgin	Jan. 1869	40,001
18S H. Z. Culver	July 1867	1,001	10S Frances Rubie	Aug. 1870	50,001
18S J. T. Ryerson	Oct. 1867	5,001	10S Gail Borden	Sept. 1871	185,001
18S H. H. Taylor	Nov. 1867	25,001	10S Dexter Street	Dec. 1871	201,001
18S G. M. Wheeler	Nov. 1867	6,001			
18S Matt Laflin	Jan. 1868	9,001	First Stem Wind	June 1873	
18S W.H. Ferry	No date	30,056	1st Nickel Movement	Aug.15, 1879	
18S J.V. Farwell	No date	30,296	Convertible	Fall 1878	
18S M.D. Ogden	No date	30,387	1st 16 Size watch	No date	600,001
18S Charles Fargo	No date	30,490	18 size with double roller	G# 214	8,400,001
18S Father Time	No date	2,300,001	16 size with double roller	G# 156	10,249,901
18S Overland	No date	6,653,401			
18S Veritas	No date	8,400,001			

B.W. Raymond retailed for $117.00 without case in 1867. First run of Advance, Age & Chief = 255,901- 256,000.

The first watch a **B.W. Raymond** was sold April 1, 1867, selling for about $115.00, and was a 18 size, KW and quick train serial # 101. This **First** Pocket Watch, Serial No. 101, **was once again sold** for **$12,000.00** in 1988 at a SALE in NEW YORK. The first stem wind model was an H. Z. Culver with serial No. 155,001, lever set and quick train. In 1874, the name was changed to the Elgin National Watch Co., and they produced watches into the 1950s. The first **WRIST WATCH** made by Elgin was sold in 1910.

Some Serial Nos. have the first two numbers replace by a letter; i.e., 49,582,000 would be F 582,000.

X= 38 & 39	F= 49
C,E,T &Y= 42	S= 50
L= 43	R= 51
U= 44	P= 52
J= 45	K= 53
V= 46	I = 54
H= 47	
N= 48	

🕐 If the letters do not match the list above; the movement was produced after 1954.

ELGIN ESTIMATED SERIAL NUMBERS
AND PRODUCTION DATES

DATE – SERIAL #	DATE–SERIAL #	DATE–SERIAL #
1867 -101= April - 9,000 =Dec	1897 – 7,000,000 Oct.28th	1927 – 30,050,000
1868 — 25,001-Nov.20th	1898 – 7,494,001 May 14th	1928 – 31,599,001-Jan.11
1869 — 40,001-May 20th	1899 – 8,000,000 Jan.18th	1929 – 32,000,000
1870 — 50,001-Aug.24th	1900 – 9,000,000 Nov.14th	1930 – 32,599,001-July
1871 – 185,001-Sep. 8th	1901 – 9,300,000	1931 – 33,000,000
1872 – 201,001-Dec.20th	1902 – 9,600,000	1932 – 33,700,000
1873 – 325,001	1903 – 10,000,000 May 15th	1933 – 34,558,001-July 24th
1874 – 400,001-Aug.28th	1904 – 11,000,000 April 4th	1934 – 35,000,000
1875 – 430,000	1905 – 12,000,000 Oct.6th	1935 – 35,650,000
1876 – 480,000	1906 – 12,500,000	1936 – 36,200,000
1877 – 520,000	1907 – 13,000,000 April 4th	1937 – 36,978,001-July 24th
1878 – 570,000	1908 – 13,500,000	1938 – 37,900,000
1879 – 625,001-Feb.8th	1909 – 14,000,000 Feb.9th	1939 – 38,200,000
1880 – 750,000	1910 – 15,000,000 April 2nd	1940 – 39,100,000
1881 – 900,000	1911 – 16,000,000 July 11th	1941 – 40,200,000
1882 – 1,000,000- March,9th	1912 – 17,000,000 Nov.6th	1942 – 41,100,000
1883 – 1,250,000	1913 – 17,339,001- Apr.14th	1943 – 42,200,000
1884 – 1,500,000	1914 – 18,000,000	1944 – 42,600,000
1885 – 1,855,001-May 28th	1915 – 18,587,001-Feb.11th	1945 – 43,200,000
1886 – 2,000,000- Aug. 4th	1916 – 19,000,000	1946 – 44,000,000
1887 – 2,500,000	1917 – 20,031,001-June 27th	1947 – 45,000,000
1888 – 3,000,000 June 20th	1918 – 21,000,000	1948 – 46,000,000
1889 – 3,500,000	1919 – 22,000,000	1949 – 47,000,000
1890 – 4,000,000 Aug.16th	1920 – 23,000,000	1950 – 48,000,000
1891 – 4,449,001-Mar.26th	1921 – 24,321,001-July 6th	1951 – 50,000,000
1892 – 4,600,000	1922 – 25,100,000	1952 – 52,000,000
1893 – 5,000,000 July 1st	1923 – 26,050,000	1953 – 53,500,000
1894 – 5,500,000	1924 – 27,000,000	1954 -- 54,000,000
1895 – 6,000,000 Nov.26th	1925 – 28,421,001-July 14th	1955 -- 54,500,000
1896 – 6,500,000	1926 – 29,100,000	1956 – 55,000,000

🕐The above list is provided for determining the **APPROXIMATE** age of your watch. Match serial number with date. Watches were not necessarily *SOLD* and *DELIVERED* in the exact order of manufactured or production dates.

It required several months for raw material to emerge as a finished movement. All the while the factory is producing all sizes, models and grades. The numbering system was basically *"consecutive"*, *due to demand a batch of movements could be side tracked, thus allowing a different size and model to move ahead to meet this demand. Therefore, the dates some movements were* **sold** *and delivered to the trade, may not be* **"consecutive"**.

NOTE: Egin starts to engrave **Adjusted to 5 Positions** about S# 15,158,001.

The B. W. Raymond grade 571 was introduced in 1950 with the following three changes. First, friction jewels; second, a solid balance wheel; third, a "DuraPower" mainspring. This was also the 47th model made by the Elgin Watch Co.. This model conformed with all railroad specifications as 16 size, 21 jewels and (8) eight adjustments; the movement is lever-set has a white enamel dial & black numbers.

Some collectors seek out low serial numbers and will usually pay a premium for them. The lower the number, the more desirable the watch. The table shown below lists the first serial number of each size watch made by Elgin.

Size	1st Serial Nos.	Size	1st Serial Nos.
18	101	10	40,001
17	356,001	6	570,001
16	600,001	0	2,889,001
14	351,001		

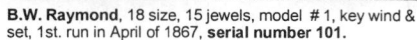

B.W. Raymond, 18 size, 15 jewels, model # 1, key wind & set, 1st. run in April of 1867, **serial number 101.**

Father Time, 18 size, 21 jewels, model #8 with wind indicator, free sprung model, serial number 22,888,020

18 SIZE

Grade or Name — Description	Avg	Ex-Fn	Mint
Advance, 11J, gilded, KW, FULL, HC .... ★	$100	$175	$300
Age, 7J, gilded, KW, FULL, OF/HC .... ★	100	175	300
Atlas Watch Co., 7J, , LS, FULL, HC (1st 7,090,001).................	70	95	195
California Watch, 15J, gilded, KW, KS, FULL, HC.......................	175	200	450
Chief, 7J, gilded, KW, FULL, HC .... ★	100	175	300
Convertible, 7J= G#98, 11J=G#99, gilded, 3/4, M#6	125	150	350
Convertible, 15J=G#100, gilded, 3/4, M#6................................	150	195	400
H.Z.Culver (Howard Z. Culver)			
H.Z.Culver, 15J, gilded, KW, KS, FULL, **ADJ**, HC, low S#	195	275	550
H.Z. Culver, 15J, gilded, KW, KS, FULL, **ADJ**, HC	150	200	400
H.Z. Culver, 15J, KW, KS, **14K, HC**	700	850	1,400
H.Z. Culver, 15J, gilded, KW, KS, FULL, HC	125	175	350
H.Z. Culver, 15J, gilded, SW, FULL, HC	70	95	195
H.Z. Culver, 15J, gilded, KW, FULL, LS, HC	95	150	300

🕐 **Generic, nameless or unmarked** grades for watch movements are listed under the Company name or initials of the Company, etc. by size, jewel count and description.

Grade or Name — Description	Avg	Ex-Fn	Mint
Elgin N. W. Co., 7J, OF, SW	$70	$95	$195
Elgin N. W. Co., 7J, KW, gilded, HC	70	95	195
Elgin N. W. Co., 11J, SW/KW, LS	70	95	195
Elgin N. W. Co., 11J, LS, SW, **HC, 9K-10K**	250	300	550
Elgin N. W. Co., 11J, LS, SW, HC, Silveroid	60	80	175
Elgin N. W. Co., 11J, LS,KW/ SW, OF	60	80	175
Elgin N. W. Co., 13J, KW/SW, PS/LS, OF	60	80	175
Elgin N. W. Co., 13J, KW/SW, PS/LS, HC	70	90	200
Elgin N. W. Co., 15J, SW, LS, OF....................................	70	95	195
Elgin N. W. Co., 15J, KW, LS, HC	125	150	400
Elgin N. W. Co., 15J, KW/SW, LS, HC	70	95	195
Elgin N. W. Co., 15J, KW, **hidden key, COIN silver case**	195	275	550

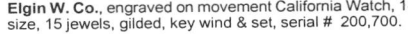

Elgin W. Co., engraved on movement California Watch, 18 size, 15 jewels, gilded, key wind & set, serial # 200,700.

Convertible, 18 size, 15 jewels, converts to either hunting or open face, Gilded, G#100, S#2,226,720.

Grade or Name — Description	Avg	Ex-Fn	Mint
Elgin N. W. Co., 15-17J, KW/SW, LS, **box–hinge YGF, HC**	$225	$300	$600
Elgin N. W. Co., 15-17J, KW/SW, LS, **box–hinge 14K, HC**	1,200	1,600	2,800
Elgin N. W. Co., 15-17, KW/SW, LS, **Multi-color box YGF, HC**	450	550	950
Elgin N. W. Co., 15-17J, KW/SW, **14K case, OF**	400	450	800
Elgin N. W. Co., 15-17J, KW/SW, **14K case, HC**	450	600	900
Elgin N. W. Co., 15-17J, KW/SW, **18K case, HC**	600	700	1,200
Elgin N. W. Co., 15-17J,KW/ SW, **Multi-color, 14K, HC**	2,000	2,500	5,000
Elgin N. W. Co., 15-17J, KW/SW, LS, **COIN Silver** 6 oz, OF	275	350	650
Elgin N. W. Co., 15-17J, KW/SW, LS, **COIN Silver**, OF	90	125	225
Elgin N. W. Co., 17J, KW/SW, LS, OF	90	125	225
Elgin N. W. Co., 17J, SW, LS or PS, HC	125	175	350
Elgin N. W. Co., 21J, SW, LS or PS, OF	195	250	500
Elgin N. W. Co., 21J, SW, LS, **box case, GF,OF**	300	350	650
Elgin N. W. Co., 21J, LS, **HC, 14K**	700	800	1,200
Elgin N. W. Co., 21J, SW, LS, Silveroid	195	250	450
Elgin N. W. Co., 21J, SW, LS, HC	295	350	600
Elgin N. W. Co., 21J, **Wind Indicator**	1,500	1,800	3,000
Elgin N. W. Co., 21J, **Wind Indicator, free sprung**	1,800	2,500	3,500
Elgin N. W. Co., 23J, SW, LS, OF	250	350	600
Elgin N. W. Co., 23J, SW, LS, HC ★	350	400	700

Above example of the *nameless* or unmarked *grades* for watch movements which are listed under the Company name or initials of the Company, (Elgin W. Co.) etc. by size, jewel count & description.

Above example of MARKED grade # which is no. 349, 21 jewel, 18 size movement which is listed under the grade by number as 18 size, **349**, 21J, OF, etc.

Above example of the *nameless* or unmarked *grades* for watch movements which are listed under the Company **name or initials** of the Company, (Elgin W. Co.) etc. by size, jewel count & description.

🕐 **Generic, nameless or unmarked** grades for watch movements are listed under the Company name or initials of the Company, etc. by size, jewel count and description.

 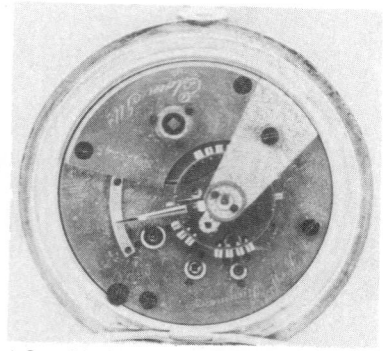

Pennsylvania Railroad Co. on dial. B.W. Raymond on movement. One of the first railroad watches commissioned by Penn. RR Co., 18 size, 15 jewels, key wind and set, serial number 123,245, Ca. 1871.

Grade or Name — Description	Avg	Ex-Fn	Mint
Charles Fargo, 7J, gilded, KW, HC..	$150	$200	$400
J. V. Farwell, 11J, gilded, KW, HC .... ★★	175	250	550
Father Time, 17J, NI, FULL, OF	125	175	400
Father Time, 17J, SW, OF, Silveroid..	125	175	400
Father Time, 17J, SW, HC	195	250	500
Father Time, **20J**, NI, FULL, HC or OF..................................... ★	295	350	650
Father Time, 21J, NI, SW, FULL, GJS, OF	195	250	550
Father Time, 21J, NI, SW, 3/4, GJS, DMK, HC	295	375	600
Father Time, 21J, NI, SW, 3/4, GJS, OF	195	250	500
Father Time, 21J, GJT, ADJ.5P, DES, **free sprung**, OF............. ★	550	700	1,000
Father Time, 21J, GJT, ADJ.5P, Diamond end stone, OF	195	250	500
Father Time, 21J, NI, SW, 3/4, OF, GJS, **wind indicator**	1,400	1,600	2,000
Father Time, 21J, SW, 3/4, GJS, **wind indicator, HC** .... ★★★	3,000	3,500	6,000
Father Time, G# 367, 21J, SW, 3/4, GJS, military style **wind indicator**, free sprung, sterling case	4,000	5,000	7,000
Father Time, G# 367, 21J, SW, 3/4, GJS, military style **wind indicator**, free sprung, **35 size with gimbals & box**	1,800	2,500	3,500
85 size, Model# **600**, 14J, **free sprung**, helical hair spring, dent escapement , **wind indicator, 85 size** with Gimbals & Box.................. ★★	3,000	3,600	6,200
W. H. Ferry, 11J, gilded, KW, HC...	95	125	225
W. H. Ferry, 15J, gilded, KW, HC...	120	175	250
Mat Laflin, 7J, gilded, KW, HC	120	175	250
National W. Co., 7J, KW, KS..	95	125	225
National W. Co., 11J, KW, KS	95	125	225
National W. Co., 15J, KW, KS	95	135	225
M. D. Ogden, 15J, KW, HC	120	175	250
M. D. Ogden, 11J, gilded, KW, HC	120	175	250
Order of Railway Conductors, 17J, LS, OF.......................... ★★★	1,500	2,000	3,000
Overland, 17J, NI, KW, HC	150	195	400
Overland, 17J, NI, SW, OF	150	195	400
Pennsylvania Railroad Co. on dial, B. W. Raymond on mvt., **must be ALL original**, 15J, KW, KS, (1st RR watches) .... ★★★	2,200	3,400	6,000
Railway Timer, 15J, FULL, HC.. ★	400	500	800

IMPORTANT NOTE: Railroad Standards, Railroad Approved & Railroad Grade **terminology,** as defined and used in this ***BOOK***.

1. **RAILROAD STANDARDS** = A commission or board appointed by the railroad companies outlined a set of **guidelines** to be accepted or approved by each railroad line.

2. **RAILROAD APPROVED** = A ***LIST*** of watches each railroad line would approve if purchased by their employee's. (this list changed through the years).

3. **RAILROAD GRADE** = A watch made by manufactures to meet or exceed the guidelines set by the railroad **standards**. Grades such as 992, Vanguard and B.W. Raymond, etc.

🕐 Some GRADES **exceeded** the R.R. standards such as 23 jewels, diamond end stone, gold train, raised gold jewel settings, double sunk dial and the list goes on. Examples: such as Veritas, Sangamo, 950 & Riverside Maximus and many others.

B.W. Raymond, 18 size, 19 jewels, wind indicator. Note small winding indicator gear next to crown wheel.

H.H. Taylor, 18 size, 15 jewels, key wind & set, serial number 288,797.

Grade or Name — Description	Avg	Ex-Fn	Mint
B. W. Raymond, 15-17J, KW, low S# under 200	$800	$1,000	$1,600
B. W. Raymond, 15-17J, KW, low S# 201 to 500	600	700	1,200
B. W. Raymond, 15-17J, KW, low S# 501 to 1,000	400	500	800
B. W. Raymond, 15J, gilded, KW, FULL, HC	150	195	350
B. W. Raymond, 17J, gilded, KW, FULL, HC	150	195	350
B. W. Raymond, 15J, SW, HC	100	150	295
B. W. Raymond, 15J, **box case 14K**	1,100	1,400	2,200
B. W. Raymond, 17J, all G#s, NI, FULL, OF	100	150	295
B. W. Raymond, 17J, NI, FULL, HC	150	200	400
B. W. Raymond, 17J, gilded, NI, SW, FULL, ADJ	100	150	295
B. W. Raymond, 17J, **Wind Indicator**	1,200	1,500	2,000
B. W. Raymond, 19J, NI, 3/4, SW, OF, GJS, G#240, GT	195	250	400
B. W. Raymond, 19J, 3/4, GJS, **jeweled barrel, Wind Indicator**	1,000	1,300	1,800
B. W. Raymond, 19J, 3/4, GJS, GT, Diamond end stone	195	250	400
B. W. Raymond, 21J, 3/4, GJS, GT, Diamond end stone, OF	195	250	450
B. W. Raymond, 21J, SW, Silveroid	150	195	300
B. W. Raymond, 21J, SW, GJS, GT, G#274, HC ★★	350	400	750
B. W. Raymond, 21J, NI, 3/4, SW, GJS, G#389 & 390, GT, OF	225	275	475
B. W. Raymond, 21J, NI, 3/4, SW, GJS, **Wind Indicator**, DMK	1,400	1,600	2,500
J. T. Ryerson, 7J, gilded, FULL, KW, HC	150	195	400
Solar W. Co., 15J, **Multi-color dial**	150	195	450
Standard, 17J, OF, LS	125	150	300
Sundial, 7J, SW, PS (1st 7,080,001)	75	95	250
H. H. Taylor, 15J, gilded, FULL, KW, HC	95	125	275
H. H. Taylor, 15J, NI, FULL, KW, DMK, HC	95	125	275
H. H. Taylor, 15J, NI, FULL, **SW**, HC, DMK, quick train	125	175	350
H. H. Taylor, 15J, SW, Silveroid	85	125	195
H. H. Taylor, 15J, SW, slow train	85	125	195

🕐 Some watch manufacturers personalize watches for jobbers or jewelry firms, with exclusive private signed or marked movements. The valuable collectable watches are listed under the signed or marked movement. Other exclusive private signed or marked movements will have equivalent value or only slightly higher value and should be compared to **Generic or Nameless** movements. Railroad signed or marked (dials & movements) are usually more collectable & higher in value.

🕐 **Generic, nameless or unmarked grades** for watch movements are listed under the Company name or initials of the Company, etc. by size, jewel count and description.

🕐 Some grades are not included. Their values can be determined by comparing with **similar** age, size, metal content, style, models and grades listed.

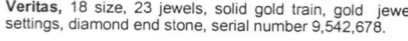

Veritas, 18 size, 23 jewels, solid gold train, gold jewel settings, diamond end stone, serial number 9,542,678.

G.M. Wheeler, Grade 369, 18 size, 17 jewels, open face, gold jewel settings, serial number 14,788,315

The word **VERITAS** translated is *"TRUTH"*.

Grade or Name — Description	Avg	Ex-Fn	Mint
Veritas, 21J, 3/4, NI, GJS, DMK, GT, G#239, OF	$265	$295	$550
Veritas, 21J, 3/4, GJS, GT, Diamond end stones	285	325	575
Veritas, 21J, SW, PS, GJS, GT, HC	285	350	625
Veritas, 21J, SW, LS, GJS, GT, HC	285	350	625
Veritas, 21J, 3/4, GJS, GT, Diamond end stones, G#274, HC	285	400	650
Veritas, 21J, 3/4, NI, GJS, **Wind Indicator**, DMK, G#239, OF	1,800	2,200	2,800
Veritas, 21J, 3/4, NI, GJS, **Wind Indicator**, DMK, G#274, HC, case ★★	3,500	4,000	6,500
Veritas, 23J, 3/4, NI, GJS, OF, DMK, GT	350	450	700
Veritas, 23J, 3/4, NI, GJS, OF, DMK, GT, Diamond end stone	350	450	700
Veritas, 23J, G#214, 3/4, NI, GJS, **Wind Indicator**, OF	1,800	2,200	2,800
Veritas, 23J, G#494, **Wind Indicator**, *"Free Sprung"*, OF.. ★★★	2,500	3,000	4,000
Veritas, 23J, **G#214**, SW, OF	350	450	700
Veritas, 23J, 3/4, SW, NI, GJS, GT, LS, HC ★★★	450	550	900
Veritas, 23J, SW, **OF, 14K**	650	800	1,200
Wabash, 21J, G # 349, Adj.5P, LS, OF ★	295	450	800
G. M. Wheeler, 11J, gilded, KW, HC	85	125	195
G. M. Wheeler, 13-15J, gilded, FULL, KW, SW	85	125	195
G. M. Wheeler, 15J, NI, FULL, KW, DMK, HC	100	125	250
G. M. Wheeler, 15J, SW, NI, FULL, DMK, OF	85	125	195
G. M. Wheeler, 17J, KW, NI, FULL, DMK, OF	100	125	250
G. M. Wheeler, 17J, SW, NI, DMK, OF	85	125	195

MOVEMENTS WITH NO NAME

Grade or Name — Description	Avg	Ex-Fn	Mint
No. 5 & No. 17, 7J, gilded, FULL, HC	$75	$100	$195
No. 23 & No. 18, 11J, gilded, FULL, HC	85	125	195
No. 69, 15J, M#1, KW, quick train, HC	85	125	195
No. 150, 20-21J, full plate, GJS, LS	195	225	425
No. 155, 17J, GJS, Adj.5P, HC	125	175	295
No. 274, 21J., marked **274**, GT, Adj.5p, diamond end stone	250	350	600
No. 316, 15J, NI, FULL, DMK, OF	85	125	195
No. 317, 15J, NI, FULL, ADJ, DMK, OF	85	125	195

⊕ Generic, nameless or unmarked grades for watch movements are listed under the Company name or initials of the Company, etc. by size, jewel count and description.

⊕ Watches listed in this book are priced at the collectable Trade Show level, as **complete** watches having an original 14k gold-filled case and *Key Wind* with silver, an original white enamel single sunk dial, and with the entire original movement in good working order with no repairs needed.

🕐 Generic, nameless or unmarked grades for watch movements are listed under the
Company name or initials of the Company, etc. by size, jewel count and description.

Grade or Name — Description	Avg	Ex-Fn	Mint
No. 326, 15J, OF	$85	$110	$200
No. 327, 15J, HC	95	125	250
No. 331, **16J**, M# 11, NI, OF ★	95	125	250
No. 335, 17J, HC	95	125	250
No. 336, 17J, NI, FULL, DMK, OF	85	125	195
No. 348, 21J, NI, FULL, GJS, DMK, HC	325	400	600
No. 349, 21J, , LS, OF	250	275	450
No. 349, 21J, , LS, **MARKED LOANER**, OF ★	350	450	700
No. 378, 17-19J, NI, FULL, DMK, HC	125	150	300
No. 379, 17-19J, OF	125	150	300
No. 411, 21J, PS, NI, 2-tone, OF ★★★	300	375	750

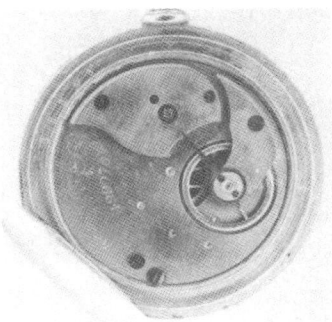

Elgin Watch Co., Leader, 17 size, 11 jewels, key wind &
set, made for English market, serial number 418,220.

Elgin Watch Co., 17 size, 7 jewels, key wind & set, serial
number 499,076. Made for Kennedy & Co.

17 SIZE

Grade or Name — Description	Avg	Ex-Fn	Mint
Avery, 7J, gilded, KW, FULL, HC (1st 400,001)	$95	$150	$250
Inter-Ocean, 7J, KWKS, HC ★★★	400	500	950
Leader, 7J, gilded, KW, FULL, HC (1st 356,001)	65	95	195
Leader, 11J, gilded, KW, FULL, HC,	65	95	195
Sunshine, 15J, KW, KS from back	95	125	225
M#11, 14, 15, 51, 59, 7J, gilded, KW, FULL, HC	95	125	225
17 Size, KW, Silveroid	50	70	165

16 SIZE

Grade or Name — Description	Avg	Ex-Fn	Mint
Braille or Blind Man's Watch, 9-17J, HC	$125	$150	$350
Convertible Model, 7J=G#47 & 11J=G#93, 13J=G#48, 3/4, gilded	75	95	195
Convertible Model, 13J=G#90, 3F BRG	125	150	250
Convertible Model, 15J=G#49, 3/4, gilded	100	125	250
Convertible Model, 15J=G#50, 3/4, NI, ADJ,	125	150	255
Convertible Model, 15J=G#50, 3/4, NI, ADJ, **14K, HC**	850	950	1,400
Convertible Model, 15J=G#85, 3F BRG, gilded	175	195	350
Convertible Model, 15J=G#86, 3F BRG, NI	175	195	350
Convertible Model, 21J=G#72, 3/4, NI, ADJ, GJS ★★★	1,500	1,800	3,000
Convertible Model, 21J=G#72, 3/4, NI, ADJ, GJS, **14K** ★★★	2,000	2,400	3,600
Convertible Model, 21J=G#91, 3F BRG, NI ★★★	1,600	1,900	3,000
Convertible Model, 21J, G#91, 3F BRG,NI, **14K** ★★★	2,100	2,500	3,700

🕐 A collector should expect to pay modestly higher prices at local shops.

Elgin Watch Co., 16 size, 21J, 3/4, Convertible Model GRADE # 72 , S# 607,061.

Elgin W. Co., Convertible Model, 16 size, 15 jewels, three-fingered bridge model, G # 86, adjusted, S # 4,907,178.

Grade or Name — Description	Avg	Ex-Fn	Mint
Doctors Watch, 13J, 4th Model, NI, GT, sweep second hand, G#89 gilded, GF	$300	$450	$700
Doctors Watch, 15J, 4th Model, NI, GT, sweep second hand, G# 83 gilded & G#84 nickel, GF case	300	450	700
Doctors Watch, 15J, 4th Model, gilded, sweep second hand, coin silver case........................	350	500	750
Doctors Watch, 15J, 4th Model, sweep second hand, 14K, OF	800	900	1,600
Elgin N. W. Co., Locomotive + diamond on lantern on case, **multi-color gold box hinged, 14K HC**	2,500	3,000	5,000

Elgin Watch Co., 16 size, Multi- Color Gold hunting case, the locomotive has a **diamond** in the lantern, the case has white, yellow, rose flowers & green leaf designs, Ca.1880.

Doctors Watch, 16 size, 15 jewels, fourth model, gold jewel settings, gold train, sweep second hand, serial number 926,458.

🕐 **The Complete Price Guide to Watches goal is to stimulate the orderly exchange of <u>Watches</u> between *"buyers"* and *"sellers"*.**

🕐 **Generic, nameless or unmarked** grades for watch movements are listed under the Company name or initials of the Company, etc. by size, jewel count and description.

Grade or Name — Description	Avg	Ex-Fn	Mint
Elgin N. W. Co., 7-9J, OF	$40	$60	$150
Elgin N. W. Co., 7-9J, HC	40	60	175
Elgin N. W. Co., 11J, OF	40	60	150
Elgin N. W. Co., 11J, HC	60	85	180
Elgin N. W. Co., 13J, OF	40	60	150
Elgin N. W. Co., 13J, OF, Silveroid	40	60	150
Elgin N. W. Co., 13J, HC	65	85	175
Elgin N. W. Co., 15J, HC	75	125	195
Elgin N. W. Co., 15J, OF	65	95	150
Elgin N. W. Co., 15J, OF **14K case**	350	425	700
Elgin N. W. Co., 15J, HC, **14K**	450	550	900
Elgin N. W. Co., 15J, **multi-color gold +diamond, HC, 14K**	1,600	2,200	3,600
Elgin N. W. Co., 16J, OF	85	125	225
Elgin N. W. Co., 16J, **Chronograph**, M # 4, LS, OF ... ★★★★★	2,000	3,000	5,000
Elgin N. W. Co., 17J, OF	75	100	195
Elgin N. W. Co., 17J, LS, **multi-color HC, YGF**	250	300	600
Elgin N. W. Co., 17J, **multi-color HC, 14K**	1,000	1,200	2,500
Elgin N. W. Co., 17J, **14K, HC**	350	450	800
Elgin N. W. Co., 17J, HC	95	150	295
Elgin N. W. Co., 19J, OF	95	150	295
Elgin N. W. Co., 21J, HC	175	250	500
Elgin N. W. Co., 21J, OF, **Silveroid**	95	150	295
Elgin N. W. Co., 21J, OF	150	195	375
Elgin N. W. Co., 23J, OF	250	295	550
3F Bridge Model, 15J, NI, DMK,, OF	95	150	295
3F Bridge Model, 15J, NI, DMK, HC	150	195	350
3F Bridge Model, 17J, NI, DMK, OF	95	150	295
3F Bridge Model, 17J, Adj.3P, NI, DMK, GJS, HC	150	195	375
3F Bridge Model, 17J, **Adj.5P**, NI, DMK, GJS, GT, OF	150	195	375
3F Bridge Model, 21J, Adj.5P, NI, DMK, GJS, GT, OF	500	600	900
3F Bridge Model, 21J, Adj.5P, NI, DMK, GJS, GT, **18K**	1,300	1,600	2,600
Father Time, 21J, 3/4, NI, GJS, DR, DMK, ADJ.5P, HC	225	250	500
Father Time, 21J, 3/4, NI, GJS, DR, **Wind Indicator**, OF	800	1,000	1,500
Father Time, 21J, 3/4, NI, GJS, DR, **pendant set**, ADJ.5P, OF ... ★	195	250	500
Father Time, 21J, NI, GJS, DR, ADJ.5P, GT, OF	195	250	500
Lord Elgin, 21J, GJS, DR, Adj.5P, 3F BRG, **14K, OF** ... ★★	1,500	1,800	2,500
Lord Elgin, 21J, GJS, DR, Adj.5P, 3F BRG, **14K, HC** ... ★★	1,800	2,100	2,900
Lord Elgin, 23J, GJS, DR, Adj.5P, 3/4, **14K, OF** ... ★★	1,800	2,100	2,900
Lord Elgin, 23J, GJS, DR, Adj.5P, 3/4, Gold filled OF ... ★★	1,200	1,400	1,900

ELGIN W. Co., <u>Chronograph</u>, 16 size, 16 jewels, model # 4, lever set.

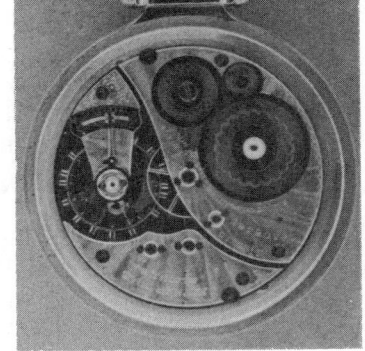

Father Time, 16 size, 21 jewels, gold train; Note model 19 up and down wind indicator movement does not show the differential wheel as does the 18 size, S# 18,106,465.

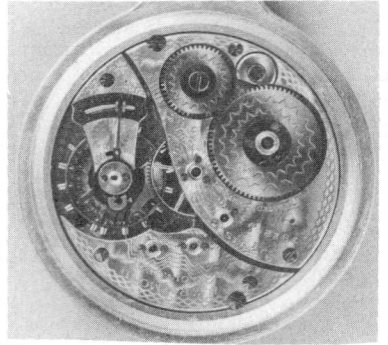

Lord Elgin, 16 size, 21 jewels, gold train, raised gold jewel settings, 3 finger bridge, grade 156, S# 10,249,819.

B.W. Raymond, 16 size, 19 jewels, gold jewel settings, Grade 350, serial number 17,822,991.

Grade or Name — Description	Avg	Ex-Fn	Mint
B. W. Raymond, 17J, 3/4, GJS, **14K, OF**	$400	$525	$850
B. W. Raymond, 17J, 3/4, GJS, SW, HC	195	295	500
B. W. Raymond, 17J, 3F BRG .... ★ ★	400	525	800
B. W. Raymond, 17J, LS, NI, **Wind Indicator** .... ★ ★	800	1,000	1,500
B. W. Raymond, 17J, GJS, SW, Adj., ALL G#s, OF	150	195	350
B. W. Raymond, 17J, 3/4, GJS, DR, Adj.5P, DMK	150	195	350
B. W. Raymond, 19J, 3/4, GJS, DR, Adj.5P, DMK, OF	175	225	400
B. W. Raymond, 19J, (Elgin **The Railroader** on dial) Adj.5P, OF	400	550	900
B. W. Raymond, 19J, OF, **14K, 30 DWT**	400	525	850
B. W. Raymond, 19J, 3/4, GJS, DR, Adj.5P, DMK, **Wind Indicator**	700	900	1,200
B. W. Raymond, 19J, M#8, G# 372, 455, Adj.5P, OF	175	195	400
B. W. Raymond, 19J, GJS, G#371, 401,Adj.5P, HC	195	250	450
B. W. Raymond, 21J, **14K, OF**	450	550	850
B. W. Raymond, 21J, G#472, 478, 506, 571, 581, 590, Adj.5P, OF	195	250	450
B. W. Raymond, 21J, 3/4, GJS, DR, Adj.5P, HC	295	350	600
B. W. Raymond, 21J, G# 391, 3/4, GJS, DR, Adj.5P, DMK, OF....	195	250	450
B. W. Raymond, 21J, **gold flashed movement**, OF	250	300	500
B. W. Raymond, 21J, 3/4, GJS, DR, Adj.5P, DMK,**Wind Indicator**	700	850	1,200
B. W. Raymond, 21J, 3/4, GJS, DR, **Adj.6P**, DMK,**Wind Indicator**	700	850	1,200
B. W. Raymond, 22J, WWII Model, sweep second hand	250	350	550
B. W. Raymond, 23J, 3/4, GJS, DR, Adj.5P, G#376, 494, 540	350	425	650
B. W. Raymond, 23J, 3/4, GJS, DR, Adj.5P, DMK, **Wind Indicator**	1,100	1,400	2,100
B. W. Raymond, 23J, 3/4, GJS, DR, **Adj.6P**, DMK, **Wind Indicator**	1,100	1,400	2,100
B. W. Raymond, 23J, 3/4, GJS, DR, Adj.5P, DMK,**Wind Indicator** military style	995	1,200	1,800

14K White or Green
Gold Filled
Specially Designed
Screw Case
Price $35.30

12K-Gold Filled
Specially Designed
Screw Case
Price $31.65

10K-Gold Filled
Specially Designed
Screw Case
Price $31.65

Winding Indicator $3.50 extra

AD
Oct. 15th, 1926

B. W. Raymond Movement
16 Size
21 Jewels
8 Adjustments, 5 of them position
Supplied with Montgomery Dial if desired

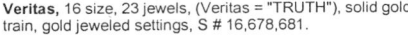

Veritas, 16 size, 23 jewels, (Veritas = "TRUTH"), solid gold train, gold jeweled settings, S # 16,678,681.

Elgin Watch Co., LORD ELGIN, Grade 351, 16 size, 23 J., gold train, gold jewel settings, S # 12,718,340. NOTE: This watch came from the first run of G # 351, 23J. Lord Elgins.

Grade or Name — Description	Avg	Ex-Fn	Mint
Veritas, 19J, G# 401, GJS, Adj. 5P., HC ....★	$400	$550	$750
Veritas, 21J, GJS, DR, Adj.5P, DMK, 3/4, **Wind Indicator**	1,400	1,700	2,100
Veritas, 21J, 3F brg, GJS, G#360..★	375	400	700
Veritas, 21J, GJS, DR, Adj.5P, DMK, 3/4, G#401, HC..................	425	475	800
Veritas, 21J, GJS, SW, Grade 360 ....★	375	400	700
Veritas, 21J, GJS, SW, Adj.5P, OF, Grade 270 & 375	295	375	650
Veritas, 23J, GJS, Adj.5P, **14K, OF**	600	675	1,000
Veritas, 23J, GJS, Adj.5P, **HC**	500	550	850
Veritas, 23J, GJS, DR, Adj.5P, 3/4, G# 375- 376- 453, OF...........	375	400	700
Veritas, 23J, GJS, DR, Adj.5P, DMK, 3/4, Diamond end stone, Grade 350 ....★	350	400	800
Veritas, 23J, GJS, DR, Adj.5P, Grade 453 & 376 DMK, 3/4, **Wind Indicator**	1,400	1,800	2,600
G. M. Wheeler, 17J, DR, Adj.3P, DMK, 3/4..............................	65	95	195
G. M. Wheeler, 17J, 3F BRG	80	125	250
G. M. Wheeler, 17J, **HC, 14K**	350	450	750
WWII Model, 17J, OF	95	150	295
WWII Model, 21J, OF	175	225	450
M#13, 9J, HC..	65	95	195
M#48, 13J, HC..	65	95	195

(Add $50 to $75 to hunting case models listed as open face)

MODELS WITH NO NAMES

Grade or Name — Description	Avg	Ex-Fn	Mint
Grade #155-160, 17J, GT, GJS, HC...	$95	$150	$250
Grade #156, 21J, 3/4, NI, DR, DMK, GT, GJS, HC ....★	350	400	700
Grade #156, 21J, 3/4, NI, DR, DMK, GT, GJS, HC, **14K** ....★	600	700	1,000
Grade #161, 21J, SW, PS, NI, GJS, GT, OF	195	250	400
Grade #162, 21J, SW, PS, NI, GJS, GT, OF	225	275	450
Grade #270, 21J, 3F BRG, GJS, **marked** 270 on mvt.	275	325	500
Grade #280, 17J, 3F BRG, **marked** 280 on mvt, OF.....................	175	225	400
Grade #290 HC& #291 , **7J**, 3/4, NI, DMK, OF	65	90	150

🕐 Generic, nameless or unmarked grades for watch movements are listed under the Company name or initials of the Company, etc. by size, jewel count and description.

🕐 Watches listed in this book are priced at the collectable Trade Show level, as complete watches having an original 14k gold-filled case and Key Wind with silver, an original white enamel single sunk dial, and with the entire original movement in good working order with no repairs needed.

Grade or Name — Description	Avg	Ex-Fn	Mint
Grade #291, 7J, 3/4, HC, **14K**	$295	$400	$600
Grade #312 & #313, 15J, 3/4, NI, DR, DMK, OF	75	95	195
Grade # 340, 17J, 3 finger bridge, OF	75	95	195
Grade #372, 19J, M#15, LS, OF, Adj.5P	195	225	350
Grade #374, 21J, M#15, LS, OF, Adj.5P	250	300	450
Grade #381 & #382, 17J, 3/4, NI, DR, DMK, OF	95	150	295
Grade#401, 19J, M#17, LS, HC	195	250	400
Grade #540, **23J**, Adj.5P, OF	275	350	550
Grade #572, 19J, Adj.5P, OF	135	175	350
Grade #573, 17J, Adj.5P, OF	125	150	275
Grade #575, 15J, Adj.3P, OF	95	125	250
Grade #581, 21J, Adj.5P, center sec, hacking, Army, OF	195	250	350
Grade # 845, 23J, Adj., (by **Buren** W. Co.) **Swiss**	65	80	195

14 SIZE

Grade or Name — Description	Avg	Ex-Fn	Mint
Lord Elgin, 15J, G# 357, OF	$65	$85	$175
Lord Elgin, 17J, G# 358-359 OF	70	95	200
7J, M#1, gilded, KW, **14K, HC**	250	325	550
7J, M#1, gilded, KW, YGF, HC	40	60	125
11J, M#1, gilded, KW, YGF, HC	40	60	125
11J, M#1, gilded, KW, YGF, OF	40	60	125
13J, M#1, gilded, KW, OF	40	60	125
15J, M#1, gilded, KW, OF	40	60	125
7J, M#2, SW, OF	40	60	125
15J, M#2, SW, OF	40	60	125
15J, M#2, SW, **14K, HC**	195	250	400
15J, M#1, grade # 46, KW, 3/4, HC	75	95	195

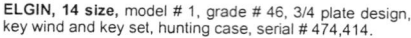

ELGIN, **14 size**, model # 1, grade # 46, 3/4 plate design, key wind and key set, hunting case, serial # 474,414.

ELGIN EIGHT DAY, **12 size**, 21 jewels, wind indicator, bridge movement, open face, serial number 12,345,678.

12 SIZE

Grade or Name — Description		Avg	Ex -Fn	Mint
Eight Day, 21J, 8-Day Wind Indicator, BRG	★ ★ ★ ★ ★	$2,700	$3,300	$4,700

☼ Generic, nameless or unmarked grades for watch movements are listed under the Company name or initials of the Company, etc. by size, jewel count and description.

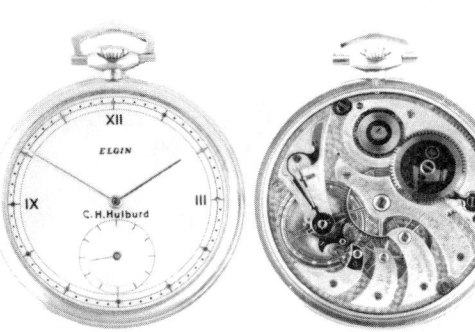

C. H. Hulburd, 19J, thin BRG model (12 /14 size), 8 Adj.
Ca. 1920-1925. Advertised as **ALL** in a **Unique case.** Mr.
Charles H. Hulburd became president in 1898.

ELGIN W. Co., 12 size, G# 190, 23J, GJS, Adj.5P, NI, DMK,
GT, M# 2, <u>Mustache lever</u>, HC, S# 7412238.

Grade or Name — Description	Avg	Ex-Fn	Mint
Elgin N. W. Co. # 30, 7J, gilded, **KW**, OF	$85	$125	$250
Elgin N. W. Co. # 89, 19J, HC...	75	95	195
Elgin N. W. Co. # 190, 23J, GJS, Adj.5P, NI, DMK, GT, M# 2,			
Mustache or **Standard** lever, **Gold Filled, HC**	225	275	500
Elgin N. W. Co. # 190, 23J, GJS, Adj.5P, NI, DMK, GT,			
M# 2, **Mustache** lever, **18K, HC** ....★	1,000	1,200	1,600
Elgin N. W. Co. # 194, 23J, GJS, Adj.5P, NI, DMK, GT, OF........	175	195	350
Elgin N. W. Co. # 236, 21J, GJS, Adj.5P, NI, DMK, GT, HC ....★	100	125	200
Elgin N. W. Co. # 237 or 273, 21J, GJS, Adj.5P, NI, GT, OF......★	125	150	250
Elgin N. W. Co. # 301 7J, HC	50	75	150
Elgin N. W. Co. # 314, 15J, HC	90	125	250
Elgin N. W. Co. # 384, 17J, OF	60	80	175
Elgin N. W. Co., 7-15J, **14K, Multi-color**	1,000	1,200	1,600
Elgin N. W. Co., 7-15J, OF, GF	60	70	150
Elgin N. W. Co., 7-15J, **HC, 14K**	250	295	550
Elgin N. W. Co., 17J, OF,GF	60	80	175
Elgin N. W. Co., 19J, OF, gold filled..................................	75	95	195
Elgin N. W. Co., 19J, HC, gold filled	75	95	195
Elgin N. W. Co., 19J, **HC, 14K**	250	300	600
Elgin N. W. Co., 19J, **14K, OF**..	150	225	450
Elgin N. W. Co., 21J, OF, gold filled case............................	95	150	295
12 size Model 2 & 3 spread to fit a "16 size"			
Elgin N. W. Co., 15-17J, Model 3 **spread to 16 size**, OF..............	$75	$95	$150
Elgin N. W. Co., 15-17J, Model 2 **spread to 16 size**, HC	85	125	195
Elgin N. W. Co., 19-21J, Model 3 **spread to 16 size**, OF..............	85	125	195
Elgin N. W. Co., 19-21J, Model 2 **spread to 16 size**, HC	95	150	250
STANDARD 12 SIZE (continued)			
Elete, 17J, GJS, Adj,4P, OF	$40	$55	$135
C. H. Hulburd, 19J, thin BRG model (12 /14 size) **14K case** ......★	800	900	1,400
C. H. Hulburd, 19J, thin BRG model (12 /14 size) **18K case** ......★	900	1,100	1,600
C. H. Hulburd, 19J, thin BRG model (12 /14 size) **Platinum**.......★	1,300	1,500	2,000
Lord Elgin, 17J, OF	60	80	150
Lord Elgin, 17J, HC..	75	95	195
Lord Elgin ,19 , ADJ, OF	75	95	195
Lord Elgin, 19J, ADJ, HC	125	150	250
Lord Elgin, 21, GJS, DR, Adj.5P, DMK, NI, OF............................	125	150	250
Lord Elgin, 21J,GJS, DR, Adj.5P, DMK, NI, **14K, OF**..................	195	250	475
Lord Elgin, 21J, GJS, DR, Adj.5P, DMK, NI, HC	150	175	350
Lord Elgin ,23, G# 194, GJS, DR, Adj.5P, DMK, NI, OF.... ★★★	150	175	350
Lord Elgin, 23J,G# 190, GJS, DR, Adj.5P, DMK, NI, HC.. ★★★	225	275	500

Lord Elgin, 12 size, 23 jewels, gold jewel settings, Adj.5p, originally sold for $110.00.

G.M. Wheeler, 12 size, 17 jewels, Adj3p, originally sold for $27.00.

Grade or Name — Description	Avg	Ex-Fn	Mint
Masonic dial, 15-17J, (with original Masonic dial), OF	$195	$275	$500
Pierce Arrow, 17J, (with original dial), OF	325	425	850
B. W. Raymond, 19J, G# 189, GJS, Adj.5P, DR, DMK, NI, HC	95	125	275
B. W. Raymond, 19J, G# 193, GJS, Adj.5P, DR, DMK, NI, OF	80	95	195
B. W. Raymond, 19J, G# 448, GJS, Adj.5P, DR, DMK, NI, OF	95	125	195
G. M. Wheeler, 17J, DR, Adj.5P, DMK, NI, OF	40	60	125
G. M. Wheeler, 17J, DR, Adj.5P, DMK, NI, HC	50	75	150

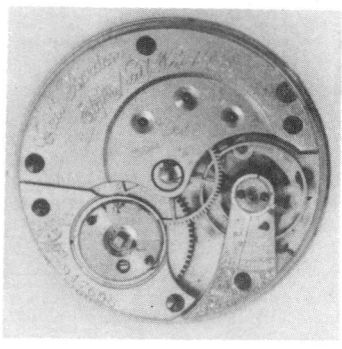

Frances Rubie, Grade 23, 10 size, 15 jewels, key wind & set.

Gail Borden, Grade 22, 10 size, 11 jewels, key wind & set, serial number 947,696.

10 SIZE
(HC)

Grade or Name — Description	Avg	Ex-Fn	Mint
Dexter St., 7J, KW, HC, **14K**	$225	$295	$500
Dexter St., 7J, KW, HC, **18K**	250	350	600
Dexter St., 7J, gilded, KW, HC, gold filled	75	100	200
Frances Rubie, 15J, gilded, KW, HC, **14K** ★	500	600	800
Frances Rubie, 15J, KW, HC, **18K** ★★	600	700	900

🕐 Watches listed in this book are priced at the collectable Trade Show level, as **complete** watches having an original 14k gold-filled case and **Key Wind** with silver, an original white enamel single sunk dial, and with the entire original movement in good working order with no repairs needed.

🕐 Pricing in this Guide are fair market price for COMPLETE watches which are reflected from the **"NAWCC"** National and regional shows.

Grade or Name — Description	Avg	Ex-Fn	Mint
Gail Borden, 11J, gilded, KW, HC, **14K**	$225	$295	$550
Gail Borden, 11J, KW, HC, gold filled	65	95	150
Gail Borden, 11J, KW, HC, **18K**	295	375	650
Lady Elgin, 15J, gilded, KW, HC, **14K**	225	275	500
Lady Elgin, 15J, KW, HC, **18K**	300	375	600
Grade # 21 or 28, 7J, gilded, KW, HC, gold filled	65	95	175
Elgin, **multi-color case, gold filled**, HC	225	295	550
Elgin, 15J, Silveroid, HC	40	55	95
Elgin, 15J, YGF, HC	65	95	150

Elgin W. Co., Grade 121, 6 size, 15 jewels, hunting, serial number 4,500,445.

Elgin W. Co., 6 size, ENGRAVED movement, enamel & gold case, fancy dial, G# 94, S# 1,886,804.

6 SIZE
(HC Only)

Grade or Name — Description	Avg	Ex-Fn	Mint
Atlas, 7J, HC	$40	$60	$150
Elgin N. W. Co. #286, 7J, HC, DMK, NI	40	60	150
Elgin N. W. Co. #295, 15J, HC, DMK, NI	40	60	150
Elgin N. W. Co. #168, **16J**, nickel, HC	95	150	275
Elgin N. W. Co., 7J, HC, **14K**	150	225	450
Elgin N. W. Co., 11J, HC, **14K**	150	225	450
Elgin N. W. Co., ENGRAVED movement, **enamel & gold case, fancy dial, G# 94, 14K** HC	650	750	1,300
Elgin N. W. Co., 15J, YGF, HC	60	80	175
Elgin N. W. Co., 15J, YGF demi-HC	60	80	175
Elgin N. W. Co., 15J, HC, **YGF** multi-color case	200	225	550
Elgin N. W. Co., 15J, HC, **10K**	175	200	400
Elgin N. W. Co., 15J, HC, **14K**	225	250	450
Elgin N. W. Co., 15J, **14K, Multi-color HC**	500	600	1,000
Elgin N. W. Co., 15J, HC, **18K**	400	500	650
Elgin N. W. Co., 15J, SW, HC, **Enamel case, 18K**	500	700	1,200
Elgin N. W. Co., **16J**, G# 230, gilded or nickel, HC	95	125	250

⊕ A collector should expect to pay modestly higher prices at local shops.

⊕ **Generic, nameless or unmarked** grades for watch movements are listed under the Company name or initials of the Company, etc. by size, jewel count and description.

Elgin W. Co., 6 size, 15 jewels

Elgin W. Co., Grade 201-HC, 205-OF, 0 size, 19 jewels, gold train.

Elgin W. Co., Grade 200-HC, 204-OF, 0 size, 17 jewels, gold jewel settings.

0 SIZE

Grade or Name — Description	Avg	Ex-Fn	Mint
Atlas W. Co., 7J, HC	$40	$95	$200
Elgin N. W. Co., 7J, NI, DR, DMK, OF	30	50	150
Elgin N. W. Co., 15J, NI, DR, DMK, OF	30	50	150
Elgin N. W. Co., 15J, NI, DR, DMK, HC	50	70	225
Elgin N. W. Co., 17J, NI, DR, DMK, ADJ, OF	50	70	175
Elgin N. W. Co., 19J, NI, DR, DMK, GJS, ADJ, OF	30	50	150
Elgin N. W. Co., 15J, OF, **14K**	150	195	400
Elgin N. W. Co., 15J, HC, **14K**	195	225	500
Elgin N. W. Co., 15J, HC, multi-color **GF**	150	195	400
Elgin N. W. Co., 15J, OF, multi-color **dial**	150	195	400
Elgin N. W. Co., 15J, HC, **10K**	150	175	295
Elgin N. W. Co., 15J, **14K**, Multi-color case	375	450	800
Elgin N. W. Co., 15J, **14K**, Multi-color case + diamond	500	600	1,000
Frances Rubie, 19J, HC ★★	250	350	600

Lady Elgin, 5/0 size, 17 jewels, gold jewel settings, originally sold for $42.50.

Lady Raymond, 5/0 size, 15 jewels, originally sold for $24.20.

3/0 and 5/0 SIZE
(HC ONLY)

Grade or Name — Description	Avg	Ex-Fn	Mint
Lady Elgin, 15J, PS, HC	$40	$70	$175
Lady Elgin, 15J, **14K**, HC	125	200	400
Lady Raymond, 15J, PS, HC	40	70	175
Elgin N. W. Co., 7J, HC	35	50	125

⊕ Generic, nameless or unmarked grades for watch movements are listed under the Company name or initials of the Company, etc. by size, jewel count and description.

⊕ Watch terminology or communication in this book has evolved over the years, in search of better and more precise language with a effort to improve, purify, adjust itself and make it easier to understand.

STYLE NO. 40
gold filled : $90 - $125 - $275
DIAL: $20 - $30 - $50

STYLE NO. 39
gold filled : $95 - $110 - $250
DIAL: $20 - $30 - $50

STYLE NO. 38
gold filled : $95- $110 - $250
DIAL: $ 20 - $30 - $50

STYLE NO. 19
gold filled : $95 - $125 - $275
wind-ind.-DIAL: $40 - $80 - $225

STYLE NO. 18
CHROME: $25 - $40 - $80
DIAL: $15 - $20 - $40

STYLE NO. 25
gold filled : $95 - $125 - $250
wind-ind.-DIAL: $40 - $80 - $225

STYLE NO. 26
gold filled : $90 - $125 - $170
wind-ind.-DIAL: $40 - $80 - $225

ANTIQUE BOW
gold filled : $95- $125 - $195
DIAL: $30 - $50 - $95

RIGID BOW
gold filled : $95- $125 - $240
DIAL: $30 - $40 - $60

NOTE: Factory Advertised as a **complete** watch and was fitted with a certain matched, timed and rated movement and sold in the factory designed case style as a **complete** watch. The factory also sold _uncased_ movements to **JOBBERS** such as Jewelry stores & they cased the movement in a case styles the **CUSTOMER requested.** All the factory advertised **complete** watches came with a enamel dial **SHOWN or CHOICE** of other **Railroad** dials.

ELGIN NATIONAL WATCH CO.

GRADES OF MOVEMENTS
WITH
CLASSIFICATION AND DESCRIPTION
AS ORIGINALLY MADE

Grade.	Class.	Size.		Style.		Model.	Sett.	Train.	Jewels.
Advance........	5	18	F. Pl.	Htg.	Gilded	1st to 4th	Key or Lever	Slow	11
Age...........	5	"	"	"	"	"	"	"	7
Avery.........	15	17	"	"	"	1st	Key	"	7
Chief.........	5	18	"	"	"	1st to 4th	Key or Lever	"	7
Culver........	2	"	"	"	"	"	"	Quick	15
Dexter St.....	48	10	¾ "	"	"	1st	Key	"	7
Father Time...	1	18	F. Pl.	"	Nickel	2d to 4th	Lever	"	20-21
Father Time...	1	"	"	"	"	"	"	"	17
Father Time...	7	"	"	O. F.	"	5th	Pend.	"	20-21
Father Time...	7	"	"	"	"	"	"	"	17
Father Time...	65	"	"	"	"	7th	Lever	"	17-21
Father Time...	90	"	¾ Pl.	"	"	8th	"	"	21
Father Time...	99	"	"	Htg.	"	9th	"	"	21
Father Time...	134	"	"	O. F.	"	8th	"	"	21
Father Time...	98	16	"	"	"	15th	"	"	21
Father Time...	126	"	"	Htg.	"	14th	"	"	21
Father Time...	126	"	"	"	"	17th	"	"	21
Fargo.........	5	18	F. Pl.	"	Gilded	1st	Key	Slow	7
Farwell........	5	"	"	"	"	"	"	"	11
Ferry.........	4	"	"	"	"	"	"	"	15
Frances Rubie..	46	10	¾ Pl.	"	"	"	"	Quick	15
Frances Rubie..	76	0	"	"	Nickel	2d	Pend.	"	19
Frances Rubie..	80	"	"	O. F.	"	3d	"	"	19
Gail Borden....	48	10	"	Htg.	Gilded	1st	Key	"	11
Lady Elgin.....	47	"	"	"	"	"	"	"	15
Lady Elgin.....	133	5/0	"	"	Nickel	"	Pend.	"	15
Lady Elgin.....	96	10/0	"	O. F.	"	"	"	"	17
Lady Elgin.....	97	"	"	"	"	"	"	"	15
Lady Raymond..	133	5/0	"	Htg.	"	"	"	"	15
Lady Raymond..	136	"	"	O. F.	"	2d	"	"	15
Laflin.........	4	18	F. Pl.	Htg.	Gilded	1st to 4th	Key or Lever	Slow	7
Leader........	15	17	"	"	"	1st to 2d	"	"	7
Lord Elgin......	36	16	¾ Pl.	Htg. Br.	Nickel	6th	Pend.	Quick	21
Lord Elgin......	41	"	"	O. F. Br.	"	7th	"	"	21
Lord Elgin......	41	"	"	O. F.	"	"	"	"	23
Lord Elgin......	67	12	"	Htg.	"	2d	"	"	23
Lord Elgin......	71	"	"	O. F.	"	3d	"	"	23
Lord Elgin......	135	"	"	"	"	"	"	"	17
Lord Elgin......	135	"	"	"	"	"	"	"	21
Ogden.........	5	18	F. Pl.	Htg.	Gilded	1st to 4th	Key or Lever	Slow	11
Overland.✦..	3	"	"	"	Nickel	2d to 4th	Lever	Quick	17
Overland......	4	"	"	"	"	"	"	"	17
Overland......	8	"	"	O. F.	"	5th	Pend.	"	17
Overland......	9	"	"	"	"	"	"	"	17
Overland......	66	"	"	"	"	7th	Lever	"	17
Overland......	123	"	"	Htg.	"	2d to 4th	"	"	17
Overland......	124	"	"	O. F.	"	7th	"	"	17
Raymond......	1	"	"	Htg.	Gilded or Nickel	1st to 4th	Key or Lever	"	15-17
Raymond......	7	"	"	O. F.	"	5th	Pend.	"	15-17
Raymond......	65	"	"	"	Nickel	7th	Lever	"	17
Raymond......	91	"	¾ Pl.	"	"	8th	"	"	19
Raymond......	91	"	"	"	"	"	"	"	21
Raymond......	99	"	"	Htg.	"	9th	"	"	21
Raymond......	134	"	"	O. F.	"	8th	"	"	17
Raymond......	98	16	"	"	"	15th	"	"	19
Raymond......	98	"	"	"	"	"	"	"	21
Raymond......	102	"	"	O. F. Br.	"	9th	"	"	17
Raymond......	102	"	"	O. F.	"	13th	"	"	17
Raymond......	102	"	"	"	"	15th	"	"	17
Raymond......	125	"	"	Htg. Br.	"	8th	"	"	17
Raymond......	126	"	"	Htg.	"	14th	"	"	19
Raymond......	126	"	"	"	"	17th	"	"	19
Raymond......	68	12	"	"	"	2d	Pend.	"	19
Raymond......	72	"	"	O. F.	"	3d	"	"	19
Ryerson........	4	18	F. Pl.	Htg.	Gilded	1st	Key	Slow	7
Taylor.........	3	"	"	"	"	2d to 4th	Lever	"	15
Taylor.........	3	"	"	"	Gilded or Nickel	1st to 4th	Key or Lever	Quick	15
Taylor.........	8	"	"	O. F.	Gilded	5th	Pend.	"	15
Veritas........	89	"	¾ Pl.	"	Nickel	8th	Lever	"	23
Veritas........	90	"	"	"	"	8th	"	"	21
Veritas...•....	99	"	"	Htg.	"	9th	"	"	21
Veritas........	98	16	"	O. F. Br.	"	"	"	"	21
Veritas........	98	"	"	O. F.	"	13th	"	"	21
Veritas........	98	"	"	"	"	"	"	"	23
Veritas........	98	"	"	"	"	15th	"	"	21
Veritas........	132	"	"	"	"	"	"	"	23
Wheeler........	4	18	F. Pl.	Htg.	Gilded	1st to 4th	Key or Lever	Slow	15
Wheeler........	4	"	"	"	Gilded or Nickel	"	Lever	Quick	13-15
Wheeler........	4	"	"	"	"	2d to 4th	"	"	15-17
Wheeler........	9	"	"	O. F.	"	5th	Pend.	"	15-17

ELGIN NATIONAL WATCH CO.

Grades of Movements with Classification and Description as Originally Made

Grade.	Class.	Size.		Style.		Model.	Sett.	Train.	Jewels.
Wheeler	122	18	F. Pl.	O. F.	Nickel	7th	Lever	Quick	17
Wheeler	123	"	"	Htg.	"	2d to 4th	"	"	17
Wheeler	124	"	"	O. F.	"	7th	"	"	17
Wheeler	130	"	¾ Pl.	Htg.	"	9th	"	"	17
Wheeler	131	"	"	O. F.	"	8th	"	"	17
Wheeler	33	16	"	Htg. Br.	"	6th	Pend.	"	17
Wheeler	38	"	"	O. F. Br.	"	7th	"	"	17
Wheeler	127	"	"	"	"	9th	Lever	"	17
Wheeler	111	12	"	Htg.	"	2d	Pend.	"	17
Wheeler	112	"	"	O. F.	"	3d	"	Lever	7
No. 1	25	16	"	Htg.	Gilded	"	Lever	"	13-15
No. 2	25	"	"	"	"	"	"	"	15
No. 3	24	"	"	"	"	"	"	"	15
No. 4	24	"	"	"	Nickel	"	"	"	11
No. 5	5	18	F. Pl.	"	Gilded	2d to 4th	"	Q. or S.	11
No. 6	6	"	"	"	"	1st	"	Slow	7
No. 7	6	"	"	"	"	"	Key	"	7
No. 8	5	"	"	"	"	2d to 4th	Lever	"	7
No. 9	5	"	"	"	"	"	"	Q. or S.	11
No. 10	5	"	"	"	"	"	"	Slow	7
No. 11	15	17	"	"	"	2d	"	"	7
No. 12	5	18	"	"	"	1st	Key	"	11
No. 13	5	"	"	"	"	"	"	"	7
No. 14	15	17	"	"	"	"	"	"	11
No. 15	15	"	"	"	"	"	"	"	7
No. 16	4	18	"	"	"	"	"	"	11
No. 17	4	"	"	"	"	"	"	"	11
No. 18	5	"	"	"	"	2d to 4th	Lever	"	11
No. 19	5	"	"	"	"	"	"	"	15
No. 20	3	"	"	"	"	1st	Key	Quick	7
No. 21	48	10	¾ Pl.	"	"	"	"	"	11
No. 22	48	"	"	"	"	"	"	"	15
No. 23	47	"	"	"	"	"	"	"	7
No. 24	45	12	"	"	"	"	"	"	11
No. 25	45	"	"	"	"	"	"	"	15
No. 26	44	"	"	"	"	"	"	"	15-17
No. 27	1	18	F. Pl.	"	Nickel	2d to 4th	Lever	"	7
No. 28	48	10	¾ Pl.	"	Gilded	1st	Key	"	11
No. 29	47	"	"	"	"	"	"	"	7
No. 30	45	12	"	"	"	"	"	"	7
No. 31	45	"	"	"	"	1st	"	"	11
No. 32	44	"	"	"	"	"	"	"	15
No. 33	3	18	F. Pl.	"	Nickel	2d to 4th	Lever	"	7
No. 34	43	14	¾ Pl.	"	Gilded	1st	Key	"	7
No. 35	43	"	"	"	"	"	"	"	11
No. 36	43	"	"	"	"	"	"	"	15
No. 37	42	"	"	"	"	"	"	Slow	15
No. 38	3	18	F. Pl.	"	"	"	"	Quick	13
No. 39	43	14	¾ Pl.	"	"	"	"	"	7
No. 40	43	"	"	"	"	"	"	"	13
No. 41	42	"	"	"	"	"	"	"	15
No. 42	42	"	"	"	"	"	Pend.	"	11
No. 43	10	18	F. Pl.	O. F.	Nickel	5th	Pend.	"	15
No. 44	9	"	"	"	"	"	"	"	13
No. 45	51	6	¾ Pl.	Htg.	"	1st	Lever	"	15
No. 46	42	14	"	"	Gilded	"	Key	"	7
No. 47	19	16	"	Htg. and O.F.	Gilded	"	Lever	"	13
No. 48	18	"	"	"	"	"	"	"	15
No. 49	17	"	"	"	Nickel	"	"	"	15
No. 50	17	"	"	"	Gilded	"	"	Slow	7
No. 51	15	17	F. Pl.	Htg.	"	1st	Key	"	11
No. 52	15	"	"	"	"	"	"	Quick	7
No. 53	48	10	¾ Pl.	"	"	"	"	"	13
No. 54	48	"	"	"	"	"	"	Slow	7
No. 55	5	18	F. Pl.	"	"	"	"	"	11
No. 56	4	"	"	"	"	"	"	"	13
No. 57	4	"	"	"	"	"	"	"	15
No. 58	3	"	"	"	"	"	"	"	7
No. 59	15	17	"	"	"	"	"	"	7
No. 60	5	18	"	"	"	2d to 4th	Lever	Quick	15
No. 61	2	"	"	"	"	1st	Key	"	15
No. 62	2	"	"	"	"	2d to 4th	Lever	Slow	13
No. 63	4	"	"	"	"	1st	"	Quick	7
No. 64	51	6	¾ Pl.	"	"	"	"	"	13
No. 65	51	"	"	"	"	"	"	"	15
No. 66	50	"	"	"	"	"	"	"	15
No. 67	50	"	"	"	Nickel	"	"	Slow	7
No. 68	5	18	F. Pl.	"	Gilded	2d to 4th	Key	Quick	15
No. 69	1	"	"	"	"	1st	Lever	"	15-17
No. 70	1	"	"	"	Nickel	2d to 4th	"	"	17
No. 71	49	6	¾ Pl.	Htg. and O.F.	Nickel	1st	"	"	21
No. 72	16	16	"	"	Gilded	"	Pend.	"	7
No. 73	11	18	F. Pl.	O. F.	Gilded	5th	Pend.	"	11
No. 74	10	"	"	"	"	"	"	"	15
No. 75	9	"	"	"	"	"	"	"	15
No. 76	8	"	"	"	"	"	"	"	15-17
No. 77	7	"	"	Htg.	Nickel	1st	Key	Q. or S.	11
No. 78	5	"	"	"	Gilded	"	"	Quick	15
No. 79	3	"	"	"	"	"	"	"	15

ELGIN NATIONAL WATCH CO.

Grades of Movement with Classification and Description as Originally Made.

Grade.	Class.	Size.	Style.		Model.	Sett.	Train.	Jewels.
No. 80	3	18	F. Pl.	Htg.	Gilded	2d to 4th	Lever	Quick	15
No. 81	4	"	"	"	"	1st	Key	"	13–15
No. 82	4	"	"	"	"	2d to 4th	Lever	"	13–15
No. 83	27	16	¾ Pl.	S. Sec.	"	4th	"	"	15
No. 84	27	"	"	"	Nickel	"	"	"	15
No. 85	22	"	"	Htg. and O.F.	Gilded	2d	"	"	15
No. 86	22	"	"	"	Nickel	"	"	"	15
No. 87	5	18	F. Pl.	Htg.	"	1st	Key	"	11
No. 88	5	"	"	"	"	2d to 4th	Lever	"	11
No. 89	28	16	¾ Pl.	S. Sec.	Gilded	4th	"	"	13
No. 90	23	"	"	Htg. and O.F.	"	2d	"	"	13
No. 91	21	"	"	"	Nickel	"	"	"	21
No. 92	26	"	"	Htg.	Gilded	3d	"	"	11
No. 93	20	"	"	Htg. and O.F.	"	1st	"	"	11
No. 94	52	6	" ·	Htg.	"	"	"	"	11
No. 95	52	"	"	"	"	"	"	"	7
No. 96	6	18	F. Pl.	"	"	2d to 4th	"	"	7
No. 97	6	"	"	"	"	1st	"	"	7
No. 98	14	"	¾ Pl.	Htg. and O.F.	"	1st	Key	"	7
No. 99	13	"	"	"	"	6th	Pend.	"	7
No. 100	12	"	"	"	"	"	"	"	11
No. 101	52	6	"	Htg.	Nickel	1st	Lever	"	11
No. 102	5	18	F. Pl.	"	"	2d to 4th	"	"	11
No. 103	4	"	"	"	"	"	"	"	15
No. 104	31	16	¾ Pl.	O. F.	Gilded	5th	Pend.	"	7
No. 105	31	"	"	"	"	"	"	"	11
No. 106	30	"	"	"	"	"	"	"	13–15
No. 107	29	"	"	"	"	"	"	"	15
No. 108	29	"	"	"	Nickel	"	"	"	15
No. 109	60	0	"	Htg.	Gilded	1st	"	"	7
No. 110	60	"	"	"	Nickel	"	"	"	11
No. 111	58	"	"	"	"	"	"	"	15
No. 112	57	"	"	"	"	"	"	"	17
No. 113	60	"	"	"	Gilded	"	"	"	11
No. 114	26	16	"	"	"	3d	"	"	7
No. 115	59	0	"	"	Nickel	1st	"	"	13
No. 116	7	18	F. Pl.	O. F.	"	5th	"	"	15–17
No. 117	56	6	¾ Pl.	Htg.	Gilded	2d	"	"	7
No. 118	56	"	"	"	"	"	"	"	11
No. 119	56	"	"	"	Nickel	"	"	"	11
No. 120	55	"	"	"	"	"	"	"	13
No. 121	54	"	"	"	"	"	"	"	15
No. 122	53	"	"	"	"	"	"	"	17
No. 123	9	18	F. Pl.	O. F.	Gilded	5th	"	"	15
No. 124	9	"	"	"	Nickel	"	"	"	15
No. 125	4	"	"	Htg.	Gilded	2d to 4th	Lever	"	15
No. 126	4	"	"	"	Nickel	"	"	"	15
No. 127	26	16	¾ Pl.	"	"	3d	"	"	11
No. 128	31	"	"	O. F.	"	5th	Pend.	"	11
No. 129	60	0	"	Htg.	Gilded	1st	"	"	15
No. 130	60	"	"	"	Nickel	"	"	"	15
No. 131	58	"	"	"	"	"	"	"	15
No. 132	56	6	"	"	Gilded	2d	"	"	15
No. 133	56	"	"	"	Nickel	"	"	"	15
No. 134	54	"	"	"	"	"	"	"	15
No. 135	26	16	"	"	Gilded	3d	Lever	"	15
No. 136	26	"	"	"	Nickel	"	"	"	15
No. 137	25	"	"	"	Gilded	"	"	"	13–15
No. 138	31	"	"	O. F.	"	5th	Pend.	"	15
No. 139	31	"	"	"	Nickel	"	"	"	15
No. 140	30	"	"	"	Gilded	"	"	"	13–15
No. 141	5	18	F. Pl.	Htg.	"	2d to 4th	Lever	"	15
No. 142	5	"	"	"	Nickel	"	"	"	15
No. 143	4	"	"	"	Gilded	"	"	"	15–17
No. 144	4	"	"	"	Nickel	"	"	"	15–17
No. 145	10	"	"	O. F.	Gilded	5th	Pend.	"	15
No. 146	10	"	"	"	Nickel	"	"	"	15
No. 147	9	"	"	"	Gilded	"	"	"	15–17
No. 148	9	"	"	"	Nickel	"	"	"	15–17
No. 149	1	"	"	Htg.	"	2d to 4th	Lever	"	20–21
No. 150	7	"	"	O. F.	"	5th	Pend.	"	20–21
No. 151	35	16	¾ Pl.	Htg.	Gilded	6th	"	"	7
No. 152	35	"	"	"	Nickel	"	"	"	15
No. 153	34	"	"	"	"	"	"	"	17
No. 154	33	"	"	"	"	"	"	"	17
No. 155	32	"	"	"	"	"	"	"	17
No. 156	36	"	"	Htg. Br.	"	"	"	"	21
No. 157	40	"	"	O. F.	Gilded	7th	"	"	7
No. 158	40	"	"	"	Nickel	"	"	"	15
No. 159	39	"	"	"	"	"	"	"	17
No. 160	38	"	"	"	"	"	"	"	17
No. 161	37	"	"	"	"	"	"	"	17
No. 162	41	"	"	O. F. Br.	"	"	"	"	21
No. 163	3	18	F. Pl.	Htg.	"	2d to 4th	Lever	"	17
No. 164	1	"	"	"	"	"	"	"	17
No. 165	8	"	"	O. F.	"	5th	Pend.	"	17
No. 166	7	"	"	"	"	"	"	"	17
No. 167	58	0	¾ Pl.	Htg.	"	1st	"	"	16
No. 168	54	6	"	"	"	2d	"	"	16

ELGIN NATIONAL WATCH CO.

Grades of Movements with Classification and Description as Originally Made.

Grade.	Class.	Size.		Style.		Model.	Sett.	Train.	Jewels.
No. 169	5	18	F. Pl.	Htg.	Nickel	2d to 4th	Lever	Quick	15
No. 170	10	"	"	O. F.	"	5th	Pend.	"	15
No. 171	6	"	"	Htg.	"	2d to 4th	Lever	"	7
No. 172	11	"	"	O. F.	"	5th	Pend.	"	7
No. 173	60	0	¾ Pl.	Htg.	"	1st	"	"	7
No. 174	57	"	"	"	"	"	"	"	17
No. 175	56	6	"	"	"	2d	"	"	7
No. 176	53	"	"	"	"	"	"	"	17
No. 177	..	"	"	"	"	"	"	"	7
No. 178	..	18	F. Pl.	"	..	2d to 4th	Lever	"	7
No. 179	..	"	"	O. F.	..	5th	Pend.	"	7
No. 180	65	"	"	"	Nickel	7th	Lever	"	17
No. 181	65	"	"	"	"	"	"	"	21
No. 182	31	16	¾ Pl.	"	Gilded	5th	Pend.	"	7
No. 183	1	18	F. Pl.	Htg.	Nickel	2d to 4th	Lever	"	17
No. 184	7	"	"	O. F.	"	5th	Pend.	"	17
No. 185	35	16	¾ Pl.	Htg.	Gilded	6th	"	"	15
No. 186	40	"	"	O. F.	"	7th	"	"	15
No. 187	70	12	"	Htg.	Nickel	2d	"	"	15
No. 188	69	"	"	"	"	"	"	"	17
No. 189	68	"	"	"	"	"	"	"	19
No. 190	67	"	"	"	"	"	"	"	23
No. 191	74	"	"	O. F.	"	3d	"	"	15
No. 192	73	"	"	"	"	"	"	"	17
No. 193	72	"	"	"	"	"	"	"	19
No. 194	71	"	"	"	"	"	"	"	23
No. 195	31	16	"	"	Gilded	5th	"	"	15
No. 196	70	12	"	Htg.	Nickel	2d	"	"	7
No. 197	74	"	"	O. F.	"	3d	"	"	7
No. 198	79	0	"	Htg.	"	2d	"	"	15
No. 199	78	"	"	"	"	"	"	"	17
No. 200	77	"	"	"	"	"	"	"	19
No. 201	76	"	"	"	"	"	"	"	7
No. 202	83	"	"	O. F.	"	3d	"	"	15
No. 203	82	"	"	"	"	"	"	"	17
No. 204	81	"	"	"	"	"	"	"	19
No. 205	80	"	"	"	"	"	"	"	7
No. 206	75	6	"	Htg.	"	2d	"	"	7
No. 207	61	18	F. Pl.	"	"	2d to 4th	Lever	"	7
No. 208	63	"	"	O. F.	"	5th	Pend.	"	7
No. 209	75	6	¾ Pl.	Htg.	Gilded	2d	"	"	7
No. 210	92	16	"	"	Nickel	6th	"	"	7
No. 211	94	"	"	O. F.	"	7th	"	"	7
No. 212	92	"	"	Htg.	Gilded	6th	"	"	7
No. 213	94	"	"	O. F.	"	7th	"	"	7
No. 214	89	18	"	"	Nickel	8th	Lever	"	23
No. 215	63	"	F. Pl.	"	Gilded	5th	Pend.	"	7
No. 216	75	6	¾ Pl.	Htg.	Nickel	2d	Lever	"	15
No. 217	61	18	F. Pl.	"	"	2d to 4th	Lever	"	15
No. 218	63	"	"	O. F.	"	5th	Pend.	"	15
No. 219	84	0	¾ Pl.	Htg.	Gilded	1st	"	"	7
No. 220	92	16	"	"	Nickel	6th	"	"	15
No. 221	94	"	"	O. F.	"	7th	"	"	15
No. 222	84	0	"	Htg.	"	1st	"	"	7
No. 223	84	"	"	"	"	"	"	"	15
No. 224	85	"	"	"	"	2d	"	"	11
No. 225	86	"	"	O. F.	"	3d	"	"	11
No. 226	5	18	F. Pl.	Htg.	Gilded	2d to 4th	Lever	"	17
No. 227	10	"	"	O. F.	"	5th	Pend.	"	17
No. 228	5	"	"	Htg.	Nickel	2d to 4th	Lever	"	17
No. 229	10	"	"	O. F.	"	5th	Pend.	"	17
No. 230	56	6	¾ Pl.	Htg.	Gilded	2d	"	"	16
No. 231	56	"	"	"	Nickel	"	"	"	16
No. 232	87	12	"	"	"	"	"	"	7
No. 233	87	"	"	"	"	"	"	"	15
No. 234	88	"	"	O. F.	"	3d	"	"	7
No. 235	88	"	"	"	"	"	"	"	15
No. 236	68	"	"	Htg.	"	2d	"	"	21
No. 237	72	"	"	O. F.	"	3d	"	"	21
No. 238	61	18	F. Pl.	Htg.	Gilded	1st	Key	"	7
No. 239	90	"	¾ Pl.	O. F.	Nickel	8th	Lever	"	21
No. 240	91	"	"	"	"	"	"	"	19
No. 241	33	16	"	Htg. Br.	"	6th	Pend.	"	17
No. 242	33	"	"	"	"	"	"	"	17
No. 243	32	"	"	"	"	"	"	"	17
No. 244	38	"	"	O. F. Br.	"	7th	"	"	17
No. 245	38	"	"	"	"	"	"	"	17
No. 246	37	"	"	Htg. Br.	"	6th	"	"	15
No. 247	93	"	"	O. F. Br.	"	7th	"	"	15
No. 248	95	"	"	"	"	"	"	"	15
No. 249	62	18	F. Pl.	Htg.	Gilded	2d to 4th	Lever	"	17
No. 250	64	"	"	O. F.	"	5th	Pend.	"	17
No. 251	61	"	"	Htg.	"	2d to 4th	Lever	"	7
No. 252	65	"	"	O. F.	Nickel	7th	Pend.	"	21
No. 253	87	12	¾ Pl.	Htg.	Gilded	2d	"	"	7
No. 254	88	"	"	O. F.	"	3d	"	"	7
No. 255	97	10/0	"	"	Nickel	1st	"	"	15
No. 256	96	"	"	"	"	"	"	"	17
No. 257	92	16	"	Htg.	"	6th	"	"	15

ELGIN NATIONAL WATCH CO.

Grades of Movements with Classification and Description as Originally Made.

Grade.	Class.	Size.		Style.		Model.	Sett.	Train.	Jewels.
No. 258	94	16	¾ Pl.	O. F.	Nickel	7th	Pend.	Quick	15
No. 259	87	12	"	Htg.	"	2d	"	"	15
No. 260	88	"	"	O. F.	"	3d	"	"	15
No. 261	61	18	F. Pl.	Htg.	"	2d to 4th	Lever	"	15
No. 262	63	"	"	O. F.	"	5th	Pend.	"	15
No. 263	77	0	¾ Pl.	Htg.	"	2d	"	"	17
No. 264	81	"	"	O. F.	"	3d	"	"	17
No. 265	66	18	F. Pl.	"	"	7th	Lever	"	17
No. 266	65	"	"	"	"	"	"	"	17–21
No. 267	85	0	¾ Pl.	Htg.	"	2d	Pend.	"	15
No. 268	86	"	"	O. F.	"	3d	"	"	15
No. 269	85	"	"	Htg.	"	2d	"	"	7
No. 270	98	16	"	O. F. Br.	"	9th	Lever	"	21
No. 271	60	0	"	Htg.	"	1st	Pend.	"	16
No. 272	56	6	"	"	"	2d	"	"	16
No. 273	65	18	F. Pl.	O. F.	"	7th	Lever	"	17
No. 274	99	"	¾ Pl.	Htg.	"	9th	"	"	21
No. 275	100	12	"	"	"	2d	Pend.	"	17
No. 276	101	"	"	O. F.	"	3d	"	"	17
No. 277	65	18	F. Pl.	"	"	7th	Lever	"	21
No. 278	4	"	"	Htg.	"	2d to 4th	"	"	17
No. 279	9	"	"	O. F.	"	5th	Pend.	"	17
No. 280	102	16	¾ Pl.	O. F. Br.	"	9th	Lever	"	17
No. 281	85	0	"	Htg.	"	2d	Pend.	"	11
No. 282	86	"	"	O. F.	"	3d	"	"	7
No. 283	66	18	F. Pl.	"	"	7th	Lever	"	17
No. 284	75	6	¾ Pl.	Htg.	Gilded	2d	Pend.	"	15
No. 285	63	18	F. Pl.	O. F.	"	5th	"	"	15
No. 286	115	6	¾ Pl.	Htg.	Nickel	2d	"	"	7
No. 287	105	18	F. Pl.	"	"	2d to 4th	Lever	"	7
No. 288	106	"	"	O. F.	"	5th	Pend.	"	7
No. 289	115	6	¾ Pl.	Htg.	Gilded	2d	"	"	7
No. 290	109	16	"	"	Nickel	6th	"	"	7
No. 291	110	"	"	O. F.	"	7th	"	"	7
No. 292	109	"	"	Htg.	Gilded	6th	"	"	7
No. 293	110	"	"	O. F.	"	7th	"	"	7
No. 294	106	18	F. Pl.	"	"	5th	"	"	7
No. 295	115	6	¾ Pl.	Htg.	Nickel	2d	"	"	15
No. 296	105	18	F. Pl.	"	"	2d to 4th	Lever	"	15
No. 297	106	"	"	O. F.	"	5th	Pend.	"	15
No. 298	116	0	¾ Pl.	Htg.	Gilded	2d	"	"	7
No. 299	109	16	"	"	Nickel	6th	"	"	15
No. 300	110	"	"	O. F.	"	7th	"	"	15
No. 301	113	12	"	Htg.	"	2d	"	"	7
No. 302	113	"	"	"	"	2	"	"	15
No. 303	114	"	"	O. F.	"	3d	"	"	7
No. 304	114	"	"	"	"	"	"	"	15
No. 305	107	16	"	Htg. Br.	"	6th	"	"	15
No. 306	108	"	"	O. F. Br.	"	7th	"	"	15
No. 307	103	18	F. Pl.	Htg.	Gilded	2d to 4th	Lever	"	17
No. 308	104	"	"	O. F.	"	5th	Pend.	"	17
No. 309	105	"	"	Htg.	"	2d to 4th	Lever	"	7
No. 310	113	12	¾ Pl.	"	"	2d	Pend.	"	7
No. 311	114	"	"	O. F.	"	3d	"	"	7
No. 312	109	16	"	Htg.	Nickel	6th	"	"	15
No. 313	110	"	"	O. F.	"	7th	"	"	15
No. 314	113	12	"	Htg.	"	2d	"	"	15
No. 315	114	"	"	O. F.	"	3d	"	"	15
No. 316	105	18	F. Pl.	Htg.	"	2d to 4th	Lever	"	15
No. 317	106	"	"	O. F.	"	5th	Pend.	"	15
No. 318	116	0	¾ Pl.	Htg.	"	2d	"	"	15
No. 319	117	"	"	O. F.	"	3d	"	"	15
No. 320	116	"	"	Htg.	"	2d	"	"	7
No. 321	111	12	"	"	"	"	"	"	17
No. 322	112	"	"	O. F.	"	3d	"	"	17
No. 323	116	0	"	Htg.	"	2d	"	"	11
No. 324	117	"	"	O. F.	"	3d	"	"	7
No. 325	115	6	"	Htg.	Gilded	2d	"	"	15
No. 326	106	18	F. Pl.	O. F.	"	5th	"	"	15
No. 327	118	"	"	Htg.	Nickel	10th	Lever	"	16
No. 328	118	"	"	"	"	"	"	"	17
No. 329	119	"	"	"	"	"	"	"	17
No. 330	119	"	"	"	"	"	"	"	21
No. 331	120	"	"	O. F.	"	11th	Pend.	"	16
No. 332	120	"	"	"	"	"	"	"	17
No. 333	121	"	"	"	"	"	Lever	"	17
No. 334	121	"	"	"	"	"	"	"	21
No. 335	105	"	"	Htg.	"	4th	"	"	17
No. 336	106	"	"	O. F.	"	5th	Pend.	"	17
No. 337	33	16	¾ Pl.	Htg. Br.	"	6th	"	"	17
No. 338	38	"	"	O. F. Br.	"	7th	"	"	17
No. 339	107	"	"	Htg. Br.	"	6th	"	"	17
No. 340	108	"	"	O. F. Br.	"	7th	"	"	17
No. 341	125	"	"	Htg. Br.	"	8th	Lever	"	17
No. 342	127	"	"	O. F. Br.	"	9th	"	"	17
No. 343	122	18	F. Pl.	O. F.	"	7th	"	"	17
No. 344	113	12	¾ Pl.	Htg.	"	2d	Pend.	"	17
No. 345	114	"	"	O. F.	"	3d	"	"	17
No. 346	111	"	"	Htg.	"	2d	"	"	17

ELGIN NATIONAL WATCH CO.

Grades of Movements with Classification and Description as Originally Made.

Grade.	Class.	Size.		Style.		Model.	Sett.	Train.	Jewels.
No. 347	112	12	¾ Pl.	O. F.	Nickel	3d	Pend.	Quick	17
No. 348	1	18	F. Pl.	Htg.	"	2d to 4th	Lever	"	21
No. 349	65	"	"	O. F.	"	7th	"	"	21
No. 350	98	16	¾ Pl.	"	"	13th	"	"	23
No. 351	41	"	"	"	"	7th	Pend.	"	23
No. 352	123	18	F. Pl.	Htg.	"	2d to 4th	Lever	"	17
No. 353	124	"	"	O. F.	"	7th	"	"	17
No. 354	116	0	¾ Pl.	Htg.	"	2d	Pend.	"	15
No. 355	117	"	"	O. F.	"	3d	"	"	15
No. 356	128	14	"	"	"	2d	"	"	7
No. 357	128	"	"	"	"	"	"	"	15
No. 358	128	"	"	"	"	"	"	"	17
No. 359	129	"	"	"	"	"	"	"	17
No. 360	98	16	"	"	"	13th	Lever	"	21
No. 361	102	"	"	"	"	"	"	"	17
No. 363	113	12	"	Htg.	Gilded	2d	Pend.	"	15
No. 364	114	"	"	O. F.	"	3d	"	"	15
No. 365	109	16	"	Htg.	"	6th	"	"	15
No. 366	110	"	"	O. F.	"	7th	"	"	15
No. 367	90	18	"	"	Nickel	8th	Lever	"	21
No. 368	130	"	"	Htg.	"	9th	"	"	17
No. 369	131	"	"	O. F.	"	8th	"	"	17
No. 370	102	16	"	"	"	15th	"	"	17
No. 371	126	"	"	Htg.	"	14th	"	"	19
No. 372	98	"	"	O. F.	"	15th	"	"	19
No. 373	126	"	"	Htg.	"	14th	"	"	21
No. 374	98	"	"	O. F.	"	15th	"	"	21
No. 375	98	"	"	"	"	"	"	"	21
No. 376	132	"	"	"	"	"	"	"	23
No. 377	116	0	"	Htg.	Gilded	2d	Pend.	"	15
No. 378	105	18	F. Pl.	"	Nickel	2d to 4th	Lever	"	17
No. 379	106	"	"	O. F.	"	5th	Pend.	"	17
No. 380	133	5/0	¾ Pl.	Htg.	"	1st	"	"	15
No. 381	107	16	"	Htg. Br.	"	6th	"	"	17
No. 382	108	"	"	O. F. Br.	"	7th	"	"	17
No. 383	113	12	"	Htg.	"	2d	"	"	17
No. 384	114	"	"	O. F.	"	3d	"	"	17
No. 385	134	18	"	"	"	8th	Lever	"	17
No. 386	109	16	"	Htg.	"	6th	Pend.	"	17
No. 387	110	"	"	O. F.	"	7th	Lever	"	21
No. 388	98	"	"	"	"	15th	"	"	21
No. 389	134	18	"	"	"	8th	"	"	21
No. 390	91	"	"	"	"	"	"	"	21
No. 391	98	16	"	"	"	15th	"	"	21
No. 392	135	12	"	"	"	4th	Pend.	"	17
No. 393	113	"	"	Htg.	Gilded	2d	"	"	7
No. 394	114	"	"	O. F.	"	3d	"	"	7
No. 395	113	"	"	Htg.	"	2d	"	"	15
No. 396	114	"	"	O. F.	"	3d	"	"	15
No. 397	33	16	"	Htg. Br.	Nickel	6th	"	"	17
No. 398	38	"	"	O. F. Br.	"	7th	"	"	17
No. 399	136	5/0	"	O. F.	"	2d	"	"	15
No. 400	131	18	"	"	"	8th	Lever	"	17
No. 401	126	16	"	Htg.	"	17th	"	"	19
No. 402	126	"	"	"	"	"	"	"	21
No. 403	133	5/0	"	"	"	1st	Pend.	"	7
No. 404	97	10/0	"	O. F.	"	"	"	"	15
No. 405	96	"	"	"	"	"	"	"	17
No. 406	116	0	"	Htg.	Gilded	2d	"	"	13
No. 407	135	12	"	O. F.	Nickel	4th	"	"	21
No. 408	133	5/0	"	Htg.	"	1st	"	"	15
No. 409	117	0	"	O. F.	Gilded	3d	"	"	7
No. 410	117	"	"	"	"	"	"	"	15
No. 411	106	18	F. Pl.	"	Nickel	5th	"	"	21
No. 412	91	"	¾ Pl.	"	"	8th	Lever	"	21
No. 413	116	3/0	"	Htg.	"	2d	Pend.	"	7
No. 414	117	"	"	O. F.	"	3d	"	"	7
No. 415	116	"	"	Htg.	"	2d	"	"	15
No. 416	117	"	"	O. F.	"	3d	"	"	15

Left Dial: 18 & 16 size=$25-$40-$100
Left Dial: 12 size=$20-$30-$60
Left Dial: 6 & 0 size=$10-$15-$45

Center: wind-ind. 18 size=$40-$65-$275
Center: wind-ind. 16 size=$35-$50-$225

Right: 24 Hr. 18 size=$25-$40-$125
Right: 24 Hr. 16 size=$25-$40-$125
Right: 24 Hr. 12 size=$20-$35-$75

196

ELGIN NATIONAL WATCH CO.
IDENTIFICATION OF MOVEMENTS
BY MODEL NUMBER

How to Identify Your Watch Size & Model: Compare the movement of your watch with the illustrations in this section. While comparing, note the location of the balance, jewels, screws, gears, and type of back plate (Full, 3/4, Bridge) these will be clues in identifying the movement you have.

Model 1, 18 size, full plate, hunting, key wind & set, first serial number 101, Apr., 1867.

Model 2-4, 18 size, full plate, hunting, lever set, first serial number 155,001, June, 1873.

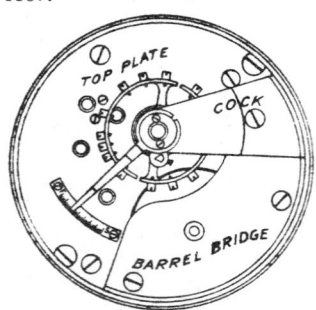

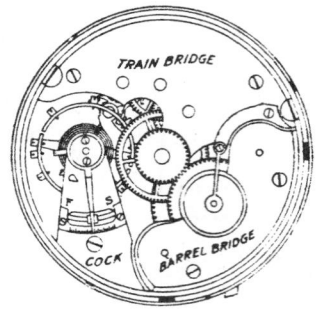

Model 5, 18 size, full plate, open face, pendant set, first serial number, 2,110,001, Grade 43, Dec., 1885.

Model 6, 18 size, three-quarter plate, hunting, open face, pendant set.

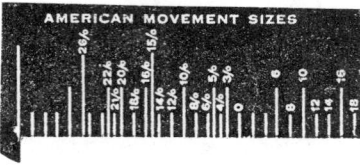

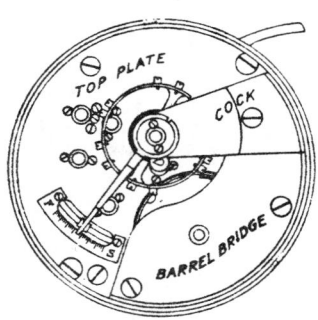

Model 7, 18 size, full plate, open face, lever set, first serial number 6,563,821, Grade 265, Apr., 1897.

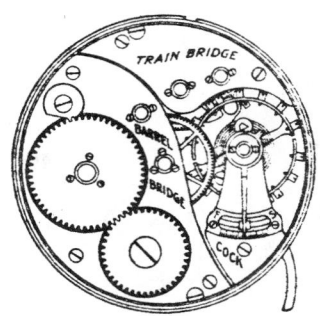

Model 8, 18 size, three-quarter plate, open face, lever set, first serial number 8,400,001, Grade 214, Dec., 1900.

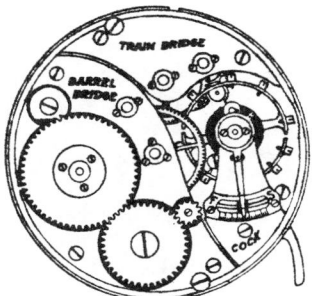

Model 8, 18 size, three-quarter plate, open face, lever set with winding indicator.

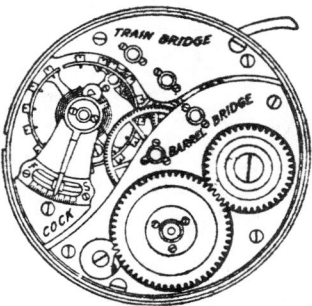

Model 9, 18 size, three-quarter plate, hunting, lever set, first serial number 9,625,001, Grade 274, May, 1904.

Model 9, 18 size, three-quarter plate, hunting, lever set with winding indicator.

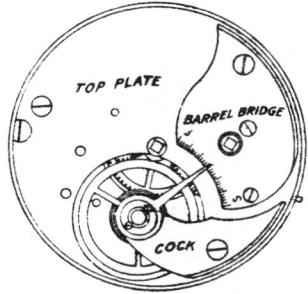

Model 1, 17 size, full plate, hunting, key wind and set.

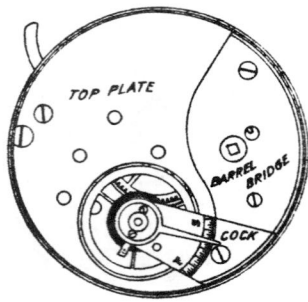

Model 2, 17 size, full plate, hunting, lever set.

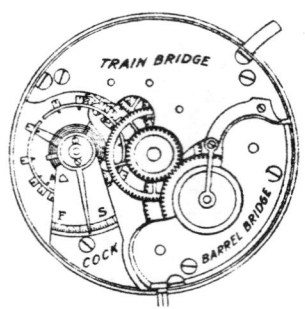

Model 1, 16 size, three-quarter plate, hunting & open face, lever set.

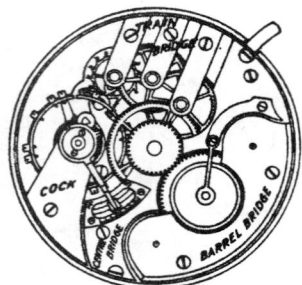

Model 2, 16 size, three-quarter plate, bridge, hunting & open face, lever set.

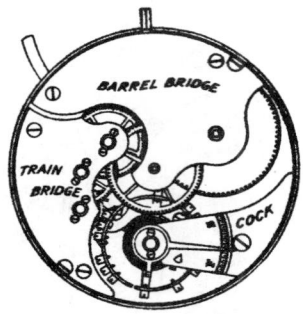

Model 3, 16 size, three-quarter plate, hunting, lever set, first serial number 625,001, Grade 1, Feb., 1879.

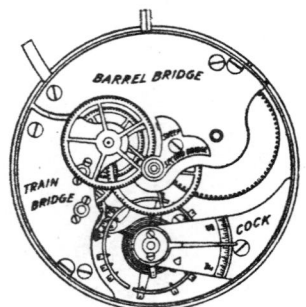

Model 4, 16 size, three-quarter plate, sweep second, hunting & open face, lever set.

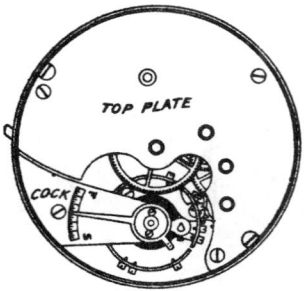

Model 5, 16 size, three-quarter plate, open face, pendant set.

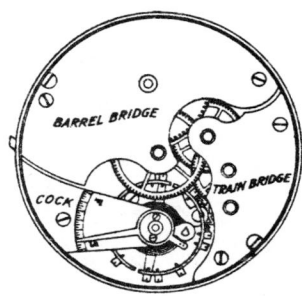

Model 5, 16 size, three-quarter plate, open face, pendant set, first serial number 2,811,001, Grade 105, Oct., 1887.

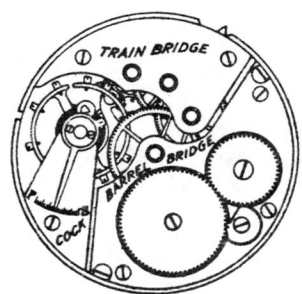

Model 6, 16 size, three-quarter plate, hunting, pendant set, first serial number 6,458,001, Grade 151, Aug., 1895.

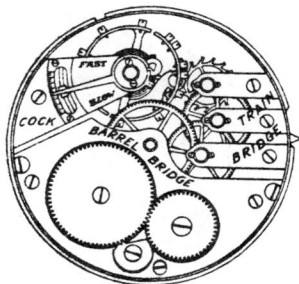

Model 6, 16 size, three-quarter plate, bridge, hunting, pendant set, first serial number 6,463,001, Grade 156, May, 1896.

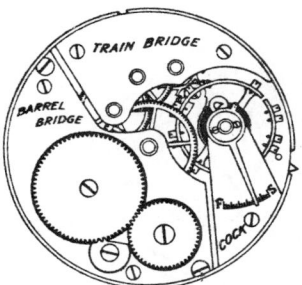

Model 7, 16 size, three-quarter plate, open face, pendant set, first serial number 6,464,001. Grade 157, Sept., 1895.

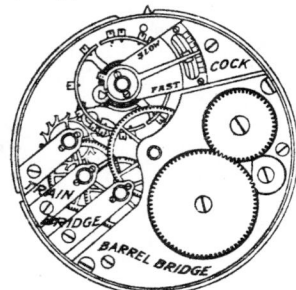

Model 7, 16 size, three-quarter plate, bridge, open face, pendant set, first serial number 6,469,001, Grade 162, Apr., 1896.

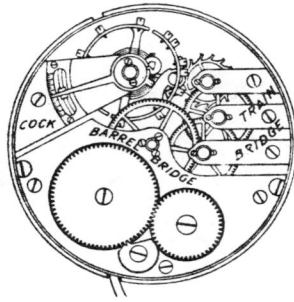

Model 8, 16 size, three-quarter plate, bridge, hunting, lever set, serial number 12,283,001, Grade 341, Jan., 1907.

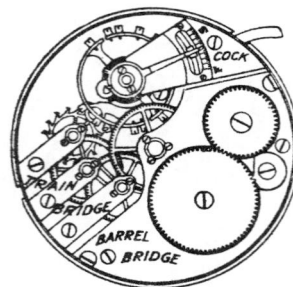

Model 9, 16 size, three-quarter plate, bridge, open face, lever set, first serial number 9,250,001, Grade 270, July, 1902.

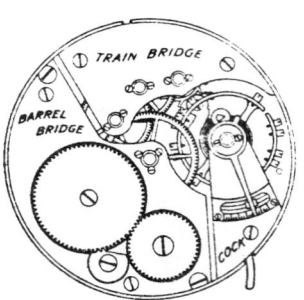

Model 13, 16 size, three-quarter plate, open face, lever set, first serial number 12,717,001, Grade 350, June, 1908.

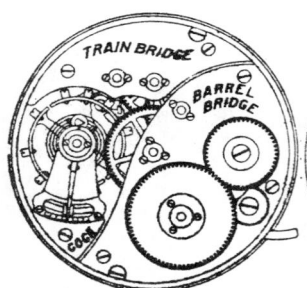

Model 14, 16 size, three-quarter plate, hunting, lever set.

Model 15, 16 size, three-quarter plate, open face, lever set.

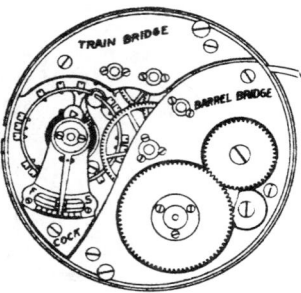

Model 17, 16 size, three-quarter plate, hunting, lever set.

Model 19, 16 size, three-quarter plate, open face, lever set with winding indicator.

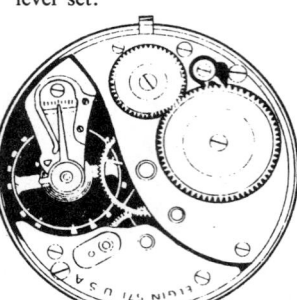

Model 20, 16 size, three-quarter plate, open face, Grades 571, 572, 573, 574, 575, 616.

Model 1, 14 size, three-quarter plate, hunting, key wind and set.

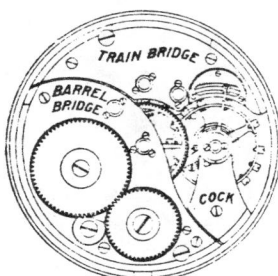

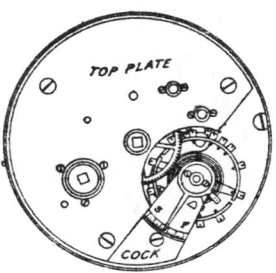

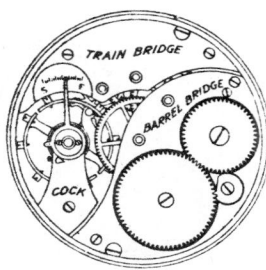

Model 2, 14 size, three-quarter plate, open face, pendant set.

Model 1, 12 size, three-quarter plate, hunting, key wind and set.

Model 2, 12 size, three-quarter plate, hunting, pendant set, first serial #7,410,001, Grade 188, Dec., 1897.

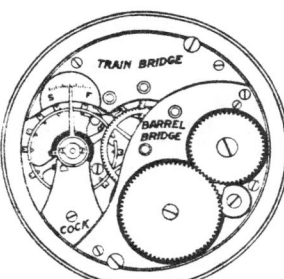

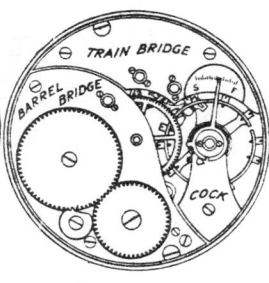

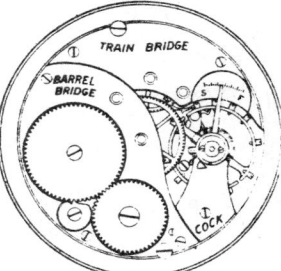

Model 2, 12 size, three-quarter plate, spread to 16 size, hunting, pendant set.

Model 3, 12 size, three-quarter plate, open face, pendant set, serial number 7,423,001, Grade 192, May 1898.

Model 3, 12 size, three-quarter plate, spread to 16 size, open face, pendant set.

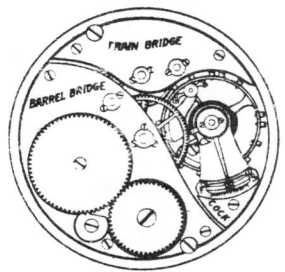

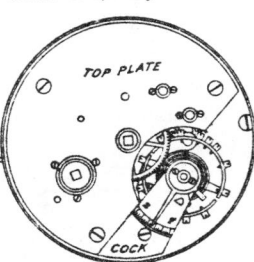

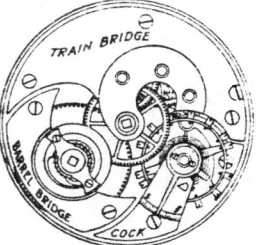

Model 4, 12 size, three-quarter plate, open face, pendant set, serial number 16,311,001, Grade 392, July, 1912.

Model 1, 10 size, three-quarter plate, style 1, hunting, key wind and set.

Model 2, 10 size, three-quarter plate, hunting, key wind and set.

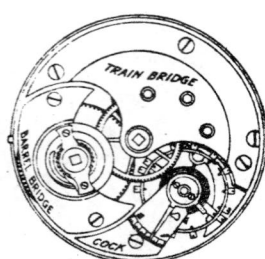

Model 3, 10 size, three-quarter plate, hunting.

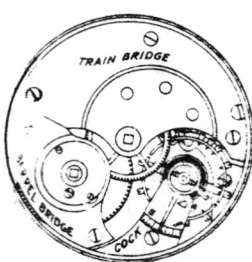

Model 4, 10 size, three-quarter plate, hunting.

Model 5 & 6, 10 size, three-quarter plate.

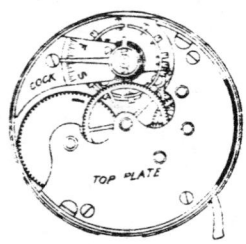

Model 1, 6 size, three-quarter plate, hunting.

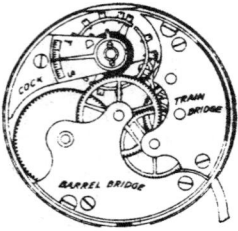

Model 1, 6 size, three-quarter plate, hunting.

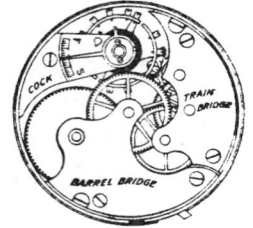

Model 2, 6 size, three-quarter plate, hunting.

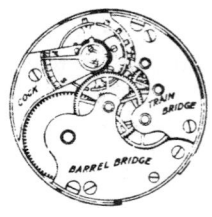

Model 1, 0 size, three-quarter plate, hunting.

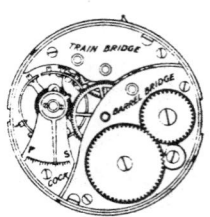

Model 2, 0 size, three-quarter plate, hunting.

Model 2, 0 size, three-quarter plate, hunting.

Model 3, 0 size, three-quarter plate, open face.

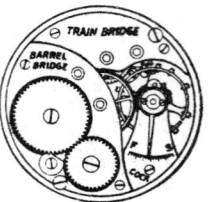

Model 3, 0 size, three-quarter plate, open face.

Model 2, 3-0 size, three-quarter plate, hunting.

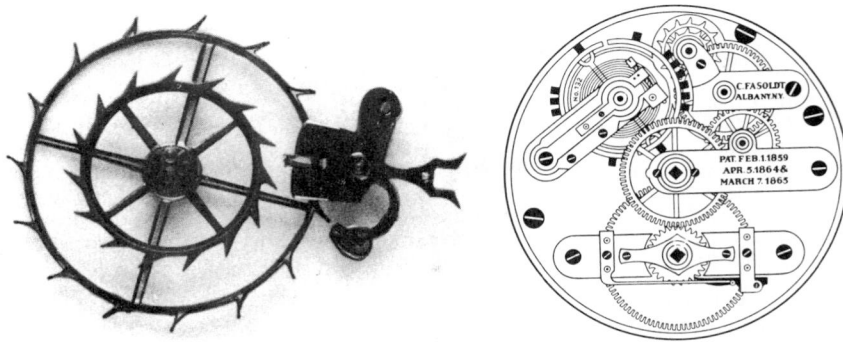

Charles Fasoldt's coaxial escape wheel with odd shaped lever. The double escape wheel was designed to eliminate the use of oil at the escapement and prevent over-banking.

Charles Fasoldt, 18-20 size, 16 jewels, coaxial double escape wheel, key wind & set, bar gilded movement, Serial # 132, note patented regulator not gold, series II.

CHARLES FASOLDT WATCH CO.
Rome, New York   1849 - 1861
Albany, New York   1861 - 1878

Charles Fasoldt came from Dresden, Germany to Rome, New York in 1848. In 1861 he moved to Albany, New York where he set up a factory to make watches and clocks and other instruments. One of his first watches, Serial No. 27, was for General Armstrong and was an eight-day movement. At about that same time, he made several large regulators and a few pocket chronometers. He displayed some of his work at fairs in Utica and Syracuse and received four First-Class Premiums and two diplomas. In 1850, he patented a micrometric regulator (generally called the Howard Regulator because Howard bought the patent). He also patented a **chronometer** escapement with a coaxial double escape wheel in 1859 & 1865, a watch regulator in 1864, and a hairspring stud in 1877.

The reliability of his coaxial double escape wheel was demonstrated when Mr. Fasoldt **strapped** one of his watches (serial # 6), along with some other brand watches, to the **drive-rod** of the Empire Express locomotive. This round trip run from Albany to New York proved his point; all the other manufacturer's watches stopped about a minute after the train started. Mr. Fasoldt's watch, serial # 6, made the entire trip running, and was within a few minutes of the correct time.

Mr. Fasoldt's coaxial double escape wheel was designed to eliminate the use of oil at the escapement and prevent over-banking. Each watch he made has minor changes making no two watches alike and these masterpieces sold for about $300.00 dollars. Mr. Fasoldt was also known for his tower clocks, for which he received many awards and medals. He made **less than 400 watches in Albany N.Y.** and **about 50 watches in Rome N.Y..** Serial numbers **200 to 299** have not been seen. Note a few movements were made **with no serial numbers**.

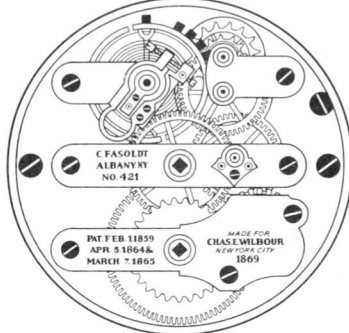

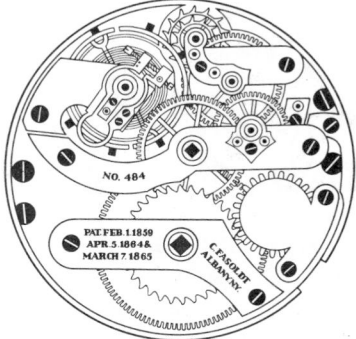

Charles Fasoldt, 18-20 size, 16 jewels, stem wind, key set, bar movement, note: the barrel ratchet wheel only having wolf tooth form, note: Single Winding Bridge, series III.

Charles Fasoldt, 18-20 size, 16 jewels, stem wind, key set, bar movement, note: the barrel ratchet wheel only having wolf tooth form, note: Double Winding Bridge, series III.

Estimated serial numbers & Production Dates
For Albany, New York MODELS (ONLY)

Year	Model	Style	Serial # Range
1861-1863	Series I	KW/KS, 1/2 plate	5-40
1864-1866	Series II	KW/KS, Bar	41-99
1867-1868	Series II	KW/KS, Bar	100-199
1868-1869	Series II	KW/KS, Bar	300-399
1869-1871	Series III	SW/KS, Bar	400-499
1872-1875	Series III	SW/KS, Bar	500-540

Serial numbers _200_ to _299_ have **not** been seen.

Serial # reported = 3, 5, 6, 27, 46, 59, 61, 64, 66, 87, 88, 90, 112, 113, 122, 124, 132, 161, 166, 174, 335, 338, 349, 350, 384, 385, 388, 390, 395, 400, 415, 421, 424, 436, 437, 438, 439, 456, 457, 481, 484, 485, 496, 500, 504, 508, 510, 512 = 12 size, 540.

Grade or Name — Description	Avg	Ex-Fn	Mint
18 - 20 SIZE, 22J, chronograph, Wind Ind., dual mainsprings & dual train, GJS, KW or SW, **18K case** ★ ★ ★ ★	$15,000	$20,000	$30,000
18 - 20 SIZE, 16J, GJS, **KW/ KS**, coaxial double escape wheel, **18K case** ★ ★ ★	8,500	12,000	22,000
* All of the above and below with a **REMONTOIRE** ★ ★ ★ ★	10,000	15,000	25,000
18 - 20 SIZE, 16J, GJS, **SW/ KS**, coaxial double escape wheel, **18K case** ★ ★ ★	8,500	12,000	22,000
18 - 20 SIZE, 16J, GJS, double escape wheel, **movement & dial**	2,500	3,000	6,000
10 - 12 SIZE, 16J, by **C. Fasoldt**, GJS, KW & SW, KS, **14K**	3,000	4,000	8,000
by **Otto H. Fasoldt**, _18S_, 15J, SW, Swiss made or American	375	450	900

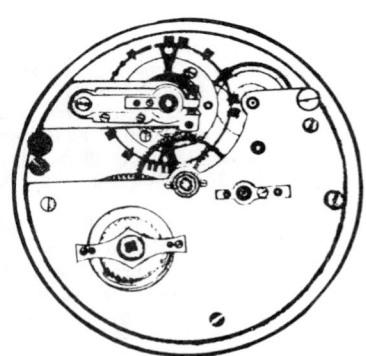

Charles Fasoldt, 18-20 size, 16 jewels, key wind, key set, half plate, coaxial double escape wheel, S. # 6, series I.

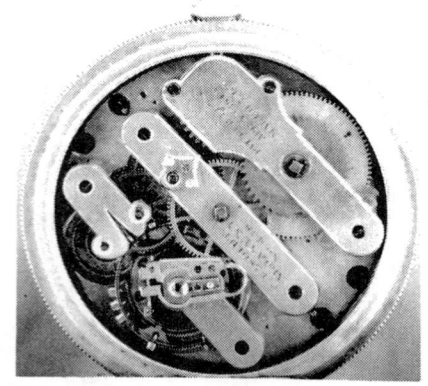

Charles Fasoldt, 18-20 size, 16 jewels, stem wind, key set, patented **chronometer** escapement with a coaxial double escape wheel, **gold regulator**, Serial No. 438, series III.

Remontoire: The constant force device is placed on the third wheel which bears two coaxial independent wheels kept in traction between themselves by a linear spring. Similar to **maintaining power** used on a fusee & clocks.

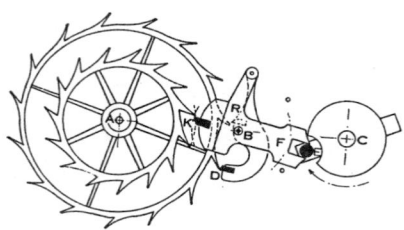

Fasoldt chronometer escapement, larger wheel for locking & smaller escape wheel for impulse to the escapement. The coaxial double escape wheel was designed to eliminate the use of oil at the escapement and prevent over-banking.

FITCHBURG WATCH CO.

Fitchburg, Massachusetts
1875 - 1878

In 1875, S. Sawyer decided to manufacture watches. He hired personnel from the U. S. Watch Company to build the machinery, but by 1878 the company had failed. It is not known how many, if any, watches were made. The equipment was sold to Cornell and other watch companies.

E. H. FLINT

Cincinnati, Ohio
1877 - 1879

The Flint watch was patented September 18, 1877, and about 100 watches were made. The serial number is found under the dial.

Grade or Name — Description		Avg	Ex-Fn	Mint
18 Size, 4–7J, KW, Full Plate, OF, Coin	★★★★	$3,500	$4,100	$8,200
18 Size, 4–7J, KW, Full Plate, **14K**, HC	★★★★	5,000	6,000	9,500

 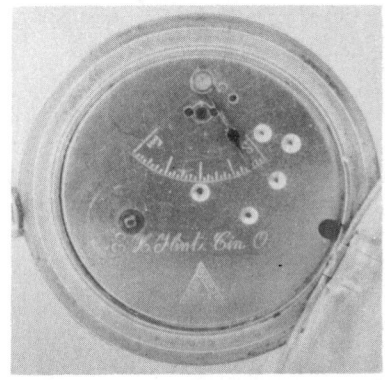

E.H. Flint dial and movement, 18 size, 4-7 jewels, open face, key wind & set, "Lancaster Pa." on dial, "Patented Sept. 18th,1877" on movement.

🕐 Watch terminology or communication in this book has evolved over the years, in search of better and more precise language with a effort to improve, purify, adjust itself and make it easier to understand.

🕐 A collector should expect to pay modestly higher prices at local shops.

🕐 Watches listed in this book are priced at the collectable Trade Show level, as complete watches having an original 14k goldfilled case & KW with a Silver case, an original white enamel single sunk dial, and with the entire original movement in good working order with no repairs needed, unless otherwise noted.

🕐 Pricing in this Guide are fair market price for **COMPLETE** watches which are reflected from the "**NAWCC**" National and regional shows.

FREDONIA WATCH CO.
Fredonia, New York
1881 - 1885

This company sold the finished movements acquired from the Independent Watch Co. These movements had been made by other companies. The Fredonia Watch Company was sold to the Peoria Watch Co. in 1885, after having produced approximately 20,000 watches. Fredonia makes a official Announcement that read as Follows:

"*Born at 2 o'clock p. m., Wednesday, Feb. 1st (1882), the "**Mark Twain**" gilt key winding movement. The child is vigorous and healthy, and there seems to be a large and increasing number of him. His parents are proud of him, and he already promises to become as universal a favorite as his illustrious namesake.*"

Chronology of the Development of Fredonia:

Independent Watch Co. 1875 –1881
Fredonia Watch Co.   1881 –1885
Peoria Watch Co.   1885 –1889

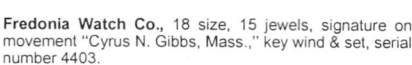

Fredonia Watch Co., 18 size, 15 jewels, signature on movement "Cyrus N. Gibbs, Mass.," key wind & set, serial number 4403.

Fredonia Watch Co., 18 size, 15 jewels, adjusted, serial number 8,368. NOTE: FREDONIA Regulator disc will have teeth all around the disc.

Fredonia Watch Co., with a reversible case; changes to either hunting or open face.

Grade or Name — Description	Avg	Ex-Fn	Mint
18S, 7J, SW, OF	$175	$225	$400
18S, 7J, SW, HC	225	300	450
18S, 9J, SW, OF	175	225	400
18S, 9J, SW, HC	225	300	450
18S, 11J, SW, OF	175	225	400
18S, 11J, KW, KS, HC, Coin	225	300	450
18S, 15J, SW, Multi-color, **14K, HC**	1,600	2,200	3,500
18S, KW, Reversible case	500	600	1,000
18S, 15J, SW, LS, **Gilt**, OF	225	300	450
18S, 15J, straight line escapement, NI, marked **Adjusted**	300	400	600
18S, 15J, SW, LS, **Gold Plated**, OF	300	400	600
18S, 15J, HC, **low** serial number	300	400	600
18S, 15J, personalized mvt.	250	325	500
18S, 15J, KW, HC, marked Lakeshore W. Co.	250	325	500
18S, 15J, Anti-Magnetic, OF	300	400	600
18S, 15J, Anti-Magnetic, HC	300	400	600
18S, 15J, Anti-Magnetic, Special, OF ★	335	450	600
18S, 15J, Anti-Magnetic, Special, HC ★	365	500	650
18S, 15J, Anti-Magnetic, Special Superior Quality, OF ★★	450	600	950
18S, 15J, Anti-Magnetic, Special Superior Quality, HC ★★	475	650	1,000
18S, Mark Twain, 11J, KW, KS ★★★	1,000	1,400	2,500

NOTE: Some of the above watches were marked **Quick Beat**.

FREEPORT WATCH CO.
Freeport, Illinois
1874 - 1875

Probably less than 20 nickel watches made by Freeport have survived. Their machinery was purchased from Mozart Co., and a Mr. Hoyt was engaged as superintendent. The building erected was destroyed by fire on Oct. 27, 1875. A safe taken from the ruins contained 300 completed brass movements which were said to be ruined.

Grade or Name — Description	Avg	Ex-Fn	Mint
18S, 19J, KW, SW, gold train, raised gold jewel settings 18K case ★★★★	$9,000	$12,000	$28,000
18S, 15J, KW, KS, gold train, friction jewels 18K case ★★★★	$8,000	$11,000	$20,000
Geo. P. Rose, Dubuque, Iowa, 18S, 15J, KW, KS, gold train, friction jewels, 18K case ★★★★	$6,000	$8,000	$12,000

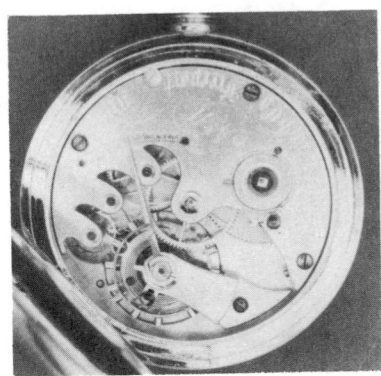 

Freeport Watch Co., Example of a basic movement, 18 size, 15 jewels, key wind & set, pressed jewels, gold train, high grade movement, serial number 11.

Freeport Watch Co., 15 jewels, gold train, damaskeened, large over coiled hairspring with a floating stud, steel lever & escape wheel with single roller.

SMITH D. FRENCH

Wabash, Indiana

1866 - 1878

On August 21, 1866, Mr. French was issued a patent for an improved escapement for watches. The escape wheel has triangular shaped pins and the lever has two hook-shaped pallets. The pin wheel escapement was probably first used by Robert Robin, about 1795, for pocket watches. Antoine Tavan also used this style escape wheel around 1800. Mr. French's improved pin wheel and hook shaped lever (about 70 total production) can be seen through a cutout in the plates of his watches.

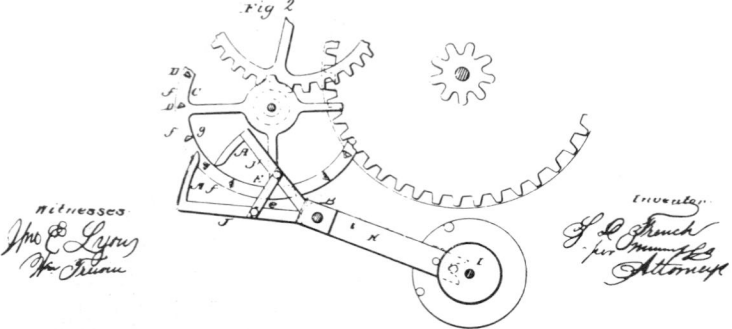

Illustration from the patent office, patent number 57,310, patented Aug. 21, 1866. Note pin wheel escapement with adjustable hook shaped lever.

Grade or Name — Description		Avg	Ex-Fn	Mint
18S, 15J, 3/4, KW, KS, gilt, pin wheel escapement, Silver case	★ ★ ★ ★	$8,000	$9,000	$15,000
18S, 15J, 3/4, KW, KS, gilt, pin wheel escapement, 18K case	★ ★ ★ ★	9,000	10,000	18,500

S.D. French, about 18 size, 15J., gilt 3/4 movement, key wind & set, with pin wheel escapement, engraved on movement "S.D. French, Wabash Ind., Aug. 21, 1866, No. 24."

L. Goddard, 55mm, 7 jewels, full plate movement with solid cock, chain driven fusee, flat steel balance, serial number 235, ca. 1809-1817.

LUTHER GODDARD

Shrewsbury, Massachusetts
1809 - 1825

The first significant attempt to produce watches in America was made by Luther Goddard. William H. Keith, who became president of Waltham Watch Co. (1861 -1866) and was once apprenticed to Goddard, said that the hands, dials, round and dovetail brass, steel wire, mainsprings and hairsprings, balance, verge, chains, and pinions were all imported. The plates, wheels, and brass parts were cast at the Goddard shop, however. He also made the cases for his movements which were of the usual style open faced, double case-and somewhat in advance of the prevalent style of thick bull's eye watches of the day. About 600 watches were made. They were of good quality and more expensive than the imported type. The first watch was produced about 1812 and was sold to the father of ex-governor Lincoln of Worcester, Massachusetts. In 1820 his watches sold for about $60.00.

Goddard built a shop one story high with a hip roof about 18' square; it had a lean-to at the back for casting. The building was for making clocks, but a need for watches developed and Goddard made watches there. He earned the distinction of establishing the first watch factory in America.

Watches **imported** from England were signed Worcester, & watches signed, Shrewsbury used brass parts (plates & wheels) & were cast at the Goddard **shop** & steel parts were all **imported** (hands, dials, mainsprings, hairsprings, balance, verge, chains, and pinions).

Frank A. Knowlton purchased the company and operated it until 1933.

Chronology of the Development of Luther Goddard:

Luther Goddard, L. Goddard, L. Goddard & Son 1809-1825
L. Goddard & Son 1817-1825
P.& D. Goddard 1825-1842
D. Goddard & Son 1842-1850
Luther D. Goddard 1850-1857
Goddard & Co. 1857-1860
D. Goddard & Co., & Benj'n Goddard 1860-1872

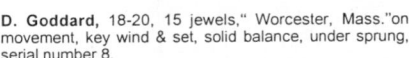

D. Goddard, 18-20, 15 jewels," Worcester, Mass."on movement, key wind & set, solid balance, under sprung, serial number 8.

L. Goddard & Co.,16-18 size, pair case, open face-thick bulls-eye type, and of high quality for the time.

NOTE: Watches listed below are with original silver cases.

Grade or Name — Description		Avg	Ex-Fn	Mint
Benj'n Goddard.. ◹ ★ ★ ★		$2,000	$2,500	$4,000
Luther Goddard, S#1-35 with eagle balance bridge ... ◹ ★ ★ ★ ★ ★		9,000	12,000	20,000
Luther Goddard without eagle on cock .... ◹ ★ ★ ★		6,000	8,000	15,000
Luther Goddard,L.Goddard, Luther Goddard & Son .... ◹ ★ ★ ★		5,000	7,000	12,000
L. Goddard & Co., D. Goddard & Son .... ◹ ★ ★ ★		4,000	6,000	9,500
Luther D. Goddard, Goddard & Co., D. Goddard & Co. .. ◹ ★ ★ ★		3,500	5,500	7,500
P. Goddard, with eagle on cock...................................... ◹ ★ ★ ★		5,000	6,500	10,000
P & D Goddard, 7J., (Worcester), fusee, KWKS, OF ...... ◹ ★ ★ ★		1,800	2,500	5,000

SEE ALSO OTHER **GODDARD** ILLUSTRATIONS ON PAGES- 208 & 210

L. Goddard & Son. Example of basic movement, about 18 size, open face, pair case; brass parts were made at the Goddard shop but steel parts were imported, CA.1815.

L. Goddard & Son, about 18 size, pair case, verge escapement, engraved on movement "L. Goddard & Son, Shrewsbury," serial number 460.

JONAS G. HALL
Montpelier, Vermont 1850 - 1870
Millwood Park, Roxbury, Vermont 1870 - 1890

Jonas G. Hall was born in 1822 in Calais, Vermont. He opened a shop in Montpelier where he sold watches, jewelry, silverware, and fancy goods. While at this location, he produced more than 60 full plate, lever style watches. Hall, later established a business in Roxbury, where he manufactured watch staking tools and other watchmaking tools. At Roxbury, he made at least one watch which was a three-quarter plate model. He also produced a few chronometers, about 20-size with a fusee and detent escapement and a wind indicator on the dial.

Hall was employed by the American Waltham Watch Co. for a short time and helped design the first lady's model. He also worked for Tremont Watch Co., E. Howard & Co., and the United States Watch Co. of Marion, New Jersey.

Style or Name–Description		Avg	Ex-Fn	Mint
18S, 15J, Full plate, KW KS	★ ★ ★	$4,000	$5,000	$9,500
18S, 15J, 3/4 plate, gilded, KW KS	★ ★ ★	5,000	6,000	10,000
20S, 15J, Detent Chronometer, KW KS	★ ★ ★ ★	6,000	8,000	15,000

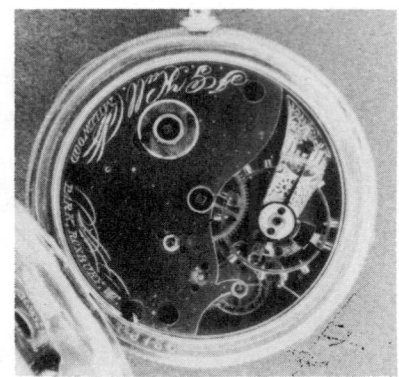

J.G. Hall, 18 size, 15 jewels, full plate, key wind & set, engraved on movement "J.G. Hall, Montpelier, VT.," serial number 25, ca. 1857.

J.G. Hall, 18 size, 15 jewels, 3/4 plate, key wind and set, engraved on movement "J.G. Hall, Millwood Park, Roxbury, VT," no serial number, ca. 1880.

HAMILTON WATCH CO.
Lancaster, Pennsylvania
December 14, 1892 - Present

Hamilton's roots go back to the Adams & Perry Watch Manufacturing Co. On Sept. 26, 1874, E. F. Bowman made a model watch, and the first movement was produced on April 7, 1876. It was larger than an 18S, or about a 19S. The movement had a snap on dial and the patented stem-setting arrangement. They decided to start making the watches a standard size of 18, and no more than 1,000 of the large-size watches were made. Work had commenced on Sept. 1, 1877, at the Lancaster Watch Co. The watches were designed to sell at a cheaper price than normal. It had a one-piece top 3/4 plate and a pillar plate that was fully ruby-jeweled (4 1/2 pairs). It had a gilt or nickel movement and a new stem-wind device designed by Mosely & Todd. By mid-1878, the Lancaster Watch Co. had made 150 movements. Four grades of watches were produced: Keystone, Fulton, Franklin, and Melrose. In September 1879 the company had manufactured 334 movements. In 1880 some 1,250 movements had been made. In mid-1882, about 17,000 movements had been assembled. All totaled, about 20,000 movements were made.

HAMILTON
No. 950 MOVEMENT

THE

Hamilton Watch

RAIL ROAD TIMEKEEPER
OF AMERICA.
LANCASTER, PA.

ABOVE: AD 1910

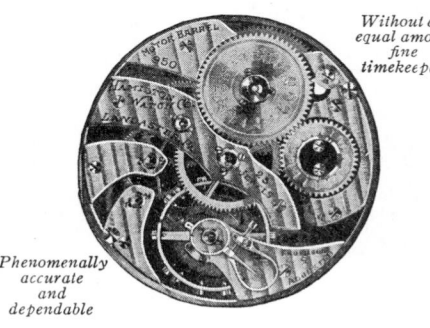

Without an equal among fine timekeepers

Phenomenally accurate and dependable

A most accurate and dependable movement designed by Hamilton to meet the most exacting standards of timekeeping.

No. 950 OPEN FACE—white gold finish, bridge movement, pendant or lever set, 23 extra fine ruby and sapphire jewels in gold settings, patent motor barrel, gold train, escapement cap jeweled, steel escape wheel, double roller escapement, sapphire pallets, Breguet hairspring, micrometric regulator, compensation balance, double sunk dial, adjusted to temperature, isochronism, and five positions.

GRADE 992 ELINVAR MOVEMENT
16 size, nickel, 3/4 plate, lever set, 21 extra fine ruby and sapphire jewels, double roller escapement, sapphire pallets, gold center wheel, steel escape wheel, micrometric regulator, ELINVAR hairspring, monometallic balance, friction set roller jewel, double sunk dial, two piece friction fit balance staff, beautifully damaskeened. Adjusted to five positions and automatically regulated to temperature. Sold cased only.

Note: Automatically regulated to temperature (1933 AD)

ABOVE: AD 1924
(TIME BOOK)

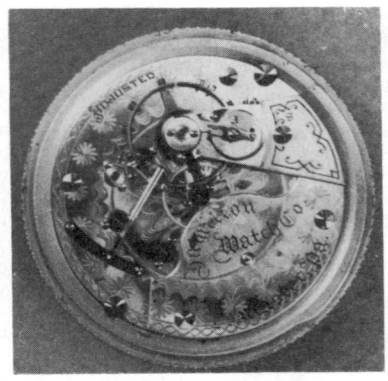 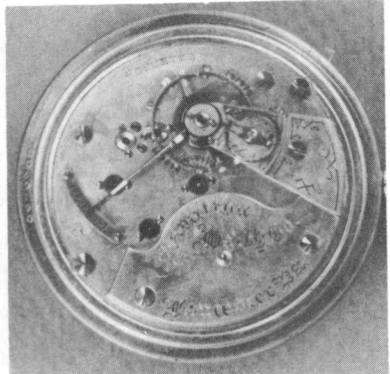

Grade 936, 18 size, 17 jewels, Note: **serial number 1.**   Grade 936, 18 size, 17 jewels, serial number 2, c. 1893.

The first Hamilton movement to be sold was No. 15 to W. C. Davis on January 31, 1893. The No. 1 movement was finished on April 25, 1896, and was never sold. The No. 2 was finished on April 25, 1893, and was shipped to Smythe & Ashe of Rochester, N. Y. serial Nos. 1 & 2 are at the N.A.W.C.C. museum.

Chronology of the Development of Hamilton:

Adams & Perry Watch Co. .... Sept. 1874 - May 1876
Lancaster Penna.Watch .... Aug. 1877 - May 1879
Lancaster Watch Co. .... May 1883 - 1886
Keystone Standard Watch Co.................... 1886-1890
Hamilton Watch Co. .... Dec. 14, 1892 - Present

In 1893 the first watch was produced by Hamilton. The watches became very popular with railroad men and by 1923 some 53 percent of Hamilton's production were railroad watches. The 940 model watch was discontinued in 1910. Most Hamilton watches are fitted with a 42-hour mainspring.

Grade 937, 18 size, 17 jewels, hunting case. Note serial   Hamilton Watch Co., 18 size, 7 jewels, serial number 2934.
number 1047. <u>Hunting case models began with **1001.**</u>   NOTE: Gilded plates.

The 950B was introduced in 1940 and by this time a total of about 25,000 grade (950) had been sold. The 992 watch sold for about $60.00 in 1929, the price remained the same $60.00 until 1940.

The Elinvar hairspring was patented in 1931 and used in all movements thereafter. Elinvar, taking its name from the words " Elasticity Invariable". On October 15, 1940, Hamilton introduced the 992B which were fitted with the Elinvar **extra** hairspring. Elinvar and Invar are trade names and are the same 36 percent nickel steel. Although the Hamilton Watch Co. is still in business today making modern type watches, they last produced American made watches in about 1969.

HAMILTON ESTIMATED SERIAL NUMBERS AND PRODUCTION DATES

Date–Serial No.	Date–Serial No.	Date–Serial No.	Date–Serial No.
1893 -1 to 2,000	1906 — 590,000	1919—1,700,000	1932—2,500,000
1894 — 5,000	1907 — 756,000	1920—1,790,000	1933—2,600,000
1895 — 11,500	1908 — 921,000	1921—1,860,000	1934—2,700,000
1896 — 16,000	1909—1,087,000	1922—1,900,000	1935—2,800,000
1897 — 27,000	1910—1,150,500	1923—1,950,000	1936—2,900,000
1898 — 50,000	1911—1,290,500	1924—2,000,000	1937—3,000,000
1899 — 74,000	1912—1,331,000	1925—2,100,000	1938—3,200,000
1900—104,000	1913—1,370,000	1926—2,200,000	1939—3,400,000
1901—143,000	1914—1,410,500	1927—2,250,000	1940—3,600,000
1902—196,000	1915—1,450,500	1928—2,300,000	1941—3,800,000
1903—260,000	1916—1,517,000	1929—2,350,000	1942—4,025,000
1904—340,000	1917—1,580,000	1930—2,400,000	
1905—425,000	1918—1,650,000	1931—2,450,000	

The above list is provided for determining the <u>APPROXIMATE</u> age of your watch. Match serial number with date. Watches were not necessarily **SOLD** in the exact order of manufactured date.

Some serial numbers have the first numbers replaced by a (date) letter such as A, B, C, E, F, G, H, J, L, M, N, R, S, T, V, W, X, Y, CY, HW. These letters were used from late 30's to about late 50's. The date letter "2B + Ser.#" found on 950B = **1941 to 1943,** the date letter "C + Ser.#" found on 992B = **1940 to 1968,** the date letter "S + Ser.#" found on 950B = **1943 to 1968** and HA = SWISS.

992B with first letter of C + serial no.
1940=   C001
1941= C75000
1942=C160000
1943=C200000
1944=C240000
1946=C300000
1947=C345000
1948=C365000
1950=C380000
1951=C400000
1954=C430000
1956=C445000
1959=C462500
1964=C495800
1969=C529200

950B with first letter of 2B + serial no.
1941=2B001
1942=2B400
1943=2B800

950B with first letter of S + serial no.
1943=S001
1944=S1500   1950=S8900
1945=S2900   1951=S10000
1946=S4000   1955=S18700
1947=S4500   1962=S20000
1948=S6500   1965=S25000
1949=S7500   1968=S30000

NOTE: *It required several months for raw material to emerge as a finished movement. All the while the factory is producing all sizes, models and grades. The numbering system was basically "consecutive", due to demand a batch of movements could be side tracked, thus allowing a different size and model to move ahead to meet this demand. Therefore, the dates some movements were <u>sold</u> and delivered to the trade, the serial numbers may not be "consecutive".*

The Hamilton Masterpiece
The adjoining illustration shows the Hamilton Masterpiece. The dial is sterling silver with raised gold numbers and solid gold hands. This watch sold for $685.00 in 1930. All 922 **MP** Models included the following: 12 size, 23 jewels, were adjusted to heat, cold, isochronism, and five positions, with a motor barrel, solid gold train, steel escape wheel, double roller, sapphire pallets and a micrometric regulator.

HAMILTON SERIAL NUMBERS AND GRADES

To help determine the size and grade of your watch, the following serial number list is provided. Serial numbers 30,001 through 32,000, which are omitted from the list, were not listed by Hamilton. To identify your watch, simply look up its serial number which will identify the grade. After determining the grade, your watch can be easily located in the pricing section.

Serial	Grade	Serial	Grade	Serial	Grade	Serial	Grade
1-20	936	27001-28000	929	56801-900	974	73001-200	975
21-30	932	28001-29000	999	56901-57000	976	73201-300	973
31-60	936	29001-800	927	57001-300	977	73301-74000	977
61-400	932	29801-30000	935	57301-500	975	74001-400	974
401-1000	936	32001-300	926	57501-600	973	74401-600	972
1001-20	937	32301-700	930	57601-800	975	74601-75000	976
1021-30	933	32701-33000	934	57801-58000	977	75001-76799	HWW*
1031-60	937	33001-500	931	58001-100	972	76002-76800	HWW*
1061-1100	933	33501-800	927	58101-200	974	77001-100	969
1101-300	937	33801-34000	935	58201-300	972	77101-300	973
1301-600	933	34001-500	928	58301-400	966	77301-500	975
1601-2000	937	34501-700	930	58401-500	976	77501-600	971
2001-3000	7J	34701-800	926	58501-600	972	77601-700	973
3001-100	931	34801-35000	934	58601-800	974	77701-900	975
3101-500	935	35001-800	931	58801-59000	976	77901-78000	977
3501-600	931	35801-36000	935	59001-300	973	78001-500	970
3601-900	935	36001-37000	928	59301-500	967	78501-700	972
3901-4000	931	37001-38000	929	59501-700	975	78701-900	974
4001-300	930	38001-500	926	59701-60000	977	78901-79000	976
4301-5100	934	38501-600	930	60001-500	976	79001-100	973
5101-400	926	38601-900	934	60501-700	974	79101-300	975
5401-600	934	38901-39000	926	60701-61000	976	79301-700	977
5601-6000	930	39001-200	931	61001-200	975	79701-900	975
6001-600	936	39201-500	935	61201-500	977	79901-80000	973
6601-700	938	39501-700	927	61501-600	973	80001-200	972
6701-800	936	39701-900	935	61601-800	975	80201-400	974
6801-7000	932	39901-40000	931	61801-62000	977	80401-600	970
7001-10	17J	40001-200	930	62001-100	972	80601-700	972
7011-600	937	40201-500	934	62101-300	974	80701-900	974
7601-700	939	40501-41000	926	62301-500	976	80901-81000	976
7701-800	937	41001-500	929	62501-700	974	81001-300	961
7801-8000	933	41501-42000	927	62701-900	972	81301-500	965
8001-700	936	42001-43000	999	62901-63000	974	81501-82000	961
8701-800	938	43001-300	941	63001-500	977	82001-300	972
8801-9000	936	43301-500	943	63501-600	975	82301-500	974
9001-300	937	43501-700	937	63601-800	977	82501-600	970
9301-600	939	43701-900	941	63801-900	975	82601-700	972
9601-800	937	43901-44000	943	63901-64000	973	82701-800	974
9801-900	933	44001-02	21J	64001-100	976	82801-900	968
9901-10000	939	44003-400	938	64101-200	972	82901-83000	976
10001-200	938	44401-500	942	64201-300	974	83001-400	977
10201-400	936	44501-45000	936	64301-600	972	83401-500	971
10401-50	932	45001-46000	929	64601-700	976	83501-700	975
10451-500	936	46001-500	926	64701-900	974	83701-800	973
10501-700	938	46501-800	934	64901-65000	976	83801-900	975
10701-900	936	46801-47000	930	65001-200	973	83901-84000	969
10901-11000	938	47001-500	927	65201-300	977	84001-400	974
11001-12000	936	47501-700	935	65301-400	975	84401-500	970
12001-200	939	47701-48000	931	65401-500	973	84501-700	972
12201-13000	937	48001-05	942	65501-700	977	84701-800	968
13001-400	999	48006-300	940	65701-900	975	84801-85000	976
13401-14000	938	48301-500	942	65901-66000	977	85001-200	937
14001-15000	999	48501-900	940	66001-200	976	85201-900	941
15001-300	939	48901-49000	942	66201-300	974	85901-86000	943
15301-15401	21J	49001-400	927	66301-500	972	86001-87000	928
15302-700	937	49401-900	925	66501-600	976	87001-88000	929
15701-16000	939	49901-50	11J	66601-700	974	88001-500	926
16001-100	931	50071-500	962	66701-800	972	88501-89000	930
16101-200	930	50501-750	960	66801-67000	074	89001-500	941
16201-300	927	50751-50850	964	67001-100	977	89501-90000	937
16301-400	931	50851-51000	960	67101-300	975	90001-100	926
16401-600	927	51001-51300	16s	67301-600	973	90101-950	999
16601-17000	931	51301-400	963	67601-800	975	91001-92000	925
17001-500	929	51401-650	961	67801-68000	977	92001-200	940
17501-18000	931	51651-750	965	68001-800	960	92201-93000	936
18001-200	928	51751-52000	961	68801-69000	964	93001-94000	927
18201-300	926	52001-300	16s	69001-100	977	94001-003	934
18301-500	928	52301-500	976	69101-200	975	94004-95000	928
18501-19500	930	52501-700	974	69201-400	973	95001-96000	923
19501-700	926	52701-800	966	69401-600	975	96001-100	942
19701-20000	930	52801-53000	976	69601-70000	977	96101-700	940
20001-300	934	53001-53070	16s	70001-200	976	96701-97000	936
20301-500	926	53071-53500	977	70201-400	970	97001-900	929
20501-21000	999	53501-600	975	70401-600	968	97901-98000	927
21001-300	935	53901-54000	967	70601-900	972	98001-99000	924
21301-500	927	54001-200	972	70901-71000	974	99001-100000	925
21501-800	935	54201-300	974	71001-200	975	100001-101000	924
21801-22500	927	54301-500	976	71201-500	971	101001-102000	925
22501-800	931	54501-700	974	71501-700	975	102001-103000	922
22801-23000	935	54701-800	968	71701-90	973	103001-104000	927
23001-200	928	54801-55000	976	71791-800	969	104001-105000	940
23201-500	7J	55001-300	973	71801-900	977	105001-500	925
24001-500	926	55301-600	977	71901-72000	975	105501-106000	927
24501-25000	934	55601-700	969	72001-100	974	106001-107000	940
25001-100	11J	55701-800	977	72101-300	976	107001-400	941
25101-400	927	55801-56000	975	72301-600	974	107401-500	943
25401-800	931	56001-300	974	72601-700	968	107501-800	941
25801-26000	935	56301-500	976	72701-900	976	107801-108000	943
26001-500	930	56501-600	966	72901-73000	972	108001-200	928
26501-27000	928	56601-800	972				

Serial No.	Grade
108201-109000	926
109001-500	927
109501-110000	925
110001-900	940
110901-111000	942
111001-500	937
111501-112000	941
112001-200	928
112201-113000	926
113001-114000	925
114001-003	940
114004-115000	936
115001-116000	927
116001-117000	940
117001-118000	925
118001-119000	999
119001-120000	925
120001-121000	924
121001-500	941
121501-122000	943
122001-300	940
122301-400	942
122401-123000	940
123001-124000	941
124001-100	942
124101-800	940
124801-125000	942
125001-126000	927
126001-127000	924
127001-128000	941
128001-129000	936
129001-130000	925
130001-500	924
130501-131000	926
131001-132000	925
132001-100	926
132101-200	934
132201-500	926
132501-133000	924
133001-134000	937
134001-135000	924
135001-136000	925
136001-137000	926
137001-100	11J
137101-138000	927
138001-139000	940
139001-140000	937
140001-300	938
140301-141000	942
141001-142000	941
142001-143000	940
143001-100	927
143101-144000	925
144001-145000	924
145001-146000	925
146001-400	934
146401-147000	924
147001-148000	927
148001-149000	940
149001-150000	925
150001-151000	924
151001-400	927
151401-500	935
151501-152000	927
152001-153000	936
153001-154000	941
154001-155000	936
155001-156000	927
156001-157000	940
157001-158000	925
158001-159000	940
159001-160000	941
160001-161000	940
161001-162000	941
162001-163000	926
163001-164000	943
164001-165000	940
165001-166000	925
166001-167000	924
167001-168000	927
168001-169000	940
169001-400	935
169401-170000	927
170001-171000	999
171001-172000	925
172001-100	934
172101-173000	926
173001-174000	925
174001-175000	924
175002-176000	HWW*
175001-699	HWW*
176001-177000	940
177001-178000	927
178001-179000	942
179001-500	935
179501-180000	927
180001-181000	940
181001-182000	941
182001-300	926
182301-400	934
182401-183000	926
183001-184000	941
184001-185000	940
185001-186000	925

Serial No.	Grade
186001-187000	942
187001-188000	927
188001-189000	924
189001-190000	925
190001-191000	926
191001-192000	927
192001-193000	924
193001-194000	925
194001-195000	926
195001-500	935
195501-196000	927
196001-197000	926
197001-198000	937
198001-199000	936
199001-200000	925
200001-201000	926
201001-202000	925
202001-500	926
202501-203000	934
203001-204000	927
204001-100	934
204101-500	926
204501-205000	934
205001-206000	941
206001-207000	940
207001-208000	927
208001-900	999
208901-209000	940
209001-210000	925
210001-211000	940
211001-212000	927
212001-213000	940
213001-500	941
213501-600	937
213601-214000	925
214001-215000	924
215001-216000	927
216001-217000	940
217001-218000	927
218001-219000	940
219001-220000	925
220001-221000	924
221001-222000	927
222001-223000	926
223001-02	927
223003-04	941
223005	937
223006-224000	927
224001-225000	924
225001-226000	927
226001-227000	940
227001-228000	925
228001-229000	924
229001-230000	925
230001-500	926
230501-231000	924
231001-565	937
231566-232000	927
232001-233000	940
233001-234000	941
234001-235000	940
235001-236000	941
236001-237000	936
237001-238000	941
238001-239000	926
239001-500	943
239501-240000	941
240001-241000	940
241001-242000	941
242001-243000	940
243001-244000	927
244001-245000	936
245001-246000	925
246001-247000	940
247001-248000	927
248001-249000	940
249001-250000	927
250001-251000	926
251001-252000	927
252001-253000	924
253001-254000	925
254001-255000	940
255001-256000	925
256001-257000	926
257001-258000	941
258001-259000	924
259001-260000	941
260001-261000	940
261001-262000	927
262001-263000	926
263001-264000	925
264001-265000	940
265001-266000	927
266001-267000	940
267001-268000	925
268001-269000	940
269001-270000	927
270001-271000	940
271001-272000	925
272001-273000	926
273001-274000	940
274001-275000	924
275002-100	HWW*
275102-200	HWW*

Serial No.	Grade
275202-460	HWW*
275462-500	HWW*
276001-277000	940
277001-278000	941
278001-279000	940
279001-280000	925
280001-281000	936
281001-282000	927
282001-283000	926
283001-284000	925
284001-500	934
284501-900	924
284901-285000	999
285001-286000	925
286001-287000	940
287001-288000	927
288001-289000	940
289001-290000	927
290001-800	936
290801-291000	938
291001-292000	925
292001-500	940
292501-293000	942
293001-294000	925
294001-295000	926
295001-296000	927
296001-297000	940
297001-298000	927
298001-299000	940
299001-300000	925
300001-300	972
300301-500	970
300501-900	974
300901-301000	968
301001-400	975
301401-500	971
301501-302000	973
302001-100	990
302101-200	992
302201-300	990
302301-900	992
302901-303000	990
303001-100	973
303101-300	971
303301-800	975
303801-304000	973
304001-100	970
304101-400	972
304401-305000	974
305001-100	973
305101-200	971
305201-300	969
305301-900	975
305901-306000	973
306001-400	972
306401-307000	974
307001-100	975
307101-300	971
307301-400	975
307401-500	973
307501-600	975
307601-700	971
307701-900	975
307901-308000	969
308001-700	990
308701-309000	992
309001-400	971
309101-400	973
309401-310000	975
310001-400	970
310401-311000	974
311001-700	975
311701-312000	973
312001-200	970
312201-500	972
312501-600	968
312601-313000	974
313001-100	973
313101-400	971
313401-600	969
313601-314000	975
314001-600	974
314601-900	972
314901-315000	970
315001-100	971
315101-400	973
315401-316000	975
316001-200	992
316201-300	972
316301-500	992
316501-317000	972
317001-600	975
317601-700	975
317701-318000	973
318001-100	972
318101-900	974
318901-319000	970
319001-100	971
319101-320000	975
320001-300	972
320301-400	968
320401-321000	974
321001-200	973
321201-322000	975

Serial No.	Grade
322001-323000	974
323001-700	975
323701-324000	973
324001-325000	960
325001-100	965
325101-326000	961
326001-327000	974
327001-300	971
327301-500	973
327501-328000	975
328001-300	992
328301-500	990
328501-329000	992
329001-330000	975
330001-100	992
330101-500	990
330501-331000	992
331001-200	973
331201-400	975
331401-500	969
331501-700	971
331701-800	973
331801-332000	975
332001-200	992
332201-800	972
332801-333000	974
333001-500	975
333501-700	971
333701-900	973
333901-334000	975
334001-200	972
334201-800	992
334801-335000	990
335001-600	975
335601-800	971
335801-900	973
335901-336000	975
336001-200	972
336201-337000	974
337001-338000	975
338001-200	974
338201-339000	990
339001-300	971
339301-500	973
339501-340000	975
340001-200	974
340201-300	972
340301-600	970
340601-341000	974
341001-200	975
341201-342000	975
342001-300	990
342301-343000	992
343001-344000	975
344001-200	970
344201-400	972
344401-345000	974
345001-346000	975
346001-300	992
346301-347000	974
347001-180	993
347181-200	991
347201-300	975
347301-400	973
347401-700	993
347701-900	991
347901-348000	993
348001-200	970
348201-800	974
348801-349000	972
349001-350000	975
350001-300	990
350301-400	974
350401-600	990
350601-351000	992
351001-352000	975
352001-100	968
352101-353000	974
353001-354000	975
354001-400	992
354401-355000	974
355001-800	975
355801-900	973
355901-356000	993
356001-500	990
356501-357000	974
357001-358000	975
358001-359000	974
359001-360000	975
360001-550	960
360801-361000	960
361001-100	993
361101-300	991
361301-400	993
361401-700	975
361701-20	973
361721-362000	975
362001-900	974
362901-363000	990
363001-364000	975
364001-365000	974
365001-100	975
365101-300	973

Serial	No.	Serial	No.	Serial	No.	Serial	No.
365301-366000	975	441001-442000	940	568001-569000	936	667001-668000	941
366001-367000	974	442001-400	946	569001-571000	924	668001-669000	926
367001-500	975	442401-500	942	571001-576000	940	669001-670000	999
367501-368000	993	442501-443000	946	576001-200	942	670001-100	937
368001-369000	974	443001-444000	926	576201-578000	940	670501-673000	925
369001-370000	992	444001-445000	924	578001-580000	924	673001-675000	926
370001-100	990	444501-446000	927	580001-582000	926	675001-677000	940
370101-400	992	446001-447000	924	582001-584000	925	677001-678000	924
370401-500	974	447001-448000	925	584001-585000	927	678001-679200	927
370501-800	990	448001-449000	940	585001-587000	999	679201-680000	926
370801-371400	992	449001-450000	924	587001-592000	940	680001-685000	924
371401-500	972	450001-451000	926	592001-593000	926	685001-687000	940
371501-373500	974	451001-452000	925	593001-594000	924	687001-688000	925
373501-700	990	452001-453000	940	594001-601000	940	688001-689000	946
373701-374000	992	453001-454000	924	B600001-601000	999 Ball	689001-694000	940
374001-200	974	454001-456000	940	601001-601800	926	694001-696000	924
374201-700	990	456001-457000	999	B601001-601800	999 Ball	696001-697000	941
374701-375000	974	457001-458000	940	601801-602000	934	697001-700000	924
375001-100	993	458001-459000	999	B601801-602000	999 Ball	700001-702000	974
375101-500	991	459001-110	946	602001-603000	926	702001-703800	992
375501-376000	975	459111-118	942	B602001-603000	999 Ball	703801-704000	990
376001-200	972	459119-200	946	603001-604000	926	704001-400	992
376201-500	974	459201-700	942	B603001-604000	999 Ball	704401-705000	990
376501-377000	992	459701-460000	946	604001-605000	926	705001-700	972
377001-200	973	460001-461900	940	B604001-605000	999 Ball	705701-706000	974
377201-378000	975	461901-462000	940	605001-606000	925	706001-707000	990
378001-379000	974	462001-463000	999	B605001-606000	999 Ball	707001-800	972
379001-380800	992	463001-500	940	606001-607000	925	707801-708000	990
380801-381000	990	463501-464000	940	B606001-607000	999 Ball	708001-709500	975
381001-382000	992	464001-466000	926	607001-608000	925	709501-710000	973
382001-100	990	466001-467000	924	B607001-608000	999 Ball	710001-800	993
382101-383000	974	467001-468000	926	608001-613000	924	710801-711000	991
383001-300	992	468001-469000	940	B608001-613000	999 Ball	711001-300	973
383301-700	990	469001-470000	924	613001-614000	925	711301-712000	975
383701-384000	972	470001-471000	992	B613001-614000	999 Ball	712001-600	993
384001-700	974	471001-472000	946	614001-616500	924	712601-713000	991
384701-900	972	472001-473000	924	B614001-616500	999 Ball	713001-714900	975
384901-385000	974	473001-474000	940	616501-617000	934	714901-715000	991
385001-600	972	474001-475000	924	B616501-617000	999 Ball	715001-716000	993
385601-800	974	475001-476000	940	617001-619000	926	716001-100	972
385801-386000	990	476001-477000	924	B617001-619000	999 Ball	716101-717000	974
386001-800	974	477001-478000	940	619001-620000	927	717001-200	991
386801-900	992	478001-479000	926	B619001-620000	999 Ball	717201-718000	975L
386901-387000	972	479001-480000	944	620001-622700	940	718001-721500	974
387001-100	990	480001-481000	926	B620001-622700	999 Ball	721501-722000	992
387101-900	992	481001-482000	924	622701-623000	942	722001-724000	974
387901-388000	972	482001-483000	972	B622701-623000	999 Ball	724001-725000	972
388001-400	990	483001-484000	926	623001-624000	941	725001-726000	974
388401-389000	992	484001-485000	940	B623001-624000	999 Ball	726001-727000	992
389001-391000	974	485001-486000	925	624001-625000	936	727001-728000	974
391001-300	972	486001-487000	999	B624001-625000	999 Ball	728001-729000	992
391301-392000	974	487001-488000	924	625001-626000	925	729001-730000	975
392001-800	992	488001-489000	999	B625001-626000	999 Ball	730001-731000	992
392801-393000	990	489001-492000	924	626001-627000	926	731001-732000	975
393001-400	975	492001-493000	940	B626001-627000	999 Ball	732001-734000	992
393401-600	973	493001-494000	946	627001-628000	924	734001-735000	975
393601-394000	993	494001-495000	944	B627001-628000	999 Ball	735001-736000	974
394001-200	972	495001-496000	972	628001-630800	925	736001-738000	975
394201-395000	974	496001-497000	925	B628001-630800	999 Ball	738001-739000	974
395001-100	993	497001-498000	999	631001-636000	940	739001-740000	975
395101-900	991	498001-499000	936	B631001-636000	999 Ball	740001-100	974
395901-396000	993	499001-501000	940	636001-637000	941	740101-200	972
396001-397000	992	501001-900	926	B636001-637000	999 Ball	740201-900	974
397001-200	990	501901-502000	934	637001-638000	936	740901-741000	975
397201-398000	992	502001-503000	926	B637001-638000	999 Ball	741001-742000	992
398001-200	972	503001-504000	999	638001-639000	926	742001-743000	974
398201-399000	992	504001-507000	940	B638001-639000	999 Ball	743001-300	975
399001-600	993	507001-508000	999	639001-640000	925	743301-400	993
399601-400000	975	508001-509900	940	B639001-640000	999 Ball	743401-744000	975
400001-401000	924	509901-511000	942	640001-642000	924	744001-500	972
401001-402000	940	510001-511500	940	B640001-644400	999 Ball	744501-745000	992
402001-404000	924	511501-700	942	644401-645000	940	745001-747000	975
404001-405000	926	511701-517000	940	645001-645500	927	747001-700	974
405001-406000	924	517001-519000	924	B645001-645500	999 Ball	747701-748000	972
406001-407000	940	519001-521000	925	645501-646000	925	748001-749500	992
407001-408000	926	521001-523000	944	B645501-646000	999 Ball	749501-750000	974
408001-416000	940	523001-524000	946	646001-647000	926	750001-100	961
416001-417000	926	524001-531000	940	B646001-647000	999 Ball	750101-200	961
417001-418000	940	531001-532000	940	647001-648000	940	750201-700	950
418001-419000	926	532001-10	934	B647001-648000	999 Ball	750701-751000	952
419001-420000	941	532011-533000	926	648001-649000	940	751001-752000	960
420001-421000	940	533001-535500	999	B648001-649000	998 Ball	752001-500	952
421001-422000	926	535501-536000	940	B649001-650000	998 Ball	752501-753000	950
422001-423000	924	536001-537000	924	B650001-651000	999 Ball	753001-500	952
423001-425000	926	537001-538000	936	651001-652000	940	753501-754000	950
425001-426000	924	538001-543000	940	B651001-652000	998 Ball	754001-100	960
426001-500	936	543001-544000	927	652001-652700	924	754101-500	952
426501-427000	944	544001-200	934	B652001-652700	998 Ball	754501-755000	960
427001-428000	924	544201-545000	926	652701-652800	924	755001-400	992
428001-429000	926	545001-546000	925	652801-652900	927	755401-500	974
429001-430000	925	546001-547000	924	652901-653000	937	755501-700	972
430001-431000	924	547001-548000	940	653001-655000	940	755701-900	974
431001-432000	925	548001-549000	999	B653001-655000	999 Ball	755901-756000	972
432001-433000	940	549001-551000	946	655001-655200	924	756001-757000	974
433001-434000	924	551001-553000	944	B655001-655200	999 Ball	757001-300	975
434001-500	940	553001-555000	940	655201-656000	924	757301-500	993
434501-600	942	555001-556000	936	656001-657000	926	757501-758000	975
434601-435000	946	556001-558000	924	657001-659000	927	758001-100	972
435001-436000	924	558001-560000	925	659001-660000	925	758101-759000	992
436001-438500	940	560001-561000	999	660001-661000	927	759001-760000	975
438501-800	946	561001-562000	926	661001-662000	924	760001-400	992
438801-900	942	562001-564000	924	662001-664000	940	760401-600	974
438901-440000	946	564001-565000	926	664001-666000	924	760601-800	974
440001-441000	924	565001-568000	940	666001-667000	940	760801-761000	992

761001-400	975	826001-500	975L	898001-899100	992	1051001-200	975
761401-600	993	826501-827000	993	899101-500	978	1051201-1052000	993
761601-762000	975	827001-828000	975P	899501-900000	974	1052001-500	972P
762001-200	992	828001-829000	974L	900001-902000	940	1052501-900	954
762201-300	972	829001-830000	974P	902001-904000	926	1052901-1053000	974
762301-763000	974	830001-500	990L	904001-906000	924	1053001-1054000	992
763001-300	993	830501-831000	992L	906001-914000	940	1054001-1056000	974
763301-600	973	831001-100	954P	914001-916000	926	1056001-1057000	975
763601-764000	975	831101-200	972P	916001-917000	927	1057001-1061200	992
764001-300	992	831201-500	954P	917001-919000	925	1061301-1062300	972
764301-400	972	831501-832000	974P	919001-921000	940	1062301-1066000	992
764401-765000	974	832001-400	974L	921001-923000	924	1066001-1068000	974
765001-300	992	832401-833000	992L	923001-500	999	1068001-1069000	975
765301-767000	974	833001-834000	990L	923501-924000	925	1069001-1070000	974
767001-600	992	834001-600	974P	924001-926000	940	1070001-1071000	992L
767601-800	972	834601-800	974L	926001-100	927	1071001-1073000	975P
767801-768000	974	834801-835000	974P	927001-929000	926	1073001-1075000	992
768001-769000	973	835001-600	992L	929001-933000	924	1075001-1076200	974L
769001-700	992	835601-800	990L	933001-935000	925	1076201-700	972L
769701-770000	972	835801-836000	974L	935001-937000	926	1076701-1077000	978L
770001-100	974	836001-500	974P	937001-939000	940	1077001-1079000	974P
770101-771200	992	836501-900	954P	939001-941000	924	1079001-1080000	992L
771201-400	972	836901-837000	974P	941001-944000	940	1080001-100	952L
771401-772000	974	837001-838000	975P	944001-949000	926	1080101-200	960L
772001-773000	975	838001-839000	975L	949001-952000	925	1080201-400	994L
773001-800	992	839001-400	974L	952001-958000	924	1080401-1081000	950L
773801-774000	972	839401-700	992L	958001-960000	926	1081001-1082000	978L
774401-775000	975	839701-840000	990L	960001-968000	940	1082001-400	993L
775001-500	952	840001-400	952L	968001-970000	926	1082401-1083000	973L
775501-776000	950	840401-900	950L	970001-971700	924	1083001-1084000	990L
776001-300	973	840901-841000	952L	971701-972000	948	1084001-1085000	992L
776301-700	993	841001-842000	975P	972001-973000	924	1085001-1086000	992L
776701-777000	975	842001-843000	974L	973001-974000	936	1086001-1088000	974P
777001-300	972	843001-844000	974P	974001-975400	924	1088001-1091000	992L
777301-778300	974	844001-200	993	975401-25 Spec.	926	1091001-200	978L
778301-800	992	844201-845000	975	975426-976000	924	1091201-1092000	974L
778801-900	972	845001-200	992	976001-979000	940	1092001-1093000	992L
778901-779300	974	845201-400	972	979001-100	942	1093001-1095000	974P
779301-780100	992	845401-700	954	979101-981000	940	1095001-1096000	992P
780101-300	972	845701-846000	972	981001-982000	948	1096001-400	974L
780301-781300	992	846001-500	952	982001-984000	924	1096401-1097000	974P
781301-400	972	846501-847000	950	984001-986000	940	1097001-1098000	992L
781401-500	974	847001-200	972	986001-987000	948	1098001-400	992P
781501-782000	992	847201-849000	972	987001-988000	936	1098401-1099000	975L
782001-783000	975	849001-850000	975	988001-992000	940	1099001-600	993L
783001-600	992	850001-300	992	992001-996000	924	1099601-1100000	975P
783601-784000	974	850301-800	990	996001-999998	940	1100001-1104000	992L
784001-785000	992	850801-851000	972	999999-1000000	947	1104001-1105000	974P
785001-500	952	851001-400	993	1000001-1000300	972	1105001-1106000	992L
785501-786000	950	851401-852000	975	1000301-1003000	992	1106001-500	978L
786001-787000	992	852001-853000	992	1003001-1004000	974	1106501-1107000	972L
787001-400	974	853001-854000	974	1004001-900	992	1107001-1109000	992L
787401-788800	972	854001-600	950	1004901-1007100	974	1109001-1111000	972L
788001-791300	992	854601-900	952	1007101-1008300	992	1111001-1112000	974L
791301-792600	974	854901-855100	960L	1008301-1009500	974	1112001-1113000	974P
792601-900	972	855101-856000	950L	1009501-1010700	992	1113001-1116000	992L
792901-793700	992	856001-857840	975	1010701-1011200	972	1116001-900	974P
793701-900	990	857841-858000	975L	1011201-1012700	974	1116901-1117000	974L
793901-794000	992	858001-500	974	1012701-1013000	992	1117001-1119000	992L
794001-200	972	858501-859000	972	1013001-1015000	978	1119001-1120000	978L
794201-795000	974	859001-860000	974	1015001-300	974	1120001-1122000	992L
795001-796400	992	860001-862300	992	1015301-1016000	992	1122001-1123000	974P
796401-800	972	862301-400	954	1016001-300	975	1123001-500	972P
796801-797200	974	862401-500	972	1016301-600	973	1123501-1125000	974P
797201-500	954	862501-600	954	1016601-1018000	993	1125001-1127000	992L
797501-798000	974	862601-800	972	1018001-1020000	992	1127001-1128000	972L
798001-500	990	862801-863000	974	1020001-1022600	950	1128001-1129000	974L
798501-800	992	863001-864000	992	1022601-1023000	952	1129001-1130500	974P
798801-799000	974	864001-865000	975	1023001-700	992	1130501-1131000	956P
799001-200	954	865001-866000	992	1023701-1024500	974	1131001-1132000	992L
799201-600	992	866001-600	974	1024501-600	974	1132001-1133000	992L
799601-800000	954	866601-700	954	1024601-1025000	972	1133001-1134000	978L
800001-802000	974	866701-867000	972	1025001-1027000	975	1134001-1135000	972L
802001-200	954	867001-868000	975	1027001-400	993	1135001-1137000	992L
802201-2	972	868001-869000	992	1027401-1029600	975	1137001-1138000	956P
802203-300	954	869001-870000	975	1029601-1030000	973	1138001-1139000	956P
802301-500	972	870001-872000	992	1030001-1032000	992	1139001-1140000	978L
802501-803700	974	872001-200	993	1032001-1033000	974	1140001-1141000	972L
803701-804200	954	872201-874000	975	1033001-200	972	1141001-1142000	956P
804201-806000	974	874001-800	974	1033201-800	954	1142001-500	974P
806001-807000	975	874801-875000	975	1033801-1035300	974	1142501-1145000	974L
807001-500	993	875001-300	952	1035301-600	972	1145001-1146000	975P
807501-808800	975	875301-876000	975	1035601-1036000	974	1146001-500	956P
808801-809000	993	876001-600	993	1036001-300	972	1146501-1149000	974P
809001-500	974	876601-877000	975	1036301-800	954	1149001-1150000	974L
809501-600	972	877001-400	992	1036801-1037000	992L	1150001-600	950L
809601-810000	974	877401-700	975	1037001-1038000	974	1150601-1151800	952L
810001-300	990	877701-878000	993	1038001-1039000	992	1151801-1152000	952P
810301-812000	974	878001-879400	975	1039001-200	972	1152001-900	950P
812001-700	992	880001-600	992	1039201-500	978	1152901-1153200	952P
812701-813000	974	880601-882400	974	1039501-1040300	974	1153201-300	
813001-814000	974P	882401-883400	992	1040301-1041000	992	1153301-500	994P
814001-800	974L	883401-884100	974	1041001-1042000	974	1153501-800	994L
814801-815900	992	884101-885300	992	1042001-700	992	1153801-1154000	960L
815901-816000	974L	885301-886000	974	1042701-1043000	972	1154001-500	950L
816001-817000	974P	886001-887000	992	1043001-700	978	1154501-1155000	950P
817001-819000	974L	887001-300	974	1043701-1044000	992	1155001-200	994P
819001-820000	974P	887301-890300	992	1044001-1045000	974	1155201-500	994L
820001-821500	974L	890301-891000	972	1045001-1046000	992	1156001-1158000	996L
821501-822000	990L	891001-600	992	1046001-1047000	975	1158001-1160000	974P
822001-700	992L	891601-892200	978	1047001-1048000	974L	1160001-1162000	992L
822701-823000	974L	892201-896200	992	1048001-1049000	992	1162001-500	993L
823001-824000	974P	896201-897800	974	1049001-500	990	1162501-1164000	992L
824001-826000	975P	897801-898000	972	1049501-1051000	992	1164001-1166000	974P

Serial No.	Grade
1166001-1167000	974L
1167001-1168000	956P
1168001-1169000	975P
1169001-1170000	974P
1170001-1174000	956P
1174001-1176000	974P
1176001-1177000	992L
1177001-1178000	956P
1178001-1179000	974P
1179001-1181000	996L
1181001-1182000	992L
1182001-1183000	996L
1183001-1184400	974P
1184401-1185400	956P
1185401-1186000	974P
1186001-1187000	992L
1187001-1188000	996L
1188001-1189000	992L
1189001-1190000	974P
1190001-1192000	996L
1192001-1193000	975P
1193001-1194000	974P
1194001-1195000	956P
1195001-1196000	974P
1196001-1199000	992L
1199001-1201000	974P
1201001-1202000	975P
1202001-1203000	992L
1203001-1204000	974P
1204001-500	956P
1204501-1206000	974P
1206001-1207000	992L
1207001-1210000	974P
1210001-1212000	992L
1212001-1213000	974P
1213001-500	996L
1213501-1214000	992L
1214001-1214600	993L
1214601-1215000	975P
1215001-1216000	974L
1216001-1219000	992L
1219001-1220000	974P
1220001-1221000	992L
1221001-1223500	974P
1223501-1224000	956P
1224001-1227000	992L
1227001-1228000	972L
1228001-700	992L
1228701-1229000	990L
1229001-500	956P
1229501-1230000	974P
1230001-1231000	974L
1231001-1232000	992L
1232001-1233000	974P
1233001-1236000	992L
1236001-500	974P
1236501-1237000	956P
1237001-500	996L
1237501-1238000	992L
1238001-1239000	956P
1239001-1241000	992L
1241001-1242000	975P
1242001-400	974L
1242401-1243000	972L
1243001-500	996L
1243501-1244000	992L
1244001-1245000	974P
1245001-1246000	992L
1246001-300	974P
1246301-800	956P
1246801-1247000	974L
1247001-1248000	992L
1248001-1249700	974P
1249701-1250000	956P
1250001-1252000	983
1252001-1253000	985
1253001-1257000	983
1257001-900	985
1260001-970	Chro.*
1260971-1265000	
1265001-1266000	956P
1266001-1267000	974P
1267001-1268200	978L
1268201-1269000	978L
1269001-600	992L
1269601-1270000	992L
1270001-1271700	956P
1271701-1272000	974P
1272001-1274000	996L
1274001-500	993L
1274501-700	992L
1274701-1275000	992L
1275001-1276000	972L
1276001-1277000	974L
1277001-1278000	992L
1278001-1279000	975P
1279001-1280000	974P
1280001-1281000	992L
1281001-800	974P
1281801-1282000	956P
1282001-1284000	996L
1284001-1285000	992L
1285001-1286000	956P
1286001-1288000	978L
1288001-500	993L
1288501-1289100	992L
1289101-700	990L
1289701-1290000	992L
1290001-1291500	974P
1291501-1292000	992P
1292001-1297000	992L
1297001-1298000	974P
1298001-1299000	992L
1299001-1300000	975P
1300001-1301000	974P
1301001-1302000	974L
1302001-500	992L
1302501-1303000	990L
1303001-500	972L
1303501-1304000	972P
1304001-1305000	978L
1305001-1306000	956P
1306001-1307000	974P
1307001-1308500	992L
1308501-1309000	993L
1309001-1310000	974L
1310001-1311000	972L
1311001-1312000	992L
1312001-800	974P
1312801-1313000	956P
1313001-1317000	992L
1317001-1318000	956P
1318001-1321000	992L
1321001-300	990L
1321301-1322000	992L
1322001-700	974L
1322701-1323000	972L
1323001-1324000	992L
1324001-1325000	996L
1325001-1326500	975P
1326501-1327000	993L
1327001-300	956P
1327301-1329000	974P
1329001-1330000	992L
1330001-1331300	974L
1331301-800	972L
1331801-1332000	978L
1332001-1334000	992L
1334001-400	974P
1334401-1335000	956P
1335001-300	978L
1335301-1336000	992L
1336001-1337000	992L
1337001-1338200	996L
1338201-1339000	996L
1339001-1340000	956P
1340001-1341000	992L
1341001-300	972L
1341301-500	974L
1341501-1342000	978L
1342001-1343000	992L
1343001-400	956P
1343401-1344000	974P
1344001-1345000	992L
1345001-600	974L
1345601-1346000	992L
1346001-1348000	975P
1348001-1349000	974P
1349001-1350000	992L
1350001-600	972L
1350601-1351000	974L
1351001-1352000	993L
1352001-1352300	974L
1352301-800	992L
1352801-1353000	974L
1353001-500	992L
1353501-1354200	972P
1354201-700	956P
1354701-1355000	974P
1355001-1356000	992L
1356001-1357000	956P
1357001-1359800	992L
1359801-1361000	996L
1361001-1362000	992L
1362001-600	974P
1362601-1363000	956P
1363001-1364000	992L
1364001-1365000	975P
1365001-800	956P
1365801-1367000	974P
1367001-1369400	992L
1369401-1370000	996L
1370001-1371000	974L
1371001-600	996L
1371601-1373000	992L
1373001-1374000	975P
1374001-1375000	992L
1375001-1376000	950L
1376001-1377000	992L
1377001-1378300	974P
1378301-1379000	956P
1379001-1380200	972L
1380201-1381000	978L
1381001-500	956P
1381501-1383000	974P
1383001-1384000	992L
1384001-1386100	974P
1386101-1387000	956P
1387001-1388000	992L
1388001-400	978L
1388401-1389000	978L
1389001-300	956P
1389301-1390000	956P
1390001-1391000	992L
1391001-500	956P
1391501-1392000	974P
1392001-1393000	992L
1393001-1394000	974P
1394001-1396000	992L
1396001-500	972L
1396501-1398000	974L
1398001-400	974P
1398401-1399000	956P
1399001-1400000	992L
1400001-1401000	936
1401001-1403000	924
1403001-1409000	940
1409001-500	946
1409501-1410000	940
1410001-1414000	924
1414001-300	941
1414501-1415000	925
1415001-1417000	924
1417001-1419000	940
1419001-1420000	924
1420001-1421000	940
1421001-1422000	924
1422001-1424000	940
1424001-1428000	924
1428001-1430000	940
1430001-200	924
1430201-400	948
1430401-1431000	924
1431001-1433000	940
1433001-1438000	924
1438001-500	926
1438501-1439500	924
1439501-1440000	926
1440001-1441000	940
1441001-1442000	924
1442001-500	926
1442501-1444000	924
1444001-1445000	940
1445001-1447000	924
1447001-1448000	940
1449001-1450500	924
1500001-600	974P
1500601-1501200	956P
1501201-1502000	974P
1502001-1503000	993L
1503001-1504000	996L
1504001-500	974L
1504501-1505200	972L
1505201-700	978L
1505701-1506000	974L
1506001-1507000	975P
1507001-1508000	992L
1508001-400	974P
1508401-1509000	956P
1509001-1510000	992L
1510001-1511000	974L
1511001-1512200	975P
1512001-1513200	992L
1513201-600	992P
1513601-1514000	992L
1514001-200	956P
1514201-1515000	974P
1515001-1516000	992L
1516001-1517000	974P
1517001-1520000	992L
1520001-1521200	974L
1521201-1522000	978L
1522001-600	974P
1522601-1525000	956P
1525001-1527000	996L
1527001-1528000	992L
1528001-1531000	974P
1531001-1533000	992L
1533001-600	974P
1533601-1534000	956P
1534001-100	992L
1535101-200	975P
1535201-600	975P
1535601-1536000	993L
1536001-1537000	972L
1537001-1538000	992L
1538001-800	956P
1538801-1539000	974P
1539001-1540000	992L
1540001-500	992P
1540501-1541000	992L
1541001-1542200	974P
1542201-800	956P
1542801-1543000	974P
1543001-1544000	996L
1544001-1545000	992L
1545001-400	978L
1545401-1546000	974L
1546001-1548000	992L
1548001-600	974L
1548601-1549000	972L
1549001-1550000	974P
1550001-500	972P
1550501-1552000	974P
1552001-1555000	992L
1555001-1557000	993P
1557001-800	972L
1557801-1558000	974L
1558001-500	956
1558501-1559700	956P
1559701-1560000	974P
1560001-1561000	975P
1561001-1563000	992L
1563001-1565000	978L
1565001-1567000	992L
1567001-1568000	974L
1568001-1569000	992L
1569001-1571000	972L
1571001-1572000	974P
1572001-1573000	975P
1573001-1575000	974P
1575001-400	950L
1575401-1576000	950P
1576001-1577000	950L
1577001-1578000	975P
1578001-1580000	992L
1580001-1581200	974L
1581201-1582000	950L
1582001-1583000	974P
1583001-1584000	992L
1584001-1585000	978L
1585001-1586000	972L
1586001-1587000	992L
1587001-500	992P
1587501-1589000	992L
1589001-500	956P
1589501-1590000	974P
1590001-1591000	974L
1591001-1592000	992L
1592001-1593000	974P
1593001-1595000	992L
1595001-200	974P
1595201-900	956P
1595901-1596000	974P
1596001-1611000	992L
1611001-1612100	974P
1612101-1613000	956P
1613001-600	996L
1614001-900	956P
1614901-1615000	974P
1615001-1625000	992L
1625001-200	950L
1625201-1626000	952L
1626001-1627000	974P
1627001-1633000	992L
1633001-1635000	950L
1635001-1636000	992L
1636001-1637000	956P
1637001-1638000	974P
1638001-1642800	992L
1642801-1643000	992P
1643001-1644000	992L
1644001-1646000	974L
1646001-1648000	972L
1648001-1649000	992L
1649001-1652000	974P
1652001-1653000	950L
1653001-1654000	956P
1654001-1657000	974P
1657001-1660000	992L
1660001-1661000	978L
1661001-1663000	974P
1663001-1664000	974L
1664001-1665000	950L
1665001-1666000	975P
1666001-1667000	956P
1667001-1669000	974P
1669001-1670000	978L
1670001-1671000	974P
1671001-300	992L
1671301-900	992P
1671901-1672000	992L
1672001-1676000	974P
1676001-1678000	992L
1678001-1679000	974P
1679001-1681000	974L
1681001-1682000	974P
1682001-1683000	956P
1683001-1685000	974P
1685001-1686000	992L
1686001-1688000	974P
1688001-500	978L
1689001-600	975P
1690001-1691000	956
1691001-1693000	992L
1693001-1696000	956P
1696001-1699000	992L
1699001-1703000	974P
1703001-1704000	992L
1704001-1705000	956P
1705001-1706000	974P
1706001-1707100	992L
1708001-1714000	974P
1714001-1715000	974P
1715001-1717000	992L
1717001-800	956
1718001-1750000	992L
1750001-1761000	900
1761001-1765000	914
1765001-1767000	920
1767001-1768000	914
1768001-1769000	900
1769001-1770000	920
1770001-1778200	914
1778201-1779000	910
1779001-1780000	920
1780001-1782000	910
1782001-500	920
1782501-1783000	900
1783001-1808000	910
1808001-1810000	914
1810001-1811000	910
1811001-1813000	900
1813001-1818000	910
1818001-1819000	914
1819001-1821000	910

Serial Range	Grade
1821001-1822000	914
1822001-1827000	910
1827001-600	914
1827601-1829100	910
1829101-500	914
1829501-1830000	910
1830001-1831000	900
1831001-1832000	920
1832001-700	910
1832701-1833300	914
1833301-1834500	910
1834501-1835400	914
1835401-1836900	910
1836901-1837400	914
1837401-1839000	910
1839001-500	914
1839501-1844700	910
1844701-1845700	914
1845701-1848300	910
1848301-1849500	914
1849501-1851900	910
1851901-1853100	914
1853101-1856800	910
1856801-1857900	914
1857901-1860300	910
1860301-1861000	914
1861001-1863000	900
1863001-700	920
1863701-1864300	900
1864301-1865000	920
1865001-500	914
1865501-1870300	910
1870301-1871500	914
1871501-1875100	910
1875101-600	914
1875601-1876500	910
1876501-1877500	914
1877501-1878700	910
1878701-1880000	914
1880001-300	920
1880301-1881500	900
1881501-700	920
1881701-900	900
1881901-1882900	920
1882901-1885000	900
1885001-1887400	910
1887401-1888600	914
1888601-1891000	910
1891001-1892200	914
1892201-1894600	910
1894601-1895800	914
1895801-1899000	910
1899001-300	900
1899301-1900000	920
1900001-400	910
1900401-1902100	914
1902101-1907000	910
1907001-1909000	914
1909001-1910000	910
1910001-500	920
1910501-1911000	900
1911001-1913000	920
1913001-1914000	900
1914001-1920000	910
1920001-1922000	920
1922001-1924000	910
1924001-1925000	900
1925001-1936000	910
1936001-1937000	920
1937001-900	900
1940001-1941000	914
1941001-1949000	910
1949001-1950000	914
1950001-1962000	910
1962001-1963000	914
1963001-1975000	910
1975001-1976000	914
1976001-1980000	910
1980001-1981000	914
1981001-1988500	910

Serial Range	Grade
1989001-400	914
2000001-2001700	988
2001701-2002400	986
2002401-800	988
2002801-2003100	986
2004001-2035000	986
2035001-2037200	981
2040001-2064900	986
2100001-2191300	986A
2200001-2248000	987
2248001-2300000	987F
2300001-2311000	992L
2311001-2312000	974L
2312001-2321700	992L
2321701-2323000	974L
2323001-2326000	992L
2326001-2327000	974P
2327001-2333000	992L
2333001-2336000	974P
2336001-2338000	992L
2338001-2339000	974P
2339001-2340000	974L
2340001-2341000	974P
2341001-2346000	992L
2346001-2347000	974P
2347001-2356000	992L
2356001-2358000	974P
2358001-2364000	992L
2364001-2365000	974P
2365001-2374000	992L
2374001-2375000	974P
2375001-2378000	992L
2378001-2380000	974L
2380001-2383000	992L
2383001-2384000	950L
2384001-2385000	992L
2385001-2396000	974P
2386001-2390000	992L
2390001-2391000	974P
2391001-2393000	992L
2393001-2395000	974P
2395001-2397000	992L
2397001-2398000	974L
2398001-2401000	992L
2401001-2402000	974P
2402001-2407000	992L
2407001-2409000	974P
2409001-2413000	992L
2413001-2414000	974P
2414001-2415000	974L
2415001-2418000	992L
2418001-2420000	974P
2420001-2422000	992L
2422001-2423000	974P
2423001-2432000	992L
2432001-2433000	974P
2433001-2434000	992L
2434001-2435000	974P
2435001-2437000	992L
2437001-2438000	974P
2438001-2442000	992L
2442001-2445000	974P
2445001-2451000	992L
2451001-2453000	974P
2453001-2455000	992L
2455001-2456000	974P
2456001-2457000	992L
2457001-2458000	950L
2458001-2459000	974L
2459001-2461000	992L
2461001-2462000	974L
2462001-2464000	992L
2464001-2466000	974P
2466001-2468000	992L
2468001-2469000	974P
2469001-2472000	992L
2472001-2473000	974P
2473001-2474000	992L
2474001-2475000	974P

Serial Range	Grade
2475001-2476000	992L
2476001-2477000	974P
2477001-2490000	992L
2490001-2492000	974L
2492001-2504000	992L
2504001-2505000	950L
2505001-300	950L
2506001-2526000	992L
2526001-2528000	974P
2528001-2533000	992L
2533001-2534000	974P
2534001-2535000	992L
2535001-2536000	974P
2536001-2537000	974L
2537001-2538000	974P
2538001-2539000	974L
2539001-2542000	974P
2542001-2543000	992L
2543001-2545000	974P
2545001-2547000	992L
2547001-2548400	974P
2548401-2548600	974L
2548601-2548700	974P
2548701-2550000	974L
2550001-2551000	992L
2551001-2552000	974L
2552001-2555000	992L
2555001-2555600	974L
2555601-2557000	974L
2557001-2558000	992L
2558001-2560000	992L
2560001-2561000	974L
2561001-2563000	992L
2563001-2564000	974L
2564001-2566000	992L
2566001-2566800	974L
2567001-2581000	992L
2581001-2583900	992E
2583901-2584300	992L
2584301-2596000	992E
2596001-2597000	974L
2597001-2608000	992E
2608001-2608800	974L
2609001-2611000	992E
2611001-2611400	950L
2611401-2613000	950E
2613001-2618000	992E
2618001-2619000	950E
2619001-2631000	992E
2631001-2631600	950E
2631801-2632000	950E
2632001-2639000	992E
2639001-2641000	950E
2641001-2649000	992E
2649001-2650600	950E
2651001-2653300	992E
2900001-2911500	979
2911601-2931900	979F
3000001-3002300	922
3002301-3002500	922M.P.
3002501-3003800	922
3003801-3004000	922M.P.
3004001-3006100	922
3006101-3006300	922M.P.
3006301-3008000	922
3008001-3008600	922M.P.
3008601-3010000	922
3010001-3010500	922
3010501-3010700	922M.P.
3010701-3011900	922
3011901-3012500	922M.P.
3012501-3013100	922
3013101-3013700	922M.P.
3013701-3015700	922
3050001-3054800	902
3054801-3056000	922
3056001-3060800	902
3061001-3065100	904
3100001-3133800	916
3135001-3152700	918
3200001-3460900	912
4000001-4447201	987F
4447301-4523000	987E

*Hamilton 36 size chronometer watch

Serial Range	Grade
A-001 to A-8900	980B
1B-001 to 1B-25300	999B
2B-001 to 2B-700	999B
2B-701 to 2B-800	950B
C-001 to C-396300	992B
E-001 to E-114000	989
E-114001 to E-140400	989E
F-101 to F-57600	995
F-57601 to F-59850	995A
F-59851 to F-62000	995
F-62001 to F-63000	995A
F-63001 to F-63800	995
F-63801 to F-286200	995A
G-001 to G-13600	980
G-13601 to G-14600	980
G-14601 to G-44500	980 & 980A
G-44501 to G-45000	980A
G-45001 to G-47400	980
G-47401 to G-48400	980A
G-48401 to G-58200	980
G-58201 to G-58700	980A
G-58701 to G-61000	980
G-61601 to G-62500	980A
G-62501 to G-67500	980
G-67501 to G-68600	980A
G-68601- to G-651700	980
H-001 to H-1000	921
H-1001 to H-1800	921
H-1801 to H-2000	400 & 921
H-2001 to H-2800	921
H-2801 to H-3500	400 & 921
H-3501 to H-51700	400
H-50001 to H-57500	401
J-001 to J-670600	982
L-001 to L-165000	997
M-001 to M-201900	982M
N-001 to N-532200	721
O-1 to O-486300	987A
R-001 to R-3600	923
S-001 to S-18700	950B
SS-001 to SS-87400	987S
T-001 to T-783000	911
V-001 to V-127200	911M
X-001 to X-197600	917
Y-001 to Y-396200	747
CY-001 to CY-176700	748
O-01A to 622700-A	750
O-01C to 126000-C	751
001E to 47400E	752
001F to 63700F	753
001H to 26800H	754

* Hayden W. Wheeler model

NOTE: The above serial number and grade listing is an actual Hamilton factory list and is accurate in most cases. However, it has been brought to our attention that in rare cases the serial number and grade number do not match the list. One example is the Hayden W. Wheeler model.

Grade 936 single roller before S# 426,001, double roller after S# 426,000.
Grade 937 single roller before S# 652,901, double roller after S# 652,900.
Grade 940 single roller before S# 512,201, double roller after S# 512,200.
Grade 941 single roller before S# 419,101, double roller after S# 419,100.
Grade 972 single roller before S# 748,001, double roller after S# 748,000.
Grade 973 single roller before S# 711,301, double roller after S# 711,300.
Grade 992 single roller before S# 377,001, double roller after S# 379,000.
Grade 993 single roller before S# 367,801, double roller after S# 367,800.
Grade 956,964,965,968,969,975,976, & 977 single roller before S# 2,477,001, double roller after S# 2,477,000.
Grade 974 & 978 single roller before S# 2,490,001, double roller after S# 2,490,000.

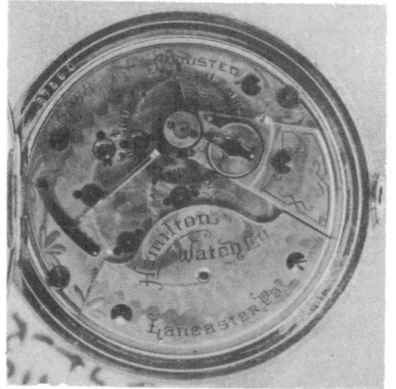

Grade 925, 18 size, 17 jewels, hunting case, serial number 101,495.

Grade 932, 18 size, 16 jewels, open face, serial number 6,888.

HAMILTON
18 SIZE

Grade or Name — Description		Avg	Ex-Fn	Mint
7J, LS, FULL, OF	★★	$1,200	$1,600	$2,500
11J, LS, FULL, HC	★★★	1,300	1,700	3,000
11J, LS, FULL, OF	★★★	1,300	1,700	3,000
922, 15J, OF	★★	400	500	900
923, 15J, HC	★★	550	700	1,000
924, 17J, NI, OF, DMK		95	150	295
925, 17J, NI, HC, DMK		95	150	295
926, 17J, NI, OF, DMK, ADJ		95	150	295
927, 17J, NI, HC, DMK, ADJ		95	150	295
928, 15J, NI, OF		150	195	400
929, 15J, NI, HC, **14K**		600	800	1,300
929, 15J, NI, HC		195	250	500
930, 16J, NI, OF		195	250	500
931, 16J, NI, HC		250	295	600
932, 16J, S#21-30 1st run , OF	★★★★	2,500	3,000	4,000
932, 16J, NI, OF (S#s less than 400)		800	1,000	1,300
932, 16J, NI, OF	★★	400	500	900
933, 16J, NI, HC	★★	500	600	1,000
933, 16J, NI, HC ((Serial #s started at 1021-30)		600	800	1,400
934, 17J, NI, DMK, ADJ, OF		125	175	350
934, 17J, NI, ADJ, Coin OF		95	150	295
934 & 935 & 937, 17J, MARKED (**Main Line**)	★	300	400	800
935, 17J, NI, DMK, ADJ, HC.	★	275	350	500
936, 17J, S# 1-20, 1st run, OF		4,000	5,000	7,000
936, 17J, NI, DMK, SR & DR, OF		95	150	295
937, 17J, NI, MARKED on Mvt.(**Official Standard**), HC	★	600	700	1,500
937, 17J, NI, DMK, SR & DR, HC		175	225	400
937, 17J, serial # 1001 to 1020 = **1st run** HC	★★	1,000	1,400	2,400
937, 17J, serial # 1031 to 1060 = **2nd run** HC	★★	600	800	1,500

FIRST Hunting Case serial # was **1001.**
Grade 937 *(Serial #s started at 1001)*

🕐 Watches listed in this book are priced at the collectable Trade Show level, as **Complete** watches having an original 14k gold-filled case for Stem Wind and *Key Wind* with silver case, an original white enamel single sunk dial, and with the entire original movement in good working order with no repairs needed.

Grade or Name — Description		Avg	Ex-Fn	Mint
938, 17J, NI, DMK, DR, OF	★★	$600	$700	$950
939, 17J, NI, DMK, DR, HC	★★	600	700	950
940, 21J, NI, Mermod Jaccards St. Louis Paragon , OF Time Keeper & a hour glass on mvt.	★	600	700	950
940, 21J, NI, DMK, SR & DR, Adj.5P, GJS, OF		195	250	400
940, 21J, NI, GF or Coin, OF		195	250	400
940, 21J, NI, SR & DR, 2-Tone, OF	★	325	375	700
940, 21J, NI, DR, Marked Extra, OF	★	500	600	900
940, 21J, NI, DR, Marked Special, OF	★	400	500	800
940, 21J, NI, DR, Marked Special for R R Service, OF	★★★	2,500	3,000	4,000
940, 21J, NI, DR, Marked Pennsylvania Special, OF	★	3,000	3,500	5,000
941, 21J, NI, DR, GJS, HC		285	350	600
941, 21J, NI, DR, GJS, Marked Special, HC	★	450	500	800
941, 21J, NI, DMK, SR & DR, Adj.5P, GJS, HC		250	350	500
942, 21J, NI, DMK, DR, Adj.5P, GJS, OF		250	350	500
942, 21J, NI, DMK, DR, Adj.5P, GJS Marked For Railroad Service. OF	★★	2,500	3,000	4,000
943, 21J, NI, DMK, DR, Adj.5P, GJS, HC	★	295	375	650
943, 21J, Marked Burlington Special	★★	2,500	3,000	4,000
944, 19J, NI, DMK, DR, Adj.5P, GJS, OF		295	400	600
946, Anderson, (jobber name on movement), 14K		1,200	1,400	2,500
946, 23J, Marked Extra, GJS, OF	★	1,000	1,200	2,000
946, 23J, Marked ''Loaner'' on case	★	800	900	1,600
946, 23J, NI, DMK, DR, Adj.5P, GJS, OF		650	750	1,200
946, 23J, NI, DMK, Adj.5P, GJS, unmarked, OF		650	750	1,200
947, 23J, NI, DMK, DR, Adj.5P, GJS, 14K, HC, NOT MARKED ''947''	★★★	3,400	4,200	6,500
947, 23J, NI, DMK, DR, Adj.5P, GJS, 14K, HC, MARKED ''947''	★★★	4,000	5,000	8,000
947, 23J, NI, DMK, DR, Adj.5P, GJS, 14K, HC, MARKED ''947'' EXTRA	★★★★	5,000	6,000	9,000

MOVEMENTS WITH ODD GRADE NUMBERS ARE HUNTING CASE example 947.
MOVEMENTS WITH EVEN GRADE NUMBERS ARE OPEN FACE example 946.
Note: Some 18 size movements are marked with grade numbers, some are not. Collectors prefer marked movement.

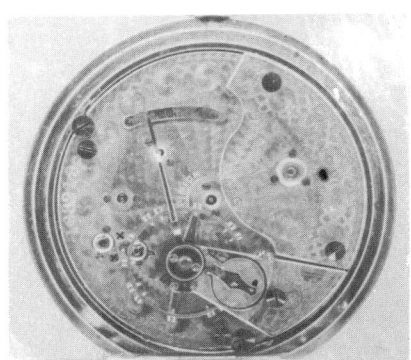

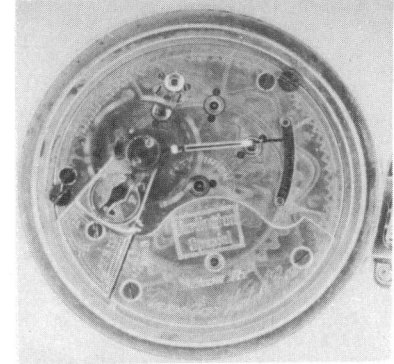

Grade 947 (marked), 18 size, 23 jewels, gold jewel settings, hunting case, Adj6p, serial number 163,219.

Burlington Special, 18 size, 21 jewels, Grade 943, open face, serial number 121,614.

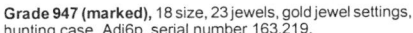 The Complete Price Guide to Watches goal is to stimulate the orderly exchange of <u>Watches</u> between *"buyers"* and *"sellers"*.

Grade or Name — Description		Avg	Ex-Fn	Mint
948, 17J, NI, DMK, DR, Adj.5P, GJS, OF	★	$350	$400	$800
948, 17J, NI, DMK, DR, Adj.5P, GJS, Coin, OF	★	350	400	800
The Banner, 928, 15J, NI, OF		175	195	400
The Banner, 940, 21J, NI, OF		275	325	500
The Banner, 940 **special**, 21J, NI, OF		375	450	800
The Banner, 941, 21J, NI, HC		325	375	600
The Banner, 17J, M#927, HC, ADJ		150	185	295
Burlington Special, 17J, Adj.5P, OF	★	1,000	1,200	2,000
Burlington Special, 17J, Adj.5P, HC	★	1,100	1,300	2,100
Burlington Special, 21J, Adj.5P, OF	★	1,200	1,400	2,200
Burlington Special, 21J, Adj.5P, HC	★	1,400	1,600	2,800
Chesapeake & Ohio, Special, (936)	★★★	2,500	3,000	4,500
Chesapeake & Ohio, Railway Special, (936)	★★★	2,500	3,000	4,500
Chesapeake & Ohio, Railway Special, (937)	★★★	2,500	3,000	4,500
Imperial Canada, GRADE 922, OF	★	550	650	1,000
Imperial Canada, GRADE 923, HC	★	600	700	1,200
Inspectors Standard, 21J, OF	★	650	750	1,400
The Union, 17J, G# 924		150	195	400
The Union Special, 17J		150	195	400
The Union, 17J, G#925, HC		195	250	500

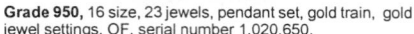

Grade 950, 16 size, 23 jewels, pendant set, gold train, gold jewel settings, OF, serial number 1,020,650.

Grade 961, 16 size, 21 jewels, gold train, gold jewel settings, HC, serial number 81,848.

16 SIZE

Grade or Name — Description		Avg	Ex-Fn	Mint
950, 23J, LS, BRG, DR, GT, **14K, OF**	★★	$1,500	$1,800	$3,000
950, 23J, DR, BRG, GJS, Adj.5P, NI, GCW, OF		700	850	1,600
950, 23J, DR, GJS, BRG, Adj.5P, NI, **Gold Train**, OF		800	950	1,700
950B, 23J, LS, Adj.6P, NI, DR, BRG, OF	◻	700	850	1,600
950B, 23J, LS, Adj.6P, NI, DR, BRG, **Gold Train,** OF	◻	800	950	1,700
950B, 23J, LS, Adj.6P, NI, DR, BRG, OF, In Hamilton original **factory** box with matching serial numbers	◻★★	1,300	1,800	2,500
950E, 23J, LS, Adj.6P, NI, DR, BRG, marked **Elinvar**, OF	◻	950	1,100	2,000
*951, 23J, LS, BRG, Adj.5P, NI, GT, GJS, DR, HC	★★★★	4,500	5,000	7,500
*951, 23J, PS, BRG, Adj.5P, NI, GT, GJS, DR, HC	★★★★	4,000	4,500	7,000
*951, 23J, PS, BRG, Adj.5P, NI, GT, GJS, DR, HC,**14K**	★★★★	5,000	5,500	9,000
952, 19J, LS or PS, BRG, Adj.5P, NI, GJS, DR, OF	★	235	275	500
952, 19J, LS or PS, BRG, Adj.5P, OF, **14K**	★	450	550	900

* NOTE: **951** movements were made from the **961 runs**. (check serial numbers list)
The last made American Pocket Watch was Hamiltons 992B, in 1969.

⊕ Watches listed in this book are priced at the collectable Trade Show level, as **Complete** watches having an original 14k gold-filled case for Stem Wind and Key Wind with silver case, an original white enamel single sunk dial, and with the entire original movement in good working order with no repairs needed.

Grade or Name — Description	Avg	Ex-Fn	Mint
954, 17J, LS or PS, 3/4, DR, Adj.5P, OF	$125	$175	$350
956, 17J, PS, 3/4, DR, Adj.5P, OF..	95	150	295
960, 21J, PS, BRG, GJS, GT, DR, Adj.5P, OF ....★	400	450	800
960, 21J, LS, BRG, GJS, GT, DR, Adj.5P, OF ....★	400	450	800
961, 21J, PS & LS, BRG, GJS, GT, DR, Adj.5P, HC ....★★	450	500	900
962, 17J, PS, BRG, OF...★★	475	550	1,000
963, 17J, PS, BRG, HC ....★★★	475	550	1,000
964, 17J, PS, BRG, OF ....★★★	500	600	1,100
965, 17J, PS, BRG, HC ....★★★	500	600	1,100
966, 17J, PS, 3/4, OF.....................................★★★	500	600	1,100
967, 17J, PS, 3/4, HC ....★★★	600	700	1,200
968, 17J, PS, 3/4, OF..★	400	450	800
969, 17J, PS, 3/4, HC...★	450	475	800
970, 21J, PS, 3/4, OF	200	275	500
971, 23J, Adj.5P, **SWISS MADE**..	55	70	175
971, 21J, PS, 3/4, HC...★	195	295	500
972, 17J, PS & LS, OF, 3/4, NI, GJS, DR, Adj.5P, DMK, OF	125	175	350
973, 17J, PS & LS, 3/4, NI, DR, Adj.5P, HC	150	195	400
974, 17J, PS or LS, 3/4, NI, single roller, Adj.3P, OF	95	150	295
974, 17J, PS or LS, 3/4, NI, double roller, Adj.3P, OF	125	175	350
974 **special**, 17J, marked Special, double roller, Adj.3P, OF	125	150	350
974 **special**, 17J, Electric Railway or Trolly Car, Adj.3P, OF........	150	195	400
974, 17J, Adj.3P, 2-tone, OF...	175	200	400
2974B, 17J, Adj.3P, **hacking, U.S. GOV.**, OF.	250	285	500
975, 17J, PS & LS, 3/4, NI, Adj.3P, HC	125	150	295
976, 16J, PS, 3/4, OF	125	150	295
977, 16J, PS, 3/4, HC	125	150	295
978, 17J, LS, 3/4, NI, DMK, OF	125	150	295
990, 21J, LS, GJS, DR, Adj.5P, DMK, NI, 3/4, GT, OF	175	225	400
991, 21J, LS, 3/4, GJS, Adj.5P, DMK, NI, GT, HC....................★	195	250	500

EARLY 16 size only made **670** - used a larger dial plate

EARLY 16 size, 17J., ADJ, 1st run = 51,001 to 51,300 ...... ★★★	$600	$675	$950
EARLY 16 size, 17J., ADJ, 2nd run = 52,001 to 52,300 ..... ★★★	500	550	850
EARLY 16 size, 17J., ADJ, 3rd run = 53,001 to 53,070...... ★★★	400	450	800

NOTE: For above see serial numbers and grades list. NO GRADE # **ASSIGNED**.

16 size NO GRADE # **ASSIGNED**, OF, PS, S# 52,135.

Grade 4992B, 16 size, 22 jewels, Adj.6p.

Note: Prefix before serial no. was Hamilton's method of I.D.,(C & serial no.= 992B railroad watch), (2B & serial no. = 950B railroad watch also **S**), (3C & serial no. = 4992B G.T.C. Canada Gov't), (4C & serial no.= 4992B for U.S.A. Gov't), (2K & serial no.= 2974B used for comparing watch).

🕐 A collector should expect to pay modestly higher prices at local shops.

Grade 992E, 21jewels, gold center wheel, gold jewel settings, Adj.5P, marked Elinvar under balance wheel, Note the wide striped style Damaskeening, serial #2,595,787.

Grade 3992B, 22J, Adj.6P, "Navigation Master", note outside chapter on dial 1–10. (NATO dial)

Grade or Name — Description	Avg	Ex-Fn	Mint
992, 21J, 3/4, Adj.5P, SR & DR, NI, OF	$175	$225	$400
992, 21J, 3/4, **gold center wheel**,GJS, Adj.5P, SR & DR, NI, OF..	195	250	450
992, 21J, 3/4, PS & LS, GJS, Adj.5P, DR, NI, DMK, **2 -Tone**, OF	250	350	600
992, 21J, **Extra**, 3/4, GJS, Adj.5P, DR, NI, DMK, OF .... ★	400	500	850
992, 21J, 3/4, DR, NI, **marked 8 Adj. for RR, Gold Flashed**, OF★	500	600	1,100
992, 21J, marked **Special**, 3/4, PS & LS, GJS, Adj.5P, DR, 2-tone NI, DMK, marked **Adj. for RR Service** on dial, OF ... ★★★	1,300	1,500	2,400
992E, 21J, marked **Elinvar, gold center wheel**, 3/4, GJS, Adj.5P .	250	295	550
992B, 21J, LS, Adj.6P, 3/4, OF	250	295	500
992B, 21J, Adj.6P, **2-Tone** .... ◲	295	375	650
992B, 21J, Adj.6P, 3/4, **Military** silver case, OF	295	375	650
992B, 21J, with a **DeLong Escapement**, ... ★★★★	2,000	2,500	4,000
3992B, 22J, Adj.6P, 12 hr. dial, (Canadian), Chrome case... ★★★	295	375	650
3992B, 22J, Adj.6P, "Navigation Master", Chrome case .... ★	400	500	800
4992B, 22J, LS, 3/4, 24-hr. dial, Greenwich Civil Time, silveroid .	195	295	500
4992B, 22J, LS, 3/4, 24-hr. dial, **Military** Silver case, OF...... ◲★	295	400	700
993, 21J, PS, GJS, Adj.5P, DR, NI, DMK, HC .... ★	195	250	450
993, 21J, LS, GJS, Adj.5P, DMK, DR, NI, HC .... ★	195	250	450
993, 21J, marked **Special**, tu-tone, GJS, Adj.5P, DMK, DR, HC ★	400	550	700
993, 21J, LS, GJS, Adj.5P, DMK, DR, NI, **14K**, HC .... ★	550	600	900
993, 21J, LS, GJS, Adj.5P, DMK, DR, (**GF multi color case**) HC★	400	475	875

ADMIRAL,16 size, 16 jewels, Damaskeened on nickel 3/4 plate, HC, serial no. 57821.

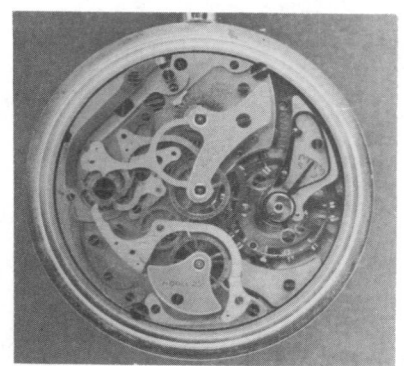

Chronograph, Grade 23, 16 size, 19 jewels, start-stop-reset to 0. Chronograph Grade 23 starts in 1943 ends in 1956 & total production = 23,146.

Grade or Name — Description	Avg	Ex-Fn	Mint
994, 21J, BRG, GJS, GT, DR, Adj.5P, DMK, PS, OF .... ★★	$800	$900	$1,600
994, 21J, BRG, GJS, GT, DR, Adj.5P, DMK, LS, OF .... ★★	900	1,000	1,700
996, 19J, LS, 3/4 GJS, DR, Adj.5P, DMK, OF	150	195	400
Admiral, 16J., 3/4 plate, OF, ...	95	150	295
Admiral,16J, 3/4, NI, ADJ., DMK, HC	150	175	350
Electric Interurban, 17J, G#974, OF	195	275	500
Official Standard, 17J, OF..	250	375	750
Union Special, 17J	150	225	400
Hayden W. Wheeler, 17J, OF ....★	350	400	650
Hayden W. Wheeler, 17J, HC ....★	400	450	700
Hayden W. Wheeler, 21J...★	400	450	750
Hayden W. Wheeler, 21J, **14K** H.W.W. case...........................★	750	900	1,300
Limited, 17J, G#974	150	195	295
Swiss Mfg., 17J, Adj.2P, G#669, OF, GF case	50	75	150
Swiss Mfg., 17J, Adj.2P, G#670, HC, GF case......................	60	95	175
Swiss Mfg., 23J, Adj.3P, (by Buren W. Co. G# 971), Ca. 1969-70s	80	125	235

CHRONOGRAPH
Grade 23

Grade or Name — Description	Avg	Ex-Fn	Mint
16S, 19J, chronograph with start-stop-reset to zero	$285	$325	$500

12 SIZE
(Some cases were octagon, decagon, cushion, etc.)

Grade or Name — Description	Avg	Ex-Fn	Mint
900, 19J, BRG, DR, Adj.5P, GJS, OF, **14K** ....★	$250	$350	$500
900, 19J, BRG, DR, Adj.5P, GJS, OF	95	150	295
902, 19J, BRG, DR, Adj.5P, GJS, OF	95	150	295
902, 19J, BRG, DR, Adj.5P, GJS, **14K** ....★	250	350	500

 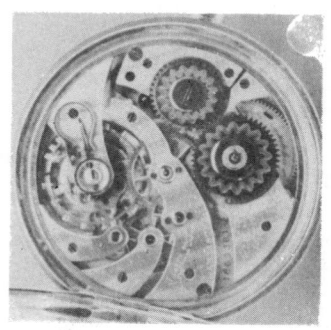

Grade **918**, 12 size, 19 jewels, Adj3p, serial number 3,136,257.

Grade **920**, 12 size, 23 jewels, gold train, gold jewel settings, serial number 1,863,381.

🕐 A collector should expect to pay modestly higher prices at local shops.

🕐 Watches listed in this book are priced at the collectableTrade Show level, as **Complete** watches having an original 14k gold-filled case for Stem Wind and *Key Wind* with silver case, an original white enamel single sunk dial, and with the entire original movement in good working order with no repairs needed.

MOVEMENTS WITH ODD GRADE NUMBERS ARE HUNTING CASE example 951.
MOVEMENTS WITH EVEN GRADE NUMBERS ARE OPEN FACE example 950.

Grade or Name — Description	Avg	Ex-Fn	Mint
904, 21J, BRG, DR, Adj.5P, GJS, GT ....★	$150	$225	$450
910, 17J, 3/4, DR, ADJ...........................	50	75	150
912, 17J, **Digital model, rotating seconds,** OF	175	250	500
912, 17J, 3/4, DR, ADJ...........................	50	75	150
914, 17J, 3/4, DR, Adj.3P, GJS	50	75	150
914, 17J, 3/4, DR, Adj.3P, GJS, **14K**........................	195	275	350
916, 17J, 3/4, DR, Adj.3P...........................	50	75	150
916, 17J, Adj.3P, silver case	50	75	150
918, 19J, Adj.3P, WGF...........................	95	125	250
918, 19J, 3/4, DR, Adj.3P, GJS, OF........................	95	125	250
920, 23J, BRG, DR, Adj.5P, GJS, GT, OF........................	225	275	450
920, 23J, BRG, DR, Adj.5P, GJS, GT, **14K**........................	425	475	650
922, 23J, BRG, DR, Adj.5P, GJS, GT, **14K**........................	425	475	650
922, 23J, BRG, DR, Adj.5P, GJS, GT, OF........................	225	275	450
922 MP, 23J, marked (MASTERPIECE), **18K case**................★	600	700	1,300
922 MP, 23J, marked (MASTERPIECE), **Iridium Platinum**......★	700	800	1,500
922 MP, **Gold Filled, Hamilton case**........................	325	450	750
400, 21J, (Illinois 13 size M#2, 5 tooth click), the Tycoon Series, **Hamilton on dial & case, 18K**, OF ....★	325	450	750

Grade 922MP, 12 size, 23 jewels, **marked** "masterpiece" serial number 3,013,390, c. 1930.

Grade 914, 10-12 size, 17J, gold jewel settings, double roller, open face, S # 1,767,782.

10 SIZE

Grade or Name — Description	Avg	Ex-Fn	Mint
917, 17J, 3/4, DR, Adj.3P...........................	$40	$60	$150
917, 17J, 3/4, DR, Adj.3P, **14K**	195	250	400
921, 21J, BRG, DR, Adj.5P...........................	125	150	295
923, 23J, BRG, DR, Adj.5P, **G.F.**...........................	150	175	350
923, 23J, BRG, DR, Adj.5P, **(spread to fit a 12 size CASE),14K** ..	225	250	450
923, 23J, **18K, and box**...........................	400	500	900
923, 23J, BRG, DR, Adj.5P, **Iridium Platinum**........................	295	400	850
945, 23J, Adj.5P, Masterpiece on DIAL...........................	95	175	295
945, 23J, Adj.5P, spread to **12 size**...........................	95	175	295

🕐 A collector should expect to pay modestly higher prices at local shops.

🕐 **The Complete Price Guide to Watches** goal is to stimulate the orderly exchange of <u>Watches</u> between *"buyers"* and *"sellers"*.

0 SIZE

Grade or Name — Description	Avg	Ex-Fn	Mint
981, 17J, 3/4, Adj.3P, DR, **18K, HC**	$175	$225	$475
982, 17-19J, same as 981 & 983 HC but no seconds bit	75	95	195
983, 17J, Adj.3P, DR, GJS, **18K, HC**	195	250	475
985, 19J, BRG, Adj.3P, DR, GJS, GT, **18K, HC**	195	250	475
Lady Hamilton, **14K** case, OF	175	200	325
Lady Hamilton, 23J, GJS, **gold filled OF**	150	175	295

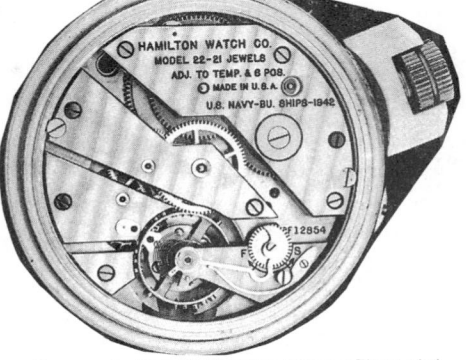

Model 22, 21 jewels, 35 Size or 70mm, wind indicator, adjusted to 6 positions, base metal case.

Chronometer Model 22, 21 jewels, 35 Size or 70mm, wind indicator, 54 hour mainspring, adjusted to 6 positions.

Above: 36 size, Sterling silver case, wind indicator.
Right: Chronometer in gimbals and box, wind indicator.

CHRONOMETER

Grade or Name — Description	Avg	Ex-Fn	Mint
35S, M#22, 21J, Wind Indicator, **Adj.6P**, in gimbals and box, lever	$900	$1,100	$1,800
35S, M#22, 21J, Wind Indicator, **Adj.6P**, in a large base metal OF case	500	600	950
36S, M#36, 21J, **Adj.5P**, Wind Indicator, in gimbals and box	1,300	1,500	2,400
36S, M#36, 21J, 56 hr.W. Ind.,"SID" (sidereal), chrome case ..... ★	1,500	1,800	2,800
36S, M#36, 21J, Wind Indicator, in Hamilton sterling pocket watch case with bow (s# 1,260,001 to 1,260,970) .... ★★★	1,700	2,000	3,000
37S, 21J, 940 movement S# range= 420,001 to 421,000, ONLY 220 made for U.S. Navy, true 24 hour black dial .... ★★★	1,500	1,800	2,800
85S, M#21, 14J, KW, KS, **Fusee, Detent Escapement** with helical hairspring, gimbals and box, (**all original**)	1,500	1,800	2,800

Baton Hands Ca.1940

CASE MODEL # A
gold filled : $95 - $150 - $325
Dial:(23J RR)$30 - $50 - $95
Note: Baton Style hands Ca.1940

CASE MODEL # 2
gold filled : $95- $125 - $325
14K Gold : $400 - $550 - $900
M# 3: 2 TONE caseGF:$150-$195-$500
Dial: RR,$20 - $40 - $80

CASE MODEL # 3
gold filled : $125 - $195 - $350
Dial: $20 - $30 - $60

Stiff Bow CASE MODEL # 4
gold filled : $125 - $195 - $350
Dial: $20 - $30 - $60

CASE MODEL #5
gold filled : $100- $120 - $275
Montgomery Dial: $30 - $45 - $100

CASE MODEL # 6
gold filled : $125- $195 - $325
Dial: $25 - $35 - $65

CASE MODEL # 7
White gold filled : $125 - $195 - $325
Montgomery Dial: $30 - $45 - $95

CASE MODEL # 8
gold filled : $135- $195 - $375
Dial: $20 - $30 - $60

CASE MODEL # 10
gold filled : $125- $195 - $350
Montgomery Dial: $35 - $50 - $95

Model "A" was advertised in a Gold-filled Case & advertised with a grade 950 movement. Models 2 & 17 came in 14K solid GOLD or gold-filled, model 2 advertised with 992 or 950. Models 3, 4, 5, 6, (7 white G.F.), 8, 10, 11, Cross Bar, & Traffic Special II all gold-filled. Model "16" gold plate and Model "15" & Traffic Special I was stainless steel case.

🕐 NOTE: Factory Advertised as a **complete** watch and was fitted with a certain matched, timed and rated movement and sold in the factory designed case style as a complete watch. The factory also sold _uncased_ movements to **JOBBERS** such as Jewelry stores & they cased the movement in a case styles the **CUSTOMER requested.** All the factory advertised complete watches came with the dial **SHOWN or CHOICE** of other **Railroad** dials.

CASE MODEL # 11
gold filled : $95 - $150 - $325
Dial: $20 - $40 - $80

CASE MODEL # 14
Nickel : $75 - $100 - $175
Dial: $20 - $40 - $80

CASE MODEL # 15
S. Steel : $35 - $45 - $95
Dial: $20 - $40 - $80

CASE MODEL # 16
gold plated : $80 - $95 - $225
M # 12 chrome:$40 - $50 - $95
Montgomery Dial: $35 - $50 - $80

CASE MODEL # 17
gold filled : $125- $175 - $375
14KGold : $425 - $550 - $900
Dial: $20 - $40 - $80

CASE MODEL Cross Bar
gold filled : $125- $195 - $400
Dial: $20 - $35 - $70

TRAFFIC SPECIAL I & #3
S. Steel : $35- $45 - $95
Montgomery Dial: $25 - $35 - $75

TRAFFIC SPECIAL II &#4
gold plated : $45- $55 - $95
Dial: $20 - $30 - $85

The MAINLINER
gold filled : $95 - $150 - $275
Dial: $30 - $45 - $80
Note: Baton style hands, Ca 1940

Railway Specials were packed & shipped in a plastic ivory cigarette style box and came in different colors. **THESE PLASTIC IVORY CIGARETTE STYLE BOX** sell for **$50 - $100 - $300.**

Model "A" was advertised in a Gold-filled Case & advertised with a grade 950 movement.
Models 2 & 17 came in 14K solid GOLD or gold-filled, model 2 advertised with 992 or 950.
Models 3, 4, 5, 6, 8, 10, 11, & Cross Bar gold-filled.
Model "16" gold plate and Model "15" & Traffic Special I was stainless steel case.
Case Model 14 = Nickel-Chrome.

HAMILTON W. CO. IDENTIFICATION OF MOVEMENTS

How To Identify Your Watch: Compare the movement with the illustration in this section. While comparing, note the location of the balance, jewels, screws, gears, and back plate (Full, 3/4, Bridge) these will be clues in identifying the movement you have. Having determined the size, the **GRADE** can also be found by looking up the serial number of your watch in the Hamilton Serial Number & Grades List. Illustrations of selected grades of the different size movements are shown to assist you in identifying movements. Hamilton movements that do not have grade numbers engraved on them <u>do</u> carry serial numbers which can be checked against the serial number list to secure the *grade number.*

Grade 936, 18 SIZE, **Full Plate, OPEN FACE** SHOWN. Also grades 922, 924, 926, 928, 930, 932, 934, 938, 940, 942, 944, 946, & 948 All look SIMILAR to the above.

Grade 925, 18 SIZE, **Full Plate, Hunting Case** SHOWN. Also grades 923, 927, 929, 931, 933, 935, 937, 939, 941, 943, 945, and 947 All look SIMILAR to the above.

NOTE: 18 Size Grades 924, 925, 926, 927, 928, 929, 930, 931, 932, 933, 934, & 935 use 90% same parts but not plates. 18 Size Grades 936, 937, 938, 939, & 948 use 90% same parts but not plates. Grades 940, 941, 942, & 943 use 90% same parts but not plates. 18 Size Grades 944 & 946 use 90% same parts.

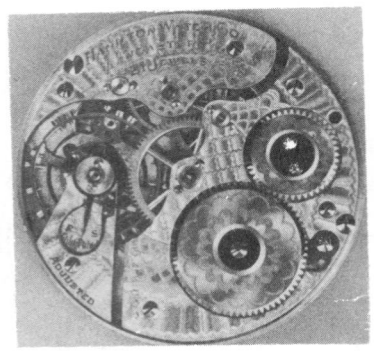 

Grade 971, 16 SIZE, **Hunting Case,** 3/4 Plate, 21 jewels, Shown. Note Crown Wheel with 2 Screws this movement uses a 4 Footed Dial. Also grades 969, 973, 975, 991, & 993 all look SIMILAR to the above. Note location of the larger ratchet wheel next to balance cock.

Grade 992, 16 SIZE, **Open Face,** 3/4 Plate, 21 jewels, **1st. model** Shown. Note Crown Wheel with 2 Screws this movement uses a 4 Footed Dial. Also grades 954, 968, 970, 972, 974, & 990 all look SIMILAR to the above. Note location of the smaller Crown wheel next to balance cock. 1st. model.

NOTE: 16 Size Grades 950, 952, & 996 use 90% same parts. 16 Size Grades 954, 962, 963, 966, 967, 972, & 973 use 90% same parts but not plates. 16 Size Grades 956, 964, 965, 968, 969, 974, 975, 976, 977, & 978 use 90% same parts. 16 Size Grades 960, 961, 970, 971, 990, 991, 992, 993, & 994 use 90% same parts but not plates. Grades 950E & 950B differ from grade 950. Grades 992E & 992B differ from grade 992.

Grade 992 Note: with narrow stripes, 16 size, 3/4 plate, 21 jewels, 5 positions, **2nd model** Shown. Note: Crown Wheel with 1 Screw. 2nd. model.

Grade 992 E = wide stripes Damaskeening with ELINVAR under balance wheel. 16 size, 3/4 plate, 21J., 5 positions, **3rd. model** Shown.

Grade 992 B, 16 size, 3/4 plate, 21J., **6 POSITIONS.** last model, model # 4.

Grade 950 16 size, BRIDGE, 23J., 5 positions. Note: with narrow stripes,

Grade 950 E = wide stripes Damaskeening with ELINVAR under balance wheel. 16 size, BRIDGE, 23J., 5 positions.

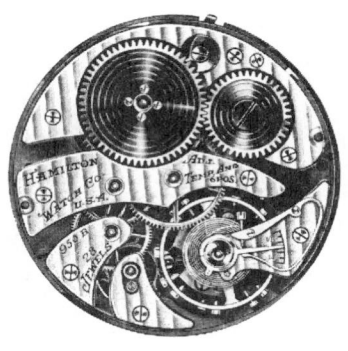

Grade 950 B, 16 size, BRIDGE, 23J., **6 POSITIONS.**

Grade 960, <u>16 SIZE</u>, **BRIDGE, OPEN FACE** SHOWN. Also GRADES 950, 952, 962, 964, 994 all look SIMILAR to the above. Note location of the smaller Crown wheel next to balance cock.

Grade 961, <u>16 SIZE</u>, **BRIDGE, Hunting Case** SHOWN. Also GRADES 951, 963, 965 all look SIMILAR to the above. Note location of the larger ratchet wheel next to balance cock.

SWISS MADE, 16 size, open face, 17 to 23 jewels, 3/4 plate.

Grade 902, 12 size
Open face, bridge movt., 19 jewels, double roller

Grade 912, 12 size
Open face, ¾ plate movt., 17 jewels, double roller

Grade 918, 12 size
Open face, ¾ plate movt., 19 jewels, double roller

Grade 922, 12 size
Open face, bridge movt., 23 jewels, double roller

Grade 917, 10 size
Open face, ¼ plate movt., 17 jewels, double roller

Grade 921, 10 size
Open face, bridge movt., 21 jewels, double roller

Grade 923, 10 size
Open face, bridge movt., 23 jewels, double roller

Grade 983, 0 size
Hunting, bridge movt., 17 jewels, double roller

Grade 979,6/0 size
Hunting, ¼ plate movt., 19 jewels, double roller

Grade 986, 6/0 size
Open face, ¼ plate movt., 17 jewels, double roller

IMPORTANT NOTE: Railroad Standards, Railroad Approved & Railroad Grade **terminology,** as defined and used in this *BOOK*.
1. **RAILROAD STANDARDS** = A commission or board appointed by the railroad companies outlined a set of **guidelines** to be accepted or approved by each railroad line.
2. **RAILROAD APPROVED** = A **LIST** of watches each railroad line would approve if purchased by their employee's. (this list changed through the years).
3. **RAILROAD GRADE** = A watch made by manufactures to meet or exceed the guidelines set by the railroad **standards**. Grades such as 992, Vanguard and B.W. Raymond, etc.
🕐 Some GRADES **exceeded** the R.R. standards such as 23 jewels, diamond end stone, gold train, raised gold jewel settings, double sunk dial and the list goes on. Examples: such as Veritas, Sangamo, 950 & Riverside Maximus and many others.

HAMPDEN WATCH CO.
(DUEBER WATCH CO.)
Springfield, Massachusetts later Canton, Ohio
1877 - 1930

The New York Watch Co. preceded Hampden, and before that Don J. Mozart (1864) produced his three-wheel watch. Mozart was assisted by George Samuel Rice of New York and, as a result of their joint efforts, the New York Watch Co. was formed in 1866 in Providence, Rhode Island. It was moved in 1867 to Springfield, Massachusetts. Two grades of watches were decided on, and the company started with a 18S, 3/4 plate engraved "Springfield." They were sold for $60 to $75. The 18S, 3/4 plate were standard production, and the highest grade was a "George Walker" that sold for about $200 and a 16S, 3/4 plate "State Street" which had steel parts and exposed balance and escape wheels that were gold plated.

John C. Dueber started manufacturing watch cases in 1864 and bought a controlling interest in a company in 1886. At about this time a disagreement arose between Elgin, Waltham, and the Illinois Watch companies. Also, at this time, an anti-trust law was passed, and the watch case manufacturers formed a boycott against Dueber. Dueber was faced with a major decision, whether to stay in business, surrender to the watch case companies or buy a watch company. He decided to buy the Hampden Watch Co. of Springfield, Mass. By 1889 the operation had moved to Canton, Ohio. By the end of the year the company was turning out 600 watches a day. The first 16 size watch was produced in 1890 (serial number 800,xxx). In 1891 Hampden introduced the **first 23J** (16 size) movement made in America. Hampden assigned serial numbers at random to the New York Watch Co. movements for years after they purchased the N.Y.W.Co.Hampden W. Co. serial numbers start at about 58,000.

HAMPDEN ESTIMATED SERIAL NUMBER
AND PRODUCTION DATES

DATE-SERIAL NO.	DATE-SERIAL NO.	DATE-SERIAL NO.	DATE-SERIAL NO.
1877 — 59,000	1890 — 740,000	1903 — 1,768,000	1916 — 3,100,000
1878 — 70,000	1891 — 805,000	1904 — 1,896,000	1917 — 3,240,000
1879 — 100,000	1892 — 835,000	1905 — 2,024,000	1918 — 3,390,000
1880 — 140,000	1893 — 865,000	1906 — 2,152,000	1919 — 3,500,000
1881 — 180,000	1894 — 900,000	1907 — 2,280,000	1920 — 3,600,000
1882 — 215,000	1895 — 930,000	1908 — 2,400,000	1921 — 3,700,000
1883 — 250,000	1896 — 970,000	1909 — 2,520,000	1922 — 3,750,000
1884 — 300,000	1897 — 1,000,000	1910 — 2,650,000	1923 — 3,800,000
1885 — 350,000	1898 — 1,120,000	1911 — 2,700,000	1924 — 3,850,000
1886 — 400,000	1899 — 1,255,000	1912 — 2,760,000	1925 — 3,900,000
1887 — 480,000	1900 — 1,384,000	1913 — 2,850,000	1926 — 3,950,000
1888 — 560,000	1901 — 1,512,000	1914 — 2,920,000	1927 — 3,980,000
1889 — 640,000	1902 — 1,642,000	1915 — 3,000,000	

The above list is provided for determining the **APPROXIMATE** age of your watch. Match serial number with date. Watches were not necessarily sold in the exact order of manufactured date.

In 1891 Hampden introduced the first "23Jewel" (16 size) watch made in America.

Left: **Teske's** patent round regulator.   Right: **Tucker's** patent square regulator _both_ were applied by **watchmakers**. Can be found on 18 size movements such as Hampden Springfield, Waltham, Elgin, Rockford and others.

Chronology of the Development of Hampden Watch Co.:
The Mozart Watch Co., Providence, R. I. (1864-1866)
New York Watch Co., Providence, R. I. (1866-1867)
New York Watch Co., Springfield, Mass. (1867-1875)
New York Watch Mfg. Co., Springfield, Mass. (1875-1876)
Hampden Watch Co., Springfield, Mass. (1877-1886)
Hampden-Dueber Watch Co., Springfield, Mass. (1886-1888)
Hampden Watch Co., Canton, Ohio. (1888–1923)
Dueber Watch Co., Canton, Ohio. (1889–1923)
Dueber-Hampden Watch Co., Canton, Ohio. (1923–1931)
Amtorg, U.S.S.R (1930)

Issued 1890

Issued 1892

Issued 1895

NR inside flag = New Railway and SR inside flag = Special Railway
D & ★ D & anchor inside flag = Dueber and H inside flag = Hampden

Dueber Watch Co., 18 size, 15 jewels, nickel movement. Model 3, hunting case.

Dueber Grand, 18 size, 17 jewels, open face, originally sold for $20.00.

HAMPDEN 18 SIZE

Grade or Name — Description	Avg	Ex-Fn	Mint
Anchor (inside flag), 17J, ADJ, GJS, DMK	$75	$95	$195
"3" Ball, 17J, ADJ, NI, DMK	90	125	275
Boston W. Co. 11J, KW/SW	60	80	175
Canadian Pacific R.W., 17J, Adj., M# 4, OF ★★	1,200	1,400	2,000
Canadian Pacific RR, 17J, OF ★★	1,000	1,200	1,800
Canadian Pacific RR, 21J, OF ★★	1,400	1,700	2,400
Champion, 7-11J, ADJ, FULL, gilded, or, NI, OF	60	80	175
Champion, 7-11J, ADJ, FULL, gilded, or, NI, HC	80	95	195
Chronometer "Dueber", 16-19-21J, **detent escapement**, (Swiss)			
Helical hairspring, LS, NI, Adj.3P, GJS, HC ★★	650	750	1,200
Correct Time, 15J, HC ★	95	150	295
Dueber, 11J, gilded, DMK	50	75	125
Dueber, 15J, gilded, DMK	60	80	175
Dueber, 16J, gilded, DMK	75	95	195
Dueber, 17J, gilded, DMK	60	80	175
Dueber Grand, 17J, OF	75	95	195
Dueber Grand, 17J, ADJ, HC	90	125	250
Dueber Grand, 21J, ADJ, DMK, NI, OF	125	200	375
Dueber Grand, 21J, ADJ, DMK, NI, HC	150	225	450
John C. Dueber, 15J, gilded, DMK, OF	60	80	175
John C. Dueber, 15J, gilded, DMK, HC	80	95	195
John C. Dueber, 17J, gilded, DMK, OF	60	80	175
John C. Dueber, 17J, NI, ADJ, DMK, OF	60	80	175
John C. Dueber, 17J, NI, ADJ, DMK, HC	90	125	250
John C. Dueber, Special, 17J, ADJ, DMK, OF	75	95	195
John C. Dueber, Special, 17J, ADJ, DMK, HC	95	150	295
John C. Dueber, 21J, HC	150	200	450

⊕ Generic, nameless or unmarked grades for watch movements are listed under the Company name or initials of the Company, etc. by size, jewel count and description.			
Dueber W. Co.,7-11J, OF	$45	$65	$125
Dueber W. Co., 15J, DMK, OF	50	75	150
Dueber W. Co., 15J, DMK, HC	65	85	195
Dueber W. Co., 16J, OF	50	75	150
Dueber W. Co., 16J, HC	65	85	195
Dueber W. Co., 17J, DMK, ADJ, OF	50	75	150
Dueber W. Co., 17J, Gilded	50	75	150
Dueber W. Co., 17J, DMK, ADJ, HC	60	85	195
Dueber W. Co., 19J, ADJ, GJS, HC ★	400	450	575
Dueber W. Co., 21J, Adj.5P, GJS, OF	150	200	295
Dueber W. Co., 21J, GJS, Adj.5P, HC	165	225	350

John C. Dueber Special, 18 size, 17 jewels, serial number 949,097.

Oriental, 18 size, 15 jewels, open face, serial number 117,825.

Grade or Name — Description	Avg	Ex-Fn	Mint
Forest City, 15J, KW	$90	$125	$250
Gladiator, 7-9J, KW, OF	75	95	195
Gladiator, 9-11J, NI, DMK, OF	75	95	295
Gulf Stream Sp., 21J, R.R. grade, LS, OF ★★	600	750	1,500
Homer Foot, gilded, KW, OF (Early)	175	250	500

🕑 Generic, nameless or unmarked grades for watch movements are listed under the Company name or initials of the Company, etc. by size, jewel count and description.

	Avg	Ex-Fn	Mint
Hampden W. Co., 7J, KW, KS, coin silver OF	$90	$125	$250
Hampden W. Co., 7J, SW, OF	50	60	150
Hampden W. Co., 11J, OF, KW	50	60	155
Hampden W. Co., 11J, HC, KW	60	80	175
Hampden W. Co., 11J, OF, SW	40	60	150
Hampden W. Co., 11J, HC, SW	75	95	195
Hampden W. Co., 15J, OF, KW	65	85	175
Hampden W. Co., 15J, HC, KW	75	95	195
Hampden W. Co., 15J, HC, SW	75	95	195
Hampden W. Co., 15J, SW, Gilded, OF	60	80	175
Hampden W. Co., 15J, SW, NI, OF	60	80	175
Hampden W. Co., 15J, **Multi-color, 14K, HC**	1,800	2,400	3,800
Hampden W. Co., 16J, OF	80	95	225
Hampden W. Co., 17J, SW, Gilded	80	95	225
Hampden W. Co., 17J, SW, NI, OF	80	95	225
Hampden W. Co., 17J, SW, HC	80	95	225
Hampden W. Co., 17J, LS, HC, **14K**	475	575	850
Hampden W. Co., 17J, LS, HC, **10K**	275	350	550
Hampden W. Co., 21J, OF, SW	150	195	400
Hampden W. Co., 21J, HC, SW	200	250	450
John Hancock, 17J, GJS, Adj., OF	75	95	195
John Hancock, 17J, GJS, Adj., HC	90	125	250
John Hancock, 21J, GJS, Adj.5P, OF	125	175	400
John Hancock, 23J, GJS, Adj.5P, OF	250	300	500
Hayward, 11J, SW	80	125	195
Hayward, 15J, KW	125	175	350

🕑 Watches listed in this book are priced at the collectable fair market value at the **Trade Show LEVEL,** as complete watches having an original 14k gold filled case, KEY WIND with silver, an original white enamel single sunk dial, and with the entire original movement in good working order with no repairs needed, unless otherwise noted.

Menlo Park, 18 size, 17 jewels, serial number 1,184,116.

New Railway, 18 size, 23 jewels, open face only, gold jewel settings, originally sold for $50.00, Model 2.

Grade or Name — Description	Avg	Ex-Fn	Mint
Lafayette, 11J, NI, HC	$125	$195	$350
Lafayette, 15J, NI, **KW** .... ★	195	250	550
Lafayette, 15J, NI, HC	125	195	350
Lakeside, 15J, NI, SW, HC	125	150	325
M. J. & Co. Railroad Watch Co., 15J, HC .... ★★	400	550	900
Menlo Park, 11-15J, ...	125	150	195
Menlo Park, 17J, NI, ADJ, OF	125	175	295
Menlo Park, 17J, gilded, ADJ, HC	150	195	400
Mermod, Jaccard & Co., 15J, KW, HC	150	195	400
Metropolis, 15J, NI, SW, OF	95	125	295
Wm. McKinley, 17J, Adj.3P, OF	75	95	195
Wm. McKinley, 17J, Adj.3P, HC	80	110	225
Wm. McKinley, 21J, GJS, Adj.5P	125	175	350
New Railway, 17J, GJS, Adj.5P, OF	125	175	350
New Railway, 19J, GJS, Adj.5P, OF	175	195	400
New Railway, 19J, GJS, Adj.5P, HC	195	250	500

Railway, 18 size, 17 jewels, key wind & set; early railroad watch.

Special Railway, 18 size, 23 jewels, Adj5p, serial number 3,357,284.

🕐 Watches listed in this book are priced at the collectable Trade Show level, as **complete** watches having an original 14k gold-filled case and *Key Wind* with silver, an original white enamel single sunk dial, and with the entire original movement in good working order with no repairs needed.

NR inside flag = New Railway and SR inside flag = Special Railway
D & ★ D & anchor inside flag = Dueber and H inside flag = Hampden

Grade or Name — Description	Avg	Ex-Fn	Mint
New Railway, 21J, GJS, Adj.5P, OF	$160	$195	$450
New Railway, 21J, GJS, Adj.5P, HC	195	250	500
New Railway, 23J, GJS, Adj.5P	250	295	500
New Railway, 23J, GJS, Adj.5P, **14K**, OF	500	550	900
North Am. RW, 21J, GJS, Adj.5P, OF	225	250	500
North Am. RW, 21J, GJS, Adj, HC	225	300	575
Order of Railroad Conductors, 17J, ADJ, OF ★★★	1,600	1,800	2,500
Pennsylvania Special, 17J, GJS, Adj.5P, DR, NI ★★★	1,800	2,200	3,200
J. C. Perry, 15J, KW, gilded, HC	95	150	275
J. C. Perry, 15J, NI, SW, OF	75	95	195
J. C. Perry, 15J, gilded, SW, OF	75	95	195
Railway, 11J, gilded, OF	100	150	295
Railway, 15-17J, NI, OF	125	175	350
Railway, 15-17J, **KW**, marked on mvt., HC ★★	700	800	1,400
Railroad with R.R. names on dial and movement:			
Private Label R.R. 17J, OF ★★	650	800	1,100
Special Railway, 17J, GJS, Adj.5P, NI, DR, OF	95	150	295
Special Railway, 21J, GJS, Adj.5P, NI, DR, OF	150	195	400
Special Railway, 21J, GJS, Adj.5P, NI, DR, **2-Tone**, OF	185	250	550
Special Railway, 21J, GJS, Adj.5P, NI, DR, HC	225	295	500
Special Railway, 23J, GJS, Adj.5P, NI, DR, OF	295	335	500
Special Railway, 23J, GJS, Adj.5P, NI, DR, **2-Tone**, OF	325	350	550
Special Railway, 23J, GJS, Adj.5P, NI, DR, HC	295	400	650
Special Railway, 23J, **14K, HC**	650	800	1,100
Springfield, 7-11J, KW, gilded, HC	95	150	295
Springfield, 7-11J, SW, NI, HC	95	150	295
Standard, 15J, gilded, HC	95	150	295
Train Service Standard, 17J, LS, M# 2, NI, HC ★	450	500	800
Theo. Studley, 9-15J, KW, KS, HC	95	150	295
Tramway Special, 17J, NI	150	195	350
Wisconsin Central R W, 17J, LS, OF ★	650	750	1,400
Woolworth, 11-15J, KW	90	125	250
Grade 30,31,45,46,54,57,65,66,70,71, **ALL =11J**	90	125	195
Grade 32,33,34,35,36,40,41,42,49,55,56,58,59,60,62, **All =15J**	90	125	195
Grade, 43,44,47,48,49,63,64,67,68,69,80,81, **ALL =16-17J**	100	135	225
Grade 85, **19J**, GJS, 2-Tone, HC ★★	500	600	1,000
Grade 95, **21J**, GJS, OF	170	195	400
Grade 125, **21J**, Adj.3P, OF	170	195	400

16 SIZE

Grade or Name — Description	Avg	Ex-Fn	Mint
Beacon, 7J, OF	$75	$95	$195
E.W. Bond & State Street models see New York W. Co. Springfield			
Champion, 7J, NI, 3/4, gilded, **coin**, OF	60	70	175
Champion, 7J, NI, 3/4, gilded, OF	60	70	175
Champion, 7J, NI, 3/4, gilded, HC	90	125	250
Chronometer, 21J, NI, Adj.3P, GJS, OF ★	500	600	750
Chronometer, 21J, NI, Adj.3P, GJS, HC ★	650	750	950
John C. Dueber, 17J, GJS, NI, Adj.5P, 3/4, LS, OF	75	95	195
John C. Dueber, 21J, GJS, NI, Adj.5P, 3/4	125	175	275
John C. Dueber, 21J, GJS, NI, Adj.5P, DR, BRG	150	195	295
Dueber Watch Co., 15-17J, ADJ, 3/4	70	95	195

NOTE: Railroad Standards, Railroad Approved & Railroad Grade **terminology**, as defined and used in this *BOOK*.
1. **RAILROAD STANDARDS** = A commission or board appointed by the railroad companies outlined a set of **guidelines** to be accepted or approved by each railroad line.
2. **RAILROAD APPROVED** = A **LIST** of watches each railroad line would approve if purchased by their employee's. (this list changed through the years)
3. **RAILROAD GRADE** = A watch made by manufactures to meet or exceed the guidelines set by the railroad **standards**. Grades such as 992, Vanguard and B.W. Raymond, etc.
☾ Some **GRADES exceeded** the R.R. standards such as 23 J,. diamond end stone, gold train, raised gold jewel settings, double sunk dial and the list goes on. Examples: such as Veritas, Sangamo, 950 & Riverside Maximus and many others.
☾ Pricing in this Guide are fair market price for **COMPLETE** watches which are reflected from the "<u>NAWCC</u>" National and regional shows.

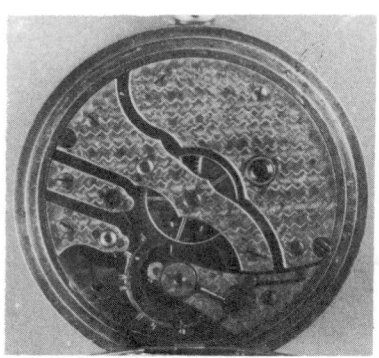 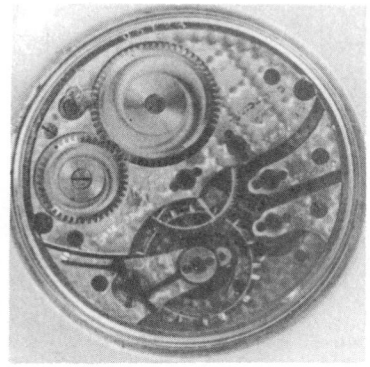

Hampden W. Co., Bridge Model, 16 size, 23 jewels, 2-tone movement, serial number 1,899,430.

Hampden W. Co., 16 size, 17 jewels, gold jewel settings, serial number 3,075,235.

⊕ Generic, nameless or unmarked grades for watch movements are listed under the Company name or initials of the Company, etc. by size, jewel count and description.

Grade or Name — Description	Av	Ex-Fn	Mint
Hampden W. Co., 7J, SW, OF	$45	$60	$125
Hampden W. Co., 7J, SW, HC	50	70	150
Hampden W. Co., 11J, SW, OF	50	70	150
Hampden W. Co., 11J, SW, HC	60	80	175
Hampden W. Co., 15J, SW, OF	60	80	175
Hampden W. Co., 15J, SW, HC	60	80	175
Hampden W. Co., 17J, SW, OF	70	85	185
Hampden W. Co., 17J, **14K, Multi-color,** HC	1,400	1,800	3,400
Hampden W. Co., 17J, SW, HC	90	125	250
Hampden W. Co., 21J, SW, HC	150	225	450
Hampden W. Co., 21J, SW, OF	150	195	400
Hampden W. Co., 23J, Adj.5P, GJS, 3/4	295	400	600
Hampden W. Co., 23J, Series 2, **Freesprung**, GJS GT, HC ★★★	700	800	1,500
Masonic Dial, 23J, GJS, 2-Tone **enamel dial**	700	800	1,500

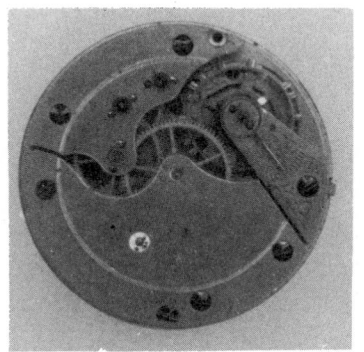 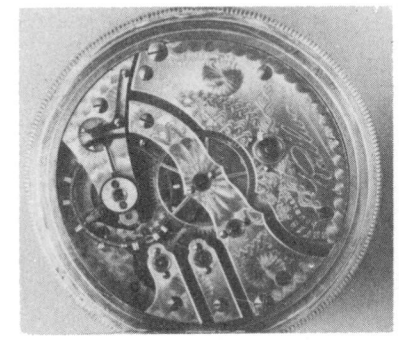

Hampden W. Co., Series 1, 16 size, 15 jewels, stem wind open face.

Railway, 16 size, 17 jewels, Adj.5P, gold jewel settings, serial number 2,271,866.

NR inside flag = New Railway and SR inside flag = Special Railway
D & ★ D & anchor inside flag = Dueber and H inside flag = Hampden

⊕ Pricing in this Guide are fair market price for **COMPLETE** watches which are reflected from the "<u>NAWCC</u>" National and regional shows.

⊕ Generic, nameless or unmarked grades for watch movements are listed under the Company name or initials of the Company, etc. by size, jewel count and description.

Grade 104, 16 size, 23 jewels, gold jewel settings, gold train, Adj5p, open face, serial number 2,801,184.

Hampden style watch produced in Russia with the machinery purchased by the Russian factory. This watch is a 16 size 7 jewel movement Ca. 1935

Grade or Name — Description

Grade or Name — Description	Avg	Ex-Fn	Mint
Wm. McKinley, 17J, GJS, Adj., NI, DR, 3/4	$75	$95	$195
Wm. McKinley, 21J, GJS, Adj.5P, NI, DR, OF	150	195	400
Wm. McKinley, 21J, GJS, Adj.5P, NI, DR, 3/4, **Coin**	150	195	400
Wm. McKinley, 21J, GJS, Adj.5P, NI, DR, HC	195	250	500
New Railway, 17J, GJS, LS, **NR** (in flag) ★★★	195	250	500
New Railway, 21J, GJS, Adj.5P	175	225	375
New Railway, 23J, GJS, Adj.5P, LS, HC	150	250	500
Ohioan, 21J, Adj., GJS, 3/4, OF & HC	150	195	450
Railway, 17-19J, GJS, Adj.5P, BRG, DR, OF	125	175	350
Special Railway, 17J, Adj, NI, BRG, DR, OF	125	175	350
Special Railway, 17J, Adj, NI, BRG, DR, HC	95	150	275
Special Railway, 23J, Adj.5P, NI, BRG, DR	295	400	650
Russian made model, 7-17J, 16 size, 3/4 plate ★	125	175	250
Garfield, 21J., Adj.5P, OF	150	195	400
Gen'l Stark, 15J, DMK, BRG	75	95	195
Gen'l Stark, 17J, DMK, BRG	75	95	195
76, 21J, LS, Adj.3P	125	150	295
94-95, 21J, **marked "94 or 95"**, GJS, Adj.5P,	225	250	475
97 HC, 98 HC, 107 OF, 108 OF, **ALL = 17J**, Adj.3P, NI, 3/4	75	95	250
99, 15J, 3/4, HC	75	95	250
103, 23J, GJS, Adj., NI,3/4, DR, free sprung, 2-tone, HC ★★★	700	800	1,500
104, 23J, GJS, Adj.5P, NI, 3\4 or BRG, DR, **marked**, OF	300	350	600
104, 23J, GJS, Adj.5P, NI, BRG, DR, **marked**, HC	350	400	700
105, 21J, GJS, Adj.5P, NI, 3/4, DR, **marked**,OF	225	250	450
105, 23J, GJS, Adj.5P, NI, 3/4, DR, HC	275	325	550
106, 107 OF, & 108, **17J**, SW, NI, **marked**,	75	95	195
109, 15J, 3/4, **marked**, OF	75	95	195
110, 11J, 3/4	50	65	150
115, 21J, SW, NI, **marked**, OF	225	250	450
120, 21J, SW, NI, OF, **marked Chronometer on dial** ★	350	400	800
340, 17J, SW, NI	80	95	225
440, 15J, 2-tone	80	95	225
555, 21J, GT, GJS, **marked 555, Chronometer on dial & mvt.** ★	600	700	1,000
555, 21J, GT, GJS, **marked 555, Chronometer on dial ONLY** ★	375	400	600
600, 17J, SW, NI, **marked, 600**	75	95	195

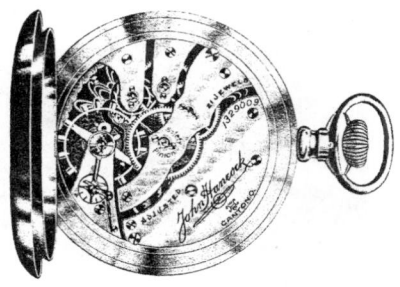

Dueber Grand, 12 size, 17 jewels, gold jewel settings, hunting case, serial number 1,737,354.

John Hancock, 21 jewels, Adj. 5P, lever set, came in HC & OF, Movement above is Hunting Case.

12 SIZE Standard Model

(SEE ALSO "12 SIZE " THIN MODEL)

Grade or Name — Description	Avg	Ex-Fn	Mint
Aviator, 17J, Adj.4P, OF .... ★★	$90	$125	$250
Aviator, 19J, Adj.4P, OF	75	95	195
Beacon, 17J, OF (only seen in ads)................... ★★★★	195	295	500
Biltmore, 17J, OF................ ★	75	95	195
Dueber Grand, 17J, BRG, OF	75	95	195
Dueber Grand, 17J, BRG, HC	95	125	250
Dueber Grand, 17J, 3/4 plate, pin set, OF............	75	100	200
Dueber Grand, 17J, 3/4 plate, lever set, OF .... ★★	95	125	250
Dueber Grand, 17J, 3/4 plate, pendent set, OF .... ★	95	125	250
Dueber Grand, 17J, 3/4 plate, HC	95	125	250
Dueber Grand, 17J, BRG, lever set, HC	95	125	250
Dueber Grand, 17J, BRG, lever or pendent set, OF	75	95	195
Dueber W. Co. 17J, Adj., 3/4, pendent set, OF	75	95	195
Dueber W. Co. 17J, Adj., 3/4, pendent set, HC .... ★	85	125	195
Duquesne, 19J, Adj., OF .... ★★	95	125	250
Gen'l Stark, 15J, M# 3 LS, HC	75	95	195
Gen'l Stark, 15J, M#3 pin or pendent set OF	65	85	150
Gen'l Stark, 15J, M# 3 lever set, OF............ ★	95	125	250
Gen'l Stark, 15J, M# 4 lever set, HC, ...	75	95	195
Gen'l Stark, 15J,M# 4 pendent set OF	65	85	150
Gen'l Stark, 15J, M# 4 lever set OF............ ★	60	75	150
Hampden W. Co., 17J, **14K, Multi-color, HC**	650	900	1,600
John Hancock, 21J, 3/4, pin set, Adj.5P, GJS, OF .... ★★	125	150	250
John Hancock, 21J, 3/4, lever set, Adj.5P, GJS, HC .... ★	150	175	295
John Hancock, 21J, BRG, pendent or lever set, Adj.5P, GJS, OF ★★	150	175	295
John Hancock, 21J, BRG, lever set, Adj.5P, GJS, HC .... ★	150	175	295
Minute Man, 17J, (standard size), OF	75	95	195
Ohioan, 21J, Adj.3P, GJS, 3/4, OF .... ★	125	150	250
Ohioan, 21J, Adj.3P, GJS, 3/4, HC .... ★★★	175	225	350
Viking, 17J, Adj, OF............ ★	75	95	195
No. 10, 7J, OF................	40	50	95
300, 7J, M# 3 LS, HC	40	50	95
300, 7J, M# 5 lever set, HC .... ★★	50	60	125
302, 7J., M# 3 LS, M# 5 stem set, OF	40	50	95
302, 7J, M#5 lever set, OF .... ★	50	60	125
304, 15J, HC	75	85	150
305, 17J, HC .... ★	75	95	195
306, 15J, OF................	60	75	125
307, 17J, Adj, OF	75	95	150
308, 17J, Adj, HC	85	125	195
310, 17J, Adj, OF	65	85	150
310, 17J, Adj, **marked, 14K** OF case	175	200	400
312, **marked,** 21J, 3/4, Adj.5P, DMK, HC .... ★★	150	175	295
314, **marked,** 21J, DR, Adj. 5P, DMK, OF .... ★	125	150	250
500, 17J, **marked,** OF .... ★	85	95	170
603, 17J, OF	85	95	170
700, 15J, **marked,** OF................	60	75	150

Example of Hampden Watch Co.'s THIN MODEL showing dial and movement, 12 size, 17-19 jewels, Adj3-5p.

12 SIZE (THIN MODEL)

Grade or Name — Description		Avg	Ex-Fn	Mint
Nathan Hale, 15J	★	$70	$95	$250
Minute Man, 17J	★	95	120	250
Relgis, 15J, OF	★	85	100	195
Paul Revere, 17J, OF, **14K**	★	225	275	550
Paul Revere, 17J	★	95	125	250
Paul Revere, 19J	★	125	150	295

Hampden 12 size (thin model) case are **not** interchangeable with other American 12 style cases.

6 SIZE

Grade or Name — Description	Avg	Ex-Fn	Mint
200, 7J (add $25 for HC)	$40	$60	$150
206, 11J (add $25 for HC)	40	60	150
213, 15J (add $25 for HC)	40	60	150
215, 16J, (add $25 for HC)	40	60	150
220, 17J (add $25 for HC)	40	60	150
Hampden W. Co., 15J, **multi-color Gold Filled, HC**	225	275	450
Hampden W. Co., 15J, **multi-color, 14K, HC**	400	500	900

The Four Hundred, 17 jewels, raised gold jewel settings, hunting case.

Molly Stark, 000 size, 7 jewels, hunting or open face, and originally sold for $12.00.

000 SIZE

Grade or Name — Description	Avg	Ex-Fn	Mint
Diadem, 11-15J, **14K**, OF Case	$125	$150	$350
Diadem, 11-15J, **14K**, HC Case	225	275	450
Diadem, 11-15J, **Gold Filled**, HC Case	75	150	250
Molly Stark, 7J, **Gold Filled**, HC Case	75	150	250
Molly Stark, 7J, **14K**, HC Case	225	275	450
Molly Stark, 7J, Pin Set, OF	75	100	200
The Four Hundred, 17J, raised gold jewel settings, HC	100	150	250
14K Multi-color, HC	400	500	800

HAMPDEN WATCH CO.
IDENTIFICATION OF MOVEMENTS

How to Identify Your Watch Size & Model: Compare the movement of your watch with the illustrations in this section. While comparing, note the location of the balance, jewels, screws, gears, and type of back plate (Full, 3/4, Bridge) these will be clues in identifying the movement you have.

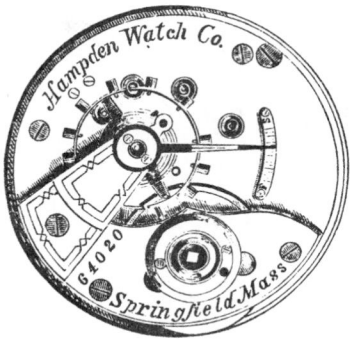

Series I, 18 size
Hunting or open face, key wind & set

Series II, 18 size
Hunting, stem wind, pendant or lever set

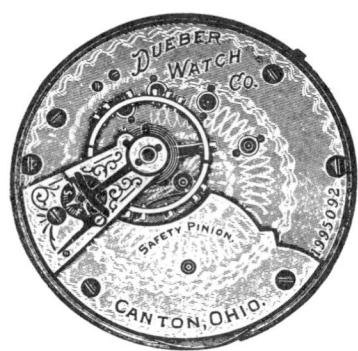

Series III, 18 size
Hunting, stem wind, pendant or lever set

Series IV, 18 size
Open face, stem wind, lever set

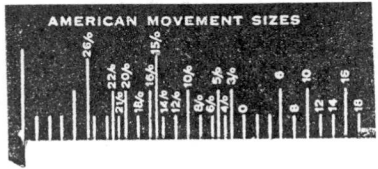

Series 1, 16 size
Open face, stem wind, pendant or lever set

Series II, 16 size
Hunting, stem wind, pendant or lever set

Series III, 16 size
Open face, stem wind, pendant set

Series IV, 16 size
Hunting, stem wind, pendant or lever set

Series V, 16 size
Open face, stem wind, pendant or lever set

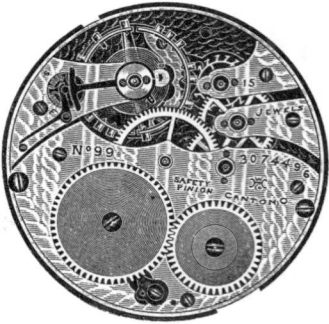

Series VI, 16 size
Hunting, stem wind, pendant set

Series VII, 16 size
Open face, stem wind, pendant set

Series III, 12 size
Open face, stem wind, pendant set

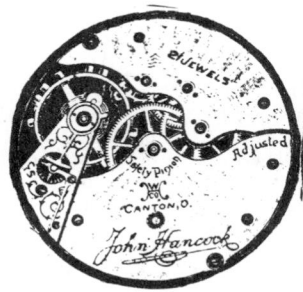

Series I, 12 size
Hunting, stem wind, lever set

Series II, 12 size
Open face, stem wind, lever set

Series IV, 12 size
Open face, stem wind, pendant

Series V, 12 size
Open face, stem wind, pendant set

Series I, 6 size
Hunting, stem wind

Series I, 3/0 size
Hunting, stem wind

⊕ Characteristics of watches differ for the same age of both case and movement, because these features vary it may not be accurate to date a watch by one single influence. Example: the second hand was _not_ commonly found on watches before 1750, but common about 1800. The first second hand appeared in 1665 and another in 1690. Therefore statements are broad rather than accurate.

Series II, 3/0 size
Open face, stem wind, pendant

Series III, 3/0 size
Hunting, lever or pendant

Series IV, 3/0 size
Hunting, stem wind, pendant

HERMAN VON DER HEYDT
CHICAGO SELF–WINDING WATCH CO.
Chicago, Illinois
1883-1895

Herman von der Heydt patented a self-winding watch on Feb. 19, 1884. A total of **35** watches were hand-made by von der Heydt. The watches were 18S, full plate, lever escapement and fully-jeweled. The wind mechanism was a gravity type made of heavy steel and shaped like a crescent. The body motion let the heavy crescent move which was connected to a ratchet on the winding arbor, resulting in self-winding. About **Five** movements were nickel and sold for about $90; the gilded model sold for about $75.

Grade or Name — Description		Avg	Ex-Fn	Mint
18S, 19J, FULL, NI .... ★★★★★		$12,000	$15,000	$20,000
18S, 19J, FULL, gilded .... ★★★★		10,000	13,000	18,000

Herman Von Der Heydt, 18 size **self winding watch,** "Chicago S. W. Co." on dial. H. VON DER HEYDT, PATENTED, FEB.19, 84 on auxiliary dial.

Herman Von Der Heydt, 18 size, 19 jewels; America's only self winding pocket watch. Note crescent shaped winding weight serial number 19.

E. HOWARD & CO.
Boston (Roxbury), Massachusetts
December 11, 1858 - 1903

After the failure of the Boston Watch Company (1853-57), Edward Howard decided to personally attempt the successful production of watches using the interchangeable machine-made parts system. He and Charles Rice, his financial backer, were unable to buy out the defunct watch company in Waltham, however, they did remove (per a prior claim) the watches in progress, the tools and the machinery to Howard and Davis' Roxbury factory (first watch factory in America), in late 1857. During their first year, the machinery was retooled for the production of a revolutionary new watch of Howard's design. Also, the remaining Boston Watch Co. movements were completed (E. Howard & Co. dials, Howard & Rice on the movement). By the summer of 1858, Edward Howard had produced his first watch. On December 11, 1858 the firm of E. Howard & Co. was formed for the manufacture of high-grade watches. Howard's first model was entirely different from any watch previously made. It introduced the more accurate "quick beat" train to American watchmaking. The top plate was in two sections and had six pillars instead of the usual four pillars in a full plate. The balance was gold or steel at first, then later it was a compensation balance loaded with gold screws. Reed's patented barrel was used for the first time. The size, based on the Dennison system, was a little larger than the regular 18 size. In 1861, a 3/4 plate model was put on the market. Most movements were being stamped with "N" to designate Howard's 18 size. On February 4, 1868 Howard patented a new steel motor barrel which was to supersede the Reed's, but not before some 28,000 had been produced. Also, in 1868 Howard introduced the stemwinding movement and was probably the first company to market such a watch in the U. S. By 1869, Howard was producing their "L" or 16 size as well as their first nickel movements. In 1870, G. P. Reed's micrometer regulator was patented for use by E. Howard & Co. The Reed style "whiplash" regulator has been used in more pocket watches, worldwide, than any other type. In 1878, the manufacturing of keywind movements was discontinued. Mr. Howard retired in 1882, but the company continued to sell watch movements of the grade and style set by him until 1903 and beyond. This company was the first to adjust to all six positions. Their dials were always a hard enamel and always bore the name "E. Howard & Co., Boston." In 1902, the company transferred all rights to use the name "Edward Howard," in conjunction with the production of watches, to the Keystone Watch Case Co. Most of their models were stamped "Howard" on the dial and "E. Howard Watch Co., Boston. U.S.A." on the movement. Edward Howard's company never produced its own watch cases, the great majority of which were solid gold or silver. Keystone, however, produced complete watches, many of which were gold filled.

CHRONOLOGICAL DEVELOPMENT OF E. HOWARD & CO.:
Howard, Davis & Dennison, Roxbury, Mass., (1850)
American Horologue Company, Roxbury, Mass., (1851)
Warren Manufacturing Company, Roxbury, Mass., (1851-53)
Boston Watch Co., Roxbury, Mass., (1853-54) & Waltham, Mass., (1854-57)
Howard & Rice, Roxbury, Mass., (1857-58) with (E. Howard & Co. on dials)
E. Howard & Co., Roxbury, Mass., (1858-1903)
Keystone Watch Case Co. (Howard line), Jersey City, N. J., (1902-30)

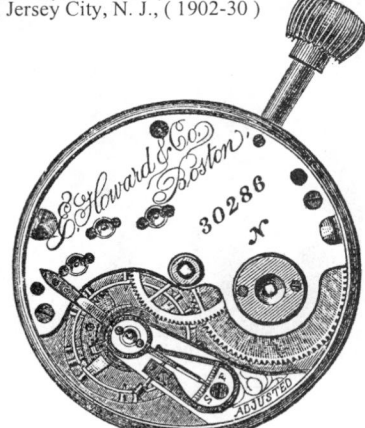

 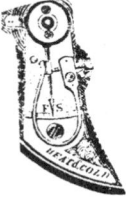 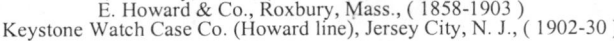

LEFT: Balance cock unmarked =UNADJUSTED
CENTER: Balance cock marked heat &cold =adjusted to TEMPERATURE
RIGHT: Balance cock on movement marked adjusted =FULLY ADJUSTED

A List of initials for **most** of the Solid Gold Watch **Case** companies used by E. Howard & Co.

A.W.C. Co.=American Watch Case Co.
B & T = Booz & Thomas
B.W.C. Co.=Brooklyn Watch Case Co.
C & M =Crosby & Mathewson
C.E.H. & Co. = C.E. Hale & Co.
C.W. Mfg. Co. = Courvoisier Wilcox Mfg. Co.
D T W & Co.= D.T. Warren & Co.
F & Co. = Fellows & Co.
F & S = Fellows & Shell
J M H = J.M. Harper
J S (intertwined)= Jeannot & Shiebler
K (inside) U = Keller & Untermeyer

K E & F. Co.= Keller, Ettinger & Fink N.Y.
M B = Margot Bros.
M & B = Mathey Bros.
N.Y.G.W.C.Co =New York Gold Watch Case Co.
P & B = Peters & Boss
S & D = Serex & Desmaison
S & M B = Serex Maitre Bros.
S & R = Serex & Robert
W & S = Warren & Spadone
W P & Co = Wheeler Parsons & Co.
W W C Mfg. Co =Western Watch Case Co.

Crescent Watch Case Co.
Dueber Watch Case Co.
Keystone Watch Case Co.

Ladd Watch Case Co.
Marsh= Marsh Watch Case Co.
Muhr Watch Case Co.

Roy = Roy Watch Case Co.

NOTE: The "E.H.& Co." marking seen on cases, was put on cases by numerous different case makers, at the request of the Howard sales offices.

NOTE: E. Howard & Co. movements will not fit standard cases properly.

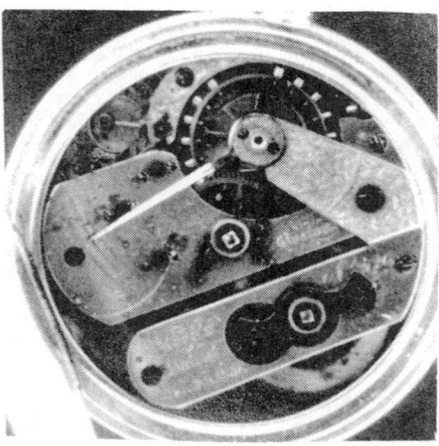

E. HOWARD & CO., Series I, helical hair-spring, detent escapement, KW KS, N (18)size, serial # 1120

E. HOWARD & CO., N (18) size, 15 jewels, chronometer escapement engraved on balance cock, Robin's escapement, serial # 3126.

E. HOWARD & CO. III, 18size, KW KS, note compensating balance above center wheel, serial # 3463.

E. HOWARD & CO., I (10) size, KW KS, **note** solid balance, unique escape wheel & pallet fork, serial # 3406.

E. HOWARD & CO.
APPROXIMATE DATES, SERIAL NOS., AND TOTAL PRODUCTION

Serial No.	Date	Series	Total Prod.
132-1,800—	1858-1860—	I (18S)—	1,600
1,801-3,000—	1860-1861—	II (18S)—	1,150
3,001-3,100—	1861-1862—	K (14S)—	100
3,101-3,300—	reserved for helicals & experimentals		
3,301-3,400—	1861-1862—	III (18S)—	100
3,401-3,500—	1861-1862—	i (10S)—	100
3,501-28,000—	1861-1871—	III (18S)—	24,500
30,001-50,000—	1868-1883—	IV (18S)—	20,000
50,001-71,500—	1869-1899—	V (16S)—	21,500
100,001-105,500—	1869-1899—	VI (6S)—	5,500
200,001-227,000—	1880-1899—	VII (18S)—	27,000
*228,001-231,000—	1895-1899—	VII (18S)—	3,000
300,001-309,000—	1884-1899—	VIII (18S)—	9,000
*309,001-310,000—	1895-1903—	VIII (18S)—	1,000
400,001-405,000—	1890-1895—	IX (18S)—	5,000
500,001-501,500—	1890-1899—	X (12S)—	1,500
*600,001-601,500—	1896-1904—	XI (16S)—	1,500
*700,001-701,500—	1896-1904—	XII (16S)—	1,500

(*) = 3/4 Split Plates & 17 J.   **Possible Total - 124,200**

The above list is provided for determining the age & help identify the Series of your watch. Match serial number with date & Series.

E. HOWARD & CO. WATCH SIZES

Letter	Inches	Approx. Size
N	1 13/16	18
L	1 11/16	16
K	1 10/16	14
J	1 9/16	12
I	1 8/16	10
H	1 7/16	8
G	1 6/16	6
F	1 5/16	4
E	1 4/16	2
D	1 3/16	0

Below: Mershon's Patent center wheel rack regulator (April 26, 1859).

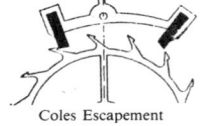

Coles Escapement

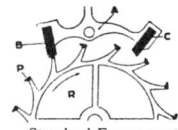

Standard Escapement

Deer
Adjusted to
Hcl6P

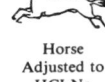

Horse
Adjusted to
HCI-No
positions

Hound
Unadjusted

Howard used a maintaining power wheel up to serial # 30,000

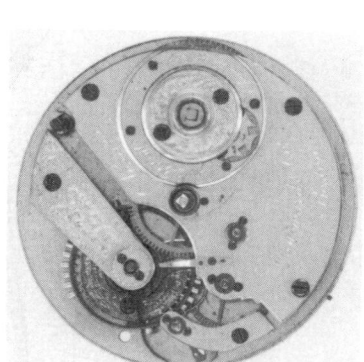

14 or K size, 15 jewels, right angle lever escapement, experimental model, serial number 3,022.

10 or I size, 15 jewels; note cut-out to view escape wheel, experimental model, serial number 3,472.

E. HOWARD & CO.
N SIZE (18) (In Original Cases)

Series or Name — Description		Avg	Ex-Fn	Mint
I, II or III, 15J, gilded, KW, helical hairspring	★★★★	$13,000	$19,000	$28,000
I, 15J, marked "Howard & Rice", S# below 130	★★★★	5,000	6,000	7,500

FOR, E. Howard & Co. on dial and movement, 15-16J, **1857 Model,**
See American Waltham Watch Co. section for 1857 Model for prices

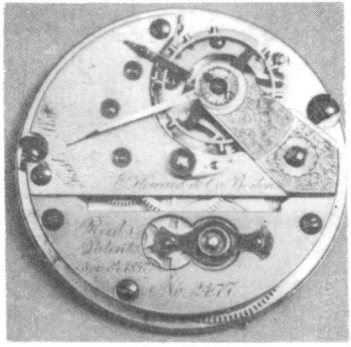

Series 1, 18 size, 17 jewels, note the compensating balance on this early movement, **low** serial number 133.

Series II, 18 size, 15 jewels, key wind & set, serial number 2,477.

Series or Name — Description		Avg	Ex-Fn	Mint
I, 15J, with serial # below 200	★★★★	$5,000	$5,800	$7,000
I, 15J, with serial # below 300	★★★★	4,500	5,000	6,000
I, 15J, gilded, KW, **18K**, HC, OF, upright or horizontal pallets	★★	4,000	5,500	8,500
I, 15J, gilded, KW, silver HC	★★	2,800	3,300	4,500
I, 15J, (movement only)	★★	900	1,000	1,700
I, 17J, with unusual plate cut (movement only)	★★★	5,000	6,500	9,000
II, 15J, gilded, KW, **18K**, HC or OF	★★	2,500	3,500	5,000
II, 15J, gilded, KW, silver HC	★★	1,500	2,000	4,000
II, 15J, (movement only)	★★	800	900	1,500
II, 17J, with screw down jewel settings (movement only).	★★★★★	3,000	3,500	5,000
III, 15J, gilded, KW, **18K**, HC		1,200	1,500	2,400
III, 15J, gilded, KW, silver case		450	550	1,000
III, 15J, **nickel**, KW, silver case	★★★★	2,000	2,700	3,600
III, 15J, gilded, KW, **18K**, Mershon's Patent		1,200	1,400	2,500
III, 15J, gilded, KW, Coles Escapement, **18K**,	★★	1,600	1,900	2,800
III, 15J, nickel Coles Movement, **18K**	★★★★	3,500	4,500	6,000
III, 15J, Gold flashed DMK, Coles Movement, **18K**	★★★★	2,200	3,200	4,500
III, 15J, NI, Private label		800	1,000	1,400
III, 15J , gold flash ray DMK screw down settings (movement only)		850	1,000	1,500
III, 15J, with RAY & nickel DMK (movement only)		450	600	1,100
III, 15J, SW, 4 OZ. hand engraved **18K CASE**		2,000	2,800	4,000

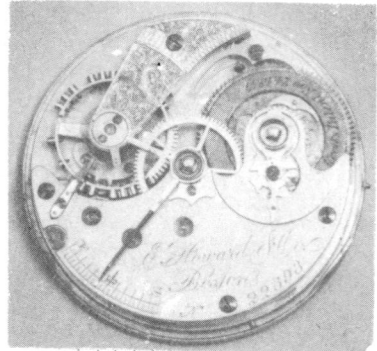

Series III, 18 size, 15 jewels, note **Mershon's Patent** center wheel rack regulator (April 26, 1859), serial # 22,693.

Series III, 18 size, 15 jewels, note high balance wheel over center wheel, serial number 7,000.

Series IV, 18 size, 15 jewels, key wind and set, serial number 37,893.

Series VII, 18 size, 15 jewels, nickel movement, note running deer on movement, "adjusted" on bridge, serial number 219,304.

Series or Name — Description	Avg	Ex-Fn	Mint
IV, 15J, gilded, KW, **18K**, HC	$900	$1,200	$2,000
IV, 15J, **nickel**, KW, **18K**, HC ★★★	2,200	2,800	3,800
IV, 15J, gilded, SW, **18K**, HC	1,000	1,200	2,000
IV, 15J, nickel, SW, **18K**, HC	1,000	1,250	2,100
IV, personalized with jobber's name, silver ★★	400	600	1,000
IV, SW, with Transitional dial, OF **14K**	1,400	1,800	2,800
IV, 15J (movement only)	100	125	300
VII, 15J, gilded or nickel, SW, **14K**, HC	650	850	1,400
VII, 15J, unusual Moorhouse dial, **14K**	1,100	1,500	2,500
VII, 15J, complex DMK (movement only)	150	200	400
VII, 15J (movement only)	125	175	350
VII, 17J, nickel, split plate, SW, **14K**, HC ★★★	1,400	1,700	2,800
VII, 17J, nickel, split plate, SW, silver, HC ★★★	700	800	1,600
VII, 19J, nickel, SW, **14K**, HC ★★★	2,500	3,000	5,000
VII, 21J, 3/4 plate (movement only) ★★★★	1,600	2,400	4,000
VIII, 15J, gilded or nickel, SW, **14K**, OF	700	800	1,400
VIII, 15J, nickel, Complex DMD (movement only)	150	200	475
VIII, 15J, unusual Moorhouse dial ★★★	1,100	1,500	2,500
VIII, 15J (movement only)	125	175	350
VIII, 17J, nickel, split plate, SW, **14K**, OF ★★★	1,800	2,200	3,200
VIII, 17J, nickel, split plate, SW, **silver**, OF ★★★	700	800	1,400
VIII, 17J, nickel or gilded, with RR on the side of balance cock, silver, OF	1,000	1,200	2,000

BALL - HOWARDS SEE **BALL W. Co.**.

Series VII, 18 size, 17J, nickel, split plate, adjusted, Stem Wind, serial number 228,055.

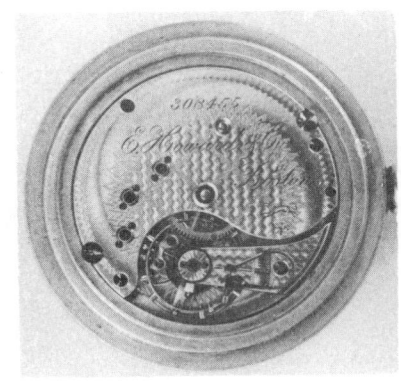

Series VIII, 18 size, 15 jewels, serial number 308,455.

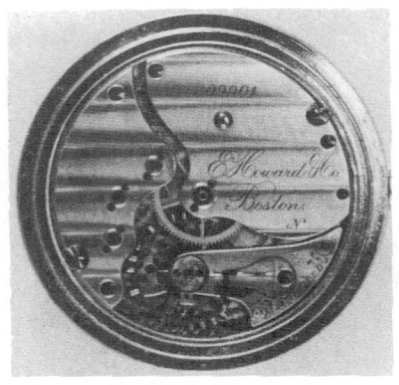

Series VIII, 18 size, 17 jewels, split plate model, gold jewel settings, serial number 309,904.

Series IX, 18 size, 15 jewels, hunting. This series is gilded only and hound grade exclusively, S # 402,873.

Series or Name — Description	Avg	Ex-Fn	Mint
IX, 15J, gilded, SW, **14K**, HC	$900	$1,100	$2,000
IX, 15J, gilded, SW, **silver**, HC	450	550	1,000
IX, 15J, gilded, SW, unusual Moorhouse dial	1,100	1,500	2,500
IX, 15J (movement only)	100	125	350

L SIZE (16)

(In Original Cases)

Series or Name — Description	Avg	Ex-Fn	Mint
V, 15J, gilded, KW, **18K**, HC	$1,100	$1,500	$2,300
V, 15J, gilded, KW, **18K**, Coles Escapement ★★	1,300	1,800	2,800
V, 15J, nickel, **18K**, Coles Escapement ★★★★	3,000	4,000	5,000
V, 15J, gilded or nickel, SW, **14K**, HC	800	1,000	1,600
V, 15J, gilded, SW, **14K**, Coles Escapement ★★	1,000	1,200	1,800
V, 15J, SW, **14K** OF, with transitional dial ★★	1,300	1,800	2,400
V, 15J, SW, **14K** OF, with Moorhouse dial ★★	1,500	2,100	3,500
V, 15J, SW, **14K**, 24 Hr. dial (red/black) ★★★	1,300	1,800	2,500
V, 15J, nickel KW, (movement only)	400	600	800
V, 15J, gilded (movement only)	90	100	300
V, **Prescott**, 15J., gilded, LS, SW, NOTE: original case may show evidence of filled key holes on dust cover ★★★	2,500	3,000	6,000
V, Prescott, 15J., gilded, SW, (Series V **movement** only).... ★★★	1,000	1,300	3,000

Series V, 16 or L size, Prescott Model, 15J., HC, S# 50,434. NOTE: Original case may show evidence of **filled key holes on dust cover.** When watches were returned to factory & converted from KW Coles movement to stem wind & lever set.

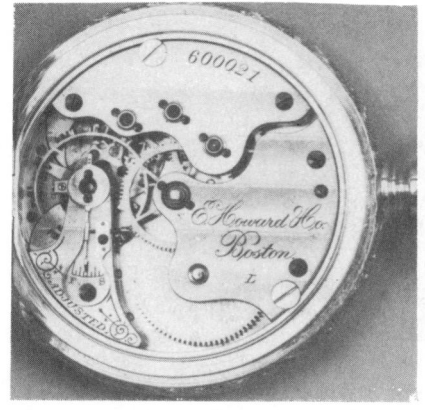

Series XI, 16 size, 17 jewels, split plate model, nickel movement, gold jewel settings, serial number 600,021.

Series XII, L-16 size, 21 jewels, split plate model, nickel movement, gold lettering, gold jewel settings, serial number 700,899.

Series or Name — Description		Avg	Ex-Fn	Mint
XI, 17J, nickel, split plate, SW, **14K**, HC	★★★	$1,100	$1,300	$2,000
XI, 17J, nickel, split plate, SW, **silver**, HC	★★★	600	800	1,600
XI, 17J (movement only)		300	400	800
XII, 17J, nickel, split plate, SW, **14K**, OF	★★★	1,000	1,200	2,000
XII, 17J, nickel, split plate, SW, **silver**, OF	★★★	500	600	1,200
XII, 17J (movement only)		100	200	500
XII, 21J, nickel, split plate, SW, **14K**, OF	★★★★	4,000	6,500	8,500

K SIZE (14)
(In Original Cases)

Series or Name — Description		Avg	Ex-Fn	Mint
K, 15J, gilded, KW, **Original case 18K**, HC	★★★★★	$9,000	$12,000	$16,000
K, 15J, gilded, (movement only)	★★★★	6,000	7,000	9,000

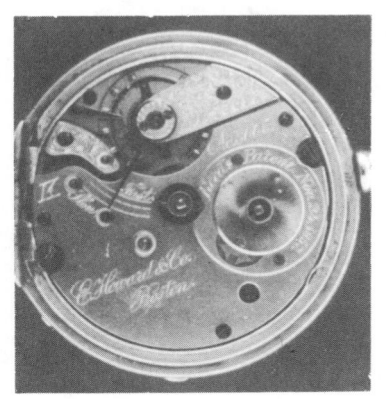

Series K, 14 or K size, 15 jewels, key wind & set, serial number 3,004.

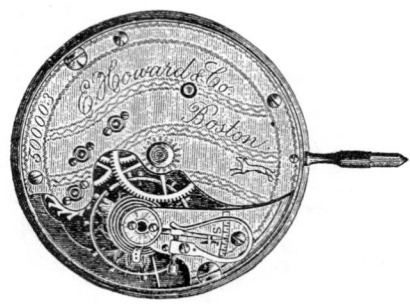

Series X, 15J, J size or 12 size, nickel, hound, SW, serial # 500,003

J SIZE (12)
(In Original Cases)

Series or Name – Description	Avg	Ex-Fn	Mint
X, 15J, nickel, hound, SW, **14K**, OF ....★	$700	$900	$1,500
X, 15J, nickel, hound, SW, fancy Moorhouse dial, **14K**, OF........	900	1,200	1,900
X, 15J, nickel, horse, SW, **14K**, OF..★	800	1,000	1,600
X, 15J, nickel, deer, SW, **14K**, OF...★	900	1,100	1,700
X, 15J, hound (movement only)..★	150	200	500

Series X, 12 or J size, 15 jewels, note deer on movement, serial number 501,361.

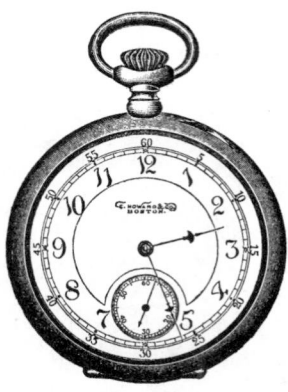

Example of *Moorhouse* style dial.

🕐 A collector should expect to pay modestly higher prices at local shops.

🕐 **The Complete Price Guide to Watches goal is to stimulate the orderly exchange of <u>Watches</u> between *"buyers"* and *"sellers"*.**

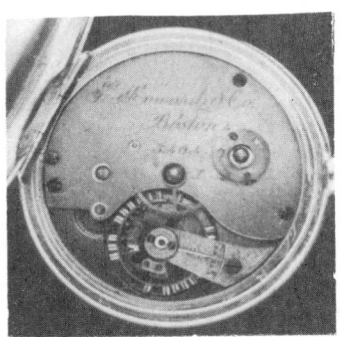

I size (10 size), 15 jewels, gilded, key wind, serial number 3,464.

I SIZE (10)   (In Original Cases)

Series or Name — Description		Avg	Ex-Fn	Mint
I size (10 size), 15J, gilded, KW, **18K** HC .... ★ ★ ★ ★		$4,000	$5,000	$9,000
I size (10 size), 15 jewels, gilded, key wind, **with unique escape wheel** & pallet fork, **18K** case		7,000	9,000	12,000

I size (10 size), 15 jewels, gilded, key wind, **unique escape wheel & pallet fork**, S# 3,414.

G SIZE (6)   (In Original Cases)

Series or Name — Description		Avg	Ex-Fn	Mint
VI, 15J, gilded, **KW, 18K**, HC .... ★ ★ ★		$2,000	$2,500	$4,600
VI, 15J, gilded or nickel, **SW, 18K**, HC.............................		1,000	1,200	1,600
VI, 15J, gilded or nickel, Moorhouse dial, **14K**		1,000	1,200	1,600
VI, 15J, (movement only)		175	200	450
VI, 15J, (movement only) **adjusted**		300	500	800

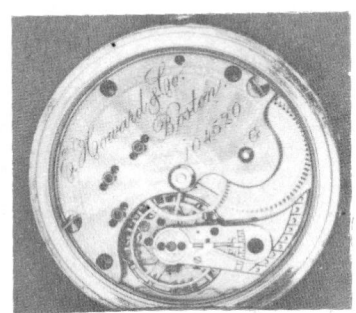

Series VI, 6 or G size, 15 jewels, stem wind, serial number 104,520.

E. HOWARD WATCH CO. (KEYSTONE)
Waltham, Massachusetts
1902 - 1930

The watches are <u>marked</u> "**E. Howard Watch Co. Boston, U. S. A.**" The Howard name was purchased by the Keystone Watch Case Co. in 1902. There were no patent rights transferred, just the Howard name. The "Edward Howard" chronometer was the highest grade, 16 size, and was introduced in 1912 for $350. All watches cased & timed at factory as a **complete** watch only.

Keystone Howard also gained control of U. S. Watch Co. of Waltham and New York Standard Watch Company.

ESTIMATED SERIAL NUMBERS
AND PRODUCTION DATES

Date	Serial No.
1902—	850,000
1903—	900,000
1909—	980,000
1912—	1,100,000
1915—	1,285,000
1917—	1,340,000
1921—	1,400,000
1930—	1,500,000

The arrows denote number of jewels and adjustments in each grade.

Cross =23 jewel, 5 positions

Star =21 jewel, Adj.5P, & 19J with V under star

Triangle =19 jewel, 5 positions

Circle =17 jewel, 3 positions

Model 1905, Series 7, 16 size, 17J., open face. This 3/4 model can be identified by the slant parallel damaskeening. This represents the 3/4 **top** grade, raised gold jewel settings, double roller, Adj.5P and sold for $115.00 in 1910.

1907 Bridge Model, Series 5, 19 jewels, **open face,** Serial # 953,733. **NOTE:** The escape wheel bridge & the fourth wheel bridge is <u>not</u> notched out.

Model 1905, Series 9, 16 size, 17 jewels, open face. This 3/4 model can be identified by the checkerboard damaskeening. This represents the 3/4 **mid** grade, GJS, double roller, Adj.3 & 5P and sold for $105.00 in 1910.

Model 1905, Series 3, 16 size, 17 jewels open face. This 3/4 model can be identified by the circular damaskeening. This represents the 3/4 **lowest** grade of the three with single roller, Adj.3P and sold for $100.00 in 1910.

E. Howard Watch Co., Model 1907, marked Series 0, 16 size, 23 jewels, in original E. Howard Watch Co. swing-out movement Keystone Extra gold filled Open Face case.

E. HOWARD WATCH CO. Model 1907, Series 0 (not marked), 16S, 23J., Hunting Case.

🕐 Model 1907= **bridge** OF & HC and Series or No., 0, 1, 2, 5 & 10 , see above illustrations, 1907 = Series or No. 0=23J, Series or No.1&10=21J, Series2=17J, Series5 or No.5 =19J. Model 1905 = **3/4 plate** OF & HC and Series 3,7,9 = 17J.

E. HOWARD WATCH CO. (KEYSTONE)
16 SIZE

Series or Name — Description	Avg	Ex-Fn	Mint
No. 0, & 1907, 23J, BRG, Adj.5P, DR, OF	$400	$475	$800
1907 model & No.0, 23J, BRG, Adj.5P, DR, HC	425	525	850
Unmarked, 23J, BRG, Adj.5P, DR, OF	350	425	700
Series 0, 23J, BRG, Adj.5P, DR, **Ruby banking pins**	450	600	1,000
Series 0, 23J, BRG, Adj.5P, DR, **jeweled barrel**	450	600	1,000
Series 0, 23J, BRG, Adj.5P, DR, **OF, 14K**	700	800	1,300
Series 0, 23J, BRG, Adj.5P, DR, **HC, 14K**	800	1,000	1,600
No. 1, 21J, BRG, Adj.5P, DR ★	350	425	800
Series 1, 21J, BRG, Adj.5P, DR	295	400	600
Series 2, 17J, BRG, Adj.5P, DR, HC	175	250	400
Series 2, 17J, BRG, Adj.5P, DR, OF	125	175	350

Series II, marked *Railroad Chronometer*, 16 size, 21 jewels, Adj5p, serial number 1,217,534.

Edward Howard Model, 16 size, 23 blue sapphire jewels, frosted gold bridge, wolfteeth wind, serial # 77.

🕐 Pricing in this Guide are fair market price for **COMPLETE** watches which are reflected from the "**NAWCC**" National and regional shows.

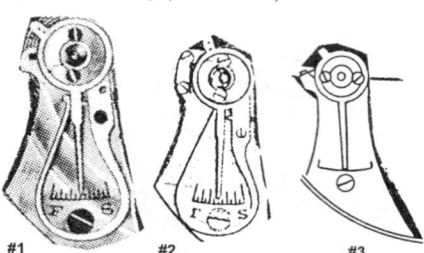

#1 #2 #3

Above: Note illustrations #1 & #2 = Howard regulators with the 2 jewel screws vertical or upright and #1 has a **square** hairspring stud also note #2 has a **sliding** stud & a bean shaped cover. Howard-**Waltham** regulators (#3) the 2 jewel screws are horizontal and **triangular** hairspring stud.

E. Howard Watch Co., 16 size, 23 jewels, by Waltham, raised gold jewel settings, gold train, Adj5p, open face, bridge style movement. NOTE: Bow, also note the Howard S# seen on bridge is 1,005,363. The **Waltham** S# seen under dial, is 605,363 .

E. Howard Watch Co., 16 size 19 jewels, by Waltham, gold jewel settings, Adj3p, hunting case, 3/4 plate movement.

Series or Name — Description	Avg	Ex-Fn	Mint
Series 3, 17J, 3/4, Adj.3P, circular DMK	$95	$150	$295
Series 3, 17J, Adj.3P, circular DMK, **14K** OF,	375	475	675
No. 5, 19J, BRG, GJS, HC ★	250	295	600
Series 5, 19J, BRG, Adj.5P, DR, **14K**	400	500	700
Series 5, 19J, BRG, Adj.5P, DR, 1907 Model	150	195	400
Series 7, 17J, 3/4, Adj.5P, DR, RGJS, slant parallel DMK, OF	95	150	300
Series 7, 17J, 3/4, Adj.5P, DR, RGJS, slant parallel DMK, HC	125	150	350
Series 9, 17J, 3/4, Adj.3P, LS, checkerboard DMK, OF	100	125	300
Series 9, 17J, 3/4, Adj.5P, DR, checkerboard DMK, RR grade,**14K**	400	500	800
Series 10, 21J, BRG, Adj.5P, DR, **Marked Non–Magnetic** ★★★	600	750	1,500
Series 10, 21J, BRG, Adj.5P, DR	295	375	675
No. 10, 21J, BRG, Adj.5P, DR	295	375	675
Series 11, 21J, **R.R. Chrono.**, Adj.5P, DR	325	400	700
Edward Howard, 23 blue sapphire pressed J, Free Sprung, Adj.5P, DR, **without box** ★★	5,500	7,000	11,000
Edward Howard, 23 blue sapphire pressed J, Free Sprung, Adj.5P, DR, **with original** box and papers, **18K** Edward Howard case ★★★	8,000	9,500	14,000
Climax,7J., (made for export), gilded, OF	75	100	200
23J, E. Howard W. Co. (mfg. by Waltham), **14K**, Brg model . ★★	1,000	1,100	1,800
23J, E. Howard W. Co. (mfg. by Waltham), gold filled, OF,	400	600	1,300
23J, E. Howard W. Co. (mfg. by Waltham), gold filled, HC	600	800	1,500
21J, E. Howard W. Co. (mfg. by Waltham), Bridge model, HC	295	400	900
21J, E. Howard W. Co. (mfg. by Waltham), 3/4, OF	195	250	450
19J, E. Howard W. Co. (mfg. by Waltham), Bridge model, HC	225	275	500
19J, E. Howard W. Co. (mfg. by Waltham), 3/4, OF	195	250	450
17J, E. Howard W. Co. (mfg. by Waltham), Bridge model, HC	195	250	450
17J, E. Howard W. Co. (mfg. by Waltham), **Equity model**, 3/4, OF .	175	200	400

12 SIZE - 1908 Model

Series or Name — Description	Avg	Ex-Fn	Mint
Series 6, 19J, BRG, DR, Adj.5P, 1908 Model, **14K**, HC	$295	$350	$600
Series 6, 19J, BRG, DR, Adj.5P, **14K**, OF....................................	195	275	475
Series 6, 19J, BRG, DR, Adj.5P, OF	70	90	195
Series 7, 17J, BRG, DR, Adj.3P, **14K**, OF	195	275	450
Series 7, 17J, BRG, DR, Adj.3P, OF	75	95	195
Series 8, 21J, BRG, DR, Adj.5P, OF	95	150	295
Series 8, 23J, BRG, DR, Adj.5P, **14K**, OF	225	295	550
Series 8, 23J, BRG, DR, Adj.5P, OF	150	195	425
Series 8, 23J, BRG, DR, Adj.5P, **14K**, HC................................	400	450	725
21J, Waltham Model, BRG, HC... ★★★	195	295	500
21J, Waltham Model, BRG, OF... ★★★	250	350	600
19J, Waltham Model, gold center wheel, BRG, HC........... ★★★	195	295	500
19J, Waltham Model, gold center wheel, BRG, OF .... ★★★	250	350	600
17J, Waltham Model, 3/4, HC... ★★★	95	150	225
17J, Waltham Model, 3/4, OF... ★★★	75	95	195

NOTE: First Serial # for 12 size with 17J.=977,001; 19J.=977,451; 21J.=1,055,851.

Series 8, 12 size, 21 jewels, open face, stop works, extra thin. **1908 MODEL** with 21 jewels engraved under balance, five positions and temperature.

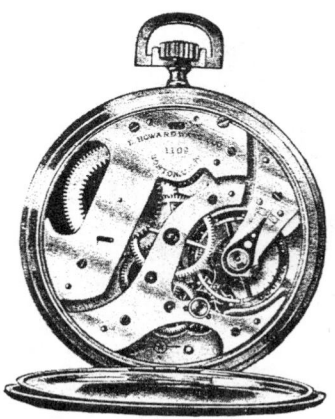

E. Howard Watch Co., 10 size, 21J, Adj.,5p. **(Serial # started at about 1,001 on this model.)**

21 Jewels 5 Positions ⟫⟶
19 Jewels 5 Positions ⟫⟶
17 Jewels 3 Positions ⟫⟶

10 SIZE

NOTE: 10 Size Serial numbers start at about **1,001** on this model.

Series or Name — Description	Avg	Ex-Fn	Mint
Thin Model, 21J, Adj.5P, **14K** case, OF......................................	$185	$225	$400
Thin Model, 21J, Adj.5P, Gold filled, OF	75	95	195
Thin Model, 19J, Adj.5P, **14K** case, OF......................................	150	195	350
Thin Model, 19J, Adj.5P, Gold filled, OF	65	85	150
Thin Model, 17J, Adj.3P, **14K** case, OF......................................	150	195	350
Thin Model, 17J, Adj.3P, Gold filled, OF	65	85	150

🕐 A collector should expect to pay modestly higher prices at local shops.

🕐 Watches listed in this book are priced at the collectable Trade Show level, as **complete** watches having an original 14k gold-filled case and *Key Wind* with silver, an original white enamel single sunk dial, and with the entire original movement in good working order with no repairs needed.

STYLE R.R. Chronometer
gold filled: $125 - $195 - $425
Dial: $25 - $40 - $80

STYLE R.R. Antique Bow
gold filled: $95 - $150 - $325
Dial: $25 - $40 - $80

STYLE R.R. Plain swing out
gold filled: $95 - $125 - $295
Dial: $25 - $40 - $80

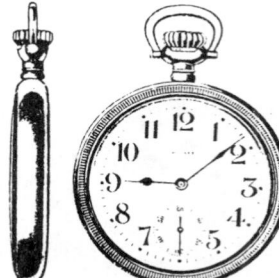

STYLE R.R. Engine Turned swing out
gold filled: $95- $125 - $295
Dial: $25 - $40 - $80

STYLE R.R. SWING OUT
gold filled: $95 - $125 - $325
14K GOLD: $295 - $325 - $600
Montgomery Dial: $35 - $50 - $95

NOTE: Factory Advertised as a **complete** watch and was fitted with a certain matched, timed and rated movement and sold in the factory designed case style as a **complete** watch. The factory advertised as *"Howard movements and cases are not sold separately"*. All the factory advertised **complete** watches came with a enamel dial **SHOWN** or **CHOICE** of other **Railroad** dials.

ILLINOIS WATCH CO.
Springfield, Illinois
1869 - 1927

The Illinois Watch Company was organized mainly through the efforts of J. C. Adams. The first directors were J. T. Stuart, W. B. Miller, John Williams, John W. Bunn, George Black and George Passfield. In 1879 the company changed all its watches to a quick train movement by changing the number of teeth in the fourth wheel. The first nickel movement was made in 1879. The first mainspring made by the company was used in 1882. The next year soft enamel dials were used.

The Illinois Watch Co. used more names on its movements than any other watch manufacturer. To identify all of them requires extensive knowledge by the collector plus a good working knowledge of watch mechanics. Engraved on some early movements, for example, are "S. W. Co." or "I. W. Co., Springfield, Ill." To the novice these abbreviations might be hard to understand, thus making Illinois watches difficult to identify. But one saving clue is that the location "Springfield, Illinois" appears on most of these watches. It is important to learn how to identify these type watches because some of them are extremely collectible. Examples of some of the more valuable of these are: the Benjamin Franklin (size 18 or 16, 25 or 26 jewels), Paillard's Non-Magnetic, Pennsylvania Special, C & O, and B & O railroad models.

The earliest movements made by the Illinois Watch Co. are listed below. They made the first watch in early 1872, but the company really didn't get off the ground until 1875. Going by the serial number, the first watch made was the Stuart. Next was the Mason, followed by the Bunn, the Miller, and finally the Currier. The first stem-wind was made in 1875.

> **STUART,** FIRST Run was serial numbers .... 1 to 100.
> **MASON,** FIRST Run was serial numbers .... 101 to 200.
> **BUNN,** FIRST Run was serial numbers .... 201 to 300.
> **MILLER,** FIRST Run was serial numbers.................................... 301 to 400.
> **CURRIER,** FIRST Run was serial numbers................................... 401 to 500.

The Illinois Watch Company was sold to Hamilton Watch Co. in 1927. The Illinois factory continued to produce Illinois watches under the new management until 1932. After 1933 Hamilton produced watches bearing the Illinois name in their own factory until 1939.

CHRONOLOGY OF THE DEVELOPMENT OF ILLINOIS WATCH CO.:
Illinois Springfield Watch Co.. 1869-1879
Springfield Illinois Watch Co... 1879-1885
Illinois Watch Co. 1885-1927
Illinois Watch Co. sold to Hamilton Watch Co. 1927

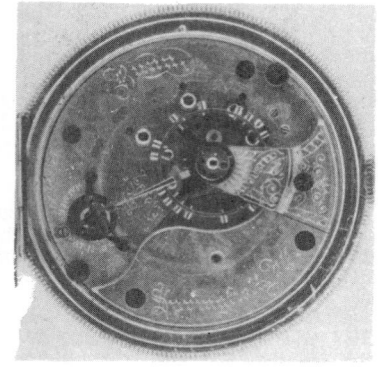

ILLINOIS WATCH CO., Bates Model, 18 size, 7 jewels, key wind & set, serial number 43,876, c.1874.

BUNN, 18 size, 16 jewels, hunting case, NOTE: Chalmer patented regulator, serial number 1,185,809.

🕐 NOTE: Numerous model 2 & 3 movements have key-wind style barrel arbors and stem wind *capabilities* they are referred to as **transition** Models. When model 2 & 3 were introduced the factory must have had a large supply of key-wind style barrel arbors so being frugal they were used.

ILLINOIS ESTIMATED SERIAL NUMBERS AND PRODUCTION DATES

DATE – SERIAL NO.	DATE – SERIAL NO.	DATE – SERIAL NO.
1872 – 5,000	1893 – 1,120,000	1914 – 2,600,000
1873 – 20,000	1894 – 1,160,000	1915 – 2,700,000
1874 – 50,000	1895 – 1,220,000	1916 – 2,800,000
1875 – 75,000	1896 – 1,250,000	1917 – 3,000,000
1876 – 100,000	1897 – 1,290,000	1918 – 3,200,000
1877 – 145,000	1898 – 1,330,000	1919 – 3,400,000
1878 – 210,000	1899 – 1,370,000	1920 – 3,600,000
1879 – 250,000	1900 – 1,410,000	1921 – 3,750,000
1880 – 300,000	1901 – 1,450,000	1922 – 3,900,000
1881 – 350,000	1902 – 1,500,000	1923 – 4,000,000
1882 – 400,000	1903 – 1,650,000	1924 – 4,500,000
1883 – 450,000	1904 – 1,700,000	1925 – 4,700,000
1884 – 500,000	1905 – 1,800,000	1926 – 4,800,000
1885 – 550,000	1906 – 1,840,000	1927 – 5,000,000
1886 – 600,000	1907 – 1,900,000	(Sold to Hamilton)
1887 – 700,000	1908 – 2,100,000	1928 – 5,100,000
1888 – 800,000	1909 – 2,150,000	1929 – 5,200,000
1889 – 900,000	1910 – 2,200,000	1931 – 5,400,000
1890 – 1,000,000	1911 – 2,300,000	1938 – 5,500,000
1891 – 1,040,000	1912 – 2,400,000	1948 – 5,600,000
1892 – 1,080,000	1913 – 2,500,000	

The above list is provided for determining the **APPROXIMATE** age of your watch. Match serial number with date. Watches were not necessarily sold in the exact order of manufactured date.

NOTE: It required several months for raw material to emerge as a finished movement. All the while the factory is producing all sizes, models and grades. The numbering system was basically "consecutive", due to demand a batch of movements could be side tracked, thus allowing a different size and model to move ahead to meet this demand. Therefore, the dates some movements were sold and delivered to the trade, may not be "consecutive".

(See Illinois Identification of Movements section located at the end of the Illinois price section to identify the movement, size and model number of your watch.)

ILLINOIS
18 SIZE (ALL FULL PLATE)

Grade or Name — Description	Avg	Ex-Fn	Mint
Alleghany, 11J, KW, gilded, OF	$80	$125	$250
Alleghany, 11J, M#1, NI, KW	80	125	250
Alleghany, 11J, M#2, NI, Transition	80	125	250
America, 7J, M#3, Silveroid ★	80	95	250
America, 7J, M#1-2, KW ★	95	150	295
America Special, 7J, M#1-2, KW ★	175	195	400
Army & Navy, 19J, GJS, Adj.5P, OF	195	250	500
Army & Navy, 19J, GJS, Adj.5P, HC	225	295	550
Army & Navy, 21J, GJS, Adj.5P, OF	195	250	500
Army & Navy, 21J, GJS, Adj.5P, HC	250	325	600
Baltimore & Ohio R.R. Special, 17J, GJS, ADJ ★ ★ ★	1,200	1,500	2,500
Baltimore & Ohio R.R. Special, 21J, GJS, NI, ADJ ★ ★ ★	1,400	1,600	2,700
Baltimore & Ohio R.R. Standard, 24J, GJS, ADJ ★ ★ ★	1,800	2,200	3,400
Bates, 7J, M#1-2, KW	175	225	500

🕐 Watches listed in this book are priced at the **collectable fair market value** at the **Trade Show** level, as **complete** watches having an original 14k gold filled case, *KEY WIND* with silver, an original white enamel single sunk dial, and with the entire original movement in good working order with no repairs needed, unless otherwise noted.

🕐 GENERIC, NAMELESS OR **UNMARKED GRADES** FOR WATCH MOVEMENTS ARE LISTED UNDER THE COMPANY NAME OR INITIALS OF THE COMPANY, ETC. BY SIZE, JEWEL COUNT AND DESCRIPTION.

🕐 Some watch manufacturers personalize watches for jobbers or jewelry firms, with exclusive private signed or marked movements. The valuable collectable watches are listed under the signed or marked movement. Other exclusive private signed or marked movements will have equivalent value or only slightly higher value and should be compared to Generic or Nameless movements. Railroad signed or marked (dials & movements) are usually more collectable & higher in value.

Illinois Watch Co., 18 size, railroad watch with a Ferguson dial with the numbers **1 through 12 in red.**
Illinois Ferguson = 18S, Dial: $100 - $200 - $500

Army and Navy, 18 size, 19 jewels, engraved on movement "Washington Watch Co.," serial number 1,606,612.

Grade or Name — Description		Avg	Ex-Fn	Mint
Benjamin Franklin U.S.A., 17J, ADJ, NI	★	$400	$500	$ 1,000
Benjamin Franklin U.S.A., 21J, GJS, **Adj.6P**, NI	★	900	1,200	1,600
Benjamin Franklin U.S.A., 21J, GJS, Adj.5P, NI	★	900	1,200	1,600
Benjamin Franklin U.S.A., 24J, GJS, Adj.6P, NI	★	2,000	2,400	4,000
Benjamin Franklin U.S.A., 25J, GJS, Adj.6P, NI	★★★★	3,800	5,000	9,000
Benjamin Franklin U.S.A., 26J, GJS, Adj.6P, NI,	★★★★	4,800	5,800	10,000
Bunn, 15J, M#1, KW, KS, **1st. run S# 201 to 300**	★★★★	2,100	2,400	4,000
Bunn, 15J, M#1, KW, KS, **2nd. run S# 2,001 to 2,500**	★★	1,800	2,200	3,300
Bunn, 15J, M#1, KW, KS, OF	★	450	500	1,000
Bunn, 15J, M#1, KW, KS, **"ADJUSTED",**	★	500	550	1,100
Bunn, 15J, KW/SW transition		250	350	800
Bunn, 15J, M#1, KW, Coin		375	425	900
Bunn, 15J, KW, M#1, HC		375	450	900
Bunn, 15J, SW, M#2, HC		375	450	900
Bunn, 16J, KW, (not marked 16J.), OF	★	400	450	900
Bunn, 16J, KW, (not marked 16J.), HC	★	400	450	900
Bunn, 16J, SW, (not marked 16J.), HC		350	400	800
Bunn, 16J, SW, **ADJ**, (not marked **16J.**), HC		375	450	850
Bunn, 17J, SW, NI, Coin		200	250	400
Bunn, 17J, SW, M#3, **5th pinion**, gilded, OF		300	350	600
Bunn, 17J, M#4, SW, NI, OF		150	195	400
Bunn, 17J, M#5, SW, NI, HC		175	250	500
Bunn, 17J, SW, M#5, **"Ruby Jewels"**, NI, Adj.5p, HC	★	500	600	1,000
Bunn, 17J, M#6, SW, NI, OF		150	195	400
Bunn, 18J, SW, NI, **ADJ.**, (not marked **18J.**), OF	★★	500	600	850
Bunn, 19J, SW, NI, DR, LS, GJS, Adj.5P, **J. barrel** , OF		195	295	500
Bunn, 19J, SW, **Adj.6P**, DR, **J. barrel**, OF		275	350	550
Bunn, 19J, SW, GJS, DR, Adj.5P, **J. barrel**, HC	★	350	500	700

IMPORTANT NOTE: Railroad Standards, Railroad Approved & Railroad Grade **terminology,** as defined and used in this *BOOK*.
1. **RAILROAD STANDARDS** = A commission or board appointed by the railroad companies outlined a set of **guidelines** to be accepted or approved by each railroad line.
2. **RAILROAD APPROVED** = A **LIST** of watches each railroad line would approve if purchased by their employee's. (this list changed through the years).
3. **RAILROAD GRADE** = A watch made by manufactures to meet or exceed the guidelines set by the railroad **standards**. Grades such as 992, Vanguard and B.W. Raymond, etc.
☉ Some GRADES **exceeded** the R.R. standards such as 23 jewels, diamond end stone, gold train, raised gold jewel settings, double sunk dial and the list goes on. Examples: such as Veritas, Sangamo, 950 & Riverside Maximus and many others.

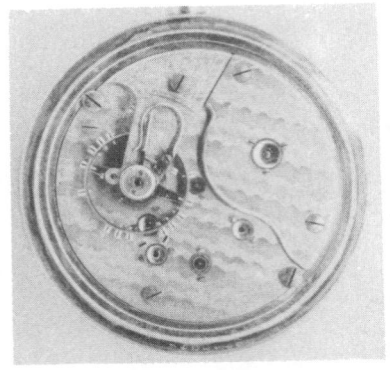

Bunn Special, 18 size, 24 jewels, adjusted, serial number 1,413,435

Bunn Special, 18 size, 26 Ruby jewels, "J. Home & Co." on dial, adjusted to six positions, gold jewel settings, serial number 2,019,415.

Grade or Name — Description	Avg	Ex-Fn	Mint
Bunn Special, 21J, SW, **Coin**	$195	$295	$500
Bunn Special, 21J, GJS, ADJ, HC	375	425	650
Bunn Special, 21J, GJS, ADJ, DR, OF	250	300	450
Bunn Special, 21J, GJS, DR, Adj.5P, OF	250	300	450
Bunn Special, 21J, GJS, DR, **Adj.6P**, OF	275	325	500
Bunn Special, 21J, GJS, Adj.5P, **HC, 14K**	650	750	1,400
Bunn Special, 21J, GJS, ADJ, 2-Tone	295	375	600
Bunn Special, 21J, GJS, Adj.5P, DR	275	325	500
Bunn Special, 21J," **EXTRA**", GJS ★★	900	1,200	2,100
Bunn Special, 23J, GJS, ADJ, DR, OF	600	750	1,000
Bunn Special, 23J, GJS, Adj.6P, DR, OF	650	750	1,000
Bunn Special, 23J, GJS, Adj.6P, DR, 2-Tone, OF ★★	700	800	1,200
Bunn Special, 23J, GJS, ADJ, DR, HC ★★★	1,800	2,200	3,600
Bunn Special, 24J, GJS, ADJ, DR, HC	900	1,100	1,500
Bunn Special, 24J, GJS, ADJ, DR, **14K, HC**	1,500	1,800	2,400
Bunn Special, 24J, GJS, ADJ, DR, OF	900	1,000	1,400
Bunn Special, 24J, GJS, **Adj.6P**, DR, OF	900	1,000	1,400
Bunn Special, 24J, GJS, **Adj.6P**, DR, HC	900	1,000	1,400
Bunn Special, 25J, GJS, **Adj.6P**, DR ★★★	5,000	6,000	9,000
Bunn Special, 26J, GJS, **Adj.6P**, DR ★★★	4,000	5,000	8,000
Central Truck Railroad, 15J, KW, KS ★★	700	900	1,600
Chesapeake & Ohio, 17J, ADJ, OF ★★	1,000	1,400	2,500
Chesapeake & Ohio Special, 21J, GJS, 2-Tone ★★	1,200	1,800	3,000
Chesapeake & Ohio Special, 24J, NI, ADJ, GJS ★★	2,400	2,800	5,400
Chronometer, 11-15J, KW, OF ★	250	295	600
Chronometer, 15J, M#2, HC ★	275	350	700
Columbia, 11J, M#3, 5th Pinion	95	150	295
Columbia, 11J, M#1 & 2, KW	95	150	295
Columbia, 11J, M#1 & 2, Silveroid	80	125	250
Columbia Special, 11J, M#1-2-3, KW	80	125	250
Columbia Special, 11J, M#1-2-3, KW/SW, transition	95	150	295
Comet, 11J, M#3, OF, LS, SW	65	95	195
Commodore Perry, 15-16J, HC	150	195	350
Criterion, 11-15J, HC	95	150	295

⊕ Some watch manufacturers personalize watches for jobbers or jewelry firms, with exclusive private signed or marked movements. The valuable collectable watches are listed under the signed or marked movement. Other exclusive private signed or marked movements will have equivalent value or only slightly higher value and should be compared to Generic or Nameless movements. Railroad signed or marked (dials & movements) are usually more collectable & higher in value.

Chesapeake & Ohio Special, 21 Ruby Jewels, Adjusted Temperature 6 Positions Isochronsim, OF, S# 1785680.

Diurnal, 18 size, 7 jewels, key wind & set, only one run, total production 2,000, serial number 86,757.

Grade or Name — Description	Avg	Ex-Fn	Mint
Currier, 11-12J, KW, OF	$70	$125	$300
Currier, 11-12J, KW, HC	95	150	325
Currier, 11-12J, **1st run S# 401 to 500** ★★★	400	500	1,000
Currier, 11-12J, KW/SW, transition, OF	75	95	195
Currier, 13–15J, M#3, OF	75	95	195
Currier, 13–15J, M#3, HC	90	125	250
Dauntless, 11J	90	125	250
Dean, 15J, M#1, KW, HC ★★	275	350	700
Diurnal, 7J, KW, KS, HC, **Coin** ★	250	325	600
Dominion Railway, with train on dial ★★★	1,500	1,900	3,300
Eastlake, 11J, SW, KW, Transition	150	195	400
Emperor, 21J, M#6, LS, SW, ADJ	175	250	400
Enterprise, M#2, ADJ	125	150	250
Eureka, 11J	95	150	250
Favorite, 16J, LS, OF	95	150	250
Forest City, 7–11J, SW, LS, HC	95	175	250
Forest City, 17J, KW/SW, gilted,	95	175	275
General Grant or General Lee, 11J, M#1, KW ★	300	350	600
Hoyt, 7-9-11J, M#1-2, KW	65	95	195

🕐 **Generic, nameless,** Personalized Jobber Watches or unmarked grades for watch movements are listed under the Company name or initials of the Company, etc. by size, jewel count and description.

	Avg	Ex-Fn	Mint
Illinois Watch Co., 7-9J, M#1-2, KW	$65	$95	$195
Illinois Watch Co., 7-9J, M#2-6, SW	65	95	195
Illinois Watch Co., 11J, M#1-2, KW	65	95	195
Illinois Watch Co., 11J, M#3, SW	50	75	150
Illinois Watch Co., 12-13J, M#1-2, KW	75	95	195
Illinois Watch Co., 15J, M#1-2, KW	75	95	195
Illinois Watch Co., 15J, KW, ADJ, NI	95	125	225
Illinois Watch Co., 15J, SW, ADJ, DMK, NI	95	125	250
Illinois Watch Co., 15J, transition	50	80	150
Illinois Watch Co., 15J, SW, **Silveroid**	40	70	150
Illinois Watch Co., 15J, SW, **9K, HC**	225	300	500
Illinois Watch Co., 16J, SW, ADJ, DMK, NI	50	80	150
Illinois Watch Co., 16J, SW, ADJ, DMK, NI, marked **ADJ**	95	150	325
Illinois Watch Co., 17J, SW, **Silveroid**	40	60	150
Illinois Watch Co., 17J, M#3, **5th Pinion**	80	125	295
Illinois Watch Co., 17J, SW, 2 tone mvt,	75	95	195

🕐 Pricing in this Guide are fair market price for **COMPLETE** watches which are reflected from the "**NAWCC**" National and regional shows.

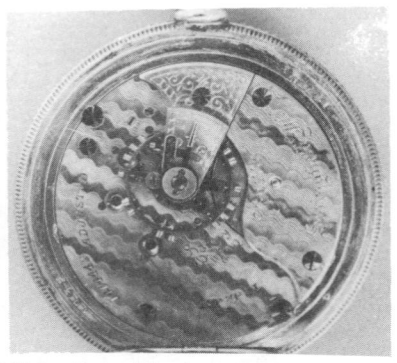

Ill. W. Co., 18 size, 17 jewels, adjusted, 2-tone movement, serial number 1,404,442.

Miller, 18 size, 17 jewels, 5th pinion model which changed hunting case to open face.

🕐 **Generic, nameless,** Personalized Jobber Watches or unmarked grades for watch movements are listed under the Company name or initials of the Company, etc. by size, jewel count and description.

Grade or Name — Description	Avg	Ex-Fn	Mint
Illinois Watch Co., 17J, SW, ADJ............................	$75	$95	$195
Illinois Watch Co., 17J, SW, **"EXTRA"**, Adj.4P .... ★	275	350	700
Illinois Watch Co., 17J, KW/SW, transition.................	75	95	195
Illinois Watch Co., 19J, ADJ. **J. Barrel**, OF	150	200	400
Illinois Watch Co., 21J, Adj.3P, OF.............................	195	250	450
Illinois Watch Co., 21J, ADJ5-6P, ...	295	350	550
Illinois Watch Co., 23J, ADJ6P, OF .... ★ ★ ★ ★	1,500	1,700	2,800
Illinois Watch Co., 24J, ADJ, ...	500	575	850
Inspector Special, 17J, LS, OF .... ★	295	400	700
Interior, 7J, KW & SW, OF......................................	60	80	125
Interstate Chronometer, 17J, HC, (sold by Sears) .... ★ ★ ★	400	450	700
Interstate Chronometer, 17J, OF .... ★ ★	295	400	600
Interstate Chronometer, 23J, Adj.5P, GJS, NI, OF......... ★ ★	900	1,000	1,500
Interstate Chronometer, 23J, Adj.5P, GJS, NI, HC .... ★ ★	1,000	1,200	1,800
Iowa W. Co., 7-11J, M#1-2, KW, ...	150	195	350
King of the Road, 16 &17J, NI, OF & HC, LS, ADJ .... ★	400	500	850
King Special, 17J, 2-tone, OF	150	195	450
King Philip Sp., 17J, (RR spur line)........................ ★ ★	295	400	700
Lafayette, 24J, GJS, Adj.6P, NI, SW, OF....................... ★	900	1,000	1,600
Lafayette, 24J, GJS, Adj.6P, NI, SW, HC .... ★ ★	1,300	1,600	2,400
Lakeshore, 17J, OF, LS, NI, SW	95	150	250
Landis W. Co., 15-17J	75	95	195
Liberty Bell, 17J, LS, NI, SW, OF	75	95	195
Liberty Bell, 17J, LS, NI, SW, HC	90	150	250
Lightning Express, 11-13J, KWKS .... ★	195	250	450
A. Lincoln, 21J, Adj.5P, NI, DR, GJS, HC	400	450	750
A. Lincoln, 21J, Adj.5P, NI, DR, GJS,OF	225	275	450
Lincoln Park, 15-17J, LS, OF..................................	75	95	195
Majestic Special, 17J, 2-tone, OF	125	150	275
Locomotive, 11J, M# 2 grade 4, Locomotive engraved on Mvt.	250	295	500
Maiden Lane, 16-17J, 5th Pinion	295	425	600
Manhattan, 11-13J, NI, KW, LS, HC or OF	95	175	295
Manhattan, 15-17J, NI, KW, LS,HC or OF	125	195	325
Mason, 7J, KW, KS, HC	95	175	295
Mason, 7J, KW, KS, HC, **1st run S# 101 to 200** .... ★ ★	450	550	850
Miller, 15J,**1st run S# 301 to 400**............................. ★ ★	400	500	800
Miller, 15J, M#1, HC, KW	95	125	250
Miller, 15J, M#1, HC, KW, ADJ	125	150	295
Miller, 15J, KW, OF	95	125	275
Miller, 17J, 5th Pinion, ADJ..................................	150	175	350
Monarch W. Co., 17J, NI, ADJ, SW	125	150	295

Paillard Non-Magnetic W. Co., 18 size, 24 jewels, gold jewel settings, serial number 1,397,812.

Pennsylvania Special, 18 size, 26 jewels, Adj6p, 2-tone movement, serial number 1,742,913.

Grade or Name — Description	Avg	Ex-Fn	Mint
Montgomery Ward, 15-17J, GJS, OF	$95	$150	$250
Montgomery Ward, 19J, GJS, OF	125	150	325
Montgomery Ward, 21J, OF	175	250	400
Montgomery Ward Timer, 21J, OF ★	200	250	450
Montgomery Ward, 24J, OF	900	1,000	1,500
Montgomery Ward, 24J, HC ★	1,100	1,300	1,800
Montgomery Ward, 24J, marked double roller, HC ★	1,100	1,300	1,800
Muscatine W. Co., 15J, LS, NI, HC	135	160	400
The National, 11J, SW, LS, OF	75	100	200
(Paillard Non-Magnetic W. Co. SEE Non-Magnetic W. Co.)			
Pennsylvania Special, 17J, GJS, ADJ ★★	850	1,000	1,500
Pennsylvania Special, 21J, DR, Adj.5P ★★	2,000	2,500	3,500
Pennsylvania Special, 24J, DR, GJS, ADJ ★★	3,000	3,500	4,500
Pennsylvania Special, 25J, DR, GJS, ADJ, NI ★★★	4,500	5,000	8,000
Pennsylvania Special, 26J, DR, GJS, ADJ, NI ★★★	5,500	6,500	9,000
Pierce Arrow, 17J, "automaker logo" ★	375	450	700
Plymouth W. Co., 15-17J, SW, (sold by Sears)	75	95	195
Potomac, 17J, ADJ, NI, OF	150	175	375
Potomac, 17J, ADJ, NI, HC ★	225	275	475
The President, 15J, NI, OF	95	150	355
The President, 17J, DMK, **14K gold case**	500	600	1,000
Rail Road Construction, 17J, OF	225	250	500
Rail Road Dispatcher Extra or Special, 15-17J, OF	250	275	550
Rail Road Dispatcher Extra, 15-17J, HC ★	250	275	550
Rail Road Employee's Special, 17J, NI, LS, HC ★	250	275	550
Rail Road Timer Extra, 17-21J, (Montgomery Ward), OF ★	225	275	500
Rail Road King, 15J, NI, ADJ, OF ★	250	275	500
Rail Road King, 15J, NI, ADJ, HC ★	295	350	550
Rail Road King, 16J, NI, ADJ, OF ★	275	325	550
Rail Road King, 16J, NI, ADJ, HC ★	325	375	575
Rail Road King, 17J, NI, ADJ, OF ★	295	350	550
Rail Road King, 17J, NI, ADJ, HC ★	350	400	575
Rail Road King, 19J, NI, ADJ, 2 tone, OF ★	350	400	575
The Railroader, 15J, OF, ADJ, NI ★	250	295	500
Railway , 11J, KW, KS, gilt ★	150	195	400
Railway Engineer, 15J ★	275	325	600
Railway Regulator, 11-15J, LS, (R.W.Sears Watch Co.) ★★	425	525	900
Remington W.Co. 17J, OF	195	225	450
Remington W.Co. 17J, HC	225	275	500
Remington Special, 21J, Adj.6P, OF	250	285	550

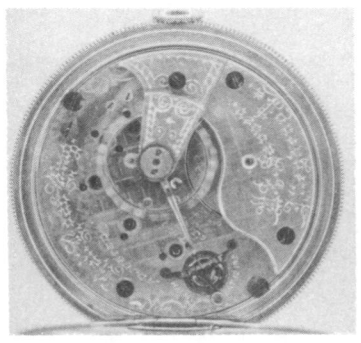

The President, 18 size, 17 jewels, Chalmer patented regulator, serial number 1,240,909.

Railroad King, 18 size, 17 jewels, Fifth Pinion Model, adjusted. Note Chalmer patented regulator, S# 1,160,836.

Grade or Name — Description	Avg	Ex-Fn	Mint
Standard W. Co., 15J, several models .... ★	$150	$200	$350
S. W. Co., 15J, M#1, KW, HC	110	150	300
R.W. Sears Watch Co. Chicago,"Defiance" model, HC........... ★ ★	600	800	1,400
Sears & Roebuck Special, 15-17J, GJS, NI, DMK, Adj	150	175	350
Senate, 17J, NI, DMK, Washington W. Co.	150	175	350
Southern R.R. Special, 21J, LS, ADJ, OF .... ★ ★	1,400	1,800	2,800
Southern R.R. Special, 21J, M#5, LS, Adj., HC .... ★ ★	1,600	2,000	2,900
Star Light, 17J, 5th pinion, Chalmers Reg. OF	150	200	400
Stewart Special, 11J	65	85	150
Stewart Special, 15J, Adj.	75	95	195
Stewart Special, 17J, Adj...	95	135	250
Stewart Special, 21J, Adj.	140	180	295
Stuart, 15J, M#1, KW, KS	300	425	850
Stuart, 15J, M#1, KW/SW, transition	250	375	650
Stuart, 15J, M#1, KW, KS, marked Adj. .... ★	300	400	750
Stuart, 15J, ADJ, KW, Abbotts Conversion, **18K, HC** .... ★	1,200	1,500	2,100
Stuart, 15J, M#1, KW, KS, Coin .... ★	500	600	1,000
Stuart, 15J, M#1, KW, KS, **1st run S# 1 to 10"** .... ★ ★ ★ ★	4,000	6,000	9,000
Stuart, 15J, M#1, KW, KS, **1st run S# 11 to 100"** .... ★ ★ ★	2,000	2,500	5,000
Stuart, 17J, M#3, 5th Pinion .... ★ ★	225	300	500
Stuart, 17J, M#3, 5th Pinion, Adj. .... ★ ★	250	325	575

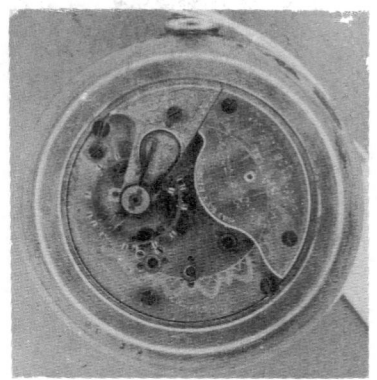

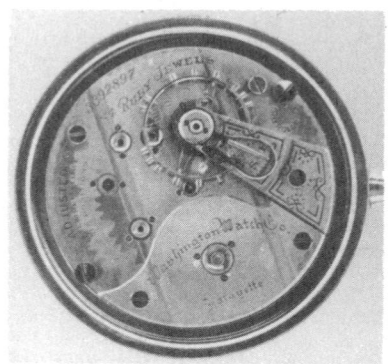

Sears & Roebuck Special, 18 size, 17 jewels, serial number 1,481,879.

Washington W. Co., Lafayette model, 18 size, 24 Ruby jewels, gold jewel settings, adjusted, serial # 3,392,897.

Grade or Name — Description	Avg	Ex-Fn	Mint
Transition Models, 17J, KW/SW, OF	$60	$95	$195
Train Dispatcher Special, 17J, (Montgomery Ward), Adj, OF ..... ★	275	325	600
Time King, 17J, OF, LS, NI	95	125	295
Time King, 21J, OF, LS,	150	225	450
Union Pacific Sp., 17J, OF ★★	450	500	1,000
Vault Time Lock for Mosler, 15J, 72 hr.	95	150	295
Ward's Special, 15J, NI, FULL, LS,	70	125	195
George Washington,11J, HC	150	225	400
Washington, 11j, also (U.S.A) sold by **Montgomery Ward,**	95	125	195
Washington, 17J, also (U.S.A) sold by **Montgomery Ward,**	125	175	295
⊙ **Washington W. Co.** (See Army & Navy, Liberty Bell, Lafayette, Senate)			
Wathiers Railway Watch, 15-17J, Adj., NI ★	450	575	1,000
N0. 5, 11J, KW KS, (**marked** No.5), HC	150	195	400
65, 15J, HC, LS, M#2	65	95	175
89, 17J, nickel, ADJ, OF	75	125	195
89, 21J, nickel, ADJ, HC	150	195	400
101, 11J, SW, KW, OF	65	90	175
101, 11J, SW, KW, Silveroid	60	80	175
101, 11J, SW, KW, HC	75	95	195
102, 13J, SW, KW, Silveroid	60	80	175
102, 13J, SW, KW, OF	75	95	195
102, 13J, SW, KW, HC	90	125	275
103, 15-16J, ADJ	80	125	250
104, 15J, M#2, HC ★★	295	400	700
104, 17J, M#3, early high grade for RR, Ca. 1885, OF ★★	350	425	775
105, 17J, M#3, early high grade for RR, Ca. 1885, OF ★★★	600	700	1,100
105, 15J, M#2, GJS, ADJ, KW, KS, HC ★★★	600	700	1,100
106, 15J, ADJ, KW, KS ★★	295	400	700
444, 17J, NI, ADJ, OF	75	95	195
445, 19J, GJS, 2-Tone, HC ★★	1,000	1,200	1,800
1908 Special, 21J, NI, Adj.5P,(**marked** 1908 special), OF	325	425	700

STUART, 17 jewels, Model #3, 5th Pinion, Transition Model.

First Model in 14K white or green gold filled Wadsworth case, showing Montgomery numerical dial.

⊕ A collector should expect to pay modestly higher prices at local shops.

⊕ Pricing in this Guide are fair market price for **COMPLETE** watches which are reflected from the "**NAWCC**" National and regional shows.

ILLINOIS
16 SIZE

Grade or Name — Description	Avg	Ex-Fx	Mint
Adams Street, 17J, 3/4, SW, NI, DMK	$195	$250	$550
Adams Street, 17J, 3/4, 2-tone, checkboard DMK, HC	250	350	700
Adams Street, 21J, 3F brg, NI, DMK ★	250	350	700
Ak-Sar-Ben (Nebraska backward), 17J, OF, GCW	150	195	350
Ariston, 11J, OF & HC	65	95	195
Ariston, 15J, OF & HC	65	95	195
Ariston, 17J, Adj, HC	125	195	400
Ariston, 17J, Adj, OF	95	175	350
Ariston, 19J, Adj.5P, OF	150	195	400
Ariston, 21J, GJS, Adj.6P, OF	195	295	600
Ariston, 21J, GJS, Adj.6P, HC	250	350	700
Ariston, 23J, GJS, Adj.6P, OF	500	600	950
Ariston, 23J, GJS, Adj.6P, HC ★★	700	800	1,100
Arlington Special, 17J, OF	100	125	275
Arlington Special, 17J, OF, Silveroid	85	125	250
Army & Navy, 19J, GJS, Adj.3P, NI, 1F brg, OF	150	195	400
Army & Navy, 19J, GJS, Adj.3P, NI, 1F brg, HC	195	275	500
Army & Navy, 21J, GJS, Adj.3P, 1F brg, OF	250	350	500
Army & Navy, 21J, GJS, Adj.3P, 1F brg, HC	350	450	600
B & M Special, 17J, BRG, Adj.4P (Boston & Main) ★	450	600	1,000
B & O Standard, 21J ★★	1,100	1,500	2,200
Benjamin Franklin, 17J, ADJ, DMK, OF	300	325	650
Benjamin Franklin, 17J, ADJ, DMK, HC ★	400	450	750
Benjamin Franklin, 21J, GJS, Adj.5P, DR, GT, OF ★	700	900	1,200
Benjamin Franklin, 21J, GJS, Adj.5P, DR, GT, HC ★★	800	1,000	1,300
Benjamin Franklin, 25J, GJS, Adj.6P, DR, GT, OF ★★★	3,000	3,500	5,000
Benjamin Franklin, 25J, GJS, Adj.6P, DR, GT, HC ★★★	4,000	5,000	7,000

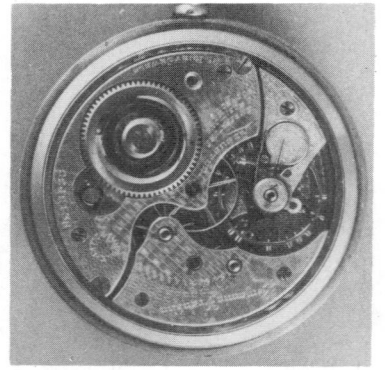

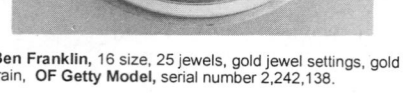

Ben Franklin, 16 size, 25 jewels, gold jewel settings, gold train, **OF Getty Model**, serial number 2,242,138.

Bunn Special, Model 163, 16 size, 23J., gold jewel settings, gold train, 60 hour movement, serial # 5,421,504.

Note: Bunn Special original cases were marked Bunn Special except for Elinvars (Hamilton cased). also GRADES 161 & 163 were made by Hamilton W. Co.

🕐 Generic, nameless or **unmarked grades** for watch movements are listed under the Company name or initials of the Company, etc. by size, jewel count and description.

🕐 Watches listed in this book are priced at the **collectable fair market value** at the Trade Show level, as complete watches having an original 14k gold filled case, KEY WIND with silver, an original white enamel single sunk dial, and with the entire original movement in good working order with no repairs needed, unless otherwise noted.

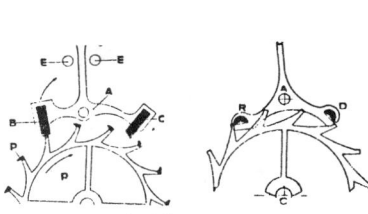

Left: Standard style escapement. **Right:** DeLong style escapement.

Illinois Watch Co., 16 size, 25J., 3 fingered bridge Getty Model, gold train, note click near balance cock = HC model, serial number S731,870.

Grade or Name — Description	Avg	Ex-Fn	Mint
Bunn, 17J, LS, OF, NI, 3/4, GJS, Adj.5P	$150	$195	$400
Bunn, 17J, LS, NI, 3/4, Adj.5P, HC ★ ★ ★	650	800	1,400
Bunn, 19J, LS, OF, NI, 3/4, GJS, Adj.5P	195	250	400
Bunn, 19J, LS, NI, 3/4, Adj.5P, HC ★ ★ ★	800	1,000	1,500
Bunn, 19J, LS, OF, NI, 3/4, GJS, Adj.5P, 60 hour	400	500	775
Bunn, 19J, **marked Jeweled Barrel**	295	350	500
Bunn Special, 19J, LS, OF, NI, 3/4, Adj.6P, GT	195	225	400
Bunn Special, 19J, LS, OF, NI, 3/4, Adj.5P, GT, 60 hour	400	500	900
Bunn Special, 21J, NI, GJS, Adj.6P, GT, HC ★ ★	575	675	1,000
Bunn Special, 21J, LS, OF, NI, 3/4, GJS, Adj.6P, GT	250	295	500
Bunn Special, 21J, LS, GJS, Adj.6P, GT, **gold plated Mvt.** ★ ★	500	600	1,000
Bunn Special, 21J, LS,OF, NI, 3/4, GJS, Adj.6P, GT, 60 hour	295	375	700
Bunn Special, 21J, LS, OF, NI, 3/4, GJS, Adj.6P, GT, 60 hr. marked Elinvar	600	800	1,200
Bunn Special, 21J, 60 hr., **14K**, OF, Bunn Special case ★	1,000	1,400	2,000
Bunn Special, 23J, LS, OF, NI, 3/4, GJS, Adj.6P, GT	500	600	1,000
Bunn Special, 23J, LS, OF, NI, 3/4, GJS, Adj.6P, GT, 60 hour	600	750	1,500
Bunn Special, 23J, LS, OF, NI, 3/4, GJS, Adj.6P, GT, with **23J, 60-hour on dial**	1,200	1,400	2,200
Bunn Special, 23J, LS, NI, GJS, GT, Adj.6P, HC ★ ★ ★ ★	2,500	3,000	5,000
161 Bunn Special, 21J, 3/4, Adj.6P, 60 hour	650	800	1,600
161 Bunn Special, 21J, 3/4, Adj.6P, 60 hour on dial & movement in Illinois original factory box with Bunn papers ★ ★ ★ ★	1,800	2,200	3,600
161 Elinvar Bunn Special, 21J, 3/4, Adj.6P, 60 hour (**Elinvar** signed at bottom of bridge)	900	1,100	1,800
161A Bunn Special, 21J, 3/4, Adj.6P, 60 hour (**Elinvar** signed under balance or on top plate)	900	1,100	1,800
161B, Bunn Special, 21J, 60 hour, pressed jewels ★ ★ ★ ★	4,500	6,000	10,000
163 Bunn Special, 23J, GJS, Adj.6P, 3/4, 60 hour	1,600	2,000	2,500
163 Elinvar Bunn Special, 23J, GJS, Adj.6P, 60 hour (**Elinvar** signed at bottom of cock, uncut balance) ★	1,600	2,000	2,500
163A Elinvar Bunn Special, 23J, GJS, Adj.6P, 3/4, 60 hour (**Elinvar** signed under balance) ◁	1,700	2,200	2,800
163A Elinvar Bunn Special, 23J, Adj.6P, 3/4, 60 hour (**Elinvar** signed on train bridge) ◁	1,800	2,400	3,000

🕑 Some grades are not included. Their values can be determined by comparing with **similar** age, size, metal content, style, models and grades listed.

Grade or Name — Description	Avg	Ex-Fn	Mint
Burlington W. Co., 11-15J, OF	$95	$150	$295
Burlington W. Co., 11- 15J, HC	125	175	350
Burlington W. Co., 17J, OF	95	150	295
Burlington W. Co., 17J, HC	125	175	350
Burlington W. Co., 19J, 3/4, NI, Adj.3P	95	150	295
Burlington W. Co., 19J, BRG, NI, Adj.3P	95	150	295
Burlington W. Co., 19J, 3/4, HC	95	150	295
Burlington W. Co., 19J, 3F brg, NI, Adj.3P	90	125	250
Burlington W. Co., 21J, 3/4, NI, Adj.3P	125	175	350
Burlington W. Co., 21J, Adj.6P, GJS	150	195	400
Burlington, Bull Dog- **on dial**, 21J, SW, LS, GJS, GT	275	295	650
C & O Special, 21J, 3/4, NI, ADJ ★★	900	1,100	1,600
Capitol, 19J, OF, 3/4, NI, Adj.3P ★	95	150	295
Central, 17J, SW, PS, OF	75	100	200
Commodore Perry Special, 21J, Adj.6P, GT, OF ★	250	295	650
Craftsman, 17J, OF	75	95	195
D. & R. G. Special, 21J, GJS, GT, Adj.5P,			
(Denver & Rio Grand RR), OF ★★★★	3,000	3,500	5,000
DeLong Escapement, 21J, GJS, (Bunn Sp. or A. Lincoln)			
Adj.6P, **14K** OF ★★★★	3,000	3,500	5,500
Dependon, 17J, (J.V.Farwell)	150	195	400
Dependon, 21J, (J.V.Farwell)	195	250	500
Diamond, Ruby, Sapphire, 21J, GJS, GT, Adj.6P, BRG, OF ★★★	1,600	2,000	3,000
Diamond, Ruby, Sapphire, 23J, GJS, GT, Adj.6P, BRG, OF ★★★	3,000	3,500	5,000
Diamond, Ruby, Sapphire, 23J, GJS, GT, Adj.6P, grade # 310,			
tall Arabic numbers on dial, BRG, DR, **HC** ★★★★	4,000	5,000	9,000
Diamond, Ruby, Sapphire, 23J, GJS, GT, Adj.6P, BRG, OF			
also marked **Greenwich** (Washington W.Co.) ★★★	3,000	3,500	5,500
Diamond, Ruby, Sapphire, 23J, GJS, GT, Adj.6P,			
3/4 plate, OF ★★★	1,800	2,200	3,200
Dispatcher, 19J, Adj.3P	150	225	400
Fifth Ave.,19J, Adj.3P,GT,OF	95	150	295
Fifth Ave., 21J, Adj.3P,GT,OF	125	175	350
Franklin Street, 15J, 3/4, NI, ADJ	95	150	295
Grant, 17J, ADJ, LS, **Getty Model,** OF	150	200	400
Getty Model # 4 &5, 17J	95	150	295
Getty Model # 4 &5, 21J	195	250	450

Interstate Chronometer, 16 size, 23 jewels, one-fingered bridge, **OF Getty Model**, serial number 2,327,614.

A. Lincoln, 16 size, 21 jewels, gold jewel settings, gold train, Adj5p, **OF Getty Model,** serial number 2,237,406.

🕐 Pricing in this Guide are fair market price for COMPLETE watches which are reflected from the **"NAWCC"** National and regional shows.

Grade or Name — Description	Avg	Ex-Fn	Mint
Great Northern Special, 17J, BRG, ADJ	$195	$250	$500
Great Northern Special, 19J, BRG, ADJ	195	250	500
Great Northern Special, 21J, BRG, ADJ, Adj.3P	250	350	600
Illinois Central, 17-21J, 2-Tone, Adj.3P, GT..................................	225	300	550

🕐 GENERIC, NAMELESS or **UNMARKED GRADES** FOR WATCH MOVEMENTS ARE LISTED UNDER THE COM-
PANY NAME OR INITIALS OF THE COMPANY, ETC. BY SIZE, JEWEL COUNT AND DESCRIPTION.

Grade or Name — Description	Avg	Ex-Fn	Mint
Illinois Watch Co., 7-9J, M#1-2-3	$40	$50	$150
Illinois Watch Co., 11J., OF...	40	60	150
Illinois Watch Co., 13J, 3/4, OF...	40	60	150
Illinois Watch Co., 11-13J, M#7, 3/4, OF.....................................	40	60	150
Illinois Watch Co., 11-13, M#6, 3/4, HC	75	100	200
Illinois Watch Co., 15J, M#2, OF	50	80	150
Illinois Watch Co., 15J, M#1, HC	90	125	250
Illinois Watch Co., 15J, M#3, OF	50	80	150
Illinois Watch Co., 15J, 3/4, ADJ...	50	80	150
Illinois Watch Co., 15J, 3F brg, GJS..	50	80	150
Illinois Watch Co., 16-17J, **14K, HC**	375	400	800
Illinois Watch Co., 16-17J, Adj.3P, OF.......................................	75	95	195
Illinois Watch Co., 16-17J, M#2-3, SW, OF	75	95	195
Illinois Watch Co., 17J, M#4-6, SW, HC	90	125	250
Illinois Watch Co., 17J, M#7, OF	75	95	195
Illinois Watch Co., 17J, M#5, 3/4, ADJ, HC	75	95	195
Illinois Watch Co., 17J, M#4, 3F brg, GJS, Adj.5P, HC	150	195	400
Illinois Watch Co., 19J, 3/4, GJS, Adj.5P, **jeweled barrel**............	150	195	400
Illinois Watch Co., 19J, 3/4, BRG, Adj.3-4P................................	95	125	225
Illinois Watch Co., 21J, Adj.3P, OF...	195	225	350
Illinois Watch Co., 21J, ADJ, OF	195	225	400
Illinois Watch Co., 21J, GJS, HC	225	250	450
Illinois Watch Co., 21J, 3/4, GJS, Adj.5P....................................	195	225	400
Illinois Watch Co., 21J, 3F brg, GJS, Adj.4P	195	225	400
Illinois Watch Co., 21J, 3F brg, GJS, Adj.5P	225	275	425
Illinois Watch Co., 23J, GJS, Adj.5P, OF................★★	400	500	850
Illinois Watch Co., 23J, GJS, Adj.5P, HC ....★★	500	600	900
Illinois Watch Co., 25J, 4th model,3F brg, GJS, Adj.5P, HC ★★★	3,500	4,000	6,000
Imperial Sp., 17J, SW, LS, Adj.4P, OF	125	150	295
Interstate Chronometer, 17J, GCW, Adj.3P, HC, (sold by Sears) ..	295	325	700
Interstate Chronometer, 17J, GCW, Adj.3P, OF	250	295	600
Interstate Chronometer, 23J, 1F brg, ADJ, OF ....★	800	1,000	1,500
Interstate Chronometer, 23J, 1F brg, ADJ, HC.....................★★	1,200	1,400	2,000
Lafayette, 23J, Washington W.Co., GJS, Adj.5P, GT, OF ... ★★★	1,000	1,200	1,900
Lafayette, 23J, Washington W.Co., GJS, Adj.5P, GT, HC ... ★★★	1,400	1,800	2,600
Lakeshore, 17J, OF..	75	95	195
Lakeshore, 17J, HC..	125	175	350
Landis W. Co., 15-17J	75	95	195
Liberty Bell, 15-17J, OF...	85	125	195
Liberty Bell, 17J, HC...★	295	350	650
A. Lincoln, 21J,3/4, GJS, Adj.5P, OF	175	225	475
A. Lincoln, 21J,3/4, GJS, Adj.5P, HC	325	375	775
The Lincoln, 15J, 3F brg, ...	125	150	295
Logan, 15J, OF..	60	80	175
Marvel, 19J, GT, GJS, Adj.3P, Of..	75	95	195
Marine Special, 21J, 3/4, Adj.3P..	150	175	350
Monarch W. Co., 17J, NI, ADJ, SW..	125	150	295
Monroe, 17J, NI,3/4, OF (Washington W. Co.)	85	125	195
Monroe, 15J, 3/4, OF (Washington W. Co.)...................................	75	95	175
Montgomery Ward, 17J, LS, Thin Model , OF	95	150	275
Montgomery Ward, 21J, "Extra RR Timer", 2 tone, G# 171 .... ★★	1,000	1,200	1,600
Our No. 1, 15J, HC, Adj., OF	95	150	295
Overland Special, 19J, Adj., OF..	95	150	295

🕐 Pricing in this Guide are fair market price for **COMPLETE** watches which are reflected from
the "**NAWCC**" National and regional shows.

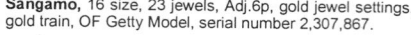

Sangamo, 16 size, 23 jewels, Adj.6p, gold jewel settings, gold train, OF Getty Model, serial number 2,307,867.

Sangamo Special, 17S, 23J., model 13, marked 60 hr. movement, Adj.6p, gold jewel settings, gold train, Serial # 4,758,199, Ca. 1926. NOTE: no red border on bal. cock.

Grade or Name Description		Avg	Ex-Fn	Mint
Pennsylvania Special, 17J, Adj.3P, HC .... ★		$400	$500	$900
Pennsylvania Special, 17J, Adj., 2 tone, G# 176, HC .... ★		800	900	1,100
Pennsylvania Special, 19J, OF .... ★		500	650	1,000
Pennsylvania Special, 21J, Getty model, 2-tone, Adj., OF .... ★		1,000	1,200	1,600
Pennsylvania Special, 21J, 2-tone, (Finely Adj.), HC .... ★ ★ ★		2,000	2,400	3,000
Pennsylvania Special, 23J, 3/4, GJS, Adj.5P .... ★		1,400	1,800	2,600
Plymouth W. Co., 15-17J, OF (Add $50 for HC), (sold by Sears) ..		95	150	295
Precise, 21J, OF, LS, Adj.3P		95	150	275
Quincy Street, 17J, 3/4, NI, DMK, ADJ		90	125	250
Railroad Dispatcher, 11-17J, DMK, 3/4		175	195	400
Railroad Dispatcher Extra or Special, 15-17J, DMK, 3/4 .... ★		225	275	500
Railroad Employee's, 17J, ...		175	225	400
Railroad King, 16-17J, M#2 or 5-Getty model, NI, PS, OF		275	295	500
Railroad Official, 23J, 3 Finger bridge .... ★ ★ ★ ★ ★		2,000	2,400	3,000
Railway King, 17J, OF		175	195	400
Remington W.Co. 11-15J, OF		95	125	195
Remington W.Co. 17J, OF		125	175	275
Remington W.Co. 17J, HC		195	250	350
Rockland, 17-19J, GJS, GT, 7th model, grade 305, OF		75	95	195
Sangamo, 19J, model # 4, GJS, GT, ADJ., HC .... ★ ★ ★		4,000	5,000	8,000
Sangamo, 21J, GJS, Adj.6P, HC		250	300	600
Sangamo, 21J, GJS, Adj., OF		195	250	500
Sangamo, 21J, 3/4, GJS, DR, Adj.6P, OF		195	250	450
Sangamo, 21J, GJS, Adj.6P, EXTRA or SPECIAL, (Getty), HC ★		525	625	1,000
Sangamo, 21J, GJS, Adj.6P, EXTRA or SPECIAL, (Getty), OF . ★		475	575	900
Sangamo, 21J, GJS, Adj., marked SPECIAL 2-tone Mvt., Adj.6P, (straight ribbon - not wavy ribbon pattern), (Getty), OF ... ★		475	575	900
Sangamo, 23J, GJS, Adj., marked SPECIAL 2-tone Mvt., Adj.6P, (straight ribbon - not wavy ribbon pattern), (Getty), OF ... ★		625	725	1,200
Sangamo, 23J,3/4, GJS, DR, Adj.6P, OF.........................		350	450	800
Sangamo, 23J, 3/4, GJS, DR, Adj.6P, HC		400	500	900
Sangamo, 25J, M#5, 3/4, GJS, DR, Adj.6P .... ★ ★ ★ ★		4,000	5,000	9,000
Sangamo, 26J, M#5, 3/4, GJS, DR, Adj.6P .... ★ ★ ★ ★		5,000	6,000	8,000
Sangamo Special, 19J, BRG, GJS, GT, Adj.6P, OF................		350	400	700
Sangamo Special, 19J, BRG, GJS, GT, Adj.6P, HC .... ★ ★ ★		1,400	1,800	2,600
Sangamo, Extra, 21J, Adj.6P, gold train, Of.............. ★ ★		425	475	900
Sangamo Special, 21J, M#7, ...		350	400	700
Sangamo Special, 21J, M#8, BRG, HC .... ★ ★ ★		1,500	2,000	2,800
Sangamo Special, 21J, M#9, BRG, GJS, GT, Adj.6P, OF		400	500	800
Sangamo Special, 21J, BRG, GJS, GT, Diamond end cap		400	500	800

Grade or Name — Description	Avg	Ex-Fn	Mint
Sangamo Special, 23J, M#9-10, BRG, GJS, GT, Adj.6P,			
Sangamo Special **HINGED** case	$800	$1,000	$1,800
Sangamo Special, 23J, BRG, GJS, GT, Adj.6P, Diamond			
end stone, **screw back,** Sangamo Special case	750	850	1,300
Sangamo Special, 23J, M#8, GJS, GT, Adj.6P, **HC** .... ★★★	1,500	1,800	3,200
Sangamo Special, 23J, BRG, GJS, GT, Adj.6P, **not marked**			
60 hour, rigid bow, Sangamo Special case	900	1,100	1,600
Sangamo Special, 23J, BRG, GJS, GT, Adj.6P,			
marked 60 hour, Sangamo Special case .... ★★★	1,600	2,200	3,300
Sangamo Special, 23J, BRG, GJS, GT, Adj.6P, 60 hour,			
rigid bow, Sangamo Special case **14K gold case**................ ★	1,800	2,400	3,500
Santa Fe Special, 17J, BRG, Adj., OF-HC	225	295	600
Santa Fe Special, 21J, 3/4, Adj., OF	400	500	700
Santa Fe Special, 21J, 3/4, Adj., **HC**	450	550	800
Sears, Roebuck & Co. Special, 15-17J, ADJ......................	75	95	195
Senate, 17J, (Washington W. Co.), NI, 3/4, ADJ	75	95	195
Standard, 15J..	75	95	195
Sterling, 17J, SW, PS, Adj.3P, OF...............................	75	95	195
Sterling, 19-21J, SW, PS, Adj.3P, OF...............................	125	150	250
Stewart, 17J..	75	95	175
Stewart Special, 21J, Adj., ...	125	150	250
Stewart Special, 19J, Adj.3P	75	95	195
Stewart Special, 15-17J, ...	60	70	150
The General, 15J, OF...	75	95	195
Time King, 17J, OF	60	80	150
Time King, 19J, Adj.3P, OF..	75	95	195
Time King, 21J, Adj, OF	125	150	295
Trainmen's Special, 17J, HC....................................★	150	195	450
Union Pacific,17J, Adj.,DR, 2-tone, DMK, OF.......................★★	500	600	1,000
Victor, 21J, 3/4, Adj.	150	175	350

   ☉ **Washington W. Co.** (See Army & Navy, Liberty Bell, Lafayette, Senate)

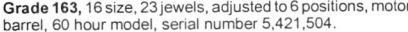

Grade 163, 16 size, 23 jewels, adjusted to 6 positions, motor barrel, 60 hour model, serial number 5,421,504.

LAFAYETTE, 23J, 16 size, WASHINGTON W.CO., GJS, Adj.5P, GT, HC. (This is Model # 6 with extra cut out.)

161 through 163A —See Bunn Special

Grade or Name — Description	Avg	Ex-Fn	Mint
167, 17J, marked..	$100	$125	$225
169, 19J, Adj.3P, OF	75	100	200
174, 17J, LS, GJS, Adj., OF...	60	80	175
174, 211, LS, GJS, Adj., OF..	165	185	300
174, 23J, LS, GJS, Adj., OF, marked .... ★★	500	600	900
175, 17J, RR grade & a (RR inspectors name on dial &mvt.) .. ★★	500	600	1,000
176, 17J, Getty model, LS, Adj.4P, 2-tone, HC ....★	125	175	300
177, 19J, SW, LS, 60 hour, Adj.5P, OF...............................★	300	400	700

Grade or Name — Description	Avg	Ex-Fn	Mint
179, 21J, 3/4, GJS, GT, Adj.6P, Getty model, **marked** Ruby Jewels			
Getty model, HC or OF .... ★ ★	$300	$400	$700
181, 21J., ADJ, GJS, marked 21 ruby jewels .... ★ ★ ★ ★	600	700	1,100
184, 17-19J, 3F brg, LS, OF	90	120	200
184, 23J, 3F brg, LS, OF	500	600	1,000
186, 23J, 3F brg, LS, OF	500	600	1,000
187, 17J, 3F brg, Adj.5P, GJS, GT, **marked** 187, HC	250	300	600
189, 21J, 3F brg, Adj.6P, GJS, DR, GT, **marked** Ruby Jewels & **6 pos.**,			
Getty model, HC or OF .... ★	300	400	700
333, 15J, HC	85	125	225
555, 17J, 3/4, ...	100	150	350
777, 17J, 3/4, ADJ .... ★	150	250	450
805, 17J, BRG, GJS, GT, DR, OF	75	95	195
809, 23J, Adj.6P, GT, **marked 809** .... ★ ★ ★	500	600	1,000
900, 19J, LS, Adj.3P	125	150	295

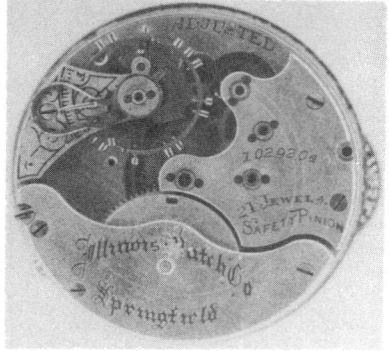

Grade **189**, 21J, 3Finger bridge, Adj.6P, GJS, DR, GT, marked "Ruby Jewels" & **6 pos.**, Getty model, Ca. 1903.

Illinois Watch Co., 14 size, 21J., adjusted, nickel movement, gold jewel settings, serial number 1,029,204.

ILLINOIS 14 SIZE

Grade or Name — Description	Avg	Ex-Fn	Mint
Illinois Watch Co., 7J, M#1, **GRADE 120, KW,** OF .... ★	$90	$125	$250
Illinois Watch Co., 7J, M#1-2-3, SW, OF	45	60	125
Illinois Watch Co., 11J, M#1-2-3, SW, OF	45	60	125
Illinois Watch Co., 15J, M#1-2-3, SW, OF	50	65	125
Illinois Watch Co., 16J, M#1-2-3, SW, OF	70	95	150
Illinois Watch Co., 21J, M#1-2-3, SW, OF .... ★	125	150	295
Illinois Watch Co., 22J, ... ★	150	195	400

NOTE: Add $35 for above watches in hunting case.

ILLINOIS

12 SIZE and 13 SIZE

Grade or Name — Description	Avg	Ex-Fn	Mint
Accurate, 21J, GJS, OF	$75	$95	$195
Aristocrat, 17J, OF..	55	85	150
Aristocrat, 19J, OF..	60	70	175
Ariston, 11-17J, OF	60	70	175
Ariston, 17J, Adj.3P, BRG, OF	75	95	200
Ariston, 19J, OF...	75	95	250
Ariston, 21J, Adj.5P, OF	95	125	350
Ariston, 21J, Adj.5P, HC .... ★ ★	225	300	600
Ariston, 23J, Adj.5P, OF.. ★	225	275	450
Ariston, 23J, Adj.5P, HC .... ★ ★	250	300	550
Ariston, 23J, Adj.6P, OF **18K** .... ★ ★ ★	400	500	900

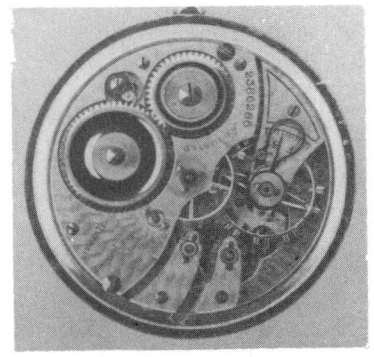

Ben Franklin, 12 size, 17J., grade 273, open face, signed on movement Benjamin Franklin USA, S # 2,386,286.

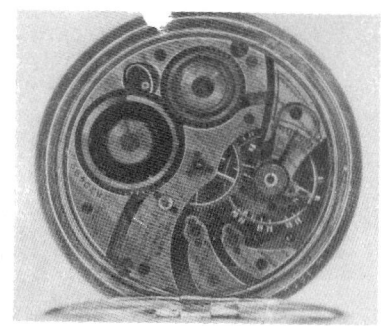

Maiden America, 12 size, 17J, serial number 2,820,499.

Grade or Name — Description	Avg	Ex-Fn	Mint
Aluminum Watch, 17J, model #3, **movement plates made of aluminum**			
G#525, S# 3,869,251 to S# 3,869,300 .... ★★★★	$1,900	$2,600	$3,600
Autocrat, 17J, Adj.3P, 3/4	60	80	150
Autocrat, 19J, Adj.3P, 3/4	65	85	175
Banker, 17J, Adj.3P, OF	60	80	150
Banker, 21J, Adj.3P, OF	75	95	195
Benjamin Franklin, 17J, OF	150	195	450
Benjamin Franklin, 21J, OF	195	250	550
Bunn Special, 21J, Adj 3P, (by Hamilton), OF .... ★★	400	450	800
Burlington Special, 19J, GT, OF..	75	95	195
Burlington Special, 19J, GT, HC	95	150	250
Burlington W. Co., 21J, GT, OF	75	95	195
Burlington W. Co., 21J, GT, HC	100	150	250
Central, 17J, OF, 2-Tone	50	80	125
Commodore Perry Special, 17J., adj.3P..★	75	95	195
Criterion, 21J, OF	75	95	195
Dependon, 17, (J.V.Farwell), HC,...	70	90	195
Elite, 19J, OF	75	95	195
Garland, 17J, Adj.,GT, OF	60	80	150
Gold Metal, 17J, OF	40	60	95

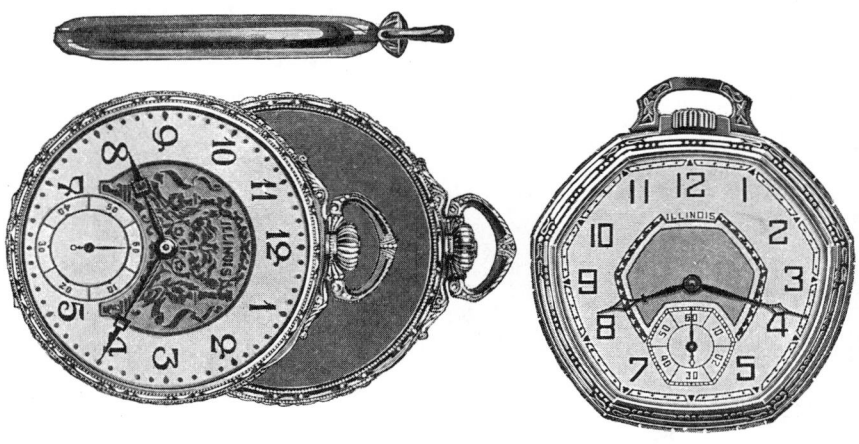

Example of Illinois Thin Model, 12 size, 17 jewels, adjusted to 3 positions.

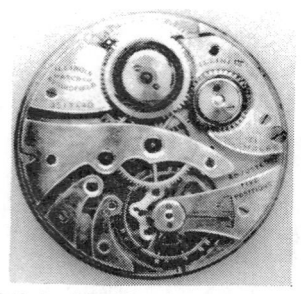

Illini, 12-13 size, 21 jewels, bridge model, serial number 3,650,129. Note five tooth pinion click & jeweled barrel.

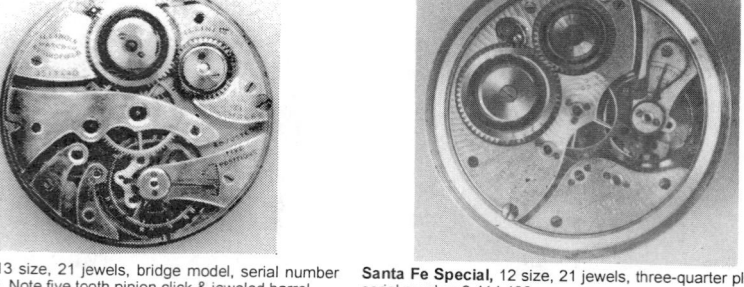

Santa Fe Special, 12 size, 21 jewels, three-quarter plate, serial number 3,414,422.

NOTE: The "Illini" 5 tooth click movement is a 13 size but advertised as 12 size.

Grade or Name — Description	Avg	Ex-Fn	Mint
Illini, 13 Size, 21J, Adj.5P, jeweled barrel, **5 tooth click**, OF, **14K** .... ★ ★	$250	$295	$550
Illini **Extra**, 13 S., 21J, Adj.5P, jeweled barrel, **5 tooth click**, OF, **14K** .... ★ ★ ★	350	450	600
Illini, 12 Size, 23J, Adj.6P, BRG, OF .... ★ ★ ★	125	175	295
Illini, 12 Size, 23J, Adj.6P, BRG, OF **14K** .... ★ ★ ★	250	295	550
Illinois Watch Co., 7-11J	35	50	95
Illinois Watch Co., 15J	35	50	95
Illinois Watch Co., 16-17J, OF, **14K**	195	250	450
Illinois Watch Co., 16-17J,OF, GF	60	75	150
Illinois Watch Co., 17J, GF, HC	80	95	195
Illinois Watch Co., 19J	80	95	195
Illinois Watch Co., 21J, OF	80	95	195
Illinois Watch Co., 21J, marked (21 SPECIAL), OF	90	125	250
Illinois Watch Co., 21J, HC	95	125	250
Illinois Watch Co., 23J, OF	150	175	295
Illinois Watch Co., 19J, EXTRA THIN MODEL, **14K**, OF ..... ★ ★	200	225	450
Illinois Watch Co., 21J, EXTRA THIN MODEL, **14K**, OF ..... ★ ★	225	250	500
Illinois Watch Co., 21J, **Marked EXTRA**, extra thin model, **14K**, OF .... ★ ★ ★	250	295	550
Interstate Chronometer, 17J, OF, (sold by Sears)............... ★ ★ ★	95	125	250
Interstate Chronometer, 21J, GJS, OF .... ★ ★ ★	175	195	350
Interstate Chronometer, 21J, GJS, HC .... ★ ★ ★	225	250	450
Governor, 17J, OF	60	75	150
A. Lincoln, 19J, Adj.5P, GJS, DR, OF	90	125	250
A. Lincoln, 21J, Adj.5P, DR, GJS, OF	90	125	250
A. Lincoln, 21J, Adj.5P, DR, GJS, HC .... ★	125	150	350
Maiden America, 17J, ADJ	60	75	125
Marquis Autocrat, 17J, OF	60	75	125
Master, 21J, GT, GJS, OF	70	90	175
Masterpiece, 19J, Adj.3P, OF.....................................	70	90	175
A. Norton, 21J, OF	95	125	250
Plymouth Watch Co., 15-17J, HC, (sold by Sears)	75	95	150
Railroad Dispatch , 11-15J, ...	50	60	150
Railroad Dispatch , 17-19J, SW, GT...........................	80	95	175
Rockland, 17J, ...	45	65	125
Roosevelt, 19J, Adj.3P, OF	250	295	550
Santa Fe Special, 21J	150	195	400
Secometer, 19J., G# 407, OF **14K** .... ★ ★	200	225	450
Sterling, 17J, OF	40	50	95
Sterling, 19-21J, OF..	60	85	175
Stewart Special, 17J, SW, Adj.3P	40	50	95
Stewart Special, 19J, SW, OF, GT.............................	50	60	125

Grade or Name — Description	Avg	Ex-Fn	Mint
Time King, 19J, SW, Adj.3P	$55	$75	$150
Time King, 21J, SW, Adj.3P	60	80	175
Transit, 19J, OF, PS	55	75	150
Vim, 17J, ADJ, BRG, GJS, DR, OF	35	50	95
Washington W. Co., **Army & Navy**, 19J ★★	90	125	250
Washington W. Co., **Monroe**, 11J, sold by Montgomery Ward	75	95	195
Washington W. Co., **Senate**, 17J, M#2, PS, ★★	60	80	175
121, 21J, Adj.3P	65	95	195
127, 17J, ADJ, (by Hamilton)	35	50	95
129, 19J, Adj.3P	45	75	150
219, 11J, M#1 ★	30	40	85
299, 21J, Adj.5P, OF ★	75	95	175
299, 23J, Adj.5P, HC ★★★	275	400	600
299, 23J, Adj.6P, HC ★★★★	300	450	700
403, 15J, BRG	35	40	90
405, 17J, BRG, ADJ, OF	40	50	125
409, 21J, BRG, Adj.5P, GJS, OF ★	225	295	500
409, 21J, BRG, Adj.5P, GJS, HC ★★	250	350	600
410, 23J, BRG, GJS, Adj.6P, DR, OF ★	175	225	400
410, 23J, BRG, GJS, Adj.6P, DR, HC ★	195	250	450
509, 21J, BRG, Adj.5P, GJS, (spread to 14 size)	65	100	195
510, 23J, BRG, GJS, Adj.6P, DR, (spread to14 size) ★★	90	125	250

ILLINOIS 8 SIZE

Grade or Name — Description	Avg	Ex-Fn	Mint
Arlington, 7J, ★	$150	$175	$350
Rose LeLand, 13J, ★★	225	275	500
Stanley, 7J, ★★	195	250	450
Mary Stuart, 15J, ★★	225	275	500
Sunnyside, 11J, ★	40	60	125
151-152-155, 7-11J, 3/4	30	40	85
Illinois W. Co. , 11-15J, (nameless unmarked grades)	40	70	125
Illinois W. Co. , 16-17J, (nameless unmarked grades)	40	70	125

Illinois Watch Co., 8 size, 7 jewels

Grade **144,** 6 size, 15 jewels, serial number 5,902,290.

ILLINOIS   6 SIZE

Grade or Name — Description	Avg	Ex-Fn	Mint
Illinois W. Co., 7J, LS, HC, **14K**	$175	$250	$400
Illinois W. Co., 7J, HC	35	45	125
Illinois W. Co., 7J, OF, Coin	30	40	95
Illinois W. Co., 11-12-13J, OF, HC	35	45	125
Illinois W. Co., 15J, OF, HC, **14K**	175	275	450
Illinois W. Co., 17J, OF, HC	35	50	125
Illinois W. Co., 19J, OF, HC	35	50	150
Plymouth Watch Co., 17J, OF, HC, (sold by Sears)	35	50	150
Sears & Roebuck Special, 15J, HC	35	50	95
Washington W. Co., 15J, Liberty Bell, HC	75	100	225
Washington W. Co., 11J, Martha Washington, HC	95	150	350

ILLINOIS
4 SIZE

Grade or Name — Description	Avg	Ex-Fn	Mint
Illinois W. Co., 7J, LS, HC	$40	$60	$125
Illinois W. Co., 11J, LS, HC	50	75	150
Illinois W. Co., 15-16J, LS, HC	50	75	150

ILLINOIS
0 SIZE

Grade or Name — Description	Avg	Ex-Fn	Mint
Accuratus, 17J, OF	$60	$70	$175
Ariste, 11-15-17J, OF & HC	95	135	225
Burlington Special, 15-17J, 3/4, OF	95	125	225
Illinois W. Co., 7 to 17J, LS, HC, **14K**	195	250	400
201, 11J, BRG, NI	40	50	125
203, 15J, BRG, NI	50	60	135
204, 17J, BRG, NI	55	65	150
Interstate Chronometer, 15J, HC, SW	95	150	350
Interstate Chronometer, 17J, HC, SW	95	150	350
Lady Franklin, 15-17J, HC	65	95	195
Plymouth Watch Co., 15-17J, HC, (sold by Sears)	75	95	125
Santa Fe Special, 15-17J ★	150	195	350
Washington W. Co., Liberty Bell, 15J, ADJ	60	80	175
Washington W. Co., Mt. Vernon, 17J, ADJ	70	95	225

Washington W. Co., Mt. Vernon, 0 size, 17J, hunting case.

Grade 203, 0 size, 15 jewels, originally sold for $10.40

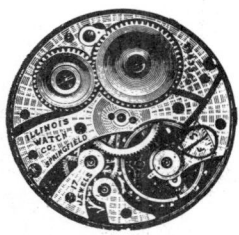

Grade 204, 0 size, 17 jewels, originally sold for $12.83.

ILLINOIS
CAPRICE

Grade or Name — Description	Avg	Ex-Fn	Mint
Caprice, 17J, handbag, pocket or desk watch, snake or ostrich	$95	$150	$350

Ca. 1929 AD

The CAPRICE
Just the watch for the handbag, pocket or desk; for sports wear or dress. It's an entirely practical timekeeper, too. In genuine coverings of snake or ostrich. 17 jewels, 14K gold filled inner case **$50**

Rigid bow 60 HR. MODEL
gold filled: $175 - $225 - $400
14K gold: $400 - $500 - $900
Dial: $35 - $50 - $95

Antique bow MODEL
gold filled: $100 - $125 - $275
14K gold: $375 - $450 - $650
Dial: $35 - $50 - $95

FIRST MODEL
gold filled: $110 - $135 - $350

Stiff bow 60 HR. MODEL
gold filled: $200 - $250 - $425
14K gold: $450 - $600 - $1,000
Dial: $40 - $60 - $95

Pyramid bow MODEL
gold filled: $95 - $150 - $295
14K gold: $400 - $500 - $750
Montgomery Dial: $40 - $60 - $125

MODEL 28
gold filled: $135 - $160 - $400
gold filled **2 tone**: $150 - $250 - $550
Bunn Special Dial: $60 - $95 - $195

MODEL 29
gold filled: $110 - $150 - $350
Montgomery Dial: $40 - $60 - $95

MODEL 107
gold filled: $110 - $150 - $325
Dial: $30 - $40 - $80

🕐 NOTE: April 1925 Factory Advertised as a **complete** watch and was fitted with a certain matched, timed and rated movement and sold in the factory designed case style as a **complete** watch. The factory also sold _uncased_ movements to **JOBBERS** such as Jewelry stores & they cased the movement in a case styles the **CUSTOMER requested.** All the factory advertised **complete** watches came with the dial **SHOWN or CHOICE** of other **Railroad** dials.

MODEL 128
gold **plated**: $60 - $75 - $175
Dial: $35 - $50 - $95

MODEL 108
gold filled: $110 - $140 - $295
Bunn Special Dial: $40 - $65 - $150

MODEL 173
gold filled: $110 - $150 - $375
gold filled **2 tone**: $175 - $250 - $500
Bunn Special Montgomery Dial: $70 - $95 - $250

MODEL 193
gold filled: $110 - $150 - $375
Dial: $40 - $60 - $95

MODEL 181
gold filled: $110 - $150 - $375
Dial: $35 - $50 - $80

MODEL 206
gold filled: $95 - $150 - $300
gold filled **2 tone**: $140 - $195 - $450
Dial: $35 - $50 - $80

BUNN SPECIALS were packed & shipped
in a ALUMINUM cigarette style box.
$90 — $150 — $275

⊕ NOTE: Aplil 1925 Factory Advertised as a **complete** watch and was fitted with a certain matched, timed and rated movement and sold in the factory designed case style as a **complete** watch. The factory also sold _uncased_ movements to **JOBBERS** such as Jewelry stores & they cased the movement in a case styles the **CUSTOMER requested**. All the factory advertised **complete** watches came with the dial **SHOWN or CHOICE** of other **Railroad** dials.

ILLINOIS SPRINGFIELD WATCH CO.
IDENTIFICATION OF MOVEMENTS
BY MODEL NUMBER

How to Identify Your Watch Size & Model: Compare the movement of your watch with the illustrations in this section. While comparing, note the location of the balance, jewels, screws, gears, and type of back plate (Full, 3/4, Bridge) these will be clues in identifying the movement you have.

THE ILLINOIS WATCH CO. MODEL CHART

Size	Model	Plate Design	Setting	Hunting or Open Face	Type Barrel	Started w/ Serial No.	Remarks
18	1	Full	Key	Htg	Reg	1	Course train
	2	Full	Lever	Htg	Reg	38,901	Course train
	3	Full	Lever	OF	Reg	46,201	Course train, 5th pinion
	4	Full	Pendant	OF	Reg	1,050,001	Fast train
	5	Full	Lever	Htg	Reg	1,256,101	Fast train, RR Grade
	6	Full	Lever	OF	Reg	1,144,401	Fast train, RR Grade
16	1	Full	Lever	Htg	Reg	1,030,001	Thick model
	2	Full	Pendant	OF	Reg	1,037,001	Thick model
	3	Full	Lever	OF	Reg	1,038,001	Thick model
	4	¾ & brg	Lever	Htg	Reg	1,300,001	Getty model
	5	¾ & brg	Lever	OF	Reg	1,300,601	Getty model
	6	¾ & brg	Pendant	Htg	Reg	2,160,111	DR & Improved RR model
	7	¾ & brg	Pendant	OF	Reg	2,160,011	DR & Improved RR model
	8	¾ & brg	Lever	Htg	Reg	2,523,101	DR & Improved RR model
	9	¾ & brg	Lever	OF	Reg	2,522,001	DR & Improved model
	10	Cent brg	Lever	OF	Motor	3,178,901	Also 17S Ex Thin RR gr 48 hr
	11	¾	Lever & Pen	OF	Motor	4,001,001	RR grade 48 hr
	12	¾	Lever & Pen	Htg	Motor	4,002,001	RR grade 48 hr
	13	Cent brg	Lever	OF	Motor	4,166,801	Also 17S RR grade 60 hr
	14	¾	Lever	OF	Motor	4,492,501	RR grade 60 hr
	15	¾	Lever	OF	Motor	5,488,301	RR grade 60 hr Elinvar
14	1	Full	Lever	Htg	Reg	1,009,501	Thick model
	2	Full	Pendant	OF	Reg	1,000,001	Thick model
	3	Full	Lever	OF	Reg	1,001,001	Thick model
13	1	brg	Pendant	OF	Motor		Ex Thin gr 538 & 539
12	1	¾	Pendant	OF	Reg	1,685,001	
Thin	2	¾	Pendant	Htg	Reg	1,748,751	
	3	Cent brg	Pendant	OF	Reg	2,337,011	Center bridge
	4	Cent brg	Pendant	Htg	Reg	2,337,001	Center bridge
	5	Cent brg	Pendant	OF	Motor	3,742,201	Center bridge
	6	Cent brg	Pendant	Htg	Motor	4,395,301	Center bridge
12T	1	True Ctr brg	Pendant	OF	Motor	3,700,001	1 tooth click, Also 13S
	2	True Ctr brg	Pendant	OF	Motor	3,869,301	5 tooth click
	3	¾	Pendant	OF	Motor	3,869,201	2 tooth click
8	1	Full	Key or lever	Htg	Reg	100,001	Plate not recessed
	2	Full	Lever	Htg	Reg	100,101	Plate is recessed
6	1	¾	Lever	Htg	Reg	552,001	
4	1	¾	Lever	Htg	Reg	551,501	
0	1	¾	Pendant	OF	Reg	1,815,901	
	2	¾	Pendant	Htg	Reg	1,749,801	
	3	Cent brg	Pendant	OF	Reg	2,644,001	
	4	Cent brg	Pendant	Htg	Reg	2,637,001	

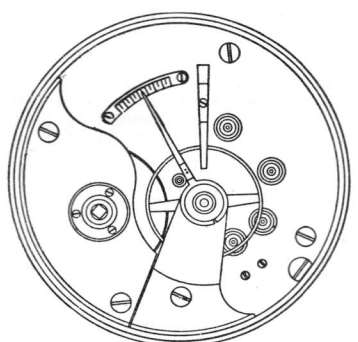

Model 1, 18 size, hunting, key wind & set.

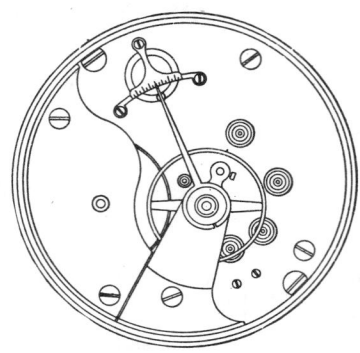

Model 2, 18 size, hunting, lever set, coarse train.

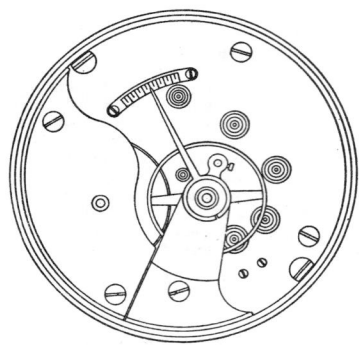

Model 3, 18 size, open face, lever set, coarse train, with fifth pinion.

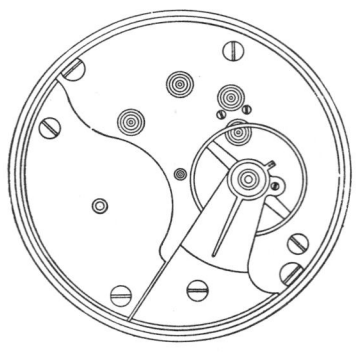

Model 4, 18 size, open face, pendant set, fine train.

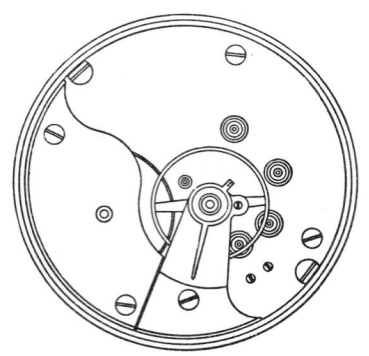

Model 5, 18 size, hunting, lever set, fine train.

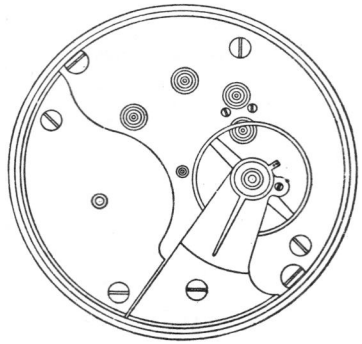

Model 6, 18 size, open face, lever set, fine train.

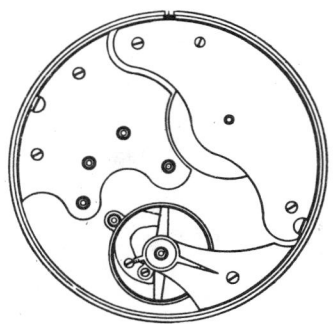

Model 1, 16 size, hunting, lever set.

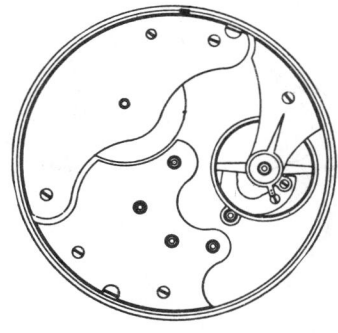

Model 2, 16 size, open face, pendant set.

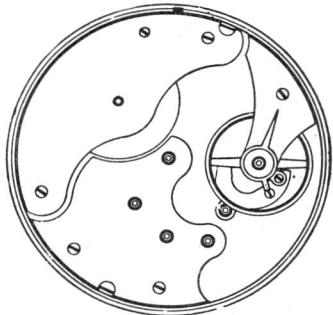

Model 3, 16 size, open face, lever set

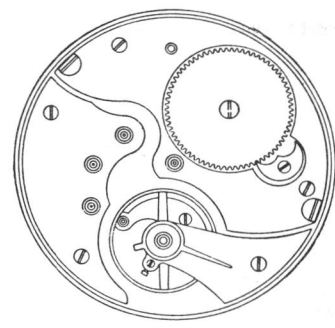

Model 4, 16 size, three-quarter plate, hunting, lever set.

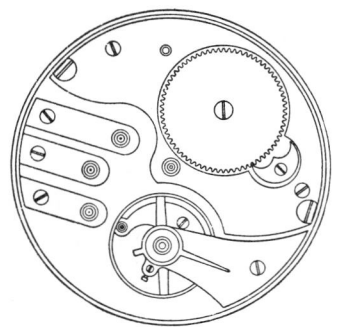

Model 4, 16 size, three-quarter plate, bridge, hunting, lever set.

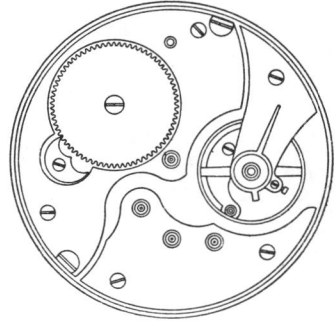

Model 5, 16 size, three-quarter plate, open face, lever set.

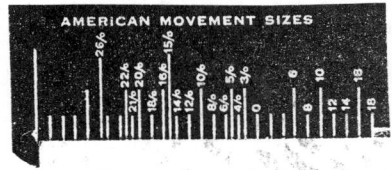

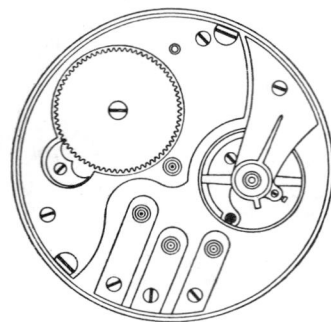

Model 5, 16 size, three-quarter plate, bridge, open face, lever set.

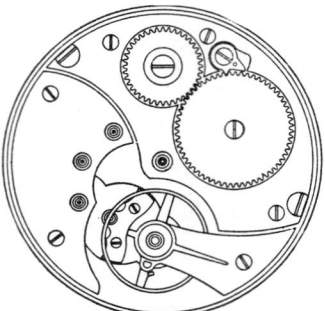

Model 6, 16 size - Pendant set
Model 8, 16 size - Lever set
hunting, three-quarter plate

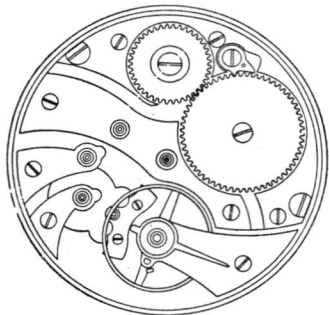

Model 6, 16 size - Pendant set
Model 8, 16 size - Lever set
hunting, bridge model

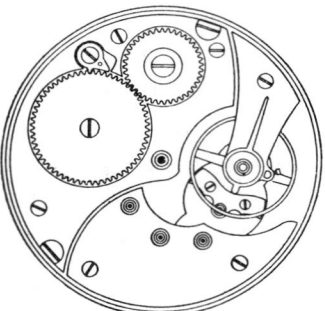

Model 7, 16 size - Pendant set
Model 9, 16 size - Lever set
open face, three-quarter plate

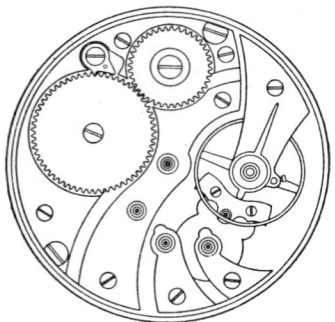

Model 7, 16 size - Pendant set
Model 9, 16 size - Lever set
open face, bridge model

Model 10, 16 size, bridge, extra thin, open face, lever set, motor barrel.

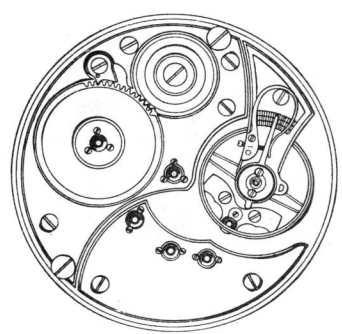

Model 11, 16 size, three-quarter plate, open face, pendant set, motor barrel.

Model 12, 16 size, three-quarter plate, hunting, pendant set, motor barrel.

Model 13, 17 size, bridge, open face, lever set, motor barrel.(no red border on bal. cock)

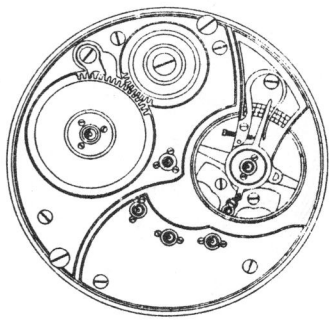

Model 14, 16 size, three-quarter plate, open face, lever set, 60-hour motor barrel.

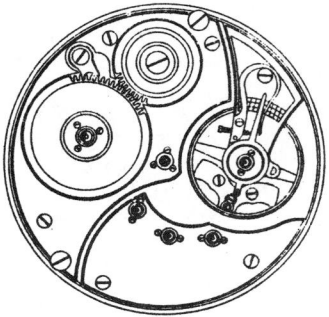

Model 15, 60 Hr. Elinvar.

Model B, 16 size, hunting case.

Model C, 16 size, open face

Model D, 16 size, open face

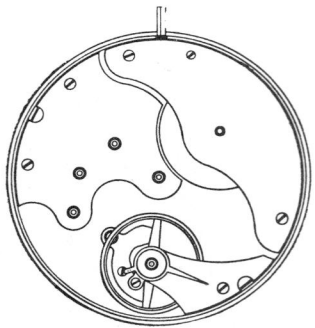

Model 1, 14 size, hunting, lever set.

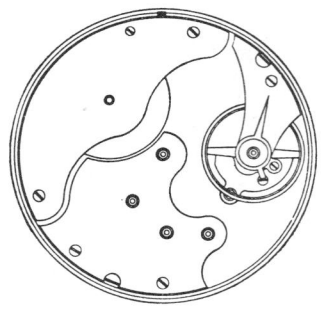

Model 2, 14 size, open face, pendant set.

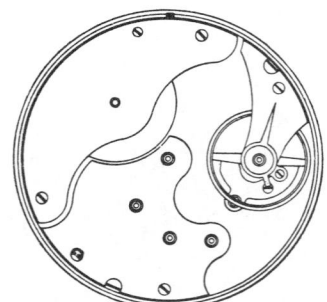

Model 3, 14 size, open face, lever set.

Model 1, 13 size, bridge, extra thin, open face, pendant set, motor barrel.

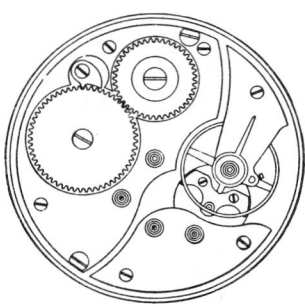

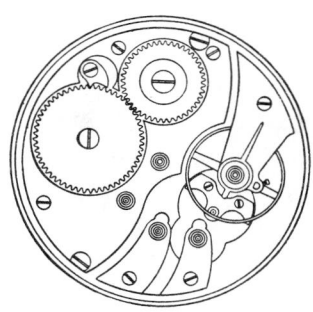

Model 1, 12 size, three-quarter plate, open face, pendant set.

Model 1, 12 size, three-quarter plate, bridge, open face, pendant set.

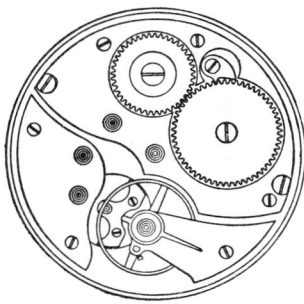

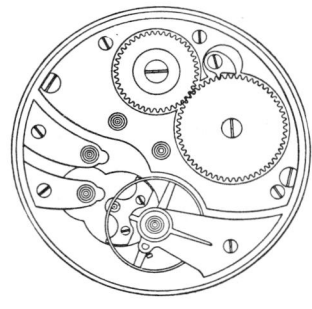

Model 2, 12 size, three-quarter plate, hunting, pendant set.

Model 2, 12 size, three-quarter plate, bridge, hunting, pendant set.

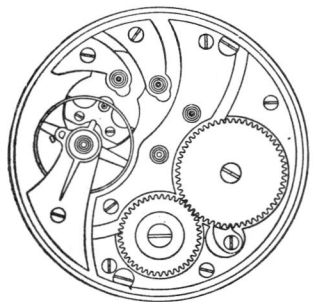

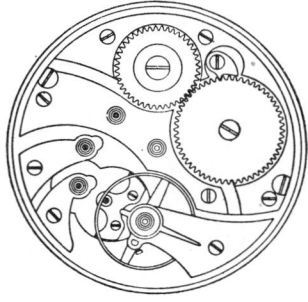

Model 3, 12 size, **Model 4**, 12 & 14 size, bridge, open face, pendant set.

Model 4, 12 size, bridge, hunting, pendant set.

Model 5, 12 size, bridge, open face, pendant set, motor barrel.

Model 1, 12 size, extra thin, bridge, open face, pendant set, motor barrel.

Model 2, 12 size, extra thin, bridge, open face, pendant set, motor barrel.

Model 3, 12 size, extra thin, three-quarter plate, open face, pendant set, motor barrel.

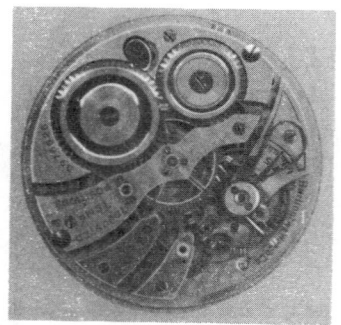

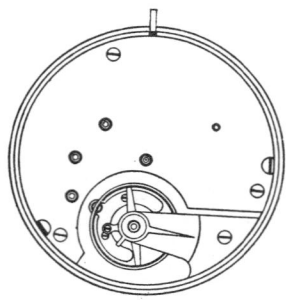

Model A, 12 size, bridge, open face.

Model 1, 8 size, hunting, key or lever set.

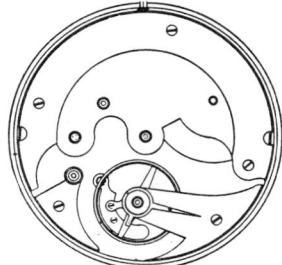

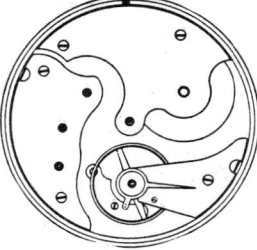

Model 2, 8 size, hunting, lever set.

Model 1, 6 size, hunting, lever set.

Model 1, 4 size, hunting, lever set.

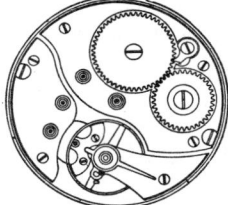

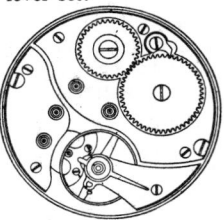

Model 1, 0 size, three-quarter plate, open face, pendant set.

Model 2, 0 size, three-quarter plate, hunting, pendant set.

Model 3, 0 size, bridge, open face, pendant set.

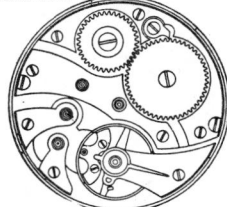

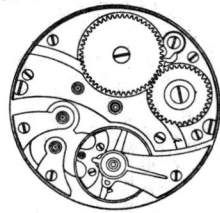

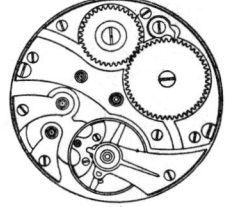

Model 4, 0 size, bridge, hunting, pendant set.

Model 3, 3/0 size, bridge, open face, pendant set.

Model 4, 3/0 size, bridge, hunting, pendant set.

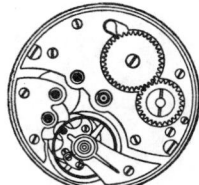

Model 1, 6/0 size, three-quarter plate, open face, pendant set.

No. 5277–269-D

18, 16, 12 Sizes S. S. & D. S.

Spread 12, 8, 6, 4, 0 & 3/0 Sizes S. S. Only

Model 2, 6/0 size, bridge, open face, pendant set.

INDEPENDENT WATCH CO.

Fredonia, New York
1875 - 1881

The California Watch Company was idle for two years before it was purchased by brothers E. W. Howard and C. M. Howard. They had been selling watches by mail for sometime and started engraving the Howard Bros. name on them and using American-made watches. Their chief supply came from Hampden Watch Co., Illinois W. Co., U. S. Watch Co. of Marion. The brothers formed the Independent Watch Co. in 1880, but it was not a watch factory in the true sense. They had other manufacturers engrave the Independent Watch Co. name on the top plates and on the dials of their watches. These watches were sold by mail order and sent to the buyer C. O. D. The names used on the movements were "Howard Bros.," "Independent Watch Co.," "Fredonia Watch Co.," "Lakeshore Watch Co., Fredonia, N. Y." and "Empire Watch Co. Fredonia"

The company later decided to manufacture watches and used the name Fredonia Watch Co., but they found that selling watches two different ways was not very good.The business survived until 1881 at which time the owners decided to move the plant to a new location at Peoria, Illinois. Approximately180,000 watches were made that sold for $16.00.

CHRONOLOGY OF THE DEVELOPMENT OF INDEPENDENT WATCH CO.

Independent Watch Co.	1875–1881
Fredonia Watch Co.	1881–1885
Peoria Watch Co.	1885–1889

18 SIZE

Grade or Name — Description	Avg	Ex-Fn	Mint
18S, 7J, KW, KS, OF, made by U.S. W. Co. Marion, with expanded butterfly cutout.......................................★	$350	$400	$650
18S, 11J, KW, KS, by Hampden.......................................	175	225	350
18S, 11J, KW, KS, Coin...	175	225	350
18S, 11J, KW, KS...	175	225	350
18S, 15J, KW, KS...	175	225	350
18S, Empire Watch Co. Fredonia, 11-15J, KWS ....★★★	350	400	650
18S, Howard Bros., 11J, KW, KS....................................	295	350	600
18S, Independent W. Co., 11J, by Illinois W. Co.............	195	250	400
18S, Independent W. Co., 15J, transition model by Illinois W. Co.	225	295	450
18S, Lakeshore W. Co., 15J, KW, HC, by N.Y. W. Co.	295	350	500

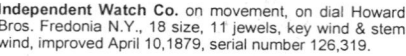

Independent Watch Co. on movement, on dial Howard Bros. Fredonia N.Y., 18 size, 11 jewels, key wind & stem wind, improved April 10,1879, serial number 126,319.

Independent Watch Co., 18 size, 15 jewels, key wind, made by U.S. Marion Watch Co., note expanded butterfly cutout, serial number 192,661.

🕐 Watches listed in this book are priced at the **collectable fair market value** at the Trade Show level, as complete watches having an original 14k gold filled case, KEY WIND with silver, an original white enamel single sunk dial, and with the entire original movement in good working order with no repairs needed, unless otherwise noted.

ROBERT H. INGERSOLL & BROS.
New York, New York
1892 - 1922

In 1892 this company published a catalog for the mail order trade. It listed men's watch chains and a "silverine" Swiss watch for $3.95. The first 1,000 said "The Universal Watch," and introduced that same year to the dealers. The watches with jewels; "Reliance" (seven) introduced about 1917. By 1899 the output was 8,000 per day and in 1901 Ingersoll advertised for sale by 10,000 dealers at $1.00 in U.S.A. and Canada. In 1916, Ingersoll's production was 16,000 a day. The slogan was "The Watch that Made the Dollar Famous." The first 1,000 watches were made by Waterbury Clock Co. Ingersoll bought the Trenton W. Co. in 1908 and the New England W. Co. in 1914. By 1922 the Ingersoll line was completely taken over by Waterbury. U. S. Time Corp. acquired Waterbury in 1944 and continued to use the Ingersoll name on certain watches.

ESTIMATED SERIAL NUMBERS
AND PRODUCTION DATES

DATE—SERIAL NO.	DATE—SERIAL NO.	DATE—SERIAL NO.	DATE—SERIAL NO.
1892 – 150,000	1902 – 7,200,000	1912 – 38,500,000	1922 – 60,500,000
1893 – 310,000	1903 – 7,900,000	1913 – 40,000,000	1923 – 62,000,000
1894 – 650,000	1904 – 8,100,000	1914 – 41,500,000	1924 – 65,000,000
1895 – 1,000,000	1905 –10,000,000	1915 – 42,500,000	1925 – 67,500,000
1896 – 2,000,000	1906 –12,500,000	1916 – 45,500,000	1926 – 69,000,000
1897 – 2,900,000	1907 –15,000,000	1917 – 47,000,000	1927 – 70,500,000
1898 – 3,500,000	1908 –17,500,000	1918 – 47,500,000	1928 – 71,500,000
1899 – 3,750,000	1909 –20,000,000	1919 – 50,000,000	1929 – 73,500,000
1900 – 6,000,000	1910 –25,000,000	1920 – 55,000,000	1930 – 75,000,000
1901 – 6,700,000	1911 –30,000,000	1921 – 58,000,000	1944 – 95,000,000

The above list is provided for determining the APPROXIMATE age of your watch. Match serial number with date. Watches were not necessarily sold in the exact order of manufactured date.

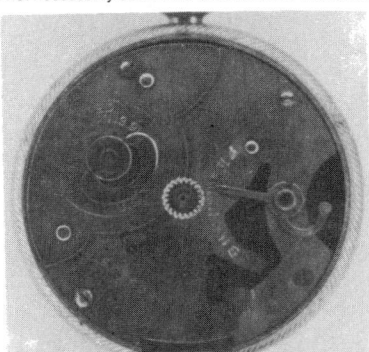

Ingersoll Back Wind & Set, patent date Dec. 23, 1890 and Jan. 13, 1891, c. late 1890s.

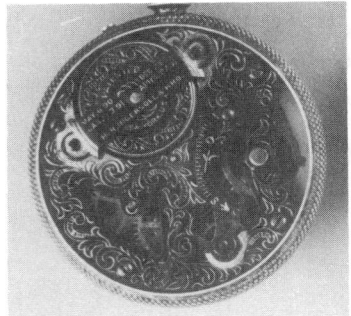

Ingersoll , engraved movement also pin set..

Ingersoll , Celluloid Case in Black or White.

Ingersoll, Blind Man's Watch.

INGERSOLL DOLLAR TYPE

NOTE: Prices are for complete watch in **good running order.** In some specialty markets, the comic character watches may bring higher prices in top condition.

Grade or Name — Description	Avg	Ex-Fn	Mint
Ingersoll Early **Back Wind** Models, (with cover plate)	$50	$75	$150
Ingersoll **Back Wind** Models	50	75	150
Ingersoll, Pin set or **Rim set** & Fancy **engraved** movement	75	95	195
Admiral Dewey, "Flagship Olympia" on back of case .... ★★★★	350	400	850
Advance, (revolving seconds)	40	45	85
American Pride	75	95	150
Are U My Neighbor	40	45	75
B. B. H. Special, Backwind	65	75	120
Blind Man Pocket Watch	50	75	150
Boer War, on dial **Souvenir of South African War 1900** .... ★★★★	900	1,200	2,000
Buck	40	45	85
Calendar (on moveable calendar on back of case)	75	85	135
Celluloid Case in Black or White	95	135	195
Champion (many models)	50	75	135
Chancery	50	75	135
Chicago Expo. 1933 ★★	295	400	850
Climax	50	65	120
Cloverine	40	55	95
Colby	40	45	75
Columbus (3 ships on back of case), 1893 ★★	295	400	800
Connecticut W. Co.	40	45	75
Cord	40	45	85
Crown	40	45	75
Dan Dee	40	45	75
Defiance	40	45	75
Delaware W. Co.	40	45	75
Devon Mfg. Co.	40	45	75
Eclipse (many models)	40	45	75
Eclipse Radiolite	45	65	85
Endura	40	45	75
Ensign	40	45	75
Escort	40	45	75

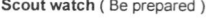

Scout watch (Be prepared)

Yankee watch with bicycle on dial.

NOTE : ADD $25 to $100 for original BOX and PAPERS

🕒 Pricing in this Guide are fair market price for **COMPLETE** watches which are reflected from the "**NAWCC**" National and regional shows.

Ingersoll Premium, early back wind & set.

Ingersoll Triumph, note pin or rim setting.

Grade or Name — Description	Avg	Ex-Fn	Mint
Fancy Dials (unfaded to be mint)	$125	$150	$400
Freedom	40	45	75
Gotham	40	45	75
Graceline	45	50	75
Gregg	40	45	75
Junior (several models)	40	45	75
Junior Radiolite	40	45	75
Kelton	40	45	75
Lapel Watches	30	45	75
Leader	30	45	75
Leeds	30	45	75
Leonard Watch Co. ★★	60	75	95
Liberty U.S.A., backwind	75	95	250
Liberty Watch Co.	50	75	175
Limited, LEVER SET ON CASE RIM OF WATCH	50	60	150
Major	45	50	75
Maple Leaf	45	50	75
Master Craft	45	50	75
Mexicana	30	45	75
Midget (several models)	40	50	85
Midget , 6 size, "patd. Jan. 29 -01," Damaskeened, fancy case	75	95	175
Monarch	45	50	75
New West	45	50	75
New York World's Fair, 1939 ★★	275	350	700
Overland	40	50	75
Pan American Expo., Buffalo, 1901 ★★	275	350	700
Paris World Expo., 1900 ★★	195	295	650
Patrol	45	50	75
Perfection	40	45	65
Pilgram	45	55	75
Premier, back wind, eagle on back, c. 1894 ★	95	150	350

NOTE : ADD $25 to $75 for original BOX and PAPERS

🕐 Pricing in this Guide are fair market price for **COMPLETE** watches
which are reflected from the "**NAWCC**" National and regional shows.

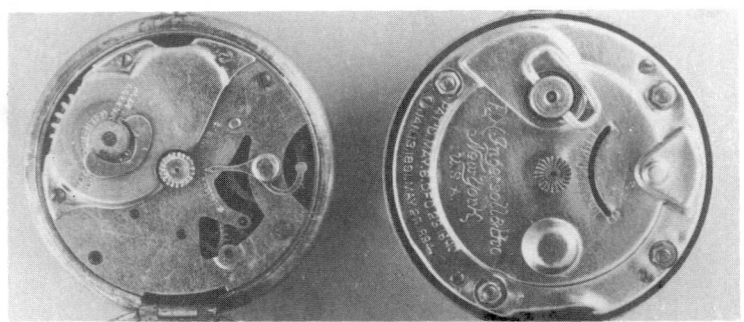

Left: Ingersoll Back Wind, c. 1895.   Right: Yankee Back Wind, c. 1893.

Grade or Name — Description	Avg	Ex-Fn	Mint
Premium Back Wind and Set	$60	$75	$150
Progress, 1933 World's Fair Chicago ★★	250	275	575
Puritan	40	50	85
Quaker	40	45	75
Radiolite	45	65	85
Reliance, 7J	60	75	95
Remington W. Co. USA	60	75	95
Rotary International, c. 1920	50	65	95
Royal	45	50	75
St. Louis World's Fair (two models) ★★	250	295	600
The Saturday Post	70	100	250
Senator	40	50	75
Senior	45	50	75
Sir Leeds	35	40	60
Solar	35	40	60
Souvenir Special	50	75	120
Sterling	35	40	60
Ten Hune	60	70	125
Traveler with Bed Side Stand	35	45	75
Triumph	95	125	150
Triumph Pin set or rim set, large crown, engine turned case (early model) with engraved barrel or movement	125	175	400
True Test	35	45	65
Trump	35	45	65
USA (two models)	50	75	95
Universal, 1st model	195	250	350
Uncle Sam	50	65	95
George Washington	150	175	295
Waterbury (several models)	40	60	95

WATERBURY **CLOCK** CO. 35 size (Duke or Duchess models)
   pat. Jan.15,1878, May 6, 90, Dec.23,90, Jan.13,91 on movement
   equivalent to Ingersoll BIG WATCH, (Waterbury on dial)... 150   195   400

NOTE : ADD $35 to $150 for original BOX and PAPERS

🕐 A collector should expect to pay modestly higher prices at local shops.

🕐 Pricing in this Guide are fair market price for **COMPLETE** watches which are reflected from the "**NAWCC**" National and regional shows.

Grade or Name — Description	Avg	Ex-Fn	Mint
Winner	$40	$45	$75
Winner , with Screw Back & Bezel.	65	75	120
Yankee Backwind	85	95	195
Yankee Bicycle Watch (sold for $1.00 in 1896)	175	195	375
Yankee Radiolite	55	65	95
Yankee Radiolite with Screw Back & Bezel.	75	95	145
Yankee Special (many models)	75	95	160
Yankee, Perpetual calendar on back of case	95	125	195

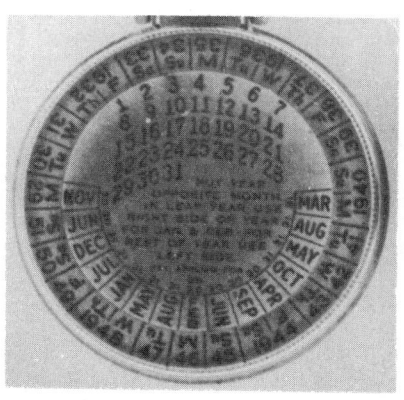

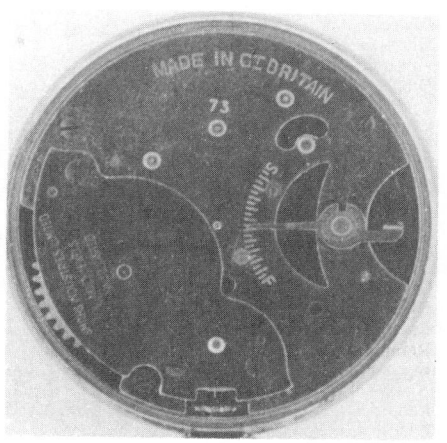

Ingersoll moveable calendar for years 1929-1951 located on back of case.

Ingersoll movement made in Great Britain.

INGERSOLL LTD.
(GREAT BRITAIN)

Grade or Name — Description	Avg	Ex-Fn	Mint
Ingersoll Ltd. (many models)	$65	$75	$95
Coronation, Elizabeth II on watch	175	195	475
Coronation, June 2, 1953 on dial	175	195	450
16S, 7J, 3F Brg	55	65	95
16S, 15J, 3F Brg	85	95	125
16S, 17J, 3F Brg, ADJ	125	145	175
16S, 19J, 3F Brg, Adj5P	150	175	325
12S, 4J	45	65	85

E. INGRAHAM CO.
Bristol, Connecticut 1912 - 1968

The E. Ingraham Co. purchased the Bannatyne Co. in 1912. They produced their first pocket watch in 1913. A total of about 65 million pocket watches and over 12 million wrist watches were produced before they started to import watches in 1968.

Grade or Name — Description	Avg	Ex-Fn	Mint
Ingraham W. Co. (many models)	$30	$40	$65
Allure	30	40	65
Aristocrat Railroad Special	50	65	95
Autocrat	30	45	75
Basketball & Football Timer	50	60	95
Beacon	30	40	65
Biltmore	30	40	75
Biltmore Radium dial	50	65	95
Bristol	30	40	65
Clipper	30	40	65
Co-Ed	30	40	65
Comet	50	60	95
Companion, sweep second hand	50	65	95
Cub	25	30	55
Dale	30	40	65
Demi–hunter style cover	65	75	150
Digital seconds dial, (no second hand but a digital seconds on dial)	60	70	95
Dixie	30	45	70
Dot	30	45	60
Endura	30	45	60
Everbrite (all models)	40	50	75
Graceline,	30	45	60
Ingraham USA	30	45	60
Jockey	30	45	60
Laddie	25	30	50
Laddie Athlete	40	45	65
Lady's Purse Watch, with fancy bezel	45	50	95
Lendix Extra	30	45	60
Master	25	30	50
Master Craft	30	45	60
Miss Ingraham	25	30	50
New York to Paris(with box for mint) ★ ★	250	295	700
Overland	45	50	80
The Pal	30	45	60

INGRAHAM, Seven Seas, shows standard time, & Nautical time.

New York to Paris, with airplane model on dial, engraved bezel, commemorating Lindbergh's famous flight.

🌐 Prices are for complete watch in **good running order.** In some specialty markets, the comic character watches may bring higher prices in top condition.

NOTE : ADD $25 to $75 for original BOX and PAPERS

Pastor Stop Watch, Sterling W. Co. printed on dial, with start stop & fly back to zero function.
The Sterling Watch Company, Inc.Waterbury, Conn. U.S.A. on movement

Grade or Name — Description	Avg	Ex-Fn	Mint
Pastor Stop Watch, (Sterling W. Co), fly back to zero.............★	$125	$175	$350
Pastor on dial & E.Ingraham on movement, fly back to zero, ...★	125	175	350
Pathfinder, compass on pendant (14 size)........................	95	125	250

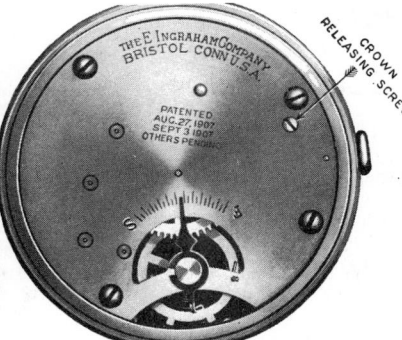

Path Finder showing compass in crown.   E. Ingraham Co. on movement **14 SIZE.**

Grade or Name — Description	Avg	Ex-Fn	Mint
Patriot	$125	$150	$275
Peerless..	30	35	60
Pilot	40	50	75
Pocket Pal..	30	45	60
Pony..	30	45	60
Pride	30	45	60
Princess..	30	45	60
Prince..	30	45	60
Professional..	30	35	60
Pup..	30	35	60
Reliance..	45	50	75
Rex	30	45	60
Rite Time..	30	45	60
St. Regis	30	45	60
Secometer..	40	50	75
Sentinel..	30	45	60
Sentinel Click	30	45	60
Sentinel Fold Up Travel	50	65	85
Sentry	30	45	60
Seven Seas, 24 hr. dial & nautical dial............................	50	80	150
Silver Star..	30	45	60

Grade or Name — Description	Avg	Ex-Fn	Mint
Sturdy	$30	$45	$60
Target	30	45	60
The Best	30	45	60
The Pal	30	45	60
Time Ball	40	50	75
Time & Time	30	40	65
Top Flight	35	45	65
Top Notch	35	45	65
Tower	30	45	60

Trail Blazer, Commemorating Byrd's Antarctic Expedition.

Showing back side of **Trail Blazer**, also depicted on box.

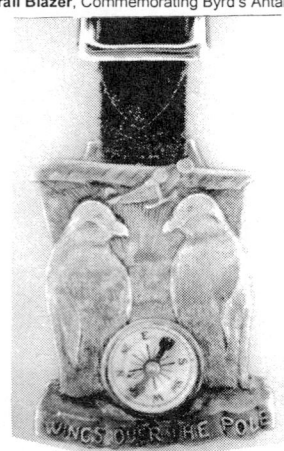

FOB

ABOVE, BOX - Same as depicted on BACK of watch.

Grade or Name — Description	Avg	Ex-Fn	Mint
Trail Blazer, Commemorating BYRD'S Antarctic Expedition ..... ★	$250	$295	$650
Trail Blazer, Commemorating BYRD'S Antarctic Expedition, *all original* **watch**, with **fob** (wings over the pole), + **box** .... ★★★	600	700	1,400
Treasure	15	20	35
Unbreakable Crystal	45	50	75
Uncle Sam (all models)	50	75	100
Uncle Sam Backwind & Set	125	150	250
United	30	35	50
Viceroy	30	45	60
Victory	30	45	60
Wings	40	50	75

Example of a basic **International Watch Co.** movement with patent dates of Aug. 19, 1902, Jan. 27, 1903 & Aug. 11, 1903.

International Watch Co., "Highland" on dial.

INTERNATIONAL WATCH CO.

Newark City, New Jersey
1902 - 1907

This company produced only non-jeweled or low-cost production type watches that were inexpensive and nickel plated. Names on their watches include: Berkshire, Madison, and Mascot.

Grade or Name — Description		Avg	Ex-Fn	Mint
18 Size, skeletonized, pinlever escape., first model	★★	$195	$250	$400
Berkshire, OF	★	80	95	225
Highland	★	80	95	225
Madison, 18S, OF	★	80	95	225
Mascot, OF	★	80	95	225

KANKAKEE WATCH CO.

Kankakee, Illinois
1900

This company reportedly became the McIntyre Watch Co. Little or no information is available.

Grade or Name — Description		Avg	Ex-Fn	Mint
16S, BRG, NI	★★★★	$6,500	$7,000	$12,000

🕐 Watches listed in this book are priced at the **collectable fair market value** at the Trade Show level, as complete watches having an original 14k gold filled case, KEY WIND with silver, an original white enamel single sunk dial, and with the entire original movement in good working order with no repairs needed, unless otherwise noted.

KELLY WATCH CO.

Chicago, Illinois
c. 1900

Grade or Name — Description		Avg	Ex-Fn	Mint
16S, aluminum movement and OF case.......................... ★ ★ ★ ★ ★		$350	$400	$700

Kelly Watch Co., 16 size, aluminum movement, straight line lever, quick train, porcelain dial, stem set, reversible ratchet stem wind, originally sold for $2.20, Ca. 1900.

KEYSTONE STANDARD WATCH CO.

Lancaster, Pennsylvania
1886 - 1891

Abram Bitner agreed to buy a large number of stockholders' shares of the Lancaster Watch Co. at 10 cents on the dollar; he ended up with 5,625 shares out of the 8,000 that were available. Some 8,900 movements had been completed but not sold at the time of the shares purchase. The company Bitner formed assumed the name of Keystone Standard Watch Co. as the trademark but in reality existed as the Lancaster Watch Co. The business was sold to **Hamilton Watch Co.** in 1891.

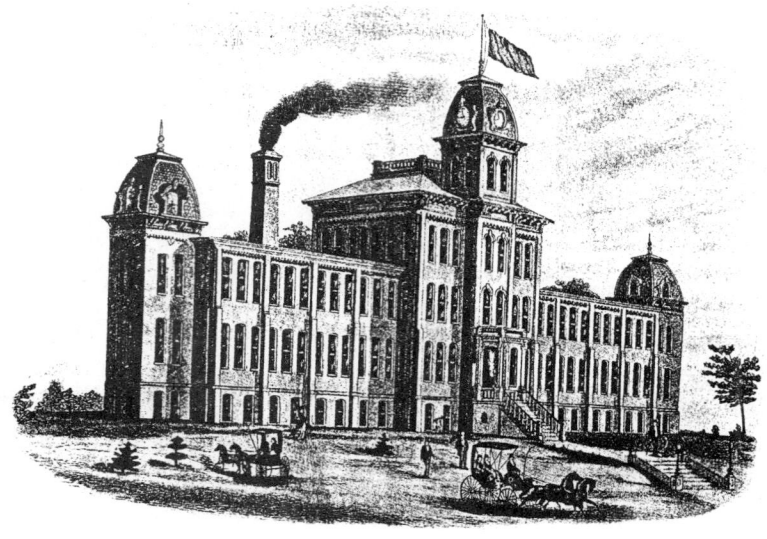

Grade or Name — Description	Avg	Ex-Fn	Mint
18S, 7-15J, OF, **KW**	$95	$125	$250
18S, 7-15J, OF, SW, 3/4, LS	70	95	175
18S, 15J, dust proof, ADJ	95	150	250
18S, 11-15J, dust proof, OF	95	125	200
18S, 11-15J, dust proof, HC	120	150	250
18S, 17J, dust proof, HC	150	175	275
18S, 20J, dust proof, HC ★ ★	295	450	750
18S, West End, 15J, HC	95	125	195
8S, 11J, dust proof	95	125	195
6S, 7-10J, HC ★	95	140	275

Keystone Watch Co., dust proof model, 18 size, 15 jewels, serial number 352,766.

Knickerbocker movement, 16-18 size, 7 jewels, duplex escapement.

KNICKERBOCKER WATCH CO.

New York, New York
1890 - 1930

This company imported and sold Swiss and low-cost production American watches.

Grade or Name — Description	Avg	Ex-Fn	Mint
18S, 7J, OF, PS, NI, duplex escapement	$50	$65	$135
16S, 7J	30	45	85
12S, 7J, OF	30	50	95
10S, Barkley **"8 Day"** ★ ★ ★	125	165	225
6S, Duplex	30	50	85

🕐 Some grades are not included. Their values can be determined by comparing with **similar** age, size, metal content, style, models and grades listed.

🕐 Watches listed in this book are priced at the collectable fair market value at the Trade Show level, as complete watches having an original 14k gold filled case, KEY WIND with silver, an original white enamel single sunk dial, and with the entire original movement in good working order with no repairs needed, unless otherwise noted.

🕐 Pricing in this Guide are fair market price for **COMPLETE** watches which are reflected from the "**NAWCC**" National and regional shows.

LANCASTER WATCH CO.
Lancaster, Pennsylvania
1879 - 1886

Work commenced on Sept. 1, 1877, at the Lancaster Watch Co. The watches produced there were designed to sell at a cheaper price than normal. They had a solid top, 3/4 plate, and a pillar plate that was fully ruby-jeweled (4 pairs). They had a gilt and nickel movement and a new stem-wind device, modeled by Mosly & Todd. By mid-1878 the Lancaster Watch Co. had produced 150 movements. Four grades of watches were made: Keystone, Fulton, Franklin, and Melrose. In September 1879 the company had made 334 movements. In 1880 the total was up to 1,250 movements, and by mid-1882 about 17,000 movements had been produced. About 200,000 watch movements were made.

CHRONOLOGY OF THE DEVELOPMENT OF THE LANCASTER WATCH CO.

Adams and Perry Watch Mfg. Co. 1874-1876
Lancaster Penna. Watch Co. 1877-1879
Lancaster Watch Co. 1879-1886
Keystone Standard Co. 1886-1891
Hamilton Watch Co. .... 1892 to present

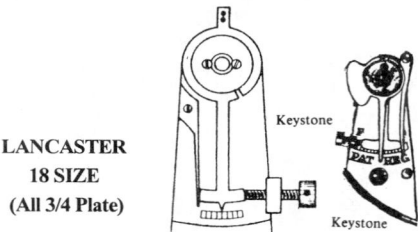

LANCASTER
18 SIZE
(All 3/4 Plate)

Grade or Name — Description	Avg	Ex-Fn	Mint
Chester, 7-11J, KW, dust proof, gilded..	$125	$150	$300
Comet, 7J, NI	125	150	300
Delaware, 20J, ADJ, SW, dust proof, gilded .... ★	295	350	600
Denver, 7J, dust proof, gilded	50	90	175
Denver, 7J, gilded, dust proof, Silveroid	50	80	150
Elberon, 7J, dust proof..	125	150	300
Ben Franklin, 7J, KW, gilded...	150	195	450
Ben Franklin, 11J, KW, gilded...	175	250	500
Fulton, 7J, ADJ, KW, gilded	70	95	250
Fulton, 11J, ADJ, KW, gilded	70	95	250
Girard, 15J, ADJ, dust proof, gilded	70	95	250
Hoosac, 11J, OF..	70	95	300
Keystone, 15J, ADJ, gilded, GJS, dust proof.................................	70	95	300
Keystone, 15J, ADJ, gilded, GJS, Silveroid	70	95	175
Lancaster, 7J, SW	70	95	175
Lancaster, 15J, SW, Silveroid	40	75	125
Lancaster, 15J, OF	55	85	195
Lancaster, 20J, OF .... ★ ★	295	350	550

"LANCASTER Watch PENNA.", **20J, ADJ, GJS, 20 size, low serial No.**
Referred to as (Adams & Perry model), **for pricing see Adams & Perry W. Co.** section.

🕘 Some grades are not included. Their values can be determined by comparing with similar age, size, metal content, style, models and grades listed.

🕘 A collector should expect to pay modestly higher prices at local shops.

🕘 Pricing in this Guide are fair market price for **COMPLETE** watches which are reflected from the "**NAWCC**" National and regional shows.

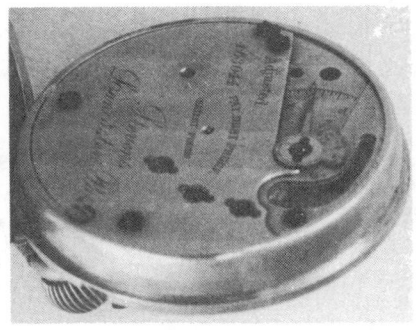

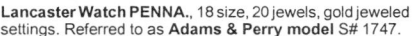

Lancaster Watch PENNA., 18 size, 20 jewels, gold jeweled settings. Referred to as **Adams & Perry model** S# 1747.

Stevens Model, 18 size, 15 jewels, adjusted, dust proof model, swing-out movement, c.1886.

Above watch is *Lancaster Watch PENNA.*, 20J, ADJ, GJS, about 19 size, low serial No. Referred to as (Adams & Perry model), **for pricing see Adams & Perry W. Co.** section.

Grade or Name — Description	Avg	Ex-Fn	Mint
Malvern, 7J, dust proof, gilded...	$60	$90	$175
Melrose, 15J, NI, ADJ, GJS	85	125	225
Nation Standard American Watch Co., 7J, HC	195	225	400
New Era, 7J, gilded, KW, HC	80	125	195
New Era, 7J, gilded, KW, Silveroid..	60	80	150
Paoli, 7J, NI, dust proof, ...	70	95	195
Wm. Penn, 20J, ADJ, NI, dust proof .... ★	400	500	800
Radnor, 7J, dust proof, gilded	60	80	195
Record, 7J, dust proof, Silveroid...	60	80	195
Record, 15J, NI	60	80	195

West End, 18 size, 15 jewels, key wind & set, serial number 158,080, c. 1878.

Lancaster movement, 8-10 size, 15 jewels, serial number 317,812.

🕐 A collector should expect to pay modestly higher prices at local shops.

🕐 Pricing in this Guide are fair market price for **COMPLETE** watches which are reflected from the "**NAWCC**" National and regional shows.

Grade or Name — Description	Avg	Ex-Fn	Mint
Ruby, 7-16J, NI	$140	$180	$295
Sidney, 15J, NI, dust proof,	95	125	250
Stevens, 15J, ADJ, NI, dust proof	150	175	295
West End, 19J, HC, **KW**, gilded	450	500	650
West End, 15J, HC, **KW**, KS	95	150	295
West End, 15J, SW	95	125	250
West End, 15J, SW, Silveroid	70	80	125

8 SIZE

Grade or Name — Description	Avg	Ex-Fn	Mint
Cricket, 11J	$40	$50	$95
Diamond, 15J	40	50	95
Echo, 11J	40	50	95
Flora, 7-11J, gilded	40	50	95
Iris, 13J	40	50	95
Lady Penn, 20J, GJS, ADJ, NI ★	300	350	600
Lancaster W. Co., 7J	40	60	95
Pearl, 7J	40	50	95
Red Rose, of Lancaster, 15J	40	50	95
Ruby, 15J	40	50	95

MANHATTAN WATCH CO.

New York, New York
1883 - 1891

The Manhattan Watch Co. made mainly low cost production watches. A complete and full line of watches was made, and most were cased and styled to be sold as a **complete** watch. The watches were generally 16S with full plate movements. The patented winding mechanism was different. These watches were both in hunter and open-face cases and later had a sweep second hand. Total production was 160,000 or more watches.

Manhattan Watch Co., stop watch, 16 size, note the escapement uses upright "D"—shaped pallets (steel), serial number 117,480.

Manhattan Watch Co., 16 size, stop watch. Note the two buttons on top; the right (at 2 o'clock) one sets the hands, the left (at 10 o'clock) starts and stops the watch.

16 SIZE

Grade or Name — Description	Avg	Ex-Fn	Mint
OF, with back wind, base metal case .... ★	$150	$195	$450
OF, 2 button stop watch, screw back & bezel, **enamel dial, gold-filled case** .... ★ ★ ★	250	400	800
OF, 2 button stop watch, snap back & bezel, paper dial, base metal case .... ★	150	195	550
HC, 2 button stop watch, snap back & bezel, paper dial, base metal case .... ★ ★	195	295	600
OF, 1 button, sweep sec., base metal case , paper dial .... ★	125	175	295
HC, 1 button, sweep sec., base metal case, paper dial.......... ★	195	250	400
Ship's Bell Time Dial, OF or HC................................ ★ ★ ★ ★	325	425	800
Twenty-Four Hour Dial, OF or HC............................ ★ ★ ★ ★	325	425	800
Stallcup, 7J, OF... ★	95	150	350

12 SIZE

Grade or Name — Description	Avg	Ex-Fn	Mint
12S... ★	$80	$125	$350

Manhattan Watch Co., 16 size, time only watch & note no second hand, the button at Right sets the hands.

Manhattan Watch Co., 16 size, time only with Sweep-Second hand, the button at Right sets the hands.

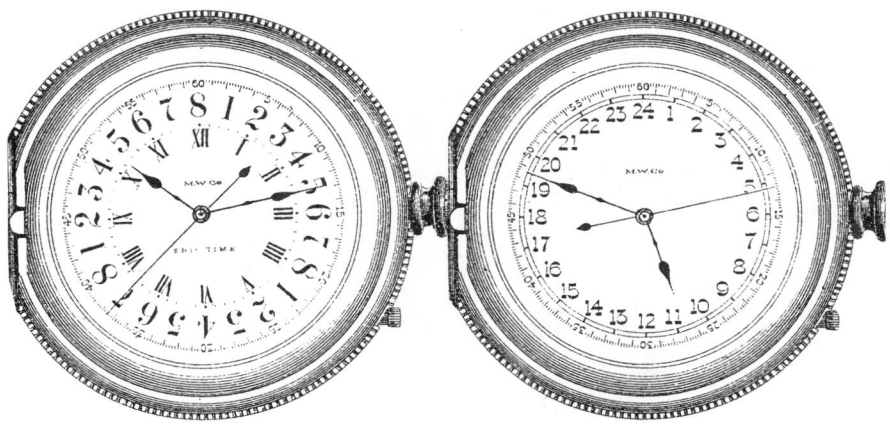

Manhattan Watch Co., 16 size, Ship's Bell Time **DIAL** for NAUTICAL USES & sweep second hand, Hunting Case.

Manhattan Watch Co., 16 size, with a 24-HOUR DIAL.& sweep second hand, Hunting Case.

MANISTEE WATCH CO.
Manistee, Michigan
1908 - 1912

The Manistee watches, first marketed in 1909, were designed to compete with the low-cost production watches. Dials, jewels, and hairsprings were not produced at the factory. The first movement was 18S, 7J, and sold for about $5. Manistee also made 5J, 15J, 17J, and 21J watches in cheap cases in sizes 16 and 12. Estimated total production was 60,000. Most were sold by Star Watch Case Co.

18 SIZE

Grade or Name —Description		Avg	Ex-Fn	Mint
18S, 7J, 3/4, LS, HC	★	$325	$375	$500
18S, 7J, 3/4, LS, OF	★	275	325	400
18S, 7J, 3/4, LS, OF, **gold train**	★★	375	425	700
18S, 7J, cut out movement	★★	275	325	400

16 TO 12 SIZE

Grade or Name —Description		Avg	Ex-Fn	Mint
16S, 7J, OF	★	$195	$250	$400
16S, 15J, OF	★	225	250	400
16S, 15J, HC	★	250	275	425
16S, 17J, OF	★	225	250	400
16S, 19J, HC	★	300	350	500
16S, 21J, OF	★	325	375	525
12S, 15J	★	150	175	295

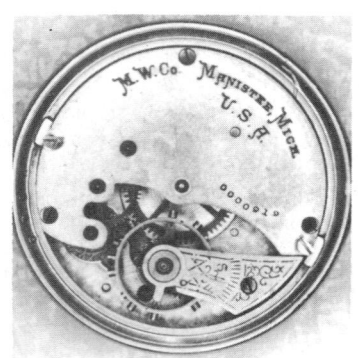

Manistee movement, 18 size, 7 jewels, 3/4 plate, open face, serial number 0000919.

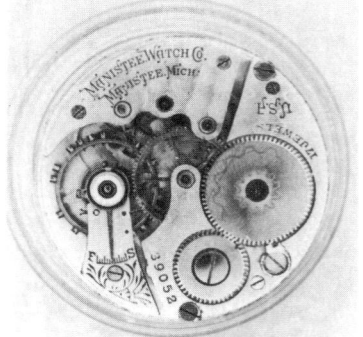

Manistee movement, 16 size, 17 jewels, three-quarter plate, open face, serial number 39,052.

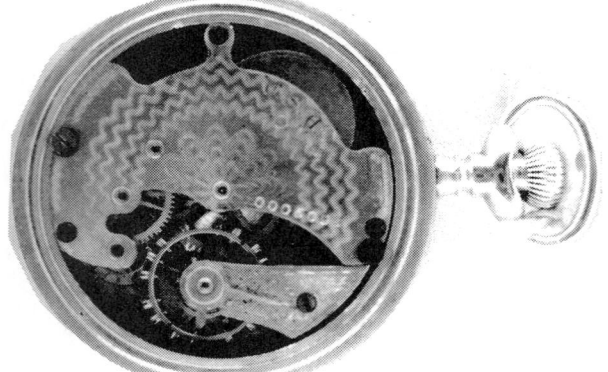

Manistee cut out movement, 18 size, 7 jewels, open face, serial number 0006094.

McINTYRE WATCH CO.

Kankakee, Illinois
1908 - 1911

This company probably bought the factory from Kankakee Watch Co. In 1908 Charles DeLong was made master watchmaker, and he designed and improved the railroad watches. Only a few watches were made, estimated total production being about **eight watches.**

Grade or Name — Description		Avg	Ex-Fn	Mint
16S, 21J, BRG, NI, WI.. ★★★★★		$4,500	$5,000	$12,000
16S, 25J, BRG, **WI**, Adj.5P, equidistant escapement .... ★★★★★		5,500	6,000	15,000
12S, 19J, BRG.. ★★★★★		2,000	2,500	5,500

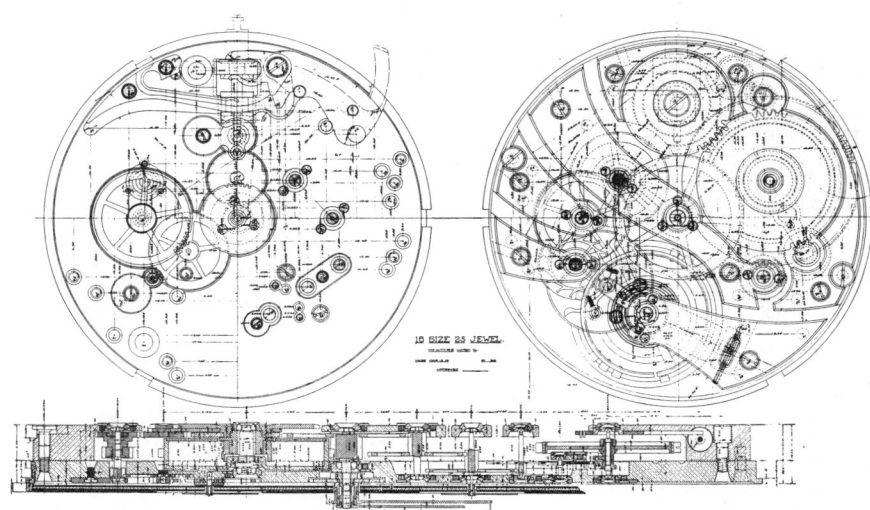

McIntyre Watch Co., 16 size, 25 jewels, adjusted to 5 positions with wind indicator, with equidistant escapement, manufactured about 1909. Above illustration taken from a blue print.

EXAMPLE OF A BREGUET STYLE DIAL   EXAMPLE OF A BOX CAR STYLE DIAL

310

MELROSE WATCH CO.

Melrose, Massachusetts
1866 - 1868

Melrose Watch Co. began as Tremont Watch Co., and imported the expansion balances and escapements. In 1866 the Tremont Watch Co. moved, changed its name to Melrose Watch Co., and started making complete watch movements, including a new style 18S movement engraved "Melrose Watch Co." About 3,000 were produced. **"Some"** watches are found with "Melrose" on the dial and "Tremont" on the movement. Serial numbers start at about 30,000.

Factory at Melrose, Mass. General Agents, Messrs. WHEELER, PARSONS & CO.,New York, Messrs. BIGELOW BROS. & KENNARD, Boston, and for sale by the trade generally. Every movement warranted.

The TREMONT WATCH CO. manufacture the only DUST-PROOF Watch movement in this country. They have a branch establishment in Switzerland, under the personal superintendence of Mr. A. L. DENNISON, (the ORIGINA-TOR of the American system of watch-making), where they produce their Balances and Escapements of a superior quality. The cheap skilled labor of Europe, working thus on the AMERICAN SYSTEM, enables them to offer a superior article at a low rate.

Example of a basic **Melrose Watch Co.** movement, 18 size, 15 jewels, key wind & set.

1867 ADVERTISEMENT

Grade or Name — Description		Avg	Ex-Fn	Mint
18S, 7J, KW, KS	★★	$250	$295	$500
18S, 11J, KW, KS, OF	★★	250	295	500
18S, 15J, KW, KS	★★	295	400	600
18S, 15J, KW, KS, Silveroid	★★	250	295	450

Note: Add $25.00 - $70.00 to values of above watches in hunting case.

MOZART WATCH CO.

Providence, Rhode Island
Ann Arbor, Michigan
1864 - 1870

In 1864 Don J. Mozart started out to produce a less expensive three-wheel watch in Providence, R. I. Despite his best efforts, the venture was declared a failure by 1866. Mozart left Providence and moved to Ann Arbor, Mich. There, again, he started on a three-wheel watch and succeeded in producing thirty. The three-wheel watch was not a new idea except to American manufacturers. Three-wheel watches were made many decades before Mozart's first effort, but credit for the first American-made three-wheel watch must go to him. The size was about 18 and could be called a 3/4 or full plate movement. The balance bridge was screwed on the top plate, as was customary. The round bridge partially covered the opening in the top plate and was just large enough for the balance to oscillate. The balance was compensated and somewhat smaller in diameter than usual. Mozart called it a chronolever, and it was to function so perfectly it would be free from friction. That sounded good but was in no way true.

The watch was of the usual American 18 size with a train that had a main wheel with the usual number of teeth and a ten-leaf center pinion, but it had a large center wheel of 108 teeth and a third wheel of 90 teeth, with a six-leaf third (escape)pinion. The escape wheel had

30 teeth and received its impulse directly from the roller on the staff, while the escape tooth locked on the intermediate lever pallet. The escape pinion had a long pivot that carried the second hand, which made a circuit of the dial, once in 12 seconds. The total number of Mozart watches produced was about 165, & 30 of these were the three-wheel type.

Grade or Name — Description		Avg	Ex-Fn	Mint
18S, 3/4, KW, KS, 3-wheel	★ ★ ★ ★ ★	$18,000	$25,000	$50,000
18S, 3/4, KW, KS	★ ★ ★ ★	12,000	18,000	30,000

Mozart Watch Co. movement, 18 size, three-quarter plate, key wind & set, three-wheel train, "Patent Dec. 24th, 1867" and Patent # was 72,528.

J. H. Mulford, 18 size, about 10 jewels, key wind, and is marked, "J. H. Mulford, patent, Albany, N.Y. S# 25".

J. H. MULFORD
Albany, New York
1842 - 1876

John Mulford started out as a jeweler and by about 1842 was listed as a watchmaker. Mulford was granted a patent on Feb. 21, 1842 (no. 2465) for his style escapement. It appears that the basic movement was imported. Most were 18 size, key wind & set with a going barrel, and he used gold jewel screwed down jewels. The verge style escapement and on the balance staff instead of pallets, he used two cylindrical jewels, and each jewel had a notch.

Grade or Name — Description		Avg	Ex-Fn	Mint
18S, 10-12J., 3/4, KW, KS	★ ★ ★ ★	$9,000	$10,000	$15,000

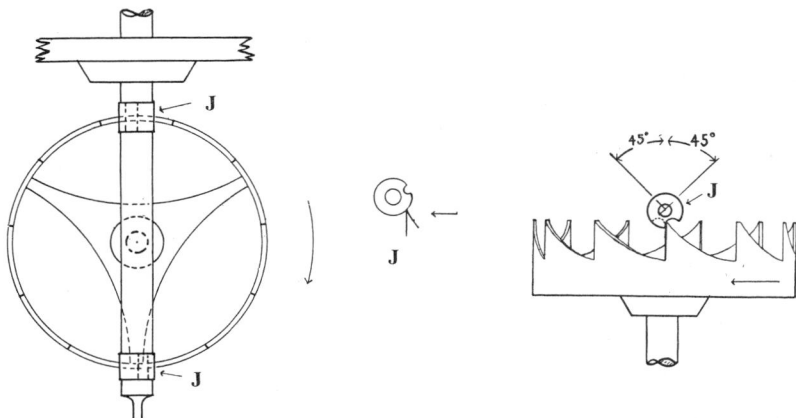

J. H. Mulford, drawing of his patented escapement. (Pat. # 2465 date Feb. 21, 1842) On the balance staff, instead of flag style pallets, there are two cylindrical jewels "J" each jewel has a notch similar to the notch of a duplex escapement. When the tip of the escape wheel tooth drops on the jewel it imparts a impulse against the side of the notched jewel.

NASHUA WATCH CO.
Nashua, New Hampshire
1859 - 1862

One of the most important contributions to the American Watch industry was made by the Nashua Watch Co. of Nashua, New Hampshire. Founded in 1859 by B. D. Bingham, the company hired some of the most innovative and creative watchmakers in America and produced an extremely high grade American pocket watch.

Since almost all the production material made by Nashua from 1859 until its incorporation into the American Watch Co. in 1862 was unfinished by Nashua, only about four examples of the 20-size keywind keyset from the back signed Nashua Watch Co. are known to exist.

NASHUA WATCH CO. (marked),
20 size, 19 jewels, gold jewel settings,
key wind & set from back,
stop work, serial number 1,219.

20-size keywind keyset from the back signed Nashua Watch Co.

Grade or Name — Description		Avg	Ex-Fn	Mint
Nashua (marked), 19J, KW, KS, 3/4, 18K .... ★★★★★		$18,000	$25,000	$35,000
Nashua (marked), 15J, KW, KS, 3/4, silver case .... ★★★★		14,000	18,000	30,000

NEWARK WATCH CO.
Newark, New Jersey
1864 - 1870

Arthur Wadsworth, one of the designers for Newark Watch Co., patented an 18 Size full plate movement. The first movements reached the market in 1867. This company produced only about 8,000 watches before it was sold to the Cornell Watch Co.

CHRONOLOGY OF THE DEVELOPMENT OF NEWARK WATCH CO.
Newark Watch Co. 1864-1870; S#s 6,501 to 12,000;
Cornell Watch Co.,Chicago, Ill. 1870-1874; S#s 12,001 to 25,000;
Cornell Watch Co., San Francisco, Calif. 1874-Jan. 1876; S#s 25,001 to 35,000;
California Watch Co., Jan. 1876-mid 1876.

⏱ A collector should expect to pay modestly higher prices at local shops.

⏱ **The Complete Price Guide to Watches goal is to stimulate the orderly exchange of <u>Watches</u> between "*buyers*" and "*sellers*".**

Newark Watch Co. Robert Fellows movement, 18 size, 15 jewels, key wind & set, serial number 12, 044.

Grade or Name — Description		Avg	Ex-Fn	Mint
18S, 15J, KW, KS, **HC**.. ★★		$325	$350	$550
18S, 15J, KW, KS, OF.. ★★		295	325	500
18S, 7J, KW, KS .... ★★		250	295	400
J. C. Adams, 11J, KW, KS .... ★★		295	325	500
J. C. Adams, 11J, KW, KS, Coin .... ★★		325	350	550
Edward Biven, 11-15J, KW, KS .... ★★		350	400	600
Robert Fellows, KW, KS.. ★★★		400	450	800
Keyless Watch Co., 15J, LS, SW .... ★★★		400	600	1,000
Newark Watch Co., 7-15J, KW, KS .... ★★		350	400	550
Arthur Wadsworth, SW .... ★★★		600	750	1,300
Arthur Wadsworth, 18S, 15J, 18K, HC ("Arthur Wadsworth, New York" on dial; "Keyless Watch, Patent #3655, June 19, 1866" engraved on movement) .... ★★★		1,500	1,900	3,200

NEW ENGLAND WATCH CO.
Waterbury, Connecticut
1898 - 1914

The New England Watch Co., formerly the Waterbury Watch Co., made a watch with a duplex escapement, gilt, 16S, open faced. Watches with the skeletonized movement are very desirable. The company later became Timex Watch Co.

Grade or Name — Description	Avg	Ex-Fn	Mint
16S, OF, duplex, **SKELETON**, good running order ....★	$295	$350	$600
12S, 16S, 18S, OF, pictures on dial: ladies, dogs, horses, trains, flags, ships, cards, etc...	150	195	500
12S, 16S, 18S, OF, duplex escapement, good running order	65	75	125
12S, 16S, 18S, OF, pin lever escapement, good running order	45	55	95

 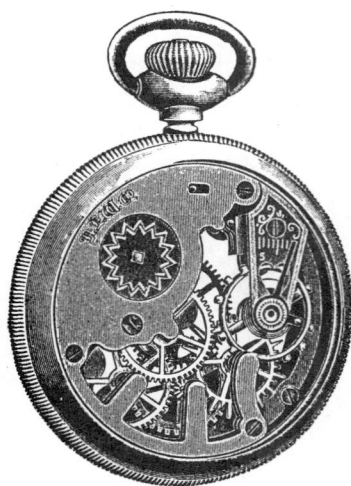

Front and back view of a **skeletonized** New England Watch Co. movement. This watch is fitted with a glass back and front, making the entire movement and wheels visible, 4 jewels, silver hands, black numbers, originally sold for $10-13.

Grade or Name — Description	Avg	Ex-Fn	Mint
6S, duplex	$40	$50	$75
0 S, 15-17 J, lever escapement	60	75	125
Addison, (all sizes)	50	60	125
Alden, (all sizes)	40	50	85
Ambassador, 12S, duplex	40	50	85
Americus, duplex	45	55	95
Berkshire, duplex, 14K, **GF**	60	75	125

New England Watch Co., 16 size, 7 jewels, open face, double roller, Dan Patch stop watch.

New England Watch Co., Scout, about 16 size, 4 jewels, duplex escapement, New England base metal case.

🕐 A collector should expect to pay modestly higher prices at local shops.

🕐 Pricing in this Guide are fair market price for **COMPLETE** watches which are reflected from the "**NAWCC**" National and regional shows.

New England Watch Co., multi-colored paper dials, showing poker style playing cards. Watches complete with these type dials bring **$350-$600-$1,200.**

New England Watch Co., Lady Mary, 0 size, 17 jewels, lever escapement, serial # 1,000,283.

Grade or Name — Description	Avg	Ex-Fn	Mint
Cadish, duplex escapement	$45	$60	$85
Cavour, duplex escapement...	45	60	85
Columbian	45	60	85
Chronograph, 7J, Start, Stop & Reset	135	150	300
Cruiser, duplex	45	60	85
Dan Patch, 7J .... ★	275	350	550
Dominion, **0 size**	40	50	75
Elf, series SS, duplex	45	60	85
Excelsior, 7J...	70	80	125
Enamel, full enamel cased watches back and bezel, blue, red,			
green, sizes from 6 size to 0 size....................................	95	125	350
Embossed, base metal cases with duplex escapement....................	80	95	200
Fancy , **"unfaded dial"**..	110	160	300
Fire Fly, about 8 size	45	60	85
Gabour...	70	80	125
General	45	60	85
Hale, 7J..	45	60	85
Jockey, duplex..	60	70	125
Lady Mary..	70	80	125
Oxford	45	60	85
Padishah, duplex	70	80	125
Putnam...	65	70	95
Queen Mab, duplex escapement - **0 size**, 4J	45	60	85
Rugby, stop watch..	70	80	125
Scout, 12 Size, duplex escapement, HC.............................	45	60	85
Senator, duplex escapement	45	60	85
Standish, about 12 size	45	60	85
Trump, duplex...	45	60	85
Tuxedo...	45	60	85
Tuxedo, DUPLEX ESCAPEMENT..	60	70	125

🕐 Some grades are not included. Their values can be determined by comparing with **similar** age, size, metal content, style, models and grades listed.

316

NEW HAVEN CLOCK AND WATCH CO.

New Haven, Connecticut

1853 - 1956

The company started making Marine clock movements with a balance wheel in about 1875, and used similar smaller movement to make watches in early 1880. The company soon reached a production of about 200 watches per day, making a total of some 40 million watches.

NEW HAVEN Clock & Watch Co., **Angelus**, with rotating dials, patented Jan 23, 1900.

NEW HAVEN, Ships Time, Ben Franklin dial. Note this watch uses only one hand.

Grade or Name – Description	Avg	Ex-Fn	Mint
Always Right	$45	$55	$85
Angelus, 2 rotating dials ★	135	195	350
Beardsley Radiant	65	75	115
Buddy	45	50	75
Bull Dog	40	45	70
Compensated	45	50	75
Captain Scout	80	95	160
Celluloid case (bold colors)	95	125	195
Chronometer	65	85	150
Earl	45	50	75
Elite	40	50	75
Elm City	45	50	75
Fancy dials, no fading	95	150	295
Football Timer ★	75	95	195
Ford Special	70	80	95
Hamilton	45	50	75
Handy Andy	55	70	125
Jerome USA	45	50	75

🕐 Note: Some styles, models and grades are not included. Their values can be determined by comparing with **similar** styles, size, age, models and grades listed.

NOTE : ADD $25 to $70 for original BOX and PAPERS

🕐 Pricing in this Guide are fair market price for **COMPLETE** watches which are reflected from the "**NAWCC**" National and regional shows.

Example of Kaiser Wilhelm.

Example of Traveler.

Grade or Name – Description		Avg	Ex-Fn	Mint
Kaiser Wilhelm	★ ★ ★	$400	$500	$900
Kermit		40	45	65
Laddie		25	30	50
Lady Clare		25	30	50
Leonard Watch Co.		25	40	60
Leonard		45	50	75
Mastercraft Rayolite		75	85	95
Miracle		45	50	75
Motor		35	40	60
Nehi		50	70	95
New Haven, pin lever, SW		65	75	125
New Haven, back wind		100	135	200
Panama Official Souvenir, 1915	★ ★ ★	295	375	750
Paul Pry, 14 size with a Locomotive on back of case		35	45	75
Pedometer, 14 size, OF		45	50	75
Pentagon-shaped case		45	50	75
Playing cards on dial	★ ★	350	500	900
Service		30	35	50
Ships Time & Franklin dial		75	95	150
Sports Timer		65	75	150
Surity		45	50	75
Tip Top		20	30	60
Tip Top Jr.		20	30	60
The American		45	50	70
Tommy Ticker		30	35	50
Tourist		45	50	75
Traveler, with travel case		40	45	70
True Time Teller Tip Top		40	45	70
United		30	35	50
USA		30	35	50
Victor		30	35	55

NOTE : ADD $25 to $70 for original BOX and PAPERS

🕐 Pricing in this Guide are fair market price for **COMPLETE** watches which are reflected from the "**NAWCC**" National and regional shows.

NEW HAVEN WATCH CO.

New Haven, Connecticut
1883 - 1887

This company was organized October 16, 1883 with the intention of producing W. E. Doolittle's patented watch; however, this plan was soon abandoned. They did produce a "Model A" watch, the first was marketed in the spring of 1884. Estimated total production is **200.** The original capital became absorbed by Trenton W. Co.

"The New Haven Watch Co. Alpha, 149, Pat. Dec. 27-81," engraved on movement, lever escapement, open face, extremely rare watch.

Grade or Name – Description		Avg	Ex-Fn	Mint
"A" Model, about 18S, pat. Dec. 27, '81 .... ★ ★ ★ ★ ★		$625	$750	$1,200
Alpha Model, pat. Dec. 27, '81 .... ★ ★ ★ ★ ★		625	750	1,200

NEW YORK CITY WATCH CO.

New York, New York
1890 - 1897

This company manufactured the Dollar-type watches, which had a pendant-type crank. The watch is wound by **cranking the pendant,** and has a pin lever escapement. The hands are set from the back of the watch movement. The" **patent number 526,871",** is engraved on movement, patent is dated October 1894, and was held by S. Schisgall. The New York City Watch Co., 20 size watch has the words "Lever Winder" printed on the paper dial.

🕑 A collector should expect to pay modestly higher prices at local shops.

🕑 Watches listed in this book are priced at the collectable fair market value at the Trade Show level, as complete watches having an original 14k gold filled case, KEY WIND with silver, an original white enamel single sunk dial, and with the entire original movement in good working order with no repairs needed, unless otherwise noted.

Grade or Name – Description	Avg	Ex-Fn	Mint
18-20S, no jewels, "**Lever Winder**" on dial .... ★ ★ ★ ★	$600	$800	$1,300
18-20S, no jewels, "**SUN DIAL**" on dial .... ★ ★ ★ ★	$700	$800	$1,200

New York City Watch Co., about 18-20 size, "**Lever Winder**" printed on paper dial. This watch is <u>**WOUND**</u> by cranking the pendant back and forth , pin lever escapement, also **back set,** & *"New York City Watch Co., patent No. 526,871"* engraved on movement.

NEW YORK CHRONOGRAPH WATCH CO.
NEW YORK, NEW YORK
1880 -1885

This company sold about 800 watches marked "New York Chronograph Watch Co." The 18 size stop watch was manufactured by Manhattan Watch Co.

Grade or Name –Description	Avg	Ex-Fn	Mint
18S, 7J, stop watch, HC .... ★	$125	$150	$275
18S, 7J, stop watch, OF .... ★	95	125	195
16S, 7J, SW, time only, OF .... ★	150	175	250
16S, 9-11J, SW, time only, OF...................................... ★	150	175	250
16S, 7-11J, SW, time only sweep sec., OF .... ★	125	150	400
16S, 7-11J, SW, **true CHRONOGRAPH**, OF............. ★ ★ ★ ★	325	500	1,000

 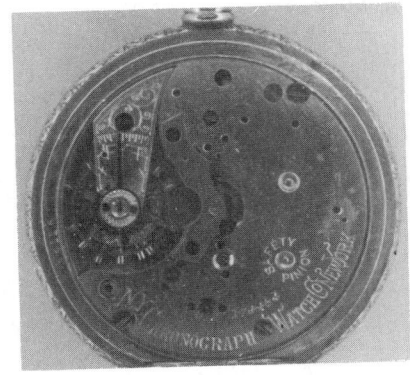

N.Y. Chronograph Watch Co., dial and movement, 16 size, 7 jewels, open face, time only, sweep second hand.

New York Chronograph Watch Co. dial and movement, 7 jewels, open face, buttons at the top of case set hands and stop watch.

NEW YORK STANDARD WATCH CO.
(CROWN WATCH CO.)
Jersey City, New Jersey
1885 - 1929

The first watch reached the market in early 1888 and was a 18S. The most interesting feature was a straight line lever with a "worm gear escapement." This was patented by R. J. Clay. All watches were quick train and open-faced. The company also made its own cases and sold a complete watch. A prefix number was added to the serial number after the first 10,000 watches were made. Estimated total production was 7,000,000.

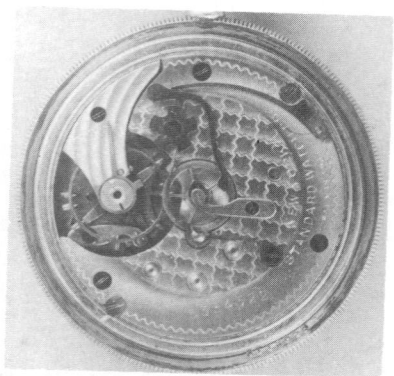 

New York Standard, Chronograph, 18 size, 7 jewels, stem wind, second hand start-stop and fly back, three-quarter plate, serial number 5,334,322.

New York Standard, converts to a hunting case movement or a open face movement, serial number 602,506.

N. Y. STANDARD
16 AND 18 SIZE

Grade or Name – Description	Avg	Ex-Fn	Mint
18S, 7J, N. Y. Standard, KW, KS	$250	$295	$395
18S, 7J, N. Y. Standard, SW	50	60	85
18S, 15J, N. Y. Standard, SW, LS, HC	95	125	175
Chronograph, 7-11J, 3/4, NI, DMK, SW, fly back hand	150	195	400
Chronograph, 10J, (marked 10J), fly back hand ★	195	250	425
Chronograph, 13J, sweep sec., stop & fly back hand	150	195	400
Chronograph, 15J, 3/4, NI, DMK, SW, fly back hand,	150	195	400
Columbus, 7J	50	60	85
Convertible, 15J., 16 size, can be changed to HC or OF .... ★★★★	295	400	750
Crown W. Co., 7J, OF or HC	50	60	75
Crown W. Co., 15J, HC	60	75	95
Dan Patch, 7J, stop watch(pat. DEC. 22 '08) ★	250	350	575
Dan Patch, 17J, stop watch(pat. DEC. 22 '08) ★★	375	450	650
Edgemere, 7J, OF & HC	50	60	85
Excelsior, 7J, OF or HC	50	60	85

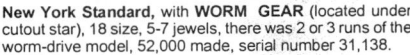

New York Standard, with **WORM GEAR** (located under cutout star), 18 size, 5-7 jewels, there was 2 or 3 runs of the worm-drive model, 52,000 made, serial number 31,138.

Remington W. Co. (marked on movement & case), 16 size, 11 jewels, 2-tone damaskeening, NOTE crown wheel & ratchet (no click), serial # CC021,331.

Grade or Name – Description	Avg	Ex-Fn	Mint
Harvard W. CO., 7–11J.,	$40	$50	$75
Hi Grade	50	60	85
Ideal	50	60	85
Jefferson, 7J.,	50	60	85
La Salle, 7J.,	35	45	65
New Era, 7J., **skeletonized** (Poor Man's Dudley) OF- HC	250	300	550
New Era, 7–11J.	40	50	75
New York Standard W. Co., 11J, 3/4	60	75	95
New York Standard, 7J, 3/4	60	75	95
New York Standard, 15J, BRG	75	95	125
N. Y. Standard, with (" WORM GEAR") ★	400	600	1,000
N. Y. Standard, with (" WORM GEAR") multi-color dial ..... ★	600	800	1,200

⊕ Note: Some styles, models and grades are not included. Their values can be determined by comparing with **similar** styles, size, age, models and grades listed.

⊕ A collector should expect to pay modestly higher prices at local shops.

⊕ Pricing in this Guide are fair market price for **COMPLETE** watches which are reflected from the "**NAWCC**" National and regional shows.

Grade or Name – Description	Avg	Ex-Fn	Mint
Pan- America, 7J, OF	$60	$85	$140
Perfection, 7J, OF or HC	50	60	75
Perfection, 15J, OF or HC, NI	60	75	95
Remington W. Co., 11J, marked mvt. & case	75	95	150
Solar W. Co., 7J	50	60	85
Special USA, 7J	45	50	65
18S Tribune USA, 23J, HC or OF, Pat. Reg. Adj.	150	175	300
Washington, 7-11J	50	60	85
William Penn, 7-11J	50	60	85
Wilmington, 7-11J	50	60	85

For watches with **O'Hara Multi-Color Dials,** add $75 -$100 to value in **mint condition;** add $40-$60 for Hunting Cases.

12 SIZE

Grade or Name – Description	Avg	Ex-Fn	Mint
N. Y. Standard, 7J-11J, OF	$25	$30	$45
N. Y. Standard, 7J-11J, HC	40	50	65
N. Y. Standard, 7J, **Multi-Color dial**	70	125	250
N. Y. Standard, 15J, OF	35	40	55
N. Y. Standard, 15J, HC	45	55	70
Crown W. Co., 7J, OF or HC	30	40	55

 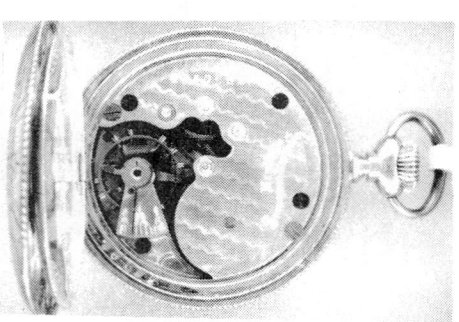

New York Standard Watch Co., 12 size, 7 jewels, open face, serial number 1,021,224.　　New York Standard W.Co., 6 size G# 144, Hunting Case.

6 SIZE - 0 SIZE - 3/0 SIZE

Grade or Name – Description	Avg	Ex-Fn	Mint
Alton, 7-15J	$35	$40	$55
American, 7J	35	40	55
Empire State W. Co., 7J	40	50	75
Excelsior, 7J, HC	40	50	65
6S, Columbia, 7J, HC	60	70	85
Crown W. Co., 7J, 6 size & 0 size, OF or HC	40	50	65
Standard USA, 7J	40	50	65
6S, N. Y. Standard, 7J, HC	60	70	85
6S, Orient, SW	30	40	60
6S, Progress, 7J, YGF	40	50	65
0S, Ideal, 7J, HC	60	70	85
0S, N. Y. Standard, 7J, HC	60	70	85

🕐 Pricing in this Guide are fair market price for **COMPLETE** watches which are reflected from the "**NAWCC**" National and regional shows.

NEW YORK STANDARD WATCH CO.
IDENTIFICATION OF MOVEMENTS

How to Identify Your Watch Size & Model: Compare the movement of your watch with the illustrations in this section. While comparing, note the location of the balance, jewels, screws, gears, and type of back plate (Full, 3/4, Bridge) these will be clues in identifying the movement you have.

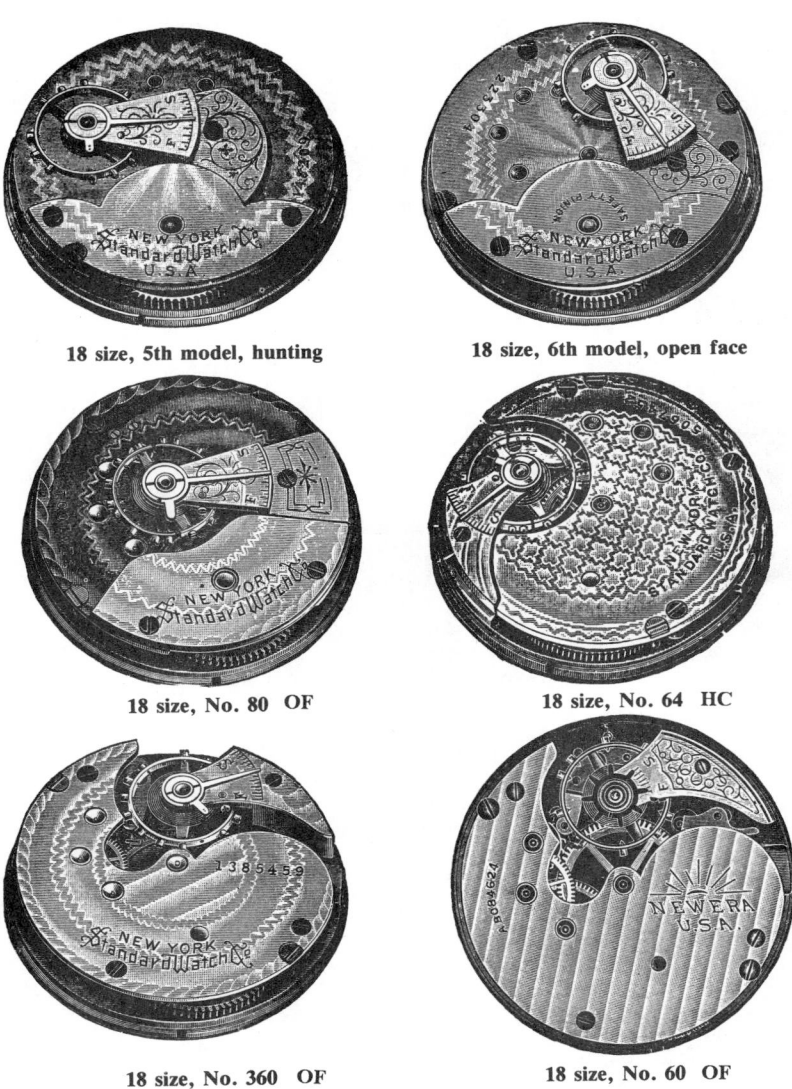

18 size, 5th model, hunting

18 size, 6th model, open face

18 size, No. 80 OF

18 size, No. 64 HC

18 size, No. 360 OF

18 size, No. 60 OF

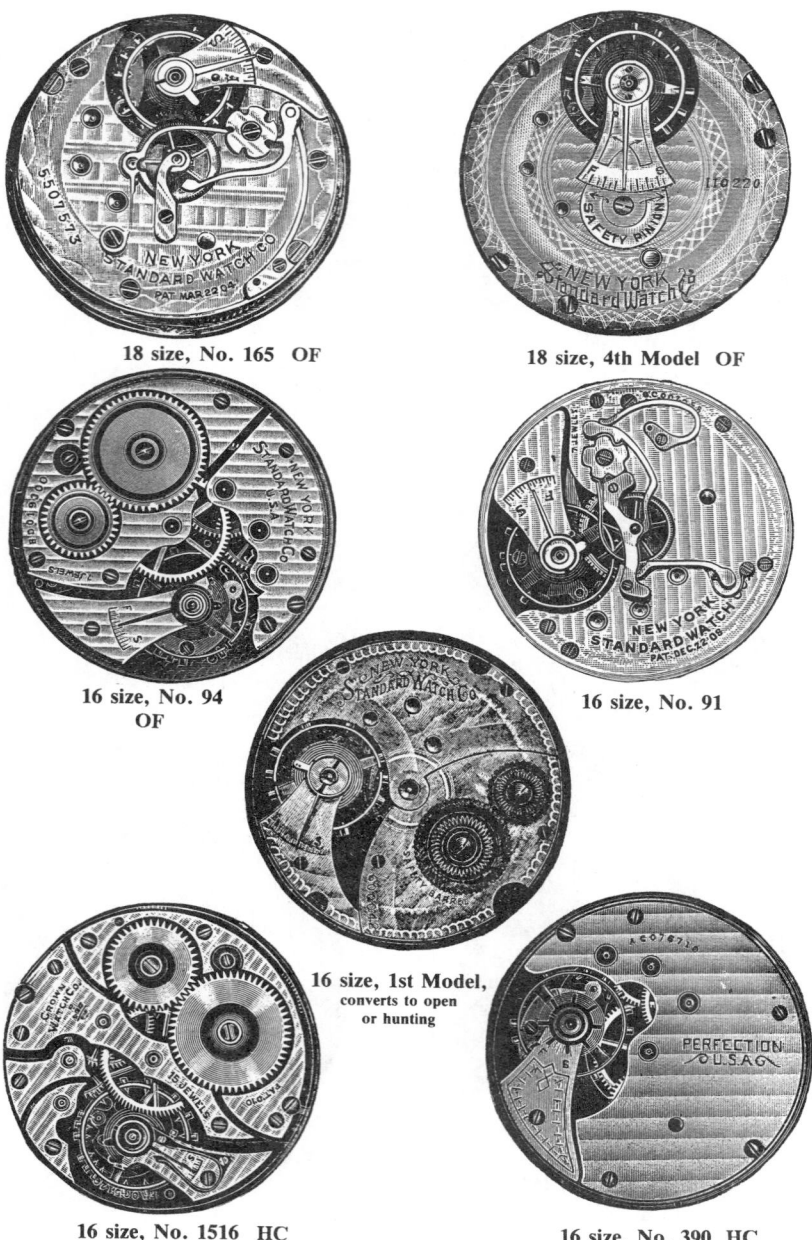

18 size, No. 165 OF

18 size, 4th Model OF

16 size, No. 94
OF

16 size, No. 91

16 size, 1st Model,
converts to open
or hunting

16 size, No. 1516 HC

16 size, No. 390 HC

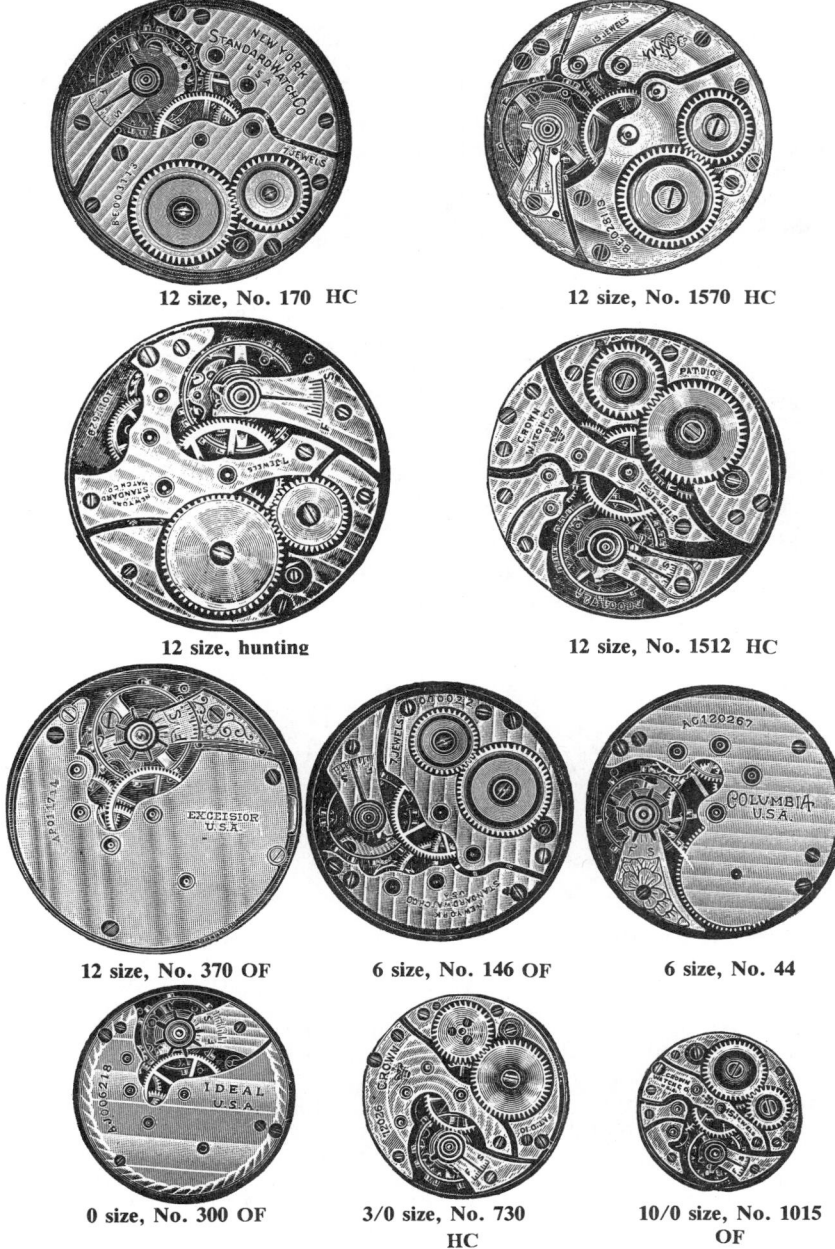

12 size, No. 170 HC

12 size, No. 1570 HC

12 size, hunting

12 size, No. 1512 HC

12 size, No. 370 OF

6 size, No. 146 OF

6 size, No. 44

0 size, No. 300 OF

3/0 size, No. 730
HC

10/0 size, No. 1015
OF

NEW YORK SPRINGFIELD WATCH CO.
Springfield, Massachusetts
1866 - 1876

The New York Watch Co. had a rather difficult time getting started. The name of the company was changed from the Mozart Watch Co. to the New York Watch Co., and it was located in Rhode Island. Before any watches had been sold, they moved to Springfield, Mass., in 1867. A factory was built there, but only about 100 watches were produced before a fire occurred on April 23, 1870. Shortly after the fire, in 1870, a newly-designed watch was introduced. The first movements reached the market in 1871, and the first grade was a fully-jeweled adjusted movement called "Frederick Billings." The standard 18S and the Swiss Ligne systems were both used in gauging the size of these watches. The New York Watch Co. used full signatures on its movements. The doors closed in the summer of 1876.

In January 1877, the Hampden Watch Co. was organized and commenced active operation in June 1877.

CHRONOLOGY OF THE DEVELOPMENT OF NEW YORK WATCH CO.

The Mozart Watch Co., Providence, R. I. 1864-1866
New York Watch Co., Providence, R. I. 1866-1867
New York Watch Co., Springfield, Mass. 1867-1875
New York Watch Mfg. Co., Springfield, Mass. 1875-1876
Hampden Watch Co., Springfield, Mass. 1877-1886
Hampden-Dueber Watch Co., Springfield, Mass. 1886-1888
Hampden Watch Co. Works, Canton, Ohio 1888-1923
Dueber-Hampden Watch Co., Canton, Ohio 1923-1930
Amtorg, U.S.S.R. 1930

NEW YORK WATCH CO.SPRINGFIELD
ESTIMATED SERIAL NUMBERS
AND PRODUCTION DATES

DATE – SERIAL NO.	DATE – SERIAL NO.
1866 – 1,000	1871 – 20,000
1867 – 3,000	1872 – 30,000
1868 – 5,000	1873 – 40,000
1869 – 7,000	1874 – 50,000
1870 – 10,000	1875 – 60,000

The above list is provided for determining the APPROXIMATE age of your watch. Match serial number with date. Watches were not necessarily sold in the exact order of manufactured date.

N. Y. W. SPRINGFIELD
SPRINGFIELD
18 TO 20 SIZE

Grade or Name – Description		Avg	Ex-Fn	Mint
Aaron Bagg, 7J, KW, KS .... ★		$225	$275	$550
Frederick Billings, 15J, KW, KS..................................... ★		225	275	550
E. W. Bond, 15-17J, 3/4 .... ★★★		500	550	950
E. W. Bond, 18J, Adj., GJS, 3/4................................. ★★★		575	700	1,200
J. A. Briggs, 11J, KW, KS, from back .... ★★		295	400	750

🕐 Some grades are not included. Their values can be determined by comparing with **similar** age, size, metal content, style, models and grades listed.

🕐 Watches listed in this book are priced at the collectable trade show level, as **complete** watches having an original 14k gold-filled case and *Key Wind* with silver, an original white enamel single sunk dial, and with the entire original movement in good working order with no repairs needed.

🕐 Pricing in this Guide are fair market price for **COMPLETE** watches which are reflected from the "**NAWCC**" National and regional shows.

E.W. Bond movement, 18 size, 15 jewels, three-quarter plate.

Chas. E. Hayward, 18 size, 15 jewels, key wind & set, note the **hidden key,** serial number 18,733.

Grade or Name – Description		Avg	Ex-Fn	Mint
Albert Clark, 11-15J, KW, KS, from back, 3/4	★★	$300	$350	$550
Homer Foot, 11-15J, KW, KS, from back, 3/4	★	225	275	475
Herman Gerz, 11J, KW, KS	★	195	250	450
John Hancock, 7J, KW, KS		95	150	295
John Hancock, 7J, KW, KS, Silveroid		85	125	250
John Hancock, 7J, KW, KS, Coin		125	150	295
Chas. E. Hayward, 11-15J, KW, KS, long balance cock		150	195	350
Chas. E. Hayward, 11-15J, KW, KS, Coin		150	195	350
J. L. King, 15-17J, KW, KS, from back, 3/4	★	400	450	800
New York Watch Co., 7 11J, KW, KS	★	195	250	450
New York Watch Co., 15-19J, KW, KS, **Wolf's Teeth winding, (Serial #s below 75)** (20 lignes)	★★★★★	1,000	1,400	2,200
New York Watch Co., 15-19J, KW, KS, **Wolf's Teeth winding,** all original (20 lignes)	★★★	800	900	1,500
New York Watch Co., 11J, KW, KS	★★	250	295	400
H. G. Norton, 15J, KW, KS, from back, 3/4	★	250	295	400
H. G. Norton, 17J, KW, KS, from back, 3/4	★	295	350	450
H. G. Norton, 19J, KW, KS, from back, 3/4	★★★	450	550	800

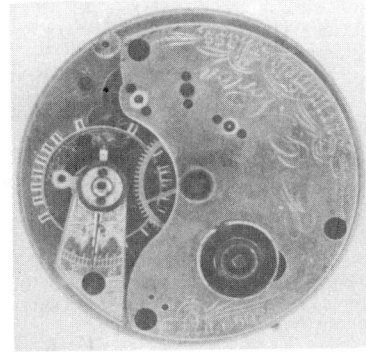

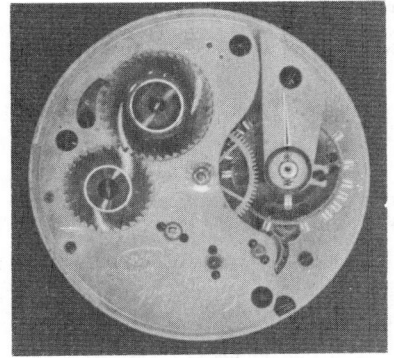

H.G. Norton, 18 size, 15 jewels, three-quarter plate, gold escape wheel, serial number 6592.

SPRINGFIELD, (20 lignes), 15-19 jewels, stem wind, hunting case, note **wolf teeth winding,** serial number 978.

State Street movement, 18 size, 15 jewels, three-quarter plate.

Theo E. Studley movement, 18 size, 15 jewels, key wind & set, full plate.

Grade or Name – Description	Avg	Ex-Fn	Mint
J. C. Perry, 15J ....★	$80	$125	$300
J. C. Perry, 15J, Silveroid ....★	75	100	200
Railway, 15J, KW, FULL, Coin ....★ ★ ★	700	800	1,500
Railway, 15J, KW, KS, FULL ....★ ★ ★	600	700	1,400
William Romp,15J,KW,KS from back,3/4 ....★ ★	300	400	750
Geo. Sam Rice, 7J, KW, KS.............................★	150	200	400
Springfield, 15J, KW, KS, from back, ADJ, **Wolf teeth winding,** serial Nos. below 1,000, (20 lignes) ....★ ★ ★	800	900	1,500
Springfield, 19J, KW, KS, from back, ADJ, **Wolf teeth winding,** serial Nos. below 1,000, (20 lignes) ....★ ★ ★	900	1,000	1,600
State Street, 11J, 3/4, SW ....★ ★	195	275	500
State Street, 15J, 3/4, SW ....★ ★	250	300	600
Theo E. Studley, 15J, KW, Coin	95	150	250
Theo E. Studley, 15J, KW, KS................................	95	150	250
George Walker, 17J, KW, 3/4, ADJ.....................★	295	350	550
Chester Woolworth, 15J, KW, KS	95	150	250
Chester Woolworth, 11J, KW, KS	75	125	225
Chester Woolworth, 11J, KW, KS, Silveroid	70	120	195
Chester Woolworth, 11J, KW, KS, ADJ....................	95	150	250
#4, 15J, ADJ, KW, KS	95	150	250
#5, 15J, KW, KS...	75	125	195
#6, 11J, KW, KS	75	125	195
#6, 11J, KW, KS, Silveroid	75	95	175

🕐 Some KW, KS watches made by the New York Watch Co. have a hidden key.If you unscrew the crown, and the crown comes out as a key, add $100 to the listed value.

🕐 Watches listed in this book are priced at the collectable trade show level, as **complete** watches having an original 14k gold-filled case and *Key Wind* with silver, an original white enamel single sunk dial, and with the entire original movement in good working order with no repairs needed.

🕐 This book endeavours to be a GUIDE or helpful manual and offers a wealth of material to be used as a tool not as a absolute document. Price Guides are like watches the worst may be better than none at all, but at best cannot be expected to be 100% accurate.

🕐 Characteristics of watches differ for the same age of both case and movement, because these features vary it may not be accurate to date a watch by one single influence. Example: the second hand was _not_ commonly found on watches before 1750, but common about 1800. The first second hand appeared in 1665 and another in 1690. Therefore statements are broad rather than accurate.

🕐 A collector should expect to pay modestly higher prices at local shops.

NON-MAGNETIC WATCH CO.

Geneva and America
1887 - 1905

The Non-Magnetic Watch Co. sold and imported watches from the Swiss as well as contracted watches made in America. Geneva Non-Magnetic marked watches appear to be the oldest type of movement. This company sold a full line of watches, high grade to low grade, as well as repeaters and ladies watches. An advertisement appeared in the monthly journal of ''Locomotive Engineers'' in 1887. The ad states that the ''Paillard's patent non-magnetic watches are uninfluenced by magnetism of electricity.'' Each watch contains the Paillard's patent non-magnetic, inoxidizable compensation balance and hairspring. An ad in 1888 shows prices for 16 size Swiss style watches as low as $15 for 7 jewels and as high as $135 for 20 jewels.

18 SIZE
(must be marked Paillard's Patent)

Grade or Name – Description	Avg	Ex-Fn	Mint
Elgin, 17J, FULL, SW, LS, OF	$90	$125	$195
Elgin, 17J, FULL, SW, LS, HC	125	175	295
Elgin, 15J, FULL, SW, LS, OF	90	125	195
Elgin, 15J, FULL, SW, LS, HC	125	175	295
Illinois, 24J, GJS, NI, Adj.5P, OF	650	750	1,300
Illinois, 24J, GJS, NI, Adj.5P, HC ★★	800	900	1,700
Illinois, 23J, GJS, NI, Adj.5P, OF	600	700	1,000
Illinois, 23J, GJS, NI, Adj.5P, HC ★★★	1,600	1,800	2,400
Illinois, 21J, GJS, NI, Adj.5P, OF	225	275	450
Illinois, 21J, GJS, NI, Adj.5P, HC	295	350	650
Illinois, 17J, NI, ADJ, OF	125	150	250
Illinois, 17J, NI, ADJ, HC	175	225	350
Illinois, 15J, NI, OF	95	125	195
Illinois, 15J, NI, HC	125	150	250
Illinois, 11J, OF	50	70	195
Illinois, 11J, HC	70	95	250

Non-Magnetic Watch Co., 18 size, 15 jewels, gold jewel settings, Adj.5p, Hunting Case, by Peoria Watch Co.

Non-Magnetic Watch Co., 18 size, 21 Ruby jewels, Adj.5p, note "Paillard" engraved on movement, made by Illinois Watch Co.

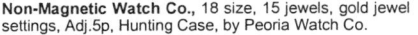

🕐 Watches listed in this book are priced at the collectabl trade show level, as **complete** watches having an original 14k gold-filled case and *Key Wind* with silver, an original white enamel single sunk dial, and with the entire original movement in good working order with no repairs needed.

Non-Magnetic Watch Co., 18 size, min repeater, jewelled through to the hammers, S # 6,870.

Non-Magnetic Watch Co., 18 size, 16 jewels, Bar bridge model, example of a Swiss Ebauche.

Grade or Name – Description	Avg	Ex-Fn	Mint
Peoria, 17J, FULL, SW, LS, Adj., OF	$175	$250	$450
Peoria, 15J, FULL, SW, LS, Adj., OF	150	195	375
Peoria, 15J, FULL, SW, LS, Adj., HC	250	300	475
Peoria, 11J, FULL, SW, LS, OF	95	150	250
Peoria, 11J, FULL, SW, LS, HC	175	200	300
Swiss, 16J, 3/4 plate, SW, LS, Adj., OF	50	70	175
Swiss, 16J, 3/4 plate, SW, LS, Adj., HC	75	100	200
Swiss, 15-16J, bar bridge, SW, LS, Adj., OF	50	70	185
Swiss, 15-16J, bar bridge, SW, LS, Adj., HC	70	100	200
Swiss, 11J, 3/4 plate, SW, LS, OF, HC	70	80	175
Swiss, 11J, bar bridge, SW, LS, OF, HC	70	80	175
Swiss, **min repeater**, jewelled through to the hammers	2,000	2,400	3,400

Non-Magnetic Watch Co., 18 size, 17 Ruby jewels, adjusted, made by Elgin Watch Co.

Non-Magnetic Watch Co., 16 size, 21 Ruby jewels, adjusted, made by Illinois Watch Co. **Model 5, G# 179**.

🕐 Watches listed in this book are priced at the collectable fair market value at the Trade Show level, as complete watches having an original 14k gold filled case, KEY WIND with silver, an original white enamel single sunk dial, and with the entire original movement in good working order with no repairs needed, unless otherwise noted.

🕐 Pricing in this Guide are fair market price for **COMPLETE** watches which are reflected from the "<u>NAWCC</u>" National and regional shows.

Non-Magnetic Watch Co., 16 size, 3/4 plate, 16 jewels, lever set, gilded, hunting case, adjusted, "Paillard's Patent, Balance And Spring" engraved on movement, S# 251568. Swiss made.

Non-Magnetic Watch Co., 16 size, 1/2 plate, 15-20 jewels, note "Paillard's Patent, Balance And Spring" engraved on movement. Swiss made.

16 SIZE

(must be marked Paillard's Patent)

Grade or Name – Description	Avg	Ex-Fn	Mint
Elgin, 21J, ADJ 5P, OF	$125	$150	$325
Elgin, 21J, ADJ 5P, HC	195	250	425
Elgin, 17J, ADJ 5P, OF	70	125	250
Elgin, 17J, ADJ 5P, HC	95	150	300
Illinois, 21J, GJS, 3/4, DR, Adj.6P, OF	175	225	450
Illinois, 21J, GJS, 3/4, DR, Adj.6P, HC	250	295	625
Illinois, 17J, 3/4, DR, ADJ, OF	70	125	275
Illinois, 17J, 3/4, DR, ADJ, HC	125	175	325
Illinois, 15J, HC	95	150	200
Illinois, 15J, OF	60	95	175
Illinois, 11J, OF	55	75	150
Illinois, 11J, HC	70	125	150
Swiss, 20J, GJS, DR, Adj.6P, NI, 1/2 ,OF	80	125	225
Swiss, 20J, GJS, DR, Adj.6P, NI, 1/2, HC	80	125	195
Swiss, 18J, GJS, DR, Adj.6P, NI, 1/2, OF	95	150	250
Swiss, 18J, GJS, DR, Adj.6P, NI, 1/2, HC	150	175	275
Swiss, 16J, GJS, DR, Adj.6P, NI, 1/2, OF	70	90	175
Swiss, 16J, GJS, DR, Adj.6P, NI, 1/2, HC	90	125	195
Swiss, 16J, DR, adjusted, gilded, 3/4, OF	50	90	150
Swiss, 16J, DR, adjusted, gilded, 3/4, HC	70	125	175
Swiss, 7-11J, gilded, 3/4, OF	40	60	95
Swiss, 7-11J, gilded, 3/4, HC	70	90	175

Non-Magnetic Watch Co., 16 size, 17J., by Elgin W. Co.   Non-Magnetic Watch Co., 16 size, 17J., by Elgin W. Co.

OTAY WATCH CO.

Otay, California
1889 - 1894

This company produced about 1,000 watches with a serial number range of 1,000 to 1,500 and 30,000 to 31,000. The company was purchased by a Japanese manufacturer in 1894. Names on Otay movements include: Golden Gate, F. A. Kimball, Native Sun, Overland Mail, R. D. Perry, and P. H. Wheeler. Machinery sold to Osaka of Japan. Only a few watches were made. Osaka watches look about the same as Otay watches.

Otay Watch Co. Dial; note hunting case style and lever for setting hands.

Otay Watch Co., F.A. Kimball, 18 size, 15 jewels, lever set, hunting, serial number 1,264.

18 SIZE

Grade or Name – Description		Avg	Ex-Fn	Mint
California, 15J., LS, HC, NI	★★★	$1,800	$2,300	$3,000
Golden Gate, 15J, LS, HC, OF, NI	★★★	2,000	2,800	4,000
F. A. Kimball, 15J, LS, HC, Gilt	★★	1,400	1,800	2,400
Native Son, 15J, LS, HC, NI	★★	2,800	3,200	4,000
Overland Mail, 15J, LS, HC, NI	★★★	2,400	2,700	4,200
R. D. Perry, 15J, LS, HC, Gilt	★★	1,400	1,800	2,400
P. H. Wheeler, 15J, LS, HC, Gilt	★★	1,400	1,800	2,400
Sunset, 7J, Gilt, HC	★★	1,600	2,000	2,800
Osaka W. Co., 15J, NI, or gilt, (made in Japan)	★★★★	3,000	3,500	4,500

D. D. PALMER WATCH CO.

Waltham, Massachusetts
1864 - 1875

In 1858, at age 20, Mr. Palmer opened a small jewelry store in Waltham, Mass. Here he became interested in pocket chronometers. At first he bought the balance and jewels from Swiss manufacturers. In 1864 he took a position with the American Watch Co. and made the chronometers in his spare time (only about 25 produced). They were,18S, 3/4 plate, gilded, key wind, and some were nickel. At first they were fusee driven, but he mainly used going barrels. About 1870, Palmer started making lever watches and by 1875 he left the American Watch Co. and started making a 10S keywind, gilded movement, and a 16S, 3/4 plate, gilt and nickel, and a stem wind of his own invention (a vibrating crown wheel). In all he made about 1,500 watches. The signature appearing on the watches was ''Palmer W. Co. Wal., Mass.''

He basically had three grades of watches: Fine-Solid Nickel; Medium-Nickel Plated; and Medium-Gold Gilt. They were made in open-face and hunter cases.

D. D. Palmer Watch Co., 18 size, 15 jewels, Palmer's Pat.
Stem Winder on movement, serial number 1,098.

Grade or name – Description		Avg	Ex-Fn	Mint
10-16S, 15-17J, 3/4 plate, spring detent chronometer .... ★★★★		$4,000	$5,000	$8,000
16-18S, 15-17J, NI, OF, **18K** .... ★★★		2,500	2,900	5,400

PEORIA WATCH CO.

Peoria, Illinois

1885 - 1895

The roots of this company began with the Independent Watch Co. (1875 - 1881). The watches marked Mark Twain were made by the Fredonia Watch Co. (1881 - 1885). Peoria Watch Co. opened Dec. 19, 1885, and made one model of railroad watches in about 1887.

Peoria watches were 18S, quick train, 15 jewel, and all stem wind. These watches are hard to find, as only about 3,000 were made. Peoria also made railroad watches for A. C. Smith's Non-Magnetic Watch Co. of America, from 1884-1888. The 18 size watches were full plate, adjusted, and had a whiplash regulator.

The Peoria Watch Co. closed in 1889, having produced about 47,000 watches.

Peoria Watch Co., 18 size, 15 jewels, nickel damaskeening plates, hunting, note patented regulator, serial number 11,532.

🕓 Watches listed in this book are priced at the collectable fair market value at the Trade Show level, as complete watches having an original 14k gold filled case, KEY WIND with silver, an original white enamel single sunk dial, and with the entire original movement in good working order with no repairs needed, unless otherwise noted.

Grade or Name – Description	Avg	Ex-Fn	Mint
18S, 9-11J, SW, OF	$150	$195	$400
18S, 15J, SW, personalized name	250	300	500
18S, Peoria W. Co., 15J, SW, OF	175	250	450
18S, Peoria W. Co., 15J, SW, HC	250	275	500
18S, Peoria W. Co., 15J, SW, low S# ★	295	400	800
18S, Anti-Magnetic, 15J, OF	250	325	450
18S, Anti-Magnetic, 15J, HC	295	375	550
18S, Anti-Magnetic, 15J, For Railway Service, OF ★	400	450	700
18S, Anti-Magnetic, 15J, For Railway Service, HC ★	425	475	850
18S, Superior Quality Anti-Magnetic, 15J, NI, SW, GJS, Adj.5P, OF ★★	500	600	900
18S, Superior Quality Anti-Magnetic, 15J, NI, SW, GJS, Adj.5P, HC ★★★	550	650	950
18S, For Railway Service, 15J, NI, GJS, Adj.5P, OF ★	350	400	800
18S, For Railway Service, 15J, NI, GJS, Adj.5P, HC ★	400	500	875

PHILADELPHIA WATCH CO.

Philadelphia, Pennsylvania

1868 - 1886

Eugene Paulus organized the Philadelphia Watch Co. about 1868. Most all the parts were made in Switzerland, and finished and cased in this country. The International Watch Co. is believed to have manufactured the movements for Philadelphia Watch Co. Estimated total production of the company is 12,000 watches.

Issued by the U. S. Patent Office, August 25, and November 3, 1868.

Philadelphia Watch Co., 16 size, 15 jewels, gold jewel settings, hunting case model. "Paulus' Patents 1868. Aug. 25th, Nov. 3rd" on movement, serial number 5,751.

NOV. 1871 advertising 15,16,19, & 21 size watches for sale at their New York City and Philadelphia offices.

Grade or Name – Description	Avg	Ex-Fn	Mint
18S, 15J, SW, HC ★	$225	$300	$500
18S, 15J, KW, KS ★	275	375	500
18S, 15J, SW, OF ★	195	250	450
18S, HC, KW, KS, **18K** original case marked Philadelphia Watch Co. ★★	1,000	1,200	1,600
18S, 11J, KW, KS ★	95	150	195
16S, 15J, KW, KS ★	150	175	250
16S, 19J, KW, KS, GJS ★	295	400	650
8S-6S, 11J, HC ★	95	125	195
8S-6S, 15J, HC ★	125	175	225
8S-6S, Paulus, 19J, KW, KS ★	150	200	475
000/S, 7J, HC, PS ★	125	195	295

JAMES & HENRY PITKIN

Hartford, Connecticut
New York, New York
1838 - 1852

Henry Pitkin was the first to attempt to manufacture watches by machinery. The machines were of Pitkin's own design and very crude, but he had some brilliant ideas. His first four workers were paid $30 a year plus their board. After much hardship, the first watches were produced in the fall of 1838. The watches had going barrels, not the fusee and chain, and the American flag was engraved on the plates to denote they were American made and to exemplify the true spirit of American independence in watchmaking.

The first 50 watches were stamped with the name "Henry Pitkin." Others bore the firm name "H. & J. F. Pitkin." The movements were about 16S and 3/4 plate. The plates were rolled brass and stamped out with dies. The pinions were lantern style with eight leaves. The movement had a slow train of 14,400 beats per hour. Pitkin's first plan was to make the ends of the pinions conical and let them run in the ends of hardened steel screws, similar to the Marine clock balances. A large brass setting was put in the plates and extended above the surface. Three screws, with small jewels set in their ends, were inserted so that they closed about the pivot with very small end shake. This proved to be too expensive and was used in only a few movements. Next, he tried to make standard type movements extend above the plates with the end shake controlled by means of a screw running down into the end of the pivots, reducing friction. This "capped jewel train" was used for a while before he adopted the standard ways of jeweling. The escape wheels were the star type, English style. The balance was made of gold and steel. These movements were fire gilded and not interchangeable. The dials, hands, mainsprings and hairsprings were imported. The rounded pallets were manufactured by Pitkin, and the cases for his watches were made on the premises. As many as 900 watches could have been made by Pitkin.

Grade or Name – Description		Avg	Ex-Fn	Mint
Henry Pitkin S#1-50 .... ★★★★★		$25,000	$40,000	$80,000
H. & J. F. Pitkin, S#50-377 .... ★★★★		15,000	20,000	40,000
Pitkin & Co., **New York**, S#378-900 .... ★★★		6,000	8,000	16,000
W. Pitkin, Hartford, Conn., S# approx. 40,000, fusee lever, KW, Coin .... ★★		1,200	1,500	2,400

H. & J. F. Pitkin, about 16 size, engraved on movement
"H. & J. F. PITKIN DETACHED LEVER", key wind & set.

Movements marked with **New York** are English made. (Imports)

ALBERT H. POTTER WATCH CO.
New York, New York
1855 - 1875

Albert Potter started his apprenticeship in 1852. When this was completed he moved to New York to take up watchmaking on his own. He made about **35 to 40 watches in USA** that sold for $225 to $350. Some were chronometers, some were lever escapements, key wind, gilded movements, some were fusee driven, both bridge and 3/4 plate. Potter was a contemporary of Charles Fasoldt and John Mulford, both horological inventors from Albany, N. Y. Potter moved to Cuba in 1861 but returned to New York in 1868. In 1872 he worked in Chicago and formed the Potter Brothers Company with his brother William. He moved to Geneva in about 1876 to make his high grade Swiss timepieces and about 600 of these watches were made.(For futher information on Potter Geneva timepieces, **SEE European Section**)

below U.S. mfg.

Grade or Name – Description	Avg	Ex-Fn	Mint
18S, BRG lever, Chronometer, signed A. H. Potter,			
NewYork, 18K Potter case, **U.S. mfg.** .... ★★★★★	$12,000	$14,000	$22,000
18S, BRG lever with wind indicator, **18K** Potter case .... ★★★	7,000	9,000	15,000
18S-20S, **Tourbillon,** signed A. H. Potter, **Boston,** gilded,			
18K Potter case, **U.S. mfg.** .... ★★★★★	25,000	35,000	50,000

below GENEVA Mfg. (Dollar Watch)

Grade or Name – Description	Avg	Ex-Fn	Mint
16S, "Charmilles," 3/4 plate, Geneva, (Dollar Watch)............. ★★	$300	$375	$750

(Note: For futher information on Potter Geneva timepieces, **SEE European Section**)

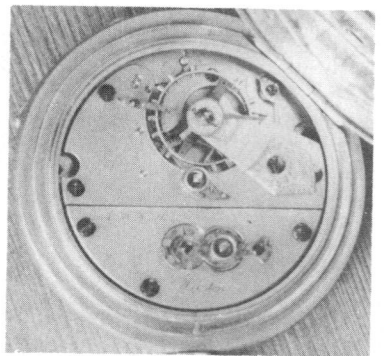

A.H. Potter Watch Co., BOSTON, 18 size, S # 5, about 6J., detent escapement. note similarity to E. Howard & Co. (early ebauche?), not a typical A.H. Potter movement.

"**Charmilles Geneva**" on dial, made in Charmilles Switzerland, 16S, 7-11 jewel count, 3/4 plate, Gun-Metal case, (dollar Watch), Ca. 1896.

THE "CHARMILLES" MOVEMENT

is made of **solid nickel**, handsomely damaskeened. The center of the case is a part of the movement, thus insuring greater strength and reducing cost. It is 16 size ¾ plate, Open Face, Stemwinding and Pendant Hand Setting; Straight line Lever Escapement; Seven Jewels; **Non-Magnetic** Balance, Hair Spring and Escapement; is non-magnetic and non-oxidizable. The wheels and pinions as well as all parts are better finished than in higher priced movements, *and guaranteed perfect timekeepers.*

"Charmilles" **AD Ca. 1896**. In Marshall Field & Co. sales catalog prices from $8.00 to $15.00.

GEORGE P. REED

Boston, Massachusetts 1865 - 1885

In 1854, George P. Reed entered the employment of Dennison, Howard and Davis, in Roxbury, Mass., and moved with the company to Waltham, Mass. Here he was placed in charge of the pinion finishing room. While there he invented and received a patent for the mainspring barrel and maintiming power combination. This patent was dated February 18, 1857. Reed returned to Roxbury with Howard who purchased his patented barrel. He stayed with the Howard factory as foreman and adjuster until 1865, when he left for Boston to start his own business.

He obtained a patent on April 7, 1868, for an improved chronometer escapement which featured simplified construction. He made about 100 chronometers with his improved escapement, to which he added a stem-wind device. His company turned out about 100 watches the first three years. Many of his watches run for two days and have up and down indicators. They are both 18S and 16S, 3/4 plate, nickel, and are artistically designed. Reed experimented with various combinations of lever and chronometer escapements. In all, about **350** watches were made.

Grade or Name – Description		Avg	Ex-Fn	Mint
18S, 15J, pivoted detent escapement, **18K case** .... ★★★★		$12,000	$15,000	$25,000
16S, 15J, LS, OF or HC, **with** chronometer, **18K case** ...... ★★★		8,000	9,000	16,000
16S, 15J, LS, OF or HC, not chronometer, **18K case** .... ★★★		7,500	8,000	15,000
16S, 15J, LS, OF, 31 day calendar, "Monitor", **18K case** ... ★★★		8,000	9,000	16,000
16S, 15-17J, Wind Indicator, "Monitor", **14K, OF** .... ★★★		6,500	7,000	13,000

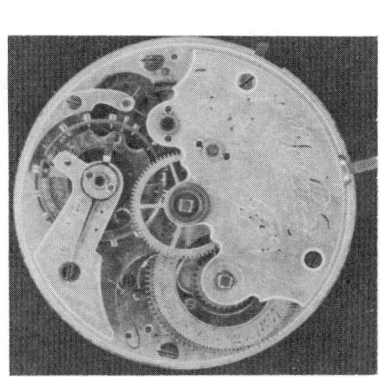
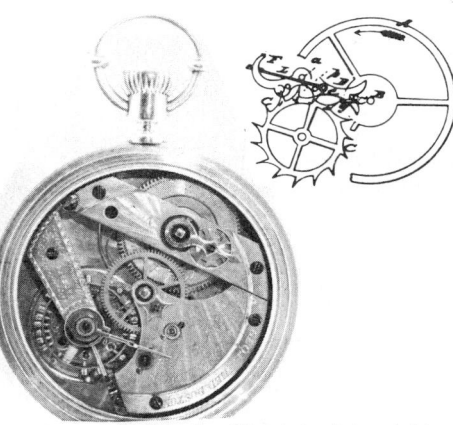

George P. Reed, 18 size, 15 jewels, key & stem wind, key & lever set, lever escapement, 48 hour up and down wind indicator, serial number 262.

George P. Reed, 18 size, 15 jewels, key & stem wind, key & lever set, Chronometer escapement, serial number 5. Note: This escapement was used on maybe 20 watches.

George P. Reed, Reeds' Two Days, Monitor, No. 335, engraved on movement, 31 calendar, 18-16 Size.

George P. Reed Boston, Monitor, 18-16 size, 15 jewels, wind indicator, serial # 322.

338

ROCKFORD WATCH CO.
Rockford, Illinois
1873 - 1915

The Rockford Watch Company's equipment was bought from the Cornell Watch Co., and two of Cornell's employees, C. W. Parker and P. H. Wheeler, went to work for Rockford. The factory was located 93 miles from Chicago on the Rock River. The first watch was placed on the market on May 1, 1876. They were key wind, 18S, full plate expansion balance & dials made by outside contract. By 1877 the company was making 3/4 plate nickel movements that fit standard size cases. Three railroads came through Rockford, and the company always advertised to the railroad and the demand was very popular with them. The company had some problems in 1896, and the name changed to Rockford Watch Co. Ltd. It closed in 1915.

ROCKFORD ESTIMATED SERIAL NUMBERS AND PRODUCTION DATES

DATE–SERIAL #	DATE–SERIAL #	DATE–SERIAL #	DATE–SERIAL #
1874 – 22,200	1884 – 226,000	1895 – 450,000	1906 – 670,000
1875 – 42,600	1885 – 247,000	1896 – 470,000	1907 – 690,000
1876 – 63,000	1886 – 267,000	1897 – 490,000	1908 – 734,000
1877 – 83,000	1887 – 287,500	1898 – 510,000	1909 – 790,000
1878 – 103,000	1888 – 308,000	1899 – 530,000	1910 – 824,000
1879 – 124,000	1889 – 328,500	1900 – 550,000	1911 – 880,000
1880 – 144,000	1890 – 349,000	1901 – 570,000	1912 – 936,000
1881 – 165,000	1891 – 369,500	1902 – 590,000	1913 – 958,000
1882 – 185,000	1892 – 390,000	1903 – 610,000	1914 – 980,000
1883 – 206,000	1893 – 410,000	1904 – 630,000	1915-1,000,000
	1894 – 430,000	1905 – 650,000	

The above list is provided for determining the APPROXIMATE age of your watch. Match serial number with date. Watches were not necessarily sold in the exact order of manufactured date.

ROCKFORD
18 SIZE

Grade or Name – Description	Avg	Ex-Fn	Mint
Belmont USA, 21J, LS, OF, NI, M#7	$225	$275	$450
Chronometer, 17J, ADJ, OF, G925.. ★	400	500	800
Dome Model, 9J, brass plates... ★	150	175	350

Rockford Watch Co., Enamel Railroad double sunk dial, with two hour hands for a second time zone the hour hand at 2 O'clock is BLUE, the hour hand at 3 O'clock is RED.

16-SIZE ROCKFORD

OUR SPECIAL No. 1000 21 JEWELS

Hunting or Open Face, nickel, 21 ruby and sapphire jewels in settings, adjusted to heat and cold. Compensating balance, Breguet hair spring, safety pinion, patent micrometric regulator, gold lettering, handsomely damaskeened, double sunk glass enameled dial, **pendant set.**

Above: 1913 AD

Note: S # 825,020, about the same as grade 645.

Watches listed in this book are priced at the collectable Trade Show level, as **complete** watches having an original 14k gold-filled case and *Key Wind* with silver, an original white enamel single sunk dial, and with the entire original movement in good working order with no repairs needed.

 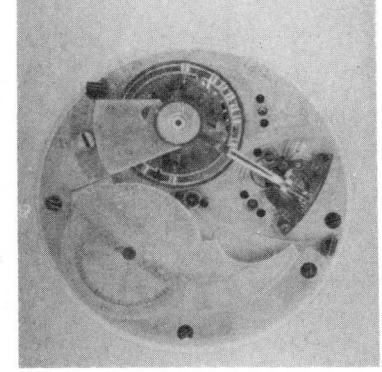

Rockford Watch Co., 18 size, 11 jewels, hunting, Model number 6, exposed escapement, serial number 190,564.

Special Railway, 18 size, 17 jewels, hunting, Model number 8, serial number 344,551.

Grade or Name – Description	Avg	Ex-Fn	Mint
King Edward, 21J, **Plymouth W. Co., 14K HC**	$650	$700	$1,200
King Edward, 21J, **(Sears)**, Plymouth W. Co. GJS, ADJ, NI, OF.	250	350	575
King Edward, 21J, **(Sears)**, Plymouth W. Co.GJS, ADJ, NI, HC .	295	400	800
Nacirema is American backward, on dial Nacirema Watch Co.	125	150	295
Paxton's, 21J, **(Special on dial)**, OF	350	400	700
Pennsylvania Special, 17J, LS, Adj., OF ★★★	2,000	2,400	3,500
Pennsylvania Special, 25J, LS, Adj.6P, tu-tone, OF ★★★★	6,000	8,000	12,000
Railway King, 21J, OF ★	425	550	1,000
The Ramsey Watch, 11J, NI, KW or SW	125	175	300
The Ramsey Watch, 15J, NI, KW or SW	125	175	295
The Ramsey Watch, M#7, 21J, OF, NI, ADJ	350	425	650

🕓 Generic, **nameless** or **unmarked** grades for watch movements are listed under the Company name or initials of the Company, etc. by size, jewel count and description.

	Avg	Ex-Fn	Mint
Rockford Early KW-KS, M#1-2, with low Serial #s less than 500 ★★	$750	$850	$1,600
Rockford Early KW-KS, M#1-2, with low Serial #s from 500-1,000 ★	400	500	900
Rockford Early KW-KS, M#1-2, with **reversible case**	400	500	900
Rockford, 7J, KW, FULL, OF	70	125	250
Rockford, 7J, KW, FULL, Silveroid	70	125	250
Rockford, 9J, SW, FULL, HC	95	150	275
Rockford, M#1, 9J, KW, FULL, HC	95	150	275
Rockford, 11J, KW, Coin HC	150	195	295
Rockford, 11J, SW, FULL, OF	60	90	195
Rockford, 13J, HC	125	150	225
Rockford, 11-13J, M#6, exposed escape wheel, FULL, HC ★	250	295	650
Rockford, M#1-2, 11J, KW, FULL	150	195	350
Rockford, M#1-2, 11J, transition case, FULL	95	150	250
Rockford, 9J,SW/ KW, **M#5, 3/4 Plate,** HC Coin	250	350	550
Rockford, 11J, SW/KW, **M#5, 3/4 Plate,** HC Coin	275	400	600
Rockford, 15J, SW/KW, **M#5, 3/4 Plate,** HC Coin	350	450	650
Rockford, 15J, SW, FULL	95	125	195
Rockford, 15J, KW, FULL, **multi-color dial**	400	550	1,100
Rockford, 15J, SW, 2-Tone movement	150	195	400
Rockford, 15J, KW, FULL, marked- **ADJ**	150	225	375
Rockford, 15J, KW/SW	95	150	275
Rockford, 15J, KW/SW, Silveroid	95	125	225

Rockford movement, 18 size, 7 jewels, model 5, hunting, lever set, three-quarter plate.

Grade 900, 18 size, 24J., Adj5p. Warning: 24J. fakes have been made from 21J. movements. The fakes are missing the eliptical jewel setting on the barrel bridge.

Grade or Name – Description	Avg	Ex-Fn	Mint
Rockford, 15J, M#6, exposed escapement wheel, FULL, HC, LS, nickel mvt. ★	$300	$350	$600
Rockford, 15J, M#6, exposed escapement wheel, FULL, HC, LS, gilded mvt. ★	225	275	500
Rockford, 15J, M#6, exposed wheel, nickel mvt., Coin	175	250	400
Rockford, M#1, 15J, KW, FULL	95	150	225
Rockford, 16J, GJS, NI, DMK, SW	125	150	250
Rockford, 16J, GJS, NI, DMK, SW, Silveroid	95	150	195
Rockford, 16J, GJS, NI, DMK, SW, Coin	125	150	225
Rockford, 17J, NI, DMK, SW, OF	95	150	225
Rockford, 17J, GJS, NI, DMK, SW, Adj.5P	95	165	275
Rockford, 17J, GJS, NI, SW, 2-Tone, OF	150	225	400
Rockford Early,19J, KW-KS, M#1-2, **nickel**, marked **Ruby Jewels**, ADJ, Serial # **less than 100** ★★★★	2,600	3,000	5,000
Rockford, M#1-2, 19J, KW, **gilt**, marked **Ruby Jewels**, ADJ, **HC** ★★	1,800	2,000	2,600
Rockford, 21J, SW, Silveroid	195	275	450
Rockford, 21J, GJS, OF, Adj.5P, **wind indicator** ★★★	3,000	4,000	5,500
Rockford, 21J, SW, DMK, ADJ, HC	350	470	600
Rockford, 21J, NI, DMK, ADJ, OF	275	350	475
Rockford, 21J, GJS, NI, DMK, Adj.5P, marked "RG" OF	325	400	550
Rockford, (**"22J"**, marked,) GJS, Adj.5P, 2 tone, **HC** ★★★	1,450	1,800	2,500
Rockford, (**"22J"**, marked,) Adj, NI, SW, "RG," OF ★★★	800	1,100	1,600
Rockford, 25J, GJS, SW, LS, Adj.5P, NI, DMK ★★★★	4,000	5,500	8,000
Rockford, 26J, GJS, SW, LS, Adj.5P, NI, DMK ★★★★	9,000	12,000	20,000

⊕ **Generic, nameless** or **unmarked** grades for watch movements are listed under the Company name or initials of the Company, etc. by size, jewel count and description.

	Avg	Ex-Fn	Mint
R.W. Co., 7-9-11J, NI or Gilded	$60	$85	$125
R.W. Co., 15J, NI or Gilded, OF	70	100	200
R.W. Co., 15J, NI or Gilded, HC	95	125	225
R.W. Co., 16-17J, Adj, NI, OF	95	125	225
R.W. Co., 16-17J, Adj, NI, HC	95	125	250
R.W. Co., 21J, Adj, NI, SW, OF	195	250	400
R.W. Co., 21J, Adj, NI, SW, HC	250	295	500

Rockford Watch Co., 18 size, 15 jewels, model # 5, 3/4 plate, key & stem wind.

Rockford Watch Co., 18 size, 15 jewels, model 4, open face, lever set, serial number 227,430.

Grade or Name – Description	Avg	Ex-Fn	Mint
Special Railway, 17J, ADJ, 2-tone, SW, HC .... ★	$425	$525	$800
The Syndicate Watch Co., M#7, 15J, LS, NI, HC	175	225	400
Winnebago, 17J, LS, GJS, Adj.5P, DR, NI, DMK, HC	250	350	600
Winnebago, 17J, LS, GJS, Adj.5P, DR, NI, DMK, OF	150	200	450
24 Hour Dial, 15J, SW or KW .... ★★	250	350	650
40, 15J, M#3, HC.. ★★	275	375	625
43, 15J, M#3, HC, 2-Tone...	125	150	295
60, 7J., 2-tone...	125	150	250
66, 11J, M#7, OF	70	80	195
66, 11J, M#7, OF, Silveroid	70	80	175
66, 11J, M#7, HC	70	80	195
72, 15J, KW-SW, **exposed escapement,** HC .... ★	600	700	1,200
81, 9J, M#3, Gilt, HC	90	125	250
82, **Special,** 21J, SW.. ★★★	700	800	1,400
83, 15J, M#8, 2-Tone, HC..	150	175	350
86, 15J, M#7, NI, OF .... ★	125	195	400
93, 9J, M#8, Gilt, HC	90	125	250
94, 9J, M#7, OF	70	100	195
200, 17J, M#9, NI, LS, HC...	95	175	250
205, 17J, M#9, NI, LS, OF...	95	150	195
800, **24J,** GJS, DR, Adj.5P, DMK, HC .... ★	1,200	1,400	2,000
805, 21J, GJS, Adj.5P, NI, DMK, **HC,** marked "RG"	350	400	775
810, 21J, NI, DMK, ADJ, HC..	335	385	600
820, 17J, SW, HC .... ★★	295	350	575
825, 17J, FULL, HC, ...	75	95	195
830, 17J, FULL, HC	75	95	195
835, 17J, FULL, HC .... ★	125	150	295
845, 21J, GJS, FULL, HC .... ★	425	500	775
870, 7J, FULL, HC	70	90	195

IMPORTANT NOTE: Railroad Standards, Railroad Approved & Railroad Grade **terminology,** as defined and used in this **_BOOK_**.
1. **RAILROAD STANDARDS** = A commission or board appointed by the railroad companies outlined a set of **guidelines** to be accepted or approved by each railroad line.
2. **RAILROAD APPROVED** = A **LIST** of watches each railroad line would approve if purchased by their employee's. (this list changed through the years).
3. **RAILROAD GRADE** = A watch made by manufactures to meet or exceed the guidelines set by the railroad **standards.** Grades such as 992, Vanguard and B.W. Raymond, etc.

⊕ Some GRADES **exceeded** the R.R. standards such as 23 jewels, diamond end stone, gold train, raised gold jewel settings, double sunk dial and the list goes on. Examples: such as Veritas, Sangamo, 950 & Riverside Maximus and many others.

Grade or Name – Description		Avg.	Ex-Fn	Mint
890, **24J**, GJS, DR, Adj.5P, NI, DMK, **HC**	★★	$1,500	$1,700	$2,200
900, **24J**, GJS, DR, Adj.5P, NI, DMK, OF	★★	1,000	1,200	1,600
900, **24J**, GJS, DR, Adj.5P, **14K**, OF case	★★	1,400	1,600	2,400
905, 21J, GJS, DR, Adj.5P, NI, DMK, OF		295	375	550
910, 21J, NI, DMK, ADJ, OF		175	195	375
912, 21J, Adj. 5P, LS, OF		475	600	800
915, 17J, M#9, SW, OF	★★★	700	800	1,300
918, **24J**, GJS, DR, Adj.5P, NI, DMK, OF	★★	1,200	1,400	2,000
918, 21J, NI, GJS, Adj.5P, DR, OF		295	350	500
918, 21J, NI, GJS, Adj.5P, DR, , OF Coin		275	325	450
920 & 930 , 17J, OF		175	225	350
925 & 935, 17J, OF		95	135	200
945, 21J, M#9, SW, OF		225	275	425
950-marked, 21J, GJS, Adj.5P, DR, OF, **Wind Indicator**	★★★	2,500	3,000	4,500
970, 7J, OF		70	90	175
970, 7J, OF Silveroid case		70	85	150

16 SIZE
(most HC grade numbers end with 0 & most OF grade numbers end with 5

Grade or Name – Description		Avg	Ex-Fn	Mint
Commodore Perry, 21J, OF, GJS, GT, marked "RG"	★	$295	$350	$600
Commodore Perry, 15-17J, ADJ		125	150	250
Cosmos, 17J, OF, GJS, LS, DMK, marked dial & mvt.		250	325	475
Cosmos, 17J, **HC**, GJS, LS, DMK, marked dial & mvt.		295	350	600
Doll Watch Co., 17J, marked dial & mvt., OF	★★★	850	1,200	2,000
Doll Watch Co., 21J, marked dial & mvt., OF	★★★	1,000	1,300	2,200
Doll Watch Co., 23J, marked dial & mvt., OF	★★★	1,500	1,700	2,600
Doll Watch Co., 23J, (G#504-M# 4), triple signed, HC	★★★★	1,700	1,900	3,000
Dome Model, 15J		75	95	195
Dome Model, 17J		85	95	195
Dome Model, 17J, 2-tone, HC		150	195	450
Herald Square, 7J, 3/4, OF		95	125	195
Iroquois, 17J, DR, **14K, HC**		550	600	1,000
Iroquois, 17J, DR, OF		150	195	400
Peerless, 17J, OF, NI, LS, DMK	★	150	195	400
Pocahontas, 17J, GJS, Adj.5P, DR, OF	★	195	250	500
Pocahontas, 17J, GJS, Adj.5P, DR, HC	★	275	350	600
Pocahontas, 21J, GJS, Adj.5P, DR, OF	★	295	450	700
Pocahontas, 21J, GJS, Adj.5P, DR, HC	★★	500	600	900
Prince of Wales (Sears), 21J, Plymouth W. Co.		275	325	550
Prince of Wales (Sears), 21J, Plymouth W. Co.**14K**		525	650	1,000

Grade 103, 16 size, 17 jewels, model 1, hunting case, serial number 384,857.

Cosmos movement, 16 size, 17 jewels, open face, gold jewel settings, grade 565, model 2.

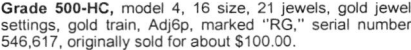

Grade 500-HC, model 4, 16 size, 21 jewels, gold jewel settings, gold train, Adj6p, marked "RG," serial number 546,617, originally sold for about $100.00.

Grade 505-OF, model 5, 16 size, 21 jewels, gold jewel settings, gold train, Adj6p, marked "RG," serial number 593,929, originally sold for about $100.00.

🕐 **Generic, nameless** or **unmarked** grades for watch movements are listed under the Company name or initials of the Company, etc. by size, jewel count and description.

Grade or Name – Description	Avg	Ex-Fn	Mint
Rockford, 7J, 3/4, HC	$60	$95	$195
Rockford, 9J, 3/4, SW, OF	60	90	185
Rockford, 9J, SW, Silveroid	60	90	165
Rockford, 9J, SW, HC	85	125	195
Rockford, 11J, SW, Silveroid	60	90	175
Rockford, 11J, 3/4, HC	60	90	225
Rockford, 15J, 3/4, ADJ, OF	60	90	195
Rockford, 15J, 3/4, ADJ, Silveroid	60	90	150
Rockford, 15J, 3/4, ADJ, HC	60	90	225
Rockford, 16J, 3/4, SW, Silveroid	60	90	150
Rockford, 16J, 3/4, ADJ, NI, DMK	60	90	175
Rockford, 17J, 3/4	60	90	175
Rockford, 17J, 3/4, **2-Tone**, marked "RG" ⋯⋯★	225	295	500
Rockford, 17J, BRG, Adj.3P, DR	125	150	250
Rockford, 17J, BRG, Silveroid	70	95	175
Rockford, 17J, 3/4, Silveroid	70	90	170
Rockford, 21J, 3/4, SW, Silveroid	250	295	400
Rockford, 21J, BRG, SW, Silveroid	250	295	400
Rockford, 21J, 3/4, GJS, Adj.5P	295	375	550
Rockford, 21J, BRG, GJS, Adj.5P, GT, DR	325	350	600
Winnebago, 17J, G#400, BRG, GJS, Adj.5P, NI, HC ⋯★	225	295	600
Winnebago, 17J, G#405, BRG, GJS, Adj.5P, NI, OF	195	250	400
Winnebago, 21J, BRG, GJS, Adj.5P, NI ⋯★	295	400	700
100, 16-17J, M#1, 3/4, 2-Tone, HC	225	275	400
100S, 21J, **Special**, 3/4, LS, HC	295	350	550
102, 15J, M#1, HC ⋯★	150	175	295
103, 15-17J, M#1, HC ⋯★★	275	325	450
104, 11J, M#1, HC	75	95	195
110, 17J, **2 tone dome** style mvt., HC ⋯★	325	350	550
115-125, 17J, **Special**, HC ⋯★★★	525	625	1,000
120-130, 17J, HC ⋯★★★	425	525	875

🕐 Pricing in this Guide are fair market price for **COMPLETE** watches which are reflected from the "<u>**NAWCC**</u>" National and regional shows.

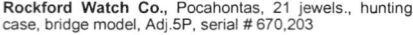

Rockford Watch Co., Pocahontas, 21 jewels., hunting case, bridge model, Adj.5P, serial # 670,203

Rockford Watch Co., 21j., Wind indicator, marked 655, adjusted to 5 positions, gold jewel settings, gold center wheel, double roller, Serial # 830,591.

Grade or Name – Description	Avg	Ex-Fn	Mint
400, 17J, NI, Adj.5P, GJS, DR, BRG, HC	$125	$150	$275
405, 17J, NI, Adj.5P, GJS, DR, BRG, OF	95	125	250
440, 17J, GJS, HC	125	150	250
445, 19J, GJS, OF ★★	900	1,000	1,300
500-501, 21J, BRG, NI, GJS, Adj.5P, GT, HC ★★★	500	575	900
505, 21J, BRG, NI, GJS, Adj.5P, GT, OF ★★★	500	575	900
510, 21J, BRG, NI, GJS, Adj.5P, GT, HC ★★★	500	575	900
515 - 525 -545, 21J, 3/4, OF	350	400	700
520, 21J, 3/4, HC	350	400	650
520 - 540, 21J, BRG, NI, GJS, Adj.5P, HC	450	500	750
525, 21J. M#5, GT, Adj.5P, OF ★	350	400	600
530, 21J, GJS, Adj.5P, marked "RG", HC ★	375	425	700
535, 21J, 3/4, OF	295	350	600
537, 21J, OF, GJS, Adj.5P ★★★	1,000	1,200	1,700
540, 21J,GT, BRG, Adj.5P, HC ★	275	325	500
545, 21J,GT, BRG, Adj.5P, OF	275	325	500
561, 17J, BRG, HC	150	175	400
566, 17J, BRG, OF	150	175	295
572, 17J, BRG, NI, HC	150	175	350
573-575, 17J, 3/4 & BRG, NI, OF	150	175	295
578-579, 17J, PS, GJS ★★	300	350	600
584 15J, 3/4 NI, HC	65	85	175
585, 15J, 3/4, NI, OF	65	75	150
620, 21J, 3/4, HC ★	325	400	650
625, 21J, 3/4, OF ★	295	350	600
640, 21J, GT, 3/4, Adj.5P, HC ★	275	325	500
645, 21J, GT, 3/4, Adj.5P, OF	275	325	500
655, 21J, **Wind Indicator**, Adj.5P, **marked 655**, OF ★★	1,100	1,500	2,200
665, 17J, **Wind Indicator**, Adj, 5P, OF ★	900	1,100	1,800
700, 21J, Adj., BRG, HC	275	325	500
705, 21J, Adj., BRG, OF	250	295	450
810, 21J, 3/4, Adj. heat & cold, OF	275	325	500
1000, 21J, 3/4, Adj. heat & cold, OF ★★	250	375	700

🕐 Watches listed in this book are priced at the collectable Trade Show level, as **complete** watches having an original 14k gold-filled case and *Key Wind* with silver, an original white enamel single sunk dial, and with the entire original movement in good working order with no repairs needed.

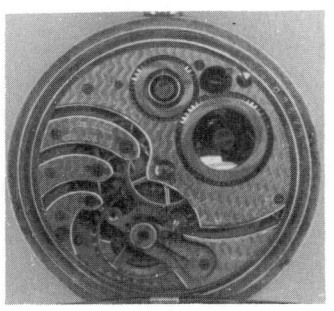

Rockford Watch Co., 12 size, 15 jewels, model 1, hunting, pendant set.

Rockford Watch Co., 12 size, 15 jewels, model 2, open face, pendant set.

12 SIZE
All 3/4 Bridge

Grade or Name – Description	Avg	Ex-Fn	Mint
Commodore Perry, 15-17J, ADJ.	$95	$125	$250
Doll Watch Co., 21J, marked on dial & movement, OF ★★	250	350	650
Iroquois, 17J, BRG, DR, ADJ	75	125	250
Pocahontas, 21J, GJS, Adj.5P, BRG, DR	175	195	350
Rockford, 15J, BRG	40	70	135
Rockford, 17J, BRG, NI, DR, ADJ	40	70	135
Rockford, 21J, BRG, NI, DR, ADJ	95	150	295
Rockford, 21J, BRG, NI, DR, ADJ, Silveroid	70	85	195
Winona, 15J, BRG	60	70	175
300, 23J, 3/4, GJS, Adj.5P, HC ★★★	295	350	600
305, 23J, BRG, NI, GJS, Adj.5P, GT, OF ★★★	295	350	600
310(HC)-315(OF), 21J, BRG, NI, GJS, Adj.5P ★★	125	150	295
320(HC)-325(OF), 17J, BRG, NI, ADJ, DR	60	70	125
330, 17J, BRG, NI, DR, HC	60	70	150
335, 17J, BRG, NI, DR, OF	60	70	125
340(HC)-345(OF), 21J, M#1 ★	225	250	400
350, 17J, OF	60	70	125
355, 17J, HC	60	70	150

Note: Add $10 to $25 to above watches with hunting case.

0 - Size movement in 12 - Size Case ("Xtremethin")

Grade or Name – Description	Avg	Ex-Fn	Mint
0 - Size movement in 12 - Size Case, 15J., Plain GF case	$60	$85	$150
0 - Size movement in 12 - Size Case, 15J., GF case & ENAMELED	125	150	250

8 SIZE

Grade or Name – Description	Avg	Ex-Fn	Mint
15J, 3/4, HC, LS, **14K, 40 DWT**	$400	$450	$700
9–15J, 3/4, KW or SW, LS, OF or HC,	65	95	175

🕐 A collector should expect to pay modestly higher prices at local shops.

🕐 Pricing in this Guide are fair market price for **COMPLETE** watches which are reflected from the "**NAWCC**" National and regional shows.

Rockford movement, 6 size, 17 jewels, quick train, straight line escapement, compensating balance, adjusted to temperature, micrometric regulator, 3/4 damaskeened plates.

6 SIZE

Grade or Name – Description	Avg	Ex-Fn	Mint
9J, NI, **HC**	$65	$85	$175
15J, 3/4, NI	75	95	195
16J, 3/4, NI	75	95	195
17J, 3/4, ADJ, NI	75	95	195

0 SIZE

Grade or Name – Description	Avg	Ex-Fn	Mint
Iroquois, 17J., HC	$125	$175	$350
Plymouth Watch Co., 15-17J, HC	195	250	375
7J, BRG, NI, DR, HC	50	70	195
11J, BRG, NI, DR, HC	50	70	195
15J, BRG, NI, DR, HC	60	95	225
17J, BRG, NI, DR, HC	75	95	225

🕐 A collector should expect to pay modestly higher prices at local shops.

🕐 Watches listed in this book are priced at the collectable Trade Show level, as **complete** watches having an original 14k gold-filled case and *Key Wind* with silver, an original white enamel single sunk dial, and with the entire original movement in good working order with no repairs needed.

🕐 This book endeavours to be a GUIDE or helpful manual and offers a wealth of material to be used as a tool not as a absolute document. Price Guides are like watches the worst may be better than none at all, but at best cannot be expected to be 100% accurate.

🕐 Characteristics of watches differ for the same age of both case and movement, because these features vary it may not be accurate to date a watch by one single influence. Example: the second hand was not commonly found on watches before 1750, but common about 1800. The first second hand appeared in 1665 and another in 1690. Therefore statements are broad rather than accurate.

ROCKFORD WATCH CO.
IDENTIFICATION OF MOVEMENTS
BY MODEL NUMBER

How to Identify Your Watch: Compare the movement of your watch with the illustrations in this section. Upon matching the movement exactly, the model number and size can be determined. While comparing, note the location of the balance, jewels, screws, gears, and type of back plate (Full, 3/4, Bridge) these will be clues in identifying the movement you have. Having determined the size and model number, you can now find your watch in the main price listing by name or number (engraved on the movement).

The Rockford Watch Company, Ltd.

JANUARY 1907
NUMBER AND GRADE

WITH

DESCRIPTION OF MOVEMENTS MANUFACTURED TO DATE

Number and Grade of Movement	GRADE	Size	Style		Jewels	Wind	Sett	Model
1 to 114,000		18	Htg.	F. Pl.		Key	Key	1
114,001 " 115,000		"	"	¾ Pl.		Stem	Lever	5
115,001 " 126,000		"	"	F. Pl.		"	"	2
126,001 " 127,000		"	"	¾ Pl.		"	"	5
127,001 " 130,000		"	"	F. Pl.		"	"	2
130,001 " 131,000		"	"	¾ Pl.		"	"	5
131,001 " 133,000		"	"	F. Pl.		"	"	3
133,001 " 134,000		"	"	¾ Pl.		"	"	5
134,001 " 138,000		"	"	F. Pl.		"	"	3
138,001 " 139,000		"	"	¾ Pl.		"	"	5
139,001 " 143,000		"	"	F. Pl.		"	"	3
143,001 " 144,000		"	"	¾ Pl.		"	"	5
144,001 " 145,000		"	"	F. Pl.		"	"	3
145,001 " 146,000		"	"	¾ Pl.		"	"	5
146,001 " 149,000		"	"	F. Pl.		"	"	3
149,001 " 151,000		"	"	¾ Pl.		"	"	5
151,001 " 153,000		"	"	F. Pl.		"	"	3
153,001 " 154,000		"	"	¾ Pl.		"	"	5
154,001 " 158,000		"	"	F. Pl.		"	"	3
158,001 " 159,000		"	"	¾ Pl.		"	"	5
159,001 " 169,000		"	"	F. Pl.		"	"	3
170,001 " 170,100		"	"	¾ Pl.	15	"	"	5
170,101 " 177,000		"	"	F. Pl.		"	"	3
177,001 " 177,800		"	"	F. Pl.		"	"	6
177,901 " 189,500		"	"	"		"	"	3
189,601 " 190,900		"	"	"		"	"	6
191,001 " 191,100		"	"	"		"	"	3
191,101 " 196,400		"	O. F.	"		"	"	4
196,501 " 197,000		"	Htg.	"		"	"	6
197,101 " 197,500		"	"	"		"	"	3
197,601 " 198,000		"	"	"		"	"	6
198,101 " 199,100		"	O. F.	"		"	"	4
199,201 " 199,500		"	Htg.	"		"	"	6
199,600 " 200,000		"	"	¾ Pl.		"	"	5
200,001 " 213,100		8	"	"		"	"	1
213,101 " 218,900		6	"	"		"	"	1
219,001 " 219,500		18	"	"		"	"	5
219,501 " 224,500		"	"	F. Pl.		"	"	3
224,501 " 228,000		"	O. F.	"		"	"	4
228,001 " 232,000		"	Htg.	"		"	"	3
232,001 " 233,000		"	"	¾ Pl.		"	"	5
233,001 " 234,000	47	"	O. F. F. Pl. Nickel		15	"	"	4
234,001 " 235,000	45	"	" " "		15	"	"	4
235,001 " 236,000	43	"	Htg. F. Pl. Gilt		"	"	"	3
236,001 " 237,000	44	"	" " Gilt		"	"	"	3
237,001 " 238,000	45	"	O. F. F. Pl. "		"	"	"	4
238,001 " 239,000		"	" " "		9	"	"	4
239,001 " 240,000	45	"	" " "		15	"	"	4
240,001 " 241,000	46	"	" " "		11	"	"	4
241,001 " 241,800	47	"	" " Nickel		15	"	"	4
241,801 " 242,000	40	"	Htg. " "		"	"	"	3
242,001 " 243,000	43	"	" " "		"	"	"	3
243,001 " 244,000	44	"	" " Gilt		"	"	"	6
244,001 " 244,300	49	"	" " Nickel		"	"	"	6
244,301 " 244,400	72	"	" " "		"	"	"	8
244,401 " 245,000	62	"	" " "		11	"	"	8
245,001 " 246,000	81	"	" " Gilt		9	"	"	3
246,001 " 247,000	44	"	" " "		15	"	"	4
247,001 " 248,000	64	"	O. F. " "		11	"	"	4
248,001 " 249,000	46	"	Htg. " "		15	"	"	6
249,001 " 250,000	49	"	" " Nickel		"	"	"	6
250,001 " 250,500	62	"	" " "		11	"	"	7
250,501 " 251,000	60	"	O. F. " "		"	"	"	7
251,001 " 252,000	66	"	" " "		"	"	"	7
252,001 " 253,000	67	"	" " Gilt		"	"	"	8
253,001 " 253,500	83	"	Htg. " Nickel		15	"	"	8
253,501 " 253,700	77	"	" " "		"	"	"	7
253,701 " 254,000	68	"	" " Gilt		11	"	"	7
254,001 " 254,600	86	"	O. F. " Nickel		15	"	"	7
254,601 " 254,800	76	"	" " "		"	"	"	7
254,801 " 255,000	78	"	" " Gilt		"	"	"	
255,001 " 256,000	89	"	" " "		"	"	"	8
256,001 " 257,000	68	"	Htg. " "		11	"	"	8
257,001 " 258,000	93	"	" " "		9	"	"	
258,001 " 259,000	69	"	" " Nickel		11	"	"	

The Rockford Watch Company, Ltd.

Number and Grade of Movement	GRADE	Size		Style		Jewels	Wind	Sett	Model
259,001 to 260,000	66	18	O. F.	F. Pl.	Nickel	11	Stem	Lever	7
260,001 " 261,000	68	"	Htg.	"	Gilt	"	"	"	8
261,001 " 262,000	86	"	O. F.	"	Nickel	15	"	"	7
262,001 " 263,000	67	"	"	"	Gilt	11	"	"	"
263,001 " 264,000	83	"	Htg.	"	Nickel	15	"	"	8
264,001 " 265,000	69	"	"	"	"	"	"	"	"
265,001 " 266,000	68	"	"	"	Gilt	11	"	"	"
266,001 " 267,000	93	"	"	"	"	9	"	"	8
267,001 " 267,800	83	"	"	"	Nickel	15	"	"	"
267,801 " 268,000	77	"	"	"	"	"	"	"	"
268,001 " 269,000	68	"	"	"	Gilt	11	"	"	"
269,001 " 270,000	67	"	O. F.	"	"	"	"	"	7
270,001 " 270,800	85	"	Htg.	"	"	15	"	"	8
270,801 " 271,000	79	"	"	"	"	"	"	"	"
271,001 " 272,000	66	"	O. F.	"	Nickel	11	"	"	7
272,001 " 272,100	77	"	Htg.	"	"	15	"	"	8
272,101 " 272,200	83	"	"	"	"	"	"	"	"
272,201 " 272,300	77	"	"	"	"	"	"	"	"
272,301 " 272,600	83	"	"	"	"	"	"	"	"
272,601 " 272,700	77	"	"	"	"	"	"	"	"
272,701 " 272,900	83	"	"	"	"	"	"	"	"
272,901 " 273,000	77	"	"	"	"	"	"	"	"
273,001 " 274,000	69	"	"	"	"	"	"	"	"
274,001 " 275,000	83	"	"	"	"	"	"	"	"
275,001 " 276,000	69	"	"	"	"	11	"	"	"
276,001 " 277,000	83	"	"	"	"	15	"	"	"
277,001 " 278,000	85	"	"	"	Gilt	"	"	"	"
278,001 " 279,000	66	"	O. F.	"	Nickel	11	"	"	7
279,001 " 279,200	76	"	"	"	"	15	"	"	"
279,201 " 280,000	86	"	"	"	"	"	"	"	"
280,001 " 281,000	66	"	"	"	"	11	"	"	"
281,001 " 282,000	85	"	Htg.	"	Gilt	15	"	"	8
282,001 " 283,000	83	"	"	"	Nickel	"	"	"	"
283,001 " 284,000	93	"	"	"	Gilt	9	"	"	"
284,001 " 285,000	89	"	O. F.	"	"	15	"	"	7
285,001 " 286,000	69	"	Htg.	"	Hickel	11	"	"	8
286,001 " 286,200	83	"	"	"	Nick.& Gilt	15	"	"	"
286,201 " 286,500	84	"	"	"	"	"	"	"	"
286,501 " 287,000	83	"	"	"	Nickel	"	"	"	"
287,001 " 288,000	66	"	O. F.	"	"	11	"	"	7
288,001 " 289,000	67	"	"	"	Gilt	"	"	"	"
289,001 " 289,500	84	"	Htg.	"	Spot Gilt	15	"	"	8
289,501 " 291,000	83	"	"	"	Nickel	"	"	"	"
291,001 " 292,000	69	"	"	"	"	11	"	"	"
292,001 " 293,000	67	"	O. F.	"	Gilt	"	"	"	7
293,001 " 294,000	85	"	Htg.	"	"	15	"	"	8
294,001 " 295,000	93	"	"	"	"	9	"	"	"
295,001 " 296,000	66	"	O. F.	"	Nickel	11	"	"	7
296,001 " 297,000	89	"	"	"	Gilt	15	"	"	"
297,001 " 298,000	69	"	Htg.	"	Nickel	11	"	"	8
298,001 " 299,000	67	"	O. F.	"	Gilt	"	"	"	7
299,001 " 300,000	93	"	Htg.	"	"	9	"	"	8
300,001 " 300,500	84	"	"	"	Nick.& Gilt	15	"	"	"
300,501 " 300,700	83	"	"	"	Nickel	"	"	"	"
300,701 " 301,000	70	"	"	"	Nick.& Gilt	16	"	"	"
301,001 " 302,000	66	"	O. F.	"	Nickel	11	"	"	7
302,001 " 303,000	93	"	Htg.	"	Gilt	9	"	"	8
303,001 " 304,000	69	"	"	"	Nickel	11	"	"	"
304,001 " 304,500	84	"	"	"	Nick.& Gilt	15	"	"	"
304,501 " 305,000	83	"	"	"	Nickel	"	"	"	"
305,001 " 305,500	84	"	"	"	Nick.&Gilt	"	"	"	"
305,501 " 306,000	83	"	"	"	Nickel	"	"	"	"
306,001 " 307,000	66	"	O. F.	"	"	11	"	"	7
307,001 " 308,000	83	"	Htg.	"	"	15	"	"	8
308,001 " 309,000	93	"	"	"	Gilt	9	"	"	"
309,001 " 310,000	83	"	"	"	Nickel	15	"	"	"
310,001 " 310,500	87	"	O. F.	"	Nick.& Gilt	"	"	"	7
310,501 " 310,700	88	"	"	"	Nickel	16	"	"	"
310,701 " 311,000	86	"	"	"	"	15	"	"	"
311,001 " 312,000	69	"	Htg.	"	"	11	"	"	8
312,001 " 313,000	93	"	"	"	Gilt	9	"	"	"
313,001 " 314,000	83	"	"	"	Nickel	15	"	"	"
314,001 " 317,000	93	"	"	"	Gilt	9	"	"	"
317,001 " 318,000	85	"	"	"	"	15	"	"	"
318,001 " 319,000	93	"	"	"	"	9	"	"	"
319,001 " 320,000	85	"	"	"	"	15	"	"	"
320,001 " 321,000	84	"	"	"	Nick.& Gilt	"	"	"	"
321,001 " 322,000	83	"	"	"	Nickel	"	"	"	"
322,001 " 323,000	84	"	"	"	Nick.& Gilt	"	"	"	"
323,001 " 325,000	83	"	"	"	Nickel	"	"	"	"
325,001 " 326,000	85	"	"	"	Gilt	"	"	"	"
326,001 " 327,000	93	"	"	"	"	9	"	"	"
327,001 " 328,000	83	"	"	"	Nickel	15	"	"	"
328,001 " 329,000	89	"	O. F.	"	Gilt	"	"	"	7
329,001 " 329,100	84	"	Htg.	"	Nick.& Gilt	"	"	"	8
329,101 " 329,200	83	"	"	"	Special	......	"	"	"
329,201 " 329,700	84	"	"	"	Nick.& Gilt	15	"	"	"
329,701 " 330,000	70	"	"	"	"	16	"	"	"
330,001 " 330,800	87	"	O. F.	"	Nickel	15	"	"	7

The Rockford Watch Company, Ltd.

Number and Grade of Movement	GRADE	Size			Style	Jewels	Wind	Sett	Model
330,801 to 331,000	88	18	O. F.	F. Pl.	Nick.& Gilt	16	Stem	Lever	7
331,001 " 332,000	68	"	Htg.	"	Gilt	11	"	"	8
332,001 " 333,000	86	"	O. F.	"	Nickel	15	"	"	7
333,001 " 334,000	69	"	Htg.	"	"	11	"	"	8
334,001 " 335,000	66	"	O. F.	"	"	"	"	"	7
335,001 " 336,000	94	"	"	"	Gilt	9	"	"	"
336,001 " 337,000	68	"	Htg.	"	"	11	"	"	8
337,001 " 338,000	94	"	O. F.	"	"	9	"	"	7
338,001 " 338,500	88	"	"	"	Nick.& Gilt	16	"	"	"
338,501 " 339,000	86	"	"	"	Nickel	"	"	"	"
339,001 " 339,500	70	"	Htg.	"	Nick.& Gilt	"	"	"	8
339,501 " 340,000	84	"	"	"	"	15	"	"	"
340,001 " 341,000	66	"	O. F.	"	Nickel	11	"	"	7
341,001 " 342,000	85	"	Htg.	"	Gilt	15	"	"	8
342,001 " 343,000	89	"	O. F.	"	"	"	"	"	7
343,001 " 344,000	94	"	"	"	"	9	"	"	"
344,001 " 345,000	84	"	Htg.	"	Nick.& Gilt	15	"	"	8
345,001 " 346,000	68	"	"	"	Gilt	11	"	"	"
346,001 " 347,000	87	"	O. F.	"	Nick.& Gilt	15	"	"	7
347,001 " 348,000	94	"	"	"	Gilt	9	"	"	"
348,001 " 348,300	88	"	"	"	Nick.& Gilt	16	"	"	"
348,301 " 348,500	87	"	"	"	"	15	"	"	"
348,501 " 349,000	86	"	"	"	Nickel	"	"	"	"
349,001 " 349,500	67	"	"	"	Gilt	11	"	"	"
349,501 " 350,000	89	"	"	"	"	15	"	"	"
350,001 " 350,500	70	"	Htg.	"	Nick.& Gilt	16	"	"	8
350,501 " 351,000	85	"	"	"	Gilt	15	"	"	"
351,001 " 352,000	87	"	O. F.	"	Nick & Gilt	"	"	"	7
352,001 " 352,500	88	"	"	"	"	16	"	"	"
352,501 " 353,000	67	"	"	"	Gilt	11	"	"	"
353,001 " 353,500	100	16	Htg.	¾ Pl.	Nick.& Gilt	16	"	"	1
353,501 " 353,800	101	"	"	"	Nickel	15	"	"	"
353,801 " 354,000	102	"	"	"	"	"	"	"	"
354,001 " 354,500	103	"	"	"	"	"	"	"	"
354,501 " 355,000	104	"	"	"	"	11	"	"	"
355,001 " 355,500	111	"	"	"	Gilt	15	"	"	"
355,501 " 356,000	112	"	"	"	"	"	"	"	"
356,001 " 356,500	113	"	"	"	"	11	"	"	"
356,501 " 357,000	114	"	"	"	"	9	"	"	"
357,001 " 358,500	68	18	"	F. Pl.	"	11	"	"	8
358,501 " 359,000	67	"	O. F.	"	"	"	"	"	7
359,001 " 359,500	87	"	"	"	Nick.& Gilt	15	"	"	"
359,501 " 360,000	86	"	"	"	Nickel	"	"	"	"
360,001 " 360,500	101	16	Htg.	¾ Pl.	Nick.& Gilt	"	"	"	1
360,501 " 361,000	102	"	"	"	Nickel	"	"	"	"
361,001 " 361,500	103	"	"	"	"	"	"	"	"
361,501 " 362,000	104	"	"	"	"	11	"	"	"
362,001 " 364,000	67	18	O. F.	F. Pl.	Gilt	"	"	"	7
364,001 " 365,000	112	16	Htg.	¾ Pl.	"	15	"	"	1
365,001 " 366,000	102	"	"	"	Nickel	"	"	"	"
366,001 " 367,000	103	"	"	"	"	"	"	"	"
367,001 " 368,000	67	18	O. F.	F. Pl.	Gilt	11	"	"	7
368,001 " 368,500	112	16	Htg.	¾ Pl.	"	15	"	"	1
368,501 " 369,000	101	"	"	"	Nick.& Gilt	"	"	"	"
369,001 " 370,000	104	"	"	"	Nickel	11	"	"	"
370,001 " 370,500	86	18	O. F.	F. Pl.	"	15	"	"	7
370,501 " 371,000	87	"	"	"	Nick.& Gilt	"	"	"	"
371,001 " 371,500	89	"	"	"	Gilt	"	"	"	"
371,501 " 372,000	94	"	"	"	"	9	"	"	"
372,001 " 372,500	113	16	Htg.	¾ Pl.	"	11	"	"	1
372,501 " 373,000	114	"	"	"	"	9	"	"	"
373,001 " 374,000	113	"	"	"	"	11	"	"	"
274,001 " 374,500	68	18	"	F. Pl.	"	"	"	"	8
374,501 " 375,000	94	"	O. F.	"	"	9	"	"	7
375,001 " 376,000	87	"	"	"	Nick.& Gilt	15	"	"	"
376,001 " 376,200	100	16	Htg.	¾ Pl.	"	16	"	"	1
376,201 " 376,700	101	"	"	"	"	15	"	"	"
376,701 " 377,000	102	"	"	"	Nickel	"	"	"	"
377,001 " 377,500	104	"	"	"	"	11	"	"	"
377,501 " 378,000	103	"	"	"	"	15	"	"	"
378,001 " 379,000	94	18	O. F.	F. Pl.	Gilt	9	"	'	7
379,001 " 379,500	86	"	"	"	Nickel	15	"	"	"
379,501 " 380,000	84	"	Htg.	"	Nick.& Gilt	"	"	"	8
380,001 " 380,500	101	16	"	¾ Pl.	"	"	"	"	1
380,501 " 381,000	104	"	"	"	Nickel	11	"	"	"
381,001 " 381,300	102	"	"	"	"	15	"	"	"
381,301 " 382,000	103	"	"	"	"	"	"	"	"
382,001 " 382,200	111	"	"	"	Gilt	"	"	"	"
382,201 " 383,000	112	"	"	"	"	"	"	"	"
383,001 " 383,500	113	"	"	"	"	11	"	"	"
383,501 " 384,000	114	"	"	"	"	9	"	"	"
384,001 " 384,500	100	"	"	"	Nick.& Gilt	16	"	"	"
384,501 " 385,000	103	"	"	"	Nickel	15	"	"	"
385,001 " 385,500	104	"	"	"	"	11	"	"	"
385,501 " 386,000	103	"	"	"	"	15	"	"	"
386,001 " 387,000	112	"	"	"	Gilt	"	"	"	"
387,001 " 387,500	93	18	"	F. Pl.	"	9	"	"	8
387,501 " 388,000	68	"	"	"	"	11	"	"	"

The Rockford Watch Company, Ltd.

Number and Grade of Movement	GRADE	Size	Style		Jewels	Wind	Sett	Model
				Description of Movement				
388,001 to 388,500	94	18 O. F.	F. Pl.	Gilt	9	Stem	Lever	7
388,501 " 389,000	89	" "	"	"	15	"	"	"
389,001 " 389,100	76	" "	"	Nickel	"	"	"	"
389,101 " 390,000	86	" "	"	"	,,	"	"	"
390,001 " 391,000	69	" Htg.	"	"	11	"	"	8
391,001 " 391,400	162	6 "	¾ Pl.	Gilt	9	"	"	2
391,401 " 391,700	161	" "	"	"	11	"	"	"
391,701 " 392,000	160	" "	"	"	15	"	"	"
392,001 " 392,300	154	" "	"	Nickel	9	"	"	"
392,301 " 392,500	153	" "	"	"	11	"	"	"
392,501 " 392,700	152	" "	"	"	15	"	"	"
392,701 " 392,900	151	" "	"	Nick.& Gilt	"	"	"	"
392,901 " 393,000	150	" "	"	"	16	"	"	"
393,001 " 393,500	154	" "	"	Nickel	9	"	"	"
393,501 " 394,000	153	" "	"	"	11	"	"	"
394,001 " 394,500	152	" "	"	"	15	"	"	"
394,501 " 394,800	151	" "	"	Nick.& Gilt	"	"	"	"
394,801 " 395,000	150	" "	"	"	16	"	"	"
395,001 " 396,000	162	" "	"	Gilt	9	"	"	"
396,001 " 396,500	161	" "	"	"	11	"	"	"
396,501 " 397,000	160	" "	"	"	15	"	"	"
397,001 " 397,800	162	" "	"	"	9	"	"	"
397,801 " 398,600	161	" "	"	"	11	"	"	"
398,601 " 399,000	160	" "	"	"	15	"	"	..
399,001 " 400,200	153	" "	"	Nickel	11	"	"	"
400,201 " 400,700	152	" "	"	"	15	"	"	"
400,701 " 401,000	152	" "	"	Nick.& Gilt	"	"	"	"
401,001 " 401,500	93	18 "	F. Pl.	Gilt	9	"	"	8
401,501 " 402,000	68	" "	"	"	11	"	"	"
402,001 " 402,500	69	,, "	"	Nickel	"	"	"	..
402,501 " 403,000	85	" "	"	Gilt	15	"	"	"
403,001 " 403,500	94	" O. F.	"	"	9	"	"	7
403,501 " 404,000	86	" "	"	Nickel	15	"	"	"
404,001 " 404,300	60	" "	"	Nick.& Gilt	11	"	"	"
404,301 " 405,000	66	" "	"	Nickel	17	"	"	"
405,001 " 405,500	86	" "	"	"	15	"	"	"
405,501 " 406,000	83	" Htg.	"	"	"	"	"	8
406,001 " 407,000	69	" "	"	"	11	"	"	"
407,001 " 407,500	68	" "	"	Gilt	"	"	"	"
407,501 " 408,000	85	" "	"	"	15	"	"	"
408,001 " 408,500	93	" "	"	"	9	"	"	"
408,501 " 409,000	94	" O. F.	"	"	"	"	"	7
409,001 " 410,000	69	" Htg.	"	Nickel	11	"	"	8
410,001 " 410,500	93	" "	"	Gilt	9	"	"	"
410,501 " 411,000	68	" "	"	"	11	"	"	"
411,001 " 411,500	94	" O. F.	"	"	9	"	"	7
411,501 " 412,000	67	" "	"	"	11	"	"	"
412,001 " 412,500	86	" "	"	Nickel	15	"	"	"
412,501 " 413,000	69	" Htg.	"	"	11	"	"	8
413,001 " 414,000	93	" "	"	Gilt	9	"	"	"
414,001 " 415,000	94	" O. F.	"	"	"	"	"	7
415,001 " 415,200	81	" Htg.	"	Plain	17	"	"	8
415,201 " 415,500	83	" "	"	Nickel	15	"	"	"
415,501 " 415,600	80	" "	"	Spot Gilt	17	"	"	"
415,601 " 416,000	82	" "	"	Plain	"	"	"	"
416,001 " 416,100	61	" O. F.	"	"	"	"	"	7
416,101 " 416,500	86	" "	"	Nickel	15	"	"	"
416,501 " 417,000	62	" "	"	Plain	17	"	"	"
417,001 " 417,500	66	" "	"	Nickel	11	"	"	"
417,501 " 418,000	83	" Htg.	"	"	17	"	"	8
418,001 " 419,000	93	" "	"	Gilt	9	"	"	"
419,001 " 419,500	94	" "	"	"	"	"	"	..
419,501 " 420,500	153	6 "	¾ Pl.	Nickel	11	"	"	2
420,501 " 421,500	161	" "	"	Gilt	"	"	"	"
421,501 " 422,500	162	" "	"	"	9	"	"	"
422,501 " 423,000	66	18 O. F.	F. Pl.	Nickel	11	"	"	7
423,001 " 424,000	93	" Htg.	"	Gilt	9	"	"	8
424,001 " 425,000	69	" "	"	Nickel	11	"	"	"
425,001 " 425,500	94	" O. F.	"	Gilt	9	"	"	7
425,501 " 426,000	66	" "	"	Nickel	11	"	"	"
426,001 " 427,000	83	" Htg.	"	"	15	"	"	8
427,001 " 428,000	69	" "	"	"	11	"	"	"
428,001 " 429,000	66	" O. F.	"	"	"	"	"	7
429,001 " 430,000	83	" Htg.	"	"	15	"	"	8
430,001 " 431,000	68	" "	"	Gilt	11	"	"	"
431,001 " 431,500	66	" O. F.	"	Nickel	"	"	"	7
431,501 " 432,000	82	" Htg.	"	Plain	17	"	"	8
432,001 " 433,000	67	" O. F.	"	Gilt	11	"	"	7
433,001 " 433,100	83	" Htg.	"	Nickel	15	"	"	8
433,101 " 433,140	82a	" "	"	"	"	"	"	"
433,141 " 433,400	82	" "	"	"	"	"	"	"
433,401 " 433,500	82	" "	"	"	17	"	"	"
433,501 " 433,600	83	" "	"	"	15	"	"	"
433,601 " 433,700	82	" "	"	Plain	17	"	"	"
433,701 " 433,750	80	" "	"	Spot Gilt	"	"	"	"
433,751 " 433,800	81	" "	"	Plain	"	"	"	"
433,801 " 434,000	83	" "	"	Nickel	15	"	"	"
434,001 " 434,500	69	" "	"	"	"	"	"	"

The Rockford Watch Company, Ltd.

Number and Grade of Movement	GRADE	Size	Style		Jewels	Wind	Sett	Model
434,501 to 434,600	86	18	O. F.	F. Pl.	Nickel	15	Stem	Lever	7
434,601 " 434,700	62	"	•	"	Plain	17	"	"	"
434,701 " 435,000	86	"	O. F.	"	Nickel	15	"	"	"
435,001 " 435,500	85	"	Htg.	"	Gilt	"	"	"	8
435,501 " 436,000	94	"	O. F.	"	"	9	"	"	7
436,001 " 436,100	67	"	"	"	"	11	"	"	"
436,101 " 436,200	89	"	"	"	"	15	"	"	"
436,201 " 436,300	67	"	"	"	"	11	"	"	"
436,301 " 437,000	89	"	"	"	"	"	"	"	"
437,001 " 437,800	82	"	Htg.	"	Nickel	17	"	"	8
437,801 " 438,000	81	"	"	"	Plain	"	"	"	"
438,001 " 438,500	83	"	"	"	"	15	"	"	"
438,501 " 438,900	62	"	O. F.	"	"	17	"	"	7
438,901 " 439,000	86	"	"	"	Nickel	15	"	"	"
439,001 " 439,500	82	"	Htg.	"	"	17	"	"	8
439,501 " 439,550	80	"	"	"	Nick.& Gilt	"	"	"	"
439,551 " 439,650	82a	"	"	"	"	"	"	"	"
439,651 " 439,700	81	"	"	"	Nickel	"	"	"	"
439,701 " 439,750	62a	"	O. F.	"	"	"	"	"	7
439,751 " 439,850	62	"	"	"	"	"	"	"	"
439,851 " 439,900	61	"	"	"	"	"	"	"	"
439,901 " 439,950	86	"	"	"	"	15	"	"	"
439,951 " 440,000	62a	"	"	"	"	17	"	"	"
440,001 " 441,000	93	"	Htg.	"	Gilt	9	"	"	8
441,001 " 441,500	62	"	O. F.	"	Nickel	17	"	"	7
441,501 " 442,000	83	"	Htg.	"	Plain	15	"	"	8
442,001 " 442,050	80	"	"	"	Nick.& Gilt	17	"	"	"
424,051 " 442,150	81	"	"	"	Plain	"	"	"	"
442,151 " 442,500	82	"	"	"	Nickel	"	"	"	"
500,001 " 500,054	930	"	O. F.	"	"	"	"	"	9
500,055	935	"	"	"	"	"	"	"	"
500,056 to 500,250	930	"	"	"	"	"	"	"	"
500,251 " 500,260	920	"	"	"	"	"	"	"	7
500,261 " 500,300	930	"	"	"	"	"	"	"	9
500,301 " 500,400	935	"	"	"	"	"	"	"	"
500,401 " 500,800	830	"	Htg.	"	"	"	"	"	10
500,801 " 500,900	835	"	"	"	"	"	"	"	"
500,901 " 501,100	830	"	"	"	"	"	"	"	"
501,101 " 501,900	835	"	"	"	"	"	"	"	"
501,901 " 502,400	830	"	"	"	"	"	"	"	"
502,401 " 502,481	930	"	O. F.	"	"	"	"	"	9
502,482 " 502,489	935	"	"	"	"	"	"	"	"
502,490 " 502 592	930	"	"	"	"	"	"	"	"
502,593	935	"	"	"	"	"	"	"	"
502,594 to 502,700	930	"	"	"	"	"	"	"	"
502,701 " 503,200	935	"	"	"	"	"	"	"	"
503,201 " 503,460	830	"	Htg.	"	"	"	"	"	10
503,461 " 503,470	820	"	"	"	"	"	"	"	8
503,471 " 503,483	830	"	"	"	"	"	"	"	10
503,484 " 503,489	820	"	"	"	"	"	"	"	8
503,490 " 503,520	830	"	"	"	"	"	"	"	10
503,521 " 503,531	820	"	"	"	"	"	"	"	8
503,532 " 503,536	830	"	"	"	"	"	"	"	10
503,537 " 503,540	820	"	"	"	"	"	"	"	8
503,541 " 503,550	825	"	"	"	"	"	"	"	10
503,551 " 503,610	830	"	"	"	"	"	"	"	"
503,611 " 503,620	820	"	"	"	"	"	"	"	8
503,621 " 503,700	830	"	"	"	"	"	"	"	10
503,701 " 504,000	835	"	"	"	"	"	"	"	"
504,001 " 504,100	830	"	"	"	"	"	"	"	"
504,101 " 505,150	835	"	"	"	"	"	"	"	"
505,151 " 505,200	830	"	"	"	"	"	"	"	"
505,201 " 505,300	835	"	"	"	"	"	"	"	"
505,301 " 505,350	830	"	"	"	"	"	"	"	"
505,351 " 505,360	835	"	"	"	"	"	"	"	"
505,361 " 505,370	830	"	"	"	"	"	"	"	"
505,371 " 505,398	835	"	"	"	"	"	"	"	"
505,399 " 505,400	830	"	"	"	"	"	"	"	"
505,401 " 505,700	835	"	"	"	"	"	"	"	"
505,701 " 506,000	830	"	"	"	"	"	"	"	"
506,001 " 506,800	935	"	O. F.	"	"	"	"	"	9
506,801 " 506,810	910	"	"	"	"	21	"	"	"
506,811 " 507,600	930	"	"	"	"	17	"	"	"
507,601 " 507,900	830	"	Htg.	"	"	"	"	"	10
507,901 " 508,500	835	"	"	"	"	"	"	"	"
508,501 " 509,000	830	"	"	"	"	"	"	"	"
509,001 " 509,100	820	"	"	"	"	"	"	"	8
509,101 " 509,700	925	"	O. F.	"	"	"	"	"	9
509,701 " 509,729	920	"	"	"	"	"	"	"	7
509,730	915	"	"	"	"	"	"	"	"
509,731 to 509,759	920	"	"	"	"	"	"	"	"
509,760	915	"	"	"	"	"	"	"	"
509,761 to 509,791	920	"	"	"	"	"	"	"	"
509,792	915	"	"	"	"	"	"	"	"
509,793 to 509,900	920	"	"	"	"	"	"	"	"
509,901 " 510,200	810	"	Htg.	"	"	21	"	"	10
510,201 " 510,700	825	"	"	"	"	17	"	"	"
510,701 " 511,300	830	"	"	"	"	"	"	"	"
511,301 " 511,600	835	"	"	"	"	"	"	"	"

The Rockford Watch Company, Ltd.

Number and Grade of Movement	GRADE	Size		Style		Jewels	Wind	Sett	Model
511,601 to 512,500	935	18	O. F.	F. Pl.	Nickel	17	Stem	Lever	9
512,501 " 512,600	910	"	"	"	"	21	"	"	"
512,601 " 512,700	920	"	"	"	"	17	"	"	7
512,701 " 512,800	930	"	"	"	"	"	"	"	9
512,801 " 512,850	920	"	"	"	"	"	"	"	7
512,851 " 512,872	830	"	Htg.	"	"	"	"	"	10
512,873	915	"	O. F.	"	"	"	"	"	7
512,874 to 512,875	920	"	"	"	"	"	"	"	"
512,876	915	"	"	"	"	"	"	"	"
512,877 to 512,900	920	"	"	"	"	"	"	"	"
512,901 " 513,101	830	"	Htg.	"	"	"	"	"	10
513,102 " 513,181	820	"	"	"	"	"	"	"	8
513,182	815	"	"	"	"	"	"	"	"
513,183 to 513,251	820	"	"	"	"	"	"	"	"
513,252 " 513,259	810	"	"	"	"	21	"	"	10
513,260 " 513,300	820	"	"	"	"	17	"	"	8
513,301 " 513,400	830	"	"	"	"	"	"	"	10
513,401 " 513,500	835	"	"	"	"	"	"	"	"
513,501 " 513,600	830	"	"	"	"	"	"	"	"
513,601 " 513,900	835	"	"	"	"	"	"	"	"
513,901 " 514,000	930	"	O. F.	"	"	"	"	"	9
514,001 " 514,100	935	"	"	"	"	"	"	"	"
514,101 " 514,150	825	"	Htg.	"	"	"	"	"	10
514,151 " 514,500	835	"	"	"	"	"	"	"	"
514,501 " 514,600	930	"	O. F.	"	"	"	"	"	9
514,601 " 514,900	935	"	"	"	"	"	"	"	"
514,901 " 515,100	835	"	Htg.	"	"	"	"	"	10
515,101 " 515,400	935	"	O. F.	"	"	"	"	"	9
515,401 " 515,500	810	"	Htg.	"	"	21	"	"	10
515,501 " 515,600	910	"	O. F.	"	"	"	"	"	9
515,601 " 516,000	935	"	"	"	"	17	"	"	"
516,001 " 516,300	925	"	"	"	"	"	"	"	"
516,301 " 516,400	935	"	"	"	"	"	"	"	"
516,401 " 516,500	925	"	"	"	"	"	"	"	"
516,501 " 517,200	825	"	Htg.	"	"	"	"	"	10
517,201 " 519,300	910	"	O. F.	"	"	21	"	"	9
519,301 " 519,400	900	"	"	"	"	24	"	"	"
519,401 " 519,500	800	"	Htg.	"	"	"	"	"	10
519,501 " 519,600	805	"	"	"	"	21	"	"	"
519,601 " 519,700	905	"	O. F.	"	"	"	"	"	9
519,701 " 520,000	835	"	Htg.	"	"	17	"	"	10
520,001 " 521,000	935	"	O. F.	"	"	"	"	"	9
521,001 " 522,000	870	"	Htg.	"	"	7	"	"	10
522,001 " 522,400	970	"	O. F.	"	"	"	"	"	9
522,401 " 523,500	870	"	Htg.	"	"	"	"	"	10
523,501 " 524,800	970	"	O. F.	"	"	"	"	"	9
524,801 " 525,000	935	"	"	"	"	17	"	"	"
525,001 " 525,100	900	"	"	"	"	24	"	"	"
525,101 " 525,400	935	"	"	"	"	17	"	"	"
525,401 " 525,900	925	"	"	"	"	"	"	"	"
525,901 " 526,700	825	"	Htg.	"	"	"	"	"	10
526,701 " 526,900	930	"	O. F.	"	"	"	"	"	9
526,901 " 527,900	935	"	"	"	"	"	"	"	"
527,901 " 528,800	930	"	"	"	"	"	"	"	"
528,801 " 529,800	935	"	"	"	"	"	"	"	"
529,801 " 530,800	925	"	"	"	"	"	"	"	"
530,801 " 531,800	835	"	Htg.	"	"	"	"	"	10
531,801 " 532,450	825	"	"	"	"	"	"	"	"
532,451 " 532,500	835	"	"	"	"	"	"	"	"
532,501 " 533,400	925	"	O. F.	"	"	"	"	"	9
533,401 " 534,000	935	"	"	"	"	"	"	"	"
534,001 " 534,012	920	"	"	"	"	"	"	"	7
534,013	915	"	"	"	"	"	"	"	"
534,014 to 534,035	920	"	"	"	"	"	"	"	"
534,036	915	"	"	"	"	"	"	"	"
534,037 to 534,039	920	"	"	"	"	"	"	"	"
534,040	915	"	"	"	"	"	"	"	"
534,041 to 534,064	920	"	"	"	"	"	"	"	"
534,065	915	"	"	"	"	"	"	"	"
534,066 to 534,112	920	"	"	"	"	"	"	"	"
534,113 " 534,115	915	"	"	"	"	"	"	"	"
534,116 " 534,119	920	"	"	"	"	"	"	"	"
534,120	915	"	"	"	"	"	"	"	"
534,121	920	"	"	"	"	"	"	"	"
534,122 to 534,123	915	"	"	"	"	"	"	"	"
534,124 " 534,127	920	"	"	"	"	"	"	"	"
534,128	915	"	"	"	"	"	"	"	"
534,129 to 534,130	920	"	"	"	"	"	"	"	"
534,131	915	"	"	"	"	"	"	"	"
534,132	920	"	"	"	"	"	"	"	"
534,133	915	"	"	"	"	"	"	"	"
534,134	920	"	"	"	"	"	"	"	"
534,135	915	"	"	"	"	"	"	"	"
534,136 to 534,138	920	"	"	"	"	"	"	"	"
534,139	915	"	"	"	"	"	"	"	"
534,140 to 534,144	920	"	"	"	"	"	"	"	"
534,145	915	"	"	"	"	"	"	"	"
534,146 to 534,147	920	"	"	"	"	"	"	"	"
534,148	915	"	"	"	"	"	"	"	"

The Rockford Watch Company, Ltd.

Number and Grade of Movement	GRADE	Size		Style		Jewels	Wind	Sett	Model
534,149	920	18	O. F.	F. Pl.	Nickel	17	Stem	Lever	7
534,150	915	"	"	"	"	"	"	"	"
534,151 to 534,155	920	"	"	"	"	"	"	"	"
534,156 " 534,157	915	"	"	"	"	"	"	"	"
534,158 " 534,163	920	"	"	"	"	"	"	"	"
534,164	915	"	"	"	"	"		"	"
534,165 to 534,171	920	"	"	"	"	"	"	"	"
534,172	915	"	"	"	"	"	"	"	"
534,173	920	"	"	"	"	"	"	"	"
534,174	915	"	"	"	"	"	"	"	"
534,175	920	"	"	"	"	"	"	"	"
534,176 to 534,179	915	'	"	"	"	"	"	"	"
534,180 " 534,182	920	"	"	"	"	"	"	"	"
534,183	915	"	"	"	"	"	"	"	"
534,184	920	"	"	"	"	"	"	"	"
534,185	915	"	"	"	"	"	"	"	"
534,186 to 534,188	920	"	"	"	"	"	"	"	"
534,189	915	"	"	"	"	"	"	"	"
534,190 to 534,196	920	"	"	"	"	"	"	"	"
534,197	915	"	"	"	"	"	"	"	"
534,198	920	"	"	"	"	"	"	"	"
534,199	915	"	"	"	"	"	"	"	"
534,200	920	"	"	"	"	"	"	"	"
534,401 to 534,600	930	"	"	"	"	"	"	"	9
534,601 " 535,200	910	"	"	"	"	21	"	"	"
535,201 " 535,400	900	"	"	"	"	24	"	"	"
535,401 " 535,600	910	"	"	"	"	21	"	"	"
535,601 " 535,700	800	"	Htg.	"	"	24	"	"	10
535,701 " 535,800	805	"	"	"	"	21	"	"	"
535,801 " 536,300	910	"	O. F.	"	"	17	"	"	9
536,301 " 536,600	930	"	"	"	"	"	"	"	"
536,601 " 536,700	945	"	"	"	"	21	"	"	Special
536,701 " 537,400	910	"	"	"	"	"	"	"	9
537,401 " 539,400	935	"	"	"	"	17	"	"	"
539,401 " 540,400	910	"	"	"	"	21	"	"	"
540,401 " 541,400	935	"	"	"	"	17	"	"	"
541,401 " 541,500	905	"	"	"	"	21	"	"	"
541,501 " 542,000	835	"	Htg.	"	"	17	"	"	10
542,001 " 542,300	800	"	"	"	"	24	"	"	"
542,301 " 542,500	810	"	"	"	"	21	"	"	"
542,501 " 542,700	900	"	O. F.	"	"	24	"	"	9
542,701 " 542,800	905	"	"	"	"	21	"	"	"
542,801 " 543,300	805	"	Htg.	"	"	"	"	"	10
543,301 " 543,500	905	"	O. F.	"	"	17	"	"	9
543,501 " 544,000	835	"	Htg.	"	"	"	"	"	10
544,001 " 544,100	560	16	"	¾ Pl.	"	"	"	"	3
544,101 " 544,200	570	"	"	"	"	"	"	"	"
544,201 " 544,400	560	"	"	"	"	"	"	"	"
544,401 " 544,500	530	"	"	"	"	21	"	"	"
544,501 " 544,800	550	"	"	"	"	17	"	"	4
544,801 " 545,000	540	"	"	"	"	21	"	"	"
545,001 " 545,500	535	"	O. F.	"	"	"	"	"	2
545,501 " 546,500	570	"	Htg.	"	"	17	"	"	3
546,501 " 546,600	540	"	"	"	"	21	"	"	4
546,601 " 546,700	500	"	"	"	"	"	"	"	"
546,701 " 546,800	510	"	"	"	"	"	"	"	"
546,801 " 546,900	520	"	"	"	"	"	"	"	"
546,901 " 547,000	530	"	"	"	"	"	"	"	3
547,001 " 548,000	560	"	"	"	"	17	"	"	2
548,001 " 549,000	565	"	O. F.	"	"	"	"	"	"
549,001 " 550,000	575	"	"	"	"	"	"	"	3
550,001 " 550,500	560	"	Htg.	"	"	"	"	"	5
550,501 " 550,600	515	"	O. F.	"	"	21	"	"	"
550,601 " 550,700	525	"	"	"	"	"	"	"	"
550,701 " 550,900	545	"	"	"	"	"	"	"	"
550,901 " 551,200	555	"	"	"	"	17	"	"	3
551,201 " 551,700	530	"	Htg.	"	"	21	"	"	2
551,701 " 552,700	575	"	O. F.	"	"	17	"	"	"
552,701 " 553,200	565	"	"	"	"	"	"	"	3
553,201 " 554,200	570	"	Htg.	"	"	"	"	"	2
554,201 " 554,700	565	"	O. F.	"	"	"	"	"	5
554,701 " 554,900	555	"	"	"	"	21	"	"	2
554,901 " 554,920	535	"	"	"	"	"	"	"	3
554,921 " 554,927	570	"	Htg.	"	"	17	"	"	2
554,928 " 554,930	575	"	O. F.	"	"	"	"	"	3
554,931 " 554,940	560	"	Htg.	"	"	"	"	"	3
554,941 " 554,960	605	"	O. F.	"	"	11	"	Pend.	Special
554,961		"	"	"	Gilt	"	"	"	"
554,962		"	"	"	"	"	"	"	"
554,963		"	Htg.	"	Nickel	17	"	"	"
554,964		"	"	"	Gilt	"	"	"	"
554,965		"	"	"	"	"	"	"	"
554,966		"	"	"	Nickel	"	"	"	"
554,967		"	"	"	Gilt	15	"	"	"
554,968		"	O. F.	"	....	"	"	"	"
554,969		"	"	"	....	"	"	"	"
554,970		"	Htg.	"	....	"	"	"	"
554,971		"	"	"	....	"	"	"	"
554,972		"	"	"		"	"	"	"

The Rockford Watch Company, Ltd.

Number and Grade of Movement	GRADE	Size		Style		Jewels	Wind	Sett	Model
				Description of Movement					
554,973................................	......	16	Htg.	¾ Pl.	Gilt	11	Stem	Pend.	Special
554,974................................	935	18	O. F.	F. Pl.	Nickel	17	"	Lever	9
554,975................................	......	16	Htg.	¾ Pl.	Nickel	11	"	Pend.	Special
554,976................................	......	"	"	".............."		"	"	"	"
554,977................................	......	"	O. F.	"		"	"	"	"
554,978................................	......	"	"	"	Nickel	17	"	"	"
554,979................................	......	"	"	"	"	"	"	"	"
554,981 to 554,992.....................	25	18	"	F. Pl.	"	25	"	Lever	"
555,001 " 556 000.....................	560	16	Htg.	¾ Pl.	"	17	"	"	3
556,001 " 558,000.....................	575	"	O. F.	"	"	"	"	"	2
558,001 " 558,500.....................	550	"	Htg.	"	"	"	"	"	4
558,501 " 559,000.....................	540	"	"	"	"	21	"	"	"
559,001 " 560,000.....................	560	"	"	"	"	17	"	"	3
560,001 " 560,500.....................	545	"	O. F.	"	"	21	"	"	5
560,501 " 561,000.....................	555	"	"	"	"	17	"	"	"
561,001 " 562,000.....................	835	18	Htg.	F. Pl.	"	"	"	"	10
562,001 " 563,000.....................	935	"	O. F.	"	"	"	"	"	9
563,001 " 565,000.....................	570	16	Htg.	¾ Pl.	"	"	"	"	3
565,001 " 566,000.....................	575	"	O. F.	"	"	"	"	"	2
566,001 " 566,500.....................	918	18	"	F. Pl.	"	24	"	"	9
566,501 " 566,600.....................	930	"	"	"	"	17	"	"	"
566,601 " 566,800.....................	935	"	"	"	"	"	"	"	"
566,801 " 566,900.....................	830	"	Htg.	"	"	"	"	"	10
566,901 " 566,940.....................	500	16	"	¾ Pl.	"	21	"	"	4
566,941 " 567,000.....................	501	"	"	"	"	"	"	"	"
567,001 " 568,000.....................	575	"	O. F.	"	"	17	"	"	2
568,001 " 570,000.....................	570	"	Htg.	"	"	"	"	"	3
570,001 " 571,000.....................	575	"	O. F.	"	"	"	"	"	2
571,001 " 571,300.....................	545	"	"	"	"	21	"	"	5
571,301 " 571,500.....................	575	"	"	"	"	17	"	"	2
571,501 " 571,530.....................	505	"	"	"	"	21	"	"	5
571,531 " 571,600.....................	515	"	"	"	"	"	"	"	"
571,601 " 571,700.....................	570	"	Htg.	"	"	17	"	"	3
571,701 " 571,900.....................	575	"	O. F.	"	"	"	"	"	2
571,901 " 572,000.....................	585	"	"	"	"	15	"	"	"
572,001 " 572,700.....................	565	"	"	"	"	17	"	"	"
572,701 " 573,000.....................	560	"	Htg.	"	"	"	"	"	3
573,001 " 573,500.....................	810	18	"	F. Pl.	"	21	"	"	10
573,501 " 573,510.....................	590	16	"	¾ Pl.	"	11	"	"	3
573,511 " 574,000.....................	584	"	"	"	"	15	"	"	"
574,001 " 574,500.....................	905	18	O. F.	F. Pl.	"	21	"	"	9
574,501 " 575,000.....................	835	"	Htg.	"	"	17	"	"	10
575,001 " 577,000.....................	570	16	"	¾ Pl.	"	"	"	"	3
577,001 " 577,500.....................	584	"	"	"	"	15	"	"	"
577,501 " 577,800.....................	565	"	O. F.	"	"	17	"	"	2
577,801 " 577,900.....................	520	"	Htg.	"	"	21	"	"	4
577,901 " 578,000.....................	525	"	O. F.	"	"	"	"	"	5
578,001 " 579,150.....................	835	18	Htg.	F. Pl.	"	17	"	"	10
579,201 " 579,370.....................	935	"	O. F.	"	"	"	"	"	9
579,401 " 579,500.....................	570	16	Htg.	¾ Pl.	"	"	"	"	3
579,501 " 579,600.....................	575	"	O. F.	"	"	"	"	"	2
579,601 " 579,700.....................	560	"	Htg.	"	"	"	"	"	3
579,701 " 579,735.....................	565	"	O. F.	"	"	"	"	"	2
579,801 " 579,900.....................	830	18	Htg.	F. Pl.	"	"	"	"	10
579,901 " 580,000.....................	930	"	O. F.	"	"	"	"	"	9
580,001 " 580,200.....................	560	16	Htg.	¾ Pl.	"	"	"	"	3
580,201 " 580,300.....................	565	"	O. F.	"	"	"	"	"	2
580,301 " 580,500.....................	570	"	Htg.	"	"	"	"	"	3
580,501 " 580,600.....................	575	"	O. F.	"	"	"	"	"	2
580,601 " 581,000.....................	930	18	"	F. Pl.	"	"	"	"	9
581,001 " 582,000.....................	585	16	"	¾ Pl.	"	15	"	"	2
582,001 " 583,000.....................	584	"	Htg.	"	"	"	"	"	3
583,001 " 584,000.....................	560	"	"	"	"	17	"	"	"
584,001 " 585,000.....................	584	"	"	"	"	15	"	"	"
585,001 " 585,500.....................	935	18	O. F.	F. Pl.	"	17	"	"	9
585,501 " 585,600.....................	515	16	"	¾ Pl.	"	21	"	"	5
585,601 " 585,700.....................	525	"	"	"	"	"	"	"	"
585,701 " 585,800.....................	830	18	Htg.	F. Pl.	"	17	"	"	10
585,801 " 585,900.....................	930	"	O. F.	"	"	"	"	"	9
585,901 " 586,000.....................	835	"	Htg.	"	"	"	"	"	10
586,001 " 588,000.....................	584	16	"	¾ Pl.	"	15	"	"	3
588,001 " 590,000.....................	835	18	"	F. Pl.	"	17	"	"	10
590,001 " 591,000.....................	570	16	"	¾ Pl.	"	"	"	"	3
591,001 " 592,000.....................	584	"	"	"	"	15	"	"	"
592,001 " 593,000.....................	835	18	"	F. Pl.	"	17	"	"	10
593,001 " 593,100.....................	560	16	"	¾ Pl.	"	"	"	"	3
593,101 " 593,200.....................	570	"	"	"	"	"	"	"	"
593,201 " 593,300.....................	100	"	"	"	"	21	"	Pend.	Special
593,301 " 593,400.....................	101	"	O. F.	"	"	"	"	"	"
593,401 " 593,600.....................	925	18	"	F. Pl.	"	17	"	Lever	9
593,601 " 593,700.....................	835	"	Htg.	"	"	"	"	"	10
593,701 " 593,800.....................	825	"	"	"	"	"	"	"	"
593,801 " 593,900.....................	520	16	"	¾ Pl.	"	21	"	"	4
593,901 " 594,000.....................	505	"	"	"	"	"	"	"	5
594,001 " 596,000.....................	590	"	O. F.	"	"	11	"	Pend.	3
596,001 " 597,000.....................	595	"	Htg.	"	"	"	"	"	2
597,001 " 598,000.....................	590	"	O. F.	"	"	"	"	"	3
598,001 " 599,000.....................	586	"	Htg.	"	"	15	"	"	5
599,001 " 599,500.....................	587	"	O. F.	"	"	"	"	"	2

The Rockford Watch Company, Ltd.

Number and Grade of Movement	GRADE	Size		Style		Jewels	Wind	Sett	Model
599,501 to 599,502	575	16	O. F.	¾ Pl.	Nickel	17	Stem	Lever	2
599,503 " 599,504	565	"	"	"	"	"	"	"	"
599,505 "	575	"	"	"	"	"	"	"	"
599,506 to 600,000	587	"	"	"	"	15	"	Pend.	"
600,001 " 601,000	935	18	"	F. Pl.	"	17	"	Lever	9
601,001 " 602,000	590	16	Htg.	¾ Pl.	"	11	"	Pend.	3
602,001 " 603,000	595	"	O. F.	"	"	"	"	"	2
603,001 " 605,000	561	"	Htg.	"	"	17	"	"	4
605,001 " 605,700	573	"	O. F.	"	"	"	"	"	5
605,701 " 605,850	845	18	Htg.	F. Pl.	"	21	"	Lever	Special
605,851 " 605,900	945	"	O. F.	"	"	"	"	"	"
605,901 " 605,950	540	16	Htg.	¾ Pl.	"	"	"	"	4
606,001 " 608,000	935	18	O. F.	F. Pl.	"	17	"	"	9
608,001 " 609,000	572	16	Htg.	¾ Pl.	"	"	"	Pend.	4
609,001 " 610,000	566	"	O. F.	"	"	"	"	"	5
610,001 " 613,000	605	"	"	"	"	11	"	"	2
613,001 " 614,000	587	"	"	"	"	15	"	"	"
614,001 " 615,000	600	"	Htg.	"	"	11	"	"	3
615,001 " 617,000	605	"	O. F.	"	"	"	"	"	2
617,001 " 617,500	586	"	Htg.	"	"	15	"	"	3
617,501 " 617,800	845	18	"	F. Pl.	"	21	"	Lever	Special
617,801 " 618,000	810	"	"	"	"	"	"	"	10
618,001 " 618,500	587	16	O. F.	¾ Pl.	"	15	"	Pend.	2
618,501 " 618,600	578	"	Htg.	"	"	17	"	"	3
618,601 " 618,700	579	"	O. F.	"	"	"	"	"	2
618,701 " 618,800	600	"	Htg.	"	"	11	"	"	3
618,801 " 618,900	586	"	"	"	"	15	"	"	"
618,901 " 618,950	120	"	"	"	"	17	"	"	Special
618,951 " 619,000	125	"	O. F.	"	"	"	"	"	"
619,001 " 619,300	525	"	"	"	"	21	"	Lever	5
619,301 " 619,700	600	"	Htg.	"	"	11	"	Pend.	3
619,701 " 619,900	565	"	O. F.	"	"	17	"	Lever	"
619,901 " 620,000	101	"	"	'	"	21	"	Pend.	Special
620,001 " 621,000	545	"	"	"	"	"	"	Lever	5
621,001 " 622,000	935	18	"	F. Pl.	"	17	"	"	9
622,001 " 622,300	160	0	Htg.	¾ Pl.	"	15	"	Pend.	1
622,301 " 622,350	140	"	"	"	"	17	"	"	"
622,351 " 622,500	150	"	"	"	"	"	"	"	"
622,501 " 623,000	160	"	"	"	"	15	"	"	"
623,001 " 623,100	200	18	O. F.	F. Pl.	"	17	"	Lever	10
623,101 " 623,500	605	16	"	¾ Pl.	"	11	"	Pend.	2
623,501 " 624,000	160	0	Htg.	"	"	15	"	"	1
624,001 " 624,200	205	18	O. F.	F. Pl.	"	17	"	Lever	10
624,201 " 624,300	945	"	"	"	"	21	"	"	Special
624,301 " 624,400	930	"	"	"	"	17	"	"	9
624,401 " 624,450	110	16	Htg.	¾ Pl.	"	"	"	Pend.	Special
624,451 " 624,500	115	"	O. F.	"	"	"	"	"	"
624,501 " 624,525	130	"	Htg.	"	Gilt	"	"	"	"
624,526 " 624,550	135	"	O. F.	"	Nickel	"	"	"	"
624,601 " 624,800	540	"	Htg.	"	"	21	"	Lever	4
625,001 " 625,400	400	"	"	"	"	17	"	Pend.	"
626,001 " 626,200	405	"	"	"	"	21	"	"	5
626,201 " 626,400	510	"	"	"	"	"	"	Lever	4
626,401 " 626,600	515	"	O. F.	"	"	"	"	"	5
626,601 " 626,700	520	"	Htg.	"	"	"	"	"	4
626,701 " 626,900	525	"	O. F.	"	"	"	"	"	5
626,901 " 627,000	845	18	Htg.	F. Pl.	"	"	"	"	Special
627,001 " 627,300	572	16	"	¾ Pl.	"	17	"	Pend.	4
628,001 " 628,100	500	"	"	"	"	21	"	Lever	"
628,101 " 628,300	520	"	"	"	"	"	"	"	5
628,301 " 628,500	515	"	O. F.	"	"	"	"	"	5
628,501 " 628,600	505	"	"	"	"	"	"	"	4
628,601 " 628,800	510	"	Htg.	"	"	"	"	"	4
628,801 " 628,950	100	"	"	"	"	"	"	Pend.	Special
628,951 " 629,000	101	"	O. F.	"	"	"	"	"	"
629,001 " 630,000	935	18	"	F. Pl.	"	17	"	Lever	9
630,001 " 630,600	835	"	Htg.	"	"	"	"	"	10
630,601 " 630,700	162	0	"	¾ Pl.	"	"	"	Pend.	1
630,701 " 630,800	150	"	"	"	"	"	"	"	"
630,801 " 631,000	160	"	"	"	"	15	"	"	"
631,001 " 632,000	586	16	"	"	"	17	"	"	3
632,001 " 632,500	825	18	"	F. Pl.	"	17	"	Lever	10
633,001 " 633,500	925	"	O. F.	"	"	15	"	"	9
634,001 " 635,000	587	16	"	¾ Pl.	"	15	"	Pend.	2
635,001 " 636,000	935	18	"	F. Pl.	"	17	"	Lever	9
636,001 " 636,500	160	0	Htg.	¾ Pl.	"	15	"	Pend.	1
636,501 " 636,600	150	"	"	"	"	17	"	"	"
636,601 " 638,000	160	"	"	"	"	15	"	"	"
638,001 " 639,000	600	16	"	"	"	11	"	"	3
639,001 " 640,000	160	0	"	"	"	15	"	Pend.	1
640,001 " 641,000	162	"	"	"	"	"	"	"	"
641,001 " 642,000	610	16	"	"	"	7	"	"	Special
642,001 " 643,000	615	"	O. F.	"	"	15	"	"	3
643,001 " 644,000	587	"	"	"	"	15	"	"	2
644,001 " 644,500	142	0	Htg.	"	"	17	"	"	1
645,001 " 646,600	162	"	"	"	"	15	"	"	"
646,001 " 647,000	610	16	"	"	"	7	"	"	Special
647,001 " 648,000	615	"	O. F.	"	"	15	"	"	3
648,001 " 649,000	160	0	Htg.	"	"	15	"	Pend.	1
649,001 " 650,000	605	16	O. F.	"	"	11	"	"	2

The Rockford Watch Company, Ltd.

Number and Grade of Movement	GRADE	Size	Style		Jewels	Wind	Sett	Model
650,001 " 651,000	573	16	O. F.	¾ Pl. Nickel	17	Stem	Pend.	5
651,001 to 656,000	160	0	Htg.	" "	15	"	"	1
656,001 " 656,100	152	"	"	" "	17	"	"	Special
657,001 " 657,200	182	"	"	" "	7	"	"	"
658,001 " 659,000	600	16	"	" "	11	"	"	3
659,001 " 659,200	930	18	O. F.	F. Pl. "	17	"	Lever	9
660,001 " 660,100	910	"	"	" "	21	"	"	"
661,101 " 661,200	810	"	Htg.	" "	"	"	"	10
662,001 " 662,600	100	16	"	¾ Pl. "	"	"	Pend.	Special
663,001 " 663,100	101	"	O. F.	" "	"	"	"	"
664,001 " 664,100	845	18	Htg.	F. Pl. "	"	"	Lever	"
665,001 " 665,100	830	"	O. F.	" "	17	"	"	10
666,001 " 666,100	900	"	"	" "	24	"	"	9
667,001 " 667,100	905	"	"	" "	21	"	"	"
668,001 " 669,000	605	16	"	¾ Pl. "	11	"	Pend.	2
669,001 " 669,100	912	18	"	F. Pl. Spot Gilt	21	"	Lever	9
670,001 " 670,100	537	16	"	¾ Pl. "	"	"	"	2
671,001 " 671,300	200	18	"	F. Pl. Nickel	17	"	"	10
672,001 " 673,000	205	"	"	" "	"	"	"	"
674,001 " 675,000	405	16	"	¾ Pl. "	"	"	Pend.	5
675,001 " 675,500	525	"	"	" "	21	"	Lever	"
676,001 " 677,000	566	"	"	" "	17	"	Pend.	"
677,001 " 678,000	573	"	"	" "	"	"	"	"
678,001 " 678,500	586	"	"	" "	15	"	"	3
679,001 " 680,500	587	"	"	" "	"	"	"	2
681,001 " 682,000	600	"	Htg.	" "	11	"	"	3
682,001 " 686,000	605	"	O. F.	" "	"	"	"	2
686,001 " 693,000	615	"	"	" "	7	"	"	2
693,001 " 694,000	610	"	Htg.	" "	"	"	"	3
694,001 " 694,500	935	18	O. F.	F. Pl. "	17	"	Lever	9
695,001 " 695,500	945	"	"	" "	21	"	"	Special

(More Serial Numbers and Grade of Movement next page.)

STYLE & NAMES OF U.S.A. HANDS

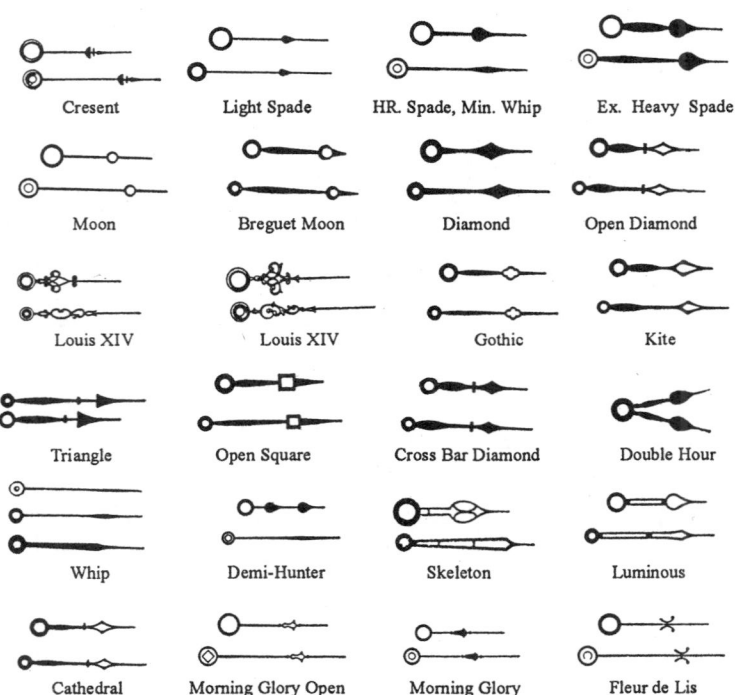

Cresent	Light Spade	HR. Spade, Min. Whip	Ex. Heavy Spade
Moon	Breguet Moon	Diamond	Open Diamond
Louis XIV	Louis XIV	Gothic	Kite
Triangle	Open Square	Cross Bar Diamond	Double Hour
Whip	Demi-Hunter	Skeleton	Luminous
Cathedral	Morning Glory Open	Morning Glory	Fleur de Lis

SERIAL NUMBER — GRADE,SIZE-STYLE,JEWELS,MODEL

695501-696000=945,18S.O.F.21J.M#SP.
696001-697000=838,18S.H.C.17J.M#10
697001-698000=938,18S.O.F.17J.M# 9
698001-699000=150, 0S. H.C.17J.M# 1
699001-700000=140, 0S. H.C.15J.M# 1
700001-702100=180, 0S. H.C. 7J.M# 1
702101-703000=160, 0S. H.C.15J.M# 1
703001-703500=170, 0S. H.C.11J.M# 1
703501-704000=160, 0S. H.C.15J.M# 1
704001-704300=935,18S.O.F.17J.M# 9
704301-704400=930,18S.O.F.17J.M# 9
704401-704500=935,18S.O.F.17J.M# 9
704501-704600=930,18S.O.F.17J.M# 9
704601-705000=935,18S.O.F.17J.M# 9
705001-706000=572,16S.H.C.17J.M# 4
706001-707000=600,16S.H.C.11J.M# 3
707001-708000=918,18S.O.F.21J.M# 9
708001-709000=586,16S.H.C.15J.M# 4
709001-710000=587,16S.O.F.15J.M# 3
710001-710100=930,18S.O.F.17J.M# 9
710101-710600=935,18S.O.F.17J.M# 9
710601-710700=930,18S.O.F.17J.M# 9
710701-711000=935,18S.O.F.17J.M# 9
711001-711100=830,18S.H.C.17J.M# 9
711101-711500=835,18S.H.C.17J.M#10
711501-711600=830,18S.H.C.17J.M#10
711601-712000=835,18S.H.C.17J.M#10
712001-712700=573,16S.O.F.17J.M# 5
712701-713000=635,16S.O.F.17J.M# 5
713001-714000=610,16S.O.F. 7J.M#SP.
714001-715000=572,16S.H.C.17J.M# 4
715001-716000=586,16S.O.F.15J.M# 3
716001-717000=587,16S.O.F.15J.M# 2
717001-718000=600,16S.O.F.11J.M# 3
718001-719000=605,16S.O.F.11J.M# 2
719001-720000=615,16S.O.F. 7J.M# 3
720001-721000=610,16S.O.F. 7J.M#SP.
721001-721500=600,16S.H.C.11J.M# 3
721501-722000=586,16S.H.C.15J.M# 3
722501-722700=573,16S.O.F.17J.M# 5
722701-722800=635,16S.O.F.17J.M# 5
722801-722900=573,16S.O.F.17J.M# 5
722901-723000=635,16S.O.F.17J.M# 5
723001-724000=935,18S.O.F.17J.M#10
724001-725000=205,18S.O.F.17J.M# 9
725001-725100=930,18S.O.F.17J.M# 9
725101-726000=935,18S.O.F.17J.M# 9
726001-727000=405,16S.O.F.17J.M# 5
727001-728000=587,16S.O.F.15J.M# 2
728001-728500=573,16S.O.F.17J.M# 5
728501-728600=635,16S.O.F.17J.M# 5
728601-728800=573,16S.O.F.17J.M# 5
728801-729000=635,16S.O.F.17J.M# 5
729001-729800=600,16S.H.C.11J.M# 3
729801-730000=586,16S.O.F.15J.M# 3
730001-730700=610,16S.O.F. 7J.M#SP.
730701-731000=586,16S.O.F.15J.M# 3
731001-732000=615,16S.O.F. 7J.M# 3
732001-732500=162, 0S.H.C.17J.M# 1
732501-733000=150, 0S.H.C.17J.M# 1
733001-734000=572, 6S.H.C.17J.M# 4
734001-735000=586,16S.O.F.15J.M# 2
735001-735200=610,16S.H.C. 7J.M#SP.
735201-736000=586,16S.O.F.15J.M# 2
736001-738000=935,18S.O.F.17J.M# 9
738001-739000=938,18S.O.F.17J.M#10
739001-740000=925,18S.O.F.17J.M# 9
740001-740200=830,18S.H.C.17J.M#10
740201-741000=835,18S.H.C.17J.M#10
741001-741100=600,16S.H.C.11J.M# 3
741101-742000=586,16S.H.C.15J.M# 3
742001-742500=605,16S.O.F.11J.M# 2
742501-743000=587,16S.O,F.15J.M# 2
743001-745000=935,18S.O.F.17J.M# 9
745001-746000=930,18S.O.F.17J.M# 9
746001-747000=586,16S.O.F.15J.M# 2
747001-748000=935,18S.O.F.17J.M# 9
748001-749000=938,18S.O.F.17J.M#10
749001-749600=572,16S.H.C.17J.M# 4
749601-750000=630,16S.O.F.17J.M# 4
750001-750200=573,16S.O.F.17J.M# 5
750201-750600=635,16S.O.F.17J.M# 5
750601-751000=573,16S.O.F.17J.M# 5
751001-751200=605,16S.O.F.15J.M# 2
752001-752100=572,16S.H.C.17J.M# 4
752101-752200=630,16S.O.F.17J.M# 4
752201-753000=572,16S.H.C.17J.M# 4
753001-754000=573,16S.O.F.17J.M# 5
754001-755000=586,16S.H.C.15J.M# 3
755001-756000=587,16S.O.F.15J.M# 2
756001-757000=935,18S.O.F.17J.M# 9
757001-758000=925,18S.O.F.17J.M# 9
758001-759000=150, 0S.H.C.17J.M# 1
759001-759500=572,16S.H.C.17J.M# 4

SERIAL NUMBER — GRADE,SIZE-STYLE, JEWELS,MODEL

759501-756000=620,16S.H.C.21J.M# 5
760001-760500=573,16S.O.F.17J.M# 5
760501-761000=625,16S.O.F.21J.M# 5
761001-762000=160, 0S.H.C.15J.M# 1
762001-762500=400,16S.H.C.17J.M# 4
762501-764000=405,16S.O.F.17J.M# 5
764001-765000=205,18S.O.F.17J.M#10
765001-765500=515,16S.O.F.21J.M# 5
765501-766000=545,16S.O.F.21J.M# 5
760010-767000=930,18S.O.F.17J.M# 9
767001-768000=572,16S.H.C.17J.M# 4
768001-769000=935,18S.O.F.17J.M# 9
769001-770000=918,18S.O.F.21J.M#10
770001-770500=938,18S.O.F.17J.M#10
770501-771000=835,18S.H.C.17J.M#10
771001-772000=586,16S.O.F.15J.M# 3
772001-772100=320,12S.H.C.17J.M# 1
772001-772200=330,12S.O.F.17J.M# 1
772201-772300=310,12S.H.C.21J.M# 1
772301-772400=300,12S.H.C.23J.M# 1
772401-772600=325,12S.O.F.17J.M# 2
772601-772800=335,12S.O.F.17J.M# 2
772801-772900=315,12S.O.F.21J.M# 2
772901-773000=305,12S.O.F.23J.M# 2
773001-773100=300,12S.H.C.23J.M# 1
773101-773200=310,12S.O.F.21J.M# 1
773201-773400=320,12S.H.C.17J.M# 1
773401-773500=305,12S.O.F.23J.M# 2
773501-773600=315,12S.O.F.21J.M# 2
773601-773800=325,12S.O.F.17J.M# 2
773801-774000=330,12S.H.C.17J.M# 1
774001-774500=335,12S.O.F.17J.M# 2
774501-774700=325,12S.O.F.17J.M# 2
774701-774000=330,12S.O.F.17J.M# 1
774901-775000=320,12S.H.C.17J.M# 1
775001-776000=587,16S.O.F.15J.M# 2
776001-777000=630,16S.H.C.17J.M# 5
777001-778000=635,16S.O.F.17J.M# 5
778001-779000=838,18S.H.C.17J.M#10
779001-779500=938,18S.H.C.17J.M#10
779501-780000=935,18S.O.F.17J.M# 9
780001-781000=835,18S.H.C.17J.M#10
781001-782000=545,16S.O.F.21J.M# 5
782001-783000=404,16S.O.F.17J.M# 5
783001-784000=561,16S.H.C.17J.M# 4
784001-785000=930,18S.O.F.17J.M# 9
785001-786000=205,18S.O.F.17J.M# 9
786001-787000=935,18S.O.F.17J.M# 9
787001-787200=310,12S.H.C.21J.M# 2
787201-788000=335,12S.O.F.17J.M# 2
788001-788100=315,12S.O.F.21J.M# 2
788101-789000=335,12S.O.F.17J.M# 2
789001-789100=330,12S.H.C.17J.M# 1
789001-789500=320,12S.O.F.17J.M# 1
789501-790000=330,12S.H.C.17J.M3 1
790001-791000=325,12S.O.F.17J.M# 2
791001-792000=330,12S.H.C.17J.M# 1
792001-792900=335,12S.O.F.17J.M# 2
792901-793000=355,12S.O.F.17J.M# 2
793001-796000=935,18S.O.F.17J.M# 9
796001-797000=930,18S.O.F.17J.M# 9
797001-798000=938,18S.O.F.17J.M# 9
798001-799000=830,18S.H.C.17J.M# 8
799001-800000=587,16S.O.F.15J.M# 2
800001-801000=572,16S.H.C.17J.M# 4
801001-802000=573,16S.O.F.17J.M# 5
802001-802500=573,16S.O.F.17J.M# 5
802501-803000=566,16S.O.F.17J.M# 5
803001-804000=573,16S.O.F.17J.M# 5
804001-805000=150, 0S.H.C.17J.M# 1
805001-806000=335,12S.O.F.17J.M# 2
806001-806100=300,12S.H.C.23J.M# 1
806101-807000=335,12S.O.F.17J.M# 2
807001-807100=305,12S.O.F.23J.M# 2
807101-808000=335,12S.O.F.17J.M# 2
808001-810000=573,16S.O.F.17J.M# 4
810001-811000=572,16S,H.C.17J.M# 4
811001-812000=160, 0S.H.C.15J.M# 1
812001-813000=330,12S.H.C.17J.M# 1
813001-814000=355,12S.O.F.17J.M# 2
814001-814500=350,12S.H.C.17J.M# 1
814501-814600=345,12S.H.C.21J.M# 1
814601-814700=340,12S.O.F.21J.M# 2
814701-815000=350,12S.H.C.17J.M# 1
815001-816000=335,12S.O.F.17J.M# 2
816001-817000=190, 0S.H.C.15J.M# 1
817001-818000=185 0S.H.C.17J.M# 1
818001-819000=335,12S.O.F.17J.M# 2
819001-820000=355,12S.O.F.17J.M# 2
820001-821000=190, 0S.H.C.15J.M# 1
821001-822000=335,12S.H.C.17J.M# 1
822001-823000=350,12S.H.C.17J.M# 1
823001-824000=330,12S.H.C.17J.M# 1

**FROM
ROCKFORD
PARTS
CATALOG
1909 - 1910**

Model 1, 18 size, full plate, hunting, key wind & set.

Model 2, 18 size, full plate, hunting, lever set.

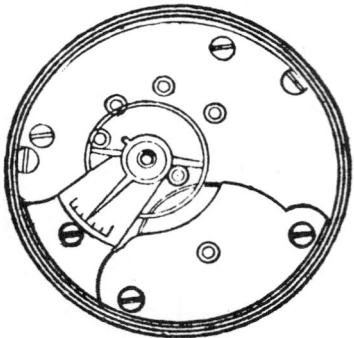

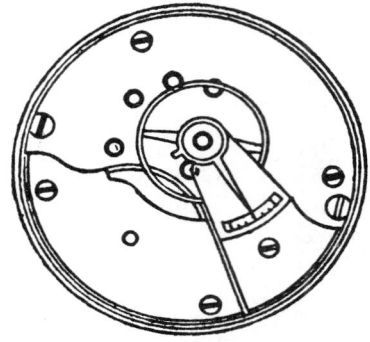

Model 3, 18 size, full plate, hunting, lever set.

Model 4, 18 size, full plate, open face, lever set.

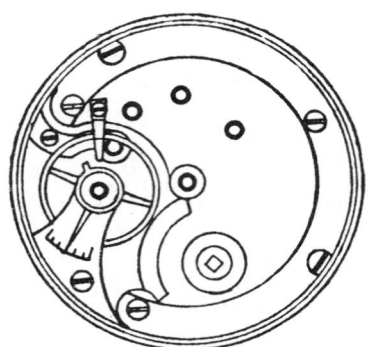

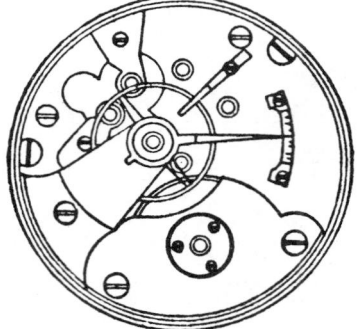

Model 5, 18 size, three-quarter plate, hunting, lever set.

Model 6, 18 size, full plate, hunting, lever set, exposed escapement.

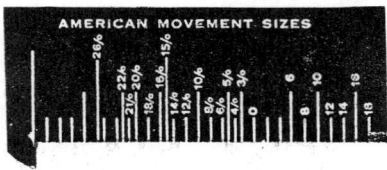

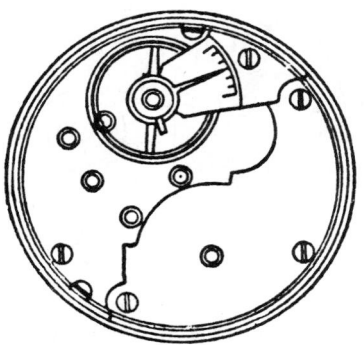

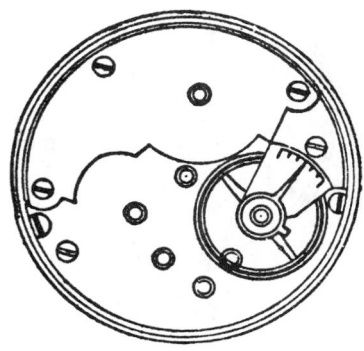

Model 7, 18 size, full plate, open face, lever set.

Model 8, 18 size, full plate, hunting, lever set.

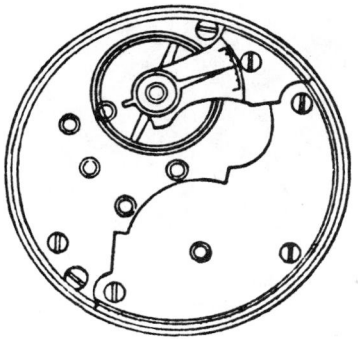

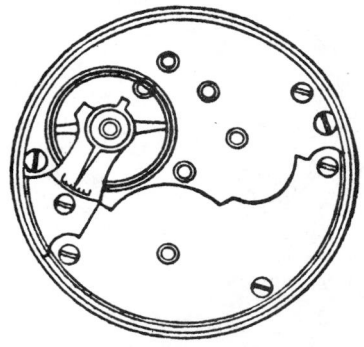

Model 9, 18 size, full plate, open face, lever set.

Model 10, 18 size, full plate, hunting, lever set.

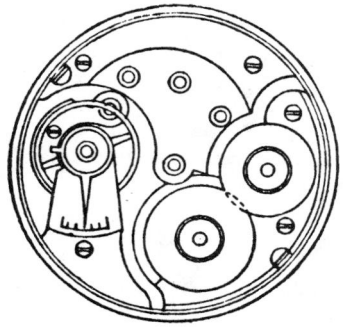

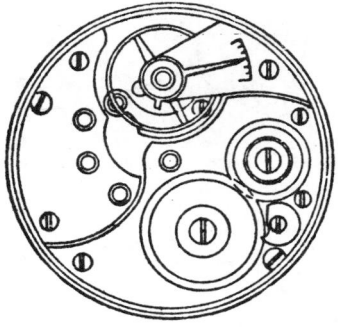

Model 1, 16 size, three-quarter plate, hunting, lever set.

Model 2, 16 size, three-quarter plate, open face, pendant & lever set.

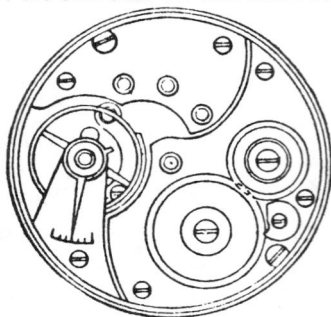

Model 3, 16 size, three-quarter plate, hunting, pendant & lever set.

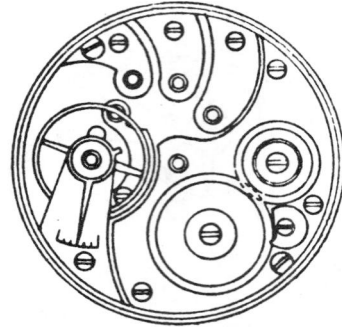

Model 4, 16 size, three-quarter plate, bridge, hunting, pendant & lever set.

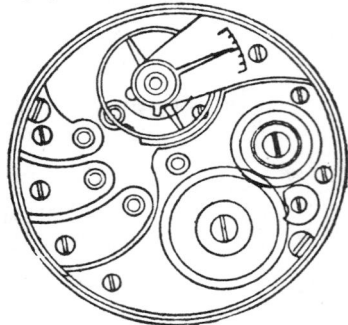

Model 5, 16 size, three-quarter plate, bridge, open face, pendant & lever set.

Model 1, 12 size, three-quarter plate bridge, hunting, pendant set.

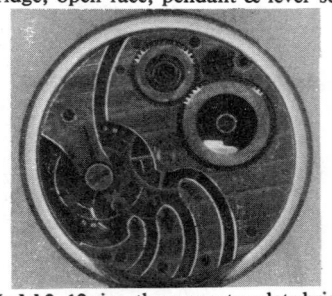

Model 2, 12 size, three-quarter plate bridge, open face, pendant set.

Model 1, 6 & 8 size, three-quarter plate, hunting, lever set.

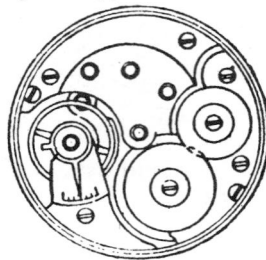

Model 2, 6 size, three-quarter plate, hunting, lever set.

Model 1, 0 size, three-quarter plate, bridge, hunting, pendant set.

Model 2, 0 size, three-quarter plate, bridge, open face, pendant set.

SAN JOSE WATCH CO.
California 1891

Very few watches were made by the San Jose Watch Co., and very little is known about them. The company purchased the Otay Watch Company and machinery and remaining watch movements. The San Jose Watch Co. produced a few dozen watches. Engraved on a San Jose Watch Co. movement S# 30,656 (First watch manufactured by San Jose Watch Co. November 1891). The San Jose W. Co was sold to Osaka, in Japan.

Grade or Name – Description		Avg	Ex-Fn	Mint
18S, 15J, LS, SW .... ★★★		$2,400	$2,800	$4,000

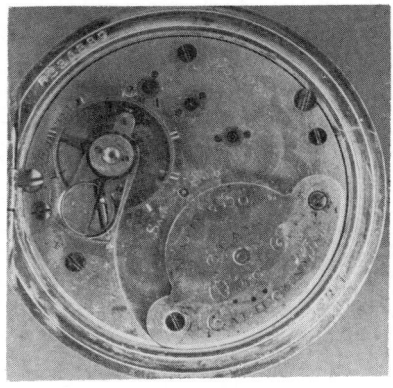
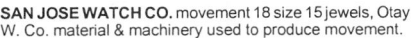

SAN JOSE WATCH CO. movement 18 size 15 jewels, Otay W. Co. material & machinery used to produce movement.

M.S. Smith & Co. movement, 18 size, 19 jewels, three-quarter plate, key wind & set.

M. S. SMITH & CO.
Detroit, Michigan 1870 - 1874

Eber B. Ward purchased the M. S. Smith & Co. which was a large jewelry firm. These watches carried the Smith name on them. A Mr. Hoyt was engaged to produce these watches and about 100 were produced before the Freeport Watch Co. purchased the firm. These watches are very similar to the **"J.H.Allison"** movements.

Grade or Name – Description		Avg	Ex-Fn	Mint
18S, 19J, 3/4, KW, KS, Freeport Model, **18K** case............ ★★★★		$3,000	$3,500	$6,500
18S, 19J, 3/4, KW, KS, Freeport Model .... ★★★★		1,800	2,200	4,500
18S, 15J, 3/4, wolf's tooth -wind, **Swiss, 14K** HC....................★		800	900	1,200
6S, 15J, KW, KS, HC **18K** case..★		500	600	850
6S, 15J, SW...★		195	295	500

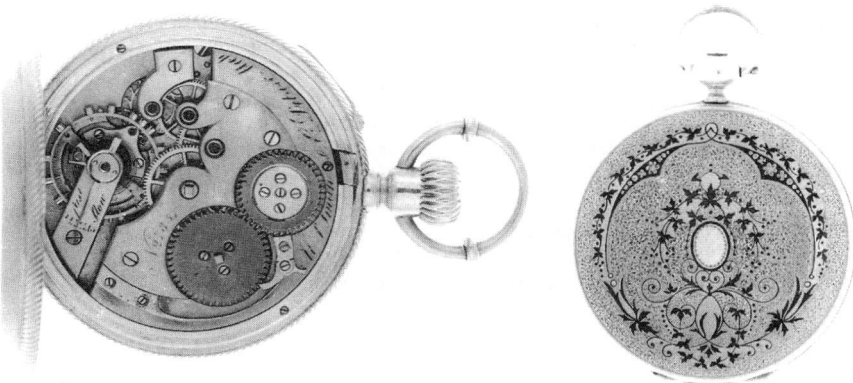

M. S. Smith & Co., 18S, 15J, 3/4, wolf's tooth -wind, **Swiss**, Ca. 1874.

M. S. Smith, 6-8 size, 15 jewels, KW KS, **Swiss**, 18K HC, Ca. 1870.

SOUTH BEND WATCH CO.
South Bend, Indiana
March 1903 - December 1929

Three brothers, George, Clement and J. M. Studebaker, purchased the successful Columbus Watch Co. The first South Bend watches were full plate and similar to the Columbus watches. The serial numbers started at 380,501 where as the Columbus serial numbers stopped at about 500,000. The highest grade watch was a ''Polaris,'' a 16S, 3/4 plate, 21 jewels, and with an open face. This watch sold for about $100. The 227 and 229 were also high grade. The company identified its movements by model numbers 1, 2, and 3, and had grades from 100 to 431. The even numbers were hunting cases, and the odd numbers were open-faced cases. The lowest grade was a 203, 7J, that sold for about $6.75. The company closed on Dec. 31, 1929.

SOUTH BEND ESTIMATED SERIAL NUMBERS
AND PRODUCTION DATES

DATE – SERIAL NO.	DATE – SERIAL NO.	DATE – SERIAL NO.	DATE – SERIAL NO.
1903 – 380,501	1910 – 600,000	1917 – 860,000	1924 – 1,070,000
1904 – 390,000	1911 – 660,000	1918 – 880,000	1925 – 1,105,000
1905 – 405,000	1912 – 715,000	1919 – 905,000	1926 – 1,140,000
1906 – 425,000	1913 – 765,000	1920 – 935,000	1927 – 1,175,000
1907 – 460,000	1914 – 800,000	1921 – 975,000	1928 – 1,210,000
1908 – 500,000	1915 – 820,000	1922 – 1,000,000	1929 – 1,240,000
1909 – 550,000	1916 – 840,000	1923 – 1,035,000	

The above list is provided for determining the APPROXIMATE age of your watch. Match serial number with date. Watches were not necessarily sold in the exact order of manufactured date.

SOUTH BEND
18 SIZE (Lever set)

Grade or Name – Description	Avg	Ex-Fn	Mint
South Bend, 15J, OF	$80	$125	$175
South Bend, 15J, HC	95	150	225
South Bend, 17J, OF	95	125	195
South Bend, 17J, HC	125	150	250
South Bend, 21J, OF	350	400	600
South Bend, 21J, HC, **14K**	600	700	1,200
South Bend, 21J, OF, HC, Silveroid	295	350	500
South Bend, 21J, SW, HC	400	450	750
The Studebaker, G#323, 17J, GJS, NI, Adj.5P, OF	400	500	800
The Studebaker, G#328, 21J, GJS, NI, FULL, Adj.5P, HC . ★ ★ ★	750	900	1,400
The Studebaker, G#329, 21J, GJS, NI, FULL, Adj.5P, OF	600	700	1,100

IMPORTANT NOTE: Railroad Standards, Railroad Approved & Railroad Grade **terminology,** as defined and used in this ***BOOK***.
1. **RAILROAD STANDARDS** = A commission or board appointed by the railroad companies outlined a set of **guidelines** to be accepted or approved by each railroad line.
2. **RAILROAD APPROVED** = A **LIST** of watches each railroad line would approve if purchased by their employee's. (this list changed through the years).
3. **RAILROAD GRADE** = A watch made by manufactures to meet or exceed the guidelines set by the railroad **standards**. Grades such as 992, Vanguard and B.W. Raymond, etc.

⊕ Some GRADES **exceeded** the R.R. standards such as 23 jewels, diamond end stone, gold train, raised gold jewel settings, double sunk dial and the list goes on. Examples: such as Veritas, Sangamo, 950 & Riverside Maximus and many others.

⊕ Generic, nameless or **unmarked** grades for watch movements are listed under the Company name or initials of the Company, etc. by size, jewel count and description.

⊕ A collector should expect to pay modestly higher prices at local shops.

⊕ Watches listed in this book are priced at the collectable Trade Show level, as **complete** watches having an original 14k gold-filled case and *Key Wind* with silver, an original white enamel single sunk dial, and with the entire original movement in good working order with no repairs needed.

⊕ Pricing in this Guide are fair market price for **COMPLETE** watches which are reflected from the "**NAWCC**" National and regional shows.

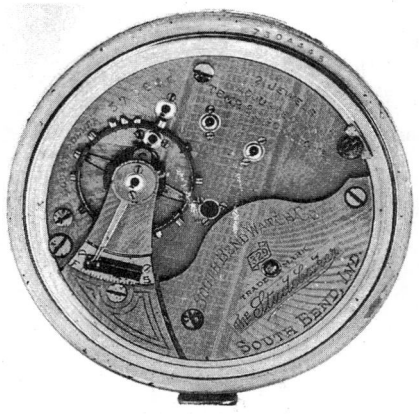

South Bend movement, 18 size, 17 jewels, stem wind, hunting, serial number 426,726.

The Studebaker in (SCRIPT), 18 size, 21 jewels, gold jewel settings, marked 329, stem wind.

Grade or Name – Description	Avg	Ex-Fn	Mint
302, 15J, M# 1, HC, (not seen) .... ★★★★★	$225	$275	$500
304, 15J, HC	95	150	250
305, 15J, OF	85	125	150
305, 15J, Silveroid, OF	75	95	125
309, 17J, OF	95	125	195
312, 17J, NI, ADJ, HC .... ★★	. 95	150	250
313, 17J, NI, ADJ, **marked 313** OF .... ★	225	275	400
313, 17J, NI, ADJ, **Not** Marked, OF	195	250	325
315, 17J, NI, Adj.3P, OF	95	125	195
For - G#s 323, 328 & 329 see **"The Studebaker"**			
327, 21J, Adj.5P, marked 327, OF .... ★★★	295	350	600
327, 21J, Adj.5P, marked 327, Silveroid, OF .... ★★★	225	250	500
330, 15J, M#1, LS, HC	95	150	250
331, 15J, M#1, LS, OF	90	125	195
332, 15J, HC	95	150	325
333, 15J, OF	90	125	195
337, 17J, OF	95	125	195
340, 17J, M#1, Adj.3P, NI, HC	125	150	275
341, 17J, M#1, ADJ, NI, Adj.3P, OF	95	125	195
342, 17J, M#1, LS	95	125	195
343, 17J, M#1, LS, OF	95	125	195
344, 17J, NI, Adj.3P, HC .... ★★	325	375	550
345, 17J, NI, Adj.3P, OF .... ★	295	350	550
346, 17J, NI, HC .... ★	350	375	500
347, 17J, NI, OF	95	125	250

Note: Gold Filled cases marked, South Bend or Pyramid - **30yr.**, =$60 - $95 - $250
      Gold Filled cases marked, South Bend or Pilgrim - **25yr.**, =$50 - $70 - $180
      Gold Filled cases marked, South Bend or Panama - **20yr.**, =$40 - $60 - $150

🕐 A collector should expect to pay modestly higher prices at local shops.

🕐 Generic, nameless or **unmarked** grades for watch movements are listed under the Company name or initials of the Company, etc. by size, jewel count and description.

🕐 Watches listed in this book are priced at the collectable trade show level, as **complete** watches having an original 14k gold-filled case and *Key Wind* with silver, an original white enamel single sunk dial, and with the entire original movement in good working order with no repairs needed.

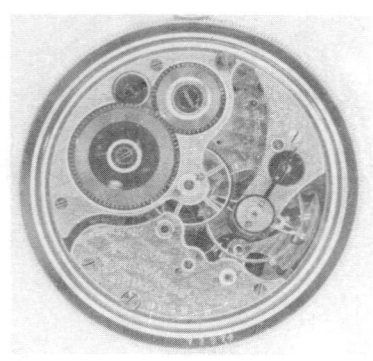

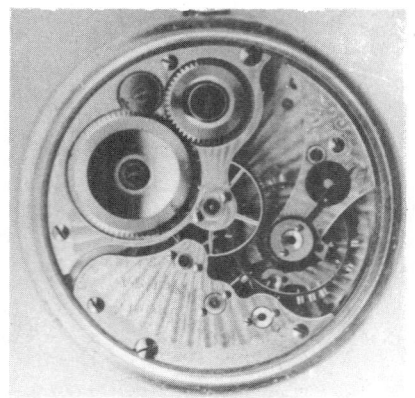

South Bend Watch Co. Polaris, 16 size, 21 jewels, model number 1, Adj.5p, gold jewel setting, gold train, open face, 14K case, serial number 518,236. (made from grade 295)

Grade marked 295, 16 size, 21 jewels, first model, gold jewel settings, gold train, open face, serial number 518,022.

16 SIZE
M#1 Lever set

Grade or Name – Description	Avg	Ex-Fn	Mint
Polaris, 21J, M#1, Adj.5P, 3/4, NI, DR, GJS, GT,			
14K South Bend case with Polaris on dial & Mvt. ..★★★★	$2,200	$3,200	$4,500
South Bend, 7J, OF	60	95	150
South Bend, 7J, HC	95	125	175
South Bend, 9J, OF	60	95	150
South Bend, 9J, HC	95	125	175
South Bend, 15J, OF	75	100	150
South Bend, 15J, HC	95	125	175
South Bend, 15J, OF, Silveroid	75	95	150
South Bend, 17J, OF	75	95	150
South Bend, 17J, HC, ADJ	125	150	195
South Bend, 17J, **14K HC**	450	500	750
South Bend, 21J, OF, Adj, 5P	250	275	450
South Bend, 21J, HC, ADJ	325	375	600
The Studebaker 223, 17J, M#2, Adj.5P, GJS, DR, GT ⬗	500	650	950
The Studebaker 229, 21J, M#2, Adj.5P, GJS, DR, GT ⬗	700	900	1,300
Studebaker, 21J, PS, Adj.5P, OF	225	250	425
203, 7J, 3/4, NI, OF	75	95	150
204, 15J, 3/4, NI, HC	85	125	195
207, 15J, PS	65	90	150
209, 9J, M#2, PS, OF	75	95	150
211, 17J, M#2, 3/4, NI, OF	75	95	165
212, 17J, M#2, LS, heat & cold, HC	125	150	250
215, 17J, M#2, LS, heat & cold, OF	75	95	150
215, 17J, M#2, SILVEROID, OF	75	95	150
217, 17J, M#2, NI, BRG, DR, GT, ADJ.3P, OF.	95	125	195
219 marked, 19J, 3 tooth click, DR, ADJ.4P, OF	150	175	350

🕐 Generic, nameless or unmarked grades for watch movements are listed under the Company name or initials of the Company, etc. by size, jewel count and description.

🕐 A collector should expect to pay modestly higher prices at local shops.

🕐 Pricing in this Guide are fair market price for **COMPLETE** watches which are reflected from the "**NAWCC**" National and regional shows.

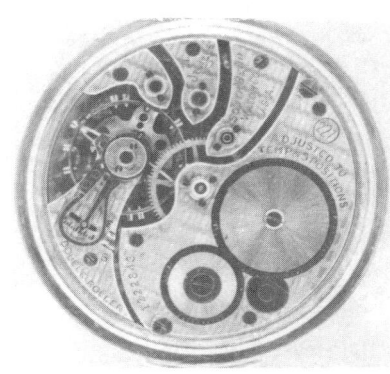

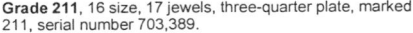

Grade 211, 16 size, 17 jewels, three-quarter plate, marked 211, serial number 703,389.

Grade 227, 16 size, 21 jewels, RR approved, gold jewel settings, Adj5p, marked 227, serial number 1,222,843.

Grade or Name – Description	Avg	Ex-Fn	Mint
223, 17J, M#2, LS, ADJ.5P, OF	$75	$95	$195
227, 21J, M#2, 3/4, NI, LS, DR, ADJ.5P, marked 227, OF	225	250	500
260, 7J, M#1, HC	75	95	150
261, 7J, M#1, OF	75	95	150
280, 15J, M#1, HC	85	95	195
281, 15J, M#1, OF	85	95	150
290, 17J, M#1, LS, Adj..3P, HC	225	275	350
291, 17J, M#1, Adj.3P, OF	195	225	295
292, 19J, M#1, 3/4, GJS, NI, DR, Adj,5P, HC ★★	275	325	500
293, 19J, M#1, 3/4, GJS, NI, DR, Adj,5P, OF ★	195	250	375
294, 21J, M#1, ADJ.5P, GJS, GT, HC, marked 294, HC ★★	600	750	1,100
295, 21J, M#1, LS, ADJ.5P, GJS, GT, marked 295, OF ★★	550	700	1,000
298, 17J, M#1, ADJ.3P, HC ★	225	275	400
299, 17J, M#1, ADJ.3P, OF ★	195	250	350

12 SIZE Extra Thin
Chesterfield Series style cases (OF Only)

Grade or Name – Description	Avg	Ex-Fn	Mint
407, 15J, DR, Gold Filled case	$60	$70	$90
411, 17J, DR, GJS, Gold Filled case	70	80	95
415, 17J, ADJ to temp, Gold Filled case.	80	90	150
417 marked, 17J, DR, Adj.5p,GJS, South Bend G. F. OF ... ★★★	90	110	195
419, 17J, Adj.3P, Gold Filled Case ★	90	110	195
429, 19J, Adj.4P, DR, GJS, Gold Filled	95	125	195
14K case	150	200	350
429, South Bend **Digital,** 19J, BRG, NI, DR, GJS, ADJ.4P (**marked 411 &429**), 12 size ◺	225	295	450
431, 21J, Adj.5P, DR, GJS, Gold Filled Case	125	150	250
14K Case	150	195	400
18K Case ★★★	250	350	600
Studebaker, 21J, 8 Adj., OF ◺	150	200	375

🕐 Chesterfield Series (OF Only) comprises of a variety of case and dial combinations. Case styles such as Delmar, Carlton, Fairfax, Girard, Savoy, Senior, Tremont, Warwick, & Wellington. Chesterfield Series were cased and timed at the factory only as complete watches. Chesterfield Series case are **not** interchangeable with other American 12 standard style cases.

🕐 Pricing in this Guide are fair market price for **COMPLETE** watches which are reflected from the "**NAWCC**" National and regional shows.

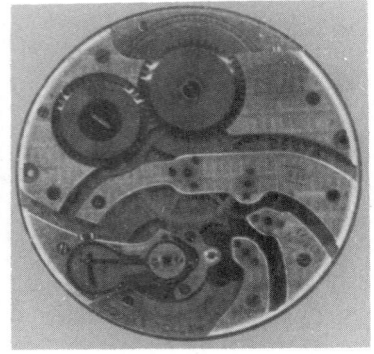

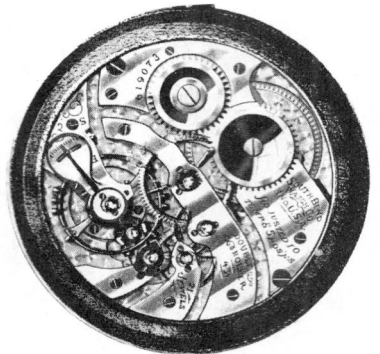

Grade 411, 12 size, 17 jewels, open face, double roller.

Chesterfield, 12 size, 21 jewels, grade # 431, bridge, gold jewel settings, pendant set, double roller, Adj5p.

6 SIZE Hunting Case

Grade or Name – Description		Avg	Ex-Fn	Mint
South Bend, 11J, G#160, HC .... ★ ★		$50	$60	$150
South Bend, 15J, G#170, HC .... ★		60	75	150
South Bend, 17J, G#180, HC .... ★ ★ ★		60	75	195
South Bend, 17J, G#180, **14K,HC**.................................... ★ ★ ★ ★		225	275	450

ALL 6 size movements were re-worked Columbus movements.

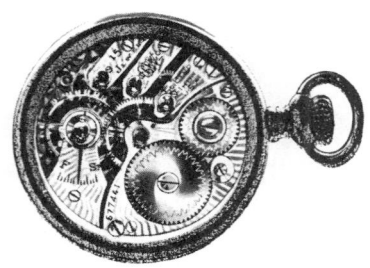

South Bend, 6 size, grade # 170, 15 jewels.

Grade 120-HC, 121-OF, 0 size, 17 jewels, bridge, nickel, double roller, pendant set.

0 SIZE

Grade or Name – Description	Avg	Ex-Fn	Mint
South Bend, 7J, M# 1, PS, HC	$75	$95	$195
South Bend, 15J, M# 1, PS, HC .... ★ ★ ★	80	125	225
Grade 100 HC & 101 OF, 7J, PS	75	95	195
Grade 110 HC & 111 OF, 15J, 3F Brg, DR..................................	75	95	195
Grade 120 HC & 121 OF, 17J, BRG, NI, DR, PS .... ★	80	125	225
Grade 150 HC & 151 OF, 17J, M# 3, BRG, NI, PS .... ★ ★	95	150	250

IDENTIFICATION OF MOVEMENTS BY MODEL NUMBER

How to Identify Your Watch: Compare the movement of your watch with the illustrations in this section. Upon matching the movement exactly, the model number and size can be determined. While comparing, note the location of the balance, jewels, screws, gears, and type of back plate (Full, 3/4, Bridge) these will be clues in identifying the movement you have. Having determined the size and model number, you can now find your watch in the main price listing by name or number (engraved on the movement).

Record of Serial and Grade Numbers of South Bend Watch Movements

Serial Number	Grade	Size	Model	Jewels	Serial Number	Grade	Size	Model	Jewels
1000 to 4000...	Htg.	18	1	7	400001 to 401200...	331	18	1	15
4001 to 7000...	"	18	1	7	401201 to 403200...	330	18	1	15
7001 to 10000...	"	16	1	15	403201 to 407200...	341	18	1	17
10001 to 21000...	"	18	1	15	407201 to 408500...	340	18	1	17
21001 to 29500...	"	16	1	7	408501 to 408700...	342	18	1	17
29501 to 37000...	"	18	1	7	408901 to 409200...	342	18	1	17
37001 to 41000...	"	16	1	15	409201 to 412200...	330	18	1	15
41001 to 52000...	"	18	1	15	412201 to 413800...	290	16	1	17
52001 to 61000...	"	16	1	7	413801 to 414800...	342	18	1	17
61001 to 76000...	"	18	1	15	414801 to 415800...	291	16	1	17
76001 to 83000...	"	16	1	15	415801 to 417700...	331	18	1	17
83001 to 92000...	"	16	1	7	417701 to 418700...	342	18	1	17
92001 to 97000...	"	18	1	7	418701 to 419700...	343	18	1	17
97001 to 105000...	"	18	1	7	419701 to 420600...	290	16	1	17
105001 to 114000...	"	16	1	17	420601 to 421900...	291	16	1	17
114001 to 127000...	"	18	1	15	421901 to 422400...	281	16	1	15
127501 to 138000...	"	18	1	17	422401 to 423200...	280	16	1	15
138801 to 156000...	"	16	1	7	423201 to 423800...	343	18	1	17
156001 to 165000...	"	18	1	15	423801 to 425800...	261	16	1	7
165001 to 171000...	"	16	1	7	425801 to 426100...	281	16	1	15
171001 to 196000...	"	16	1	17	426101 to 428100...	342	18	1	17
196001 to 201000...	"	18	1	7	428101 to 431100...	260	16	1	7
201001 to 214000...	"	16	1	15	431101 to 431600...	290	16	1	15
214001 to 218000...	"	16	1	7	431601 to 432100...	281	16	1	15
218001 to 220000...	"	18	1	15	432101 to 433100...	342	18	1	17
220001 to 232000...	"	16	1	15	433101 to 435100...	340	18	1	17
232001 to 250000...	"	18	1	7	435101 to 436600...	280	16	1	15
250001 to 261000...	"	16	1	7	436601 to 437900...	281	16	1	15
261001 to 267000...	"	16	1	15	437901 to 438200...	280	16	1	15
267001 to 271000...	"	18	1	15	438201 to 438500...	290	16	1	17
271001 to 274000...	"	16	1	15	438501 to 439500...	293	16	1	19
274001 to 281000...	"	16	1	7	439501 to 440500...	280	16	1	15
281001 to 292000...	"	16	1	7	440501 to 441500...	290	16	1	17
292001 to 294000...	"	16	1	17	441501 to 441600...	260	16	1	7
294001 to 295500...	"	18	1	17	441601 to 441700...	261	16	1	7
295501 to 299100...	"	16	1	7	441701 to 441800...	290	16	1	17
299101 to 302000...	"	18	1	7	441801 to 441850...	293	16	1	17
302001 to 311000...	"	16	1	7	441901 to 445900...	280	16	1	15
311001 to 314000...	"	16	1	15	445901 to 446000...	Htg.	16	1	21
314001 to 321000...	"	18	1	15	446001 to 447000...	261	16	1	7
321001 to 329000...	"	16	1	7	447001 to 450000...	260	16	1	7
329001 to 334000...	"	18	1	7	450001 to 451000...	261	16	1	7
334001 to 341000...	"	16	1	15	451001 to 453000...	260	16	1	7
341001 to 347000...	"	16	1	7	453001 to 455000...	261	16	1	7
347001 to 349500...	"	16	1	17	455001 to 457000...	343	18	1	17
349501 to 354000...	"	16	1	15	457001 to 461000...	260	16	1	7
354001 to 361000...	"	18	1	7	461001 to 462500...	331	18	1	15
361001 to 366000...	"	16	1	7	462501 to 464000...	281	16	1	15
366001 to 368000...	"	18	1	17	464001 to 465300...	331	18	1	15
368001 to 371000...	"	16	1	15	465301 to 467300...	261	16	1	7
371001 to 374000...	"	18	1	15	467301 to 468800...	331	18	1	15
374001 to 376000...	"	16	1	17	468801 to 469300...	290	16	1	17
376001 to 377000...	"	16	1	15	469301 to 469800...	294	16	1	21
377001 to 378000...	"	18	1	17	469801 to 470100...	295	16	1	21
378001 to 379500...	"	18	1	15	*470101 to 470200...	295	16	1	21
379501 to 380500...	"	16			15	470201 to 470300...	295	16	1	21
380501 to 381000...	160	6	1	11	470301 to 471300...	281	16	1	15
381001 to 381500...	170	6	1	15	471301 to 472300...	280	16	1	15
381501 to 382500...	330	18	1	15	472301 to 473300...	281	16	1	15
382501 to 383000...	160	6	1	11	473301 to 474800...	330	18	1	15
383001 to 383500...	170	6	1	15	474801 to 475800...	331	18	1	15
383501 to 384000...	302	18	1	15	475801 to 476800...	290	16	1	17
384001 to 384500...	160	6	1	11	477001 to 478000...	261	16	1	7
384501 to 384900...	291	16	1	17	478001 to 479000...	330	18	1	15
384901 to 385200...	281	16	1	15	479001 to 480000...	261	16	1	7
385201 to 385500...	291	16	1	17	480001 to 480200...	295	16	1	21
385501 to 386400...	290	16	1	17	*480201 to 480500...	295	16	1	21
386401 to 386900...	280	16	1	15	480501 to 481500...	290	16	1	17
386901 to 387400...	170	6	1	15	481501 to 483500...	291	16	1	17
387401 to 387900...	330	18	1	15	483501 to 485000...	280	16	1	15
387901 to 388400...	331	18	1	15	485001 to 486000...	331	18	1	15
388401 to 389400...	180	6	1	17	486001 to 487000...	330	18	1	15
389401 to 389900...	170	6	1	15	487001 to 489000...	331	18	1	15
389901 to 390400...	341	18	1	17	489001 to 490000...	341	18	1	17
390401 to 390900...	331	18	1	15	*490001 to 490500...	294	16	1	21
390901 to 391200...	330	18	1	15	490501 to 490800...	293	16	1	19
391201 to 391700...	341	18	1	17	*490801 to 490900...	293	16	1	19
391701 to 392600...	330	18	1	15	490901 to 491000...	293	16	1	19
392601 to 394100...	331	18	1	15	491001 to 492000...	281	16	1	15
394101 to 396000...	330	18	1	15	492001 to 493000...	330	18	1	15
396001 to 400000...	340	18	1	17	493001 to 494000...	340	18	1	17

Although grade numbers appear in this list some of the earlier watches did not have grade numbers stamped upon them. In all instances odd grade numbers indicate open face movement, even grade numbers indicate hunting movement.

*Watches with these serial numbers have double roller.

Serial Number	Grade	Size	Model	Jewels	Serial Number	Grade	Size	Model	Jewels
494001 to 495000...	290	16	1	17	570001 to 571000...	261	16	1	7
495001 to 497000...	331	18	1	15	*571001 to 572000...	313	18	2	17
497001 to 498000...	261	16	1	7	572001 to 573000...	280	16	1	15
498001 to 499000...	291	16	1	17	573001 to 574000...	347	18	2	17
499001 to 500000...	261	16	1	7	*574001 to 575000...	323	18	2	17
500001 to 501000...	281	16	1	15	*575001 to 576000...	217	16	2	17
501001 to 502000...	290	16	1	17	576001 to 577000...	333	18	2	15
502001 to 503000...	331	18	1	15	577001 to 578000...	281	16	1	15
503001 to 503500...	341	18	1	17	*578001 to 579000...	223	16	2	17
503501 to 504000...	343	18	1	17	*579001 to 580000...	329	18	2	21
504001 to 505000...	290	16	1	17	*580001 to 581000...	212	16	2	17
505001 to 505100...	293	16	1	19	*581001 to 582000...	333	18	2	15
*505101 to 505500...	293	16	1	19	582001 to 583000...	261	16	1	7
505501 to 506500...	261	16	1	7	*583001 to 584000...	227	16	2	21
506501 to 507500...	280	16	1	15	*584001 to 585000...	229	16	2	21
507501 to 508500...	261	16	1	7	585001 to 586000...	207	16	2	15
508501 to 509500...	280	16	1	15	586001 to 587000...	211	16	2	17
509501 to 510500...	281	16	1	15	*587001 to 588000...	215	16	2	17
510501 to 511400...	291	16	1	17	588001 to 589000...	260	16	1	7
511401 to 511500...	299	16	1	17	*589001 to 590000...	217	16	2	17
511501 to 511900...	292	16	1	19	590001 to 591000...	204	16	2	15
*511901 to 512000...	292	16	1	19	591001 to 592000...	203	16	2	7
512001 to 513000...	333	18	2	15	592001 to 593000...	207	16	2	15
513001 to 514000...	280	16	1	15	*593001 to 594000...	212	16	2	17
514001 to 515000...	261	16	1	7	594001 to 595000...	203	16	2	7
515001 to 516000...	260	16	1	7	595001 to 596000...	332	18	2	15
516001 to 516500...	298	16	1	17	*596001 to 597000...	215	16	2	17
*516501 to 516600...	298	16	1	17	*597001 to 598000...	223	16	2	17
516601 to 516800...	298	16	1	17	*598001 to 599000...	229	16	2	21
*516801 to 516900...	298	16	1	17	599001 to 600000...	260	16	1	7
516901 to 517000...	298	16	1	17	600001 to 601000...	211	16	2	17
517001 to 517700...	345	18	2	17	*601001 to 602000...	313	18	2	17
*517701 to 518000...	345	18	2	17	602001 to 603000...	203	16	2	7
*518001 to 518500...	295	16	1	21	603001 to 604000...	204	16	2	15
518501 to 519000...	294	16	1	21	604001 to 605000...	207	16	2	15
519001 to 520000...	347	18	2	17	605001 to 606000...	333	18	2	15
520001 to 521000...	332	18	2	15	606001 to 607000...	347	18	2	17
*521001 to 522000...	329	18	2	21	*607001 to 608000...	215	16	2	17
*522001 to 523000...	293	16	1	19	608001 to 609000...	211	16	2	17
523001 to 523400...	299	16	1	17	609001 to 610000...	203	16	2	7
*523401 to 524000...	299	16	1	17	*610001 to 611000...	215	16	2	17
524001 to 524300...	344	18	2	17	611001 to 612000...	207	16	2	15
*524301 to 524800...	344	18	2	17	612001 to 613000...	203	16	2	7
524801 to 525000...	344	18	2	17	*613001 to 614000...	212	16	2	17
525001 to 526000...	346	18	2	17	614001 to 615000...	305	18	2	15
526001 to 527000...	333	18	2	15	615001 to 616000...	204	16	2	15
527001 to 528000...	347	18	2	17	616001 to 617000...	207	16	2	15
528001 to 529000...	346	18	2	17	617001 to 618000...	203	16	2	7
*529001 to 530000...	292	16	1	19	*618001 to 619000...	415	12	1	17
530001 to 531000...	260	16	1	7	*619001 to 620000...	431	12	1	21
531001 to 532000...	281	16	1	15	620001 to 621000...	211	16	2	17
532001 to 533000...	333	18	2	15	*621001 to 622000...	223	16	2	17
*533001 to 534000...	323	18	2	17	*622001 to 623000...	229	16	2	21
*534001 to 535000...	345	18	2	17	*623001 to 624000...	411	12	1	17
535001 to 536000...	347	18	2	17	*624001 to 625000...	215	16	2	17
536001 to 537000...	333	18	2	15	625001 to 626000...	203	16	2	7
537001 to 538000...	312	18	2	17	626001 to 627000...	305	18	2	15
538001 to 539000...	332	18	2	15	627001 to 628000...	207	16	2	15
*539001 to 539500...	298	16	1	17	*628001 to 629000...	419	12	1	17
539501 to 539700...	298	16	1	17	629001 to 630000...	260	16	1	7
*539701 to 540000...	298	16	1	17	*630001 to 631000...	407	12	1	15
540001 to 540400...	299	16	1	17	*631001 to 632000...	217	16	2	17
540401 to 541000...	299	16	1	17	632001 to 633000...	204	16	2	15
*541001 to 542000...	328	18	2	21	633001 to 634000...	347	18	2	17
*542001 to 543000...	313	18	2	17	*634001 to 635000...	329	18	2	21
543001 to 544000...	261	16	1	7	635001 to 636000...	203	16	2	7
544001 to 545000...	260	16	1	7	*636001 to 637000...	217	16	2	17
545001 to 546000...	333	18	2	15	*637001 to 638000...	411	12	1	17
546001 to 547000...	332	18	2	15	638001 to 639000...	211	16	2	17
547001 to 548000...	333	18	2	15	*639001 to 640000...	212	16	2	17
548001 to 549000...	346	18	2	17	*640001 to 641000...	217	16	2	17
549001 to 550000...	261	16	1	7	*641001 to 642000...	415	12	1	17
550001 to 551000...	280	16	1	15	642001 to 643000...	203	16	2	7
551001 to 552000...	281	16	1	15	*643001 to 644000...	229	16	2	21
552001 to 553000...	347	18	2	17	644001 to 645000...	260	16	1	7
*553001 to 554000...	313	18	2	17	*645001 to 646000...	215	16	2	17
554001 to 555000...	323	18	2	17	646001 to 647000...	207	16	2	15
*555001 to 556000...	327	18	2	21	*647001 to 648000...	407	12	1	15
556001 to 557000...	298	16	1	17	*648001 to 649000...	419	12	1	17
*557001 to 558000...	299	16	1	17	649001 to 650000...	207	16	2	15
558001 to 559000...	347	18	2	17	650181 to 655200...	Htg.	0	1	7
559001 to 560000...	346	18	2	17	655201 to 656200...	"	0	1	15
*560001 to 561000...	313	18	2	17	656201 to 659700...	"	0	1	7
561001 to 562000...	333	18	2	15	659701 to 662400...	"	0	1	7
562001 to 563000...	332	18	2	15	662401 to 662500...	O.F.	0	2	7
563001 to 564000...	261	16	1	7	662501 to 665400...	Htg.	0	2	7
564001 to 565000...	347	18	2	17	665401 to 665500...	O.F.	0	2	7
565001 to 566000...	260	16	1	7	665501 to 666000...	Htg.	0	2	7
566001 to 567000...	211	16	2	17	666001 to 666500...	"	0	2	17
567001 to 569000...	333	18	2	15	666501 to 666600...	"	0	2	15
*569001 to 570000...	215	16	2	17	666601 to 666650...	O. F.	0	2	15

Although grade numbers appear in this list some of the earlier watches did not have grade numbers stamped upon them. In all instances odd grade numbers indicate open face movement, even grade numbers indicate hunting movement.
*Watches with these serial numbers have double roller.

Serial Number	Grade	Size	Model	Jewels
666651 to 667500...	Htg.	0	2	15
667501 to 671500...	"	0	2	7
671501 to 671600...	O. F.	0	2	7
671601 to 672800...	Htg.	0	2	7
672801 to 672900...	O. F.	0	2	7
672901 to 673000...	Htg.	0	2	7
673001 to 674000...	"	0	2	15
674001 to 675000...	"	0	2	17
675001 to 676000...	"	0	2	7
676001 to 679400...	"	0	2	15
679401 to 679500...	O. F.	0	2	15
679501 to 680400...	Htg.	0	2	15
680401 to 680500...	O. F.	0	2	15
680501 to 681000...	Htg.	0	2	15
681001 to 682000...	"	0	2	17
682001 to 682800...	"	0	2	15
682801 to 682900...	O. F.	0	2	15
682901 to 683000...	Htg.	0	2	15
683001 to 684000...	"	0	2	17
684001 to 684600...	"	0	2	7
684601 to 684700...	O. F.	0	2	7
684701 to 685000...	Htg.	0	2	7
685001 to 686000..	*	0	2	15
686001 to 686100...	101	0	2	7
686101 to 687000...	100	0	2	7
686701 to 687100...	111	0	2	15
687101 to 688000...	110	0	2	15
688001 to 688100...	101	0	2	7
688101 to 689000...	100	0	2	7
689001 to 689100...	111	0	2	15
689101 to 690000...	110	0	2	15
690001 to 690100...	101	0	2	7
690101 to 691000...	100	0	2	7
691001 to 691100...	101	0	2	7
691101 to 692000...	100	0	2	7
692001 to 692100...	111	0	2	15
692101 to 693000...	110	0	2	15
693001 to 693100...	101	0	2	7
693101 to 694000...	100	0	2	7
*694001 to 695000...	217	16	2	17
695001 to 696000...	305	18	2	15
696001 to 696100...	111	0	2	15
696101 to 697000...	110	0	2	15
697001 to 697100...	101	0	2	7
697101 to 698000...	100	0	2	7
*698001 to 699000...	215	16	2	17
*699001 to 700000...	415	12	1	17
*700001 to 701000...	431	12	1	21
*701001 to 702000...	313	18	2	17
702001 to 702100...	111	0	2	15
702101 to 703000...	110	0	2	16
703001 to 704000...	211	16	2	17
*704001 to 705000...	212	16	2	17
705001 to 706000...	305	18	2	15
*706001 to 707000...	215	16	2	17
707001 to 708000...	203	16	2	7
*708001 to 709000...	407	12	1	15
709001 to 710000...	204	16	2	15
710001 to 711000...	305	18	2	15
711001 to 712000...	260	16	1	7
712001 to 713000...	207	16	2	15
*713001 to 713100...	111	0	2	15
713101 to 714000...	110	0	2	15
*714001 to 714500...	227	16	2	21
715001 to 716000...	211	16	2	17
*716001 to 717000...	411	12	1	17
*717001 to 717100...	101	0	2	7
717101 to 718000...	100	0	2	7
*718001 to 719000...	215	16	2	17
719001 to 720000...	309	18	2	17
720001 to 721000...	203	16	2	7
*721001 to 722000...	227	16	2	21
722001 to 723000...	204	16	2	15
723001 to 724000...	207	16	2	15
724001 to 725000...	211	16	2	17
*725001 to 726000...	217	16	2	17
*726001 to 727000...	227	16	2	21
*727001 to 728000...	223	16	2	17
*728001 to 729000...	212	16	2	17
729001 to 730000...	305	18	2	15
730001 to 731000...	304	18	2	15
*731001 to 732000...	313	18	2	17
732001 to 733000...	309	18	2	17
733001 to 734000...	211	16	2	17
*734001 to 735000...	215	16	2	17
*735001 to 736000...	217	16	2	17
*736001 to 737000...		0	2	17
*737001 to 738000...	227	16	2	21
*738001 to 739000...	215	16	2	17

Serial Number	Grade	Size	Model	Jewels
*739001 to 740000...	217	16	2	17
*740001 to 740200...	101	0	2	7
*740201 to 741000...	100	0	2	7
*741001 to 741200...	111	0	2	15
*741201 to 742000...	110	0	2	15
742001 to 743000...	207	16	2	15
743001 to 744000...	203	16	2	7
*744001 to 745000...	212	16	2	17
*745001 to 746000...	227	16	2	21
746001 to 746100...	111	0	2	15
*746101 to 747000...	110	0	2	15
747001 to 748000...	305	18	2	15
748001 to 749600...	309	18	2	17
*749601 to 750000...	223	16	2	17
750001 to 751000...	207	16	2	15
*751001 to 751100...	101	0	2	7
*751101 to 752000...	100	0	2	7
752001 to 753000...	211	16	2	17
*753001 to 754000...	229	16	2	21
754001 to 755000...	203	16	2	7
*755001 to 756000...	215	16	2	17
*756001 to 757000...	313	18	2	17
*757001 to 758000...	323	18	2	17
758001 to 759000...	204	16	2	15
*759001 to 759500...	Htg.	0	2	17
759501 to 759510...	150	0	3	17
759511 to 759520...	103	0	3	7
759521 to 759530...	102	0	3	7
759531 to 759540...	151	0	3	17
759541 to 760000...	Htg.	0	2	17
760001 to 761000...	305	18	2	15
761001 to 762000...	207	16	2	15
*762001 to 762100...	111	0	2	15
762101 to 763000...	110	0	2	17
763001 to 764000...	203	16	2	7
*764001 to 765000...	215	16	2	17
*765001 to 766000...	217	16	2	17
766001 to 767000...	211	16	2	17
*767001 to 768000...	217	16	2	17
*768001 to 769000...	212	16	2	17
*769001 to 770000...	217	16	2	17
*770001 to 771000...	151	0	3	17
*771001 to 772000...	217	16	2	17
*772001 to 773000...	150	0	3	17
*773001 to 774000...	215	16	2	17
*774001 to 775000...	107	0	3	15
*775001 to 776000...	106	0	3	15
776001 to 777000...	207	16	2	15
*777001 to 778000...	102	0	3	7
*778001 to 779000...	103	0	3	7
779001 to 780000...	211	16	2	17
780001 to 781000...	203	16	2	7
781001 to 782000...	305	18	2	15
*782001 to 783000...	217	16	2	17
*783001 to 784000...	215	16	2	17
784001 to 785000...	207	16	2	15
*785001 to 786000...	215	16	2	17
786001 to 787000...	227	16	2	21
*787001 to 788000...	407	12	1	15
*788001 to 789000...	217	16	2	17
789001 to 790000...	211	16	2	17
*790001 to 791000...	215	16	2	17
*791001 to 792000...	217	16	2	17
*792001 to 793000...	407	12	1	15
*793001 to 794000...	215	16	2	17
*794001 to 795000...	212	16	2	17
*795001 to 796000...	411	12	1	17
796001 to 797000...	203	16	2	7
*797001 to 798000...	407	12	1	15
*798001 to 799000...	429	12	1	19
*799001 to 800000...	411	12	1	17
*800001 to 801000...	219	16	2	19
*801001 to 802000...	429	12	1	19
*802001 to 804000...	219	16	2	19
*804001 to 805000...	411	12	1	17
*805001 to 806000...	407	12	1	15
*806001 to 808000...	429	12	1	19
*808001 to 809000...	219	16	2	19
*809001 to 810000...	411	12	1	17
*810001 to 811000...	429	12	1	19
*811001 to 812000...	211	16	2	17
*812001 to 814000...	219	16	2	19
*814001 to 815000...	429	12	1	19
*815001 to 816000...	407	12	1	15
*816001 to 817000...	219	16	2	19
*817001 to 818000...	429	12	1	19
*818001 to 819000...	219	16	2	19
*819001 to 820000...	429	12	1	19

Although grade numbers appear in this list some of the earlier watches did not have grade numbers stamped upon them. In all instances odd grade numbers indicate open face movement, even grade numbers indicate hunting movement.

*Watches with these serial numbers have double roller.

A-112

(below all double roller)

SERIAL NUMBER-GRADE-SIZE-M#- Jewels

820001-821000 = 215 - 16 - 2 - 17j
821001-822000 = 415 - 12 - 1 - 17j
822001-823000 = 411 - 12 - 1 - 17j
823001-825000 = 429 - 12 - 1 - 19j
825001-826000 = 209 - 16 - 2 - 9j
826001-827000 = 207 - 16 - 2 - 15j
827001-828000 = 407 - 12 - 1 - 15j
828001-830000 = 429 - 12 - 1 - 19j
830001-831000 = 211 - 16 - 2 - 17j
831001-832000 = 407 - 12 - 1 - 15j
832001-833000 = 207 - 16 - 2 - 15j
833001-834000 = 429 - 12 - 1 - 19j
834001-835000 = 219 - 16 - 2 - 19j
835001-837000 = 429 - 12 - 1 - 19j
837001-838000 = 219 - 16 - 2 - 19j
838001-839000 = 209 - 16 - 2 - 9j
839001-840000 = 211 - 16 - 2 - 17j
840001-841000 = 219 - 16 - 2 - 19j
841001-842000 = 209 - 16 - 2 - 9j
842001-843000 = 207 - 16 - 2 - 15j
843001-844000 = 429 - 12 - 1 - 19j
844001-845000 = 411 - 12 - 1 - 17j
845001-846000 = 429 - 12 - 1 - 19j
846001-847000 = 209 - 16 - 2 - 9j
847001-848000 = 227 - 16 - 2 - 21j
848001-849000 = 429 - 12 - 1 - 19j
849001-850000 = 407 - 12 - 1 - 15j
850001-851000 = 211 - 16 - 2 - 17j
851001-852000 = 209 - 16 - 2 - 9j
852001-853000 = 429 - 12 - 1 - 19j
853001-854000 = 219 - 16 - 2 - 19j
854001-855000 = 429 - 12 - 1 - 19j
855001-856000 = 207 - 16 - 2 - 15j
856001-857000 = 209- -16 - 2 - 9j
857001-858000 = 407 - 12 - 1 - 15j
858001-859000 = 429 - 12 - 1 - 19j
859001-860000 = 204 - 16 - 2 - 15j
860001-861000 = 211 - 16 - 2 - 17j
861001-862000 = 411 - 12 - 1 - 17j
862001-863000 = 209 - 16 - 2 - 9j
863001-864000 = 429 - 12 - 1 - 19j
864001-865000 = 219 - 16 - 2 - 19j
865001-866000 = 209 - 16 - 2 - 9j
866001-867000 = 429 - 12 - 1 - 19j
867001-868000 = 411 - 12 - 1 - 17j
868001-869000 = 211 - 16 - 2 - 17j
869001-871000 = 227 - 16 - 2 - 21j
871001-872000 = 207 - 16 - 2 - 15j
872001-873000 = 209 - 16 - 2 - 9j
873001-874000 = 219 - 16 - 2 - 19j
874001-875000 = 407 - 12 - 1 - 15j
875001-876000 = 411 - 12 - 1 - 17j
876001-877000 = 429 - 12 - 1 - 19j
877001-878000 = 207 - 16 - 2 - 15j
878001-879000 = 211 - 16 - 2 - 17j
879001-880000 = 219 - 16 - 2 - 19j
880001-882000 = 407 - 12 - 1 - 15j
882001-883000 = 217 - 16 - 2 - 17j
883001-884000 = 209 - 16 - 2 - 9j
884001-885000 = 411 - 12 - 1 - 17j
885001-886000 = 229 - 16 - 2 - 21j
886001-887000 = 429 - 12 - 1 - 19j
887001-888000 = 209 - 16 - 2 - 9j
888001-889000 = 217 - 16 - 2 - 17j
889001-890000 = 219 - 16 - 2 - 19j
890001-891000 = 209 - 16 - 2 - 9j
891001-892000 = 207 - 16 - 2 - 15j
892001-893000 = 227 - 16 - 2 - 21j
893001-894000 = 315 - 18 - 2 - 17j
894001-895000 = 211 - 16 - 2 - 17j
895001-896000 = 204 - 16 - 2 - 15j
896001-897000 = 219 - 16 - 2 - 19j

SERIAL NUMBER-GRADE-SIZE-M#- Jewels

897001-898000 = 315 - 18 - 2 - 17j < last 18 size
898001-899000 = 207 - 16 - 2 - 15j
899001-900000 = 429 - 12 - 1 - 19j
900001-901000 = 227 - 16 - 2 - 21j
901001-902000 = 219 - 16 - 2 - 19j
902001-903000 = 211 - 16 - 2 - 17j
903001-904000 = 227 - 16 - 2 - 21j
904001-905000 = 411 - 12 - 1 - 17j
905001-906000 = 407 - 12 - 1 - 15j
906001-907000 = 429 - 12 - 1 - 19j
907001-908000 = 411 - 12 - 1 - 17j
908001-910000 = 209 - 12 - 1 - 9j
910001-911000 = 207 - 16 - 2 - 15j
911011-912000 = 219 - 16 - 2 - 19j
912001-913000 = 429 - 12 - 1 - 19j
913001-914000 = 207 - 16 - 2 - 15j
914001-915000 = 209 - 16 - 2 - 9j
915001-916000 = 219 - 16 - 2 - 19j
916001-917000 = 211 - 16 - 2 - 17j
917001-918000 = 207 - 16 - 2 - 15j
918001-919000 = 407 - 12 - 1 - 15j
919001-920000 = 219 - 16 - 2 - 19j
920001-921000 = 209 - 16 - 2 - 9j
921001-923000 = 429 - 12 - 1 - 19j
923001-924000 = 407 - 12 - 1 - 15j
924001-925000 = 227 - 16 - 2 - 21j
925001-926000 = 219 - 16 - 2 - 19j
926001-927000 = 429 - 12 - 1 - 19j
927001-928000 = 227 - 16 - 2 - 21j
928001-929000 = 204 - 16 - 2 - 15j
929001-930000 = 209 - 16 - 2 - 9j
930001-931000 = 217 - 16 - 2 - 17j
931001-932000 = 219 - 16 - 2 - 19j
932001-933000 = 407 - 12 - 1 - 15j
933001-934000 = 411 - 12 - 1 - 17j
934001-935000 = 211 - 16 - 2 - 17j
935001-937000 = 429 - 12 - 1 - 19j
937001-938000 = 207 - 16 - 2 - 15j
938001-939000 = 227 - 16 - 2 - 21j
939001-940000 = 407 - 12 - 1 - 15j
940001-941000 = 209 - 16 - 2 - 9j
941001-942000 = 211 - 16 - 2 - 17j
942001-943000 = 219 - 16 - 2 - 19j
943001-944000 = 209 - 16 - 2 - 9j
944001-946000 = 429 - 12 - 1 - 19j
946001-947000 = 219 - 16 - 2 - 19j
947001-948000 = 207 - 16 - 2 - 15j
948001-949000 = 411 - 12 - 1 - 17j
949001-950000 = 429 - 12 - 1 - 19j
950001-951000 = 407 - 12 - 1 - 15j
951001-952000 = 219 - 16 - 2 - 19j
952001-953000 = 211 - 16 - 2 - 17j
953001-954000 = 209 - 16 - 2 - 9j
954001-955000 = 227 - 16 - 2 - 21j
955001-956000 = 429 - 12 - 1 - 19j
956001-957000 = 209 - 16 - 2 - 9j
957001-958000 = 227 - 16 - 2 - 21j
958001-959000 = 407 - 12 - 1 - 15j
959001-960000 = 411 - 12 - 1 - 17j
960001-961000 = 429 - 12 - 1 - 19j
961001-962000 = 207 - 16 - 2 - 15j
962001-963000 = 211 - 16 - 2 - 17j
963001-964000 = 407 - 12 - 1 - 15j
964001-965000 = 429 - 12 - 1 - 19j
965001-966000 = 204 - 16 - 2 - 15j
966001-967000 = 219 - 16 - 2 - 19j
967001-968000 = 407 - 12 - 1 - 15j
968001-969000 = 209 - 16 - 2 - 9j
969001-970000 = 431 - 12 - 1 - 21j
970001-971000 = 227 - 16 - 2 - 21j
971001-972000 = 411 - 12 - 1 - 17j
972001-973000 = 219 - 16 - 2 - 19j

SERIAL NUMBER GRADE-SIZE-M# -Jewels

973001-974000 = 207 - 16 - 2 - 15j
974001-975000 = 209 - 16 - 2 - 9j
975001-977000 = 429 - 12 - 1 - 19j
977001-978000 = 219 - 16 - 2 - 19j
978001-979000 = 211 - 16 - 2 - 17j
979001-980000 = 227 - 16 - 2 - 21j
980001-981000 = 429 - 12 - 1 - 19j
981001-982000 = 407 - 12 - 1 - 19j
982001-983000 = 209 - 16 - 2 - 9j
983001-984000 = 219 - 16 - 2 - 19j
984001-985000 = 207 - 16 - 2 - 15j
985001-986000 = 411 - 12 - 1 - 17j
986001-987000 = 429 - 12 - 1 - 19j
987001-988000 = 211 - 16 - 2 - 17j
988001-989000 = 219 - 16 - 2 - 19j
989001-990000 = 209 - 16 - 2 - 9j
990001-991000 = 207 - 16 - 2 - 15j
991001-992000 = 211 - 16 - 2 - 17j
992001-993000 =   ? - ? - ? - ?
993001-994000 = 411 - 12 - 1 - 17j
994001-995000 = 407 - 12 - 1 - 15j
995001-996000 = 219 - 16 - 2 - 19j
996001-999000 = 429 - 12 - 1 - 19j
999001-1001000 = 209 - 16 - 2 - 9j
1001001-1002000 = 411 - 12 - 1 - 17j
1002001-1003000 = 207 - 16 - 2 - 15j
1003001-1004000 = 211 - 16 - 2 - 17j
1004001-1005000 = 407 - 12 - 2 - 15j
1005001-1006000 = 204 - 16 - 2 - 15j
1006001-1007000 = 219 - 16 - 2 - 19j
1007001-1008000 = 227 - 16 - 2 - 21j
1008001-1009000 = 207 - 16 - 2 - 15j
1009001-1010000 = 209 - 16 - 2 - 9j
1010001-1011000 = 429 - 12 - 1 - 19j
1011001-1012000 = 209 - 16 - 2 - 9j
1012001-1014000 = 429 - 12 - 1 - 19j
1014001-1015000 = 407 - 12 - 1 - 15j
1015001-1016000 = 219 - 16 - 2 - 19j
1016001-1018000 = 429 - 12 - 1 - 19j
1018001-1019000 = 209 - 16 - 2 - 9j
1019001-1020000 = 227 - 16 - 2 - 21j
1020001-1021000 = 411 - 12 - 1 - 17j
1021001-1022000 = 211 - 16 - 2 - 17j
1022001-1023000 = 429 - 12 - 1 - 19j
1023001-1024000 = 411 - 12 - 1 - 17j
1024001-1025000 = 207 - 16 - 2 - 15j
1025001-1026000 = 227 - 16 - 2 - 21j
1026001-1027000 = 219 - 16 - 2 - 19j
1027001-1029000 = 429 - 12 - 1 - 19j
1029001-1030000 = 407 - 12 - 1 - 15j
1030001-1031000 = 204 - 16 - 2 - 15j
1031001-1032000 = 209 - 16 - 2 - 9j

SERIAL NUMBER GRADE-SIZE-M# -Jewels

1032001-1033000 = 429 - 12 - 1 - 19j
1033001-1034000 = 227 - 16 - 2 - 21j
1034001-1036000 = 429 - 12 - 1 - 19j
1036001-1037000 = 411 - 12 - 1 - 17j
1037001-1038000 = 219 - 16 - 2 - 19j
1038001-1040000 = 429 - 12 - 1 - 19j
1040001-1041000 = 227 - 16 - 2 - 21j
1041001-1046000 = 429 - 12 - 1 - 19j
1046001-1047000 = 411 - 12 - 1 - 17j
1047001-1049000 = 429 - 12 - 1 - 19j
1049001-1050000 = 411 - 12 - 1 - 17j
1050001-1051000 = 429 - 12 - 1 - 19j
1051001-1052000 = 407 - 12 - 1 - 15j
1052001-1053000 = 429 - 12 - 1 - 19j
1053001-1054000 = 211 - 16 - 2 - 17j
1054001-1056000 = 429 - 12 - 1 - 19j
1056001-1062000 = 219 - 16 - 2 - 19j
1062001-1069000 = 211 - 16 - 2 - 17j
1069001-1072000 = 209 - 16 - 2 - 9j
1072001-1075000 =Studbaker12 -1 - 21j
1075001-1075100 =for directors12 -1 - 19j
1075101-1076000 = 429 - 12 - 1 - 19j
1076001-1083000 =Studbebaker12 -1 - 21j
1083001-1088000 = 411 - 12 - 1 - 17j
1088001-1093000 = 227 - 16 - 2 - 21j
1093001-1098000 =Studbebaker12 -1 - 21j
1098001-1103000 = 429 - 12 - 1 - 19j
1103001-1108000 =Studbaker12 -1 - 21j
1108001-1113000 = 211 - 16 - 2 - 17j
1103001-1108000 = 411 - 12 - 1 - 17j
1118001-1128000 =Studbebaker12 -1 - 21j
1128001-1133000 = 227 - 16 - 2 - 21j
1133001-1138000 = 429 - 12 - 1 - 19j
1138001-1143000 =Studbebaker12 -1 - 21j
1143001-1153000 =Studbebaker12 -1 - 21j
1153001-1158000 = 411 - 12 - 1 - 17j
1158001-1163000 =Studbebaker12 -1 - 21j
1163001-1168000 =Studbebaker12 -1 - 21j
1168001-1173000 =Studbebaker12 -1 - 21j
1173001-1178000 = 429 - 12 - 1 - 19j
1178001-1183000 =Studbebaker12 -1 - 21j
1183001-1188000 =Studbebaker12 -1 - 21j
1188001-1193000 = 227 - 16 - 2 - 21j
1193001-1198000 =Studbebaker12 -1 - 21j
1198001-1203000 =Studbebaker12 -1 - 21j
1203001-1208000 = 211 - 16 - 2 - 17j
1208001-1213000 =Studbebaker12 -1 - 21j
1213001-1218000 = 429 - 12 - 1 - 19j
1218001-1223000 = 227 - 16 - 2 - 21j
1223001-1228000 = 211 - 16 - 2 - 17j
1228001-1233000 = 411 - 12 - 1 - 17j
1233001-1238000 =Studbebaker12 -1 - 21j
1238001-1241000 = 429 - 12 - 1 - 19j

For information about the South Bend W. Co. complete serial & grade BOOK contact:

**Lyle and Donna Stratton
1314 N. Gay St.
Longmont, CO 80501
303-776-7531**

The authors of "The Complete Price Guide to Watches" recomend this BOOK.

18 SIZE—MODEL 1
Open Face and Hunting Lever Set

No. 302—Hunting, 15 Jewels, Lever Set. (Factory listed but never seen)
No. 341—Open Face, 17 Jewels, Lever Set, Adjusted to Temperature & 3 Positions.
No. 340—Hunting, 17 Jewels, Lever Set, Adjusted to Temperature & 3 Positions.
No. 343—Open Face, 17 Jewels, Lever Set.
No. 342—Hunting, 17 Jewels, Lever Set.
No. 331—Open Face, 15 Jewels, Lever Set.
No. 330—Hunting, 15 Jewels, Lever Set.

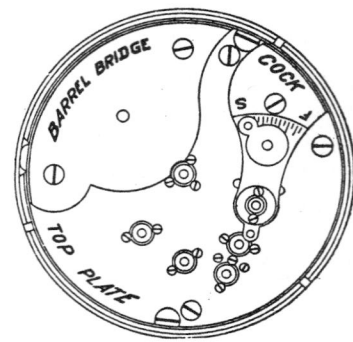 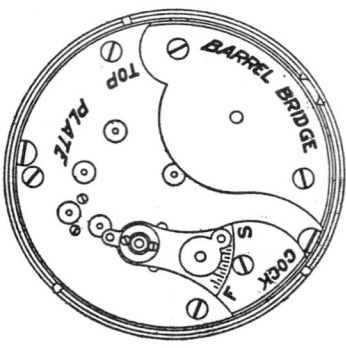

Model 1, Full Plate, Open face.   Model 1, Full Plate, Hunting

18 SIZE—MODEL 2
Open Face and Hunting, Lever Set

No. 329—21J, Open Face, "Studebaker," Adjusted to Temperature and 5 Positions.
No. 328—21J, Hunting, "Studebaker," Adjusted to Temperature and 5 Positions.
No. 327—21J, Open Face, Adjusted to Temperature and 5 Positions.
No. 323—17J, Open Face, "Studebaker," Adjusted to Temperature and 5 Positions.
No. 345—17J, Open Face, Adjusted to Temperature and 3 Positions.
No. 344—17J, Hunting, Adjusted to Temperature and 3 Positions.
No. 313—17J, Open Face, Adjusted to Temperature.
No. 312—17J, Hunting, Adjusted to Temperature.
Nos. 309, 337, 347—17J, Open Face.
No. 346—17J, Hunting.
Nos. 333, 305—15J, Open Face.
Nos. 332, 304—15J, Hunting.

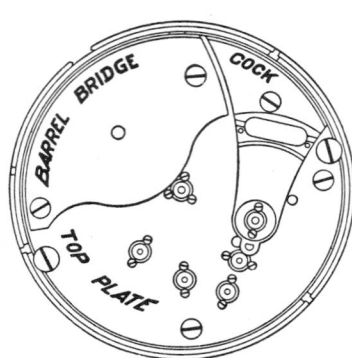 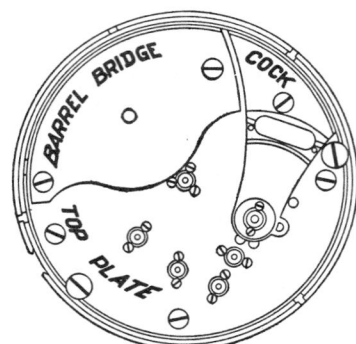

Model 2, Full Plate, Open face.   Model 2, Full Plate, Hunting.

16 SIZE—MODEL 1
Open Face and Hunting, Lever Set

No. 295—Open Face, 21 Jewels, Adjusted to Temperature and 5 Positions.
No. 294—Hunting, 21 Jewels, Adjusted to Temperature and 5 Positions.
No. 293—Open Face, 19 Jewels, Adjusted to Temperature and 5 Positions.
No. 292—Hunting, 19 Jewels, Adjusted to Temperature and 5 Positions.
No. 299—Open Face, 17 Jewels, Adjusted to Temperature and 3 Positions.
No. 298—Hunting, 17 Jewels, Adjusted to Temperature and 3 Positions.
No. 291—Open Face, 17 Jewels, Adjusted to Temperature and 3 Positions.
No. 290—Hunting, 17 Jewels, Adjusted to Temperature and 3 Positions.
No. 281—Open Face, 15 Jewels, & No. 280—Hunting, 15 Jewels.
No. 261—Open Face, 7 Jewels, & No. 260—Hunting, 7 Jewels.

Model 1, 3/4 Plate, Open Face.   Model 1, 3/4 Plate, Hunting.

16 SIZE—MODEL 2
Open Face and Hunting, Pendant and Lever Set.

No. 229—21J, Open Face, Lever Set, "Studebaker," Adjust. to Temp. and 5 Positions.
No. 227—21J, Open Face, Lever Set, Adjusted to Temperature and 5 Positions.
No. 219—19J, Open Face, Pendant Set, Adjusted to Temperature and 4 Positions.
No. 223—17J, Open Face, Lever Set, "Studebaker," Adjust. to Temp. and 5 Positions.
No. 217—17J, Open Face, Lever Set, Adjusted to Temperature and 3 Positions.
No. 215—17J, Open Face, Pendant Set, Adjusted to Temperature.
No. 212—17J, Hunting, Lever Set, Adjusted to Temperature.
No. 211—17J, Open Face, Pendant Set
No. 207—15J, Open Face, Pendant Set, & **No. 204—15J, Hunting, Lever Set.**
No. 209—9J, Open Face, Pendant Set, & **No. 203—7J, Open Face, Pendant Set.**

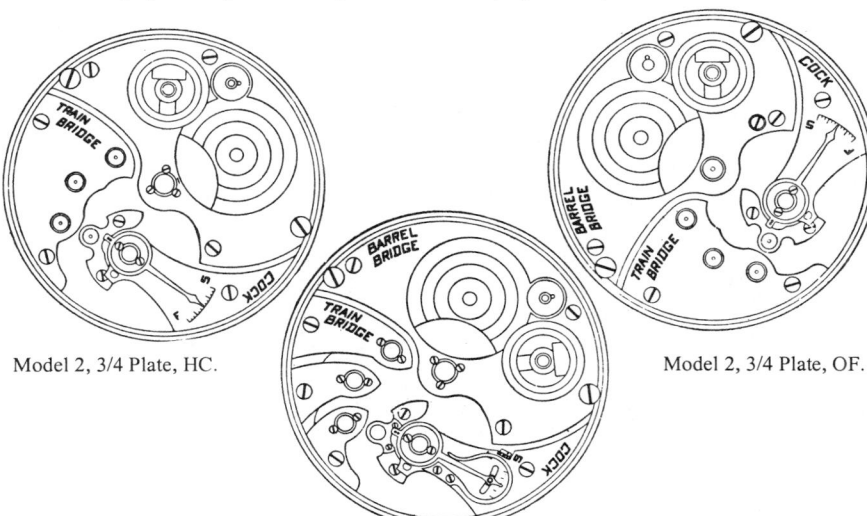

Model 2, 3/4 Plate, HC.   Model 2, 3/4 Plate, OF.

Model 2, Bridges, Open Face.

12 SIZE—MODEL 1
Chesterfield Series and Grade 429 Special
Made in Pendant Set, Open Face Only

No. 431—21J, Adjusted to Temperature and 5 Positions.
No. 429—19J, Adjusted to Temperature and 4 Positions.
No. 419—17J, Adjusted to Temperature and 3 Positions.
No. 415—17J, Adjusted to Temperature.
No. 411—17J.
No. 407—15J.

Model 1, Bridges, Open Face.

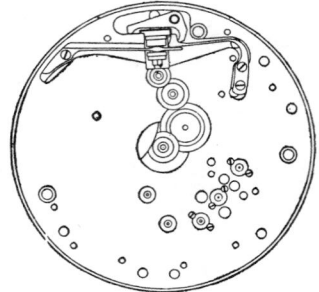

Model 1, Lower Plate, Dial Side.

6 SIZE— MODEL 1
Hunting
Grade No. 180, 17 Jewels
Grade No. 170, 15 Jewels
Grade No. 160, 11 Jewels

Serial Number Range
380,501 to 389,900

Model 1, 3/4 Plate, 6 size

0 SIZE—MODEL 1
Open Face, No second hand, Hunting has second hand

Model numbers 1 & 2 serial numbers under 659,700. All open face and hunting parts for this model except dial and fourth pinion are interchangeable.

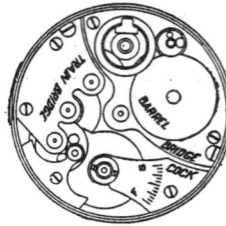

Model 1, Open Face, 3/4 Plate, 7 jewels.

Model 1, Hunting, Bridges, 15-17 jewels.

0 SIZE—MODEL 2
Open Face, No second hand, Hunting has second hand

No. 100— 7 Jewels, Hunting, 3/4 Bridge.
No. 101— 7 Jewels, Open Face, 3/4 Plate.
No. 110— 15 Jewels, Hunting, 3/4 Bridge.
No. 111— 15 Jewels, Open Face, 3/4 Plate.
No. 120— 17 Jewels, Hunting, 3/4 Bridge.
No. 121— 17 Jewels, Open Face, 3/4 Plate.

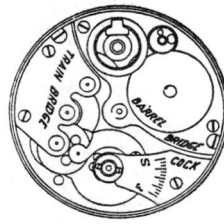

Model 2, Open Face, 3/4 Plate.   Model 2, Hunting, 3/4 Bridge.

Model numbers 1 & 2 serial numbers under 659,700. All open face and hunting parts for this model except dial and fourth pinion are interchangeable.

0 SIZE—MODEL 3
Both Open Face and Hunting have second hand

No. 151— 21J, Open Face, Bridge Model.
No. 150— 21J, Hunting, Bridge Model.
No. 121— 17J, Open Face, Bridge Model.
No. 120— 17J, Hunting, Bridge Model.

Model 3, Open Face, Bridges.   Model 3, Hunting, Bridges.

🕒 Pricing in this Guide are fair market price for **COMPLETE** watches which are reflected from the "**NAWCC**" National and regional shows.

J. P. STEVENS & CO.

J. P. STEVENS & BRO.
J. P. STEVENS WATCH CO.
Atlanta, Georgia
1882 - 1887

In mid-1881 J. P. Stevens bought part of the Springfield Watch Co. of Massachusetts; and some unfinished watch components from E. F. Bowman. He set up his watchmaking firm above his jewelry store in Atlanta, Ga., and started to produce the Bowman unfinished watches which were 16 size and 18 size, to which was added the "Stevens Patent Regulator." This regulator is best described as a simple disc attached to the plate which has an eccentric groove cut for the arm of the regulator to move in. This regulator is a prominent feature of the J. P. Stevens, and only the top is jeweled. These watches were 16S, 3/4 plate, stem wind and had a nickel plate with damaskeening. The pallets were equidistant locking and needed greater accuracy in manufacturing. About 50 of these watches were made. A line of gilt movements was added. The pallet and fork are made of one piece aluminum. The aluminum was combined with 1/10 copper and formed an exceedingly tough metal which will not rust or become magnetized. The lever of this watch is only one-third the weight of a steel lever. The aluminum lever affords the least possible resistance for overcoming inertia in transmitting power from the escape wheel to the balance. In 1884, the company was turning out about ten watches a day at a price of $20 to $100 each. In the spring of 1887 the company failed. Only 169 true Stevens watches were made, but other watches carried the J. P. Stevens name.

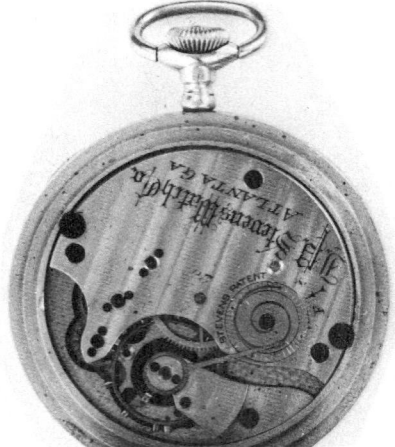

Original "J. P. Stevens Atlanta, Ga.", nickel movement, 16 size, 3/4 plate, lever set, gold jewel settings, note patented spiral grooved regulator, serial number 26.

J.P. Stevens Watch Co. movement by Columbus Watch Co., 18 size, 11-15 jewels.

16 TO 18 SIZE

Grade or Name – Description		Avg	Ex-Fn	Mint
Original Model, Serial Nos. 1 to 174, (recased)	★ ★ ★	$1,500	$2,000	$3,000
Original Model, Serial Nos. 1 to 174, ALL original with J. P. Stevens dial & 18K case	★ ★ ★ ★	6,000	7,000	12,000
Aurora, 15-17J	★	350	400	900
Chronograph, 17J, Swiss made, fly back hand	★ ★	500	550	1,000
Columbus W. Co., 15-17J	★	400	500	850

⊕ A collector should expect to pay modestly higher prices at local shops.

⊕ Watches listed in this book are priced at the collectable Trade Show level, as **complete** watches having an original 14k gold-filled case and *Key Wind* with silver, an original white enamel single sunk dial, and with the entire original movement in good working order with no repairs needed.

J. P. Stevens & Bro., on movement & dial, made by Aurora, 18 size, 15 jewels, Hunting Case, S # 39806.

J. P. Stevens & Bro., Swiss chronograph movement, about 18 size, with fly back hand.

Grade or Name – Description	Avg	Ex-Fn	Mint
Elgin, 15-17J ....★	$300	$350	$500
Hamilton, 17J ....★	400	450	700
Hampden, 15-17J	295	350	500
Illinois, 15-17J ....★	600	650	900
N. Y. W. Co., 17J, Full Plate, S#s range in 500s ....★	700	750	1,200
N. Y. W. Co. "Bond" Model, S#s range in 500s ....★★	900	1,000	1,600
A. Potter, **14K case**, Swiss made ....★★★	3,000	3,500	6,000
Rockford, 15J, Full Plate, HC ....★	400	450	800
18S Swiss, 15-17J, by "Vacheron & C.", wolf teeth winding..........	400	450	675
16S Swiss, 15-17J, Longines..	175	195	350
16S Swiss, 15-17J, 3/4 plate..	175	195	350
Waltham, 11-15-17J..★	400	450	775

J.P. Stevens & Bro., about 18 size, 17 jewels, Note: by "Vacheron & Constantin", wolf teeth winding, Ca. 1889.

J.P. Stevens Watch Co. movement by Waltham, 18 size, 11 jewels, serial number 1,240,058.

J.P. Stevens movement made by Hampden, 18 size, 17 jewels, note eccentric style regulator, serial # 515.

J.P. Stevens & Bro., movement made by Hampden, model 4, 18 size, 17jewels, model 4, S#732,085.

6 SIZE

Grade or Name – Description	Avg	Ex-Fn	Mint
Ladies Model, 15J, LS, HC, **14K** ....★	$500	$575	$900
Ladies Model, 15J, LS, GF case, HC	225	275	450
Ladies Model, 15J, LS, GF cases, OF	195	250	325
Ladies Model, 15J, LS, GF cases, Swiss made	150	175	275

J.P. Stevens Watch Co., 16 size, 15 jewels, Adjusted to temperature & positions, serial number 21,814.

J.P. Stevens Watch Co., 6 size, 11 jewels, exposed winding gears.

🕐 Generic, nameless or **unmarked** grades for watch movements are listed under the Company name or initials of the Company, etc. by size, jewel count and description.

🕐 Watches listed in this book are priced at the collectable Trade Show level, as **complete** watches having an original 14k gold-filled case and *Key Wind* with silver, an original white enamel single sunk dial, and with the entire original movement in good working order with no repairs needed.

🕐 Pricing in this Guide are fair market price for **COMPLETE** watches which are reflected from the "**<u>NAWCC</u>**" National and regional shows.

SUFFOLK WATCH CO.

Waltham, Massachusetts 1899 - 1901

The Suffolk Watch Company officially succeeded the Columbia Watch Company in March 1901. However, the Suffolk 0-size, 7-jewel nickel movement with lever escapement was being manufactured in the Columbia factory before the end of 1899. More than 25,000 movements were made . The factory was closed after it was purchased by the Keystone Watch Case Company on May 17, 1901. The machinery was moved to the nearby factory of the United States Watch Company (purchased by Keystone in April 1901), where it was used to make the United States Watch Company's 0-size movement,introduced in April 1902. Both the Columbia Watch Company and the Suffolk Watch Company made 0-size movements only.

Grade or Name – Description		Avg	Ex-Fn	Mint
0S, 7J, NI, HC .... ★		$75	$95	$175

Suffolk Watch Co., 0 Size, 7 jewels, serial number 216,841.   Seth Thomas, *Colonial U.S.A.* on movement, 18 size, 7 jewels, model # 11.

SETH THOMAS WATCH CO.

Thomaston, Connecticut

1883 - 1915

Seth Thomas is a very prominent clock manufacturer, and in early 1883, the company made a decision to manufacture watches. The watches were first placed on the market in 1885. They were 18S, open face, stem wind, 3/4 plate, and the escapement was between the plates. The compensating balance was set well below the normal. They were 11J, 16,000 beats per minute train, but soon went to 18,000 or quick train. In 1886, the company started to make higher grade watches and produced four grades: 7J, 11J, 15J, and 17J. That year the output was 100 watches a day.

SETH THOMAS ESTIMATED SERIAL NUMBERS AND PRODUCTION DATES

DATE – SERIAL NO.	DATE – SERIAL NO	DATE–SERIAL NO.	DATE – SERIAL NO.
1885 – 5,000	1893 – 510,000	1901 – 1,230,000	1909 – 2,500,000
1886 – 20,000	1894 – 600,000	1902 – 1,320,000	1910 – 2,725,000
1887 – 40,000	1895 – 690,000	1903 – 1,410,000	1911 – 2,950,000
1888 – 80,000	1896 – 780,000	1904 – 1,500,000	1912 – 3,175,000
1889 – 150,000	1897 – 870,000	1905 – 1,700,000	1913 – 3,490,000
1890 – 235,000	1898 – 960,000	1906 – 1,900,000	1914 – 3,600,000
1891 – 330,000	1899 – 1,050,000	1907 – 2,100,000	
1892 – 420,000	1900 – 1,140,000	1908 – 2,300,000	

The above list is provided for determining the APPROXIMATE age of your watch. Match serial number with date. Watches were not necessarily sold in the exact order of manufactured date.

Seth Thomas movement, 18 size,17 jewels, Molineux model, 2 tone yellow gold, heavy damaskeening, H. C.

Seth Thomas 18 size,"Molineux" 17 J., 2 tone yellow gold gilt & nickel heavy damaskeening model #2 ,HC

18 SIZE

Grade or Name – Description	Avg	Ex-Fn	Mint
Century, 7J, OF	$55	$70	$150
Century, 7J, HC	70	90	175
Century, 15J, OF	50	70	150
Century, 15J, HC	60	80	175
Chautauqua, 15J, GJS, M#5 ★	150	195	400
Colonial U.S.A., 7J, model # 11	55	65	125
Cordnia Watch Co., 7J	55	65	125
Early model # 1, low serial # under **1,000** ★	275	350	750
Eagle Series, No. 36, 7J, OF	95	125	150
Eagle Series, No. 37, 7J, HC	125	150	195
Eagle Series, No. 106, 11J, OF	95	125	150
Eagle Series, No. 107, 11J, HC	125	150	195
Eagle Series, No. 206, 15J, OF	95	125	150

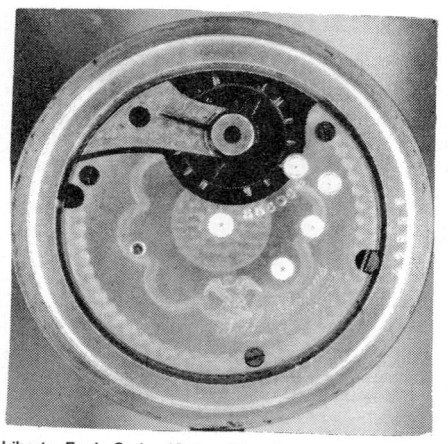
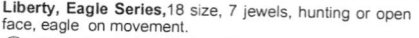

Liberty, Eagle Series,18 size, 7 jewels, hunting or open face, eagle on movement.

Maiden Lane, 18 size, 28 jewels, gold jewel settings, Adj5p, engraved dated as =8,1,99. No serial number.

⊕ Pricing in this Guide are fair market price for **COMPLETE** watches which are reflected from the "**NAWCC**" National and regional shows.

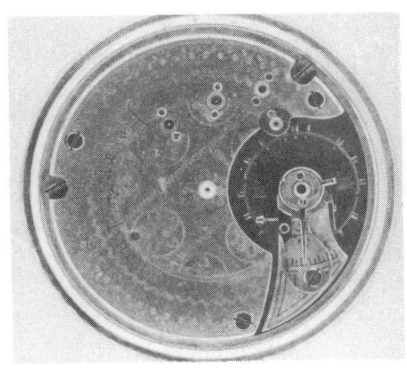 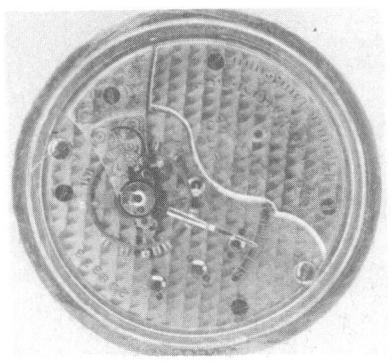

Henry Molineux, 18 size, 17 jewels, "Corona W. Co. USA" on dial, open face, serial number 54,951. **Seth Thomas**, 18 size, 23 jewels, gold jewel settings, adjusted, serial number 298,333.

Grade or Name – Description	Avg	Ex-Fn	Mint
Eagle Series, No. 207, 15J, HC	$150	$175	$250
Eagle Series, 15J, M# 2, HC	125	150	225
Eagle Series, No. 210, 17J, OF	125	150	195
Eagle Series, No. 211, 17J, HC	175	195	325
Eagle Series, 17J, NI, 3/4, OF	125	150	195
Edgemere, 11J	50	65	150
Edgemere, 17J	50	65	175
Keywind M#2, 7J, 11J, & 15J, 3/4	175	225	400
Keywind M#4, 7J, 11J, & 15J, 3/4	175	225	400
Lakeshore, 17J, GJS, ADJ, NI	150	195	350
Liberty, 7J, 3/4, eagle on back plate	100	125	295
Maiden Lane, 17J, GJS, DR, Adj.6P, NI, marked, OF ★★★	1,200	1,400	2,000
Maiden Lane, 19J, GJS, DR, Adj.6P, NI, marked, OF ★★★	1,300	1,500	2,200
Maiden Lane, 21J, GJS, DR, Adj.6P, NI, marked, OF ★★★	1,400	1,600	2,400
Maiden Lane, 24J, GJS, DR, Adj.6P, marked, OF ★★★	1,600	1,800	2,500
Maiden Lane, 25J, GJS, DR, Adj.6P, NI, marked, OF ★★★	2,000	2,400	3,000
Maiden Lane, **28J**, GJS, DR, Adj.5P, NI, marked, OF ★★★★★	15,000	18,000	25,000
Henry Molineux, M#3, 20-21J, 3/4, GJS, ADJ,, OF ★★	575	675	900
Henry Molineux, M#2, 17J, GJS, ADJ, HC ★★	500	600	850
Henry Molineux, M#2, 19-21J, GJS, ADJ, HC ★★★	700	900	1,500
Monarch Watch Co., 7-15J, 2-tone	90	125	250
R. R. Special USA, 7J, with a locomotive on dial	125	150	295
Republic USA, 7J, OF	50	65	125

🕐 Generic, nameless or **unmarked** grades for watch movements are listed under the Company name or initials of the Company, etc. by size, jewel count and description.

S. Thomas, 7J, 3/4, **multi-color dial**	$175	$225	$600
S. Thomas, 7J, 3/4	50	75	150
S. Thomas, 11J, 3/4, HC	50	75	175
S. Thomas, 11J, 3/4, OF	50	75	150
S. Thomas, 15J, 3/4, HC	50	75	195
S. Thomas, 15J, 3/4, gilded, OF	50	75	150
S. Thomas, 15J, 3/4 , OF	50	75	150
S. Thomas, 16J, 3/4	50	75	175
S. Thomas, 17J, 3/4, OF, nickel	50	75	195

🕐 A collector should expect to pay modestly higher prices at local shops.

🕐 Pricing in this Guide are fair market price for **COMPLETE** watches which are reflected from the "**NAWCC**" National and regional shows.

Grade or Name – Description	Avg	Ex-Fn	Mint
S. Thomas, 17J, 3/4, 2-Tone	$125	$175	$400
S. Thomas, 17J, 3/4, OF, gilded	50	70	175
S. Thomas, 17J, 3/4, HC	70	90	195
S. Thomas, 19J, GJS, DR, Adj.5P, OF ★★	700	850	1,100
S. Thomas, 21J, GJS, DR, Adj.5P	500	600	800
S. Thomas, 23J, GJS, DR, Adj., OF ★★★	1,200	1,500	2,000
S. Thomas, G# 33, 7J, 3/4, gilded, OF	60	80	150
S. Thomas, G# 34, 7J, 3/4, gilded, HC	60	80	175
S. Thomas, G# 37, 7J, 3/4, NI, HC	60	80	175
S. Thomas, G# 44, 11J, 3/4, gilded, OF	60	80	150
S. Thomas, G# 47, 7J, gilded, FULL, OF	60	80	150
S. Thomas, G# 58, 11J, FULL, gilt, OF	60	80	150
S. Thomas, G# 70, 15J, 3/4, gilded, OF	60	80	150
S. Thomas, G# 71, 15J, 3/4, gilded, HC	60	80	175
S. Thomas, G# 80, 17J, 3/4, gilded, ADJ, HC	90	125	195
S. Thomas, G# 101, 15J, 3/4, gilded, ADJ, OF	60	80	150
S. Thomas, G# 149, 15J, gilded, FULL, OF	60	80	150
S. Thomas, G# 159, 15J, NI, FULL, OF	60	80	150
S. Thomas, G# 169, 17J, NI, FULL, OF	60	80	150
S. Thomas, G# 170, 15J, 3/4, NI, OF	60	80	150
S. Thomas, G# 171, 15J, 3/4, NI, HC	60	80	175
S. Thomas, G# 179, 17J, 3/4, NI, ADJ, OF	95	125	175
S. Thomas, G# 180, 17J, 3/4, NI, HC	135	175	250
S. Thomas, G# 182, 17J, DR, NI, FULL, OF	95	125	175
S. Thomas, G# 201, 15J, 3/4, NI, ADJ, OF	95	135	175
S. Thomas, G# 202, 15J, 3/4, NI, ADJ, HC	95	135	195
S. Thomas, G# 245, 19J, GJS, 2-Tone, HC ★★	1,000	1,200	1,600
S. Thomas, G# 248, 17-21J, FULL, DR, Adj.3P, OF, 2-tone	195	250	400
S. Thomas, G# 260, 21J, DR, Adj.6P, NI, FULL, OF	400	500	800
S. Thomas, G# 281, 17J, FULL, DR, Adj.3P, OF, 2-tone	195	250	400
S. Thomas, G# 282, 17J, FULL, DR, Adj.5P, OF	195	250	350
S. Thomas, G# 382, 17J, FULL, DR, Adj.5P, OF, 2-tone	195	275	500
S. Thomas, G# 406-408, 17J, FULL, Adj., OF	195	250	350
S. Thomas, G# 408-508, 17J, FULL, Adj., HC	225	275	375
Special Motor Service,17J, 2 tone, LS, OF ★★	350	400	700
Trainsmen Special, **fake "17-23"J Adj**, seen in model 10, 12, 13	75	125	250
20th Century (Wards), 11J	75	95	175
20th Century (Wards), 11J, 2-Tone	75	95	200
Wyoming Watch Co., 7J, OF	90	125	250

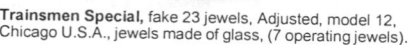

Trainsmen Special, fake 23 jewels, Adjusted, model 12, Chicago U.S.A., jewels made of glass, (7 operating jewels).

Grade 36, 16 size, 7 jewels, open face, three-quarter nickel plate.

16 SIZE
(OF Only)

Grade or Name – Description	Avg	Ex-Fn	Mint
Centennial, 7J, 3/4, NI, OF	$50	$70	$125
Locust, 7J, NI, 3/4, OF	50	70	125
Locust, 17J, NI, ADJ, 3/4, OF	60	80	150
Republic USA, 7J, OF	50	70	125

🕐 Generic, nameless or **unmarked** grades for watch movements are listed under the Company name or initials of the Company, etc. by size, jewel count and description.

	Avg	Ex-Fn	Mint
S. Thomas, G# 25, 7J, BRG, OF	$40	$60	$125
S. Thomas, G# 26, 15J, BRG, GJS, OF	40	60	125
S. Thomas, G# 27, 17J, BRG, GJS, OF	40	60	125
S. Thomas, G# 28, 17J, BRG, Adj.3P, GJS, OF	75	95	195
S. Thomas, G# 326, 7J, 3/4, NI, OF	40	60	125
S. Thomas, G# 328, 15J, 3/4, NI, OF	40	60	125
S. Thomas, G# 332, 7J, 3/4, NI, OF	40	60	125
S. Thomas, G# 334, 15J, NI, ADJ,3/4, DMK, OF	40	60	125
S. Thomas, G# 336, 17J, ADJ, 3/4, DMK, OF	70	95	150

Seth Thomas, 12 size, 7 jewels, open face, pendant set.

Seth Thomas, 12 size, 17 jewels, gold jewel settings, gold center wheel, open face, Adj3p.

12 SIZE
(OF Only)

Grade or Name – Description	Avg	Ex-Fn	Mint
Centennial, 7J	$35	$55	$95
Republic USA, 7J, OF	35	55	95
S. Thomas, G# 25, 7J, BRG, OF	35	55	95
S. Thomas, G# 26, 15J, BRG, GJS, OF	35	55	95
S. Thomas, G# 27, 17J, BRG, GJS, OF	35	55	95
S. Thomas, G# 28, 17J, OF, BRG, Adj.3P, GJS	45	75	150
S. Thomas, G# 326, 7J, OF, 3/4, NI	35	55	95
S. Thomas, G# 328, 15J, OF, 3/4, NI	35	55	95

🕐 Watches listed in this book are priced at the collectable Trade Show level, as complete watches having an original 14k gold-filled case and Key Wind with silver, an original white enamel single sunk dial, and with the entire original movement in good working order with no repairs needed.

🕐 Generic, nameless or unmarked grades for watch movements are listed under the Company name or initials of the Company, etc. by size, jewel count and description.

Seth Thomas movement, 6 size, 7 jewels, serial number 441,839. Sometimes appears in a 12 size case.

SETH THOMAS, 0 size, 15 jewels, pendant set, hunting case, serial number 200,449.

6 SIZE
(Some 6 Size were spread to fit 12 Size cases)

Grade or Name – Description	Avg	Ex-Fn	Mint
Century, 7J, NI, 3/4	$35	$55	$95
Countess Janet, 17J, Adj., HC	75	125	150
Eagle Series, 7J, No. 45, 3/4, NI, DMK, OF	65	85	95
Eagle Series, 7J, No. 205, 3/4, HC	60	125	150
Eagle Series, 15J, No. 35, 3/4, NI, DMK, OF	65	85	125
Eagle Series, 15J, No. 245, 3/4, HC	70	125	150
Edgemere, 7-11J,	35	50	125
Republic USA, 7J	35	50	95
Seth Thomas, 7J, 3/4, **14K, 26 DWT, HC**	250	275	500
Seth Thomas, 11J, 3/4, HC	70	80	150
Seth Thomas, 11J, 3/4, OF	35	45	125
S. Thomas, G# 35, 7J, NI, DMK,3/4, HC	35	45	150
S. Thomas, G# 119, 16J, GJS, NI, DMK, 3/4, HC	70	125	150
S. Thomas, G# 205, 15J, HC	70	125	150
S. Thomas, G# 320, 7J, NI, DMK, 3/4, OF	35	50	95
S. Thomas, G# 322, 15J, OF	35	50	95

NOTE: Add $25 to $50 for HC.

0 SIZE

Grade or Name – Description	Avg	Ex-Fn	Mint
Seth Thomas, 7J, No. 1, OF	$40	$60	$95
Seth Thomas, 7J, No. 1, HC	50	70	125
Seth Thomas, 15J, GJS, No. 3, OF	50	70	150
Seth Thomas, 15J, No. 3, HC	55	75	165
Seth Thomas, 17J, GJS, PS, No. 9, OF	50	70	150
Seth Thomas, 17J, GJS, PS, No. 9, HC	55	75	165

🕒 A collector should expect to pay modestly higher prices at local shops.

🕒 Pricing in this Guide are fair market price for **COMPLETE** watches which are reflected from the "<u>NAWCC</u>" National and regional shows.

Number		Model
1 to	10900	1
10901 "	25100	3
25101 "	25200	2
25201 "	25300	3
25301 "	25400	2
25401 "	28000	3
28001 "	29000	2
29001 "	34900	3
34901 "	35000	2
35001 "	36200	4
36201 "	40000	2
40001 "	41200	3
41201 "	41500	2
41501 "	42100	3
42101 "	44800	2
44801 "	46000	4
46001 "	47200	2
47201 "	47300	3
47301 "	48200	2
48201 "	48300	3
48301 "	48600	2
48601 "	49000	3
49001 "	50300	2
50301 "	50400	4
50401 "	51100	2
51101 "	52000	4
52001 "	53300	2
53301 "	54500	4
54501 "	54900	2
54901 "	55000	3
55001 "	55400	2
55401 "	55700	4
55701 "	56600	3
56601 "	57700	4
57701 "	58900	2
58901 "	59200	3
59201 "	59300	2
59301 "	60500	4
60501 "	60800	2
60801 "	61800	2
61801 "	62400	2
62401 "	63800	4
63801 "	64800	2
64801 "	65100	3
65101 "	65700	2
65701 "	65800	4
65801 "	66200	2
66201 "	67300	2
67301 "	68100	2
68101 "	68200	2
68201 "	68800	2
68801 "	69800	3
69801 "	70540	2
70541 "	70550	3
70551 "	71700	2
71701 "	71950	3
71951 "	72000	2
72001 to	73200	2
73201 "	73500	3
73501 "	74900	2
74901 "	75700	3
75701 "	77000	2
77001 "	78000	3
78001 "	79900	2
79901 "	80100	3
80101 "	80500	2
80501 "	81000	3
81001 "	82100	2
82101 "	82300	3
82301 "	84000	2
84001 "	84500	4
84501 "	84900	2
84901 "	85500	3
85501 "	86000	2
86001 "	87000	2
87001 "	87500	4
87501 "	87600	2
87601 "	87900	3
87901 "	89100	2
89101 "	89600	4
89601 "	90800	2
90801 "	90900	4
90901 "	91500	2
91501 "	92000	4
92001 "	94400	2
94401 "	94600	3
94601 "	95200	2
95201 "	95300	3
95301 "	95500	2
95501 "	95800	3
95801 "	96500	2
96501 "	97100	3
97101 "	98200	2
98201 "	98225	3
98226 "	98700	2
98701 "	99300	3
99301 "	100000	2
100001 "	128000	14
128001 "	137000	15
137001 "	138000	14
138001 "	139000	15
139001 "	141000	14
141001 "	142000	15
142001 "	144000	14
144001 "	160000	15
160001 "	165000	16
165001 "	166000	14
166001 "	200000	16
200001 "	400000	5
400001 "	420000	16
420001 "	500000	17
500001 "	500500	2
500501 "	502400	3
502401 "	505500	2
505501 to	505600	3
505601 "	506200	2
506201 "	507900	3
507901 "	508000	2
508001 "	509000	7
509001 "	509800	2
509801 "	510000	4
510001 "	512300	2
512301 "	513500	7
513501 "	514300	2
514301 "	514800	3
514801 "	515300	2
515301 "	516100	6
516101 "	516600	7
516601 "	516800	4
516801 "	517400	7
517401 "	517500	3
517501 "	518200	6
518201 "	519300	7
519301 "	519800	6
519801 "	521800	7
521801 "	523300	6
523301 "	523800	4
523801 "	523834	6
523835 "	528100	7
528101 "	528600	6
528601 "	528900	7
528901 "	529900	6
529901 "	530500	7
530501 "	530700	6
530701 "	530800	2
530801 "	531000	6
531001 "	531100	7
531101 "	532600	6
532601 "	535000	7
535001 "	536000	2
536001 "	537000	7
537001 "	538000	6
538001 "	539000	7
539001 "	540000	6
540001 "	541000	2
541001 "	542000	6
542001 "	544000	2
544001 "	547000	6
547001 "	549000	2
549001 "	551000	7
551001 "	556000	6
556001 "	558000	7
558001 "	559000	2
559001 "	562000	6
562001 "	568000	7
568001 "	569000	6
569001 "	570000	7
570001 "	571000	6
571001 "	575000	7
575001 "	577000	6
577001 "	579000	7
579001 to	581000	6
581001 "	582600	7
582601 "	582800	4
582801 "	584100	7
584101 "	585000	6
585001 "	585400	7
585401 "	585600	4
585601 "	586000	7
586001 "	590000	6
590001 "	591000	7
591001 "	592000	6
592001 "	592300	7
592301 "	592800	4
592801 "	593000	7
593001 "	607000	6
607001 "	608000	7
608001 "	610000	6
610001 "	612000	7
612001 "	615000	6
615001 "	616000	7
616001 "	617000	6
617001 "	618000	7
618001 "	620000	6
620001 "	621800	7
621801 "	622000	4
622001 "	632000	6
632001 "	633000	7
633001 "	640000	6
640001 "	640100	7
640101 "	640800	6
640801 "	641100	7
641101 "	641700	6
641701 "	642000	7
642001 "	642400	6
642401 "	642500	7
642501 "	647100	6
647101 "	647300	7
647301 "	647600	6
647601 "	647800	7
647801 "	700000	6
700001 "	700100	8
700101 "	700300	9
700301 "	700800	8
700801 "	700900	9
700901 "	701900	8
701901 "	702400	9
702401 "	702900	8
702901 "	703200	9
703201 "	703300	8
703301 "	703800	9
703801 "	703900	8
703901 "	704300	9
704301 "	705800	8
705801 "	706000	9
706001 "	707400	8
707401 "	708000	9
708001 "	709100	8
709101 "	709300	9
709301 "	710200	8
710201 "	710600	9
710601 "	712400	8
712401 "	713700	9
713701 "	715200	8
715201 to	715300	8
715301 "	715600	8
715601 "	717000	9
717001 "	718000	8
718001 "	718100	9
718101 "	718200	4
718201 "	721500	8
721501 "	722000	9
722001 "	722200	8
722201 "	722900	9
722901 "	725600	8
725601 "	725700	9
725701 "	727000	8
727001 "	728600	8
728601 "	729500	8
729501 "	730100	9
730101 "	730300	8
730301 "	730800	9
730801 "	731000	8
731001 "	731200	9
731201 "	734900	8
734901 "	735100	9
735101 "	736700	8
736701 "	737800	9
737801 "	738400	8
738401 "	738600	9
738601 "	740500	8
740501 "	741200	9
741201 "	743100	8
743101 "	744200	9
744201 "	747000	8
747001 "	747300	8
747301 "	747500	8
747501 "	747600	8
747601 "	747700	9
747701 "	747800	9
747801 "	748000	8
748001 "	748200	9
748201 "	749100	8
749101 "	749200	8
749201 "	750000	8
750001 "	752600	9
752601 "	753300	9
753301 "	754100	9
754101 "	758400	8
758401 "	758700	9
758701 "	759600	8
759601 "	760600	9
760601 "	761800	8
761801 "	762000	8
762001 "	769000	9
769001 "	769200	9
769201 "	770100	8
770101 "	770600	9
770601 "	777600	8
777601 "	778700	9
778701 "	778900	9
778901 "	784600	8
784601 "	784700	9
784701 "	785800	8
785801 "	786400	9
786401 "	786800	8
786801 "	786900	9
786901 to	788700	8
788701 "	790000	9
790001 "	795300	9
795301 "	795350	9
900001 to	950000	17
950001 "	1000000	18

SETH THOMAS WATCH CO.
IDENTIFICATION OF MOVEMENTS
BY MODEL NUMBER

How to Identify Your Watch Size & Model: Compare the movement of your watch with the illustrations in this section. While comparing, note the location of the balance, jewels, screws, gears, and type of back plate (Full, 3/4, Bridge) these will be clues in identifying the movement you have.

Model 1, 18 size, Open Face

Model 2, 18 size, Hunting

Model 3, 18 size, Open Face

Model 4, 18 size, Key Wind

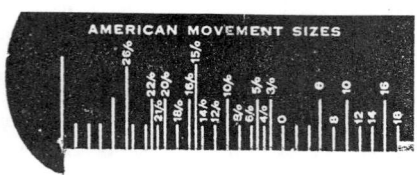

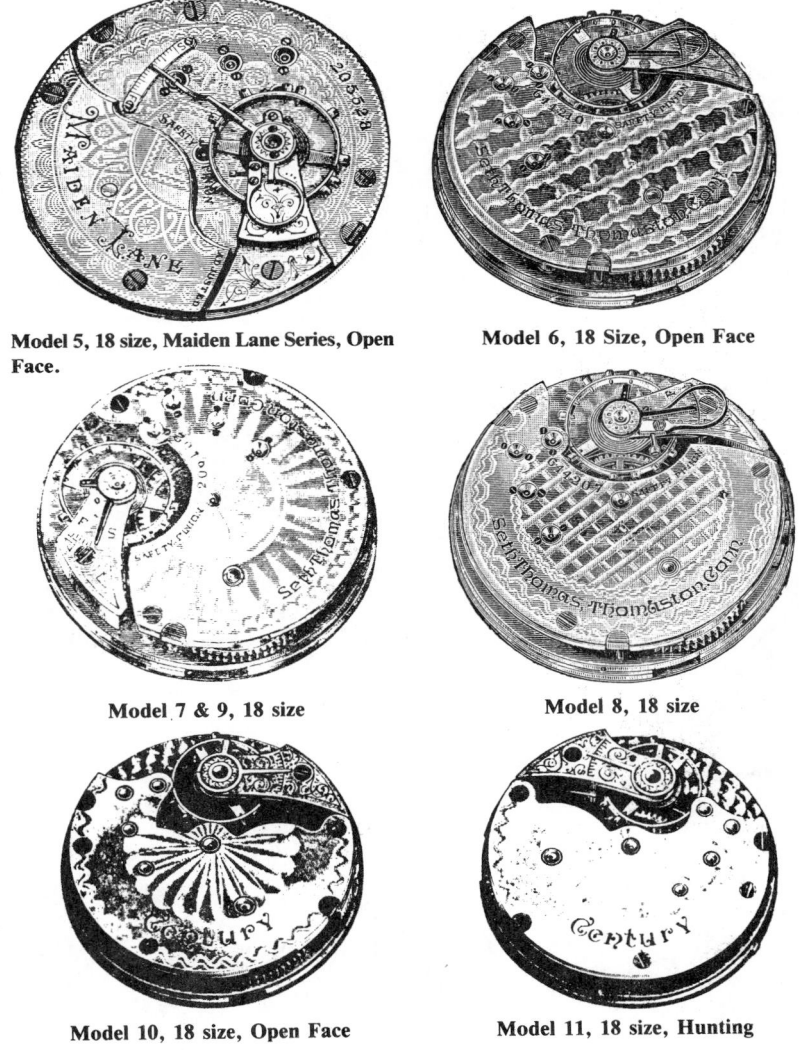

Model 5, 18 size, Maiden Lane Series, Open Face.

Model 6, 18 Size, Open Face

Model 7 & 9, 18 size

Model 8, 18 size

Model 10, 18 size, Open Face

Model 11, 18 size, Hunting

🕐 This book endeavours to be a GUIDE or helpful manual and offers a wealth of material to be used as a tool not as a absolute document. Price Guides are like watches the worst may be better than none at all, but at best cannot be expected to be 100% accurate.

🕐 Characteristics of watches differ for the same age of both case and movement, because these features vary it may not be accurate to date a watch by one single influence. Example: the second hand was not commonly found on watches before 1750, but common about 1800. The first second hand appeared in 1665 and another in 1690. Therefore statements are broad rather than accurate.

Model 13, 18 size, Hunting

16 Size

16 Size, Open Face

12 Size, Open Face

6 Size, Open face

Model 14, 6 size

Model 16 & 17, 6 size

TREMONT WATCH CO.

Boston, Massachusetts
1864 - 1866

In 1864 A. L. Dennison thought that if he could produce a good movement at a reasonable price, there would be a ready market for it. Dennison went to Switzerland to find a supplier of cheap parts, as arbors were too high in America. He found a source for parts, mainly the train and escapement and the balance. About 600 sets were to be furnished. Dials were first made by Mr. Gold and Mr. Spurr, then later by Mr. Hull and Mr. Carpenter. Tremont had hoped to produce 600 sets of trains per month. In 1865, the first movements were ready for the market. They were 18S, key wind, fully jeweled, and were engraved "Tremont Watch Co." In 1866, the company moved from Boston to Melrose. The Tremont Watch Co. produced about 5,000 watches before being sold to the English Watch Co.

Tremont Watch Co., with "Washington Street Boston" engraved on movement, 18 size, 15 jewels, key wind and set, serial number 5,264.

Tremont movement, 18 size, 15 jewels, key wind & set, serial number 8,875.

Grade or Name – Description	Avg	Ex-Fn	Mint
18S, 7J, KW, KS	$250	$275	$425
18S, 11J, KW, KS	250	275	425
18S, 7-11-15J, KW, KS, gilded Silveroid	200	225	400
18S, 7-11-15J, KW, KS, gilded, marked LONDON	250	300	450
18S, 15J, KW, KS, gilded	250	275	450
18S, 15J, KW, KS, HC, **14K**	775	850	1,300
18S, 15J, KW, KS, gilded, Washington Street ★★	500	600	1,000
18S, 17J, KW, KS, gilded	300	325	500
18S, 15J, KW, **Key Set from back**, 3/4 plate ★★★	1,800	2,400	3,400

🕐 Watches listed in this book are priced at the collectable Trade Show level, as **complete** watches having an original 14k gold-filled case and *Key Wind* with silver, an original white enamel single sunk dial, and with the entire original movement in good working order with no repairs needed.

🕐 A collector should expect to pay modestly higher prices at local shops.

🕐 Pricing in this Guide are fair market price for **COMPLETE** watches which are reflected from the "**NAWCC**" National and regional shows.

TRENTON WATCH CO.
Trenton, New Jersey
1885 - 1908

Trenton watches were marketed under the following labels: Trenton, Ingersoll, Fortuna, Illinois Watch Case Company, Calumet U.S.A., Locomotives Special, Marvel Watch Co., and Reliance Watch Co.

Serial numbers started at 2,001 and ended at 4,100,000. Total production was about 1,934,000.

CHRONOLOGY OF THE DEVELOPMENT OF TRENTON WATCH CO.:

New Haven Watch Co., New Haven, Conn. 1883-1887
Trenton Watch Co., Trenton, N. J. 1887-1908
Sold to Ingersoll 1908-1922

TRENTON MODELS AND GRADES
With Years of Manufacture and Serial Numbers

Date	Numbers	Size	Model	Date	Numbers	Size	Model
1887-1889	2,001-61,000	18	1	1900-1903	2,000,001-2,075,000	6	2
1889-1891	64,001-135,000	18	2	1902-1905	2,075,001-2,160,000	6	3 LS
1891-1898 *1	135,001-201,000	18	3	"	"	12	2 LS
1899-1890	201,001-300,000	18	6	1905-1907	2,160,001-2,250,000	6	3 PS
1891-1900	300,001-500,000	18	4	"	"	12	2 PS
1892-1897	500,001-600,000	6	1	1899-1902	2,500,001-2,600,000	3/0	1
1894-1899	650,001-700,000	16	1	ca. 1906	2,800,001-2,850,000	6	3 PS
1898-1900	700,001-750,000	6	2	"	"	12	2 PS
1900-1904 * 2	750,001-800,000	18	4	1900-1904	3,000,001-3,139,000	16	2
1896-1900	850,001-900,000	12	1	1903-1907	3,139,001-3,238,000	16	3 OF
1898-1903	900,001-1,100,000	18	5	1903-1907	3,500,001-3,600,000	16	3 HC
1902-1907	1,300,001-1,400,000	18	6	1905-1907	4,000,001-4,100,000	0	1

1—7 jewel grades made only during 1891; 9 jewel chronograph Pat. Mar. 17, 1891, made 1891-1898.
2—A few examples are KWKS for export to England.

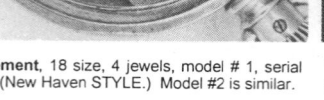

Trenton movement, 18 size, 4 jewels, model # 1, serial number 4,744. (New Haven STYLE.) Model #2 is similar.

Trenton movement, 18 size, 7 jewels, 4th model, serial number 788,313.

⊕ A collector should expect to pay modestly higher prices at local shops.

⊕ Pricing in this Guide are fair market price for **COMPLETE** watches which are reflected from the "**NAWCC**" National and regional shows.

18 SIZE

Grade or Name – Description	Avg	Ex-Fn	Mint
Trenton W. Co., M#1-2, gilded, OF.. ★	$150	$175	$300
Trenton W Co., 7J, KW, KS.. ★	175	225	500
Trenton W. Co., M#3, 7J, 3/4...	60	75	125
Trenton W. Co., M#3, 9J, 3/4...	60	75	125
Trenton W. Co., M#4, 7J, FULL..	60	75	125
Trenton W. Co., M#4, 11J, FULL..	60	75	125
Trenton W. Co., M#4, 15J, FULL..	60	75	125
Trenton W. Co., M#4-5, FULL, OF, NI	60	75	125
Chronograph, 9J, start, stop, & fly back, **DMK** .... ★★★★	275	350	750
Chronograph, 9J, start, stop, & fly back, **GILDED** .... ★★★★	275	350	750
Locomotive Special, tu-tone, **marked 23J,** also 17J., 7 working jewels,			
a locomotive on dial & movement (fake jewels)................. ★	95	150	325
Marvel W. Co. **Marked 23 jewels** (fake jewels) 7 working jewels	60	75	150
New Haven Watch Co. STYLE, M#1, 4J .... ★★★	250	325	500

Note: Add $25 to value of above watches in hunting case.

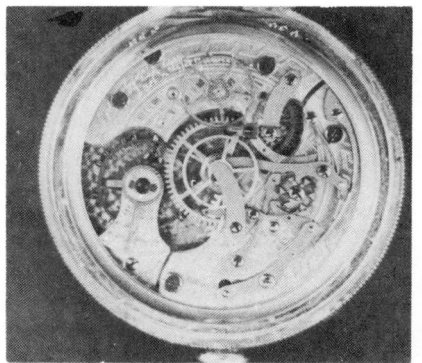

Chronograph, **18** size, 9 jewels, **third model**; Gilded, start, stop & fly back, S# 200,835, pat.mar.17.91.

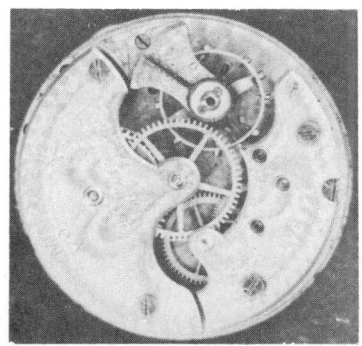

Trenton movement, 18 size, 7 jewels, model #3, serial number 148,945.

16 SIZE

Grade or Name – Description	Avg	Ex-Fn	Mint
Trenton W. Co., M#1-2, 7J, 3/4, NI, OF...	$30	$50	$125
Trenton W. Co., M#3, 7J, 3F BRG	30	50	125
Trenton W. Co., M#3, 11J, 3F BRG	30	50	125
Trenton W. Co., M#3, 15J, 3F BRG	30	50	135
Trenton W. Co., 7,11,15J, 3F BRG, NI	30	50	135
Trenton W. Co., Grade #30 & 31, 7J	50	75	125
Trenton W. Co., Grade #35, 36 & 38, 11J	50	75	125
Trenton W. Co., Grade #45, 16J..	60	70	150
Trenton W. Co., Grade #125, 12J..	50	75	125
Trenton W. Co., 7J., **convertible model** converts			
to open face or hunting case .... ★★	95	125	295

🕐 Generic, nameless or **unmarked** grades for watch movements are listed under the Company name or initials of the Company, etc. by size, jewel count and description.

🕐 A collector should expect to pay modestly higher prices at local shops.

🕐 Watches listed in this book are priced at the collectable trade show level, as **complete** watches having an original 14k gold-filled case and *Key Wind* with silver, an original white enamel single sunk dial, and with the entire original movement in good working order with no repairs needed.

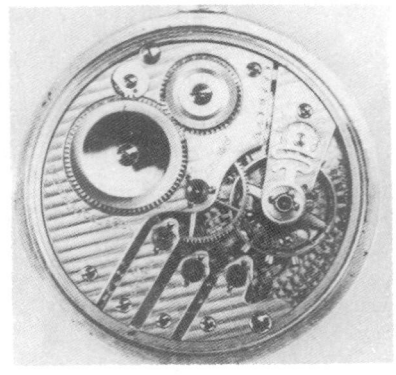

Ingersoll Trenton movement, 16 size, 19 jewels, three fingered bridge, adjusted, serial number 3,419,771.

Ingersoll Trenton movement, 16 size, 12 jewels; "Edgemere" engraved on movement.

Grade or Name – Description	Avg	Ex-Fn	Mint
Ingersoll Trenton, 7J, 3F BRG	$40	$50	$125
Ingersoll Trenton, 15J, 3F BRG, NI, ADJ	75	95	150
Ingersoll Trenton, 17J, 3F BRG, NI, ADJ	85	110	160
Ingersoll Trenton, 19J, 3F BRG, NI, Adj.5P, OF .... ★	150	250	350
Ingersoll Trenton, 19J, 3F BRG, NI, Adj.5P, HC..................... ★★	150	250	400
Peerless, 7J, SW, LS...	50	65	80
Railroad Reliance, 17J, OF.. ★	95	125	225
Reliance, 7J	40	65	80

Note: Add $25 to value of above watches in hunting case.

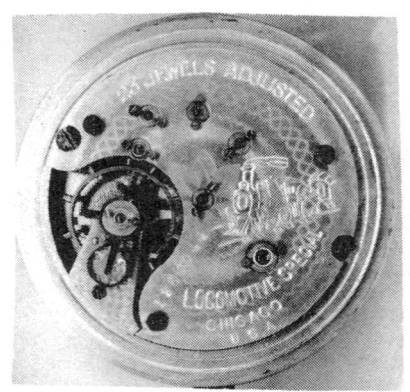

Railroad Special, 18 size, 23 jewels, tu-tone, locomotive on dial & movement, model # 6, S# 1,3660,044.

Trenton movement, convertible model converts to open face or hunting case, 16 size, 7 J.

🕐 A collector should expect to pay modestly higher prices at local shops.

🕐 Pricing in this Guide are fair market price for **COMPLETE** watches which are reflected from the "**NAWCC**" National and regional shows.

10 - 12 SIZE

Grade or Name – Description	Avg	Ex-Fn	Mint
"Fortuna," 7J, 3 finger BRG	$30	$50	$65
Trenton W. Co., M#1, 7J, 3/4	30	50	65
Monogram, 7J, SW	30	40	55

Trenton Watch Co. movement, 12 size, *Fortuna*, 7 jewels, 3 finger BRG., quick train, cut expansion balance.

Trenton Watch Co. movement, 6 size, 7 jewels, open face & hunting, nickel damaskeened.

6 SIZE

Grade or Name – Description	Avg	Ex-Fn	Mint
Trenton W. Co., 7J, 3/4, NI	$20	$40	$55
Trenton W. Co., 7J, 3Finger BRG	20	40	55
Trenton W. Co., 15J, 3Finger BRG	30	50	65
"Fortuna," 7J, 3 Finger Bridge	20	40	55

Note: Add $25 to value of above watches in hunting case.

0 SIZE

Grade or Name – Description	Avg	Ex-Fn	Mint
Trenton W. Co., 7J, 3F BRG	$25	$50	$65
Trenton W. Co., 15J, 3F BRG	30	60	75

Note: Add $25 to value of above watches in hunting case.

Trenton Chronograph, 18 size, 9J, start, stop, & fly back, **Model # 3.**

UNITED STATES WATCH CO.
Marion Watch Co.
Marion, New Jersey
1865 - 1877

The United States Watch Company was chartered in 1865, and the factory building was started in August 1865 and was completed in 1866. The first watch, called the "Frederic Atherton," was not put on the market until July 1867. It was America's first mass produced stem winding watch. This first grade was 18S, 19J, full plate and a gilt finish movement. A distinctive feature of the company's full plate movements was the butterfly shaped patented opening in the plate which allowed escapement inspection. That same year a second grade called the "Fayette Stratton" was introduced. It was also a gilt finish, full plate movement.

Most of these were 15J, but some of the very early examples have been noted in 17J. In 1868 the "George Channing," "Edwin Rollo," and "Marion Watch Co." grades were introduced. All were 18S, 15J, full plate movements in a gilt finish. In February 1869 the gilt version of the "United States Watch Co." grade was introduced. It was 18S, 19J, full plate and was the company's first entry into the prestige market. Later that year the company introduced their first nickel grade, a 19J, 18S, full plate movement called the "A. H. Wallis." About this same time, in December 1869, they introduced America's most expensive watch, the first nickel, 19J, 18S, full plate "United States Watch Co." grade. Depending on case weight, these prestige watches retailed between $500 and $600, more than the average man earned in a year at that time. The company also introduced damaskeening to the American market; first on gilt movements and later on the nickel grades. The damaskeening process was later improved by using **IVORY** disc in place of wooden disc. The United States and Wallis 19J prestige grades were beautifully finished with richly enameled engraving including a variety of unique designs on the balance cock. It is significant to note that no solid gold trains have been seen with these prestige items in the extant examples presently known.

pin set

FREDERIC ATHERTON & CO., 18 size, 19 J., gold jewel settings, key wind, also note the pin set on rim which will bring a HIGHER price. Note butterfly cut-out.

United States Watch Co. Marion,N.J.,1871 advertisement.

In 1870 the company introduced their first watch for ladies, a 10S, 15J, plate, cock & bridge movement which was made to their specifications in Switzerland. This model was first introduced in two grades, the "R. F. Pratt" and "Chas. G. Knapp," both in a 15J, gilt finish movement. Later it was offered in a high grade, 19J "I. H. Wright" nickel finish movement. During 1870 and 1871 several other full plate grades in both gilt and nickel finish were introduced. In 1871 development on a new line of full plate, 3/4 plate, and plate & bridge was started but not introduced to the market until late in 1872 and early 1873. The 10S and 16S new grades in 3/4 plate and bridge were probably delayed well into 1873 and were not available long, just before the "Panic of 1873" started in September; this explains their relative scarcity.

By July 1874 the "Panic" had taken its toll and it was necessary for the company to reorganize as the Marion Watch Company, a name formerly used for one of their grades. At this time jewel count, finish standards, and prices were lowered on the full plate older grades, but this proved to be a mistake. That same year they introduced a cased watch called the "North Star", their cheapest watch at $15 retail.

The year of 1875 hit the watch industry the hardest; price cutting was predatory and the higher priced watches of the United States Watch Co. were particularly vulnerable. Further lowering of finish standards and prices did not help and in 1876 the company was once again reorganized into the Empire City Watch Co. and their products were displayed at the Centennial that year. The Centennial Exhibition was not enough to save the faltering company and they finally closed their doors in 1877. The Howard brothers of Fredonia, New York (Independent and Fredonia Watch Co.) purchased most of the remaining movements in stock and machinery. In the ten year period of movement production, current statistical studies indicate an estimated production of only some 60,000 watches, much smaller than the number deduced from the serial numbers assigned up to as high as 289,000.

NOTE: The above historical data and estimated production figures are based on data included in the new NAWCC book **MARION, A History of the United States Watch Company,** by William Muir and Bernard Kraus. This definitive work is available from NAWCC, Inc., 514 Poplar St., Columbia, PA. (Courtesy, Gene Fuller, MARION book editor.) This book is recommended for your library.

EMPIRE CITY W. CO. & EQUIVALENT U.S.W. CO. GRADES

Empire City W. Co. .... United States W. Co.

Empire City W. Co.	United States W. Co.
W. S. Wyse	A. H. Wallis
L. W. Frost	Henry Randel
Cyrus H. Loutrel	Wm. Alexander
J. L. Ogden	S. M. Beard
E. F. C. Young	John W. Lewis
D. C. Wilcox	George Channing
Henry Harper	Asa Fuller
Jesse A. Dodd	Edwin Rollo
E. C. Hine	J. W. Deacon
New York Belle	A. J. Wood
The Champion	G. A. Read
Black Diamond	Young America

NOTE: Courtesy Gene Fuller, NAWCC "MARION" book editor.

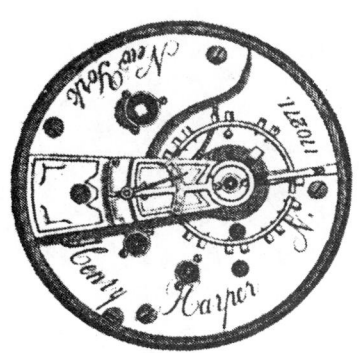

Empire City W. Co., Henry Harper, note: movement does not have **Butterfly Cut-out**.

United States Watch Co. movement, 18 size, 19 jewels, gold jewel settings, key wind. Their highest grade watch.

United States Watch Co., Henry Randel, 15 jewels, KWKS, FROSTED plates, S.# 24,944

MARION
18 SIZE
(All with Butterfly Cut-out Except for 3/4 Plate)

Grade or Name – Description	Avg	Ex-Fn	Mint
Wm. Alexander, 15J, NI, KW, HC .... ★	$225	$295	$550
Wm. Alexander, 15J, NI, KW, OF .... ★	195	295	500
Wm. Alexander, 15J, NI, SW, OF .... ★	195	295	500
Frederic Atherton & Co., 15J, SW, gilded	275	325	500
Frederic Atherton & Co., 17J, KW, gilded, HC	325	375	600
Frederic Atherton & Co., 17J, KW, gilded, OF	275	350	500
Frederic Atherton & Co., 17J, SW, gilded, HC	275	350	500
Frederic Atherton & Co., 17J, SW, gilded, OF	250	325	475

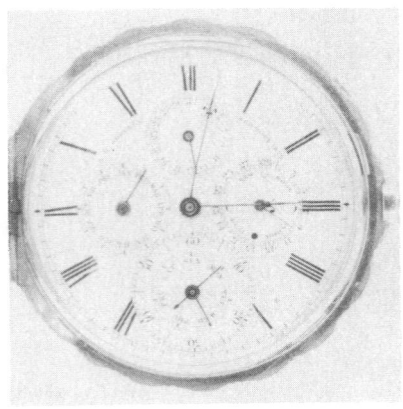

U.S. Watch Co., dial and movement, 18 size, 20 jewels, hunting case, 3/4 plate, engraved on movement "N.D. Godfrey," serial number 72,042. Painted on the dial "New York 1873." The dial consists of day-date-month and moon phases.

NOTE: The **PIN** or **NAIL** set feature is considered more desirable & will bring a **HIGHER** price.

Grade or Name – Description	Avg	Ex-Fn	Mint
Frederic Atherton & Co., 19J, SW, gilded, ... ★★	$600	$700	$1,200
Frederic Atherton & Co., 19J, KW, gilded .... ★★	650	750	1,300
BC&M R.R., 11J, KW... ★★★★	1,800	2,000	4,000
BC&M R.R., 15J, gilded, KW .... ★★★★	1,800	2,000	4,000
S. M. Beard, 15J, KW, NI, OF .... ★	175	250	400
S. M. Beard, 15J, SW, NI, OF .... ★	175	250	400
S. M. Beard, 15J, SW or KW, HC .... ★	250	295	450
Centennial Phil., 11-15J, SW or KW, NI .... ★★★★	2,400	3,000	5,000
George Channing, 15J, KW, NI	225	295	400
George Channing, 15J, KW, gilded	225	295	400
George Channing, 15J, KW, NI, 3/4 Plate	250	350	500
George Channing, 17J, KW, NI	250	350	475
J. W. Deacon, 11-13J, KW, gilded...............................	150	225	300
J. W. Deacon, 15J, KW, gilded	175	250	400
J. W. Deacon, 11-15J, KW, 3/4 Plate........................... ★	300	350	650
Empire City Watch Co., 11J, SW, **NO butterfly cut-out.** ★★★★	1,400	1,800	3,300
Empire City Watch Co., 15-19J, KW, **butterfly cut-out**... ★★★★	2,400	3,000	5,500
Empire Combination Timer, 11J, FULL, time & distance on dial.. ★★★	1,600	2,000	4,000
Empire Combination Timer, 15J, 3/4, time & distance on dial.. ★★★	1,500	1,800	3,800
Fellows, 15J, NI, KW .... ★	400	450	700
Benjamin Franklin, 15J, KW...................................... ★★	400	450	800
Asa Fuller, 7-11J, gilded, KW....................................	150	225	350
Asa Fuller, 15J, gilded, KW	150	225	350
Asa Fuller, 15J, gilded, KW, 3/4 Plate....................... ★★	300	325	500
N. D. Godfrey, 20J, NI, 3/4 plate, day date month, moon phases, c. 1873, HC, 18K .... ★★★★	5,000	6,000	13,000
John W. Lewis, 15J, NI, KW .... ★	150	200	375
John W. Lewis, 15J, NI, SW .... ★	250	300	500

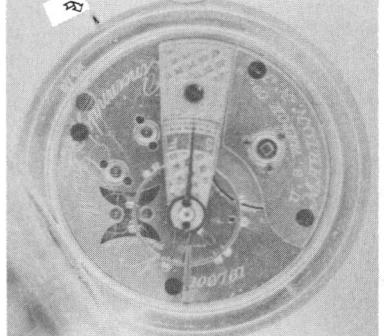

Edwin Rollo, 18 size, 15 jewels, gilded, key wind & set, note butterfly cut-out, serial number 110,214.

Marion Watch Co. personalized Watch, 18 size, about 15J., pin set, note butterfly cut-out, serial # 106,761.

🕐 Watches listed in this book are priced at the collectable Trade Show level, as **complete** watches having an original 14k gold-filled case and *Key Wind* with silver, an original white enamel single sunk dial, and with the entire original movement in good working order with no repairs needed.

🕐 Pricing in this Guide are fair market price for **COMPLETE** watches which are reflected from the "**NAWCC**" National and regional shows.

🕐 A collector should expect to pay modestly higher prices at local shops.

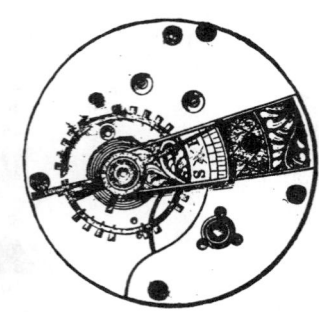

Empire City Watch Co. on movement, U.S. Marion Watch Co. on dial, 18 size, 15 jewels, note **NO butterfly cut-out** on this model. **Second Quality**

United States Watch Co., 18 size, 19 jewels, gold jewel settings, key wind & pin set, serial number 24,054.

Grade or Name – Description	Avg	Ex-Fn	Mint
John W. Lewis, 15J, NI, 3/4 Plate ★	$295	$350	$500
Marion Watch Co., 11J, KW, gilded ★	150	250	400
Marion Watch Co., 15J, KW, gilded ★	150	250	400
Marion Watch Co., 15J, SW, gilded, 3/4 Plate ★ ★	295	350	500
Marion Watch Co., 17-19J, KW, gilded ★	400	425	650
N.J. R.R.&T. Co., 15J, gilded, KW ★ ★ ★	1,200	1,400	2,600
Newspaper Special Order, 11-15J, gilded, SW or KW ★	400	500	900
North Star, 7J, KW, NI case ★	350	450	550
North Star, 7J, SW, KS ★	295	375	500
North Star, 7J, 3/4 Plate ★	425	475	600
Pennsylvania R.R., 15J, NI, KW, HC ★ ★ ★ ★	2,400	3,000	5,400
Personalized Watches, 7-11J, KW, 3/4 Plate ★	250	325	500
Personalized Watches, 11J, KW, gilded ★	250	325	500
Personalized Watches, 15J, KW, gilded ★	250	325	500
Personalized Watches, 15J, KW, NI ★	275	325	500
Personalized Watches, 15J, KW, 3/4 Plate ★	300	350	500
Personalized Watches, 19J, KW, Full Plate ★	400	450	800
Henry Randel, 15J, KW, NI ★	250	295	450
Henry Randel, 15J, KW, **frosted plates** ★	295	375	550
Henry Randel, 15J, SW, NI ★	250	300	450
Henry Randel, 15J, 3/4 Plate ★	295	350	600
Henry Randel, 17J, KW, NI ★	275	325	600
G. A. Read, 7J, gilded, KW	135	225	400
G. A. Read, 7J, 3/4 Plate	175	250	425
Edwin Rollo, 11J, KW, gilded	150	195	400
Edwin Rollo, 15J, KW, gilded	150	195	400
Edwin Rollo, 15J, SW, gilded	150	195	400
Edwin Rollo, 15J, 3/4 Plate ★	225	350	475
Royal Gold, 11J, KW ★	400	500	800
Royal Gold, 15J, KW ★	450	550	900
Royal Gold, 15J, 3/4 Plate ★ ★	500	600	1,100

🕐 A collector should expect to pay modestly higher prices at local shops.

🕐 Watches listed in this book are priced at the collectable Trade Show level, as **complete** watches having an original 14k gold-filled case and *Key Wind* with silver, an original white enamel single sunk dial, and with the entire original movement in good working order with no repairs needed.

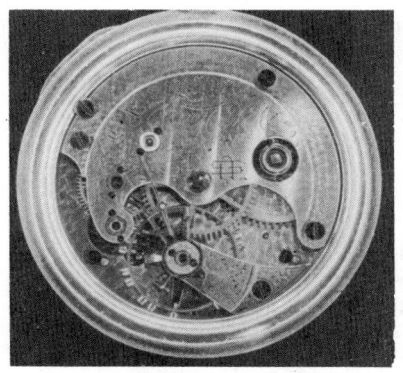 

A.H. Wallis on movement, Empire City Watch Co. on dial, 18 size, 19 jewels, three-quarter plate, hunting. This combination timer has listed on the dial, 16 cities showing the time of day and distance in comparison with New York City, serial number 54,409.

Grade or Name – Description		Avg	Ex-Fn	Mint
Rural New York, 15J, gilded	★	$400	$475	$775
Fayette Stratton, 11J, gilded	★	225	275	425
Fayette Stratton, 15J, KW, gilded	★	250	325	425
Fayette Stratton, 15J, SW, gilded	★	250	325	400
Fayette Stratton, 17J, KW, gilded	★	275	350	500
Fayette Stratton, 17J, SW, gilded	★	300	350	500
Union Pacific R.R., 15J, KW, gilded	★★★	2,000	2,400	4,000
United States Watch Co., 15J, NI, KW	★	700	800	1,000
United States Watch Co., 15J, NI, SW	★	800	850	1,200
United States Watch Co., 15J, 3/4 Plate, NI	★	800	850	1,200
United States Watch Co., 15J, 3/4 Plate, gilded	★	800	850	1,200
United States Watch Co., 19J, GJS, Adj.5P, 18K HC, dial mvt. & case all marked, Pin Set, SW	★★★	3,500	4,000	7,000
United States Watch Co., 19J, NI, KW	★★	1,200	1,500	2,400
United States Watch Co., 19J, NI, SW	★★	1,350	1,650	2,500
A. H. Wallis, 15J, KW, NI	★	250	295	400
A. H. Wallis, 15J, SW, NI	★	250	295	400
A. H. Wallis, 17J, KW, NI	★	275	325	450
A. H. Wallis, 17J, SW, NI	★	295	350	450
A. H. Wallis, 19J, KW, NI	★★★	450	500	850
A. H. Wallis, 19J, SW, NI	★★★	450	500	850
D. C. Wilcox, 15J, SW, **NO** butterfly cut-out	★	295	400	700
I. H. Wright, 11J, KW, gilded	★	225	275	400
I. H. Wright, 15J, KW, gilded	★	225	275	400

🕐 A collector should expect to pay modestly higher prices at local shops.

🕐 Watches listed in this book are priced at the collectable Trade Show level, as **complete** watches having an original 14k gold-filled case and *Key Wind* with silver, an original white enamel single sunk dial, and with the entire original movement in good working order with no repairs needed.

🕐 Some grades are not included. Their values can be determined by comparing with **similar** age, size, metal content, style, models and grades listed.

🕐 Pricing in this Guide are fair market price for **COMPLETE** watches which are reflected from the "**NAWCC**" National and regional shows.

16 SIZE
1/4 Plate

Grade or Name – Description		Avg	Ex-Fn	Mint
S. M. Beard, 15J, NI, KW,	★ ★ ★	$400	$450	$600
Marion Watch Co., 11-15J., KW	★ ★ ★	400	450	600
John W. Lewis, 15J, NI, KW	★ ★ ★	400	450	600
Personalized Watches, 15J, NI, SW	★ ★ ★	400	450	600
Edwin Rollo, 15J, KW	★ ★ ★	400	450	600
United States Watch Co., 15J, NI, SW	★ ★ ★	700	800	1,600
A. H. Wallis, 19J, NI, SW,	★ ★ ★	700	800	1,600

Note: 16S, 1/4 plate are the scarcest of the U.S.W.Co.–Marion watches.

Asa Fuller, 16 size, 15 jewels, stem wind, one-quarter plate, serial number 280,018. Note: 3 screws on barrel bridge.

United States Watch Co., 14 size, 15 jewels, three-quarter plate, engraved on movement "Royal Gold American Watch, New York, Extra Jeweled."

14 SIZE
3/4 Plate

Grade or Name – Description		Avg	Ex-Fn	Mint
Centennial Phil., 11J, KW, gilded	★ ★ ★ ★	$800	$1,000	$2,000
J. W. Deacon, 11J,	★ ★	250	325	400
Asa Fuller, 15J,	★ ★	295	375	500
John W. Lewis, 15J, NI	★ ★	295	375	500
Marion Watch Co., 15J., KW	★	250	325	450
North Star, 15J,	★ ★	295	325	500
Personalized Watches, 7-11J,	★ ★	375	425	550
Edwin Rollo, 15J,	★	325	375	500
Royal Gold, 15J,	★	375	450	700
Young America, 7J, gilded	★	250	300	500

🕐 A collector should expect to pay modestly higher prices at local shops.

🕐 Watches listed in this book are priced at the collectable Trade Show level, as **complete** watches having an original 14k gold-filled case and *Key Wind* with silver, an original white enamel single sunk dial, and with the entire original movement in good working order with no repairs needed.

🕐 Some grades are not included. Their values can be determined by comparing with **similar** age, size, metal content, style, models and grades listed.

10 SIZE
1/4 Plate

Grade or Name – Description	Avg	Ex-Fn	Mint
Wm. Alexander, 15J, KW, NI	$125	$150	$375
S. M. Beard, 15J, KW, NI, 1/4 Plate	125	150	375
Empire City Watch Co., 15J, KW .... ★★	400	550	950
Chas. G. Knapp, 15J, **Swiss**, 1/4 Plate, KW	100	150	275
Marion Watch Co., 11-15J., 1/4 Plate	125	150	350
Personalized Watches, 11-15J, 1/4 Plate	195	250	350
R. F. Pratt, 15J, **Swiss**, 1/4 Plate, KW	95	150	250
Edwin Rollo, 11-15J, 1/4 Plate...	150	175	400
A. H. Wallis, 17-19J, KW, 1/4 Plate .... ★	195	275	450
A. J. Wood, 15J, 1/4 Plate, KW .... ★★	295	350	500
I. H. Wright, 19J, **Swiss**, NI, Plate, KW .... ★★	250	295	475

S. M. Beard, 10 size, 15 jewels, key wind, quarter plate, serial number 248,407. Note: 2 screws on barrel bridge.

Chas. G. Knapp, 10 size, 15 jewels, Swiss, quarter plate, key wind.

U. S. WATCH CO.
OF WALTHAM
Waltham, Massachusetts
1884-85 - 1905

The business was started as the Waltham Watch Tool Co. in 1879. It was organized as the United States Watch Co. in about 1884-85. The first watches were 16S, 3/4 plate pillar movement in three grades. They had a very wide mainspring barrel (the top was thinner than most) which was wedged up in the center to make room for the balance wheel. These watches are called dome watches and are hard to find. The fork was made of an aluminum alloy with a circular slot and a square ruby pin. The balance was gold at first, as was the movement which was a slow train, but the expansion balance was changed when they went to a quick train. The movement required a special case which proved unpopular. By 1887, some 3,000 watches had been made. A new model was then produced, a 16S movement that would fit a standard case. These movements were quick train expansion balance with standard type lever and 3/4 plate pillar movement. This company reached a top production of 10 watches a day for a **very short period.** The company was sold to the E. Howard Watch Co. (Keystone) in 1903. The United States Watch Co. produced watches with serial number as high as 890,000 so **possible** total is 890,000. Its top grade watch movement was the **"The President."**

🕐 Pricing in this Guide are fair market price for **COMPLETE** watches which are reflected from the "<u>**NAWCC**</u>" National and regional shows.

U. S. WATCH CO. OF WALTHAM
ESTIMATED SERIAL NUMBERS AND PRODUCTION DATES

Date	Serial No.	Date	Serial No.
1887	3,000	1896	300,000
1888	6,500	1897	350,000
1889	10,000	1898	400,000
1890	30,000	1899	500,000
1891	60,000	1900	600,000
1892	90,000	1901	700,000
1893	150,000	1902	750,000
1894	200,000	1903	800,000
1895	250,000		

U.S. Watch Co. of Waltham, **The President** on dial & movement,18 size,17J, hunting case, marked Adjusted, serial # 150,020, produced in late 1893 or early 1894.

U.S. Watch Co. of Waltham, **The President**, 18 size, 17 jewels, open face, 2-tone, adj., note regulator, serial number 150,350. Note: A.C. Roebuck 17J. similar to President.

18 SIZE

Grade or Name – Description	Avg	Ex-Fn	Mint
A.C. Robuck 17J., Adjusted Special (similar to The President) ★ ★	$375	$450	$775
Express Train, 15J, ADJ, OF	195	295	450
Express Train, 15J, ADJ, HC	225	350	575
The President, 17J, GJS, Adj.6P, DR, NI, DMK, HC ★ ★ ★	375	450	775
The President, 17J, GJS, Adj.6P, DR, NI, DMK, OF ★ ★	350	400	700
The President, 21J, GJS, Adj.6P, DR, NI, DMK, OF ★ ★ ★ ★ ★	800	900	1,400
The President, 21J, GJS, Adj.6P, DR, 14K ★ ★ ★ ★	1,000	1,200	1,800

Note: A Feb. 1st; 1894 ad states the only 18 size **Double Roller**, Lever set movement on the market & guarantees that this (The President) movement will vary less than SIX-SECONDS a Month.

Washington Square, 15J, HC ★	$195	$225	$350

Generic, **nameless** or unmarked grades for watch movements are listed under the Company name or initials of the Company, etc. by size, jewel count and description.

U. S. Watch Co., 15J, OF, **2-tone, stem attached** ★	$295	$350	$550
U. S. Watch Co., 39 (HC) & 79 (OF), 17J, GJS, ADJ, NI, DMK, Adj.5P, BRG	95	175	225
U. S. Watch Co., 40 (HC) & 80 (OF), 17J, GJS	95	175	225
U. S. Watch Co., 48 (HC) & 88 (OF), 7J, gilded, FULL	95	175	225
U. S. Watch Co., 48 (HC) & 88 (OF), 7J, gilded, FULL, Silveroid	55	85	150
U. S. Watch Co., 52 (HC)	90	125	195
U. S. Watch Co., 92 (OF), 17J, Silveroid	60	95	125

⊕ Some grades are not included. Their values can be determined by comparing with **similar** age, size, metal content, style, models and grades listed.

Grade or Name – Description	Avg	Ex-Fn	Mint
U. S. Watch Co., 52 (HC) & 92 (OF), 17J	$70	$90	$195
U. S. Watch Co., 53 (HC) & 93 (OF), 15J, NI, FULL, DMK	70	90	195
U. S. Watch Co., 54 (HC) & 94 (OF), 15J	70	90	195
U. S. Watch Co., 56 (HC) & 96 (OF), 11J	70	90	195
U. S. Watch Co., 57 (HC) & 97 (OF), 15J	70	90	195
U. S. Watch Co., 58 (HC) & 98 (OF), 11J, NI, FULL, DMK	70	90	195

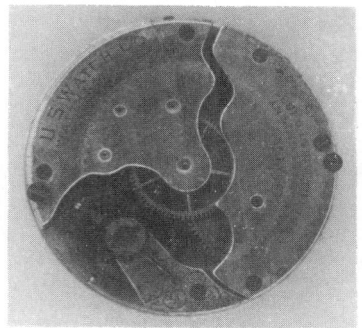

U.S. Watch Co. of Waltham, 16 size, 7 jewels, gilded, note **raised dome** on center of movement, engraved on movement "Chas. V. Woerd's Patents," serial number 3,564.

U.S. Watch Co. of Waltham, 16 size, 7 jewels, "A New Watch Company At Waltham, Est'd 1885" on movement, serial number 770,771.

16 SIZE

Grade or Name – Description	Avg	Ex-Fn	Mint
Dome plate style movement, 7J, gilded	$95	$150	$295
U. S. Watch Co., 103, 17J, NI, 3/4, ADJ	60	80	150
U. S. Watch Co., 104, 17J, NI, 3/4	60	80	150
U. S. Watch Co., 104, 17J, NI, 3/4, Silveroid	60	80	150
U. S. Watch Co., 105, 15J, NI, 3/4, HC	75	95	195
U. S. Watch Co., 105, 15J, NI, 3/4, OF	60	80	150
U. S. Watch Co., 105, 15J, NI, 3/4, Silveroid	60	80	150
U. S. Watch Co., 106, 15J, gilded, 3/4, Silveroid	60	80	150
U. S. Watch Co., 106, 15J, gilded, 3/4	60	80	150
U. S. Watch Co., 108, 11J, gilded, 3/4	60	80	150
U. S. Watch Co., 109, 7J, NI, 3/4	60	80	150
U. S. Watch Co., 110, 7J, 3/4, HC	75	95	195
U. S. Watch Co., 110, 7J, 3/4, OF	60	80	150

Note: Add $20 - $40 to value of above watches in hunting case.

🕐 Generic, **nameless** or **unmarked** grades for watch movements are listed under the Company name or initials of the Company, etc. by size, jewel count and description.

🕐 Watches listed in this book are priced at the collectable Trade Show level, as complete watches having an original 14k gold-filled case and Key Wind with silver, an original white enamel single sunk dial, and with the entire original movement in good working order with no repairs needed.

🕐 Pricing in this Guide are fair market price for **COMPLETE** watches which are reflected from the "**NAWCC**" National and regional shows.

U.S. Watch Co., 16 size, 15 jewels, three-quarter plate.

6 SIZE

Grade or Name – Description	Avg	Ex-Fn	Mint
U. S. Watch Co., 60, 17J, GJS, NI, 3/4, Adj.3P	$30	$40	$150
U. S. Watch Co., 60, 17J, GJS, NI, 3/4, Adj.3P, **HC, 14K**	200	275	500
U. S. Watch Co., 62, 15J, NI, 3/4	40	55	95
U. S. Watch Co., 63, 15J, gilded	40	55	95
U. S. Watch Co., 64, 11J, NI	40	55	95
U. S. Watch Co., 65, 11J, gilded	40	55	65
U. S. Watch Co., 66, 7J, gilded	40	55	65
U. S. Watch Co., 66, 7-11J, NI, 3/4	40	55	95
U. S. Watch Co., 68, 16J, GJS, NI, 3/4	45	60	125
U. S. Watch Co., 69, 7J, NI, HC	45	60	150
U. S. Watch Co., 69, 7J, NI, OF	40	55	95

Grade 64, 6 size, 11 jewels

U.S. Watch Co. of Waltham, 0 size, 7 jewels, serial number 808,231. Engraved on movement United States Watch Co. New York U.S.A., 808,231.

0 SIZE

Grade or Name – Description	Avg	Ex-Fn	Mint
Betsy Ross, HC, GF case	$95	$125	$295
U. S. Watch Co., 15J, HC, GF case	70	90	195
U. S. Watch Co., 7-11J, HC, GF case	70	90	195

THE WASHINGTON WATCH CO.
Washington, D. C.
1872 - 1874

NOTE: **First** check your watch for a **grade** name as Liberty Bells, Potomac, Lafayette, Army & Navy, Senate, Monroe, and others which are listed under **Illinois** section. Washington Watch Co. was Montgomery Ward's private label and made by Illinois Watch Co.

J. P. Hopkins, though better known as the inventor of the Auburndale Rotary Watch, was also connected with the Washington Watch Co., they may have produced about 50 watches. They were 18S, key wind, 3/4 plate and had duplex escapements. Before Hopkins came to Washington Watch Co. he had handmade about six fine watches. The company had a total production of 45 movements with duplex escapements.

Grade or Name – Description		Avg	Ex-Fn	Mint
18S, 15J, 3/4, KW, KS..★★★★		$5,000	$6,000	$13,000

WATERBURY WATCH CO.
Waterbury, Connecticut
1880 - 1898

The Waterbury Watch Co. was formed in 1880, and D. A. A. Buck designed the first watch. The **rotary** long wind watches were simple with about 54 to 58 parts. The rotary **long wind** takes about **120** to **140** turns of the crown to fully wind. It had a two-wheel train rather than the standard four-wheel train. The Waterbury rotary long wind movement revolved once every hour and has a duplex escapement. The dials were made of paper, and the watch was priced at $3.50 to $4.00. Some of these dollar type watches were used as give aways (not long wind). The Waterbury Watch Co. was reorganized and renamed the New England Watch Company in 1898. Ingersoll bought the New England Watch Co. in 1914. The Waterbury Watch Co. took over Ingersoll in 1922, and became part of the US Time Corp. in 1944 and is now the TIMEX Corp.

WATERBURY WATCH CO.

Waterbury, Conn., Nov. 1, 1881.

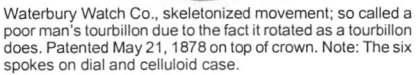

Waterbury Watch Co., skeletonized movement; so called a poor man's tourbillon due to the fact it rotated as a tourbillon does. Patented May 21, 1878 on top of crown. Note: The six spokes on dial and celluloid case.

Waterbury Watch Co., rotary long wind movement. Note **six** spokes on dial.

CHRONOLOGY OF THE DEVELOPMENT OF THE WATERBURY WATCH CO.:

Waterbury Watch Co., Waterbury, Conn. 1880-1898
re-named New England Watch Co 1898-1912
Purchased Ingersoll 1922
Became U. S. Time Corp. (maker of Timex) 1944

Waterbury Watch Co., ROTARY long wind movement, note **Three** spokes.

Waterbury Watch Co., ROTARY Long wind movement, note **four** spokes.

18 TO 16 SIZES

Grade or Name – Description	Avg	Ex-Fn	Mint
Series A, **rotary long wind**, skeletonized, 3 spokes .... ★ ★ ★	$400	$450	$1,000
Series A, **rotary long wind**, skeletonized, 4 spokes .... ★ ★ ★	400	450	1,000
Series A, **rotary long wind**, skeletonized, 6 spokes .... ★	300	350	700
Series A, **rotary long wind, skeletonized**, 6 spokes, celluloid case .... ★ ★ ★	400	450	900
Series B, **rotary long wind** .... ★	150	225	295
Series C or E, **rotary long wind** .... ★	150	225	295
Series C or E, **rotary long wind** (with advertising embossed on backs) .... ★	195	225	400
Series D, patented Feb. 5, 1884 engraved on Mvt. (4 times) .... ★	295	350	500

Waterbury Watch Co. "ROTARY" movement, Series C.

Series L, Waterbury W. Co. Duplex Escapement, about 16 size.

Series I, The Trump, about 18 size, no jewels, pin lever escapement.

Series T, Oxford Duplex Escapement, about 18 size, no jewels.

18 to 0 Size

Grade or Name – Description	Avg	Ex-Fn	Mint
Series F, Duplex escapement	$60	$75	$150
Series G, 3/4 lever escapement ★	150	225	300
Series H, Columbian, Duplex ★★	295	350	600
Series I, Trump, Duplex,	50	75	125
Series I, Trump, 3/4	50	75	125
Series J, Americus, Duplex	50	75	125
Series K, Charles Benedict, Duplex	125	150	350
Series L, Waterbury W. Co., Duplex	85	100	125
Series N, Addison, Duplex	65	70	110
Series P, Rugby, Duplex	60	70	150
Series R, Tuxedo, Duplex	60	70	125
Series S, Elfin	60	70	85
Series T, Oxford, Duplex	60	70	95
Series W, Addison	60	70	135
Series Z	60	70	95
Free Press Watch, Series E ★	195	250	500
Old Honesty, Series C, rotary longwind ★	250	300	575
Oxford,	40	60	95
The Trump	40	60	90
Waterbury W. Co., 7J, 3/4, low Serial No.	295	375	500
18size, Waterbury W. Co., KW, LS. ★	350	425	600

NOTE: Dollar -watches must be in **Running** condition to bring these prices.

Old Honesty, Series C, rotary longwind.

Waterbury Watch Co. **"ROTARY"** movement

E. N. WELCH MFG. CO.
Bristol, Connecticut
1834 - 1897

Elisha Welch founded this company about 1834. His company failed in 1897, and the Sessions Clock Co. took over the business in 1903. E. N. Welch Mfg. Co. produced the large watch which was displayed at the Chicago Exposition in 1893. This watch depicted the landing of Columbus on the back of the case.

E.N. Welch Mfg. Co., 36 size, back wind & set, made for the Chicago Exposition in 1893. Die debossed back depicting the landing of Columbus in America, Oct, 12th, 1492.

Grade or Name – Description	Avg	Ex-Fn	Mint
36S, Columbus Exhibition watch ....★	$375	$450	$750

WESTCLOX
United Clock Co. – Western Clock Mfg. Co.– General Time Corp.
Athens, Georgia
1899 - Present

The first Westclox pocket watch was made about 1899; however, the Westclox name did not appear on their watches until 1906. In 1903 they were making 100 watches a day, and in 1920 production was at 15,000 per day. This company is still in business in Athens, Georgia.

Grade or Name – Description	Avg	Ex-Fn	Mint
M#1, SW, push to set, GRO	$50	$65	$135
M#2, SW, back set, GRO	50	60	95
18S, Westclox M#4, OF, GRO	50	60	75
1910 Models to 1920, GRO	35	45	60
Anniversary	35	45	60
Antique	20	30	45
Boy Proof	60	70	90
Bingo	30	40	55
Bulls Eye (several models)	15	20	25
Campus	15	20	25
Celluloid case, 70mm	30	35	45
Coronado	15	20	25
Country Gentleman	40	50	70

Boy Proof Model, about 16 size, designed to be tamper proof.

Westclox movement, stem wind, back set.

Grade or Name – Description	Avg	Ex-Fn	Mint
Dax (many models)	$10	$15	$20
Dewey	10	15	30
Elite	25	30	40
Everbrite (several models)	30	45	65
Explorer	150	195	375
Farm Bureau	65	75	95
Glo Ben	65	75	95
Glory Be	20	25	35
Johnny Zero (several models)	100	150	250
Ideal	30	35	45
Lighted Dial	25	30	40
Magnetic	20	25	30
Major	25	30	40
Man Time	15	20	25
Mark IV	35	45	55
Mascot	20	25	30
Maxim	30	40	50

Zep, about 16 size with radiant numbers and hands, c. 1929.

Explorer, back of case and dial, "Wings Over The Pole, The Explorer" on back of case.

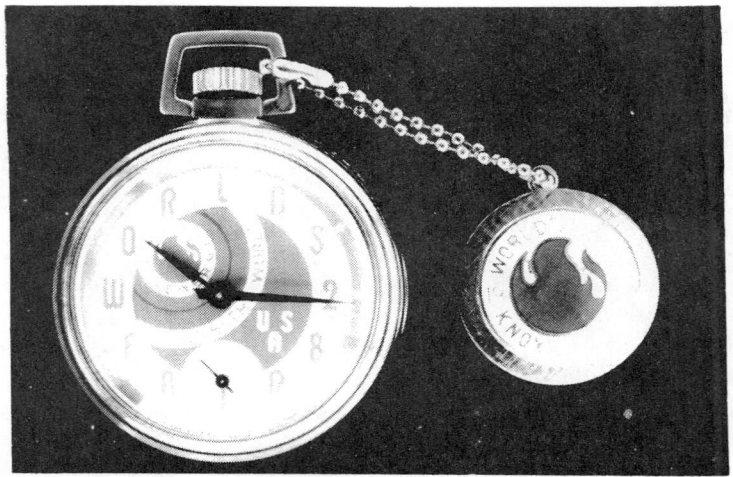

World's Fair watch & fob, (1982 -Knoxville Tn.){Wagner Time Inc.}, total production for watch 4,200 and 200 for the FOB, Ca. 1982 .

Grade or Name – Description	Avg	Ex-Fn	Mint
Military Style, 24 hour	$65	$75	$95
Monitor	15	20	25
Mustang	40	45	60
NAWCC, TOTAL PRODUCTION = 1,000 ★★	65	85	125
above wth box	85	95	175
Panther	45	50	60
Pocket Ben (many models)	10	15	30
Ruby	25	30	45
Scepter	20	25	40
Scotty (several models)	15	20	30
Silogram	15	20	30
Smile	25	30	45
Solo	15	20	30
St. Regis	20	25	35
Sun Mark	30	35	40
Team Mate (various major league teams)	25	35	50
Tele Time	25	30	45
Texan	35	45	65
The Airplane	45	50	65
The American, **back SET**	50	80	180
The Conductor	45	55	85
Tiny Tim	150	195	295
Trail Blazer	50	95	250
Uncle Sam	40	45	60
Victor	80	95	130
Vote	25	30	45
Westclox	15	20	25
World's Fair (1982 -Knoxville Tn.){Wagner Time Inc.}	60	75	95
above wth box & (FOB TOTAL PRODUCTION=200) . ★★	95	150	300
Zep, (Zepplin)	200	225	500
Zodiak Time	35	40	50

⊕ Pricing in this Guide are fair market price for **COMPLETE** watches which are reflected from the "**NAWCC**" National and regional shows.

WESTERN WATCH CO.

Chicago, Illinois
1880

Albert Trotter purchased the unfinished watches from the California Watch Co. Mr. Trotter finished and sold those watches. Later he moved to Chicago and, with Paul Cornell and others, formed the Western Watch Company. Very few watches were completed by the Western Watch Co.

Grade or Name – Description		Avg	Ex-Fn	Mint
Western Watch Co., 18S, FULL .... ★★★★		$2,000	$2,500	$4,400

Western Watch Co. movement, 18 size, 15 jewels, key wind & set.

WICHITA WATCH CO.

Wichita, Kansas
July, 1887 - 1888

This company completed construction of their factory in Wichita, Kansas in June 1888, and only a half dozen watches were produced during the brief period the company was in operation. The president was J. R. Snively. These watches are 18S, 1/2 to 3/4 plate, adjusted, 15 jewels.

Grade or Name – Description		Avg	Ex-Fn	Mint
18S, 15J, 3/4 plate, ADJ .... ★★★★		$3,500	$4,500	$7,500

🕐 Watches listed in this book are priced at the collectable trade show level, as **complete** watches having an original 14k gold-filled case and *Key Wind* with silver, an original white enamel single sunk dial, and with the entire original movement in good working order with no repairs needed.

🕐 Pricing in this Guide are fair market price for **COMPLETE** watches which are reflected from the "<u>NAWCC</u>" National and regional shows.

🕐 A collector should expect to pay modestly higher prices at local shops.

COMIC AND CHARACTER WATCHES

When discussing the topic of watches and someone mentions Comic Character Watches, we immediately picture a watch with Mickey Mouse. Isn't Mickey Mouse the most famous of all watches in the world? Before Mickey appeared in the 1930's there were a handful of lesser known comic watches with characters like Skeezix, Smitty and Buster Brown, but it was the Mickey Mouse Watch that paved the way for all other comic character watches. As a collaboration between Walt Disney (the creator of Mickey Mouse) and Robert Ingersoll and his brother the founders of the Ingersoll-Waterbury Watch Company, the Mickey Mouse Watch was one of this century's greatest marketing concepts. In a two year period Ingersoll had sold nearly 2.5 million Mickey Mouse wrist and pocket watches. Throughout the 1930's they also introduced other watches with Disney characters such as Big Bad Wolf in 1934, as well as, the Donald Duck wrist watch. The Donald Duck pocket watch was produced several years later in 1939. The Mickey Lapel and Mickey Deluxe Wrist were produced in the late 1930's.

Ingersoll dominated the character watch market in the early 1930's due to the incredible popularity of the Disney characters, however by the mid 1930's other companies mainly Ingraham and New Haven secured the rights to other popular characters. Throughout the 1930's kids fell in love with these watches featuring their favorite comic character or hero, such as, Popeye, Superman, Buck Rogers, Orphan Annie, Dick Tracy and The Lone Ranger. There was also a couple of other well known characters, Betty Boop and Cowboy Tom Mix produced, but for some reason these watches did not become popular like all the others, so very small quantities were produced.

During World War II production of comic watches ceased, but after the war comic watches came back stronger than ever. Once again Disney was the overall leader. The Ingersoll name only appeared on some watches to keep the trade name still familiar, as Ingersoll was sold to U.S. Time Watch Co.

The late 1940's was very good to the character watch market and proof being the many character watches produced as the Twentieth Birthday Series for Mickey in 1948 that included with Mickey, Donald Duck, Pinocchio, Pluto, Bambi, Joe Carioca, Jiminy Cricket, Bongo Bear and Daisy Duck. Other watches from this time include Porky Pig, Puss-N-Boots, Joe Palooka, Gene Autry, Captain and Mary Marvel and others featuring characters of the comic and cartoons, space and western heroes.

The early to mid 1950's was also a vibrant time for character watch production with more Disney characters, western heroes and comic characters than ever before, but by 1958 manufacturing of character watches had almost completely stopped as manufacturing costs went up, popularity of some characters faded and many other circumstances led to a complete stop of any of these watches until the late 1960's. The watches were never the same again.

In the 1970's Comic Character Watch once again made it's come back with the Bradley Watch Company (Elgin W. Co.) leading the way just as Ingersoll did in the first years of comic watches. Today there are hundreds of character watches to choose from, Disney Super Hero movie characters like E.T., and Roger Rabbit and a wealth of others, but today's fascination is not just with the new but with the old as we see in the re-issue of the original Mickey watches. There is a growing awareness and appreciation for all the originals. It is a very unusual attraction that draws people to love and collect the character watches of the past. Collectors appreciate the original boxes (that are fascinating works of art) and the face of the watch that features the character that we love. The manufacturing method of these simple pin lever movements were not the best of timekeepers, but were solidly constructed. All in all, when you put together the watches and boxes they are pieces of functional art and history that brings back memories of our youth. Something that no other kind of watch can do.

Tom Mix pocket watch on back "Always Find Time For A Good Deed / Tom Mix", & BOX inside color illo. of Tom on Tony.

Babe Ruth, by Exact Time, ca. 1948.

Betty Boop, by Ingraham, ca. 1934.

Style or Grade – Description	Avg	Ex-Fn	Mint	Mint +Box
Alice in Wonderland, WW, c. 1951, by U.S. Time $40		$50	$150	$350
Alice, Red Riding Hood, & Marjory Daw, WW,				
c. 1953, by Bradley.. 40		50	150	350
Alice in Wonderland, WW, c. 1958, by Timex 40		50	95	295
Alice in Wonderland & Mad Hatter, WW, c. 1948,				
by New Haven 65		95	195	400
All * Stars, c.1965, autograped by Mickey Mantel, Rodger Maris,				
Willie Mays, Sandy Koufax, Swiss, GREEN DIAL 125		195	295	600
All * Stars, c.1965, autograped by Mickey Mantel, Rodger Maris,				
Willie Mays, Sandy Koufax, Swiss, BLACK DIAL 95		150	250	500
Annie Oakley, WW, (Action Gun) c. 1951, by New Haven 150		195	295	500
Archie, WW, c.1970s, Swiss... 50		60	95	250
Babe Ruth, WW, c. 1948, by Exact Time, box,				
baseball, pledge card.. ★ 175		325	775	1,900
Ballerina, WW, c.1955, Ingraham, Action legs, ... 40		50	60	95
Bambi, WW, c. 1949, by U.S. Time, Birthday series.................. 95		195	350	600
Barbie, WW, c.1964, by Bradley, facing "3", ... 75		95	250	350
Barbie, WW, c.1970, by Bradley, action arms 75		95	250	295
Batman, WW, c. 1966 by Gilbert (band in shape of bat) 95		195	400	900
Batman, WW, c. 1978, by Timex.. 95		125	195	350
Betty Boop, PW, c. 1934, by Ingraham, (all original)				
(with **diedebossed back**)................................... ★ ★ ★ ★450		750	2,000	4,000
Betty Boop, WW, c.1980s, with hearts on dial & band................ 40		50	60	95
Bert & Ernie, WW, c.1970s, swiss.. 40		50	60	95
Big Bad Wolf & 3 Pigs, PW, c. 1936, by Ingersoll .... ★ 400		600	1,200	2,200
Big Bad Wolf & 3 Pigs, WW, c. 1936, by Ingersoll .... ★ 500		700	1,400	2,800
Big Bird, WW, c.1970s, Swiss, action arms, (pop up box).......... 40		50	60	95
Blondie & Dagwood, WW, c.1950s, Swiss 150		195	250	500
Bongo Bear, WW, c.1946, Ingersoll, Birthday series.................. 95		150	195	400
Boy Scout,PW, c.1937, by Ingersoll, be prepared hands 250		275	400	800
Boy Scout,WW, c.1938, by New Haven....................................... 75		85	150	295
Buck Rogers, PW, c.1935, Ingraham (lightning bolt hands)..... 350		500	1,000	2,100
Bud Man, WW, Swiss, c.1970s... 40		50	60	95
Bugs Bunny, WW, c. 1951, Swiss, (carrot shaped hands) 95		195	295	600
Bugs Bunny, WW, c. 1951, Swiss, (without carrot hands) 70		95	195	300
Bugs Bunny, WW, c. 1970, Swiss, (standing bugs) 45		50	75	150

🕐 NOTE: Beware (**COLOR COPY DIALS**) are being faked as Buck Rodgers, Babe Ruth, Hopalong Cassidy and others. ***BUYER BEWARE***

   The Complete Price Guide to Watches goal is to stimulate the orderly exchange of <u>Watches</u> between "*buyers*" and "*sellers*".

BIG BAD WOLF & 3 PIGS, + FOB INGERSOLL

BUSTER BROWN, INGERSOLL, Ca. 1925

BUGS BUNNY, EXACT TIME, Ca. 1949
3 styles of hands.

BUCK ROGERS, INGRAHAM, Ca. 1935

Ingersoll (1934)
BIG BAD WOLF & 3 PIGS

– DICK TRACY, NEW HAVEN, Ca.1948

– DICK TRACY, (six shooter action arm) Ca.1952

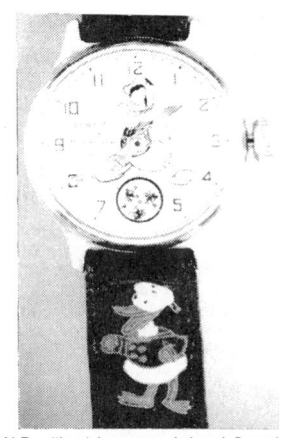

DIZZY DEAN, By Everbright W. Co.

DONALD, with mickey seconds hand, 3 grades.

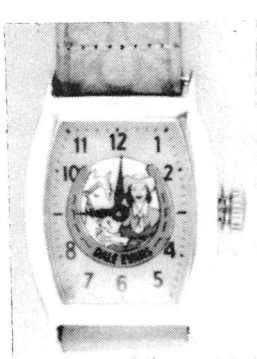

Left: DONALD DUCK, by INGERSOLL, C. 1947.   Center; Snoopy, Ca.1968   DALE EVANS, INGRAHAM

DAN DARE, INGERSOLL made in England

FROM OUTER SPACE, INGERSOLL made in England

Style or Grade – Description	Avg	Ex-Fn	Mint	Mint +Box
Buster Brown, PW, c. 1928, by Ingersoll	$125	$175	$295	$650
Buster Brown, PW, c. 1928, by Ingersoll (Buster in circle)	125	175	400	700
Buster Brown, WW, c.1930, engraved case	125	150	195	500
Buzz Corey, WW, c. 1952, by U.S. Time	75	125	195	450
Buzzy the Crow, in red hat	40	50	60	125
Captain Liberty, WW, c. 1950, by U.S.Time, multi-color band	50	80	150	450
Captain Marvel, PW, c. 1945, by New Haven	195	250	550	1,000
Captain Marvel,WW, c.1948, New Haven (small w.w.)	85	95	295	700
Captain Marvel, WW, c. 1948, by New Haven (larger size)	95	150	350	800
Captain Marvel, WW, c. 1948, Swiss made	95	195	400	850
Captain Marvel **Jr.**, c. 1948, Swiss, small size	150	295	500	1,300
Captain Midnight, PW, c. 1948, by Ingraham	250	295	500	1,300
Casper, WW, c.1970s, Swiss, action arms	40	50	60	150
Cat In The Hat, WW, c.1970s, Swiss, Action arms	40	50	60	125
Cinderella, WW, c. 1950, by Timex (slipper box)	40	45	65	350
Cinderella, WW, c. 1955, by Timex (box with imitation cel)	40	50	60	350
Cinderella, WW, c. 1958, by Timex (box with plastic statue)	25	30	60	350
Cinderella, WW, c. 1958, by Timex (box & porcelain statue)	40	50	75	350
Coca Cola, PW, c. 1948, by Ingersoll	125	150	195	400
Cowboy, WW, c.1955, by Muros, Swiss, action gun	40	50	60	150
Cowgirl, WW, c.1951, by New Haven, Action Gun	40	45	65	150
Cub Scout, WW, by Timex	40	50	60	150
Daisy Duck, WW, c. 1947, by Ingersoll (tonneau style)	95	175	250	500
Daisy Duck, WW, c. 1948, by U.S. Time (fluted bezel, birthday series)	95	175	250	500
Daisy Duck, WW, c. 1949, by U.S. Time, (grooved bezel)	95	135	175	400
Dale Evans, WW, c.1949,by Ingraham,Dale standing, (tonneau)	80	95	175	400
Dale Evans, WW, c. 1950, by Bradley (western style leather band & necklace &lucky horseshoe), tonneau style case	75	95	150	400
Dale Evans, WW, c. 1960, by Bradley (round)	40	50	65	200
Dan Dare, PW, c. 1950, by *Ingersoll Ltd. England*, action arm	195	295	400	1,100
Davy Crockett, WW, c. 1951, by Bradley (round dial)	80	95	195	600
Davy Crockett, WW, c. 1954, Action gun, (round dial)	75	95	195	500
Davy Crockett, WW, c. 1954, Liberty , (round dial)	50	90	150	400
Davy Crockett, WW, c. 1955, by U.S. Time (& powder horn)	125	195	295	700
Davy Crockett, WW, c. 1956, by Bradley (barrel shaped dial)	40	70	195	400
Dennis the Menace, WW, c. 1970, by Bradley	45	55	75	150
Dick Tracy, PW, c. 1948, by Ingersoll	250	350	500	1,400
Dick Tracy, WW, c. 1948, by New Haven (round dial)	95	110	195	500
Dick Tracy, WW, c. 1948, by New Haven (small tonneau)	75	95	195	450
Dick Tracy, WW, c. 1935, by New Haven (large)	150	225	295	600
Dick Tracy, WW, c. 1951, by New Haven (6 shooter action)	195	275	350	700
Dizzy Dean, PW, c. 1935, by Ingersoll ★★	195	350	500	1,200
Dizzy Dean, WW, c. 1938, by Everbright W.Co. ★★	195	295	500	1,200

🕐Note: To be mint condition, character watches must have **unfaded dials**, and boxes must have ALL inserts. (PW=Pocket Watch; WW=Wrist Watch)

COCA COLA, PW, Ca. 1948, by Ingersoll.

ADOLF HITLER, character wrist watch, Swiss movement "Roskopf" caliber, Ca. 1935.

Dizzy Dean, Ingersoll, ca. 1935   Donald Duck, Ingersoll, ca. 1940. Mickey on back of case.

Style or Grade – Description	Avg	Ex-Fn	Mint	Mint +Box
Donald Duck, PW, c. 1939, by Ingersoll (Mickey on back) .... ★★	$350	$500	$1,000	$2,000
Donald Duck, PW, Ward W. Co., c. 1954, Swiss made 75		150	250	500
Donald Duck, WW, c. 1935, by Ingersoll (Mickey on second hand) .... ★★ 500		800	1,200	2,500
Donald Duck, WW, c. 1942, by U.S. Time (tonneau style, silver tone) 95		150	350	800
Donald Duck, WW, c. 1948, by U.S. Time (tonneau style, gold tone) 150		195	400	850
Donald Duck, WW, c. 1948, by Ingersoll (fluted bezel, birthday series) with metal mickey bracelet 150		175	295	750
Donald Duck, WW, c. 1955, by U.S. Time, (plain bezel, pop-up in box) with leather band & Donald metal decal..... 75		95	250	550
Dopey, WW, c. 1948, by Ingersoll (fluted bezel, birthday series) 95		150	295	700
Dudley Do-Right, WW, 17J (Bullwinkle & Rocky) .... ★ 195		250	450	900
Elmer Fudd, WW, c.1970s, Swiss 55		95	150	375
Elvis, WW, c.1970s, Bradley 55		60	75	200
Flash Gordon, PW, c. 1939, by Ingersoll .... ★ 350		475	900	1,800
Flash Gordon,WW, c.1970, Precision 95		225	400	800
From Outer Space, PW, Ingersoll G.Britian, ... 95		150	225	500
Fred Flintstone, WW, (Fred on dial) 95		125	195	350
Garfield,WW, (The Cat Jumped Over The Moon) 40		45	95	195
Gene Autry, WW, c. 1939, by Ingersoll (Gene and Champion on dial) 95		195	350	800

Mickey, 32MM, Ca.1930.   – Gene Autry, (action gun), by Ingersoll, ca.1950. – Howdy with moving eyes Ca.1954.
Maybe HOAX ??

MICKEY MOUSE, by Ingersoll, original band, Ca.1933-34

MICKEY MOUSE, by Ingersoll, Ca. 1947

MICKEY MOUSE by Ingersoll, center LUGS, Ca. 1938.

MICKEY MOUSE, by Bradley, 1972 -1985

MICKEY MOUSE, made in England by Ingersoll, Ca.1934

Who's afraid of the Big Bad Wolf.
Maybe "Proto Type"

Hopalong Cassidy, U.S. Time, ca. 1950s. Maybe HOAX ?? Hopalong Cassidy, Ingersoll, ca. 1955.

Style or Grade – Description	Avg	Ex-Fn	Mint	Mint +Box
Gene Autry, WW, c. 1939, by Ingersoll	$95	$125	$295	$700
Gene Autry, WW, c. 1950, by New Haven, (action gun)	200	275	350	750
Gene Autry, WW, c. 1956, Swiss made	65	75	195	400
Girl Scouts, WW, c.1955, by Timex	40	50	60	125
Goofy, WW, c. 1972, by Helbros, 17J (watch runs backward)	400	500	750	1,400
Hoky Poky, WW, c.1950, **action arm**	35	50	75	195
Hopalong Cassidy, WW, by U.S. Time (metal watch, box with saddle)	40	70	225	500
Hopalong Cassidy, WW, by U.S. Time (plastic watch, box with saddle)	45	75	225	500
Hopalong Cassidy, WW, by U.S. Time (small watch, leather Western band, flat rectangular box)	45	55	195	450
Hopalong Cassidy, WW, by U.S. Time (regular size watch, black leather cowboy strap), flat box	45	55	195	475
Hopalong Cassidy, PW, c. 1955, by U.S. Time (rawhide strap and fob)	125	225	295	700
Hot Wheels, WW, c.1971, Bradley -Swiss, checkered hands	45	55	75	150
Hot Wheels, WW, c.1971, Bradley -Swiss, rotating bezel	35	45	65	150
Hot Wheels, WW, c.1983, Swiss, LCD QUARTZ	25	35	45	85
Howdy Doody, WW, c. 1954, Swiss (with moving eyes)	95	195	400	800
Howdy Doody, WW, c. 1954, by Ingraham (with friends)	85	150	400	750
Jamboree, PW, c. 1951, by Ingersoll, Ltd.	75	95	250	450

Robin Hood, Ca.1958 — BUD MAN Ca.1970s — Li'l Abner (waving flag)

LONE RANGER, New Haven, ca.1939

LONE RANGER, New Haven, ca.1939. 2 styles of backs

MICKEY MOUSE Ingersoll, ca.1933

MICKEY MOUSE Ingersoll, ca.1933

HOAX ??

LEFT: Mickey Mouse, Ingersoll, w/ Mickey seconds, ca.1938. **CENTER:** Mickey Mouse, 1947 Ingersoll dial in a 1938 Ingersoll case. **RIGHT:** Mickey Mouse, Ingersoll, grooved bezel NOT birthday series, ca.1948

Note: To be **mint** condition, character watches must have unfaded dials, and boxes must have all inserts. (PW=Pocket Watch; WW=Wrist Watch)

Style or Grade – Description	Avg	Ex-Fn	Mint	Mint +Box
James Bond 007, WW, c. 1972, by Gilbert............................$90		$150	$250	$700
Jeff Arnold, PW, c. 1952, by Ingersoll (English watch with moving gun)... 150		195	325	600
Jiminy Cricket, WW, c.1948, Ingersoll, Birthday series (fluted) 75		95	295	600
Jiminy Cricket, WW, c.1949, Ingersoll, Not Birthday (grooved) 75		95	295	600
Joe Carioca, WW, c. 1948, by U.S. Time (fluted bezel, birthday series)... 75		95	295	500
Joe Palooka, WW, c. 1948, by New Haven 150		195	295	600
Li'l Abner, WW, c. 1948, by New Haven (waving flag) 150		175	250	600
Li'l Abner, WW, c. 1948, by New Haven (moving mule) 150		175	250	500
Li'l Abner, WW, c. 1955, all black dial....................................... 95		135	195	350
Little King, WW, c. 1968, by Timex.. 55		125	225	425
Little Pig Fiddler, WW, c.1947, by Ingersoll............................ 125		195	295	600
Lone Ranger, PW, c. 1939, by New Haven (with fob) .... ★ 150		250	400	1,000
Lone Ranger, WW, c. 1938, by New Haven (large).................... 95		185	350	600
Lone Ranger, WW, c. 1948, New Haven, (Fluted lugs)............... 75		125	250	500
Lone Ranger, WW, c. 1950's, round case 65		95	195	400
Louie, WW, c.1940s, by Ingersoll, (Donalds nephew) 95		150	250	450
Mary Marvel, WW, c. 1948, by U.S. Time (paper box).............. 65		85	175	500
Mary Marvel, WW, c. 1948, by U.S. Time (plastic box) 65		85	125	400
Mickey Mouse, PW, c.1933, by Ingersoll, #1&2 (tall stem)...... 285		400	650	1,000
Mickey Mouse, PW, c.1936, by Ingersoll, #3 & 4(short stem).. 195		295	450	900
Mickey Mouse, PW, c. 1936, by Ingersoll, #4 lapel watch (short stem) with **rare FOB**... 195		295	700	1,200
Mickey Mouse, PW, c. 1938, by Ingersoll (Mickey decal on back)... 275		400	700	1,000
Mickey Mouse, PW, c. 1933, by Ingersoll Ltd. (English).......... 295		450	750	1,400
Mickey Mouse, PW, c. 1934, by Ingersoll (Foreign) 275		325	450	650
Mickey Mouse, PW, c.1976, by Bradley (bicentennial model) ... 40		50	95	250
Mickey Mouse, PW, c. 1974, by Bradley (no second hand)........ 40		50	60	95
Mickey Mouse, PW, c. 1974, by Bradley ("Bradley" printed at 6)... 40		50	60	95
Mickey Mouse, small 32MM PW, Ingersoll, s. steel, Ca.1930s.. 95		150	250	400

MICKEY MOUSE, Ingersoll, model no.3 on the left.   Right: Model no.4 is called a lapel watch, Very RARE FOB.

NOTE: Beware (**COLOR COPY DIALS**) are being **FAKED** as Buck Rodgers, Babe Ruth, Hopalong Cassidy and others. *BUYER BEWARE*

The Complete Price Guide to Watches goal is to stimulate the orderly ex-change of <u>Watches</u> between "*buyers*" and "*sellers*".

Style or Grade – Description	Avg	Ex-Fn	Mint	Mint +Box
Mickey Mouse, WW, c. 1933, by Ingersoll (metal band with 3 Mickeys' on seconds disc)	$195	$295	$500	$1,000
Mickey Mouse, WW, c. 1933, by Ingersoll (English Mickey with 3 Mickeys' on seconds disc, 24 hr. outer dial)	195	295	450	1,000
Mickey Mouse, WW, c. 1938-9, by Ingersoll (one Mickey for second hand)	125	195	350	900
Mickey Mouse, WW, c. 1939, by Ingersoll, plain seconds	85	125	250	450
Mickey Mouse, WW, c. 1938-9, by Ingersoll (girl's and boys style watch, 1 Mickey for second hand)	175	195	350	900
Mickey Mouse, WW, c. 1948, by Ingersoll (fluted Bezel, birthday series, 2 styles Mickey in a circle & no circle)	150	175	400	600
Mickey Mouse, WW, c. 1949, by Ingersoll, **grooved** bezel	125	150	250	400
Mickey Mouse, WW, c. 1946, by U.S. Time (10k gold plated)	95	125	225	400
Mickey Mouse, WW, c. 1946, **Kelton**	95	125	225	400
Mickey Mouse, WW, c. 1947, by U.S. Time (tonneau, plain, several styles)	75	95	175	375
Mickey Mouse, WW, c. 1947, by U.S. Time (same as above, gold tone)	85	95	195	375
Mickey Mouse, WW, c. 1950s, by U.S. Time (round style)	40	50	125	325
Mickey Mouse, WW, c. 1958, by U.S. Time (**statue** of Mickey in box)	75	95	195	400
Mickey Mouse, WW, c. 1965 to 1970, by Timex (Mickey Mouse electric)	95	125	250	400
Mickey Mouse, WW, c. 1965-70s, Timex (manual wind)	55	65	125	175
Mickey Mouse, WW, c. 1975, Elgin (**ELECTRIC MODEL**), **14K** GOLD CASE & leather band, 13 jewels	400	500	750	1,300
Mickey Mouse, WW, c. 1970s, by Bradley	40	50	60	95
Mickey Mouse, WW, c. 1980, by Bradley (colored min. chapter)	60	70	85	150
Mickey Mouse, WW, c. 1983, by Bradley (limited commemorative model)	60	75	95	175

Mickey Mouse, Bradley, ca. 1969.

Mickey Mouse, with wide bezel, Ingersoll, it is believed dealers have used a Wrist Watch dial in a Hopalong case, ca. 1955. **Maybe HOAX ??**

Note: To be **mint** condition, character watches must have unfaded dials, and boxes must have all inserts. (PW=Pocket Watch; WW=Wrist Watch)

Left: Captain Marvel, Ca. 1948. **Center:** Minnie Mouse, U.S.Time, Ca.1968. **Right:** Orphan Annie, New Haven, Ca.1939

ORPHAN ANNIE, New Haven, in 1940 sold for $5.95. 2 case styles of POPEYE & friends, New Haven, Ca. 1936

POPEYE, New Haven, (with friends), Ca. 1935   POPEYE, New Haven, Ca. 1936, (Wimpy only), originally sold for .80 in 1936.

Note: To be **mint** condition, character watches must have unfaded dials, and boxes must have all inserts. (PW=Pocket Watch; WW=Wrist Watch)

LEFT: GOOFY watch runs backward.   CENTER: Little Pig & fiddle.   RIGHT: Porky Pig

Left: Pluto, Birthday Series, by Ingersoll.   **Center:** Rocky Jones, Ca.1955.   **Right:** Speedy Gonzales, Swiss

Ingraham tonneau-shaped movement Ca. 1934.

DONALD DUCK, Ward W. Co. made for the Austria market, Ca. 1940s.   Rare Dan Winslow watch front and back.

Style or Grade – Description	Avg	Ex-Fn	Mint	Mint +Box
Mickey Mouse, WW, c. 1985, by ETA (clear plastic bezel and band)	$40	$50	$65	$95
Mickey Mouse, WW, c.1980s, Bradley, (Tachometer dial)	45	50	60	85
Mighty Mouse, WW, c.1980s, Swiss, (Plastic case)	25	30	35	50
Minnie Mouse, WW, c. 1958, by U.S. Time (statue of Minnie in box)	40	50	195	450
Moon Mullins, PW, c. 1930, by Ingersoll	★ 195	295	500	1,000
Orphan Annie, WW, c. 1939, by New Haven (fluted bezel)	75	95	195	500
Orphan Annie, WW, c. 1935, by New Haven (large style)	95	120	195	450
Orphan Annie, WW, c. 1948, by New Haven smaller model)	50	65	150	295
Orphan Annie, WW, c. 1968, by Timex	45	55	75	125
Pee Wee Herman, WW, (Swiss), FLIP TOP	25	35	75	125
Peter Pan, PW, c. 1948, by Ingraham	150	195	295	700
Pinocchio, WW, c. 1948, by Ingersoll (fluted bezel, birthday series)	125	150	295	500
Pinocchio, WW, c. 1948, by U.S. Time (Happy Birthday cake box)	125	150	325	625
Pluto, WW, c. 1948, by U.S. Time(birthday series)	95	150	250	500
Popeye, PW, c. 1935, by New Haven (with friends on dial)	★ 275	450	650	1,200
Popeye, PW, c. 1936, by New Haven (plain dial)	225	375	550	1,100
Popeye, WW, c. 1936, by New Haven (tonneau style, with friends on dial)	★ 250	375	650	1,300
Popeye, WW, c. 1966, by Bradley (round style)	75	95	125	195
Popeye, WW, c. 1948, Swiss, Olive Oyl at 3	75	150	250	450
Porky Pig, WW, c. 1948, by Ingraham (tonneau)	95	175	250	500
Porky Pig, WW, c. 1949, by U.S. Time (round)	95	175	250	500
Punkin Head, WW, c.1946, Ingraham,	55	65	85	150
Puss-N-Boots, WW, c. 1959, by Bradley	95	175	250	400
Quarterback, WW, c.1965, Swiss, (Football action arm)	65	75	85	150
Red Ryder, WW, c.1949, Swiss, (with Little Beaver)	95	150	300	750
Robin, WW, c. 1978, by Timex	40	45	85	150
Robin Hood, WW, c. 1955, by Bradley (tonneau style)	85	125	275	500
Robin Hood, WW, c. 1958, by Viking (round)	75	125	275	500
Rocky Jones Space Ranger, WW, c. 1955, by Ingraham	125	235	350	750
Roy Rogers, PW, c. 1960, by Ingraham, (stop watch) rim set	150	350	650	1,200
Roy Rogers, WW, c. 1954, by Ingraham (Roy and rearing Trigger)	55	125	275	600

Joe Palooka, Ca.1948.　— Snow White U.S.Time. —　Roy Rogers, Ingraham, ca. 1954.

ROY ROGERS, Ingraham, note rim set, Ca. 1960.

ROY ROGERS, Ingraham (large), Ca. 1951.

Left: ROY ROGERS, Note: This watch is a 1950's Ingraham dial in a 1938 Ingersol case.

Center: Tom Corbett, Space Cadet, New Haven, Ca. 1935

Right: SKEEZIX, Ingraham, Ca. 1936.

Left: Smitty, New Haven, Ca.1936. Center: Superman, New Haven, Ca.1939. Right: Superman, New Haven, Ca.1939.

Style or Grade – Description	Avg	Ex-Fn	Mint	Mint +Box
Roy Rogers, WW, c. 1954, by Ingraham (Roy and Trigger)	$70	$125	$250	$600
Roy Rogers, WW, c. 1954, by Ingraham (expansion band)	70	125	250	600
Roy Rogers, WW, c. 1956, by Ingraham (round dial)	70	125	195	500
Rudolf the Red Nose Reindeer, c.1946, Ingraham	85	125	295	600
Rudy Nebb, PW, c. 1930, by Ingraham ★★	150	195	500	900
Shirley Temple, PW, c.1958, by Westclox ★★	275	375	450	800
Skeezix, PW, c. 1928, by Ingraham ★★	295	400	600	1,000
Sky King, WW, (action gun)	75	95	150	400
Smitty, PW, c. 1928, by New Haven	225	275	350	700
Smitty, WW, c. 1936, by New Haven	150	195	295	600
Smokey Stover, WW, c. 1968, by Timex	75	95	150	295
Snoopy, WW, c. 1958 (tennis racket)	30	40	80	150
Snoopy, WW, c. 1958 (Woodstock)	30	40	80	150
Snow White, WW, c. 1938, by Ingersoll (tonneau)	100	125	250	550
Snow White, WW, c. 1952, by U.S. Time (round)	45	50	65	295
Snow White, WW, c. 1956, by U.S. Time (statue in box)	40	45	70	400
Snow White, WW, c. 1962, by U.S. Time (plastic watch)	40	45	65	295
Space Explorer, c.1953, COMPASS watch	75	95	175	400
Speedy Gonzales, WW, Swiss	75	95	150	275
Spiro Agnew, WW,c.1970s, Swiss	60	80	150	275
Superman, PW, c. 1956, by Bradley (stop watch)	150	195	400	700
Superman, WW, c. 1938, by New Haven	195	250	400	800
Superman, WW, c.1946, by Ingraham(lightning bolt hands)	150	195	295	500
Superman, WW, c. 1978, by Timex (large size)	50	65	95	175
Superman, WW, c. 1978, by Timex (small size)	45	50	75	150
Superman, WW, c.1975, Dabs & Co., yellow min. chapter	45	50	75	150
Superman, WW, c.1965, Swiss, rotating superman	55	75	150	225
Superman, WW, c.1976, Timex, sweep sec. hand	60	65	95	195
Texas Ranger, WW, c.1950, by New Haven, action gun	95	125	195	400
Three Little Pigs, PW, c. 1939, by Ingersoll ★★	400	600	1,000	1,800
Tom Corbett, WW, c. 1954, by New Haven ★	195	295	600	1,200
Tom Mix, PW, c. 1934-5, by Ingersoll (with fob) ★★★	1,000	1,500	2,000	3,600
Tom Mix, WW, c. 1934-5, by Ingersoll ★★★	400	600	900	3,200
Winnie the Pooh Bear, c.1970s, Swiss	40	50	60	125
Wizard of Oz, c.1972, swiss	40	55	70	150
Wonder Woman,WW, c.1975, stars at 1,2,4,5,7,8,10,11	65	70	150	175
Wonder Woman,WW, c.1975, Dabs & Co.	65	65	150	175
Woody Woodpecker, WW, c. 1948, by Ingersoll (tonneau)	95	125	250	700
Woody Woodpecker, WW, c. 1952, by Ingraham (round dial)	95	125	195	600
Yogi Bear, WW, c. 1964, by Bradley	50	55	75	150
Zorro, WW, c. 1956, by U.S. Time	60	75	150	400

Left: Tom Mix wrist watch, came with metal link band.

Center: Tom Mix, Ingersoll, ca. 1934-5. TOM MIX on TONY

Right: Woody Woodpecker, U.S. Time, ca. 1948.

Moon Mullins, by Ingersoll, ca. 1928
Reproductions seen

Rudy Nebb, by Ingersoll, ca. 1928

Shirley Temple, by Westclox, ca. 1958

1952 AD, by Ingersoll, Dan Dare Watch and Box.

CUB SCOUT by Timex   BOY SCOUT by New Haven   DAVY CROCKETT, by Ingraham

MICKEY MOUSE WRIST WATCH with metal or leather strap bearing Mickey's picture. The watch itself is smartly styled ... round and therefore entirely practical for a very little girl's wrist. Packed in Mickey Mouse display carton. Retails $2.75.
List **$3.90**

MICKEY MOUSE WATCH AND FOB— a wonderful buy at $1.50 complete. Mickey on the dial of the watch pointing out the time—Mickey on the fob—three little Mickies on the second-circle chasing each other around. List $2.20

New Mickey Mouse Lapel Watch. A handsome lapel model with Mickey's hands telling time on small dial. Mickey on dial and back of a black glossy finished case with nickel trim. Black lapel cord and button. Each in a display box.

No. 1W61. Each......................$2.10

LONE RANGER FOB WATCH

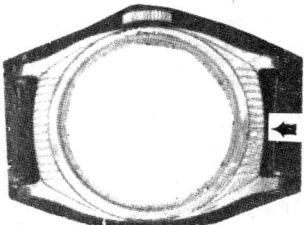

ABOVE: 20th Birthday series style case note **fluted** bezel. The Birthday series used ten different characters & sold for $6.95. The TEN CHARACTERS are: Mickey Mouse, Daisy Duck, Pluto, Bambi, Joe Carioca, Bongo, Donald Duck, Pinnochio, Dopey, and Jiminy Cricket.

New De Luxe Mickey Mouse Wrist Watch. A smarter thinner chromium plated rectangular case. Mickey appears in bright colors on the dial. Fitted with a perspiration proof leather band. Each in display box.

No. 11W440. Each.................$5.54

Above: From a 1938 ad

EARLY ANTIQUE WATCHES

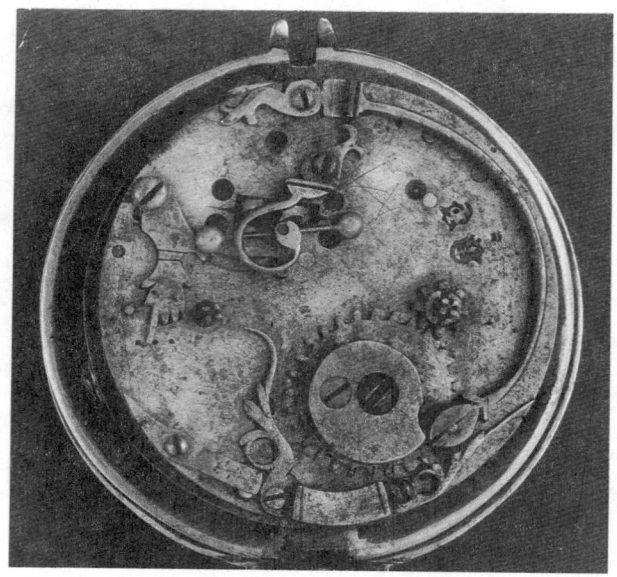

Early German Alarm Iron movement, note Stackfreed with contoured cam, dumbbell foliot, scroll cock, hand-form index arm with a bristle regulator, 70MM, made in Augsburg, Ca. 1570.

The early antique watches looked quite similar to small table clocks. The **mainspring** was introduced to clocks in about **1450**. These drum-shaped watches were about two inches in diameter and usually over one-half inch thick. The drum-shaped watch lost popularity in the late 1500s. The earliest portable timepieces did not carry the maker's name, but initials were common. The cases generally had a hinged lid which covered the dial. This lid was pierced with small holes to enable ready identification of the position of the hour hand. They also usually contained a bell. The dial often had the numbers "I" to "XII" engraved in Roman numerals and the numbers "13" to "24" in Arabic numbers with the "2" engraved in the form of a "Z." Even the earliest of timepieces incorporated striking. The oldest known watch with a date engraved on the case was made in 1548. A drum-shaped watch with the initials "C. W.," it was most likely produced by Casper Werner, a protege of Henlein.

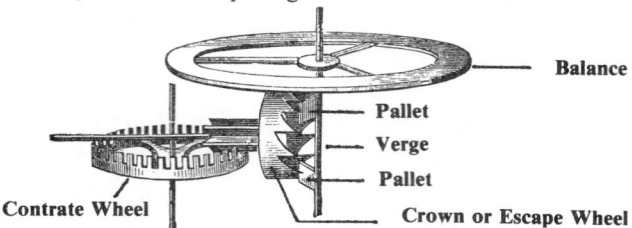

Balance
Pallet
Verge
Pallet
Contrate Wheel
Crown or Escape Wheel

Early pocket watches were designed to run from 12 to 16 hours. The pinions usually bore five leaves, the great wheel 55 teeth, the second wheel 45 teeth, the third wheel 40 teeth, and the escape wheel 15 teeth. With one less pinion and wheel the escape wheel ran reverse to a standard four-wheel watch. During the 1500s, 1600s, and much of the 1700s, it was stylish to decorate not only the case and balance cock but all parts including the clicks, barrel, studs, springs, pillars, hands, and stackfreed.

The plates themselves were decorated with pierced and engraved metal scrolls, and in some instances the maker's name was engraved in a style to correspond with the general decoration of the movement. During these periods the most celebrated artists, designers, and engravers were employed. The early watches were decorated by famous artists such as Jean Vauquier 1670, Daniel Marot 1700, Gillis l'Egare 1650, Michel Labon 1630, Pierre Bourdon 1750, and D. Cochin 1750. Most of the artists were employed to design and execute pierced and repousse cases.

Alarm watch made by Bockel of London Ca. 1648.

THE MID-1700s

In the mid-1700s relatively minor changes are noticed. Decoration became less distinctive and less artistic. The newer escapements resulted in better time keeping, and a smaller balance cock was used. The table and foot became smaller. The foot grew more narrow, and as the century and the development of the watch advanced, the decoration on the balance cock became smaller and less elaborate. About 1720 the foot was becoming solid and flat. No longer was it hand pierced; however, some of the pierced ones were produced until about 1770. Thousands of these beautiful hand pierced watch cocks have been made into necklaces and brooches or framed. Sadly, many of the old movements were destroyed in a mad haste to cater to the buyers' fancy.

THE 1800s

As the 1800s approached the balance cocks became less artistic as the decoration on movements gradually diminished. Breguet and Berthoud spent very little time on the beauty or artistic design on their balance cocks or pillars. But the cases were often magnificent in design and beauty, made with enamels in many colors and laden with precious stones. During this period the movements were plain and possessed very little artistic character.

As early as 1820 three-quarter and one-half plate designs were being used with the balance cock lowered to the same level as the other wheels. The result was a slimmer watch. **Flat enamel** dials are being used in about 1810.

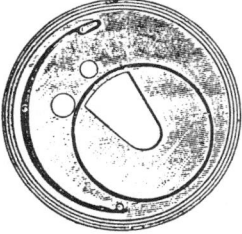

The DUST CAP Ca. 1680 to 1875 Popular in England.
Note: To remove dust cap from Movement, Slide crescent shaped catch or latch **right to Left.**

WATCH-MAKER

The term watch-maker might originally denote the *maker* of *watches* from base material or one who manufactures watches. But as we shall see a watch-maker may better be described as the expert in charge of producing watches. One other note before we move on, a watch may be considered as a miniature spring driven clock, so early on many **clock-makers** were also watch-makers.

There are surviving artifacts that make it possible to make certain assumptions. Thomas Tompion (also a English clock-maker) born 1639, death 1713, used a production system for making watches. About 1670 Tompion divided and sub-divided laborers into various branches of manufacturing of watches. This meant each craftsman specialized in making single watch parts, thus the division of labor led to a faster rate of production, with higher quality and a lower cost to the ebauche movement. About 1775 John Elliott and John Arnold had much of their work done by other sub-divided workers. The quality of the employees work depends upon the watch-maker. Thus, the **PRICE depends** on the **reputation** of the master (watch-maker). The same holds true for todays prices, the reputation of the maker helps to determine the price they can fetch for the timepieces. The parts and materials are of little value in their original state, but the various pieces require such delicacy of manipulation and the management of production of watches, thus the responsibility for the action of the watch depends on the committee in the house of the maker. Prior to 1870 rough movements were mainly produced in the **Prescot** area then finished in London, Liverpool, & etc.

In about 1760 to 1765 Lepine introduced the French or Lepine style calibre of ebauche movements. The Lepine style used separate bridges instead of the single top plate design. Frederic Japy (Japy Freres & Cie.) of Beaucourt, France, later manufactured ebauche Swiss bar style movements in the early 1770's. About 1776, Japy aids in setting up a factory in the LeLocle area and latter in England. Japy Freres & Co. were producing 30,000 movements each year by 1795, and over 60,000 ebauche style movements each year by 1860. Other "BAR" style Ebauche Companies: 1804-Sandoz & Trot of Geneva, 1840-G.A. Leschot with Vacheron & Constantin and about 1850- LeCoultre. These bar style ebauche movements were imported into the U.S.A. about 1850 and were used in the jewelry trade with the jewelers name on the case and dial until about 1875.

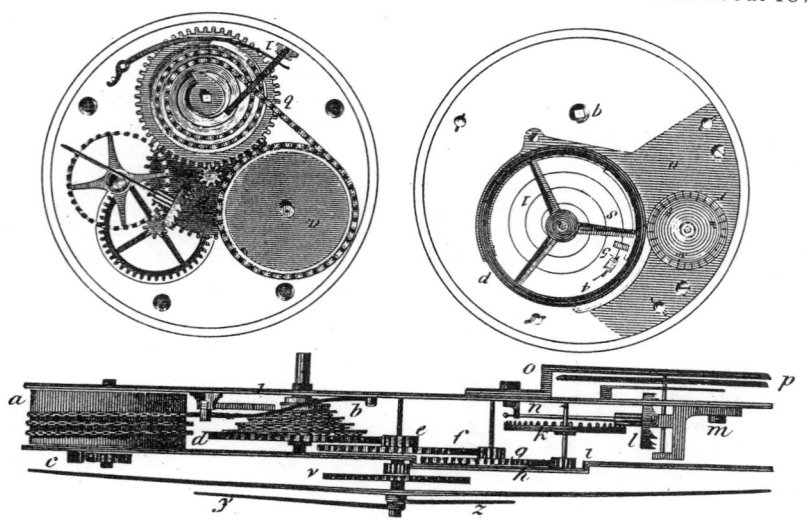

MOVEMENTS " IN THE GRAY "
Movements in an early stage of manufacture.

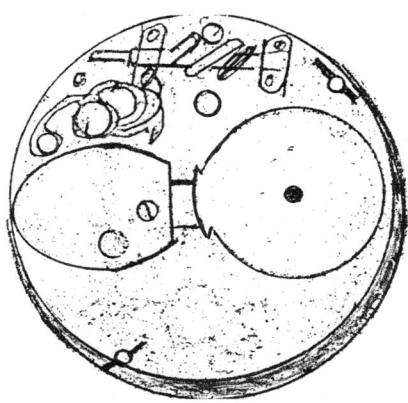

ABOUT MID 1600'S

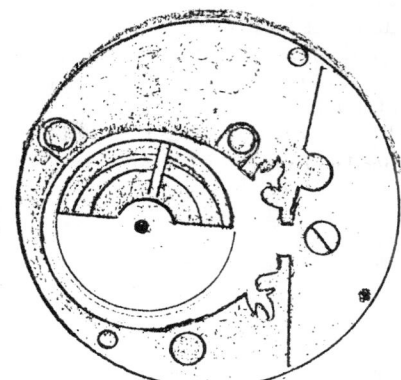

ABOUT 1700'S

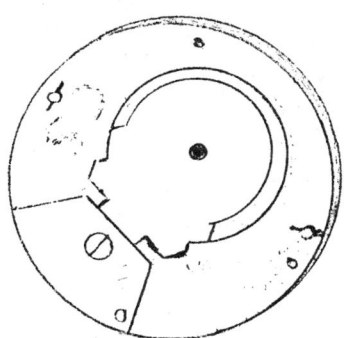

ABOUT 1790—1830
ENGLISH STYLE

EBAUCHE style movement with verge, chain driven fusee, under sprung, KW, **ABOUT 1810 — 1860.**

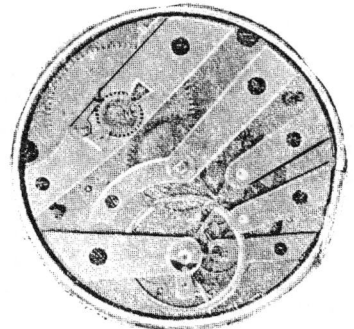

BAR STYLE movement, cylinder, **ABOUT 1840 t0 80.**

Le Locle style EBAUCHE **ABOUT 1870 to 1890.**

🕐 **Multi-color** cases became popular by 1800, 1st. used in 1760 & **Engine Turning** rarely found before early 1760s. **Tortoise Shell** 1st. used in 1620, but did not become popular till about 1780.

The ebauche makers and the cottage industry made different models designed to conform or answer the needs of each country to which they were trying to do business with such as French style, English style, Chinese style, etc. This makes it hard to determine the origin of the ebauche watch. The case may be made in England, the movement Swiss, and the dial French.

Below are some of the principle workmen employed in the sub-divided production of plain parts or ebauche simple watch movements (in the rough) from about 1800s. Some of these were small family specialist that formed a **cottage industry**, (some being females) they usually produced only one product.

1. Cock-maker (made brass blanks)
2. Pillar-maker (turn the pillars, etc.)
3. Frame-maker (full plates, bars, bridges, etc.)
4. Wheel-maker (small and large)
5. Wheel-cutter (cuts the teeth on the wheels)
6. Balance-makers (made of steel or brass)
7. Spring-maker(hair & main springs)
8. Fusee-maker
9. Verge-makers
10. Chain-makers
11. Pinion- maker
12. Escapement-maker
13. Hand-maker
14. Dial-maker

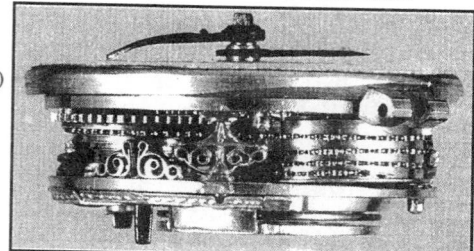

Below a list of craftsman making cases.
1. Case-maker (makes cupped lids for cases)
2. Side-maker (makes the side of the case)
3. Cap-maker (makes the lids of the case)
4. The joint-finisher (joints for cases)
5. Glass-maker (made crystals for bezels)
6. Bezel-makers & Pendant-maker

RIGHT: A English made movement,
Ca. 1750s.

These blank movements, parts, dials and cases were bought, then shipped on to the final destination. The *watch-maker* or *finisher,* such as, the house of (CARTIER). The Finisher would often house or contract decorators to finish the cases. The Finisher completed, polished, engraved, timed, regulated and made all the adjustments to the movements. They added and fitted the case to the movement. They added and fitted the complications such as repeaters to the movements. The *finished* watch is now ready for sale.

This type of system of producing watches left time for the Master watch-makers or famous watch-makers to invent, design new and better ways to make watches, such as, Abraham Louis Breguet. In early 1800's Breguet firm received parts and Swiss ebauches from 18 different suppliers. Thus the more famous the maker the higher the price of the watch even though the watch-maker may not have **made** the smallest piece for the *finished* watch.

The cottage industry with its one man, one task system, make it difficult to establish who, when and where some watches were actually made. It is some what simpler to determine the origin or area, as Swiss, English, French or American, however it is rewarding with further research to unmask the disguise of watch-making. Close study, inspection and comparing movements over the years will prove helpful and may reveal the origin and age of your watch.

Most Swiss manufactures do not make the complete watch on their own premises. Some parts are supplied by specialized firms, such as; balance wheels, escape wheels, jewels, hairsprings, mainsprings, pendant bows and crowns, crystals, hands, cases, screws, pins and other small parts. There were a few factories in Le Locle, Switzerland that manufactured the Cylinder and escape wheel but most were made in the *Maiche district of **France***. Brass plates were plated with RHODIUM for the most part in Swiss Industry. Ebauche or rough movements were made in the Valley of Joux and the Val-de-Ruz regions, in and around towns such as Granges, Bienne, Solothurn, La Chaux- de-Fonds also near by Le Locle, in the Bernese Jura, the Valley of St.Imier, and elsewhere.

CLUES TO DATING YOUR WATCH

To establish the age of a watch there are many points to be considered. The dial, hands, pillars, balance cock and pendant, for example, contain important clues in determining the age of your watch. However, no one part alone should be considered sufficient evidence to draw a definite conclusion as to age. The watch as a whole must be considered. For example, an English-made silver-cased watch will have a hallmark inside the case. It is quite simple to refer to the London Hallmark Table for hallmarks after 1697. The hallmark will reveal the age of the case only. This does not fix the age of the movement. Many movements are housed in cases made years before or after the movement was produced.

An informed collector will note that a watch with an **enamel dial**, for instance, could not have been made before 1635. **A pair of cases** indicates it could not have been made prior to 1640. A **dust cap** first appeared in 1680. The **minute hand** was introduced about 1680. The presence of a **cylinder escapement** would indicate it was made after 1710. **1750 the duplex escapement** was first used. *1776 Lepine* introduced the **thin** watch. **Flat enamel dial** being used in about 1810. **Keyless winding** came into being after 1820, but did not gain widespread popularity until *after* about 1860. All of these clues and more must be considered before accurately assessing the age of a watch. *Some watches were also updated such as minute hand added, enamel dial or new style escapement added.*

Example of an early pocket watch (**Ca. 1548**) with a stackfreed tear shaped cam design to equalize power much as a fusee does. Note dumbbell shaped foliot which served as a balance for verge escapement.

Thomas Tompion started to number his watches in about **1680** & apparently being the **first maker to do so**. Tompion had *three* series of numbers, Time only ordinary watches up to about serial number 4600, repeaters and alarms had a separate series of numbers. Some watches signed Tho. Tompion Edwd. Banger from 1701-08 also T. Tompion & G. Graham from 1711-13. George Graham continued the series after Tompion's death. Daniel Quare also started to number his production of watches about the same time. Therefore, for **time only ordinary watches** there are no earlier serial numbers higher than the Tompion serial numbers listed below for **approximated** year produced.

T. Tompion (time only watch)

Year — Serial #
1682 — 400
1685 — 900
1690 — 1,600
1695 — 2,100
1700 — 2,800
1705 — 3,500
1710 — 4,000

G. Graham Continues

Year — Serial #
1715 — 4,600
1725 — 5,200
1735 — 5,600
1745 — 6,100
1750 — 6,400

IMPORTANT NOTE: **FORGED** Watches signed T. Tompion and G. Graham, watches were Forged in their life-time. These watches are the same age, style, hallmarks and difficult to tell from the true authentic watches.

PILLARS

Pillars are of interest and should be considered as one of the elements in determining age. Through the years small watches used round pillars, and the larger watches generally used a square type engraved pillar.

(*Illus.* 1) This pillar is one of the earliest types and used in the 1800s as well. This particular pillar came from a watch which dates about 1550. It is known that this type pillar was used in 1675 by Gaspard Girod of France and also in 1835 by James Taylor of England.

(*Illus.* 2) This style pillar is called the tulip pattern. Some watchmakers preferred to omit the vertical divisions. This style was popular between 1660 and 1750 but may be found on later watches. It was common practice to use ornamentation on the tulip pillar.

(*Illus.* 3) The ornament shown was used by Daniel Quare of London from 1665 to 1725 and by the celebrated Tompion, as well as many others.

(*Illus.* 4) This type pillar is referred to as the Egyptian and dates from 1630 to the 1800s. The squared Egyptian pattern was introduced about 1630 and some may be found with a wider division with a head or bust inserted. This style was used by D. Bouquet of London about 1640 and by many other watchmakers.

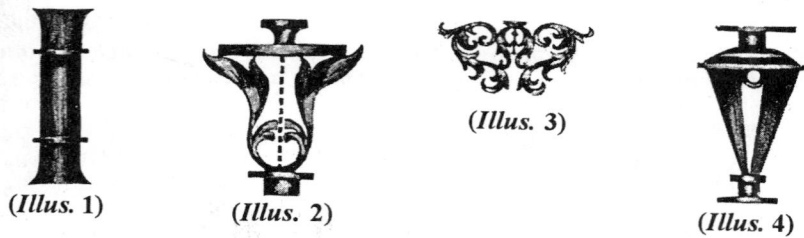

(*Illus.* 1)   (*Illus.* 2)   (*Illus.* 3)   (*Illus.* 4)

(*Illus.* 5) This pillar was used by Thomas Earnshaw of London about 1780. The plain style was prominent for close to two hundred years 1650 to 1825.

(*Illus.* 5)   (Illus. 6)   (Illus. 7)   (Illus. 8)

(Illus. 6) This style was popular and was used by many craftsmen. Nathaniel Barrow of London put this in his watches about 1680.

(Illus. 7) This pillar may be seen in watches made by Pierre Combet of Lyons, France, about 1720. It was also used by many others.

(Illus. 8) This style pillar and the ornament were used by John Ellicott of England and other watchmakers from 1730 to 1770.

These illustrations represent just a few of the basic pillars that were used. Each watchmaker would design and change details to create his own individual identity. This sometimes makes it more difficult to readily determine the age of watches.

⊕ **Multi-color** cases became popular by 1800, 1st. used in 1760 & **Engine Turning** rarely found before early 1760s. **Tortoise Shell** 1st. used in 1620, but did not become popular till about 1780. **Flat enamel** dials are being used in about 1810.

Example of 2 Egyptian pillars left & right also a hand pierced ornament that is not a pillar. (Ca.1700)

BALANCE COCKS OR BRIDGES

The first balance cocks or bridges used to support the balance staff were a plain ''S'' shape. The cocks used on the old three-wheel watches were very elaborate; hand-pierced and engraved. At first no screws were used to hold the cock in place. It is noteworthy that on the three wheel watch the regulator was a ratchet and click and was used on these earlier movements to adjust the mainspring. About 1635 the balance cock was screwed to the plate and pinned on its underside, which helped steady the balance. The first cock illustrated is a beautifully decorated example made by Josias Jeubi of Paris about 1580. Note that it is pinned to a stud which passes through a square cut in the foot of the cock. Next is a balance cock made by Bouquet of London about 1640. The third balance cock is one made by Jean Rousseau and dates around 1650. The fourth one dates around 1655.

The next two bridges are supported on both sides of the balance bridge by means of screws or pins. They are strikingly different and usually cover much of the plate of the movement. This French & Swiss style of balance bridge was used around 1665 and was still seen as late as 1765.

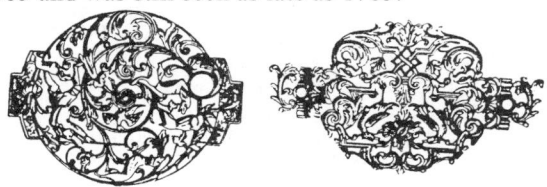

438

The beautiful balance cock below at left, with the ornate foot, dates about 1660. The next illustrated balance cock with the heavy ornamentation was used from about 1700 to 1720 or longer. By 1720 a face was added to the design. The face shows up where the table terminates on most balance cocks.

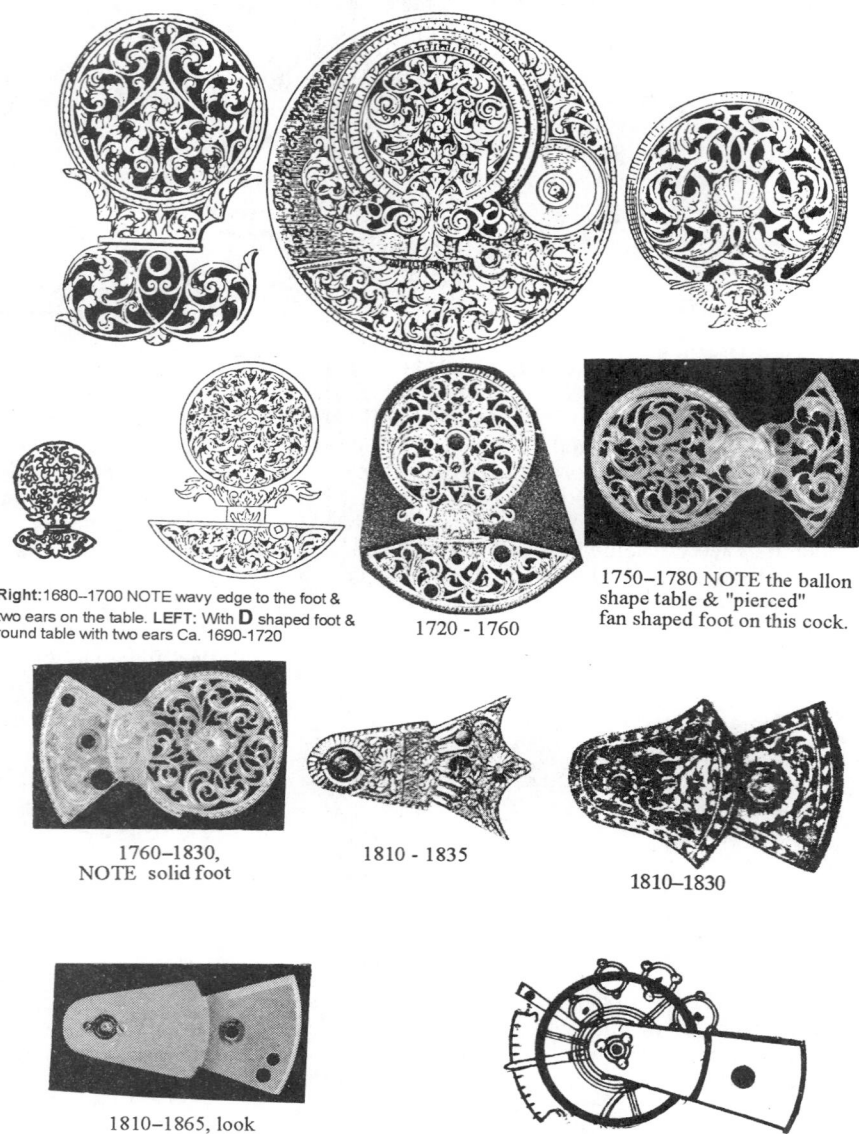

Right:1680–1700 NOTE wavy edge to the foot & two ears on the table. LEFT: With **D** shaped foot & round table with two ears Ca. 1690-1720

1720 - 1760

1750–1780 NOTE the ballon shape table & "pierced" fan shaped foot on this cock.

1760–1830, NOTE solid foot

1810 - 1835

1810–1830

1810–1865, look for barrel bridge

1850 NOTE under-sprung

⊕ Characteristics of watches differ for the same age of both case and movement, because these features vary it may not be accurate to date a watch by one single influence. Example: the second hand was not commonly found on watches before 1750, but common about 1800. The first second hand appeared in 1665 and another in 1690. Therefore statements are **broad** rather than absolute.

Lepine style movement Ca. 1790 to 1820, with free standing barrel, also note the horse shoe shaped bridge, this denotes center seconds. (Virgule Escapement)

Lepine, or FRENCH style ebauche caliber, NOTE the step shaped and tapered bridges, also note the free standing barrel, Ca. 1800 to1825.

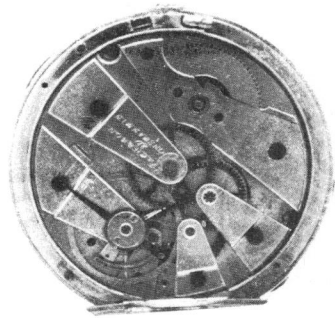

Lepine, or FRENCH style ebauche caliber, NOTE the step shaped and tapered bridges, also note the COVERED barrel bridge, this style movement was popular from Ca.1820 to 1840.

Lepine, or FRENCH style ebauche caliber, NOTE the step shaped and tapered bridges, also note the CURVED barrel bridge, this style movement was popular from Ca.1830 to 1845.

🕐 Characteristics of watches differ for the same age of both case and movement, because these features vary it may not be accurate to date a watch by one single influence. Example: the second hand was not commonly found on watches before 1750, but common about 1800. The first second hand appeared in 1665 and another in 1690. Therefore statements are **broad** rather than absolute.

Muti-colored cases became popular by 1800, 1st. used in 1760 & **Engine Turning** rarely found before early 1760s. **Tortoise Shell** 1st. used in 1620, but did not become popular till about 1780. An informed collector will note that a watch with an enamel dial, for instance, could not have been made before 1635. A pair of cases indicates it could not have been made prior to 1640. The minute hand was introduced in 1650. The presence of a cylinder escapement would indicate it was made after 1710. 1750 the duplex escapement was first used. A dust cap first appeared in 1774. 1776 Lepine introduced the thin watch. **Flat enamel** dials are being used in about 1785. Keyless winding came into being after 1820 but did not gain widespread popularity until after about 1860. All of these clues and more must be considered before accurately assessing the age of a watch. Some watches were also **updated** such as minute hand added or new style escapement added.

Bar (Le Coultre) SWISS style ebauche caliber, NOTE the flat straight bridges and parallel design, also the CURVED barrel bridge this movement was popular Ca.1830 to 1875.

Bar (Le Coultre) SWISS style ebauche caliber, NOTE the flat straight bridges and parallel design, also the STRAIGHT barrel bridge this movement was popular Ca.1840 to 1885.

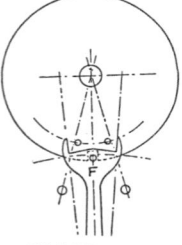

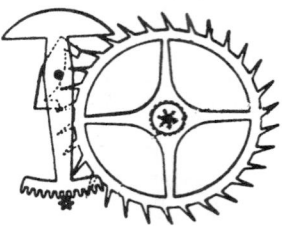

JULES JURGENSEN Style Bar SWISS La Chaux de Fonds ebauche caliber, Ca.1870 to 1895.

SAVAGE, two pin.

Rack and lever escapement

Invented in 1722

ESCAPEMENTS

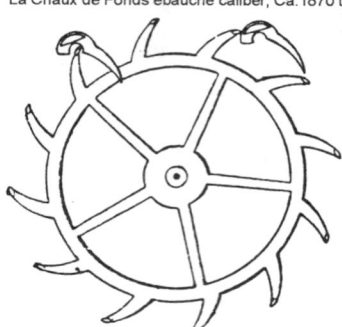

Virgule Escapement

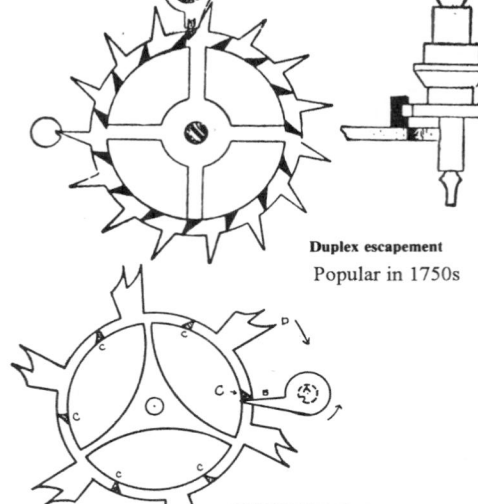

Duplex escapement

Popular in 1750s

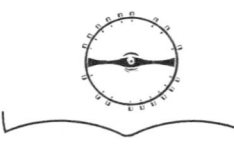

The "Glucydur" Balance can be recognized by the **shape** of its spokes.

CHINESE DUPLEX or CRAB LEG DUPLEX

CHRONOLOGICAL LIST TO HELP ESTABLISH THE AGE OF YOUR WATCHES
DATES BELOW ARE WHEN COMPONENTS WERE FIRST INTRODUCED OR BECAME POPULAR.

1450 - Mainspring also large watches made entirely of **IRON** & were round in shape.

1525 - Fusee by Jacob of Prague.

1530-1545 - Brass plates.

1550 - Screws & Oval shaped watches.

1564 - Swiss Watchmaking begins.

1570 - Hexagonal and octagonal shaped watches.

1590 - Rock Crystal & Form style watches.

1590 - Fusee CHAIN being used.

1590 - English Watchmaking.

1615 - **Glass** crystal to protect dials.

1620 - Tortoise shell covered cases & used till 1800.

1625 - Colored enamel cases.

1635 - Enamel dial invented by Paul Viet, of Blois, France.

1640 - Pair cased watches.

1650 - Repousse Cases & Form watches.

1657 - Balance spring by Hooke.

1660 - Virgule escapement.

1670 - Large Bulb shaped or Oignon watches, shagreen cases being seen.

1670 - Minute hand on watches.

1675 - Watchmaking in Scotland.

1677 - Subdivision of labor, cottage industry.

1680 - Serial number first appear on movements. Watches now run for about 24 hours; before 1680 for about 15 hours only.

1687 - Repeating watches.

1690 to 1700 - All white Enamel watch dials now being used in ENGLAND.

1695 - Cylinder escapement by Tompion.

1700 - Pinchbeck "Gold" (Zink & Copper)

1704 - Watch JEWELS invented.

1715 - Repousse, dust band also seconds hand with tails.

1720 - Improved cylinder escapement by Graham, but not popular.

1722 - Rack lever escapement.

1724 - Duplex escapement invented.

1750 - Duplex escapement **popular**.

1760 - Engine Turning & multi- color gold found on cases.

1761 - John Harrison's chronometer # 4 went to sea for first trial.

1765 - Center seconds.

1765 - Lever escapement by Mudge.

1766 - Compensation balance by Le Roy.

1767 - Virgule escapement.

1770 - Ebauche style watches by Japy.

1775 - Helical balance spring by Arnold.

1776 - Thin modern watches by Lepine.

1782 - Spring detent by Arnold & Earnshaw.

1790 - Musical works & Automaton style watches, 4 color gold dials.

1800 - Watches decorated with pearls.

1800-10 - Flat Enamel dials being used.

1820 - Reproduction of **1600 Form** watches.

1825 - Single sunk Dial.

1830 - Club tooth escape wheel. Min repeater

1835 - Chinese Duplex.

1844 - Heart shaped cam for chronograph.

1848 - Rocking bar keyless winding.

1867 - Roskopf (Dollar) watches.

1896 - Invar "Guillaume" balance.

1900 - Wrist Watches being used.

1924 - Auto-wind Wrist Watch.

1957 - 1st electric W. W. sold by Hamilton.

1960 - First Electronic Wrist Watch by Max Hetzel & sold by Bulova "Accutron".

1967 - Quartz crystal watch developed.

⊕ Characteristics of watches differ for the same age of both case and movement, because these features vary it may not be accurate to date a watch by one single influence.

442

EARLY EUROPEAN WATCHMAKERS

NOTE ABBREVIATIONS USED
art = maker used this enamel case painter
enamel = enamel case painter or artist
pat. = patent or inventor
ca. = circa or about
since = founded to present

Achard, J. Francois (Geneva, ca. 1750)
Addison, J. (London, 1760-1780)
Adamson, Gustave (Paris, 1775-1790)
Alfred, W. Humphreys (London, ca. 1905)
Alibut (Paris, ca. 1750s)
Alliez, Buchelard & Teron Co. (French, ca. 1830)
Amabric, Abraham (Geneva, ca. 1750-1800)
Amabric, Freres (Geneva, ca. 1760-1795)
Amon (Paris, 1913)
Andre, Jean (enamel) (Geneva, 1660-1705)
Anthony, Willams (London, 1785-1840)
Antram, J. (London, ca. 1700-1730)
Appleby, Edward (London, ca. 1675)
Appleby, Joshua (London, ca. 1720-1745)
Ardin, Coppet (ca. 1710)
Arlaud, Benjamin (London, c. 1680)
Arlaud, Louis (Geneva, ca. 1750)
Anord & Dent (London) ca. 1839
Arnold & Frodsham, Charles (London, 1845)
Arnold, Henery (London, ca. 1770-1780)
Arnold, John (London, ca. 1760-1790)
Arnold, John Roger, son of (London, ca. 1800-1830)
Arnold, Nicolas (ca. 1850)
Arnold & Lewis, Lote Simmons (Manchester, ca. 1860)
Arnold & Son (London, ca. 1787-1799)
Assman, Julius (Glasshutte, 1850-1885)
Auber, Daniel (London, ca. 1750)
Aubert, D. F. (Geneva, ca. 1825)
Aubert, Ferdinand (1810-1835)
Aubert & Co. (Geneva, ca. 1850)
Aubry, Irenee (Geneva, 1885-1910)
Audebert (Paris, 1810-1820)
Audemars, Freres (Swiss, 1810 until Co. splits in 1885)
Audemars, Louis-Benjamin (Swiss, 1811-1867)
Aureole (Swiss, 1921)
Auricoste, Jules (Paris, ca. 1910)
Bachhofen, Felix (Swiss, 1675-1690)
Badollet, Jean-Jacques (Geneva, 1779-1891)
Baillon, Jean-Hilaire (Paris, ca. 1727)
Baird, Wm. (London, 1815-1825)
Balsiger & Fils (ca. 1825)
Barberet, J. (Paris, ca. 1600)
Barbezat, Bole (Swiss, 1870)
Baronneau, Jean-Louis (France, 1675-1700)
Barnett, John (England) 1690
Barraud & Lunds (England) 1872
Barraud & Lunds (1812-1840)
Barraud, Paul-Philip (London, 1752-1820)
Barrow, Edward (London, ca. 1650-1710)
Barrow, Nathaniel (London, 1653-1689)
Barry, M. (French, ca. 1620)
Bartholony, Abraham (Paris, 1750-1752)
Barton, J. (London, 1760-1780)
Barwise J.(London, 1800)
Bassereau, Jean-Hilaire (Paris, ca. 1800-1810)
Bautte, Jean-Francois (Geneva, 1800-1835)
Bautte & Moynier (Geneva, ca. 1825)
Beaumarchais, Caron (Paris, 1750-1795)
Beauvais, Simon (London, ca. 1690)
Beckman, Daniel (London, 1670-1685)
Beckner, Abraham (London, ca. 1640)
Beliard, Dominique (Paris, ca. 1750)
Bell, Benj. (London, 1650-1668)
Bennett, John (London, 1850-1895)
Benson, J. W. (London, 1825-1890)
Benson, J. W. (London, 1850-1900)
Bergstein, L. (London, ca. 1840)
Bernard, Nicholas (Paris, 1650-1690)

Bernoulli, Daniel (Paris, 1720-1780)
Berrollas, J. A. (Denmark, 1800-1830)
Berthoud, Augusta-Louis (Paris, ca. 1875)
Berthoud, Ferdinand (Paris, 1750-1805)
Beihler & Hartmann (Geneva, ca. 1875)
Blanc, Henri (Geneva, ends 1964)
Blanc, Jules (Geneva, 1929-1940)
Blanc & Fils (Geneva, 1770-1790)
Bock, Johann (German, 1700-1750)
Bockel (London, ca. 1650)
Bolslandon, Metz (ca. 1780)
Bolviller, Moise (Paris, 1840-1870)
Bommelt, Leonhart (Nuremburg, Ger., ca. 1690)
Bonney (London, ca. 1790)
Bonniksen, Bahne (England, 1890-1930) invented karrusel
Booth, Edward (name change to Barlow)
Bordier, Denis (France, ca. 1575)
Bordier, Freres (Geneva, 1787-1810)
Bordier, Jacques (enamel) (ca. 1670)
Bornand, A. (Geneva, 1895-1915)
Boubon (Paris, 1810-1820)
Bouquet, David (London, ca. 1630-1650)
Bovet (England) 1815 (used J.L.Richer Art)
Bovet, Edouard (Swiss, 1820-1918)
Bovier, G. (enamel painter) (Paris, c. 1750)
Brandt, Iacob (Swiss, ca. 1700)
Brandt, Robert & Co. (Geneva, ca. 1820)
Breitling, "Leon" (Swiss, since 1884)
Brookbank (London, 1776)
Brocke (London, ca. 1640)
Brodon, Nicolas (Paris, 1674-1682)
Bronikoff, a Wjatka (Russia, 1850 "watches of wood")
Bruguier, Charles A. (Geneva, 1800-1860)
Bull, Rainulph (one of the first British) (1590-1617)
Burgis, Eduardus (London, 1680-1710)
Burgis, G. (London, 1720-1740)
Burnet, Thomas (London, ca. 1800)
Busch, Abraham (Hamburg, Ger., ca. 1680)
Buz, Johannes (Augsburg, Bavaria, ca. 1625)
Cabrier, Charles (London, ca. 1690-1720)
Capt, Henry Daniel (Geneva, 1802-1880)
Caron, Augustus (Paris, ca. 1750-1760)
Caron, Francois-Modeste (Paris, 1770-1788)
Caron, Pierre (Paris, ca. 1700)
Caron, Pierre Augustin (pat. virgule escap.) (Paris,1750-1795)
Carpenter, William (London, 1750-1800)
Carte, John (England, 1680-1700)
Champod, P. Amedee (enamel) (Geneva, 1850-1910)
Chapeau, Peter (England) 1746
Chapponier, Jean (Geneva, 1780-1800)
Charlton, John (England) 1635
Charman (London, 1780-1800)
Charrot (Paris, 1775-1810)
Chartiere (enamel) (France, ca. 1635)
Chaunes (Paris, ca. 1580-1600)
Chauvel, J. (England) 1720-25
Chavanne & Pompejo (Vienna, 1785-1800)
Cheneviere, Louis (Geneva, 1710-1740)
Cheneviere, Urbain (Geneva, 1730-1760)
Cheriot or Cherioz, Daniel (ca. 1750-1790)
Cheuillard (Blois, France, ca. 1600)
Chevalier & Co. (Geneva, 1795-1810)
Cisin, Charles (Swiss, 1580-1610)
Clark, Geo. (London, 1750-1785)
Clay, Charles (England) 1750
Clerc (Swiss, ca. 1875)
Clouzier, Jacques (Paris, 1690-1750)
Cochin, D. (Paris, ca. 1800)

Cocque, Geo. (ca. 1610)
Cogniat (Paris, ca. 1675)
Coladon, Louis (Geneva, 1780-1850)
Cole, James Ferguson (London, 1820-1875)
Cole, Thomas (London, 1820-1864)
Collins, Clement (London, ca. 1705)
Collins, John (London, ca. 1720)
Collins, R. (London, ca. 1815)
Colondre & Schnee (ca. 1875)
Combret, Pierre (Lyons, France, ca. 1610-1625)
Cooper, T.F. (England) 1842-80 later "T.M."
Cotton, John (London, ca. 1695-1715)
Coulin, Jaques & Bry, Amy (Paris & Geneva, 1780-1790)
Court, Jean-Pierre (ca. 1790-1810)
Courvosier, Freres (Swiss, 1810-1852)
Courvoisier & Houriet (Geneva, ca. 1790)
Cox, James (London, 1760-1785)
Crofswell J.N. (London), ca. 1825
Csacher, C. (Prague, Aus., ca. 1725)
Cumming, Alexander (London, 1750-1800)
Cummins, Charles (London, 1820)
Cuper, Barthelemy (French, 1615-1635)
Curtis, John (London, ca. 1720)
Cusin, Charles (Geneva, ca. 1587)
Darling, William (British, ca. 1825)
Daniel, de St. Leu (England) 1815
De Baghyn, Adriaan (Amsterdam, ca. 1750)
Debaufre, Peter (French, 1690-1720) (Debaufre escap.)
Debaufre, Pierre (Paris, London, Geneva, 1675-1722)
De Bry, Theodore (German, 1585-1620)
De Charmes, Simon (London, France, 1690-1730)
De Choudens (Swiss & French, 1760-1790)
Decombaz, Gedeon (Geneva, 1780-1820)
Degeilh & Co. (ca. 1880-1900)
De Heca, Michel (Paris, ca. 1685)
De L Garde, Abraham (Paris, "Blois," ca. 1590)
Delynne, F. L. (Paris, ca. 1775)
"Dent", (Edward John)(London, 1815-1850)
Denham, Go. (London, 1750)
Derham, William (English, ca. 1677-1730)
Deroch, F. (Swiss, 1730-1770)
Des Arts & Co. (Geneva, 1790-1810)
Desquivillons & DeChoudens (Paris, ca. 1785)
Destouches, Jean-Francois-Albert (Holland, ca. 1760)
Devis, John (London, 1770-1785)
Dimier & Co. (Geneva, 1820-1925)
Dinglinger (enamel) (Dresden, Ger., ca. 1675)
Ditisheim & Co. "Maurice" (Swiss, 1894)
Ditisheim, Paul (Swiss, 1892)
Dobson, A. (London, 1660-1680)
Droz, Daniel (Chaux-de-Fonds, Sw., ca. 1760)
Droz, Henri (Chaux-de-Fonds, Sw., ca. 1775)
Droz, Pierre Jacquet (Chaux-de-Fonds, Sw., 1750-1775)
Droz, Pierre (Swiss, 1740-1770)
Droz & Co. (Swiss, ca. 1825)
Dubie (enamel) (Paris, ca. 1635)
Dubois & Fils (Paris, ca. 1810)
Duchene & Co. "Louis" (Geneva, 1790-1820)
Ducommun, Charles (Geneva, ca. 1750)
Duduict, Jacques (Blois, France, ca. 1600)
Dufalga, Philippe (Geneva, 1730-1790)
Dufalga, P. F. (Geneva, ca. 1750)
Dufour, Foll & Co. (Geneva, 1800-1830)
Dufour, J. E. & Co. (ca. 1890)
Dufour & Ceret (Ferney, Fr., ca. 1770-1785)
Dufour & Zentler (ca. 1870)
Duhamel, Pierre (Paris, ca. 1680)
Dunlop, Andrew (England) 1710
Dupin, Paul (London, 1730-1765)
Dupont (Geneva, ca. 1810-1830)
Dupont, Jean (enamel) (Geneva, 1800-1860)
Duru (Paris, ca. 1650)
Dutertre, Baptiste (ca. 1730) (pat. duplex escapement)
Dutton, William (London, 1760-1840)

Dyson, John & Sons (England) 1816
Earnshaw, Thomas (London, 1780-1825)
East, Edward (London, 1630-1670)
Edmonds, James (London to U.S.A., 1720-1766)
Edward, George & Son (London, ca. 1875)
Ekegren, Henri-Robert (Geneva, 1860)
Ellicott, John (London, 1728-1810)
Emanuel, E.& E (England) 1861
Emery, Josiah (Geneva, 1750-1800)
Etherington, George (England) 1700
Esquivillon & De Choudens (Paris, 1710-1780)
Ester, Jean Henry (Geneva, 1610-1665)
Etherington, George (London, 1680-1730)
Etienne Guyot & Co. (Geneva, ca. 1880)
Facio De Duillier, Nicholas (British, 1665-1710)
Fallery, Jacques (Geneva, ca. 1760)
Farmer, G. W. (wooden watches) (Germany, 1650-1675)
Fatio, Alfred (Geneva, 1920-1940)
Fatton, Frederick Louis (London, ca. 1822)
Favre Marius & Fils (Geneva, 1893)
Fenie, M. (ca. 1635)
Ferrero, J. (ca. 1854-1900)
Fiarce, Clement (Paris, ca. 1700)
Fitter, Joseph (London, ca. 1660)
Fontac (London, ca. 1775)
Forfaict, Nicolas (Paris, 1573-1619)
Fowles, Allen (Kilmarnock, Scot., ca. 1770)
French (London, 1810-1840)
Fureur (Swiss, 1910)
Gallopin "Henri Capt" (Geneva, 1875)
Gamod, G. (Paris, ca. 1640)
Garnier, Paul (Paris, 1825) (pat. Garnier escapement)
Garon, Peter (England) 1700
Garrault, Jacobus (Geneva, ca. 1650)
Garty & Constable (London, ca. 1750)
Gaudron, Antoine (Paris, 1675-1707)
Gaudron, Pierre (Paris, 1695-1740)
Geissheim, Smod (Augsburg, Ger., ca. 1625)
Gent, James & Son (London, 1875-1910)
Gerbeau, V. (Paris, 1900-1930)
Gerrard (British, 1790-1820)
Gibs, William (Rotterdam, ca. 1720)
Gibbons Joshua (London), ca. 1825
Gibson & Co., Ltd. (Ireland, ca. 1875-1920)
Gidon (Paris, ca. 1700)
Gillespey, Charles (Ireland, 1774-1171)
Girard, Perregaux (Swiss, 1856)
Girard, Theodore (Paris, 1623-1670)
Girardier, Charles (Geneva, 1780-1815)
Girod, B. (Paris, ca. 1810)
Girod, Gaspard (Paris, ca. 1670-1690)
Godod, E. (Paris, ca. 1790)
Godon, F. L. (Paris, ca. 1787)
Golay, A. Leresche & Fils (Geneva, 1844-1857)
Golay, H. (Swiss, 1969-1911)
Golay, Stahl & Fils (1878-1914)
Gollons (Paris, ca. 1663)
Gould, Christopher (England) 1650
Gounouilhou, P. S. (Geneva, 1815-1840)
Gout, Ralph (London, 1790-1830)
Graham, George (London, 1715-1750)
Grandjean, Henri (Swiss, 1825-1880)
Grandjean, L. C. (Swiss, 1890-1920)
Grant, John & Son (English, 1780-1867)
Grantham, William (London, ca. 1850-60)
Grasset, Isaac (Geneva, ca. 1896)
Gray & Constable (London, ca. 1750-90)
Grazioza (Swiss, ca. 1901)
Grebauval, Hierosme (ca. 1575)
Gregory, Jermie (London, ca. 1652-1680)
Gregson, Jean P. (Paris, 1770-1790)
Grendon, Henry (England) 1645
Griblin, Nicolas (French, 1650-1716)
Griessenback, Johann G. (Bavaria, ca. 1660)

Grignion "family" (London, 1690-1825)
Grignion, Daniel & Thomas (London, 1780-1790)
Grinkin, Robert (England) 1625
Grosclaude, Ch. & Co. (Swiss, ca. 1865)
Grosjean, Henry (French, ca. 1865)
Gruber, Hans (Nurnberg, Ger., ca. 1520-1560)
Gruber, Michel (Nurnberg, Ger., ca. 1605)
Gruet (Geneva, Sw., ca. 1664)
Gubelin, E. (Lucern, Switzerland, ca. 1832)
Guillaume, Ch. (pat. Invar, Elinvar)
Haas Nevevx & Co. (founder B. J. Haas) (Swiss, 1828-1925)
Hagen, Johan (German, ca. 1750)
Haley, Charles (London, 1781-1825)
Hallewey (London, 1695-1720)
Hamilton & Co. (London, 1865-1920)
Hamilton G.(London), Ca.1800s
Harper, Henry (London, ca. 1665-1700)
Harrison, John (England, b.1693-1776) **Marine No.1-2-3-4**
Hasluck Brothers (London, ca. 1695)
Hautefeuille, Jean (Paris, 1670-1722)
Hautefeuille, John (Paris, 1660-1700)
Hawley, John (London, ca. 1850)
Hebert, Juliette (enamel) (Geneva, ca. 1890)
Helbros (Geneva, since 1918)
Hele or Henlein, Peter (Nurnberg, 1510-1540)
Heliger, J. (Zug, Sw., ca. 1575)
Henner, Johann (Wurtzburg, Ger., ca. 1730)
Henry, F. S. (Swiss, ca. 1850)
Hentschel, J. J. (French, ca. 1750)
Hess, L. (Zurich, Sw., ca. 1780)
Hessichti, Dionistus (ca. 1630)
Higgs & Evans (London, 1775-1825)
Hill, Ben. (London, 1640-1670)
Hindley, Henry (England) 1758
Hoddell, James, & Co. (England) 1869
Hoguet, Francois (Paris, ca. 1750)
Hooke, Robert (England, 1650-1700)
Hoseman, Stephen (London, ca. 1710-1740)
Houghton, James (England, ca. 1800-1820)
Houghton, Thomas (Chorley, England, ca. 1820-1840)
Houriet, Jacques Frederic (Paris 1810-1825)
Howells & Pennington (England) 1795
Huaud, Freres (enamel) (Geneva, ca. 1685)
Huber, Peter (German, ca. 1875)
Hubert, David (London, 1714-1747)
Hubert, James (England) 1760
Hubert, Oliver (London, ca. 1740)
Hubert, Etienne (French, 1650-1690)
Hues, Peter (Augsburg, Ger., ca. 1600)
Huguenin, David L. (Swiss, 1780-1835)
Humbert-Droz, David (Swiss, ca. 1790)
Hunt & Roskell (England) 1846
Huygens, Christian (Paris, 1657-1680)
Iaquier or Jacquier, Francois (Geneva, 1690-1720)
Ilbery, *William* (London, 1800-35) (used J.L. Richer art)
Ingold, Pierre-Frederic (Swiss, Paris, London, 1810-1870)
Invicta ("R. Picard") (Swiss, 1896)
Jaccard, E. H. & Co. (Swiss, ca. 1850)
Jacot, Charles-Edouard (Swiss, 1830-1860) (pat. Chinese duplex)
Jaeger, Edmond (Paris, 1875-1920)
Jaeger Le Coultre & Co. (Swiss, since 1833)
Jamison, Geo. (London, 1786-1810)
Janvier, Antide (Paris, 1771-1834)
Japy, Frederic & Sons "family" (French, Swiss, ca. 1776)
Jaquet, Pierre (Swiss, 1750-1790)
Jean Richard, Daniel (Swiss, 1685-1740)
Jean Richard, Edouard (Swiss, 1900-1930)
Jeannot, Paul (ca. 1890)
Jefferys & Gildert (London, 1790)
Jessop, Josias (London, 1780-1794)
Jeubi, Josias (Paris, ca. 1575)
Joly, Jacques (Paris, ca. 1625)
Jovat (London, ca. 1690)

Johnson Joseph. Liverpool (English), ca.1805-1855
Jones, Henry (London, ca. 1665-1690)
Jump, Joseph (English, ca. 1827-1850)
Junod, Freres (Geneva, ca. 1850)
Jurgensen, Urban & Jules (Copenhagen, Swiss,1745-1912)
Just & Son (London, 1790-1825)
Juvet, Edouard (Swiss, 1844-1880)
Juvet, Leo (Swiss, 1860-1890)
Keates, William (London, ca. 1780)
Keely, W. (London, ca. 1790)
Kendall, Larcum (London, ca. 1786)
Kendall, James (London, 1740-1780)
Kessels, H. J. (Holland, 1800-1845)
Kirkton, R. (London, ca. 1790)
Klein, Johann Heinr (Copenhagen, Den., ca. 1710)
Klentschi, C. F. (Swiss, 1790-1840)
Koehn, Edward (Geneva, 1860-1908)
Kreizer, Conard (German, 1595-1658)
Kuhn, Jan Hendrik (Amsterdam, 1775-1800)
Kullberg, Victor (Copenhagen to London, 1850-1890)
Lamy, Michel (Paris, 1767-1800)
Lang & Padoux (ca. 1860)
Larcay (Paris, ca. 1725)
Lardy, Francois (Geneva, ca. 1825)
Larpent, Isacc & Jurgensen (Copenhagen, 1748-1811)
Laurier, Francois (Paris, 1654-1675)
Le Baufre (Paris, ca. 1650)
Lebet (Geneva, ca. 1850)
Lebet & Fils (Swiss, 1830-1892)
Le Coultre, Ami (Geneva, ca. 1887)
Le Coultre, Eugene (Geneva, ca. 1850)
Leekey, C. (London, ca. 1750)
Leeky, Gabriel (London, ca. 1775-1820)
Lepaute, Jean-Andre (Paris, 1750-1774)
Lepine, Jean-Antoine (Paris, 1744-1814)
Le Prevost (Swiss), ca.1810
Le Puisne, Huand (enamel) (Blois, Fr., ca. 1635)
Leroux, John (England, 1758-1805)
Le Roy & Co. (Paris, ca. 1853)
Le Roy, Charles (Paris, 1733-1770)
Le Roy, Julien (Paris, 1705-1750)
Le Roy, Pierre (French, 1710-80) (improved duplex escap.)
Levy, Hermanos (Hong Kong, "Swiss," 1880-1890)
L'Hardy, Francois (Geneva, 1790-1825)
Lichtenauer (Wurzberg, Ger., ca. 1725)
Lindesay, G. (London, ca. 1740-1770)
Lindgren, Erik (England, 1735-1775) (pat. rack lever)
Litherland, Peter (English, 1780-1876)
Loehr, (Von) (Swiss, ca. 1880)
Long & Drew (enamel) (London, ca. 1790-1810)
Losada, Jose R. (London, 1835-1890)
Lowndes, Jonathan (London, ca. 1680-1700)
MacCabe, James (London, 1778-1830)
Maillardet & Co. (Swiss, ca. 1800)
Mairet, Sylvain (Swiss, 1825-1885) (London, 1830-1840)
Malignon, A. (Geneva, ca. 1835)
Marchand, Abraham (Geneva, 1690-1725)
Margetts, George (London, 1780-1800)
Markwick Markham, "Perigal" "Recordon" (London, 1780-1825)
Marshall, John (London, ca. 1690)
Martin (Paris, ca. 1780)
Martin, Thomas (London, ca. 1870)
Martineau, Joseph (London, 1765-1790)
Martinot, "family" (Paris, 1570-1770)
Martinot, James (London, ca. 1780)
Mascarone, Gio Batt (London, ca. 1635)
Massey, Edward (England, 1800-1850)
Massey, Henry (London, 1692-1745)
E. Mathey-Tissot & Co. (Swiss, 1886-1896)
Matile, Henry (Swiss, ca. 1825)
Maurer, Johann (Fiessna, Ger., ca. 1640-1650)
May, George (English, 1750-1770)
Mayr, Johann Peter (Augsburg, Ger., ca. 1770)

McCabe, James (London, 1780-1710)
McDowall, Charles (London, ca. 1820-1860)
Meak, John (London, ca. 1825)
Mecke, Daniel (ca. 1760)
Melly, Freres (Geneva, Paris, 1791-1844)
Mercier, A. D. (Swiss, 1790-1820)
Mercier, Francois David (Paris, ca. 1700)
Meuron & Co. (Swiss, ca. 1784)
Meylan, C. H. "Meylan W. Co." (Swiss, ca. 1880)
Michel, Jean-Robert (Paris, ca. 1750)
Miller, Joseph (London, ca. 1728)
Milleret & Tissot (ca. 1835)
Miroir (London, ca. 1700-1725)
Mistral (Swiss, ca. 1902)
Mobilis (Swiss, ca. 1910)
Modernista (Swiss, ca. 1903)
Moillet, Jean-Jacques (Paris, 1776-1789)
Molina, Antonio (Madrid, Spain, ca. 1800)
Molinie (Swiss, ca. 1840)
Molyneux, Robert (London, ca. 1825-1850)
Montandon, Chs. Ad. (Swiss, 1800-1830)
Morand, Pierre (Paris, ca. 1790)
Moricand & Co. (Swiss, ca. 1780)
Moricand & Desgranges (Geneva, 1828-1835)
Moricand, Christ (Geneva, 1745-1790)
Morin, Pierre (English, French & Dutch style, ca. 1700)
Morliere (enamel) (Blois, Fr., ca. 1636-1650)
Moser, George Michael (London, ca. 1716-1730)
Motel, Jean Francois (French, 1800-1850)
Moulineux, Robert (London, 1800-1840)
Moulinier, Aine & Co. (Swiss, 1828-1851)
Moulinier, Freres & Co. (Swiss, ca. 1822)
Mudge, Thomas (London, 1740-1790)
Mulsund (enamel) (Paris, ca. 1700)
Munoz, Blas (Madrid, Spain, ca. 1806-1823)
Mussard, Jean (Geneva, 1699-1727)
Musy Padre & Figlo (Paris, 1710-1760)
Myrmecide (Paris, ca. 1525)
Nardin, Ulysse (Swiss, ca. 1846)
Nelson, W. (London, 1777-1818)
Nocturne (ca. 1920)
Noir, Jean-Baptiste (Paris, 1680-1710)
Norris, J. (Dutch, 1680-1700)
Norton (London), ca.1805
Nouwen, Michael (1st English, 1580-1600)
Noyean (ca. 1850)
Oldnburg, Johan (German, ca. 1648)
Oudin, Charles (Paris, 1807-1900)
Owen, John (English, ca. 1790)
Palmer, Samuel (London, ca. 1790-1810)
Panier, Iosue "Josue" (Paris, ca. 1790)
Papillon (ca. 1690)
Papillon, Francesco (Florence, ca. 1705)
Parr, Thomas (London, ca. 1735-1775)
Payne, H. & John (London, ca. 1735-1775)
Pellaton, Albert (Swiss, ca. 1873)
Pellaton, James (Swiss, 1903) (Tourbillon)
Pendleton, Richard (London, 1780-1805)
Pennington, Robert (English, 1780-1816)
Perigal, Francis (English, 1770-1790)
Pernetti, F. (Swiss, ca. 1850)
Perrelet, Abram (Swiss, 1780) (self wind)
Perret, Edouard (Swiss, 1850)
Perrin, Freres (Swiss, 1810)
Phillips, Edouard (Paris, ca. 1860)
Phleisot (Dijon, Fr., ca. 1540)
Piaget, George (Swiss, ca. 1881)
Picard, James (Geneva, ca. 1850)
Piguet & Capt (Geneva, 1802-1811)
Piguet & Meylan (Geneva, 1811-1828)
Piguet, Victorin-Emile (Geneva, 1870-1935)
Plairas, Solomon (Blois, Fr., ca. 1640)
Plumbe, David (ca. 1730)
Poitevin, B. (Paris, 1850-1935)

Poncet, J. F. (Dresden, 1750)
Poncet, Jean-Francois (Swiss, 1740-1800)
Potter, Harry (London, 1760-1800)
Pouzait, Jean-Moise (Geneva, 1780-1800)
Poy, Gottfrey (London, ca. 1725-1730)
Prest, Thomas (English, 1820-1855)
Prevost, Freres (ca. 1820)
Prior, Edward (London, 1825-1865)
Prior, George (London, 1800-1830) (used J.L. Richer art)
Pyke, John (English, 1750-1780)
Quare, Daniel (London, 1700-1724)
Quarella, Antonio (ca. 1790)
Racine, Cesar (Swiss, ca. 1902)
Racine, C. Frederic (la Chaux-de-Fonds, Swiss, ca.1810-32)
Raillard, Claude (Paris, 1662-1675)
Raiss (1890-1910) (enamel)
Rait, D. C. (German, ca. 1866)
Ramsay, David (Scotland, France, London, 1590-1654)
Ramuz, Humbert U. & Co. (Swiss, ca. 1882)
Ratel, Henri (Paris, 1850-1900)
Recordon, Louis (London, 1778-1824)
Redier, Antoine (Paris, 1835-1883)
Renierhes (London, ca. 1850)
Rey, Jn. Ante, & Fils (Paris, 1790-1810)
Reynaud, P. & Co. (1860)
Rich, John (Geneva, London, 1795-1825)
Richard, Daniel Jean (1685-1740)
Richer, J. L. (outstanding enamel artist) (Geneva, 1786-1840)
Rigaud, Pierre (Geneva, 1750-1800)
Rigot, Francois (Geneva, ca. 1825)
Robert & Courvoisier & Co. (Paris, 1781-1832)
Robin, Robert (Paris, 1765-1805)
Robinet, Charles (Paris, ca. 1640)
Robinson, Olivier & Fredmahn (Naples, 1727-1790)
Robinson William (Liverpool), ca.1850
Rogers, Isaac (London, 1770-1810)
Romilly, Sieur (Geneva, ca. 1750-1775)
Rooker, Richard (London, 1790-1810)
Rose, Joseph (London, 1752-1795)
Rosier, John (Geneva, ca. 1750)
Roskell, Robert (London, 1798-1830) (rack-lever)
Roskopf, G. (German to Swiss, 1835-1885)
Rosselet, Louis (Geneva, 1855-1900) (enamel)
Rousseau, Jean (Paris, 1580-1642)
Roux, Bordier & Co. (Geneva, ca. 1795)
Ruegger, Jacques (ca. 1800-1840)
Ruel, Samuel (Rotterdam, ca. 1750)
Rugendas, Nicholas (Augsburg, Ger., ca. 1700-1750)
Rundell & Bridge (London, ca. 1772-1825)
Russel, Thomas & Son (England) 1898
Sailler, Johann (Vienna, Aus., ca. 1575)
Sanchez, Cayetano (Madrid, Spain, c. 1790-1800)
Sandoz, Henri F. (Tavannes W. Co.) (ca. 1840)
Savage, George (London, 1808-1855) (Inv. pin lever)
Savage, William (London (1800-1850)
Savile, John (London, ca. 1656-1679)
Schatck, Johann Engel (Prague, ca. 1650)
Schultz, Michael (ca. 1600-1650)
Schuster, Caspar (Nunburg, ca. 1570)
Sermand, J. (Geneva, ca. 1640)
Sellar - Reading (England) 1854
Shepherd, Thomas (England) 1632
Sherman De Neilly (Belfort, ca. 1910)
Sherwood, J. (London, ca. 1750-1775)
Sidey, B. (England) 1770
Solson (London, 1750)
Soret (Geneva, ca. 1810)
Soret, Frederic II (1735-1806)
Soret, Isaac & Co. (1690-1760)
Sleightholm & Co. (England) 1800
Smith, C. (England) 1829
Smith, George (England) 1630
Smith, S, & Son (England) 1910
Snelling,J.50

Speakman, Edward (England) 1690
Spencer & Perkins (London, 1770-1808)
Stadlin, Francois (Swiss, 1680-1735)
Staples, James (1755-1795)
Stuffer, M. T. (Swiss, 1830-1855)
Stauffer "Stauffer Son & Co." (London, 1880)
Strasser & Rohde (Glashutte, 1875)
Sudek, J. (ca. 1850)
Sully, Henry (French, London, 1700-1725)
Swift, Thomas (London, ca. 1825-1865)
Tavan, Antoine (Geneva, 1775-1830)
Tavernier, Jean (Paris, 1744-1795)
Tempor Watch Co. (1930) (Masonic watch)
Terond, Allier & Bachelard (ca. 1805-1830)
Terrot & Fazy (ca. 1767-1775)
Terrot, Philippe (Geneva, ca. 1732)
Terroux (ca. 1776)
Theed & Pikett (ca. 1750)
Thierry, J. (London, ca. 1760)
Thierry, Niel (ca. 1810)
Thiout, Antoine (Paris, 1724-1760)
Tobias & Co. M.I. (England) 1805-68 (Michael Isac)
Tobias large family very active in exporting watches
Thomlinson, George (England) 1675
Thorne, Robert (London, 1850)
Thoroton, James (London, 1860)
Thuret, Jacques (Paris, ca. 1695)
Thomason J.N. (Edinburgh), ca.1830
Timing & Repeating W. Co. (Geneva, 1900)
Tompion, Thomas (English, 1671-1715)
Tonkin, Tho. (London, ca. 1760)
Torin, Daniel (England) 1750
Toutaia, Henri (French, 1650) (enamel)
Toutin, Jean (enamel) (Blois, Fr., ca. 1630)
Treffler, Sebastain (ca. 1750)
Tregent, J. (English, 1765-1800)
Truitte, Louis & Mourier (Geneva, ca. 1780)
Tupman (England) 1828
Tyrer, Thomas (London, ca. 1782)
Uhren Fabrik Union (Glashutte, 1893-1970)
Ullman, J. & Co. (Swiss, 1893)
Ulrich, Johann (London, 1820-1870)
Upjohn, W. J. (London, 1815-1824)
Vacheron, Abraham Girod (German, 1760-1843)
Valere (Paris, 1860)

Vallier, Jean (Lyons, Fr., ca. 1630)
Valove, James (London, ca. 1740)
Vanbroff, James (Germany, ca. 1600)
Van Ceule, J. (ca. 1799-1725)
Vandersteen (ca. 1725)
Vaucher, C. H. (Geneva, ca. 1835)
Vaucher, Daniel (Paris, 1767-1790)
Vaucher, Freres (Swiss, 1850)
Vauquer, Robert (French, ca. 1650) (enamel)
Veigneur, F. I. (ca. 1780)
Verdiere A. (Paris), ca.1810
Vernod, Henriette (Paris, ca. 1790)
Vigne, James (London, ca. 1770)
Viner (England) 1834
Vrard, L., & Co. (Pekin, 1860-1872)
Vulliamy, *Justin* (London, ca. 1830-1854)
Vully, Jaques (ca. 1890-1900)
Vuolf (Swiss, ca. 1600)
Waldron, John (London, 1760)
Wales, Giles & Co. (Swiss, ca. 1870)
Walker, Allen (England) 1784
Waltrin (Paris, ca. 1820)
Webb, Benjamin (England) 1799
Weston, D. & Willis (enamel) (London, ca. 1800-1810)
Welldon, I. (England) 1731
Wichcote, Samuel (England) 1733
Widenham (England) 1824
Windmills,J. (England) 1710
Whitney, A. (Enniscorthy- S.of Dublin) Ca. 1810-1830
Whitthorne, James (Dublin, since 1725)
Willats, John (London, ca. 1860)
Williamson, Timothy (London, 1770-1790)
Wilter, John (London, ca. 1760)
Winckles, John (London, 1770-1790)
Winnerl, Joseph Thaddeus (Paris, 1829-1886)
Wiss, Freres & Menu (Swiss, ca. 1787-1810)
Wiss, G. (Geneva, ca. 1750)
Wood, William (England) 1860
Wright, Charles (London, 1760-1790)
Wright, Thomas (English, ca. 1770-1790)
Yates, Thomas (England) 1855
Young, Richard (London, 1765-1785)
Zech, Jacob (Prague, Aus. 1525-1540)
Zolling, Ferdinand (Frankfurt, Ger. ca. 1750)

Tambour style case, probably Nuremburg, ca. 1575, hinged cover, pierced to reveal engraved Roman chapter I-XII and Arabic 13-24 Central chapter, 60mm.

HALLMARKS OF ENGLAND

Hallmarks were used only on gold and silver **cases** made in England. These **case** marks, when interpreted, will help determine **age** of the **case** and location of the assay office. Hallmarks were used to denote information for the **case only**. The Maker's Mark (*W.C.Co.*) when interpreted is who made the **case only**.

The *London* date-marks (a single letter) used 20 letters, A-U, never using the letters W, X, Y, or Z. The letters J & I or U & V, because of their similarity in shape, were never used together within the same 20-year period.

A total of four marks maybe found on English **cases**, which are:

The **CASE MAKER'S MARK** with two or more letters was used to denote the manufacturer of the case **ONLY.**
The **STANDARD MARK** was used to denote a guarantee of the quality of the metal.
The **ASSAY OFFICE MARK** (also known as the town mark) was used to denote the location of the assay office.
The **DATE LETTER MARK** was a letter of the alphabet used to denote the year in which the article was stamped.
The stamp was used on gold and silver cases by the assay office.

Case Maker's Mark   The Standard Mark

The Assay Office Mark   The Date Letter Mark   DUTY MARK

1822 - UP
NO CROWN   1478 to 1821   With George looking to the right 1786 to 1789 are uncommon.

Chester   Birmingham   Edinburgh   Dublin   Glasgow

SWISS HALLMARKS

18k .750   14k .585   Platinum .950

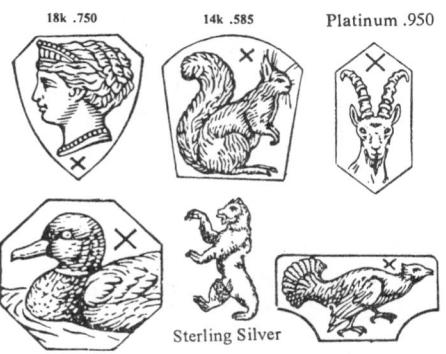

Sterling Silver

Sterling Silver .925   Silver .800

Lucerne   Neuchatel. Poinçons d'essai de décembre 1852.

German silver mark   German gold mark

.800

FRENCH Combination Silver & Gold

FRENCH .800

FRENCH .950

TROY WEIGHT = 24 grains=1dwt., 1 Grain= 0.0648 grams, 20dwt = 1 OZ., 12oz = 1 LB.
NOTE: Gold & Silver Standards Vary from Country to Country. U.S.A. Coin Gold =.900 or 21 3/5K, Silver Coin=.900.
Gold Standards: 24K=1,000%or 1.0, 23K=.958 1/3, 22K=.916 2/3, 21K=.875, 20K=.833 1/3, 19K=.791 2/3, 18K=.750,
17K=.708 1/3, 16K=.666 2/3, 15K=.625, 14K=.583 1/3, 13K=.541 2/3, 12K=.500, 11=.458 1/3, 10K=.416 2/3, 9K=. 375.
8K=.333 1/3, 7K=.291 2/3, 6K=.250, 5K=.208 1/3, 4K=.166 2/3, 3K=.125, 2K=.83 1/3, 1K=.41 2/3.

LONDON DATE LETTER MARKS

Letter	Year	Letter	Year	Letter	Year	Letter	Year
O	1551	M	1589	k	1627	J	1666
P	1552	N	1590	l	1628	R	1667
Q	1553	O	1591	m	1629	L	1668
R	1554	P	1592	n	1630		1669
S	1555	Q	1593	o	1631		1670
T	1556	R	1594	p	1632		1671
V	1557	S	1595	q	1633	P	1672
a	1558	T	1596	r	1634		1673
b	1559	V	1597	S	1635	R	1674
c	1560	X	1598	t	1636	S	1675
d	1561	B	1599	u	1637	T	1676
e	1562	C	1600	A	1638		1677
f	1563	D	1601	B	1639	a	1678
g	1564	E	1602		1640	b	1679
h	1565	F	1603		1641	c	1680
i	1566	G	1604		1642	I	1681
k	1567	h	1605	m	1643	e	1682
l	1568	I	1606		1644	f	1683
m	1569	K	1607		1645	g	1684
n	1570	L	1608		1646	h	1685
o	1571	M	1609	B	1647	u	1686
p	1572	N	1610	e	1648	B	1687
q	1573	O	1611		1649	J	1688
r	1574	P	1612	P	1650	m	1689
s	1575	Q	1613	b	1651	n	1690
t	1576	R	1614	P	1652	o	1691
u	1577	S	1615		1653	p	1692
A	1578	T	1616		1654	q	1693
B	1579	V	1617		1655	r	1694
C	1580	a	1618		1656	s	1695
D	1581	b	1619		1657	t	1696
E	1582	C	1620		1658	u	1697
F	1583	d	1621		1659		1698
G	1584	e	1622		1660		1699
H	1585	f	1623	D	1661		1700
I	1586	g	1624	E	1662		1701
K	1587	h	1625	F	1663		1702
L	1588	i	1626	G	1664		1703
					1665		1704
							1705
							1706
							1707
							1708

Letter	Year	Letter	Year	Letter	Year	Letter	Year
	1709	r	1752	B	1797	J	1841
	1710		1753	C	1798		1842
	1711	t	1754	D	1799		1843
	1712	u	1755	E	1800	J	1844
	1713	a	1756	F	1801	k	1845
	1714	B	1757	G	1802	l	1846
	1715	C	1758	H	1803		1847
A	1716	D	1759	I	1804		1848
B	1717	E	1760	K	1805		1849
C	1718	J	1761	L	1806		1850
D	1719		1762	M	1807		1851
E	1720	h	1763	N	1808	R	1852
F	1721		1764	O	1809		1853
G	1722	k	1765	P	1810	c	1854
H	1723	L	1766	Q	1811		1855
I	1724	M	1767	R	1812	a	1856
K	1725	N	1768	S	1813	b	1857
L	1726	O	1769	T	1814	c	1858
M	1727	P	1770	U	1815	d	1859
N	1728	Q	1771	a	1816	e	1860
O	1729	R	1772	b	1817	f	1861
P	1730		1773	c	1818	g	1862
Q	1731		1774	d	1819	h	1863
R	1732		1775	e	1820	i	1864
S	1733	a	1776	f	1821	k	1865
T	1734	b	1777	g	1822	l	1866
V	1735	c	1778	h	1823	m	1867
a	1736	d	1779	i	1824	n	1868
b	1737	e	1780	k	1825	o	1869
c	1738	f	1781	l	1826	p	1870
d	1739	g	1782	m	1827	q	1871
d	1739	h	1783	n	1828	r	1872
e	1740	i	1784	O	1829	s	1873
f	1741	k	1785	P	1830	t	1874
g	1742	l	1786	q	1831	u	1875
h	1743	m	1787	r	1832	A	1876
i	1744	n	1788	s	1833	B	1877
k	1745	O	1789	t	1834	C	1878
l	1746	P	1790	u	1835	D	1879
m	1747	q	1791	a	1836	E	1880
n	1748	r	1792		1837	F	1881
o	1749	s	1793	c	1838	G	1882
p	1750	t	1794		1839	H	1883
q	1751	u	1795	e	1840		
		A	1796				

Letter	Year
I	1884
K	1885
L	1886
M	1887
N	1888
O	1889
P	1890
Q	1891
R	1892
S	1893
T	1894
U	1895
a	1896
b	1897
c	1898
d	1899
e	1900
f	1901
g	1902
h	1903
i	1904
k	1905
l	1906
m	1907
n	1908
o	1909
p	1910
q	1911
r	1912
s	1913
t	1914
u	1915
a	1916
b	1917
c	1918
d	1919
e	1920
f	1921
g	1922
h	1923
i	1924
k	1925
l	1926

DATE LETTER MARKS FOR
BIRMINGHAM & CHESTER

BIRMINGHAM ASSAY OFFICE DATE LETTERS

A 1773	a 1798	A 1824	A 1849	a 1875
B 1774	b 1799	B 1825	B 1850	b 1876
C 1775	c 1800	C 1826	C 1851	c 1877
D 1776	d 1801	D 1827	D 1852	d 1878
E 1777	e 1802	E 1828	E 1853	e 1879
F 1778	f 1803	F 1829	F 1854	f 1880
G 1779	g 1804	G 1830	G 1855	g 1881
H 1780	h 1805	H 1831	H 1856	h 1882
I 1781	i 1806	J 1832	I 1857	i 1883
K 1782	J 1807	K 1833	J 1858	k 1884
L 1783	k 1808	L 1834	K 1859	l 1885
M 1784	U 1809	M 1835	L 1860	m 1886
N 1785	m 1810	N 1836	M 1861	n 1887
O 1786	n 1811	O 1837	N 1862	o 1888
P 1787	o 1812	P 1838	O 1863	p 1889
Q 1788	p 1813	Q 1839	P 1864	q 1890
R 1789	q 1814	R 1840	Q 1865	r 1891
S 1790	r 1815	S 1841	R 1866	s 1892
T 1791	s 1816	T 1842	S 1867	t 1893
U 1792	t 1817	U 1843	T 1868	u 1894
V 1793	u 1818	U 1844	U 1869	v 1895
W 1794	V 1819	W 1845	V 1870	w 1896
X 1795	w 1820	X 1846	W 1871	x 1897
Y 1796	x 1821	Y 1847	X 1872	y 1898
Z 1797	y 1822	Z 1848	Y 1873	z 1899
	z 1823		Z 1874	

CHESTER ASSAY OFFICE DATE LETTERS

A 1701	A 1726	a 1751	a 1776	A 1797	A 1818	N 1839	a 1864
B 1702	B 1727	b 1752	b 1777	B 1798	B 1819	O 1840	b 1865
C 1703	C 1728	c 1753	c 1778	C 1799	C 1820	P 1841	c 1866
D 1704	D 1729	d 1754	d 1779	D 1800	D 1821	Q 1842	d 1867
E 1705	E 1730	e 1755	e 1780	E 1801	E 1822	R 1843	e 1868
F 1706	F 1731	f 1756	f 1781	F 1802	F 1823	S 1844	f 1869
G 1707	G 1732	g 1757	g 1782	G 1803	G 1824	T 1845	g 1870
H 1708	H 1733	h 1758	h 1783	H 1804	G 1825	U 1846	h 1871
I 1709	I 1734	i 1759	i 1784	I 1805	H 1826	V 1847	i 1872
K 1710	K 1735	k 1760	K 1785	K 1806	I 1827	W 1848	k 1873
L 1711	L 1736	l 1761	l 1786	L 1807	K 1828	X 1849	l 1874
M 1712	M 1737	m 1762	m 1787	M 1808	L 1829	Y 1850	m 1875
N 1713	N 1738	n 1763	n 1788	N 1809	M 1830	Z 1851	n 1876
O 1714	O 1739	o 1764	O 1789	O 1810	N 1831	a 1852	o 1877
P 1715	P 1740	p 1765	P 1790	P 1811	O 1832	b 1853	p 1878
Q 1716	Q 1741	q 1766	q 1791	Q 1812	P 1833	c 1854	q 1879
R 1717	R 1742	r 1767	r 1792	R 1813	Q 1834	R 1855	r 1880
S 1718	S 1743	s 1768	S 1793	S 1814	R 1835	S 1856	s 1881
T 1719	T 1744	t 1769	t 1794	T 1815	S 1836	t 1857	t 1882
U 1720	U 1745	u 1770	u 1795	U 1816	T 1837	u 1858	u 1883
V 1721	V 1746	u 1771	V 1796	V 1817	U 1838	v 1859	A 1884
W 1722	W 1747	v 1772				w 1860	B 1885
X 1723	X 1748	w 1773				x 1861	C 1886
Y 1724	Y 1749	x 1774				y 1862	D 1887
Z 1725	Z 1750	y 1775				z 1863	E 1888
							F 1889

English Watch-Making Evolution

In about 1750 the watch trade divided into two segments. (1.) Ebauche or rough movements were made at Prescot in Lancashire. (2.) These rough movements were then sold to finishers (watchmakers) in London, Liverpool, Coventry also to **America** and **Ireland**. This style of manufacturing of the movements, made the different components not inter-changeable. By 1790 they were producing about 200,000 rough movements per year. This type of system, the quality of the watch depends on the watchmaker thus his reputation helped to determine the price of the finished product.

By mid 1870s watchmaking changed to factory-made watches. Larger volumes of watches were made and to dispose of their product. There were wholesalers who dealt with the retail trade. It is common to find identical retail watches from such firms as English Watch Co. (1874-95), William Ehrhardt (1874-1924), Rotherham & Sons (1880-1930), P. & A. Guye (1880-1900), Nicole, Nielson & Co. (1887-1914), Lancashire Watch Co. (1888-1910), Coventry Watch Movement Co. (1892-1914), J.W. Benson (1892-1941) and H. Williamson (1897-1931). Below are some of the trademarks for identification of the factory-maker. Most often found under dial.

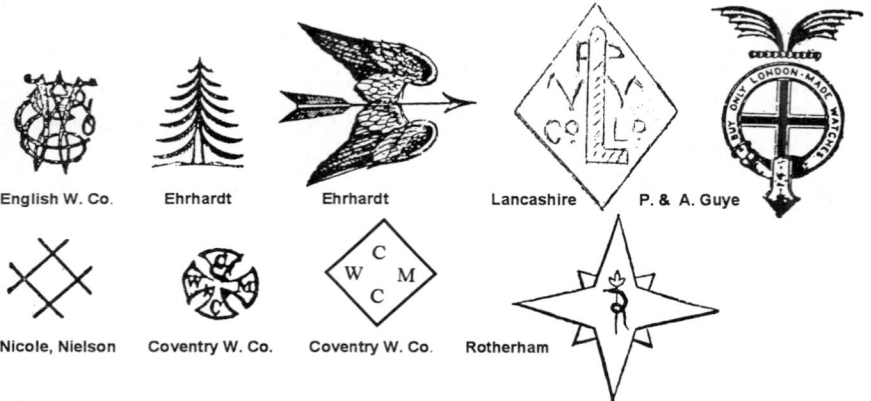

English W. Co.   Ehrhardt   Ehrhardt   Lancashire   P. & A. Guye

Nicole, Nielson   Coventry W. Co.   Coventry W. Co.   Rotherham

In 1814 Edward Massey invented a form of detached escapement. The Massey styles of escapement became popular and widely used. They became known as Massey style or type levers 1, 2, 3, 4, & 5. Below are some illustrations of the right angle lever with different forms of the impulse pin.

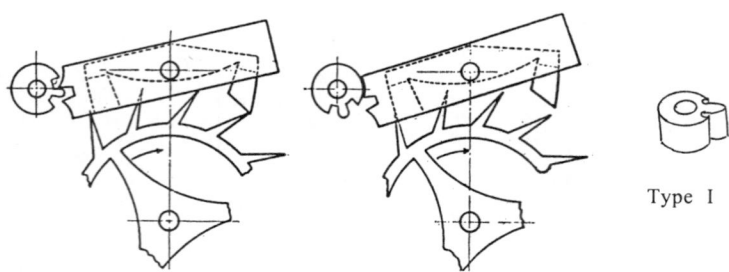

Type I

Original **Massey** (type I) one tooth pinion (on balance staff) & the impulse slot at one end of lever.

II   III   IV   V
Left To Right: **Massey**, type rollers II, III, IV & V in use from 1814 - 1850.

REPEATING WATCHES

Repeaters are those watches with an attachment added that will sound the time at the wish of the user. The repeating mechanism is operated by either a slide, plunger, or button in the case of the watch. There are basically five types of repeating mechanisms, some more common than others:

(1). **QUARTER REPEATERS**– The quarter repeater strikes the previous hour and quarter hour. In the older watches, usually verge, the striking is on a single bell attached to the inside of the case and the hour and quarter striking uses the same tone. There is first a series of hammer blows on the bell to indicate the hours, followed, after a short pause, by up to three twin strikes to denote the number of quarters elapsed. In later watches the striking is on wire gongs attached to the movement itself. The hours are struck on a single deep gong and the quarters on a higher-pitched gong followed by the deeper gong, producing a "ting-tang" sound.

(2). **HALF-QUARTER REPEATERS** -These strike the hours, the last quarter (ting-tang) and the previous half-quarter; i.e., seven and a half minutes. Half-quarter repeaters are mostly all verge escapement watches and are rarely seen by the average collector.

(3). **FIVE-MINUTE REPEATERS**– These fall into two types. One system is similar to the half-quarter repeater but follows the 1/4 "ting-tang" by a single higher-pitched strike for each 5 minute interval elapsed since the last quarter. The other system strikes the hours on a deep gong and follows this with a single higher note for each 5 minute period after the hour, omitting a 1/4 striking.

(4).**MINUTE REPEATERS**– The most complicated of the repeater is similar to the 1/4 repeater with the addition of the minutes. The minute repeater strikes the last recorded hour, quarter and minutes. At 10:52; a minute repeater will strike 10 deep chimes for the hour, 3 double chimes (deep & high) producing a "ting-tang for 3/4 hours & 7 high pitched chimes for 7 minutes (45+7=52).

Example of Split Second & Fly-Back Movement with a minute repeater, c. 1890. Note: ♂ Showing Hammer.

Example of English Clock Watch, 20 size, jeweled through hammers, minute repeater.

(5). **CLOCK WATCHES**– The clock watch is essentially a repeater with the features of a striking clock. Where as the above-mentioned repeaters are all operated by a plunger or slide which winds the repeating function and runs down after the last strike, the clock watch is wound in the same way as the going train usually with a key and is operated by the touch of a button in the case. The repeat function can be operated many times before the watch needs to be rewound. The **CLOCK** part of the name comes from the watch also striking the hours and sometimes the quarters or half hour in passing. The clock watch is easily recognizable by the two winding holes in either the case or the dial.

In addition to the five types described above, the features of striking are sometimes found with not only two but three and even four gongs, this producing a peal of notes. These repeaters are known as **"CARILLONS."**

At the other end of the scale from the carillon is the ''dumb'' repeater. This strikes on a block of metal in the case or on the movement and is felt rather than heard. It is said that the idea was to produce a watch that would not embarrass its owner when he wished to know when to slip away from boring company. Although the dumb repeater is less desirable for the average collector, it certainly should not be avoided– Breguet himself made dumb repeaters.

Grande Sonnerie and **Petite Sonnerie** have been used since early 1700's. The clock watch striking system at first was called *Dutch Striking* because it was used in clock making in about 1665. The older system used striking on bells and struck the hours of the day. Then came the Dutch Striking which also struck the half-hour. This system later developed into a chiming function called **Grande Sonnerie** (grand strike or tone) which struck <u>both</u> the hour and quarter hours are struck ever 15 minutes (thus the hour is repeated every 15 minutes). The **Petite Sonnerie** is a simpler variation of *Grande Sonnerie* in which the 1/4 hour are struck, but the hour is struck only at the o'clock (not repeated).

L.Audemars 2 train Grande or Petite Sonnerie minute repeating clock watch. Note: Marked on bezel sonne & silence at 12 o'clock also Petite Sonnerie & Grande Sonnerie at 6 o'clock, Ca. 1870's.

L. Audemars 2 train Grande or Petite Sonnerie 1/4 repeating clock watch. Note: The push button in the pendant that activate the repeating gongs, Ca. 1850.

A BIT OF HISTORY

Now that we have seen what repeaters are supposed to do, it might be in order to look briefly at their origins. Before the days of electric light, it was a major project to tell the time at night, since striking a tinderbox was said to have taken up to fifteen minutes to accomplish. Clocks, of course, had striking mechanisms, but they tended to keep the occupants of the house awake listening for the next strike. The repeating addition to the clock meant that the master of the house could silence the passing strike at night and, at his whim, simply pull a cord over his bed to activate the striking in another part of the house and thus waking everyone. To silence those members of the household who did not appreciate a clock booming out in the early hours of the morning, the horologists of the day turned their thoughts to the idea of a repeating watch.

The first mention of repeating watches is in the contest between Daniel Quare (1649-1724) and the Rev. Edward Barlow (1639-1719) to miniaturize the repeating action of a clock. Barlow, who for some reason had changed his name from Booth, was a theoretical horologist of outstanding ability. Barlow's design made for him by Thomas Tompion and Quare's watch were both submitted to King James II and the Privy Council for a decision as to whom should be granted a patent. The King chose Quare's design because the repeating mechanism was operated by a single push-button, whereas Barlow's required two. Quare was granted a patent in 1687. Barlow had had his share of fame earlier, however, with the invention of rack-striking for clocks in 1676.

Quare went into production with his new repeater watches, but changed the design to replace the push-button in the case with a pendant that could be pushed in. The first of these watches showed a fault that is still found on the cheaper repeaters of this century – that is, if the pendant was not pushed fully in, then the incorrect hours were struck. To overcome this problem, he invented the so-called "all-or-nothing" piece. This is a mechanism whereby if the pendant was not pushed fully home, then the watch would not strike at all.

The half-quarter appeared shortly after the all-or-nothing piece, and then by about 1710 the five-minute repeater was on the market. Some five years after this, a "deaf-piece" was often fitted to the watch. This was a slide or pin fitted to the case which, when activated, caused the hammers to be lifted away from the bell and had the same effect as a dumb repeater.

Sometime around 1730, Joseph Graham decided to dispense with the idea of a bell and arranged for the hammers to strike a dust-cover, thus making the watch slimmer and preventing dust from entering the pierced case.

About the middle of the century, the French master Le Roy carried the idea a stage further and dispensed with both bells and dust covers, and used a metal block which revolutionized the thickness of the repeating watch and introduced the dumb repeater. Breguet used wire gongs around 1789 and the pattern for the modern repeater was set. The minute repeater came into more common use after 1800, and earlier examples are definitely very rare, although it is known that Thomas Mudge made a complicated watch incorporating minute repeating for Ferdinand VI of Spain about 1750.

By the last quarter of the 1700s, Switzerland had gone for the repeater in a big way and the center of fine craftsmanship for complicated watches was in the Vallee de Joux. Here the principle of division of labor was highly refined and whole families were hard at work producing parts for repeating and musical watches. Since one person concentrated only on one part of the watch, it is hardly surprising that parts of excellent quality were turned out. The basic movements were then sold to watchmakers/finishers all over the Continent and even to England, where the principle of one man, one watch, among the stubborn majority eventually led to the downfall of what had once been the greatest watchmaking nation in history. Minute repeaters first appeared about 1830.

The greatest popularity of the repeater came, however, in the last quarter of the 1800s, when Switzerland turned them out in the tens of thousands. Although there were many different names on the dials of the watches, most seem to have been produced by the company "Le Phare" and only finished by the name on the dial. The production of repeaters in quantity seems to have ground to a finish in about 1921 due to (a) the invention of luminous dials and universal electric or gas lighting, and (b) a lack of watchmakers willing to learn the highly demanding skills. The interest in horology over the past decade has, however, revived the idea of the repeater and several companies in Switzerland are now producing limited editions of expensive models.

BUYING A REPEATER

Since so many repeaters seem to have been repaired at some time in the past by incompetent watchmakers, it is often too expensive a purchase if the buyer does not know what he is doing. **Important: only SET hands clockwise.**

Rule One should be: if it does not work perfectly, avoid it like the plague unless a competent repairer first gives you an estimate which suits your pocket. All too often in the past the repairer was under the impression that metal grows with age and he has filed the teeth of a rack in order to get the full striking to work again. When it dawned on him that the problem was a worn bearing, the tooth was stretched with a punch and refiled, making it weak. It was then goodbye to a fine piece of craftsmanship. **Important only: SET hands clockwise.**

A better quality repeater is usually one which is ''jeweled to the hammers.'' This simply means that the hammers have jeweled bearings which can be seen by searching the movement for the hammers, locating the pivots around which they swing, and looking for the jeweled bearing in which they sit.

All repeaters have some system for regulating the speed of the repeating train. On the older fusee types, there was usually a rather primitive arrangement of a pinion in an eccentric bushing which could be turned to increase or decrease the depth of engagement of the pinion with the next wheel. Another system, a little better, uses an anchor and a toothed wheel as in an alarm clock. This system is usually located under the dial but can be detected by the buzzing sound it makes when the train is operated. The far superior system is the centrifugal governor that can be seen whizzing around in the top plate of the watch when the repeating action is operated. On the whole, the watch with the centrifugal governor is more desirable, although it must be mentioned that the Swiss turned out some inferior watches with this system.

Minute repeating movement by Dent of London. Minute repeating on two gongs and slide activated. Also note the watch has a split second chronograph, Ca. early 1900s.
IMPORTANT NOTE: If possible & it should be possible if you are investing a lot of money have a watchmaker check it.

Test the watch by operating the repeating train over a full hour, seeing that the quarters and minutes function correctly, then test each individual hour. Finally, set the hands to just before 1 o'clock (about 12:45) and test the striking. Any defect due to dirt or worn bearings will show up by the final blow(s), being either sluggish or not striking at all. If there is incorrect striking, have an expert look at it before you buy. **Important: only set hands clockwise.**

Try a partial operation of the slide or push-piece. If the watch has an all-or-nothing piece (as a reasonable grade movement should have), then the watch will not strike. Partial striking indicates either a low grade watch or a non-functioning all-or-nothing piece.

Note: Additional features such as chronograph functions, calendar, moon phase, etc., and will obviously affect the price of the watch.

Important note: Remember Rule One, if any function does not work, **BUYER BEWARE!**

⊕ The earth's orbit around the sun is 365 days, 5 hours, 48 minutes and 45.967685 seconds.

TOURBILLON

Breguet invented the tourbillon in 1795. A tourbillon is a device designed to reduce the position errors of a watch. This device has the escape wheel, lever and balance wheel all mounted in a **carriage** of light frameworks. The carriage turns 360 degrees at regular intervals (usually once per minute). The fourth wheel is **fixed** and is concentric with the carriage pinion and arbor. The escape wheel pinion meshes with the fourth wheel and will **rotate** around the fixed fourth wheel in the manner of a satellite. The escape wheel and lever are mounted on the carriage, and the third wheel drives the carriage pinion, turning the carriage once every minute. This rotation of the escapement will help reduce the position errors of a watch. One of the major objections is that the carriage and escapement weight mass must be stopped and started at each release of the escapement. The tourbillon design requires extreme skill to produce and is usually found on watches of high quality. Somewhat similar to the tourbillon is the *karrusel*, except it rotates about once per hour and the fourth wheel is **not** fixed. The escape pinion in a karrusel watch is driven in the normal manner by the fourth wheel.

Charles Frodsham, TOURBILLON escapement, minute repeating, split second chronograph, about 600 to 700 tourbillons are known to exist. About 85 % of the English tourbillon movements were made by Albert Pellaton, Favre and Nicole Nielson & Co. as in this watch. The TOURBILLON escapement, is located near the top of this movement.

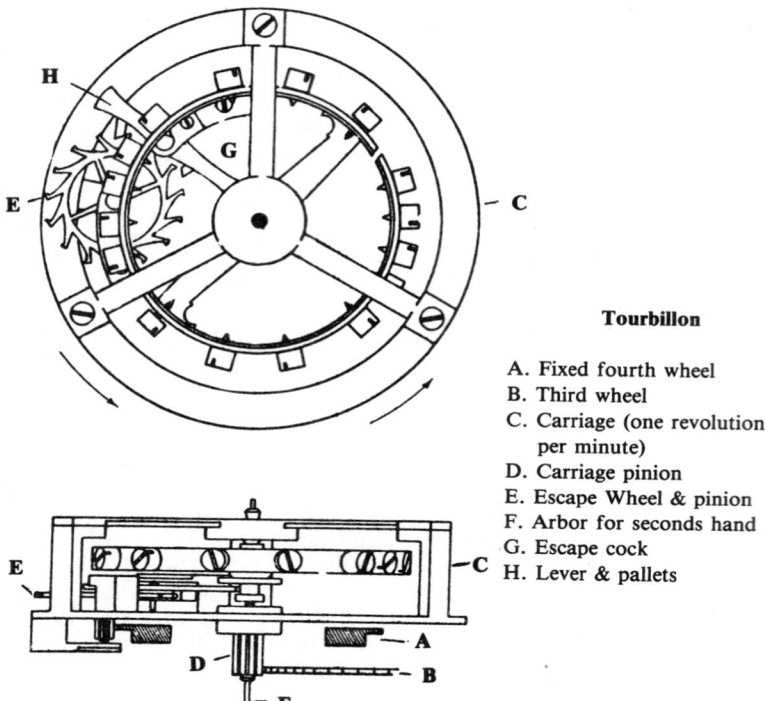

Tourbillon

A. Fixed fourth wheel
B. Third wheel
C. Carriage (one revolution per minute)
D. Carriage pinion
E. Escape Wheel & pinion
F. Arbor for seconds hand
G. Escape cock
H. Lever & pallets

MUSICAL WATCHES
(Three basic types)

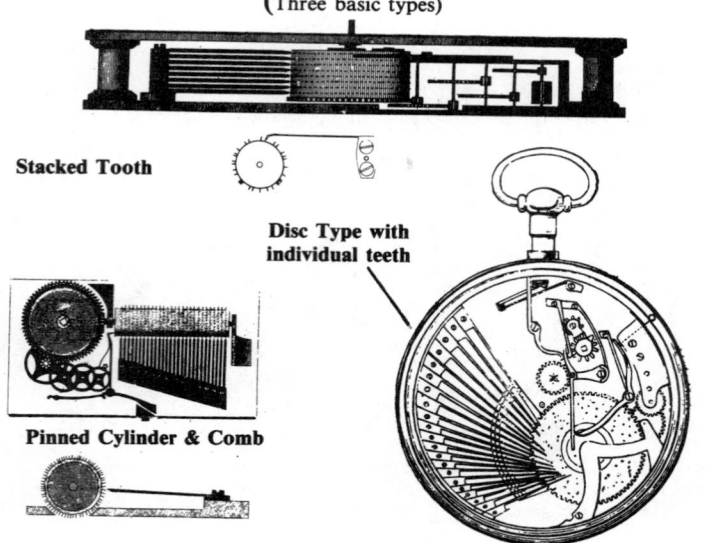

Stacked Tooth

Disc Type with individual teeth

Pinned Cylinder & Comb

Bonniksens' Karrusel

The *watch* has two *distinct* frames, one of which takes all parts but the escapement, the other taking the escapement.   The *escapement frame* is made to *revolve* in the main frame at a uniform rate of about once per hour.   The position of the escapement frame's bearing in the main frame is the same as that of the fourth wheel,—the axle of the escapement frame being large and having a hole through it of such a size that it admits the fourth pinion through freely, in order that the fourth wheel can run in its own jewelled holes without *interference*.   The fourth wheel, C, will be seen inside the *escapement frame*, while the pinion of the fourth wheel A goes outside, so as to be *geared with* and *driven by* the 3rd wheel H.

F F B B is the *bed-plate* of the escapement frame : B B being its axle ; F F B B is turned out of *one piece* ; B B goes through a hole in the main frame, and to the end of B B is screwed the wheel D D, making this wheel *practically* one with F F B B.

Now as D D has teeth upon it and is just large enough to make a correct gearing with G, the third pinion, it follows that as the *third* pinion turns round it will take the wheel D D with it, and thus the *whole escapement* must go round for D D is fixed to the axle of the escapement frame.

All will now be plain on merely naming the parts in the illustration, which are as follows :—

P P is the pillar plate.

H and G are third wheel and pinion respectively.

M is the bar under dial.

L is the third wheel top cock.

D D is the wheel fixed to B B, and driven by G.

F F B B bed-plate of the escapement frame.

K is the fourth top cock which also takes bottom balance pivot.

S is the escape-cock, the escapement is left out of the illustration.

E the balance.

N the balance cock.

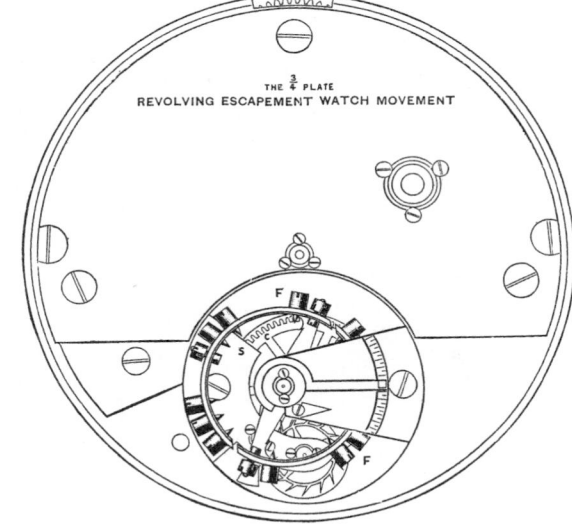

THE ¾ PLATE
REVOLVING ESCAPEMENT WATCH MOVEMENT

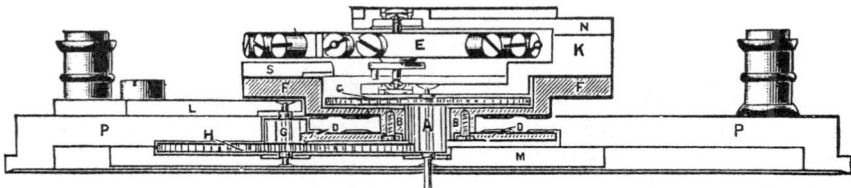

The karrusel rotates slower than a tourbillon but the object is the same to average errors in the vertical position. A tourbillon uses a carriage which forms part of the train, in a karrusel the escapement is mounted on a revolving platform like a carousel, which is driven separately by the train. A tourbillon has a fixed fourth wheel and a karrusel does not have a fixed wheel. Other watch makers used ebauche movements made by Bonniksen.

Where Watches Are Born

A trip to *"Where Watches Are Born,"* is recommended. In this area persists a strong cottage industry where in every small village and almost every street corner, a famous watch-maker or watch factory was born, and after this modern age of electronic and quartz watches still some survive. This area is the Jura Mountain chain which borders the French & Swiss countries.

A micro-techniques route may start at Montbeliard, France and go south to Geneva Switzerland. This micro-techniques route adjacent to the French & Swiss borders should include Factories, Museums, Workshops, and *Antique watch shops galore.* In Besancon, France its Fine Arts Museum with a collection that includes the LeRoy watch that has 25 indicators in addition to the time, also the Museum of Time to be finished in the year 2000, this is also home of the Lip watch factory. Next to Beaucourt, France to see the Frederic Japy Museum. Japy, a very productive maker which at one time produced 3,500 Ebauches a month. On to Valdahon and Morteau (Villers-le-Lac) and visit the Museum of Clock and Watch Making (Musee de Horlogerie du Haut-Doubs). Next LeLocle, Switzerland, home of Cyma, Ulysse Nardin, Tissot and Zenith also see the Watch Museum of the Chateau des Monts. Then La Chaux-de-Fonds home of Corum, Ebel, Girard-Perregaux and many more watch factories. Also visit the International Museum of Horology with a wealth of items also near by Antique Watch & Clock shops. In Neuchatel the Art Museum with the Jaquet Droz collection of mechanical dolls. Now go North to the area of Solothurn, Grenchen & Biel (Bienne) where the Rolex, Omega movement factory and many more as Mido, Urban Jurgensen, Swatch, Breitling, Movado and ETA factory. Further south the Vallee de Joux to see watch factories as Jaeger-LeCoultre, also smaller watch-makers as Daniel Roth & Philippe Dufour in LeSentier. Near by Le Brassus to see Audemars Piguet, Blancpain, and Breguet. On south to Geneva home of Patek Philippe, Rolex, Vacheron Constantin and many more also the see the Clock and Watch Museum Geneva. You may wish to start in Geneva and reverse the above trip. (*Basel Watch Fair usually in the Spring .*)

NOTE: **Nick Lerescu of Advantage Tours** has a Horological tour & seminar each year in late Spring or early Summer. *ADVANTAGE TOURS - P.O. BOX 401 - Glenwood, NJ 07418* or call Nick at 1-800-262-4284. Ask about the trip for the **TIME TRIPPERS**.

EUROPEAN POCKET WATCH LISTINGS
Pricing at Collectable Fair Market Retail Level
(Complete Watches Only)

Unless otherwise noted, watches listed in this section are priced at the collectable **fair market** retail level and as **complete** watches having an original 14k gold-filled case with an original white enamel single sunk dial, and the entire original movement in good working order with no repairs needed. Watches listed as 14k and 18k are solid gold cases. Coin or silveroid type and stainless steel cases will be listed as such. Keywind and keyset pocket watches are listed as having original coin silver cases. Dollar type watches, or low cost production watches, are listed as having a base metal type case and a composition dial.

The prices shown were averaged from dealers' lists just prior to publication and are an indication of the Trade Show level or what collectors will pay. Prices are provided in three categories: average condition, extra fine, and mint condition, and are shown in whole dollar amounts only. The values listed are a guide for the *collectable* retail level and are provided for your information only. Dealers will not necessarily pay FULL RETAIL PRICE. Prices listed are for watches with *original cases* and *dials*.

⊕ Descriptions and serial number ranges listed for early watches cannot be considered 100 percent accurate due to the manner in which records were kept by these companies. Watches were not necessarily sold in the exact order of manufactured date.

Important Notice. All of the information, including valuations, in this book has been compiled from the most reliable sources, and every effort has been made to eliminate errors and questionable data. Nevertheless, the possibility of error, in a work of such immense scope, always exists. The publisher or authors will not be held responsible for losses which may occur in the purchase, sale, statements of its advertisers, or other transaction of items, because of information contained herein. Readers who feel they have discovered errors are invited to write and inform us, so they may be corrected in subsequent editions.

The Complete Price Guide to Watches goal is to stimulate the orderly exchange of Watches between *"buyers"* and *"sellers"*.

⊕ WATCH terminology or communication in this book has evolved over the years, in search of better and more precise language with a effort to improve, purify, adjust itself and make it easier to understand.

INFORMATION NEEDED

This price guide is interested in any facts and information you might have that should possibly be considered for future editions. Documented facts are needed. Please send photo or **sources** of information to:

**COOKSEY SHUGART
P.O. BOX 3147
CLEVELAND, TENNESSEE
37320-3147**

(WHEN CORRESPONDING, PLEASE INCLUDE A 🖃
SELF-ADDRESSED, STAMPED ENVELOPE.)

AGASSIZ
Swiss

Auguste Agassiz of Saint Imier & Geneva started manufacturing quality watches in 1832. They later became interested in making a flat style watch which proved to be very popular. Some of these movements can be fitted inside a $20 gold piece. The company was inherited by Ernest Francillion who built a factory called **Longines.**

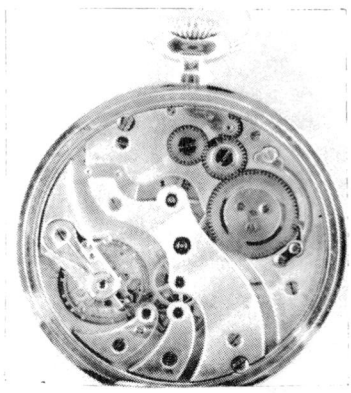

Agassiz, 43mm, 17 jewels, World Time, 42 Cities, ca. 1940.   Agassiz, 40mm, 21 jewels, 8 day with wind indicator.

TYPE – DESCRIPTION	Avg	Ex-Fn	Mint
Early, KW KS, Swiss bar Mvt., time only, Ca.1870, Silver case ...	$75	$95	$150
Time only, gold, 25-38mm, OF	175	250	325
Time only, gold, 40–44mm, 10-12 size, OF	175	250	350
HC	225	295	400
Time only, gold, 45- 50mm, OF	195	295	450
Time only, gold & **enamel**, 45- 50mm, OF	400	650	950
HC	450	700	1,100
Cole's Resilient Escapement, 20J, gold, 45mm, Of	700	900	1,300
8 day, 21J, wind indicator, **18K gold**, 44mm, OF	700	1,000	1,700
14K gold, OF	500	700	1,300
S. S. case, OF	350	500	900

Agassiz, Time only, gold & **enamel**, 45- 50mm, OF   Agassiz, $20 gold 22 / 18K coin watch, Ca. 1950s.

🕐 Watches listed in this book are priced at the collectable fair market **value** at the Trade Show level, as complete watches having an original case, an original white enamel dial, and with the entire original movement in good working order with no repairs needed, unless otherwise noted.

TYPE – DESCRIPTION	Avg	Ex-Fn	Mint
$20 gold 22 to **18K coin** watch, 34mm, Ca. 1950s.	$1,200	$1,800	$2,300
World Time, 42 Cities, gold, 43mm, OF	3,000	4,500	5,500
Chronograph, gold, 45-50mm, register, OF	475	600	700
HC	675	800	1,000
Split second chronograph, register, gold, OF	700	900	1,200
HC	800	1,100	1,500
1/4 hr. repeater, gold, 46-52mm, OF	650	1,000	1,200
HC	1,000	1,250	1,600
Minute repeater, gold, 46-52mm, OF	1,500	1,800	2,500
HC	2,000	2,400	3,100
Minute repeater, w/chrono., gold, 46-52mm, OF	2,000	2,400	3,200
HC	2,400	3,000	4,500
Minute repeater, Split sec. chrono & register, gold, 46-52mm, OF.	3,000	4,000	6,000
HC	4,000	6,000	8,000

ASSMANN
Glasshute - Dresden

Julius Assmann began producing watches with the help of Adolf Lange in 1852. His watches are stylistically similar to those produced by Lange. Later on he adopted his own lever style. Assmann made highly decorative watches for the South American market that are highly regarded by some collectors.

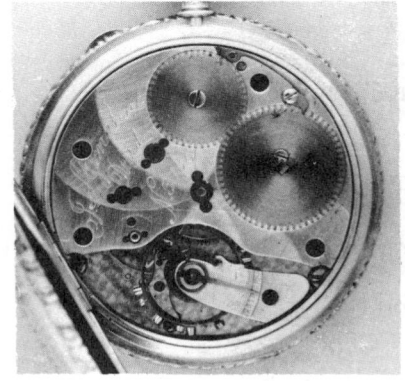

Assmann, 50mm, 19 jewels, diamond cap jewels, gold jewel settings, gold lever escapement, serial number 3,086, BRIDGE MODEL, 1st Quality, Ca. 1875.

Assmann, 50mm, 19 jewels, diamond cap jewels, gold jewel settings, gold lever escapement, serial number 3,739, 1st Quality, Ca. 1877.

TYPE – DESCRIPTION	Avg	Ex-Fn	Mint
Time only, 45- 50mm, **1st Quality**, 18K OF	$2,500	$3,000	$4,000
18K HC	3,000	3,500	4,500
Time only, 45- 50mm, **2nd Quality**, 14K OF	2,000	2,500	3,500
14K HC	2,200	3,000	4,000
Chronograph, **1st Quality**, 55mm, 18K OF	4,000	5,500	8,500
18K HC	5,000	7,000	8,900
Split second chronograph, **1st Quality**, 57mm, 18K OF	5,000	7,000	10,000
18K HC	6,000	9,000	12,000
1/4 hr. repeater, gold, 50-55mm, OF	8,000	10,000	15,000
HC	8,500	11,000	16,000
Minute repeater, gold, 50-55mm, OF	10,000	12,000	18,000
HC	12,000	14,000	20,000
Perp. moonph. cal. w/min. repeater, gold, HC	50,000	70,000	100,000

🕐 A collector should expect to pay modestly higher prices at local shops.

AUDEMARS, PIGUET & CIE

Swiss

Audemars, Piguet & Cie was founded in 1875 by Jules Audemars and Edward Piguet, both successors to fine horological families. This company produced many fine high grade and complicated watches, predominantly in nickel and, with a few exceptions, fully jeweled. Their complicated watches are sought after more than the time only pocket and wrist watches.

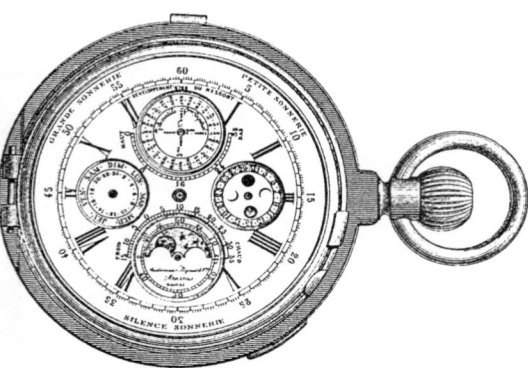

Audemars Piguet, 40mm, about 10 size, 19 jewels, cabochon on winding stem, Platinum, OF.

Audemars Piguet, 50mm, hunting case, Grand, Petite & Silence Sonnerie, minute repeater on demand, split-second Chronograph, Perpetual Calendar, wind indicator & thermometer, taken from a French ad, ca. 1900.

TYPE – DESCRIPTION	Avg	Ex-Fn	Mint
Early, KW KS, Swiss bar Mvt., time only, Ca.1870, **Gold case**	$300	$425	$600
Time only, gold, 25-38mm, OF	300	425	600
Time only, gold, 40-44mm, OF	500	700	1,000
HC	700	800	1,100
Platinum, OF	800	1,000	1,500
Platinum, Diamond Dial & on hands, OF	1,200	1,500	2,200
Time only, gold, 45- 50mm, OF	750	900	1,200
HC	800	1,000	1,500
Jumping hour w/ day-date-month, gold, 43mm., ca. 1925.	3,000	4,500	7,000
Rising Arms (Bras en L'Air), 44mm, one arm points to the hours & the other to the minute, 18K, OF	5,000	7,000	10,000
Chronograph, gold, 45-50mm, OF	1,500	2,000	3,000
HC	2,000	2,500	3,500
OF w/register	2,000	2,500	3,500
HC w/register	2,500	3,000	4,000

Audemars Piguet, (Bras en L'Air) a push-piece on rim of watch, lifts the arms of the bronze, one points to the hour and the other points to the minutes, 44mm, 18K, OF.

Audemars Piguet, Perpetual moon phase calendar, Astronomic watch showing the moon phases, and perpetual calendar showing day, date, & month, Ca.1920s.

AUDEMARS PIGUET, 46mm, 36 jewels, minute repeater, split-second chronograph, serial # 3853, Ca.1888.

AUDEMARS PIGUET, 46mm, Min. repeater, moon-phase, Chronograph, 18K, HC, Ca.1928.

TYPE – DESCRIPTION	Avg	Ex-Fn	Mint
Split second chronograph, gold, 45-52mm, OF	$4,500	$5,000	$6,000
HC	5,000	6,000	8,000
OF w/register	4,000	5,500	8,000
HC w/register	5,000	6,500	9,000
5 minute repeater, gold, 46-52mm, OF	3,500	4,000	5,000
HC	4,000	4,500	5,750
Minute repeater, gold, 46-52mm, OF	4,000	5,500	7,000
HC	5,000	6,500	9,000
OF w/chrono.	4,000	5,000	7,500
HC w/chrono.	5,000	6,500	9,000
OF w/chrono. & register	5,500	7,000	8,500
HC w/chrono. & register	5,250	6,750	10,000
OF w/split chrono. & register	7,000	10,000	15,000
HC w/split chrono. & register	8,000	15,000	20,000
Perpetual moonphase calendar, gold, OF	7,000	9,000	12,000
HC	8,000	10,000	15,000
Perp. moonphase cal. w/min.repeater, chronograph, gold, OF	30,000	40,000	50,000
HC	32,000	50,000	65,000
Grand & Petite Sonnerie, min. repeater, split-second Chron., Perp. Calendar, wind ind. & thermometer, 52-54mm, HC ★★★★	100,000	135,000	175,000

PRODUCTION TOTALS

Date- Serial #	Date- Serial #	Date- Serial #	Date- Serial #	Date- Serial #
1882 - 2,000	1905 - 9,500	1925 - 33,000	1945 - 48,000	1965 - 90,000
1890 - 4,000	1910-13,000	1930 - 40,000	1950 - 55,000	1970-115,000
1895 - 5,350	1915-17,000	1935 - 42,000	1955 - 65,000	1975-160,000
1900 - 6,500	1920-25,000	1940 - 44,000	1960 - 75,000	1980-225,000

REPEATER IDENTIFICATION

Calibre SMV

Calibre SMS

BARRAUD & LUNDS
LONDON (1750-1929)

The Barraud family (of which) there were several makers, one of them being Paul Philip Barraud. Paul was in the trade at 86 Cornhill from about 1796 to 1813. His sons John and James, traded at 41 Cornhill as Barraud & Sons from 1813 till 1838. After 1838 the firm became known as Barraud & Lunds. About 1885 their address was 49 Cornhill and 14 Bishopsgate about 1895. Advertised "machine-made" watches in about 1880 until 1929.

TYPE – DESCRIPTION	Avg	Ex-Fn	Mint
Time only, gold, 45- 50mm, OF	$450	$550	$700
HC	550	650	850
Time only, gold, 45- 50mm, (wind indicator), OF	550	900	1,200
Chronograph, gold, 45-50mm, OF	800	1,000	1,400
HC	900	1,100	1,500
Split second chronograph, gold, 45-52mm, OF	1,500	1,900	2,500
HC	1,600	2,200	3,000
1/4 hr. repeater, gold, 46-52mm, OF	1,000	1,400	2,000
HC	1,250	1,600	2,200
Minute repeater, gold, 46-52mm, OF	1,800	2,400	3,000
HC	2,200	3,000	4,500
OF w/chrono.	2,800	3,500	4,500
HC w/chrono.	3,000	4,500	6,500
OF w/clock watch	8,000	10,000	15,000
HC w/clock watch	10,000	12,000	20,000

Barraud & Lunds, English lever and movement signed *"Barraud & Lunds 49 Cornhill London 3/3333"*, 3/4 plate with a fusee and chain, stem wind, Note: Engraved and raised barrel. With a white enamel signed *"Barraud & Lunds-Cornhill London 3/3333"*, with wind-indicator, Ca. 1886.

⊕ Some models and grades are not included. Their values can be determined by comparing with similar age, size, metal content, style, models and grades listed.

⊕ Watches listed in this book are priced at the collectable fair market **value** at the Trade Show level, as complete watches having an original case, an original white enamel dial, and with the entire original movement in good working order with no repairs needed, unless otherwise noted.

BARWISE
LONDON

John Barwise a leading watchmaker born 1790 died 1843. Dealer at 29 St.Martin's Lane, and with Weston Barwise from 1820 to 1842. John Barwise was also the chairman of British Watch Co., 1842 to 1843. The firm moved back to 29 St.Martin's Lane, 1845 to 1851, and 69 Piccadilly from 1856 to 1875.

TYPE – DESCRIPTION	Avg	Ex-Fn	Mint
Time only, gold, 45- 50mm, OF	$800	$1,000	$1,400
HC	1,000	1,300	1,800
Chronograph, gold, 45-50mm, OF	1,200	1,400	1,800
HC	1,500	1,700	2,000
7-1/2 Min. Repeater, gold, 46-52mm, **18K**, OF ★	4,800	5,400	7,000
1/4 hr. repeater, gold, 46-52mm, OF	2,000	2,600	3,500
HC	2,500	3,000	4,000
Minute repeater, gold, 46-52mm, OF	3,000	3,500	4,500
HC	3,500	4,500	6,000
Detent Chronometer, gold, 48-52mm, OF	5,000	6,000	8,000
HC	6,000	7,000	9,000

BARWISE, Rare 7-1/2 MINUTE REPEATER with ruby cylinder escapement, open face, key wind & key set, Signed BARWISE LONDON No. 5369, Ca. 1800.

COMPARISON OF WATCH SIZES

U. S. A.	EUROPEAN
10-12 SIZE	40—44 MM
16 SIZE	45—49 MM
18 SIZE	50—55 MM

J. W. BENSON
London (1749)

The Benson signature is found on many medium to extremely high grade gilt movements. Factory English machine-made market circa 1870-1930. "Makers to the Admiralty" & "By Warrant to H.M. the Queen" can be found signed on the movements. Named models ("Bank", "Field", "Ludgate") 16 or 14 size.

TYPE – DESCRIPTION	Avg	Ex-Fn	Mint
KWKS, side lever, Silver hallmarked, 48-52mm, OF, C. 1875	$125	$150	$185
SW, 15-17J, side lever, ("Bank", "Field", "Ludgate")			
Silver, 49mm, C. 1870-1930	150	175	225
Gold, 49mm, C. 1870-1930	200	250	400
Fusee, lever escape., high grade, SW, 18K, 54mm, OF, C.1875	500	600	800
Fusee w/indicator, KWKS, side lever, Silver, 54mm, OF, C.1870	450	550	750
Fusee, w/indicator, free spring, lever escape.,18K, 50mm, OF	750	1,000	1,500
Time only, gold, 45-48mm, OF	450	550	700
HC	550	700	1,000
Chronograph, gold, 45-52mm, OF	1,000	1,100	1,500
HC	1,200	1,300	1,800
Split second chronograph, gold, 45-52mm, OF	1,200	1,600	2,500
HC	1,500	2,000	3,000
Perpetual moonphase calendar, gold, OF	8,000	10,000	14,000
HC	10,000	12,000	18,000
Minute repeater, gold, 46-52mm, OF	3,000	3,500	5,000
HC	3,500	4,000	6,000
Minute, Clock Watch, OF	10,000	13,000	17,000
Minute, Clock Watch, HC	12,000	15,000	20,000
Minute, Perpetual, Clock Watch, OF	60,000	90,000	125,000
HC	90,000	110,000	150,000
Karrusel, gold, 48-55mm, OF	4,000	5,000	8,000
Karrusel, silver, 48-55mm, OF	3,000	3,500	4,500

J. W. Benson, 13-15 jewels, 3/4 plate, "The Field, Best London Make, By Warrant to H.M. the Queen" engraved on Movement. Serial Number C8764.

J. W. Benson, 45mm, Split Second Chronograph, 20 jewels, 3/4 plate, free sprung, hunting case, Ca. 1890.

COMPARISON OF WATCH SIZES

U. S. A.	EUROPEAN
10-12 SIZE	40—44 MM
16 SIZE	45—49 MM
18 SIZE	50—55 MM

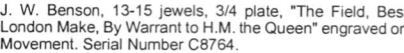

BOREL & COURVOISIER
NEUCHATEL, SWITZERLAND

Founded in 1859 by Jules Borel & first introduced into the United States in 1860. For some of their higher grade movements they used Girard - Perregaux.

BOREL & COURVOISIER, 15J, nickel movement with counterpoised lever, HC, Ca. 1889.

TYPE – DESCRIPTION	Avg	Ex-Fn	Mint
Time only, KW, **SILVER**, 45- 50mm, OF	$125	$150	$200
HC	135	175	225
Time only, KW, **Gold**, 45- 50mm, OF	300	350	475
HC	300	350	525
Time only, SW, nickel, **GF**, 45- 50mm, OF	175	200	275
HC	200	225	325
Time only, SW, nickel, **Gold**, 45- 50mm, OF	325	350	495
HC	350	375	550
Captains Watch, **SILVER**, 2 hour dials, 2 trains, Key Wind, center seconds, 50mm, OF	500	575	700
(SAME AS ABOVE) HC	550	625	750
Captains Watch, **GOLD**, 2 hour dials, 2 trains, Key Wind, center seconds, 50mm, OF	900	1,100	1,500
(SAME AS ABOVE) HC	1,000	1,300	1,700
1/4 hr. repeater, **SILVER**, 46-52mm, OF	600	750	1,000
1/4 hr. repeater, **GOLD**, 46-52mm, OF	850	1,000	1,400
Detent Chronometer, gold, 48-52mm, OF	1,800	2,000	2,500
HC	2,000	2,200	2,700

BOREL & COURVOISIER, both KW movements came in 15 - 21 lignes and four grades, extra, 1st, 2nd, and 3rd quality, Ca. 1860-75.

BOVET
FRENCH & SWISS

Edouard Bovet starts a company in the village of Fleurier Switzerland about 1818 and another firm in Besancon in 1832. The Bovet firm specialized in watches for the chinese market. The Bovet Companies was purchased by Leuba Freres (Cesar & Charles). Bovet also signed watches "TEVOB" making his signature easily read by the Chinese. The new Bovet firm discontinued making watches for the Chinese market. The company was purchased by the Ullmann & Co. in 1918. **Fleurier** a village in Switzerland with **Superior Enamel** artist.

Above: *Superior* FLEURIER *quality* finely painted turquoise enamel watch set in pearls, 18K, 58mm, time only, Duplex Escapement, signed BOVET - FLEURIER, Ca. 1845.

TYPE – DESCRIPTION	Avg	Ex-Fn	Mint
Time only, LEVER escapement, KW, Silver, 58mm, OF	$195	$250	$375
HC	225	295	400
Time only, DUPLEX escapement, KW, Silver, 58mm, OF	225	295	400
HC	250	350	475
Time only, DUPLEX escapement, KW, GOLD, 58mm, OF	700	900	1,200
HC	800	1,000	1,300
Enamel, Time only, DUPLEX, KW, **Silver/gilded,** 58mm, OF	1,200	1,700	2,500
HC	1,500	2,000	3,000
(below *SUPERIOR FLEURIER QUALITY* **Gold & Enamel,** on OF & HC watches)			
Gold &Enamel, Time only, Landscape or Floral, 55- 58mm, OF	6,500	9,500	14,000
HC	9,500	12,500	17,500

⊕ Some models and grades are not included. Their values can be determined by comparing with similar age, size, metal content, style, models and grades listed.

⊕ Watches listed in this book are priced at the collectable Trade Show level, as complete watches having an original case, an original dial, and with the entire original movement in good working order with no repairs needed.

The Complete Price Guide to Watches goal is to stimulate the orderly exchange of Watches between "buyers" and "sellers".

ABRAHAM-LOUIS BREGUET
also BREGUET ET FILS
Paris

Abraham-Louis Breguet, one of the worlds most celebrated watchmakers.

ABRAHAM-LOUIS BREGUET was born at Neuchatel in 1747 and died in 1823. He was perhaps the greatest horologist of all time in terms of design, elegance, and innovation. He is responsible for the development of the tourbillon, the perpetual calendar, the shock-proof parachute suspension, the isochronal overcoil, and many other improvements. It is difficult to include him in this section because of the complexity surrounding identification of his work which was frequently forged, and the fact that so many pieces produced by his shop were unique. Suffice it to say that the vast majority of watches one encounters bearing his name were either marketed only by his firm or are outright fakes made by others for the export market. Much study is required for proper identification. **The first SOUSCRIPTION watch was sold in 1796.**

Abraham-Louis Breguet died on 17th day of September, 1823. The Breguet firm continues today with the tradition started by Abraham-Louis. At first in the hands of his immediate successors and later under the guidance of the "Browns", when the interest of the Breguet family diversified. Today the firm of Breguet continues to produce high quality and exclusive range of watches based on the *classic style* that has made the Breguet name so famous. The Company makes jewelry, wrist watches, clocks, as well as, fine pocket watches. They produce choice examples, with complicated movements and should be signed on dial, case and movement.

Abraham-Louis Breguet, Production Totals

Date —	Serial #	Date —	Serial #
1795 —	150	1815 —	2700
1800 —	500	1820 —	3500
1805 —	1500	1825 —	4000
1810 —	2000	1830 —	4500

The year a watch was **sold** may differ from the year it was **produced**.

Above: Reprints (Reduced) issued by the firm Breguet Ca. 1820s.

60 to 62mm. Example of Breguet **SOUSCRIPTION** style face and movement. Gilt movement with central winding arbor, balance with parachute suspension, HANGING ruby cylinder escapement. White enamel dial with secret signature at 12 o'clock. NOTE: Winds from center either front or back, also most had a silver case and gold bezel. Total production of SOUSCRIPTION style watches about 1,600. **"The above Example is actual size"**.

TYPE – DESCRIPTION	Avg	Ex-Fn	Mint
1/4 repeater, **not** by Breguet, silver, OF, fusee, 54mm C.1825	$500	$700	$1,000
1/4 repeater, **not** by Breguet, fusee, 18K, 54mm, OF, C.1825........	800	1,000	1,300
1/4 repeater, **not** by Breguet, verge, automated, 18K, 55mm, OF ...	3,500	4,000	5,500
1/4 repeater, **Hanging ruby cylinder**, 18K, 60-65mm, C.1795	8,000	11,000	16,000
Hanging ruby cylinder, parachute, KW, 18K, 49mm, OF, C. 1800.	3,000	4,000	6,000
Repeater Horologer De La Marine , silver dial,			
Hanging ruby cylinder escapement	8,000	11,000	15,000
Min. repeater, split sec. chrono., min. register			
18K, 2 tone case, 53mm, OF, C. 1945	15,000	18,000	25,000
Jump hr.w/ aperture, revolving min.disc, 18K, 46mm, OF, C.1930	6,500	8,500	12,000
Hanging ruby cylinder, enamel **"SOUSCRIPTION"** dial,			
center wind, all original,18K, 60 to 62mm, OF, C. 1800	8,000	10,000	14,000
Montre'a tact, 6J ruby cylinder, pearl & enamel case,			
18K, 36mm, C. 1790-1800	15,000	19,000	25,000

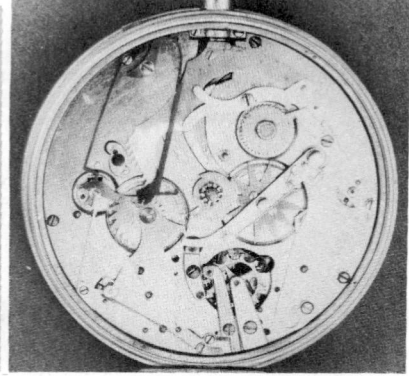

Abraham Louis Breguet, repeating, ruby cylinder watch. Left: gilt movement with standing barrel. Note jeweled parachute suspension. Right: Dial side of movement, repeating train with exposed springs.

Important repeater Horologer De La Marine by Breguet. Left: Guilloche silver dial with roman numerals and typical Breguet hands. Right: Gilt brass movement with ruby cylinder escapement and triple arm balance.

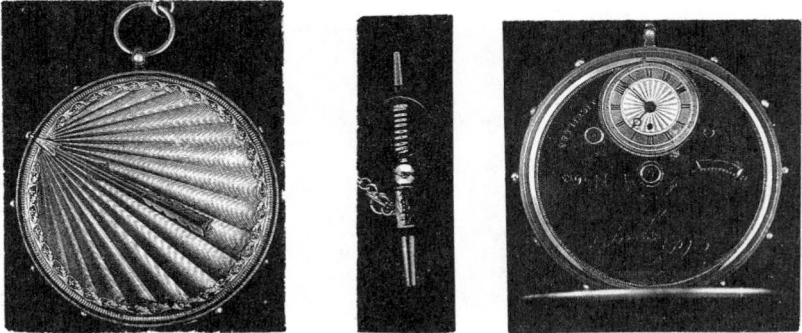

Breguet "montre a tact" or touch time watch, 36mm. Case embellished with 12 pearls for tactile hours (Braille style watch). The arrow on case revolves. Souscription movement with 6 jewels, central barrel, ruby cylinder escapement.

BREGUET, 51mm, chronograph with perpetual calendar and minute repeater. Note sector style wind indicator.

BREGUET, 53mm, minute repeating, split-second chronograph. Chronograph activated by crown and button on band. Repeater activated by slide.

Generic Breguet, 45-48mm, ruby cylinder, KW KS, Swiss bar Mvt., time only, Ca.1830, 18K case

TYPE – DESCRIPTION	Avg	Ex-Fn	Mint
Min. repeater, perpetual calendar chronograph,			
wind indicator, 18K, 51mm, OF, C. 1932	$50,000	$70,000	$120,000
Min. repeater, split sec. chronograph,			
two tone gold case, 53mm, C.1948	12,000	15,000	20,000
Perpetual calendar, thin digital watch, 18K case, 45mm	7,500	9,000	14,000
Tactile braille watch, 18K enamel case w/ pearls, 36mm	15,000	18,000	25,000
Small keyless watch, platinum balance, gold case, 18mm	12,000	15,000	20,000
Early, KW / KS, **generic Swiss bar Mvt.**, time only, Ca.1830,			
18K case, (NOT TRUE BREGUET)	200	300	550

BULOVA
U. S. A. & Swiss

Bulova was a leader in the mass production of quality wristwatches; however, their pocket watch output was small and limited to mostly basic time only varieties. The ultra thin "Phantom" was one of their limited production models.

Joseph Bulova started with a wholesale jewelry business in 1875. The first watches were marketed in the early 1920s. Bulova manufactured millions of movements in their own Swiss plant. The company cased these movements in the U.S.A. and imports all production today. The ACCUTRON was introduced in 1960 and sold about 5 million watches.

Some models and grades are not included. Their values can be determined by comparing with similar age, size, metal content, style, models and grades listed.

Watches listed in this book are priced at the collectable Trade show level, as complete watches having an original case, an original dial, and with the entire original movement in good working order with no repairs needed.

The Complete Price Guide to Watches goal is to stimulate the orderly exchange of **Watches** between *"buyers"* and *"sellers"*.

TYPE – DESCRIPTION	Avg	Ex-Fn	Mint
GF, 17J, 42mm, OF, C. 1940	$50	$60	$85
Rose GF, art deco, 17J, 42mm, OF, C. 1930	70	90	125
14K, 17J, 42mm, OF, C. 1950	150	195	250
Platinum, ultra-thin, "Phantom", 18J, 43mm, OF, C. 1920	400	475	600
Accutron, date, GF, 43mm, **pocket watch**, HC	125	150	195

BULOVA Accutron, with date, gold filled hunting case, about 43mm, ca. 1970s.

HENRY CAPT, 52mm, 32 jewels, minute repeater, serial number 34,711, ca. 1900.

HENRY CAPT
Geneva

Henry Daniel Capt of Geneva was an associate of Isaac Daniel Piguet for about 10 years from 1802 to 1812. Their firm produced quality watches and specialized in musicals, repeaters and chronometers. By 1844, his son was director of the firm and around 1880 the firm was sold to Gallopin.

TYPE – DESCRIPTION	Avg	Ex-Fn	Mint
Early, KW KS, Swiss bar Mvt., time only, Ca.1870, Silver case	$125	$150	$195
Early, KW KS, Swiss bar Mvt., time only, Ca.1870, Gold	300	400	600
Time only, gold, 45- 50mm, OF	400	450	600
HC	500	575	750
Chronograph, gold, 45-50mm, register, OF	700	850	1,000
HC	750	900	1,100
Split second chronograph, gold, 45-52mm, register, OF	1,000	1,300	1,700
HC	1,100	1,400	1,800
1/4 hr. repeater, gold, 46-52mm, OF	1,400	1,700	2,200
HC	1,500	1,800	2,500
Minute repeater, gold, 46-52mm, OF	2,000	2,800	3,500
HC	2,200	3,200	4,500
OF, w/split chrono.	5,000	6,000	8,000
HC, w/split chrono.	6,000	7,500	9,000
Minute repeater, w/ clock watch, OF	8,000	9,000	12,000
HC	10,000	12,000	15,000
Perpetual moonphase calendar, gold, OF	7,500	8,500	10,000
HC	8,000	9,000	11,000
Perp. moonphase cal., w/min.repeater, gold, OF	18,000	27,000	35,000
Perp. moonphase cal. ,w/min.repeater and chrono., gold, HC	20,000	37,000	45,000

CARTIER
Paris

CARTIER was a famous artisan from Paris who first made powder flasks. By the mid-1840s the family became known as the finest goldsmiths of Paris. Around the turn of the century the Cartier firm was designing watches and in 1904 the first wrist watches were being made.

Cartier, 52mm, 40 jewels, triple complicated-perpetual calendar, minute repeater, split-second chronograph.

Cartier, 45mm, 18 jewels, flat, astronomic with moon phases triple calendar, platinum watch, Ca. 1930s.

TYPE – DESCRIPTION	Avg	Ex-Fn	Mint
Time only, gold, 40- 44mm, signed E.W.C., OF	$1,400	$1,650	$2,000
HC	1,500	1,750	2,200
Time only, gold, 45- 50mm, signed E.W.C., OF	1,600	1,800	2,200
HC	1,750	2,000	2,400
Flat, astronomic w/ moon ph. triple calendar, signed E.W.C., platinum,OF	8,000	9,000	12,000
Chronograph, gold, 45-50mm, signed E.W.C., OF	2,500	3,200	4,500
5 minute repeater, gold, 46-52mm, signed E.W.C., OF	3,500	4,000	6,500
HC	4,000	5,000	7,000
Minute repeater, gold, 46-52mm, signed E.W.C., OF	7,500	9,500	12,000
HC	8,000	10,000	12,500
Triple complicated, astronomical moon ph. perpetual triple cal., signed E.W.C. min. repeater, split sec. chron. w/min. recorder, 18 K	70,000	95,000	125,000

Above: **Cartier,** 43mm, 18 jewels, dial has raised gold Arabic numbers, 18k, OF, Ca.1930s.

T. F. COOPER
Liverpool

The Cooper name is usually marked on inner dust covers which protect Swiss ebauche keywind bar movements. Numerous watches produced from 1850-1890 are found with this Liverpool name. The T.F. Cooper & later the T.W. Cooper firms supplied the U.S. market with low cost silver-cased keywinds.

TYPE – DESCRIPTION	Avg	Ex-Fn	Mint
KWKS, "full-jeweled" , Silver, 44-48mm, OF, Ca.1850-1875	$75	$95	$135
KWKS, 15J, Silver, 46-50mm, HC, Ca.1850-1870	85	125	175
KW, Fusee, lever, silver, 48mm, OF, C. 1870	130	150	225
KW, 15J, metal dust cover, gilt dial, **18K**, OF, C. 1875	250	295	400
KW, 15J, **Lady's** , **18K,** 44mm, fancy HC, C. 1875	295	350	500
KW, gold dial, bar movement w/side lever escap., parachute shock on balance, **18K**, 50mm, OF, C. 1870	285	325	400
Captains double time, 15J, KWKS, **silver**, 48mm, OF, C.1865	400	465	800
18K, OF	600	800	1,200
18K, HC	800	1,100	1,500

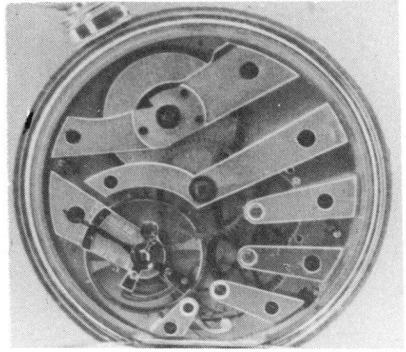

T.F. Cooper, KW, bar movement with right angle lever escapement, parachute shock on balance, 18K, 50mm, OF, Ca. 1852.

Courvoisier, Freres, 37mm, cylinder escap. with wolf-tooth winding, front & back view, 18K & enamel HC, Ca.1880.

COURVOISIER, Freres
SWISS (La Chaux de Fonds)

Started as Courvoisier & Cie in 1810-11, by 1845 Henri-Louis and Philippe-Auguste became owners. In 1852 name changes to Courvoisier, Freres. The watches circa 1810 are signed with the older signature. They exported very ornate pieces for the Chinese market (Lepine bar caliber).

TYPE – DESCRIPTION	Avg	Ex-Fn	Mint
Time only, KW, **SILVER**, 45- 50mm, OF	$125	$150	$195
HC	135	175	225
Time only, KW, **Gold**, 45- 50mm, OF	195	325	400
HC	295	350	500
Time only, **SW**, **Gold**, 45- 50mm, OF	225	325	400
HC	295	350	500
Captains Watch, **SILVER**, 2 hour dials, 2 trains, Key Wind, center seconds, 50mm, OF	500	575	700
HC, (SAME AS ABOVE)	550	625	750
Captains Watch, **GOLD**, 2 hour dials, 2 trains, Key Wind, center seconds, 50mm, OF	900	1,200	1,500
HC, (SAME AS ABOVE)	1,000	1,300	1,700
1/4 hr. repeater, **SILVER**, 46-52mm, OF	600	750	1,000
1/4 hr. repeater, **GOLD**, 46-52mm, OF	850	1,000	1,400
Detent Chronometer, gold, 48-52mm, OF	1,800	2,000	2,500
HC	2,000	2,200	2,700

E. J. Dent
LONDON

Edward John Dent, born in 1790 died in 1853. Edward was in partnership with J.R.Arnold, at 84 Strand, from 1830-1840 and worked alone at 82 Strand from 1841 to 1849. Then moved to 61 Strand 1850 till 1853. The year before his death the Westminster Palace gave Dent the contract for making BIG BEN with a big bell weighing over 13 tons. The clock was built by Frederick Rippon Dent. E. Dent & Co. Ltd. was in business until about 1968 at 41 Pall Mall London.

DENT, PIVOTED Detent chronometer, about 15 jewels, fusee, gold, 48-52mm, Ca. 1870, open face.

DENT, 1/4 hr. repeater, marked " Dent Watch Maker to the Queen 61 Strand London", S# 30077, gold, 46-52mm, OF

TYPE – DESCRIPTION	Avg	Ex-Fn	Mint
Time only, gold, 45- 50mm, OF	$550	$650	$800
HC	650	800	1,000
Chronograph, gold, 45-50mm, OF	750	900	1,200
HC	800	1,100	1,500
Split second chronograph, gold, 45-52mm, OF	1,000	1,400	2,000
HC	1,100	1,600	2,500
1/4 hr. repeater, gold, 46-52mm, OF	1,800	2,300	3,000
HC	2,000	2,800	4,000
HC w/chrono., cal. & moonphase	5,700	7,000	10,000
Minute repeater, gold, OF	3,000	3,800	5,000
HC	3,200	4,000	6,000
OF w/chrono.	3,500	4,500	6,000
HC w/split chrono.	5,500	6,500	9,000
HC w/cal. & moonphase	8,000	12,000	20,000
Minute, w/clock watch	12,000	15,000	20,000
Detent chronometer, fusee, gold, 48-52mm, OF	3,500	4,500	6,000
Perpetual moonphase calendar, gold, OF	8,000	10,000	14,000
HC	9,000	11,000	15,000
Perp. moonphase cal. w/**min. repeater**, OF	22,000	28,000	35,000
HC	24,000	30,000	45,000
w/split sec., OF	40,000	55,000	75,000
w/split sec., HC	50,000	65,000	100,000

⊕ Some models and grades are not included. Their values can be determined by comparing with similar age, size, metal content, style, models and grades listed.

PAUL DITISHEIM
La Chaux de Fonds - Swiss

In 1892 Paul Ditisheim founded his own firm, which later became Vulcain. He made precision and novelty type watches. He gained many Prizes and awards also wrote many articles for improving watches. His research of new ideas were successful with oil and balances. Found on some watches, a balance, he called "**affix**". In about 1920 he formed the Solvil movement and later Titus .

TYPE – DESCRIPTION	Avg	Ex-Fn	Mint
Time only, gold, 40-44mm, OF	$300	$350	$500
HC	450	500	650
Time only, gold, 40-50mm, **Flat or Thin**, OF	450	500	650
Time only, gold, "**Affix**" balance, 45- 50mm, OF	600	650	800
HC	700	750	900
Time only, **platinum & diamond**, art deco, 41-42mm, OF	1,500	1,800	2,500
Chronograph, gold, 45-50mm, OF	700	850	1,100
HC	775	950	1,200
Split second chronograph, gold, 45-52mm, OF	900	1,100	1,500
HC	1,000	1,200	1,600
Deck chronometer **w/box**, detent chronometer, C. 1905	1,400	1,600	2,200
Pocket chronometer, **wind-indicato**r, 21J., GJS, OF, C.1920	1,200	1,400	1,800
Pocket chronometer, **pivoted detent,** gold, 57mm	3,000	3,500	5,500
Pocket chronometer, with **TOURBILLON**	25,000	32,000	45,000
1/4 hr. repeater, gold, 46-52mm, OF	1,800	2,250	2,750
HC	2,000	2,500	3,500
Minute repeater, gold, OF	3,000	3,800	5,000
HC	3,200	4,400	6,000

AFFIX Balance

Art Deco-style, 41mm, black onyx bezel and diamonds, Ca. 1920.

Pocket chronometer, Wind-Indicator, 21J., OF, C.1920   **Solvil**, 17J., with "**Affix**" balance, 49mm, OF, Ca. 1920s.

DUBOIS et FILS
Le Locle (SWISS) 1760

Merchant and Watchmaker, one of the most active in the Le Locle region. Founded in 1785. They exported all over the world and specialized in repeater, automaton watches, skeleton watches and watches with false pendulums. They provided the Courvoisier Freres with movements.

TYPE – DESCRIPTION	Avg	Ex-Fn	Mint
Verge, KW, pair case, silver, 48-52mm	$275	$325	$400
Verge, enamel w/scene & automata windmill, silver or gilt, 48-52mm...	1,100	1,400	1,800
Verge w/mock pendulum, chain & fusee, silver, OF, 48-52mm......	650	850	1,150
with **large** seconds-beating balance wheel, **Pirouette** gearing and **double** escape wheel .... ★★★★	4,000	5,000	7,500
Verge, KW, GOLD, OF, 50-54mm..	600	750	950
Verge, KW, GOLD w/enamel, OF,52mm	900	1,400	2,200
1/4 hr. repeater, SILVER, OF, 50-54mm..	650	850	1,150
1/4 hr. repeater, GOLD, OF, 50-54mm...	850	1,050	1,350
1/4 hr. repeater w/automaton, 18K, OF, 50-52mm..........................	3,000	3,800	4,500
Minute **pump** repeater, gold, OF, 50-52mm .... ★★	8,000	10,000	15,000

DuBois & Fils, **Verge** with mock pendulum, chain & fusee, silver, OF, enamel dial, 48-52mm, Ca. 1800. **Note:** This movement used a large seconds-beating balance wheel, with **pirouette** gearing and double escape wheel.

DuBois et Fils, Verge, enamel w/scene, silver or gilt, OF, painted enamel scene with windmill automata, 48-52mm. Ca. 1810.

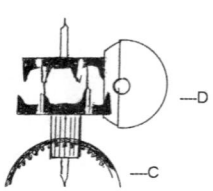

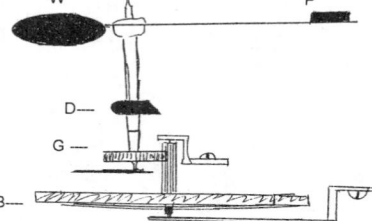

Frictional rest escapement, Double escape wheel with 6 teeth on each escape wheel for a total of 12, also note the pinion to drive double escape wheel.

D = D-shaped **pallet**, inclined for impulse. B = Balance.
C = **Contrate** wheel.   G= gear with 26 teeth at bottom.
W = counter **Weight**.   P = false pendulum.

Note: Movement has a large seconds-beating balance wheel, **pirouette** gearing, double escape wheel & a single pallet . This DuBois **pirouette** is unlike most DeBaufre or Pauzait ect. where balance wheel was central to movement.

DUCHENE L., & Fils
GENEVA

Watchmaker, well known for their large and small pieces, including coach clocks, calendar watches and minute repeater watches. The firm was known also for decorative work with polychrome champleve enamel and painted enamel, and fantasy watches. The movements are classically-designed, with fusee & verge escapements. Cases are in "Empire-style", engraved or guilloche.

TYPE – DESCRIPTION	Avg	Ex-Fn	Mint
KW, cylinder, silver, 46mm, OF	$85	$125	$175
HC	95	150	195
KW, verge fusee, silver, 46-52mm, OF	275	325	450
KW, verge fusee, enamel case ,gilt, 52mm, OF	600	900	1,500
1/4 hr. repeater, silver, 54mm, OF	500	700	1,000
1/4 hr. repeater, gold, 52mm, OF	900	1,100	1,500
1/4 hr. repeater, w/**automata**, gold, 52mm, OF	3,000	4,000	5,500
Ball form, KWKS, cylinder, 29mm, 18K OF	450	600	900

Duchene L. & Fils, 1/4 Hour Repeater, fusee and cylinder escapement, repeats on gongs, 52mm, Ca. 1820.

Dunand, 1/4 hour repeater, about 15 jewels, repeater is slide activated, 49MM, OF, Ca. 1905

DUNAND
Swiss

The Dunand factory produced repeaters, timers & chronographs during the 1890-1930 time period.

TYPE – DESCRIPTION	Avg	Ex-Fn	Mint
Time only, gold, 45-50mm, OF	$195	$250	$300
HC	300	350	500
Chronograph, gold, 45-50mm,OF	400	450	600
HC	450	500	700
Split second chronograph, gold, 45-52mm, OF	800	950	1,200
HC	900	1,100	1,500
1/4 hr. repeater, gold, 46-52mm, OF	750	900	1,100
HC	850	1,000	1,200
OF w/chrono.	950	1,100	1,300
HC w/chrono.	1,100	1,250	1,500
Minute repeater, gold, 46-52mm, OF	1,500	1,800	2,500
HC	1,800	2,200	3,000

The Complete Price Guide to Watches goal is to stimulate the orderly exchange of **Watches** be-**tween** "*buyers*" and "*sellers*".

EARNSHAW, THOMAS
LONDON

Thomas Earnshaw born in 1749 died in 1829. In about 1781 he improves the spring detent. Earnshaw also contributed to the development of the chronometer. He pioneered the method of fusing brass and steel together to form a laminate of the compensation rims as in the modern method of today. Known for his chronometers he also made 1/4 and 1/2 hour repeaters with cylinder and duplex escapements.

THOMAS EARNSHAW, chronometer, KWKS, spring detent, Z or S balance with trapezoidal weights, helical hairspring, serial # 589, silver case, Ca.1810.

Signed: "T. EARNSHAW Invt et Fecit 665 London 9117" KW KS, spring detent chronometer, NOTE: compensation curb so called "sugar-tongs", silver case, Ca.1803.

TYPE – DESCRIPTION	Avg	Ex-Fn	Mint
Time only, KW, **SILVER**, 45- 48mm, OF	$800	$900	$1,200
Time only, KW, **GOLD**, 45- 48mm, OF	1,500	2,000	3,000
1/4 hr. repeater, **GOLD**, 46-52mm, OF	4,000	5,000	6,000
Spring detent escapement, chronometer, gold, 48-54mm, OF	5,000	7,000	9,000
Spring detent escapement, chronometer, **(Sugar-Tongs)**, OF	7,000	9,000	12,000

H. R. EKEGREN
Copenhagen & Geneva

Henry Robert Ekegren, a Swiss maker of quality watches, started in business around 1870. The firm specialized in flat watches, chronometers and repeaters. Ekegren became associated with F. Koehn in 1891.

TYPE – DESCRIPTION	Avg	Ex-Fn	Mint
Time only, gold, 45- 50mm, register, OF	$550	$700	$900
HC	650	850	1,100
Chronograph, gold, 45-50mm, register, OF	800	1,000	1,500
HC	900	1,200	1,700
Split second chronograph, gold, 45-52mm, OF	1,200	1,500	1,800
HC	1,300	1,500	2,000
FIVE-Minute repeater, gold, 46-52mm, OF	1,800	2,100	2,700
HC	2,000	2,400	3,000

⊕ A collector should expect to pay modestly higher prices at local shops.

⊕ Some models and grades are not included. Their values can be determined by comparing with similar age, size, metal content, style, models and grades listed.

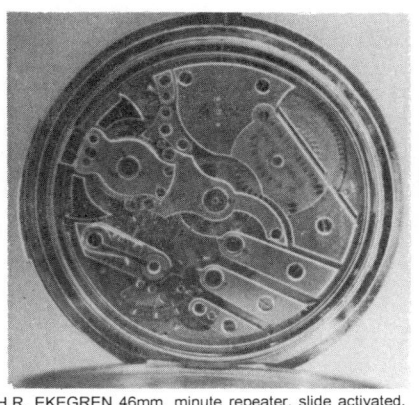
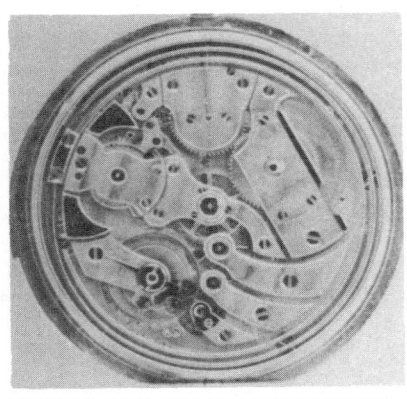

H.R. EKEGREN 46mm, minute repeater, slide activated, jeweled through hammers, open face, serial no. 78,268.

H.R. EKEGREN, 47mm, minute repeater, jeweled through hammers, hunting case.

TYPE – DESCRIPTION	Avg	Ex-Fn	Mint
Minute repeater, gold, 46-52mm, OF	$2,400	$2,900	$3,500
HC	2,700	3,500	5,000
OF w/chrono.	2,500	3,200	4,000
HC w/chrono.	3,000	3,500	5,000
OF w/split chrono.	4,000	4,500	7,000
HC w/split chrono.	4,500	6,500	10,000
Perpetual moonphase calendar, gold, OF	8,000	9,500	12,500
Perpetual moonphase cal. w/ min. repeater, OF	18,000	24,000	30,000
HC	20,000	25,000	35,000
Perp. moonphase cal. w/min. rep. and chrono., OF	22,000	24,000	32,000
HC	25,000	32,000	45,000
Karrusel, gold, 48-55mm, OF	8,000	9,500	12,000
Tourbillon, gold, 48-55mm, OF	40,000	50,000	70,000
Detent chronometer, gold, 48-52mm, OF	4,500	5,750	7,000
World time watch, gold, 48-52mm, OF	4,000	5,000	8,000

FAVRE–LEUBE
Le Locle & Geneva

Favre-Leube firm is still active and production has covered more than eight generations of watchmakers. The company has made watches since 1815.

FAVRE-LEUBE, 53mm, Minute repeater, 15 jewels, slide on rim activates the repeater mechanism, Ca.1895.

TYPE – DESCRIPTION	Avg	Ex-Fn	Mint
Early, KW KS, Swiss bar Mvt., time only, Ca.1870, Silver case ...	$100	$125	$175
KW, Gold w/enamel, 35-40mm, HC	700	800	1,000
KW, silver w/enamel, 45mm, HC	195	295	400
KW, Gold w/enamel, 45-48mm, OF	500	700	1,000
Chronograph, gold, 45-50mm, OF	500	600	800
HC	600	750	1,000
Split second chronograph, gold, 45-52mm, OF	700	850	1,100
HC	800	950	1,200
1/4 hr. repeater, gold, 46-52mm, OF	700	900	1,200
HC	900	1,100	1,400
Minute repeater, gold, 46-52mm, OF	1,200	1,400	1,800
HC	1,500	1,900	2,500

CHARLES FRODSHAM
London

Charles Frodsham followed in the footsteps of his father, William, whose father was close with Earnshaw. Charles became the most eminent of the family, producing very fine chronometers and some rare tourbillon and complicated watches. He died in 1871. His quality movements endorse the letters A.D. FMSZ. Originally Arnold & **Frodsham** was located at 84 Strand, London until 1858. He later moved to New Bond Street, London.

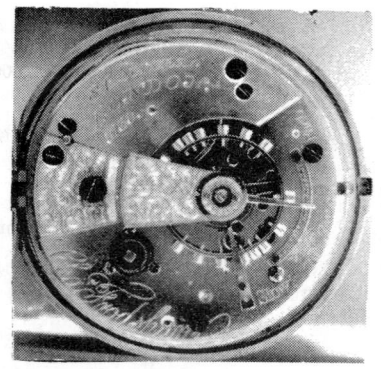

Frodsham, 84 Strand, London engraved on movement, 16-18 jewels, platinum balance screws, Ca. 1850s

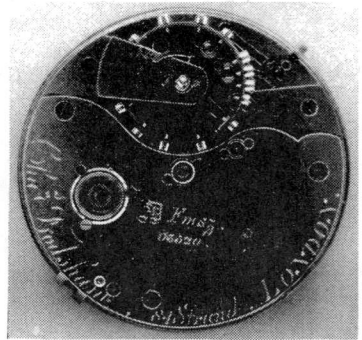

Chas. Frodsham, 84 Strand London, 25 jewels, Fusee, Freesprung, Diamond end stone, serial number 3520.

TYPE – DESCRIPTION	Avg	Ex-Fn	Mint
Time only, early mvt. 84 Strand, silver, 45- 48mm, OF, C.1850 ...	$250	$350	$475
Time only, early mvt. 84 Strand, gold, 45- 48mm, OF, C.1850	700	900	1,200
Time only, gold, 45- 50mm, OF	700	900	1,300
HC	900	1,100	1,500
Chronograph, gold, 45-50mm, OF	1,600	1,800	2,500
HC	1,800	2,400	3,000
Split second chronograph, gold, 45-52m, OF	2,800	4,000	6,000
HC	3,000	4,200	7,000

⊕ The Complete Price Guide to Watches goal is to stimulate the orderly exchange of **Watches** between *"buyers"* and *"sellers"*.

Frodsham, 46-50mm, jeweled through the center wheel, stem wind, 18K case, Ca. 1895.

Frodsham, 59mm, 60 minute Karrusel, 15 jewels, stem wind, open face, 18K gold case, Ca. 1895.

TYPE – DESCRIPTION	Avg	Ex-Fn	Mint
Minute repeater, gold, 46-52mm,OF	$4,500	$5,500	$7,000
HC	5,000	6,000	8,000
OF w/split chrono.	12,000	16,000	22,000
HC w/split chrono.	15,000	18,000	25,000
Perpetual moonphase calendar, gold, OF	18,000	22,000	28,000
Perp. moonphase cal. w/min. repeater, OF	35,000	45,000	60,000
HC	40,000	52,000	75,000
Karrusel, 16J, (59 to 60 Min. Karrusel), 18K, C.1895	5,500	8,500	12,000
Tourbillon, gold, 48-55mm, OF	45,000	65,000	90,000
Marine chronometer, Parkinson-Frodsham, helical hairspring, w/ detent escape., 48 hr. WI, C. 1840, 97mm deck box	2,400	2,800	3,500
Detent chronometer, w/wind ind., silver, OF, KWKS, C. 1850	1,800	2,500	3,300
Clock Watch, Minute repeater, OF	10,000	12,000	18,000
HC	12,000	15,000	22,000

GIRARD-PERREGAUX
La Chaux-de-Fonds Switzerland

In 1856, The Constant Girard and Henry Perregaux families founded the Swiss firm of Girard-Perregaux. About 1860, the firm made a tourbillon with three golden bridges. A replica of this watch was made in 1982. Both were a supreme expression of horological craftsmanship. Girard-Perregaux **said** about 1880 the first wrist watches were made for the German Navy officers. In 1906, the company purchased the Hecht factory in Geneva. Girard-Perregaux has been recognized many times and still makes prestigious watches.

TYPE – DESCRIPTION	Avg	Ex-Fn	Mint
Skeletonized "Shell" (Shell Oil Co. advertising watch), 7J, Base metal display case, total production = 30,000 Ca.1940	$125	$150	$250

Skeletonized **"Shell Watch"** (Golden Shell Oil) advertising a watch filled with Shell car motor oil they wanted to prove even a watch would run on this top quality car motor oil. Most stopped with heavy car oil, so the oil was removed from some watches. Girard-Perregaux used a ebauche by A. Scheld calibre 1052, Base metal display case, only 7J, total production = 30,000, & sold for $5.00, Ca. June 5, 1940.

GIRARD-PERREGAUX, three golden bridges movement patented March 25th, 1884.

GIRARD-PERREGAUX, Chronometer, with pivoted dentent, gold train, 20 jewels, nickel movement, Ca. 1878.

Note: Watches with Gold embosed dial add $200.

TYPE – DESCRIPTION	Avg	Ex-Fn	Mint
Time only, gold 40-44mm, OF	$250	$300	$400
HC	350	475	600
Time only, gold 45- 50mm, OF	325	395	500
HC	475	550	750
3 gold bridges, with **silver** case, C. 1884,	3,500	4,500	6,500
with **gold** case	6,000	8,000	12,000
Chronometer, pivoted detent, 20J., gold train, 18K, C.1878	4,000	5,000	7,000
Chronograph, gold, 45-50mm, OF	800	1,000	1,300
HC	1,000	1,200	1,500
1/4 hr. repeater, gold, 45-52mm, OF	1,400	1,700	2,200
HC	1,600	2,000	3,000
HC w/chrono., cal. & moonphase	2,400	2,800	4,000
Minute repeater, gold, 46-52mm, OF	2,500	2,800	3,200
HC	2,700	3,000	3,500
OF w/chrono.	2,800	3,200	4,000
OF w/split chrono.	4,000	4,500	5,500
HC w/cal. & moonphase	4,500	5,800	7,000
Detent chronometer, gold, 48-54mm, OF	3,500	4,000	5,000
HC	4,500	5,000	6,000

⊕ Note: Some models and grades are not included. Their values can be determined by comparing with similar age, size, metal content, style, models and grades listed.

⊕ This book endeavors to be a GUIDE or helpful manual and offers a wealth of material to be used as a tool not as a absolute document. Price Guides are like watches the worst may be better than none at all, but at best cannot be expected to be 100% accurate.

COMPARISON OF WATCH SIZES

U. S. A.	EUROPEAN
10-12 SIZE	40—44 MM
16 SIZE	45—49 MM
18 SIZE	50—55 MM

GOLAY A., LERESCHE & Fils

SWISS

Manufactured under the name Golay-Leresche from 1844-1857, then his son changed the name to Golay A., Leresche & Fils, he worked until the beginning of the 20th Century. Watches were primarily exported to U.S.A., he was well known for watches of all kinds and "grande complications".

TYPE – DESCRIPTION	Avg	Ex-Fn	Mint
Time only, gold, 45- 50mm, OF	$400	$450	$600
HC	500	550	700
Chronograph, gold, 45-50mm, OF	600	700	900
HC	700	800	1,000
Split second chronograph, gold, 45-52mm, OF	750	925	1,200
HC	900	1,100	1,400
1/4 hr. repeater, gold, 46-52mm, OF	1,400	1,800	2,200
HC	1,600	2,000	2,500
HC w/chrono., cal. & moonphase	4,000	5,200	6,500
Minute repeater, gold, OF	2,000	2,500	3,200
HC	2,200	2,800	3,500
OF w/chrono.	2,200	2,800	3,500
HC w/split chrono.	3,500	5,000	7,500
HC w/cal. & moonphase	6,000	7,500	9,500
Detent chronometer, gold, 48-52mm, OF	2,200	2,600	3,500
Perpetual moonphase calendar, gold, OF	8,000	10,000	12,500
HC	8,500	10,500	13,500
Perp. moonphase cal. w/min. repeater, OF	15,000	19,000	25,000
HC	18,000	22,000	28,000
Clock Watch, gold, 48-52mm, OF	6,000	7,500	10,000
HC	10,000	12,000	15,000

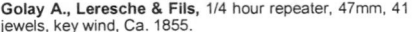

Golay A., Leresche & Fils, 1/4 hour repeater, 47mm, 41 jewels, key wind, Ca. 1855.

Golay A., Leresche & Fils, minute repeater, split seconds chronograph, moon phases, day date month, open face, Ca. 1896.

COMPARISON OF WATCH SIZES

U. S. A.	EUROPEAN
10-12 SIZE	40—44 MM
16 SIZE	45—49 MM
18 SIZE	50—55 MM

H. GRANDJEAN

The son of David-Henri (1774-1845), this respected maker produced high quality complicated watches, chronometers and ornately decorated watches for the South American market. A Grandjean specialty was magnificent enamel and gem set ladies watches.

Note: Watches with Gold embossed dial add $200.

TYPE – DESCRIPTION	Avg	Ex-Fn	Mint
Time only, gold, 45- 50mm, OF	$500	$600	$800
HC	600	800	1,200
Chronograph, gold, 45-50mm, OF	650	750	950
HC	750	900	1,100
Split second chronograph, gold, 45-52mm, OF	1,100	1,400	1,800
HC	1,200	1,600	2,200
1/4 hr. repeater, gold, 46-52mm, OF	1,400	1,600	2,000
HC	1,600	1,800	2,200
HC w/chrono., cal. & moonphase	2,500	3,000	4,000
Minute repeater, gold, OF	2,200	2,800	3,500
HC	2,800	3,500	5,000
OF w/chrono.	2,400	2,800	3,500
HC w/split chrono.	3,800	4,800	6,000
HC w/cal. & moonphase	5,800	7,000	9,000
Detent chronometer, gold, 48-52mm, OF	3,000	3,600	4,500
Perpetual moonphase calendar, gold, OF	8,000	10,000	13,000
HC	8,500	10,500	14,000
Perp. moonphase cal. w/min. repeater, OF	20,000	26,000	35,000
HC	24,000	30,000	40,000
Grande & Petite Sonnnerie repeating clock watch, 38J, fancy dial, 18k gold, 53mm, HC	10,000	13,000	20,000

H. GRANDJEAN, Grande & Petite Sonnnerie repeating clock watch, 38J, with tandem wind mechanism, fancy dial, 18k gold, 53mm, HC

🕐 A collector should expect to pay modestly higher prices at local shops.

GRUEN WATCH CO.

Swiss & U. S. A. (1874 - 1953)

The early roots of the Gruen Company are found in Columbus, Ohio where Dietrich Gruen and W.J. Savage formed a partnership in 1876. The D. Gruen & Son legacy began in 1894 and flourished with the introduction of fine quality "Precision" movements. Curvex movements, ultra-thins and the prestigious 50th anniversary model are highlights of this prolific company.

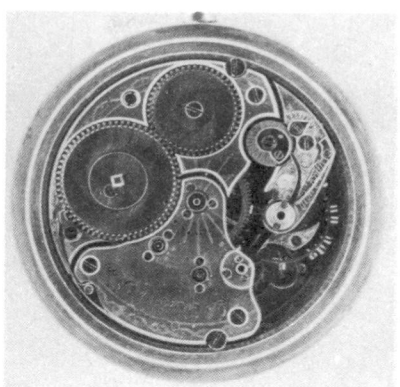 

D. Gruen & Son, OF, 44mm, 19-21J., by Assmann, plates are Argentan (silver & nickel), *Adj.to HCIP* on bal. bridge, gold mustache lever & escape wheel,S# 62,428,Ca.1895.

Gruen 50th Anniversary Watch, 10 size, 23J., 12K gold plates engraved, 600 made-1 for each month & marked *all adjts 8 eight*, 50 made later 1 for each year (S# 01-050).

TYPE – DESCRIPTION	Avg	Ex-Fn	Mint
17-21J, veri-thin or precision, 40-43mm, OF, C. 1920-40, ... Grades, V1 - V2 - V3 - V4 - V5, OF-**GF** case	$100	$125	$225
17-21J, veri-thin or precision, 40-43mm, OF, C.1920-40, ... Grades, V1 - V2 - V3 - V4 - V5, OF-**14K** case.....................	200	275	475
Pentagon case ,17-21J, **GF**, 40-43mm, OF, C.1920-40	125	150	250
Pentagon case, 17-21J, precision, **14K**, 40-43mm, C.1920-40	275	350	600
23J., GJS, 47mm, wind indicator, micrometer regulator, **14K**	500	600	900
Madretsch Model, 21J., 16 size, **GF** OF ....★	250	350	500
21-23J, D. Gruen & Son, Swiss, **Gold**, 45-54mm, OF, C. 1900-20	250	350	600
21J, D. Gruen, (by **Assmann**), **14K**, OF, C. 1905..........................	500	600	900
21J, D. Gruen, (by **Assmann**), **14K**, HC, C. 1905	750	1,000	1,500
50th anniversary , 12K gold movement, 21J + 2 diamonds = 23J, pentagon case, **18K**, 40mm, OF, C. 1924 ....★ ★	2,000	2,600	3,500

Gruen W. Co., Swiss made, 23 jewels in screwed settings, 47mm, wind indicator, micrometer regulator, Ca.1900's.

D. Gruen & Son, "Madretsch marked", 16 size, 21 jewels, open face, with end-less screw style regulator, Ca.1905.

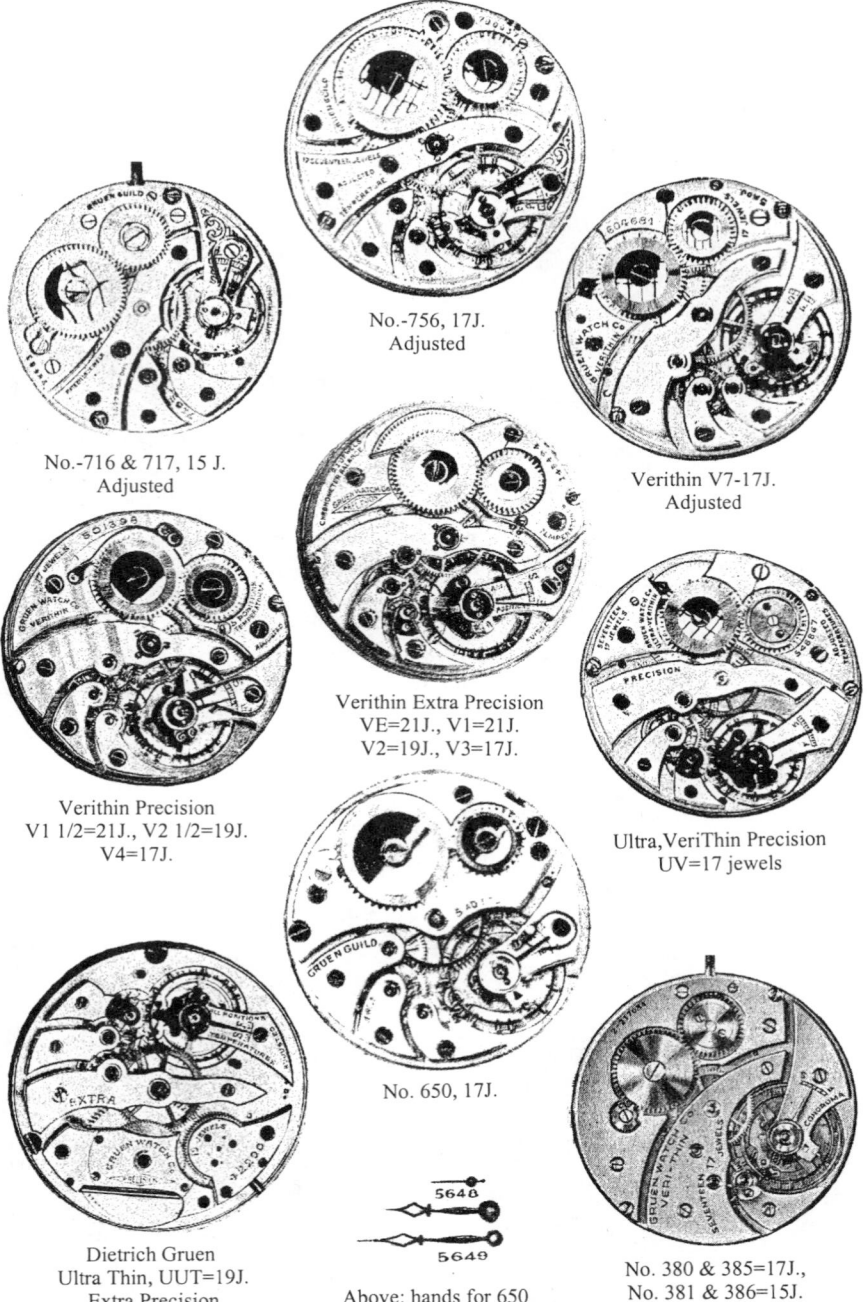

No.-756, 17J.
Adjusted

No.-716 & 717, 15 J.
Adjusted

Verithin V7-17J.
Adjusted

Verithin Extra Precision
VE=21J., V1=21J.
V2=19J., V3=17J.

Verithin Precision
V1 1/2=21J., V2 1/2=19J.
V4=17J.

Ultra,VeriThin Precision
UV=17 jewels

No. 650, 17J.

Dietrich Gruen
Ultra Thin, UUT=19J.
Extra Precision

Above: hands for 650

No. 380 & 385=17J.,
No. 381 & 386=15J.

E. GUBELIN
Swiss

Jacques Edouard Gubelin joined the firm of Mourice Brithschmid in Lucerne around 1854. By 1919, Edouard Gubelin headed the firm. In 1921 they opened an office in New York & produced fine jewelry and watches for 5 generations.

E. GUBELIN, 50mm, 29J., minute repeater, chronograph, Perpetual day-date-month-moon phase.

E. GUBELIN, 48mm, world time with 68 cities on outside bezel 24 hour on inter bezel, Gold Filled open face.

TYPE – DESCRIPTION	Avg	Ex-Fn	Mint
Time only, gold, 40- 44mm, OF	$300	$350	$450
HC	400	450	600
Time only, gold, 45- 50mm, OF	325	400	500
HC	500	650	750
Chronograph, gold, 45-50mm, OF	500	575	700
HC	600	675	800
Split second chronograph, gold, 45-52mm, OF	750	850	1,200
HC	850	1,100	1,500
1/4 hr. repeater, gold, 46-52mm, OF	1,200	1,600	2,200
HC	1,400	1,900	2,600
OF w/chrono.	1,300	1,700	2,300
HC w/chrono.	1,500	2,100	3,000
HC w/chrono., calendar & moonphase	3,200	3,800	4,500
5 minute repeater, gold, 46-52mm, OF	1,800	2,200	2,800
HC	2,000	2,400	3,200
Minute repeater, gold, 46-52mm, OF	2,200	2,700	3,500
OF w/chrono.	2,500	3,200	4,000
OF w/split chrono.	4,000	5,000	8,000
OF w/chrono., calendar & moonphase	4,800	6,000	9,000
World time watch, **Gold Filled**, 48-52mm, OF	500	650	900
World time watch, **18K Gold**, 48-52mm, OF	3,500	3,900	5,000
Perpetual moonphase calendar, gold, OF	8,500	10,000	12,500
Perp. moonphase cal. w/min. repeater, OF	24,000	28,000	35,000
Perp. moonphase cal. w/min.rep. and chrono., OF	26,000	32,000	40,000
Gold Clock Watch, OF	5,000	7,000	10,000
HC	7,000	9,000	12,000

The following will explain the French days of the week abbreviations, Sunday =**DIM** (Dimanche), Monday = **LUN** (Lundi), Tuesday = **MAR** (Mardi), Wednesday = **MER** (Mercedi), Thursday = **JEU** (Jeudi), Friday = **VEN** (Vendredi), Saturday = **SAM** (Samedi).

C. L. GUINAND & CO.

Swiss

Founded Ca. 1865 and became know for their Timers and Chronographs.

TYPE – DESCRIPTION	Avg	Ex-Fn	Mint
Timer, with register, base metal, OF, 46mm	$50	$60	$75
Timer, split second, register, base metal, OF, 46mm	65	75	95
Chronograph, 30 min. register,14K, 50mm, OF, C. 1910	400	550	800
HC	600	700	900
Split sec. chrono., 30 min. register, 14K, OF, 50mm, C. 1915	1,000	1,200	1,600
Minute repeater, **18K,** OF, 50mm, C. 1915	2,200	2,500	3,500
HC	3,000	3,400	4,000
Minute repeater, split sec. chrono., 18K, OF, 50mm, C. 1915	4,000	4,700	6,000

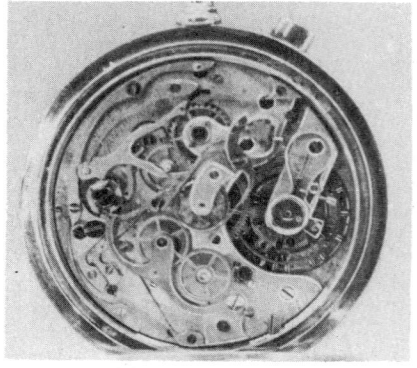

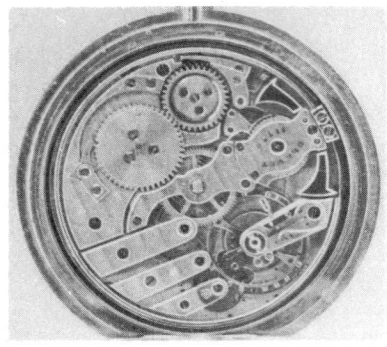

C.L. Guinand, 50mm, split-second chronograph, serial number 44,109.

Haas, Neveux & Co., 40mm, 31 jewels, minute repeater, 18k open face case, serial number 11,339.

HAAS, NEVEUX

Swiss

The Haas Neveux firm is one of the oldest in Switzerland, founded by Leopold & Benjamin Haas in 1848. High grade precision timepieces and chronometers were characteristic of this reputable firm's output.

TYPE – DESCRIPTION	Avg	Ex-Fn	Mint
Time only, gold, 40- 44mm, OF	$300	$375	$500
HC	400	475	600
Time only, gold, 45- 50mm, OF	400	475	600
HC	600	750	900
Chronograph, gold, 45-50mm, OF	700	750	900
HC	800	950	1,100
Split second chronograph, gold, 45-52mm, OF	1,000	1,300	1,700
HC	1,200	1,500	2,200
1/4 hr. repeater, gold, 46-52mm, OF	900	1,100	1,500
HC	1,100	1,300	1,700
Minute repeater, gold, 46-52mm, OF	1,500	1,800	2,500
OF w/split chrono.	3,500	4,200	5,000
OF w/cal. & moonphase	4,000	4,400	5,000
Perpetual moonphase calendar, gold, OF	7,000	8,000	10,000
Perp. moonphase cal. w/min. repeater, OF	25,000	28,000	35,000
HC	26,000	30,000	37,000
Perp. moonphase cal. w/min. rep. and chrono., OF	28,000	32,000	40,000
Clock Watch, Gold, OF	5,000	6,500	9,000
HC	7,000	8,500	12,000

HEBDOMAS
Swiss

The Hebdomas name is commonly found on imported Swiss novelty "8" day watches. Produced from the early 1900's to the 1960's, these popular timepieces featured fancy colored dials with an opening at the bottom of dial to expose the balance wheel and pallet-fork. This style watch is now being made by Arnex Time Corp. under the name of (Lucien Piccard) & other Co. names.

Hebdomas, 8 day (JOURS) 6 jewels, balance seen from the face of the watch, Ca.1920s. This style watch is now being made by Arnex Time Corp. (Lucien Piccard).

Hebdomas, 8 day (JOURS), 6 jewels, 1 adjustment, exposed balance, day date, center seconds, Ca.1920s

TYPE – DESCRIPTION	Avg	Ex-Fn	Mint
8 day, exposed balance, 7J, gun metal, 50mm, OF, C. 1920............	$150	$175	$225
8 day, exposed balance, 7J, base metal, fancy dial, 50mm, OF, C.1920	195	235	300
8 day, exposed balance, 7J, silver, 50mm, OF, C. 1920....................	195	235	300
8 day, exposed balance, 7J, silver, 50mm, HC, C. 1920's .... ★	250	300	400
8 day, exposed balance, 7J, **day date calendar,** center sec., with fancy dial, silver, 55mm, OF, C. 1920's........................	350	400	500

🕐 Note: Some models and grades are not included. Their values can be determined by comparing with similar age, size, metal content, style, models and grades listed.

🕐 Watches listed in this book are priced at the collectable fair market **value** at the Trade Show level, as complete watches having an original case, an original white enamel dial, and with the entire original movement in good working order with no repairs needed, unless otherwise noted.

The Complete Price Guide to Watches goal is to stimulate the orderly exchange of **Watches** between **"buyers"** and **"sellers".**

COMPARISON OF WATCH SIZES

U. S. A.	EUROPEAN
10-12 SIZE	40—44 MM
16 SIZE	45—49 MM
18 SIZE	50—55 MM

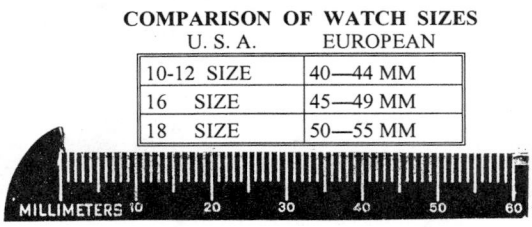

HUGUENIN & CO.

Swiss

Founded by Adolphe Huguenin and the firm name registered in 1880. Purchased by Hamilton W. Co. in March of 1959.

Huguenin & Co., 2-Train 1/4 second jump watch, center sweep hand, enamel dial, 54mm, KW KS, 18K, Ca. 1880.

Huguenin & Co., 2-Train 1/4 second jump watch, 2 main barrels & 2 gear trains, 54mm, KW KS, Ca. 1880.

TYPE – DESCRIPTION	Avg	Ex-Fn	Mint
KW, cylinder, silver, 46- 48mm, OF, C. 1870s	$85	$95	$125
KW, silver, 46- 48mm, HC, C. 1870s	125	150	185
KW, cylinder escapement, **18K**, 48mm, OF, C.1870s	250	325	425
KW, fancy engraved, **18K**, 47mm, HC, C. 1870s	500	600	800
1/4 Sec. Jump, 2-train, **silver**, 50-54mm	1,500	1,800	2,500
1/4 Sec. Jump, 2-train, **gold**, 50-54mm	2,500	2,800	3,500
Chronograph, gold, 45-52mm, OF	800	950	1,200
HC	1,000	1,200	1,500
1/4 hr. repeater, gold, 46-52mm, OF	1,400	1,600	2,000
HC	1,500	1,800	2,400
Minute repeater, gold, 46-52mm, OF	1,800	2,200	2,800
HC	2,500	2,800	4,000
OF, w/ chrono.	2,200	2,400	2,800
OF, w/ split chrono.	4,500	5,200	6,000
HC, w/ split chrono.	5,000	5,600	7,000
HC, w/ chrono., cal. & moonphase	4,500	5,000	6,500
Minute Clock Watch, Gold, OF	5,000	6,000	8,000
HC	7,000	8,000	10,000

 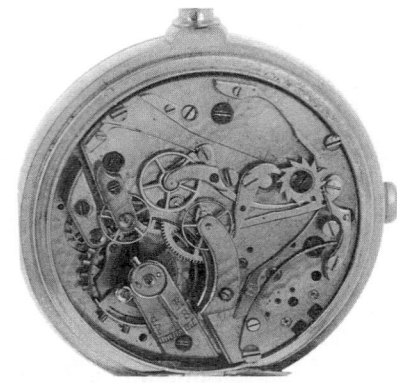

Huguenin & Co., Chronograph, enamel dial, 51mm, 18K, Hunting Case, Ca. 1890.

Huguenin & Co., Chronograph, 3/4 plate movement, 51mm, 18K, Hunting Case, Ca. 1890.

International Watch Co.
Swiss

The founder of the prestigious Swiss International Watch Co. was an American engineer F.A. Jones from Boston and previously worked for E. Howard Watch & Clock Company. F.A. Jones and C. L. Kidder for 3 years worked together from about 1869 to 1872 building up a new firm which was the only North-eastern watch factory founded in Switzerland by **Americans**. Mr. C. L. Kidder returned to U.S.A. in 1872 and took on a position with Cornell Watch Co. as first Superintendent in the new Newark factory. Mr. Jones stayed to continue building up the factory which was completed in spring of 1875. F.A. Jones in December of 1875 filed for bankruptcy and soon returned to U.S.A. in 1876. The I.W.Co., factory started by F.A. Jones was short lived and produced about 5,000 watches. In 1877 the production of the factory (now called "Internationale Uhrenfabrik") was delegated to F.F. Seeland of New York. In 1879 Mr. Seeland was removed from his position by managing director Johann Rauschenbach. The company today is still making precision, hand crafted watches.

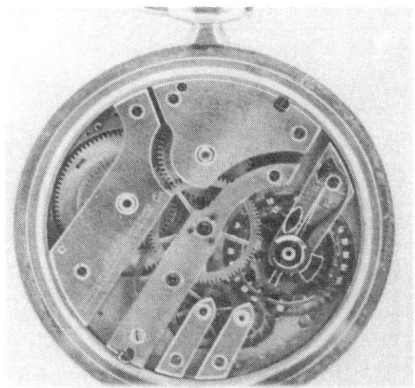

International W. Co., apertures for jump hr. & min. disc, 11-15J., enamel dial, **Pallweber** movement, Ca.1880-90.

International Watch Co., 54mm, 17 jewels, adj.6P, serial number 741,073.

TYPE – DESCRIPTION

	Avg	Ex-Fn	Mint
Early, KW, Time only, Swiss bar, silver case	$150	$175	$225
Time only, gold, 40-44mm, OF	400	485	550
HC	600	700	850
Time only, gold, 45-50mm, OF	600	675	800
HC	800	1,000	1,500
Jones Caliber, 13-16J., grades H, D, S, R, B ★★	650	750	1,000
Jones Caliber, **20J., grade E**, GJS, 3/4, SW ★★★	900	1,100	1,500
Caliber 71-72, 16J., GJS, OF ★★	625	750	900
Caliber 72-72, 16J., GJS, HC ★★	700	850	1,100
Pallweber, 11-15J., jump hr. & min. disc, enamel dial, **Niello**, HC	1,500	1,800	2,200
silver, HC	1,500	1,800	2,200
14K, HC	2,200	2,800	3,800
Chronograph, gold, 45-50mm, OF	1,800	2,000	2,500
HC	2,000	2,500	3,000
Split second chronograph, gold, 45-52mm, OF	3,000	3,400	4,000
HC	4,000	4,400	5,000
Minute repeater, gold, 46-52mm, OF	2,800	3,500	4,500
HC	3,200	4,500	6,000
OF, w/split chrono.	6,500	7,200	8,500
HC, w/split chrono	8,000	8,500	10,000
OF, w/cal. & moonphase	7,000	8,000	10,000
HC, w/chrono., cal. & moonphase	9,000	10,000	12,000
Detent chronometer, gold, 48-52mm, OF	7,000	7,500	9,000
World Time watch, gold, 48-52mm, OF	10,000	12,000	15,000
Perpetual moonphase calendar, gold, OF	7,000	7,500	9,000
Perpetual moonphase calendar, w/minute repeater, HC	30,000	40,000	60,000
Clock Watch, Gold, 48-52mm, OF	8,000	9,000	12,000
HC	10,000	12,000	15,000

A new numbering system was started with serial # 01 in **1884**. The old register can not be found and the new uninterrupted serial numbers list started on the 9th of January 1885 with serial number 6,501. The highest known serial number for the "JONES" Caliber is 42,327, & the lowest "SEELAND" Caliber serial number is 26,211, the highest number for "SEELAND" Caliber is 60,014.

PRODUCTION TOTALS

OLD DATE – SERIAL #	DATE – SERIAL #	DATE – SERIAL #	DATE – SERIAL #
1875 — 7,000	1901 - 253,500	1926 - 845,000	1951 - 1,253,000
1877 — 25,000	**1902 - 276,500**	**1927 - 866,000**	**1952 - 1,291,000**
1879 — 50,000	1903 - 298,500	1928 - 890,500	1953 - 1,316,000
1881 — 80,000	1904 - 321,000	1929 - 919,500	1954 - 1,335,000
1883 — 100,000	1905 - 349,500	1930 - 929,000	**1955 - 1,361,000**
NEW	1906 - 377,500	1931 - 937,500	1956 - 1,399,000
DATE – SERIAL #	1907 - 406,000	1932 - 938,000	1957 - 1,436,000
1884 — 6,500	1908 - 435,000	1933 - 939,000	1958 - 1,480,000
1885 — 15,500	1909 - 463,500	1934 - 940,000	1959 - 1,513,000
1886 — 23,500	1910 - 492,000	1935 - 945,000	1960 - 1,553,000
1887 — 29,500	1911 - 521,000	1936 - 955,500	1961 - 1,612,000
1888 — 37,500	1912 - 557,000	1937 - 979,000	1962 - 1,666,000
1889 — 49,000	1913 - 594,000	1938 - 1,000,000	1963 - 1,733,000
1890 — 63,000	1914 - 620,500	1939 - 1,013,000	1964 - 1,778,000
1891 — 75,500	1915 - 635,000	1940 - 1,019,500	1965 - 1,796,000
1892 — 87,500	1916 - 657,000	1941 - 1,039,000	1966 - 1,820,000
1893 — 103,000	1917 - 684,000	1942 - 1,062,000	1967 - 1,889,000
1894 — 117,000	1918 - 714,000	1943 - 1,078,000	1968 - 1,905,000
1895 — 133,000	1919 - 742,000	1944 - 1,092,000	1969 - 1,970,000
1896 — 151,500	1920 - 765,000	1945 - 1,106,000	1970 - 2,026,000
1897 — 170,500	1921 - 780,000	1946 - 1,131,000	1971 - 2,113,000
1898 — 194,000	1922 - 783,500	1947 - 1,153,000	1972 - 2,218,000
1899 — 212,000	1923 - 793,500	1948 - 1,177,000	1973 - 2,230,000
1900 — 231,000	1924 - 807,000	1949 - 1,205,000	1974 - 2,265,000
DATE – SERIAL #	1925 - 827,500	1950 - 1,222,000	1975 - 2,275,000

The above list is provided for determining the APPROXIMATE age of your watch. Match serial number with date. Watches were not necessarily sold in the exact order of manufactured date.

OLD STYLE MOVEMENTS

NOTE: **"Jones"** Caliber, had 6 different grades, the highest grade was E = 20J, SW, 3/4 plate in nickel, 3 sets of screwed gold settings; next was grade H = 16J, SW, 3/4 plate in nickel; grade D =16J, SW, 3/4 plate in nickel; grade S = 15J, SW, 3/4 plate in nickel; grade R = 15J, 3/4 plate; grade B = 13J, 3/4 plate. The **"Jones"**model used a stem- wind & *set*, a long index regulator & exposed winding gears. The *key- wind* models did not have exposed winding gears but used long index regulator. **"SEELAND"** Caliber, usually were full or 3/4 plate, with short index regulator, and lever or pin set.

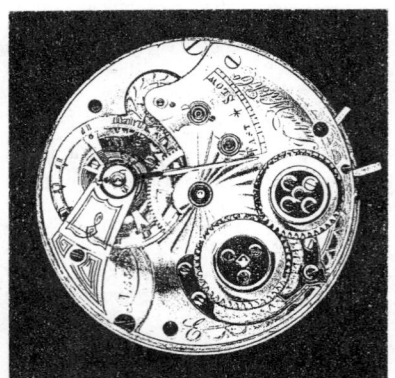

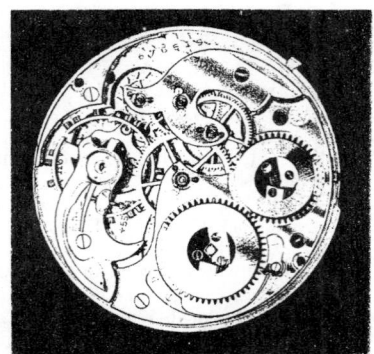

"Jones" Caliber, grade "E", HC, 20J., long index regulator, exposed wolf tooth wind gears, gold train, 3 sets of screwed in gold jewel settings, SW, 3/4 plate, overcoil hair-spring, (may have a pat. date on movement of Sept. 15th, 1868) Ca. 1876.

"71" Caliber, 16J., OF, 4 sets of screw style gold jewel settings, 300 made in 1904 & 300 in 1917, also HC Caliber **"72"**, 300 made in 1904 & 300 in 1917, 71 & 72 total=1,200.

Ⓑ Some models and grades are not included. Their values can be determined by comparing with similar age, size, metal content, style, models and grades listed.

Ⓑ The year a watch was **sold** may differ from the year it was **produced**.

INVICTA
Swiss

Founded by R. Picard in 1837. Invicta trade-mark was registered on May 18, 1896 by Files de R. Picard, of La Chaux-de-Fonds. Other names used Seeland Watch Co. and Eno Watch Co.

TYPE – DESCRIPTION	Avg	Ex-Fn	Mint
1/4 hr. repeater, gun metal ,48mm, OF, C. 1900s	$425	$485	$600
1/4 hr. repeater, silver, 48mm, OF, C. 1900s	500	600	750
1/4 hr. repeater, silver, 50mm, HC, C. 1900s	700	800	950
1/4 hr. repeater, **gold**, 58mm, HC, C. 1900s	800	1,100	1,500
with chronograph	1,200	1,500	2,000
Min. repeater, gun metal, 52mm, HC, C. 1900s	700	900	1,300
silver, HC	800	1,100	1,500
gold, HC	1,200	1,500	2,200
W/chronograph, gold, HC	1,500	2,000	2,800

INVICTA, 1/4 hour repeater with chronograph, 18 jewels, Hunting Case about 58MM, Ca. 1895.

JACOT, HENRI
PARIS

Henri Jacot settled in Paris in 1820 and developed the carriage clock industry. He also invented and improved watchmaking and clock making tools. Henri Jacot died July 31, 1867.

TYPE – DESCRIPTION	Avg	Ex-Fn	Mint
KW, cylinder, silver, 46mm, OF	$85	$100	$125
HC	125	150	185
KW, LADIES, **18K,** 40-44mm, OF	225	275	350
HC	300	350	425
KW, GENTS, **18K,** 48mm, OF	400	450	550
HC	500	550	650
1/4 hr. repeater, SILVER, 50mm, OF	800	950	1,200
1/4 hr. repeater, GOLD, 50mm, OF	1,500	1,700	2,000

CHARLES E. JACOT

New York & Swiss

In 1837 Charles worked with his uncle, Louis Matthey in New York City. During the 20 year period of working in the U.S.A. he was sold a interest in the firm and the name was changed to Jacot, Courvoisier & Co. Charles E. Jacot had a patent for a star duplex escapement on July 20, 1852. He had about 12 or more watch patents.

In 1857 he returned to Switzerland he forms a company of Jacot & Saltzman. 1876 the name of the firm was Charles E. Jacot. He remained in close contact with his New York connections and in 1897 he died. In 1925 the firm Chas.E. Jacot was listed in Le Locle.

TYPE – DESCRIPTION	Avg	Ex-Fn	Mint
Early, KW, Time only, silver case	$150	$200	$300
Time only, gold, 40-44mm, OF	300	400	550
HC	400	550	800
Time only, gold, 45-50mm, OF	400	550	800
HC	700	800	1,000
Time only, 30J., independent 1/4 seconds, 2 train, gold, OF	1,000	1,500	2,200
HC	1,500	2,200	3,500
3 or 4 star duplex, Patented July 1852, gold case .... ★★★★	2,500	3,500	5,000

Cha's E. Jacot, Patents, Sept. 64, Nov. 67, Apr, 70; 50mm, lever escapement, SW, HC, Ca. 1871, S# 8133.

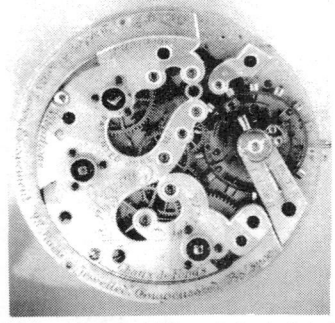

Cha's E. Jacot, on movement "Chaux de Fonds, Indep't Quarter Seconds Lever Escapement 28 Ruby Jewels Compensated Balance. Isochronal Vibrations. Patented June, 1858, S# 7715", 2 train, KW & KS from back.

Cha's E. Jacot, on movement "Chaux de Fonds, Improved Straight Line Lever, full jeweled in Ruby & Sapphire, Pat. Sept. 1859, S# 1637", KW & KS.

Cha's E. Jacot, on movement, " Pat, Oct. 1867, N=25338", KW & KS from back, 15 jewels, 40mm.

RIGHT: Cha's E. Jacot's STAR DUPLEX escapement with 3 pointed star, escapement with 4 pointed star PATENTED JULY 20, 1852.

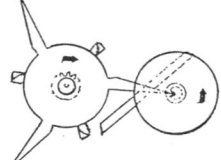
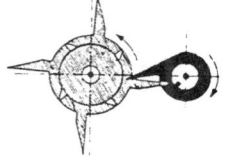

JOSEPH JOHNSON
LIVERPOOL, (1810-1850)

Josh. Johnson of Liverpool started his firm in the early 1800's and lasted till mid 1800's. The Johnson firm supplied the U.S. market with low to medium cost key-wind watches.

TYPE – DESCRIPTION	Avg	Ex-Fn	Mint
KW, 7-15J, fusee, silver, 47mm, OF	$125	$200	$300
KW,7- 15J, fusee, silver, 47mm, HC	150	250	350
KW,7-15J, swiss, **gilt dial,** fancy case, **18K,** 48mm,OF	265	300	375
KW, lever, fusee, **gold dial, Heavy 18K,** 52mm, HC	800	950	1,200
KW, **rack lever** escapement, **Silver,** 56mm, OF	300	350	500
HC	400	450	600
KW, **rack lever** escapement, **Gold,** 56mm, OF	700	850	1,100
HC	1,100	1,200	1,500
KW, verge fusee, **multi-color gold dial & THIN case,** 52mm, OF	400	450	600
HC	700	800	950
KW, **15 sec. dial,** detached lever, fusee, multi-color gold dial & case, 50mm, OF	800	950	1,200

Signed on movement *Josh. Johnson Liverpool Detached Patent*, Key wind Key Set, diamond end stone, Massey style side lever, the escape wheel coverts the second hand to rotate once every 15-seconds rather than the normal 60-seconds. Multi-color gold case and dial with carved decorations on the back of case and outer rim of the case, S # 5563, 50mm open face case, Ca. 1850.

🕐 Note: Some models and grades are not included. Their values can be determined by comparing with similar age, size, metal content, style, models and grades listed.

🕐 Watches listed in this book are priced at the collectable fair market **value** at the trade show level, as **complete** watches having an original case, an original white enamel dial, and with the entire original movement in good working order with no repairs needed, unless otherwise noted.

COMPARISON OF WATCH SIZES

U. S. A.	EUROPEAN
10-12 SIZE	40—44 MM
16 SIZE	45—49 MM
18 SIZE	50—55 MM

JULES JURGENSEN
Swiss

The firm of Jules Jurgensen was an extension of the earlier firm of Urban Jurgensen & Sons, which was located, at various times, in Copenhagen and Le Locle. Jules ultimately established his firm in Le Locle after his father's death in the early 1830's. From that time forward the company produced, generally speaking, very fine watches that were high grade and complicated. It appears that by 1850 the company had already established a strong market in America, offering beautiful heavy 18K gold watches of exemplary quality. Until around 1885, most stem-winding watches exhibited the **bow-setting feature.**

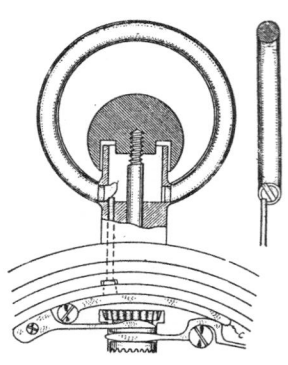

The Jules Jurgensen famous **bow-setting** feature, was Patented in 1867.

Jules Jurgensen, 27 jewels, 1/5 second jump watch, 2 main barrels & 2 gear trains, 54mm, Ca. 1890.

Jules Jurgensen, LEFT: fully signed dial *"Jules Jurgensen Copenhagen"*; RIGHT: movement signed on barrel bridge *"Jules Jurgensen Copenhagen No.6319"*, 18K Hunting Case, 17 jewels, with gold escape wheel & chronometer pivoted detent escapement, KWKS, Ca. 1875.

Almost any collectible Jurgensen watch will be fully signed on the dial and movement, with an impressively embossed "JJ" stamping on all covers of the case. Watches not so marked should be examined carefully; and untypical or inelegant stamping should be viewed suspiciously, as there have been some forgeries of these fine watches. Frequently one finds the original box and papers accompanying the watch, which enhances the value. After 1885, as the firm started to buy movements from other companies, we begin to see variations in Jurgensen watches. By 1930, Jurgensen watches barely resembled the quality and aesthetics of the early period, and they are not as desirable to the collector.

JULES JURGENSEN, 46mm, 21J., hands set by inclination of pendant ring, serial # 14,492, ca.1890.

JULES JURGENSEN, 46-52mm, Minute repeater, 32 jewels, Ca.1887.

TYPE – DESCRIPTION	Avg	Ex-Fn	Mint
Time only, gold, 35- 44mm, Ca. 1930, OF	$600	$750	$1,000
HC	800	900	1,200
Time only, gold, 45- 55mm, OF	900	1,100	1,500
HC	1,000	1,600	2,000
Time only, gold, 45- 55mm, **BOW SET**, OF	2,000	2,500	3,500
HC	3,000	3,400	4,000
Flat digital watch, 18J., gold, 40-44mm, OF, Ca. 1930	4,000	4,300	5,000
1/5 second jump watch, 2 main barrels & 2 gear trains, 18K OF	3,500	4,500	6,000
Chronograph, gold, 45-50mm, OF	3,000	3,500	5,000
HC	4,000	4,500	6,000
HC w/register	4,500	4,800	6,500
Split second chronograph, gold, 45-52mm, OF	5,500	5,800	7,000
HC	6,500	6,800	8,000
5 minute repeater, gold, 46-52mm, OF	4,000	4,500	6,000
HC	5,000	5,500	6,500
Minute repeater, gold, 46-52mm, OF	5,000	6,000	7,500
HC	6,000	6,500	8,000
OF, w/ chrono.	6,500	7,000	8,500
HC, w/ chrono.	8,000	9,000	11,000
OF, w/split chrono.	10,000	12,000	18,000
HC, w/split chrono.	11,000	14,000	20,000
Detent chronometer, gold, 48-52mm, OF	6,000	8,000	10,000
HC	7,000	9,000	12,000
Perpetual moonphase calendar, gold, OF	20,000	24,000	30,000
HC	25,000	28,000	35,000
Perp. moonphase cal. w/min. repeater, OF	45,000	55,000	70,000
HC	50,000	60,000	75,000
Tourbillon ★ ★ ★	100,000	150,000	225,000
Clock Watch, OF	10,000	14,000	20,000
HC	12,000	17,000	25,000

EDWARD KOEHN

Swiss

Koehn was an innovative watchmaker and a specialist in the design of thin calibre watches. Formerly associated with Patek Phillipe and H. R. Ekegren, he produced watches under his own name from 1891-1930.

TYPE – DESCRIPTION	Avg	Ex-Fn	Mint
Time only, gold, 40- 44mm, OF	$400	$450	$550
HC	550	650	800
Time only, gold, 45- 50mm, OF	800	850	1,000
HC	1,000	1,200	1,500
Chronograph, gold, 45-50mm, OF	1,200	1,400	1,800
HC	1,400	1,600	2,000
Split second chronograph,gold, 45-52mm, OF	1,800	2,000	2,500
HC	2,500	2,900	3,500
5 minute repeater, gold, 45-52mm, OF	3,000	3,400	4,000
HC	3,500	3,800	4,500
Minute repeater, gold, 46-52mm, OF	2,200	2,700	3,500
HC	2,800	3,200	4,000
OF, w/split chrono.	4,000	4,500	5,500
HC, w/split chrono.	6,000	6,500	7,500

E. Koehn, of Geneve, 46mm, 18 jewels, note: **free standing barrel,** lever escapement, Ca. 1900.

🕐 Note: Some models and grades are not included. Their values can be determined by comparing with similar age, size, metal content, style, models and grades listed.

🕐 Watches listed in this book are priced at the collectable fair market **value** at the trade show level, as complete watches having an original case, an original white enamel dial, and with the entire original movement in good working order with no repairs needed, unless otherwise noted.

COMPARISON OF WATCH SIZES

U. S. A.	EUROPEAN
10-12 SIZE	40—44 MM
16 SIZE	45—49 MM
18 SIZE	50—55 MM

The Complete Price Guide to Watches goal is to stimulate the orderly exchange of **Watches** between *"buyers"* and *"sellers"*.

A. LANGE & SOHNE
Germany

A. Lange & Sohne was established with the aid of the German government at Glashutte, Germany in 1845. Lange typically produced 3/4 plate lever watches in gilt finish for the domestic market, and in nickel for the export market. High grade and very practical, these watches had a banking system for the pallet that was later used briefly by E. Howard in America. Lange complicated watches are scarce and very desirable. On May 8, 1945 Russian bombers destroy workshops.

All A. Lange & Sohne must be **triple signed** (Dial, Case, Movement) to bring top prices

PRODUCTION TOTALS

DATE– SERIAL #	DATE– SERIAL #	DATE– SERIAL #
1870— 5,000	1895— 35,000	1920— 75,000
1875— 10,000	1900— 40,000	1925— 80,000
1880— 20,000	1905— 50,000	1930— 85,000
1885— 25,000	1910— 60,000	1935— 90,000
1890— 30,000	1915— 70,000	1940—100,000

TYPE – DESCRIPTION	Avg	Ex-Fn	Mint
Time only, **A.L.S.** first. quality , GJS, **18k gold**, 45- 52mm, OF	$4,000	$5,500	$8,000
HC	5,500	7,000	9,000
Time only, **D.U.F.** grade, pressed jewels, **14k gold**, 45- 52mm, OF	1,500	2,000	3,000
HC	2,000	2,500	3,500
Time only, **O.L.I.W.** grade, pressed jewels, not adjusted	500	600	800
World War II model, wind indicator, 52mm, OF (before 1945)	1,500	1,900	2,500
Chronograph, gold, 45-50mm, OF	9,000	14,000	18,000
HC	10,000	15,000	20,000
Split second chronograph, gold, 45-52mm, OF	15,000	22,000	30,000
HC	17,000	24,000	32,000
1/4 hr. repeater, gold, 45-52mm, OF	10,000	15,000	20,000
HC	12,000	18,000	25,000
Minute repeater, gold, 45-52mm, OF	17,000	24,000	30,000
HC	18,000	28,000	40,000
OF, w/split chrono.	20,000	35,000	50,000
HC, w/split chrono.	23,000	37,000	55,000
Detent chronometer, gold, 48-52mm, OF	20,000	25,000	35,000
Perpetual moonphase calendar, gold, OF	30,000	42,000	60,000
Karrusel, 14J., 60 min. carriage driven by **center wheel**, 18K ..... ★ ★ ★	50,000	65,000	90,000

Right: To identify a Glashutte movement note balance cock.

A. LANGE & SOHNE, 52mm, serial number 87250, hunting case, Ca. 1926. The A.L.S. top grade watches had gold jewel settings which are screwed to the plates, diamond end stone, gold lever, Adj. to 5 positions, a second A.L.S. grade the gold settings are not screwed into plates, and most had no diamond end stone, both A.L.S. grades are in 18K cases.

D. U. F. grade by Lange, 50mm, 3/4 plate, engraved on movement **"Deutsche Uhren Fabrikation Glashutte,"** serial number 58,398. The D. U. F. grade had pressed jewels, brass & nickel balance, adjusted to 3 positions, the D.U. F. grades came in 14K cases and introduced in about 1885 with lower production cost to compete with other Co.'s.

TYPE – DESCRIPTION	Avg	Ex-Fn	Mint
Perp. moonphase cal. w/min. repeater, OF	$45,000	$80,000	$125,000
Perp. moonphase cal. w/min. rep. and chronograph, HC .... ★	100,000	135,000	175,000
Perp. moonphase cal. w/min. rep., leap year indicator, 30 minutes recorder			
2 button split chronograph, 60mm, HC .... ★★★★	185,000	200,000	275,000

A. Lange & Sohne, 60mm Hunter Cased Minute Repeating instantaneous Perpetual calendar with day, date, month and leap year indicator, full split second chronograph operated by two buttons with minute recorder and the phases of the moon. The white enamel dial has Arabic numbers, pierced gold hands, four subsidiary dials indicating day, date and the month is combined with leap year indicator and 30 minutes recorder, and the moon phases is combined constant seconds.

A. Lange & Sohne, the movement made in the typical Glashutte 3/4 plate style with a nickel finish, gold lever escapement with convex entry pallet & concave exit pallet, compensation balance, diamond endstone, gold escape wheel, gold lever, repeating on two gongs. This type of watches have 40 to 60 jewels, 75 wheels, over 300 screws and 24 bridges. The movement was supplied by Audemars Piguet in 1908-1909 & may be one of fourteen with a two button chronograph finished & cased by A. Lange & Sohne. Audemars Piguet supplied about 35 watches of this type to the Glashutte market.

LE COULTRE & CO.
Swiss

Antoine Le Coultre in 1833 formed a company to make ebauches. He created a machine to cut pinions from solid steel as well as other machines for manufacturing clocks and watches. By 1900 they were making flat or thin watches. 1936 Jaeger & Le Coultre officially merge. The signed watches with Jaeger - Le Coultre logo may fetch more money, but have the same quality grade movement as the signed Le Coultre dial & movement. They make movements & parts for Vacheron & Constantin, P. P. & Co., Omega, Longines & many more.

TYPE – DESCRIPTION	Avg	Ex-Fn	Mint
Early, KW, Time only, Swiss bar, Pre. 1870, silver case	$75	$100	$175
Time only, gold, 40- 44mm, OF	200	250	400
HC	250	350	500
Time only, gold, 45- 50mm, OF	225	300	400
HC	375	450	575
8 day, 15J, wind indicator, 45mm, **18K**, OF	600	750	1,100
8 day, 14K, OF	500	650	900
8 day, S.S., OF	300	400	600
Roulette wheel style bezel, gold, 40mm, OF	500	700	1,100
World time watch, gold, 48-52mm, OF	4,000	5,200	7,000
Chronograph, gold, 45-50mm, OF	700	850	1,100
HC	800	1,000	1,300
OF, w/register	700	900	1,200
Split second chronograph,gold, 45-52mm, OF	1,000	1,200	1,500
HC	1,400	1,600	2,000

Le Coultre & Co., 52mm, 32J., minute repeater, exposed winding gears, high grade movement, 14K HC.

Le Coultre & Co., runs on one winding for **8 DAYS**, wind-indicator at 6 0'clock, 45mm, OF, Ca. 1930.

TYPE – DESCRIPTION	Avg	Ex-Fn	Mint
1/4 hr. repeater, gold, 46-52mm, OF	$1,000	$1,300	$1,800
HC w/chrono., cal. & moonphase	2,400	3,500	5,000
Minute repeater, gold, 46-52mm, OF	2,200	2,500	3,200
HC	2,300	2,800	3,500
OF, w/chrono. & register	2,500	2,800	3,400
HC, w/chrono. & register	2,700	3,400	4,000
HC, w/split chrono.	3,500	4,000	5,500
HC w/chrono., cal. & moonphase	5,000	6,000	8,000
Perpetual moonphase calendar, gold, OF	7,000	8,000	10,000
HC	7,500	8,500	11,000
Perp. moonphase cal. w/min. repeater, OF	15,000	18,000	25,000
HC	17,000	22,000	30,000
Perpetual moonphase cal. w/ min. rep. & chrono., OF	18,000	24,000	30,000
HC	20,000	26,000	35,000
Clock Watch, gold, 46-52mm, OF	6,000	7,500	10,000
HC	8,000	9,000	12,000

Note: Ebauche movements look under hammers for initials **L.C. & Co.**(not on all movements)

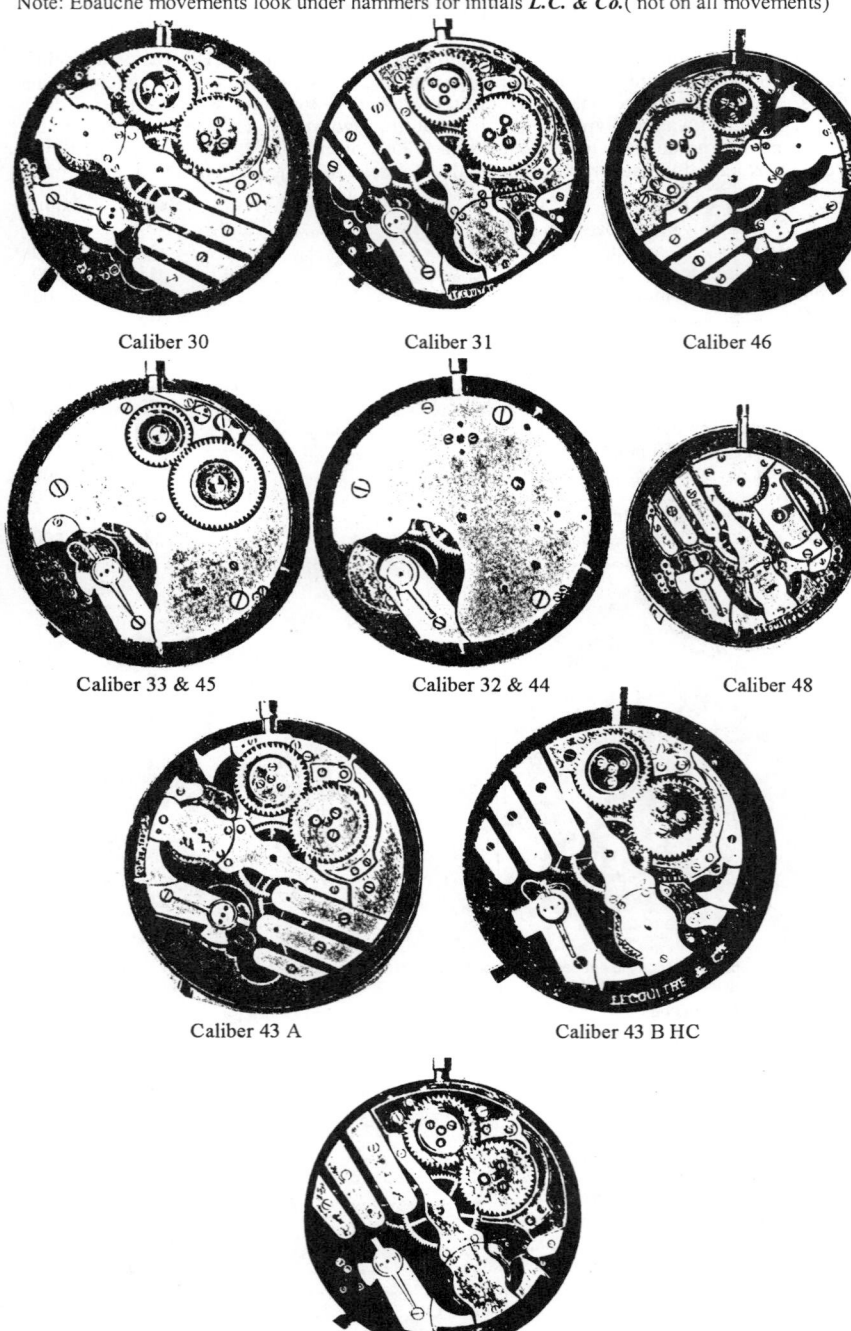

Caliber 30   Caliber 31   Caliber 46

Caliber 33 & 45   Caliber 32 & 44   Caliber 48

Caliber 43 A   Caliber 43 B HC

Caliber 49

LE PHARE
Swiss

Le Phare specialized in the production of repeater ebauches from 1890-1940. They were the first to mass produce or manufacture inexpensive repeaters with interchangeable parts. Le Phare *patented* a **centrifugal force governor**.

TYPE – DESCRIPTION	Avg	Ex-Fn	Mint
Chronograph, gold, 45-50mm, OF	$600	$750	$1,000
HC	700	850	1,100
Split second chronograph, gold, 45-52mm, OF	1,100	1,300	1,600
HC	1,200	1,400	1,800
1/4 hr. repeater, gold, 46-52mm, OF	900	1,000	1,300
HC	1,000	1,200	1,500
HC w/chrono., cal. & moonphase	2,200	2,700	3,500
Minute repeater, gold, 46-56mm, OF	1,500	1,800	2,200
high grade min. repeater with **helical** balance spring	2,500	3,000	4,000
HC	1,800	2,200	2,800
OF w/chrono. & register	1,800	2,400	3,000
HC w/chrono.	1,900	2,500	3,200
HC w/chrono., cal. & moonphase	2,800	3,400	4,800

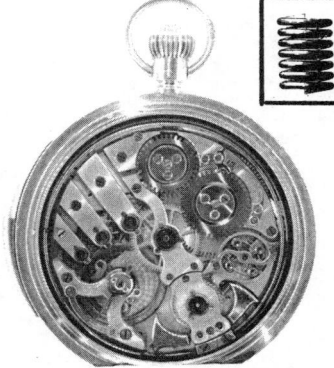

Le Phare, 56mm, minute repeater, chronograph and calendar with moon phases, Note the governor at 6 0'clock..

Le Phare, high grade min. repeater with **helical** balance spring, 5mm, Ca. 1910.

Below: Centrifugal style governor.

Le Phare, Min. repeater, 54mm, HC, 17J., 3/4 plate, push button, Ca. 1895, Note centrifugal force governor at 6 o'clock.

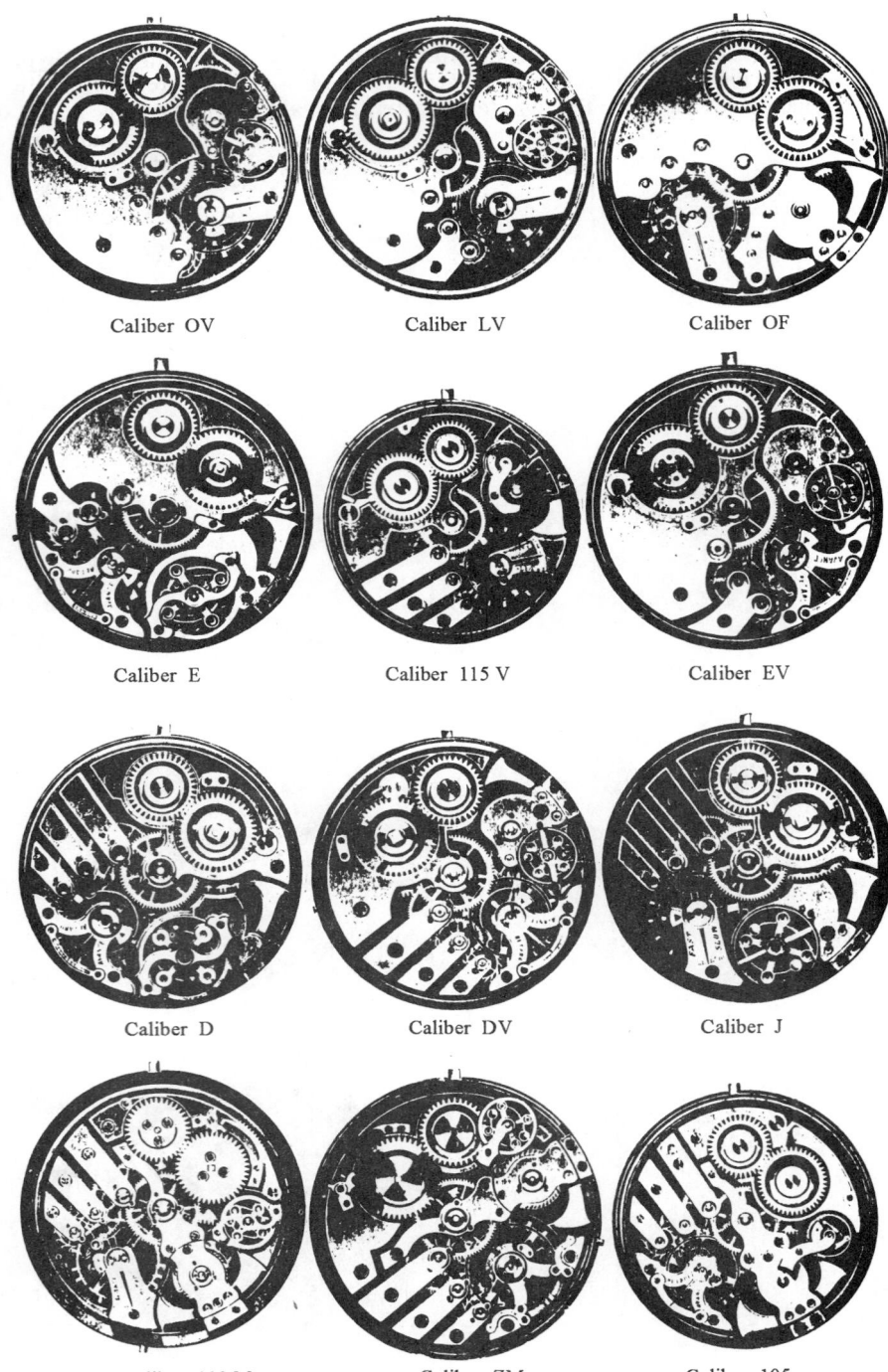

Caliber OV   Caliber LV   Caliber OF

Caliber E   Caliber 115 V   Caliber EV

Caliber D   Caliber DV   Caliber J

Caliber 110 M   Caliber ZM   Caliber 105

L'Epine or Lepine
Paris France (1720 - 1814)

Jean-Antoine L'Epine more than any other one man, revolutionized the **form** of the watch. He developed and first used the following list of improvements in 1770 to 1790, bar bridges, suspended use of the fusee, free-standing **going** barrel, new style virgule, cylinder and lever escapements, stylized arabic numbers, center seconds, moon style hands, wolf's teeth gearing, gongs for repeaters, much thinner watches about 12-13mm, concealed case hinge, cuvette dust cover, engine turned cases, back wind & back set of the hands, pump wind, and open faced style case which is called L'Epine calibre by the Swiss watch makers. The House of Lepine was sold in 1914.

George Washington was the owner of a L'Epine *Gold Watch*. Governor Morris was commissioned to acquire for his friend, the President, a reliable watch while on a business trip to Paris, France. On April 23, 1789, Governor Morris selected a Lepine large gold watch with Virgule escapement as the best. Thomas Jefferson was asked to deliver the watch due to the fact the Governor had a delay in Paris. The watch is on exhibit in the Museum of the Historical Society of Pennsylvania, Pittsburgh, Pa.

TYPE – DESCRIPTION	Avg	Ex-Fn	Mint
Time only, **Silver,** KW, verge or cylinder escap., 46-52mm OF	$200	$300	$600
Time only, **Silver,** KW, virgule escap., 46-52mm OF	600	700	1,000
Time only, **Gold,** KW, verge or cylinder escap, , plain, 50mm, OF	500	650	900
Time only, **Gold,** KW, virgule escap., enamel & scene, 50mm, OF	2,000	2,500	3,800
Time only, **Gold,** KW, *lever with 40 tooth gold escape wheel,* Ca. 1778-1790, 50mm, OF .... ★★★	2,500	3,500	5,000
1/4 repeater, **SILVER,** 52mm, OF..	800	1,100	1,500
1/4 repeater, **GOLD,** 54mm, OF..	1,100	1,500	2,000
Minute Pump Repeater, Gold .... ★★★	6,000	8,000	12,000

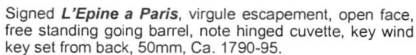

Signed *L'Epine a Paris*, virgule escapement, open face, free standing going barrel, note hinged cuvette, key wind key set from back, 50mm, Ca. 1790-95.

Lepine, virgule escapement, note horse-shoe shaped centerbridge for center seconds, free standing going barrel, Ca. 1790-95.

LE ROY ET CIE
Paris

Le Roy et Cie was the final product of a dynasty of great watchmakers, starting with Julien Le Roy and his son Pierre, whose credits are numerous in the development of horology in the 18th century. There is, however, much confusion and hoopla over "Le Roy" watches. Frequently, you will see watches signed "Le Roy" that have nothing to do with the original family. These watches are unimportant. You have to distinguish between the works of Julien, of Pierre, of Charles, and of their contemporary namesakes. The modern firm, Le Roy et Cie., established in the late 19th century, contracted and finished some very fine and, in some cases, extremely important complicated watches, using imported Swiss ebauches.

TYPE – DESCRIPTION	Avg	Ex-Fn	Mint
Verge, KW, paircase, silver, 49-50mm, C. 1775	$325	$400	$500
Verge, fusee, Enamel w/scene, 18K, 38- 40mm, C. 1760	2,400	3,000	3,800
Miniature, 22mm, diamonds & pearls on enamel, OF	800	1,000	1,300
Time only, gold, 45- 50mm, OF	600	750	1,000
1/4 hr. repeater, gold, 46-52mm, OF	1,200	1,800	2,400
Min. repeater, two train, tandem winding wheels, fully jeweled jump center seconds, gold, 50mm	6,000	7,000	9,000

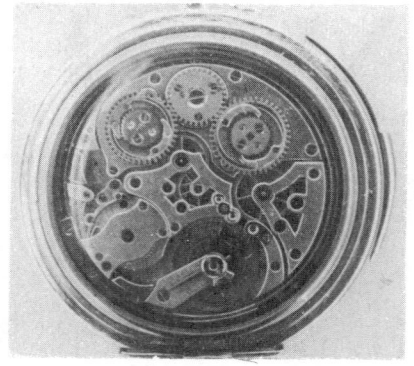

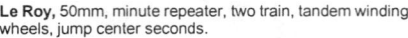

Le Roy, 50mm, minute repeater, two train, tandem winding wheels, jump center seconds.

Le Roy, 22mm, miniature watch with enamel, pearls, with Diamonds on the pin, 18K, OF, Ca. 1910.

⊕ This book endeavours to be a GUIDE or helpful manual and offers a wealth of material to be used as a tool not as a absolute document. Price Guides are like watches the worst may be better than none at all, but at best cannot be expected to be 100% accurate.

⊕ Characteristics of watches differ for the same age of both case and movement, because these features vary it may not be accurate to date a watch by one single influence. Example: the second hand was not commonly found on watches before 1750, but common about 1800. The first second hand appeared in 1665 and another in 1690. Therefore statements are broad rather than accurate.

⊕ A collector should expect to pay modestly higher prices at local shops.

The Complete Price Guide to Watches goal is to stimulate the orderly exchange of **Watches** between *"buyers"* and *"sellers"*.

LONGINES
Swiss

The beautiful Fabrique des Longines is situated in St. Imier, Switzerland. The company was founded by Ernest Francillon in 1866. They manufactured all grades of watches. Winged hour-glass trademark registered in May 1890.

PRODUCTION TOTALS
LONGINES DATE OF MOVEMENT MANUFACTURE

DATE – SERIAL #	DATE – SERIAL #	DATE – SERIAL #
1867 — 1	1911 - 2,500,000	1937 - 5,500,000
1870 — 20,000	1912 - 2,750,000	1938 - 5,750,000
1875 — 100,000	1913 - 3,000,000 - Aug.	1940 - 6,000,000 - June
1882 — 250,000	1915 - 3,250,000	1945 - 7,000,000 - July
1888 — 500,000	1917 - 3,500,000	1950 - 8,000,000 - May
1893 — 750,000	1919 - 3,750,000	1953 - 9,000,000 - July
1899 - 1,000,000 - Feb.	1922 - 4,000,000 - Oct.	1956-10,000,000 - May
1901 - 1,250,000	1925 - 4,250,000	1959-11,000,000 - April
1904 - 1,500,000	1926 - 4,500,000	1962-12,000,000 - May
1905 - 1,750,000	1928 - 4,750,000	1966-13,000,000 - June
1907 - 2,000,000 - July	1929 - 5,000,000 - Oct.	1967-14,000,000 - Feb.
1909 - 2,250,000	1934 - 5,250,000	1969-15,000,000 - Feb.

The above list is provided for determining the APPROXIMATE age of your watch. Match serial number with date. Watches were not necessarily sold in the exact order of manufactured date.

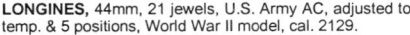

LONGINES, 44mm, 21 jewels, U.S. Army AC, adjusted to temp. & 5 positions, World War II model, cal. 2129.

LONGINES, 59mm, 21 jewels, Railroad Model , gold filled open face case, Ca. 1910-1925.

TYPE – DESCRIPTION	Avg	Ex-Fn	Mint
15 -17J, GF, 40- 50mm, OF, C. 1930	$55	$65	$85
15 -17J, **Gold**, 40- 50mm, OF, C. 1930	150	175	300
21J, GF, 40- 50mm, OF, C. 1930	125	150	250
15 -17J, silver, 48- 50mm, HC, C. 1890	100	125	165
15-17J, for Tiffany, Sterling, 45- 50mm OF, C. 1905	135	155	195
KW, for Turkish market, .800 silver, HC, C. 1900	100	125	175
17J, "Express Leader", Adj., LS, **GF**, 48- 50mm, OF	125	150	250
19J, "Express Leader", Adj., LS, **GF**, 48- 50mm, OF	150	175	300
19J, "Express Monarch", LS, **GF**, 48- 50mm, OF	165	200	325
21J, "Express Monarch", LS, **GF**, 48- 50mm, OF	200	250	400
23J, "Express Monarch", Adj., LS, **GF**, 48- 50mm, OF	225	300	500
24J, "Express Monarch", LS, **GF**, 48- 50mm, OF	250	350	600
21J, Trans-Continental Express, LS, **GF**, 48- 50mm, OF	200	250	350
23J, Trans-Continental Express, LS, **GF**, 48- 50mm, OF	225	250	450
U.S. Army AC, World War II, 21J., silver, 44mm, **WI.**, OF	600	800	1,200
U.S. Army, World War II, 17-21J., silver, 44mm, OF	350	450	600
Time only, gold, 40- 44mm, OF	250	325	425
HC	350	400	500
Time only, gold, 45- 48mm, OF	300	375	500
HC	450	550	800
World time watch, gold, 48-52mm, OF	4,000	5,000	7,000

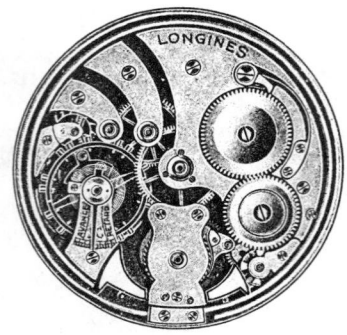

Longines, open face minute repeater movement

Longines, 46mm, Min. repeater, 24 jewels, 3/4 plate design, open face, Ca. 1915.

TYPE – DESCRIPTION	Avg	Ex-Fn	Mint
8 day watch with wind-indicator, **14K OF**	$1,200	$1,500	$2,000
Chronograph w/register, silver, OF, 48- 50mm, C. 1905	250	300	400
Chronograph, gold, 45-50mm, OF	450	500	700
HC	700	800	1,000
Split second chronograph, gold, 45-52mm, OF	1,000	1,200	1,600
HC	1,200	1,400	1,800
Chronograph, Lugrin's Pat., fly back, silver OF case	375	400	500
1/4 hr. repeater, gold, 46-52mm, OF	1,200	1,400	1,800
HC	1,500	1,700	2,000
HC w/chrono., cal. & moonphase	3,500	4,500	6,000
Minute repeater, gold, 46-52mm, OF	2,000	2,500	3,500
HC	2,500	3,000	4,000
OF w/chrono.	2,500	3,000	4,000
HC w/chrono.	3,000	3,500	4,500
OF w/split chrono.	3,500	4,000	5,000
HC w/split chrono.	4,500	5,000	7,000
HC w/cal. & moon- phase	5,000	6,000	7,500
Perpetual moonphase calendar, gold, OF	6,000	8,000	10,000
Perp. moonphase cal. w/min.repeater & chrono., OF	15,000	18,000	25,000
HC	18,000	25,000	30,000
Clock Watch, gold, 46-52mm, OF	6,000	7,000	10,000
HC	8,000	9,000	12,000

Longines, Chronograph, H.A. Lugrin's Pat. June 13, Oct. 3, 1876, Start, Stop, Fly Back.

Longines, 8 day with wind-indicator, Ca. 1930.

MARKWICK, MARKHAM

LONDON (1725-1825)

They enjoyed selling clocks and watches to the Turkish Market. Watches can be found with his name & that of another maker added, Example: Markwick, Markham "Perigal", or "Recordon". Also watches with the names "Story" Ca.1780, "Borrel" Ca.1813 and "Perigal" Ca.1825 are known.

TYPE – DESCRIPTION	Avg	Ex-Fn	Mint
Pair case, verge, silver plain, 50mm, OF	$300	$375	$500
GOLD	800	1,000	1,300
Pair case, verge, silver w/ **repousee**, 50mm, OF	450	650	1,000
GOLD	1,100	1,400	1,850
Triple cased, verge, silver & **Tortoise shell** outer case,	750	1,000	1,500
Triple cased, verge, Painted enamel on first & second case, for Turkish Market, 18K gold cases, Ca. 1800	7,500	8,500	10,000
Four cases, verge fusee, Silver Gilt and Tortoise, KW/KS, for Turkish Market, 45mm, Ca. 1820	1,500	2,000	2,800
1/4 hr. repeater, SILVER, 54mm, OF	700	900	1,200
GOLD	1,100	1,300	1,600
Pair case, verge, **20K Gold repousee**, 50mm, OF	6,000	7,000	9,000

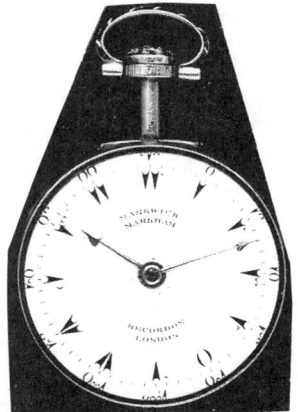

Markwick, Markham, Triple cased , 18K gold cases, Painted enamel on first & second case, made for Turkish Market, Ca. 1800.

Markwick, London, 20K pair case, both cases hand pierced, 1/4 hour repeating on a bell, 55MM, Ca. 1720

512

MATHEY – TISSOT
Swiss

Firm founded in June 1886 by Edmond Mathey-Tissot. Makers of complicated and simple watches of good quality.

TYPE – DESCRIPTION	Avg	Ex-Fn	Mint
Early, KW, Time only, Swiss bar, Pre 1870, silver	$100	$125	$195
Time only, gold, 40- 44mm, OF	285	350	425
HC	425	500	585
Time only, gold, 45- 50mm, OF	435	500	650
HC	600	700	850
1/4 hr. repeater, gold, 46-52mm, OF	1,200	1,300	1,600
HC	1,500	1,600	2,000
OF w/chrono., cal. & moonphase	2,200	2,400	3,000
HC w/chrono., cal. & moonphase	2,500	2,800	3,500

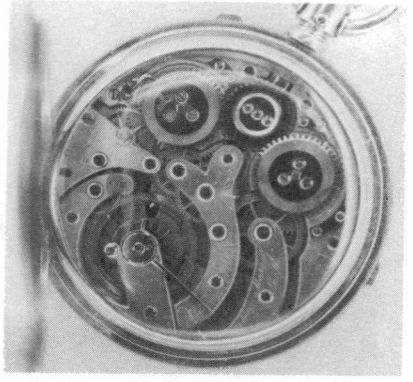 

Mathey-Tissot, 52mm, 27 jewels, quarter jump sweep second chronograph, two train, 18k HC.

Mathey-Tissot, min. repeater with chronograph, day date month & moon phases, HC.

TYPE – DESCRIPTION	Avg	Ex-Fn	Mint
Minute repeater, gold, 46-52mm, OF	$1,800	$2,200	$2,800
HC	2,000	2,400	3,000
OF w/chrono. & register	2,000	2,400	3,000
HC w/chrono. & register	2,200	2,700	3,400
HC w/chrono. & moon ph,. day date month,	4,000	4,800	6,500
OF w/split chrono.	4,200	4,500	5,500
HC w/split chrono.	4,700	5,200	6,000
OF w/cal. & moonphase	3,800	4,200	5,000
HC w/cal. & moonphase	4,000	4,800	6,000
World time watch, gold, 48-52mm, OF	4,000	4,800	6,000
Perpetual moonphase calendar, gold, OF	6,000	7,000	9,000
Perp. moonphase cal. w/min. repeater, OF	15,000	18,000	25,000
HC	20,000	24,000	30,000
Perp. moonphase cal. w/min. rep. and chrono., OF	20,000	22,000	28,000
HC	22,000	26,000	32,000
Clock Watch, Gold, 48-52mm, OF	6,000	7,500	10,000
HC	8,000	8,500	12,000

⊕ Note: Some models and grades are not included. Their values can be determined by comparing with **similar** age, size, metal content, style, models and grades listed.

⊕ A collector should expect to pay modestly higher prices at local shops.

⊕ Pricing in this Guide are fair market price for **COMPLETE** watches which are reflected from the "**NAWCC**" National and regional shows.

McCabe
London

William McCabe of Ireland was a clock & watch-maker who moved to London. This long lived firm has a good reputation for making watches. The son of William, James McCabe became the owner in about 1822. The business was carried on by nephew, Robert Jeremy till about 1883.

TYPE – DESCRIPTION	Avg	Ex-Fn	Mint
Time only, Verge escapement, KW, Silver, 58mm, OF	$200	$275	$400
HC	225	325	450
Time only, DUPLEX escapement, KW, Silver, 58mm, OF	225	295	500
HC	250	375	550
Time only, DUPLEX escapement, KW, GOLD, 58mm, OF	700	900	1,200
HC	800	1,000	1,400
Enamel, Time only, DUPLEX escap., KW, Silver, 58mm, OF	900	1,200	1,500
HC	1,000	1,300	1,700
Gold &Enamel, Time only, Duplex escap., KW, 55- 58mm, OF	5,000	6,500	9,000
HC	6,000	8,000	12,000
Time only, Lever escapment, gold, 45- 50mm, OF	600	750	1,000
HC	800	900	1,200
1/4 hr. repeater, gold, 46-52mm, OF	1,800	2,000	2,500
HC	2,500	2,800	3,200
Detent Chronometer, gold, 48-52mm, OF	4,000	5,000	7,000
HC	5,000	6,000	7,500

Ja. McCabe, "Royal Exchange London", key-wind with fusee, diamond stone, three arm gold balance, right angle lever, Ca. 1835.

⊕ A collector should expect to pay modestly higher prices at local shops.

⊕ Pricing in this Guide are fair market price for **COMPLETE** watches which are reflected from the "**NAWCC**" National and regional shows.

The Complete Price Guide to Watches goal is to stimulate the orderly exchange of **Watches** between **"buyers"** and **"sellers".**

514

MEYLAN WATCH CO.
Swiss

Meylan Watch Co., founded by C.H. Meylan in 1880, manufactured fine watches, with complications, in Le Brassus, Switzerland.

TYPE – DESCRIPTION	Avg	Ex-Fn	Mint
Time only, gold, 40- 44mm, OF	$350	$425	$500
HC	450	525	650
Time only, **platinum**, + diamonds, 40- 44mm, OF	900	1,200	1,800
Time only, gold, 40- 44mm, 18K case & **enamel on bezel**, OF	1,200	1,500	2,000
Time only, gold, 45- 50mm, OF	500	550	700
HC	850	950	1,100
Chronograph, gold, 45-50mm, OF	600	700	900
HC	800	950	1,200
Split second chronograph, gold, 45-52mm, OF	1,000	1,200	1,600
HC	1,500	1,700	2,200

C. H. **Meylan**, 42mm, 21 jewels, straight line lever escapement, 18K case with enamel on bezel.

C. H. **Meylan**, Minute Repeater, split second Chronograph, minute register, 18K gold OF case, Ca. 1895

TYPE – DESCRIPTION	Avg	Ex-Fn	Mint
5 minute repeater, gold, 46-52mm, OF	$1,700	$2,000	$2,400
HC	1,900	2,200	2,600
Minute repeater, gold, OF	2,400	2,700	3,200
HC	2,600	2,900	3,400
OF w/chrono.	2,600	2,900	3,300
HC w/chrono.	2,700	3,000	3,500
OF w/split chrono.	3,800	4,500	5,500
HC w/split chrono.	4,000	4,800	6,000
OF w/cal. & moonphase	4,000	4,800	6,000
HC w/cal. & moonphase	5,000	5,500	7,000
HC w/chrono., cal. & moonphase	5,500	6,000	7,500
Tourbillion, gold, 48-55mm, OF	25,000	30,000	40,000
Detent chronometer, gold, 48-52mm, OF	3,000	3,500	5,000
World time watch, gold, 48-52mm, OF	4,000	4,300	5,000
Perpetual moonphase calendar, gold, OF	7,000	8,000	10,000
HC	8,000	9,000	12,000
Perp. moonphase cal. w/min. rep. and chrono., OF	16,000	18,000	22,000
HC	20,000	22,000	25,000
Clock Watch, gold, 48-52mm, OF	6,000	7,500	10,000
HC	8,000	9,500	12,000

MORICAND, CH.
GENEVA

Firm specialized in making verge watches with cases highly decorated with stones and enameled portraits. Associates with brother Benjamin and Francois Colladon from 1752 to 1755, with a firm name of Colladon & Moricand. Later, with Jean Delisle then later in 1780 as Moricand.

Delisle & Moricand, 36MM, 1/4 hour repeater pendant activated, two-footed balance bridge, Ca.1775.

Ch. Moricand, 46mm, gilt and enamel with two ladies in a floral garden, KW KS, Ca.1800.

TYPE – DESCRIPTION	Avg	Ex-Fn	Mint
Verge, KW, paircase, **silver**, 50mm, OF	$250	$375	$500
Verge, enamel w/ portrait, **silver/ gilt**, 49-52mm, OF	700	900	1,300
Verge, KW, **gold**, 50-54mm, OF	800	950	1,200
Verge, KW, **gold** w/ enamel, 52mm, OF	1,600	2,200	3,000
1/4 hr. repeater, **silver**, 54mm, OF	600	700	1,000
1/4 hr. repeater, **gold**, 50-54mm, OF	900	1,100	1,400
1/4 hr. repeater, **gold** w/ enamel, 54mm, OF	2,500	3,500	4,500

C. MONTANDON
Swiss

This 19th century maker was associated with Perret & Company as well as other Le Locle and Chaux-de-Fonds factories. Montandon specialized in low cost keywind watches for the American market.

TYPE – DESCRIPTION	Avg	Ex-Fn	Mint
KW, cylinder escap., silver, 46mm, OF, C. 1870	$85	$95	$125
KW, silver, 46-48mm, HC, C. 1875	100	125	150
KW, 15J, lady's , **18K**, 40-44mm, OF, C. 1870	175	200	250
HC, C. 1870	250	300	385
KW, 15J, gent's, **18K**, 48mm, OF, C. 1875	275	325	395
Chronograph, gold, 45-50mm, OF	600	750	1,000
HC	700	800	1,100
1/4 hr. repeater, gold, 46-52mm, OF	800	900	1,200
HC	1,000	1,300	1,800
Minute repeater, gold, 46-52mm, OF	2,200	2,400	2,800
HC	2,600	2,900	3,500
Minute repeater, w/cal. & moonphase, OF	3,500	3,800	5,500
HC	4,500	5,000	6,000
Minute repeater, **w/chrono.**, cal. & moonphase, HC	5,000	5,300	6,500

MOVADO (Swiss)

L. A. I. Ditesheim & Freres (L.A.I. the initials of the 3 Ditesheim brothers) formed their company in 1881. The name Movado ("always in motion") was adopted in 1905. The Swiss company invented a system of watch making which they called "Polyplan." This was an arrangement of three different angles to the watch movement which produced a curve effect to the case so as to fit the curvature of the arm. Another unusual watch produced by this company in 1926-27 was the "Ermeto." This watch was designed to be protected while inside a purse or pocket and each time the cover was opened to view the time, the watch was partially wound. L., A. & I. Ditesheim (before Movado) used trade names as Ralco, Tanit, Ultra, Apogee, Record, Talma, Noblesse, Salud, Negus, Bonne, Belgravia, Surete and Mintral in about 1895.

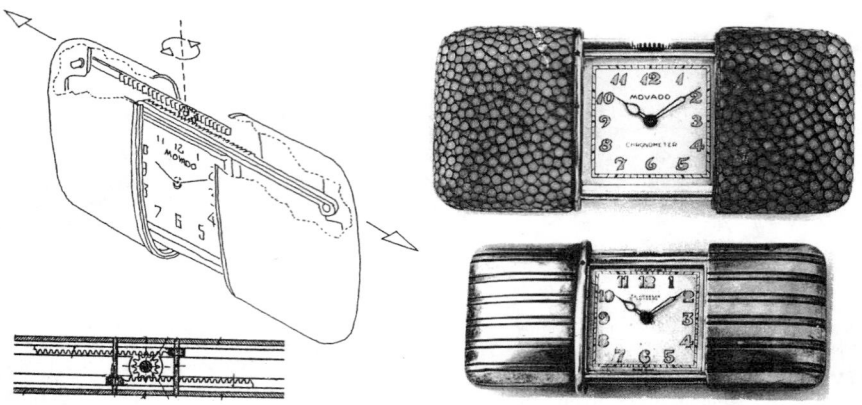

Above: Movado, Automatic RACK-WINDING mechanism, a single opening provides winding for about 4 hours.

Top: **Movado,** Purse watch, **Sting Ray** leather, 17 jewels.
Bottom: **Movado,** Purse watch, **silver** case, 17 jewels.

TYPE – DESCRIPTION

	Avg	Ex-Fn	Mint
SW, 17J, LS, Silver, 43mm, OF, C. 1920	$125	$150	$185
SW, 15J, LS, Silver, 47mm, HC, C. 1920	150	175	200
Time only, gold, 40-44mm, OF	225	250	325
HC	350	400	500
Time only, gold, 45-50mm, OF	425	500	600
HC	625	700	850
Purse watch, black leather, 50 x 33mm, C. 1930's	200	250	350
Alarm	275	325	500
silver	250	300	450
Sting Ray leather	275	325	475
leather, **moonph. & calendar**	800	900	1,200
Coin form, 17J, St. Christopher coin, 18K, closed case, 29mm	600	700	900
Chronograph, gold, 45-50mm, OF	800	900	1,200
Minute repeater, gold, 46-52mm, OF	2,200	2,600	3,200
HC	2,500	3,000	3,600
HC w/split chrono. & register	5,000	5,500	7,000

Movado, Purse watch with moonph. & calendar, auto-wind by opening & closing case, leather.

ULYSSE NARDIN

Swiss

Ulysse Nardin was born in 1823. The company he started in 1846 produced many fine timepieces and chronometers, as well as repeaters and more complicated watches. This firm, as did Assmann, found a strong market in South America as well as other countries. Ulysse's son, Paul David Nardin, succeeded him, as did Paul David's sons after him.

Ulysse Nardin, Key wind, 18 jewels, pivoted detent, bridge movement, 48mm, Ca. 1860.

Ulysse Nardin, pocket chronometer with date, 19J. pivoted detent, gold jewel settings, Ca.1890.

TYPE – DESCRIPTION	Avg	Ex-Fn	Mint
Early KW, 18J., pivoted detent, bar style mvt., gold, HC, C.1860 ..	$1,200	$1,500	$2,000
Time only, gold, 40-44mm, OF	300	350	500
HC	450	500	650
Time only, gold, 45- 50mm, OF	600	650	700
HC	750	800	850
Chronograph, gold, 45-50mm, OF	800	1,000	1,250
HC	1,000	1,200	1,500
Deck chronometer **w/box**, detent chronometer, C. 1905	1,400	1,600	2,000
Pocket chronometer, lever escape., 21J., GJS, **18K**, HC, C.1910....	900	1,100	1,400
Pocket chronometer, **pivoted detent, with date**, gold, 57mm	4,000	4,500	5,500
World time watch, gold, 48-52mm, OF	4,000	4,400	5,000
Karrusel, 52 Min. karrusel, free sprung balance, silver case	4,000	6,000	8,500

Ulysse Nardin, 53mm, 52 minute karrusel, free sprung balance, ca. 1905.

Ulysse Nardin, pocket chronometer, lever escapement, 21 jewels, gold jewel settings, Ca. 1910

TYPE – DESCRIPTION	Avg	Ex-Fn	Mint
1/4 hr. repeater, gold, 46-52mm, OF	$1,400	$1,600	$2,250
OF w/chrono., cal. moonphase	2,200	2,600	3,400
HC	1,600	2,000	2,700
HC w/chrono., cal. & moonphase	2,600	3,000	3,800
Minute repeater, gold, 46-52mm, OF	2,800	3,200	4,000
HC	3,200	3,600	4,500
OF w/split chrono.	3,800	4,400	5,500
HC w/split chrono.	4,200	4,800	6,000
OF w/cal. & moonphase	7,000	9,000	12,000
HC w/cal. & moonphase	7,500	9,000	12,000
HC w/chrono., cal. & moonphase	8,500	10,500	14,000
Perpetual moonphase calendar, gold, OF	9,000	10,000	12,000
HC	10,000	11,000	14,000
Perp. moonphase cal. w/min . repeater, OF	22,000	26,000	35,000
HC	24,000	30,000	38,000
Perp. moonphase cal. w/min. rep. and chrono. , OF	23,000	28,000	37,000
HC	25,000	32,000	40,000
Clock Watch, gold, 46-52mm, OF	6,000	7,500	10,000
HC	8,000	9,000	12,000

NICOLE, NIELSEN & CO.
London

Adolphe Nicole in 1840 came to London from Switzerland and joined Henry Capt. In 1876 Emil Nielsen became a partner in the firm. The company was purchased by S. Smith & Sons in 1904. Tourbillons were made by V. Kullberg and Nicole, Nielsen for the England market. Last watches made Ca. 1933.
(Made ebauche for Dent, Frodsham, and Smith)

Nicole, Nielsen, 50mm, chronograph, 15 jewels, 3/4 plate, gilded movement, Ca. 1890.

Nicole, Nielsen, 64mm, min. repeater, split-second chronograph, tourbillon, free sprung escapement , most were made for Frodsham.

TYPE – DESCRIPTION	Avg	Ex-Fn	Mint
Time only, gold, 45- 50mm, OF	$600	$800	$1,200
HC	700	900	1,300
Chronograph, gold, 45-50mm, HC	1,200	1,400	1,800
Minute repeater, gold, 46-52mm, OF	2,700	3,200	4,000
HC	3,000	3,800	5,000
OF w/chrono. & register	3,500	4,300	6,000
HC w/chrono. & register	4,000	4,800	6,500

TYPE – DESCRIPTION	Avg	Ex-Fn	Mint
Minute repeater, **tourbillon**, split-second chronograph, free sprung escapement, gold, 64mm,	$100,000	$140,000	$200,000
Karrusel, gold, 48-55mm, OF	6,000	7,000	10,000
Tourbillon, gold, 48-55mm, OF	28,000	32,000	55,000
Perpetual moon phase calendar, gold, OF	12,000	14,000	18,000
HC	14,000	16,000	22,000
Perp. moonphase cal. w/min.rep. and chrono., OF	24,000	28,000	35,000
HC	26,000	33,000	40,000
Clock Watch, gold, 48-55mm, OF	10,000	12,000	15,000
HC	12,000	15,000	20,000

NON–MAGNETIC WATCH CO.
Swiss
(NOT MARKED PAILLARD'S PATENT)

TYPE – DESCRIPTION	Avg	Ex-Fn	Mint
Time only, gold, 45- 50mm, OF	$275	$325	$400
HC	350	400	500
Chronograph, gold, 45-50mm, OF	500	650	800
HC	600	750	1,000
Split second chronograph, gold, 45-52mm, OF	750	850	1,100
HC	850	950	1,200
1/4 hr. repeater, gold, 46-52mm, OF	1,100	1,200	1,500
HC	1,300	1,500	2,000
Minute repeater, gold, 46-52mm, OF	2,200	2,400	2,800
HC	2,400	2,600	3,250
OF w/split chrono.	4,000	4,500	5,500
HC w/split chrono.	4,500	5,000	6,000
HC w/chrono., cal. & moonphase	5,000	5,500	6,500

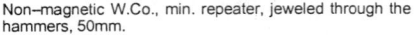

Non–magnetic W.Co., min. repeater, jeweled through the hammers, 50mm.

Omega pocket watch movement, 45-48mm, 15 jewels, serial number 9,888,934.

Watches listed in this book are priced at the collectable fair market **value** at the Trade Show level, as complete watches having an original case, an original white enamel dial, and with the entire original movement in good working order with no repairs needed, unless otherwise noted.

The Complete Price Guide to Watches goal is to stimulate the orderly exchange of **Watches** between **"buyers"** and **"sellers".**

OMEGA WATCH CO.
Swiss

Omega Watch Co. was founded by Louis Brandt in 1848. They produced watches of different grades. In 1930, they began to produce different lines with Tissot under the name Societe Sussie pour l'Industrie Horlogere. Omega is now part of the SMH (Societe Suisse de Microelectronique et d' Horlogerie).

PRODUCTION TOTALS

DATE- SERIAL #	DATE- SERIAL #	DATE- SERIAL #	DATE- SERIAL #
1895 –1,000,000	1935 - 8,000,000	1956-15,000,000	1965-22,000,000
1902 - 2,000,000	1939- 9,000,000	1958-16,000,000	1966-23,000,000
1908 - 3,000,000	1944-10,000,000	1960-17,000,000	1967-25,000,000
1912 - 4,000,000	1947-11,000,000	1961-18,000,000	1968-26,000,000
1916 - 5,000,000	1950-12,000,000	1962-19,000,000	1969-28,000,000
1923 - 6,000,000	1952-13,500,000	1963-20,000,000	1970-29,000,000
1929 - 7,000,000	1954-14,000,000	1964-21,000,000	

The above list is provided for determining the APPROXIMATE age of your watch. Match serial number with date. Watches were not necessarily sold in the exact order of manufactured date.
Note: By 1980 ETA Calibers were being used by Omega.

TYPE – DESCRIPTION	Avg	Ex-Fn	Mint
15J, SW, gilt, silver, 48mm, OF, C.1900	$75	$95	$150
15J, SW, gilt, silver, 48mm, HC, C.1900	100	135	200
Time only, gold, 45- 48mm, OF	400	475	600
HC	500	575	700
Chronograph, gold, 45-50mm, OF	700	900	1,100
HC	800	1,000	1,200
Pulsation (Doctor Watch), gold HC	900	1,100	1,400
Chronograph, gold, 45-50mm, **Double-Dial**, OF	2,200	3,000	4,000
Minute repeater, gold, 46-52mm, OF	2,000	2,500	3,200
HC	2,200	2,700	3,500
OF w/split chrono.	4,000	4,500	6,000
HC w/split chrono.	4,200	4,700	6,500
HC w/chrono., cal. & moonphase	5,000	6,000	8,000

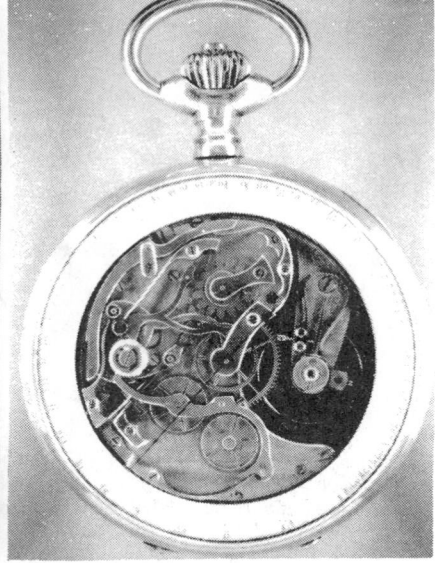

Omega, Chronograph, gold, 45-50mm, **Double-Dial**, open face, Multi-color enamel dials.

In 1894 the creation of the Omega **"19"** caliber, remarkable for the perfection of its construction, the ingenuity of certain mechanisms (time-setting) and its modest price, owing to new manufacturing methods. The **19** caliber resulted from the **FIRST** introduction in Switzerland of the ***DIVIDED ASSEMBLY SYSTEM*** based on the interchange-ability of standard parts, a system which would be adopted progressively by the entire Swiss watch industry. This was also the year when Omega chronometers began receiving official rating certificates from the Neuchatel, Geneva and Kew/Teddington (London) observatories. That year the owners of the company registered the word **Omega** as the new trademark.

The source of information from the book OMEGA The History of a Great Brand.

Omega 19 Grade DDR, 23 jewels with 2 diamond end stones, jeweled barrel arbor, **18** screwed gold jewel settings, a swan-neck regulator with graduated snail. Signed *Ls Brandt & frere SA*, grade DDR, 23 jewels, Adjusted to 5 positions and movement serial number is 2584692.

16 - 18 SIZE (19-20 lignes) 50-55MM

TYPE – DESCRIPTION	Avg	Ex-Fn	Mint
23J, grade **DDR** = RR grade, **18** GJS+2 diamond end stones, **GF** OF	$400	$550	$950
19J, grade **DR** = RR grade, **15** GJS, **GF** OF	325	425	650
23J, grade **CCCR** = RR grade, **15** GJS, **GF** OF	350	450	750
19J, grade **CCR** = RR grade, **10** GJS, **GF** OF	300	400	600

16 size Movement

Omega 19 Grade CCCR, 16-18 size, 23 jewels, signed Omega Watch Co. Swiss, 15 gold settings, S# 3,658,546.

Omega 19 caliber, basic MOVEMENT open face 16 size, & 20 caliber = 18 size. (used for official chronometers)

CHARLES OUDIN
PARIS

Oudin was a pupil of Breguet and became a talented maker from 1807-1830. He produced quality timepieces and invented an early "keyless" watch. He signed some of his Watches "Eleve de Breguet" = Student of Breguet.

Charles Oudin, Dial & Movement, 51mm, 32J., Minute repeater with Chronograph, Ca.1910.

TYPE – DESCRIPTION	Avg	Ex-Fn	Mint
Verge, KW, silver single case, 45mm, OF, C. 1865......................	$300	$350	$500
Early, KW, Time only, Swiss bar, silver , OF	75	95	125
GOLD, OF	300	400	600
Split sec. chrono., 29J, w/ register,18K, 51mm, HC, C. 1900	800	900	1,200
Minute repeater, gold, 46-52mm, OF...	2,000	2,400	3,000
HC	2,200	2,700	3,500
OF w/chrono. & register...	2,500	2,800	3,500
HC w/chrono. & register	3,000	3,400	4,000

"CHs. OUDIN, Paris," engraved on movement, Key Wind, cylinder escapement, Swiss bar, Ca. 1865.

PATEK, PHILIPPE & CIE.
Swiss

Patek, Philippe & Cie. has produced some of the world's most desirable factory-made watches. Antoine Norbert de Patek began contracting and selling watches in the 1830's, later became partners with Francois Czapek and generally produced lovely decorative watches for a high class of clientele. In 1845 Adrien Philippe, inventor of the modern stem-winding system, joined the firm of Patek & Cie., and in 1851, the firm established its present name. Between Philippe's talent as a watchmaker and Patek's talent as a businessman with a taste for the impeccable, the firm rapidly established an international reputation which lasts to this day. Early Patek, Philippe & Cie. watches are generally signed only on the dust cover, but some are signed on the dial and cuvette. It was not until the 1880's that the practice began of fully signing the dial, movement and case-perhaps in response to some contemporary forgery but more likely a necessity to conform to customs' regulations for their growing international market. Many early and totally original Patek watches have suffered from the misconception that all products of the company are fully signed. Never the less, collectors find such pieces more desirable. It requires more experience, however, to determine the originality of the earlier pieces. As with Vacheron & Constantin, some watches were originally cased in U.S.A., but this lowers their value in general.

PRODUCTION TOTALS

DATE—SERIAL #	DATE—SERIAL #	DATE—SERIAL #
1840— 100	1950—700,000	1940— 900,000
1845— 1,200	1955—725,000	1945— 915,000
1850— 3,000	1960—750,000	1950— 930,000
1855— 8,000	1965—775,000	1955— 940,000
1860— 15,000	1970—795,000	1960— 960,000
1865— 22,000		1965— 975,000
1870— 35,000	DATE—SERIAL #	1970— 995,000
1875— 45,000	1920— 800,000	
1880— 55,000	1925— 805,000	DATE—SERIAL #
1885— 70,000	1930— 820,000	1960—1,100,000
1890— 85,000	1935— 824,000	1965—1,130,000
1895—100,000	1940— 835,000	1970—1,250,000
1900—110,000	1945— 850,000	1975—1,350,000
1905—125,000	1950— 860,000	1980—1,450,000
1910—150,000	1955— 870,000	1985—1,600,000
1915—175,000	1960— 880,000	1990—1,850,000
1920—190,000	1965— 890,000	
1925—200,000	1970— 895,000	

The above list is provided for determining the APPROXIMATE age of your watch. Match serial number with date. Watches were not necessarily sold in the exact order of manufactured date.

EARLIER KEY WIND
NOTE: Watches signed *PATEK & CIE.* usually have serial numbers from about 1,129 to 3,729, Ca. 1845 to 1850. Usually signed on cuvette with serial number & Patek & Cie., and not on the movement. *"Patek et Czapek"* found signed on cuvette for earlier KEY WIND watches.

Important note: From about 1880 forward all watches were signed on dial, case & movement .

1854 Tiffany & Co. became a official customer of the Patek firm.

Patek, Philippe & Cie., 15-17J., KWKS, gilt movement, lever escapement ("moustache lever"), **signed on 18K cuvette**, 47mm, Ca. 1865-69.

Patek, Philippe & Cie., 18 jewels, engraved gold dial with enamel center, 18K, 43mm, Ca. 1920's.

Patek, Philippe & Cie. 43mm, time only, 18K, open face.

Patek, Philippe & Co., Perpetual calendar, moonphase, min. repeater & split second chronograph, 18K, OF.

Patek, Philippe & Co.,signed "Chronometro Gondolo", 24 hr. dial, 19J, lever escapement, 55mm, Ca. 1908.

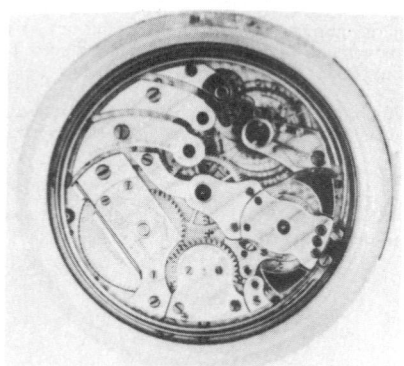

Patek, Philippe & Co., dial & movement, min. repeater, 29J, perpetual calendar, day, date, month, moon-phases, 18K.

TYPE – DESCRIPTION	Avg	Ex-Fn	Mint
EARLY Time only, KWKS, gilt mvt., lever or cylinder escapement			
pre 1865, signed on gold case, 40-45mm, ...	$1,200	$1,500	$2,000
Time only, gold, 25- 30mm, ladies, OF	700	850	1,100
HC	1,000	1,300	1,800
Time only, gold, 32- 44mm, OF.........................	1,800	2,000	2,500
HC	2,500	2,800	3,500
Time only, **Platinum**, 32- 44mm, OF.........................	2,500	3,000	4,000
Time only, **enameled bezel**, gold, 32- 44mm, OF	2,700	3,000	4,000
Time only, gold, 45- 55mm, OF.........................	2,500	2,800	3,500
HC	3,000	3,200	4,000
Time only, with **Wind Indicator**, gold, 45- 50mm, OF	4,000	5,000	7,000
Military, Silver deck Watch with Wind Indicator.........................	6,500	8,000	11,000
Time only, Chronometro **Gondolo**, gold, 38mm, OF	2,000	2,700	3,500
Time only, Chronometro **Gondolo**, gold, 50-55mm, OF	2,500	3,200	4,000
Time only, Chronometro **Gondolo**, gold, 24 Hr. dial, 52mm, OF ★	2,900	3,500	4,200

Patek, Philippe & Co., enameled bezel, 18K OF, 42mm

Patek, Philippe & Co., perpetual calendar & moon phases, signed, 18 jewels, 49mm, Ca. 1949

TYPE – DESCRIPTION	Avg	Ex-Fn	Mint
Chronograph, gold, 45-50mm, OF	$3,200	$3,400	$4,500
HC	4,000	4,400	5,000
OF w/register	3,600	4,200	5,500
HC w/register	4,200	5,000	6,000
Split second chronograph, gold, 45-52mm, OF	5,200	6,200	8,000
HC	5,800	6,800	9,000
OF w/register	5,500	6,500	10,000
HC w/register	6,500	7,500	11,000
1/4 hr. repeater, gold, 46-52mm, OF...............★	4,500	6,000	8,000
HC ....★	5,000	7,000	10,000
5 minute repeater, gold, 46-52mm, OF	3,500	4,500	7,000
HC	4,000	5,500	8,000
OF w/split chrono.	8,000	9,500	12,000
HC w/split chrono.	9,000	11,000	15,000
Minute repeater, gold, 46-52mm, OF...............	5,000	7,000	10,000
HC	10,000	12,000	16,000
OF w/chrono.	10,000	12,000	15,000
HC w/chrono.	12,000	15,000	20,000
OF w/chrono. & register...............	11,000	14,000	18,500
HC w/chrono. & register	14,000	16,000	20,000
Minute repeater, **2 train**, self contained, 18K, OF	15,000	18,000	25,000

TYPE – DESCRIPTION	Avg	Ex-Fn	Mint
Minute repeater, w/split chrono., gold, 46-52mm, OF	$15,000	$18,000	$22,000
HC w/split chrono.	16,000	22,000	30,000
OF w/split chrono. & register	16,000	20,000	25,000
HC w/split chrono. & register	20,000	26,000	35,000
Perpetual moonphase calendar, gold, OF	25,000	30,000	35,000
HC	27,000	32,000	40,000
Perp. moonphase cal. w/min. repeater, OF	40,000	55,000	75,000
HC	50,000	60,000	80,000
Perpetual moonphase cal. w/ min. rep. & chrono. , OF	50,000	80,000	120,000
HC	65,000	75,000	90,000
Perpetual moonphase cal. w/ min. rep. & split sec. chrono. , OF	70,000	100,000	150,000
HC	90,000	120,000	175,000
Clock Watch, gold, 48-52mm, OF	18,000	28,000	40,000
HC	20,000	32,000	50,000

Patek, Philippe & Co., Digital Jump Hour, with minute hand & second hand, 18 jewels, 45mm, 18K.

Patek, Philippe & Co., gold coin watch, 100 pesetas, secret push-piece opens lid to disclose dial, 35mm, Ca.1928.

TYPE – DESCRIPTION	Avg	Ex-Fn	Mint
Lady's pendant watch w/ brooch,18K & small diamonds, 27mm	$2,400	$2,800	$3,500
Gold Coin, 100 pesetas 18K, 18J., coin opens to disclose dial	4,000	4,300	5,000
Digital Jump Hour, W/minute hand & sec. hand, 45mm, 18K	30,000	38,000	50,000
Karrusel, gold, 48-55mm, OF	85,000	95,000	100,000
Tourbillon, gold, 48-55mm, OF	80,000	120,000	150,000
HC	110,000	130,000	175,000
Detent chronometer, gold, 48-52mm, OF	25,000	30,000	40,000
HC	30,000	35,000	50,000
World time watch, gold, 48-52mm, OF	20,000	28,000	40,000

⊕ Pricing in this Guide are fair market price for **COMPLETE** watches which are reflected from the "**NAWCC**" National and regional shows.

COMPARISON OF WATCH SIZES

U. S. A.	EUROPEAN
10-12 SIZE	40—44 MM
16 SIZE	45—49 MM
18 SIZE	50—55 MM

PICARD, JAMES
GENEVA

Watch dealer and finisher in the latter part of the 19th Century. Known for his complicated watches and pocket chronometers of high quality.

TYPE – DESCRIPTION	Avg	Ex-Fn	Mint
Time only, gold, 45- 50mm, OF	$450	$550	$700
HC	600	700	850
Chronograph, gold, 45-50mm, OF	750	850	1,000
Split sec. chronograph, 27J., independent jumping 1/5 seconds,			
Tandem wind, 2 gear train, 56mm, 18K , OF	2,200	2,800	3,500
Split second chronograph, gold, 45-52mm, OF	1,500	1,700	2,000
HC w/register	2,200	2,500	3,000
5 minute repeater, gold, 45-52mm, OF	3,000	3,400	4,000
HC	3,500	3,700	4,500
Minute repeater, gold, 45-52mm, OF	3,500	3,700	4,200
HC	3,700	4,200	4,700
OF w/split chrono.	4,800	5,200	6,000
HC w/split chrono.	7,000	7,500	8,200
OF w/cal. & moonphase	9,000	9,500	11,000
HC w/chrono., cal. & moonphase	10,000	11,000	13,000
Tourbillon, gold, 48-55mm, OF	30,000	35,000	45,000
Detent chronometer, gold, 48-52mm , OF	4,000	4,500	6,000
HC	5,000	5,500	7,000
Perp. moonphase cal. w/min.rep. and chrono, OF	20,000	25,000	35,000
HC	25,000	30,000	45,000
Clock Watch, gold, 48-52mm, OF	6,000	7,500	10,000
HC	8,000	9,500	12,000

James Picard, 27J, Split sec. chronograph, independent jumping 1/5 seconds, 2 gear train, 56mm, **Tandem wind,** Ca. 1885.

🕐 A collector should expect to pay modestly higher prices at local shops.

The Complete Price Guide to Watches goal is to stimulate the orderly exchange of **Watches** between **"buyers"** and **"sellers".**

ALBERT H. POTTER & CO.

(Note: For further information on Potter timepieces, see U.S. Watch Section.)

Albert Potter was born in Saratoga county, New York. He started his apprenticeship in 1852 with Wood & Foley Albany (N.Y.). When this was completed he moved to New York to take up watchmaking on his own. He made about 35 watches in USA that sold for $225 to $350. Some were chronometers, some were lever escapements, key wind, gilded and movements, some were fusee driven, both bridge and 3/4 plate. Potter was a contemporary of Charles Fasoldt and John Mulford, both horological inventors from Albany, N. Y. Potter moved to Cuba in 1861 but returned to New York in 1868. In 1872 he worked in Chicago and formed the Potter Brothers Company with his brother William. He moved to Geneva about 1876. His Geneva ultra high grade ebauches timepieces may have been made by the maker Charles Ami LeCoultre of Le Sentier, Le Brassus area. In 1896 the firm failed with about 600 watches being made.

TYPE – DESCRIPTION	Avg	Ex-Fn	Mint
Time only, gold, 45- 48mm, OF	$4,000	$5,000	$7,000
HC	4,500	5,500	7,500
Pocket chronometer, pivoted detent ,free-spring balance, porcelain dial, bridge mvt., **re-cased** (silver), 58mm, C.1879	4,000	4,500	5,000
Calendar, nickel, offset seconds and days of week dials, SW, 18K, 50mm, OF, C.1800	8,000	9,000	12,000
Regulator dial (center minute hand, offset hours, offset seconds), half moon- shaped nickel mvt., 18K, 50mm, OF, C.1880	10,000	12,000	18,000
Minute repeater, gold, 46-52mm, OF	15,000	18,000	22,000
HC	20,000	22,000	26,000
Detent chronometer, gold, 48-52mm, OF	15,000	18,000	25,000
HC	18,000	22,000	27,000
Perp. moonphase cal. w/min. repeater, HC	30,000	38,000	50,000
Perp. moonphase cal. w/min. rep. & chrono.,HC	32,000	40,000	55,000
4 SIZE, 21J., hour repeater, **original** 18K HC ★★	4,000	5,000	7,000

Below trade mark found on some cases.

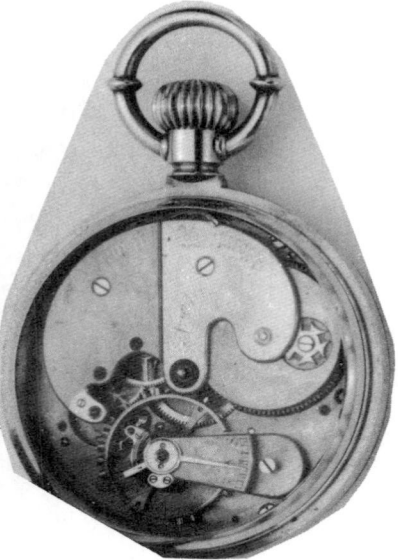

Albert Potter, 22 jewels, hunting case, helical hair spring, Free sprung, detent escapement. Note: The style bridge used for his pocket Chronometer, 58mm, Ca. 1880.

Albert Potter, 21 jewels, Note kidney-form bridge, Serial # 22, Ca. 1880. Note: A. H. Potter used a unique patented style of stem-wind & stem-set for his Geneva watches.

PRIOR, GEORGE & EDWARD PRIOR
LONDON

George Prior born in 1793 and died in 1830. He was a recipient of two prestigious awards and well known for his pieces for the turkish market. He also produced tortoise shell and triple-case watches with the outer case featuring wood with silver inlay. He made gold watches with Oriental chased cases, watches with pierced outer cases and triple-cased enamel engraved and repeaters.

Edward Prior born in 1800 and died in 1868. Well known for his pieces for the turkish market.

TYPE – DESCRIPTION	Avg	Ex-Fn	Mint
Verge, pair case, plain silver, 50mm, OF	$450	$500	$600
Verge, pair case w/ repousee, silver, 50mm, OF	1,000	1,200	1,500
Verge, Triple case w/Shagreen outer case, Gilded case, 57mm	1,200	1,500	1,800
Verge, Triple case w/ tortoise shell, silver, 56mm, OF	1,500	1,700	2,000
Verge, Quadruple cases w/ tortoise shell, silver, 56mm, OF	2,000	2,400	2,900
Verge, pair case, GOLD, 48-52mm, OF	2,000	2,300	2,800
Verge, pair case, GOLD & enamel, 48-54mm, OF	2,800	3,000	3,500
1/4 hr. repeater, pair case, GOLD & enamel, 50mm, OF	6,000	6,500	7,500

Left: **Edward Prior**, 57mm, Triple Shagreen case, white enamel signed dial, verge with fusee, KW KS, Ca. 1820.

Right: **George Prior, Quadruple** case with third case made of **tortoise** shell, fourth outer case of embossed silver, the first two cases made of silver, verge escapement, note the stag beetle hour hand and poker minute hand, Ca. 1810.

ROLEX WATCH CO.
Swiss

Rolex was founded by Hans Wilsdorf in 1905 & in <u>1908</u> the trade-mark "**Rolex**" was officially registered. In 1926, they made the first real waterproof wrist watch and called it the "**Oyster.**" In 1931, Rolex introduced a self-wind movement which they called "**Perpetual**". In 1945, they introduced the "**Date-Just**" which showed the day of the month. The "**Submariner**" was introduced in 1953 and in 1954 the "**GMT Master**" model. In 1956, a "Day-Date" model was released which indicates the day of the month (in numbers) and the day of the week (in letters.)

Rolex, SPORTING PRINCE, 17 jewels, Adjusted to six positions, silver & leather case.

Rolex, 42-43mm, 17 jewels, three adjustments, cam regulator, exposed winding gears.

ROLEX ESTIMATED PRODUCTION DATES

IMPORTANT:
The following is a *guide* to help determine the age of your Rolex watches. However on **some** Oyster style watches Rolex added **inside** the case a Roman number (I,II,III,IV) to denote first, second, third, or fourth quarter + "53", "54", "55", "56" to denote the year of production. Example outside Oyster case # 955454 inside case IV-53 which = last quarter of 1953. Example outside Oyster case # 282621 inside case III-55 which = third quarter of 1955. Rolex went back to 100,000 in 1954 on some cases.

ROLEX ESTIMATED PRODUCTION DATES

DATE–SERIAL #	DATE–SERIAL #	DATE–SERIAL #	DATE–SERIAL #	DATE–SERIAL #	DATE–SERIAL #	DATE–SERIAL #
1925 - 25,000	1937- 99,000	1949 - 608,000	1961-1,480,000	1973-3,741,000	1985 - 8,815,000	1992 1/4-C000,001
1926 - 28,500	1938-118,000	1950 - 673,500	1962-1,557,000	1974-4,002,000	1986 - 9,292,000	1993 3/4-S000,001
1927 - 30,500	1939-136,000	1951 - 738,500	1963-1,635,000	1975-4,266,000	1987 - 9,765,000	1995 — W000,001
1928 - 33,000	1940-165,000	1952 - 804,000	1964-1,713,000	1976-4,538,000	1987 1/2-R999,999	1996 — T000,001
1929 - 35,500	1941-194,000	1953 - 950,000	1965-1,792,000	1977-5,005,000	1987 3/4-R000,001	1997 3/4-U000,001
1930 - 38,000	1942-224,000	1954 - 999,999	1966-1,870,000	1978-5,481,000	1988 - R999,999	1999 — A000,001
1931 - 40,000	1943-253,000	1955 - 200,000	1967-2,164,000	1979-5,965,000	1989 - L000,001	2000 — P000,001
1932 - 43,000	1944-285,000	1956 - 400,000	1968-2,426,000	1980-6,432,000	1990 - L999,999	2001— K000,001
1933 - 47,000	1945-348,000	1957 - 600,000	1969-2,689,000	1981-6,910,000	1990 1/2-E000,001	
1934 - 55,000	1946-413,000	1958 - 800,000	1970-2,952,000	1982-7,385,000	1991 1/4-E999,999	
1935 - 68,000	1947-478,000	1959-1,100,000	1971-3,215,000	1983-7,860,000	1991 1/2-X000,001	
1936 - 81,000	1948-543,000	1960-1,401,000	1972-3,478,000	1984-8,338,000	1991 3/4-N000,001	

The above list is provided for determining the APPROXIMATE age of your watch. Match serial number with date. Watches were not necessarily sold in the exact order of manufactured date.The above list was furnished with the help of TOM ENGLE.

Hans Wilsdorf started in 1905 with his brother-in-law using the name of Wilsdorf & Davis. They used movement supplier **Aegler** in Bienne and bought cases in London. In 1919 Wilsdorf started the "Manufacture des Montres Rolex", the movements were manufactured in Bienne but finished in Geneva. 1950 the **Turn-o-graph** was used, the forerunner of the **SUBMARINER**.

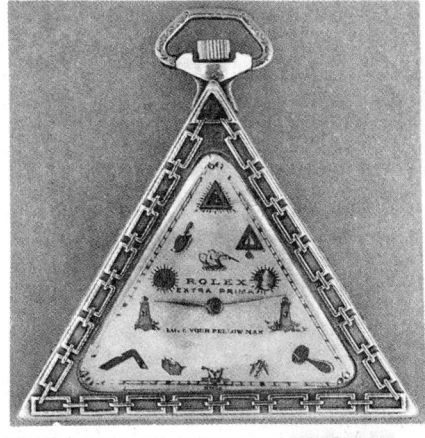

ROLEX, split seconds Chronograph, register, S.S. case.   ROLEX, Masonic watch, mother of pearl dial, 15J.

TYPE – DESCRIPTION	Avg	Ex-Fn	Mint
17J, silver, 45mm, OF, C. 1920's	$400	$550	$800
17J, 3 adj., CAM regulator, **14K,** 43mm, OF, C. 1920	600	800	1,200
1/4 Century Club, 17J, **14K,** 41mm, OF, C. 1940	700	850	1,200
Thin line, 17J, **18K,** 42mm, OF, C. 1940	700	850	1,200
Time only, gold, 40-44mm, **18K,** OF	700	850	1,200
HC	800	1,000	1,500
Time only, gold, 45-50mm, **18K,** OF	1,000	1,200	1,700
HC	1,200	1,500	2,000
Rolex, **SPORTING PRINCE,** 17J, Adj. 6P ★★	3,000	3,500	4,500
Duo dial, fancy-shaped, 17J, **18K/WG,** OF, 41mm, C. 1930	2,000	2,500	3,500
$20 dollar coin watch in closed case, triple signed, C.1950	2,500	3,000	4,000
World time watch, gold, 45-52mm	9,000	10,000	12,000
Chronograph, split seconds, register, S.S. case, 50mm	3,000	4,000	6,000
Masonic, mother of pearl dial, silver case, Ca.1930s ★★★	4,000	4,200	5,000

Romilly, Gold , verge, pair case with polychrome enamel & scene, 52mm, OF, Ca.1730.

ROMILLY, JEAN
PARIS

Became a master Watchmaker in 1752 after studying in Geneva and Paris. In 1755, he completed a repeater with beating seconds and a large balance (at one oscillation per second). He also made watches with a 8 day power reserve. Also known for his very ornate paintings on enamel.

TYPE – DESCRIPTION	Avg	Ex-Fn	Mint
Time only, KW, verge, silver, 46-52mm OF	$700	$900	$1,200
Time & Calendar, verge, silver, 50mm, OF	1,500	1,600	1,800
Gold , verge, pair case, plain, 48mm, OF	2,000	2,100	2,300
Gold , verge, pair case w/ enamel & scene, Ca.1730, 52mm, OF....	4,000	4,200	4,800
1/4 repeater, **SILVER**, 52mm, OF	2,500	2,800	3,500
1/4 repeater, **GOLD**, 54mm, OF	3,500	3,800	4,500

ROBERT ROSKELL
Liverpool

Roskell was active from 1798-1830 and worked in both Liverpool and London. He made fine rack lever fusees and gold dial watches. Other family members also produced watches for many years in Liverpool.

R. Roskell, 47mm, bar style movement, cylinder escapement, Ca. 1850.

Roskell, Monochrome Scene, Hour & Min. Hand removed to show scene, KW KS, Ca. 1810-20.

TYPE – DESCRIPTION	Avg	Ex-Fn	Mint
KW, (Swiss ebauche) 15J, silver, 48mm, OF, C. 1830-70	$75	$95	$125
KW, (Swiss) 15J, silver, 46-48mm, HC, C. 1830-70	100	125	150
KW, 13J, dust cover, fancy gold dial, **18K**, 47mm, OF, C.1830-70	275	350	500
KW, Tortoise shell case	525	700	950

Roskell, 48mm, lever escapement, KW KS, Ca.1830.   Roskell, 55mm, KW KS, Ca. 1825

TYPE – DESCRIPTION	Avg	Ex-Fn	Mint
Rack lever fusee, porcelain dial, **silver**, about 1800, OF	$350	$400	$600
Rack lever fusee, gold dial, **Gold**, about 1800, OF	500	650	900
2 day marine chronometer fusee, spring detent escapement, helical hairspring, 54 hr. wind ind., gimbal & box	1,800	2,000	2,500
Debaufre escapement, KW KS, silver, 55mm, OF .... ★ ★	3,000	3,300	4,000

Debaufre escapement,
D-shaped & inclined pallet.

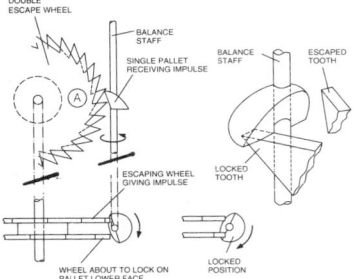

Roskell, 55mm, movement with **Debaufre escapement,** D-shaped and inclined pallet, KW KS, Ca. 1840.

Robert Roskell, 52mm, London, fusee, spring detent escapement, helical hairspring, 54 hr. wind ind., KW KS.

534

ROSKOPF
Swiss

Maker of pin lever, early low cost stem wind watches, often found with fancy dials. A **true** Roskopf watch has only *3 wheels* in its train of gears.

Roskopf, multi-colored blue enamel dial, nail set.

Roskopf, 45mm, pin lever escapement, 3 wheel train.

TYPE – DESCRIPTION	Avg	Ex-Fn	Mint
4J, pin lever, 3 wheel train, nail set, base metal, OF, Ca. 1885	$65	$75	$100
Fancy dial, oversize plain case, 55mm, OF, Ca. 1880	75	95	125
Fancy enamel dial, **fancy enamel case**, 55mm, OF, Ca. 1880	125	150	250

Roskopf, multi-colored enamel with blue & purple Butterflies & silver case, nail set.

THOMAS RUSSELL & SONS
London

Thomas Russell & Sons produced quality early keyless watches including Karrusels and chronometers. (Circa 1870-1910)

TYPE – DESCRIPTION	Avg	Ex-Fn	Mint
Time only, gold, 45-48mm, OF	$600	$700	$900
Chronograph, gold, 45-50mm, OF	1,200	1,300	1,600
Split second chronograph, gold, 45-52mm, OF	1,800	2,000	2,500
Minute repeater, gold, 46-52mm, OF	2,500	3,000	4,000
HC	3,000	3,500	4,500
Karrusel, 18K, 51mm, OF, C. 1890	4,000	4,200	5,000

Signed *Thomas Russell & Sons Liverpool,* KW KS, lever with a club foot escape wheel, Ca. 1905.   Sandoz, 52mm, KW, nickel bridge, gold train, Ca.1880.

SANDOZ & FILS
SWISS

Large family of watchmakers in the La Chaux-de-Fonds area. Known for repeating watches and pocket chronometers of fine quality.

TYPE – DESCRIPTION	Avg	Ex-Fn	Mint
Time only, gold, 40- 44mm, OF	$325	$375	$450
HC	400	435	500
Time only, gold, 45- 50mm, OF	500	535	600
HC	600	635	800
Chronograph, gold, 45-50mm, OF	700	750	800
Split second chronograph, gold, 45-52mm, OF	1,600	1,800	2,000
HC w/register	2,250	2,500	2,750
5 minute repeater, gold, 45-52mm, OF	2,000	2,400	3,000
HC	2,200	3,000	4,000
Minute repeater, gold, 45-52mm, OF	2,000	2,700	3,500
HC	2,500	3,300	4,500
OF w/split chrono.	4,000	4,800	6,000
HC w/split chrono.	6,000	7,000	8,500
OF w/cal. & moonphase	7,000	8,000	10,000
HC w/chrono., cal. & moonphase	8,000	9,500	12,000
Tourbillion, gold, 48-55mm, OF	20,000	25,000	35,000
Detent chronometer, gold, 48-52mm , OF	4,000	4,500	6,000
HC	5,000	5,800	6,500
World time watch, gold, 48-52mm, OF	5,000	6,000	8,000
Perp. moonphase cal. w/min.rep. and chrono, OF	20,000	24,000	30,000
HC	24,000	27,000	32,000

TAVANNES
Swiss

Created watches in 1895, other names used Dvina, La Tavannes, Obi, Lena Azow, and Kawa.

TYPE – DESCRIPTION	Avg	Ex-Fn	Mint
15J, GF, 35mm, HC, C. 1910	$80	$95	$125
15J, **14K**, 35mm, HC, C. 1910	195	225	275
17J, **14K**, 45mm, OF, C. 1915	225	250	300
21J, **14K**, 45mm, OF, C. 1920	250	275	325
Enamel Bezel & gold, 14K, 40mm, OF	400	500	650
Enamel Scene & gold, 18K, 45mm, OF, C. 1925	4,000	5,500	7,000

TAVANNES, Enamel Scene, 45mm, 18K, OF, C. 1925.

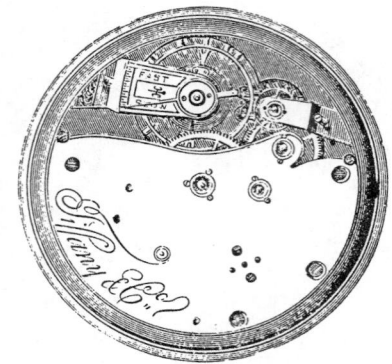

Tiffany & Co. 21J., HC, manufactured by Tiffany, Ca. 1875.

TIFFANY & CO.

In 1837 Charles Lewis Tiffany opened a store with John P. Young. They enlarged this operation in 1841, with the help of J.L. Ellis, and imported fine jewelry, watches and clocks from Europe. They incorporated as Tiffany & Co. in 1853. Tiffany made clocks, on special order, in New York around the mid-1800's. In 1874 Tiffany & Co. started a **watch** factory in Geneva, which lasted about 4 years (low production). Patek, Philippe & Co. assumed the management of their Geneva watch business. The watch machinery was returned to America. Tiffany, Young & Ellis had been a client of Patek, Philippe & Co. since 1849. Tiffany & Co. introduced Patek, Philippe to the American market in 1885. Audemars, Piguet and International Watch Co. also made watches for this esteemed company. Tiffany & Co. sells watches of simple elegance as well as watches with complications such as chronographs, moon phases, repeaters, etc.

engraved on cuvette **"Tiffany, Young & Ellis,** by Jules Jurgensen, fully jeweled, S # 5526, Ca. 1850s.

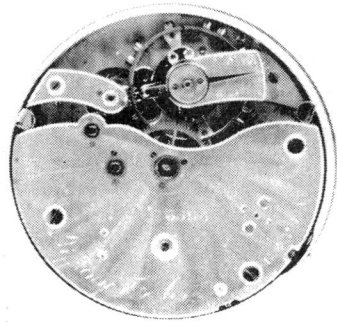

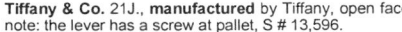

Tiffany & Co. 21J., **manufactured** by Tiffany, open face, note: the lever has a screw at pallet, S # 13,596.

Tiffany & Co.,21J., manufactured by Tiffany, HC, S# 1516, some models engraved on balance cock **Wilmot** patent.

TYPE – DESCRIPTION	Avg	Ex-Fn	Mint
Tiffany, Young & Ellis, KW KS, gold, 48MM, OF	$1,500	$1,600	$2,000
Tiffany 21J., **manufactured** by Tiffany, gold, 50-55MM, OF ★	400	500	650
Tiffany 21J., **manufactured** by Tiffany, gold, 50-55MM, HC ★	500	650	800
Time only, gold, 40- 44mm, OF	300	375	500
HC	450	500	700
Time only, gold, 40-44mm, (P.P.Co.), 18K, **enamel on bezel**, OF.	1,000	1,300	2,000
Time only, gold, 45- 55mm, OF	600	750	950
HC	700	900	1,200
Chronograph, gold, 45-50mm, OF	1,000	1,300	1,800
HC	1,500	1,700	2,200
OF w/register	1,200	1,500	2,000
Split second chronograph, gold, 45-52mm, OF	2,400	2,800	3,400
HC	2,800	3,400	5,000
5 minute repeater, gold, 46-52mm, OF	2,500	3,200	4,500
HC	3,000	3,500	5,000
OF w/split chrono.	4,000	5,000	7,000
HC w/split chrono.	5,000	6,000	7,500
Minute repeater, gold, 46-52mm, OF	2,500	3,100	4,000
HC	3,500	5,000	7,000
by **P. P. & Co.**, flat, 29J., gold, 45mm, OF, C.1912	8,000	9,000	12,000
OF w/split chrono. & register	6,000	7,500	10,000
HC w/split chrono. & register	7,000	9,000	12,000
HC w/chrono., cal. & moonphase	9,000	12,000	16,000
World time watch, gold, 48-52mm, OF	10,000	12,000	16,000
8 day watch with wind indicator, enamel dial, gold OF	800	950	1,200
Perpetual moonphase calendar, gold, OF	8,000	9,500	12,000
Perp. moonphase cal. w/**min. rep**. and chrono, OF	30,000	38,000	50,000
HC	35,000	48,000	60,000

Tiffany & Co., 50mm, 25J., split-second chronograph.

Tiffany & Co., flat minute repeater, 45mm, 29 jewels, made by Patek, Philippe & Co., ca. 1911

TISSOT
Swiss

The firm of Chs. Tissot & Fils was founded in 1853 in Le Locle by Charles Tissot. This skilled watchmaker worked from his home and in 1907 a factory was started. In 1971 the worlds first plastic wrist watch was made.

TYPE – DESCRIPTION	Avg	Ex-Fn	Mint
Early, KW, Time only, Swiss bar, Pre. 1870, silver case	$75	$100	$175
Time only, gold, 40- 44mm, OF	350	400	500
HC	450	500	600
Time only, gold, 45- 50mm, OF	500	550	700
HC	600	700	850
2-Train 1/4 second jump watch, silver, 50mm,	700	800	1,000
2-Train 1/4 second jump watch, gold, 50mm,	1,700	2,200	3,000
Chronograph, gold, 45-50mm, OF	800	850	900
Split second chronograph, gold, 45-52mm, OF	1,600	2,000	3,000
HC w/register	2,500	3,000	3,500
5 minute repeater, gold, 45-52mm, OF	2,200	2,800	3,300
HC	2,500	3,200	4,000
Minute repeater, gold, 45-52mm, OF	2,500	2,800	3,500
HC	3,000	3,500	4,000
OF w/split chrono.	3,500	4,500	6,000
HC w/split chrono.	5,500	7,000	8,500
OF w/cal. & moonphase	8,000	8,500	10,000
HC w/chrono., cal. & moonphase	9,000	9,500	11,000
Tourbillon, gold, 48-55mm, OF	38,000	40,000	55,000
Detent chronometer, gold, 48-52mm , OF	4,000	5,000	7,000
HC	5,000	6,000	7,500
World time watch, gold, 48-52mm, OF	8,000	9,000	12,000
Perp. moonphase cal. w/min.rep. and chrono, OF	20,000	25,000	35,000
HC	25,000	30,000	40,000
Clock Watch, gold, 48-52mm, OF	6,000	7,000	10,000
HC	8,000	9,000	12,000

Tissot, 2-Train 1/4 second jump watch, center sweep hand, enamel dial, 28 J., gold train, 44mm, KW KS, 18K, Ca. 1880.

Tissot, Minute repeater, with chronograph, day date month, moonphase, 27 jewels, 18K, HC, Ca. 1910.

The Complete Price Guide to Watches goal is to stimulate the orderly exchange of **Watches** between *"buyers"* and *"sellers"*.

TOBIAS & CO.

M. I. Tobias started a watchmaking career in Liverpool, about 1805. He specialized in exporting watches to U.S.A. About 1820 the company started using movements made in Switzerland the watches were engraved, *Liverpool*. The script M.I.Tobias can be misleading the script letter (I) may look like a **(J)**. The watches with a (J style) are made in the Swiss manner with a club-tooth escape-wheel made of steel and straight line lever, the Liverpool or English style watches used a (I) & a "ratchet" (sharp-pointed) escape wheel made of brass and right angle lever. The Tobias family activity extends from about 1805 to 1868.

 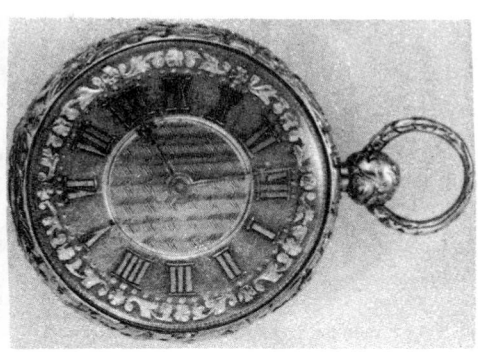

M. I. Tobias & Co., Lord Street, Liverpool, 2 train independent sec., Pat.21 Feb, 1848, 52mm, right angle lever.

M. I. Tobias, multi-color gold dial & thin gold case, 52mm.

TYPE – DESCRIPTION	Avg	Ex-Fn	Mint
KW, 7-15J, silver, 47-52mm, OF	$75	$95	$135
KW,7- 15J, silver, 47-52mm, HC	100	125	175
KW,7-15J, swiss, **gilt dial,** fancy case, **18K,** 48mm,OF	265	300	375
KW, lever, fusee, **gold dial, Heavy 18K,** 52mm, HC	700	900	1,200
KW, **2 train** independent sec., **Silver,** 56mm, OF	350	400	500
KW, **rack lever** escapement, **Silver,** 56mm, OF	350	400	500
HC	400	450	600
KW, verge fusee, **multi-color gold dial & THIN case,** 52mm, OF	450	500	700
HC	600	700	950
KW, **rack** lever escapement, **Gold,** 56mm, OF	700	800	1,000
HC	900	1,000	1,200
Captain's watch, center sec., sub-sec., gold dial, **18K,** 51mm, OF..	1,300	1,600	2,000
18K, 51mm, HC	1,500	1,800	2,500

Tobias, (Liverpool), 51mm, OF, 18K, Captain's watch, center & sub-seconds, gold dial.

TOUCHON & CO.
Swiss

Touchon & Co. started using this name as a trade mark in 1907. They manufactured complex and simple watches. In 1921 they associated with the firm of Wittnauer & Co.

Touchon & Co., 47mm, 29 jewels, minute repeater, open face, jeweled through hammers.

Touchon & Co., 47mm, 29 jewels, split-second chronograph and minute repeater, ca. 1910.

TYPE – DESCRIPTION	Avg	Ex-Fn	Mint
Time only, gold, 45- 50mm, OF	$450	$500	$600
HC	550	600	750
1/4 hr. repeater, gold, 46-52mm, OF	800	1,000	1,100
HC	1,000	1,400	2,000
OF w/chrono.	900	1,100	1,500
HC w/chrono.	1,100	1,500	2,200
OF w/chrono., cal. & moonphase	2,200	2,600	3,500
HC w/chrono., cal. & moonphase	2,400	2,800	3,700
5 minute repeater, gold, 46-52mm, OF	1,800	2,200	3,000
HC	2,000	2,400	3,200
Minute repeater, gold, 46-52mm, OF	2,500	3,000	4,000
HC	2,700	3,200	4,200
OF w/chrono. & register	2,700	3,200	4,200
HC w/chrono. & register	2,900	3,400	4,400
OF w/split chrono.	4,500	5,000	6,000
HC w/split chrono. & register	4,800	5,500	7,000
HC w/chrono., cal. & moonphase	5,500	6,000	7,500
HC, **Perp.** moonphase cal.	22,000	24,000	28,000
HC, **Perp.** moonphase cal. and chrono.	25,000	28,000	32,000
World time watch, gold, 48-52mm, OF	4,500	5,000	6,500
Perpetual moonphase calendar, gold, OF	7,000	8,000	10,000
Clock Watch, gold, 46-52mm, OF	6,000	7,500	10,000
HC	8,000	9,500	12,000

COMPARISON OF WATCH SIZES

U. S. A.	EUROPEAN
10-12 SIZE	40—44 MM
16 SIZE	45—49 MM
18 SIZE	50—55 MM

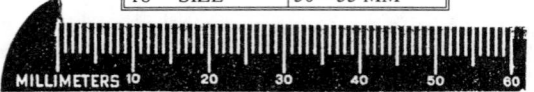

VACHERON & CONSTANTIN
Swiss

The oldest Swiss factory, founded by Jean-Marc Vacheron, in 1775. The firm of Vacheron & the firm of Constantin were in business about the same date 1785, but the association bearing the name today did not come into being until 1819. In these early periods, different grades of watches produced by Vacheron & Constantin bore different names.

The association with Leschot, around 1840, catapulted the firm into its position as a top quality manufacturer. Before that time, their watches were typical of Genevese production. Vacheron & Constantin exported many movements to the United States to firms such as Bigelow, Kennard & Co., which were cased domestically, typically in the period 1900-1935. In its early period the firm produced some lovely ladies' enameled watches, later it produced high grade timepieces and complicated watches, and to this day produces fine watches.

ESTIMATED PRODUCTION DATES

DATE-SERIAL #	DATE-SERIAL #	DATE-SERIAL #
1830 - 30,000	1880-170,000	1925-400,000
1835 - 40,000	1885-180,000	1930-410,000
1840 - 50,000	1890-190,000	1935-420,000
1845 - 60,000	1895-223,000	1940-440,000
1850 - 75,000	1900-256,000	1945-464,000
1855 - 95,000	1905-289,000	1950-488,000
1860-110,000	1910-322,000	1955-512,000
1865-125,000	1915-355,000	1960-536,000
1870-140,000	1920-385,000	1965-560,000
1875-155,000		1970-585,000

The above list is provided for determining the APPROXIMATE age of your watch. Match serial number with date. Watches were not necessarily sold in the exact order of manufactured date.

The date a watch **sold** is not an indication of the date it was **produced**.

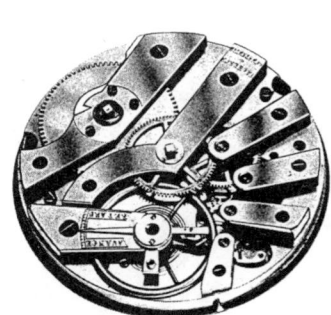

Early movements manufactured with the machines invented by George-Auguste Leschot. The machines were built in the Vacheron Constantin factory Ca. 1839 to 1840. In about 1863 to 1865 V. & C. manufactured a inexpensive watch using the names Abraham Vacheron or Abm. Vacheron also the name of Chossat & Cie.

Vacheron & Constantin, 44mm, 18 jewels, enamel bezel, 18K, Ca. 1930.

Early Vacheron & Constantin's With Different Names

1755 - Jean-Marc Vacheron
1785 - Abraham Vacheron
1786 - Abraham Vacheron - Girod
1810 - Vacheron - Chossat & Cie.
1819 - Vacheron & Constantin

1857 - C'esar Vacheron
1869 - Charles Vacheron & Cie
1870 - Veuve C'esar Vacheron & Cie
1887 - Ancienne Fabrique Vacheron & Constantin SA
1896 - Vacheron & Constantin SA

Early bar movement, lever escap., **signed "VACHERON & CONSTANTIN"** time only, KW KS, silver case, Ca.1840-1875.

TYPE – DESCRIPTION	Avg	Ex-Fn	Mint
Early bar movement, lever escap., **signed Vacheron & Constantin**			
time only, KW KS, silver case, 30-39mm, OF	$135	$175	$250
(same as above) 40-44mm, OF	185	235	325
(same as above) 45-48mm, OF	200	250	350
(same as above) 45-48mm, **HC**...	250	300	400
Early Le-Pine bar movement, duplex escap., **GOLD & ENAMEL**			
KW KS, **signed Vacheron & Constantin**, 49mm, OF	4,500	5,500	7,000
Time only, 18K gold & **enamel bezel**, 40-44mm, OF	1,200	1,300	1,800

Vacheron & Constantin, 49mm, Early Lepine bar style movement, duplex escapement, GOLD & ENAMEL, KW KS, **signed Vacheron & Constantin**, 49mm, OF, Ca. 1840.

Vacheron & Constantin, Gold coin 50 pesos 900 fine, coin hollowed out to receive watch, LEFT view shows dial & movement.

TYPE – DESCRIPTION	Avg	Ex-Fn	Mint
Time only, 18K gold, 40-44mm, OF	$600	$800	$1,000
HC	900	1,100	1,500
Time only, gold, 45-50mm, OF	1,000	1,200	1,800
HC	1,600	1,800	2,400
X-thin, 17J., **Aluminum,** weight =20 grains, OF, C. 1940	1,400	1,600	2,200
Desk chronometer, wooden box, 21J., silver, 60mm,OF, C.1943	2,000	2,800	3,500
Gold coin 50 pesos 900 fine, coin hollowed out to receive watch	2,500	3,200	4,000

V. & C., Chronograph, for the corps of engineers USA, 20 jewels, enamel dial, nail set, 50mm, 3,000 made, Ca.1917.

V. & C., Astronomic with moon phases, perpetual calendar, minute repeater, split-second chronograph, 1905.

TYPE – DESCRIPTION	Avg	Ex-Fn	Mint
Chronograph, 20J, corps of engineers USA, **Silver**, 45-50mm, OF	$1,000	$1,200	$1,800
Chronograph, gold, 45-50mm, **V& C case**, OF	2,200	2,700	3,000
HC	2,500	3,000	3,500
OF w/register	2,500	3,000	3,500
HC w/register	3,200	3,600	4,000

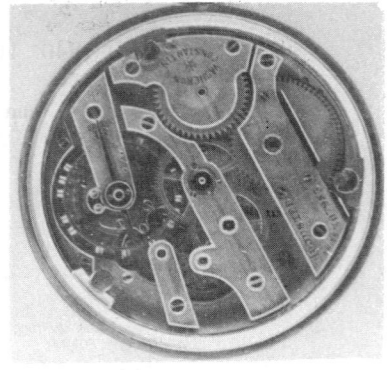 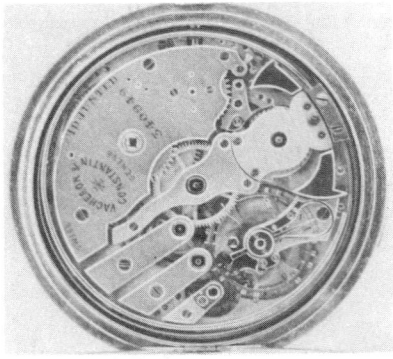

V. & C., 40mm, wolf tooth winding, open face. V. & C., 40mm, 31J., Min. repeater, slide activated, OF.

TYPE – DESCRIPTION	Avg	Ex-Fn	Mint
Split second chronograph, gold, 45-52mm, OF	$4,500	$5,200	$6,500
HC	5,500	6,200	7,500
OF w/register	5,000	6,000	7,000
HC w/register	7,000	7,200	8,500
Minute repeater, gold, 46-52mm, OF	5,000	6,200	8,000
HC	6,000	8,000	11,000
OF w/chrono.	6,000	7,500	10,000
HC w/chrono.	9,000	12,000	17,000
OF w/chrono. & register	6,000	8,000	11,000
HC w/chrono. & register	10,000	12,000	18,000
OF w/split chrono.	8,000	9,500	13,000
HC w/split chrono.	10,000	14,000	20,000
OF w/split chrono. & register	8,000	10,000	15,000
HC w/split chrono. & register	12,000	16,000	22,000
OF w/chrono., cal. & moonphase	12,000	16,000	22,000
Tourbillon, gold, 48-55mm, OF	45,000	70,000	100,000
World time watch, gold, 48-52mm, OF	20,000	25,000	35,000
Perp. moonphase cal. w/min. repeater, OF	40,000	50,000	65,000
HC	45,000	55,000	70,000
Perp. moonphase cal. w/min. rep. and split sec. chrono., OF	50,000	65,000	90,000
Perp. moonphase cal. w/min. rep. and split sec. chrono., HC	60,000	75,000	100,000
Clock Watch, gold, 46-52mm, OF	15,000	18,000	25,000
HC	20,000	24,000	30,000

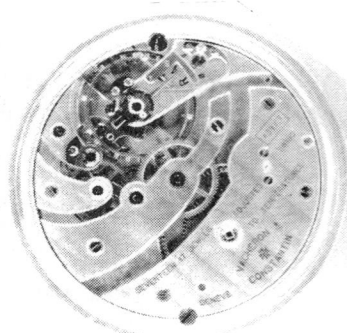 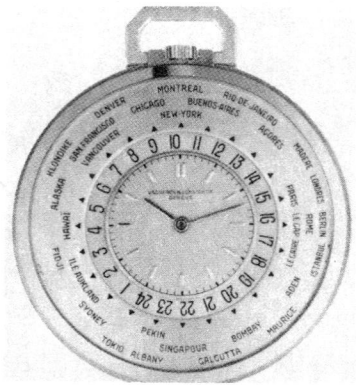

V. & C., extra thin and light weight **Aluminum,** (20 grains), about 12 size, 44mm, OF, 17 jewels, Ca. 1940.

V. & C., World time, revolving 24 hour dial, 31 citys of the world, 18 jewels, 45mm, Ca. 1945

VINER
LONDON

Charles Viner apprenticed in about 1802 and in records till 1840. The company continued after his death as Viner & Co. Viner also made clocks.

TYPE – DESCRIPTION	Avg	Ex-Fn	Mint
VINER, Verge Fusee / Alarm, 50MM, Silver, OF, Ca.1835	$1,000	$1,300	$1,800

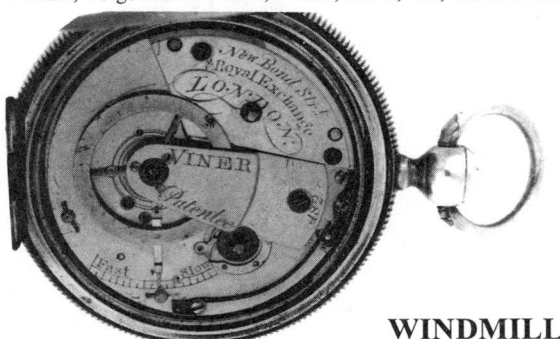

VINER, Verge Fusee with Alarm, marked on cuvette for the two arbors *"wind up"* & the other marked *"warning"*, under sprung hairspring, 50MM, Silver Open Face Case, Ca. 1835.

WINDMILL
LONDON

Joseph and his son Thomas made clocks and watches and at one time employed 10 workers. Started in business in 1671 and lasted till about 1732.

TYPE – DESCRIPTION	Avg	Ex-Fn	Mint
Tho. WINDMILL, 1/4 hr. repeater, 55MM, silver, OF, Ca.1690 ...	$5,500	$7,000	$9,000
Tho. WINDMILL, 1/4 hr. repeater, 55MM, **gold**, OF, Ca.1690.....	7,000	10,000	15,000

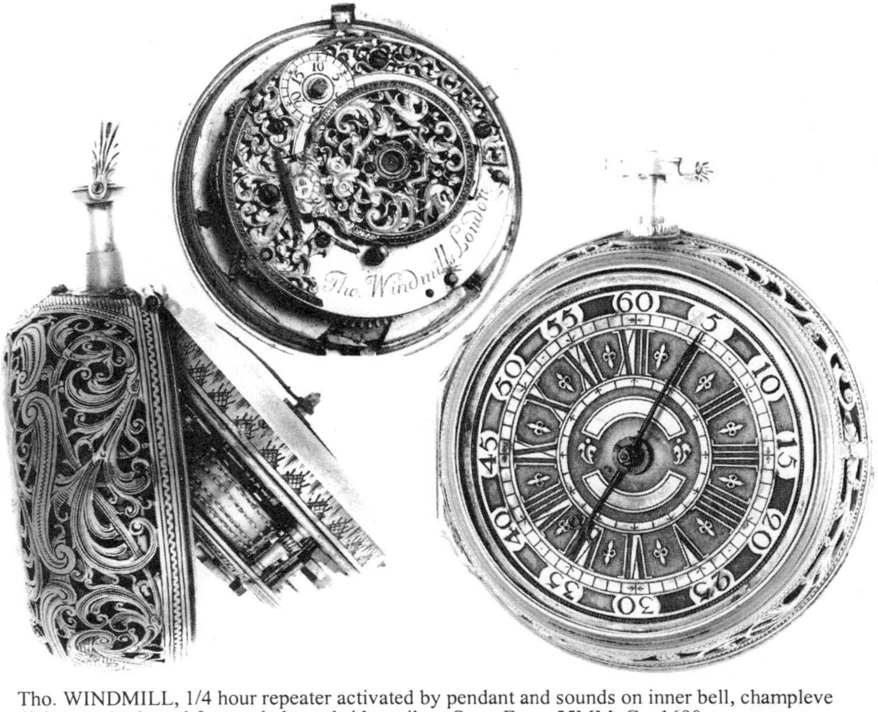

Tho. WINDMILL, 1/4 hour repeater activated by pendant and sounds on inner bell, champleve dial, note D shaped foot on balance bridge, silver Open Face, 55MM, Ca. 1690.

ZENITH
Le Locle Swiss

Founded in 1865 by Georges Favre- Jacot. The name *Zenith* was registered in 1897 & by 1920 they had made 2,000,000 watches.

ZENITH, alarm watch, enamel dial, 17J., 50mm, Ca. 1930

ZENITH, Military Deck Watch, 51mm, nickel case, Ca.1940.

TYPE – DESCRIPTION	Avg	Ex-Fn	Mint
Time only, gold, 40-44mm, OF	$250	$300	$400
HC	400	450	500
Time only, gold, 40-44mm, with **enamel** on bezel, **18K**, OF	600	650	800
Time only, gold, 45-50mm, OF	450	500	600
HC	550	600	700
RR Extra, 21J., **Grade 56**, (16 size), **Gold Filled** OF	175	225	325
Military Deck Watch, 51mm, nickel case, Ca.1940	250	300	375
Alarm watch, 17J., nail set, **two barrels**, gold, 50mm, C.1930	1,200	1,400	1,800
Chronograph, gold, 45-50mm, OF	800	900	1,100
HC	900	1,000	1,200
Minute repeater, gold, 46-52mm, OF	2,500	2,800	3,500
HC	3,200	3,500	4,000
OF w/split chrono.	4,000	4,500	5,200
HC w/split chrono.	4,500	5,000	6,500
OF w/chrono., cal. & moonphase	5,000	5,500	7,000
HC w/chrono., cal. & moonphase	6,000	6,500	8,000
Perp. moonphase cal. w/min. rep. and chrono., OF	20,000	22,000	30,000
HC	22,000	26,000	32,000

ZENITH, 42mm, 18K, enamel on case, open face, 17J., signed ZENITH, Ca. 1930's.

PRE–1850 REPEATERS

Swiss 1/4 hr. repeater, verge or cylinder, silver, 55mm, Ca. 1820, OF. **Note: Parachute (illo.1)**

Swiss 1/4 hr. rep., pump, verge or cylinder, 18K, 52mm, OF, Ca.1800s. **(illo.2)**

TYPE – DESCRIPTION	Avg	Ex-Fn	Mint
Swiss 1/4 hr. rep., verge, silver, 55mm, OF (illo.1)	$1,200	$1,400	$1,800
Swiss 1/4 hr. rep., cylinder, silver, 55mm, OF (illo.1)	1,000	1,200	1,500
Swiss 1/4 hr. rep., **pump**, verge, 18K, 52mm, OF, C.1800s (illo.2)	2,000	2,500	3,500
Swiss 1/4 hr. rep., **pump**, cylinder,18K, 52mm, OF, C.1800s (illo.2)	1,500	2,000	3,000
Swiss 1/4 hr., automaton on dial (2 figures), gilt, verge, KW, 55mm, OF, early 1800s	2,500	3,000	3,700
Swiss 1/4 hr. musical repeater disc-driven, KW KS, cylinder,**18K**, 57mm, OF, C. 1825 (illo.3)	4,000	4,500	6,000
Swiss 1/4 hr. repeater, 32-35mm, KW KS, **gold**, Ca. 1850 (illo.4) .	1,800	2,200	2,800

Swiss 1/4 hr. musical repeater disc-driven, cylinder, Kw KS, 18k, 57mm, OF, C. 1825, **(illo.3)**

Swiss 1/4 hr. repeater, 32-35mm, cylinder escapement, Swiss bar movement, KW KS, gold, Ca. 1850, **(illo.4)**

French, 1/4 hr. repeater, gold and enamel superior quality, enameled scene, outer case with pearls, verge, 20K, 52mm, OF, C.1785. (illo.5)

1/4 hr. repeater, Virgule escap., KW, 18K, 46mm, OF, Ca. 1840. (illo.6)

TYPE – DESCRIPTION	Avg	Ex-Fn	Mint
Skeletonized 1/4 hr., cylinder, Swiss, 18K, 58mm, OF, C.1810......	$3,200	$3,500	$4,500
French 1/4 hr. repeater, **20K** gold and enamel, verge, enameled scene, superior quality, outer pearls, 52mm, OF, C.1785 (illo.5)	5,000	6,000	7,500
1/4 hr. repeater, Virgule escap., KW, 18K, 46mm, OF (illo.6)........	2,500	3,000	3,600
1/4 hr. rep., erotic scene (concealed in cuvette), automated, multi-color gold figures, verge, pump 1/4 hr., 18K, 54mm, OF, C.1800...	3,500	4,200	5,000
French or Swiss pump 1/4 hr. repeater, free standing barrel, **Thin gold** case, cylinder escape., tapered bridges , Ca.1790-1835 (illo.7)......	2,000	2,500	3,200
Early 1/4 hr. rep., Paris (Clouzier) gilt dial w/ enamel hour cartouches, verge, gilt & shagreen case, 58mm, OF, C.1700....................	5,500	6,500	8,500
1/4 hr. repeater, London, gilt & shagreen paircase, verge, extremely fine, 56mm, OF, C.1700s	5,000	5,800	7,000

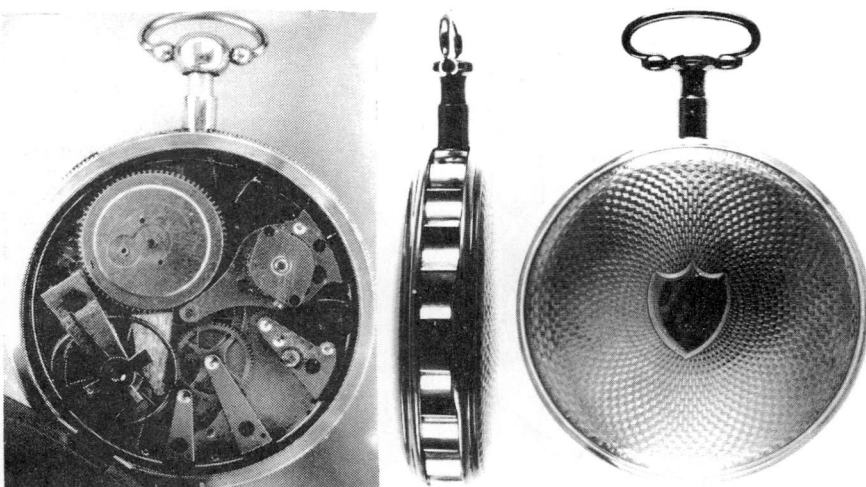

French or Swiss pump 1/4 hr. repeater, free standing barrel, cylinder escapement, tapered bridges, **Thin** gold engine turned case, Ca. 1790-1835. (illo.7)

1/4 hour verge repeater, 49mm, 22K gold repousse pair case, repeating on an inner bell, repeat mechanism is activated from the pendant, ca. 1700-1750, **(illo.8)**

1/4 hour repeater, musical, 25 musical tines, cylinder, center seconds, KW, 18K, 58mm, OF, Ca.1820, **(illo.9)**

1/4 hour repeater, verge (London, Dutch), pierced inner case, repousee outer case, gold, 49mm, C.1700, **(illo.10)**

1/4 Hr. repeating coach watch, with alarm, about 120 MM, verge fusee, silver repousse case, ca.1700-40. **(illo. 11)**

TYPE – DESCRIPTION	Avg	Ex-Fn	Mint
1/4 hr. repeater, repousse pair case, verge, **22K**, 49mm (illo.8)	$4,500	$4,800	$6,500
1/4 hr. repeater, musical, 25 musical tines, cylinder, center seconds, KW, 18K, 58mm,OF, C. 1820 (illo.9)	5,000	6,000	7,500
1/4 hr. rep., verge (London, Dutch), pierced inner case, repousee outer case, gold, 49mm, C.1700 (illo.10)	5,000	6,500	9,000
1/4 hr. repeating coach watch w/alarm, verge, fusee, silver repousee case, large, C. 1700-40 (illo. 11)	7,500	8,500	11,000
1/4 hr. repeater with automaton dial, verge, Swiss, KW, 3 automated figures on dial and carillon chimes, silver, 52mm, OF, C. 1790.	2,000	2,600	3,500
Gold & enamel, 1/4 hr. repeater, London, cylinder, Fusee, paircase, enamel on outer case, 18K, 48mm, C. 1790	3,500	4,300	5,500
Swiss, 1/4 hr. pump repeater, w/ automaton, verge, 18K, 54mm, OF, C. 1800	3,500	4,500	6,000
Virgule escapement, 1/4 hr. repeater, fancy gold & multi-dial, London, KW, 18K, OF, C. 1840	2,200	2,800	3,500

REPEATERS

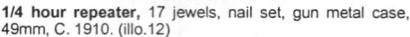

1/4 hour repeater, 17 jewels, nail set, gun metal case, 49mm, C. 1910. (illo.12)

1/4 hour repeater with chronograph, gun metal base-metal or gold filled, 49-50mm, (illo.13)

TYPE – DESCRIPTION	Avg	Ex-Fn	Mint
1/4 hr. repeater, 17J, gun metal, 49-50mm, C. 1910 (illo.12)	$450	$500	$600
1/4 hr. repeater, 17J, silver, 49-50mm, OF, C. 1910	550	600	700
1/4 hr. repeater, 17J, silver, 49-50mm, HC, C. 1910......................	600	650	800
1/4 hr. rep. **w/chrono.**,17J, base metal, gun metal or GF, **OF** 49-50mm, C.1910 (illo.13)...	650	700	800
1/4 hr. rep. **w/chrono.**,17J, base metal, gun metal or GF, **HC** 49-50mm, C.1910	750	800	1,000

🕐 Pricing in this Guide are fair market price for **COMPLETE** watches which are reflected from the "**NAWCC**" National and regional shows.
The Complete Price Guide to Watches goal is to stimulate the orderly exchange of **Watches** between "*buyers*" and "*sellers*".

1/4 hr. repeater with Calendar, 17J, gold filled, 3/4 plate, open face, 50mm, C. 1910 (illo.14)

1/4 hour repeater, 55mm, 2 Jacquemarts, gilt case, Ca. 1820. (illo.15)

TYPE – DESCRIPTION	Avg	Ex-Fn	Mint
1/4 hr. repeater with Calendar, 17J, gun metal or gold filled, 3/4 plate, OF, 49-50mm, C. 1910 (illo.14)	$700	$950	$1,200
Swiss 1/4 hr. repeater w/moonphase & calendar, 17J, 18K, 53mm, HC, C. 1900	3,000	3,200	4,000
55mm, 1/4 repeater, 2 Jacquemarts, gilt case, Ca. 1820 (illo.15) ...	2,200	2,800	3,500
Swiss, 1/4 repeater, **musical,** pinned cylinder & comb, 18K, 50-55mm, Ca. 1800. (illo.16)	5,000	5,500	6,500
Swiss 1/4 hr. repeater, **Erotic Scene,** 14K, HC, 50-54mm, ALL ORIGINAL, (note: beware of fakes) (illo.16A)	7,500	9,000	12,000

Swiss 18K, 1/4 repeater, musical, pinned cylinder & comb, 50-55 mm, Ca. 1800. (illo.16)

Swiss 1/4 hour repeater, Erotic Scene with automaton action dial, 14K, HC, 50-54mm, (illo.16A) This watch has CONVERSION not original (note: beware of fakes)

A bit of musical history in 1796, Antoine Favre of Geneva invented a comb with **vibrating strips.** This innovation lead to the production the musical pocket watch.

COMPARISON OF WATCH SIZES

U. S. A.	EUROPEAN
10-12 SIZE	40—44 MM
16 SIZE	45—49 MM
18 SIZE	50—55 MM

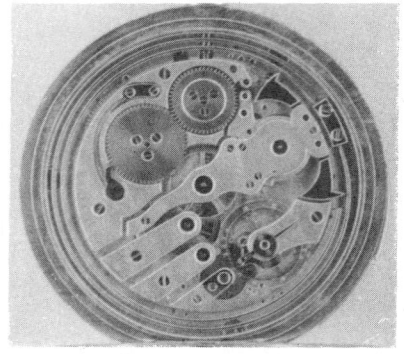

Minute Repeater, 48 jewels, 2 train Independent seconds TANDEM wind, 55mm, Ca. 1890, 18K HC. (illo.17)

Swiss minute repeater, 54mm, jeweled through hammers, 14k case. (illo.18)

TYPE – DESCRIPTION	Avg	Ex-Fn	Mint
Min. rep., 20J, Swiss, gilt mvt., gun metal, 52mm, **OF**, 1910	$700	$900	$1,200
Min. rep., 48 jewels, 2 train Independent seconds **TANDEM** wind, 55mm, Ca. 1890, 18K HC. (illo.17).......................................	6,000	7,200	9,000
Min. rep., 17J, Swiss, gilt, 18K, 52mm, HC, C. 1910	2,500	2,800	3,500
Min. rep., 32 J, Swiss, gilt, 18K, 54mm, HC, C. 1910	2,700	3,200	4,000
Min. rep., 32 J, Swiss, NI, porc. dial, 14K, OF, C. 1905 (illo.18) ...	2,200	2,700	3,500
Min. rep., 32 J, Swiss, NI, porc. dial, 18K, OF, C. 1905 (illo.19) ...	2,500	2,900	3,800
Min. repeater, Self contained, (activated from button on crown) 25J, 14K, OF, C. 1915..	3,500	4,100	5,000
Min. repeater, Swiss, ultra thin, 32J, 18K, OF, C. 1930..................	4,000	4,200	6,000
18K, 54mm (illo.20)	5,000	6,900	8,500

Minute Repeater, 32 jewels., Swiss, enamel dial, wolf tooth winding, 18K, Ca. 1905, (illo.19)

Father & Baby Time, automated min. repeater, 54mm, note father and baby striking bell, 18K. (illo.20)

Minute repeating **Clock Watch,** 3/4 plate, a on or off strike activated mechanism, three gongs, tandem-winding barrels, 18K, 48-50mm, HC, Ca.1900 (illo.21)

Minute repeater, split second chronograph, Swiss, 18K, 47-50mm, OF, Ca.1900 . (illo.22)

TYPE – DESCRIPTION	Avg	Ex-Fn	Mint
Min. repeating Clock Watch, 18K, 48-50mm, HC, Ca.1900 (illo.21)	$8,000	$9,500	$12,000
Min.rep. w/ chrono, Swiss ,SW, 18K, large 58mm, OF, C.1900	2,000	2,300	3,000
Min. repeater w/chrono. register, 32J, nickel, very high quality, 18K, 50mm, OF, C. 1900	3,500	4,200	5,000
Min. rep.w/chrono, 30 min. register, Swiss, 36J, 18K ,HC, C.1895	3,500	4,200	5,000
Min. rep., split sec. chrono, Swiss, 18K, 47-50mm, OF, C.1900 (illo.22)	5,000	5,600	7,000
Min. rep., split sec. chrono, Swiss, 18K, 47-50mm, HC,C.1900	6,000	6,700	8,000
Swiss min. repeater, chrono, moonphase and calendar, 30J or more, 18K, 60mm, HC, C. 1895	5,500	6,200	7,000
Swiss min. repeater, moonphase and **perpetual calendar,** 30J or more, 18K, 60mm, HC, C. 1895 (illo.23) ....★	14,000	16,000	22,000
Swiss min. rep., 4 hammers & Westminster carillon on gongs, 32J, 18K, 53mm, HC, C. 1910 (illo.24)...................................	8,500	13,000	17,000

Swiss minute repeater, moonphase and **perpetual calendar,** 30J or more, 18K, 60mm, HC, C. 1895. (illo.23)

Swiss min. rep., 4 hammers & Westminster carillon on gongs, 32J, 18K, 53mm, HC, C. 1910. (illo.24)

PRE–1850 ALARMS

TYPE – DESCRIPTION	Avg	Ex-Fn	Mint
Alarm, (**Blois, France**), double silver case pierced and engraved, gilt mvt., cut gut cord fusee, 2 wheel train + verge escape. w/foliot, silver balance cock, 44mm, Ca. 1640 (illo.25)	$13,000	$16,000	$22,000
Alarm, 2 cases pierced, 3 wheel train, Egyptian pierced pillers, verge & foliot, 51mm, Ca. 1675 (illo.26)	9,000	12,000	18,000

ALARM, **from BLOIS,** FRANCE, double silver case pierced and engraved, silver crown dial with roman numbers, alarm center dial with arabic numbers, gilt movement, cut gut cord fusee, 2 wheel train plus verge escapement with foliot, silver balance cock, 44mm, Ca. 1640. It is believed French watch-making started in the town of **Blois, France.** (illo.25)

ALARM, 2 cases pierced & engraved, roman outer dial, alarm center dial, blued hands , 3 wheel train, Egyptian pierced pillers, verge & foliot, endless screw adjustment, Paris, 51mm, Ca. 1675. (illo.26)

ALARM, strikes on bell, pair cased, verge, C. 1650. (illo.27)   Alarm, pair cased, first case pique nailed skin, second case pierced, 4 wheel train, verge, amphora pillers, 56mm, Ca. 1680. (illo.28)

TYPE – DESCRIPTION	Avg	Ex-Fn	Mint
Alarm, strikes on bell, pair cased, verge, C. 1650 (illo.27).............	$7,000	$9,000	$12,000
Alarm, pair cased, first case pique nailed skin, 4 wheel train, verge, 56mm, Ca. 1680 (illo.28)	9,000	12,000	18,000
Alarm, Rotterdam, silver pierced case, gilt, tulip pillars, verge, fusee, 48mm, Ca. 1685 (illo.29)...	7,000	9,000	12,000
Alarm, "oignon", verge, fusee, large pierced bal. bridge (illo.30) ...	6,500	7,500	10,000

ALARM, Rotterdam, silver pierced case, gilt, tulip pillars, verge, fusee, 48mm, Ca. 1685. (illo.29)

ALARM, "oignon", verge, fusee, large pierced balance bridge. (illo.30)

ALARM, nailed pique shagreen skin, second case pierced silver, balance cock has short feet, 4 wheel train verge, 60mm, London, Ca. 1685. (illo.31)

ALARM, nailed pique shagreen (**Sting-Ray**) skin, triple cases, entirely pierced throughout, richly decorated, 4 wheel train, verge, fusee, English-Swiss, Ca. 1700. (illo.32)

TYPE – DESCRIPTION	Avg	Ex-Fn	Mint
Alarm, nailed pique shagreen skin, second case pierced silver, 4 wheel train verge, 60mm, London, Ca. 1685 (illo.31)	$6,500	$7,200	$9,000
Alarm, nailed pique shagreen (**Sting-Ray**) skin, English-Swiss, verge, fusee, Ca.1700s, (illo.32)	5,500	6,800	8,500
Oignon alarm, verge, French, silver and animal skin cover, movement wound from center arbor on dial, silver champleve dial, 60mm, OF, C. 1710	6,500	7,200	9,000

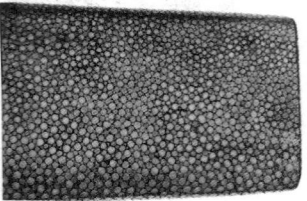

Right Example of
Sting-Ray skin

ALARMS

The most common Swiss and German alarms are usually in base metal or gun metal cases. Early makes with porcelain dials are more desirable than later (post 1920's) metal dial alarms.

TYPE – DESCRIPTION	Avg	Ex-Fn	Mint
Swiss alarm sounding on bell,7J, base metal, 49mm,OF, C.1915	$95	$110	$150
Swiss alarm sounding on gongs, 15J, tandem wind, gun metal, 50mm, OF, C. 1900	175	200	275
Cricket alarm, w/cricket design, Swiss , SW, silver case, 48mm, OF, C.1890	500	600	750

TIMERS & CHRONOGRAPHS

Timer, 1/5 sec., 7J, register, base metal, 48mm, OF.   Timer, **split second,** register, base metal, 56mm, Ca. 1970

TYPE – DESCRIPTION	Avg	Ex-Fn	Mint
Timer, 1/5 sec., register,7J, base metal, 48mm, OF, C. 1940	$35	$45	$65
Timer, 1/5 sec. register, **17J,** base metal, 48mm, OF, C. 1940	40	55	95
Timer, **split sec.,** register, base metal, 46mm, OF, C. 1940	55	75	125
Timer,15-17J, **split sec.**, register, base metal, 56mm, OF, C. 1970.	55	75	125
Timer and Watch, **silver,** 48mm, **HC,** 1925	125	150	185
Chronograph, **7J, GF or silver,** 48mm, OF, C. 1905......................	130	150	195
HC	155	175	200
Chronograph, **15-17J, porcelain** dial, GF or silver, 50mm, OF, ...	200	225	300
HC, ...	250	275	350
Chronograph, **20J, 18K,** 52mm, OF, C. 1895	500	600	750
HC	600	700	850

Timer and Watch, **silver,** 48mm, HC.   Chronograph, 7-17J, GF, 48mm, OF, C. 1905.

Chronograph, w/register, porc. dial, **20J, 14K**, 52mm, HC, Ca. 1890. (illo.A)

Chronograph, Split Seconds, w/register, porc. dial, **20J, 18K**, 52mm, OF, Ca. 1910. (illo.B)

TYPE – DESCRIPTION	Avg	Ex-Fn	Mint
Chronog. w/register, porc. dial, **15J, silver,** 52mm, OF, C. 1890....	$250	$300	$400
HC (illo.A)	300	350	450
Chronog. w/register, porc. dial, **20J, 14K**, 52mm, OF, C. 1890	400	450	550
HC	500	550	650
Chronog. w/register, porc. dial, **20J, 18K**, 52mm, OF, C. 1890	600	650	750
HC	800	850	1,100
Split sec. chronograph, 15-17J, **.800 silver,** 52mm, OF, C. 1900..	300	325	400
Split sec. chronograph, 19-32J, **18K**, 52mm, OF, C. 1900	800	900	1,200
HC (illo.B)	1,000	1,200	1,500
Double dial (time on front, chrono. on back), Swiss , 17J, **14K** display case , 51mm, OF, Ca. 1885 (illo.C)	800	1,200	1,800
1/4 second jump watch, 26J, two gear train, SW , **18K**, HC, C.1880 (illo.D)	2,200	2,700	3,500

Double dial (time on front, Chronograph on back), Swiss, 17J, 14K display case, 51mm, OF, Ca. 1885. (illo.C)

1/4 second jump watch, 26J, two gear train, two main spring barrels, KW , 18K, 53mm, HC, C.1880. (illo.D)

POCKET CHRONOMETER

JOHN ARNOLD, chronometer, KWKS, spring detent, Z balance with adjustable weights, helical hair spring, 18K case, serial # 14, upright escape wheel, "INV ET FECT" engraved on movement (made by), his chronometer factory was located in Chigwell (London), #36 pocket chronometers sold for about $500.00 in 1776. (illo.33)

TYPE – DESCRIPTION	Avg	Ex-Fn	Mint
Chronometer, KWKS, spring detent, Z bal., helical hair-spring, "JOHN ARNOLD", 18K case, C. 1776 (illo.33)	$15,000	$22,000	$32,000
Chronometer, KWKS, spring detent, Z bal., helical hair-spring, silver case, C. 1795 (illo.34)	5,000	6,000	9,000
Chronometer, KWKS, spring detent, Z bal., helical hair-spring, "J. R. ARNOLD", 18K case, C. 1805 (illo.35)	10,000	15,000	22,000

Chronometer, 13 jewels, KWKS, spring detent, Z balance with screw counterpoise on terminal curves, helical hair-spring, silver case, Ca. 1795. (illo.34)

J. R. ARNOLD, chronometer, KWKS, spring detent, Z balance with screw counterpoise on terminal curves, helical hair-spring, 18K case, 58mm, C. 1805. (illo.35)

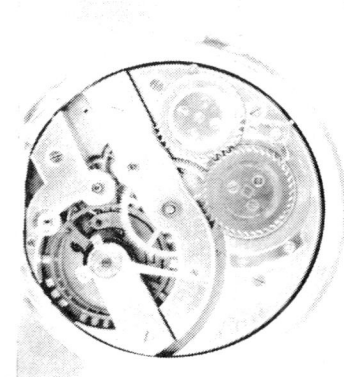

JOHANNES KESSELS "ALTON", deck chronometer, KWKS, spring detent, fusee, silver case, C. 1830 . (illo.36)

Detent chronometer, Helical hairspring, Swiss, SW, 18K, wolf teeth winding, 56mm, HC, C. 1900. (illo.37)

TYPE – DESCRIPTION	Avg	Ex-Fn	Mint
Chronometer, KWKS, spring detent, Z bal., helical hair-spring, "KESSELS", **silver case**, C. 1830 (illo.36)	$2,000	$3,200	$4,500
Chronometer, KW, spring detent, **coin**, OF, C. 1875	600	700	900
Detent chronometer, Swiss, SW, **18K**, 56mm, HC, Ca.1900 (ill0.37)	1,500	1,900	2,500
Detent chronometer, English, w/ wind indicator, **18K**, 48mm, OF .	3,500	4,500	6,500
Chronometer, pivoted detent, helical hairspring, (French), SW, **silver,** 56mm, OF (illo.38)	300	400	550
Pocket chronometer, Swiss, 20 jewel, fancy case, silver and gilt dial, detent, w/ helical spring, **18K**, 49mm, HC, C. 1890 (illo.38A)	2,600	3,200	4,500

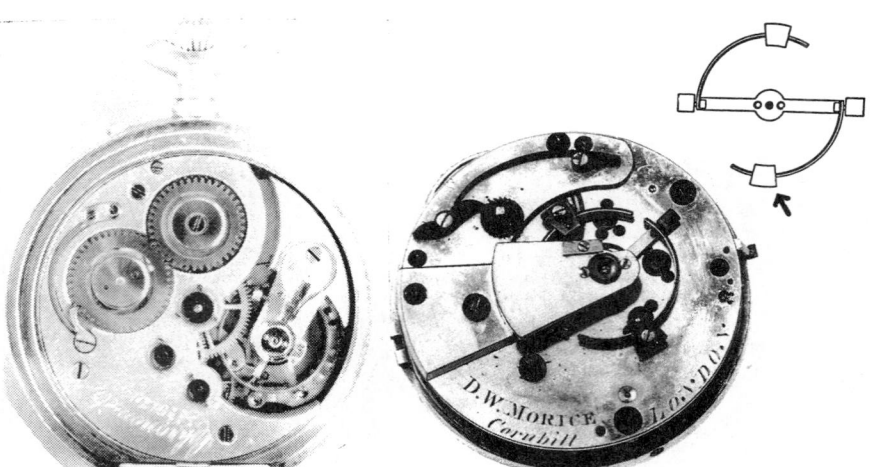

Engraved on movement "*Chronome'tre*" (French), 16 jewels, pivoted detent, helical hairspring, stem wind, manufactured by **LIP** in **Besancon France**, silver, 56mm, OF, Ca. 1910-30. (illo.38)

Detent chronometer, English, w/ fusee, helical hairspring, note: Trapezoidal weights on balance. (illo.38A)

⊕ Note: Some models and grades are not included. Their values can be determined by comparing with **similar** age, size, metal content, style, models and grades listed.

⊕ Note: Watches listed in this book are priced at the **collectable trade show** level, as **complete** watches having an original case, an original dial, and with the entire original movement in good working order with no repairs needed.

TOURBILLON, KARRUSEL, RARE & UNUSUAL MOVEMENTS

One minute so called "Poor Man's Tourbillon", center seconds silver watch with centered dial & visible Tourbillon carriage from back of watch. Swiss, 54mm. (illo.39)

Singed **Mobilis**,Visible Tourbillon, 53mm, 13 to 15 jewels, tourbillon carriage is visible from dial side, Pat. No. 30754 (made by Courvoisier Freres), ca. 1905. (illo.40)

TYPE – DESCRIPTION	Avg	Ex-Fn	Mint
Tourbillon, Swiss, base metal, 54mm, OF (illo.39).................★	$1,500	$2,400	$3,500
Tourbillon, 53mm, 13J, **Mobilis**, Ca. 1905 (illo.40) ....★	2,000	2,800	4,000
Tourbillon, **4 min.**, 15J, enamel dial, silver, C.1910 (illo.41).......★	2,800	3,500	5,000
Karrusel, **52 min.**, English, 3/4, gilt, 16J, SW, silver case, 56mm, OF, C.1885 (illo.42)	2,500	3,200	4,500
Karrusel, **52 min.**, English, 3/4, gilt, 16J, SW, **18K case**, 56mm, OF, C.1885 (illo.42)....................................	3,500	4,200	5,500
Helicoil mainspring, Swiss, 15J , cylinder esc., base metal, 51mm, OF, C. 1910 (illo.43)........................★★	2,000	2,600	3,500

signed **TOURBILLON**, one complete turn in 4-5 minutes, 15 jewels, enamel dial, silver case, Ca.1930. (illo.41)

52 minute **KARRUSEL**, 57mm, 14J., English, silver case, Ca.1885. (illo.42)

NOTE:
The Tourbillon **Mobilis** is signed "Mobilis Pat. no. 30754" the Pat. date was June 11,1904 and was Patented by Paul Loichet of Charquemont, France, Tourbillon movement was made by Courvoisier Freres of La Chaux de Fonds Switzerland from 1905 to about 1910.

Helicoil Mainspring, 51mm, 15J., rare winding system, cylindrical spring replaces standard mainspring. (illo.43)

Lever with Fusee, KW KS, (Liverpool), hallmarked, silver, **undersprung**, 46mm, OF, Ca. 1850-70.(illo.44)

EARLY PRE–1850 NON—GOLD

TYPE – DESCRIPTION	Avg	Ex-Fn	Mint
Lever, Fusee, (Liverpool), silver, 46mm, OF, Ca. 1850-70 (illo.44)	$135	$185	$275
Lever or cylinder, BAR, KW KS, silver, 46-52mm, OF (illo.45)...	95	125	150
Lever or cylinder, **engraved** BAR, KW KS, silver, 46-52mm, OF, Ca. 1840-85 (illo.46)	135	150	200
Lever or cylinder, **Le-PINE**, KW KS, silver, 46-52mm (illo.47)...	135	150	200
Rack & pinion escap., KW KS, silver, 46-52mm, OF (illo.48).....	250	325	475

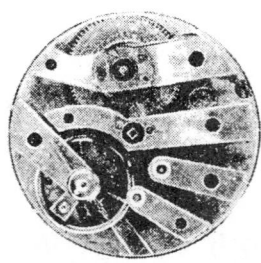

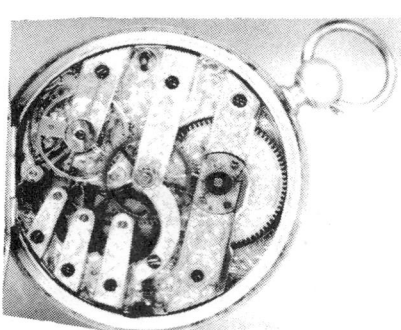

Lever, KW KS, bar style movement, note **curved barrel bridge,** silver, 46-52mm, OF, C. 1830-50. (illo.45)

Lever, **Lepine style bar, engraved,** KW KS, silver, 46-52mm, OF, Ca. 1840-85. (illo.46)

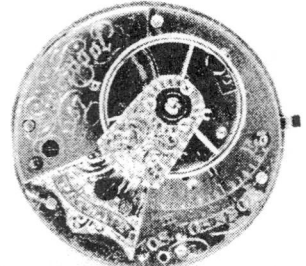

Lever, **Lepine style tapered bar movement,** KW KS, silver, 46-52mm, OF, Ca. 1820-35. (illo.47)

Rack & pinion escapement, KW KS, silver, 46-52mm, Ca. 1830. (illo.48)

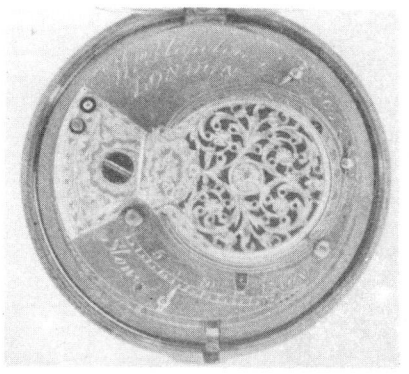
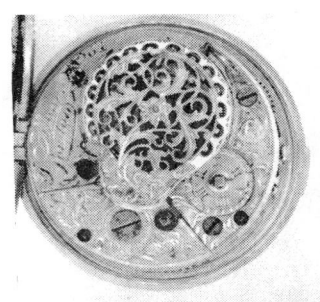

Verge, chain driven fusee, (English) paircase, 52mm, OF, C.1800- 40. (illo.49)

Verge, fusee, (English) paircase, hallmarked, KW, 52mm, OF, Ca. 1780-90. (illo.50)

TYPE – DESCRIPTION	Avg	Ex-Fn	Mint
Verge, Fusee (Swiss), KW, (unmarked) single case, silver, 49mm, OF, C. 1810-40	$250	$300	$400
Verge (English) paircase, 52mm, OF, C.1800- 40 (illo.49)	250	300	400
Painted "farmer's dial," verge, Swiss / London, silver, 52-55m, OF	500	600	800
Cylinder, Fusee, silver, 48-52mm, OF, C. 1830s	250	300	400
Verge, Fusee (Swiss), KW, silver single case, 49mm OF, C. 1810-1840	250	300	400
Verge (English) paircase, hallmarked, KW, 52mm, OF, C. 1780-90 (illo.50)	275	325	450
Miniature, verge, lady's, plain, porcelain dial, hallmarked silver, 24mm, OF, C. 1810	700	800	1,100
Gilt & enamel, verge, Swiss or French, 46mm, OF, C. 1800	800	1,000	1,500
Skeletonized, verge, Swiss, double case, hand-carved movement, case silver & horn, 53mm,OF, C. 1800	700	900	1.200
Repousee paircase, fancy dial, verge, London, hallmarked silver, 49mm, OF, C. 1800 (illo.51)	800	1,100	1,600
Erotic Repousee paircase, Swan & Lady, verge, London (illo.52)	1,000	1,400	2,000

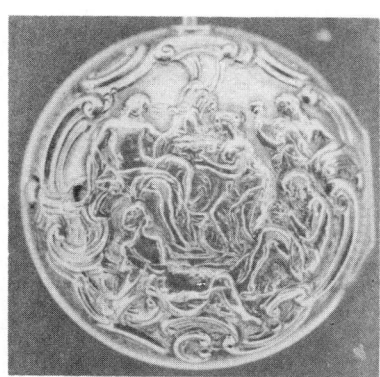
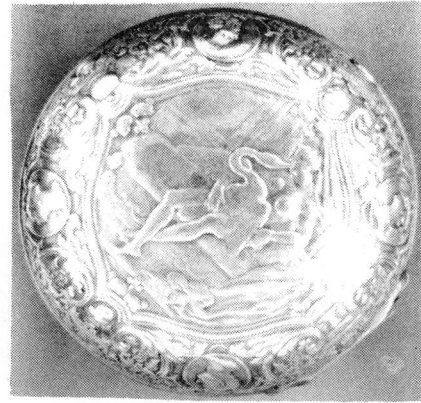

Repousee paircase, fancy dial, verge, English hallmarked silver case, 49mm, OF, C. 1800. (illo.51)

Erotic Repousee silver paircase, Swan & Lady, verge, Fusee, London. (illo.52)

OIGNON watch with mock pendulum, 58mm, Ca. 1700-1720. (illo.53)

Lady & mock pendulum, mock pendulum can be seen at top of Lady's head , 58mm, Ca. 1690 (illo.54)

TYPE – DESCRIPTION	Avg	Ex-Fn	Mint
Oignon watch with mock pendulum, 58mm, ca. 1700-20 (illo.53) .	$2,800	$4,000	$6,000
Lady & mock pendulum, enamel Lady, 58mm, Ca. 1690 (illo.54) .	3,200	4,500	6,500
Verge w/ calendar, repousee paircase, London hallmarked, silver, 51mm, OF, C. 1690	2,500	3,200	4,000
Dublin, early verge, silver paircase, champleve silver dial (signed), 54mm, OF, C. 1720	1,800	2,200	2,800
Early verge, large winged cock, signed silver dial, London, Egyptian pillars, silver, 55mm, OF, C. 1700 (illo.55)	2,000	2,400	3,000
Viennese enamel on gilt, verge, fusee, multi-scenes on case, KW, 55mm, HC, C. 1780	2,200	2,700	3,500
English, verge w/ calendar, signed champleve dial, silver & horn, 54mm OF, C. 1680	2,500	3,200	4,000

Early verge, large D shaped foot on the cock, London, signed silver dial, Egyptian pillars, silver, 55mm, OF, C. 1700 . (illo.55)

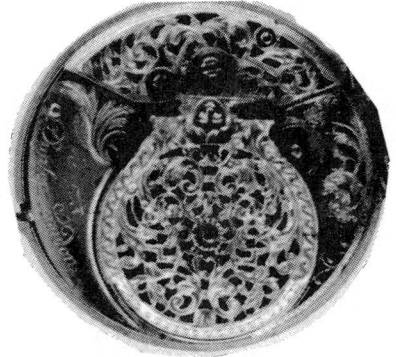

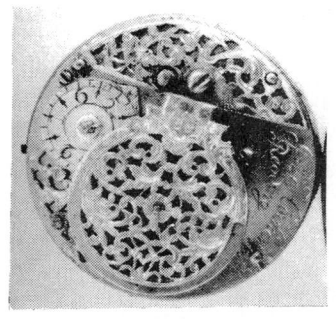

Tortoise shell case, verge with chain driven fusee, calendar, D shaped foot balance cock, C. 1700, (illo.56)

English, verge, hand pierced cock, fusee, silver, note face on balance cock, C. 1720, (illo.57)

TYPE – DESCRIPTION

	Avg	Ex-Fn	Mint
Tortoise shell, verge, calendar, Ca. 1700 (illo.56)...............	$1,900	$2,500	$3,500
English, verge, hand pierced cock, fusee, silver, Ca. 1720, (illo.57)	1,200	1,400	2,200
Pumpkin Form Case, verge, silver, 40mm, Ca. 1775 (illo.58)........	1,800	2,400	3,500
Garooned Case, verge, fusee, 44mm, silver, Ca. 1650 (illo.59).......	8,000	10,000	15,000
Painted scene on horn, verge, gilt, 57mm, OF, Ca. 1780 (illo.60)..	1,800	2,400	3,500

Pumpkin Form Case, verge, silver, Ca. 1775. (illo.58)

Garooned Case, verge, fusee, 44mm, Ca. 1650. (illo.59)

Painted horn (full scene in color) London, verge, gilt, 57mm, OF, C. 1780. (illo.60)

EARLY NON—GOLD

Early Astronomic watch with day date month calendar, lunar calendar, 57mm, Ca. 1680. (illo.61)

TYPE – DESCRIPTION	Avg	Ex-Fn	Mint
Early Astronomic watch with day date month calendar, lunar calendar, 57mm, Ca. 1680 (illo.61)	$10,000	$14,000	$20,000
Early Astronomic watch with moon phases and triple date, fusee with cut-gut cord, 3 gear train, foliot, Ca.1660 (illo.62)	15,000	19,000	25,000

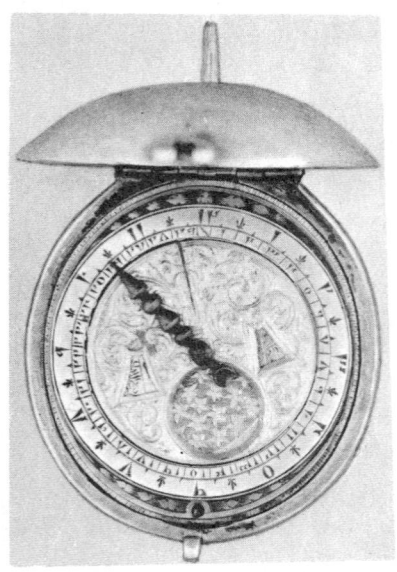
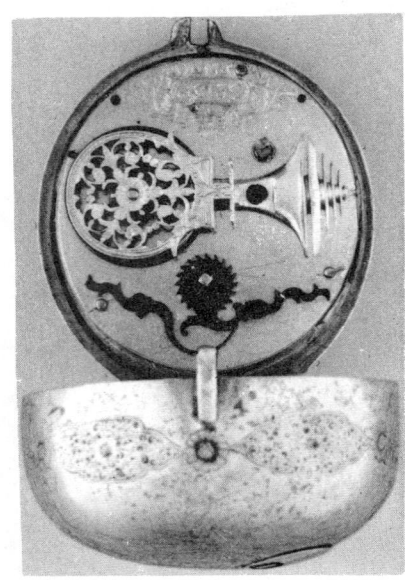

Early Astronomic watch with moon phases and triple date, fusee with cut-gut cord, 3 gear train, 6 armed foliot, Ca.1660. (illo.62)

Early German made silver watch, verge and foliot, silver pierced dial, "Hamburg", Ca. 1660. (illo.63)

TYPE – DESCRIPTION	Avg	Ex-Fn	Mint
Early German made silver watch, verge and foliot, silver pierced dial, "Hamburg", Ca. 1660 (illo.63)	$6,000	$8,000	$12,500
Early silver watch, blued steel hand, cut-gut fusee, foliot, rosette for adj., 53mm, Ca.1660 (illo.64)	12,000	15,000	20,000

Early silver watch, silver dial with blued steel hand, cut gut fusee, 3 wheel train, foliot, rosette for adjustment of the motor-spring tension, 53mm, Ca.1660. (illo.64)

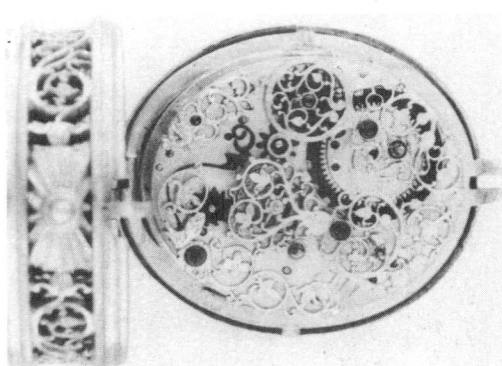

Pair cased, first case silver covered with nailed skin, verge, cut-gut cord fusee, 3 wheel train, foliot, pierced cock, endless screw adjustment for main spring tension, 45mm, Ca. 1660. (illo.65)

Early French watch movement with hour and minute hand, striking bell each hour, hand pierced case & gilt brass movement, cut-gut fusee, c. 1600s. (illo.66)

TYPE – DESCRIPTION	Avg	Ex-Fn	Mint
Pair cased, first case silver & nailed skin, verge, fusee, 3 wheel train, foliot, pierced cock, 45mm, Ca. 1660 (illo.65)	$7,000	$9,000	$12,500
Early French watch hour and minute hand, striking on bell, cut-gut fusee, c. 1600s (illo.66)	12,000	16,000	22,000
Early Drum Clock, iron plates, 4 wheel train, brass fusee on a steel great wheel, steel contrate wheel with brass teeth, steel verge and foliot balance w/ T-shaped ends, 34mm high (illo.67)	25,000	35,000	50,000

43mm, Early Drum Clock, iron plates, 4 wheel train, brass fusee on a steel great wheel, steel contrate wheel with brass teeth, steel verge and foliot balance with T-shaped ends . The cylindrical gilt brass case is finely engraved and is 34mm high, Ca. 1550 - 1560. (illo.67)

🕐 Pricing in this Guide are fair market price for **COMPLETE** watches which are reflected from the "**NAWCC**" National and regional shows.

Lever or verge, Fusee, (Liverpool), 18K, multi-colored gold dial, 52mm, OF, C.1820-75. (illo.68).

Lever or cylinder, BAR style movement, GOLD, 45-52mm, OF, 1840-1865. (illo.69)

TYPE – DESCRIPTION	Avg	Ex-Fn	Mint
Lever, (Liverpool), **18K,** 52mm, OF, C.1820-75 (illo.68)	$300	$350	$500
Verge, (Liverpool), **18K,** 52mm, HC, C. 1820-75	400	500	700
Lever or cylinder, BAR, GOLD, 45-52mm, OF(illo.69).................	250	325	425
(same as above) w / skeletonized movement,**18K** (illo.70) ...	350	425	575
Lever or cylinder, Le-Pine style, GOLD, 45-52mm, OF (illo.71) ...	250	300	425
Cylinder Fusee, paircase, London, plain case, porcelain dial,**18K**, 48mm, OF, C. 1880	1,100	1,500	1,900
Verge, multi-color case, Swiss/ French, porcelain dial, **18K**, 42mm,OF, Ca. 1770-1800	1,200	1,600	2,000
Verge, French, gold & enamel patterns on case, KWKS, OF, C. 1805	1,400	1,700	2,200
Verge, (Swiss), **18K,** 52-54mm, plain case, OF, C. 1790-1820	550	700	1,000
Verge ,Swiss, gold scene, high quality ,**18K**, 50mm, OF, C.1790...	1,200	1,600	2,200

Lever or cylinder, skeletonized & engraved bar movement, Swiss, 45-52mm, OF,18K. (illo.70)

Lever or cylinder escapement, Lepine style movement, Ca. 1820-1835, GOLD, 45-52mm, OF. (illo.71)

Verge, repousee paircase, 20K gold case, 43mm, Open Face, Ca.1720 to 1750, (illo.72)

Early verge, D shaped balance cock, signed dial, London, Egyptian pillars, gold, 55mm, OF, Ca. 1690 to 1720. (illo.73)

TYPE – DESCRIPTION	Avg	Ex-Fn	Mint
Verge, repousee paircase, 20K, 43mm, OF, C.1730 (illo.72)	$1,800	$2,300	$3,200
Early verge, large winged cock, signed dial, London,Egyptian pillars, gold, 55mm, OF, C. 1700 (illo.73)..............................	2,000	2,400	3,000
Virgule, Fusee, Swiss or French, 18K, 50-55mm, OF, C. 1790	1,200	1,400	1,800
Fusee, made in HOLLAND, Ca. 1800, GOLD case (illo.74)	450	550	800
Skeletonized French, diamonds on bezel, 39mm, C.1780 (illo.75) .	1,400	1,700	2,500
Rack & Pinion lever escapement, 18K, OF, Ca. 1830 (illo.75A)	600	775	1,000

Fusee, movement made in HOLLAND, GOLD case, note the bridge style, 60mm, OF, Ca. 1800 (illo.74)

Skeletonized French watch, diamonds on bezel, 39mm, C.1780 (illo.75)

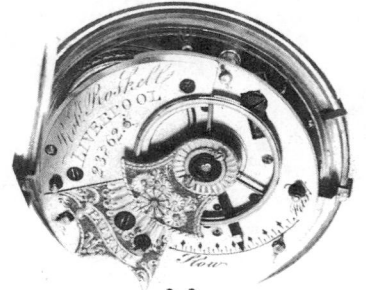

Rack and Pinion Lever Escapement, 18K, OF, Ca. 1830 (illo.75A)

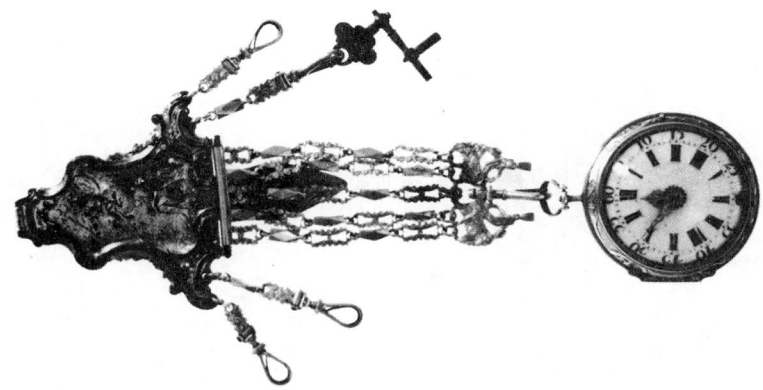

CHATELAINE, verge, fusee, 22k pair case, 45mm, (illo.76)

TYPE – DESCRIPTION	Avg	Ex-Fn	Mint
Chatelaine, verge, fusee, 22k pair case (illo.76)..............................	$3,200	$3,800	$4,500
Early gold & nailed double case watch, foliot, C.1670 (illo.77)......	20,000	24,000	30,000

Early gold & nailed double case watch, Champleve gold dial, 3 wheel train, verge, foliot, rosette adjustment and endless screw, 50mm, C.1670 (illo.77)

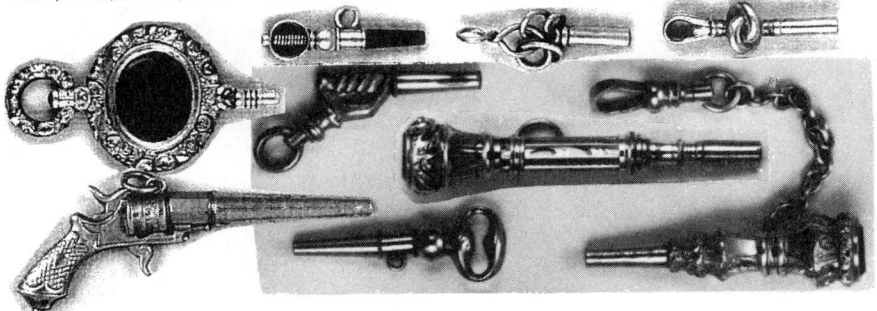

GOLD KEYS, the tops are all gold and the bottom key shaft is base metal, PRICES= **$85 to $165** each.

MISC. MEN'S GF / SILVER / BASE METAL

Dollar watch **German**, base metal ,OF, C.1895. (illo.78)

German, with camera, back wind, **waterproof style model,** base metal, OF, C.1885. (illo.79)

TYPE – DESCRIPTION	Avg	Ex-Fn	Mint
Dollar watch **German**, base metal ,OF, C.1895 (illo.78)	$40	$50	$75
German, back wind, **waterproof**, OF, C.1885 (illo.79)	250	300	350
Base metal, 7-17J, SW, 43-48mm, OF, C. 1900-1930	40	50	75
GF or silver, 7-17J, SW, 43-48mm, OF, C. 1895-1940	60	70	95
GF or silver, 7-17J, SW, 43-52mm, **HC**, C. 1895-1940..................	85	100	150
Swiss Fakes , 7J, KW, base metal, OF, 52mm, C. 1870-90	65	85	100
Non-magnetic, pat.# 7546/780, **Moeris**, base metal (illo.80)	95	125	165
Cylinder, (Liverpool), 1/2 plate design (illo.81).............................	85	100	125

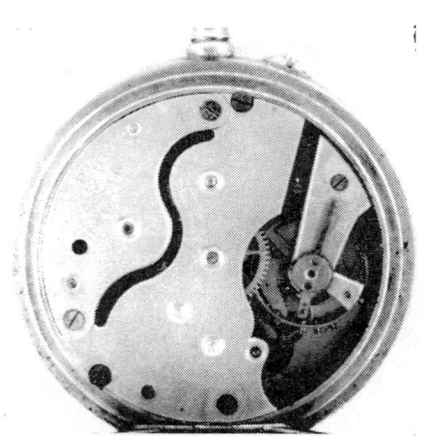

Non-magnetic, pat.#7546-780, **Moeris**, base metal, thumb-nail set, SW, OF. (illo.80)

Cylinder escapement, (Liverpool), 1/2 plate design, marked 4 hole jeweled=8 jewels. (illo.81)

COMPARISON OF WATCH SIZES

U. S. A.	EUROPEAN
10-12 SIZE	40—44 MM
16 SIZE	45—49 MM
18 SIZE	50—55 MM

KW KS, **Chinese Duplex** escapement, 3/4 plate design, note **BAT** style weights on balance, OF. (illo.82)

KW KS, with a **Compass** on movement, lever escapement, Ca. 1855. (illo.83)

TYPE – DESCRIPTION	Avg	Ex-Fn	Mint
KWKS, **Chinese Duplex,** 3/4 plate design, OF (illo.82)	$250	$300	$400
KWKS, **Compass** on movement, lever escap., (illo.83)	100	125	175
KWKS, 6-15J, silver, 45-52mm, OF, C. 1860-85	65	80	100
KWKS, 8-17J, silver, 45-52mm, HC, C. 1860-85	75	90	130
Engraved movement, KWKS, 15J, silver, 46mm, HC, C.1870	90	100	150
KWKS, marked railway, pin lever, Swiss (illo.84)	45	55	90
21J, RR type, GF, 48mm, OF, C. 1910-30	80	100	150
25J, Waltham (Swiss made), GF, 48mm, OF, C. 1950	100	125	175
Niello enamel, 17J, SW, silver, 45mm, HC, C. 1940	150	200	300
Niello enamel & **embossed** hunting scene on **base metal** case, enamel dial, 3/4 plate, made in **Beaucourt France,** OF (illo.85)	100	125	200

KWKS, marked railway, pin lever, Swiss, Ca. 1889. (illo.84)

Niello enamel & embossed hunting scene on case, enamel dial, 3/4 plate, made in Beaucourt France, made by Japy Freres et Cie, OF, Ca. 1890. (illo.85)

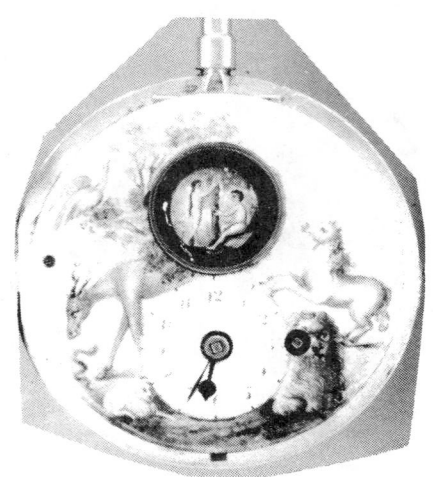

1/4 repeater early rim activated, Swiss or French, silver, OF, Ca.1820. (illo.86)

Automaton, **Adam & Eve**, note snake circles Adam & Eve, hand painted enamel dial, KW KS, OF. (illo. 87)

TYPE – DESCRIPTION	Avg	Ex-Fn	Mint
1/4 repeater early rim activated, silver, OF, Ca.1820 (illo.86).........	$900	$1,200	$1,800
Automaton, **Adam & Eve**, w/ snake, KW KS, OF (illo. 87)..........	3,800	4,500	5,500
Spring detent chronometer w/**Tandem** wind, fusee, 56mm, Ca.1875 (illo.88)...	700	900	1,200
Gamblers playing cards on dial porcelain, Swiss, silver, OF (illo.89)	285	400	600

Spring Detent chronometer with **Tandem** wind, chain driven fusee, Helical hair spring, 56mm, Ca.1875. (illo.88)

Gamblers playing cards on porcelain dial, Swiss, silver, OF. (illo.89)

Exposed Skeletonized Balance from dial, enamel painted dial, verge, fusee, KW KS, large advance-retard index, Ca.1790. (illo.90)

TYPE – DESCRIPTION	Avg	Ex-Fn	Mint
Exposed Balance from dial, enamel painted dial, Ca.1790 (illo.90)	$1,600	$1,900	$2,600
Wandering Digital Jump Hour Hand, 45mm, Ca. 1880 (illo.91)....	3,500	4,400	6,000
Jump Digital Hour, W/ Date at 6, sec. hand at 3, Ca. 1820 (illo.92)	1,200	1,500	2,000

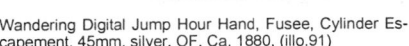

Wandering Digital Jump Hour Hand, Fusee, Cylinder Escapement, 45mm, silver, OF, Ca. 1880, (illo.91)

Jump Digital Hour, W/ Date at 6, sec. hand at 3, silver, engine turned dial, OF, Ca. 1820 (illo.92)

COMPARISON OF WATCH SIZES

U. S. A.		EUROPEAN
10-12 SIZE		40—44 MM
16 SIZE		45—49 MM
18 SIZE		50—55 MM

Day, date, moon phases, Swiss, fancy dial, lever set at rim of case, GF, 46mm (illo.93)

Day, date, Swiss, fancy dial, **base metal**, 46mm. (illo.94)

TYPE – DESCRIPTION	Avg	Ex-Fn	Mint
Day, date, moon phases, Swiss, fancy dial, **GF**, 46mm (illo.93).....	$200	$275	$375
Day, date, moon phases, Swiss, fancy dial, **gun metal**, 46mm	150	225	350
Day, date, Swiss, fancy dial, **base metal**, 46mm (illo.94)	85	125	175
Self winding, (Loehr patent), KW, set from back (illo.95)	400	500	700
Mock pendulum (dial side), **all original**, duplex escap. (illo.96) ..	350	400	500

Self winding, (Loehr patent), KW, set from back. (illo.95)

Mock pendulum (seen from face side), duplex escap. Multi-color dial. **FAKES** SEEN (illo.96)

MISC. MEN'S *GOLD* / PLATINUM

TYPE – DESCRIPTION	Avg	Ex-Fn	Mint
SW, 17J, **14K**, 43-46mm, OF, C. 1910-1940	$200	$225	$275
SW, 17J-19J, **18K**, 43-46mm, OF, C. 1910-1940	250	275	350
SW, 17J, **14K**, 48mm, HC, C. 1910-1940	375	400	500
SW, 17J, **Platinum**, 42mm, OF, C. 1940's	500	550	650
KWKS, 15J, lever, fancy ,gilt dial, **18K**, 45mm, C. 1870...............	275	300	400
KWKS, 15-20J, lever **18K**, 49-53mm, C. 1870-1885	400	500	650
Lever, Fusee, (Liverpool), 15J, porcelain dial, **18K**, 52mm, C.1860	450	550	700

UNUSUAL NON—GOLD

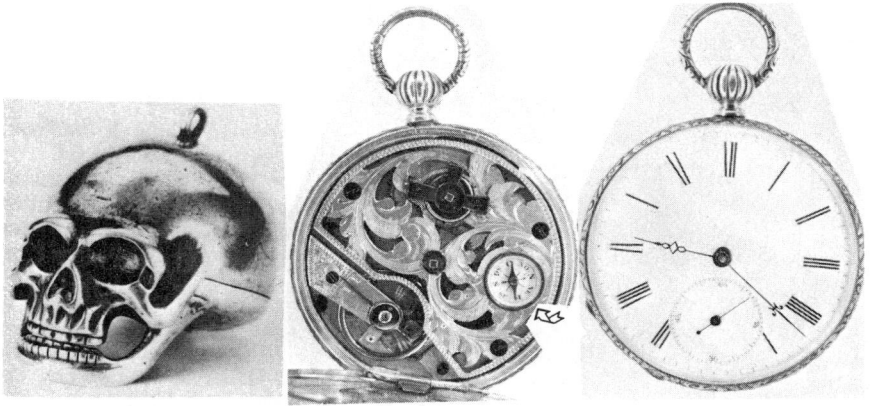

Skull (miniature) form watch, fusee, cylinder escapement, 25mm. Reproduction Ca. 1950 w/ early movement. (illo.97)

Silver Compass Watch, a small compass set into the movement can be seen through a hole in cuvette, (illo.98)

TYPE – DESCRIPTION	Avg	Ex-Fn	Mint
Skull (miniature) form, fusee, cylinder escape., 25mm, (illo.97)	$350	$550	$900
Silver Compass Watch, a small compass set into the movement can be seen through a hole in cuvette, 43mm, OF (illo.98)	300	350	450
Blinking Eyes, pin set animated eyes, 46mm, (illo.99)	250	275	375
8 day, exposed balance, 7J, gun metal, 50mm, C. 1920s (illo.100) .	125	175	275
8 day, exposed balance, 7J, Swiss, **DAY & DATE,** gun metal, 50mm, C. 1920s	200	250	400

Blinking Eyes, pin set animated eyes, 46mm. (illo.99)

8 day, exposed balance, 7J, by Hebdomas but with other name, gun metal, 50mm, C. 1920s. (illo.100)

⊕ Note: Some models and grades are not included. Their values can be determined by comparing with **similar** age, size, metal content, style, models and grades listed.

⊕ Note: Watches listed in this book are priced at the collectable trade show level, as **complete** watches having an original case, an original dial, and with the entire original movement in good working order with no repairs needed.

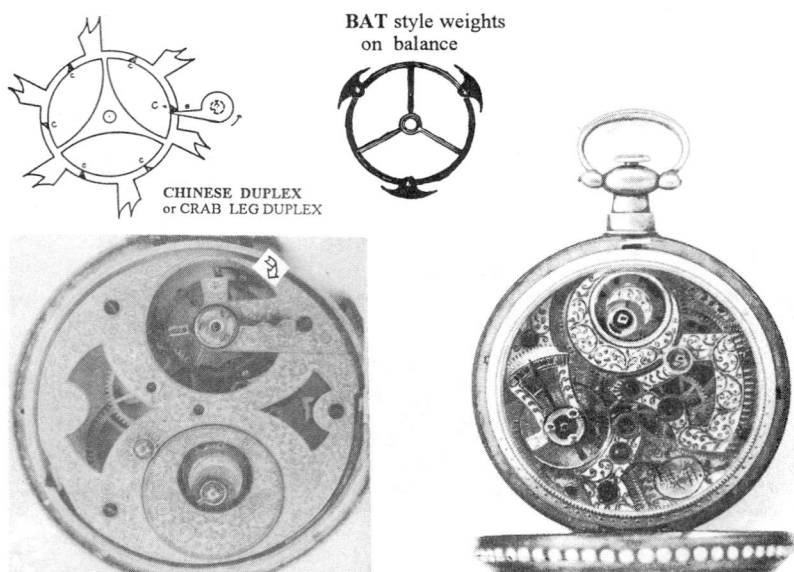

BAT style weights
on balance

CHINESE DUPLEX
or CRAB LEG DUPLEX

Chinese market, KWKS, duplex esc. silver, 58mm, OF, note **BAT** style weights on balance, C.1870. (illo.101)

Chinese market, KW, duplex esc. silver, 58mm, OF, C.1870. (illo.102)

TYPE – DESCRIPTION	Avg	Ex-Fn	Mint
For Chinese market, lever esc., 12J, KWKS, silver, **BAT** style balance, 55mm, OF, C. 1880	$175	$225	$325
Chinese market, KW, duplex esc. silver, 58mm, OF, C.1870 (illo.101)	200	250	350
Chinese market, KW, duplex esc. silver, 58mm, OF, C.1870 (illo.102)	200	250	350
same as above with a **GOLD CASE**	450	550	700
same as above with a **GOLD CASE** + pearls	500	650	1,000
Chinese market, KW, duplex esc. silver, carved movement, 58mm, OF, C.1870 (illo.103)	250	300	450
Carved movement, lever escap., KWKS, silver, 58mm, OF(illo.104)	95	125	200
KW, for Turkish market, 15J, .800 silver, 47mm, HC, C. 1880	95	150	225

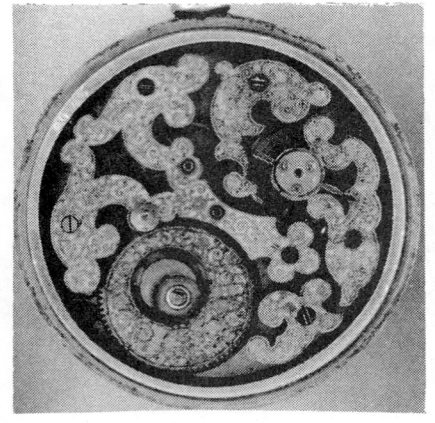

Chinese market, KW, duplex esc. silver, carved movement,58mm, OF, Ca.1850-70. (illo.103)

Carved movement, lever escap., KW KS, silver, 58mm, OF, Ca.1850-70. (illo.104)

Oversize, moon phase & calendar, silver, 65-70mm, Ca.1900. (illo.105)

Moonphase triple cal., Swiss, gun metal, 50mm, OF, Ca. 1905. (illo.106)

TYPE – DESCRIPTION	Avg	Ex-Fn	Mint
Oversize PW, 15J, base metal, 65-70mm, C. 1900-1915	$125	$175	$250
Oversize, moon ph. & calendar, silver,65-70mm, Ca.1900 (illo.105)	750	950	1,250
Moonphase triple cal., Swiss, gun metal , 50mm, OF, C.1905(illo.106)	300	350	425
Moonphase triple cal., Swiss, silver or GF, 50mm, OF, C.1905	350	450	575
Moonphase triple cal., Swiss, silver, 52-54mm, **HC**, C. 1905	550	700	900
Moonphase calendar, sterling, , oversize 65mm, OF, C. 1895	700	950	1,300
Verge (Swiss) skeletonized KW movement, silver & horn pair-case, 61mm, C. 1800	650	800	1,000
Captain's watch, 2 hour dials, 1 train, KW KS, center second, silver, 50mm, HC, C. 1870 (illo.107)	325	425	600
Digital enamel dial, 15J, SW, Swiss, jump hr. & min. discs, silver,HC, C. 1900 (illo.108)	350	475	700

Captain's watch, 2 hour dials, 1 train, KW KS, center second, silver, 50mm, HC, C. 1870. (illo.107)

Digital dial (porcelain), 15J, SW, Swiss, jump hr. & min. discs, silver,HC, C. 1900. (illo.108)

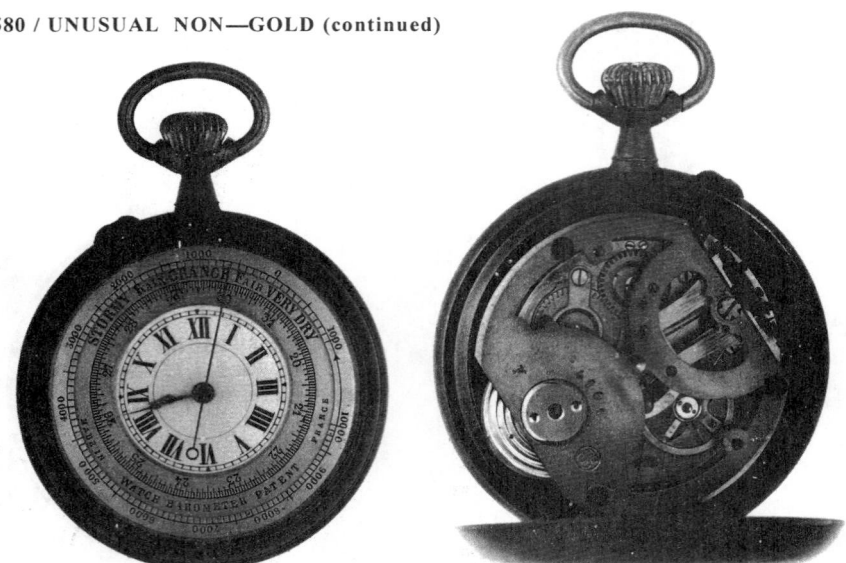

Swiss Pocket Watch with **BAROMETER**, Left: White enamel dial and outer Barometer chapter is signed "Made in France, Watch Barometer Patent", Right: Barometer is attached to movement, 7 jeweled, Cylinder escapement, 54MM, Gun Metal, Ca. 1890. (illo.108A)

TYPE – DESCRIPTION	Avg	Ex-Fn	Mint
Swiss Pocket Watch with **BAROMETER**, Made in France, 54MM, Gun Metal, Ca. 1890. (illo.108A)	$900	$1,250	$2,000
Oversized 1/4 Hour Repeater, 3-1/4" diameter Gun Metal Watch Case, leather box, Ca. 1890. (illo.108B)	500	800	1,200

Oversized 1/4 Hour Repeater, 3-1/4" diameter Gun Metal Case, 29 jewels, 3/4 plate gilt movement, large white enamel dial, velvet-lined leather box , Ca. 1890. (illo.108B)

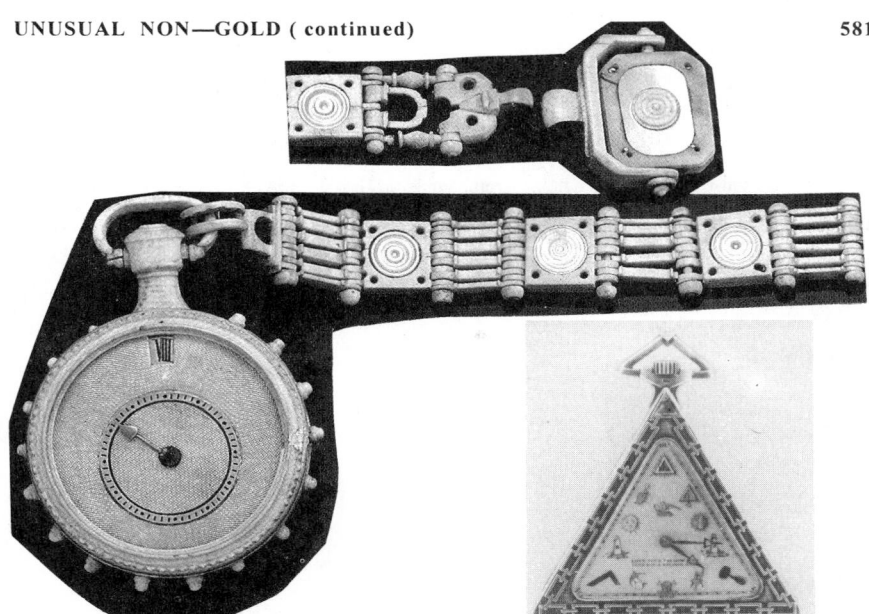

Ivory Case with matching ivory chain, verge movement, digital dial, key wind and key set, Ca. 1800. (illo.109)

Masonic triangular watch, Swiss ,17J, mother of pearl masonic dial, sterling, C. 1920's. (illo.110)

TYPE – DESCRIPTION	Avg	Ex-Fn	Mint
Ivory Case with matching ivory chain, verge movement, digital dial, key wind and key set, Ca. 1800. (illo.109)	$5,000	$6,200	$8,000
Automated w/moving windmill on dial, Swiss, colored scene, exposed balance, 8 day , base metal, OF, C.1910	400	500	625
Masonic triangular watch, Swiss ,17J, mother of pearl masonic dial, sterling, C. 1920's (illo.110)	1,100	1,500	2,000
Masonic, as above, with blue stone in crown, 1905	1,500	2,200	3,000
World time w/ 6 zones, Swiss, Gun Metal, OF, C. 1900 (illo.111)	500	650	800
World time w/ 6 zones, Swiss, silver, 52mm, OF, C. 1900	700	800	1,000
World time, 24 Cities, w/ coded color rotating dial, 18K GOLD, 61mm (illo.112)	2,500	4,000	6,500

World time, with 6 zones, Swiss, GUN METAL, 52mm, OF, Ca.1900. (illo.111)

World time, 24 Cities, with coded color rotating dial, Ca. 1895, 61mm. (illo.112)

582 / UNUSUAL NON—GOLD (continued)

TYPE – DESCRIPTION	Avg	Ex-Fn	Mint
Mysterieuse watch, Swiss, see-through dial, hidden movement			
silver, 52mm, OF, Ca. 1895 (illo.113-114)............................	$1,000	$1,500	$2,500
GOLD, 52mm, OF, Ca. 1895 (illo.113-114).................... ★★	2,000	2,900	3,500
Wooden works, wooden wheels, wooden case, (illo.115)...... ★★	2,800	3,500	4,500
above w/ wooden **chain** and wooden storage style box ★★★	4,500	5,200	6,500
Sector watch, fan-shaped, fly back hour & min. hands, 17J,			
"Record Watch Co.," silver, 49x34mm, Ca. 1900 (illo.116)...	1,800	2,500	4,000
Musical, play's 2 tunes, silver, HC, 50mm, Ca. 1900 (illo.117)......	2,400	3,000	4,000

Mysterieuse watch, Swiss, see-through dial, showing dial side of watch, 52mm, OF, Ca. 1895. (illo.113)

Mysterieuse watch, Swiss, see-through dial, showing the hidden movement, 52mm, OF, Ca. 1895. (illo.114)

Wooden works, wooden wheels, wooden case, all wooden watch, 50mm, made in **Russia**, Ca. 1860. (illo.115)

Sector watch, fan-shaped, fly back hour & min. hands, 17J, "Record Watch Co.," silver, 49x34mm, Ca. 1900. (illo.116)

Musical, play's 2 tunes, silver, 30 Tines, HC, 50mm, 1900. (illo.117)

Wandering hour hands, 12 hands appear one at a time and move across minute sector, the 12 hands are on 3 star wheels, pin lever escapement, **gun metal** case, Ca. 1900. (illo.M1)

TYPE – DESCRIPTION		Avg	Ex-Fn	Mint
Wandering hour hands, 12 hands are on 3 star wheel, **gun metal**, pin lever escapement, Ca. 1900. (illo.M1) .... ★★		$1,000	$1,500	$2,500
Wandering hour hands and **1/4 repeater**, 12 hands are on 3 star wheel, cylinder escapement, **18K gold,** Ca. 1800. (illo.M2) ... ★★★		6,000	8,000	12,000

Wandering hour hands and **1/4 repeater**, 12 hands appear one at a time and move across minute sector, the 12 hands are on 3 star wheels, cylinder escapement, **18K** gold case. Ca. 1800. (illo.M2)

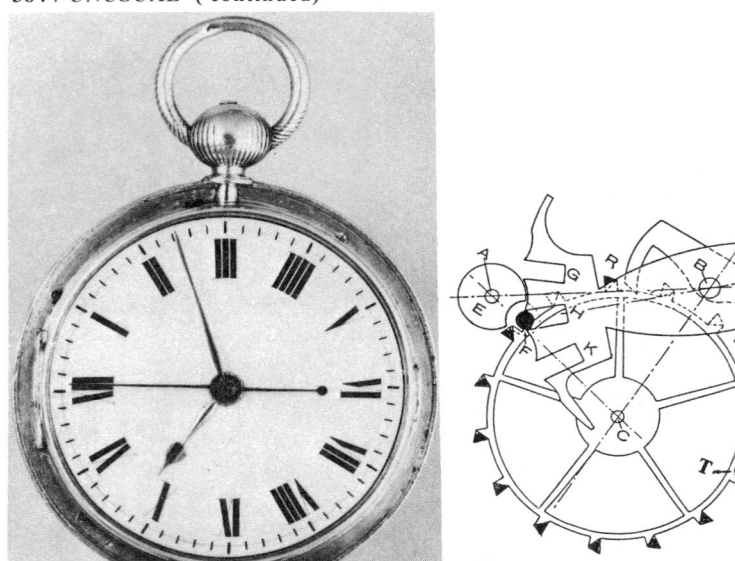

Pouzait style escape wheel, with 15 upright teeth (see"T" on escapement illo.), the center seconds hand jumps (dead seconds), silver 60 MM hunting case, Ca. 1885.(illo. M3)

TYPE – DESCRIPTION	Avg	Ex-Fn	Mint
Pouzait style escape wheel, with 15 upright teeth, dead seconds, **silver**, 60 MM, hunting case, Ca. 1885 (illo. M3)...............★	$1,200	$2,200	$3,500
Pouzait, 15 upright teeth on the escape wheel, large 5 arm balance, by Du Bois et Fils, **gold**, 57MM, Ca. 1800 (illo. M4)..... ★★	8,000	9,000	12,000

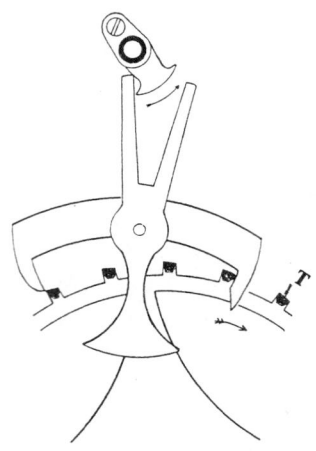

Pouzait style lever with 15 upright teeth on the escape wheel, each swing of the large 5 arm balance is one second, J.M. Pouzait lever escapement was introduced in 1786, the escape wheel with upright teeth are seen in 15 and 30 teeth, escapement seen through plate, many watches of this style were signed and made by Du Bois et Fils, also seen signed Breguet et Fils, Ca. 1800 (illo. M4)

Unique winding design (Each time the hunting case style watch is opened to view the time, the mainspring is partially wound) Patented in 1873 by B. Haas.

TYPE – DESCRIPTION	Avg	Ex-Fn	Mint
Unique winding design (Each time the hunting case style watch is opened to view the time, the mainspring is partially wound) Patented in 1873 by B. Haas, 42mm, **gold HC**	$2,200	$2,600	$3,500
Peculiar Endless screw winding system, stem wind, pin set, 15 jewels, pat. by Lehmann, Ca. 1885, 42mm, **silver HC**	400	600	1,000

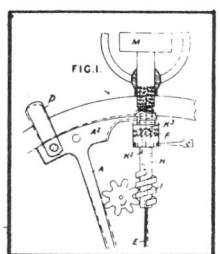

Peculiar Endless screw winding system, stem wind, pin set, 15 jewels, pat. by Lehmann, Ca. 1885

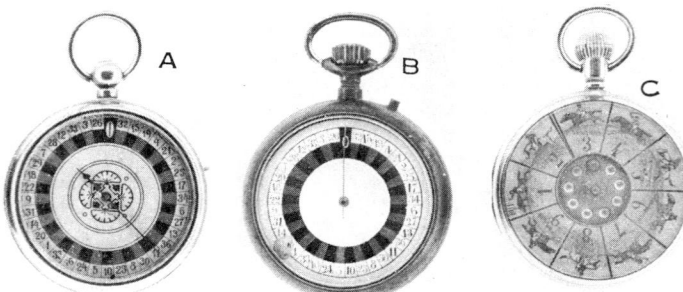

A. Roulette wheel style dial, press a lever & the center pointer spins to a red or black number.
B. Roulette wheel style dial, press a button & the center pointer spins to a red or black number.
C. Horse Race dial, twist the crown & a tiny ball spins & falls into a indentation at one of 9 horses.

TYPE – DESCRIPTION	Avg	Ex-Fn	Mint
A. Roulette wheel style dial, press a lever & the center pointer spins to a red or black number.	$125	$175	$300
B. Roulette wheel style dial, press a button & the center pointer spins to a red or black number.	125	175	300
C. Horse Race dial, twist the crown & a tiny ball spins & falls into a indentation at one of 9 horses.	200	275	400
D. Roulette wheel style dial, press a button & the center pointer spins to a red or black number.	125	175	300
E. Horse Race dial, push the crown & 8 horses rotate , the winner appears in an aperture (window).	200	275	400
F. Dice Game, press a lever & the platform spins causing 5 dice to roll and come up randomly.	125	175	300

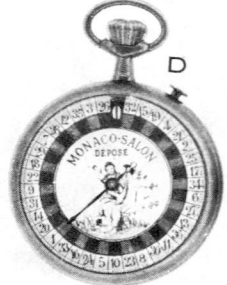
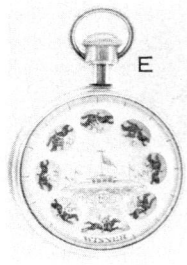

D. Roulette wheel style dial, press a button & the center pointer spins to a red or black number.
E. Horse Race dial, push the crown & 8 horses rotate , the winner appears in an aperture (window).
F. Dice Game, press a lever & the platform spins causing 5 dice to roll and come up randomly.

NIELLO WATCH CASES

Niello (nye-el-oh) is a black or dark blue composition of lead, silver, copper, sulfur and ammonium chloride. The mixture is fused onto an engraved or cut out metal base by firing the mix in a process similar to **champleve** enameling. Silver was the most often used metal for Niello cases. Rose gold inlay is also seen in combination with Niello. Niello cases appeared in the early 1900s about the same time Art Nouveau and Art Deco was popular. Huegenin Brothers of Le Locle, Favre of Le Locle, Duchene of Geneva, Rene Lalique of Paris and Longines of St. Imier played prominent roles in the design and marketing of Niello cases. Niello cases were never made in quantity by the American case factories.

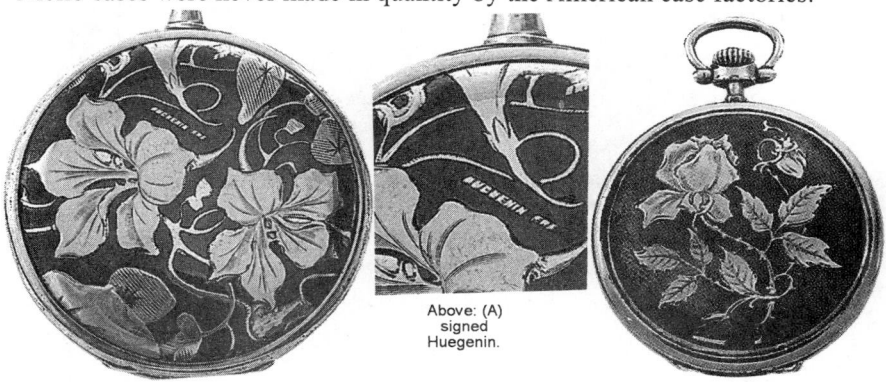

Above: (A)
signed
Huegenin.

(A) Niello, silver only, floral motif, signed, 46mm OF, Ca.1905.   (B) Niello, silver & rose gold, floral motif, 40mm HC, Ca.1910.

TYPE – DESCRIPTION	Avg	Ex-Fn	Mint
(A) Niello, silver only, floral motif, signed, 46mm OF	$300	$500	$850
HC	400	600	950
(B) Niello, silver & rose **gold**, floral motif, Ca. 1910, 40mm OF	200	325	575
HC	250	400	650
(C) Niello, silver only, Floral motif, signed, 46mm OF	325	550	825
HC	400	600	950
(D) Niello, silver only, Floral motif, **NOT** signed, OF	225	375	700
HC	300	450	800

(C) Niello, silver only, floral motif, signed, 46mm HC.   (D) Niello, silver only, floral motif, **NOT** signed, HC.

(E) Niello, silver only, portrait motif (**Lady Liberty**), 50mm HC.   (F) Niello, silver & gold, portrait+floral+scene, 47mm HC.

TYPE – DESCRIPTION	Avg	Ex-Fn	Mint
(E) Niello, silver only, portrait Lady Liberty, 50mm OF	$400	$700	$1,150
HC	500	800	1,250
(F) Niello, silver & gold, portrait+floral+scene, 47mm OF	400	675	1,100
HC	500	800	1,250
(G) Niello, silver & gold, with a portrait, (Omega), 47mm OF	400	700	1,150
HC	500	800	1,250
(H) Niello, silver, **equestrian** motif, 47mm OF	325	575	875
HC	400	600	950

(G) Niello, silver & gold, portrait motif, (Omega), 47mm HC.   (H) Niello, silver, **equestrian** motif, 47mm HC.

Art Nouveau: A style of art decoration popular from about 1890 to 1910, depicted as curves & flowing intertwining floral designs, Gazelles & female with long hair. Designs by Tiffany & Coco Channel.
Art Deco: Derived from the discovery of King Tut's tomb in 1922. A style of art decoration using Cubism, Egyptian, Aztec & Mayan themes. The angle was in & curves were out.

(J) Niello, silver & rose gold, hunting Motif, 47mm HC.   (K) Niello, silver & gold, hunting motif, 47mm HC.

TYPE – DESCRIPTION	Avg	Ex-Fn	Mint
(J) Niello, silver & **rose** gold, hunting scene, 47 mm OF	$350	$500	$875
HC	400	650	950
(K) Niello, silver & **gold**, hunting scene, 47mm OF	425	725	1,150
HC	500	800	1,250
(L) Niello, silver, **owl**, animal motif, 47mm OF	300	500	800
HC	400	600	900
(M) Niello, silver & **rose** gold, **tiger**, animal motif, 48mm OF	425	725	1,000
HC	500	775	1,100

(L) Niello, silver, owl, animal motif, 47mm HC.   (M) Niello, silver & rose gold, **tiger**, animal motif, 48mm HC.

Art Nouveau: A style of art decoration popular from about 1890 to 1910, depicted as curves & flowing intertwining floral designs, Gazelles & female with long hair. Designs by Tiffany & Coco Channel. Art Deco: Derived from the discovery of King Tut's tomb in 1922. A style of art decoration using Cubism, Egyptian, Aztec & Mayan themes. The angle was in & curves were out.

(N) Niello, silver & gold, automobile motif, 47mm HC.

(P) Niello, silver, **signed** pattern motif, 47mm HC.

TYPE – DESCRIPTION	Avg	Ex-Fn	Mint
(N) Niello, silver & gold, automobile motif, 47mm OF	$400	$650	$1,000
HC	500	700	1,100
(P) Niello, silver, **signed** pattern motif, 47mm OF	100	275	475
HC	175	300	550
(R) Niello, silver, dot pattern motif, 47mm OF	100	225	500
HC	200	325	600
(S) Niello, silver, wavy line pattern motif, 43mm OF	100	225	500
HC	200	325	600

(R) Niello, silver, dot pattern motif, 47mm HC.

(S) Niello, silver, wavy line pattern motif, 43mm HC.

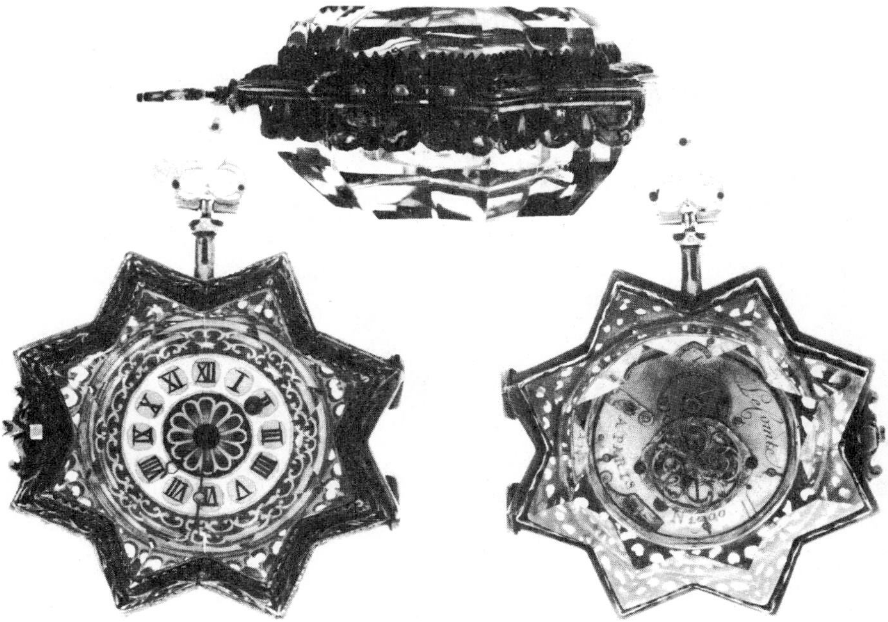

Rock crystal & enamel, star shape case, champleve enameled dial, verge, gilt & crystal case, 57x27mm, original French form Ca. 1600-1660, **Shown** Viennese form Ca. 1780-1800. (illo.118)

TYPE – DESCRIPTION	Avg	Ex-Fn	Mint
Rock crystal & enamel, star shape case, champleve dial, **Shown** Viennese verge, gilt & crystal case, 57x27mm, C.1800 (illo.118)	$4,000	$4,500	$6,000
Crucifix form 1/4 hr. repeater & musical, crystal & silver form case, **Shown** Viennese (illo.119)...	6,500	8,500	12,000

Crucifix form 1/4 hr. repeater & musical, crystal & silver form case, original French form Ca. 1600-1660, **Shown** Viennese form Ca. 1780-1800. (illo.119)

MEN'S UNUSUAL *"GOLD"*

Above note thin watch.
Extra flat watch, **1.5mm thick,** Swiss, 18K, HC, <u>ACTUAL SIZE</u>,50mm. (illo.120)

TYPE – DESCRIPTION	Avg	Ex-Fn	Mint
Extra flat watch, 1.5mm thick, Swiss, **18K**, HC, 50mm (illo.120)..	$2,000	$2,600	$3,500
Jump 1/4 seconds, 2 train, 30J, KW, nickel, (Swiss),			
18K, 56mm, HC, C. 1870-90	2,000	2,600	3,500
Captain's watch, enameled portraits on case, Maharaja & Queen			
Victoria, KW, lever movement, **18K**, 44mm, HC, C.1870	2,500	3,100	4,000
Captain's watch, KW, 15J, engraved case & enamel dial, **2 train,**			
18K, 52-58mm, OF, C. 1870 (illo.121)	1,000	1,700	3,000
1776-1876 centennial watch, H.O. Stauffer, bridges in 1776 form,			
17J, **18K**, 53mm, HC, C. 1876 (illo.122)...............................	1,500	2,200	3,500

Captain's watch, KW, 15J, engraved case & enamel dial,
2 train,18K, 52-58mm, OF, Ca. 1870. (illo.121)

1776-1876 Centennial watch, H.O. Stauffer, bridges in 1776
form, 17J, 18K, 53mm, HC, Ca. 1876. Made by Georges
Favre- Jacot of le Locle later became *Zenith* (illo.122)

Above: Hour and Minute hands **CONTRACTED.**

Extremely RARE oval watches with hands that **EXPAND** and **CONTRACT**. The hands work much like scissors with cams to expand and contract the hands. The case has 60 pearls and the watch is thought to be made by William Anthony of London, Ca. 1795. William Anthony was famous for his verge watches and watches set in pearls and diamonds. Wwith many of his watches being made for the Chinese market.

TYPE – DESCRIPTION		Avg	Ex-Fn	Mint
Oval watch with hands that **EXPAND** and **CONTRACT**				
Gold case .... ★★★★★		$90,000	$110,000	$150,000
above with 60 pearls .... ★★★★		95,000	120,000	175,000

Above: Hour and Minute hands **EXPANDED.**

Moonphase, double dial, calendar, Swiss, 17J, back lid opens to reveal cal. dial, 14K, HC, C.1890. (illo.123)

TYPE – DESCRIPTION	Avg	Ex-Fn	Mint
Captain's watch, KW KS, 15J, ornate case, Swiss, single train, **18K,** 52mm, HC, C. 1870	$800	$1,000	$1,500
Digital dial, hrs. & min. on digital jump discs, Swiss, 15J, SW, **18K**, 51mm, HC, C. 1905	1,000	1,300	1,800
Moonphase, double dial, calendar, Swiss, 17J, back lid opens to reveal cal. dial, **14K**, HC, C.1890 (illo.123)	1,500	2,400	3,500
Two train, center independent sec.,2 going barrels, lever escap., KW KS, GOLD, 42mm, Ca. 1880, HC (illo. 124)	1,000	1,200	1,800
Art Deco dial, Swiss, **18K**, 45mm,OF (illo.125)	600	800	1,200

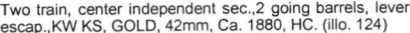

Two train, center independent sec.,2 going barrels, lever escap.,KW KS, GOLD, 42mm, Ca. 1880, HC. (illo. 124)

Art Deco style with **exaggerated** numbers on dial, Swiss, 18K, 45mm,OF. (illo.125)

TYPE – DESCRIPTION	Avg	Ex-Fn	Mint
Double dials, world time & moon ph. triple date,**18K** (illo.126)	$4,500	$5,500	$8,000
Perpetual calendar with moonphase and chrono., Swiss , 20J, porcelain dial, 3/4 plate, 18K, 51mm, OF, C.1890-1900	5,500	7,000	9,000
Rare verge, w/ automaton "Serpent, Adam & Eve" on dial with moving serpent, verge, French , 18K, OF, C. 1800	4,500	5,300	6,500
Musical, two train of gears, pin cylinder & 24 blades, one tune, 18K (illo.127)	2,500	3,200	5,500
Waterproof watch w/wind ind. 17J., C.1885 (illo.128)	1,000	1,300	2,000
Cigarette lighter & Swiss watch, Dunhill, Silver, C.1926 (illo.129)	300	350	500
9K case	900	1,100	1,400
14K case	1,200	1,400	1,700
$20.00 U.S. gold coin, 17J, mvt. in coin, 35mm, Ca.1920's (illo.130)	1,200	1,600	2,000

Double dials, world time & moon ph. triple date,18K. (illo.126)

Musical, two train of gears, pin cylinder & 24 blades, one tune, 18K. (illo.127)

Waterproof watch w/wind ind. 17J., C.1885. (illo.128)

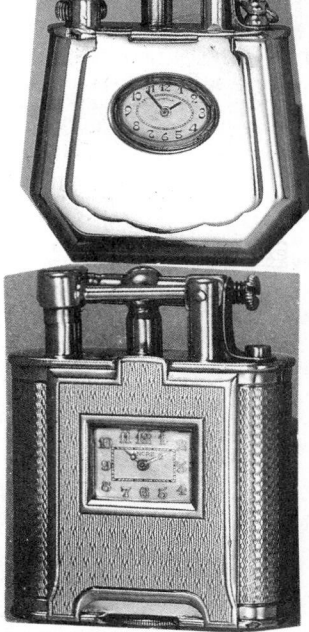

Cigarette lighter & Swiss watch, Dunhill, Silver, Ca.1926. (illo.129)

$20.00 U.S. gold coin, 17J, Swiss mvt. in coin, 35mm, Ca.1920's. (illo.130)

Skeletonized Verge & Fusee (*French*), Multi-color 18K Case & rose cut diamonds, horseshoe shaped plate, balance end stone is a large Cabochon Ruby,45MM, KW KS, Ca. 1785.(illo.130A)

TYPE – DESCRIPTION	Avg	Ex-Fn	Mint
Skeletonized Verge & Fusee movement, 45MM, KWKS with Multi-color 18K Case, Ca. 1785 (illo.130A)	$2,800	$3,200	$4,000
Lorgnette Form Watch, 3/8" x 7/8 x 3-1/4", *18K Closed Case*, KWKS, Ca. 1850. (illo.130B)	3,700	4,700	6,500

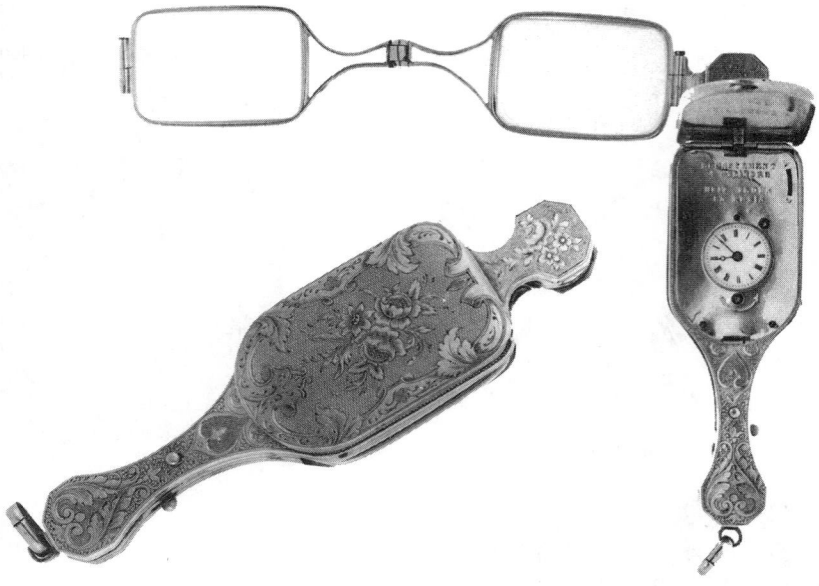

Lorgnette Form Watch, 3/8" x 7/8 x 3-1/4", *18K Closed Case*, the case is chased with leaf patterns and arabesque, signed "Echappement a Cylindre Huit Trous en Rubis", the looking frames are rose gold and flip out with a push button, KWKS, Ca. 1850. (illo.130B)

MISC. SWISS LADY'S Ca. 1850–1950 SILVER or GOLD FILLED

TYPE – DESCRIPTION	Avg	Ex-Fn	Mint
GF or silver, 7-17J, SW, 35mm, OF, C. 1900-1930	$45	$55	$85
GF or silver, 10-15J, SW, 35mm, fancy dial, OF, C. 1910	65	75	125
GF or silver, 7-17J, SW, 35- 40mm, HC, C. 1890-1930	75	95	135
Enamel or silver, cylinder, pinset, 35mm, OF, C. 1910	85	95	125
KWKS, silver, 40- 45mm, OF, C. 1865-1885	75	90	125
KWKS, silver, 37- 45mm, **HC**, C. 1865-1885	100	125	175
Ball shaped, 17J, 35mm, SW, GF or silver with chain	125	150	200

MISC. LADYS Ca. 1850–1950 *GOLD* (NO ENAMEL)

TYPE – DESCRIPTION	Avg	Ex-Fn	Mint
SW, 7-15J, 14K, 35- 40mm, OF, C. 1910-1930	$100	$135	$195
SW, 7-15J, 14K, 35- 40mm, HC, C. 1910-1930	200	250	325
KWKS, 10J, cylinder, 18K, 34- 40mm, OF, C.1865-90	150	200	275
KWKS, 10J, cylinder, 18K, 38- 43mm, HC, C. 1865-85	200	300	400
Fusee, lever, fancy dial, 18K, 38- 43mm, OF, C. 1845-75	300	375	500
Fusee, lever, fancy dial, 18K, 38- 43mm, HC, C. 1850s	400	500	600
Ball shaped w/pin, 10J, 14K, 25mm, OF, C. 1890	500	600	650

MISC. LADYS Ca. 1850–1950 ENAMEL ON *GOLD*

TYPE – DESCRIPTION	Avg	Ex-Fn	Mint
KW, enamel (black outlines) 18K, 40- 42mm HC, C. 1860	$250	$375	$475
KW, enamel & dia., Swiss, 10J, 18K, OF, C. 1860	350	450	650
Pattern enamel & demi-hunter, 15J, 18K , 35mm, HC, C.1885	400	550	800
Portrait enamel, KWKS, Swiss, 14K, 34- 42mm, OF, C. 1870	400	600	900
Enamel , with pearls and/ or dia., 10-17J, w/ matching pin, 18K, 23-26mm, OF	700	900	1,400
Enamel, w/dia. or pearls, w/ pin, 18K, 26-30mm, HC, C. 1895	900	1,250	1,700
Miniature verge, gold & enamel w/ pearls, superior enamel, Swiss, KW, gold case, 27mm, OF, C. 1770	2,500	3,500	5,000
Miniature HC enamel & dia., 17J, Swiss, with orig. pin, 18K, 23mm, HC, C. 1890	1,200	1,800	2,500
Ball-shaped (Duchene) Geneva, verge, KW, enamel and gold, 25mm, C. 1800	1,200	1,800	2,500

⊕ Note: Some models and grades are not included. Their values can be determined by comparing with similar age, size, metal content, style, models and grades listed.

⊕ Note: Watches listed in this book are priced at the collectable retail level, as complete watches having an original case, an original dial, and with the entire original movement in good working order with no repairs needed.

COMPARISON OF WATCH SIZES

U. S. A.	EUROPEAN
10-12 SIZE	40—44 MM
16 SIZE	45—49 MM
18 SIZE	50—55 MM

LADY'S UNUSUAL *GOLD* & ENAMEL

LEFT; Ball-shaped, bezel wind, 18K, enamel & diamonds, Swiss, 16mm, OF, C. 1920. (illo.131) CENTER: Ring watch w/enamel & dia., Swiss, 18K, 18mm, C.1910. (illo.132) RIGHT: Padlock form enamel and gold, Swiss, KW. (illo.133)

TYPE – DESCRIPTION	Avg	Ex-Fn	Mint
Ball-shaped, bezel wind, Swiss, enamel & diamonds on 18K case, size of a marble, 16mm, OF, C. 1920 (illo.131)	$900	$1,300	$2,000
Ring watch w/enamel & dia., Swiss, 18K, 18mm, C.1910 (illo.132)	750	1,000	1,500
Cherry form enamel & 18K, 17J, closed case, bezel wind, Swiss, 22mm,	1,500	2,300	3,500
Flower basket form, enamel and 18K, Swiss, KWKS, with heart form movement, 10J, 18K, 30x24mm, HC, C. 1860	2,500	3,300	4,500
Padlock form enamel and gold, Swiss, KW (illo.133)	900	1,400	2,000
Padlock form enamel and gold (cover over dial,) Swiss, KW, diamonds on case, heart shaped mvt.,18K, 28x51mm, HC, C.1870	1,200	1,600	2,500
Form watch in shape of **leaf**, gold & enamel, Bar mvt. (illo.134)	1,200	1,600	2,500

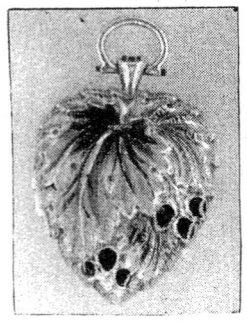 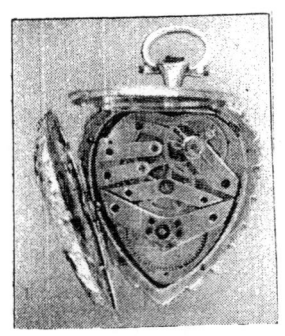

Form watch in shape of **leaf**, gold & enamel, cylinder escapement, Bar movement., KW KS, Ca.1865. (illo.134)

🕐 Pricing in this Guide are fair market price for **COMPLETE** watches which are reflected from the "**NAWCC**" National and regional shows. The Complete Price Guide to Watches goal is to stimulate the orderly exchange of **Watches** between *"buyers"* and *"sellers"*.

Scarab form gold & enamel, 10J, cylinder, diamonds, closed case w/wings that open, 18K, 54x23mm, C.1885. (illo.135)

Rare enamel & gold harps, matched pair w/ music, verge, diamonds, lapis and enameled scenes, 3 3/4" high, C.1830. (illo.136)

TYPE – DESCRIPTION	Avg	Ex-Fn	Mint
Scarab form gold & enamel, 10J, cylinder, diamonds, closed case w/wings that open, 18K, 54x23mm, C.1885 (illo.135)	$4,000	$5,200	$7,000
Lorgnette with enamel & gold, KW, 10J, Swiss, 3 1/4" x 1" cover ornamented w/dia., 18K	3,500	4,500	6,000
Rare enamel &gold harps, matched pair w/ music, verge, diamonds, lapis and enameled scenes, 3 3/4" high, C.1830 (illo.136)	18,000	24,000	32,000
Rock crystal case, silver dial, **Viennese** made, C. 1830 (illo.137) ..	3,500	4,700	7,500

Rock crystal case, silver dial, Viennese made, C. 1830. (illo.137)

ENAMEL WATCHES

Floral enamel watch. Bouquet of flowers within a champleve border of scrolls enclosing panels of flowers. (illo.E-2)

Floral enamel watch. Finely painted floral enamel panel within border of seed pearls. (illo.E-1)

SIZE AND DESCRIPTION	Avg	Ex-Fn	Mint
55mm, finely painted floral, seed pearls, (Bovet also Ilbery),18K (illo.E.1)	$7,500	$10,000	$15,000
47mm, gold enamel repeater, with chatelaine of pierced gold links & enamel plaques with enamel key & fob seals (illo.E.2)	5,000	6,500	9,000
Enamel & pearls, hunting scene of lion, for China market, silver gilt duplex escapement, 62mm, Ca. 1845 (illo.E-3)	4,000	5,500	8,000
Enamel and 18K case, automated horseman and windmill also fountain, horse drinks water (illo.E-4)	25,000	29,000	35,000
Enamel floral scene, enamel and pearls on gold case, finely painted floral bouquet, 55mm (illo.E-5)	20,000	28,000	40,000
Enamel and 18K case, MINUTE- REPEATER, HC, surrounded with pearls, 55mm, (illo.E-5A)	12,000	15,000	20,000
VIENNESE enamel watch, the front cover shows a lady and gentleman in a scene, the back cover pictures three boys in a scene, 55mm (illo.E-6 & E-6A)	1,500	1,900	2,500
54mm, 29J., 1/4 repeater, pearls & enamel, silver case (illo.E-8)	1,800	2,200	3,000
VIENNESE Lapis Lazuli enamel watch, verge fusee, top and bottom covers are finely cut solid lapis stone, champleve enamel dial, Ca. 1830 (illo.E-9)	2,600	4,200	6,000

⊕ French watch-making believed to have started in town of Blois, France. French Enamel Watches also believed to have started in Blois, in early 1600's.

Enamel & pearls, hunting scene of lion, for China market, duplex escapement, 62mm, Ca. 1845. (illo.E-3)

Enamel and 18K case, automated horseman and windmill also fountain, horse drinks water. (illo.E-4)

Enamel floral scene, enamel and pearls on gold case, finely painted floral bouquet, 55mm (illo.E-5)

Enamel and 18K case, MINUTE- REPEATER, Hunting Case, surrounded with pearls, 55mm, Ca.1890. (illo.E-5A)

VIENNESE enamel watch, the front cover shows a lady and gentleman in a scene, the back cover pictures three boys in a scene, 55mm. see movement below. (illo.E-6)

VIENNESE enamel watch, same watch as above, two-footed balance bridge, the inner lids are decorated with polychrome enamelled scenes. (illo.E-6A)

54mm, 29J, 1/4 hour repeater, Pearls and enamel on a silver case, ca. 1885. (illo.E-8)

VIENNESE Lapis Lazuli enamel watch, verge fusee, top and bottom covers are finely cut solid lapis stone, champleve enamel dial, Viennese made, Ca. 1830 (illo.E-9)

Floral enamel watch, 57mm, bouquet of flowers within a gold case set with split pearls. (illo.E-10)

Enamel scene watch, 58mm, finely painted scene of ships in harbor. (illo.E-11)

SIZE AND DESCRIPTION	Avg	Ex-Fn	Mint
57mm, floral enamel, duplex, (Bovet), pearls, 18K, (illo.E-10)	$6,500	$8,000	$10,000
58mm, harbor scene enamel, duplex, 18k, Ca. 1790 (illo.E-11)	18,000	25,000	35,000
43mm, basket form champleve enamel, 18k, Ca.1800 (illo.E.12) ...	2,600	4,000	6,000
42mm, champleve border, finely painted flowers, (Le Roy), gold case & chain..	2,500	2,800	3,500
37mm, rose gold guilloche enamel demi-hunter.............................	350	450	600
36mm, gold enamel & champleve enamel, verge, Ca. 1800	1,500	2,200	3,000
35mm, gold champleve enamel, (L'Epine), cylinder	650	900	1,200
35mm, gold enamel & seed pearls, rose cut diamonds	275	400	600
34mm, gold egg-shaped form enamel, verge, (Austrian)	1,200	1,800	2,500
30mm, gold miniature enamel, verge, seed pearls, Ca. 1800	750	900	1,200
27mm, gold enamel lapel brooch with seed pearls & rose cut diamonds, Ca. 1890	550	700	900
27mm, gold fine enamel lapel brooch with cut diamonds by C. H. Meylan (illo.E.13)	1,500	1,900	2,500

Enamel form tapered oval basket with rising rope handle, enhanced with panels of flowers, 18K case. (illo.E-12)

A chased enamel gold lady's pendant watch. Enamel portrait of a lady. (illo.E-13)

(ILLO. A)　　　　(ILLO. B)　　　　　　(ILLO. D)

Size and Description	Avg	Ex-Fn	Mint
27mm, Art Noveau design, multi-colored flowers gold & diamond pendant watch & pin, 18K, OF, Ca.1890 (illo. A)..................	$800	$1,100	$1,500
25mm, Enamel & pearls & diamonds, star shaped gold settings , pendant and pen, 18K, OF, Ca. 1890 (illo. B)	650	900	1,200
25mm, enamel pendant with pin, golden frame of vines around a scene of a lady , 14K, OF, Ca. 1900	900	1,100	1,400
24mm, pearl pendant watch with pin, seed pearls also on classic fleur-de-lis designed pin, 14K OF, Ca.1885 (illo. C)	800	1,000	1,300
24mm, enamel and gold pendant watch with a starburst gold and pearl pin, 10 J, cylinder movement, 18K, OF, Ca.1900 (illo. D)...	700	900	1,200
22mm, ball-shaped enamel & pearl pendant watch, exposed balance, lever escapement can be seen back crystal (illo. E)	1,400	1,700	2,200
20mm, 17J, three-finger bridge miniature movement, Adj.5P, by Didsheim platinum OF case, Ca.1930s (illo. F)	1,100	1,400	1,800

(ILLO. E)

(ILLO. C)　　　　　　　　　　　　(ILLO. F)

Am. Waltham W. Co.

Date	Serial #
1852	50
1853	400
1854	1,000
1855	2,500
1856	4,000
1857	6,000
1858	10,000
1859	15,000
1860	20,000
1861	30,000
1862	45,000
1863	65,000
1864	110,000
1865	180,000
1866	260,000
1867	330,000
1868	410,000
1869	460,000
1870	500,000
1871	540,000
1872	590,000
1873	680,000
1874	730,000
1875	810,000
1876	910,000
1877	1,000,000
1878	1,150,000
1879	1,350,000
1880	1,500,000
1881	1,670,000
1882	1,835,000
1883	2,000,000
1884	2,350,000
1885	2,650,000
1886	3,000,000
1887	3,400,000
1888	3,800,000
1889	4,200,000
1890	4,700,000
1891	5,200,000
1892	5,800,000
1893	6,300,000
1894	6,700,000
1895	7,100,000
1896	7,450,000
1897	8,100,000
1898	8,400,000
1899	9,000,000
1900	9,500,000
1901	10,200,000
1902	11,100,000
1903	12,100,000
1904	13,500,000
1905	14,300,000
1906	14,700,000
1907	15,500,000
1908	16,400,000
1909	17,600,000
1910	17,900,000
1911	18,100,000
1912	18,200,000
1913	18,900,000
1914	19,500,000
1915	20,000,000
1916	20,500,000
1917	20,900,000
1918	21,800,000
1919	22,500,000
1920	23,400,000
1921	23,900,000
1922	24,100,000
1923	24,300,000
1924	24,550,000
1925	24,800,000
1926	25,200,000
1927	26,100,000
1928	26,400,000
1929	26,900,000
1930	27,100,000
1931	27,300,000
1932	27,550,000
1933	27,750,000
1934	28,100,000
1935	28,600,000
1936	29,100,000
1937	29,400,000
1938	29,750,000
1939	30,050,000
1940	30,250,000
1941	30,750,000
1942	31,050,000
1943	31,400,000
1944	31,700,000
1945	32,100,000
1946	32,350,000
1947	32,750,000
1948	33,100,000
1949	33,500,000
1950	33,560,000
1951	33,600,000
1952	33,700,000
1953	33,800,000
1954	34,100,000
1955	34,450,000
1956	34,700,000
1957	35,000,000

AURORA W. Co.

Date	Serial #
1884	10,001
1885	60,000
1886	101,000
1887	160,000
1888	200,000
1889	215,000
1891	230,901

COLUMBUS W. Co.

Date	Serial #
1875	1,000
1876	3,000
1877	6,000
1878	9,000
1879	12,000
1880	15,000
1881	18,000
1882	21,000
1883	25,000
1884	30,000
1885	40,000
1886	53,000
1887	75,000
1888	97,000
1889	119,000
1890	141,000
1891	163,000
1892	185,000
1893	207,000
1894	229,000
1895	251,000
1896	273,000
1897	295,000
1898	317,000
1899	339,000
1900	361,000
1901	383,000

SPECIAL BLOCK OF SERIAL NOS.

Date	Serial #
1894	500,001
1896	501,500
1898	503,000
1900	504,500
1902	506,000

ELGIN WATCH Co.

Date	Serial #
1867	10,000
1868	25,001 Nov,20th
1869	40,001 May, 20th
1870	50,001 Aug. 24th
1871	185,001 Sep. 8th
1872	201,001 Dec. 20th
1873	325,001
1874	400,001 Aug.28th
1875	430,000
1876	480,000
1877	520,000
1878	550,000
1879	625,001 Feb.8th
1880	750,000
1881	900,000
1882	1,000,000 March,9th
1883	1,250,000
1884	1,500,000
1885	1,855,001 May,28th
1886	2,000,000 Aug.4th
1887	2,500,000
1888	3,000,000 June 20th
1889	3,500,000
1890	4,000,000 Aug.16th
1891	4,449,001 Mar.26th
1892	4,600,000
1893	5,000,000 July 1st
1894	5,500,000
1895	6,000,000 Nov.26th
1896	6,500,000
1897	7,000,000 Oct. 28th.
1898	7,494,001 May,14th
1899	8,000,000 Jan.18th
1900	9,000,000 Nov.14th
1901	9,300,000
1902	9,600,000
1903	10,000,000 May 15th
1904	11,000,000 April 4th
1905	12,000,000 Oct.6th
1906	12,500,000
1907	13,000,000 April 4th
1908	13,500,000
1909	14,000,000 Feb.9th
1910	15,000,000 April 2nd
1911	16,000,000 July 11th
1912	17,000,000 Nov.6th
1913	17,339,001 Apr.14th
1914	18,000,000
1915	18,587,001 Feb.11th
1916	19,000,000
1917	20,031,001 June,27th
1918	21,000,000
1919	22,000,000
1920	23,000,000
1921	24,321,001 July,6th
1922	25,100,000
1923	26,050,000
1924	27,000,000
1925	28,421,001 July,14th
1926	29,100,000
1927	30,050,000
1928	31,500,000
1929	32,000,000
1930	32,599,001 July
1931	33,000,000
1932	33,700,000
1933	34,558,001 July,24th
1934	35,000,000
1935	35,650,000
1936	36,200,000
1937	36,978,001 July,24th
1938	37,900,000
1939	38,200,000
1940	39,100,000
1941	40,200,000
1942	41,100,000
1943	42,200,000
1944	42,600,000
1945	43,200,000
1946	44,000,000
1947	45,000,000
1948	46,000,000
1949	47,000,000
1950	48,000,000
1951	50,000,000
1952	52,000,000
1953	53,500,000
1954	54,000,000
1955	54,500,000
1956	55,000,000

HAMILTON WATCH Co.

Date	Serial No.
1893	1-2,000
1894	5,000
1895	11,500
1896	16,000
1897	27,000
1898	50,000
1899	74,000
1900	104,000
1901	143,000
1902	196,000
1903	260,000
1904	340,000
1905	425,000
1906	590,000
1907	756,000
1908	921,000
1909	1,087,000
1910	1,150,500
1911	1,290,500
1912	1,331,000
1913	1,370,000
1914	1,410,500
1915	1,450,500
1916	1,517,000
1917	1,580,000
1918	1,650,000
1919	1,700,000
1920	1,790,000
1921	1,860,000
1922	1,900,000
1923	1,950,000
1924	2,000,000
1925	2,100,000
1926	2,200,000
1927	2,250,000
1928	2,300,000
1929	2,350,000
1930	2,400,000
1931	2,450,000
1932	2,500,000
1933	2,600,000
1934	2,750,000
1935	2,800,000
1936	2,900,000
1937	3,000,000
1938	3,200,000
1939	3,400,000
1940	3,600,000
1941	3,800,000
1942	4,025,000

DATE LETTERS
2B on 950B=1941-43
C on 992B=1940-59
S on 950B=1943-68
OTHER DATE LETTERS = 1930s to 1950s

HAMPDEN W. Co.

Date	Serial #
1877	59,000
1878	70,000
1879	100,000
1880	140,000
1881	180,000
1882	215,000
1883	250,000
1884	300,000
1885	350,000
1886	400,000
1887	480,000
1888	560,000
1889	640,000
1890	740,000
1891	805,500
1892	835,000
1893	865,000
1894	900,000
1895	930,000
1896	970,000
1897	1,000,000
1898	1,120,000
1899	1,255,000
1900	1,384,000
1901	1,512,000
1902	1,642,000
1903	1,768,000
1904	1,896,000
1905	2,024,000
1906	2,152,000
1907	2,280,000
1908	2,400,000
1909	2,520,000
1910	2,650,000
1911	2,700,000
1912	2,760,000
1913	2,850,000
1914	2,920,000
1915	3,000,000
1916	3,100,000
1917	3,240,000
1918	3,390,000
1919	3,500,000
1920	3,600,000
1921	3,700,000
1922	3,750,000
1923	3,800,000
1924	3,850,000
1925	3,900,000
1926	3,950,000
1927	3,980,000

E. HOWARD & Co.

Date	Serial #
1858-60)	113-1,900
1860-61)	1,901-3,000
1861)	3,001-3,100
1861)	3,101-3,250
1861)	3,401- 3,500
1861-71)	3,501-28,000
1868-83)	30,001-50,000
1869-99)	50,001-71,000
1869-90)	100,001-105,000
1880-99)	200,001-227,000
1895)	228,001-231,000
1884-99)	300,001-309,000
1895)	309,001-310,000
1890-95)	400,001-405,000
1890-99)	500,001-501,500
1896-1903)	600,001-601,500
1896-1903)	700,001-701,500

HOWARD WATCH Co. (KEYSTONE)

Date	Serial #
1902	850,000
1903	900,000
1909	980,000
1912	1,100,000
1915	1,285,000
1917	1,340,000
1921	1,400,000
1930	1,500,000

ILLINOIS WATCH Co.

Date	Serial #
1872	5,000
1873	20,000
1874	50,000
1875	75,000
1876	100,000
1877	145,000
1878	210,000
1879	250,000
1880	300,000
1881	350,000
1882	400,000
1883	450,000
1884	500,000
1885	550,000
1886	600,000
1887	700,000
1888	800,000
1889	900,000
1890	1,000,000
1891	1,040,000
1892	1,080,000
1893	1,120,000
1894	1,160,000
1895	1,220,000
1896	1,250,000
1897	1,290,000
1898	1,330,000
1899	1,370,000
1900	1,410,000
1901	1,450,000
1902	1,500,000
1903	1,650,000
1904	1,700,000
1905	1,800,000
1906	1,840,000
1907	1,900,000
1908	2,100,000
1909	2,150,000
1910	2,200,000
1911	2,300,000
1912	2,400,000
1913	2,500,000
1914	2,600,000
1915	2,700,000
1916	2,800,000
1917	3,000,000
1918	3,200,000
1919	3,400,000
1920	3,600,000
1921	3,750,000
1922	3,900,000
1923	4,000,000
1924	4,500,000
1925	4,700,000
1926	4,800,000
1927	5,000,000
(Sold to Hamilton)	
1928	5,100,000
1929	5,200,000
1931	5,400,000
1938	5,500,000
1948	5,600,000

ROCKFORD W.Co.

Date	Serial #
1874	22,200
1875	42,600
1876	63,000
1877	83,000
1878	103,000
1879	124,000
1880	144,000
1881	165,000
1882	185,000
1883	206,000
1884	226,000
1885	247,000
1886	267,000
1887	287,500
1888	308,000
1889	328,500
1890	349,000
1891	369,500
1892	390,000
1893	410,000
1894	430,000
1895	450,000
1896	470,000
1897	490,000
1898	510,000
1899	530,000
1900	550,000
1901	570,000
1902	590,000
1903	610,000
1904	630,000
1905	650,000
1906	670,000
1907	690,000
1908	734,000
1909	790,000
1910	824,000
1911	880,000
1912	936,000
1913	958,000
1914	980,000
1915	1,000,000

SOUTH BEND W. Co.

Date	Serial #
1903	380,501
1904	390,000
1905	405,000
1906	425,000
1907	460,000
1908	500,000
1909	550,000
1910	600,000
1911	660,000
1912	715,000
1913	765,000
1914	800,000
1915	720,000
1916	840,000
1917	860,000
1918	880,000
1919	905,000
1920	935,000
1921	975,000
1922	1,000,000
1923	1,035,000
1924	1,070,000
1925	1,105,000
1926	1,140,000
1927	1,275,000
1928	1,210,000
1929	1,240,000

SETH THOMAS W. Co.

Date	Serial #
1885	5,000
1886	20,000
1887	40,000
1888	80,000
1889	150,000
1890	235,000
1891	330,000
1892	420,000
1893	510,000
1894	600,000
1895	690,000
1896	780,000
1897	870,000
1898	960,000
1899	1,050,000
1900	1,140,000
1901	1,230,000
1902	1,320,000
1903	1,410,000
1904	1,500,000
1905	1,700,000
1906	1,900,000
1907	2,100,000
1908	2,300,000
1909	2,500,000
1910	2,725,000
1911	2,950,000
1912	3,175,000
1913	3,490,000
1914	3,600,000

BALL WATCH Co.

Date	Serial #
(Hamilton)	
1895	13,000
1897	20,500
1900	42,000
1902	170,000
1905	462,000
1910	600,000
1915	603,000
1920	610,000
1925	620,000
1930	637,000
1935	641,000
1938	647,000
1939	650,000
1940	651,000
1941	652,000
1942	654,000
(Waltham)	
1900	060,700
1905	202,000
1910	216,000
1915	250,000
1920	260,000
1925	270,000
(Illinois)	
1929	800,000
1930	801,000
1931	803,000
1932	804,000

(Elgin) 1904-1906
S # range
11,853,000-12,282,000

(E. Howard & C0.)
1893-1895
S # range
226,000-308,000

(Hampden) 1890-1892
S # range
626,750-657,960-759,720

Audemars Piguet

DATE	SERIAL #
1882	2,000
1890	4,000
1895	5,350
1900	6,500
1905	9,500
1910	13,000
1915	17,000
1920	25,000
1925	33,000
1930	40,000
1935	42,000
1940	44,000
1945	48,000
1950	55,000
1955	65,000
1960	75,000
1965	90,000
1970	115,000
1975	160,000
1980	225,000

International W.Co. (Schaffhausen)

DATE	SERIAL #
1884	6,500
1886	23,500
1888	37,500
1890	63,000
1892	87,500
1894	117,000
1896	151,500
1898	194,000
1900	231,000
1902	276,500
1904	321,000
1906	377,500
1908	435,000
1910	492,000
1912	557,000
1914	620,500
1916	657,000
1918	714,000
1920	765,000
1922	783,500
1924	807,000
1926	845,000
1928	890,500
1930	929,000
1932	938,000
1934	940,000
1936	955,500
1938	1,000,000
1940	1,019,000
1942	1,062,000
1944	1,092,000
1946	1,131,000
1948	1,177,000
1950	1,222,000
1952	1,291,000
1954	1,335,000
1956	1,399,000
1958	1,480,000
1960	1,553,000
1962	1,666,000
1964	1,778,000
1966	1,820,000
1968	1,905,000
1970	2,026,000
1972	2,218,000
1974	2,265,000
1975	2,275,000

A. Lange & Sohne

DATE	SERIAL #
1870	5,000
1875	10,000
1880	20,000
1885	25,000
1890	30,000
1895	35,000
1900	40,000
1905	50,000
1910	60,000
1915	70,000
1920	75,000
1925	80,000
1930	85,000
1935	90,000
1940	100,000

LONGINES

DATE	SERIAL #
1867	1
1870	20,000
1875	100,000
1882	250,000
1888	500,000
1893	750,000
1899	1,000,000
1901	1,250,000
1904	1,500,000
1905	1,750,000
1907	2,000,000
1909	2,250,000
1911	2,500,000
1912	2,750,000
1913	3,000,000
1915	3,250,000
1917	3,500,000
1919	3,750,000
1922	4,000,000
1925	4,250,000
1926	4,500,000
1928	4,750,000
1929	5,000,000
1934	5,250,000
1937	5,500,000
1938	5,750,000
1940	6,000,000
1945	7,000,000
1950	8,000,000
1953	9,000,000
1956	10,000,000
1959	11,000,000
1962	12,000,000
1966	13,000,000
1967	14,000,000
1969	15,000,000

OMEGA

DATE	SERIAL #
1895	1,000,000
1902	2,000,000
1908	3,000,000
1912	4,000,000
1916	5,000,000
1923	6,000,000
1929	7,000,000
1935	8,000,000
1939	9,000,000
1944	10,000,000
1947	11,000,000
1950	12,000,000
1952	13,000,000
1956	15,000,000
1958	16,000,000
1961	18,000,000
1963	20,000,000
1965	22,000,000
1967	25,000,000
1968	26,000,000
1970	29,000,000

PATEK PHILIPPE & Co.

DATE	SERIAL #
1840	100
1845	1,200
1850	3,000
1855	8,000
1860	15,000
1865	22,000
1870	35,000
1875	45,000
1880	55,000
1885	70,000
1890	85,000
1895	100,000
1900	110,000
1905	125,000
1910	150,000
1915	175,000
1920	190,000
1925	200,000
1950	700,000
1955	725,000
1960	750,000
1965	775,000
1970	795,000
1920	800,000
1925	805,000
1930	820,000
1935	824,000
1940	835,000
1945	850,000
1950	860,000
1955	870,000
1960	880,000
1965	890,000
1970	895,000
1940	900,000
1945	915,000
1950	930,000
1955	940,000
1960	960,000
1965	975,000
1970	995,000
1960	1,100,000
1965	1,130,000
1970	1,250,000
1975	1,350,000
1980	1,450,000
1985	1,600,000
1990	1,850,000

ROLEX (Case S #)

DATE	SERIAL #
1925	25,000
1926	28,500
1927	30,500
1928	33,000
1929	35,500
1930	38,000
1931	40,000
1932	43,000
1933	47,000
1934	55,000
1935	68,000
1936	81,000
1937	99,000
1938	118,000
1939	136,000
1940	165,000
1941	194,000
1942	224,000
1943	253,000
1944	285,000
1945	348,000
1946	413,000
1947	478,000
1948	543,000
1949	608,000
1950	673,500
1951	738,500
1952	804,000
1953	950,000
1954	999,999
1955	*200,000
1956	*400,000
1957	*600,000
1958	*800,000
1959	1,100,000
1960	1,401,000
1961	1,480,000
1962	1,557,000
1963	1,635,000
1964	1,713,000
1965	1,792,000
1966	1,870,000
1967	2,164,000
1968	2,426,000
1969	2,689,000
1970	2,952,000
1971	3,215,000
1972	3,478,000
1973	3,741,000
1974	4,002,000
1975	4,266,000
1976	4,538,000
1977	5,005,000
1978	5,481,000
1979	5,965,000
1980	6,432,000
1981	6,910,000
1982	7,385,000
1983	7,860,000
1984	8,338,000
1985	8,815,000
1986	9,292,000
1987	9,765,000
1987 1/2	9,999,999
1987 3/4	R000,001
1988	R999,999
1989	L000,001
1990	L999,999
1990 1/2	E000,001
1991 1/4	E999,999
1991 1/2	X000,001

VACHERON

DATE	SERIAL #
1830	30,000
1835	40,000
1840	50,000
1845	60,000
1850	75,000
1855	95,000
1860	110,000
1865	125,000
1870	140,000
1875	155,000
1880	170,000
1885	180,000
1890	190,000
1895	223,000
1900	256,000
1905	289,000
1910	322,000
1915	355,000
1920	385,000
1925	400,000
1930	410,000
1935	420,000
1940	440,000
1945	464,000
1950	488,000
1955	512,000
1960	536,000
1965	560,000
1970	585,000

The above list is provided for determining the **approximate** age of your watch. Match serial number with date. Watches were not necessarily sold in the exact order of manufactured date.

ROMANCING THE WRIST WATCH

The wrist watch is considered by many watch collectors to be "today's collectable." This phenomenon is due, in part, to the development of the quartz movement which began in the 1970's and virtually revolutionized the watch market. Although these quartz watches are quiet, accurate timekeepers, and are inexpensive to manufacture, the watches of the past hold a special fascination in the heart of the collector. They enjoy collecting the timepieces with jeweled and moving parts that produce a rhythmic heartbeat inside their gold cases.

The watch collector has seen the prices of wrist watches soar in the past years, as wrist watches have become more and more in demand as an object of fashion, function and jewelry. A Patek Philippe man's platinum minute repeater wrist watch sold for the record price of 345,000 Swiss francs, about $250,000 U.S. Not far behind this record setting sale was a Patek Philippe "Calatrava" that brought $198,000. A Patek Philippe enameled white gold "World Time" man's wrist watch sold for about $130,000. Some collectors have seen the values of their wrist watches double and, in many cases, triple in recent years. For example, in the early 1980s, a Patek Philippe perpetual calendar chronograph watch would have sold for $10,000. In 1987, the same watch would have sold for $50,000, and in 1988 for $80,000. In 1989, the price was up to $100,000. Such dramatic increases in values have brought about a feverish demand for wrist watches. The Swiss wrist watch has the attention of the wealthiest collectors, with Patek, Philippe & Co. at the top of their list and Audemars Piguet, Cartier, Rolex, and Vacheron & Constantin close behind. Other wrist watches showing appreciable value are Ebel, A. Lange, Gubelin, International Watch Co., Le Coultre, Ulysse Nardin, and Piaget. Next are Jules Jurgensen, Baume & Mercier, Gerard Perregaux, Movado, and Omega; then Benrus, Bulova, Agassiz, Elgin, Gruen, Hamilton, Illinois, Longines, and Waltham, the character watches, chronographs, and complicated watches.

Many wrist watch collectors have focused on fashion and take pride in wearing their unique watches. Women have been buying high fashion men's watches to wear, making women candidates for collecting. Young men appear to enjoy collecting wrist watches rather than pocket watches. The intense competition within their increasing numbers has influenced the rising prices.

*   *   *

European and Japanese collectors are making the biggest impact on the wrist watch market with their volume of buying, as well as, the higher prices being paid. The American collector has been inspired by the heated market which has been, in part, fueled by the weakened U.S. dollar. The general appearance of a wrist watch seems to be the main factor in the price of the watch, but high mechanical standards, along with the various functions of the watch, also determine the price. Some of these features include repeaters, chronographs, duo-dials, bubble backs, curvex, flip-up tops, reverso, day-date-month moon phase, jump hour, diamond dial, world time, sector, skeletonized, character, first versions as early auto winds, very early electronics, unusual shapes, and enamel bezels.

EBEL WATCH CO., chronograph with triple day & moon phases, outside chapter shows tachymeter, 18k gold.

Today's watches are a "mixed bag," ranging from gold luxury watches priced at $10,000, and mid-priced watches at $1,000, to the low-end plastic quartz watches at $30, and all keep time equally well. The gold watch is still a status symbol today; a mark of affluence and of appreciation for the finer things in life. The Swiss control about 85 percent of the luxury watch market, while the Japanese have about the same percentage of the market for more moderately-priced watches. The predominant companies producing the "top of the line" watches are Patek, Philippe & Co., Cartier, Gubelin, Audemars Piguet, Piaget, Vacheron Constantin. Just below in price, but higher in volume, are names like Rolex, International Watch Co., Girard Perregaux, and Le Coultre. Collectors are also wearing high grade new watches by Ebel, Blancpain, Gerald Genta, Hublot, Raymond Weil, and watches produced for and bearing the names of Chanel, Christian Dior, and Dunhill. Prices of Ebel watches start at about $1,000 and go upward to $24,000. This company also manufactures watches for Cartier. Patek, Philippe watches range in price from $3,000 to $100,000.

NOTE: **Sapphire** glass has a hardness of 9 (Mohs.), **Mineral** glass has a hardness of 5 (Mohs.).

The following will explain the French days of the week abbreviations, Sunday =**DIM** (Dimanche), Monday = **LUN** (Lundi), Tuesday = **MAR** (Mardi), Wednesday = **MER** (Mercedi), Thursday = **JEU** (Jeudi), Friday = **VEN** (Vendredi), Saturday = **SAM** (Samedi).

Audemars Piguet produces a tourbillon wrist watch. Blancpain, owned by Omega, produces only about 100 ultra-thin handmade watches per year. Rolex is the most recognizable name in today's luxury wrist watch market. The Rolex Cosmograph Daytona is one of the most sought-after wrist watches and has been for years. Cosmograph Daytona fans have known that Rolex have not used its own complete movement but relied on Zenith and Valjoux for chronograph movements. The new 2001 Rolex Cosmograph Daytona is now manufactured in house. Due to good marketing this large robust watch is able to compete with slender elegant named brand in the watch market. Sport style wrist watch fans are learning the inner workings such as balance wheels and rotors are now acquiring other quality sport style watches.

The Warhol collection, which included about 200 watches, was sold on April 27, 1988 at Sotheby's for a reported price of $461,000. The artist collected watches of various styles and types. A set of three vinyl quartz character watches brought the price of $2,400. A stainless steel Gene Autry watch listed and pre-determined to bring about $100 sold for $1,700. The so-called "heavy weight" wrist watches such as Patek Philippe, Cartier, Rolex, and Vacheron Constantin sold for two to three times the estimated prices.

The trend or vogue for older watches has motivated some watch companies to reproduce favorite watches from their past models. Companies have searched their archives to find older models that sold well, and are now marketing replicas of those watches. Hamilton Classics Authentic Reproductions From America's Past include the Ventura (1957), Wilshire City (1939), Cabot (1935), and Ardmore (1934). Jaeger LeCoultre's Reverso has been reintroduced, as well as, Longines' hour angle watch developed and worn by Charles Lindbergh. Also, the Lorus Company has marketed a close look-a-like to the Mickey Mouse wrist watch first sold by Ingersoll in the early 1930s.

The romancing of the wrist watch is moving at a steady upward pace. Price adjustments may be needed, but should hold for a few more years. The quality American movements may still be undervalued, and the novelty or comic character wrist watches may still be a good value for the investor.

Left: Movado designed by Andy Warhol the "Times Five" were made in Quartz and limited to 250 pieces. The dials have New York scenes in black and white with red hands. The five time zones cases are black with black links Ca. 1988.

A SHORT HISTORY OF WRIST WATCHES

While no one is sure who invented the first wrist watch or when the first wrist watch was ever worn. Watch-bracelets were created by great makers for ladies of great wealth and a few ladies wrist watches began to appear around 1790. Small miniature watches had been made earlier than this, however. David Rosseau made a watch which was about 18mm in diameter (the size of a dime) in the late 1600s.

 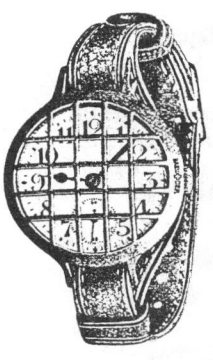

Early BRACELET that holds a small pendant-watch, a lid opens on this 18K & enamel case to view the watch, Ca.1840.

Girard-Perregaux **said** they produced wrist watches which were to be used by officers of the German Navy about 1880. The 1,000 watches used a protective mesh guard.

Miniaturization was a great challenge to many of the famous watch makers including Louis Jaquet, Paul Ditisheim, John Arnold and Henri Capt. The smallest watch in semi-mass production was 12mm by 5mm. In early 1930, the American Waltham Watch Co. made a 9mm by 20mm Model 400 watch.

Wrist watches were at first thought to be too small and delicate to be practical for men to wear. However, during World War I a German officer was said to have strapped a small pocket watch to his wrist with a leather webbed cup. This arrangement freed both hands and proved to be most useful. After the war, the wrist watch gained in popularity. **Girard - Perregaux** factory **said** they made wrist watches around 1880 and were designed to be used by officers of the German Navy. The Swiss introduced wrist watches to the United States around 1895, but they did not prove to be very popular at first. Around 1907 the Elgin and Illinois watch companies were manufacturing wrist watches and by 1912 Hampden and Waltham had started.

  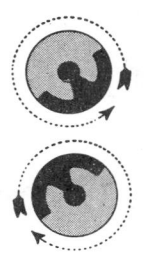 

Miniaturized wrist watch by Waltham model # 400. Note size comparison to dime.

Oscillating weight for self winding Wrist Watch.

HARWOOD self-winding wrist watch, RIM SET, Ca.1928.

By 1920 the round styles were being replaced with square, rectangular and tonneau shapes and decorated with gems. By 1928 wrist watches were outselling pocket watches, and, by 1935, over 85 percent of the watches being produced were wrist watches.

Self-wind pocket watches were first developed by Abraham Louis Perrelet in 1770 and by Abraham Louis Breguet about 1777. Louis Recordon made improvements in 1780, but is was not until 1923 that the principle of self-winding was adapted to the wrist watch by John Harwood, an Englishman who set up factories to make his patented self-wind wrist watches in Switzerland, London, France, and the United States. His watches first reached the market about 1929. The firm A. Schild manufactured about 15,000 watches in Switzerland. Mr. Harwood's watch company removed the traditional stem or crown to wind the mainspring, but in order to set the hands it was necessary to turn the bezel. The Harwood Watch Co. failed around 1931 and the patent expired.

Snap on protector used on some early Wrist Watches.   Rolex Oyster Perpetual, BUBBLE BACK, Ca. 1940.

Early in 1930 the Rolex Watch Co. introduced the Rolex Oyster Perpetual, the first waterproof and self-winding wrist watch. In 1933 the first "Incabloc" shock protection device was used. By 1940 wrist watches came in all shapes and types including complicated chronographs, calendars, and repeaters. Novelties, digital jump hour and multi-dial were very popular, as well.

A dramatic change occurred in 1957 when the Hamilton Watch Co. eliminated the mainspring and replaced it with a small battery that lasted well over one year. In 1960 the balance wheel was removed in the Accutron by Bulova and replaced by a tuning fork with miniature pawls.

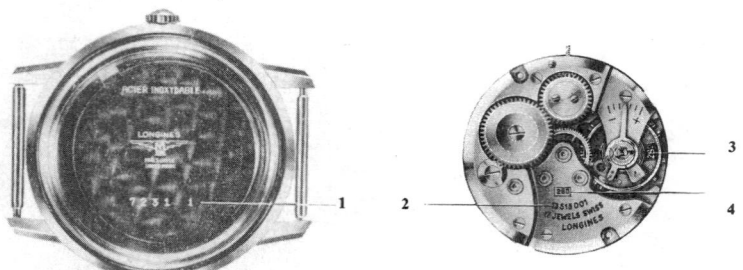

1. Case number.   2. Movement serial number.   3. Caliber number.   4. Caliber number.

NOTE: Some wrist watches have a grade, reference or caliber number engraved on the case, or movement. For example, Patek, Phillipe & Co. has a caliber number 27-460Q. The '27' stands for 27mm; the '460Q' is the grade; the 'Q' designates Quantieme (Perpetual calendar and moon phases).

AUTOMATIC WINDING

The self-winding watch uses the movements of the body in order to wind up the mainspring slowly and nearly continuously. The first pocket self-winding watches were executed by a watchmaker from Le Locle, Abraham-Louis Perrelet, around 1770.

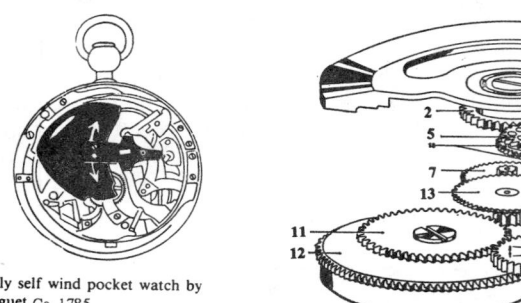

Early self wind pocket watch by Breguet Ca. 1785.

ETERNA-MATIC automatic winding mechanism with rotor oscillating on *5 ball bearings 1st introduced in 1949*. 1.–Oscillating weight. 2. –Oscillating gear. 3. –Upper wheel of auxiliary pawl-wheel. 4. –Lower wheel of auxiliary pawl-wheel. 5. –Pawl-wheel with pinion. 6. –Lower wheel of pawl wheel with pinion. 7. –Transmission-wheel with pinion. 8. –Crown-wheel yoke. 9. –Winding pinion. 10. –Crown-wheel. 11. –Ratchet-wheel. 12. –Barrel. 13. –Driving runner for ratchet-wheel. 14. –Winding stem. 15. –Winding button.

They were improved soon after by Abraham-Louis Breguet. In the case of the pocket watch, the movements causing the winding of the watch were essentially the result of walking. This system of winding was never widely adopted. The watch was a fancy model and not a really useful one. Herman von der Heydt was the only maker in America to work with the self-winding pocket watch. However, inventors always kept the idea of the self-winding watch in mind.

In 1923, the British firm Harwood took up once again the solution of the problem of automatic winding, for wrist watches. This was the spark which rapidly resulted in research to improve and simplify this type of mechanism. A company was formed in London to manufacture Harwood's watch, and before long over 500 jewelers in the United Kingdom were selling his automatic watch. A second company was formed in France, and a third in the United States. The business flourished about two and one-half years. Then, in 1931, these companies were liquidated.

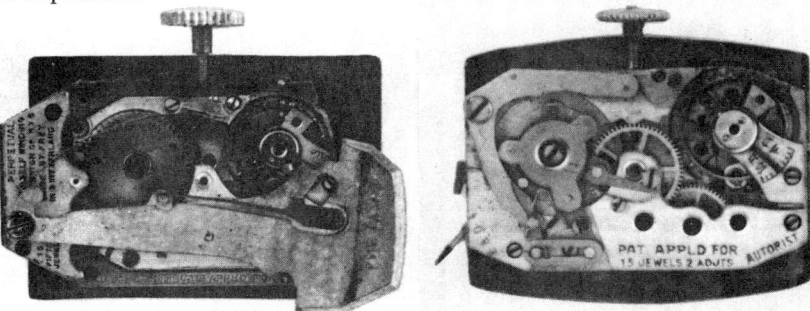

Early self-winding wrist watch by FREY W. Co., Ca. 1930's. NOTE: The pendulum style weight for self-winding.

Early self-winding wrist watch by AUTORIST W. Co. Ca.1930's. Winding by moving flexible lugs.

CHRONOGRAPH

The term chronograph is derived from the Greek words chronos which means "time" and grapho which means "to write." The first recording of intervals of time was around 1821 by the inventor Rieussec. His chronograph (*Time-Writer*) made dots of ink on a dial as a measure of time. Around 1862 Adolph Nicole introduced the first chronograph with a hand that returned to zero. The split second chronograph made its appearance around 1879. Today a chronograph can be described as a timepiece that starts at will, stops at will, and can return to zero at will. A mechanical chronograph had a sweep or center second hand that will start, stop, and fly back to zero. The term chronometer should not be confused with chronograph. A chronometer is a timepiece that has superior time keeping qualities at the time it is made. The CHRONOGRAPH 1 **button** wrist watch was 1st. advertised in 1910 & a 2 **button** CHRONOGRAPH in 1939 by Breitling.

A. Day window. **B.** Split second hand. **C.** Calendar pusher. **D.** Register for seconds. **E.** Calendar pusher. **F.** Date hand. **G.** Register for total hours. **H.** Sweep center second hand. **I.** Month window. **J.** Start/stop pusher. **K.** Register for total minutes. **L.** Return pusher. **M.** Date of month.

TRADE MARK	MANUFACTURER	TRADE MARK	MANUFACTURER

 VALJOUX
Now part of the **ETA** group

 LANDERON

 VENUS

 FONTAINEMELON

CHRONOGRAPH MECHANISM
NUMBERS & NAMES USED IN THE EBAUCHE BOOK
" TECHNOLOGICAL DICTIONARY OF WATCH PARTS " Ca. 1953

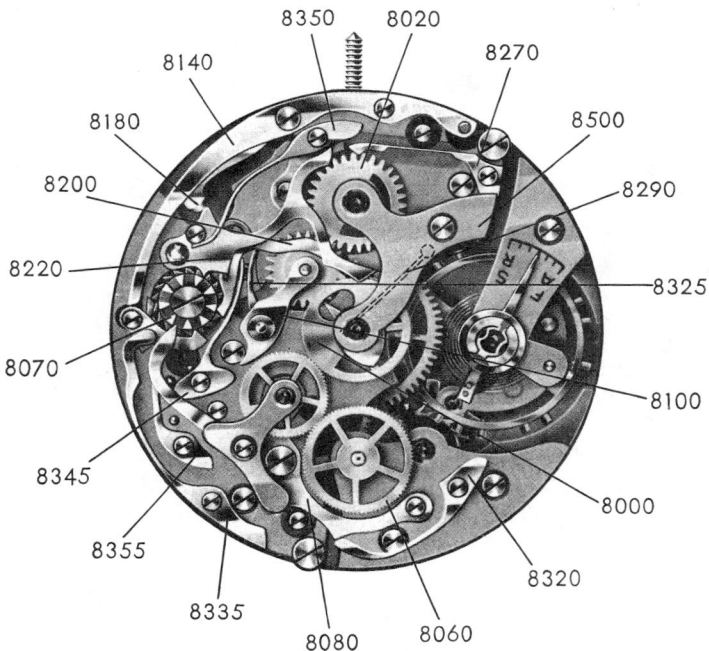

8000 = Chronograph central wheel, w/ finger.
8020 = Minute-recording wheel, register.
8060 = Driving wheel.
8070 = Pillar or Crown wheel, 3 functions.
8080 = Coupling clutch w/ transmission wheel, 2 functions.
8100 = Sliding or star gear, 2 functions.
8140 = Operating or starting lever, 2 functions.
8180 = Fly-back lever, reset to zero.
8200 = Blocking lever, 2 functions.
8220 = Hammer or heart piece striker, 2 functions.
8270 = Minute-recording jumper spring.
8290 = Friction spring , for chronograph central wheel.
8320 = Coupling clutch spring.
8325 = Sliding gear spring, 2 functions.
8335 = Operating or starting lever spring.
8345 = Blocking lever spring.
8350 = Hammer or heartpiece lever spring, 2 functions.
8355 = Pillar or crown wheel jumper or block.
8500 = Chronograph bridge, for center & min. recording wheels.

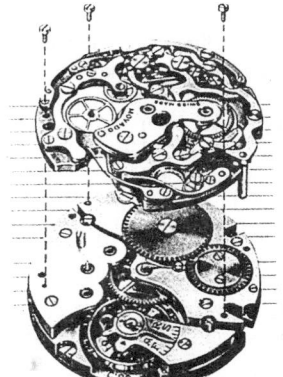

ABOVE: Illustration of a
Modular construction or
a chronograph Attachment.

The chronograph is a fitted attachment to a time only watch movement, with a additional function that can be used independently of the time indication. The chronograph ebauche factories who make 80% of the raw chronograph attachments (about 10 ebauche manufacturers), are rarely known by the public. The chronograph modular or attachment are made to be fitted or added to a time only movement. The same is true of repeaters. Companies as Patek Philippe, Audemars Piguet, Rolex and many more are fitted with ebauche chronograph attachments to their own time only movement. Watch Companies as Breitling, Heuer, Eberhard and many more are finished with ebauche chronograph attachments fitted to raw movements made by other wrist-watch ebauche factories.

LEFT: CHRONOGRAPH with 1 push piece & CENTER 2 push pieces. RIGHT: CHRONOGRAPH module or attachment

Chronograph with two push pieces:

Action and movement of hands : The pusher No .1 sets the hands in action and second action stops the same hands.

Pusher No. 2 brings the hands back to zero. During their movement this pusher is a fixture, thus preventing the accidental return of the hands to zero. The double pusher chronograph permits an interruption in the reading, the hands are set going again from the position they stopped, thus indispensable for any time lost during a control of any description.

HOW TO READ THE TACHOMETER-TELEMETER DIAL

The **TACHOMETER** may have a spiral scale around center of dial, this indicates miles per hour, based on a trial over one mile. It indicates speeds from 400 to 20 miles per hour on three turns. Each turn of spiral corresponds to one minute (scale for first 8 seconds being omitted), the outer turn from 400 to 60 (0 to 1 minute) and the center turn from 30 to 20 miles per hour (2 to 3 minutes).

When passing the first marker of mile zone, start chronograph hand by pressing push piece. When passing following mile marker, press push piece again. The chronograph hand now indicates the speed in miles per hour on the spiral. If a mile has been made in less than one minute the speed will be indicated on outside turn of spiral; from 1 to 2 minutes on middle turn and 2 to 3 minutes on center turn.

EXAMPLE: If a mile has been made in 1 minute and 15 seconds the chronograph hand indicates 48 miles per hour on middle turn of spiral.

The **TELEMETER** scale around margin of dial is based on the speed of sound compared with the speed of light. Each small division is 100 meters. The scale is read in kilometers & hundreds of meters. Approximately 16 divisions equal 1 mile.

To determine the distance of a storm: When you see the flash of lightning press push piece of chronograph. When hearing thunder press again, the chronograph hand will indicate on the Telemeter scale the distance in kilometers and hundreds of meters. One kilometer equals 5/8 of a mile.

NOTE: The chronograph is a fitted attachment to a time only watch movement, with a additional function that can be used independently of the time indication. The chronograph ebauche factories who make 80% of the raw chronograph attachments (about 10 ebauche manufacturers), are rarely known by the public. The chronograph module or attachment are made to be fitted or added to a time only movement. The same is true of repeaters. Companies as Patek Philippe, Rolex, Audemars Piguet and many more are fitted with ebauche chronograph attachments to their own time only movement. Watch Companies as Breitling, Heuer, Eberhard and many more are finished with ebauche chronograph attachments fitted to raw movements made by other wrist-watch ebauche factories.

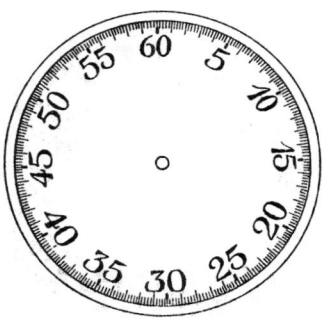
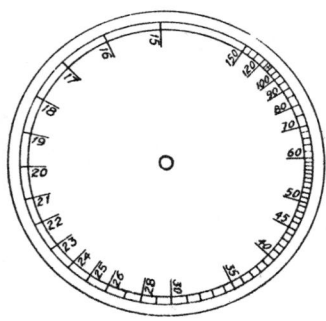

Dial No. 1 is a simple stop watch and chronograph dial. Graduated into fifths of seconds.

Dial No. 2 is used to time a car over a quarter-mile track and read the numbers of miles per hour directly from dial.

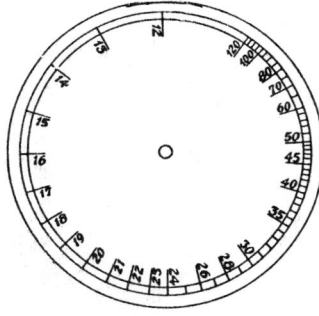
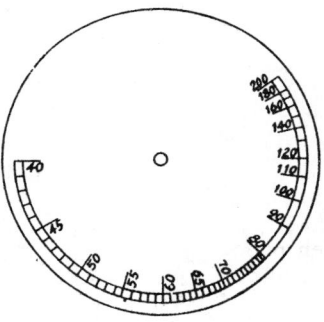

Dial No. 3 is used to measure speed in kilometers per hour over a course of one fifth of a kilometer.

Dial No. 4 used by physicians to count the pulse beats of a patient.

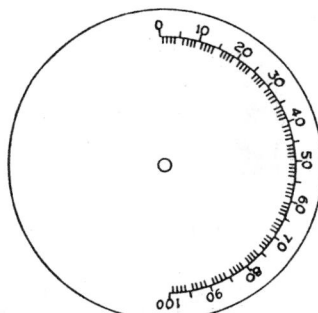
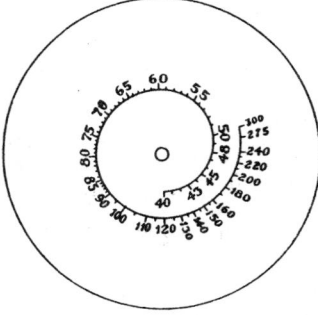

Dial No. 5 is used by artillery officers for determining distance by means of sound in kilometers.

Dial No. 6 shows a tachometer: many watches are made with several scales on the same dial in order to cover a greater range of functions. The figures are sometimes grouped in a spiral form or in several circles, thus the hand may make more than one complete revolution.

WRIST WATCH CASE AND DIAL STYLES

Barrel

Maxine

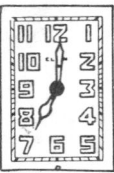

Square

Round

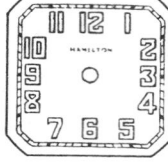

Square Cut Corner

Cushion

Rectangle

Flared

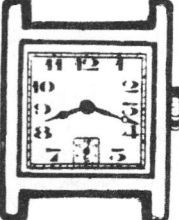

Round
(Ladies style; con-
verts to lapel or
wrist)

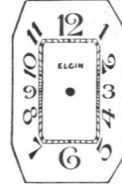

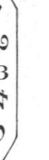

Curved or Curvex

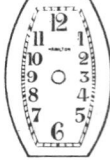

**Rectangle
Cut Corner**

Tonneau

Baguette

Oval

**EXAGGERATED
NUMBERS**

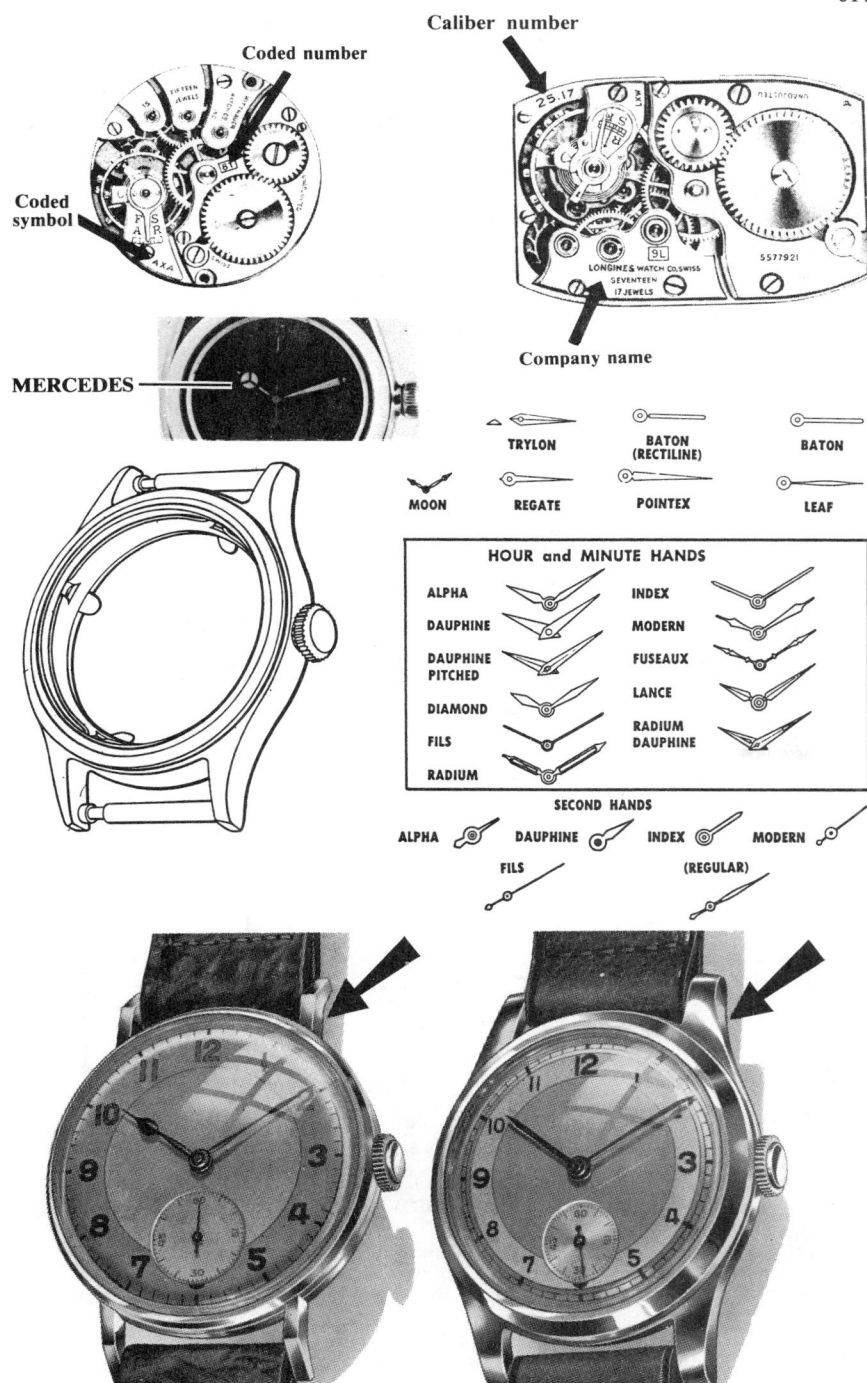

Coded number

Caliber number

Coded symbol

Company name

MERCEDES

TRYLON

BATON (RECTILINE)

BATON

MOON

REGATE

POINTEX

LEAF

HOUR and MINUTE HANDS

ALPHA

INDEX

DAUPHINE

MODERN

DAUPHINE PITCHED

FUSEAUX

DIAMOND

LANCE

FILS

RADIUM DAUPHINE

RADIUM

SECOND HANDS

ALPHA   DAUPHINE   INDEX   MODERN

FILS   (REGULAR)

LEFT: Watch has SOLDERED lugs. **RIGHT**: Watch has SOLID lugs or ONE PIECE lug.

SWISS CODE INITIALS

Between the years of 1880 & 1927 over 8,000 trademarks and brand names were registered in Switzerland. Some Swiss watches have three initials on the balance bridge. These initials are not model identification but are for house identification. Following is a list of import initials with the name of the firm.

AOC–Roamer
AOL–Adolph Schwarcz & Son
AOX–Alstate W. Co.
AXA–Wittnauer
AXZ–Benrus
AYP–Audemars Piguet
BOL–Lemania
BXC–Avia
BXJ–Midland
BXN–Benrus
BXP–Imperial, Bayer, Pretzfelder & Mills
BXW–Bulova
COC–Crawford
COW–Croton
CXC–Concord
CXD–Cypres
CXH–Clinton
CXV–Cort
CXW–Central; Benrus
DOB–Dreffa W. Co.
DOW–Deauville
EOE–Elrex
EON–Avalon
EOP–Harvel
EOT–Lavina
EXA–ETERNA
EXC–Everbrite
FXE–Provis
FXU–Louis Aisenstein & Bros.
FXW–Louis
GXC–Gruen
GXI–Gotham (Ollendorff)
GXM–Girard-Perregaux
GXR–Grant
GXW–Gothic
HOM–Homis
HON–Tissot; A. Hirsch
HOR–Lanco; Langendorf

HOU–Oris
HXF–Harman
HXM–R. H. Macy & Co.
HXN–Harvel
HXO–Harold K. Oleet
HXW–Helbros
HYL– Hamilton
HYO–Hilton W Co.
JXE–Normandie
JXJ–Jules Jurgensen
JXR–Gallet
KOT–Landau
KXJ–Wm. J. Kappel
KXV–Louis
KXZ–Kelton; Benrus, Central
LOA–Emil Langer
LOD–Latham
LOE–Packard
LXA–Laco, Winton, Elbon
LXE–Evkob
LXJ–Jaegar-LeCoultre
LXW–Longines
MOG–Mead & Co.; Boulevard
MOU–Tower; Delbana
MXE–Monarch
MXH–Seeland
MXI–Movado
MXT–Mathey-Tissot
NOA–U.Nardin
NOS–Heritage
NOU–Louvic
NXJ–National Jewelers Co.
NXO–Oris
OXG–Omega
OXL–Wyler
OYT–Shriro (Sandoz)
POY–Camy; Copley
PXA–Pierce
PXP–Patek, Philippe

PXT–Paul Breguette
PXW–Parker
PYS–Langel
QXO–Kelbert
ROC–Raleigh
ROL–Ribaux
ROP–Rodania
ROR–Audemars Piguet
ROW–Rolex
RXG–R. Gsell & Co.
RXM–Galmor
RXW–Rima
RXY–Liengme
RYW–Ritex
SOA–Felca
SOE–Semca
SOW–Seeland
SOX–Cortebert, Orvin
SXE–Savoy; Banner
SXK–S. Kocher & Co.
SXS–Franco
UOA–Actua
UOB–Aero
UOW–Universal
UXM–Medana
UXN–Marsh
UYW–Stanley W. Co.
VOS–Sheffield
VXN–V & C & LeCoultre
VXT–Kingston
WOA–Tower
WOB–Wyler
WOG–Breitling
WOR–Creston
WXC–Buren
WXE–Welsbro
WXW–Westfield
ZFX–Zenith W.Co.
ZOV–Titus
ZYV–Hampden (new company)

Between the years 1880 & 1927 over 8,000 trade-mark titles were registered in Switzerland. Such as ALPHA, BULOVA, CAMY, JAEGER, REVERSO, SUBMARINER, VALJOUX, ZODIAC & ETC.

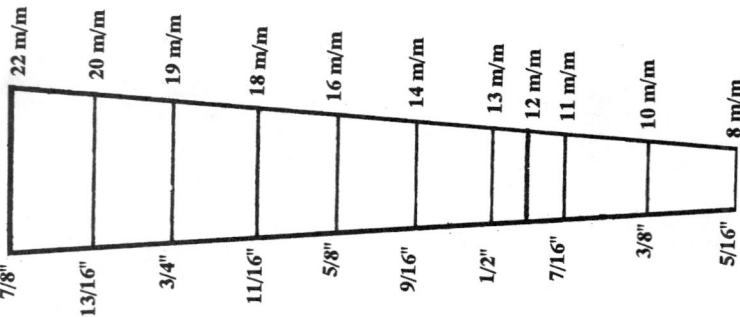

To determine your wrist watch band size use the **ABOVE GAUGE** and measure between the lugs. The band sizes are listed on each side of the gauge.

When performing any underwater activity, the dynamic pressure generated through movement is greater than the static pressure. Below a ranking of water resistance for most watches.

1 **meter** = 3.28 ft., 330 ft. =about 100 **meters**. 33.89 ft. =1 **atmosphere**, 100 ft. = about 3 **atmospheres**.

30M = sweat-resistant
50M = shower only, rain (1 AT.)
100M = swimming (**no diving**) -330 ft.
200M = snorkeling, skin diving -600 ft.
1000M =scuba diving -3,300 ft.

Like many industries consolidation of the major market brands increase vendors market share and higher volume to increase profitability. Many of the famous names of the past are no longer independent, but owned by a larger company. Concentration is bad when boarders between various brands become indistinct; it lessons their unique character. Interesting to note is that Swatch Group owns 90% of movements. Below are some of the conglomerates and a list of the watch brands under their control.

OWNER	BRAND NAME
Artime	Philip Watch
	Sector No Limits
Audemars,Piguet	Audemars Piguet
Bottinelli Families	Jaeger Le Coultre 40%
+ shareholders	
Chung Nam Group	ISA
	Roamer
Citizen	Citizen
	Miyota
Desco	Maurice Lacroix
Diehl family	Junghans
Dixi Paul Castella	Mondia
Egana	Benetton
	Caravelles
	Chromachron
	Dugena 70%
	Esprit
	Morellato
	Pierre Cardin
	ZenRa
Eterna SA	Eterna
	Porche Design
Frey family	Minerva
Hour Glass	Daniel Roth
	Gerald Genta
Gerd-R. Lang	Chronoswiss
Dr. Luigi Macaluso	
(Lorane Holding SA,	Girard-Perregaux
Sowind SA)	
LVMH	Chaumet
(Louis Vuitton,	Ebel
Moet, Hennessy)	Givenchy
	Gucci 20%
	Tag Heuer
	Zenith
Maddox AG	Bernini
	BWC
	Cerutti
NAWC (North	Concord
American W. Co.)	Movado
Renley W. Co.	Le Phare-Jean d'Eve
	Sultana

OWNER	BRAND NAME
Richmont Group	Alfred Dunhill
	A. Lange & Sohne
(Cartier family)	Baume & Mercier
	Cartier
	IWC (International W. Co.)
	Jaeger Le Coultre
	Montblanc
	Officine Panerai
	Piaget
	Vacheron Constantin
	Van Cleef & Arpels 80%
	Yves Saint Laurent
SAB	St. John
(Swiss Army Brands)	Swiss Air Force
	Swiss Army Watches
	Victorinox
	Wenger
Scheufele	Chopard
Schneider Family	Breitling
	Kelek
Seiko	Lassale
	Lorus
	Pulsar
	Spoon
Stern family	Patek Philippe
Swatch Group	Blancpain
	Breguet
	Calvin Kline (CK)
	Certina
	Endura
	ETA (movements)
	Flick Flak
	Glashutte Original
	Hamilton
	Jaquet-Droz
	Lanco
	Lemania (movements)
	Longines
	Mido
	Nivarox - FAR
	Omega
	Pierre Balmain
	Piguet (movement)
	Frederic
	Rado
	Renata (movements)
	Swatch
	Tissot
	Unitas (movements)
	Valjoux (movement)
Wilsdorf Foundation	Rolex & Tudor

The table below list the brand name alphabetically and who is the owner of the company.

Brand Name .... Owners	Brand Name .... Owners
A. Lange & Sohne — Richemont Group	Lorus — Seiko (Hattori)
Alfred Dunhill — Richemont Group (Cartier Family)	Marvin — Revue-Thommen
Audemars Piguet — Audemars, Piguet, Bottinelli families, + Shareholders	Maurice Lacroix — Desco von Schulthess, Bodmer family
Baume & Mercier — Richemont Group (Cartier Family)	Mido — Swatch Group
Benetton — Egana	Minerva — A. & J.J. Frey
Bernini — Maddox AG	Miyota — Citizen
Blancpain — Swatch Group	Mondia — Dixi Paul Castella
Bovet — Thierry Oulevay & Roger Guye	Montblanc — Richemont Group (Cartier Family)
Breguet — Swatch Group	Morellato (49%) — Egana
Breitling — Schneider Family - Kelek	Movado — NAWC (North American Watch Co.)
Bulgari — Bulgari family	Muhle Glashutte — Nautische Instrument
BWC — Maddox AG	Officine Panerai — Richemont Group (Cartier Family)
Calvin Kline (CK) — Swatch Group	Omega — Swatch Group
Caravelles — Egana	Parmigiani — Sandoz foundation 90%, Michel Parmigiani
Cartier — Richemont Group (Cartier Family)	Patek Philippe — Stern family
Certina — Swatch Group	Philip Watch — Artime
Cerutti — Maddox AG	Piaget — Richemont Group (Cartier Family)
Chaumet — LVMH (Louis Vuitton, Moet, Hennessy)	Pierre Balmain — Swatch Group
Chopard — Scheufele Family	Pierre Cardin — Egana
Christ — Douglas AG	Frederic Piguet (mvm't) — Swatch Group
Chromachron — Egana	Porche Design — Eterna SA
Chronoswiss — Gerd-R. Lang ?	Pulsar — Seiko (Hattori)
Citizen — Miyota	Rado — Swatch Group
Concord — NAWC (North American Watch Co.)	Raymond Weil — Weil family
Corum — Jean-Rene Bannwart 10% Severin Wundermann 90%	Renata (mvm't) — Swatch Group
Daniel Roth — Hour Glass	RGM — Roland Murphy
Dunhill — Richemont Group (Cartier Family)	Roamer — Chuung Nam Group
Ebel — LVMH (Louis Vuitton, Moet, Hennessy)	Rolex — Wilsdorf Foundation
Endura — Swatch Group	Sector No Limits — Artime
ETA (mvm't) — Swatch Group	Speidel — Hisch
Eterna — Eterna SA	Spoon — Seiko (Hattori)
Favre-Leuba — Benedom SA	St. John — SAB (Swiss Army Brands)
Flik Flak — Swaych Group	Sultana — Renley Watch Co.
Fortis — Rolf Voght family; Prince Ernst August von Hannover	Swatch — Swatch Group
Franck Muller — Vartan Sirmakes, Franck Muller	Swiss Air Force — SAB (Swiss Army Brands)
Gerald Genta — Hour Glass	Swiss Army Watches — SAB (Swiss Army Brands)
Girard-Perregaux — Dr.L. Macaluso, Lorane Holding SA, Sowind SA	Tag Heuer — LVMH (Louis Vuitton, Moet, Hennessy)
Givenchy — LVMH (Louis Vuitton, Moet, Hennessy)	Tissot — Swatch Group
Glashutte Original — Swatch Group	Tudor — Wilsdorf Foundation
Gucci Watches - Gucci, LVMH, PPR	Tutima — Tutima Uhrenfabik
Hamilton — Swatch Group	Ulysse Nardin - Rolf W. Schnyder, Dieter Meier, Balthasar Meier
Hermes — Hermes family	Unitas (mvm't) — Swatch Group
IWC Schaffhausen — Richemont Group	Universal Geneve — Stelux Holdings
Jaeger-LeColture — Richemont Group 60%	Vacheron Constantin — Richemont Group (Cartier Family)
Jaquet-Droz — Swatch Group	Valjoux (mvm't) — Swatch Group
Jughans — Diehl family	Van Cleef & Arpels — Richemont Group 80% (Cartier Family)
Kelek — Schneider family	Ventura — Ventura Design on time SA
Lanco — Swatch Group	Victornox — SAB (Swiss Army Brands)
Lassale — Seiko (Hattori)	Wenger — SAB (Swiss Army Brands)
Le Phare- Jean d'Eve — Renley Watch Co.	Xemex — Xemex Swiss watch
Lemania (mvm't) — Swatch Group	Yves Saint Laurent — Richemont Group (Cartier Family)
Limes — Ickler Gmbh	Zeneth — LVMH (Louis Vuitton Moet, Hennessy)
Longines — Swatch Group	ZentaRa — Egana

WRIST WATCH LISTINGS

Priced At The Collectable Fair Market Trade Show Level
(Complete Watches Only)

Unless otherwise noted, wrist watches listed in this section are priced at the *collectable* fair market **TRADE SHOW** level (What a collector may expect to pay for a watch from a watch dealer) and as **complete** watches having an original gold-filled case and stainless steel back, also with original dial, and the entire original movement in good working order with no repairs needed. They are also priced as having a watch band made of **leather** except where a bracelet is described. Watches listed as 14k and 18k are solid gold cases. Coin or base-metal and stainless steel cases will be listed as such. Low cost production watches, are listed as having a base metal type case and a composition dial.

Many of the watch manufacturers were commissioned to put jewelers' or jobbers' **names** on their movements in place of their own. Because of this practice, the true manufacturers of these movements are difficult to identify. Between the years 1880 & 1927 over 8,000 trade-mark titles were registered in Switzerland, such as Alpha, Bulova, Camy, Jaeger, Reverso, Submariner, Valjoux, Zodiac, etc.

The prices shown were averaged from dealers' trade show display's just prior to publication and are an indication of the trade show level or what collectors will pay. **Prices** are provided in three categories: **average condition, extra fine, and mint condition,** and are shown in whole dollar amounts only. The values listed are a guide for the *collectable* trade show level and are provided for your information only. **Dealers** will not necessarily pay full trade show price. Prices listed are for watches with **original** cases, movement and dials and in good running order.

Warning: There are currently fake wrist watches being sold on the world-wide market. These watches have the appearance of authenticity but are merely cheap imitations of prestigious companies such as Rolex (all types), Gucci, Cartier, & Piaget.

Important Notice. All of the information, including valuations, in this book has been compiled from the most reliable sources, and every effort has been made to eliminate errors and questionable data. Nevertheless, the possibility of error, in a work of such immense scope, always exists. The publisher or authors will not be held responsible for losses which may occur in the purchase, sale, statements of its advertisers, or other transaction of items, because of information contained herein. Readers who feel they have discovered errors are invited to write and inform us, so they may be corrected in subsequent editions.

🕐 Wrist Watch terminology or communication in this book has evolved over the years, in search of better & more precise language with a effort to improve, purify, adjust itself & make it easier to understand.

INFORMATION NEEDED — The authors are interested in any facts and information you might have that should possibly be considered for future editions. Documented facts are needed, so please send photo or sources of information. Send to:

COOKSEY SHUGART
P.O. BOX 3147
CLEVELAND, TN. 37320-3147

When **CORRESPONDING**, Please send a 🖃 self addressed, stamped **ENVELOPE**.

ABERCROMBIE & FITCH, 17J., chronog.by Valj.,3 reg.
14K..................................$700 $900 $1,200
s.steel $250 $350 $500

Abercrombie & Fitch, 17J., **Seafarer**, chronog., waterproof
18k $900 $1,200 $1,600
s. steel $300 $400 $600

Abercrombie & Fitch, 17J., chronog.by Valj.,3 reg., Ca.1950
s.steel $275 $325 $500

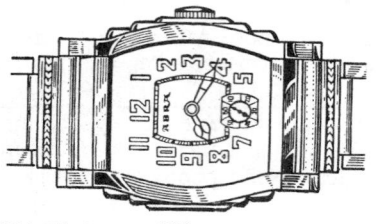

ABRA, 17J., step case, c.1930s
base metal $30 $40 $65

 Pricing in this Guide are trade show fair market price for
COMPLETE watches which are reflected from the "**NAWCC**"
National and regional shows.

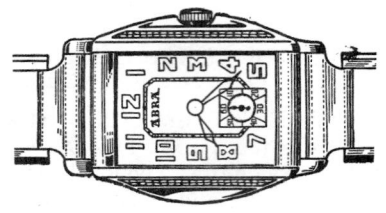

ABRA,17J., carved case, c.1930s
base metal $30 $40 $65

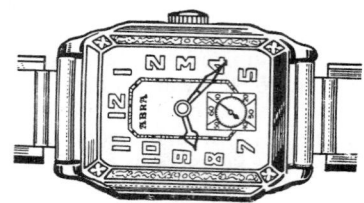

ABRA, 17J., engraved case
base metal $30 $40 $65

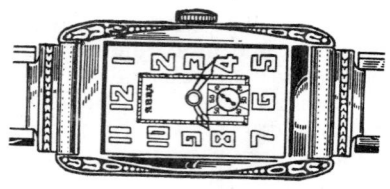

ABRA,15J., curved case, c.1930s
base metal $30 $40 $65

ABRA, 17J., **jump hour**
s. steel $175 $195 $300

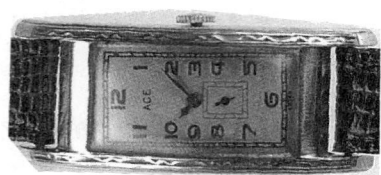

ACE, 17 jewels, Ca. 1936
gold filled $50 $60 $75

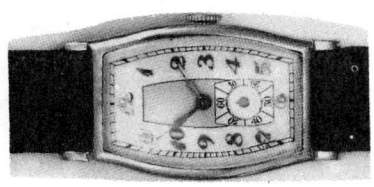

ACRO W. CO., 17 jewels, **hinged back**
18k $175 $225 $350

ADMES, 17 jewels, self wind, waterproof, center sec.,
14K..$95 $125 $175
  gold filled................................ $40 $50 $100

AGASSIZ, 17 jewels, **World Time**
18k $4,000 $4,500 $6,000

AGASSIZ, 17 jewels, fancy bezel,
18k $450 $550 $800

AGASSIZ, 18 jewels, for Tiffany & Co., 48mm, oversize
18k $800 $900 $1,100

AGASSIZ,17J., C. 1940s
18K(W).......................................$500 $600 $800

AGASSIZ, 18 jewels, barrel shaped dial, 40mm,
18k $300 $400 $600

AGASSIZ, 17 jewels, for Tiffany & Co., 45mm
18k $700 $800 $1,000

ALAVENTE, 7J., "Mystery", **simulated** jewels, ca.1965
base metal $55 $75 $175

ALPHA, 17J., chrono. 2 reg., cal.48, c.1950s
14K $350 $450 $600
s.steel $200 $250 $400

ALPHA, 17J., **Fancy lugs**, sweep sec., c. 1948
18k $200 $225 $300

ALPHA, 17J, autowind, c.1950s
18K.. $175 $200 $250

ALPINA, 17 jewels, automatic, ca. 1950
18k $175 $200 $250

ALPINA, 17J., chronograph, ca. 1940
14k $400 $450 $525

ALPINA, 17 jewels, automatic, water proof, aux. sec.
18k $150 $175 $250

ALSTA, 17J., **chronograph**, 3 reg.
14K $325 $375 $500
base metal $175 $225 $300

ALSTA, 17 jewels, **wrist alarm**
gold filled $85 $100 $125

ALTON, 17J., fancy lugs, c.1950s
14K $125 $150 $225

ALTUS, 17 jewels, ref. 827
18k $150 $175 $250

AM. WALTHAM, 21J., "Adair", ca.1941
gold filled..................................$60 $75 $125

AM. WALTHAM, 21J., "Albright", ca.1940
14k $125 $150 $225

AM. WALTHAM, 17J., "Allen", ca.1940
gold filled..................................$60 $75 $125

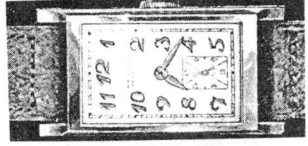

AM. WALTHAM, 21J., "Boxford", gold numbers, ca.1941
18k yellow $175 $200 $250
18K red $200 $250 $350

AM. WALTHAM, 17J., "Braintree", **Side Wrist**, ca.1940
gold filled..................................$75 $85 $150

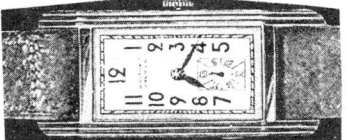

AM. WALTHAM, 17J., "Camden", ca.1941
gold plate $45 $55 $85

🕐 A collector should expect to pay modestly higher prices at local shops

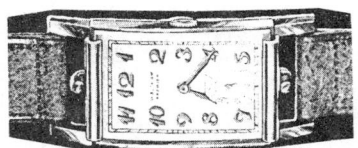

AM. WALTHAM, 21J., "Campton", **note** bezel, c.1940
14k $175 $200 $250

AM. WALTHAM, 17J., "Canton", gold numbers, ca.1941
gold filled $60 $75 $125

AM. WALTHAM, 10J., "Chandler", sweep sec., ca.1941
gold plate $40 $50 $75

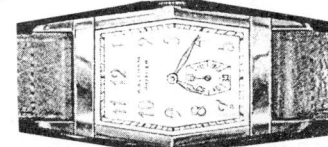

AM. WALTHAM, 17J., "Charlton", ca.1940
gold plate $40 $50 $85

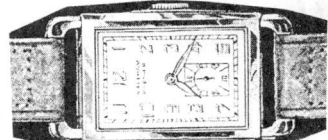

AM. WALTHAM, 9J., "Conway", ca.1941
gold plate $40 $50 $75

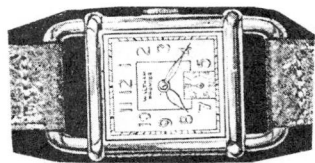

AM. WALTHAM, 17J., "Creston", ca.1941
gold filled $60 $75 $125

AM. WALTHAM, 17J., "Cronwell", ca.1940
gold filled $60 $75 $125

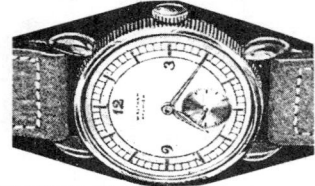

AM. WALTHAM, 17J., "Danbury", coin edge, ca.1941
gold filled...................................$60 $75 $125

AM. WALTHAM, 17J., "Dighton", thin model, ca.1941
gold filled yellow or red..........$60 $75 $135

AM. WALTHAM, 9J., "Duxbury", ca.1941
gold plate $45 $55 $80

AM. WALTHAM, 17J., "Fairmont", ca.1940
gold filled...................................$75 $100 $145

AM. WALTHAM, 17J., "Fremont", gold numbers, ca.1941
14k $150 $175 $250

AM. WALTHAM, 21J., "Gardner", gold numbers, ca.1940
gold filled...................................$60 $75 $125

AM. WALTHAM, 17J., "Goodwin", ca.1941
gold filled...................................$60 $75 $125

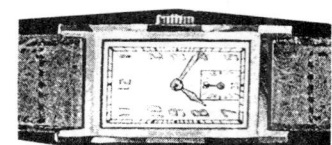

AM. WALTHAM, 17J., "Granby", gold numbers, ca.1941
14k $150 $175 $250

AM. WALTHAM, 17J., "Heath", ca.1941
gold filled $60 $75 $125

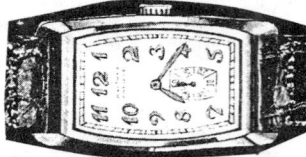

AM. WALTHAM, 21J., "Hingham", gold numbers, ca.1941
14k $150 $175 $250

AM. WALTHAM, 17J., "Hollis", applied numbers, ca.1941
14k $150 $175 $250

AM. WALTHAM, 21J., "Hubbard", 13 rubies or sapphires
set in gold on dial, ca.1941
14k yellow $125 $150 $200
14k red $175 $200 $275

AM. WALTHAM, 17J., "Jeffery", ca.1941
gold filled $65 $85 $125

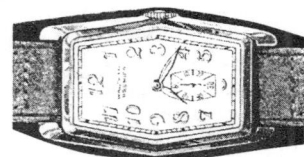

AM. WALTHAM, 17J., "Lebanon", ca.1941
gold filled $60 $75 $125

AM. WALTHAM, 17J., "Mendon", ca.1941
gold filled.................................$60 $75 $125

AM. WALTHAM, 17J., "Norton", ca.1941
gold filled.................................$60 $75 $125

AM. WALTHAM, 17J., "Oberlin", ca.1941
gold filled.................................$60 $75 $125

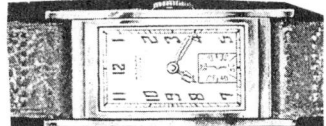

AM. WALTHAM, 17J., "Pacer", ca.1941
gold filled.................................$60 $75 $125

AM. WALTHAM, 17J., "Patten", hidden lugs, ca.1941
14k yellow $125 $150 $200
14K red $175 $200 $275

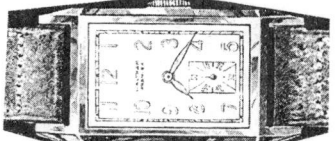

AM. WALTHAM, 17J., "Paxton", ca.1941
gold plate $40 $50 $75

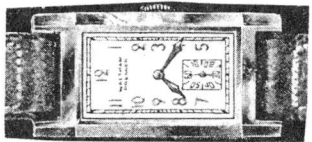

AM. WALTHAM, 17J., "Peabody", ca.1941
gold plate $45 $55 $75

AM. WALTHAM, 17J., "Penton", ca.1941
gold filled $60 $75 $125

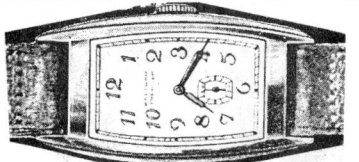

AM. WALTHAM, 17J., "Preston", ca.1941
gold filled yellow $60 $75 $135
gold filled red $75 $95 $175

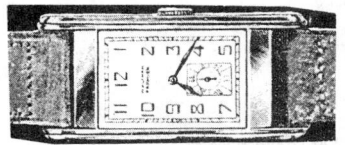

AM. WALTHAM, 17J., "Quincy", ca.1941
gold filled $60 $75 $125

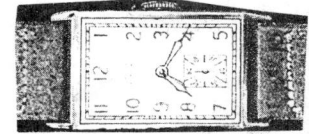

AM. WALTHAM, 17J., "Reading", ca.1941
gold filled $60 $75 $125

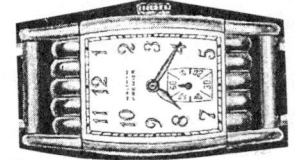

AM. WALTHAM, 17J., "Regal", ca.1941
gold plate $40 $50 $75

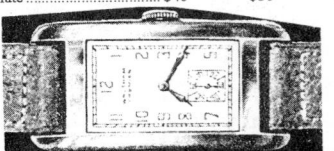

AM. WALTHAM, 17J., "Richford", ca.1941
gold filled $60 $75 $125

AM. WALTHAM, 17J., "Rowe", ca.1941
gold filled $60 $75 $125

AM. WALTHAM, 21J., "Sheraton", ca.1941
14k $125 $150 $225

AM. WALTHAM, 17J., "Side-wrist", ca.1941
gold filled...............................$125 $150 $225

AM. WALTHAM, 17J., "Stan Hope", ca.1941
gold filled..................................$60 $75 $125

AM. WALTHAM, 9-17J., "Submarine", ca.1941
gold filled=17J........................$60 $75 $125
Chrome=9J...............................$35 $45 $75

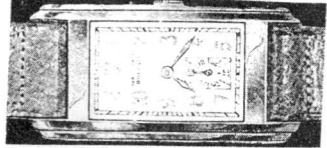

AM. WALTHAM, 17J., "Townsend", ca.1941
gold plate yellow $40 $50 $75
gold plate red $50 $60 $125

AM. WALTHAM, 17J., "Tulane", ca.1941
gold filled..................................$60 $75 $125

AM. WALTHAM, 18J., "Upton", ca.1941
gold filled $60 $75 $125

AM. WALTHAM, 18J., "Upton", **pulse computing dial**
gold filled $75 $100 $150

AM. WALTHAM, 21J., "Wachusett", gold numbers, ca.1941
gold filled $60 $75 $125

AM. WALTHAM, 17J., "Wesley", ca.1941
gold plate red $40 $50 $85

AM. WALTHAM, 17J., "Windfield", ca.1941
gold filled $60 $75 $125

AM. WALTHAM, 9J., "Wollaston", ca.1941
gold plate yellow or red $45 $55 $95

AM. WALTHAM, 21J., "Woodland", gold numbers, ca.1941
14k $150 $175 $250

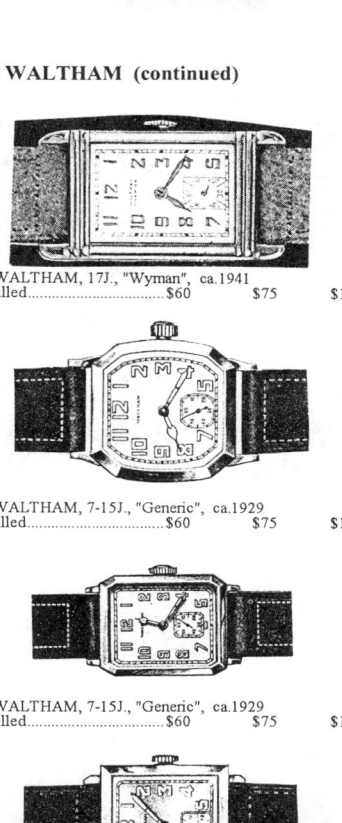

AM. WALTHAM, 17J., "Wyman", ca.1941
gold filled.................................$60 $75 $125

AM. WALTHAM, 7-15J., "Generic", ca.1929
gold filled.................................$60 $75 $125

AM. WALTHAM, 7-15J., "Generic", ca.1929
gold filled.................................$60 $75 $125

AM. WALTHAM, 7-15J., "Generic", ca.1929
gold filled.................................$60 $75 $125

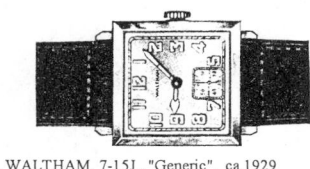

AM. WALTHAM, 7-15J., "Generic", ca.1929
gold filled.................................$60 $75 $125

AM. WALTHAM, 7-15J., "Generic", ca.1929
gold filled.................................$60 $75 $125

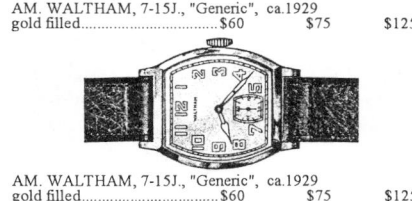

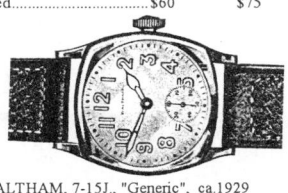

AM. WALTHAM, 7-15J., "Generic", ca.1929
gold filled.................................$60 $75 $125

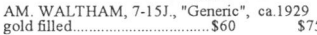

AM. WALTHAM, 15J.,"Harley-Davidson", c.1935
gold filled $75 $95 $150

AM. WALTHAM, 17J., aux, sec. c.1930s
14k $150 $175 $295

AM. WALTHAM, 17J., Driver style, Ca. 1935
gold filled $80 $90 $125

AM. WALTHAM, 21J., cal.750B, GJS, c.1950s
14k $125 $150 $275

AM. WALTHAM, 17J., cal.750B, c.1951
gold filled $60 $75 $125

AM. WALTHAM, 15J., "Masonic" model, c.1925
14k (original dial)...................$150 $200 $300

AM. WALTHAM, 15 jewels, engraved bezel
gold filled $50 $75 $125

AM. WALTHAM, 15-17J, **solid lugs**, c.1920s
sterling silver $175 $200 $300

AM. WALTHAM, 17J., **enamel dial**, for Tiffany & Co.
14k $200 $250 $400

AM. WALTHAM, 15-17J, "Ruby", enamel dial, c.1920s
gold filled................................$100 $125 $225

AM.WALTHAM, 19J., **enamel dial**, C. 1905
silver $135 $165 $250

AM. WALTHAM, 17 J, barrel shaped dial, c. 1920
14k $150 $175 $225

AM. WALTHAM, 17 jewels, **enamel dial**, wire lugs
14k $250 $350 $500

A collector should expect to pay modestly higher prices
at local shops

AM. WALTHAM, 17 J, Premier, diamond dial, Ca. 1938
14K (rose)..............................$700 $800 $1,000

AM. WALTHAM, 21J, stepped case, curved back
14k $150 $175 $275

AM. WALTHAM, 7-15 jewels, **wandering sec.**, c. 1930
gold filled............................... $75 $100 $175

AM. WALTHAM, 17 jewels, **wandering sec.**, c. 1930
gold filled................................ $75 $100 $175

AM. WALTHAM, wandering min., **jumping hour.**, c. 1933
gold filled............................... $375 $500 $750

AM. WALTHAM, 17J., center sec.
gold filled................................. $60 $75 $125

AM. WALTHAM, 17 jewels, center sec.
gold filled $60 $75 $125

AM. WALTHAM, 15 jewels, **winds at 12**, wire lugs, c. 1916
silver & enamel dial $250 $325 $500

AM. WALTHAM, 15 J., case by **Rolland Fischer**
silver $500 $600 $800

AM. WALTHAM, 15J., **enamel dial, center lugs**, c.1915
silver $200 $275 $450

AM. WALTHAM, 17J., **multi-color enamel dial**, c.1910s
gold filled..............................$125 $175 $300

AM. WALTHAM, 15J, **multi-color enamel dial**, Ca. 1920
base metal $125 $175 $300

AM. WALTHAM, 7-15J., **pulsations**, solid lugs, c.1925
silver $300 $375 $525

AM. WALTHAM, 17J.,"**Riverside**", **GJS**, c.1918
silver $400 $500 $650

AM. WALTHAM, 15 jewels, c. 1930
gold filled $60 $75 $125

AM. WALTHAM, 7J., **oxidized bezel**, c.1930s
gold filled $65 $100 $150

AM. WALTHAM, 7-15J., **cut corner dial**, c.1930s
gold filled $60 $85 $125

AM. WALTHAM, 15 jewels,
gold filled $60 $75 $125

AM. WALTHAM, 15J., **engraved oxidized bezel**,c.1930s
gold filled $75 $85 $135

AM. WALTHAM, 15J.,engraved case
gold filled $50 $65 $135

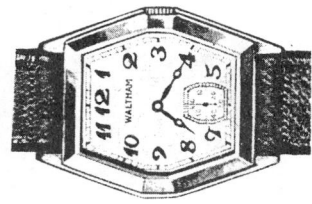

AM. WALTHAM, 17 jewels, 18K applied #s
silver $125 $150 $225

AM. WALTHAM, 7-15 jewels, engraved case
gold filled $75 $85 $125

AM. WALTHAM, 7-15 jewels, carved case
gold filled $75 $85 $135

AM. WALTHAM, 15 jewels, curved back
14k $150 $175 $235

AM. WALTHAM, 7-15 jewels, engraved case
gold filled $75 $85 $135

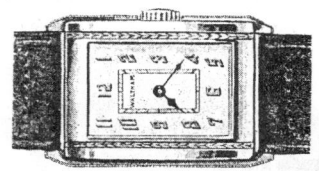

AM. WALTHAM, 17 jewels, 18K applied #s
14kw $175 $200 $275

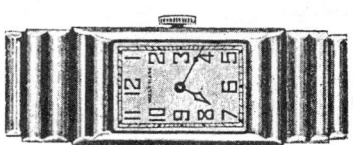

AM. WALTHAM, 15-17 jewels,
gold filled $60 $75 $125

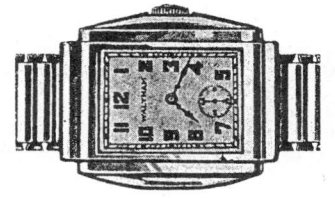

AM. WALTHAM, 7-15 jewels,
gold filled $60 $75 $125

AM. WALTHAM, 15J., case by Rolland Fischer,
silver $400 $500 $850

AM. WALTHAM, 15 jewels, "Depollier," early water
proof, (Canteen style), c. 1917
silver $350 $450 $900

AM. WALTHAM, 15 jewels, protective grill, c. 1907
gold filled...............................$250 $300 $425
14k $650 $750 $900

AM. WALTHAM, 15 jewels, protective grill, c. 1907
silver $250 $300 $450

AM. WALTHAM, 17 jewels, military with **hack setting**
s. steel $85 $125 $175

AM. WALTHAM, 17J., luminous dial, cut-corner style.
14k $150 $175 $250

AM. WALTHAM, 17 jewels, **WINDS at 12,** wire lugs
gold filled...............................$175 $200 $350

AM. WALTHAM, 17 jewels, **center lugs**
14k..$175 $200 $275

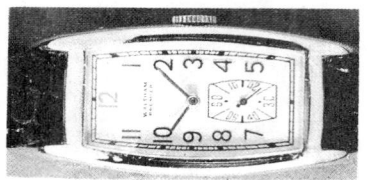

AM. WALTHAM, 17 jewels, **curvex, 42mm**
14k..$300 $350 $550

AM. WALTHAM, 17 jewels, **curvex, 52mm**
14k..$400 $500 $800

AM. WALTHAM, 17 jewels, **curvex, 42mm**
gold filled..............................$75 $100 $150

AM. WALTHAM, 17-21 jewels, curved
14k $150 $175 $250
gold filled $60 $75 $125

AM. WALTHAM, 17 jewels, curved, aux. sec.
gold filled $60 $75 $125

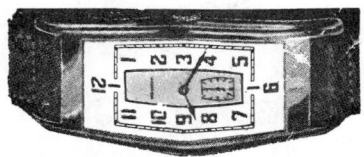

AM. WALTHAM, 17 jewels, curved
gold filled $60 $75 $125

AM. WALTHAM, 21 jewels, C.1938
14K..$150 $175 $250

AM. WALTHAM, 17 jewels, curved
gold filled $60 $75 $125

AM. WALTHAM, 17 jewels, curved
gold filled $60 $75 $125

AM. WALTHAM, 15J., **note bow swings, screw back case,
solid lugs, enamel dial, early water proof** , c. 1920s
14K...................★★★★★$1,000 $1,100 $1,500

AM. WALTHAM, 17 jewels, enamel bezel
14k..$550 $750 $950
14k (w) $500 $700 $800
gold filled $150 $225 $300

AM. WALTHAM,21J., enamel bezel,**"ruby"** model,c.1928
14k(w) $450 $575 $800

AM. WALTHAM,17J., **stepped case**
gold filled $60 $75 $125

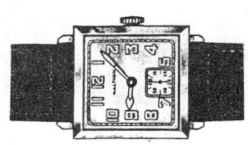

AM. WALTHAM, 15 jewels, square, 1929
gold filled $60 $75 $125

AM. WALTHAM, 7-15 jewels, cut corner, ca. 1929
gold filled.................................$50 $65 $100

AM. WALTHAM, 7J., luminous dial, c.1928
base metal................................$40 $50 $75

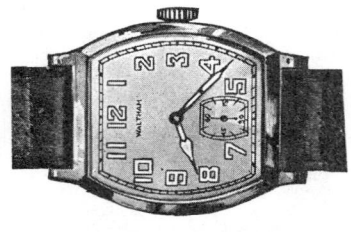

AM. WALTHAM, 17J., triangular, masonic symbols
fancy hands, **mother of pearl dial**, Ca. 1950
gold filled..............................$700 $850 $1,200

AM. WALTHAM, 7J., luminous dial, c. 1928
gold filled.................................$50 $65 $100

AM. WALTHAM, 7-15J., luminous dial, c.1928
base metal $40 $50 $75

AM. WALTHAM, 17J., luminous dial, c.1929
gold filled.................................$55 $70 $100
14k(w).....................................$165 $185 $250

AM. WALTHAM, 7-15J., cushion case, c.1928
gold filled.................................$50 $65 $100

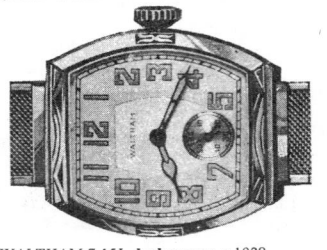

AM. WALTHAM, 17J., aux. sec., c. 1928
14k(w) $125 $150 $225

AM. WALTHAM, 7-15J., tonneau case, c. 1928
gold filled.................................$50 $65 $100

AM. WALTHAM, 7-15J., **lugless case**, c.1928
gold filled.................................$60 $75 $125

AM. WALTHAM,15J., generic, luminous dial, c.1928
14k $150 $175 $225

AM. WALTHAM,15J., generic style brush finish, c.1928
14k $175 $200 $275

AM. WALTHAM,7J., luminous dial, c.1928
gold plate $60 $75 $125

AM. WALTHAM,17J.,GJS, ca.1940
14K..$125 $150 $225

AM. WALTHAM,7-15J., cut corner case, c.1929
gold filled..................................$60 $75 $125

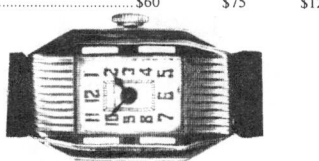

AM. WALTHAM,15J., **fluted case for men**, GJS, c.1925
14k(w)+enamel......................$150 $175 $250

AM. WALTHAM,7-15J., **Butler finish** = (smooth), c.1928
gold filled.................................$50 $65 $110

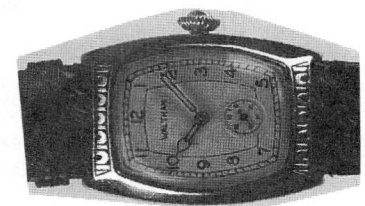

AM. WALTHAM, 7-15J., GJS, Ca.1927
14K(w) $150 $175 $225

AM. WALTHAM,7-15J., engraved case, etched dial, c.1929
14k(w) $50 $70 $100
gold filled..................................$20 $40 $70

AM. WALTHAM,15J., engraved case, etched dial, c.1928
14K(W) $95 $125 $175
gold filled..................................$20 $40 $65

AM. WALTHAM,7-15J., enamel case, c. 1928
14k(w) $70 $100 $150

AM. WALTHAM,15J., enamel case, c.1929
gold filled (w) $45 $75 $125

AMERICAN WALTHAM WATCH CO. IDENTIFICATION BY MOVEMENT

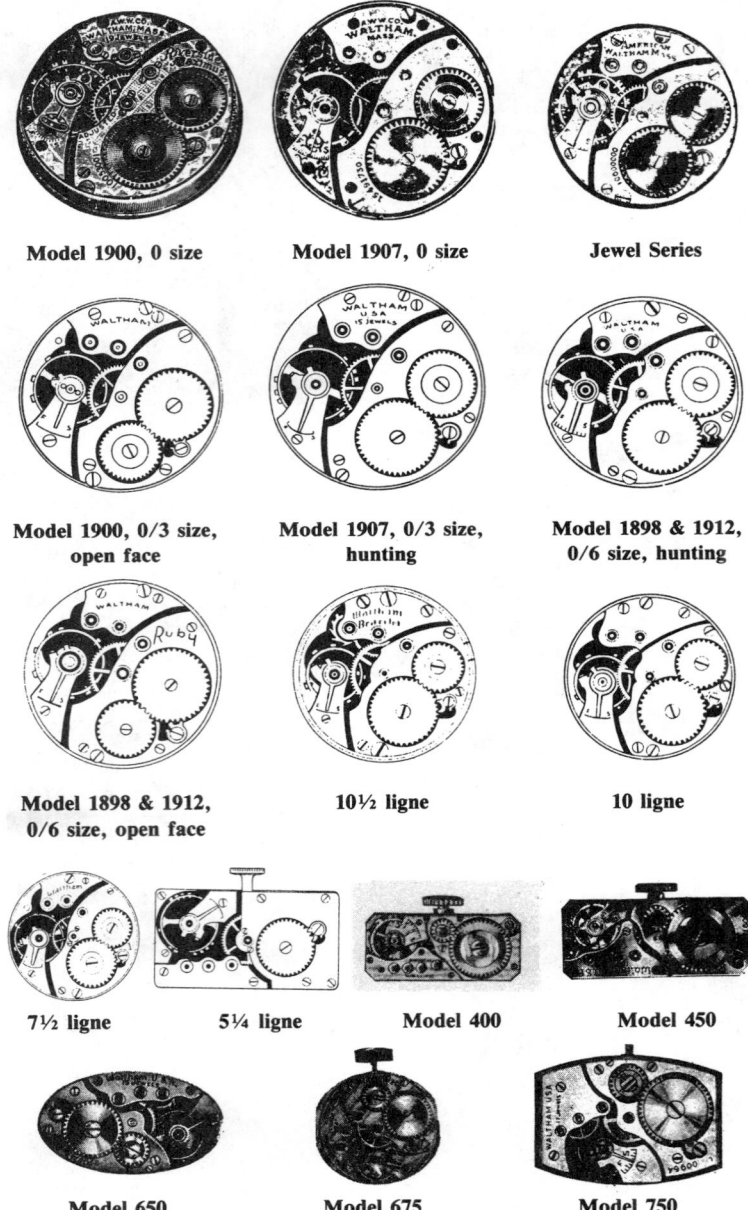

Model 1900, 0 size   Model 1907, 0 size   Jewel Series

Model 1900, 0/3 size,   Model 1907, 0/3 size,   Model 1898 & 1912,
open face   hunting   0/6 size, hunting

Model 1898 & 1912,   10½ ligne   10 ligne
0/6 size, open face

7½ ligne   5¼ ligne   Model 400   Model 450

Model 650   Model 675   Model 750

AMERICUS, 17 jewels, **8 day** movement, c. 1933

18k	★★★★$700	$800	$1,000
gold filled	★★$200	$300	$500
s. steel	★★$200	$300	$500

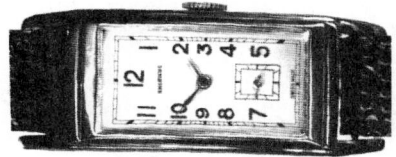

AMERICUS, 7 jewels, curved, c.1935

gold filled	$45	$60	$100

ANGELUS, 17 jewels, chronograph, 2 reg., c. 1943

18k	$450	$550	$800
14k	$300	$400	$650
gold filled	$150	$175	$250

ANGELUS, 17J., chronograph, **triple date,** C. 1949

s. steel	$300	$400	$500
14k	$600	$750	$1,000
18k	$1,000	$1,200	$1,600

ANGELUS, 17J., day, date, moon ph.,C. 1949

s. steel	$300	$350	$500

ANGELUS, 17 jewels, chronograph, 2 reg., water proof

14k	$400	$550	$700
18k	$500	$650	$900
s. steel	$200	$250	$350

ANGELUS, 17J., **date and alarm**, c.1955

s. steel	$75	$100	$200

ANGELUS, 27 jewels, **1/4 hour repeater**

s. steel	$2,500	$3,000	$4,000

ARAMIS, 15 jewels, **early self wind, lug action winding
by back & forth motion of watch case**, c. 1933
s. steel .... ★★$500 $650 $900

ARCTOS, 17J., "PARAT", world map on dial, c.1955
base metal................................$90 $125 $200

ARBU, 17 jewels, triple date, **moon phase**
18k $500 $650 $900
s. steel $180 $200 $300

ARDATH, 17J., chronograph, triple date, c.1947
s. steel....................................$200 $300 $450

ARBU, 17 jewels, chronograph, 3 reg., day-date-month
18k $500 $650 $900
s. steel $250 $300 $450

ARISTO, 17 jewels, chronog., water proof
14k...$400 $500 $750
s. steel....................................$125 $175 $225

ARBU, 17 jewels, **split second chronograph**
18k $2,500 $3,300 $4,500

ARISTO, 17J., chronog., 3 reg., **triple date**
14k...$800 $900 $1,200
s. steel....................................$250 $350 $600

ARISTO, 17 jewels, day-date-month, moon phase
s. steel $200 $300 $450

ARSA, 17 jewels, chronog., day-date-month, Ca. 1950
18k $600 $800 $1,200

ARSA, 17 jewels, day-date-month, moon phase
18k $600 $800 $1,100
s. steel $200 $325 $450

ARSA, 15 jewels, day-date-month, moon phase
18k $600 $750 $1,000
s. steel $200 $275 $400

ASPREY, 16 jewels, **curved hinged back**
9k...$125 $150 $250

ASPREY, 17J., **date,** ca. 1930s
14k...$250 $300 $400
gold filled................................$100 $125 $200

ASPREY, 15 jewels, **duo dial**
18k...$900 $1,100 $1,600

ASPREY, 17 jewels, **enamel dial, center lugs**
9k...$125 $150 $250

AUDAX, 15J., Ca.1938
9k...$75 $125 $200

🕐 Some grades are not included. Their values can be determined by comparing with **similar** age, size, metal content, style, grades, or models such as **time only,** chronograph, repeater etc. listed.

AUDEMARS PIGUET, 33J., **minute** repeater, gold train,
platinum & 18K with **40** diamond bezel, diamond dial & diamonds on band
18K & platinum.................$60,000 $70,000 $90,000

AUDEMARS PIGUET, Royal Oak Offshore, auto wind,
Chronograph, 10 atmospheres
s. steel................................$5,500 $6,000 $7,000

AUDEMARS PIGUET, 29 J., **minute repeater**, c. 1917
18k $55,000 $65,000 $80,000

AUDEMARS PIGUET, 33J., day date, moon ph., c.1989
18k.......................................$2,500 $2,800 $3,500

AUDEMARS PIGUET, 29 J., **minute repeater**, c. 1925
platinum $65,000 $75,000 $100,000

AUDEMARS PIGUET, day date, moon ph., C. 1980s
18k.......................................$2,200 $2,400 $3,000

AUDEMARS PIGUET, 19 J., **tourbillon**, self-winding
tourbillon can be seen from dial side
18k $6,000 $7,000 $9,000

AUDEMARS PIGUET, chronograph, triple date, moon ph.,
tear drop lugs, Ca. 1940s
18k.......................................$16,000 $18,000 $22,000

AUDEMARS PIGUET, 36 jewels, gold rotor, day-date
month, moon phase, perpetual
18 k C&B $9,000 $10,000 $11,500

AUDEMARS PIGUET, skeletonized, triple date,
moon phase, perpetual , C. 1980s
platinum $16,000 $18,000 $22,000

AUDEMARS PIGUET, 17 J., chronog., 3 reg., c. 1945
s.steel $8,000 $9,000 $11,000
18k $12,000 $13,000 $15,000

AUDEMARS PIGUET, 18 J., "Le Brassus," **chronog.**
skeletonized
18k C&B $7,000 $8,000 $10,000

AUDEMARS PIGUET, 22 jewels, chronog., 2 reg.,
s.steel $7,000 $8,000 $10,000
18k $14,000 $15,000 $16,000

AUDEMARS PIGUET, 18 jewels, skeletonized
18k $3,500 $4,000 $5,500

AUDEMARS PIGUET, 18 J., triple date, moonphase
18k $3,500 $4,000 $5,000

AUDEMARS PIGUET, **Star Wheel**, showing the passing of
time on Sapphire discs bearing the hours and moving over a
concentric circular aperture showing the minutes
18k $3,500 $4,500 $6,000

AUDEMARS PIGUET, 36 jewels, skeletonized
18k $4,000 $5,000 $7,000

AUDEMARS PIGUET, 17 J., center lugs, skeletonized
18k $3,500 $4,500 $6,500

AUDEMARS PIGUET, 17J., Dodecagonal, black dial
18k $1,200 $1,300 $1,600

AUDEMARS PIGUET, 17J., diamond dial, c. 1970
18k $1,500 $1,600 $1,900

AUDEMARS PIGUET, 12 diamond dial c.1960
platinum $2,000 $2,200 $2,500

AUDEMARS PIGUET, 11 diamond dial
18k $1,400 $1,600 $2,000

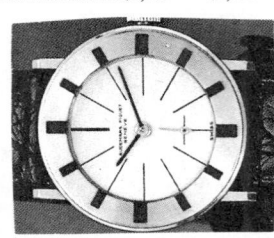

AUDEMARS PIGUET, 12 sapphire dial, c.1950
18k $2,000 $2,200 $2,600

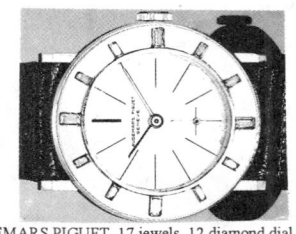

AUDEMARS PIGUET, 17 jewels, 12 diamond dial
18k (w) $2,200 $2,400 $2,800

AUDEMARS PIGUET, 36 jewels, self-winding
18k $1,200 $1,400 $1,700

AUDEMARS PIGUET, 17 jewels, adj. to 5 positions
18k C&B.............................$1,400 $1,600 $2,000

AUDEMARS PIGUET, 17 jewels, rope style bezel
18k C&B $1,500 $1,700 $2,000

AUDEMARS PIGUET, 36 jewels, self-winding
18k $1,500 $1,700 $2,000

AUDEMARS PIGUET, 17J., diamond bezel, center lugs
18k $2,000 $2,200 $2,500

AUDEMARS PIGUET, 36 jewels, lazuli dial
18k C&B $2,000 $2,200 $2,600

AUDEMARS PIGUET, 20J., rope style bezel, c. 1980s
18k case, 14k band $1,000 $1,100 $1,300

AUDEMARS PIGUET, 17 jewels, thin style
18k C&B $2,000 $2,200 $2,600

AUDEMARS PIGUET, 20J., "Le Brassus," c. 1970
18k C&B $2,000 $2,200 $2,600

AUDEMARS PIGUET, 17 jewels, fancy bezel, c. 1950
18k $1,800 $2,000 $2,500

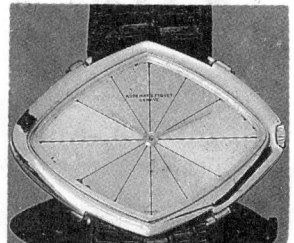

AUDEMARS PIGUET, fancy shaped, c.1960s
18k $4,000 $4,500 $6,000

AUDEMARS PIGUET, 17J., "Philosopher", hour hand only
18k $3,000 $3,500 $4,500

AUDEMARS PIGUET, 20 jewels, thin model
18k $800 $1,000 $1,300

AUDEMARS PIGUET, 17J., engraved bezel, c. 1963
18k $1,200 $1,400 $1,800

AUDEMARS PIGUET, 17J., wide bezel, thin model
14k C&B $1,200 $1,400 $1,800

AUDEMARS PIGUET, 21J., auto wind, center sec.
18k $1,600 $1,800 $2,200

🕐 Pricing in this Guide are fair market price for **COMPLETE** watches which are reflected from the "**NAWCC**" National and regional shows.
🕐 A collector should expect to pay modestly higher prices at local shops.

AUDEMARS PIGUET, **painted world time**, fancy lugs
s. steel $7,000 $8,000 $10,000

AUDEMARS PIGUET, **painted world time**, c. 1940s
14k $8,000 $9,000 $10,000

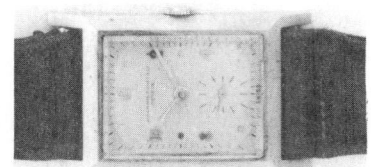

AUDEMARS PIGUET, 18 jewels, gold train
18k $2,500 $2,800 $3,500

AUDEMARS PIGUET, 18J., **hidden lugs**, Ca. 1950
18k $1,000 $1,200 $1,600

AUDEMARS PIGUET, 18 jewels, aux. sec. c. 1940
18k $1,200 $1,400 $1,800

AUDEMARS PIGUET, 17 jewels, for Tiffany & Co.
18k C&B $2,000 $2,200 $2,600

AUDEMARS PIGUET, 18 jewels, aux. sec.
18k $1,600 $1,700 $2,000

AUDEMARS PIGUET, 18 jewels, tank style, c. 1960
18k (w).................................$1,400 $1,500 $1,800

AUDEMARS PIGUET, 18 jewels, hooded lugs
18k $1,800 $2,000 $2,400

AUDEMARS PIGUET, 17J., engraved bezel, c.1966
18k $900 $1,000 $1,200

AUDEMARS PIGUET, 18J., no second hand, Ca. 1965
18k $800 $900 $1,100

AUDEMARS PIGUET, 18 jewels, center sec., c. 1950
18k $1,400 $1,500 $1,800

AUDEMARS PIGUET,18J., straight line lever escape.
18k $900 $1,000 $1,300

AUDEMARS PIGUET, 17 jewels, mid-size
18k $500 $600 $800

AUDEMARS PIGUET, 18J., mid size, **flat bezel**, Ca. 1969
18k $900 $1,000 $1,300

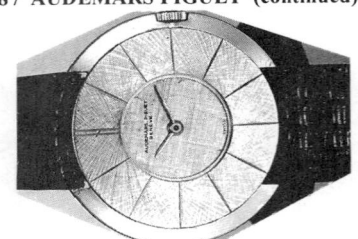

AUDEMARS PIGUET, gold textured dial, c.1960s
18k $900 $1,000 $1,200

AUDEMARS PIGUET,18J., aux. sec., c. 1950s
18k $1,000 $1,200 $1,500

AUDEMARS PIGUET, 18J., auto wind, waterproof
18k $1,600 $1,800 $2,200

AUDEMARS PIGUET, 18 jewels, **painted dial**, c. 1970
18k $800 $900 $1,100

AUDEMARS PIGUET, 21J., sweep sec., automatic -18k rotor
18k $1,700 $1,900 $2,300

AUDEMARS PIGUET, 19J., center sec.
18k $1,400 $1,600 $2,000

AUDEMARS PIGUET, 18J., Manual wind, waterproof
18k $1,500 $1,700 $2,000

AUDEMARS PIGUET, 17 jewels, gold train
18k $1,000 $1,200 $1,500

AUDEMARS PIGUET, **triple date, moon ph.**, c.1930s
18k $12,000 $14,000 $18,000

AUDEMARS PIGUET, 18 J.," **top hat**", aux. sec., c. 1950
platinum.............................$3,000 $3,500 $4,500

Wrist Watches listed in this section are priced at the collectable fair market **Trade Show** level as **complete** watches having an original gold-filled case and stainless steel back, also with original dial, leather watch band, and the entire original movement in good working order with no repairs needed.

AUDEMARS PIGUET, 17J., gold train, 2 tone case in platinum & gold
18k (w) C&B $2,500 $2,700 $3,000

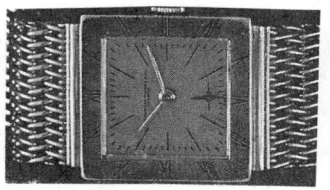

AUDEMARS PIGUET, engraved bezel, c.1950s
18k $1,500 $1,800 $2,500

AUDEMARS PIGUET, 17 jewels, gold train
14k C&B $1,200 $1,400 $2,000

AUDEMARS PIGUET, 18 J., textured bezel, c. 1950
18k $1,200 $1,400 $1,800

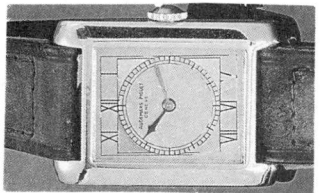

AUDEMARS PIGUET, 2 tone dial, c.1930s
18k $2,500 $3,000 $4,000

🕐 Some grades are not included. Their values can be determined by comparing with **similar** age, size, metal content, style, grades, or models such as **time only**, chronograph, repeater etc. listed.

AUDEMARS PIGUET, 18J, curvex, large bezel, c. 1950
18k $1,500 $1,700 $2,000

AUDEMARS PIGUET, 18 jewels, tank style, c. 1950's
18k $1,500 $1,700 $2,000

AUDEMARS PIGUET, Royal Oak, **date,** auto wind, c.1973
18K & s. steel $2,500 $2,800 $4,000
18K C&B $5,000 $5,500 $7,000
18K C&B,day/date/moonphase. $6,000 $6,500 $8,000
18K C&B,perpetual/moonph. $12,000 $13,000 $15,000
s. steel, auto wind $1,700 $1,800 $2,000
s. steel, LARGE, auto wind $2,100 $2,200 $2,400
2-tone, LARGE, auto wind . $2,500 $2,800 $3,400
Ladies 18K C&B, ... $2,500 $3,000 $4,000
Ladies 18K C&B,day/date/ auto $3,500 $4,000 $5,500
Note: Add 20% for new style button release clasp.

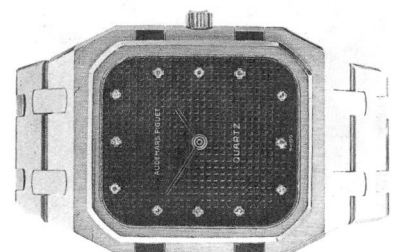

AUDEMARS PIGUET, quartz, 12 diamonds, c. 1981
s. steel $1,200 $1,300 $1,600

AUDEMARS PIGUET, Ladies, 72 small diamonds, C. 1930's
plat. case & band $1,800 $2,000 $2,500

AUTORIST, 15 jewels, **lug action wind**, c. 1930
gold filled $400 $450 $600

AUDEMARS PIGUET, ladys, 36 diamonds, c.1930s
plat.case $1,500 $1,700 $2,000

AUTORIST, 15 jewels, **lug action wind**, (lady's)
s. steel $150 $200 $300

AUTOMATIQUE, 17J., cal.F699, c. 1955
s. steel $40 $50 $75

AVALON,17J., aux.sec.
gold filled $30 $45 $75

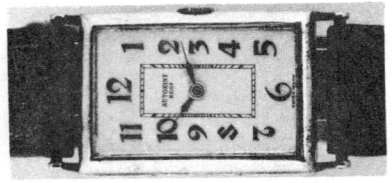

AUTORIST, 15 jewels, **lug action wind**, enamel dial
s. steel $300 $350 $500

AVALON,17J., aux.sec.
gold filled $35 $45 $75

AUTORIST, 15 jewels, **lug action wind**, c. 1930
s. steel $300 $350 $500

BALL W. CO., 25 jewels, "Trainmaster", auto wind,
adj. to 5 pos., E.T.A.
10k $250 $300 $400

BALL W. CO., 25 jewels, "Trainmaster"auto wind,
adj. to 5 pos., E.T.A.
gold filled.................................$125 $150 $225

BALL W. CO., 25 jewels, "Trainmaster"auto wind,
adj. to 5 pos., E.T.A.
s. steel $125 $150 $225
s. steel (manual wind)............$125 $165 $250

BAUME & MERCIER, 18J., triple date, moon phase
s. steel $400 $450 $600

BAUME & MERCIER, 17J., chronog., 2 reg., c.1949
gold filled................................$250 $300 $400

BAUME & MERCIER, 17J., chronog., 2 reg.,c.1950s
18k $500 $600 $750

BAUME & MERCIER, 18J., chronog., 3 reg. & dates
s. steel $350 $400 $550

BAUME & MERCIER, 18 J., chronog., 3 reg. & dates
18k $1,000 $1,200 $1,400

BAUME & MERCIER, 18 jewels, **tachymeter**, c. 1940
s. steel, original black dial $500 $600 $800

BAUME & MERCIER, 17J., triple date, chronog.
moon ph., c.1950s
18k $1,300 $1,500 $1,900

BAUME & MERCIER, 17J., 2 dials, 2 time zones &
2 movements
18k $500 $600 $800

BAUME & MERCIER, 18 J., chronog., fancy lugs
18k $1,800 $2,100 $2,600

BAUME & MERCIER, 18 jewels, gold dial, date
14k C&B................................ $500 $600 $800

BAUME & MERCIER, 17J., chronog., triple date
18k $1,000 $1,200 $1,500

BAUME & MERCIER, 18 jewels, thin model
14k C&B................................ $400 $450 $550

BAUME & MERCIER, 18J., triple date, moon phase
18k $800 $1,000 $1,300

BAUME & MERCIER, 17 jewels, center sec., c. 1956
14k $200 $250 $350

BAUME & MERCIER, 17J, fancy lugs, aux. sec., c. 1955
14k $250 $300 $400

BAUME & MERCIER, 17J., RF#49300, c. 1965
14k $150 $175 $225

BAUME & MERCIER, 18 J., "Riviera", date, c. 1980s
18k & s. steel $400 $450 $525

BAUME & MERCIER, **quartz**, enamel dial, tank, c.1990s
14k $300 $350 $550

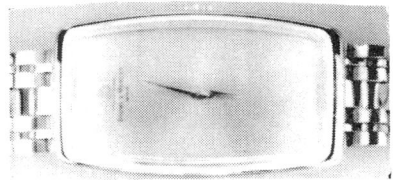

BAUME & MERCIER, 17J., curved, c. 1990s
14k C&B $500 $600 $800

BAUME & MERCIER,17J., sec. window, auto-w., c.1950s
base metal $100 $125 $175

BAUME & MERCIER, 17J.,diam. mystery dial, c.1950s
14k(W)....................................$500 $600 $800

BAYLOR, 17J., hidden lugs
gold filled $40 $55 $75
14k $125 $150 $200

BAYLOR, 17J., diamond on bezel & dial, c.1948
14k $175 $200 $275

BELTONE, 17J., fancy hidden lugs
14k $135 $150 $175

BEMONTOIR, 15J., enamel dial, c.1920
14k $100 $125 $175

BENRUS, 15 jewels, quick change date
gold filled $65 $75 $125

BENRUS,17J., day date
base metal $25 $30 $60

BENRUS,17J.,"Sky Chief", chronog., 3-reg., c.1945
s. steel $225 $250 $325

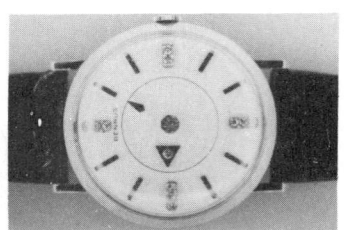

BENRUS, 18J., mystery-diamond dial
18k $250 $300 $400
gold filled................................$75 $100 $175

BENRUS,17J.,"Sky Chief",**triple date**,chronog.,c.1940s
s. steel $300 $325 $400

BENRUS, 15 jewels, day, date, c. 1948
s. steel $55 $65 $100

🕐 Pricing in this Guide are fair market price for **COMPLETE** watches which are reflected from the "**NAWCC**" National and regional shows.
🕐 A collector should expect to pay modestly higher prices at local shops

BENRUS,17J.,Wrist Alarm c.1945
base metal $100 $150 $225

BENRUS, 15 jewels, calendar, auto wind, fancy lugs, c.1950

14k	$100	$125	$200
gold filled	$60	$75	$125

BENRUS, 15 jewels, jumping hour, wandering min.

gold filled	$125	$150	$225
s. steel	$100	$125	$175

BENRUS, 15J., auto wind, fancy bezel, by ETA, c. 1950

gold filled	$40	$50	$95
14k	$100	$125	$200

BENRUS,17J., fancy lugs

gold filled	$50	$75	$125

BENRUS,17J., jumping hour, wandering min., Ca. 1958
Chevron style case

gold filled	$150	$175	$300

BENRUS,17J., fancy lugs

gold filled	$50	$60	$95

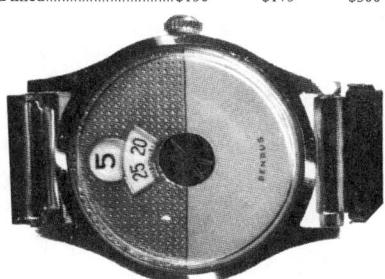

BENRUS,17J., dial-0-rama, direct read, c. 1958

gold filled	$150	$175	$300

Wrist Watches listed in this section are priced at the collectable fair market **Trade Show** level as **complete** watches having an original gold-filled case and stainless steel back, also with original dial, leather watch band, and the entire original movement in good working order with no repairs needed.

BENRUS,21J., Diamond Dial, Ca. 1956

14K	$100	$125	$195

⏱ Some grades are not included. Their values can be determined by comparing with **similar** age, size, metal content, style, grades, or models such as **time only**, chronograph, repeater etc. listed.

BENRUS, 15 jewels, fancy lugs, **recased**, c. 1948
14k $75 $100 $150
gold filled.................................$55 $65 $95

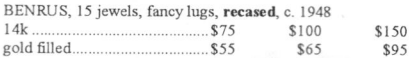

BENRUS, 15J., auto-wind, **water-proof**
gold filled..................................$50 $60 $95

BENRUS, 15 jewels, fancy bezel, cal. BB14
14k $150 $175 $225
gold filled..................................$75 $100 $150

BENRUS, 21J., aux. sec., c. 1950s
14k $90 $125 $195

🕐 Pricing in this Guide are fair market price for **COMPLETE** watches which are reflected from the "**NAWCC**" National and regional shows.

🕐 Some grades are not included. Their values can be determined by comparing with **similar** age, size, metal content, style, grades, or models such as **time only**, chronograph, repeater etc. listed.

BENRUS, 17J., **wind indicator,** c.1955
gold filled $60 $70 $125

BENRUS, 21J., aux. sec., fancy lugs, c.1950
gold filled $50 $65 $100

BENRUS, 17J., hidden lugs
14K $100 $125 $200

BENRUS, 17J., cadillac logo, c.1950s
gold plate $40 $50 $85

BENRUS, 17J., by ETA, c.1955
gold filled $40 $50 $95

BENRUS, 15J., engraved bezel, c.1935
14k $100 $125 $175

BENRUS, 17J., rhinestone dial, c. 1945
gold filled...................................$50 $65 $95

BENRUS, 17J., date, fancy lugs, c.1950
gold filled...................................$55 $75 $125

BENRUS, 17J., aux. sec., c.1940
14k $100 $125 $175

BENRUS, 15J.,aux sec.
gold filled...................................$50 $60 $95

Ⓛ Pricing in this Guide are fair market price for **COMPLETE**
watches which are reflected from the "**NAWCC**" National and
regional shows.

BENRUS,17J., **flared case**, cal.180, c. 1951
gold filled $50 $75 $125

BENRUS, 7J., rhinestone dial, fancy lugs, c. 1948
base metal $30 $40 $60

BENRUS,17J., rhinestone dial, cal. bb1, c. 1945
gold plate $30 $40 $60

BENRUS, 15J.,stepped case
gold filled $30 $40 $60

BENRUS, 15J.,fancy lugs
14K $150 $175 $225

BENRUS, 17J., hidden lugs, cal.11ax, Ca.1951
14k $125 $150 $225

BENRUS, 15J., fancy hooded lugs, cal#ax11, Ca.1946
14K..$125 $150 $225

BENRUS, 15J., **enamel bezel,** c. 1930
14k (w)................................$200 $250 $325

BENRUS, 15 jewels, 26 diamond bezel
14k (w)................................$250 $275 $350

BENRUS,17J., aux sec., Ca.1935
gold filled..............................$40 $50 $85

BENRUS, 15 jewels, **flip-top case,** c. 1940
gold filled $250 $300 $400

BENRUS,17J., hooded lugs, c.1948
14k $125 $150 $200

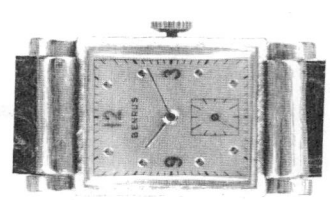

BENRUS,17J., hooded lugs, cal.AX11, c. 1950
14k $150 $175 $225

BENRUS, 15 jewels, hooded lugs
gold filled $60 $70 $95

BENRUS, 15 jewels, cal. AX, 3 small diam. dial, c. 1950
14k $125 $150 $225

Wrist Watches listed in this section are priced at the collectable
fair market **Trade Show** level as **complete** watches having an
original gold-filled case and stainless steel back, also with
original dial, leather watch band, and the entire original movement in good working order with no repairs needed.

BENRUS, 17 jewels, curved, rhinestones , hooded lugs
14k $150 $175 $225

BENRUS, 15 jewels, curved back, c. 1942
gold filled................................$60 $70 $90

BENSON, 15 jewels, of London, aux sec. c.1930s
9k $95 $125 $175

BENSON, 15J., of London, Ca.1938
9k $95 $125 $175

BENSON, 15 jewels, enamel dial, tank style case
9k $195 $235 $300

♕ Some grades are not included. Their values can be determined by comparing with **similar** age, size, metal content, style, grades, or models such as **time only**, chronograph, repeater etc. listed.

BENSON, 15 jewels, enamel dial, flared case
9k $200 $250 $350

BENSON, 15 jewels, enamel dial, 2-tone flared case
9k $275 $325 $425

BERG, 25J., auto-wind, c.1959
14k $125 $140 $175

BLANCPAIN, 23J, day-date-month, perpetual, auto-wind
s. steel- perpetual................$3,000 $3,500 $4,500
18K - perpetual...................$4,000 $5,500 $7,000

BLANCPAIN, 17J.,hooded lugs, c.1945
14k $195 $225 $300

BLANCPAIN, 16J., fancy lugs, Ca.1958
14K..$150 $175 $250

BOILLAT FRERES, 17 jewels, "Blita," waterproof
s. steel $35 $45 $60

E. BOREL, 17 jewels, chronometer, aux. sec.
18k $175 $225 $300
gold filled..................................$30 $40 $65

E. BOREL, 17J., cocktail style, c.1960s
gold filled..................................$50 $60 $90
s. steel $45 $50 $80

⊕ A collector should expect to pay modestly higher prices at local shops.

⊕ Some grades are not included. Their values can be determined by comparing with **similar** age, size, metal content, style, grades, or models such as **time only**, chronograph, repeater etc. listed.

E. BOREL, 17J., cocktail dial, date, c. 1969
base metal $30 $40 $65

E. BOREL, 15J., hour dial, min. dial, center sec., c.1940
s. steel $95 $125 $195

E. BOREL, 17 jewels, auto wind, date
gold filled $55 $65 $95

BOUCHERON, 17J., c.1930s
18k $400 $500 $700

Wrist Watches listed in this section are priced at the collectable fair market rade Trade Show **retail** level as **complete** watches having an original gold-filled case and stainless steel back, also with original dial, leather watch band, and the entire original movement in good working order with no repairs needed.

⊕ Pricing in this Guide are fair market price for **COMPLETE** watches which are reflected from the "**NAWCC**" National and regional shows.

BOULEVARD, 17J., "STOP", c.1950s
s. steel $75 $95 $195

BOVET, 17 jewels, chronog., 2 reg., c. 1940
s. steel $150 $175 $250

BOVET, 17 jewels, chronog., triple date & 3 reg.
14k $700 $800 $1,000
gold filled................................$375 $425 $500

BREGUET, 21 jewels, skeletonized
18k C&B $6,000 $7,000 $9,000

BREGUET, 17J., chronog., triple date, Ca.1950
s. steel $6,000 $7,000 $9,000

BREGUET, auto-w., triple date, moon ph., perpetual
18k $15,000 $16,000 $20,000

BREGUET, jump hour, c.1980s, **total made =50**
18k $9,000 $10,000 $12,000

BREGUET,37J., auto-w.,date, moon ph.,45 hr.wind ind.
18k $12,000 $13,000 $15,000

BREGUET, 17 jewels, silver dial, thin model
18k $1,200 $1,300 $1,600

BREGUET, 17 jewels, curvex
platinum...............................$3,000 $3,500 $5,000

P. BREGUETTE, 17J., gold jewel settings, Ca.1948
14k $125 $150 $225

P. BREGUETTE, 17J., gold jewel settings, flared case
14k $175 $200 $250

P. BREGUETTE, 17 jewels, top hat, diamond dial, c. 1940
14k $500 $600 $750

P. BREGUETTE, 17J., triple date, c.1960s
gold filled $125 $150 $200
s. steel $100 $125 $175

Breitling, 17 J., Precision, red & blue Tacky.-rings, Ca1940h
s. steel $1,200 $1,300 $1,500

Breitling, 17 J., "Chronomat," slide rule bezel
18k $2,000 $2,200 $2,500
gold filled $900 $1,000 $1,200
s. steel $800 $900 $1,100

Breitling, 17 J., **Navitimer,** date, slide rule bezel, RF 7806
s. steel $1,100 $1,200 $1,400

BREITLING, 17J., **Chronomat.**, RF 808, c.1950
gold filled.................................$900 $1,000 $1,200

BREITLING, 18J., date, moon ph., split chronog. 3 reg.
18k $8,000 $9,000 $11,000

BREITLING, 17J., chronog., RF#1199, sq. button, c.1958
s. steel $400 $450 $525

BREITLING, 17 J., chronog., "Navitimer," RF 806
18K C&B............................$5,000 $5,500 $6,000
18K case only $4,000 $4,500 $5,500
gold filled $1,100 $1,200 $1,500
s. steel $1,000 $1,100 $1,400

BREITLING, 17J., chronog., "Cosmonaute", **24 hour,** 3 reg.
18k $4,500 $5,000 $6,500
s. steel $1,000 $1,100 $1,400

BREITLING, 17 J., chronog., "Cosmonaute," 24 HR.
s. steel $1,000 $1,100 $1,400

AOPA logo ☞

A.O.P.A., the initials of Aircraft Owners & Pilots Association,
This logo first appeared in 1952 on the "*Navitimer*", a word
derived from <u>Navi</u>gation, **Navi** + the word Timer. The AOPA
logo and other logos are being collected such as Blue Angles
(*U.S.Navy*), Red Arrow (*Royal Air Force*), Frecce Tricolori
(*Aeronautica Militare Italiana*), Patrouille Suisse (*Escadre de
Surveillance*), Thunderbirds (*U.S. Air Force*), Blue Impulse
(*Japan Self Defense Force*), Team 60 (*Swedish Air Force*)
Patrouille de France (*French Air Force*) and others.

BREITLING, 17 jewels, split sec. chronog., 2 reg.
s. steel $4,000 $5,000 $6,500

BREITLING, 17 J., chronog., "Chronomat," 3 reg.
s. steel $600 $700 $900

BREITLING, 17 J., telemeter, 1 button, hinged lugs
s. steel- 44mm......................... $850 $950 $1,150

BREITLING, 17 J., **AOPA** logo Navitimer, Ca. 1952
s. steel $1,100 $1,200 $1,500

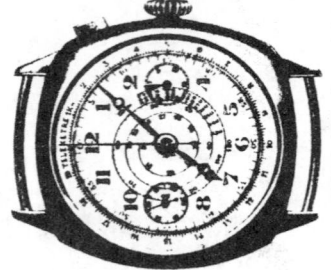

BREITLING, 17 jewels, tachymeter, Ca.1925
s. steel $1,200 $1,500 $2,000

BREITLING, 17 jewels, chronog., pulsations
s. steel $600 $700 $850

BREITLING, 17 jewels, chronog., 2 reg.
s. steel :................................. $1,000 $1,100 $1,300

BREITLING, 17 jewels, tachymeter, center hinged lugs
s. steel - 35mm $800 $900 $1,200

BREITLING, 17J., chronog., RF#765, c.1960
14k $1,400 $1,600 $2,000
s. steel $700 $900 $1,200

BREITLING, 17 jewels, chronog., Toptime, 24 HR.
s. steel $425 $550 $800

BREITLING, 17 jewels, chronog., 2 reg. RF#790
18K **refinished dial**...............$800 $900 $1,100
18K original dial.................$1,200 $1,400 $1,700

BREITLING, 17J., chronog., 2 reg., "Premier", RF#790
18k $1,600 $1,800 $2,200

BREITLING, 17J., chronog., 3 reg., RF#787, c.1942
14k C&B $1,200 $1,400 $1,800

BREITLING, 17 jewels, chronog., "Premier," 3 reg.
s. steel $500 $600 $800

BREITLING, 17 J., chronog., day-date-month, 3 reg.
18k.......................................$2,000 $2,200 $2,500
s. steel $800 $900 $1,100

BREITLING, 17 jewels, chronog., 2 reg. RF # 178
s. steel $375 $450 $550

BREITLING, 17 jewels, chronog., 2 reg. RF # 769
18k $1,200 $1,300 $1,500
s. steel $275 $325 $425

BREITLING, 17 J., **split sec.** chronog., "Duograph", C.1945
18k $7,000 $8,000 $10,000
s. steel $4,000 $5,000 $7,000

BREITLING, 17J., **Super Ocean**, RF # 2005, c.1960
s. steel $1,000 $1,200 $1,500

BREITLING, 17J., chronog., 3 reg., RF#815, c.1968
gold filled..............................$600 $700 $900

BREITLING, 17J., chronog., RF#2110, c.1970
s. steel $400 $450 $550

BREITLING, 17J., **AOPA** logo , Toptime, RF#810, c.1968
s. steel $650 $750 $950

BREITLING, 17J., chronog., RF#2009-33, c. 1975
s. steel $325 $350 $400

BREITLING, 17J., **Tour de France**, c. 1945
18K...$1,200 $1,400 $1,700

BREITLING, 17J., **Co-Pilot**, enamel bezel, RF # 765, c. 1960
s. steel $1,300 $1,500 $2,000

BREITLING, 17J., **Cosmonaute II**, 24 hr., Ca.1990
s.steel C&B..........................$1,100 $1,200 $1,400

BREITLING,17J., "Blue Angel 92", **total production 1,000**
S. steel & gold bezel $1,800 $2,000 $2,400

BREITLING, 17J., **Old Navitimer II**, gold bezel, Ca.1990
s.steel & G-Bezel....................$900 $1,000 $1,200

BREITLING, 17J., **Corono QP**, day date moon ph., Ca.1990
18K C&B.............................$6,000 $7,000 $9,000

BREITLING, 17J., **Navitimer 92**, self-wind, Ca.1992
s.steel case $1,200 $1,300 $1,500
18K case $3,500 $4,000 $4,800

BREITLING, 17J., **Corono 1461**, day date moon ph., c.1990
s.steel C&B.........................$2,100 $2,300 $2,600

BREITLING, 17J., **Chronomat**, date, self-wind, Ca.1990
s.steel $1,200 $1,300 $1,600
18K & s.steel C&B..............$2,300 $2,400 $2,600

BREITLING, 17J., **Chrono Longitude**, date, Ca.1990
s.steel & gold C&B $1,500 $1,600 $1,800

BREITLING, 17J., **Chronomat Yachting**, date, Ca.1990
s.steel C&B..........................$1,100 $1,200 $1,400

BREITLING, 17J., **Navitimer Airborne**, date, Ca.1990
s.steel case $1,300 $1,500 $1,800

BREITLING, 17J., **Chrono Cockpit**, date, Ca.1990
18K & s.steel C&B..............$1,500 $1,600 $1,800

BREITLING, 17J., **Navitimer AVI**, date, Ca.1990
s.steel case $700 $800 $1,000
Note: **UTC** (Universal Time Coordinated), small Quartz that is
fitted between lugs & used for second time zone = **$300 to $400**

BREITLING, "Golden Knights", only 50 made, **only 20 made available to general public**, to bring top price watch should have a factory letter, papers & 2 boxes. (**U.S. Army**)
s. steel $1,500 $1,600 $2,000

BREITLING, "Blue Angels Limited Edition", only 100 made, **only 25 made available to general public**, to bring top price watch should have a factory letter, papers & 2 boxes.
Sonic Minute Repeater   (**U.S. Navy**)
Titanium.............................. $3,000 $3,200 $4,000

BREITLING, "Top Gun", Limited Edition, 1,000 made
s. steel & gold bezel $1,250 $1,400 $1,800

BREITLING,"Blue Angels Limited Edition 96", Montbrillant
18K...................................... $4,000 $4,500 $6,000

BLUE ANGELS
U.S. Navy
NAS Pensacola,
McDonnell Douglas
F/A-18 Hornet
MONTBRILLANT – 1996

BREITLING, "Team 60", Limited Edition, 1,000 made,
Pluton model, Ca. 1995
s. steel $550 $650 $900

BUCHERER,17 jewels, note: day date in lugs
18k $400 $500 $700

BREITLING, 17J., chronog., RF#1450, 3 reg., c.1970
s. steel $300 $350 $450

BREITLING, 17J., day date month,
18k $300 $350 $450

BUCHERER,17 jewels, chronog., 2 reg.
18k $475 $500 $600

BREITLING, 21J., "UNITIME", date, 24 hour, c.1958
gold filled.............................. $900 $1,100 $1,500
18k $1,800 $2,000 $2,500

BUCHERER, 17J., chronog., 2 reg., C.1959
18k $400 $450 $600
s. steel $250 $300 $375

BUCHERER, 25 J., triple date moon ph., cal.693, c.1950
18k $700 $800 $1,000

BREITLING, 21J., auto-wind, rf#2528, c.1959
s. steel $50 $75 $125

BUCHERER, 21 J., 3 dates, moon ph., diamond dial
18k $2,000 $2,200 $2,500

BUECHE-GIROD, 17J., dual time movements,
18k $500 $600 $800

BUCHERER, 15 jewels, **8 day** movement
18k $700 $800 $1,000
gold filled...............................$300 $350 $500

BUECHE-GIROD, 17 jewels, tank style case
18k $500 $550 $650

BUECHE-GIROD, 17 J., day-date-month, moon ph.
s. steel $325 $375 $500

BUECHE-GIROD, 17 jewels
18k C&B..............................$500 $550 $650

P. BUHRE, 17 jewels, aux. sec.
gold filled $40 $50 $75

BUECHE-GIROD, 17J., by Piguet, cal.99, c.1975
18k $350 $400 $500

🕐 Some grades are not included. Their values can be
determined by comparing with **similar** age, size, metal
content, style, grades, or models such as **time only**,
chronograph, repeater etc. listed.

Wrist Watches listed in this section are priced at the collectable
fair market **Trade Show** level as **complete** watches having an
original gold-filled case and stainless steel back, also with
original dial, leather watch band, and the entire original movement in good working order with no repairs needed.

P. BUHRE, 17J., alarm, C.1956
s. steel $50 $75 $100

BULOVA WATCH CO.

In 1875 Joseph Bulova starts a wholesale jewelry business. Basically, it was always a Swiss-USA company & in 1930 Bulova sets up to make bridges and plates at Woodside, NY. By 1934 the company manufactured watches by the millions, using ebauches manufactured in its own Swiss plant. The New York Plant by now was making escapements, dials, plates and other parts and also cased and assembled the watches. About 1940 or sooner they were able to make complete watches. By the early 1950s they produced over a million watches a year of which over half were imported movements & the remaining were domestic. The *Accutron* was introduced on October 25, 1960, it was the **first** electronic watch made. The watch used a tuning fork that vibrated 360 times a second using a transistorized electronic circuit and a battery which would last for about a year. Micro-miniaturization of components was a technical achievement. The tuning fork vibrates, a jewel-tipped (pawl spring) index finger advancing the index wheel. The index wheel is only 0.0945 inches in diameter ● (about the size of a pin head) yet it has 320 ratchet teeth. The coil is less than a 1/4 inch long but contains 8,000 turns of wire that is 0.0006 inches in diameter. The original **214** model, (identified by absence of a crown) was produced until about 1966 and about a 2,000,000 were made. The newer **218** model has a crown at the 4 0'clock position. By 1975- 76 the Accutron production ended and about 5,000,000 were sold.

The "**Spaceview**" so named due to the conventional dial was left off so the **tuning fork** can be viewed from the top using a transparent crystal. With the conventional dial missing it had to be replaced with a dial spacer. The "**Spaceview Alpha**", as delivered from factory, used a transparent crystal with **dots** and a dial spacer only. The "**Spaceview H**" used a crystal and a dial reflector (chapter ring) not a dial spacer. There are many different **original factory** combinations of the "**Spaceview**" crystals with many different styles of hands. **Spaceviews** came in both 214 & 218 models.

 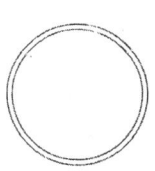  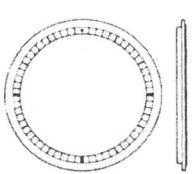

"Spaceview Alpha" with **dots** on crystal & dial spacer   "Spaceview H" with chapter ring & dial reflector

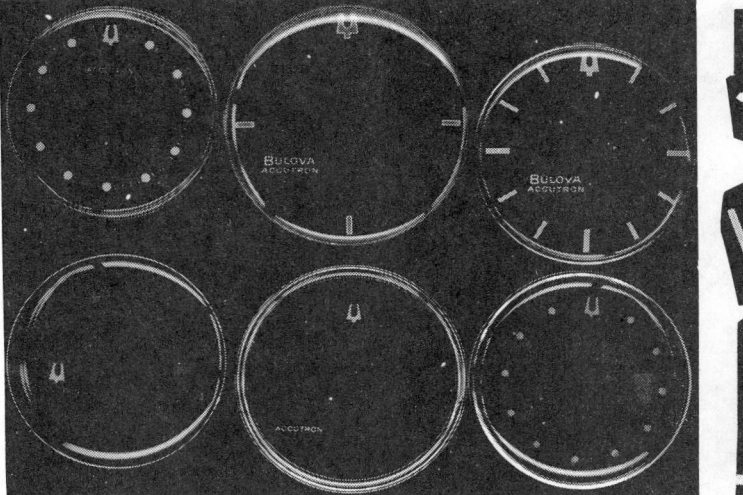

Different Spaceview transparent dot crystals   Above: Different Hands

Different Hands -   tuning fork (white-red-gold) seconds hands -   also orange second hand

Spaceview "Alpha", was the 1st model, Ca 1960
1963 ad **Alpha** model sold for **$200**

BULOVA, Accutron, "Spaceview **Alpha**" Ca. 1960
Accutron the first transistorized watch was sold Oct. 25, 1960.
14k $600 $700 $1,000

BULOVA, Accutron, "Spaceview B", yellow dots & hands,
sold for $150 in 1964.
s.steel $250 $275 $425

BULOVA, Accutron, "Spaceview H"
gold filled............................... $275 $325 $425

BULOVA, Accutron, "Spaceview T", clearview dial,
orange second hand, sold for $135.00 in 1967.
s. steel $250 $275 $425
Note: model **214** = back set & model **218** = crown at 4.

BULOVA, Accutron, RF # 202, RR approved,
sold for $125.00 in 1964.
s. steel $150 $175 $300
gold filled $175 $200 $325

BULOVA, Accutron, RF # 210, **gold bezel** & s.steel case
s.steel & **14k** $275 $325 $450

BULOVA, Accutron, RF # 213, sold for $125.00 in 1964.
s.steel $150 $175 $250

BULOVA, Accutron, RF # 214
s.steel $150 $175 $250

BULOVA, Accutron, RF # 216, sold for $175.00 in 1964.
s.steel $150 $175 $250

BULOVA, Accutron, RF # 218, **bow tie** lugs
s.steel $200 $250 $325

BULOVA, Accutron, RF # 223
s.steel $200 $250 $325
14k $450 $500 $600

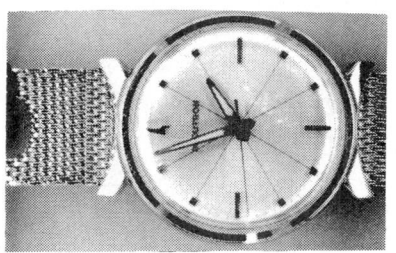

BULOVA, Accutron, RF # 241, **bow tie** lugs,
sold for $125.00 in 1967.
s.steel $200 $250 $325

BULOVA, Accutron, RF # 252, red second hand,
sold for $110.00 in 1967.
s. steel $150 $175 $250

BULOVA, Accutron, RF # 254, red second hand,
sold for $125.00 in 1967.
s. steel $100 $125 $200

BULOVA, Accutron, RF # 301, basketweave band,
sold $150.00 in 1967.
gold filled $150 $175 $250

BULOVA, Accutron, RF # 400
gold filled $150 $175 $250

BULOVA, Accutron, RF # 401, sold for $150.00 in 1964.
s.steel $150 $175 $250

BULOVA, Accutron, RF # 403, sold for $175.00 in 1964.
gold filled $150 $175 $250

BULOVA, Accutron, RF # 411
gold filled $150 $175 $250

BULOVA, Accutron, RF # 412 gold filled bezel & s.steel
gold filled & s.steel case $150 $175 $250

BULOVA, Accutron, RF # 413, GF bezel & s. steel case
gold filled & s.steel case $100 $125 $225

BULOVA, Accutron, RF # 417
gold filled..............................$175 $225 $275

BULOVA, Accutron, RF # 420
gold filled..............................$200 $225 $275

BULOVA, Milady's Accutron, RF # 430,
sold for $185.00 in 1967.
gold filled................................$85 $100 $150

Note: model 214 = back set & model 218 = crown at 4.

BULOVA, Accutron, RF # 500, center lugs,
sold for $300.00 in 1964.
14k $500 $550 $750

BULOVA, Accutron, RF # 505, Ca. 1960
14k yellow or white...............$525 $575 $750

BULOVA, Accutron, RF # 513
14k $350 $400 $550

BULOVA, Accutron, RF # 514, Florentine engraved case
14k $400 $450 $600

BULOVA, Accutron, RF # D515, 20 diamonds on case,
sold for $750.00 in 1967.
14K (w) C&B $400 $450 $600

⊕ NOTE: Some Bulova cases are stamped with a year date
code letter & number . L = 1950s, M = 1960s, N = 1970s,
P = 1980s, T = 1990s.
example: L3=1953, M4=1964, N5=1975, P6=1986, T7=1997.

BULOVA, Accutron, RF # 560
14k $325 $375 $550

BULOVA, Accutron, RF # 602
18k $700 $750 $900

BULOVA, Accutron, RF # AK, Day & Date,
sold for $200.00 in 1967.
gold filled.................................$150 $175 $250

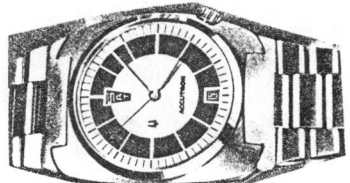

BULOVA, Accutron, RF # AG, Day at 12 & Date at 6,
sold for $185.00 in 1967.
s. steel $175 $200 $275

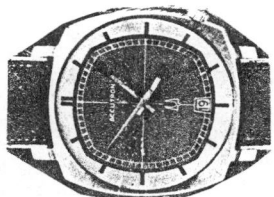

BULOVA, Accutron, RF # CK, date at 6,
sold for $135.00 in 1967.
s. steel $175 $200 $275

Note: A small **predictable** position error can be taken into
consideration in the daily regulation of your Accutron. In the 12
- down **vertical** position the rate is about 5 seconds per day faster
conversely in the 6-down **vertical** position a rate of 5 seconds
per day slower. You can take advantage of this, if slow place it
in the 12-down vertical position at night and it will gain back
lost time, if fast use the 6-down vertical position to slow it down.

BULOVA, Accutron, RF # CL, tortoise-toned dial,
sold for $250.00 in 1967.
14K $350 $400 $525

BULOVA, Accutron, "Mickey" day & date, **RARE** (218)
s. steel(214) $400 $500 $700
14k C&B(original dial) ★ ★ ★$700 $850 $1,200

BULOVA, Accutron, date, "M 8" on back - Ca. 1968
14k $350 $400 $575

BULOVA, Accutron, Ca. 1969-70.
14K $500 $550 $700

Note Below: Bulova Accutron regulator, to regulate use a
tooth pick and move regulator up or down.

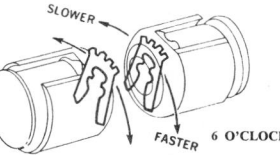

12 O'CLOCK   SLOWER

FASTER   6 O'CLOCK

NOTE: Some Bulova cases are stamped with a year date code letter & number . **L** = 1950s, **M** = 1960s, **N** = 1970s **P** =1980s, **T** = 1990s. example: L3=1953, M4=1964, N5=1975, P6=1986, T7=1997.

BULOVA, Accutron, "Spaceview"
s. steel $250 $300 $450

BULOVA, Accutron, **"Not Factory"**, cal. 214, c.1963
gold filled.................................. $75 $100 $150

BULOVA, Accutron, cal. 214, c. 1963
s. steel $200 $225 $350

BULOVA, Accutron, "Spaceview," c. 1960
18K... $750 $850 $1,200
14k $600 $650 $850
gold filled................................. $250 $275 $400
s. steel $250 $275 $400

BULOVA, Accutron, "Spaceview"
s. steel $250 $300 $400

BULOVA, Accutron, "Spaceview"
18k $800 $900 $1,200
14k $500 $600 $750
s. steel $250 $300 $400

BULOVA, Accutron, "Spaceview," Accutron second hand
gold filled $200 $250 $400

BULOVA, Accutron, "Spaceview," c. 1961
gold filled $225 $250 $350

BULOVA, Accutron, "Spaceview," c. 1967
gold filled...............................$250 $275 $425
s. steel $250 $275 $425
14k $450 $500 $675

BULOVA, Accutron, "Spaceview," center lugs
14k C & B.............................$700 $800 $1,200

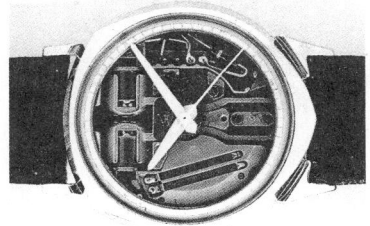

BULOVA, Accutron, **Not Factory,** Alpha, waterproof
14k $200 $225 $275

BULOVA, Accutron, **Not Factory** dial, date, cal.218
14k 2 tone $200 $225 $250

BULOVA, Accutron, Skeletonized, date, cal.218, Ca.1967
14k $550 $600 $750

BULOVA, Accutron, "Spaceview," **Bowtie** lugs
gold filled...............................$300 $350 $450

BULOVA, Accutron, day, date, sold for $135.00 in 1976
gold filled $95 $135 $200

BULOVA, Accutron, center lugs
s. steel $275 $300 $375
gold filled...............................$275 $300 $375

Accutron the **first** electronic watch was sold Oct. 25, 1960.
**By 1966 Accutron had sold over 1 1/2 million,
and by 1976, 5 million watches.**

🕐 Some grades are not included. Their values can be determined by comparing with **similar** age, size, metal content, style, grades, or models such as **time only,** chronograph, repeater etc. listed.

🕐 A collector should expect to pay modestly higher prices at local shops.

BULOVA, Accutron, "Spaceview," RED second hand.
s. steel $275 $300 $425

BULOVA, Accutron, "Spaceview," **Not Factory**
s. steel $100 $125 $175

BULOVA, Accutron, 2 tone, Ca. 1967
gold filled...............................$275 $300 $450

BULOVA, Accutron, "Spaceview," gold bezel
14k $450 $500 $650
gold bezel & s. steel case $300 $325 $425

BULOVA, Accutron, oval, "Spaceview" Ca. 1962
18K...$600 $700 $950
14K...$350 $400 $525
gold filled................................$225 $250 $325
s. steel $225 $250 $325

BULOVA, Accutron, M# 214, railroad approved, Ca. 1962
gold filled $175 $200 $300
s. steel $175 $200 $300

BULOVA, Accutron, "Spaceview,"
s. steel $225 $250 $350

BULOVA, Accutron, M# 218, RR approved, **red** 24 hr. #s,
sold for $125.00 in 1976
gold filled $175 $200 $300

BULOVA, Accutron, RR approved
gold filled................................$175 $200 $300

BULOVA, Accutron, RR approved
s. steel $175 $200 $300

BULOVA, Accutron," **Mark IV" / RR approved,** date
Crown at 2 sets the hour hand, Crown at 4 sets Time & Date
two hour hands for two time zones
s. steel $250 $300 $425

BULOVA, Accutron, cal. 214," Pulsation", c. 1966
gold filled................................$250 $300 $400
14k ....★ $700 $750 $900

BULOVA, Accutron, cal. 214," Pulsation", c. 1966
14k ....★ $700 $750 $900

BULOVA, Accutron, "Alpha", model 214, 6 diamond dial
14k $650 $700 $900
18K ....★ $1,000 $1,200 $1,500

BULOVA, Accutron, sweep sec. hand
gold filled $150 $175 $250

BULOVA, Accutron, masonic dial (all original dial)
NOTE: This dial can be printed for about $35.00.
14k $335 $365 $450

BULOVA, Accutron, asymmetric
14k $550 $575 $750

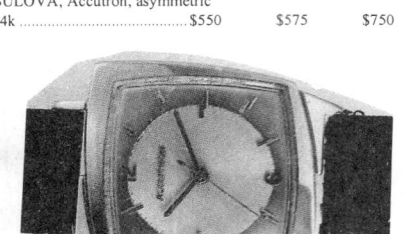

BULOVA, Accutron, asymmetric, 2- tone dial, Ca.1963
14k $600 $650 $750

BULOVA, Accutron, "ASTRONAUT A", 24 hour dial,
the s. steel case & band sold for $175.00 in 1964.
18kC&B $1,500 $1,600 $2,100
14k $800 $1,000 $1,400
gold filled...............................$350 $400 $600
s. steel $300 $350 $550

BULOVA, Accutron, "ASTRONAUT B", rotating bezel
s. steel $300 $350 $475

BULOVA, Accutron, "ASTRONAUT C", 18k case & band,
sold for $1,000.00 in 1964.
18k C & B..........................$1,400 $1,600 $2,100
also made with a gold filled case & 14K bezel
GF case & 14K bezel $500 $600 $850

BULOVA, Accutron, "Astronaut Mark II", time zone, window
at six o'clock, date at 12, note: on back N2 = 1972
14k $500 $550 $650
s. steel $250 $275 $375

BULOVA, Accutron, "Astronaut Mark II", time zone, original sales price was $275.00 in S. Steel.
14k $450 $500 $650
gold filled $250 $325 $450
s. steel $250 $325 $450

BULOVA, Accutron, "Astronaut Mark II", auxiliary time
zone window at 6-o'clock & date at 12-o'clock.
14k $500 $550 $700

BULOVA, Accutron, "Astronaut Mark II", time zone with a
extra red hour hand, date at 3 o'clock, on back M9 = 1969
gold filled.................................$250 $300 $400

BULOVA, Accutron, "Spaceview"
gold filled $250 $275 $375

BULOVA, Accutron,"Astronaut Mark II E", travel time zone
sold for $185.00 in 1967, orange sec. hand & hour markers
s. steel $250 $300 $400

BULOVA, Accutron, **4 diamond** dial, Ca. 1967
gold filled $225 $250 $375

BULOVA, Accutron, Ca. 1966
gold filled................................$150 $200 $250

BULOVA, Accutron, "spaceview", sold for $180.00 in 1976
gold filled $150 $200 $300

BULOVA, Accutron, date, gold filled bezel
s. steel $100 $125 $175

BULOVA, Accutron, fancy lugs
gold filled................................$150 $175 $250

BULOVA, day, date, sold for $150.00 in 1976
gold filled $100 $125 $175

BULOVA, Accutron, date, **Tiffany & Co.** M7=1967,
note: accutron **tuning fork** second hand.
14K.. $450 $525 $650

BULOVA, Accutron, day, date, sold for $185.00 in 1976,
gold filled $125 $150 $225

BULOVA, Accutron, date
18K.. $450 $550 $700
gold filled $150 $175 $250

BULOVA, Accutron, date, Ca.1972
base metal $75 $100 $150

Note: Designed the shape of Accutron tuning fork.
BULOVA, Accutron, **Spaceview Anniversary**, model 214
14k(large case)....................... $500 $525 $675

BULOVA, Accutron, gold filled bezel, day date
gold filled $125 $150 $200

BULOVA, Accutron, red second hand, Ca. 1970
s. steel $275 $300 $425

BULOVA, day date
s. steel $100 $125 $175
14k diamond bezel $350 $400 $450

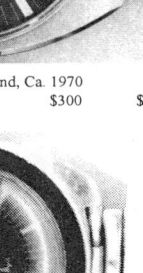

BULOVA, Accutron, **wood bezel,** day date
gold filled...............................$100 $125 $175

BULOVA, Accutron, day date
gold filled $125 $150 $200

BULOVA, Accutron, red dial, date
gold filled...............................$125 $150 $225

BULOVA, Accutron, day date, Ca.1972
gold filled $100 $125 $175

BULOVA, Accutron, numbered bezel, day date
14k $350 $400 $575

BULOVA, Accutron, date
gold plate $100 $125 $175

BULOVA, Accuquartz, note band with **accutron symbol**
18k C&B $700 $800 $1,000

BULOVA, Accutron, day date, c. 1970
s. steel $125 $150 $200

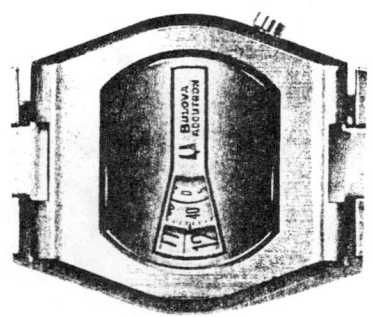

BULOVA, Accutron, model 2186, direct read
gold filled $200 $250 $350

BULOVA, Accutron, **Accutron 14k Gold Band**, Ca. 1972
14k C & B $600 $650 $800

BULOVA, Accutron, **DEEP SEA**, 666 ft. depth, day date, 12
& 24 hr. dial, crown at 2 rotates outside dial to locate city.
s. steel $375 $425 $550

BULOVA, Accutron, **DEEP SEA "A"**, 666 feet, day date,
crown at 2 rotates elapsed for REMAINING time dial,
sold for $195.00 in 1967.
s. steel $275 $325 $450

BULOVA, Accutron, **DEEP SEA**, 666 feet, date
rotating enamel bezel for REMAINING time.
s. steel $250 $300 $450

BULOVA, Accutron, day date, note <u>Accutron style sec. hand</u>
s. steel $175 $200 $275

BULOVA, Accutron, date, Ca. 1968
gold filled $100 $125 $175

BULOVA, Accutron, day, date, sold for $125.00 in 1976
gold filled.............................. $125 $150 $225

BULOVA, Accutron, day, date, sold for $450.00 in 1976
14k $300 $350 $500

BULOVA, Accutron, **"Spaceview", Bowtie lugs**
18K.. $800 $900 $1,200

BULOVA, Accutron, cal. #221, textured bezel
sterling & 14k........................ $100 $125 $175

BULOVA, Accutron, model "AO", asymmetrical,
Sold for $225.00 in 1971.
gold filled.............................. $100 $125 $175

BULOVA, Accutron, day, date, sold for $125.00 in 1976
gold filled $100 $150 $225

🕐 NOTE: Some Bulova cases are stamped with a year date
code letter & number . L = 1950s, M = 1960s, N = 1970s
P =1980s, T = 1990s.
example: L3=1953, M4=1964, N5=1975, P6=1986, T7=1997.

BULOVA, digital,
s. steel $95 $125 $225

BULOVA, 17J., chronog., "660 feet" dive watch, c.1972
s. steel $95 $125 $195

BULOVA, enamel bezel
s. steel $75 $95 $150

BULOVA, 16 jewels, military style
s. steel $250 $300 $375

BULOVA, 15J., one button chronog.,1/5 sec.,C.1946
14k $400 $500 $650
gold filled................................$250 $300 $400

BULOVA, 17J., **Alarm**, cal.11aerc, c.1967
s. steel $95 $125 $195

BULOVA, 17J., one button chronog., cal.10BK, c.1947
gold filled................................$250 $300 $400

BULOVA, self winding, c. 1960
14k $150 $175 $195
gold filled $50 $65 $95

BULOVA, 17J., fancy lugs
gold filled..................................$60 $75 $150

BULOVA, 23 jewels, waterproof
14k $95 $125 $225

BULOVA, 23 jewels, date, 6 adj., c. 1951
gold filled..................................$75 $85 $150

BULOVA, 17J., cal.11 af, ca.1959
gold filled..................................$50 $65 $95
14K...$95 $125 $225

BULOVA, 17jewels, fancy long lugs, c. 1954
gold filled $75 $95 $150

BULOVA, 17J., crisscrossed hidden lugs, c.1958
14k $150 $175 $250

BULOVA, 21J., fancy lugs, c.1950
gold filled $60 $75 $135

BULOVA, 17J., center sec., c.1942
gold filled $50 $65 $95

BULOVA, 15J., military style, c.1940
s. steel $50 $65 $95

BULOVA, cal. 700, **canteen** style, c. 1946
s. steel .... ★ ★ ★ $400 $500 $700

BULOVA, 15J., military style, cal.10 bnch, c.1940
s. steel $55 $65 $95

BULOVA, 17J., U.S.A. military, c.1945
s. steel $55 $65 $95

BULOVA, 17J., 20 diamond dial
14k(w)...................................$175 $195 $300

BULOVA, 23J., 12 diamond dial, c. 1959
14k(w)...................................$175 $195 $325

BULOVA, 30J., diam. dial, cal#10B2AC, C.1960s
14k(w)...................................$175 $195 $300

BULOVA, diamond dial, c. 1939
platinum..................................$600 $700 $900
14k (w) $400 $500 $700

BULOVA, 21 jewels, hidden lugs, diamond dial, c. 1935
14k $400 $500 $700

BULOVA, hidden lugs, diamond dial, c. 1945
14k $300 $350 $500

BULOVA, 21 jewels, diamond dial, long lugs, c. 1941
14k (w) $250 $300 $400

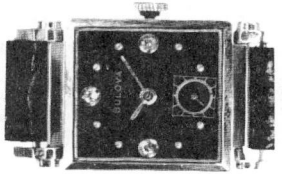

BULOVA, 17J., 3 diamond dial, cal.8ae, c.1949
14k $150 $175 $250

BULOVA, **early auto wind** movement see Champ below

BULOVA, **early auto wind,** by Champ, c. 1930
gold filled .... ★★★$400 $450 $625

BULOVA, 17 jewels, curved, cal. 7AP, c. 1939
14k $250 $275 $375

BULOVA, 17J., drivers watch, c.1935
gold filled $225 $275 $400

BULOVA, 17J., engraved, Ca. 1928
gold filled $50 $60 $90

BULOVA, 17J., 5th ave., cal.6am, engraved bezel, c.1935
gold filled $50 $60 $90

BULOVA, 21J., stepped bezel, curved,
gold filled $75 $85 $125

BULOVA, 21J., plain bezel, curved,
gold filled $75 $85 $125

BULOVA, 17J., cal. 7ap, c.1937
gold filled $75 $85 $125

BULOVA, 17J., curved, cal.7ap, c.1936
gold filled...............................$75 $85 $125

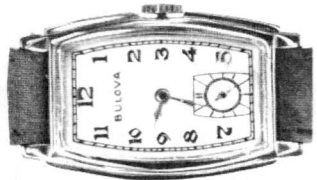

BULOVA, 17J., cal.13al,c.1935
14k $125 $150 $225

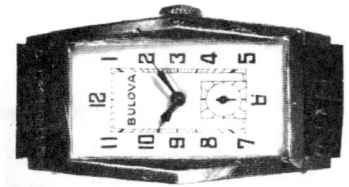

BULOVA, 17J., cal.9af, c.1929
s. steel $40 $50 $75

BULOVA, 17J., cal.7ap, c.1934
gold filled...............................$50 $65 $95

BULOVA, 15J., cal.10ae, c.1938
gold filled...............................$50 $65 $95

BULOVA, 17 jewels, curved, c. 1939
gold filled...............................$75 $85 $125

BULOVA, 21 jewels, curved, c. 1939
gold filled $75 $85 $135

BULOVA, 21J., cal# 6AE,
14k $125 $150 $250

BULOVA, 17 jewels, duo dial, c. 1935
gold filled(S.S.back) $175 $200 $350
s. steel $175 $200 $350

BULOVA, 17 jewels, **2 tone**, duo dial
gold filled(S.S.back) $175 $200 $350
s. steel $175 $200 $350

BULOVA, 17 jewels, 2 tone dial, **flexible lugs,** fancy bezel
s. steel $75 $100 $150
Wrist Watches listed in this section are priced at the collectable
fair market Trade Show level as **complete** watches having an
original gold-filled case and stainless steel back, also with
original dial, leather watch band, and the entire original movement in good working order with no repairs needed.

BULOVA, 21 J., **President, wandering sec.,** c. 1932
gold filled..............................$125 $150 $225

BULOVA, 17 jewels, cal. 10GM, fancy lugs, c. 1953
gold filled................................$75 $100 $150
14k $150 $175 $250

BULOVA, 15J., fancy lugs, c.1952
gold filled................................$75 $85 $135

BULOVA, 21J., fancy lugs, c.1952
14k $150 $175 $250
gold filled................................$75 $95 $150

BULOVA, 17J., fancy lugs, cal.8an, c.1951
14k $195 $225 $300
gold filled................................$75 $95 $150

BULOVA, 17J., cal.8ad, fancy lugs, c.1939
gold plate $40 $50 $85

BULOVA, 21J., cal. 7ak, c.1945
gold filled $50 $75 $95

BULOVA, 21J., c.1950s
gold filled $60 $75 $125

BULOVA, 21J., scalloped case, c.1950s
gold filled $65 $75 $125

BULOVA, 7J., c.1945
gold filled $50 $65 $95

🕐 Pricing in this Guide are fair market price for **COMPLETE**
watches which are reflected from the "**NAWCC**" National and
regional shows.

BULOVA, 17J., fancy lugs, c.1950 code on case=(LO)
gold filled..................................$50 $65 $95

BULOVA, 17J., gold jewel settings, Ca.1923
gold filled..................................$50 $65 $95

BULOVA, 21J., **carved case**, c.1948
14k $150 $175 $250

BULOVA, 21J., cal.7ak, c.1945
gold filled..................................$50 $65 $95

BULOVA, 17J., cal.8ae, fancy hidden lugs, c.1941
gold filled..................................$60 $85 $125

BULOVA, 21J., hooded lugs, c.1945
14k $150 $175 $250

BULOVA, 21 jewels, cal. 7AK, c. 1950
14k $135 $175 $250

BULOVA, 17 jewels, fancy long lugs, c. 1942
14k $125 $165 $225

BULOVA, 17 jewels, cal. 10BM, Ca. 1954
gold filled $85 $100 $150

BULOVA, 17J., cal. 8AC, **flip top, photo watch,** c. 1940
gold filled $250 $300 $375
14k $350 $400 $500

🕘 Some grades are not included. Their values can be determined by comparing with **similar** age, size, metal content, style, models and grades listed.

BULOVA, 15 jewels, wandering hr. min. sec., c. 1928
s. steel $150 $200 $300

BULOVA, 17J., rite angle, cal. 8AZ, c. 1938
gold filled................................ $150 $175 $300
14k $250 $325 $500

BULOVA, 17 jewels, aux. sec.
14k $125 $150 $225

BULOVA, 17 jewels, fancy bezel
gold filled................................. $95 $125 $200

BULOVA, 17 jewels, bell shaped lugs
14k $150 $175 $250

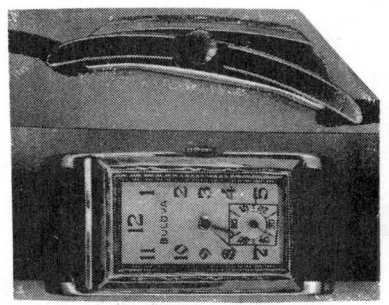

BULOVA, 17J., rite angle case
gold filled $150 $175 $250

BULOVA, 17J., center sec., cal.10bac, c.1935
gold filled $50 $60 $95

BULOVA, 17J., cal.8ac, fancy lugs, c.1940
gold plate $40 $50 $75

BULOVA, 17J., flared top of case & sides,
gold filled $60 $75 $100

BULOVA, 21J., hidden lugs, c.1961
gold filled $65 $85 $125

BULOVA, 21J., hidden lugs, c.1950s
14k .,...$95 $150 $225

BULOVA, 21J., hidden lugs, c.1945
gold filled.................................$55 $75 $125

BULOVA, 17J., BMW- logo, c.1957
gold filled.................................$55 $75 $100

BULOVA, 17J., FORD logo, c.1947
base metal $40 $50 $75

BULOVA, 17J., engraved lugs & bezel, cal.10an,c.1928
s. steel $40 $50 $75

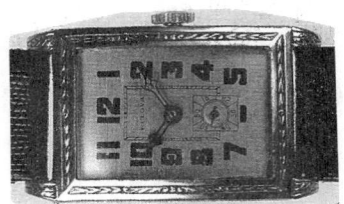

BULOVA, 17J., engraved bezel only
base metal $30 $40 $60

BULOVA, 15J., cal.11ac, c.1958
gold filled $60 $75 $125

BULOVA, 15J., cal.10ae, c.1935
gold filled $50 $60 $95

BULOVA, 7J., cal.10bc, c.1949
gold filled $50 $60 $95

BULOVA, **Masonic** dial, Ca. 1944
gold filled $95 $125 $195

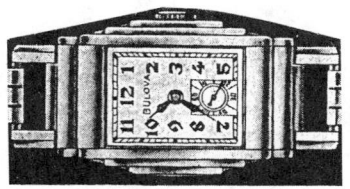

BULOVA, 15 jewels, **Senator,**
gold filled...............................$50 $60 $95

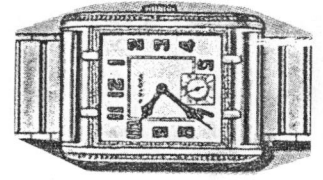

BULOVA, 15 jewels, **Ambassador,**
gold filled $50 $60 $95

BULOVA, 17 jewels, **Oakley,**
gold filled...............................$50 $60 $95

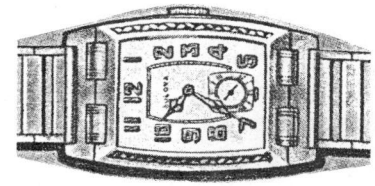

BULOVA, 17 jewels, **Argyle,**
14K $125 $150 $225

BULOVA, 17 jewels, **LONE EAGLE,** stepped style case
gold filled $75 $95 $150

BULOVA, 15 jewels, **Norman,**
gold filled $50 $60 $95

BULOVA, 15 jewels, **LONE EAGLE,** tonneau style case
gold filled $75 $95 $150

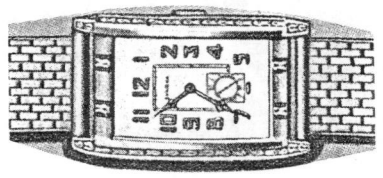

BULOVA, 15 jewels, **Spencer,**
gold filled $50 $60 $95

BULOVA, 17J., **LONE EAGLE,** radium & cut corner dial
gold filled $65 $85 $125

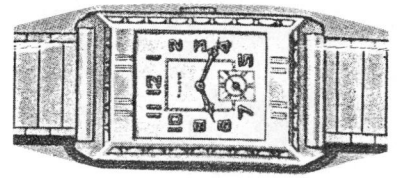

BULOVA, 17 jewels, **Wellington,**
14K $125 $150 $225

BULOVA, 17 jewels, fancy lugs
14k $150 $175 $225

BUREN, 17 jewels, day-date-month, moon phase
s. steel $195 $250 $350

BULOVA, 17 jewels, "The Ambassador"
gold filled $50 $60 $95

BUREN, 17 jewels, long lugs
14k $125 $150 $195

BULOVA, 17 jewels, "The Curtis," tank style
gold filled $50 $65 $95

BUREN, 17 jewels, center lugs, c.1940
9k $95 $125 $175

BULOVA, 15 jewels, "The Athelete"
gold filled $50 $65 $95

BUTEX, 17J., triple date, moon ph.
gold filled $125 $150 $195

BULOVA, 17 jewels, "The Governor,"
14K $125 $150 $195

CARLTON, 15 jewels, **"Rite angle"** case, c. 1939
gold filled $125 $175 $250
14k $250 $300 $400

CARTIER, "Pasha", automatic, 300ft, **recent**
18k C & B..........................$6,500 $7,000 $8,000
18k leather $3,000 $3,500 $4,500

CARTIER, "Golf", automatic, 100 ft., **4 counters, recent**
18k C & B.......................$14,500 $15,000 $16,500
18k leather $9,500 $10,000 $12,000

CARTIER, "Pasha", automatic, 300 ft., rotating bezel, **recent**
18k C & B..........................$7,000 $7,500 $8,500
18k leather $3,200 $3,600 $4,500

CARTIER, "Diabolo", automatic, 100ft, **tourbillon, recent**
18k leather $35,000 $38,000 $42,000

CARTIER, "Pasha", automatic, 300ft, W/grill, **recent**
18k C & B..........................$8,000 $9,000 $11,000
18k leather $4,000 $4,500 $5,500

CARTIER, "Diabolo", manual wind, **Min. Repeater, recent**
18k leather $40,000 $45,000 $55,000

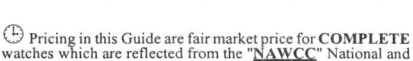

Pricing in this Guide are fair market price for **COMPLETE** watches which are reflected from the "**NAWCC**" National and regional shows.

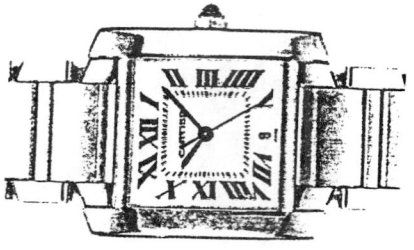

CARTIER, "Tank Francaise", automatic, date, 100 ft., **recent**
18k C & B..........................$7,500 $8,000 $9,000
18k leather $3,000 $3,300 $4,000

CARTIER, "Pasha", automatic, rotating bezel, 100 ft., **recent**
18k C & B..........................$13,000 $13,500 $15,000
18k leather $9,000 $9,500 $11,000

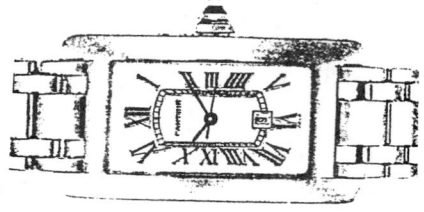

CARTIER, "Tank Americaine", automatic, date, **recent**
18k C & B..........................$9,000 $9,500 $10,000
18k leather $3,000 $3,300 $4,000

CARTIER, "Pasha", automatic, moon phases, 100 ft., **recent**
18k C & B..........................$11,000 $12,000 $14,000
18k leather $7,500 $8,000 $10,000

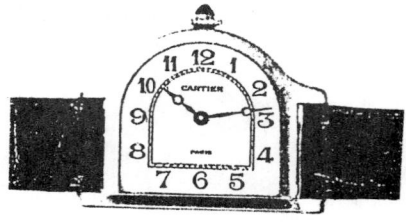

CARTIER, "Cloche", manual wind, **recent**
18k leather $4,000 $4,500 $5,500

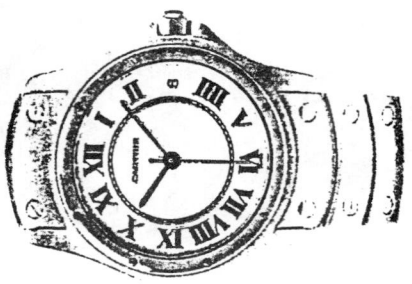

CARTIER, "Pasha", **Min. Repeater**, moon phases, **recent**
18k C & B..........................$60,000 $68,000 $75,000
18k leather $55,000 $62,000 $70,000

CARTIER, "Pasha", automatic, rotating bezel, 100 ft., **recent**
18k C & B..........................$4,000 $4,500 $5,500

⊕ Pricing in this Guide are fair market price for **COMPLETE** watches which are reflected from the "<u>NAWCC</u>" National and regional shows.

CARTIER, 18 J., **8 day** Mvt., tank style, by E. W. Co.
18k $25,000 $27,000 $32,000

CARTIER, 18 J., sapphire crown & bezel, c. 1970
18k $3,000 $3,500 $4,500

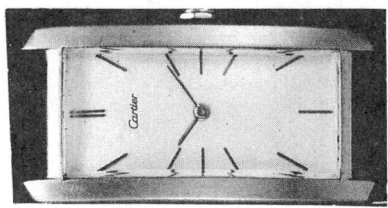

CARTIER, 18 jewels, curved, tank style
18k $6,000 $6,500 $8,000

CARTIER, 18 jewels, curved, signed E. W. Co., c.1930s
18k $5,000 $5,500 $6,500

CARTIER, 18 J., tank style, platinum case & band
platinum C&B...................$10,000 $11,000 $14,000

NOTE: With original Cartier 18K Deployment clasp
ADD $400 to $600.

CARTIER, 18 jewels, tank style case, c. 1970s
18k $1,800 $2,000 $2,500

CARTIER, 20 jewels, tank style case, c. 1950
18k $2,500 $2,800 $3,200

CARTIER, Must de, **quartz,** tank style case, c.1980s
Vermeil =(gold over sterling)
G.P. vermeil...........................$300 $325 $400
SAME STYLE CASE AS ABOVE
CARTIER, Must de, **Mechanical,** tank style case, c.1980s
Vermeil =(gold over sterling)
G.P. vermeil...........................$300 $325 $400

CARTIER, 18 jewels, tank style, European W. Co.
platinum..............................$8,000 $9,000 $12,000

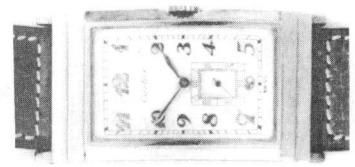

CARTIER, 18 jewels, by Movado
14k $1,000 $1,100 $1,400

CARTIER, 18 jewels, duo plan, European W. Co.
18k C&B $2,500 $2,800 $3,500

CARTIER, 18J., by Le Coultre, long lugs
18k $1,200 $1,300 $1,600

CARTIER, 18 jewels, curved, hidden lugs
18k $3,500 $3,800 $4,500

CARTIER, 18 jewels, by Universal, c. 1960
18k $800 $900 $1,200

CARTIER, 18 jewels, center lugs, c. 1930
18k $2,800 $3,000 $3,600

CARTIER, 18 J., Prince, by Le Coultre, C.1930
18k $16,000 $18,000 $22,000

CARTIER, 18 J., reversible to view 2nd time zone
18k $20,000 $22,000 $26,000

CARTIER, 18 jewels, by European W. Co. c. 1927
18k $4,000 $4,500 $5,500

CARTIER, 18 J., early E.W.Co., C. 1928
18k $3,500 $3,800 $4,500

CARTIER, 18 J., lady's watch by European W. Co.
18k C&B..............................$2,500 $2,800 $3,500

CARTIER, 18 J., sovonnette (hunter case style), C. 1928
18k $6,000 $6,500 $8,000

CARTIER, 18 J., E.W.Co., Tank Normale, Ca. 1925
18k $4,000 $4,500 $5,500

CARTIER,18 J., guichet tank, jump hr. & min. by E.W.Co.
18k $30,000 $34,000 $40,000

CARTIER, 18 jewels, "Santos," octagonal, date
18k & s. steel C&B $800 $900 $1,100

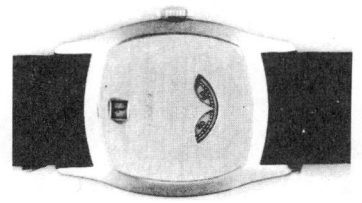

CARTIER, 18 J., jump hr. & min., E. W. Co. c. 1930
platinum $35,000 $38,000 $45,000

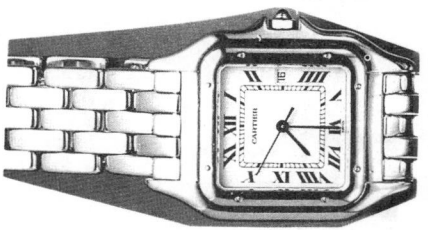

CARTIER, Panthere, date, water resistant, Medium size

s. steel band	$900	$1,000	$1,300
1 stripe of gold, quartz	$800	$900	$1,200
2 stripes of gold, quartz.......	$1,400	$1,700	$2,200
3 stripes of gold, quartz.......	$2,000	$2,200	$2,600
18k **reg**. C & B....................	$5,000	$5,800	$6,800
18k **large** C & B..................	$6,000	$6,800	$7,800
lady's, s. steel band	$900	$1,000	$1,200
lady's, 1 stripe of gold, ...	$800	$900	$1,100
lady's, 2 stripe of gold, ...	$1,700	$1,800	$2,000
lady's, 3 stripe of gold, ...	$1,800	$2,000	$2,300
lady's, 18k C & B	$5,000	$5,500	$6,500

CARTIER, 18 J.,"Santos", mechanical, cal.21
mens18k.............................. $2,500 $2,800 $3,500
ladies 18k........................... $2,000 $2,200 $2,700

CARTIER, 18 J., "Santos," 18k & s. steel case, band, **Lady's**
platinum & 18k C&B $9,000 $10,000 $12,500
18k & s. steel C&B................ $800 $900 $1,200

CARTIER, 25 jewels, chronog., European W. Co.
18k $60,000 $65,000 $80,000

CARTIER, 18 jewels, "Santos," date, Gents, Ca. 1980's
18k & s. steel C&B.............. $1,000 $1,100 $1,400

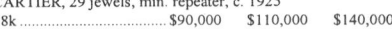

CARTIER, 29 jewels, min. repeater, c. 1925
18k $90,000 $110,000 $140,000

CARTIER, 18 jewels, c. 1925
18k $3,000 $3,300 $4,000

CARTIER, 18 jewels, asymmetric, E. W. Co., c. 1928
18k $6,000 $7,000 $9,000

CARTIER, 18 J., oval maxi, C. 1968
18k $7,000 $8,000 $10,000

CARTIER, 18 jewels, by Le Coultre
18k $2,000 $2,300 $3,000

CARTIER, 18 J., large cut corner bezel, C.1970s
18k $3,000 $3,300 $4,000

CARTIER, 18 J., "Helm", single lug, C. 1950s
18k $10,000 $12,000 $15,000
platinum.........................$20,000 $22,000 $28,000

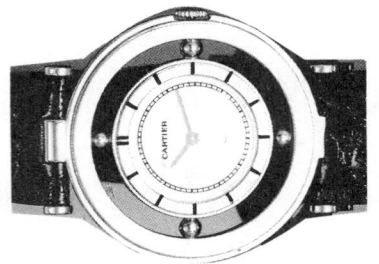

CARTIER, 18 J.,by E.W.CO., single lug, C. 1949
18k $7,000 $8,000 $10,000

CARTIER, 29 J., **min. repeater, by Le Coultre**, c. 1930
platinum............................$70,000 $75,000 $85,000

CARTIER, 18 J., bamboo style bezel, Gents, C.1970s
18k $4,000 $4,300 $5,000

NOTE: With original Cartier 18K Deployment clasp
ADD $400 to $600.

CARTIER, 18 J., **triple date, moon ph.**, tear-drop lugs, marked European Watch & clock Co., Ca.1945
s. steel $4,000 $4,500 $5,500
18K..$6,000 $6,500 $7,500

CARTIER, 18 J., **Ca. 1985**
18K..$1,500 $1,700 $2,000

CARTIER, 18J, day of week & date chapter, by Le Coultre
14k $1,000 $1,200 $1,500

CARTIER,Quartz, 296 diamonds on bezel & 18k Band
18k $18,000 $19,000 $22,000

CARTIER, 18 J., lady's, back wind, E.W.CO., c.1940s
18k $2,000 $2,200 $3,000

CARTIER, 18J., tonneau, Ca. 1920
platinum...............................$3,500 $4,000 $5,000

CARTIER, 18 J., lady's, E.W.Co., C.1949
14k(w) C&B $600 $650 $800

CERTINA, 17J., "NEWART", auto-wind, date, c.1965
14k $100 $110 $150

CENTRAL, 7J., cal.39, c.1937
gold filled $35 $40 $70

CHEVROLET, 6J., in form of car radiator, C. 1927
silver $450 $600 $900

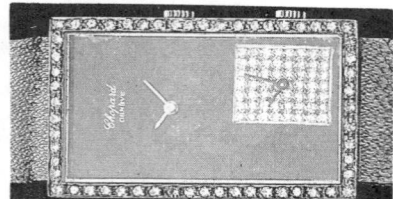

CHOPARD, 18 J., 2 dial , 2 time zones, diam.bezel
18k C&B..............................$2,000 $2,800 $3,000

CLEBAR, 17 jewels, chronog., 2 reg., cal.2248, c.1952
gold filled $125 $250 $325
base metal $100 $150 $275

CHOPARD, 18 J., skeletonized, diamonds on case & hands
18k $2,000 $2,200 $3,000

CLEBAR, 17 jewels, chronog., 3 reg. c.1950s
gold filled $200 $250 $350
s. steel $150 $200 $325

CHOPARD, 28J., triple date moon ph., cal.900, c.1980
18k $900 $1,000 $1,200

CLEBAR, 17J., chronog.,triple date, moon ph.
gold filled $450 $650 $800
s. steel $400 $600 $750

CHOPARD, 20 J., RF#2113, c.1978
18k $300 $350 $400

CHOPARD, 17J., RF#2134, c.1978
18k $275 $325 $375

CLEBAR, 17 jewels, center lugs, chronog., c. 1938
s. steel $250 $300 $400

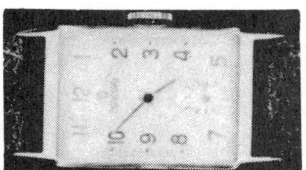

CONCORD, 17J., aux. sec., ca. 1947
14k $95 $125 $175

CONCORD, 17 jewels, center sec.
14k $95 $125 $175

CONCORD, 17 jewels, chronog. 2 reg., c.1940s
s. steel $175 $225 $300

CONDAL,15J. **hunter style**, flip top, C.1928
silver $250 $350 $500

CONTINENTAL, 17J., 3 diamond dial
14k $110 $125 $195

CORNAVIN, 17J., day date, c. 1960
gold filled $55 $65 $95

CORNAVIN, 17J., date, auto, RF#1243, C.1963
gold filled $30 $40 $75
s. steel $30 $40 $75

CORONET, 17J., chronog.
s. steel $175 $200 $250

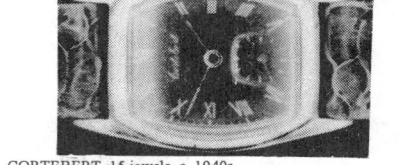

CORTEBERT, 15 jewels, c. 1940s
gold filled $45 $55 $95

CORTEBERT, 15 jewels, c. 1941
gold filled $45 $55 $95

CORTEBERT, 17 J., "Sport," triple date, moon phase
18k $400 $500 $700
gold filled................................$100 $125 $200

CORUM, 17 J., twenty dollar gold piece= 22K
22k leather band (quartz) $2,400 $2,600 $3,200
22k, leather band (M. wind) $2,600 $2,800 $3,500
22k, **gold** band, (M. wind) . $3,500 $4,000 $5,000

CORTEBERT, 17 jewels, center sec.
s. steel $35 $45 $65

CORUM, 24k gold ingot, 15 Grams, manual wind
24k $1,100 $1,300 $1,600

CORTEBERT, **quartz**, U.K. military, (CWC)
s. steel $75 $95 $135

CORUM, 17 J., in form of Rolls-Royce car Grill
18k (reg.) $2,000 $2,200 $2,600
18k (large) $2,600 $2,800 $3,200

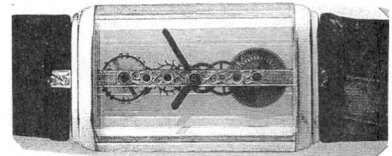

CORUM, 17 jewels, "Golden Bridge", in line train, **recent**
18k $2,200 $2,600 $3,500

CORTEBERT, (CWC), chronog., by Valjoux, c.1971
s. steel $175 $200 $295

CORUM, 17 jewels, rope style bezel
18k C&B.............................. $1,000 $1,200 $1,500

CORUM, 17 jewels, peacock feather dial
18k $700 $800 $1,000

CRAWFORD, 17J., hooded lugs, c. 1940
14k $100 $110 $150

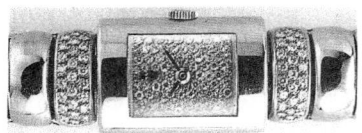

CORUM, 21 jewels, "pave" diamond dial, c.1990
18k C&B $2,200 $2,500 $3,000

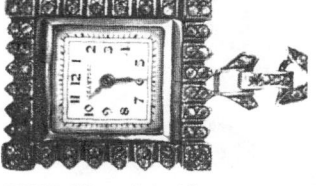

CRAWFORD, 17J., pendant watch
base metal $35 $40 $55

CORUM, 21 jewels, gold dial
18k $250 $300 $375

CROTON, 17 jewels, day date
gold filled $35 $40 $55

CRAWFORD, 17J., triple date, c. 1942
s. steel $85 $100 $150

CROTON, 17 jewels, diamond bezel & dial
14k (w) $175 $225 $300

CRAWFORD, 17J., chronog.engraved bezel
base metal $125 $150 $195

CROTON, 17 jewels, chronog., c. 1948
s. steel $175 $200 $250

CROTON, 17 jewels, chronog., c. 1946
s. steel $175 $195 $250

CROTON, 17 jewels, cal.630, c.1943
gold filled................................$35 $45 $85

CROTON, 17 jewels, Ca.1937
14k $95 $110 $195

CROTON, 17 jewels, fancy lugs
14k $150 $195 $275

CROTON, 7J., **drivers** style, **winds at 12** o'clock, c.1938
gold filled................................$95 $135 $195

CROTON, 17 jewels, swinging lugs, cal.f3x, c.1940
14k $95 $125 $175

CROWN, 7J., luminous dial
base metal...............................$35 $45 $65

CROWN, 7J., luminous dial
gold filled $30 $40 $55

CYMA, 15J., aux. sec., ca. 1935
nickel $30 $40 $55

CYMA,7J.,enamel dial, wire lugs,(signal corp.USA),c.1928
silver $250 $300 $375

CYMA, 17 jewels, aux. sec.

18k	$175	$195	$250
14k	$95	$110	$150
gold filled	$30	$40	$55

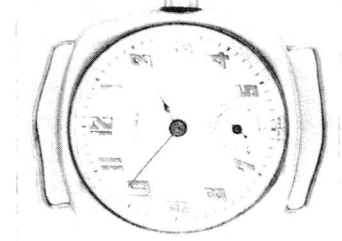

CYMA, 15J., enamel dial, (Tacy W. Co.), c. 1925

silver	$50	$60	$75

CYMA, 15J., military style, cal.234, Ca.1945

s. steel	$95	$120	$150

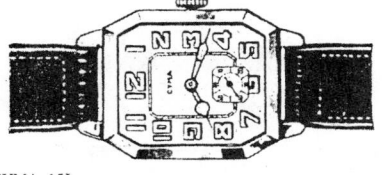

CYMA, 15J.,

base metal	$20	$30	$45

🕐 Some grades are not included. Their values can be determined by comparing with **similar** age, size, metal content, style, models and grades listed.

🕐 A collector should expect to pay modestly higher prices at local shops

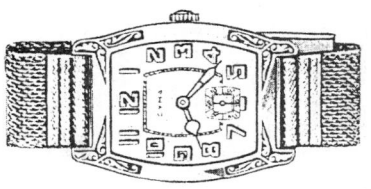

CYMA, 15J., engraved case

chromium	$20	$30	$45

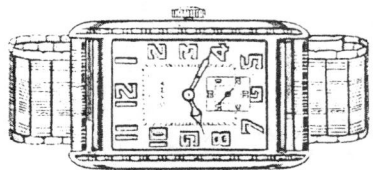

CYMA, 15J., engraved case

chromium	$20	$30	$45

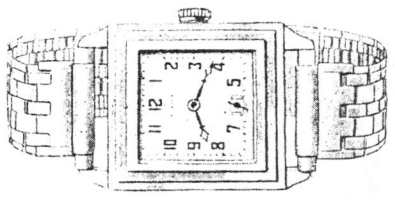

CYMA, 15J., 2-tone case

chromium	$20	$30	$45

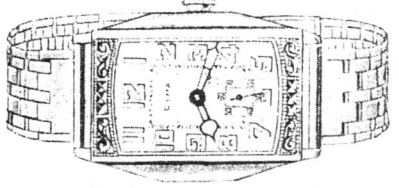

CYMA, 15J., engraved case

chromium	$20	$30	$45

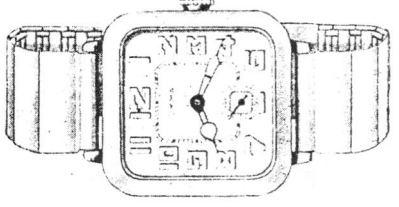

CYMA, 15J.,

chromium	$20	$30	$45

🕐 Pricing in this Guide are fair market price for **COMPLETE** watches which are reflected from the "**NAWCC**" National and regional shows.

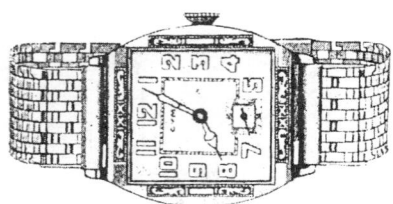

CYMA, 15J., engraved case
chromium.................................$20 $30 $45

DAU, 15J., wire lugs, c.1915
14k $75 $90 $125

DAYNITE, 7J., **8 day movement by Hebdomas**, Ca. 1920
s. steel $250 $300 $450

DELBANA, 17J., fancy hooded lugs, c.1951
14k $95 $125 $175

DIDISHEIM, 15J., "Winton", enamel art deco bezel, c.1927
14k(w)....................................$250 $275 $350

P. DITISHEIM, 16 J., "Solvil,"fancy bezel, c. 1935
18k $300 $350 $425

P. DITISHEIM, 17 J., "Solvil," diamond dial, c. 1947
18K $275 $325 $400

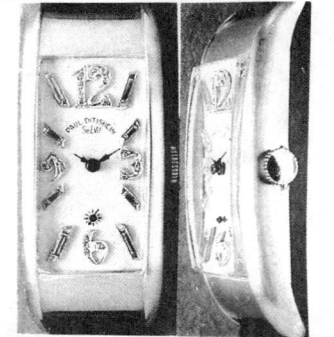

P. DITISHEIM, 17 J., "Solvil," diamond dial, c. 1948
platinum................................$600 $650 $800

P. DITISHEIM, 17 J., "Solvil," curved, diamond dial
platinum..............................$1,000 $1,100 $1,400

P. DITISHEIM, 17 jewels, diamond dial, curved
platinum..............................$1,000 $1,100 $1,400

P. DITISHEIM, 17 J., baguette diamonds, fancy bezel
platinum $1,400 $1,500 $1,800

DOXA, 17 jewels, center sec., fancy lugs
14k $125 $150 $195

P. DITISHEIM, 17 jewels, hinged lugs, enameled bezel
14k $700 $750 $900

DOME, 25 jewels, triple dates, moon ph., auto wind
18k $400 $450 $550

DOXA, 17 jewels, chronog., fluted lugs
14k $350 $400 $475

DORIC, 17J., fancy lugs, two tone case, c.1935
gold filled.................................. $60 $75 $125

DOXA, 17J., chronog., date, 3 reg., by Valjoux
gold filled $300 $350 $425
14k $500 $550 $650

DOXA, 17 jewels, aux sec.
gold filled.................................. $40 $50 $75

DOXA, 17 jewels, chronog., triple dates, moon phase
14k $1,000 $1,200 $1,500

DOXA, 17 jewels, chronog., 2 reg., c. 1942
gold filled.............................$300 $400 $600

DOXA, 17 jewels, chronog., cal. 1220, c. 1940
gold filled.............................$175 $200 $275
s. steel $175 $200 $275

DOXA, 17 jewels, center sec
s. steel $45 $50 $75

DOXA, 17 jewels, center sec., c. 1949
gold filled.................................$50 $65 $95

DOXA, 17J., "Grafic" date,
14k $95 $125 $195

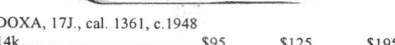

DOXA, 17J., cal. 1361, c.1948
14k $95 $125 $195

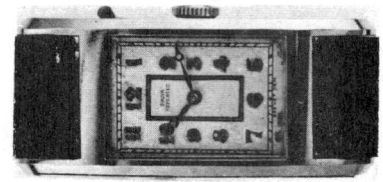

DRIVA, 15 jewels, repeater, repeats on gong, 1/4 repeater
activated by bolt above hand, c. 1930
s. steel $3,000 $3,500 $4,000

DRIVA, 15 jewels, 5 min. repeater, activated by bolt
14k $2,500 $3,000 $3,500

DRIVA, 17 jewels, double teardrop lugs, c.1945
14k $125 $150 $195

DUGENA, 17J., cal.985, c.1960
14k $95 $110 $175

DUNHILL, 17J., date, auto w., alarm by Le Coultre, c. 1965
s. steel $700 $800 $1,000

DUNHILL, 15J., by Bulwark W.Co., engraved bezel,c.1930
gold filled................................. $30 $40 $55

DUODIAL, 15 jewels, c. 1934
9k $400 $500 $700

EBEL, 21 jewels, chronog., self winding, perpetual cal.
18k $7,000 $8,000 $10,000

EBEL, 18 jewels, Ca.1959
18k $175 $195 $275

EBEL, 18 jewels, applied gold numbers, c. 1950
18k $250 $300 $375

EBEL, 18 jewels, Ca. 1958
14k $150 $175 $225

EBEL, 17 jewels, slide open to wind
leather $195 $250 $325

EBEL, 17 jewels, chronog., 2 reg., enamel dial
s. steel $195 $250 $325

EBEL, 17J., cal.119, auto-wind, c.1950
s. steel $60 $75 $125

EBEL, 17 jewels, chronog., c. 1955
14k $350 $400 $500
gold filled.............................. $195 $250 $325

EBEL, 17J., cal.93, center sec., c.1950
18k $195 $225 $300

EBEL, 17 jewels, chronog., "pulsation", c. 1943
s. steel $250 $275 $350

EBEL, 17J., lady's watch, c.1948
14k C&B................................. $195 $225 $300

EBEL, 17 jewels, chronog., 3 reg., c. 1941
14k $500 $550 $650
s. steel $300 $350 $425

EBERHARD, 18 jewels, split sec. chronog., 3 reg.
18k $4,500 $5,000 $6,000

🕐 Pricing in this Guide are fair market price for **COMPLETE** watches which are reflected from the "**NAWCC**" National and regional shows.

🕐 Some grades are not included. Their values can be determined by comparing with **similar** age, size, metal content, style, grades, or models such as **time only**, chronograph, repeater etc. listed.

EBEL, 17J., "Sport", c.1949
gold filled................................. $60 $75 $125

EBERHARD, 17 J., tele-tachymeter, enamel dial, c. 1930
18k $1,400 $1,600 $2,000

EBERHARD, 17J., water proof, auto wind, triple date, moon phases
18k rose $900 $1,000 $1,600

EBERHARD, 17 jewels, "Extra Fort", chronog., 2 reg.,
note: Button at 4 slides to **lock** chronograph action.
18k $1,200 $1,500 $2,000

EKEGREN, 18 jewels, **jumping hr.**, c. 1920
platinum..............................$5,000 $6,000 $8,000
18k $3,000 $3,500 $4,500

EBERHARD, 17 J., chronog., center lugs, 1 button, enamel
dial
s. steel $550 $650 $800

ELECTRA W. Co., 17J, chronog., 1 button, hinged back,
enamel dial
silver $450 $600 $800

EBERHARD, 17 J., wire lugs, enamel dial, c.1928
early waterproof case
silver $400 $450 $550

ELECTRA W. Co., 17J, chronog., 1 button, hinged back,
wire lugs, enamel dial
silver $650 $750 $1,000

ELGIN, 17J., Fancy hidden lugs, Ca. 1950
gold filled................................$125 $150 $225

LORD ELGIN, 21J., extended lugs, Ca.1955
14k $125 $150 $225

LORD ELGIN, 21J., extended lugs,
gold filled................................$95 $125 $225

LORD ELGIN, 21J., hooded bezel, Ca. 1953
14K..$125 $150 $225

ELGIN, 19J., fancy bezel, c.1950s
gold filled................................$95 $125 $195

ELGIN, 17J., **hidden lugs, 7 diamonds & 8 baguettes**
14K $300 $350 $550

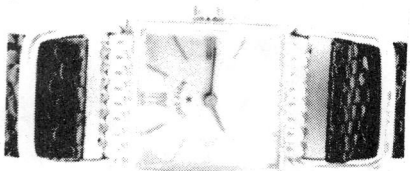

LORD ELGIN, 21J., hinged lugs
gold filled $75 $95 $150

ELGIN, 15-17J., hooded lugs, gold jewel settings, Ca. 1925
gold filled $125 $175 $225
14k(w)....................................$300 $350 $550

LORD ELGIN, 21J., Ca. 1948
14K $95 $125 $195

LORD ELGIN, 21J., **3 diamonds**, cal.626, c.1950
14k(w)....................................$150 $175 $225

ELGIN, 21J., cal.626, 3 diamonds, Ca.1950's
14k $150 $175 $225

ELGIN, 17J., stepped hooded lugs, c.1925
gold filled $75 $85 $150

ELGIN, 17J., stepped case, Ca. 1935
gold filled................................$60 $75 $125

ELGIN, 17J., side lugs, Ca. 1958
gold filled $95 $125 $175

ELGIN, 15J., cal. 554, Ca. 1950's
gold filled................................$60 $75 $125

ELGIN, 7-15J., stepped case, sold for $25.00 in 1936
gold filled $60 $75 $125

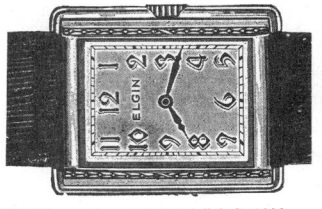

ELGIN, 15J., spur lugs, embossed dial, Ca.1929
gold filled................................$60 $75 $125

ELGIN, 21J., Lord Elgin, Ca. 1945
14k $95 $125 $195

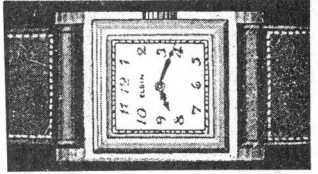

ELGIN, 15J., Crown Guard, Ca.1929
gold filled................................$60 $75 $125

ELGIN, 17J., **Dollar markers,** Ca. 1955
gold filled $75 $95 $135

ELGIN, 19J., cal. 626, Ca. 1946
14k $95 $125 $225

ELGIN, engraved case, Ca. 1924
14k $95 $125 $195

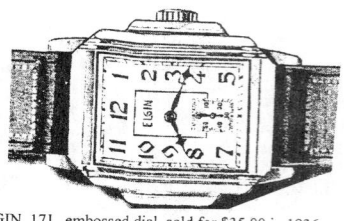

ELGIN, 17J., embossed dial, sold for $35.00 in 1936,
gold filled.................................. $60 $75 $125

LORD ELGIN, 21J., cal.625, c.1950
14k $95 $125 $225

LORD ELGIN, 21J., **11 diamonds,** Ca. 1946
14K.. $195 $225 $350

LORD ELGIN, 21J., cal. 713, GJS, c.1958
14k $125 $150 $225

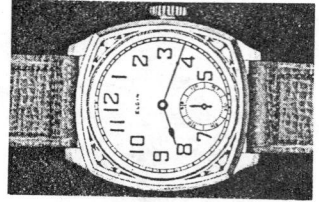

LORD ELGIN, 21J.,
gold filled.................................. $60 $75 $125

ELGIN, 17J., deluxe, Ca. 1955
gold filled $60 $75 $125

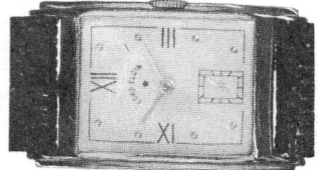

LORD ELGIN, 21J., cal.559, c.1942
gold filled $60 $75 $125

ELGIN, 15J., Legionnaire, Ca. 1929
gold filled.................................. $60 $75 $125

LORD ELGIN, 21J., GJS, c. 1936
14k $95 $125 $225

LORD ELGIN, 21J., GJS, cal.626, c.1940
14k $95 $125 $225

ELGIN, 17J., **Adonis**, engraved, Ca. 1929
gold filled............................... $75 $85 $150

ELGIN, 17J., "Dura Power" mainspring LOGO,
gold plate $30 $40 $75

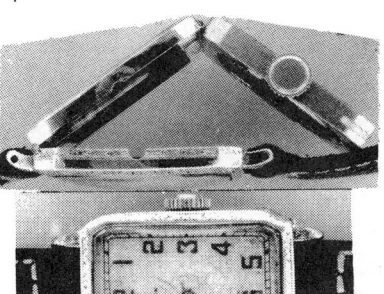

ELGIN, 7J., **hinged case**, engraved case, c.1920s
gold filled................................. $75 $95 $150

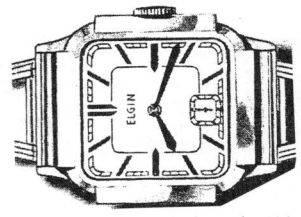

ELGIN,17J., embossed dial, sold for $25.00 in 1936
gold filled $60 $75 $125

ELGIN, 17 jewels, raised numbers
14k $95 $125 $225

LORD ELGIN, 21 jewels, curved, raised numbers
14k $125 $150 $225

ELGIN, 17 jewels, embossed dial
14k $95 $125 $225

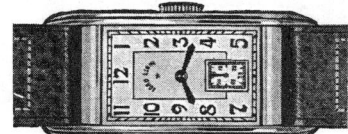

LORD ELGIN, 21 jewels, curved
gold filled $60 $75 $125

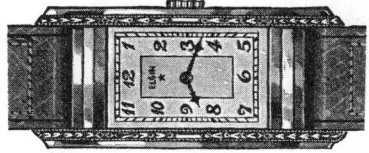

ELGIN, 17 jewels, curved, "Streamlined"
gold filled $75 $95 $150

 Some grades are not included. Their values can be
determined by comparing with **similar** age, size, metal
content, style, grades, or models such as **time only**,
chronograph, repeater etc. listed.

ELGIN, 17 jewels, raised numbers
gold filled...................................$60 $75 $125

ELGIN, 15 jewels, curved, fancy bezel
gold filled...................................$75 $95 $150

LORD ELGIN, 21 jewels, curved
platinum..................................$250 $300 $450

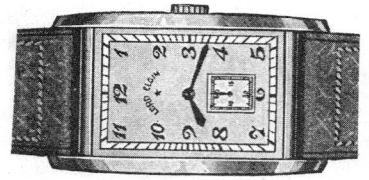

LORD ELGIN, 21 jewels, curved
14k..$175 $195 $250

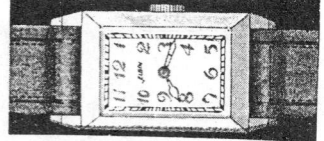

ELGIN, 15 jewels, Ca. 1929
Sterling.....................................$95 $125 $175

ELGIN, 17 jewels, curved
gold filled...................................$60 $75 $125
Wrist Watches listed in this section are priced at the collectable
fair market **Trade Show** level as **complete** watches having an
original gold-filled case and stainless steel back, also with
original dial, leather watch band, and the entire original movement in good working order with no repairs needed.

A collector should expect to pay modestly higher prices
at local shops

ELGIN, 15 jewels, drivers style, winds at 12 O'clock
gold filled $125 $150 $275

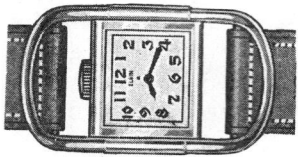

ELGIN, 17 jewels, "Ristflo" winds at 12 O'clock
gold filled $125 $150 $275

ELGIN, 17 jewels
gold filled $60 $75 $125

ELGIN, 17 jewels, hidden lugs
gold filled $60 $75 $125

ELGIN, 17 jewels, embossed dial, thin model
gold filled $60 $75 $135

Pricing in this Guide are fair market price for **COMPLETE**
watches which are reflected from the "**NAWCC**" National and
regional shows.

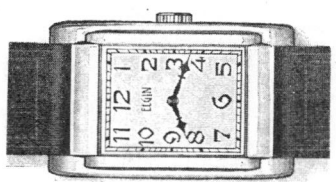

ELGIN, 17 jewels, curved, thin model
gold filled..................................$60 $75 $125

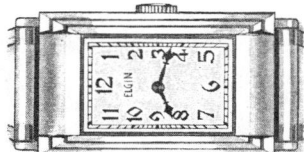

ELGIN, 17 jewels, stepped case
gold filled..................................$60 $75 $125

ELGIN, 17J., center sec., cal.11553, c.1928
gold filled..................................$75 $95 $150

ELGIN, 15 jewels, ''William Osler'' recess crown
gold filled..................................$75 $95 $150

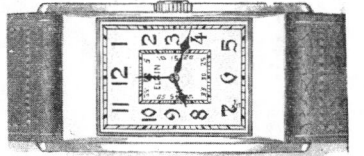

ELGIN, 7 jewels, center sec., recess crown
gold filled..................................$75 $95 $150

ELGIN, 17J., engraved case, c.1928
gold filled..................................$60 $75 $125

ELGIN, 17J., sold for $47.50 in 1936
gold filled $60 $75 $125

ELGIN,7-15J., engraved case, c. 1928
14K $95 $125 $225
gold filled $60 $75 $125

ELGIN, 15J., engraved **Mermaid** design case, c.1928
gold filled $195 $275 $375

ELGIN, 15J., engraved case, c. 1928
gold filled $60 $75 $125

ELGIN, 15J., curved engraved case, c. 1928
gold filled $60 $75 $125

ELGIN, 7J., Ca. 1925
nickel..$55 $65 $85

ELGIN, 17 jewels, "Crusade"
gold filled $75 $85 $125

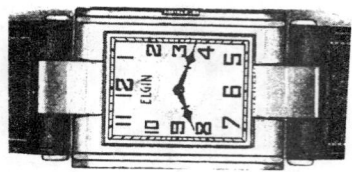

ELGIN, 15 jewels, center lugs
gold filled................................$95 $125 $175

ELGIN, 7 jewels
gold filled $60 $70 $95

ELGIN, 7 jewels, fancy bezel
s. steel $45 $55 $95

ELGIN, 7 jewels, stepped bezel
s. steel $60 $75 $95

ELGIN, 7 jewels, fancy bezel
gold filled................................$50 $60 $95

ELGIN, 15J., wire lugs, stem at "12", c.1920s
silver $95 $150 $275

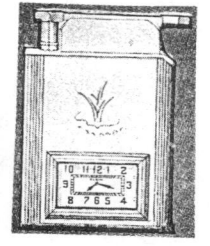

ELGIN, 15J.,combination lighter and Elgin Watch
Sterling....................................$195 $225 $275

ELGIN, 15J., cut-corner case, Ca. 1925
gold filled $60 $75 $125

ELGIN, 15J., engraved case, c.1925
gold filled..................................$55 $65 $95

LORD ELGIN, 21J., stepped case, c.1930
gold filled..................................$60 $75 $150

LORD ELGIN, 21J., stepped case, c.1930
gold filled..................................$60 $75 $150

ELGIN, 7J., stepped case, c.1925
gold filled..................................$60 $75 $95

ELGIN, 17J., **BMW** logo, Ca.1955
gold filled..................................$60 $75 $125

LORD ELGIN, 21J., GJS, c.1937
14k $125 $150 $225

ELGIN, 17J., stepped case, c.1930
gold filled $60 $75 $125

ELGIN, 17J., curved, stepped case, c.1927
gold filled $40 $50 $95

ELGIN, 17 jewels, raised numbers
gold filled $60 $75 $125

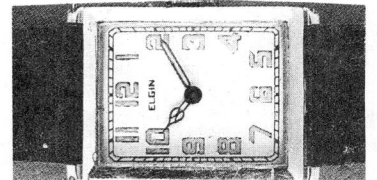

ELGIN, 17 jewels, c. 1927
14k $95 $125 $195

🕐 A collector should expect to pay modestly higher prices at local shops

🕐 Some grades are not included. Their values can be determined by comparing with **similar** age, size, metal content, style, models and grades listed.

LORD ELGIN, 21 jewels, diamond dial
14k (w).....................................$150 $195 $275

ELGIN, 19 jewels, flared case
14k $195 $250 $325

ELGIN, 19 jewels, c. 1947
14k $95 $125 $225
gold filled..................................$60 $75 $125

ELGIN, 19 jewels, flared case, fancy lugs
14k $195 $225 $275

LORD ELGIN, 21 jewels, diamond dial
14k (w)....................................$150 $175 $275

ELGIN, 7J., **star** dial, cushion case, c.1930
gold filled $65 $75 $125

LORD ELGIN, 21 jewels, aux. sec., fancy lugs
14k $150 $175 $250

ELGIN, 7-15J., cushion case, c.1930
chromium..................................$30 $40 $65

LORD ELGIN, 21J., cal.670, c.1948
gold filled..................................$75 $95 $150
14k $195 $250 $325

Wrist Watches listed in this section are priced at the collectable
fair market **Trade Show** level as **complete** watches having an
original gold-filled case and stainless steel back, also with
original dial, leather watch band, and the entire original movement in good working order with no repairs needed.

ELGIN, 7-15J., **star** dial, solid lugs, Ca. 1925
s. steel $65 $75 $125

ELGIN, 15J., **pierced** shield, **star** dial, wire lugs, c.1918
silver $300 $350 $450

ELGIN, 15J., U.S.GOV'T grade II, c.1960s
s. steel $75 $85 $125

ELGIN, 15J., **pierced** shield, c.1918
silver $300 $350 $450

ELGIN, 15J., military style, 24 hr. dial, c.1942
s. steel $85 $95 $125

ELGIN, 15J., **canteen** style case, **star** dial, wire lugs, c.1919
nickel.............................. ★ ★ $400 $450 $550

ELGIN, 15J., military style, cal.539, c.1940
s. steel $75 $85 $125

ELGIN, 15 jewels, "Official Boy Scout" model
s. steel $125 $150 $235

🕐 A collector should expect to pay modestly higher prices at local shops

🕐 Some grades are not included. Their values can be determined by comparing with **similar** age, size, metal content, style, grades, or models such as **time only**, chronograph, repeater etc. listed.

ELGIN, 16J., **canteen** style case, U.S.N.234C, c.1930s
s. steel .... ★ ★ ★ $400 $500 $700

ELGIN, 7 jewels, "Official Boy Scout" model
s. steel $60 $75 $125

ELGIN, 15 jewels, enamel dial, wire lugs, c. 1915
silver $95 $150 $250

ELGIN, 15 jewels, enamel dial, wire lugs, c. 1915
silver $95 $125 $175

ELGIN, 15 jewels, center lugs
gold filled.................................$95 $125 $175

ELGIN, 15 jewels, center lugs, c. 1922
silver $95 $150 $250

ELGIN, 15J., case by **Rolland Fischer,** c. 1928
silver $400 $500 $700

ELGIN, 7J., center sec., sold for $27.50 in 1936
gold filled $60 $70 $95

ELGIN, 21 jewels, "Black / Golden Knight"
gold filled $75 $95 $175
14k $150 $175 $250

ELGIN, 7 jewels, "Avigo ", Ca. 1929
base metal $65 $75 $125

Wrist Watches listed in this section are priced at the collectable
fair market Trade Show level as **complete** watches having an
original gold-filled case and stainless steel back, also with
original dial, leather watch band, and the entire original movement in good working order with no repairs needed.

ELGIN, 21J., center sec., wire lugs, cal. 680, c.1952
gold filled.................................$30 $40 $95

ELGIN, 30J., auto-wind, grade 760
gold filled $60 $75 $125

ELGIN, 17 jewels, **Alarm**, Ca. 1960
gold filled.................................$95 $125 $195

ELGIN, 19J.,cal.681 , c.1959
gold filled $30 $40 $75

ELGIN, 21J., water-proof, c.1952
s. steel $40 $50 $95

LORD ELGIN, 21J., **enamel bezel**, cal.688, c.1948
gold filled $75 $95 $175

LORD ELGIN, 21J., **shockmaster**, aux. sec., ca. 1955
14K...$95 $125 $195

ELGIN, 23 J., ''B. W. Raymond,'' R.R. approved
14k $300 $350 $550
gold filled $150 $195 $300
s. steel $150 $195 $300

Some grades are not included. Their values can be
determined by comparing with **similar** age, size, metal
content, style, grades, or models such as **time only**,
chronograph, repeater etc. listed.

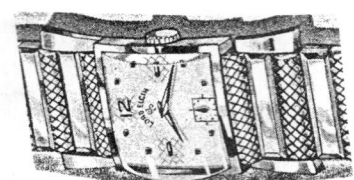

LORD ELGIN, 21J., "Oxford", sold for $100.00 in 1954
gold filled.................................$75 $95 $135

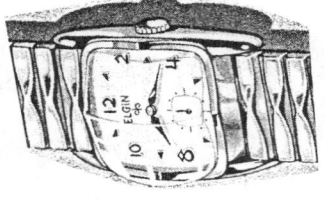

ELGIN, 17J., "Sinclair", sold for $39.75 in 1954
gold filled $70 $90 $125

LORD ELGIN, 21J., "Thornton", sold for $71.50 in 1954
gold filled.................................$85 $95 $150

ELGIN, 19J., "Gulfport", sold for $69.55 in 1954
gold filled $70 $90 $125

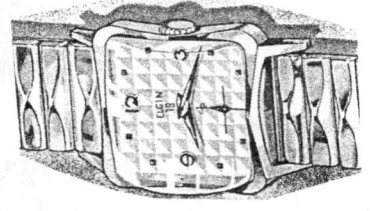

ELGIN, 19J., "Garfield", sold for $69.50 in 1954
gold filled.................................$75 $95 $135

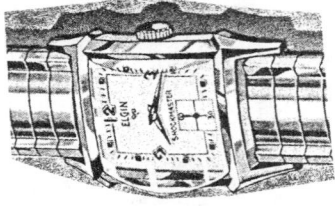

ELGIN, 17J., "Edgewater", sold for $62.55 in 1954
gold filled $70 $90 $125

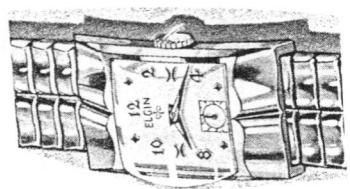

ELGIN, 17J., "Milburn", sold for $59.50 in 1954
gold filled.................................$70 $90 $125

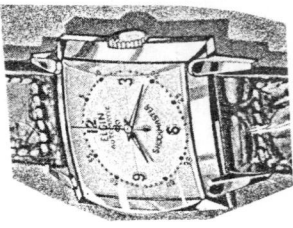

ELGIN, 17J., "Windsor", auto-wind, sold for $95.00 in 1954
gold filled $70 $90 $125

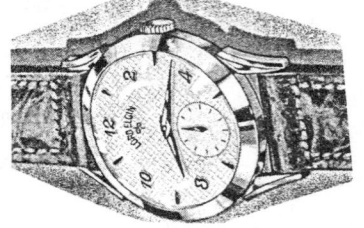

LORD ELGIN, 21J., "Wakefield", sold for $71.50 in 1954
gold filled.................................$65 $75 $125

ELGIN, 17J., "Dante", auto-wind, sold for $71.50 in 1954
s. steel $70 $90 $125

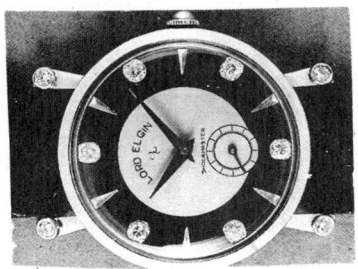

LORD ELGIN, 21J., **diamond on lugs not factory**, c. 1958
14k (w)....................................$195 $225 $275

LORD ELGIN, 21 jewels, mystery dial, c. 1957
14k (w)....................................$150 $195 $275

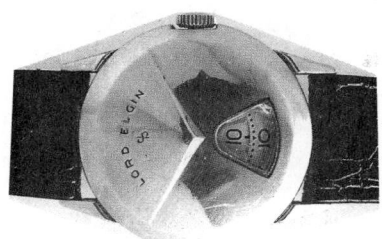

LORD ELGIN, 21J., direct reading, Chevron style, Ca.1957
gold filled................................$250 $300 $400

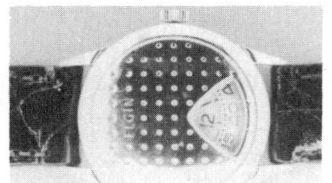

ELGIN, 17 J., in form of golf ball, rotating hr. & min.
gold filled................................$300 $350 $500

LORD ELGIN, 21 jewels, applied numbers, c. 1946
14k $125 $150 $225

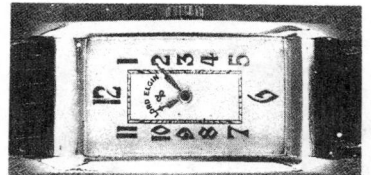

LORD ELGIN, 21 jewels, curved, applied numbers
14k $150 $175 $250

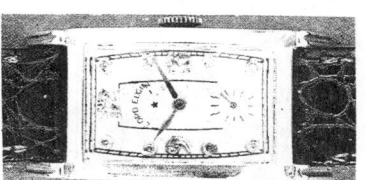

LORD ELGIN, 21 jewels, diamond dial, faceted crystal
14k $150 $175 $250

ELGIN, 17 jewels, hinged back
14k (w) $125 $150 $225

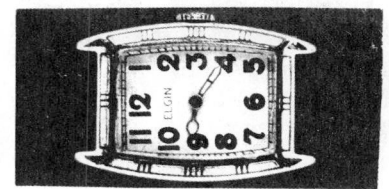

ELGIN, 17 jewels, enamel bezel, Ca. 1930
14k (w) $195 $250 $350

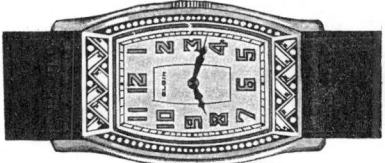

ELGIN, 15 jewels, Art Deco bezel, c. 1935
gold filled $85 $95 $150

⌛ A collector should expect to pay modestly higher prices at local shops

⌛ Some grades are not included. Their values can be determined by comparing with **similar** age, size, metal content, style, grades, or models such as **time only**, chronograph, repeater etc. listed.

ELGIN, 15 jewels, 2 tone, c. 1930
gold filled.................................$75 $85 $125

ELGIN, 7 jewels, engraved bezel
s. steel $40 $50 $95

ELGIN, 15 jewels, enamel bezel, c. 1920
14k (w)....................................$250 $300 $450

ELGIN, 17 jewels, aux. sec., curved
gold filled $50 $60 $95

ELGIN, 17 jewels, raised numbers
gold filled.................................$75 $95 $150

ELGIN, 17 jewels, curved
gold filled $50 $60 $95

ELGIN, 15-21J., enamel bezel, 2 tone, in 1929 sold for
$24.00
14k $350 $400 $500
 gold filled..............................$150 $175 $250

ELGIN, 17 jewels, curved
gold filled $50 $60 $95

ELGIN, 15J., Luminous hands, sold for $27.50 in 1929
gold filled (Y or W)................$75 $95 $135

ELGIN, 21 jewels, blue enamel bezel, c. 1920
14k(yellow gold) $700 $800 $950

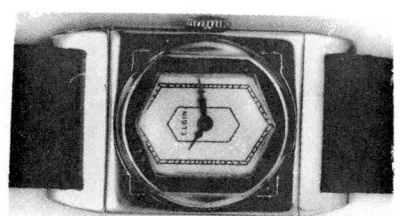

ELGIN, 15 jewels, enamel bezel
14k $900 $1,000 $1,200

LORD ELGIN, 21J, grade 670, large lugs, anniversary of 50
million watches made serial # 50,000,000 to 50,000,999,
gold plated movement, Ca. 1951
18k .... ★ ★ ★$1,000 $1,200 $1,500

LORD ELGIN, 21J., Jump Hr. & Wandering Min., curved
gold filled...............................$325 $400 $600

ELGIN, 17 jewels, double dial
gold filled...............................$350 $400 $500

LORD ELGIN, 21 jewels, curved, c. 1957
14k $195 $250 $350

LORD ELGIN, 21 jewels, hooded lugs, c. 1950s
14k $150 $175 $250

ELGIN, 15 jewels, waterproof
s. steel $30 $40 $75

ELGIN, 15 jewels, center sec.
gold filled $30 $40 $75

ELGIN, 7 jewels, aux. sec.
gold filled $30 $40 $75

LORD ELGIN, 21 jewels, hooded lugs, c. 1952
14k $200 $225 $350

LORD ELGIN, 21 jewels, stepped case
18k $250 $275 $325

LORD ELGIN, 21 jewels, stepped case, curved
14k $125 $150 $195

ELGIN, 17 jewels, stepped case
14k $125 $150 $195

LORD ELGIN, 21 jewels, curved
gold filled................................$70 $80 $125

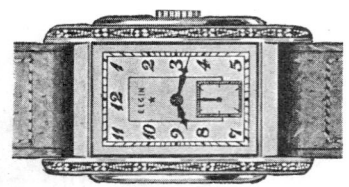

ELGIN, 17 jewels, curved, fancy bezel
gold filled................................$60 $70 $95

ELGIN, 17 jewels, curved, stepped case
gold filled................................$80 $90 $125

ELGIN, 17 jewels, curved, stepped case
gold filled................................$60 $75 $125

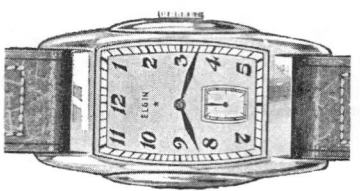

ELGIN, 17 jewels, curved
gold filled $60 $75 $125

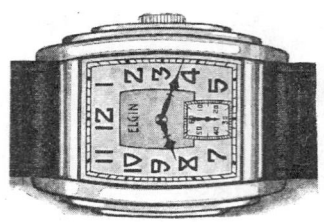

ELGIN, 19 jewels, stepped case
gold filled $60 $75 $125

ELGIN, 15 jewels
gold filled $60 $75 $125

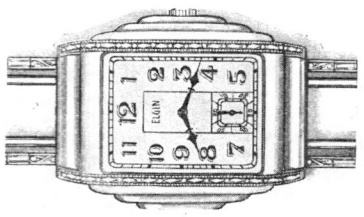

ELGIN, 7 jewels, fancy bezel
base metal $30 $45 $75

ELGIN, 7 jewels, fancy bezel
gold filled $55 $65 $95

LORD ELGIN, 21 jewels, curved, c. 1938
14k $150 $175 $225

ELGIN, 15 jewels, fancy bezel
gold filled.................................$60 $70 $95

ELGIN, 21 jewels, curved
gold filled.................................$60 $75 $125

LORD ELGIN, 21 jewels, raised numbers
14k $125 $150 $225

LORD ELGIN, 21 jewels, curved
14k $125 $150 $225

LORD ELGIN, 21 jewels, curved
14k $150 $175 $225

LORD ELGIN, 21 jewels, aux. sec.
gold filled.................................$60 $75 $125

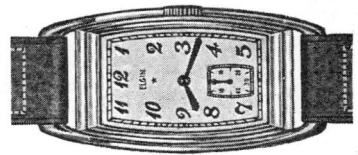

LORD ELGIN, 21 jewels, curved
14k..$150 $175 $235

ELGIN, 17 jewels, curved
gold filled.................................$60 $70 $95

ELGIN, 17 Jewels, raised numbers
14k..$150 $175 $225

LORD ELGIN, 15 jewels, **electric**, 6 adj., Ca. 1962, (sold
for $89.50, July of 1962), grade 725, in **good running order**
gold filled........................★★$200 $250 $325

**Elgin pioneering effort in electric watches
started in 1955.**

LORD ELGIN, 15 jewels, **electric**, c. 1962
(back–set)
s. steel .... ★★$200 $250 $325

LORD ELGIN, 15 jewels, **electric**, c.1962
(grade 725, 6 adj.)
gold filled......................... ★★$200 $250 $325

ELGIN, 17 Jewels, Lady Elgin, flared case, cal. 650, c.1950
14k $100 $125 $175

ELGIN, 15 Jewels, art deco, c.1925
gold filled...................................$40 $50 $75

ELGIN, 15 Jewels, art deco, c.1928
14k $90 $125 $150

ELGIN, 17 Jewels, art deco, c.1928
18k(w)......................................$125 $150 $200

ELGIN, 15J., art deco, Tiger & Lady, Ca. 1929
14K(W) $100 $125 $175

ELGIN, 15 jewels, art deco, Ca. 1928
gold filled...................................$40 $50 $75

ELGIN, 15 jewels, art deco, Ca. 1928
gold filled...................................$25 $30 $45

ELGIN, 15 jewels, art deco, Ca. 1928
gold filled...................................$25 $30 $45

ELGIN, 15 jewels, sports model, Ca. 1928
14k...$75 $85 $125

ELGIN, 17J., 20 diamonds, art deco, Ca. 1928
18k...$225 $275 $350

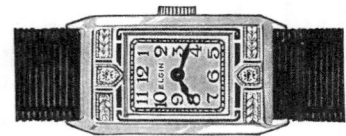

ELGIN, 15 jewels, 2 diamonds, art deco, Ca. 1928
gold filled...................................$75 $85 $125

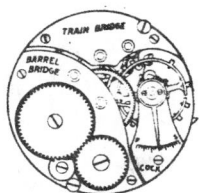   

Model 3, 3-0 size, three-quarter plate, open face, pendant set, first serial number 18,179,001, Grade 414, March, 1915.

Model 1, 5-0 size, three-quarter plate, hunting, pendant set, first serial number 14,699,001, Grade 380, Feb., 1910.

Model 2, 5-0 size, three-quarter plate, open face, pendant set, first serial number 17,890,001, Grade 399, Feb., 1914.

Model 2, 8-0 size, Grade 532, 539, sweep second.

Model 7, 8-0 size, Grades 554, 555,

Model 20, 8-0 size, Grades 681, 682.

Model 1, 10-0 size, three-quarter plate, open face

Model 2, 15-0 size, Grades 623, 624, 626.

15-0 Size, movement, Grades 670, 672, 673.

15-0 size, movement. Grade 674.

15-0 size, movement, Grades 557, 558, 559.

Model 2, 21-0 size, Grade 541, 533, 535.

Model 3, 21-0 size, Grade 547, sweep second.

Model 4, 21-0 size, Grades 617, 617L, 619, 619L.

Model 9, 21-0 size, Grades 650, 651.

Model 9, 21-0 size, Grades 655, 656.

 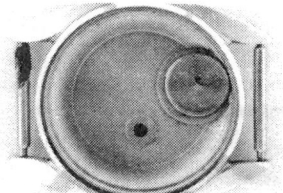

GRADE 725, 15 jewels,"electric" model movement

"ELECTRIC", case showing back—set

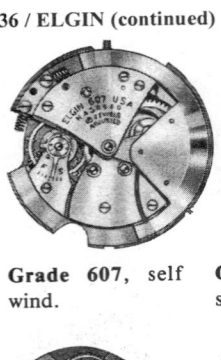

Grade 607, self wind.

Grade 630, sweep second.

Grade 641, 642

Grade 643, self wind.

Grades 644, 645, self wind.

Grade 647, sweep second.

Grade 661

Grade 666, sweep second.

Grade 668, sweep second.

Grade 685

Grade 687

Grade 700

GRADE 710 & 719
719 = DIRECT READ TRAIN SIDE

719 = DIAL SIDE OF MOVEMENT

Grade 716

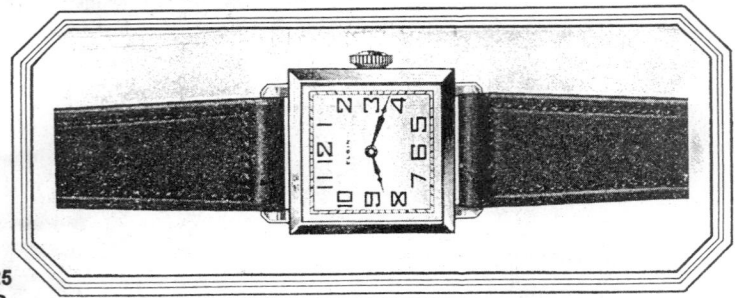

1925 AD

Elgin strap watches for men, in gold and gold-filled cases of yellow, white or green; also silver and nickel. Prices ranging from $20 to $75.

ELOGA, triple calendar,
gold filled bezel $75 $95 $150

EMERSON, 17J., hooded lugs,
gold filled $50 $60 $85

ENICAR, 17 jewels, center sec.
18k $150 $175 $235

ENICAR, 17J., chronograph, 2 reg. Ca. 1955
s. steel $175 $225 $300

ENICAR, 17 jewels, center sec.
s. steel $30 $40 $65

ENICAR, 17 jewels, triple date, moon phase
gold filled $195 $250 $325

ENICAR, 15 jewels, egg shaped with compass, c. 1918
silver $375 $450 $500

ENICAR, 17J., autow., date, 24 hour dial, C.1970
s. steel $95 $125 $195

ESKA, 17J.,chronog., triple date, moon phase
14k $1,200 $1,400 $1,700

ESKA, 17 jewels, chronog., 2 reg., C. 1950s
s. steel $150 $175 $235

ETERNA, 19 jewels, day-date-month
18k...$195 $225 $300

ESKA, 17 jewels, chronog., 2 reg., c. 1940
s. steel $900 $1,000 $1,200

ETERNA, 17 jewels, chronog., triple date, 3 reg.
s.steel.....................................$275 $300 $350
18k...$600 $700 $850

ESKA, 17 jewels, multi-colored enamel dial
18k $1,800 $2,000 $2,600

ETERNA, 21 jewels, date, cal. 14390, c.1960
18k...$150 $195 $300

ETERNA, quartz, date, by ETA, cal#954, C.1975
s. steel $30 $40 $65

⊕ Pricing in this Guide are fair market price for **COM-
PLETE** watches which are reflected from the "<u>**NAWCC**</u>" National and regional shows.

ETERNA, 19 jewels, c.1944
14k...$95 $120 $160

ETERNA, 16 jewels, aux. sec., c.1945
gold filled................................$55 $60 $95

ETERNA, 19 jewels, c.1938
gold filled................................$55 $60 $95

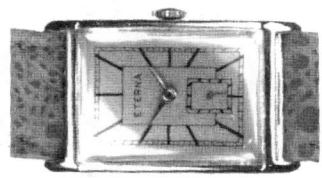

ETERNA, 17 jewels, gold jewel settings, c.1935
14k $95 $125 $195

EVANS, 17 jewels, rhinestones on bezel & dial, c. 1948
gold plate $50 $60 $95

EVANS, 17 jewels, chronog., 2 reg., c. 1940
18k $300 $350 $450

EXACTUS, 17 J., chronog.,triple-date, moon ph.
s. steel....................................$450 $500 $650

EXCELSIOR, 17 jewels, chronog., 2 reg.
14k..$300 $350 $450
gold filled...............................$150 $175 $250

EXCELSIOR, 17 jewels, chronog.
gold filled...............................$150 $175 $250
s. steel....................................$150 $175 $250

EXCELSIOR PARK, 17 jewels, chronog.
s. steel....................................$175 $195 $250

FAIRFAX, 6J, engraved case, c.1929
base metal $30 $35 $55

FAIRFAX, 6J, engraved case, c.1929
base metal $30 $35 $55

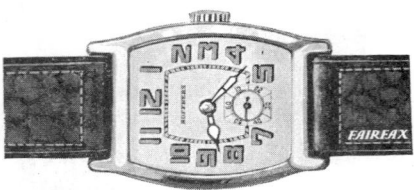

FAIRFAX, 6J, butler finish case, c.1929
base metal $30 $35 $55

FAITH, 17J, **flip top case** HC style, by Hyde Park, c.1950
gold filled............................$195 $225 $300

FAVRE LEUBA,17J., triple date, cal.Valj.89, c.1948
s. steel $125 $150 $195

⏱ A collector should expect to pay modestly higher prices
at local shops

⏱ Some grades are not included. Their values can be determined by comparing with **similar** age, size, metal content,
style, grades, or models such as **time only**, chronograph,
repeater etc. listed.

FAVRE LEUBA,17J., "Bivouac", altimeter with aneroid cap-
sule transmitting variations of atmospheric pressure to the baro-
metric mechanism, revolving bezel, Ca. 1968.
s. steel.....................................$275 $325 $450

FAVRE LEUBA,17J., "Bathy 50", depth reading to about 165
feet, waterproof to 470 feet, Ca. 1968
s. steel.....................................$275 $325 $450

FERRARI, quartz, chronog., c.1988
base metal...............................$150 $175 $250

FELCA, 17 jewels, auto wind
gold filled..................................$40 $50 $80
14k...$95 $125 $195
18k..$175 $195 $300

FONTAINEMELON, S. A., 17 J., gold train, digital
14k $1,100 $1,200 $1,500

FREY,15J., engraved case, c.1933
base metal................................$30 $35 $60

FRAMONT, 17J, timer, date, cal. 290, c.1970
s. steel $75 $95 $150

FREY,15J., engraved stepped case, c.1933
base metal................................$30 $35 $60

FREY, 25J., rotating outside chapter, c.1970
s. steel $45 $55 $80

FREY,15J., engraved case, c.1933
base metal................................$30 $35 $60

FRIEDLI, 17 jewels, auto wind, center sec.
gold filled................................$40 $55 $70
18k..$175 $195 $250

FREY,17J., GJS, c.1970
s. steel $30 $35 $60

Wrist Watches listed in this section are priced at the collectable
fair market **Trade Show** level as **complete** watches having an
original gold-filled case and stainless steel back, also with
original dial, leather watch band, and the entire original movement in good working order with no repairs needed.

FRODSHAM, 17J., Ca. 1935
18k(w) $350 $450 $600

GALLET, 15 jewels, wire lugs, Ca. 1925
silver $75 $95 $150

GALLET, 17 jewels, chronog., 3 reg., c. 1945
s. steel....................................$250 $300 $400

GALLET, 15 jewels, waterproof, auto wind
s. steel $30 $35 $60

GALLET, 17 jewels, chronog., 3 reg., c. 1942
gold filled..............................$250 $300 $400

GALLET, 17 jewels, chronog., single button, c. 1950
s. steel $195 $295 $450

GALLET, 17J., chronog., 2 reg.,single button, C.1925,
silver"small size" $600 $700 $900

GALLET, 17J., chronog., by Racine, US air force, c. 1978
s. steel $175 $250 $350

🕐 Pricing in this Guide are fair market price for **COM-PLETE** watches which are reflected from the **"NAWCC"** National and regional shows.

GALLET, 17J., chronog., 3 reg., triple date, moon ph.
18k.......................................$1,300 $1,500 $2,000

GALLET, 17J., chronog., 3 reg., triple **date**
14k	$650	$750	$1,000
s. steel	$350	$450	$700

GALLET, 17 jewels, chronog., 3 reg., c. 1955
s. steel $275 $325 $500

GALLET, 17 jewels, 2 reg., Ca. 1958
s. steel $175 $195 $300

GALLET, 17 jewels, chronog., 2 reg.
14k	$300	$350	$525
s. steel	$175	$195	$275

GALLET, 17 jewels, chronog., mid size, c. 1940
s. steel...................................$250 $300 $400

GALLET, 17J., chronog., flying officer, cal.149, c. 1958
s. steel...................................$350 $450 $650

GALLET, 17 jewels, chronog., waterproof
s. steel...................................$275 $350 $500

GALLET, 17 jewels, chronog., 2 reg.
s. steel...................................$195 $225 $300

⊕ Some grades are not included. Their values can be determined by comparing with **similar** age, size, metal content, style, grades, or models such as **time only**, chronograph, repeater etc. listed.

GALLET, 17 jewels, chronog., 2 reg.
s.steel $325 $400 $575

GALLET, 17 jewels, time dial at 12 , chronog.
s. steel.....................................$300 $325 $400

GALLET, 17 jewels, chronog., 2 reg.
gold filled...............................$195 $225 $275

P. GARNIER, 17 jewels, minu-stop, c. 1965
s. steel.....................................$50 $60 $90

GALLET, 17 jewels, chronog., 2 reg.
s. steel $175 $195 $250

P. GARNIER, 17 jewels, world time, c. 1968
s. steel.....................................$95 $125 $175

GALLET, 17 jewels, chronog., 2 reg., c. 1939
s. steel $195 $250 $375

⊕ Pricing in this Guide are fair market price for COM-
PLETE watches which are reflected from the "NAWCC" National and regional shows.

GARLAND, 17J., center sec., water-proof.
s. steel.....................................$35 $45 $70

Wrist Watches listed in this section are priced at the collectable
fair market Trade Show level as **complete** watches having an
original gold-filled case and stainless steel back, also with
original dial, leather watch band, and the entire original movement in good working order with no repairs needed.

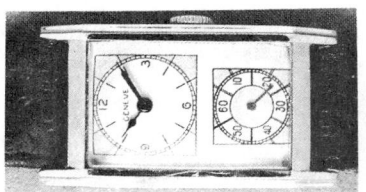

GENEVE, 15 jewels, dual dial, c. 1939
s. steel $400 $500 $650

GENEVE, 15 jewels, dual dial, c. 1937
s. steel $400 $500 $650

GENEVE, 17 jewels, curly lugs, c.1950
14k $150 $175 $225

GERMINAL, 17 J., center sec.
s. steel 60   70   95
14k $95 $125 $175

GERMINAL, 15 J., early auto wind, lug action, c. 1933
s. steel $550 $650 $750

GERALD GENTA, 29J., skeletonized, auto wind,
perpetual calendar
18k C&B $8,000 $9,000 $11,000

GIRARD-PERREGAUX, 17J., auto wind, C.1951
s. steel $60 $80 $125

GIRARD-PERREGAUX, 17J., alarm, c.1960
gold filled................................$125 $150 $250

GIRARD-PERREGAUX, 39J., center sec. c.1955
14k..$150 $175 $225

⊕ Some grades are not included. Their values can be
determined by comparing with **similar** age, size, metal
content, style, grades, or models such as **time only**,
chronograph, repeater etc. listed.

GIRARD-PERREGAUX, 17J., auto w., center sec., c.1948
18k $250 $275 $325

GIRARD-PERREGAUX, 17J., aux. sec., c.1958
gold filled.................................$65 $80 $125

GIRARD-PERREGAUX, 17J., Gyromatic, center sec., c.1960
s. steel $65 $80 $125

GIRARD-PERREGAUX, 17J., "Sea Hawk", aux. sec., c.1950
s. steel.......................................$95 $125 $175

GIRARD-PERREGAUX, 17J., Gyromatic, cal.47ae, c.1953
14k $150 $175 $225

GIRARD-PERREGAUX, 17J., Gyromatic, date, c.1960
gold filled.................................$65 $80 $125

GIRARD-PERREGAUX, 17J., Sea Hawk, c.1960
gold filled.................................$65 $80 $125

GIRARD-PERREGAUX, 39J., Gyromatic, "HF", date, c.1960
18k..$225 $250 $325

🕐 Some grades are not included. Their values can be
determined by comparing with **similar** age, size, metal
content, style, grades, or models such as **time only**,
chronograph, repeater etc. listed.

GIRARD-PERREGAUX, 39J., chronometer "HF", c.1970
s. steel $70 $90 $150

GIRARD-PERREGAUX, 17 jewels, triple date, aux. sec.
s.steel......................................$150 $175 $225

GIRARD-PERREGAUX,17J.,"Gyromatic",date
gold filled.................................$65 $80 $125

GIRARD-PERREGAUX, 17J., chronog., 2 reg., waterproof
s. steel......................................$275 $325 $400

GIRARD-PERREGAUX, 39J.,"Gyromatic",date, Ca. 1960
18k $195 $225 $300

GIRARD-PERREGAUX, 17J., by Valjoux cal.72, c.1955
s. steel......................................$400 $450 $600

GIRARD-PERREGAUX, 17J., triple date, autow.
s. steel $150 $175 $225

GIRARD-PERREGAUX, 17J., chronog cal.285, c.1940
gold filled................................$195 $250 $350

GIRARD-PERREGAUX, 17J., pulsations, c.1948
14k $400 $450 $550

GIRARD-PERREGAUX, 17 J., chronog., 3 reg., c. 1952
s. steel $325 $350 $475

GIRARD-PERREGAUX, 17J, chronog., triple date, moon phase
18k $1,500 $1,700 $2,200

GIRARD-PERREGAUX, 39 J., Ca. 1955
14k $95 $125 $195
18k $125 $150 $285

GIRARD-PERREGAUX, 17J., aux. sec., Ca.1960
14k $150 $175 $225

GIRARD-PERREGAUX, 17J., "gyromatic",
14k..$150 $175 $225

GIRARD-PERREGAUX, 17J., RF#2459, c.1970
14k...$95 $125 $195

GIRARD-PERREGAUX, 17J., cal.a6 3606, GJS, c.1955
14k..$150 $175 $225

GIRARD-PERREGAUX, 17J., recess crown, GJS, c.1954
14k..$175 $195 $250

GIRARD-PERREGAUX, 17J., cal.86, GJS, Ca.1948
14k $95 $125 $195

GIRARD-PERREGAUX, 17J., recess crown, GJS, c.1947
gold filled.................................$65 $80 $125

GIRARD-PERREGAUX, 17J., cal.86ae, GJS, c.1940
s. steel $60 $80 $125

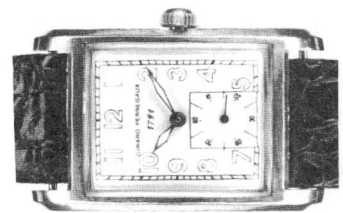

GIRARD-PERREGAUX, 17J., "1791", GJS, c.1942
s. steel......................................$75 $95 $150

GIRARD-PERREGAUX, 17J., two tone case, GJS, Ca.1942
14k $195 $250 $300

GIRARD-PERREGAUX, 17J., cal.91ae220, GJS, c.1948
gold filled.................................$65 $80 $125

GIRARD-PERREGAUX, 17J., GJS, c.1953
14k $125 $150 $195

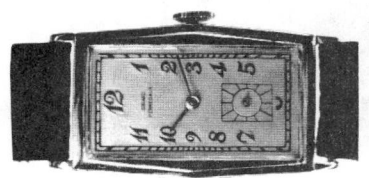

GIRARD-PERREGAUX, 17J., GJS, c.1936
gold filled.................................$65 $80 $125

GIRARD-PERREGAUX, 17J., cal. 86ae, GJS, c.1942
s. steel $65 $80 $125

GIRARD-PERREGAUX, 17J., cal.86ae, GJS, c.1942
14k..$125 $150 $195

Wrist Watches listed in this section are priced at the collectable fair market **Trade Show** level as **complete** watches having an original gold-filled case and stainless steel back, also with original dial, leather watch band, and the entire original movement in good working order with no repairs needed.

🕐 A collector should expect to pay modestly higher prices at local shops

GIRARD-PERREGAUX, 39 jewels, aux. sec.
14k $150 $175 $225

GIRARD-PERREGAUX, 17 jewels, aux. sec.
gold filled..................................$65 $80 $125

GIRARD-PERREGAUX, 17 jewels,Ca. 1948
14k $150 $175 $225

GIRARD-PERREGAUX, 17 J., C. 1948
14k $150 $175 $225

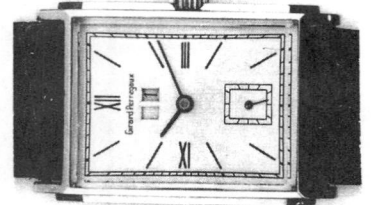

GIRARD-PERREGAUX, 17 J., date, stepped case,
18k $500 $550 $700
14k $300 $350 $500

GLASHUTTE, 17J., 2 reg., fluted bezel, c.1942
s. steel....................................$800 $950 $1,200

GLASHUTTE, 17J., signed Uhrenfabrik Glashutte, c.1935
18k..$500 $550 $700

GLASHUTTE, 15J., signed "GUB", Ca.1950's
gold filled...............................$200 $250 $350

GLYCINE, 17J., **Airman** ,auto-wind, 24hr., date, c.1970
s. steel....................................$125 $150 $250

GLYCINE, 17J., 15 diamond dial, cal.4645, c.1945
14k..$450 $550 $700

GLYCINE, 17J., 3 diamond dial, c.1950
14k(w).....................................$95 $125 $195

GLYCINE, 17 J., airman, 24 hr. dial, autow, date, C.1960s
s. steel $175 $250 $450

GLYCINE, 17 jewels, **curved,** c. 1938
18k $195 $225 $300

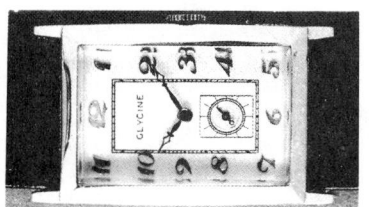

GLYCINE, 17 jewels, aux. sec., c. 1934
14k (w)....................................$135 $165 $225

GLYCINE, 18 jewels, faceted crystal & bezel
gold filled...............................$65 $80 $125

GOERING W. Co., jump hr., wandering sec.,C.1935
14k.......................................$1,000 $1,200 $1,500

GOERING W. Co., **jump hr.**, wandering sec.,C.1935
chrome....................................$195 $250 $350

GOERING W. Co., 15J., center sec., C.1935
base metal................................$30 $40 $65

GOERING W. Co., 15J., engraved case, C.1935
gold filled...............................$30 $40 $65

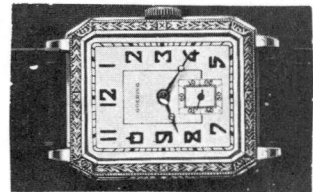

GOERING W. Co., 15J., engraved case, C.1935
gold filled...............................$30 $40 $65

GOERING W. Co., 15J., engraved case, C.1935
gold filled...............................$30 $40 $65

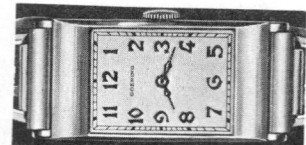

GOERING W. Co., 15J., rectangular, C.1935
gold filled................................$30 $40 $75

GOERING W. Co., 15J., **ladies** engraved case, C.1935
gold filled................................$30 $40 $65

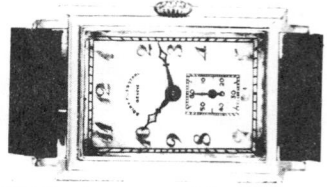

GOLAY, 18 jewels, aux. sec., c. 1928
18k & platinum...................$1,500 $1,700 $2,200

GOLAY, 32 jewels, **min.** repeater, adj. to 5 positions
18k $15,000 $18,000 $23,000

GRANA, 16J., **Masonic dial**, original dial, GJS, ca. 1948
14k $175 $195 $250

GRUEN, 17J., curved, precision, cal. 330, Ca. 1937
platinum.............................$1,200 $1,400 $2,000

GRUEN, 15J., enamel dial, wire lugs, c. 1915
silver $150 $175 $250

GRUEN, 17J., **driver's** watch, winds at **12**, cal.400, c.1938
gold filled $195 $225 $300

GRUEN,17J., curved, drivers, cal.401, RF#352, c.1932
gold filled $500 $600 $850

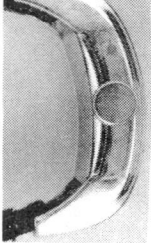

GRUEN, 17J., extremely curved, drivers, c. 1932 , and
side view of watch
gold filled $600 $700 $900

GRUEN, 17 J., extremely curved, driver's watch
gold filled..............................$600 $700 $950

GRUEN, 17J., driver's watch , flexible long lugs , RF # 641
gold filled..............................$700 $900 $1,400

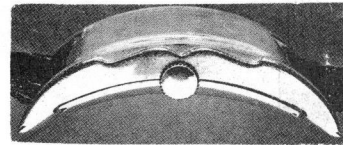

GRUEN, 17 jewels, curvex, c. 1949
gold filled..............................$250 $300 $400

GRUEN, 17 jewels, curvex, 35mm long
gold filled..............................$250 $300 $400

GRUEN, 17J, curvex **Majesty**, 52mm long, C.1937
gold filled..........................$1,000 $1,200 $1,600
14k ....★★$2,500 $3,000 $4,000

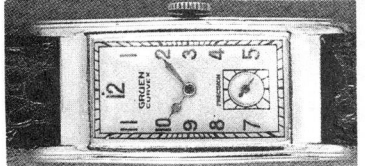

GRUEN, 17J.,curvex, precision, C. 1936
14k $400 $450 $600

GRUEN, 17 jewels, curvex, c. 1937
gold filled..............................$195 $250 $350

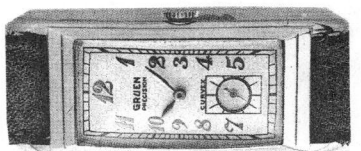

GRUEN, 17 jewels, curvex, RF# 228, c. 1935
gold filled $195 $250 $350

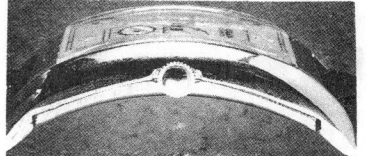

GRUEN, 17 jewels, curvex, 50mm long, c. 1937
gold filled $500 $600 $800

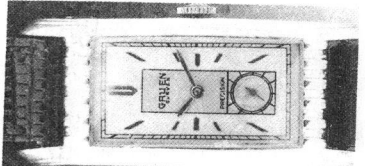

GRUEN, 17 jewels, curvex, c. 1937
s. steel $300 $350 $500

GRUEN, 15-17 jewels, curvex, 46mm lug to lug, Ca 1940s.
gold filled $250 $300 $450

GRUEN, 17J., note bezel, curvex, ca.1936
gold filled $200 $250 $325

GRUEN, 17 jewels, curvex, RF# 334, Ca. 1939
gold filled $195 $250 $350

⊕ First **CURVEX** was introduced on October 26, 1935, it was
series # 311, the 2nd series was 330 in 1939, and in 1940 series
440 was issued.

GRUEN, 17 jewels, Precision, 2 Tone, Ca. 1933
18K 2 tone $300 $350 $500

GRUEN, 17J., curvex, RF#266, cal.165, c. 1935
gold filled $95 $125 $175

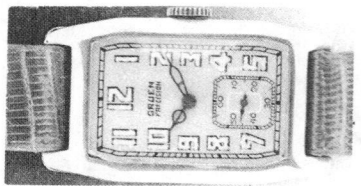

GRUEN, 17 jewels, Precision
gold filled................................$125 $150 $195

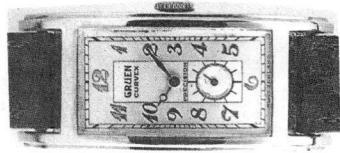

GRUEN, 17J., curvex, RF#280, cal.330, c. 1936
gold filled $175 $195 $250

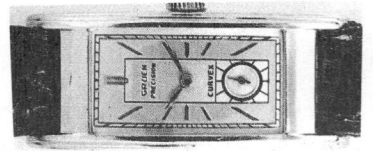

GRUEN, 17J., curvex, RF#202, cal.311, c. 1936
gold filled............................. $200 $250 $350

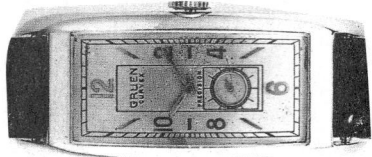

GRUEN, 17J., curvex, stepped case, RF#280, c. 1937
14k $300 $350 $500
gold filled $175 $225 $300

GRUEN, 15J., curvex, RF#226, c. 1936
gold filled............................. $175 $195 $250

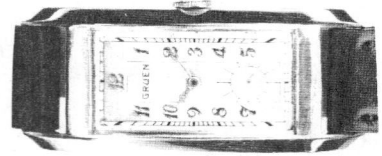

GRUEN, 17J., curvex, precision, RF#292, cal.330, c. 1937
gold filled $195 $225 $375

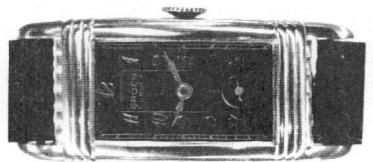

GRUEN, 15J., curvex, stepped case, RF#278, c. 1936
gold filled................................ $150 $195 $325

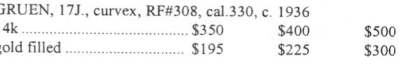

GRUEN, 15J., curvex, RF#324, cal.500, c. 1936
gold filled $175 $195 $300

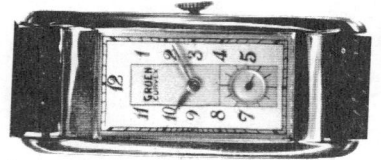

GRUEN, 15J., curvex, RF#255, cal.500, c. 1936
gold filled................................ $150 $175 $250

GRUEN, 17J., curvex, RF#308, cal.330, c. 1936
14k $350 $400 $500
gold filled $195 $225 $300

"Curved to fit the wrist"

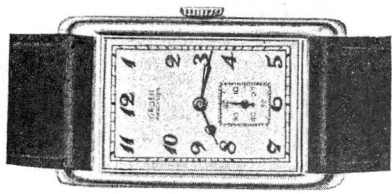

GRUEN, 17J., curved, aux. sec., curved crystal, precision,
sold for $135.00 in 1931
14k (w).....................................$125 $150 $250

GRUEN, 17J., curvex, cal#440, hooded lugs, ca.1943
14k $175 $195 $325

GRUEN, 17 jewels, curvex, fancy lugs
14k $150 $195 $300

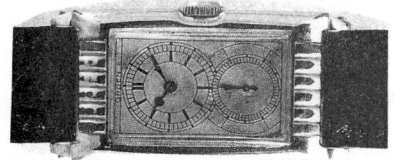

GRUEN, 17 jewels, curvex, long lugs
14k $250 $300 $400

GRUEN, 15 jewels, **tu-tone case**, double dial, Ca. 1937
14k W & Y $3,000 $3,500 $4,500

GRUEN, 17 jewels, **jumping hr**., double dial
s. steel $4,000 $5,000 $6,500
14k $5,000 $6,000 $8,000

GRUEN, 17 jewels, double dial
gold filled $1,200 $1,300 $1,800

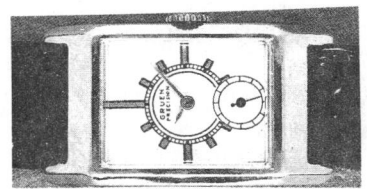

GRUEN, 17 jewels, curved, c.1930s
gold filled $250 $275 $350

GRUEN, 17 jewels, double dial, curved, c. 1938
gold filled $900 $1,000 $1,600

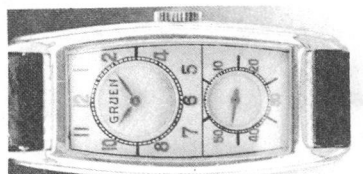

GRUEN, 17 jewels, double dial
gold filled $900 $1,000 $1,500

GRUEN, 17 jewels, double dial, c. 1932
gold filled $900 $1,000 $1,600

GRUEN, 15 jewels, in form of car radiator, curved nickel......................................$700 $900 $1,200

GRUEN, 17J., **diamond** dial & bezel, RF # 568, Ca. 1946
14k $250 $300 $500

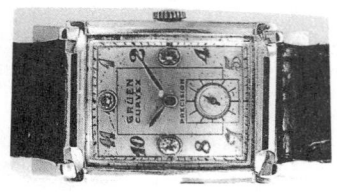

GRUEN, 17J., curvex, 3 diam., RF#568, cal.440, c. 1945
14k(w)......................................$195 $250 $350

GRUEN, 17J., curvex, 5 diam., RF#615, cal.370c. 1945
14k(w).......................................$195 $250 $350

GRUEN, 21J., stepped case, 3 diam., RF#798, c. 1950
14k(w)......................................$195 $250 $350

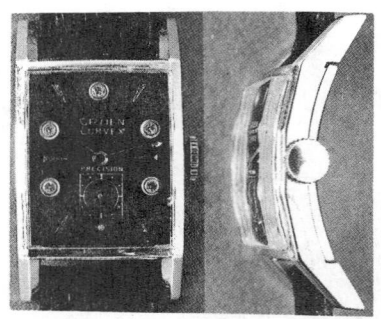

GRUEN, 17J., curvex, diamond dial, faceted crystal
14k $250 $300 $450

GRUEN, 17 jewels, veri-thin model, fancy lugs
14k $195 $225 $300

GRUEN, 17 jewels, auto wind, cal. 840, c. 1952
18k $250 $300 $400

GRUEN, 17 jewels, curvex, fancy lugs
gold filled $95 $125 $175

GRUEN, 17 jewels, curvex, diamond dial, fancy lugs
14k (w) $195 $250 $350

Note: 21 jeweled Gruen wrist watches are **American** Made.

GRUEN, 21 jewels, diamond dial, fancy center lugs, Ca. 1947
14k $225 $275 $400

GRUEN, 21 jewels, fancy lugs, c. 1945
14k $250 $275 $350

GRUEN, 17 jewels, curvex, fancy lugs, c. 1943
gold filled................................$95 $125 $195
14k $150 $195 $300

GRUEN, 17 jewels, curvex, diamond dial, Ca. 1947
14k $195 $250 $350

GRUEN, 17J., **flared**, diamond dial,
14k(w)....................................$300 $375 $550

GRUEN, 17 jewels, curvex, diamond dial, c.1945
14k $195 $250 $350

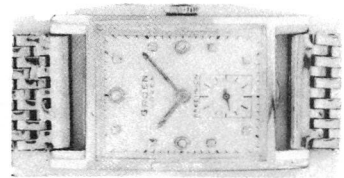

GRUEN, 17 jewels, curvex, diamond dial, c. 1951
14k(w)C&B $300 $400 $600

 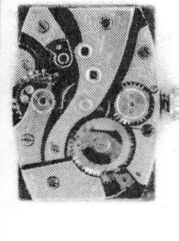

GRUEN, 17J., so called **50th Anniversary, with a engraved**
quadron precision extra **mvt. G# 119,** Adj., also used **G# 123.**
14k(w)............................. ★★$700 $800 $1,000

GRUEN, 17 jewels, curvex, c.1951
14k $150 $175 $225

GRUEN, 17 jewels, curvex, "Belmont"
14k $195 $250 $350

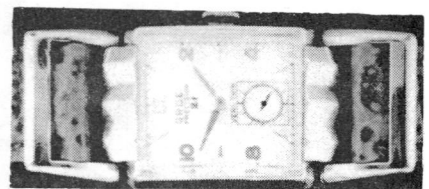

GRUEN, 21J., veri-thin, precision, swinging lugs
gold filled..................................$95 $125 $195

GRUEN, 15J., RF#467, cal.431, c. 1948
gold filled $65 $80 $125

GRUEN, 15J., RF#93, cal.179, c. 1925
gold filled................................ $70 $85 $125

GRUEN, 17J., curvex, RF#498, cal.440, c. 1945
gold filled $95 $125 $195

GRUEN, 17J., curvex, stepped lugs, RF#449, cal.440, c.1945
gold filled................................ $95 $125 $195

GRUEN, 17J., curvex, RF#498, cal.440, c. 1945
gold filled $95 $125 $175

GRUEN, 17J., curvex, large lugs, RF#449, cal.440, c. 1945
gold filled.............................. $175 $195 $250

GRUEN, 17J., curvex, RF#530, cal.335, c. 1948
gold filled $75 $95 $135

GRUEN, 17J., curvex, RF#449, cal.440, c. 1943
gold filled.............................. $125 $150 $195

GRUEN, 17J., veri-thin, RF#530, cal.430, c. 1945
14k $125 $150 $225

🕐 A collector should expect to pay modestly higher prices at local shops

GRUEN, 17J., curvex, RF#544, cal.440, c. 1942
gold filled................................. $95 $110 $175

GRUEN, 17J., fancy lugs, curvex, RF#610, c. 1945
14k $195 $250 $425

GRUEN, 17J., veri-thin **3 diam**., RF#558, cal.335, c. 1945
14k(w)................................. $150 $175 $250

GRUEN, 17J., curvex, RF#610, cal.1370, c. 1945
14k $195 $250 $425

GRUEN, 17J., curvex, RF#576, cal.440, c. 1942
gold filled..................................$95 $125 $175
14k $150 $175 $225

GRUEN, 17J., 3 diam., curvex, RF#615, cal.370, c. 1945
14k $150 $175 $250

GRUEN, 17J., curvex precision, RF#600, Ca. 1940
gold filled................................. $95 $125 $175

GRUEN, 17J., curvex, RF#642, "Marshall", c. 1945
gold filled $95 $125 $175

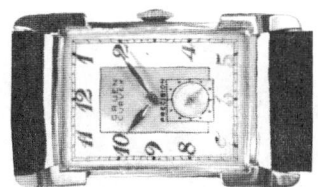

GRUEN, 17J., curvex, RF#607, "Citadel", c. 1943
gold filled................................. $95 $125 $175

GRUEN, 17J., curvex, RF#650, cal.370, c. 1948
gold filled $125 $150 $225

Pricing in this Guide are fair market price for **COM-PLETE** watches which are reflected from the "**NAWCC**" National and regional shows.

GRUEN, 21J., twisted bezel, RF#657, cal.335, c. 1953
gold filled............................... $125 $150 $225

GRUEN, 17J., curvex, faceted crystal, cal.440, c. 1947
14k $175 $195 $250

GRUEN, 21J., precision, RF#674, cal.430, c. 1947
gold filled............................... $65 $80 $125

GRUEN, 21J., precision, RF#801, ca.1335., c. 1953
14k $175 $195 $250

GRUEN, 21J., precision, RF#738, cal.335, c. 1948
14k $150 $175 $225

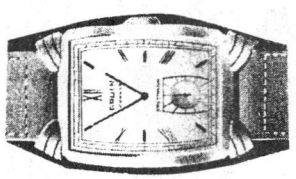

GRUEN, 17J., "Collegian", curvex - precision, Ca. 1944
gold filled $200 $225 $300

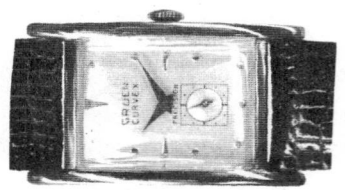

GRUEN, 17J., curvex, RF#750, cal.370, c. 1940
gold filled................................. $80 $95 $150

GRUEN, 17J., RF # 578, Curvex Precision, Ca. 1943
gold filled $75 $95 $150

GRUEN, 17J., curvex, RF#773, cal.370, c. 1945
gold filled................................$75 $95 $150

GRUEN, 17J., RF # 755, stepped bezel, Auto wind, Ca. 1950
gold filled $125 $150 $200

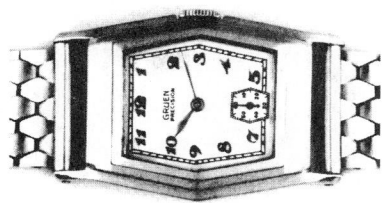

GRUEN, 19 jewels, precision, c. 1920
14k $200 $250 $350

GRUEN, 17 jewels, Curvex, RF#610, 3 diam.dial, Ca.1945
14k(w) 6 diam.case $250 $300 $500

GRUEN, 17 jewels, curvex
14k $150 $195 $250

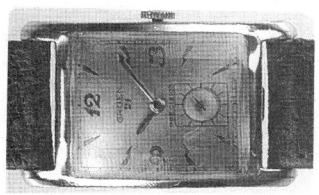

GRUEN, 21J., "Precision", RF#709, cal.335, Ca.1945
gold filled $75 $85 $125

GRUEN, 17J., RF # 575, Curvex Precision, Ca.1945
gold filled................................$80 $95 $175

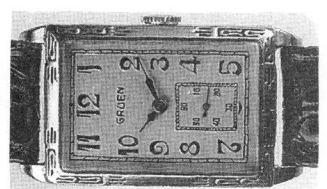

GRUEN, 15 jewels, RF#8w, cal.157, Ca. 1929
gold filled $75 $95 $150

GRUEN, 17 jewels, curvex, c. 1943
14k $150 $175 $250

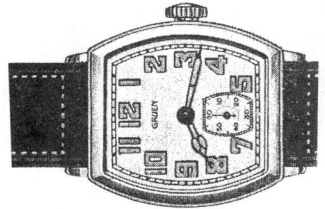

GRUEN, 15 jewels, 3 Adj., sold for $25.00 in 1930
nickel $55 $65 $95

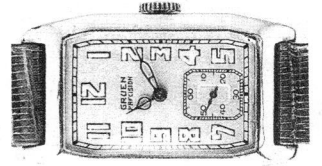

GRUEN, 17 jewels, Ca. 1925
14k $150 $175 $250

Some grades are not included. Their values can be determined by comparing with **similar** age, size, metal content, style, grades, or models such as **time only**, chronograph, repeater etc. listed.

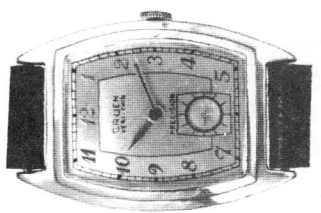

GRUEN, 17J., veri-thin, cal.405, c. 1946
gold filled $70 $90 $135

GRUEN, 17J., curvex, RF#450, cal.440, c. 1938
gold filled................................ $95 $125 $175

GRUEN, 17J., curvex, RF#448, cal.440, c. 1941
gold filled $95 $125 $175
14K $150 $200 $300

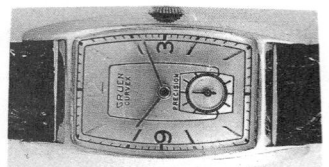

GRUEN, 17J., curvex, RF#450, cal.440, c. 1938
14k $195 $225 $325

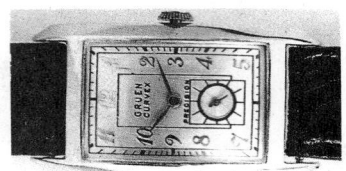

GRUEN, 17J., curvex, RF#448, cal.440, c. 1944
gold filled $95 $125 $175
14k $150 $200 $300

GRUEN, 17J., curvex, RF#450, cal.440, c. 1942
14k ....$ 195 $225 $325

GRUEN, 17J., curvex, RF#879, cal.370, c. 1942
14k $150 $200 $300

GRUEN, 17J., curvex, RF#364, cal.400, c. 1935
gold filled................................ $95 $125 $175

GRUEN, 17J., curvex, RF#293, cal.330, c. 1940
gold filled $95 $125 $175

GRUEN, 17J., precision, RF#271, cal., c. 1936
gold filled................................ $95 $125 $175

Note:Different dial styles were used on same RF# and Caliber.

GRUEN, 17J., fluted bezel, RF#240, cal.335, c. 1935
14k $195 $250 $300

GRUEN, 17J., curvex, RF#602, cal.370, c. 1943
14k $125 $200 $300

GRUEN, 17J., curvex, RF#449, cal.440, c. 1945
14k $125 $150 $275

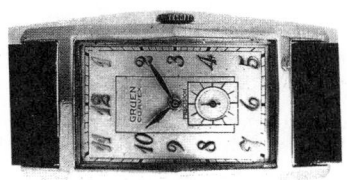

GRUEN, 17J., Curvex Precision, RF # 601, Ca. 1949
gold filled................................ $95 $125 $175

GRUEN, 17 jewels, curvex, RF # 271, c. 1936
gold filled................................$125 $150 $195

GRUEN, 17 jewels, precision, fancy lugs
14k $200 $250 $400

⊕ Some grades are not included. Their values can be determined by comparing with **similar** age, size, metal content, style, grades, or models such as **time only**, chronograph, repeater etc. listed.

GRUEN, 17 jewels, curvex, c. 1947
14k $175 $195 $250

GRUEN, 17J., Curvex Precision, RF # 600, Ca.1945
gold filled $95 $125 $175

GRUEN, 17 jewels, curvex, fancy lugs
14k $150 $175 $300

GRUEN, 17 jewels, curvex, c. 1939
14k $250 $300 $450
gold filled $125 $150 $195

GRUEN, 17 jewels, curvex, fancy lugs, c. 1961
14k $250 $300 $400

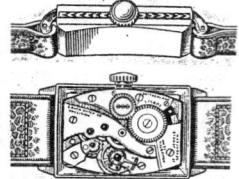

Gruen Quadron rectangular movement

GRUEN, 15J., enamel on nickel case, mvt# 158, Ca. 1927
nickel $195 $225 $275

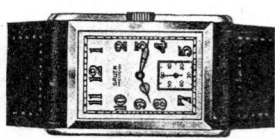

GRUEN, 17J., crown-guard, quadron mvt# 59, Ca. 1927
18K..$250 $275 $325

GRUEN, 15-17J., enamel Art Deco, Ca. 1927
gold filled $195 $225 $275

GRUEN, 15-17J., inlaid enamel case, quadron mvt, Ca. 1927
gold filled.................................$95 $115 $150

GRUEN, 15-17J., center sec., radium dial, Ca. 1927
14K $150 $175 $225

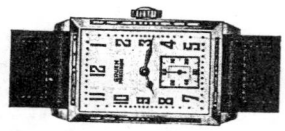

GRUEN, 15-17J., engraved case, quadron mvt# 47, Ca. 1927
gold filled.................................$60 $85 $125

GRUEN, 15-17J., engraved case, radium dial,, Ca. 1927
nickel $70 $80 $95

GRUEN, 17J., crown-guard, quadron mvt, Ca. 1927
14K..$175 $200 $205

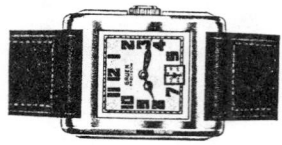

GRUEN, 15-17J., tank w/crown-guard, Ca. 1927
14K $150 $200 $250

GRUEN, 17J., crown-guard, quadron mvt, Ca. 1927
gold filled.................................$95 $115 $150

GRUEN, 15-17J., tank engraved case, mvt # 13, Ca. 1927
14K $150 $200 $250

The *Adjutant* features a case
and crystal curved to fit the
wrist

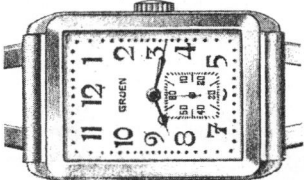

GRUEN, 15J., "Adjutant", curved case,1931 sold @ $57.50
gold filled................................$60 $75 $125

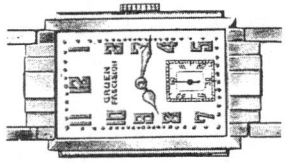

GRUEN, 17J., "Annapolis", Quadron mvt., 1931 @ $90.00
gold filled................................$75 $95 $150

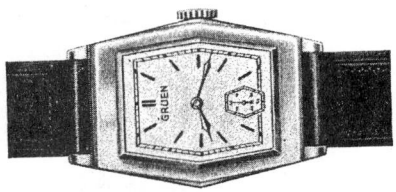

GRUEN,"Arlington or Fleetwood"=17J., 1931 sold @ $67.50
& "Carlton"=21J. ",1931 sold @ $92.50, all 3 Quadron mvt.
gold filled................................$60 $75 $125

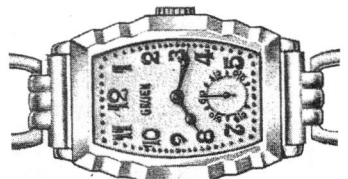

GRUEN, 17J., "Ascot", 1931sold for $55.00
gold filled................................$60 $75 $125

GRUEN, 15J., "Aviator", 1931 sold for $42.50
gold filled(W) $135 $150 $175

GRUEN, 15J., "Chief or Courier", 1931 sold for $27.50
nickel..$50 $60 $90

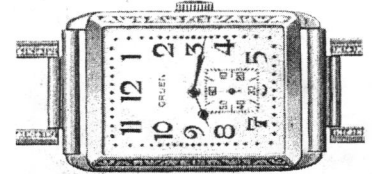

GRUEN, 15J., "Commander", 1931 sold for $50.00
gold filled (W) $60 $75 $125

GRUEN, 15J., "Courier or Chief", 1931 sold for $27.50
nickel..$50 $60 $90

GRUEN, 15J., "Culver", 1931 sold for $57.50
gold filled................................$60 $75 $125

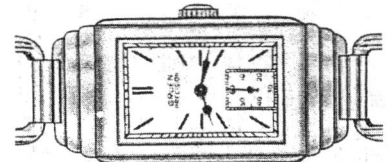

GRUEN, 17J., "Dartmouth", Quadron mvt.,1931@ $85.00
gold filled................................$60 $75 $125

GRUEN, 17J., "Kensington", 1931 sold for $45.00
gold filled................................$60 $75 $125

GRUEN, 15J., "Lakehurst", 1931 sold for $47.50
gold filled................................$60 $75 $125

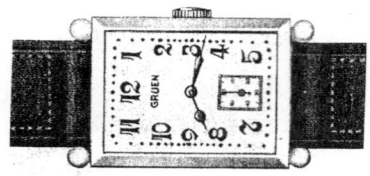

GRUEN, 21J., "Longacre", Quadron mvt., 1931 @ $100.00
14K(Y)...................................$150 $175 $225
14K(W)..................................$150 $175 $225

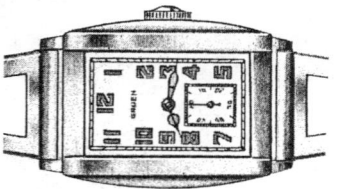

GRUEN, 17J., "Marcus", 1931 sold for $47.50
gold filled................................$60 $75 $125

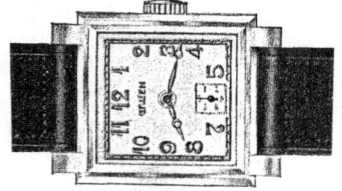

GRUEN, 15J., "Rutgers", 1931 sold for $35.00
gold filled................................$60 $75 $125

GRUEN, 15J., "Scout or Trooper", 1931 sold for $25.00
nickel.......................................$50 $60 $90

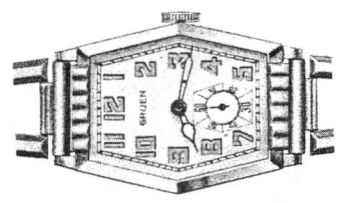

GRUEN, 15J., "Stadium", 1931 sold for $42.50
gold filled (2 tone)....................$75 $95 $150

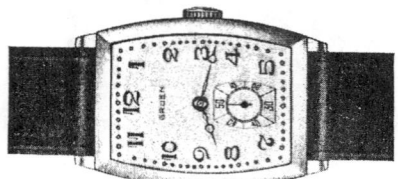

GRUEN, 15J., "Stanford", 1931 sold for $35.00
gold filled................................$60 $75 $125

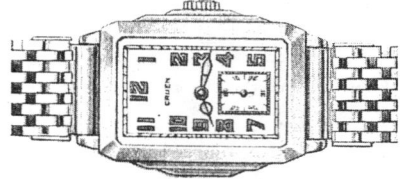

GRUEN, 15-17J., "Varsity", 1931 15J@ $55.00, 17J@$60.00
gold filled................................$60 $75 $125

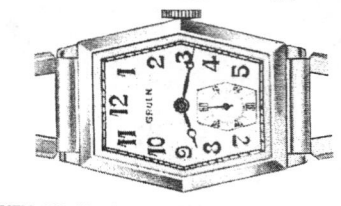

GRUEN, 15J., "Wesleyan", 1931 sold for $37.50
gold filled(W) $60 $75 $125

GRUEN, 15J., "West Point", 1931 sold for $52.50
gold filled (2 tone) $75 $95 $150

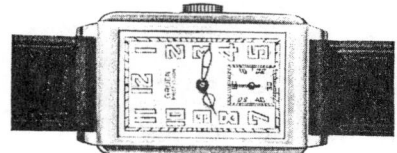

GRUEN, 17J., "Whitehall", Quadron mvt.1931 @ $75.00
gold filled................................$60 $75 $125

GRUEN, 17J., pulsemeter,
s. steel $400 $500 $650

GRUEN, 17J., triple date, cal.415, c. 1953
s. steel.................................... $150 $200 $300
gold filled.............................. $150 $200 $300

GRUEN, 17 jewels, physicians chronog., screw back
18k $1,000 $1,200 $1,500

GRUEN, 17 jewels, rope style bezel with diamonds
14k...$195 $225 $300

GRUEN, 17J., jump 24 hour, c. 1970
s. steel $175 $250 $350

GRUEN, 17J., "Day-Night", cal.n510, waterproof, Ca. 1960
The "Day-night" markers have a self-powered illumination system.
base metal.......................... ★ $150 $185 $275

GRUEN, 17J., alarm, date, c. 1964
s. steel $125 $150 $195

GRUEN, 17J., **Airflight**, jumping hours, c. 1960
base metal...............................$225 $250 $350

GRUEN, 17 jewels, 17 diamonds, RF# 744, Ca. 1955
14k(w)....................................$250 $275 $350

GRUEN, 17 jewels, veri-thin model, fancy lugs
14k $150 $175 $250

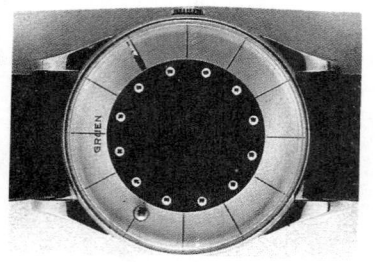

GRUEN, 17J., mystery dial, cal#215, ca.1965
gold filled...............................$150 $175 $225

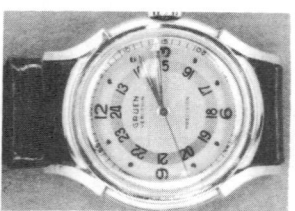

GRUEN, 17J., veri-thin model, fancy lugs, 24 hr. dial
14k $195 $225 $275

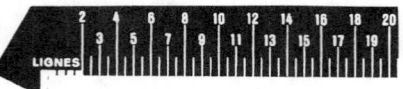

GRUEN, 17J., mystery dial, Ca. 1950
14k(w)....................................$450 $500 $600

GRUEN, 15J., cushion, luminous dial, c. 1930s
gold filled.................................$95 $125 $175

GRUEN, 15-17J., barrel shaped, Ca. 1939
gold filled...............................$75 $95 $150

GRUEN, 17J., veri-thin, fancy bezel, Ca. 1948
gold filled...............................$75 $95 $135

GRUEN, 15-17J., curvex, RF# 544, Ca. 1949
gold filled.................................$95 $125 $175

GRUEN, 17J., fluted center lugs, cal.343, c. 1936
gold filled................................ $90 $100 $125

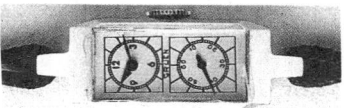

GRUEN, 17J., nurse style double dial, ca.1937
s. steel $125 $150 $250

E. GUBELIN, 29 jewels, min. repeater
18k C&B $30,000 $33,000 $40,000

E. GUBELIN, 17 jewels, chronog. 3 reg., Valj.72, c. 1950
18k (waterproof).................$1,000 $1,100 $1,500

E. GUBELIN, 25J., ipso-matic, triple date, moon ph.
14k & steel back $1,000 $1,200 $1,500
18k.......................................$1,800 $2,200 $2,800

E. GUBELIN, 19 jewels, chronog., day-date-month
18k $1,300 $1,500 $1,900

E. GUBELIN, 15J., triple date, c.1945
s. steel...................................$250 $300 $400

E. GUBELIN, 19J., chronog.by Valjoux, waterpf, 3 reg.
18k $1,000 $1,100 $1,500

E. GUBELIN, 19 jewels, 18k case, 14k band
18k & 14k C&B....................$400 $450 $550

E. GUBELIN, 17J., ca. 1970s
18k $195 $225 $300

E. GUBELIN, 25J., cal#F690, autow., center sec., ca. 1950s
18k $250 $275 $400
s. steel $195 $225 $300

E. GUBELIN, 17J., autow., ca. 1952
s. steel $195 $225 $300

E. GUBELIN, 25J., ipso-matic, c.1955
14k $250 $275 $350

E. GUBELIN, 17-25J., alarm, autow., ipso-vox, c.1960
18k $1,400 $1,600 $2,000

E. GUBELIN, 17-25J., ipso-vox, date, autow., alarm, c.1960
s. steel $700 $800 $1,100

E. GUBELIN, 17J., carved lugs, center sec., c.1944
18k $300 $350 $450

E. GUBELIN, 17J., 8 baguettes, 3 diamonds, autow., c.1948
platinum $650 $750 $1,000

E. GUBELIN, 15J., back wind duoplan, c.1935
s. steel.................................... $250 $300 $450

E. GUBELIN, 15J., ca. 1935
18k(W)..................................$700 $750 $900

E. GUBELIN, 19 J., hunter style pop-up lid, c. 1930
18k (w)................................$2,500 $2,800 $3,500

E. GUBELIN, 17jewels, jumping hr., c. 1924
14k $5,500 $6,000 $7,000

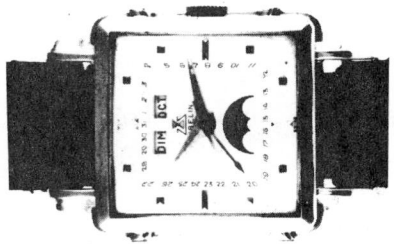

E. GUBELIN, 25J., triple date, moon phase, autow., c. 1950
18k $3,200 $3,500 $4,500

E. GUBELIN, triple date & moon ph., by Audemars-Piguet,
Ca. 1930
18k $12,000 $15,000 $20,000

E. GUBELIN, 25J., milled bezel, autow., center sec., c. 1955
18k..$350 $400 $550

E. GUBELIN, 19 jewels, fancy hooded lugs
18k..$700 $800 $1,000

E. GUBELIN, 19 jewels, curvex, 2 tone
18k......................................$1,000 $1,100 $1,300

E. GUBELIN, 19J., center sec., flared case, c. 1950
18k..$350 $400 $600

E. GUBELIN, 17-21J., milled bezel, center sec., Ca. 1958
18k..$250 $300 $400

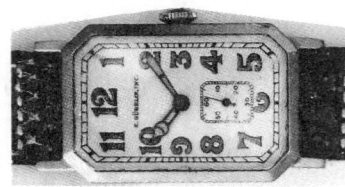

E. GUBELIN, 17 jewels, by Vacheron & Constantin
18k $1,800 $2,200 $2,800

E. GUBELIN, 18 jewels, curved, stepped case, c. 1940
18k $600 $700 $1,000

GUINAND, 17J., chronog., day-date-month, 3 reg.
18k $600 $700 $900
s. steel $250 $300 $400

GUINAND, 17 J., chronog., triple date, moon phase
18k $1,000 $1,100 $1,400
s. steel $500 $600 $750

HAFIS, 15J., center sec., cushion style
gold plate $30 $35 $50

HAFIS, 15J., luminous dial
gold plate.................................$30 $35 $50

HAFIS, 15J., engraved case
gold plate.................................$40 $50 $75
14k...$125 $135 $175

HAFIS, 15J., engraved case
gold plate.................................$40 $50 $70

HAFIS, 17J., "Queen Druga", 52 diamonds
Platinum $300 $350 $450

HALLMARK, 17 jewels, day-date-month, autowind
gold filled.................................$75 $95 $150

Prices for electric watch to be in **good running order.**

Prices for electric watch to be in **good running order.**

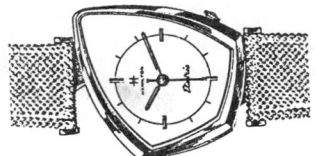

HAMILTON, electric, "Altair", Ca. 1962
gold filled......................... ★$1,200 $1,500 $2,000

HAMILTON, electric, "Converta I", Ca.1958
18k bezel & s.s. case. $200 $300 $450

HAMILTON, electric, "Aquatel", Ca. 1961
gold filled.................................$75 $95 $175

HAMILTON, electric, "Converta II", Ca.1958
14k bezel & s.s. case. $125 $195 $325

HAMILTON, electric, "Aquatel B" , Ca. 1962
gold filled.................................$75 $95 $175

HAMILTON, electric, "Converta III", Ca.1958
GF bezel & s.s. case. $125 $175 $275

HAMILTON, electric, "Atlantis", Ca. 1958
gold filled.................................$95 $125 $195

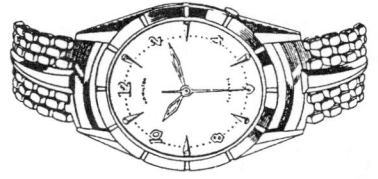

HAMILTON, electric, "Converta IV", Ca.1958
S.S. bezel & case...................$95 $125 $225

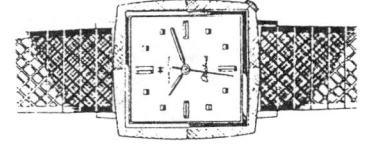

HAMILTON, electric, "Centaur" , Ca. 1965
gold filled.................................$60 $95 $135

HAMILTON, electric, "Everest", Ca.1958
gold filled $225 $325 $450

HAMILTON, electric, "Clearview" **display back,**
sold for $100.00 in 1965
s.steel case & GF bezel ... ★★$300 $400 $650

HAMILTON, electric, "EverestII", sold for $99.50 in 1964
gold filled $95 $125 $195

Prices for electric watch to be in **good running order.**

HAMILTON, electric, "Gemini" Ca.1962
gold filled..................................$95 $125 $225

HAMILTON, electric, "Gemini II", sold for $125.00 in 1964
gold filled..................................$95 $125 $225

HAMILTON, electric, "Lord Lancaster E" , Ca.1963
14k, 12 diamonds $400 $500 $650

HAMILTON, electric, "Lord Lancaster J" , Ca.1965
gold filled, 8 diamonds..........$275 $375 $550

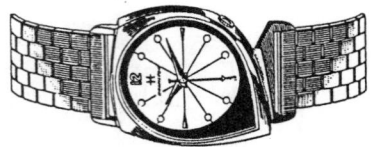

HAMILTON, electric, "Meteor," c. 1960
gold filled........................... ★$300 $400 $600

HAMILTON, electric, "Nautilus" 200, single lugs, Ca.1962
14k $150 $225 $350

HAMILTON, electric, "Nautilus" 201, Ca.1964
14k $150 $225 $350

HAMILTON, electric,"Nautilus" 202,sold for $160.00 in 1964
14k $125 $195 $300

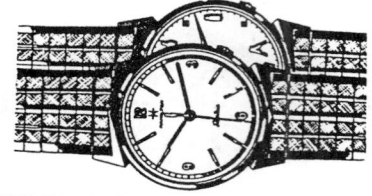

HAMILTON, electric, "Nautilus" 400, Ca.1962
gold filled $60 $80 $125

HAMILTON, electric, "Nautilus" 401, Ca.1964
gold filled $60 $80 $125

HAMILTON, electric, "Nautilus" 402, Ca.1963
gold filled $60 $80 $125

HAMILTON, electric, "Nautilus" 403, pocket watch, Ca.1965
gold filled .... ★ ★$400 $500 $800

Prices for electric watch to be in **good running order.**

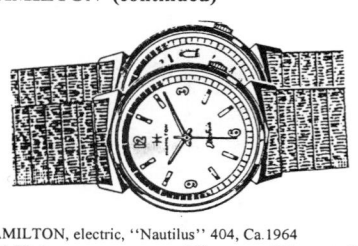

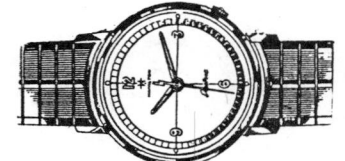

HAMILTON, electric, "Nautilus" 404, Ca.1964
gold filled.................................$60 $80 $125

HAMILTON, electric, "Nautilus" 503, Ca.1964
s. steel $60 $80 $125

HAMILTON, electric, "Nautilus" 405, Ca.1966
gold filled.................................$60 $80 $125

HAMILTON, electric, "Nautilus" 506, Ca.1965
s. steel $60 $80 $125

HAMILTON, electric, "Nautilus" 450, Ca.1963
gold filled bezel $60 $80 $125

HAMILTON, electric, "Nautilus" 507, Ca.1966
s. steel $60 $80 $125

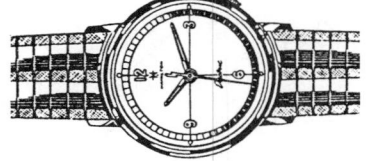

HAMILTON, electric, "Nautilus" 500, Ca.1962
s. steel $60 $80 $125

HAMILTON, electric, "Nautilus" 508, Ca.1962
s. steel $60 $80 $125

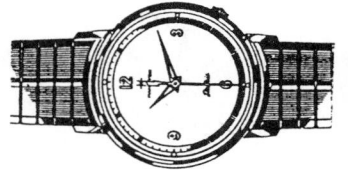

HAMILTON, electric, "Nautilus" 501, Ca.1962
s. steel $60 $80 $125

HAMILTON, electric, "Nautilus" 509, Ca.1966
s. steel $60 $80 $125

HAMILTON, electric, "Nautilus" 502, Ca.1963
s. steel $60 $80 $125

HAMILTON, electric, "Nautilus" 600, Ca.1963
rolled gold.................................$50 $70 $95

Prices for electric watch to be in **good running order**.

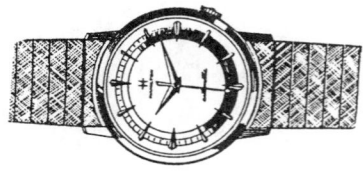

HAMILTON, electric, "Nautilus" 601, Ca. 1963
rolled gold..............................$50 $70 $95

HAMILTON, electric, "Nautilus" 602, Ca. 1965
rolled gold..............................$50 $70 $95

HAMILTON, electric, "Nautilus" 604, Ca. 1965
rolled gold..............................$50 $70 $95

HAMILTON, electric, "Nautilus" 605, Ca. 1965
rolled gold..............................$50 $70 $95

HAMILTON, electric, "Pacer," 2 tone , Ca. 1957
14k .... ★ ★ ★$1,500 $1,800 $2,200
gold filled...............................$250 $350 $500

Wrist Watches listed in this section are priced at the collectable
fair market **Trade Show** level as **complete** watches having an
original gold-filled case and stainless steel back, also with
original dial, leather watch band, and the entire original movement in good working order with no repairs needed.

HAMILTON, electric, "Pegasus", engraved bezel,
sold for $125,00 in 1965
gold filled $250 $325 $400

HAMILTON, electric, "Polaris", Ca. 1960
14k Y $300 $350 $450
14k W $350 $400 $500

HAMILTON, electric,"Polaris II", Ca. 1965
14k $250 $300 $400

HAMILTON, electric, "Regulus" , Ca. 1958
s. steel $450 $550 $700

HAMILTON, electric, "Regulus" II, Ca. 1962
s. steel $75 $95 $195

🕐 A collector should expect to pay modestly higher prices
at local shops

Prices for electric watch to be in **good running order.**

HAMILTON, electric, "R. R. Special", Ca. 1962
model#52 = all 10k GF $150 $195 $300
model#51 = GF bezel only $150 $195 $300
model#50 = all s. steel...........$150 $195 $300

HAMILTON, electric, "Sea-Lectric II", Ca. 1962
s. steel $75 $125 $195

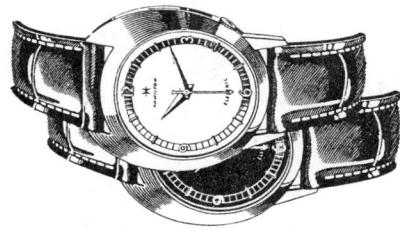

HAMILTON, electric, "Saturn", Ca. 1960
gold filled............................ ★$350 $400 $550

HAMILTON, electric, "Skip Jack", Ca. 1961
s. steel $60 $80 $125

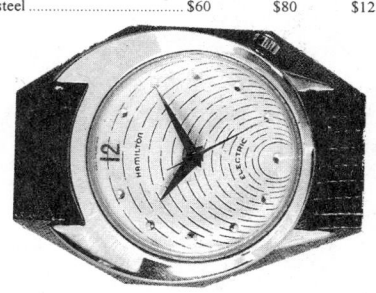

HAMILTON, electric, "Savitar", Ca. 1961
14k .... ★$425 $500 $675

HAMILTON, electric, "Spectra", Ca. 1957
18k **Rose gold** .... ★ ★ ★ ★$1,200 $1,400 $1,800
18k .... ★ ★ ★$700 $900 $1,200
14k .... ★$550 $650 $800

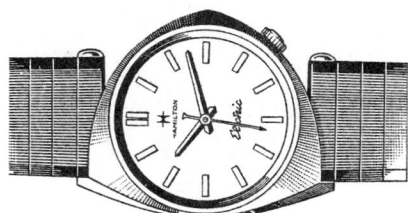

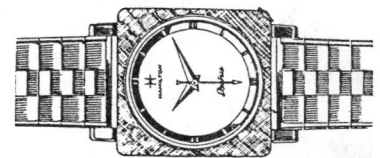

HAMILTON, electric, "Savitar 11", Ca.1965
gold filled................................$200 $300 $450

HAMILTON, electric, "Spectra" II, Ca. 1963
gold filled $95 $150 $250

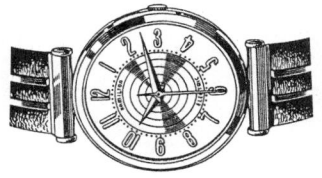

HAMILTON, electric, "Sea-Lectric I", GF bezel, Ca. 1965
s. steel $125 $150 $275

HAMILTON, electric, "Summit", Ca. 1961
14k $195 $225 $325

Prices for electric watch to be in **good running order.**

HAMILTON, electric, "Summit" II, Ca. 1964
gold filled............................ ★ $200 $225 $325

HAMILTON, electric, "Titan IV-B" , Ca. 1966
14kC&B.................. ★ ★ ★ ★ $600 $800 $1,000

HAMILTON, electric, "Taurus" , Ca. 1962
gold filled.................................. $75 $95 $150

HAMILTON, electric, "Uranus" , Ca. 1959
gold filled $150 $225 $350

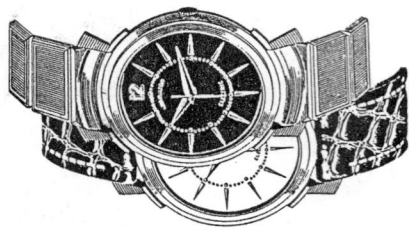

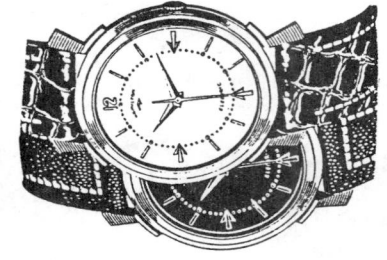

HAMILTON, electric, "Titan", Ca. 1958
gold filled............................... $125 $200 $325

HAMILTON, electric, "Van Horn", Ca.1957
14k $250 $325 $475
14k +diam. dial........................ $400 $500 $650

HAMILTON, electric, "Titan II" , Ca. 1961
gold filled............................... $125 $200 $325

HAMILTON, electric, Vantage , ca.1958
gold filled $125 $150 $250

HAMILTON, electric, "Titan III" , Ca. 1964
gold filled............................... $125 $200 $325

HAMILTON, electric, "Vega" , Ca. 1961
gold filled .... ★ $500 $600 $800

Prices for electric watch to be in **good running order.**

HAMILTON, electric, "Vela" , sold for $115.00 in 1966
gold filled..................................$150 $175 $250

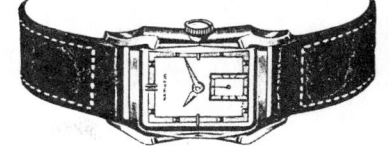

HAMILTON, 19 jewels, "Adrian", ca. 1953
gold filled $85 $125 $175

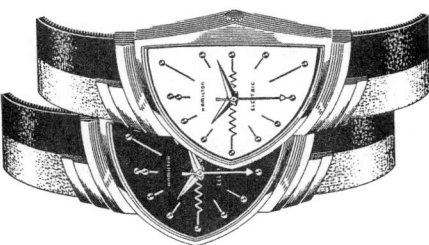

HAMILTON electric, "Ventura",
14k sold for $200.00 in 1957

18k rose................ ★ ★ ★ ★$2,600	$3,000	$3,500
18k ....★ ★ ★$1,600	$1,800	$2,300
14k(w)..........................★ ★$1,800	$2,000	$2,500
14k(Y)..................................$1,000	$1,300	$1,800

HAMILTON, 17 jewels, "Alan", ca.1942
gold filled $75 $95 $150

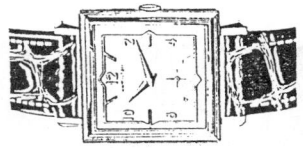

HAMILTON, 22 jewels, " Aldrich", Ca, 1958
14k $125 $150 $195

HAMILTON electric, "Ventura", **6 diamond dial**, Ca. 1957
14K.....................................$1,500 $1,800 $2,200

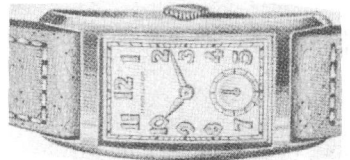

HAMILTON, 19 jewels, "Allison" , Ca. 1937
14k $150 $195 $300

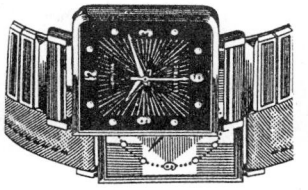

HAMILTON, electric,"Victor", ca.1957
gold filled...............................$175 $250 $400

HAMILTON,17J., " Amherst", 14k markers , Ca. 1956
gold filled $70 $95 $135

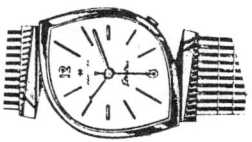

Hamilton, electric, "Victor II" , Ca. 1961
gold filled...............................$250 $350 $475

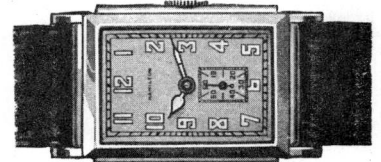

HAMILTON, 19 jewels, "Andrews", ca.1930
14k(y & w) ....★$250 $275 $400

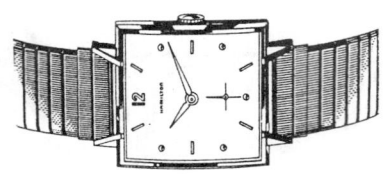

HAMILTON, 22J., " Ansley" , 14k markers, Ca. 1960
gold filled................................$60 $80 $125

HAMILTON, 17J., "Aqualine ", 14k markers, Ca. 1957
gold filled................................$50 $60 $95

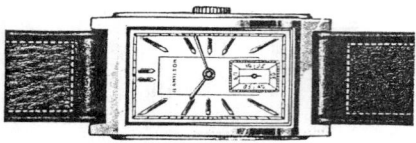

HAMILTON, 19J., " Ardmore", Ca. 1935
14k $350 $400 $500

HAMILTON, 17J., " Arnold", Ca. 1957
rolled gold................................$40 $50 $75

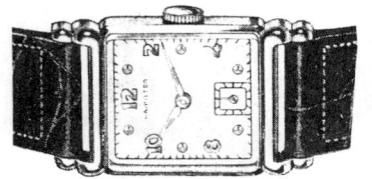

HAMILTON, 19J., " Ashley", grade 982, Ca. 1948
gold filled................................$70 $95 $135

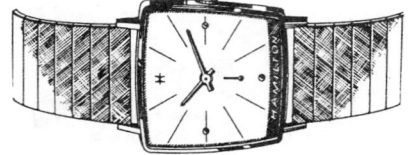

HAMILTON, 22J., "Attache", 14k markers, c.1961
gold filled................................$175 $225 $325

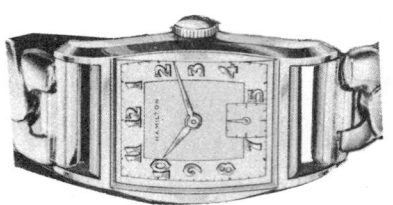

HAMILTON, 17J.," Austin ", Ca. 1949
gold filled $85 $95 $145

HAMILTON, 17J, "Bagley," applied numbers, Ca. 1939
gold filled $90 $125 $175

HAMILTON, 19J.," Bailey ", c.1949
gold filled $75 $95 $135

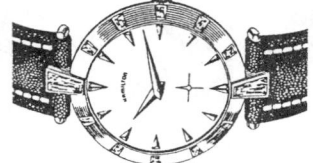

HAMILTON, 22J., " Barbizon", diam. bezel, Ca.1957
18k(w)................ ★ ★ ★ ★ ★$3,000 $4,000 $5,500

HAMILTON, 22J., " Baron" , 5 diam. dial, BIG lugs, c.1960
14k $175 $225 $300

HAMILTON, 22J., " Baron II" , 5 diamond dial, ca. 1961
14k $175 $225 $300

HAMILTON, 22J, "Barry", sterling silver dial, ca.1957
gold filled..................................$70 $95 $125

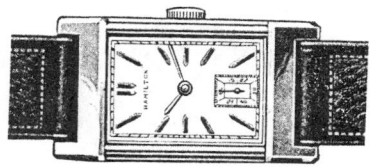

HAMILTON, 17J.," Bartley", Ca.1936
gold filled..............................$125 $175 $250

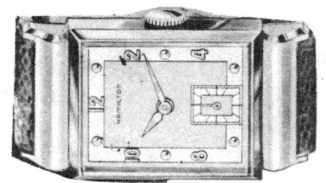

HAMILTON, 19J.,"Barton", tu tone dial, c.1948
14k $150 $200 $275

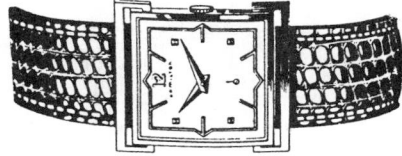

HAMILTON, 22J., "Baton", 14k markers, ca.1958
14k $125 $150 $225

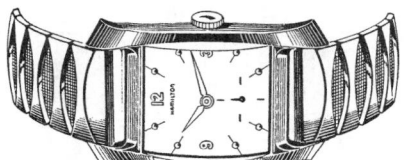

HAMILTON, 17J., "Baxter", sterling silver dial, ca.1957
gold filled..................................$75 $95 $135

HAMILTON,17J.,"Beldon", 2 tone dial, sealed case, c.1949
gold filled..................................$75 $95 $150

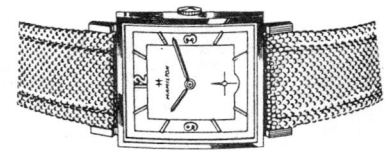

HAMILTON, 22J., " Bentley", 14k markers, ca. 1961
gold filled $70 $85 $125

HAMILTON, 19J., " Bentley", 14k markers, Ca. 1937
14k $700 $850 $1,000

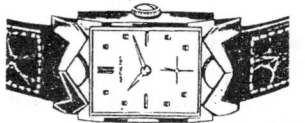

HAMILTON, 17-19J., "Benton" , 14k markers, c. 1952
14k $200 $275 $400

HAMILTON, 17J., "Berkshire" , 14k markers, Ca. 1953
14k $150 $200 $325

HAMILTON, 22J.,"Blade", asymmetrical, note lugs, Ca.1962
gold filled ....★$225 $300 $400

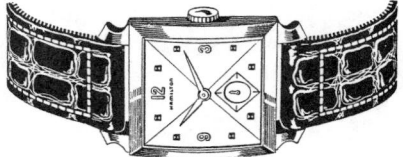

HAMILTON, 22J.," Blair ", sterling silver dial, c.1957
gold filled $70 $95 $135

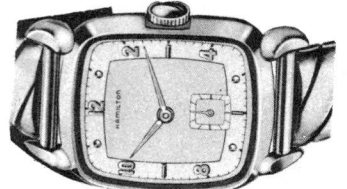

HAMILTON, 17-21J.," Blake", c.1949
gold filled $70 $95 $135

HAMILTON, 17J., " Boatswain", center sec., c. 1958
rolled gold...............................$40 $50 $75

HAMILTON, 17J., " Boatswain II" , c. 1961
rolled gold...............................$40 $50 $75

HAMILTON, 17J.," Boone ", Curved, Ca.1936
gold filled...............................$95 $125 $200

HAMILTON, 19 jewels, "Boulton" , Ca. 1941
gold filled...............................$75 $95 $135

HAMILTON, 22J., " Boulton II" , 14k markers, c. 1961
gold filled...............................$60 $70 $125

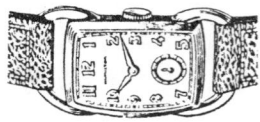

HAMILTON, 17J.,"Bowman", c.1939
gold filled...............................$175 $200 $300

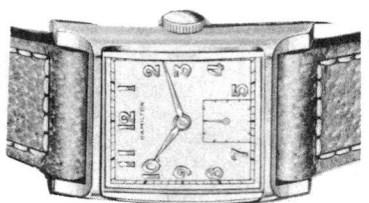

HAMILTON, 17J.,"Boyd", c.1949
gold filled...............................$75 $95 $135

HAMILTON, 22J., "Bradford " , 14k markers, c. 1954
14k...............................$95 $125 $195

HAMILTON, 22J., "Bradford B" , 11 diam. dial, c. 1954
14k...............................$150 $175 $275

HAMILTON, 17J., "Brandon", swing lugs, ca. 1946
gold filled...............................$80 $95 $150

HAMILTON, 17 jewels, "Brandon", Ca. 1948
gold filled...............................$75 $95 $135

HAMILTON, 19J.,"Brent ", faceted crystal, c.1949
gold filled...............................$75 $95 $135

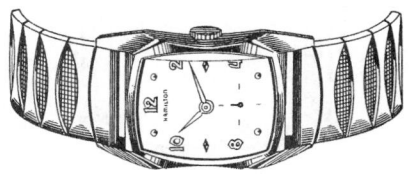

HAMILTON, 22J.," Brewster ", sterling silver dial, Ca.1957
gold filled................................$65 $85 $125

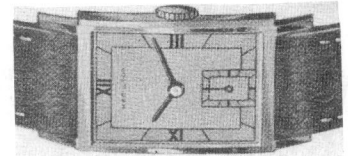

HAMILTON, 19 jewels, "Brock" , c. 1939
14k(coral).................... ★ ★ ★$600 $750 $900
14k(yellow).............................$150 $175 $250

HAMILTON, 19 jewels, " Brockton", c. 1952
10k $95 $125 $175

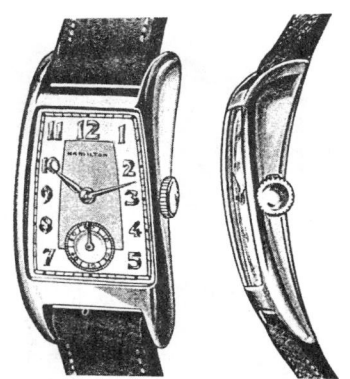

HAMILTON, 19J.," Brooke ", Curved, Ca.1938
gold filled...........................★$350 $425 $550

HAMILTON, 19 jewels, "Byrd" ca.1930
18k ....★ ★ ★ ★$1,000 $1,200 $1,500
14k(y).........................★ ★ $750 $800 $900
14k(w).............................★ ★ $750 $800 $900

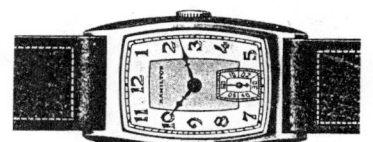

HAMILTON, 17J.,"Cabot", cal.960, Ca. 1938
gold filled $75 $95 $150

HAMILTON, 17J.,"Cabot", luminous, Ca. 1957
s.steel $40 $50 $80

HAMILTON, 17J.,"Cadet", Ca. 1957
rolled gold................................$40 $50 $70

HAMILTON, 17J., "Calvin", applied gold numbers, ca.1936
gold filled $95 $125 $195

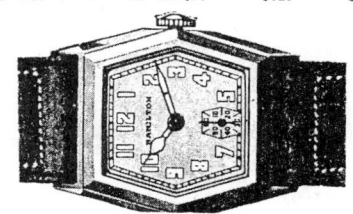

HAMILTON, 17J.,"Cambridge", ca.1930
14k(w)....................... ★ ★ ★$700 $850 $1,000
14k(y) .... ★ ★ ★$750 $900 $1,100

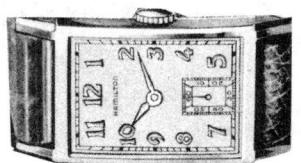

HAMILTON, 19J.," Cambridge ", c.1949
platinum..............................★ $600 $700 $900

HAMILTON, 19 jewels, "Cameron", c. 1937
14k $150 $200 $300

HAMILTON, 17J.," Carlton ", c.1949
gold filled $85 $125 $175

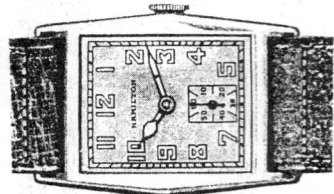

HAMILTON, 17J.,"Captain Rice", Ca. 1930
14k(w or y) .... ★ ★ ★ $600 $650 $800

HAMILTON, 17J., " Carlyle ", c. 1958
rolled gold................................ $40 $50 $65

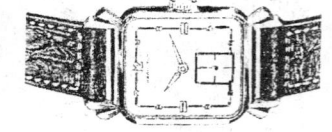

HAMILTON, 17J.," Carl ", Ca.1953
gold filled.................................$75 $95 $150

HAMILTON, 17J., " Carteret" 14k markers, Ca. 1958
14k $95 $125 $200

HAMILTON, 17J.," Carlisle ", 44mm, cal. 937, Ca.1937
gold filled................................$150 $200 $300

HAMILTON, 17J.,"Casino", 5 diamond, Ca. 1957
14kYorW $175 $200 $275

HAMILTON, 17J.," Carson ", Ca.1935
gold filled.................................$70 $95 $150

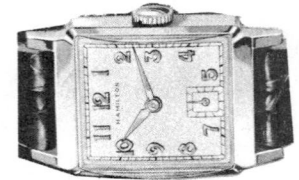

HAMILTON, 19J.," Cedric ", c.1949
gold filled $75 $95 $135

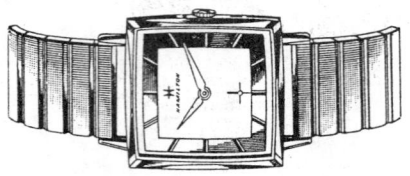

HAMILTON, 17J., " Carson ", c. 1961
rolled gold.................................$40 $50 $75

Wrist Watches listed in this section are priced at the collectable
fair market **Trade Show** level as **complete** watches having an
original gold-filled case and stainless steel back, also with
original dial, leather watch band, and the entire original movement in good working order with no repairs needed.

🕐 A collector should expect to pay modestly higher prices
at local shops

HAMILTON, 22J., "Chadwick ", 14k markers, c. 1959
14k ....$125 · $150 $200

HAMILTON, 18J., "Clearview" , left = 1958, right = 1961
14k (1958).............................$150 $175 $250
14k (1961).............................$125 $150 $225

HAMILTON,17J.,"Chanticleer", alarm & power reserve, c.1957
gold filled..............................$100 $125 $175

HAMILTON, 17J.," Clinton ", c.1949
s. steel $50 $60 $95

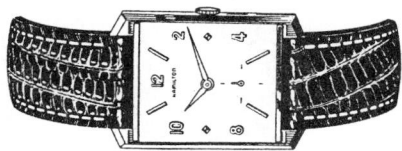

HAMILTON, 22J., "Chapman", 14k markers, Ca. 1958
gold filled...................................$60 $75 $125

HAMILTON, 17J.," Clyde ", c.1950
gold filled $75 $95 $135

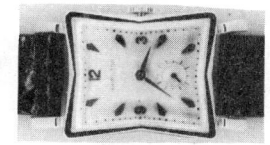

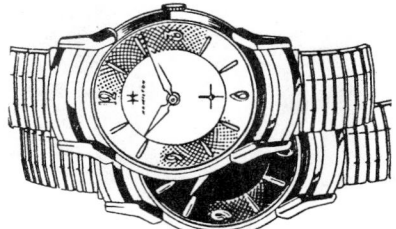

HAMILTON, 17-19J., "Chatham", Ca. 1953
14k $250 $300 $450

HAMILTON, 17J., "Clark", Ca. 1936
gold filled...............................$125 $150 $200

HAMILTON, 17J., "Coburn " , c. 1958
rolled gold................................$40 $50 $70

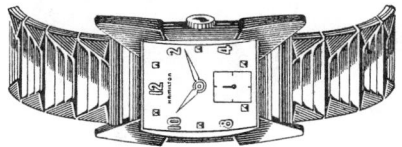

HAMILTON, 17-18J., "Clark", sterling silver dial, Ca. 1957
gold filled...................................$95 $110 $150

HAMILTON, 17J., "Colby " , c. 1957
rolled gold................................$45 $55 $75

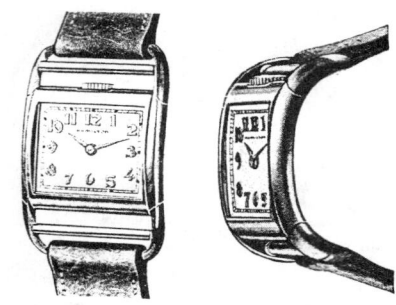

HAMILTON, 17J.,"Contour", Drivers, Crown at 12, c. 1938
gold filled..............................$350 $400 $550

HAMILTON, 17J., "Conway ", c. 1961
rolled gold...............................$50 $60 $75

HAMILTON, 17J., " Cordell", Ca. 1961
14k C&B.................................$250 $300 $400

HAMILTON,17J., "Coronado ", black enamel bezel, ca.1928
14k(w or y) $1,000 $1,200 $1,500

HAMILTON, 22J., "Corvet " , 14k markers, c. 1961
gold filled................................$50 $60 $85

HAMILTON, 17J., "Courtney " , 14k markers, c. 1958
14k $125 $150 $195

HAMILTON, 22J., "Courtney " , 6 diamond dial, c. 1958
14k $200 $225 $300

HAMILTON, 17J.," Craig ", c.1949
gold filled $75 $95 $135

HAMILTON, 19J., "Cranston ", gold markers, c. 1952
gold filled $75 $95 $135

HAMILTON, 22J., "Crispin", sterling silver dial, c. 1957
14k $125 $150 $200

Wrist Watches listed in this section are priced at the collectable
fair market **Trade Show** level as **complete** watches having an
original gold-filled case and stainless steel back, also with
original dial, leather watch band, and the entire original movement in good working order with no repairs needed.

5 Time Zones, Introduced Jan. 6th, 1956, the G hand = Greenwich
Pacific - Mountain - Central - Eastern

HAMILTON, 17J., "Cross Country", 5 time zones, ca. 1956
gold filled...............................$250 $350 $450

HAMILTON, 18J.,"Cross Country II", 5 time zones,
sold for $85.00 in 1957
gold filled...............................$250 $350 $450

HAMILTON, 18J., "Croydon", sweep seconds, ca.1953
s.steel $40 $50 $70

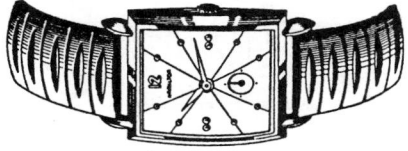

HAMILTON, 22J., " Cullen" , 14k markers, c. 1957
gold filled.................................$75 $95 $135

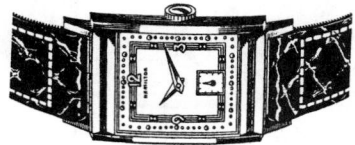

HAMILTON, 22J., " Curtiss", hinged lugs, Ca. 1953
14k $150 $175 $250

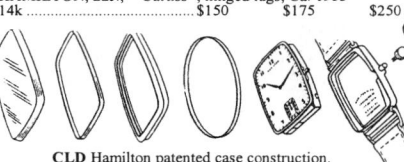

CLD Hamilton patented case construction.

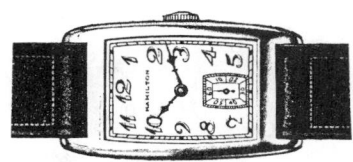

HAMILTON, 19J., " Custer", Ca. 1936
14k $200 $250 $350

HAMILTON, 17J., "Cyril", Ca. 1957
gold filled $70 $80 $125

HAMILTON, 17J., "Darrell", cal#747, c. 1951
gold filled $80 $90 $145

HAMILTON, 17J., "Dawson " , c. 1959
gold filled $60 $80 $125

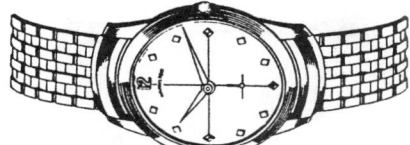

HAMILTON, 17J., "Dean " , c. 1957
gold filled $60 $70 $95

HAMILTON, 17J., "Deauville ", c. 1962
rolled gold.................................$40 $50 $75

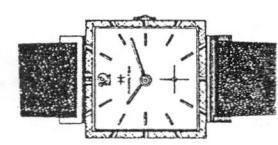

HAMILTON, 17J.," Dennis", Ca.1961
14k $95 $125 $200

HAMILTON, 17J.," Dennis ", Ca.1948
gold filled.................................. $75 $95 $135

HAMILTON, 17J.," Dewitt ", c.1950
gold filled.................................. $75 $85 $125

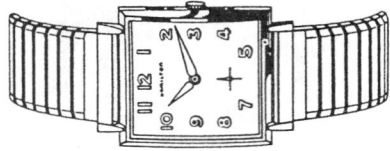

HAMILTON, 17J., " Dexter", c. 1959
rolled gold.................................. $50 $60 $75

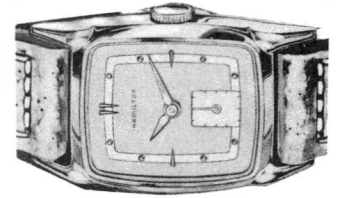

HAMILTON, 17J.," Dexter ", c.1950
gold filled.................................. $80 $90 $125

HAMILTON, 17J.," Dickens ", 44MM long, Ca.1937
Note: Also see **Gilman** = 14k (**look-a-like**)
gold filled.................................. $175 $195 $300

HAMILTON, 17J.,"Dixon", left = Ca.1936, right = Ca. 1953
gold filled = 1936 .... $95 $110 $135
gold filled = 1953 .... $95 $110 $135

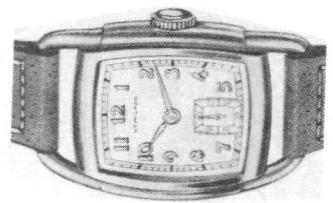

HAMILTON, 17 jewels, "Dodson" , c. 1939
gold filled $95 $125 $175

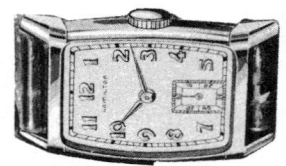

HAMILTON, 19J.," Donald ", c.1941
note: Turner 10K (look-a-like)
14k $195 $250 $350

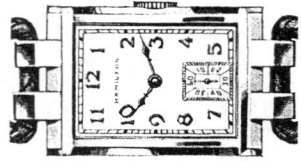

HAMILTON, 19J.," Donavan ", center lugs, Ca. 1935
14k $500 $600 $800

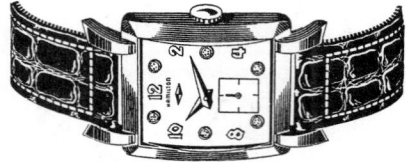

HAMILTON, 22J.,"Donavan II", 6 diamonds, Ca.1956
14k $175 $200 $300

HAMILTON, 22J.," Donavan II", Ca.1955
14k $150 $175 $250

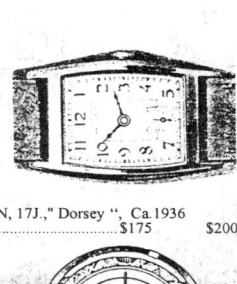

HAMILTON, 17J.," Dorsey ", Ca.1936
14k $175 $200 $250

HAMILTON, 17J.," Doublet ", Ca.1962
14k $175 $200 $275

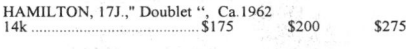

HAMILTON, 17J.," Drake ", Ca.1951
14k $175 $225 $300

HAMILTON, 17J.," Drake ", Ca.1935
gold filled $95 $150 $200

HAMILTON, 17J.,"Drew", Ca.1957
rolled gold $40 $50 $65

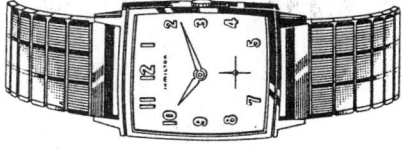

HAMILTON, 17J., "Drummond ", 14k markers, c. 1959
gold filled $75 $95 $125

HAMILTON, 17J.," Dunham ", c.1951
gold filled $95 $125 $175

HAMILTON, 19 jewels, "Dunkirk" , c. 1937
14k $275 $325 $400

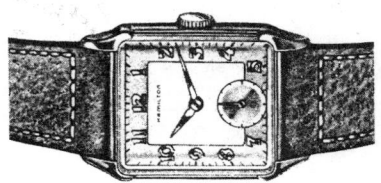

HAMILTON, 17J., "Dwight", gold numbers, ca. 1948
gold filled $75 $95 $135

HAMILTON, 17 jewels, "Dyson" , c. 1951
gold filled $75 $95 $135

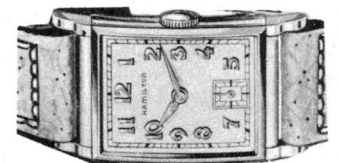

HAMILTON, 17J.," Eaton ", c.1948
gold filled $75 $95 $135

HAMILTON, 22J.,"Edgemere B", sterling silver dial, c.1957
gold filled $60 $70 $85

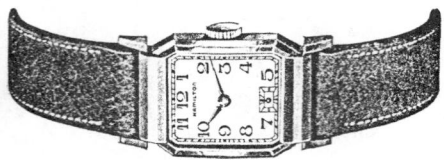

HAMILTON, 17J.," Eliott ", Cal.980, Ca. 1936
gold filled................................$95 $125 $200

HAMILTON, 17J.," Emery ", c.1949
gold filled................................$75 $95 $135

HAMILTON, 17 jewels, "Eric" , c. 1948
gold filled................................$75 $95 $135

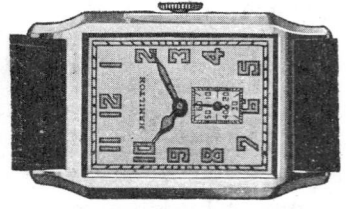

HAMILTON, 17 jewels, "Ericsson" , Ca. 1930
18k .... ★★★★$1,000 $1,300 $1,700
14k Y or W .... ★★★$500 $700 $900

HAMILTON, 17 jewels, "Emerson" , c. 1941
gold filled................................$95 $110 $150

Wrist Watches listed in this section are priced at the collectable
fair market **Trade Show** level as **complete** watches having an
original gold-filled case and stainless steel back, also with
original dial, leather watch band, and the entire original movement in good working order with no repairs needed.

🕑 A collector should expect to pay modestly higher prices
at local shops.

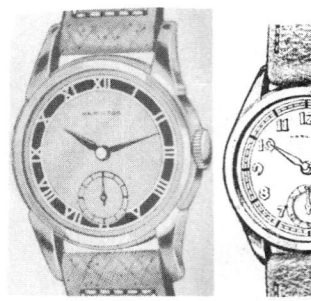

HAMILTON, 17 jewels, "Endicott" , c. 1941
gold filled yellow $75 $100 $150
gold filled coral .... ★★★★$700 $900 $1,100

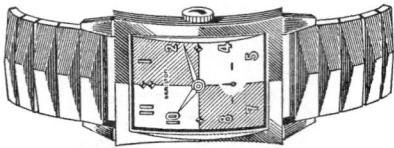

HAMILTON, 17J., "Errol", 2-tone sterling silver dial, c.1957
gold filled $75 $95 $135

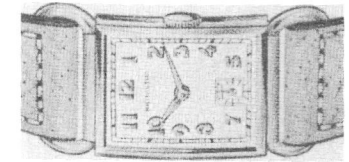

HAMILTON, 17 jewels, "Essex" , c. 1941
gold filled yellow $100 $125 $175
gold filled coral .... ★$195 $275 $375

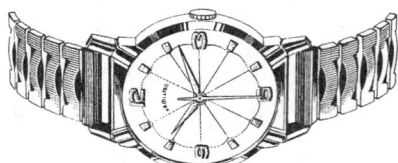

HAMILTON, 17J., "Essex", c.1957
rolled gold................................$40 $50 $70

HAMILTON, 17J., "Farrell", 14k # s, c.1959
rolled gold................................$40 $50 $70

HAMILTON, 17J., " First Mate'', c.1960
rolled gold..............................$40 $50 $70

HAMILTON, 18J.,"Fleetwood ", c.1949
14k $125 $150 $225

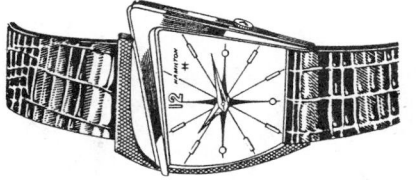

HAMILTON, 22J., "Flight I" / 14k marks & # 12, ca. 1960
14k case ....★★$2,500 $3,200 $4,000

HAMILTON, 22J., "Flight II",14k dots & #s 12,3,6,9, c.1961
gold filled case................★$1,200 $1,400 $1,700

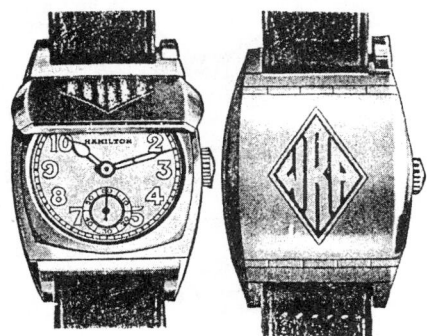

HAMILTON, "Flint Ridge", flip top is lug activated,
Grade 987=17J, Grade 979=19J, Ca. 1930
14k (w or y) ....★★$2,200 $2,500 $2,800

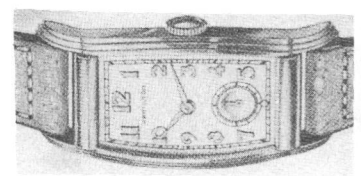

HAMILTON, 19 jewels, "Foster" , c. 1939
14k $250 $300 $425

HAMILTON, 17J., "Franklin", c.1949
gold filled $75 $95 $135

HAMILTON, 17J., "Fulton", sterling silver dial; c.1957
gold filled $80 $95 $125

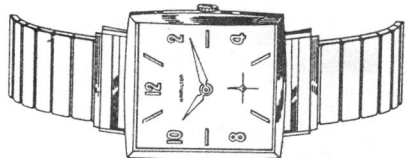

HAMILTON, 17J., " Gardner'', c.1961
rolled gold................................$50 $55 $70

HAMILTON, 17J.," Gary ", c.1949
gold filled $75 $95 $135

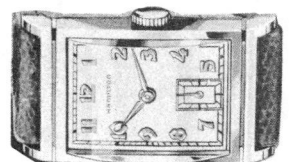

HAMILTON, 19J.," Gilbert ", c.1941
14k $175 $195 $250

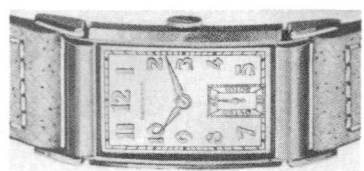

HAMILTON, 19 jewels, "Gilman" , 44mm long, c. 1937
Note: Also see **Dickens** = *Gold Filled* (**look-a-like**)
14k .... ★$350 $450 $600

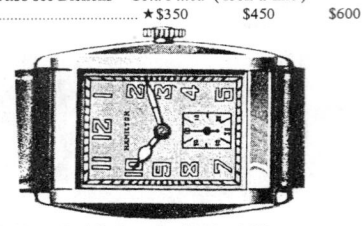

HAMILTON, 17J.,"Gladstone", cal.981, c.1931
gold filled **W**..........................$125 $150 $250
gold filled **Y**...........................$125 $150 $250

HAMILTON, 19J.," Glendale ", engraved case, Ca. 1928
14k **W** .... ★ ★ ★$1,200 $1,500 $2,000
14K **Y**.................. ★ ★ ★ ★$1,200 $1,500 $2,000

HAMILTON, 17J., " Glendon", c.1961
rolled gold..................................$40 $45 $65

HAMILTON, 17J.," Glenn ", c.1948
14k $150 $175 $225

HAMILTON, 19 jewels, "Glenn Curtis", Ca.1931
14k(Y or W) .... ★ ★$300 $350 $500

HAMILTON, 18J., "Golden Tempus", c.1957
14k regular style dial............. $300 $325 $400
14k time zones dial................. $500 $550 $800

HAMILTON, 18J., "Diamond Tempus", (masterpiece),
NOTE: **Both with 11 diamond** dial, c.1957
14k regular style dial............. $600 $700 $1,000
14k time zones dial................. $700 $900 $1,200

HAMILTON, 18J., " Golden Tempus II", 14k #s, c.1959
gold filled $75 $85 $125

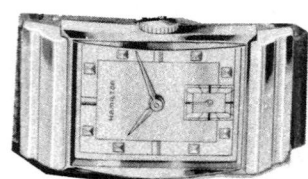

HAMILTON, 19J.," Gordon ", c.1941
platinum..............................$1,000 $1,400 $1,800
18k $450 $500 $650

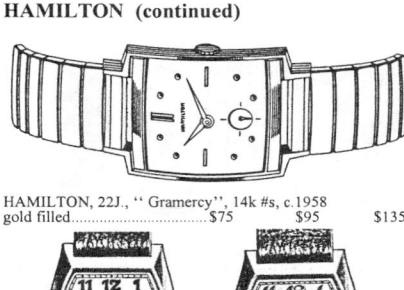

HAMILTON, 22J., " Gramercy", 14k #s, c.1958
gold filled..................................$75 $95 $135

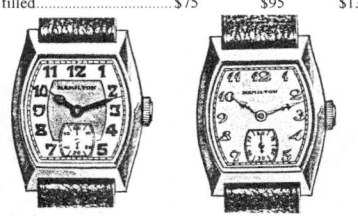

HAMILTON, 17 jewels, "Grant", Ca. 1933
sterling $200 $325 $400
gold filled $150 $200 $350

HAMILTON, 17 jewels, "Grant", Ca. 1957
rolled gold................................$50 $60 $80

HAMILTON, 17 jewels, "Greenwich" Ca. 1931
gold filled..................................$95 $125 $175

HAMILTON, 18J.,"Grenadier I", sterling silver dial, c.1957
gold filled................................$40 $50 $80

HAMILTON, 18J.,"Grenadier II", sterling silver dial, c.1957
gold filled................................$40 $50 $80

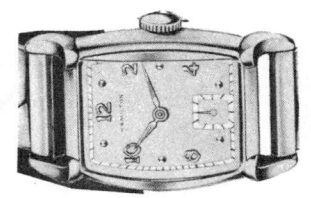

HAMILTON, 17J.,"Grover", c.1949
gold filled $75 $95 $135

HAMILTON, 18J.,"Guardsman I", sterling silver dial, c.1957
gold filled $50 $60 $95

HAMILTON, 17J.,"Guardsman II", c.1957
gold filled $50 $60 $95

HAMILTON, 17J., "Haddon", sold for $69.50 in 1952
gold filled $70 $80 $125

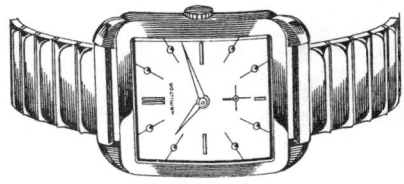

HAMILTON, 17J.,"Halesworth B", sterling silver dial, c.1957
gold filled $60 $70 $95

HAMILTON, 17J.," Harris ", Ca.1937
gold filled $75 $95 $135

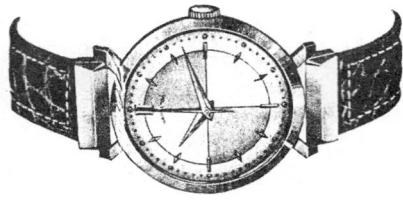

HAMILTON, 18J., "Hartman", **hinged lugs**, Ca.1953
18k, sold for $225.00 .. ★ ★ ★ $350 $500 $650
14k, sold for $175.00 ...... ★ ★ $235 $275 $325

HAMILTON, 17J.,"Hastings", **14k** sold for $75.00 in 1928
14k (Y or W) $175 $200 $300
gold filled (Y or W)................. $75 $95 $135

HAMILTON, 19J.," Hayden ", c.1948
gold filled................................ $95 $110 $150

HAMILTON, 17J., "Heyward", sold for $37.50 in 1936
gold filled................................ $95 $125 $195

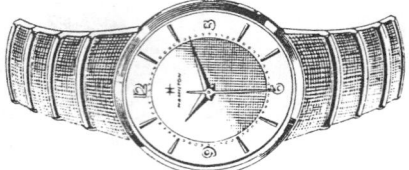

HAMILTON, 18J., "Holden", ca.1961
gold filled................................ $60 $75 $95

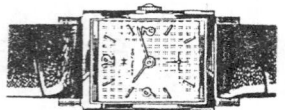

HAMILTON, 17J.," Huntley ", Ca.1961
14k $125 $150 $225

HAMILTON, 17J., **"Howard"**, on dial & movement, c.1939
gold filled .... ★ ★ $325 $400 $500

HAMILTON, 17J.,"Jason", sold for $55.00 in 1957
s.steel $40 $50 $70

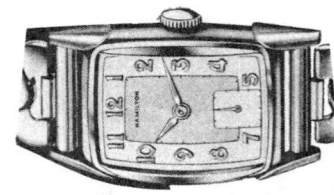

HAMILTON, 17J.," Jeffrey ", c.1949
'gold filled $75 $95 $135

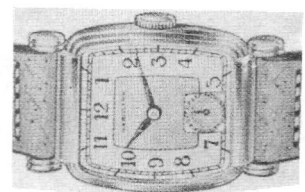

HAMILTON, 19 jewels, "Judson" Ca. 1935
gold filled $75 $95 $135

HAMILTON, 17J., " Keane", c.1958
rolled gold................................ $40 $45 $65

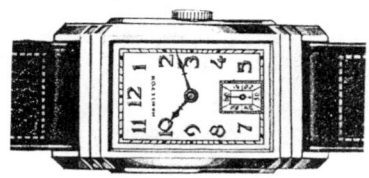

HAMILTON, 17J., " Nelson", Ca.1936
gold filled............................$150 $175 $225

HAMILTON, 17J., " Newton", cal.747, Ca.1954
gold filled................................$95 $125 $175

HAMILTON, 17J, Norde is 14k, Nordon,18J, is gold filled
Ca. 1949
14k $150 $175 $225
gold filled................................$60 $75 $125

HAMILTON, 19 jewels, "Norman" , c. 1949
gold filled................................$95 $110 $150

HAMILTON, 17J., " Norman", 14k #s, c.1958
gold filled................................$50 $65 $85

🕐 A collector should expect to pay modestly higher prices
at local shops

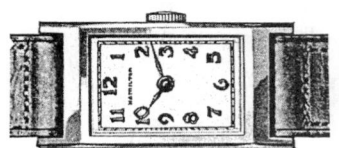

HAMILTON, 17 jewels, "Norfolk", Ca. 1936
gold filled $100 $110 $150

HAMILTON, 22J., " Norton", 14k #s, c.1961
14k $125 $150 $195

HAMILTON, 19 jewels, "Oakmont"
14k (y) ....★$350 $400 $550
14k (w) $250 $300 $450

HAMILTON, 17J., "Orson ", c.1961
gold filled $50 $60 $80

HAMILTON, 19J., "Otis", reversible, sold for $67.50 in1938
14k ....★ ★ ★ ★$5,000 $6,500 $9,000
gold filled ....★$1,100 $1,300 $1,600

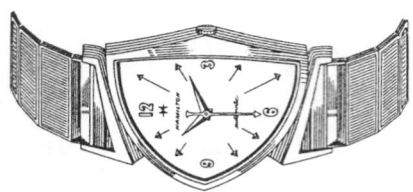

HAMILTON,17J., "Pacermatic", **automatic** on dial, cal. 667
swiss movement, tu-tone case, Ca. 1961, beware of **FAKES**
gold filled................. ★★★$1,000 $1,200 $1,600

HAMILTON, 17 jewels, "Perry" , Ca. 1933
gold filled **Y** $125 $200 $300
gold filled **W** .... ★★$175 $275 $400

HAMILTON, 19 jewels, "Paige" , c. 1941
gold filled.................................$80 $95 $135

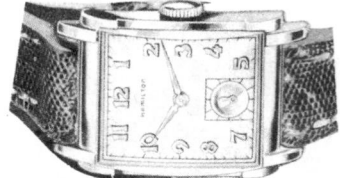

HAMILTON, 19J.," Perry ", c.1948
gold filled $95 $110 $150

HAMILTON, 22 jewels, "Paige", sterling silver dial, c. 1957
14k $150 $175 $225

HAMILTON, 22J., "Peyton ", c.1959
gold filled $50 $60 $85

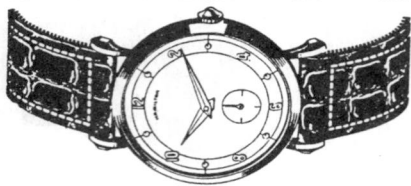

HAMILTON, 22J., " Parker B", 14k #s, anti-magnetic,
sold for $95.00 in 1957
10k $95 $125 $185

HAMILTON, 19 jewels, "Pierre" Ca. 1936
14k $400 $500 $650

HAMILTON, 17J.," Pinehurst " CA. 1930
14K (y) .... ★★★$1,000 $1,100 $1,400
14k (w) .... ★★$700 $800 $1,000

HAMILTON, 17 jewels, "Paxton", c. 1957
rolled gold.................................$40 $50 $70

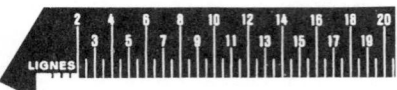

HAMILTON, 19J.,"Piping Rock", enamel bezel, ca.1928
14k (y) $800 $900 $1,200
14k (w) $700 $800 $1,000
See Ca. 1948 Piping Rock next page

HAMILTON, 17J.,"Piping Rock", grade 747, ca.1948
14k **Y** $900 $1,000 $1,300
14k **W** .... ★★★$1,200 $1,400 $1,700

HAMILTON, 17J.,"Powell", ca.1957
gold filled..................................$50 $60 $80

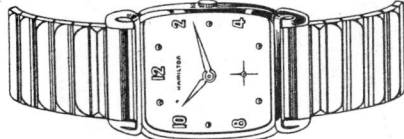

HAMILTON, 17J., '' Prentice'', c.1959
rolled gold..................................$40 $45 $65

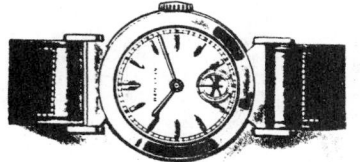

HAMILTON, 17J., ''Prescott '', sold for $45.00 in 1936
gold filled..................................$75 $100 $125

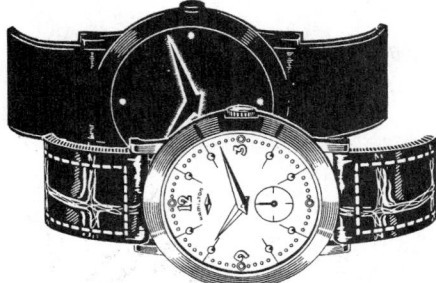

HAMILTON, 22J., "Prescott B", sterling silver dial, Ca. 1957
14k $125 $150 $200

HAMILTON, 17J, "Putnam", sold for $50.00 in 1932
gold filled (w or y) $175 $200 $300

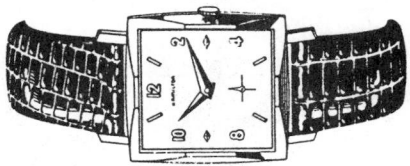

HAMILTON, 22J., '' Radburn'', 14k #s, c.1959
14k $125 $150 $200

HAMILTON, 17J.,'' Raleigh '', Plain, ca.1931
gold filled **Y** $150 $200 $250
gold filled **W** $95 $125 $175

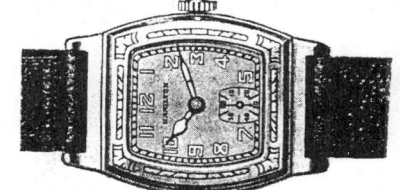

HAMILTON, 17J.,"Raleigh", Engraved, ca.1931
gold filled **Y** $175 $225 $300
gold filled **W** $95 $125 $175

HAMILTON, 19J.,"Raleigh", gold numbers, , ca.1953
gold filled $60 $80 $125

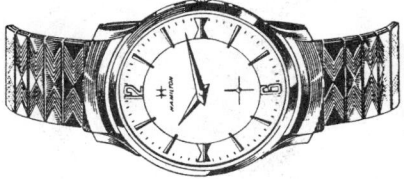

HAMILTON, 17J., '' Ramsey'', c.1961
rolled gold................................$40 $50 $70

HAMILTON, 17 jewels, "Randolph" , c. 1935
14k $95 $150 $225

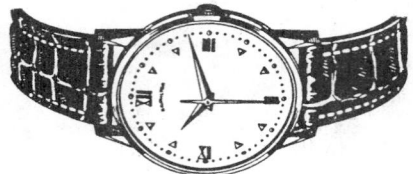

HAMILTON, 18J., " Randolph", 14k #s, c.1958
14k $125 $135 $175

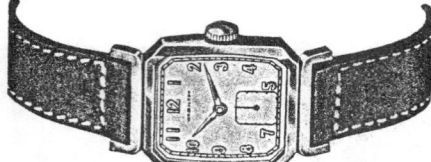

HAMILTON, 17J., "Raymon", ca.1950
s.steel $70 $90 $125

HAMILTON, 17 jewels, "Reagan" , c. 1937
gold filled................................$75 $95 $135

HAMILTON, 17J., "Reardon", ca.1949
14k $125 $150 $200

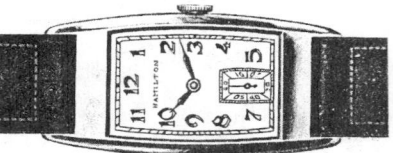

HAMILTON, 19J., " Richmond", curved, Ca.1933
18k Y $400 $500 $600
18k W ....★★$600 $750 $900

HAMILTON, 17J., " Robert", Ca.1953
14k ....$300 $400   . $550

HAMILTON, 18J., " Rodney", 14k #s, Ca.1953
Masonic dial $95 $125 $165
gold filled $50 $60 $85

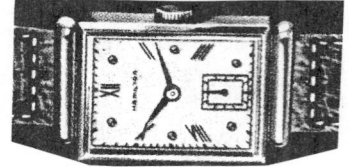

HAMILTON, 19J., "Rodney", ca.1941
14 k coral ....★$325 $350 $400
14k Y $150 $195 $250

HAMILTON, 17J., "Roland", Ca.1937
gold filled $95 $110 $150

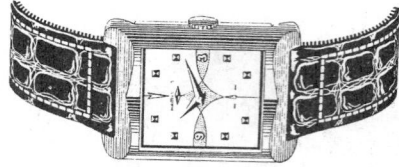

HAMILTON, 17J., "Roland", sterling silver dial, Ca.1955
14k $250 $275 $350

HAMILTON, 22J., " Romanesque M", c.1960
14k $125 $175 $250

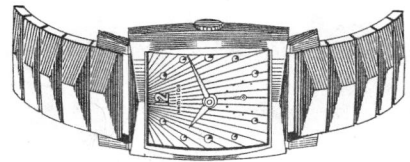

HAMILTON, 17J., "Romanesque N ", c.1960
gold filled...............................$50 $65 $95

HAMILTON, 17 jewels, "Russell", c. 1957
gold filled $65 $75 $95

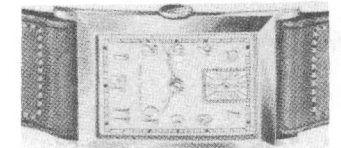

HAMILTON, 22J., " Romanesque R", c.1960
gold filled...............................$50 $60 $95

HAMILTON, 19 jewels, "Rutledge" , c. 1935
platinum.................................$800 $950 $1,200

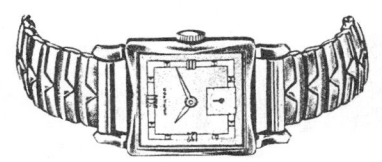

HAMILTON, 22J., "Romanesque S ", c.1960
gold filled...............................$75 $95 $125

HAMILTON, 17J., "Ryan", sold for $65.00 in 1952
gold filled $75 $95 $135

HAMILTON, 17J., " Romanesque T", c.1960
rolled gold...............................$50 $60 $95

HAMILTON, 17 jewels, "Samson", c. 1957
gold filled $50 $60 $95

HAMILTON, 19 jewels, "Ross" , c. 1939
gold filled yellow....................$75 $95 $135
gold filled Coral................. ★$150 $200 $300

HAMILTON, 17J., " Sawyer", 14k #s, c.1955
gold filled $70 $80 $110

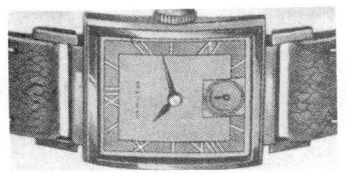

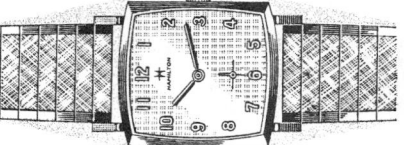

Scott 17J., sold for 79.50 in 1966
gold filled $50 $60 $75

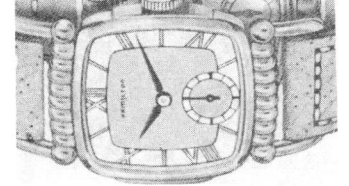

HAMILTON, 17 jewels, "Russell", hinged lugs , c. 1941
gold filled...............................$75 $95 $135

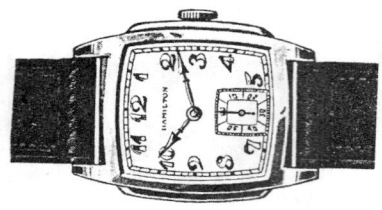

HAMILTON, 17J.," Scott ", GJS, Ca..1935
gold filled **Y**.............................$75 $95 $135
gold filled **W**.....................★$150 $195 $300

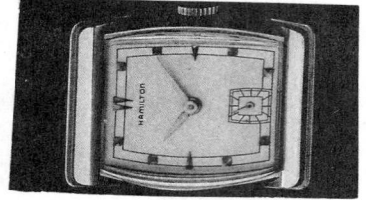

HAMILTON, 19J.," Scott ", GJS, 982, Ca.1949
14k $350 $400 $500

HAMILTON, 17J., " Sea Breeze", c.1961
rolled gold................................$30 $35 $60

HAMILTON, 17J., " Seabrook", c.1961
rolled gold................................$30 $35 $60

HAMILTON, 17J., " Sea-cap ", c.1961
rolled gold................................$30 $35 $60

HAMILTON, 22J., " Sea Cliff ", 14k #s, c.1961
gold filled $40 $50 $75

HAMILTON, 17J., " Sea - crest", c.1961
s. steel $30 $40 $65

HAMILTON, 17J., " Sea- glo ", c.1961
s. steel $30 $40 $65

HAMILTON, 17J., " Sea - guard", c.1962
s. steel $30 $40 $65

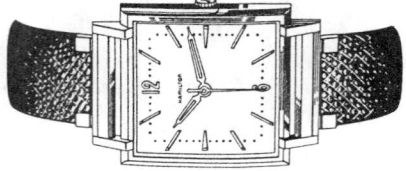

HAMILTON, 17J., " Sea - mate", c.1961
rolled gold................................$30 $35 $65

HAMILTON, 22J., " Sea Ranger", 14K #s, c.1961
gold filled $75 $95 $135

HAMILTON, 17J., " Sea Rover B", c.1961
s. steel $40 $55 $70

HAMILTON, 17J., " Sea- scape ", c.1961
gold plate $30 $35 $70

HAMILTON, 17J., " Sea- scout B ", c.1961
s. steel $30 $35 $70

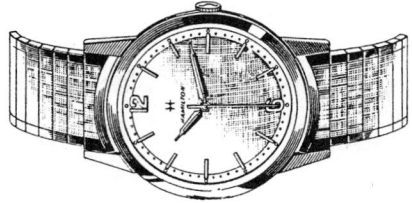

HAMILTON, 17J., " Sea - skip", c.1962
s. steel $30 $35 $70

HAMILTON, 17J., " Seaview", 14k #s, c.1961
14k $95 $125 $195

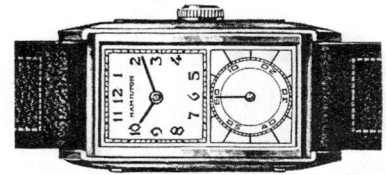

HAMILTON, 17J.,"Seckron", dual dial, grade 980, c.1935
gold filled $600 $700 $850

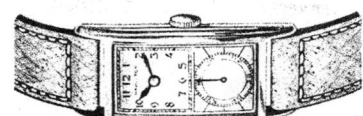

HAMILTON, 17J.,"Seckron", grade 980B, dual dial, c.1940
gold filled $700 $800 $950

HAMILTON, 17J., "Sectometer", sweep sec., ca.1945
gold filled $55 $75 $125

HAMILTON, 18J.,"Sectometer B", sweep sec., ca.1948
gold filled $55 $75 $125

HAMILTON, 18J.,"Sectometer C", sweep sec., ca.1951
14k $125 $150 $195

Wrist Watches listed in this section are priced at the collectable
fair market **Trade Show** level as **complete** watches having an
original gold-filled case and stainless steel back, also with
original dial, leather watch band, and the entire original movement in good working order with no repairs needed.

HAMILTON, 18J., " Sedgman'', Ca. 1952
14k $150 $195 $275

HAMILTON, 17 jewels, ''Sentinel,'' hack setting , Ca. 1941
gold filled..................................$55 $75 $125

HAMILTON, 18J., "Seville", c.1958
gold filled..................................$50 $75 $110

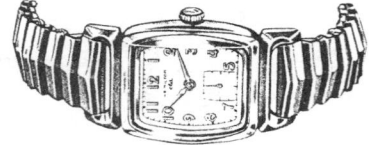

HAMILTON, 19J., "Sheldon", sold for $89.50 in 1953
gold filled..................................$75 $95 $135

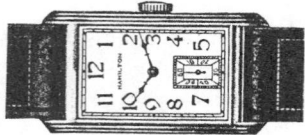

HAMILTON, 19J., "Sherwood", (also - Seneca), Ca.1935
14k $195 $225 $300

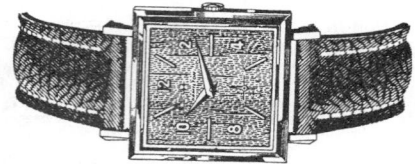

HAMILTON, 22J., " Sherwood M'', 14k #s, wood dial,
American walnut wood dial, c.1961
14k .... ★$700 $1,000 $1,500

HAMILTON, 17J., "Sherwood N"', 14k #s, auto-wind, wood
dial, Mexican Mahogany wood dial, c.1961
14k .... ★$600 $900 $1,400

HAMILTON, 22J.," Sherwood R", dial is made of wood,
(dial is American walnut) c.1961
14k .... ★$600 $850 $1,300

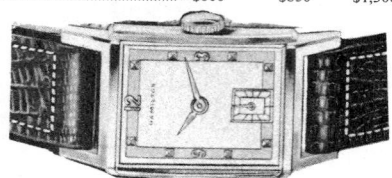

HAMILTON, 19J.," Sherwood", c.1949
gold filled $75 $95 $135

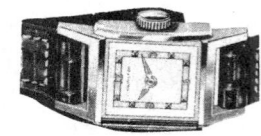

HAMILTON, 17J.,"Sheryll", matched styling to the Sherwood for men, Sheryll = ladies watch, Ca. 1949
gold filled $75 $95 $135

HAMILTON, 22 jewels, "Sinclair" , c. 1957
14k $125 $150 $195

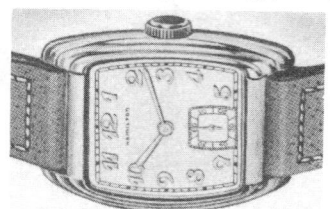

HAMILTON, 17 jewels, ''Sidney'' , c. 1937
gold filled $150 $175 $250

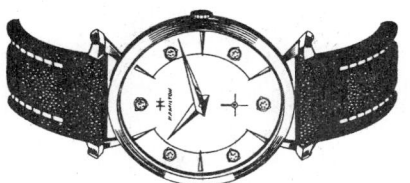

HAMILTON, 22J., " Sir Echo" ,14K #s, 6 diamond, c.1957
14k (W)...................................$150 $175 $250

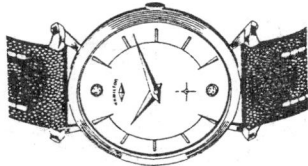

HAMILTON, 22J., " Sir Echo", 2 diamonds, 14K #s, c.1957
14k (W)...................................$125 $150 $225

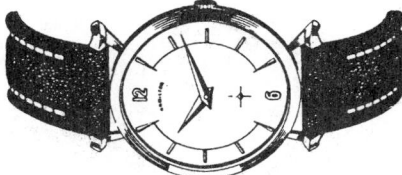

HAMILTON, 22J., " Sir Echo" , 14K #s, c.1957
14k (W)................................ $125 $150 $225

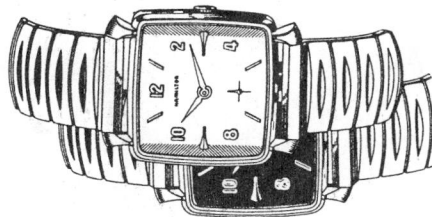

HAMILTON, 17J., "Sloane " , c.1959
rolled gold................................ $45 $55 $75

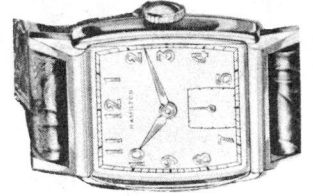

HAMILTON, 17J.,"Spencer", gold numbers, ca.1951
10k,With Masonic symbols... $150 $175 $200
10k $95 $125 $175

🕐 A collector should expect to pay modestly higher prices
at local shops

HAMILTON, 19J., "Spur", enamel bezel, ca.1928
14k (y) .... ★ ★ ★ $1,800 $2,200 $2,500
14k(w)...................... ★ ★ ★ $1,600 $1,800 $2,300

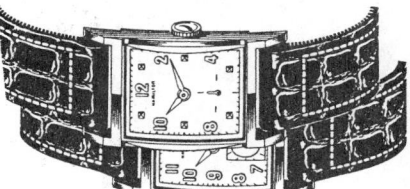

HAMILTON, 22J., " Stafford" , 14K #s, c.1952
14k $125 $150 $225

HAMILTON, 18 jewels, "Steeldon" , c. 1949
s. steel $40 $65 $95

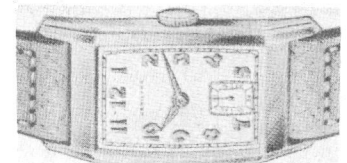

HAMILTON, 17 jewels, "Stanford" , c. 1940
gold filled $75 $95 $135

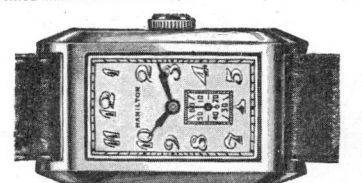

HAMILTON, 19 jewels, "Stanley" Ca. 1930
gold filled $150 $195 $325

HAMILTON, 22 jewels, "Staunton", c. 1957
14 k $125 $150 $195

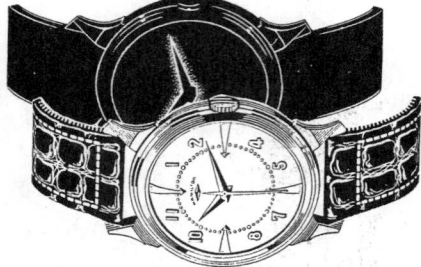

HAMILTON, 18J., "Stormking I", sterling silver dial, c.1957
18K..$250 $300 $425

HAMILTON, 18J., "Stormking II", sterling silver dial, c.1957
14k $125 $150 $195

HAMILTON, 18J.,"Stormking III", sterling silver dial, c.1957
14k $125 $150 $195

HAMILTON,18J.,"Stormking IV ", 14K#, c.1957
gold filled................................$65 $75 $95

HAMILTON,18J., "Stormking IV Military", c.1957
s.steel 24 hour Cycle dial $95 $125 $165

HAMILTON, 18J., "Stormking V", sterling silver dial, c.1957
s.steel $40 $50 $95

HAMILTON, 18J., " Stormking VI" , c.1955
gold filled $50 $60 $95

HAMILTON, 18J., " Stormking VII" , c.1961
gold filled $50 $60 $95

HAMILTON, 18J., " Stormking VIII" , 14K #s, c.1961
10k $95 $125 $165

HAMILTON, 17J., " Stormking IX" , 14K #s, c.1961
14k $125 $150 $195

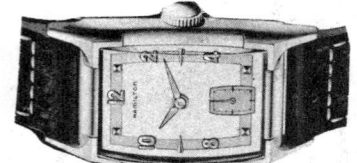

HAMILTON, 19J.," Stuart ", c.1949
gold filled $75 $95 $135

HAMILTON, 17J., "Surf", c.1957
s.steel $40 $50 $75

HAMILTON, 22J., " Thor" , 14K #s, c.1959
gold filled $200 $250 $350

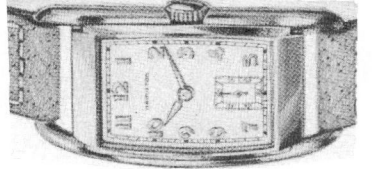

HAMILTON, 17-19 jewels, "Sutton" , Ca. 1936
gold filled...............................$175 $195 $225

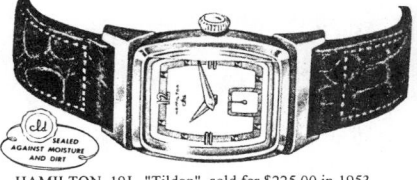

HAMILTON, 19J., "Tildon", sold for $225.00 in 1953
14k $200 $250 $350

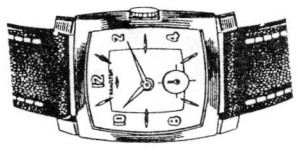

HAMILTON, 22 jewels, "Sutton " , Ca. 1957
14k $125 $150 $195

HAMILTON, 18J.," Todd ", c.1951
gold filled $50 $70 $95

HAMILTON, 17J., " Talbot" , Ca.1937
gold filled..................................$90 $110 $135

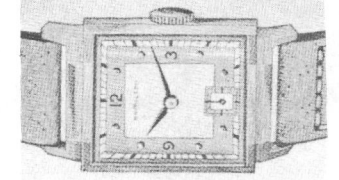

HAMILTON, 19 jewels, "Touraine" , c. 1935
14k $150 $175 $250

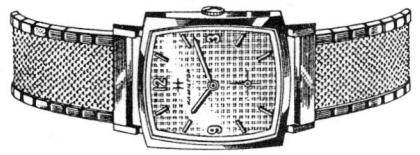

HAMILTON, 17J., " Talbot" , c.1961
gold filled..................................$60 $70 $95

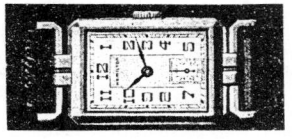

HAMILTON, 17J., " Taylor", hinged lugs, Ca.1935
gold filled..............................$150 $175 $250

HAMILTON, 17J, "Transcontinental A", Time Zone, Ca.1957
gold filled $250 $300 $450
Transcontinental B next page

HAMILTON, 17J, "Transcontinental B", Time Zone, Ca.1957
14k $600 $700 $900

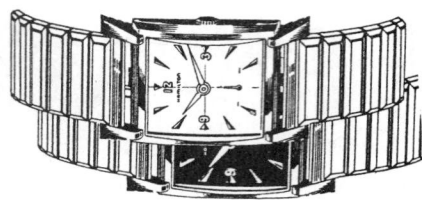

HAMILTON, 22J., " Trent" , sterling silver dial, c.1955
gold filled................................ $90 $95 $125

HAMILTON, 17J, "Turner", Ca.1936
gold filled Y............................$100 $125 $200
gold filled W.................. ★ ★$150 $300 $400

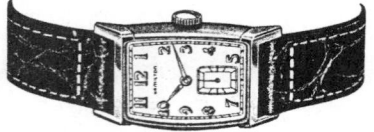

HAMILTON, 19J., "Turner", sold for $100.00 in 1953
(look-a-like) Donald, 14k
10k(w or y) $125 $150 $250

HAMILTON,22J., "Tuxedo B " , 44 diamonds,14K #s,
Ca. 1956
14k(w)................................. $250 $300 $375

HAMILTON, 22J., " Tuxedo II" , 44 diamonds,14K #s,
Ca. 1961
14k(w)................................... $250 $300 $375

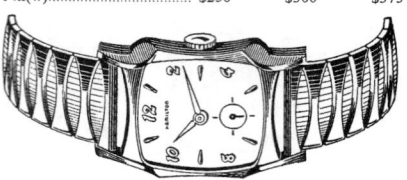

HAMILTON, 17J, "Tyrone", 14k markers, Ca.1957
gold filled $75 $95 $135

HAMILTON, 17J.," Vardon ", sealed. c.1949
s. steel $35 $45 $80

HAMILTON, 22J., " Valiant" , 14K #s, c.1959
gold filled $250 $300 $400

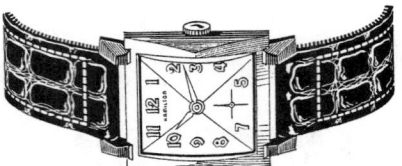

HAMILTON, 17J, "Vernon", sterling silver dial, Ca.1957
10 k $95 $125 $195

Wrist Watches listed in this section are priced at the collectable
fair market **Trade Show** level as **complete** watches having an
original gold-filled case and stainless steel back, also with
original dial, leather watch band, and the entire original movement in good working order with no repairs needed.

🕀 A collector should expect to pay modestly higher prices
at local shops

HAMILTON, 17J., " Viking" , c.1961
rolled gold................................$50 $60 $80

HAMILTON, 17J., " Viking II" , c.1961
rolled gold................................ $40 $50 $70

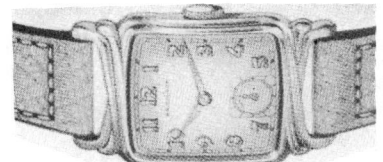

HAMILTON, 17 jewels, "Vincent" , c .1941
gold filled..................................$95 $125 $175

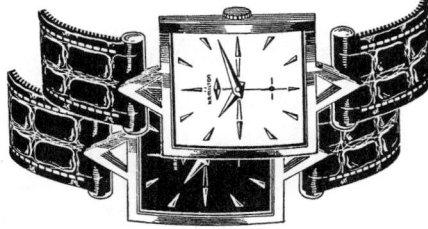

HAMILTON, 22J., "Viscount", sterling silver dial, ca.1955
14k .... ★★$400 $500 $650

HAMILTON, 17J., "Ward", ca.1957
gold filled..................................$75 $95 $135

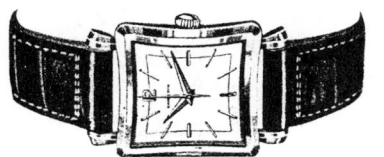

HAMILTON, 18J., "Warwick", sold for $150.00 in 1953
gold filled..................................$95 $110 $150

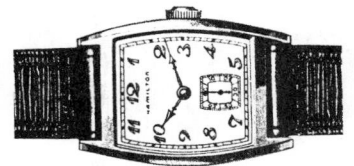

HAMILTON, 17 jewels, "Watson", Ca. 1930
gold filled plain $95 $125 $175
gold filled engraved .... ★★★$195 $250 $400

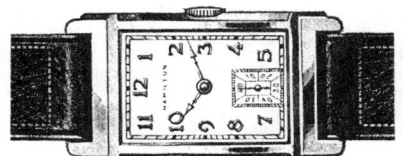

HAMILTON, 19 jewels, "Wayne", Ca. 1935
14k $175 $195 $275

HAMILTON, 17 jewels, "Webster", Ca. 1932
14k W .... ★★★★$500 $600 $800
gold filled $95 $125 $175

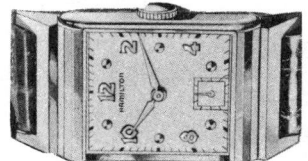

HAMILTON, 19J.," Wesley ", c.1941
14k $150 $175 $225

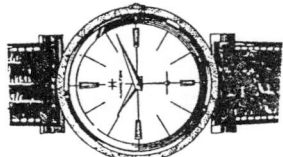

HAMILTON, 17 jewels, "Whitford", Ca. 1960
14k $95 $125 $225

⊕ A collector should expect to pay modestly higher prices
at local shops

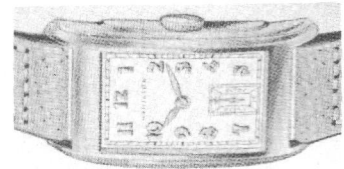

HAMILTON, 17 jewels, "Whitman" , c. 1940
gold filled..................................$75 $95 $135

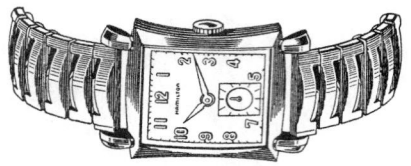

HAMILTON, 17 jewels, "Wilson", **flared**, Ca. 1954
gold filled $95 $120 $150

HAMILTON, 17J, "Whitman", sterling silver dial, Ca. 1957
gold filled..................................$50 $60 $75
gold filled Masonic dial............$65 $75 $125

HAMILTON, 19J., "Windsor", sold for $87.50 in1953
gold filled $75 $95 $125

HAMILTON, 17 jewels, "Whitney" , Ca. 1932
gold filled(w or y)........ ★ ★ $250 $300 $400

HAMILTON, 18 jewels, "Winfield", Ca. 1957
14k $125 $150 $195

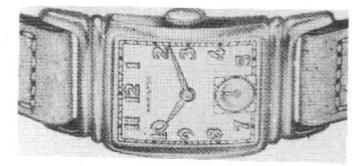

HAMILTON, 19 jewels, "Wilkinson", Ca. 1930
14k (w or y) .... ★ ★ ★ ★ $750 $800 $900

HAMILTON, 19 jewels, "Winthrop" , c. 1939
gold filled $85 $125 $175

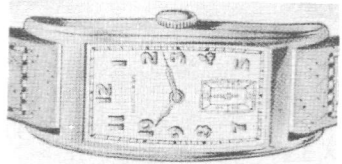

HAMILTON, 17 jewels, "Yorktown" , c. 1940
gold filled $125 $175 $275

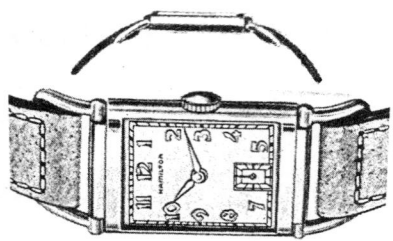

HAMILTON, 19 jewels, "Wilshire", hinged lugs, c. 1941
gold filled yellow...................$175 $200 $275
gold filled coral...................★ $200 $250 $350

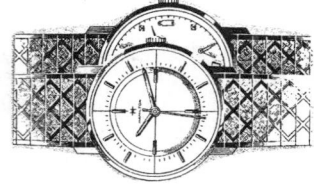

HAMILTON, 17 jewels,"Yeoman II
gold filled $50 $60 $75

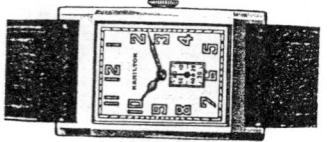

HAMILTON, 17 jewels, "Accumatic II" , c. 1957
rolled gold..................................$40 $50 $75

HAMILTON, 17 jewels, ''Accumatic **X**''
s. steel $40 $50 $75

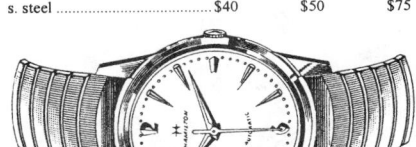

HAMILTON, 17 jewels, ''Accumatic **XI**''
s. steel $40 $50 $75

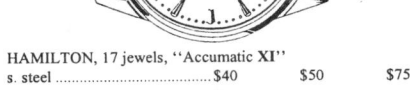

HAMILTON, 17J, "Accumatic **A-201**", Ca. 1968
shaped like a early TV screen dial.
14k $150 $175 $250

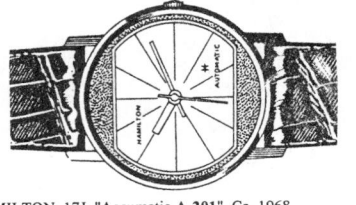

HAMILTON, 17 jewels, ''Accumatic **A-575**'', date
s. steel $40 $50 $75

HAMILTON, 17 jewels, ''Accumatic **A-650**''
rolled gold $40 $50 $75

HAMILTON, 17 jewels, ''Accumatic **A-651**''
gold plate $40 $50 $75

HAMILTON, 17 jewels, ''Automatic **K-203**''
14k $95 $125 $175

HAMILTON, 17 jewels, ''Automatic **K-303**''
10k $80 $95 $150

HAMILTON, 17 jewels, ''Automatic **K-304**''
10k $80 $95 $150

Note: Hamilton acquired the Buren
Watch Factory of Switzerland in 1966
and adapted a ultra thin self-winding
movement for the **Thin-o-matic.**

HAMILTON, 17 jewels, "Automatic **K-414**"
gold filled...................................$60 $70 $95

HAMILTON, 17 jewels, "Automatic **K-417**"
gold filled $60 $70 $95

HAMILTON, 17 jewels, "Accumatic **VII**"
rolled gold..............................$40 $50 $75

HAMILTON, 17 jewels, "Automatic **K-418**"
gold filled $60 $70 $95

HAMILTON, 17 jewels, "Automatic **K-415**"
gold filled...................................$60 $70 $95

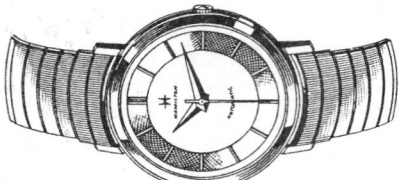

HAMILTON, 17 jewels, "Automatic **K-419**"
gold filled $60 $70 $95

HAMILTON, 17 jewels, "Automatic **K-416**"
gold filled..............................$60 $70 $95

HAMILTON, 17 jewels, "Automatic **K-420**"
gold filled $60 $70 $95

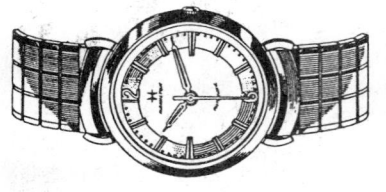

HAMILTON, 17 jewels, "**Kinematic II**"
rolled gold..............................$40 $50 $75

HAMILTON, 17 jewels, "Automatic **K-458**"
gold filled $60 $70 $95

Pricing in this Guide are fair market price for **COM-PLETE** watches which are reflected from the "**NAWCC**" National and regional shows.

Some grades are not included. Their values can be determined by comparing with **similar** age, size, metal content, style, grades, or models such as **time only**, chronograph, repeater etc. listed.

HAMILTON, 17 jewels, "Automatic **K-459**"
gold filled...................................$60 $70 $95

HAMILTON, 17 jewels, "Automatic **K-460**"
gold filled...................................$60 $70 $95

HAMILTON, 17J, "Automatic **K-475**", with date,
Swiss movement, sold for $100.00 in 1960
gold filled................ ★ ★ ★ $1,200 $1,500 $1,850

HAMILTON, 17 jewels, "Automatic **K-503**" Ca.1962
s. steel $50 $60 $85

HAMILTON, 17 jewels, "Automatic **K-507**"
s. steel $50 $60 $85

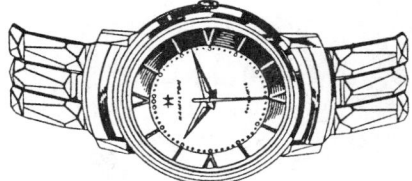

HAMILTON, 17 jewels, "Automatic **K-650**"
gold plate $40 $50 $75

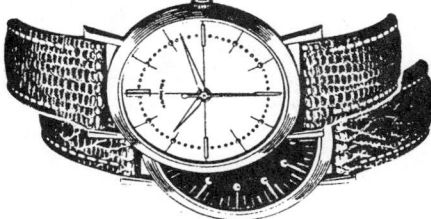

HAMILTON, 18 jewels, "Thincraft **II**"
gold filled $50 $60 $85

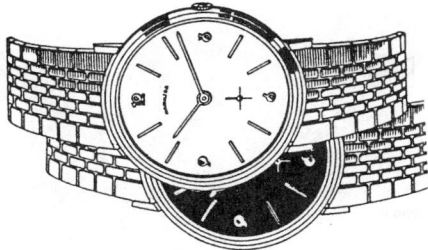

HAMILTON, 17 jewels, "Thinline **2000**"
14k $95 $125 $195

HAMILTON, 17 jewels, "Thinline **2001**"
14k $95 $125 $195

HAMILTON, 17 jewels, "Thinline **3000**"
10k $80 $95 $165

HAMILTON, 17 jewels, "Thinline **4000**"
gold filled................................$50 $60 $85

HAMILTON, 17 jewels, "Thinline **4001**"
gold filled................................$50 $60 $95

HAMILTON, 17 jewels, "Thin-o-matic", **date**
rolled gold................................$50 $60 $85

HAMILTON, 17 jewels, "Thin-o-matic", **Masterpiece**
14k $95 $125 $195

HAMILTON, 17 jewels, "Thin-o-matic **T-200**"
14k $95 $125 $195

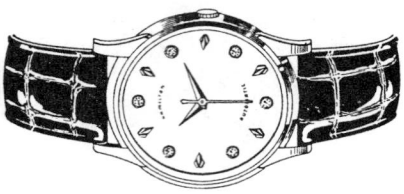

HAMILTON, 17 jewels, "Thin-o-matic **T-201**", **6- diamonds**
14k $150 $175 $225

HAMILTON, 17 jewels, "Thin-o-matic **T-201**"
14k $95 $125 $195

HAMILTON, 17 jewels, "Thin-o-matic **T-202**"
14k $95 $125 $195

HAMILTON, 17 jewels, "Thin-o-matic **T-300**"
10k $80 $100 $150

HAMILTON, 17 jewels, "Thin-o-matic **T-400**"
gold filled $40 $50 $75

Pricing in this Guide are fair market price for **COM-PLETE** watches which are reflected from the "**NAWCC**" National and regional shows.

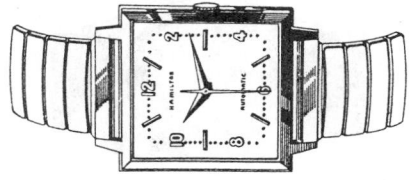

HAMILTON, 17 jewels, "Thin-o-matic **T-401**"
gold filled.................................$70 $80 $95

HAMILTON, 17 jewels, "Thin-o-matic **T-402**"
gold filled.................................$40 $60 $95

HAMILTON, 17J, "Thin-o-matic **T-403**", Swiss movement
Ca. 1960
rolled gold (with date). ★ ★ ★$500 $650 $850
gold filled **W**.................★ ★$450 $525 $650
gold filled **Y**.......................★$350 $425 $550

HAMILTON, 17 jewels, "Thin-o-matic **T-404**"
gold filled.................................$40 $60 $95

HAMILTON, 17 jewels, "Thin-o-matic **T-405**"
gold filled.................................$40 $60 $95

Wrist Watches listed in this section are priced at the collectable fair market **Trade Show** level as **complete** watches having an original gold-filled case and stainless steel back, also
with original dial, leather watch band, and the entire original
movement in good working order with no repairs needed.

HAMILTON, 17 jewels, "Thin-o-matic **T-450**"
gold filled $40 $60 $95

HAMILTON, 17 jewels, "Thin-o-matic **T-451**"
gold filled $40 $60 $95

HAMILTON, 17 jewels, "Thin-o-matic **T-475**"
gold filled $40 $50 $95

HAMILTON, 17 jewels, "Thin-o-matic **T-476**", date
gold filled $40 $50 $95

HAMILTON, 17 jewels, "Thin-o-matic **T-500**"
s. steel $40 $50 $95

🕐 Some grades are not included. Their values can be
determined by comparing with **similar** age, size, metal
content, style, grades, or models such as **time only**,
chronograph, repeater etc. listed.

HAMILTON, 17 jewels, "Thin-o-matic **T-501**"
s. steel $40 $50 $95

HAMILTON, 17 jewels, "Thin-o-matic **T-502**"
s. steel $40 $50 $95

HAMILTON, 17 jewels, "Thin-o-matic **T-575**" date
s. steel $40 $50 $95

HAMILTON, 17 jewels, "Thin-o-matic **T-650**"
rolled gold.............................. $40 $50 $75

HAMILTON, 17 jewels, "Thinline **5000**"
s. steel $40 $50 $95

HAMILTON, 17 jewels, "Cushion ", **(round)**, grade 987,
ca.1927
gold filled $75 $95 $150

HAMILTON, 17 jewels, "Cushion", plain, grade 987,
ca.1927
14k $195 $250 $325
gold filled $75 $95 $150

HAMILTON, 17J.,"Cushion" , no sec., grade 986, c.1923
gold filled $75 $95 $125

HAMILTON, 17 jewels, "Cushion", **engraved**, grade 987,
ca.1927
14k $195 $250 $350
gold filled $95 $125 $150

HAMILTON, 17 jewels, tonneau engraved
14k $225 $275 $350
gold filled $95 $125 $150

HAMILTON, 17J.,"Tonneau" plain
14k $195 $225 $300
gold filled................................... $75 $95 $150

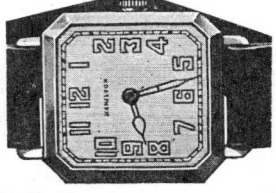

HAMILTON, 17J., "Square", cut corner, no sec., ca.1927
gold filled................................... $75 $95 $150
14k $95 $125 $225

HAMILTON, 17J., "Square B", cut corner, with sec., ca.1927
gold filled................................... $70 $90 $125
14k $125 $175 $275

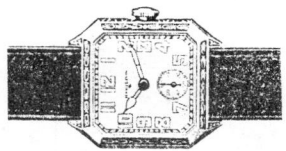

HAMILTON, 17J., "Square", cut corner, enameled, ca.1927
gold filled................................... $75 $95 $150
14k $125 $150 $250

HAMILTON, 17J., Square cut corner, engraved LUGS
gold filled................................... $75 $95 $150

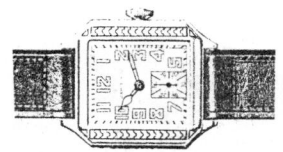

HAMILTON, 17J., "Square B", engraved, ca.1931
gold filled $75 $95 $150
14k $95 $150 $225

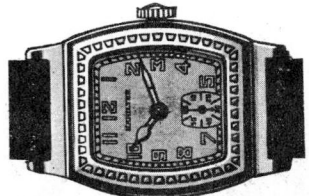

HAMILTON, 17 jewels, Raleigh, engraved fancy, Ca. 1930
gold filled $95 $125 $175

HAMILTON, 17J., "Barrel", Plain bezel, ca.1928
gold filled $75 $95 $150
14k $95 $125 $225

HAMILTON, 17J., "Barrel", engraved, ca.1927
gold filled $75 $95 $150
14k $125 $150 $250

HAMILTON, 17J., grade 987, w gold or Platinum buckle
sold for $485.00 in 1927
Platinum................... ★★★$2,000 $2,200 $2,600

HAMILTON, 17J., cal.987, **enamel** on case, c.1930
gold filled..................................$95 $125 $165

HAMILTON, 17 jewels, engraved bezel, hinged back
14k(w).....................................$250 $275 $325

HAMILTON, 17J., "Oval", plain or engraved, grade 987
sold for in1927 $70.00 GF & $105.50 14K
gold filled..........................★$350 $400 $500
14K..............................★★★$700 $900 $1,200

HAMILTON, 17 jewels, engraved bezel, c. 1920
14k $150 $175 $225

HAMILTON, 17J, *Hamilton Illinois* on dial, sold by Hamilton & Illinois marked on case with Illinois mvt. (**crossover**).
gold filled $95 $125 $165

HAMILTON, 19 jewels
platinum C&B $900 $1,000 $1,200

HAMILTON, 19J., gold numbers, **large lugs**, Ca.1950
14K $195 $225 $250

HAMILTON, 19J.,"bomb timer", c.1944
base metal $300 $350 $450

HAMILTON, 15 J., military frogman style, waterproof
(USN BU SHIPS on dial), canteen style
base metal $400 $650 $850

HAMILTON, 17 J., military issue, hack setting, c.1960s
base metal $80 $95 $150

HAMILTON, 17 J., British issue note broad arrow symbol,
Grade 649, swiss movement
base metal $80 $95 $140

HAMILTON, 7 J., military issue, hack setting, note "H3" for
Hydrogen 3 and radioactive symbol, c.1970s
base metal $80 $95 $150

HAMILTON, 17J., "Aqua-date", autow, waterproof - 600 feet
elapsed time indicator, sold for $115.00 in 1966
s. steel $50 $60 $95

HAMILTON, 17J., chronograph Valjoux cal.7733, ca.1971
s. steel $195 $225 $350

HAMILTON, 17J., **Date**, chrono.Valjoux cal.7733, ca.1971
s. steel $225 $275 $385

HAMILTON, 17J., chronograph screw back
s. steel $195 $225 $350

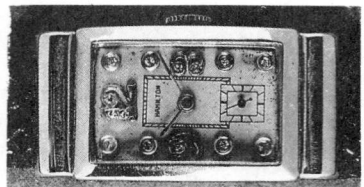

HAMILTON, 17-19 jewels, diamond dial, hooded lugs
14k $800 $900 $1,100

HAMILTON, 17-19 jewels, diamond dial
14k(w).....................................$800 $900 $1,100

HAMILTON, 17-19 jewels, diamond dial , curved
platinum..............................$1,000 $1,100 $1,300
14k $800 $900 $1,100

HAMILTON, 17-19 jewels, diamond dial, c. 1940
14k $800 $900 $1,100

HAMILTON, 17-19 jewels, diamond dial
14k $400 $450 $550

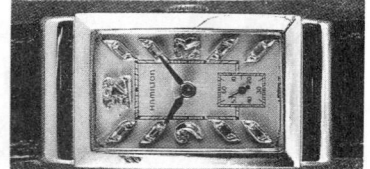

HAMILTON, 17-19 jewels, diamond dial, hooded lugs
14k $500 $550 $600

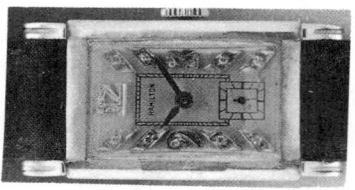

HAMILTON, 17-19 jewels,diamond dial
14k $500 $550 $600

HAMILTON, 17-19 jewels, diam. dial, c.1948, top hat
platinum..............................$1,200 $1,300 $1,500
14k (w) $900 $1,000 $1,200

HAMILTON, 17-19 jewels, diamond dial
14k (w) $400 $450 $550

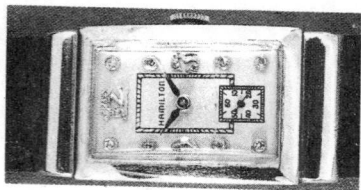

HAMILTON, 17-19 jewels, diamond dial, hooded lugs
14k $450 $500 $600

HAMILTON, 17-19 jewels, diamond dial
platinum..............................$1,100 $1,200 $1,400
14k (w) $900 $1,000 $1,200

Wrist Watches listed in this section are priced at the collectable
fair market **Trade Show** level as **complete** watches having an
original gold-filled case and stainless steel back, also with
original dial, leather watch band, and the entire original movement in good working order with no repairs needed.

HAMILTON, 17-19J., mystery dial with diamonds & **bezel**
Swiss Model
18k $550 $650 $800
14k $450 $550 $650

HAMILTON, 17-19 jewels, diamond dial, **Not Factory**
14k $200 $250 $325

HAMILTON, 17-19 jewels, diamond dial, **Not Factory**
14k (w)......................................$175 $225 $300

HAMILTON, 19 jewels, diamond dial, fancy **knotted** lugs
14k (w)......................................$200 $225 $300

HAMILTON,17J., " Belmont ", cal.955 , c.1933
gold filled..................................$30 $35 $50

HAMILTON,17J., 40 diamond bezel, Ca. 1955
18k (w)....................................$300 $350 $450

HAMILTON,17J., "Bianca", diamond & sapphire, c.1933
18k(w) $150 $175 $250

HAMILTON,17J., " Bryn Mawr ", c.1933
14k...$60 $70 $100

HAMILTON,17J., " Briarcliffe ", c.1933
gold filled..................................$30 $35 $50

HAMILTON,17J., " Caroline ", cal.955, c.1933
gold filled..................................$20 $25 $35

HAMILTON,17J., " Cedarcrest ", cal.955, c.1933
14k...$50 $60 $80

HAMILTON,17J., " Chevy Chase A ", cal. , c.1933
14k(w) $60 $70 $90

HAMILTON,17J., " Chevy Chase B ", cal.989 , c.1933
14k $70 $80 $100

HAMILTON,17J., " Chevy Chase C ", cal. , c.1933
14k(w)......................................$60 $70 $90

HAMILTON,17J., " Chevy Chase E ", c.1933
14k(w)......................................$70 $80 $100

HAMILTON,17J., " Diane ", c.1933
14k $60 $70 $90

HAMILTON,17J., " Drexel ", cal.955 , c.1933
14k $70 $75 $90

HAMILTON,17J., " Edgewood ", c.1933
gold filled...................................$30 $35 $45

HAMILTON,17J., " Eugenie ", 44 diamonds, c.1933
platinum.....................................$250 $275 $350

HAMILTON,17J., " Glenwood ", cal.955, c.1933
gold filled...................................$30 $35 $50

HAMILTON,17J., " Linden Hall ", c.1933
gold filled...................................$30 $35 $50

HAMILTON,17J.," Maritza ", 6 diamonds, cal.955 , c.1933
18k(w)......................................$80 $90 $120

HAMILTON,17J., " Mayfield ", cal.955 , c.1933
gold filled...................................$30 $35 $50

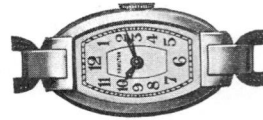

HAMILTON,17J., " Newcomb ", cal.989, c.1933
gold filled...................................$30 $35 $50

HAMILTON,17J., " Nightingale ", 40 diamonds, c.1933
18k(w) $200 $225 $300

HAMILTON,17J., " Portia ", 8 diamonds, c.1933
18k(w) $200 $225 $300

HAMILTON,17J., " Trudy ", c.1948
14k...$50 $60 $80

Grade 986A, 6/0 size
Open face, ¾ plate movt., 17 jewels, double roller

Grade 987, 6/0 size
Hunting, ¾ plate movt., 17 jewels, double roller

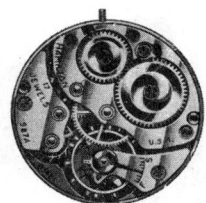

Grade 987A, 6/0 size
Open face, ¾ plate movt., 17 jewels, double roller

Grade 987S, 6/0 size
Hunting, ¾ plate movt., 17 jewels, double roller

Grade 747, 8/0 size
Open face, ¾ plate movt., 17 jewels, double roller

Grade 980, 14/0 size
Open face, ¾ plate movt., 17 jewels, double roller

Grade 982, 14/0 size
Open face, ¾ plate movt., 19 jewels, double roller

Grade 982M, 14/0 size
Open face, ¾ plate movt., 19 jewels, double roller

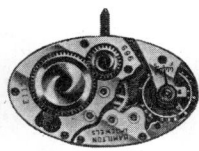

Grade 989, 18/0 size
Open face, ¾ plate movt., 17 jewels, double roller

Grade 997, 20/0 size
Open face, ¾ plate movt., 17 jewels, double roller

Grade 721, 21/0 size
Open face, ¾ plate movt., 17 jewels, double roller

Grade 995, 21/0 size
Open face, ¾ plate movt., 17 jewels, double roller

Grade 911, 22/0 size
Open face, ¾ plate movt., 17 jewels, double roller

Grade 911M, 22/0 size
Open face, ¾ plate movt., 17 jewels, double roller

Grade 780, 21/0 size
17 jewels

Grade 770, 12/0 size
22 jewels

Grade 761, 21/0 size
22 jewels

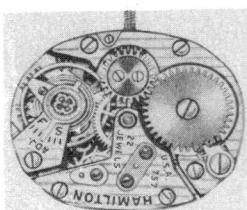

Grade 757, 21/0 size
22 jewels

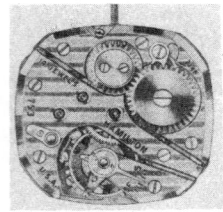

Grade 753, 12/0 size, 19 jewels
Grade 752, 12/0 size, 17 jewels

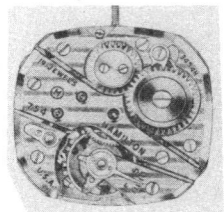

Grade 754, 12/0 size, 19 jewels
Grade 770, 12/0 size, 17 jewels

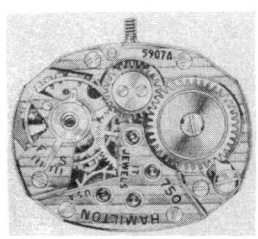

Grade 750 & 751, 21/0 size
17 jewels

Grade 748, 8/0 size
18 jewels

Grade 747, 8/0 size
17 jewels

LIGNE GAUGE

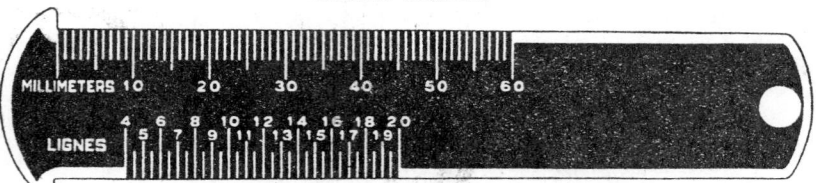

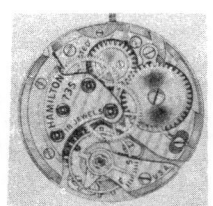

Grade 735, 8/0 size
18 jewels

Grade 730, 8/0 size
17 jewels

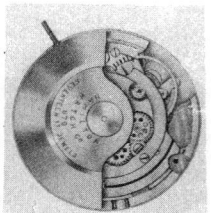

Grade 679, 17 jewels
Grade 692, 694 - calendar

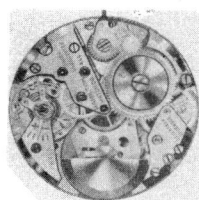

Grade 666 & 663, 17 jewels
Grade 668 - calendar

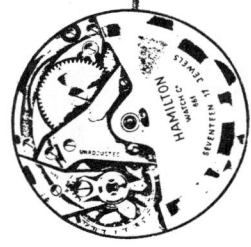

Grade 658, 661, 667, 17 jewels
Grade 665, 23J, Grade 664, 25J
Grade 662, 690 - calendar, 17J

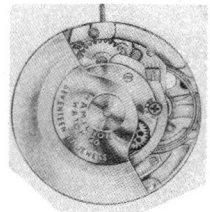

Grade 623 & 624, 17 jewels

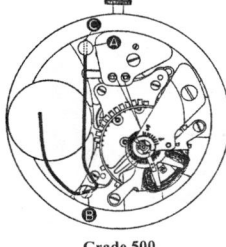

Grade 500
Electric

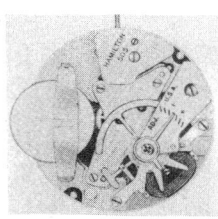

Grade 505, electric, 11 jewels

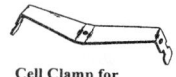

Cell Clamp for
500A or 501

THE SPUR

1930 AD

A Hamilton the true Sportsman will
love. In either 14K yellow or white
gold with numerals of gold in a black
enamel circlet on the outside of the
case—19 jewel movement, $125

HAMPDEN,15J., old stock, all original, engraved case, c.1925
gold filled..............................$75 $95 $175

HAMPDEN,11=15J., "LEVER SET" , 3/0 size, old stock, all
original, c.1928
silver......................................$125 $150 $225

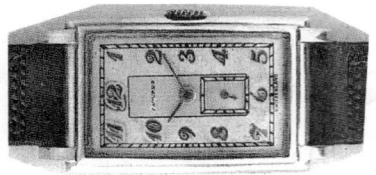

HAMPDEN, 17 jewels., c. 1936
14k $125 $150 $225

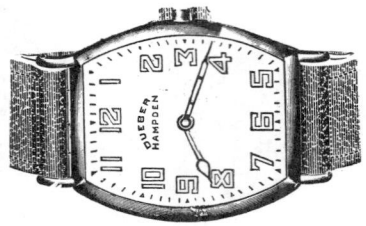

HAMPDEN, 15j, old stock, all original, c. 1928
14k..$125 $150 $200
gold filled.................................$75 $95 $135

HAMPDEN, 17J., by Lonville W. Co., c. 1936
gold filled................................$50 $65 $95

HAMPDEN, 17 jewels, double dial, c. 1938
gold filled.................................$75 $95 $125

HAMPDEN, 11J., Molly Stark, old stock, all original, c. 1928
base metal.................................$40 $50 $75

HAMPDEN, 7J., tonneau shaped, old stock, all original, c. 1928
gold filled.................................$75 $85 $135

HAMPDEN, 15J, old stock, all original, c. 1928
14k $125 $150 $225
gold filled.................................$95 $125 $165

🕐 Some grades are not included. Their values can be
determined by comparing with similar age, size, metal
content, style, grades, or models such as time only,
chronograph, repeater etc. listed.

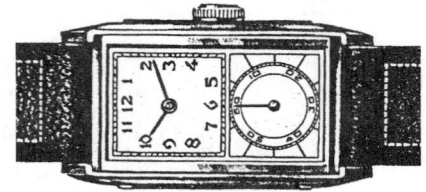

HARMAN,7J.,doctor style duo-dial,
gold filled..............................$200 $225 $350

HARMAN, 17J., **one button** chronog., mid size, c.1940s
s. steel $250 $275 $325

HARVARD, 17 jewels, chronog., tach-telemeter
s. steel $195 $250 $325

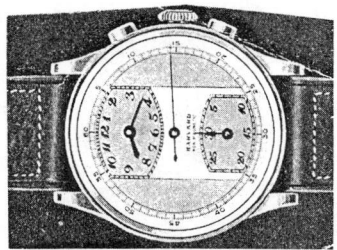

HARVARD, 17 jewels, 1/5 sec. chronog.
s. steel $250 $275 $375

HARVEL, 17 jewels, date-o-graph
s. steel $75 $95 $150

Wrist Watches listed in this section are priced at the collectable
fair market **Trade Show** level as **complete** watches having an
original gold-filled case and stainless steel back, also with
original dial, leather watch band, and the entire original movement in good working order with no repairs needed.

Pricing in this Guide are fair market price for **COM-
PLETE** watches which are reflected from the "**NAWCC**" National and regional shows.

HARVEL, 17J.,center sec.
gold filled................................$25 $35 $55

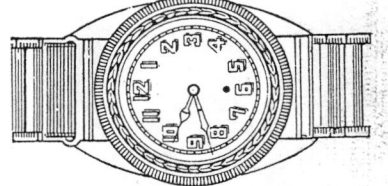

HARWOOD, 15 jewels, early self winding, c. 1928
18k (w) $600 $750 $1,000
14k..$450 $550 $750
gold filled..............................$195 $250 $400
s. steel....................................$195 $250 $400

HARWOOD, 15 J., rim set by turning bezel clockwise
9k...$300 $350 $525

HARWOOD, 15 jewels, back set, c. 1925
18k...$350 $450 $650

HASTE, 17J., triple calendar moon ph.
gold filled...............................$250 $300 $400

HAYDEN, 7J., by Solomax W.Co., hinged case
gold filled..............................$60 $70 $95

HELBROS, 17 jewels, aux. sec.
gold filled................................$40 $50 $75

HEBDOMAS, 7-15 J., visible escapement, 8 day movement
s. steel $400 $500 $650

HELBROS, 17 jewels,
14k...$95 $125 $175

HEBDOMAS, 7-15 J., **8 day** movement, Ca. 1915
s. steel $200 $250 $325

HELBROS, 7J., "Federal", c. 1929
base metal.................................$25 $30 $45

HELBROS,17J., 24 hour dial
base metal.................................$40 $50 $85

HELBROS, 17 jewels, aux.sec., alarm
gold filled.................................$75 $110 $150

HENDA, 15J., direct read, c. 1930
nickel...$95 $110 $175

HELBROS, 7 jewels, "Fairfax", Ca 1928
gold filled.................................$50 $60 $85

Pricing in this Guide are fair market price for **COM-PLETE** watches which are reflected from the "**<u>NAWCC</u>**" National and regional shows.

HERMES, 17J., big wire lugs, enamel dial
14k $95 $125 $195

HELVETIA, 15 jewels, Ca. 1935
9k $80 $95 $125

HELVETIA, 21 jewels, auto wind
gold filled.................................. $30 $45 $75

HEUER, 15 jewels, chronog., 2 reg., one button,
14k $1,100 $1,300 $1,600

🕐 Some grades are not included. Their values can be determined by comparing with **similar** age, size, metal content, style, grades, or models such as **time only**, chronograph, repeater etc. listed.

🕐 Pricing in this Guide are fair market price for **COMPLETE** watches which are reflected from the "**NAWCC**" National and regional shows.

HEUER, 17J., chronog., 3 reg., 3 dates, moon phase
18k.................................... $1,600 $1,800 $2,200
s. steel.................................. $900 $1,000 $1,200

HEUER, 17 J., chronog., 3 reg., "Carrera", c.1960
s. steel.................................. $600 $800 $1,200

HEUER, 17 jewels, chronog., 3 dates, 3 reg. c.1948
14k.................................... $800 $1,000 $1,400
s. steel.................................. $600 $700 $900

HEUER, 17 jewels, "Carrera," chronog., 2 reg., c.1960s
14k.................................... $900 $1,100 $1,400
s. steel.................................. $550 $700 $1,000

HEUER,17J., "Carrera", RF# 2547, day date month, Ca. 1970
14k $1,200 $1,400 $1,800
s. steel $900 $1,100 $1,400

HEUER,17J., "Camaro", by Valjoux #7730, c. 1965
14k $700 $900 $1,200
s. steel $500 $600 $800

HEUER,17J., "Autavia", cal.72, micro rotor, c. 1972
s. steel $350 $450 $600

Wrist Watches listed in this section are priced at the collectable
fair market **Trade Show** level as **complete** watches having an
original gold-filled case and stainless steel back, also with
original dial, leather watch band, and the entire original movement in good working order with no repairs needed.

🕐 A collector should expect to pay modestly higher prices
at local shops

🕐 Some grades are not included. Their values can be
determined by comparing with **similar** age, size, metal
content, style, grades, or models such as **time only**,
chronograph, repeater etc. listed.

HEUER,17J., "Monaco", date, c. 1974
base metal............................$1,000 $1,200 $1,600

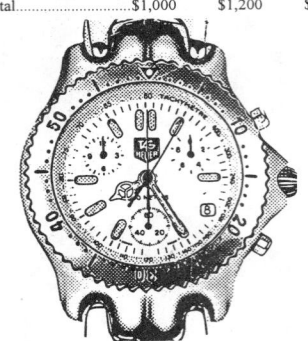

HEUER,17J., **TAG**, split sec., date, 600 ft., gold & s. steel,
sold new for $1,895.00 in Ca.1991
gold tone $200 $250 $350
s. steel & gold tone $200 $250 $350

HEUER, 17 jewels, day-date-month, moon phase
s. steel....................................$350 $450 $650

HEUER, 17 jewels, day-date-month
14k..$450 $550 $700
s. steel....................................$150 $200 $350

HILTON W. Co.,17J., chronog. by Venius W.Co.
18k $300 $325 $450

ILLINOIS, 17J., GJS, 207 on Mvt., model 250 on case
14K .... ★ ★ ★ ★$1,200 $1,300 $1,500

E. HUGUENIN, 17J., "Black Star", Ca. 1940
14k $300 $350 $425

ILLINOIS, 17J., **direct read**, Aluminum, case & band, c.1925
Chrome,case & band $225 $250 $325
Aluminum case & Aluminum band
.... ★ ★ ★ ★ ★ $2,000 $2,200 $2,500

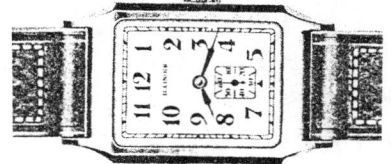

ILLINOIS, 17J., "Andover", Ca. 1929
gold filled $175 $200 $250

HYDEPARK, 17 jewels, flip up top for photo
14k $400 $450 $550

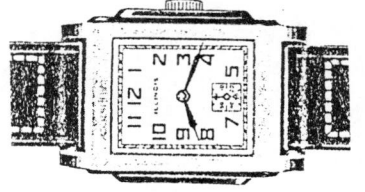

ILLINOIS, 15J., "Arlington also Hawthorne", Ca. 1929
gold filled $175 $200 $250

ILLINOIS, 17J., case # 196, "Art Deco", cal.207, c.1925
gold filled................................$250 $300 $400

🕐 Some grades are not included. Their values can be
determined by comparing with **similar** age, size, metal
content, style, grades, or models such as **time only**,
chronograph, repeater etc. listed.

ILLINOIS, 17J., "Ardsley", Ca. 1929
gold filled $150 $175 $225

ILLINOIS, 17 jewels, "Aviator"
gold filled...............................$195 $225 $300

ILLINOIS, 17-21J.= Beau Monde=14k, Beau Gest =WGF
14k $400 $450 $525
gold filled W $195 $250 $325

ILLINOIS, 21J., " BARONET ", GJS, cal.601, c.1925
14k $500 $650 $800
gold filled.............................$195 $225 $300

ILLINOIS, 15J., "Beau Royal "
gold filled $225 $250 $325

ILLINOIS, 19J., " Beau Brummel"
14k $700 $800 $950

ILLINOIS, 17J., " Blackstone"
gold filled $125 $150 $250

ILLINOIS, 17-19 jewels, "Beau Brummel"
gold filled.............................$275 $325 $400

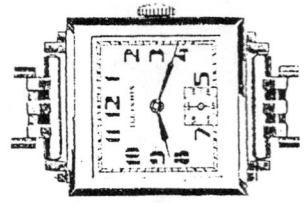

ILLINOIS, 15J., showing as advertised the "Bostonian" with
metal band also look a like "Commodore" came in leather.
gold filled $150 $175 $225

ILLINOIS, 17J., " Beau Brummel", also aux.sec @ 6, c.1929
gold filled.............................$250 $275 $425

ILLINOIS, 17J., " Cavalier "
gold filled $175 $195 $250

ILLINOIS, 15 jewels, "Champion"
gold filled............................$150 $175 $250

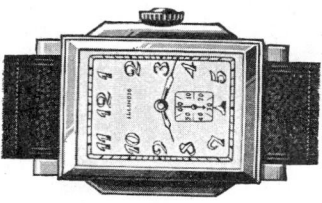

ILLINOIS, 15 jewels, "Chatham"
gold filled............................$150 $175 $300

ILLINOIS, 17J., " The Chief's", chased bezel
gold filled (w).........................$175 $195 $275

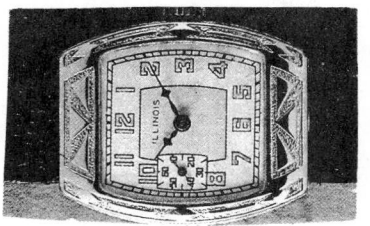

ILLINOIS, 15-17 jewels, "Chieftain"
gold filled............................$400 $500 $650

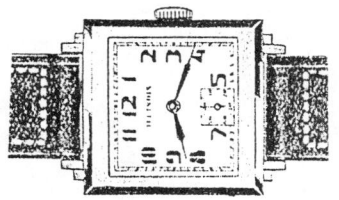

ILLINOIS, 15-17J., showing as advertised the "Commodore"
with leather band also look a like "Bostonian" came in metal.
gold filled............................$150 $175 $225

ILLINOIS, 19-21 jewels, "Consul"
14k $600 $700 $800

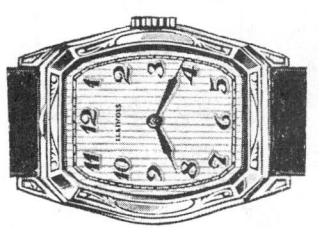

ILLINOIS, 19-21 jewels, "Consul"
14k ....★$650 $750 $900
14k smooth bezel......... ★★★$750 $900 $1,200

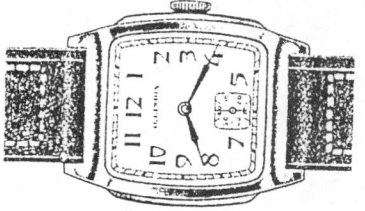

ILLINOIS, 17J., " Derby also Pimlico"
gold filled $150 $175 $350

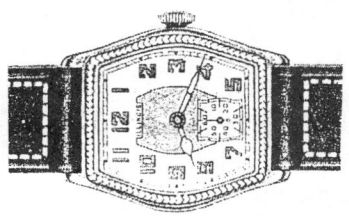

ILLINOIS, 15-17 jewels, "Ensign", aux.sec. at 6
gold filled plain bezel.............$225 $275 $375
gold filled engraved bezel......$250 $300 $400

ILLINOIS, 15-17 jewels, "Ensign" engraved bezel
gold filled $250 $300 $400

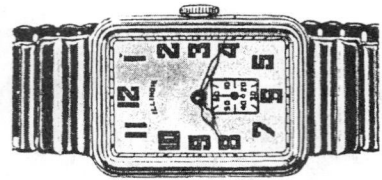

ILLINOIS, 17J., " Frontenac "
gold filled..............................$175 $195 $250

ILLINOIS, 17 jewels, "Hudson
gold filled ....,....................... $175 $195 $275

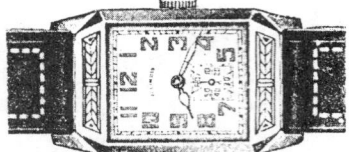

ILLINOIS, 17J., " Finalist also Chesterfield"
gold filled..............................$300 $350 $400

ILLINOIS, 17 jewels, ''Jolly Roger'' engraved bezel
gold filled (smooth bezel) $450 $550 $800
gold filled (engraved bezel) .. $350 $450 $600

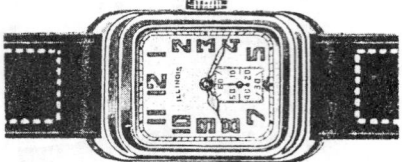

ILLINOIS, 17J., " Futura ", rect. mvt.
gold filled..............................$195 $225 $350

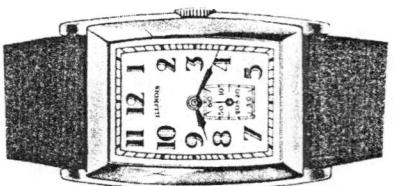

ILLINOIS, 17J., " Kenilworth " also "Gallahad"
gold filled $175 $195 $275

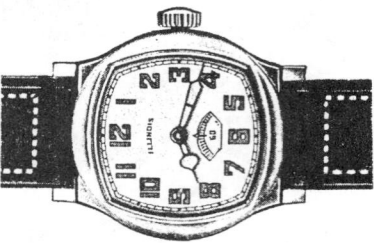

ILLINOIS, 17J., " Guardsman ", plain, rotor second dial
gold filled..............................$350 $400 $475

ILLINOIS, 17 jewels, "Larchmont also Vernon",
gold filled $175 $195 $275

ILLINOIS, 17J., ''Guardsman '', engraved, cal.307, c.1929
gold filled..............................$350 $400 $475

Note: Many Illinois look the same but with two names old ads
show same **style case** but with different bands. Example in 1931
a advertisement for a New Yorker with leather band grade
607,17J., priced at $50.00 & Manhattan with metal band grade
607,17J., priced at $55.00. The same 1931 ad a New Yorker
with leather band grade 601, 21J., priced at $75.00 & Manhattan
with metal band grade 601, 21J., priced at $85.00. Larchmont
leather & Vernon metal, Commodore leather Bostonian metal
and others with same **style case** & different bands.

ILLINOIS, 17J, "Major", engraved bevel & plain lugs
gold filled plain lugs $250 $300 $400
gold filled engraved lugs........ $250 $300 $400
gold filled plain bezel............. $250 $300 $400

ILLINOIS, 17-21J., "Manhattan or New Yorker", aux. sec. at 9
14k $375 $425 $525

ILLINOIS, 17-21J., **Yorktown** or New Yorker", with smooth
bezel & aux. sec. at 9, also came with aux. sec. at 6
gold filled................................$195 $250 $325

ILLINOIS, 17-21J., "Manhattan", aux. sec. at 6, metal band
14k $375 $425 $525

ILLINOIS, 17-21J, "New Yorker", aux. sec. at 6, leather band
gold filled................................$195 $250 $325

ILLINOIS, 17-19 jewels, "Marquis", engraved, curved case
gold filled................................$250 $300 $375

ILLINOIS, 17-19J., " Marquis ", plain, curved case
gold filled $195 $225 $300

ILLINOIS, 17J., " Mate ", engraved
gold filled $175 $195 $275

ILLINOIS, 17J., "Mate" , plain
gold filled $150 $175 $250

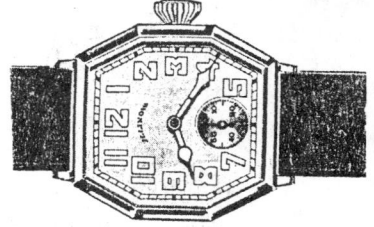

ILLINOIS, 17J., engraved case in "Maxine", plain, ladies
gold filled $75 $95 $135

ILLINOIS, 17 jewels, "Maxine", wire lugs, ladies
14k $135 $150 $195

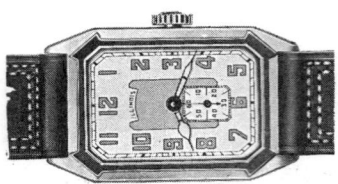

ILLINOIS, 17J., "Medalist also Wembley", rect. mvt, c.1929
gold filled..............................$150 $175 $250

ILLINOIS, 17 jewels, "Piccadilly" in white or yellow G.F.
came with Luminous or Modern as a option
gold filled plain......................$750 $900 $1,300
gold filled engraved...............$875 $1,000 $1,400

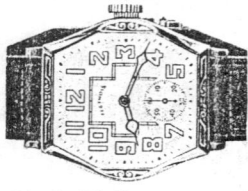

ILLINOIS, 17 jewels, "Pilot"
gold filled..............................$195 $225 $275

ILLINOIS, 17 jewels, "Prince"
gold filled..............................$150 $175 $225

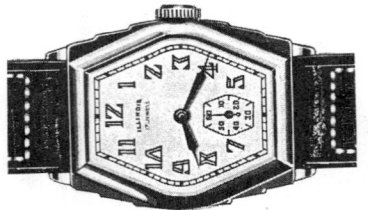

ILLINOIS, 17J., "Ritz", white bezel & yellow center case
also called "Valedictorian"
gold filled..............................$400 $500 $800

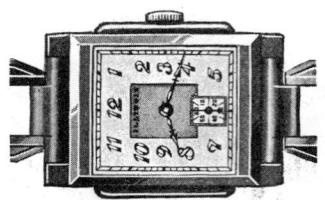

ILLINOIS, 15 jewels, "Rockingham also Potomac"
gold filled $200 $250 $325

ILLINOIS, 17J., " Rockliffe ", cal.805, c.1925
14k $350 $400 $500

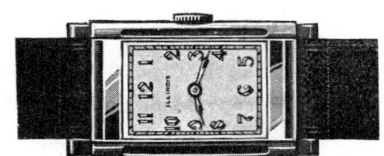

ILLINOIS, 15 jewels, "Sangamo"
gold filled $200 $250 $450

ILLINOIS, 17J., " Skyway ", engraved case, G#307
gold filled .... ★ ★ ★$1,200 $1,300 $1,500

ILLINOIS, 17J., "Special", plain bezel, ca.1929
nickel $250 $300 $450

Note: Auxiliary seconds = (aux. sec.), aux. sec. at 6 o'clock
position is a hunting model, aux. sec. at 9 is a open face
model.

ILLINOIS, 17J., "Special", engraved bezel, ca.1929
nickel.......................................$250 $300 $400

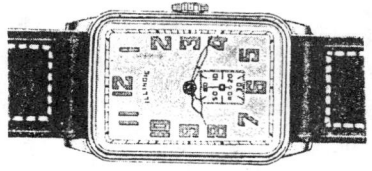

ILLINOIS, 17J., "Trophy also Westchester"
gold filled $125 $150 $225

ILLINOIS, 17 jewels, "Speedway"
gold filled..............................$250 $300 $500

ILLINOIS, 17 jewels, "Tuxedo", 2 tone
14k $500 $600 $1,000

ILLINOIS, 15 jewels, "Standish"
gold filled..............................$150 $175 $250

ILLINOIS, 17J., " Viking "
gold filled $195 $225 $450

ILLINOIS, 17J., " Sterling ", direct read, c.1929
sterling silver $225 $275 $350

ILLINOIS, 17 jewels, "Off Duty", stars on bezel, Ca. 1927
gold filled .... ★★★$900 $1,000 $1,200

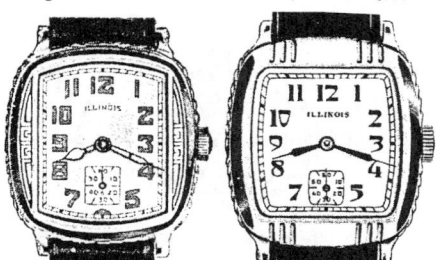

ILLINOIS, 15-17J., left "Townsman" carved case
right "Metropolitan", 2-tone carved case
gold filled Townsman............$250 $275 $350
gold filled Metropolitan $275 $300 $375

ILLINOIS, 15J., "Urbana",
gold filled $150 $195 $350

Note: Auxiliary seconds = (aux. sec.), aux. sec. at 6 o'clock
position is a hunting model, aux. sec. at 9 is a open face model.

ILLINOIS, 17J., Debonair model "A", ca.1953
base metal $40 $50 $70

ILLINOIS, 17J., Debonair model "B", ca.1953
base metal $40 $50 $70

ILLINOIS, 17J., Debonair model "C", ca.1953
base metal $40 $50 $70

ILLINOIS, 17J., Debonair model "D", ca.1953
base metal $40 $50 $70

ILLINOIS, 17J., Debonair model "E", ca.1953
base metal $40 $50 $70

ILLINOIS, 17J., Debonair model "F", ca.1953
base metal $40 $50 $70

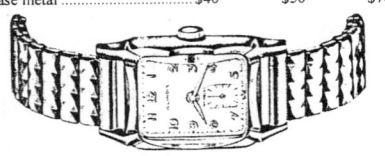

ILLINOIS, 17J., Topper model "A", ca.1953
base metal $40 $50 $70

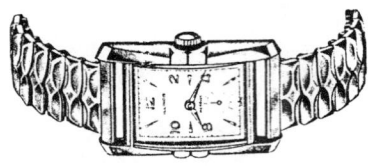

ILLINOIS, 17J., Topper model "B", ca.1953
base metal $40 $50 $70

ILLINOIS, 17J., Automatic model "A", ca.1953
gold filled $50 $65 $85

ILLINOIS, 17J., Automatic model "B", ca.1953
base metal $40 $50 $70

ILLINOIS, 17J., Automatic Signamatic / wind ind., ca.1953
base metal $50 $65 $85

ILLINOIS, 17J., Automatic Nautilus "A", ca.1953
waterproof anti-magnetic
s. steel $50 $60 $75

ILLINOIS, 15-17J., Generic, Telephone Dial, enamel dial
14k $700 $800 $1,000

ILLINOIS, 15-17J., Generic, Admiral Evans, enamel dial
sterling $500 $600 $800

ILLINOIS, 15J., Generic, seconds at "9" c.1929
gold filled.................................$95 $125 $175

ILLINOIS, 15-17-19J., Generic, Square cut corner **plain**
gold filled.................................$95 $125 $175

ILLINOIS, 15-17-19J., Generic, Square cut corner **engraved**
gold filled.................................$95 $125 $175

ILLINOIS, 17J., Generic Cushion Form, round dial
gold filled $95 $135 $185

ILLINOIS, 19J., Generic Cushion Form, plain, sec. at 6
gold filled $95 $135 $185

ILLINOIS, 19J., Generic Cushion Form, engraved, sec. at 9
gold filled $95 $145 $195

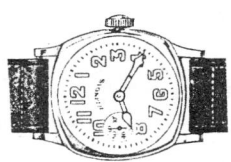

ILLINOIS, 19J., Generic Cushion Form, plain, sec. at 9
gold filled $95 $135 $185
14k $150 $175 $250

ILLINOIS, 15-17J., Generic, Ca.1929
sterling silver $300 $375 $650

Note: *Generic* period about 1915 to about 1927 is a period
ILLINOIS advertised "Only delivered fitted in cases supplied
by jobbers". July 1st 1924 ad **retail** selling price "Movement
only NO. 907, 19 jewels at $35.00, & NO. 903, 15 jewels
$26.50". Jewelers **cost** "Movement only NO. 907, $20.00 &
NO. 903, $14.50". After about 1934 Illinois wrist watch ads fade
away and not seen again till about 1953, ads state cased & timed
by Hamilton. See July 1926 Illinois ad and jobbers ad this book.

ILLINOIS, 17J., Generic, Cushion round, engraved, c.1929
gold filled.................................$95 $135 $185

ILLINOIS, 17J., GENERIC, tonneau style, hand engraved,
14k (W)...................................$125 $150 $195

ILLINOIS, 17J., Generic, Cushion round, plain, c.1929
nickel..$80 $90 $125

ILLINOIS, 15-19J., GENERIC, square, c.1925
gold filled $95 $125 $175

ILLINOIS, 17J., Generic, Barrel & side of case engraved
base metal $80 $90 $125

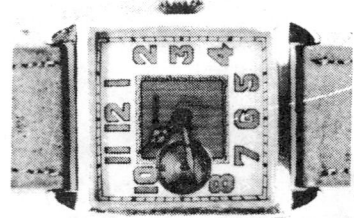

ILLINOIS, 17J., GENERIC, double hinged, GJS, c.1929
gold filled $95 $125 $175

ILLINOIS, 17J., Generic, Barrel engraved, sec at 9, ca. 1929
gold filled.................................$95 $125 $175

ILLINOIS, 15J., GENERIC, c.1926
gold filled $95 $125 $175

ILLINOIS, 17 jewels, GENERIC, hand engraved, wire lugs
14k (W)...................................$150 $175 $225

ILLINOIS, 17J., GENERIC, engraved case
silver $125 $150 $195

ILLINOIS, 15J., GENERIC, engraved bezel, GJS, c.1926
14k (w)...................................$150 $175 $225

ILLINOIS, 15J., **GENERIC, winds at 12:00 o'clock**
silver $195 $225 $300

ILLINOIS, 17J., Golden Treasure "A", ca.1953
14k $65 $75 $95

ILLINOIS, 17J., Golden Treasure "B", ca.1953
14k $65 $75 $110

ILLINOIS, 17J., Kimberly "A", 8 diamonds, ca.1953
gold filled................................$75 $95 $150

ILLINOIS, 17J., Kimberly "B", 2 diamonds, ca.1953
gold filled................................$70 $80 $110

ILLINOIS, 15-17J., lady's watch, black enamel on bezel
14k $100 $125 $175
gold filled................................$30 $40 $60

BELOW A JULY 1926 AD
By The ILLINOIS WATCH CO.

6-0 SIZE OR ELEVEN LIGNE

Only delivered fitted in cases supplied by Jobbers

Illustrations simply indicate some of the different styles of cases, made by
various watch case manufacturers, for these movements.

No. 907, 19 Jewels   No. 903, 15 Jewels
$35.00   Movements Only $26.50

19 and 15 ruby and sapphire jewels: compensating balance with timing
screws; double roller escapement; Breguet hairspring; steel escape wheel;
polished winding wheels; recoil click; silvered or gilt metal dials; full or
three-quarter open.

BELOW GENERIC or JOBBERS AD Ca. 1926
ADVERTISING ILLINOIS WATCHES FOR SALE

No. 1045   The Ace $37.30
3/0 Illinois 17 Jewel
White Engraved Stellar Quality Star Case
Silver Dial Luminous Figures and Hands
Established retail price with each

No. 1047   The Whippet $36.20
3/0 Illinois 17 Jewel
Stellar White Plain Barrel Case
Silver Dial Luminous Figures and Hands
Established retail price with each

ILLINOIS, 17J., " Eliza ", c.1929
gold filled.................................$65 $75 $90

ILLINOIS, 17J., " Long Beach ", c.1929
gold filled.................................$55 $65 $80

ILLINOIS, 17J., " Lynette ", c.1929
gold filled.................................$50 $60 $75

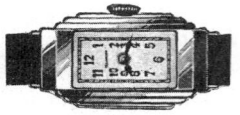

ILLINOIS, 17J., " Mariette ", c.1929
gold filled.................................$50 $60 $75

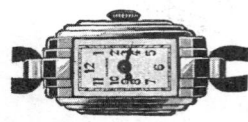

ILLINOIS, 17J., " Marionette ", c.1929
gold filled.................................$50 $60 $75

ILLINOIS, 17J., " Marlette ", c.1929
gold filled.................................$50 $60 $75

ILLINOIS, 16J., " Mary Todd ", c.1929
18k(w)....................................$150 $200 $250

ILLINOIS, 16J., " Mary Todd ", black enamel bezel, c.1929
18k(w)..........................$150 $200 $250

ILLINOIS, 16J., " Mary Todd ", c.1929
18k $150 $200 $250

ILLINOIS, 17J., " Mateel ", c.1929
14k(w)......................................$90 $100 $140

ILLINOIS, 17J., " Miami ", c.1929
gold filled $55 $65 $85

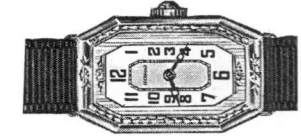

ILLINOIS, 17J., " Narragansett ", c.1929
14k $85 $95 $110

ILLINOIS, 17J., " Newport ", engraved case, c.1929
gold filled $55 $65 $80

ILLINOIS, 16J., " Queen Wilhelmina ", 22 diamonds and
8 synthetic sapphires
18k(w)....................................$200 $275 $350

ILLINOIS, rectangular, Grade 207, 17 jewels

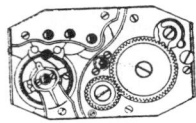

ILLINOIS, rectangular, 1st, 2nd & 3rd model

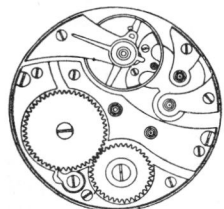

ILLINOIS, Model #4, 3/0 size, bridge, hunting, movement.

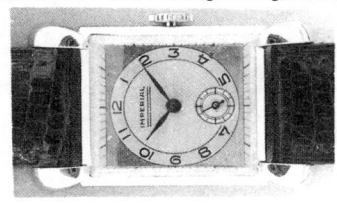

IMPERIAL, 17J., fancy lugs
14k(W) $135 $150 $175

IMPERIAL, 17J., center sec.
s. steel $30 $40 $55

⊕ Some grades are not included. Their values can be determined by comparing with **similar** age, size, metal content, style, grades, or models such as **time only**, chronograph, repeater etc. listed.

INGERSOLL, 2 J.," Rist-Arch", stepped case
base metal $20 $25 $40

INGERSOLL, "Swagger",
base metal $20 $25 $40

INGERSOLL, 7 jewels
base metal $20 $25 $35

INGERSOLL, 7 jewels, radiolite dial wire lugs
W/ original band $30 $40 $60
base metal $20 $30 $40

INGERSOLL, 7 J., military style, **protective grill cover
wire lugs, all original band and cover**
base metal $95 $110 $150

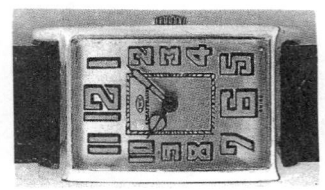

INTERNATIONAL W. CO., 17J., Ca. 1926
18k $600 $700 $900

INTERNATIONAL W. CO., 16J., enamel dial, c. 1920
silver $400 $500 $700

INTERNATIONAL W. CO., 16J., cal.53, c. 1920
18k $600 $700 $900

INTERNATIONAL W. CO., 17 jewels, c. 1920
18k $600 $700 $900

INTERNATIONAL W. CO., 17 jewels, **curved**
14k $700 $850 $1,200

INTERNATIONAL W. CO., 17 jewels, c. 1925
18k $600 $700 $900

INTERNATIONAL W. CO., 17 jewels
14k $400 $500 $700

INTERNATIONAL W. CO., 21 J., **auto-w**, center sec.,
Ca. 1940
18k $800 $900 $1,200

INTERNATIONAL W. CO., 17J., "Art Deco", Ca. 1925
TU-TONE case w/ enamel on bezel
18k $1,200 $1,400 $1,800

INTERNATIONAL W. CO., 17 jewels
14k C&B..................................$600 $700 $900

INTERNATIONAL W. CO., 17 jewels, c. 1940
18k $400 $500 $700

INTERNATIONAL W. CO., 17J., RF # 1160, auto wind, Ca. 1964
18k $500 $600 $800

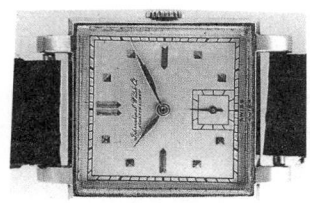

INTERNATIONAL W. CO., 17J., c. 1945
14k $300 $400 $600

INTERNATIONAL W. CO., 17J., tank style, c. 1937
18k $500 $600 $800

INTERNATIONAL W. CO., 17J., Tiffany on dial, c. 1942
14k $350 $450 $650

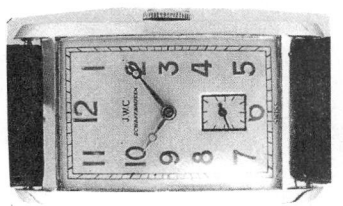

INTERNATIONAL W. CO., 17J., c. 1926
s. steel $300 $400 $550

INTERNATIONAL W. CO., 17 jewels, hidden lugs
14k $400 $500 $700

INTERNATIONAL W. CO., 17 J., on dial "Yard"
18k $800 $900 $1,200

INTERNATIONAL W. CO., 17J., aux. sec.
14k $300 $400 $600

Wrist Watches listed in this section are priced at the collectable fair market Trade Show level as **complete** watches having an original gold-filled case and stainless steel back, also with original dial, leather watch band, and the entire original movement in good working order with no repairs needed.

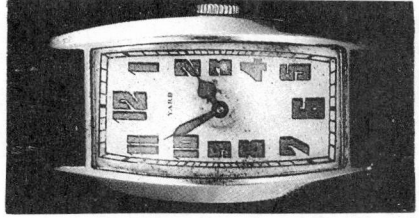

INTERNATIONAL W. CO., 17 J., curved, on dial "Yard"
platinum $1,200 $1,300 $1,600

INTERNATIONAL W. CO., 17 jewels, **hinged back**
14k $400 $500 $700

INTERNATIONAL W. CO., 17 jewels, curved
14k $600 $800 $1,100

INTERNATIONAL W. CO., 17J, date, auto-wind,
waterproof
18k $1,000 $1,100 $1,500

INTERNATIONAL W. CO., 21 jewels, auto wind, date
18k $900 $1,000 $1,400

INTERNATIONAL W. CO., 17 jewels, center sec.
18k $500 $550 $675

INTERNATIONAL W. CO., 17 jewels, center sec.
18k..$550 $600 $725

INTERNATIONAL W. CO., 17J., cen. sec., auto-w., date
platinum $1,800 $2,000 $2,400

INTERNATIONAL W. CO.,17J., RF# 802a, cal.8541, auto
wind, Ca.1960
s. steel....................................$550 $650 $900

INTERNATIONAL W. CO., 21J., "Ingeneur", date, c.1976
18k non-magnetic.... ★ ★ $2,000 $2,400 $3,000
s. steel non-magnetic ...... ★ $1,200 $1,400 $1,800

⊕ Some grades are not included. Their values can be
determined by comparing with **similar** age, size, metal
content, style, grades, or models such as **time only**,
chronograph, repeater etc. listed.

INTERNATIONAL W. CO., 21J., date, auto wind, c. 1960
18k $900 $1,100 $1,400

INTERNATIONAL W. CO., 21J., cal.853, auto wind,
Ca. 1961
18k $700 $800 $1,000

INTERNATIONAL W. CO.,17J.,fancy lugs,cal.C89, c.1952
18k $600 $700 $850

INTERNATIONAL W. CO., 21J., cal.853, auto wind,
Ca. 1958
18k $700 $800 $1,000

INTERNATIONAL W. CO., 17J., center sec.cal.89, c.1957
18k...$550 $650 $800

INTERNATIONAL W. CO., 17J., wide lugs, c. 1960
18k...$600 $700 $900

INTERNATIONAL W. CO., 21J., cal.C852, auto wind,
Ca. 1952
18k...$700 $800 $1,000

INTERNATIONAL W. CO., 17J., cal.89, c. 1962
s. steel....................................$400 $450 $700

INTERNATIONAL W. CO., 17J., ca.1960s
18k C & B $800 $900 $1,100

INTERNATIONAL W. CO., 17J., auto wind, Ca. 1960
18k..$700 $750 $900

INTERNATIONAL W. CO., 17J., center sec.
18k $600 $700 $900

INTERNATIONAL W. CO., 17 jewels, center sec.
18k..$500 $550 $675

INTERNATIONAL W. CO., 17J., fancy lugs, cen. sec.
18k $600 $700 $900

INTERNATIONAL W. CO., 17 jewels, center sec., cal.402
18k..$500 $550 $675

INTERNATIONAL W. Co., 18 jewels, center sec.
18k $550 $650 $800

INTERNATIONAL W. CO., 17 jewels, center sec., cal. 89
18k..$500 $550 $675

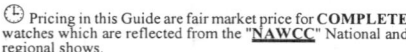
Pricing in this Guide are fair market price for **COMPLETE** watches which are reflected from the "**NAWCC**" National and regional shows.

Wrist Watches listed in this section are priced at the collectable fair market **Trade Show** level as **complete** watches having an original gold-filled case and stainless steel back, also with original dial, leather watch band, and the entire original movement in good working order with no repairs needed.

INTERNATIONAL W. CO., 17 jewels, center sec., cal.89
18k $500 $550 $675

INTERNATIONAL W. CO., 36J., "Da Vinci," chronog.
auto wind, triple date, moon ph., center lugs
18k C & B.............................$8,000 $8,500 $10,000
18k $6,000 $6,500 $8,000

INTERNATIONAL W. CO., "Porsche Design", date, auto-
wind, compass, sapphire mirror, RF#3510-LMW, Ca.1988
Titanium.................................$800 $900 $1,200
base metal $400 $450 $550

INTERNATIONAL W. CO., 17J, for Royal Navy, ca.1950
s. steel....................................$700 $800 $1,000

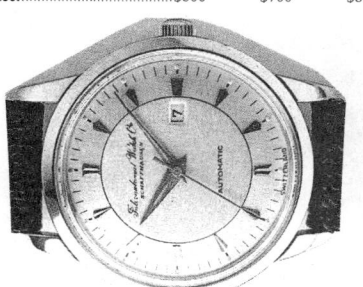

INTERNATIONAL W. CO., 17J., winds at 12 o'clock
s. steel....................................$600 $700 $850

INTERNATIONAL W. CO., 17 jewels, Autowind, Ca. 1958
s. steel....................................$400 $450 $500

INTERNATIONAL W. CO., 17J., anti-magnet, Ca. 1942
s. steel....................................$200 $250 $325

⊕ A collector should expect to pay modestly higher prices
at local shops

INTERNATIONAL W. CO., 17 jewels, c. 1948
18k $500 $550 $650

INTERNATIONAL W. CO., 17J.,date, 30 ATM=1,000 ft.
s. steel $450 $550 $750

INTERNATIONAL W. CO., 17J., aux sec., cal.83, c.1938
14k $500 $550 $650

INTERNATIONAL W. CO., 17J., fancy lugs, Ca.1952
18k..$600 $700 $900

INTERNATIONAL W. CO., 17J., aux. sec., cal., c.1948
s. steel $400 $500 $700

INTERNATIONAL W. CO., 15J., cal. 83, ca.1945
14k..$500 $600 $750

INTERNATIONAL W. CO., 17J., mid-size, Ca.1945
s. steel..................................$400 $500 $700

INTERNATIONAL W. CO., 17J., cal.461, c.1962
18k $500 $600 $800

INTERNATIONAL W. CO., 17J., 36 small diamonds
platinum $450 $550 $700

INTERNATIONAL WATCH CO.
MOVEMENT IDENTIFICATION

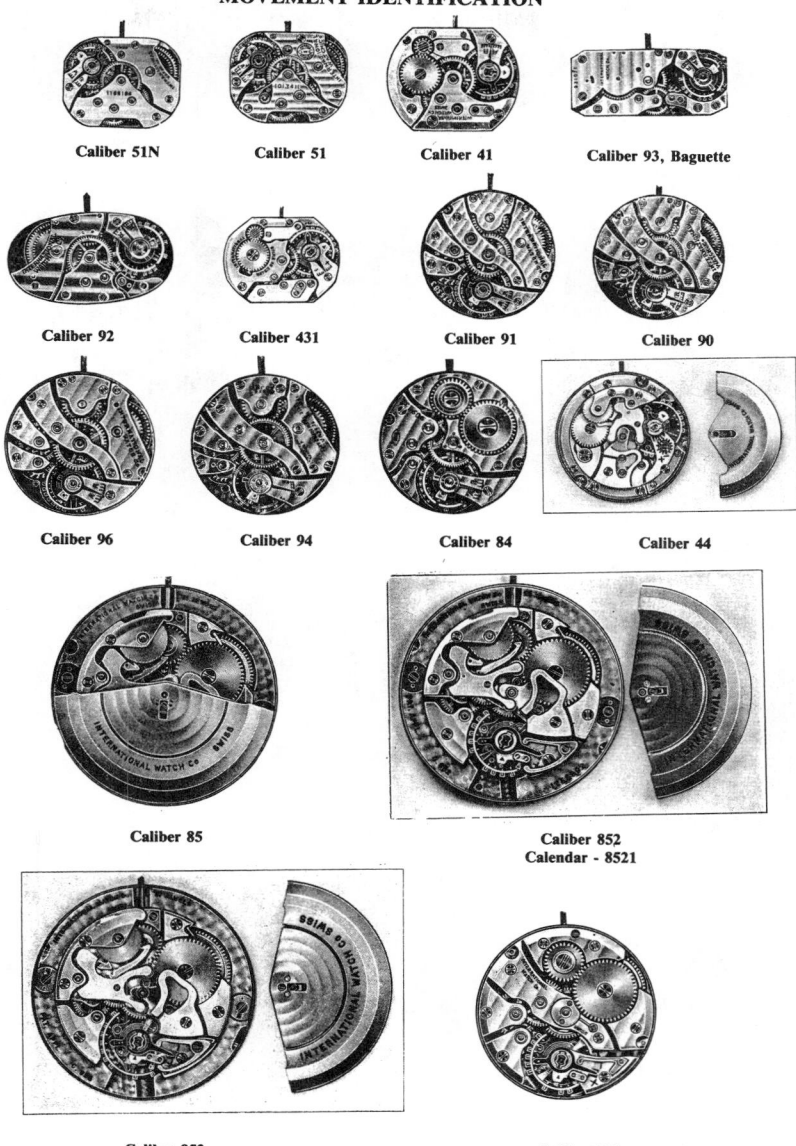

Caliber 51N — Caliber 51 — Caliber 41 — Caliber 93, Baguette

Caliber 92 — Caliber 431 — Caliber 91 — Caliber 90

Caliber 96 — Caliber 94 — Caliber 84 — Caliber 44

Caliber 85

Caliber 852
Calendar - 8521

Caliber 853
Calendar - 8531

Caliber 401

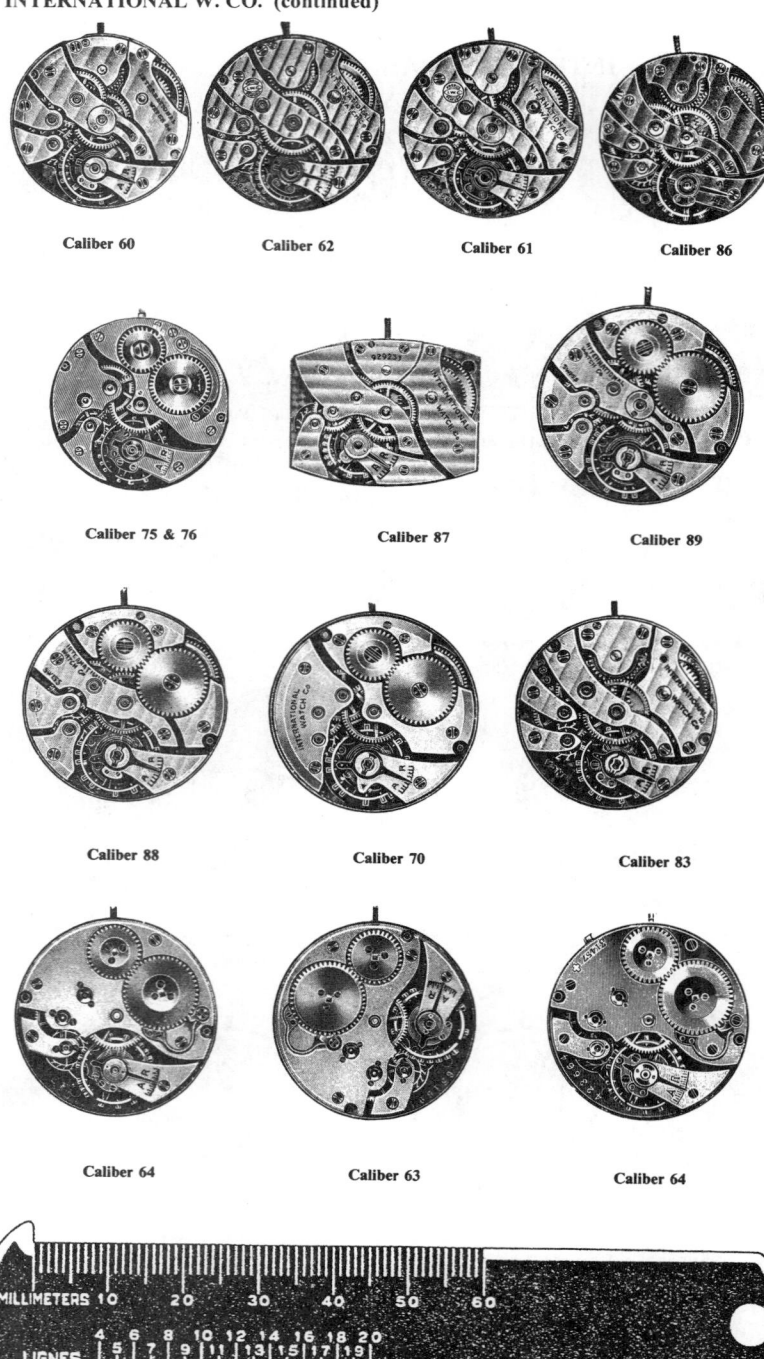

Caliber 60

Caliber 62

Caliber 61

Caliber 86

Caliber 75 & 76

Caliber 87

Caliber 89

Caliber 88

Caliber 70

Caliber 83

Caliber 64

Caliber 63

Caliber 64

INVICTA, 15 jewels, chronograph, min. reg. at 6 o'clock, decimal aperture for sec. at 12 o'clock
18k $2,000 $2,400 $2,900

INVICTA, 17 jewels, date, center sec.
18k $195 $250 $425
s. steel $40 $50 $95

INVICTA, 17 jewels, day-date, waterproof
18k $150 $175 $250
s. steel $60 $70 $125

INVICTA, 17 jewels, day-date-month
18k $195 $250 $325
s. steel $75 $100 $150

⊕ Some grades are not included. Their values can be determined by comparing with **similar** age, size, metal content, style, grades, or models such as **time only**, chronograph, repeater etc. listed.

⊕ A collector should expect to pay modestly higher prices at local shops

INVICTA, 17 jewels, day-date-month, moon phase
18k $400 $500 $650
s. steel $195 $300 $450

INVICTA, 17 jewels, waterproof
18k $125 $150 $225
s. steel $40 $50 $70

INVICTA, 17 jewels, auto wind, waterproof
18k $125 $150 $225
s. steel $50 $60 $70

JAEGER W. CO., 17J., RF#5184, chronog., Ca. 1942
s.steel $300 $350 $425
18k $600 $650 $725

⊕ Pricing in this Guide are fair market price for **COMPLETE** watches which are reflected from the "**NAWCC**" National and regional shows.

JAEGER W. CO., 15J., **duoplan, backwind,** c.1935
s steel $300 $350 $550

JOHNSON-MATTHEY, 15 J., 5-10-15 gram ingot 24k gold
24k 5 gram $200 $250 $325
24k 10 gram $600 $650 $750
24k 15 gram $850 $900 $1,000

JARDUR W. CO., 17J., RF#29840, c.1950
s. steel $300 $350 $425

JUNGHANS, 16J., chronometer, c.1965
14k...$95 $110 $150

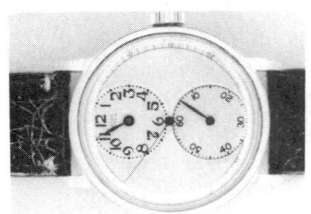

JEAN LOUIS, 17 jewels, double dial, c. 1930
14k $200 $250 $350

JUNGHANS, electronic "Ato Chron" , C.1978
14k...$90 $100 $140

J. E. Watch Co., 17J., tank style, c.1950
gold plate $40 $50 $65

JUNGHANS , 17J., cal.J88, c.1980
s. steel...................................$195 $250 $350

Wrist Watches listed in this section are priced at the collectable fair market **Trade Show** level as **complete** watches having an original gold-filled case and stainless steel back, also with original dial, leather watch band, and the entire original movement in good working order with no repairs needed.

JEWEL, 15 jewels, dual dial, c. 1938
gold filled...............................$250 $300 $400

J. JURGENSEN, 31J, 5 min. repeater, **recased**, c.1906
18k $7,000 $8,000 $10,000

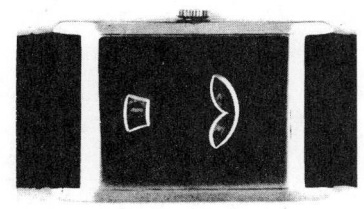

J. JURGENSEN, 15J, jumping hr., revolving min., c.1930s
18k $2,500 $3,000 $4,000

J. JURGENSEN,17J., large lugs, recess crown, c.1950
14k $195 $250 $350

J. JURGENSEN,17J., long lugs, c.1948
18k $175 $195 $275

J. JURGENSEN,17J., recess crown, fancy lugs, c.1952
14k $195 $225 $300

J. JURGENSEN,17J., 2 tone, center lugs, c.1940
14k...$300 $350 $425

J. JURGENSEN, 17 jewels, fancy lugs, ca.1949
14k...$300 $350 $425

J. JURGENSEN, 17 jewels, fancy lugs
14k...$300 $350 $425

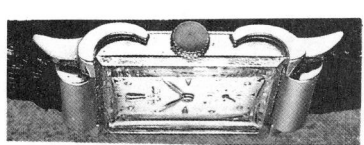

J. JURGENSEN, 17 jewels, extra fancy lugs, c. 1946
18k...$500 $550 $650

J. JURGENSEN, 17 jewels, c. 1950
18k...$150 $195 $300

🕐 Pricing in this Guide are fair market price for **COMPLETE**
watches which are reflected from the "**NAWCC**" National and
regional shows.

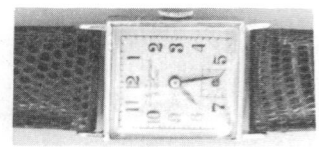

J. JURGENSEN, 17 jewels
18k $150 $175 $235

J. JURGENSEN,17J., center sec., c.1946
14k $95 $125 $195

J. JURGENSEN,17J., aux. sec., c.1948
14k $95 $125 $195

J. JURGENSEN,17J., aux. sec., c.1940
14k $95 $125 $195

J. JURGENSEN,17J., textured bezel, c.1960
14k $95 $125 $175

J. JURGENSEN,17J., hidden lugs, c.1948
14k $150 $175 $225

J. JURGENSEN,17J., hidden lugs, c.1940
14k $150 $175 $225

J. JURGENSEN,17J., hidden lugs, c.1952
14k $300 $350 $450

J. JURGENSEN,17J., hidden lugs, c.1950
14k $300 $350 $450

J. JURGENSEN,17J., hidden lugs, c.1948
14k $150 $175 $225

J. JURGENSEN, 17 J., flared case, Ca. 1954
14k $175 $200 $250

🕐 Some grades are not included. Their values can be determined by comparing with **similar** age, size, metal content, style, grades, or models such as **time only**, chronograph, repeater etc. listed.

J. JURGENSEN,17J., by Valjoux, cal. 69, c.1944
14K..$400 $500 $700
s. steel $250 $300 $400

J. JURGENSEN, 17 J., auto-w., cen. sec., ca. 1954
14k $150 $175 $250

J. JURGENSEN,17J., cal.8273, extended lugs, c.1958
14k $175 $195 $250

J. JURGENSEN,17J., aux, sec., c.1968
14k $95 $125 $175

Wrist Watches listed in this section are priced at the collectable fair market **Trade Show** level as **complete** watches having an original gold-filled case and stainless steel back, also with original dial, leather watch band, and the entire original movement in good working order with no repairs needed.

J. JURGENSEN,17J., extended bezel, c.1950
14k..$300 $325 $400

J. JURGENSEN,17J., cal.1139, c.1950
18k..$225 $250 $300

J. JURGENSEN,17J., center sec., date, c.1960
14k..$150 $175 $225

J. JURGENSEN,17J., center sec., mid size, c.1940
14k..$150 $175 $225

⊕ Some grades are not included. Their values can be determined by comparing with **similar** age, size, metal content, style, grades, or models such as **time only**, chronograph, repeater etc. listed.

J. JURGENSEN,17J., 3 diamond dial, date, c.1960
14k(w)..................................$150 $175 $225

J. JURGENSEN,17J., 40 diamond bezel, c.1960
14k(w)..................................$300 $350 $450

J. JURGENSEN, 17 J., 12 diamond dial, ca. 1960s
14k(W)..................................$150 $175 $225

JUVENIA,17J.,3 dates, moon ph., screw on back c. 1950s
18k $400 $500 $700

Wrist Watches listed in this section are priced at the collectable
fair market **Trade Show** level as **complete** watches having an
original gold-filled case and stainless steel back, also with
original dial, leather watch band, and the entire original movement in good working order with no repairs needed.

JUVENIA, 21 jewels, **gold movement**
18k..$225 $250 $350

JUVENIA, 17J.,
s. steel.....................................$30 $35 $55

JUVENIA, 17J.,
s. steel.....................................$30 $40 $65

JUVENIA, 17J.,
s. steel.....................................$30 $40 $65

JUVENIA, 17J.,
s. steel.....................................$30 $40 $65

⏱ Some grades are not included. Their values can be
determined by comparing with **similar** age, size, metal
content, style, grades, or models such as **time only**,
chronograph, repeater etc. listed.

JUVENIA, 17J.,
s. steel $40 $50 $75

JUVENIA, 17J.,
s. steel $40 $50 $75

JUVENIA, 17J.,
s. steel $35 $40 $70

KELBERT, 17J., triple date, moon ph., ca.1945
gold filled............................... $200 $250 $350
s. steel $250 $300 $400

KELBERT, 17 jewels, fancy lugs, c. 1949
gold filled............................... $50 $60 $85

KELEK,17J., tachymeter, auto-wind, c.1970
s. steel $85 $95 $150

Kelton, 7 jewels, curved, stepped case
gold filled $30 $40 $60

KELTON, 7 jewels, "Drake"
gold filled $30 $35 $55

KENT W. CO.,17J., Continental W.Co.(french),chronog.
s. steel $95 $125 $200

KINGSTON, 17 jewels, day-date-month, moon phase
gold filled $250 $275 $375

KINGSTON,17J., cal.G10, hidden lugs, c.1943
gold filled..............................$50 $60 $85

LANCEL (Paris),17J., **one** button chronog. by Nicolet, c.1960
gold filled $225 $250 $300

KORD, day date month, moon ph., auto wind
s. steel $150 $200 $275

A.LANGE & SOHNE,17J., 55mm., c.1940
s. steel $1,200 $1,400 $1,800

KURTH, 17 jewels, "Certina"
gold filled..............................$30 $35 $65

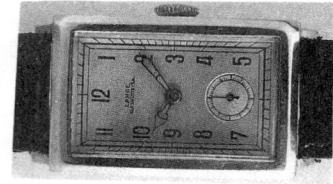

A.LANGE & SOHNE, 17J, (Glashutte), c.1936
14k $700 $800 $950

LACO, 17J., center sec., c.1955
gold plate $20 $30 $50

🕐 Some grades are not included. Their values can be determined by comparing with **similar** age, size, metal content, style, grades, or models such as **time only**, chronograph, repeater etc. listed.

🕐 Pricing in this Guide are fair market price for **COMPLETE** watches which are reflected from the "**NAWCC**" National and regional shows.

LANGE "UHR" (Glashutte),15J., c.1936
14k $800 $850 $950

LANGE "UHR" (Glashutte),17J., c.1937
s. steel $500 $600 $800

LANGE, 17J, (Glasshutte), date, auto wind, waterproof
18k $600 $650 $750

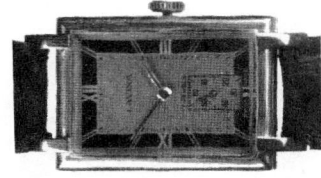

LAVINA, 17J., ca.1937
9K...$95 $110 $150

LE COULTRE, 15 jewels, wire lugs, c. 1919
silver $175 $195 $250

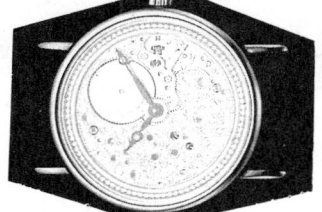

LE COULTRE, 18J., skeletonized,
18k $1,400 $1,600 $2,000

LE COULTRE, 19 jewels, alarm
18k $800 $900 $1,300
14k $600 $700 $1,000
gold filled..............................$195 $250 $375
s. steel $195 $250 $375

LE COULTRE, 19 jewels, alarm, sold for $99.00 with gold
filled case & $235.00 with 18K case in1950
18k $700 $850 $1,200
14k $500 $650 $950
gold filled $195 $250 $375
s. steel $195 $250 $375

LE COULTRE, 17J., alarm, cal.815, c.1960
gold filled $195 $250 $375

LE COULTRE, 17J., ruby dial, alarm, auto wind, c.1960
gold filled $400 $500 $700

LE COULTRE, 17J.,cal.814, memovox, alarm, c.1960
14k $700 $800 $1,000
gold filled $250 $300 $400

LE COULTRE, 17J., cal.p815, alarm, c.1960
gold filled................................$250 $300 $400

LE COULTRE, 17J.,memovox , alarm, auto wind,c.1973
14k & s.s................................ $500 $600 $800

LE COULTRE, 17J., RF#3025, wrist-alarm, c.1948
gold filled................................$250 $300 $400

LE COULTRE, 17J., RF#2676, date, memovox, c.1960
gold filled $250 $300 $400

LE COULTRE, 17J., wrist alarm, Ca.1949
gold filled................................$195 $250 $350

LE COULTRE, 17J., date, auto-w., memovox, c.1975
s. steel $250 $300 $500

LE COULTRE, 17J., "Polaris", memovox, underwater alarm
tested to 600 feet, date, Ca. 1968, s.s. band by Le Coultre.
s. steel $1,000 $1,200 $1,600

LE COULTRE, 17J., auto wind, date, memovox, c.1976
gold filled $400 $450 $550

LE COULTRE, 19J., date, Memovox, ca. 1959
18k $750 $800 $1,000
gold filled..............................$250 $300 $400
s. steel $250 $300 $400

LE COULTRE, 17J., Powermatic Nautilus "S", wind-ind.,
auto-w., sold for $85.00 with gold filled case in 1950
gold filled $225 $250 $350

LE COULTRE, 19J., alarm, date, autowind
14k $900 $1,000 $1,200

LE COULTRE, 17J., cal. 481, wind-ind., auto-w., c.1954
the cal. 481,up & down wind-ind. has **Differential Gearing**
gold filled $225 $250 $350

LE COULTRE, 19 jewels, alarm, date, autowind, ca. 1950
18k $1,000 $1,100 $1,400
gold filled..............................$500 $600 $800
s. steel $600 $700 $900

LE COULTRE, 17J., auto wind, wind indicator, sold for
$150.00 with a 14K case in 1951
14k $550 $600 $750

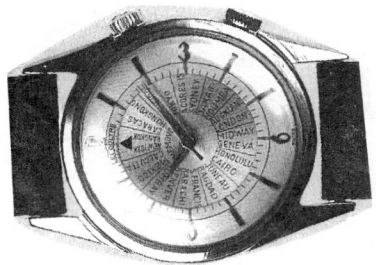

LE COULTRE, 17-19J., **World Time,** Memovox, ca. 1956
s. steel $800 $900 $1,300

LE COULTRE, 17 jewels, auto wind, screw back
18k $195 $250 $325

LE COULTRE, 17J., "Master Mariner, auto wind, c.1960
14k $250 $300 $400

LE COULTRE, 17J., "Master Mariner", autow., date, Ca.1960
gold filled $125 $150 $195

LE COULTRE, 17J., cal.p478, center sec.c.1947
s. steel $95 $125 $195

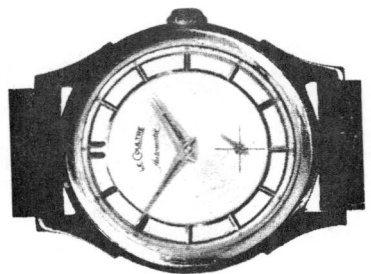

LE COULTRE, 17J., auto-wind, cal.p812, c.1955
gold filled $95 $125 $150

LE COULTRE, 17J., "Master Mariner", auto wind, c.1952
14k $250 $300 $450

LE COULTRE, 17J., RF#.480-C-380, autow., Ca.1955
14k $150 $175 $275

LE COULTRE, 17J., "Master Mariner", auto-wind, c.1960
s. steel $125 $150 $225

LE COULTRE, 17J., RF#555-149, Ca.1955
14k $150 $175 $275

🕐 A collector should expect to pay modestly higher prices
at local shops

Wrist Watches listed in this section are priced at the collectable
fair market **Trade Show** level as **complete** watches having an
original gold-filled case and stainless steel back, also with
original dial, leather watch band, and the entire original movement in good working order with no repairs needed.

LE COULTRE, 17J., cal. 812, auto-wind, c.1952
s. steel $95 $125 $225

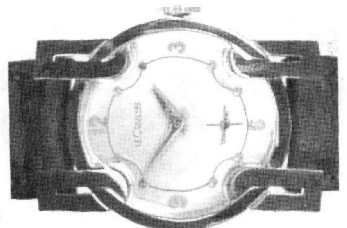

LE COULTRE, 17J.,"Coronet", cal.480cw, c.1951
gold filled................................ $225 $250 $350

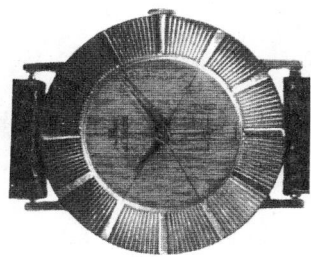

LE COULTRE, 17J., cal.480, wide bezel, c.1958
gold filled.................................. $95 $125 $195

LE COULTRE, 17J., cal.480, c.1955
14k $150 $175 $300

LE COULTRE, 17J., RF#7534, c.1960
14k $195 $250 $350

LE COULTRE, 17J., 11 diamond dial, RF#197, c.1955
14k(w)................................... $195 $250 $400

LE COULTRE, 17 jewels, center lugs, c. 1960
18k $400 $500 $700

LE COULTRE, 17 jewels, "Pershing", fancy lugs, c. 1950
14k $195 $250 $350

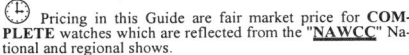 Pricing in this Guide are fair market price for **COM-PLETE** watches which are reflected from the "**NAWCC**" National and regional shows.

🕐 Some grades are not included. Their values can be determined by comparing with **similar** age, size, metal content, style, grades, or models such as **time only**, chronograph, repeater etc. listed.

LE COULTRE, 17J., fancy lugs
14k $195 $250 $350

LE COULTRE, 17J., fancy lugs, ca. 1950s
18k $300 $350 $500

LE COULTRE, 17 jewels, fancy lugs, c. 1952
14k $300 $325 $400

LE COULTRE, 17 jewels, fancy bezel & lugs
14k $600 $700 $900

LE COULTRE, 17 jewels, fancy bezel & lugs, Ca.1953
14k $325 $350 $450

LE COULTRE, 17J., fancy bezel, Ca.1952
gold filled $95 $125 $175

LE COULTRE, 17J., auto wind, textured bezel, c. 1950
18k $250 $300 $400

LE COULTRE, 17 jewels, center sec., c. 1949
18k $300 $400 $700
s. steel $195 $250 $400

LE COULTRE, 17J., cen. sec., 24 hr dial, c. 1940
s. steel $195 $250 $350

This book endeavours to be a GUIDE or helpful manual and offers a wealth of material to be used as a tool not as a absolute document. Price Guides are like watches the worst may be better than none at all, but at best cannot be expected to be 100% accurate.

LE COULTRE, 17J., "Quartermaster", 24 hr dial, auto-w.,
RF#114
s.steel $400 $450 $600

LE COULTRE, 17J., auto-w., cal.813, RF#388-870, Ca.1959
gold filled..................................$95 $125 $175

LE COULTRE, 17J., center sec., cal.468/ACa.1940
s.steel $95 $125 $175

LE COULTRE, 17J., center sec., ca. 1930s
silver $250 $300 $375

LE COULTRE, 17J., alarm, auto-w., date, ca.1964
s. steel $195 $250 $375

LE COULTRE, 17J., **quartz**, cal.352, c.1970
gold filled $50 $60 $80

LE COULTRE, 17J., date alarm, auto-w., c.1975
gold filled $195 $250 $375

LE COULTRE, 17 jewels, alarm, date, auto wind
s.steel $195 $250 $375

LE COULTRE, 17J., chronog., 2 reg.
14k $700 $800 $1,000
s. steel $350 $400 $475

LE COULTRE, 17J., chronog., cal.281, c.1940
s. steel $300 $350 $425

LE COULTRE, 17J., chronog., FR#2644, blue dial,
s. steel $600 $650 $800

LE COULTRE, 17J., chronog. 3 reg., ca. 1958
14k $1,500 $1,800 $2,500
s. steel $700 $800 $1,000

LE COULTRE, 17 jewels, chronog., 3 reg.
18k $2,000 $2,200 $2,800

LE COULTRE, 17 jewels, mystery dial, c. 1955
14k yellow $400 $450 $600

LE COULTRE, 17J., 15 diamond mystery dial, RF # 182
14k(W) $650 $750 $900

LE COULTRE, 17J., 2 diamond mystery dial, RF # 182
14k(W)..................................$450 $550 $700

LE COULTRE, 17J., 36 diamond mystery dial, waterproof,
auto wind, **"Vacheron Galaxy"**
14k(w) $1,200 $1,400 $1,800

LE COULTRE, 17J, diamond dial, textured bezel, c. 1960s
14k (w) $150 $200 $300

LE COULTRE, 17J., date, cal.810, c.1952
14k $300 $350 $425

LE COULTRE, 17J., date, center sec., c.1950
14k $325 $375 $450

🕐 Some grades are not included. Their values can be
determined by comparing with **similar** age, size, metal
content, style, grades, or models such as **time only**,
chronograph, repeater etc. listed.

LE COULTRE, 15 jewels, triple-date, c. 1945
s. steel $400 $450 $600
14k $700 $800 $1,000
18k $900 $1,000 $1,400

LE COULTRE, 17J, triple date, moon ph., c. 1940s
18k $1,500 $1,700 $2,000
gold filled $500 $600 $700

LE COULTRE, 17J., triple date, moon ph., fancy lugs
14k $1,700 $1,900 $2,400

LE COULTRE, 17J., auto-w., Memovox, world time, c.1960
14k $1,500 $1,700 $2,000

LE COULTRE, 17J., weems style, cal.450, c.1942
s. steel $600 $650 $800

LE COULTRE, 17J., rotating chapters, date, c.1960
s. steel $1,000 $1,200 $1,800

LE COULTRE, 17J., "Futurematic", cal.817, c.1952
gold filled...............................$400 $500 $750
14k $600 $700 $950

LE COULTRE, 17 jewels, "Futurematic" power-reserve
18k $700 $750 $850
14k $550 $600 $700

LE COULTRE, 17J, "Futurematic", auto- w., W. Ind.
sold for $95.00 with s. steel case in 1950
18k $550 $600 $850
gold filled $250 $300 $450
s. steel .... ★ $400 $500 $600

LE COULTRE, 23 J., auto-w., date cen. sec.
14k $150 $195 $250

LE COULTRE, 17J., Master Mariner, auto-w., date
gold filled $95 $150 $195
14k $150 $195 $250

LE COULTRE, 17J., day date, mid size, ca. 1940s
gold filled $95 $150 $195
Wrist Watches listed in this section are priced at the collectable
fair market **Trade Show** level as **complete** watches having an
original gold-filled case and stainless steel back, also with
original dial, leather watch band, and the entire original movement in good working order with no repairs needed.

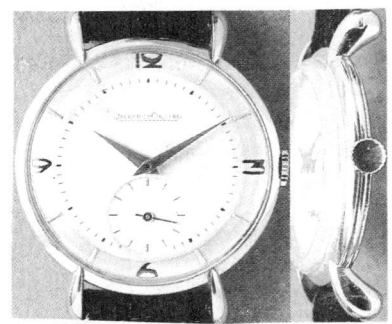

LE COULTRE, 17J., fancy lugs, aux. sec., ca. 1948
14k $400 $450 $600

LE COULTRE, 17J., auto-w., ca. 1950s
14k $150 $195 $250

LE COULTRE, 17J., fancy lugs
14k $175 $225 $325

LE COULTRE, 17J., aux. sec. ca.1950s
14k $125 $150 $250

LE COULTRE, 17 jewels, fancy wide bezel, ca.1955
14k (W)....................................$95 $125 $225

LE COULTRE, 17J., alarm, date,
14k $500 $600 $850

LE COULTRE, 15J., drivers style wind at 12, c.1960s
s. steel $250 $300 $375

LE COULTRE,17J.,drivers style crown at 6, RF#9041
s. steel $250 $300 $375

LE COULTRE, 17J., RF#9041, cal.818, crown at 6, c.1960s
18k $500 $600 $800

LE COULTRE, 17J, ''Reverso,'' center sec., c. 1930
18k $6,000 $7,000 $8,500
s. steel $2,200 $2,500 $3,200

LE COULTRE, 17J., ''Reverso,'' c. 1940s
18k $5,500 $6,500 $8,000
s. steel $2,000 $2,400 $3,000

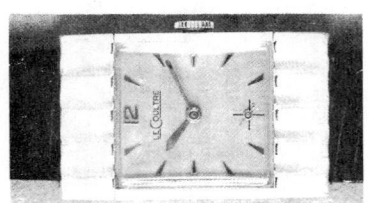

LE COULTRE, 17 jewels, fancy hooded lugs, c. 1952
14k $225 $250 $350

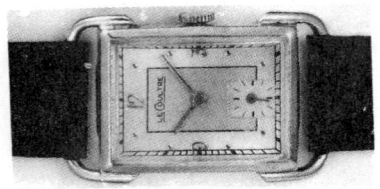

LE COULTRE, 17 jewels, fancy lugs
14k $225 $250 $300

LE COULTRE, 17 jewels, large fancy lugs
14k $450 $500 $600

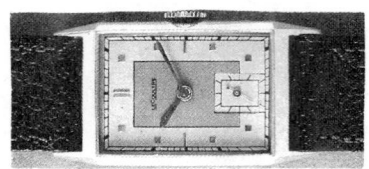

LE COULTRE, 17J., curvex,
14k $195 $225 $300

LE COULTRE, 17J., curvex, ca. 1940s
14k $195 $225 $300

LE COULTRE, 17J., stepped lugs, ca. 1944
gold filled $75 $95 $150

LE COULTRE, 17J., aux. sec., ca. 1940s
gold filled $75 $95 $150

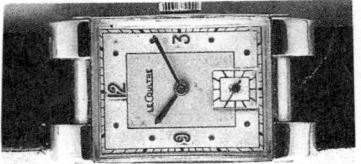

LE COULTRE, 17J., square lugs, ca. 1948
14k $300 $350 $500

LE COULTRE, 17J., extended lugs, c.1938
gold filled.................................$75 $95 $150

LE COULTRE, 17J., aux. sec., c.1940
14k $135 $165 $250

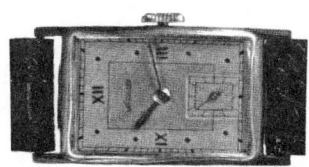

LE COULTRE, 17J., tu tone dial, c.1940
gold filled.................................$75 $95 $150

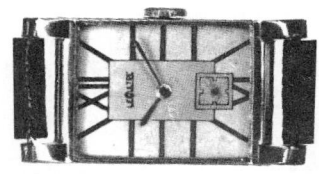

LE COULTRE, 17J., large lugs, c.1938
gold filled.................................$95 $125 $175

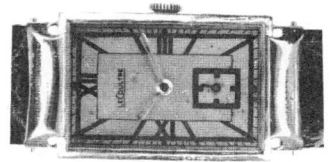

LE COULTRE, 17J.,hidden lugs, c.1942
14k $150 $195 $300
gold filled..............................$95 $125 $165

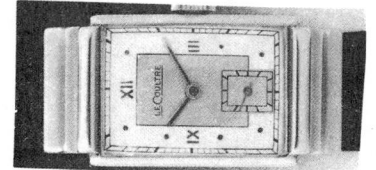

LE COULTRE, 17J., hooded lugs, ca. 1940s
14k $225 $250 $325

LE COULTRE, 17J., fluted bezel, Ca. 1949
gold filled $75 $95 $150

LE COULTRE, 17J., fancy bezel, ca. 1940s
14k $400 $450 $600

LE COULTRE, 17J., RF # 2406, 15 diamonds, Ca. 1957
14k $350 $375 $450

LE COULTRE, 17J., Asymmetric, cal.438.4cw, Ca.1957
gold filled $150 $175 $225

LE COULTRE, 17J., Asymmetric, diamond dial, RF#2406,
Ca.1960
14k $300 $325 $400

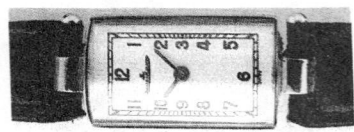

LE COULTRE, 15J., **Duoplan, back-wind,** c. 1930
18k $900 $1,000 $1,200

LE COULTRE, 17 jewels, **uniplan,** c. 1938
14k (w)....................................$400 $450 $550

LE COULTRE, 15J., **Duoplan, back-wind,** c. 1930
14k $1,200 $1,400 $1,800

LE COULTRE, 17 jewels, fancy lugs, c. 1948
14k $400 $500 $700

LE COULTRE, 17J., fancy lugs, cal.438-4cw, c.1951
18k $600 $700 $900

LE COULTRE, 17 jewels, fancy lugs
14k $700 $800 $1,000

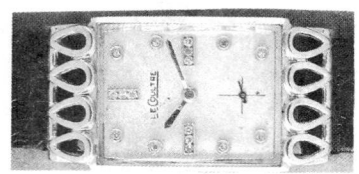

LE COULTRE, 17 jewels, diamond dial, fancy lugs
14k...$800 $900 $1,200

LE COULTRE, 17J., diamond dial, ca. 1940s
14k $250 $300 $450

LE COULTRE, 17J., 12 diamond dial, cal.4870cw, c.1958
14k(w)....................................$150 $175 $225

LE COULTRE, 17J., 15 diamond mystery dial ca.1940s
14k $1,000 $1,200 $1,500

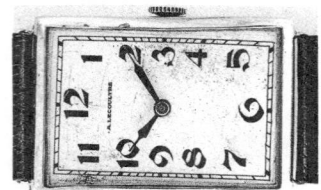

LE COULTRE, 15J., hinged case, c.1920
14k $400 $450 $550

Pricing in this Guide are fair market price for **COM-PLETE** watches which are reflected from the "**NAWCC**" National and regional shows.

LE COULTRE, 17J., stepped case & lugs, cal., c.1950
gold filled................................$75 $95 $150

LE COULTRE, 17J., aux. sec., c.1940
14k $95 $125 $175

LE COULTRE, 17J., cal.493, auto wind, c.1955
14k $250 $275 $350

LE COULTRE, 17J., cal.438-4cw, wide bezel, c.1950
14k $250 $275 $350

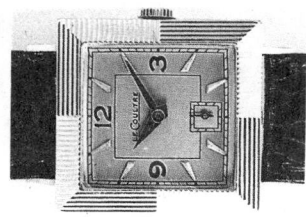

LE COULTRE, 17J., textured bezel, c.1952
14k $250 $275 $350

◷ Pricing in this Guide are fair market price for **COM-PLETE** watches which are reflected from the "**NAWCC**" National and regional shows.

LE COULTRE, 17J., textured bezel, c.1950
14k $250 $275 $350

LE COULTRE, 17J., RF#7540,engraved bezel, cal., c.1960
14k $250 $300 $400

LE COULTRE, 17J., auto wind, cal.p812, c.1948
gold filled $95 $125 $175

LE COULTRE, 17 jewels, Ca.1958
18k $450 $500 $600

LE COULTRE, 17J., textured bezel, cen. sec.
18k $350 $400 $500

LE COULTRE, 17J., aux. sec., auto wind, ca. 1940s
14k $250 $300 $450

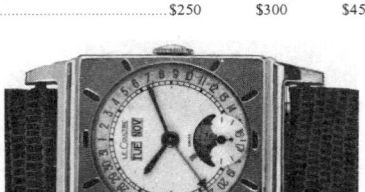

LE COULTRE, 17J, triple date, moon ph., fancy bezel
sold for $99.50 with gold filled case in 1951
18k .... ★ ★ $3,200 $3,700 $4,500
14k $2,400 $2,800 $3,500
gold filled $1,600 $1,800 $2,200

LE COULTRE, 17 jewels, c. 1945
18k $195 $225 $300

LE COULTRE, 17 jewels, fancy lugs, c. 1948
14k $250 $300 $375

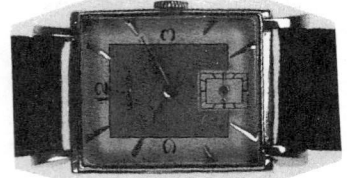

LE COULTRE, 17 jewels, Ca. 1940
14k(rose) $150 $175 $225

LE COULTRE, 17 jewels, center lugs, c. 1945
14k $175 $195 $250

LE COULTRE, 17 jewels, c. 1950s
14k $195 $225 $275

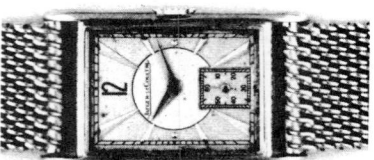

LE COULTRE, 17 jewels, 18k case & band
18k C&B $700 $750 $850

LE COULTRE, 17 jewels, date cal. 810, c. 1952
14k $300 $350 $450

LE COULTRE, 17 jewels, two tone dial
14k $150 $195 $325
18k $250 $275 $475

🕒 Some grades are not included. Their values can be determined by comparing with **similar** age, size, metal content, style, grades, or models such as **time only**, chronograph, repeater etc. listed.

LE COULTRE, 15 jewels, by Blancpain, c.1925
gold filled.................................$40 $50 $75

LE COULTRE, quartz, date, waterproof, c. 1960s
18k $175 $195 $250

LE COULTRE, electric, digital calendar (good running order)
silver & gold filled $150 $175 $225

LE COULTRE, 17J, "Aristocrat", sold for $71.50 with gold
filled case either Gents or Ladies model in 1951
gold filled...............................$350 $425 $550

LE COULTRE, 17 jewels, small, "Aristocrat", c. 1953
gold filled................................$300 $375 $475

LE COULTRE, 15J., lady's
14k(W).....................................$95 $125 $175

LE COULTRE, 15J., lady's art deco, by Blancpain, c.1925
silver $195 $250 $350

LE COULTRE, 15J., lady's REVERSO, c.1940
s. steel $700 $800 $1,000

LE COULTRE, 15J., Duoplan, back-wind, c. 1930
silver $550 $600 $725

LE COULTRE, 17J., lady's MYSTERY dial, c.1959
gold filled $95 $125 $175

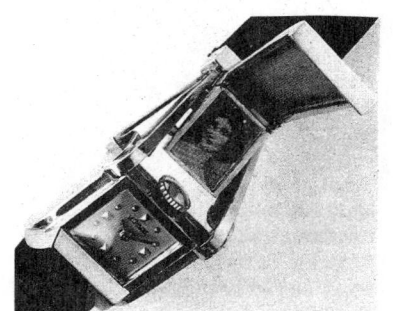

LE COULTRE, 17J., photo-watch, winds at 12, Ca. 1950
14k $450 $500 $600

LEMANIA, 17 jewels, auto wind
s. steel $50 $60 $75

LEMANIA, 17 jewels, chronog., military, ca.1970s
s. steel $400 $450 $600

LEMANIA,17J., chronog., 3 reg., c.1946
14k $450 $550 $700

LEONIDAS,17J., chronog., triple date, c.1945
gold filled $300 $350 $450

LEMANIA, 17 jewels, chronog., 2 reg., auto wind, c. 1950
18k $400 $500 $650

LEONIDAS, 17 jewels, triple date, 3 reg.
18k $600 $700 $900
s. steel $350 $400 $500

LEMANIA, 17 jewels, chronog., waterproof
s. steel $350 $450 $600

LEONIDAS, 17 jewels, auto wind, triple date, moon phase
s. steel $300 $350 $425

LEONIDAS, 17 jewels, chronog., 2 reg.
s. steel $95 $125 $195

LEVRETTE,17J., chronog., (fly back), center lugs, c.1935
18k(1 button)........................ $1,000 $1,100 $1,300

LE PHARE, 17J., chronog., triple date, 3 reg., antimagnetic
14k $500 $550 $700

LIBELA,7J., direct read, c.1952
base metal $75 $95 $125

LE PHARE, 17 jewels, chronog., 2 reg., antimagnetic
18k $375 $425 $500
14k $275 $325 $400
s. steel $100 $150 $200

LIP,15J., chronog., tu-tone, center lugs, (French), c.1940
gold filled & s.steel. $450 $500 $700

LIP, electric, bulbous crown, (French)
s. steel $195 $225 $300

LE PHARE, 17J., triple date, moon ph., waterproof, autow.
18k $500 $600 $800
gold filled...............................$200 $250 $500

Wrist Watches listed in this section are priced at the collectable
fair market Trade Show level as **complete** watches having an
original gold-filled case and stainless steel back, also with
original dial, leather watch band, and the entire original movement in good working order with no repairs needed.

LONGINES, 15J., center lugs, enamel dial, ca.1923
silver $275 $300 $375

LONGINES, 15J., wire lugs, enamel dial, c.1927
silver $195 $225 $275

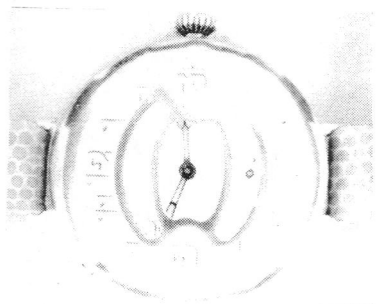

LONGINES,15J., enamel dial, pierced grill , c.1923
silver $325 $350 $450

LONGINES, 15J., wire lugs, ca. 1930s
silver $250 $275 $350

LONGINES,15J., metal dial, GJS, c.1925
14k $150 $175 $225

LONGINES,17J., tu-tone, GJS, c.1936
14k & s.s. $195 $225 $300

LONGINES,17J., double dial, cal.932, c.1937
s. steel $900 $1,100 $1,500

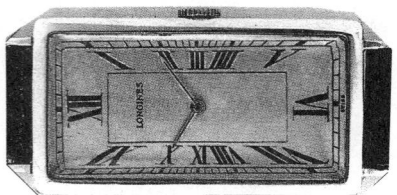

LONGINES, 18J.,wire lugs, ca.1928
14k $300 $325 $400

🕐 Some grades are not included. Their values can be
determined by comparing with **similar** age, size, metal
content, style, grades, or models such as **time only**,
chronograph, repeater etc. listed.

LONGINES,17J., large & curved, GJS, exaggerated numbers
gold filled $225 $250 $350

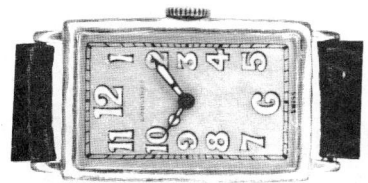

LONGINES, 15J., GJS, c.1922
silver $225 $250 $325

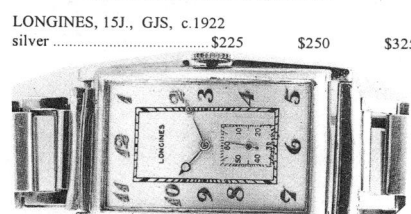

LONGINES, 17J., GJS, cal.940, c.1931
18k $450 $500 $600

LONGINES, 17J., GJS, cal.1086, c.1928
14k $400 $500 $700

LONGINES, 17J., cal.101, c.1947
14k $95 $125 $195

LONGINES, 17J., large Lindberg model 47mm., movable
center dial (weem's second setting), Ca. 1930s
18k .... ★ ★ ★ $10,000 $12,000 $15,000
silver $4,000 $4,500 $6,000
nickel................................... $3,000 $3,500 $5,000

LONGINES, 17J., small Lindberg model, original retail price
for gold filled $97.50, movable center dial, Ca. 1930s
18k .... ★ ★ $6,000 $7,000 $8,500
14k $4,000 $5,000 $6,500
gold filled $1,100 $1,200 $1,500
s. steel $1,400 $1,600 $2,000

LONGINES, 17J., Weems U.S. Patent 2008734 on dial
s. steel $450 $500 $650
14k $700 $800 $1,000

LONGINES, 17J., "Weems", revolving bezel, Ca. 1940s
s. steel $475 $550 $750

LONGINES, 17J., "Weems", revolving bezel, Ca. 1940s
s. steel $500 $600 $800

LONGINES,17J., fly back hand, center recording, c.1945
s. steel(1 button) $900 $1,100 $1,500

LONGINES, 17 jewels, chronog., 1 button, 2 reg., c. 1923
silver $1,400 $1,500 $1,800

LONGINES,17J., 1 button chronog., 2 reg., c.1946
14k $1,900 $2,200 $2,600

LONGINES, 17J., chronog., one button
gold filled $600 $700 $900
14k $1,400 $1,700 $2,000

LONGINES,17J., 1 button, fly back hand, center recording,
RF# 5034, Ca. 1940
s. steel $900 $1,100 $1,500

LONGINES, 17J. chronog., ref. 1333, enamel dial, Ca. 1925
silver(1 button) $1,200 $1,400 $1,700

LONGINES, 17J., one button chronog., 2 reg., Ca. 1928
18k $2,300 $2,500 $3,000

LONGINES, 17J., chronog. 2 reg., tach.
14k $2,000 $2,200 $2,800

LONGINES,17J., chronog., c.1942
s. steel $1,300 $1,500 $1,900

LONGINES,17J., RF#6474, c.1955
s. steel $1,600 $1,800 $2,200

LONGINES, 17 jewels, chronog., 2 reg., Telemeter
Anti Magnetic, Ca. 1940s
18k $2,500 $2,800 $3,500

LONGINES, 17 jewels, chronog., 2 reg.
14k $2,000 $2,200 $2,600
s. steel $1,500 $1,700 $2,000

LONGINES, 17J., 1 button, chronog., ca. 1945
gold filled $300 $350 $425

LONGINES, 17 jewels, chronog. 1 button
14k $1,200 $1,400 $1,700

LONGINES,17J., chronog., cal.539, c.1969
s steel $195 $225 $275

LONGINES,17J., Valjoux 726, cal.332, c.1972
s. steel $225 $275 $350

LONGINES, 16J., military issue, waterpr., ca. 1940s
s. steel $400 $500 $700

LONGINES,17J., GJS, c.1965
18k $150 $175 $275

LONGINES,17J., GJS, cal.23z, c.1958
gold filled..................................$50 $70 $125

LONGINES, 17J., GJS, cal.194, c.1963
gold filled..................................$50 $70 $125

🕐 A collector should expect to pay modestly higher prices at local shops

LONGINES,17J., GJS, cal.352, auto wind, c.1960
14k $95 $125 $195

LONGINES,17J., GJS, cal., c.1960
14k $95 $125 $195

LONGINES,17J., aux. seconds, Ca. 1960
gold filled $50 $70 $125

LONGINES,17J., Aux. seconds, gold jewel settings,
automatic, Ca. 1957
14k $95 $125 $195

🕐 Some grades are not included. Their values can be determined by comparing with **similar** age, size, metal content, style, grades, or models such as **time only**, chronograph, repeater etc. listed.

LONGINES,17J., RF#2033p, GJS, cal., c.1958
14k $125 $150 $225

LONGINES,17J., RF#2021, GJS, cal.23z, c.1955
14k $195 $225 $300

LONGINES,17J., GJS, cal.23z, c.1955
14k $125 $150 $225

LONGINES,17J., large fluted lugs, GJS, c.1940
14k $300 $325 $425

LONGINES,17J., large lugs, GJS, c.1952
18k $300 $350 $425

LONGINES,17J., GJS, cal.18LN, c.1952
14k $225 $275 $350

LONGINES,17J., one lug at 11 & one at 5, GJS, 1955
14k $250 $275 $350

LONGINES,17J., GJS, cal.22a, auto-wind, c.1958
14k $225 $275 $350

Wrist Watches listed in this section are priced at the collectable
fair market **Trade Show** level as **complete** watches having an
original gold-filled case and stainless steel back, also with
original dial, leather watch band, and the entire original movement in good working order with no repairs needed.

A collector should expect to pay modestly higher prices
at local shops

Pricing in this Guide are fair market price for **COM-
PLETE** watches which are reflected from the "**NAWCC**" National and regional shows.

LONGINES,17J., GJS, cal.10L, c.1952
14k $95 $125 $195

LONGINES, 17 jewels, fancy lugs, c. 1954
14k $300 $325 $425

LONGINES,17J., GJS, cal.23z, c.1954
18k $275 $325 $400

LONGINES, 17 jewels, fancy lugs, c. 1949
14k $300 $325 $425

LONGINES, 15 jewels, c. 1940s
18k $225 $250 $300
14k $150 $175 $225
s. steel $75 $95 $150

LONGINES, 19J.,"Conquest", auto-wind,
14k $400 $475 $650

LONGINES,17J., GJS, cal.22ls, c.1950
14k $195 $225 $275

LONGINES, 17J., fancy lugs, diamond dial,
14k $325 $350 $450

⊕ Some grades are not included. Their values can be
determined by comparing with **similar** age, size, metal
content, style, grades, or models such as **time only**,
chronograph, repeater etc. listed.

LONGINES,17J., "Flagship", GJS, cal.340, autow., c.1960
18k $195 $225 $300

LONGINES,17J., RF#3759, GJS, cal.22as, autow., c.1949
14k $225 $250 $300

LONGINES,17J., center sec., GJS, c.1948
14k $150 $175 $225

LONGINES,17J., GJS, center sec., c.1958
gold filled $95 $125 $195

LONGINES,17J., GJS, cal.19as, autow., c.1955
gold filled..................................$50 $70 $125

LONGINES,17J., center sec., GJS, cal., c.1940
14k $150 $175 $225

LONGINES,17J., "Admiral", GJS, cal.340, autow., c.1960
14k $95 $125 $195

LONGINES,17J., GJS, center sec., c.1943
14k $95 $125 $195

Wrist Watches listed in this section are priced at the collectable fair market Trade Show level as **complete** watches having an original gold-filled case and stainless steel back, also with original dial, leather watch band, and the entire original movement in good working order with no repairs needed.

Pricing in this Guide are fair market price for **COMPLETE** watches which are reflected from the "NAWCC" National and regional shows.

LONGINES, 17J., military, Ca.1942
s. steel $195 $250 $325

LONGINES,17J., a-wind, "5 star Admiral", date, Ca.1963
gold filled $65 $75 $135

LONGINES,17J., GJS, "Flagship", date, autow., c.1964
gold filled................................$75 $85 $95

LONGINES,17J., "5 star Admiral", cal.506, autow., c.1965
14k $125 $150 $195

LONGINES,17J., 36,000 (beat), auto-wind, "Ultra-Chron"
14k $195 $225 $275

LONGINES,17J., high frequency, date, autow., c.1972
s. steel $50 $65 $85

LONGINES,17J., RF#9003, date, GJS, "Conquest", autowind, Ca.1958
18k $500 $550 $650

LONGINES, 17 jewels, ''Flagship'' autowind
14k $125 $150 $225

LONGINES, 17 jewels, gold jewel settings, Ca. 1950
s. steel $75 $85 $125

LONGINES, 17J., "Grand Prize", auto-w., date, Ca. 1950
gold filled $85 $110 $150
14k $250 $300 $350

LONGINES, 17 jewels, center seconds
14k $175 $195 $250

LONGINES, 17J., aux. seconds, large lugs
14k $150 $185 $250

LONGINES, 17J., "Conquest", auto-w., date, w.-indicator
s. steel $375 $425 $500

LONGINES, 17J., auto wind
14k $125 $150 $225

LONGINES, 17J., date, ca. 1940s
14k $275 $300 $350

LONGINES, 19J., "Conquest", auto-w., date, ca.1962
s. steel $400 $450 $600

LONGINES,17J., mystery dial, cal.232 c.1960
gold filled $125 $150 $225

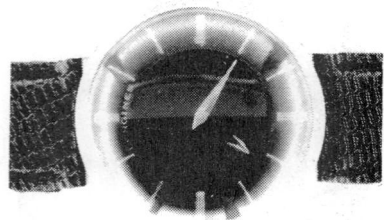

LONGINES,17J., mystery dial,
gold filled...............................$125 $150 $225

LONGINES, 17 jewels, mystery hand, ca.1962
gold filled...............................$125 $150 $225

LONGINES, 17 jewels, mystery hand, autowind
14k $300 $350 $450

LONGINES, 17 jewels, mystery hand, 12 diamond dial
14k $500 $550 $700

LONGINES,17J., mystery 39 diamond dial, RF#1017
14k(w)...................................$700 $750 $850

LONGINES, 17 jewels, diamond dial, center lugs
14k $400 $425 $500

LONGINES, 17J., "Ultra Chron," diamond dial, autow.
14k $195 $250 $350

LONGINES, 17 jewels, "Ultra Chron," date, autow., c.1949
14k $125 $175 $225

LONGINES, 17J., auto-w., aux. sec.
14k $125 $150 $195

🕐 Some grades are not included. Their values can be determined by comparing with **similar** age, size, metal content, style, grades, or models such as **time only**, chronograph, repeater etc. listed.

LONGINES, 17J., auto-w., aux. sec.
14k $175 $195 $250

LONGINES, 17J., aux sec.
14k $150 $175 $225

LONGINES, 17J., diamond dial
14k(W)...................................$150 $175 $225

LONGINES, 17J.,diamond bezel
gold filled...............................$175 $200 $275

LONGINES, 17J.,3 diamond dial
gold filled $90 $110 $135

LONGINES, 17J., diamond dial,
14k(W)...................................$150 $175 $225

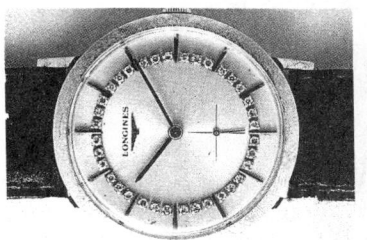

LONGINES, 17 jewels, cocktail style, 36 diamond dial
14k(W)...................................$275 $300 $375

LONGINES, 17J., 12 diamond dial, textured case
14k (w) $175 $225 $275

LONGINES,17J., GJS, 34 diamond dial, date, autow., c.1962
14k $300 $325 $375

LONGINES,17J., 44 diamonds bezel, GJS, cal.22L, c.1952
18k(w)...................................... $450 $500 $600

LONGINES, 17J., 14 diamond dial, Ca. 1960
14k $150 $175 $225

LONGINES,17J., 14 diamonds,GJS, cal.370, c.1960
14k $150 $175 $225

LONGINES,17J., "Admiral", GJS, auto-wind, Ca. 1960
14k $275 $300 $400

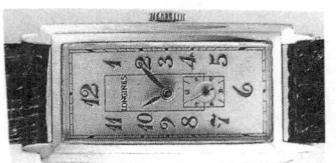

LONGINES, 17J., GJS, Ca. 1935-
14k (rose)................................ $250 $275 $350

LONGINES,17J., 4 diamonds, cal.194, c.1958
gold filled.................................. $95 $125 $175

LONGINES, 17J., GJS, faceted crystal, Ca.1951
gold filled $50 $75 $125

LONGINES,17J., 37 diamonds on bezel 24 on dial, c.1958
14k(w)...................................... $350 $400 $500

LONGINES, 17J., GJS, cal.9L, Ca.1939
gold filled $75 $95 $150

LONGINES, 17J., 4 diamonds, GJS, cal.23z, c.1948
14k $125 $150 $225

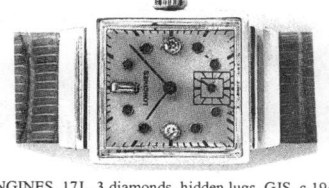

LONGINES, 17J., 3 diamonds, hidden lugs, GJS, c.1943
gold filled $75 $95 $135

LONGINES, 17J., 5 diamonds, GJS, cal.8ln, c.1940
14k(w)..................................... $125 $150 $225

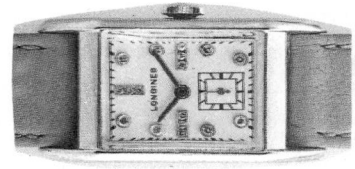

LONGINES, 17J., 17 diamonds, GJS, c.1951
14k $250 $300 $400

LONGINES, 17J., 8 diamonds, GJS, cal.22L, c.1958
14k $125 $150 $225

LONGINES, 17J., 15 diamonds, GJS, cal.9L, c.1945
platinum................................. $750 $850 $1,100
14k $300 $350 $450

LONGINES,17J.,4 diamonds, textured bezel,cal.194, c.1955
gold filled................................. $75 $95 $125

LONGINES, 17J., 18 diamonds, RF#176, GJS, c.1950
14k(w)..................................... $300 $350 $450

LONGINES, 17J., 6 diamonds, GJS
14k $125 $150 $225

LONGINES, 17J., 16 diamonds, cal.9LT, c.1958
14k(w)..................................... $225 $275 $350

 Pricing in this Guide are fair market price for **COMPLETE**
watches which are reflected from the "**NAWCC**" National and
regional shows.

LONGINES, 17J., 4 diamonds, GJS, cal.L8474, c.1960
gold filled...................................$75 $95 $150

LONGINES, 17J., 6 diamonds, RF#2763, GJS, c.1955
14k $175 $225 $300

LONGINES, 17J., 8 diamonds, GJS, cal.9LT, c.1958
14k(w)...................................$175 $225 $300

LONGINES, 17J., 5 diamonds, GJS, c.1945
14k C&B.................................$450 $500 $550

LONGINES, 17J., 5 diamonds, GJS, cal.9L, c.1952
14k $250 $275 $350

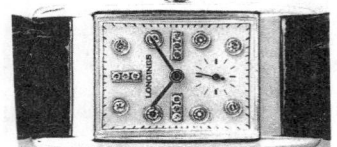

LONGINES, 17 jewels, 17 diamond dial, c. 1951
14k(w)...................................$300 $350 $425

LONGINES, 17 jewels, diamond dial, hidden lugs, c. 1938
s. steel $125 $150 $225

LONGINES, 17 jewels, fancy hidden lugs, diamond dial
14k (w) $400 $450 $600

LONGINES, 17 jewels, diamond dial, c. 1944
14k $300 $350 $450

LONGINES, 17 jewels, 17 diamond dial, c. 1951
14k $200 $250 $350

LONGINES, 17 jewels, diamond dial, c. 1935
platinum..............................$1,100 $1,200 $1,500
14k $750 $800 $900

LONGINES, 17 jewels, 18 diamond dial
14k (w) $150 $200 $275

LONGINES, 17 jewels, flared, 6 diamond dial
14k $600 $650 $750

LONGINES, 17 jewels, 4 diamond dial
14k $175 $225 $300

LONGINES, 17 jewels, 12 diamond dial
s.steel $150 $175 $225

LONGINES, 17 jewels, stepped case, Ca. 1951
14k $175 $225 $300

LONGINES, 17 jewels, c. 1923
gold filled.................................$75 $95 $125

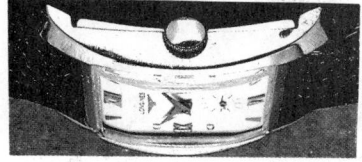

LONGINES, 17 jewels, flared, c. 1959
14k $600 $650 $750

LONGINES, 17 jewels, flared
14k C&B...............................$750 $850 $1,000

LONGINES, 17 jewels, fancy lugs, c. 1943
14k $300 $350 $450

LONGINES, 17 jewels, torpedo shaped numbers
14k $150 $175 $225

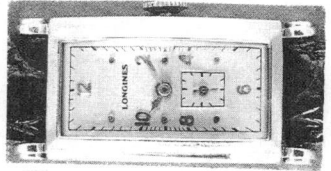

LONGINES, 17 jewels, curved, fancy lugs, c. 1939
14k $300 $350 $450

LONGINES, 17 jewels, center lugs, c. 1955
14k $175 $195 $250

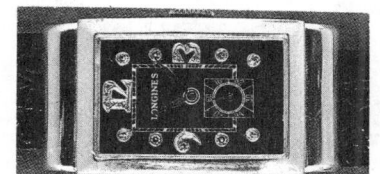

LONGINES, 17 jewels, hooded lugs, diamond dial
14k(w)....................................$700 $800 $950

LONGINES, 17 jewels, hooded lugs
14k $195 $225 $275

LONGINES, 17 jewels, diamond dial, fancy lugs
14k $450 $500 $600

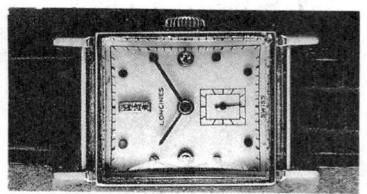

LONGINES, 17 jewels, diamond dial, c. 1944
14k $175 $195 $250

LONGINES, 17 jewels, fancy lugs
14k $175 $195 $250

LONGINES, 17 jewels, c. 1930
18k $700 $750 $900
14k $400 $450 $600
gold filled $175 $195 $275

LONGINES, 17 jewels, 20 diamond dial, Ca. 1932
platinum $1,000 $1,200 $1,500

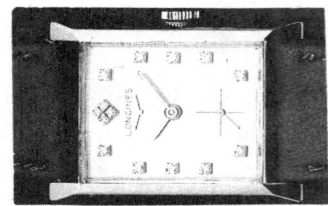

LONGINES, 17 jewels, diamond dial
14k(W) $250 $300 $375

LONGINES, 17J., curved,
14k $150 $175 $250

LONGINES, 17J., stepped case,
14k $300 $325 $400

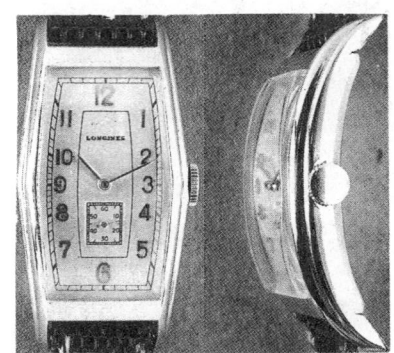

LONGINES, 17J., curvex, 52mm, ca. 1930
gold filled $300 $350 $450

LONGINES, 15J., tonneau, GJS, c.1925
silver $300 $350 $450

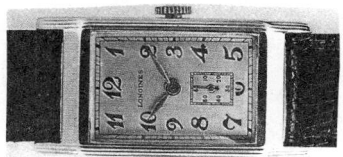

LONGINES, 17J., stepped case, GJS, cal.9L, c.1939
14k $250 $275 $325

LONGINES, 17J., extended lugs, GJS, cal.9L, c.1942
14k $175 $195 $300

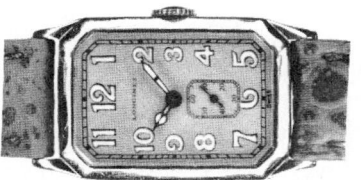

LONGINES, 17J., cut corner, cal.94w, c.1929
gold filled.................................$95 $125 $165

LONGINES, 17J., tonneau, cal.9L, c.1948
gold filled.................................$150 $175 $225

Wrist Watches listed in this section are priced at the collectable
fair market **Trade Show** level as **complete** watches having an
original gold-filled case and stainless steel back, also with
original dial, leather watch band, and the entire original movement in good working order with no repairs needed.

LONGINES, 17J., carved bezel, GJS, cal.9LT, c.1950
gold filled $75 $95 $150

LONGINES, 17J., butler finish, GJS, cal., c.1951
gold filled $75 $95 $150

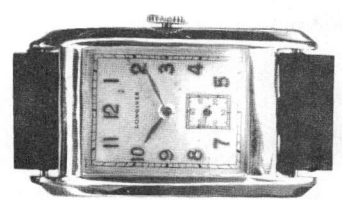

LONGINES, 17J., beveled bezel, GJS, cal., c.1935
gold filled $95 $125 $165

LONGINES, 17J., aux. sec., GJS, cal.9L, c.1948
gold filled $75 $95 $150

LONGINES, 17J., carved case, GJS, cal.9LT, c.1950s
14k $200 $225 $275

⊕ A collector should expect to pay modestly higher prices
at local shops

⊕ Some grades are not included. Their values can be
determined by comparing with **similar** age, size, metal
content, style, grades, or models such as **time only**,
chronograph, repeater etc. listed.

LONGINES, 17J., butler finish, GJS, cal.9LT, c.1957
14k $150 $175 $250

LONGINES, 17J., fluted lugs, GJS, cal.9L, c.1949
gold filled $95 $125 $175

LONGINES, 15-17J., butler finish, c.1926
gold filled................................. $75 $95 $150

LONGINES, 17J., carved case, GJS, cal.9LT, c.1959
gold filled $95 $125 $175

LONGINES, 17J., stepped case, GJS, cal.9LT, c.1958
14k $195 $225 $300

LONGINES, 17J., spur lugs, GJS, cal., c.1948
gold filled $95 $125 $175

LONGINES, 17J., right angle, GJS, curved, c.1938
gold filled...............................$175 $195 $275
s. steel $350 $400 $600
14k $500 $600 $900

LONGINES, 17J., extended lugs, GJS, cal.9LT, c.1955
14k $195 $225 $275

LONGINES, 17J., fancy bezel, GJS, Ca. 1950
14k $175 $195 $275

LONGINES, 17J., fancy lugs, GJS, cal.9LT, c.1957
14k $175 $200 $250

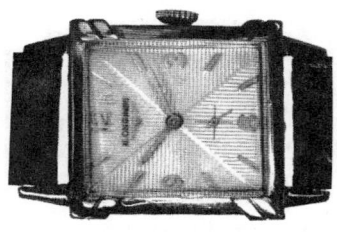

LONGINES, 17J., fluted sides, GJS, cal.9LT, c.1950
gold filled.................................$95 $125 $175

LONGINES, 17J., carved case, GJS, cal.9LT, c.1955
14k $250 $275 $350

LONGINES, 17J., U shaped lugs, GJS
14k $250 $300 $400

LONGINES, 17J., gold jewel settings, Ca. 1951
gold filled.................................$75 $95 $150
14k (w)....................................$175 $195 $250

LONGINES, 17J., RF#8475, GJS, cal.10L, c.1948
14k $175 $195 $250

LONGINES,17J., GJS, c.1958
14k $175 $195 $250

LONGINES, 17J., RF#3327, GJS, cal.10L c.1948
gold filled $95 $125 $165

LONGINES, 17J., extended lugs, GJS, cal.9LT, c.1951
14k $225 $250 $300

LONGINES, 17J., aux. sec., GJS, Ca.1951
14k $125 $150 $225

LONGINES, 17J., butler finish, GJS, cal.9L, c.1955
14k $95 $125 $195

🕐 Some grades are not included. Their values can be
determined by comparing with **similar** age, size, metal
content, style, grades, or models such as **time only**,
chronograph, repeater etc. listed.

LONGINES, 17J., aux. sec., GJS, cal.9LT, c.1950
14k $150 $175 $225

LONGINES, 17J., fancy lugs, GJS, cal.10L, c.1951
gold filled $75 $95 $150

LONGINES, 17J., butler finish, GJS, cal.8LN, c.1942
14k $125 $150 $225

LONGINES, 17J., GJS, cal. 23Z, Ca. 1950
gold filled $75 $95 $150

LONGINES, 17J., beveled lugs, GJS, cal.8LN, c.1947
14k $125 $150 $225

LONGINES, 17J., beveled case, GJS, cal.9LT, c.1955
gold filled $75 $95 $150

LONGINES, 17J., wide bezel, GJS, cal.23z, c.1950
gold filled $75 $95 $110

LONGINES, 17J., curly lugs, GJS, cal.23z, c.1950
gold filled $75 $95 $150

LONGINES, 17J., GJS, cal.23z, c.1957
14k $150 $175 $250

⊕ Pricing in this Guide are fair market price for **COMPLETE** watches which are reflected from the "**NAWCC**" National and regional shows.

LONGINES, 17J., checked dial, GJS, cal.22L, c.1957
14k $125 $150 $225

LONGINES, 17J., RF#1050, mystery dial, cal.23z, c.1960
14k $300 $325 $400

LONGINES, 17J., center seconds, GJS, hidden lugs, Ca.1942
14k (rose)..............................$150 $175 $250

LONGINES, 17J., textured bezel, GJS, cal.22L, c.1950
14k $225 $250 $350

LONGINES, 17J., stepped case, GJS, cal.23z, c.1955
14k $125 $150 $225
gold filled................................$75 $95 $150

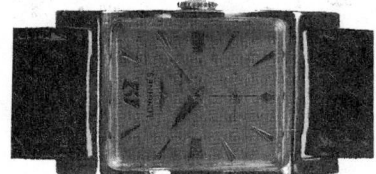

LONGINES, 17J., carved case, GJS,
gold filled................................$75 $95 $150

LONGINES, 17J., hooded lugs, GJS, cal.8LN, c.1942
gold filled $75 $95 $150

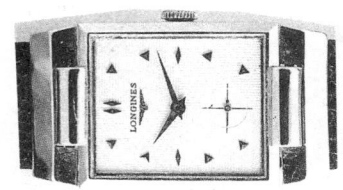

LONGINES, 17J., RF#2288, hidden lugs, GJS, c.1955
14k $250 $275 $350

LONGINES, 17J., hidden lugs
14k (rose)..............................$500 $550 $700

LONGINES, 17J., **contract** case or recent case,
14k $75 $95 $150

LONGINES, 17 jewels, 42mm
14k (w) $300 $350 $500

Wrist Watches listed in this section are priced at the collectable
fair market **Trade Show** level as **complete** watches having an
original gold-filled case and stainless steel back, also with
original dial, leather watch band, and the entire original movement in good working order with no repairs needed.

🕐 A collector should expect to pay modestly higher prices
at local shops

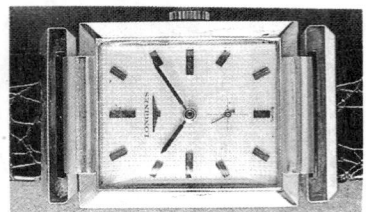

LONGINES, 17 jewels, fancy lugs
14k $195 $225 $300

LONGINES, 17 jewels, c. 1939
14k $200 $225 $325

LONGINES, 17 jewels, curvex, slanted lugs
14k (w)...................................$150 $175 $225

LONGINES, 17 jewels, fancy lugs, c. 1942
14k $250 $275 $350

LONGINES, 17 jewels, fancy lugs, c. 1947
14k $250 $275 $350

LONGINES, 17 jewels, curved, flared
14k $150 $175 $250

LONGINES, 15 jewels, chased bezel
14k $600 $650 $800

LONGINES, 15 jewels, engraved bezel, c. 1928
14k (w) $350 $400 $550

LONGINES, 17J., faceted crystal, center seconds
14k $125 $150 $225

LONGINES, 17J., fancy lugs & diamond bezel
14k(W)....................................$400 $450 $600

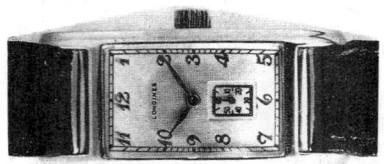

LONGINES, 17J., curved case, Ca. 1930s
14k $250 $275 $350

🕐 Pricing in this Guide are fair market price for **COMPLETE** watches which are reflected from the "**NAWCC**" National and regional shows.

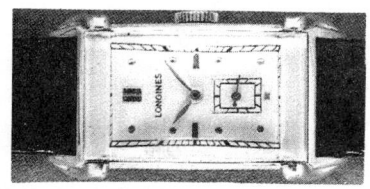

LONGINES, 17J., fancy lugs
14k $275 $300 $375

LONGINES, 17J., fancy lugs,
14k $275 $300 $375

LONGINES, 17J., cal#232, ca. 1948
14k $125 $150 $225

LONGINES, 17J., aux. sec.
14k $175 $195 $275

LONGINES, 17J., ca. 1952
14k $175 $195 $275

⊕ Some grades are not included. Their values can be
determined by comparing with **similar** age, size, metal
content, style, grades, or models such as **time only**,
chronograph, repeater etc. listed.

LONGINES, 17J., cal#10L, center sec.,
14k $175 $195 $275

LONGINES, 17J., center sec., fancy lugs, ca.1946
14k $175 $195 $275

LONGINES, 17J., fancy lugs, cal#10L
14k $150 $175 $225

LONGINES, 17J., aux. sec.
14k $125 $150 $225

LONGINES, 17J., offset lugs
14k $225 $250 $300

⊕ A collector should expect to pay modestly higher prices
at local shops

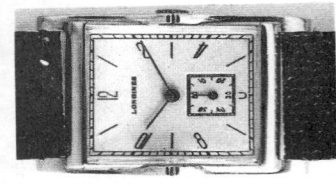

LONGINES, 17J., fancy lugs, ca. 1951
14k $175 $195 $275

LONGINES, 17J., hidden lugs, Ca. 1940
14k(rose)................................. $400 $425 $500

LONGINES, 17J., fancy bezel
14k $125 $150 $225

LONGINES, 17 jewels, enameled bezel, c. 1928
14k $400 $425 $500

LONGINES, 17 jewels, formed case
14k $200 $250 $350

LONGINES, 17J., flared case, GJS, c.1955
gold filled...............................$175 $195 $275

LONGINES, 17J., flared case, GJS, cal.9LT, c.1950
gold filled...............................$150 $195 $275

LONGINES, 17J.,antimagnetic
s. steel $350 $450 $600

Wrist Watches listed in this section are priced at the collectable
fair market **Trade Show** level as **complete** watches having an
original gold-filled case and stainless steel back, also with
original dial, leather watch band, and the entire original movement in good working order with no repairs needed.

LONGINES, 17J., flared case, textured dial
14k $450 $500 $600

Some grades are not included. Their values can be
determined by comparing with **similar** age, size, metal
content, style, grades, or models such as **time only**,
chronograph, repeater etc. listed.

LONGINES MOVEMENT IDENTIFICATION

Cal. No. 4.21, Ca.1930

Cal. No. 5.16, Ca.1922

Cal. No. 6.22, Ca.1932

Cal. No. 7.45, Ca.1916

Cal. No. 7.48, Ca.1925

Cal. No. 8.23, Ca.1931

Cal. No. 8.47, Ca.1916

Cal. No. 9.32, Ca.1932

Cal. No. 9.47, Ca.1922

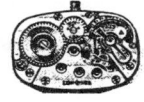

Cal. No. 12.19, Ca.1934

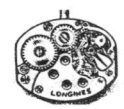

Cal. No. 13.15, Ca.1936

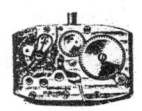

Cal. No. 25.17, Ca.1935

PRODUCTION TOTALS
LONGINES DATE OF MOVEMENT MANUFACTURE

DATE– SERIAL #	DATE– SERIAL #	DATE– SERIAL #
1867 — 1	1911 - 2,500,000	1937 - 5,500,000
1870 — 20,000	1912 - 2,750,000	1938 - 5,750,000
1875 — 100,000	1913 - 3,000,000	1940 - 6,000,000
1882 — 250,000	1915 - 3,250,000	1945 - 7,000,000
1888 — 500,000	1917 - 3,500,000	1950 - 8,000,000
1893 — 750,000	1919 - 3,750,000	1953 - 9,000,000
1899 - 1,000,000	1922 - 4,000,000	1956-10,000,000
1901 - 1,250,000	1925 - 4,250,000	1959-11,000,000
1904 - 1,500,000	1926 - 4,500,000	1962-12,000,000
1905 - 1,750,000	1928 - 4,750,000	1966-13,000,000
1907 - 2,000,000	1929 - 5,000,000	1967-14,000,000
1909 - 2,250,000	1934 - 5,250,000	1969-15,000,000

The above list is provided for determining the APPROXIMATE age of your watch. Match serial number with date. Watches were not necessarily sold in the exact order of manufactured date.

LONGINES date of movement manufacture

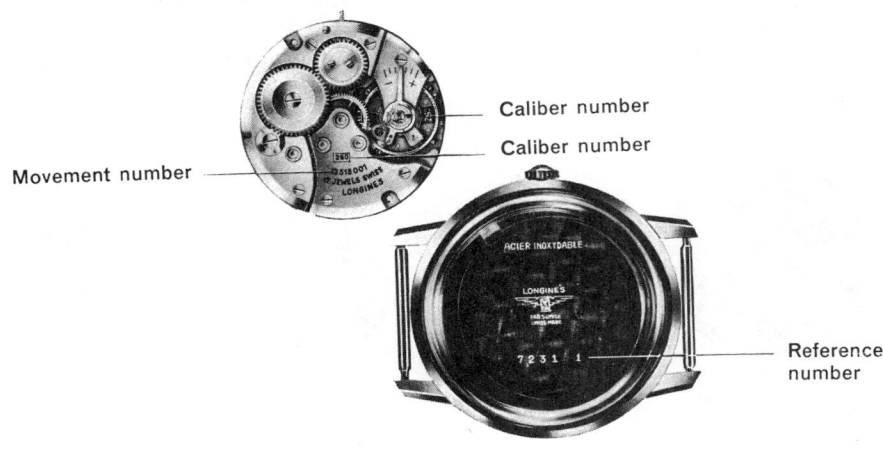

Caliber number

Caliber number

Movement number

Reference number

Cal. No. 10.68, Ca.1932   Cal. No. 10.68, Lindburg   Cal. No. 12.68, Ca.1938   Cal. No. 12.68 Z, Ca.1939

Cal. No. 14.16, Ca.1951   Cal. No. 14.16 S, Ca.1954   Cal. No. 14.17, Ca.1952   Cal. No. 15.18, Ca.1941

Cal. No. 19 A, Ca.1952   Cal. No. 19.4, Ca.1953   Cal. No. 19.4 S, Ca.1953   Cal. No. 22 A, Ca.1945

Cal. No. 22 L, Ca.1946   Cal. No. 23 Z, Ca.1948   Cal. No. 23 ZD, Ca.1954   Cal. No. 25.17, Ca.1935

Cal. No. RR 280, Ca.1963   Cal. No. 290, Ca.1958   Cal. No. 310   Cal. No. 312

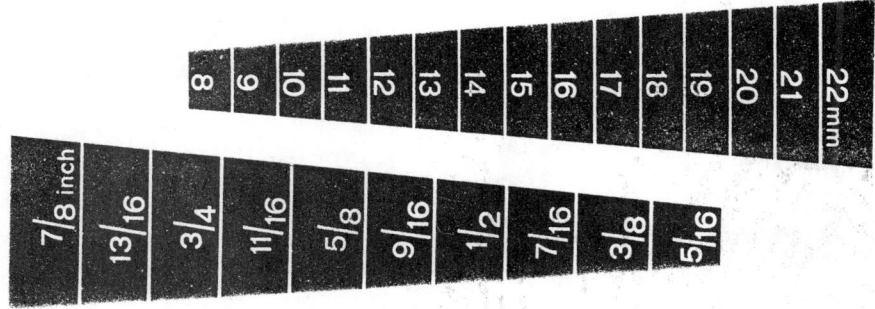

Cal. No. 380

Cal. No. 420

Cal. No. 430, Ca.1967

Cal. No. 320

Cal. No. 450

Cal. No. 460

Cal. No. 470

Cal. No. 30 CH, Ca.1947

Cal. No. 30 ZN

Cal. No. 330

To determine your Wrist watch **band** size use the ABOVE GAUGE and measure between the lugs.

LONGINES, 17J., "COMET", cal.702, c.1972
s. steel $150 $195 $275

LONGINES, 17J., lady's style, center lugs, c.1948
14k C&B $175 $195 $275

LONGINES, 15J., lady's style,
14k C&B $175 $195 $275

LORTON, 17 jewels, chronog., c. 1950
s. steel $150 $175 $225

LOUIS, 17J., center sec.,
14k $95 $110 $135

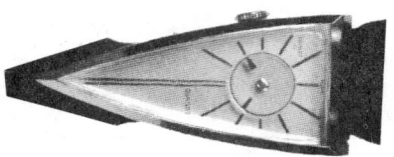

LOUVIC, 17J., mystery dial, long triangular case, c.1950
base metal $60 $70 $95

LOUVIC, 17J., hunter style case, ca. 1965
s. steel $75 $95 $150

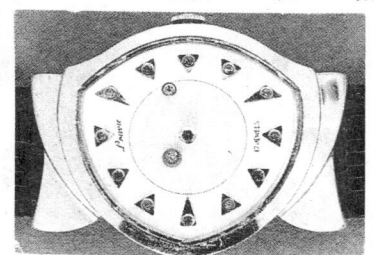

LOUVIC, 17J., mystery diamond dial, ca.1960
s. steel $125 $150 $225

LUCERNE, 17 jewels, 14k case & band , 3 diamonds
14k C&B $195 $225 $275

LUCIEN PICCARD, 17J., movement by Ditisheim
14k $125 $135 $175

LUCIEN PICCARD, 17 jewels, gem set bezel
14k $125 $150 $195

LUSINA, 17 jewels, aux. sec., fancy lugs
gold filled $40 $50 $75

LUCIEN PICCARD, 17 jewels, "Seahawk," auto wind
18k C&B................................ $300 $350 $425

LYCEUM, 17J., beveled case, aux. sec.
14k $95 $120 $175

LUCIEN PICCARD, 17J., auto wind, wind indicator, c. 1958
s. steel $75 $95 $125

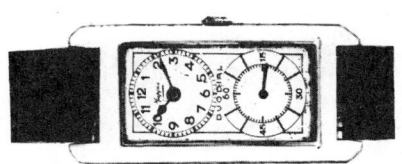

MAPPIN, 15 jewels, duo dial, c. 1930
9k $500 $550 $700

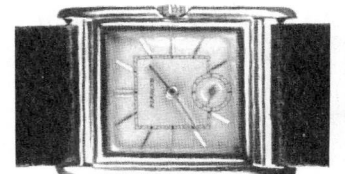

MARLYS, 15J., G.J.S., c.1935
14k $125 $135 $175

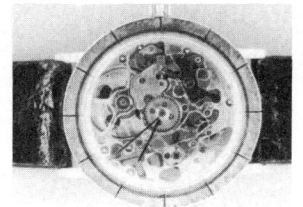

LUCIEN PICCARD, 17 jewels, skeletonized
18k $550 $600 $700

🕐 Some grades are not included. Their values can be determined by comparing with **similar** age, size, metal content, style, grades, or models such as **time only**, chronograph, repeater etc. listed.

MARS, 17J, "Dateur," date on lugs, hinged back, c. 1934
gold filled $250 $275 $350

MARVIN, 17J., center sec., cal.520s, c.1943
14k $95 $125 $195

MARVIN, 17J., non magnetic,
gold filled..................................$50 $55 $95

MARVIN, 17J., c.1943
base metal $40 $50 $70

MASTER, 17J., tonneau case, c.1943
gold plate $30 $35 $50

MASTER, 17J., stepped case, c.1943
gold plate $30 $35 $50

⊕ Pricing in this Guide are fair market price for **COMPLETE**
watches which are reflected from the "**NAWCC**" National and
regional shows.

C.H. MEYLAN, 17 jewels, c. 1940s
18k $195 $250 $350

C.H. MEYLAN, 18 jewels, jumping hr., c. 1920
18k $3,000 $3,500 $4,500

C.H. MEYLAN, 16 jewels, wire lugs
14k $225 $250 $325

C.H. MEYLAN, 27J, 1 button chronog., 2 reg., enamel dial
18k $2,500 $2,800 $3,500

C.H. MEYLAN, 18J., ladies , Octagon case, c.1917
platinum..................................$300 $325 $400

J.E. MEYLAN, 17J., chronograph, 2 reg., ca. 1937

14k	$600	$700	$900
s. steel	$195	$250	$400

MIDO, 17 jewels, chronog., "Multi-centerchrono"

s. steel	$400	$450	$550
with telemeter dial	$450	$500	$600

J.E. MEYLAN,17J., stop watch,

s. steel	$175	$225	$350

MIDO, 17J., choronog., Pulsations, cal.1300, c.1954

gold filled	$400	$500	$700
14k	$500	$650	$900
18k	$700	$800	$1,100

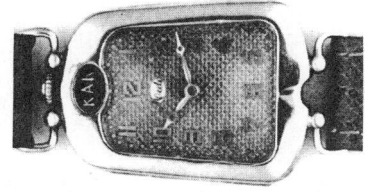

MIDO, 15 jewels, in form of car radiator, c. 1940s

silver	$2,000	$2,200	$2,800

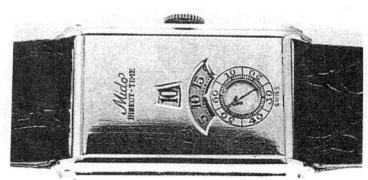

MIDO, 15J., "DIRECT-TIME", jump hour, Ca. 1932

14k (w)	$500	$550	$800
18k (w)	$600	$700	$1,000
s. steel	$350	$400	$550

MIDO, 17 jewels, chronog., "Multi-centerchrono", c. 1952

s. steel	$300	$450	$600

Wrist Watches listed in this section are priced at the collectable fair market **Trade Show** level as **complete** watches having an original gold-filled case and stainless steel back, also with original dial, leather watch band, and the entire original movement in good working order with no repairs needed.

🕐 A collector should expect to pay modestly higher prices at local shops

MIDO, 17J., carved case, cal.2m, c.1947

14k	$150	$175	$225

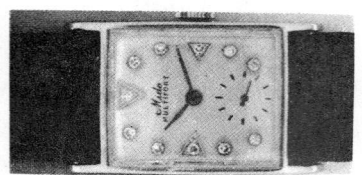

MIDO, 17 jewels, diamond dial
platinum $300 $400 $650
14k $175 $195 $250

MIDO, 17 jewels "Multifort," diamond dial
s. steel $100 $125 $175

MIDO, 17 jewels, fancy lugs, c. 1945
14k $150 $175 $225

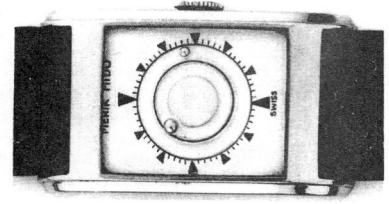

MIDO, 15 jewels, mystery dial, c. 1935
s. steel $400 $450 $650

MIDO, 17J., multifort grand luxe, autow., date, ca. 1950s
18k C&B $300 $400 $650

MIDO, 17J., RF#7204, cal.d917b, autow., c.1958
s. steel $60 $70 $95

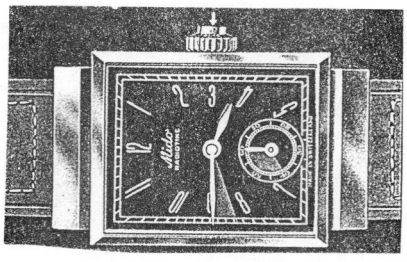

MIDO, 17J., RF#228, mid size case, autow., c.1943
s. steel $40 $55 $75

MIDO, 17J., **"Radiotime"**, to correct time push button on
crown advances minutes & seconds hand, Ca. 1939
gold filled .... ★★$350 $450 $600

MIDO, 17J., mid size case, cal.917r, autow., c.1949
s. steel $40 $55 $75

Some grades are not included. Their values can be
determined by comparing with **similar** age, size, metal
content, style, grades, or models such as **time only**,
chronograph, repeater etc. listed.

MIDO, 17J., super auto-wind, muiltfort extra,
14k $95 $110 $175
s. steel $50 $60 $85

MIDO, 17J., "power wind", c.1955
s. steel $50 $55 $75

MIDO, 17J., rotating bezel, autow., c.1960
s. steel $150 $195 $300

MIDO, 17J., multifort grand luxe, extra-flat
s. steel $50 $55 $75

MILDIA, 17 jewels
s. steel $30 $40 $65

MIMO, 15 jewels, date
gold filled $65 $75 $125

MIMO, 17J., "De Frece", date, c.1935
14k(w) $125 $150 $195

MIMO, 17 jewels, jumping hr., wandering min. & sec.
gold filled $300 $350 $450

MIMO, 17 jewels, **8 day**, 6 gear train, c. 1950s
gold filled $400 $500 $650

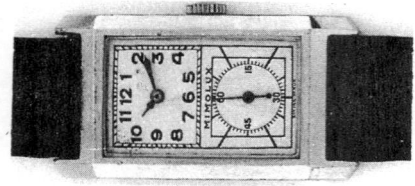

MIMO, 17 jewels, duo dial
s. steel $325 $375 $500

MIMO, 15 jewels, engraved bezel
gold filled.................................$35 $40 $65

MIMO, 15 jewels, ''Mimomatic,'' c. 1932
s. steel $60 $70 $95

MINERVA, 29J., min. repeater, repeats on 2 gongs
18k $12,000 $14,000 $18,000

MINERVA, 17 jewels, chronog., 2 reg. telemeter km
18k $700 $900 $1,400
s. steel $275 $350 $500

MINERVA, 17 jewels, chronog., 2 reg.
18k $300 $350 $500

MINERVA, 17 jewels, waterproof, chronog., c. 1950s
14k $400 $450 $675
s. steel $250 $275 $400

MINERVA, 17J., chronog., Valjoux cal.723, c.1955
14k $750 $850 $1,100
s. steel $500 $550 $750

MINERVA, 19 jewels, chronog., 3 reg.
s. steel $195 $250 $375

MINERVA, 17 jewels, one button chronog., c. 1942
s. steel $300 $350 $450

MINERVA, 17J., chronog., day-date-month, 3 reg.
18k $1,000 $1,100 $1,400

MINERVA, 17 jewels, center sec., auto wind
gold filled................................ $40 $50 $65

MISC. SWISS, 15J., hunter style, wire lugs, ca. 1926
silver $450 $500 $600

Watches listed in this BOOK as Misc. Swiss are just a few
examples of miscellaneous jobbers, distributors & jewelry
firms. Example Abc Watch Co., to Zuma Watch Co., etc. with
the name xxxx out.

Watches listed in this BOOK as Misc. Swiss are just a few
examples of miscellaneous jobbers, distributors & jewelry
firms. Example Abc Watch Co., to Zuma Watch Co., etc. with
the name xxxx out.

MISC. SWISS, 15J., shield cover, enamel dial, ca. 1927
silver $600 $650 $750

MISC. SWISS,15J., **rim wind,** wire lugs, cal., c.1920
s. steel .... ★$250 $300 $400

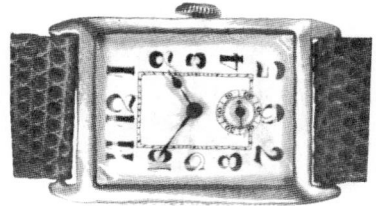

MISC. SWISS,15J., mother of pearl dial, c.1925
s. steel $150 $195 $275

MISC. SWISS,15J., wire lugs, exaggerated no.s, c.1925
silver $195 $250 $350

⊕ Some grades are not included. Their values can be
determined by comparing with **similar** age, size, metal
content, style, grades, or models such as **time only,**
chronograph, repeater etc. listed.

MISC. SWISS, 15J., wire lugs, Ca. 1918
silver $95 $125 $165

MISC. SWISS, 15J., wire lugs, Ca. 1917
silver $70 $95 $125

MISC. SWISS, 15J., wire lugs, Ca. 1918
silver $95 $135 $175

MISC. SWISS, 15J., wire lugs, Ca. 1917
silver $95 $110 $165

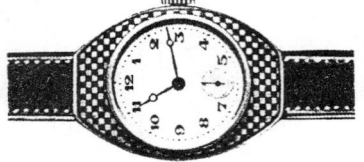

MISC. SWISS, 15J., wire lugs, Ca. 1917
base metal $55 $65 $95

MISC. SWISS, 15J., wire lugs, Ca. 1917
silver $95 $110 $165

MISC. SWISS, 15J., wire lugs, Ca. 1917
silver $95 $125 $175

MISC. SWISS, 15J., wire lugs, Ca. 1917
silver $250 $300 $375

MISC. SWISS, 15J., wire lugs, Ca. 1917
base metal $65 $75 $95

Watches listed in this BOOK as Misc. Swiss are just a few
examples of miscellaneous jobbers, distributors & jewelry
firms. Example Abc Watch Co., to Zuma Watch Co., etc. with
the name xxxx out.

MISC. SWISS, 15J., wire lugs, Ca. 1919
base metal $50 $55 $65

Watches listed in this BOOK as Misc. Swiss are just a few examples of miscellaneous jobbers, distributors & jewelry firms. Example Abc Watch Co., to Zuma Watch Co., etc. with the name xxxx out.

MISC. SWISS, 15J., wire lugs, Ca. 1917
silver $70 $95 $125

MISC. SWISS, 15J., wire lugs, Ca. 1917
14K..$95 $110 $150

MISC. SWISS, 15J., wire lugs, Ca. 1917
14K..$125 $150 $195

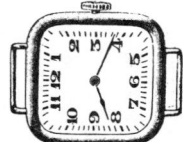

MISC. SWISS, 15J., wire lugs, Ca. 1917
14K..$95 $125 $165

MISC. SWISS, 15J., wire lugs, Ca. 1917
14K..$95 $125 $165

MISC. SWISS, 15J., wire lugs, Ca. 1917
14K..$95 $125 $165

MISC. SWISS, 15J., wire lugs, Ca. 1917
14k $95 $125 $165

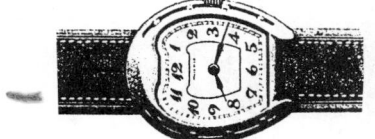

MISC. SWISS, 15J., wire lugs, Ca. 1917
14K $95 $125 $165

MISC. SWISS, 15J., horseshoe style, Ca. 1935
base metal $95 $125 $195

MISC. SWISS, 17J., nail set, 31 X 43mm, exaggerated no.s, ca.1915
18k $1,200 $1,400 $2,000

MISC. SWISS, 15J., exaggerated no.s,   ca.1916
silver $600 $650 $850

MISC. SWISS, 15J., exaggerated no.s, Ca.1916
18K...................................$900 $1,000 $1,200

MISC. SWISS, 15J., exaggerated no.s, Ca.1916
18K...................................$800 $1,000 $1,400

MISC. SWISS, 15J., exaggerated no.s, Ca.1920
14K...................................$300 $350 $600

MISC. SWISS, 15J., exaggerated no.s, Ca.1916
18K...................................$800 $900 $1,200

MISC. SWISS, 15J., exaggerated no.s, wire lugs, Ca.1916
14K...................................$200 $250 $400

Watches listed in this BOOK as Misc. Swiss are just a few examples of miscellaneous jobbers, distributors & jewelry
firms. Example Abc Watch Co., to Zuma Watch Co., etc.
with the name xxxx out.

MISC. SWISS, 15J., exaggerated no.s, Ca.1916
18K $400 $450 $600

MISC. SWISS, 15J., exaggerated no.s, Ca.1916
18K $1,400 $1,500 $1,800

MISC. SWISS, 15J., exaggerated no.s, wire lugs, Ca.1916
silver $95 $125 $195

MISC. SWISS, 15J., exaggerated no.s, wire lugs, Ca.1916
silver $95 $125 $195

MISC. SWISS, 15J., exaggerated no.s, Ca.1916
silver $85 $110 $165

MISC. SWISS, 15J., wire lugs, Ca.1917
silver $70 $80 $125

MISC. SWISS, 15J., wire lugs, Ca.1917
silver ....$95　　$125　　$175

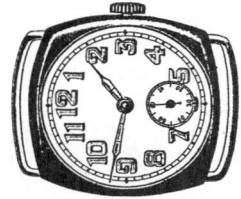

MISC. SWISS, 15J., wire lugs, Ca.1917
silver ....$95　　$125　　$175

MISC. SWISS, 15J., wire lugs, Ca.1917
14k ....$95　　$125　　$175

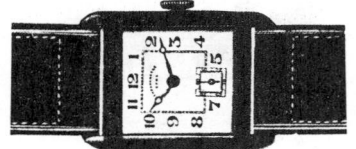

MISC. SWISS, 15J., Ca.1925
14K..$125　　$150　　$195

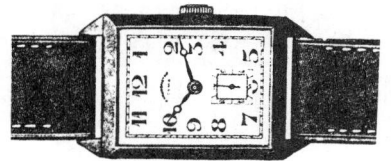

MISC. SWISS, 15J., Ca.1925
14K..$125　　$150　　$195

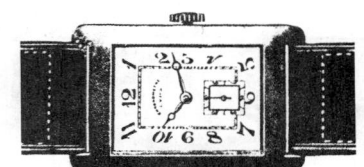

MISC. SWISS, 15J., Ca.1925
14K ....$125　　$150　　$195

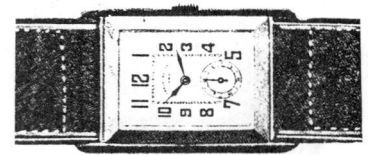

MISC. SWISS, 15J., Ca.1925
14K ....$125　　$150　　$195

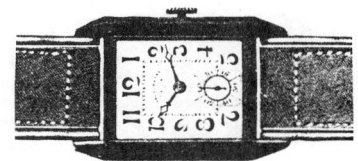

MISC. SWISS, 15J., Ca.1925
14K ....$125　　$150　　$195

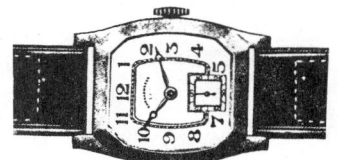

MISC. SWISS, 15J., Ca.1925
14K ....$125　　$150　　$195

MISC. SWISS, 15J., Ca.1925
14K ....$125　　$150　　$195

🕐 A collector should expect to pay modestly higher prices
at local shops

Wrist Watches listed in this section are priced at the collectable
fair market **Trade Show** level as **complete** watches having an
original gold-filled case and stainless steel back, also with
original dial, leather watch band, and the entire original movement in good working order with no repairs needed.

Watches listed in this BOOK as Misc. Swiss are just a few examples of miscellaneous jobbers, distributors & jewelry firms. Example Abc Watch Co., to Zuma Watch Co., etc. with the name xxxx out.

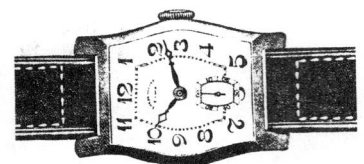

MISC. SWISS, 15J., Ca.1925
14K..$125 $150 $195

MISC. SWISS, 15J., Ca.1925
14K..$125 $150 $195

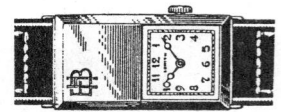

MISC. SWISS, 15J., Ca.1930
14K..$195 $250 $325

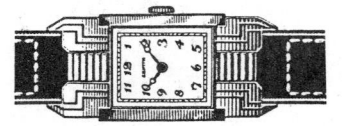

MISC. SWISS, 15J., Ca.1930
18K..$250 $300 $375

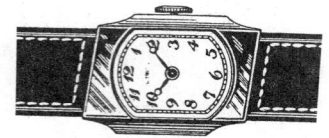

MISC. SWISS, 15J., Ca.1930
18K..$250 $300 $375

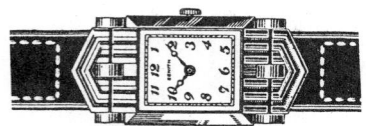

MISC. SWISS, 15J., Ca.1930
18K..$250 $300 $375

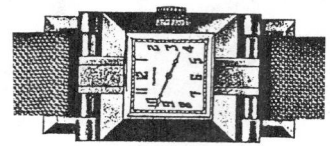

MISC. SWISS, 15J., Ca.1930
18K..$250 $300 $375

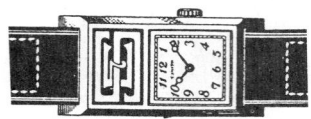

MISC. SWISS, 15J., Ca.1930
14K..$150 $175 $225

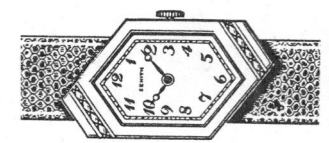

MISC. SWISS, 15J., Ca.1930
18K..$250 $300 $375

MISC. SWISS, 15J., Ca.1930
18K..$175 $195 $250

MISC. SWISS, 15J., flex lugs, Ca.1930
18K..$250 $300 $375

⏱ Some grades are not included. Their values can be determined by comparing with **similar** age, size, metal content, style, grades, or models such as **time only**, chronograph, repeater etc. listed.

MISC. SWISS, 15J., enamel dial, wire lugs, ca. 1925
silver $150 $195 $300

MISC. SWISS, 15J., wire lugs, nail set, ca.1925
silver $125 $150 $225

MISC. SWISS, 15J., aux. sec., ca. 1930s
gold filled................................ $75 $95 $135

MISC. SWISS, 17 jewels, picture watch "Flip up''
gold filled............................... $300 $350 $450

MISC. SWISS, 17J, Flip Top **winds by opening lid**, Ca.1932
gold filled.............................. $600 $700 $900
base metal $400 $500 $700

MISC. SWISS, 17J., watch top flips up to view photo, c.1950
gold filled $195 $250 $325

MISC. SWISS, 17J., day date month moon phase, Ca. 1955
gold filled $500 $600 $850
14K $1,200 $1,400 $1,800

MISC. SWISS, 17J., jump hr., wandering min., c. 1930
9k $350 $400 $500
14k $500 $600 $750

MISC. SWISS, 17J., wandering min., hr. by red mark
s. steel $150 $200 $300

MISC. SWISS, 17 jewels, fancy bezel
14k $125 $150 $195
18k $175 $195 $250

MISC. SWISS, 17 jewels, masonic symbols, c. 1950s
s. steel & gold filled $900 $1,000 $1,200

MISC. SWISS, 17 jewels, masonic symbols, c. 1975
base metal $300 $350 $425

MISC. SWISS, 15 jewels, early auto wind, c. 1930s
s. steel $400 $500 $650

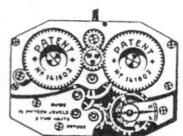

(note tandem wind)
(see watch below for prices)
MISC. SWISS, 15J, 2 barrels, 8 day movement , (8 JOURS)

MISC. SWISS, 15 jewels, 2 barrels, 8 day watch, Ca. 1935
base metal $225 $250 $350
s. steel $275 $325 $400
silver $350 $550 $650

MISC. SWISS, 17 jewels, digital hr., min.& sec.
s. steel $250 $300 $375
gold filled $275 $325 $400
s. steel (8 day) $300 $350 $550

MISC. SWISS, 15 jewels, double dial, c.1935
9K $375 $475 $625

MISC. SWISS, 15 jewels, center lugs, c.1936
9K $95 $125 $175

MISC. SWISS, 17J, drivers style winds at 12, Ca. 1930
gold filled $150 $200 $300

MISC. SWISS, 7J, "Corvette or Mercedes Benz", c.1970
base metal $60 $70 $95

Watches listed in this BOOK as Misc. Swiss are just a few examples of miscellaneous jobbers, distributors & jewelry firms. Example Abc Watch Co., to Zuma Watch Co., etc. with the name xxxx out.

MISC. SWISS, 29J, repeater, 2 jacquemart, **all original**
18k $6,000 $7,000 $8,500

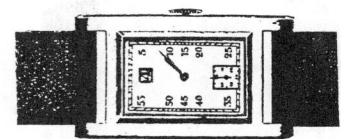

MISC. SWISS, 17J., jump hour at 12:00, Ca. 1930
14k $1,000 $1,200 $1,500
18K $1,200 $1,400 $1,800

MISC. SWISS, 17J., silver coin, Ca. 1960
silver $200 $250 $350

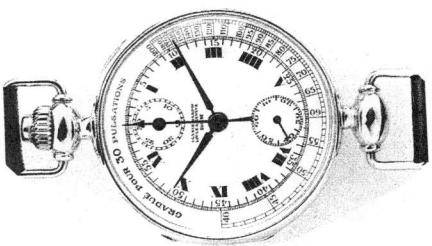

MISC. SWISS,15J., one button chronog. wind and sets at 12, center hinged lugs, enamel dial, c.1920s
silver $1,200 $1,400 $1,700

MISC. SWISS, 17J., world time, date, Ca. 1965
s. steel $75 $95 $135

MISC. SWISS,15J., 1 button chronog., enamel dial, wire lugs, Ca.1923
silver $700 $800 $1,000

MISC. SWISS, 27J., perpetual calendar, Ca. 1970
base metal $50 $60 $80

MISC. SWISS, 15-17J, enamel dial, one button chronog.
s. steel $800 $900 $1,200

MISC. SWISS, 17J.,early 1 button chronog., ca.1929
18k $1,200 $1,400 $1,800

MISC. SWISS, 15J., one button chronog., ca. 1925
silver $600 $700 $900

MISC. SWISS,15-17J, enamel dial, 1 button chronog., 2 reg.
s. steel $500 $600 $800

MISC. SWISS, 17J., one button, chronog., ca. 1950
gold filled................................$250 $300 $450

MISC. SWISS, 17J., 2 reg., chronograph
s. steel $175 $195 $250

MISC. SWISS, 17J, chronog., 2 reg.
gold filled $195 $225 $275

MISC. SWISS,17J., "chronographe" on dial, c.1940
base metal $125 $150 $195

MISC. SWISS,17J., by Venus
s. steel $125 $150 $195
14k $225 $250 $300
18K $275 $300 $350

Watches listed in this BOOK as Misc. Swiss are just a few examples of miscellaneous jobbers, distributors & jewelry
firms. Example Abc Watch Co., to Zuma Watch Co., etc.
with the name xxxx out.

MISC. SWISS, 17J., triple date, chronog., 2 reg., c.1955
s. steel $350 $400 $500

MISC. SWISS, 17J., chronog., triple date, moon ph., c. 1945
14k $900 $1,000 $1,200
s. steel $500 $600 $800

MISC. SWISS, 17 jewels, split sec. chronog., 2 reg.
18k $3,200 $3,800 $5,000
s. steel $2,000 $2,200 $2,600

MISC. SWISS, 18 jewels, Jaeger,chronog., c. 1930s
18k $600 $700 $900

MISC. SWISS, 17J., triple date, moon ph., ca. 1967
gold filled $250 $300 $400

MISC. SWISS, 17 jewels, early auto wind, c. 1930s
14k $300 $350 $500

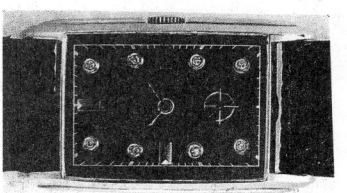

MISC. SWISS, 17J., diamond dial, Ca. 1945
14K $195 $225 $275

MISC. SWISS, 17J., diamond dial, top hat, Ca. 1945
platinum.................................$900 $1,000 $1,200

MISC. SWISS, 17J., mystery diamond dial, Ca. 1960
gold filled $175 $225 $275

MISC. SWISS, 17J., Rhinestone dial & bezel, Ca. 1950
gold filled..................................$60 $70 $95

MISC. SWISS, 17J., Rhinestone dial & bezel, Ca. 1950
gold filled..................................$60 $70 $95

MISC. SWISS, 17J., hidden lugs, Ca. 1934
gold filled..................................$50 $60 $75

MISC. SWISS, 17J., fancy lugs, Ca. 1945
14k $150 $175 $225
18K..$175 $195 $325

MISC. SWISS, 17J., fancy lugs, Ca. 1940
gold filled..................................$35 $45 $60

Watches listed in this BOOK as Misc. Swiss are just a few examples of miscellaneous jobbers, distributors & jewelry
firms. Example Abc Watch Co., to Zuma Watch Co., etc.
with the name xxxx out.

MISC. SWISS, 17J., fancy bezel, Ca. 1938
14K $125 $150 $195

MISC. SWISS, 17J., fancy bezel, Ca. 1947
gold filled $70 $80 $95
14K $125 $150 $195

MISC. SWISS, 17J., fancy bezel, Ca. 1930
18K (W)................................$150 $195 $250

MISC. SWISS, 7J., stepped case, Ca. 1935
gold filled $40 $50 $70

MISC. SWISS, 17J., wandering minute & hour, Ca. 1938
base metal $150 $195 $275

Watches listed in this BOOK as Misc. Swiss are just a few examples of miscellaneous jobbers, distributors & jewelry firms. Example Abc Watch Co., to Zuma Watch Co., etc. with the name xxxx out.

MISC. SWISS, 15J., Ca. 1938
14K...$125 $135 $175

MISC. SWISS, 17J., Fancy lugs, Ca. 1950
gold filled $95 $125 $175

MISC. SWISS, 15J., Ca. 1925
silver $70 $75 $95

MISC. SWISS, 17J., Fancy lugs, Ca. 1950
14K $150 $175 $225

MISC. SWISS, 21J., curved, Ca. 1938
gold filled................................$125 $150 $195

MISC. SWISS, 21J., Fancy lugs, Ca. 1955
Note: **After Market lugs add on**
18K $175 $200 $275

MISC. SWISS, 17J., Fancy lugs, Chronometer, Ca. 1950
14K...$150 $175 $225

MISC. SWISS, 17J., Fancy lugs & bezel, Ca. 1950
gold filled................................$75 $95 $125

MISC. SWISS, 17J., Fancy lugs, Ca. 1948
gold filled $75 $95 $135

🕐 Pricing in this Guide are fair market price for **COMPLETE** watches which are reflected from the "**NAWCC**" National and regional shows.

🕐 Some grades are not included. Their values can be determined by comparing with **similar** age, size, metal content, style, grades, or models such as **time only**, chronograph, repeater etc. listed.

MISC. SWISS, 22J., Military, Ca. 1941
base metal $400 $500 $700

MISC. SWISS, 15J., Military, Ca. 1942
s. steel $75 $90 $125

MISC. SWISS, 16J., Military, Ca. 1940
base metal $60 $70 $95

Watches listed in this BOOK as Misc. Swiss are just a few examples of miscellaneous jobbers, distributors & jewelry
firms. Example Abc Watch Co., to Zuma Watch Co., etc.
with the name xxxx out.

MISC. SWISS, 17J., enamel & gold bezel, pin set, c.1925
18k $175 $195 $250

MISC. SWISS, 15J., wire lugs, Ca. 1930
14K rose $75 $95 $120

MISC. SWISS, 15J., Ruby on case, Ca. 1950
14K $75 $95 $120

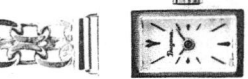

MISC. SWISS, 15J., Ca. 1930
14K case & band $195 $225 $275

MISC. SWISS, 15J., **Ring watch**, Ca. 1955
14K $85 $95 $125

MISC. SWISS, 21J., horseshoe shaped, Ca. 1939
gold filled $95 $125 $175

MONARCH, 7 jewels, stepped case
gold filled.................................$40 $50 $65

MONARCH, 7 jewels,
gold filled.................................$40 $50 $65

MONARCH, 7 jewels, engraved bezel, curved
gold filled.................................$40 $50 $65

MONARCH, 7 jewels , curved
14k $125 $150 $195
gold filled.................................$70 $95 $125

MONTBRILLANT, 15J., one button chronog. Ca 1915-20
MONTBRILLANT = early **BREITLING**
18k $1,500 $1,800 $2,500

MONTE, 16J., "Ancre", ca.1938
14k $95 $125 $175

MORIVA,17J., auto-w. with wind indicator,
s. steel $60 $70 $95

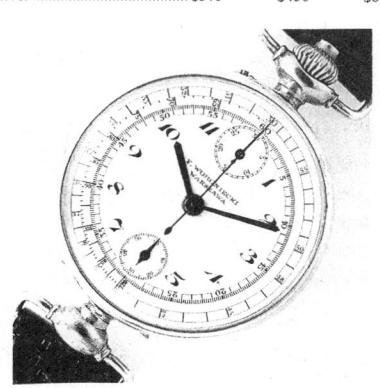

HY. MOSER & CIE., 14J., "Signal Corps USA", ctr. lugs
silver $375 $450 $600

HY. MOSER & CIE., 14-18J., one button chronograph, wind
and set at 12, center lugs, 2 reg. Ca. 1920s
silver $1,400 $1,500 $1,800

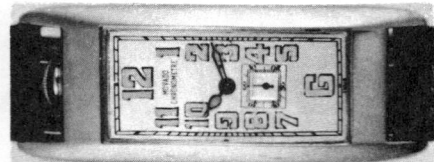

MOVADO, 15J., polyplan, winds at 12 o'clock, 46mm,
curved, c. 1910
18k $4,000 $4,500 $6,000

MOVADO, 15J., polyplan, winds at 12 o'clock,
14k $3,000 $3,500 $4,500

MOVADO, 15J., polyplan, winds at 12 o'clock,
silver $2,000 $2,400 $3,000

Movado, Purse Watches See P.W. section Movado

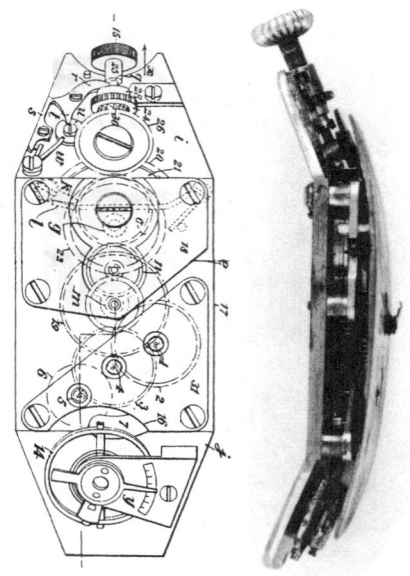

ABOVE: **Polyplan**
MOVADO, side view of movement with three inclined plans.

MOVADO, 15J., "Chronometre", c.1930
14k $175 $250 $325

MOVADO, 17J., day date month, "Sportsman"
14k $300 $350 $450

MOVADO, 17J., day date month, snap back
18k $500 $550 $700

MOVADO, 17J., triple date, snap back ," calendomatic"
18k $600 $650 $800

MOVADO, 28J., date, "Kingmatic", c.1959
s. steel $80 $95 $120
14k(w)..................................$195 $225 $300

MOVADO, 17J., month date, ca. 1950s
14k $195 $225 $325

MOVADO, 17J., 1 button chronog., c.1948
s. steel $450 $500 $600

MOVADO, 17 jewels, day-date-month, c. 1945
18k	....$400	$500	$700
14k	....$200	$250	$325
s. steel	....................................$175	$195	$250

MOVADO, 17J., chronog., 2 reg., c.1940
14k $800 $900 $1,200

MOVADO, 17J, triple date, moon phases, Ca. 1959
pink GF & s.s.	.....................$1,000	$1,100	$1,400
s. steel	....................................$900	$1,000	$1,200

MOVADO, 17J., 3 reg. chronog.
s. steel $800 $900 $1,200

MOVADO, 17J., 3 reg. chronog.,
18k	....................................$2,000	$2,200	$2,600
14k	....................................$1,500	$1,700	$2,200
s. steel	....................................$800	$900	$1,200

MOVADO, 17J., "tempograf, chronog., 2 reg., c.1935
s. steel $1,000 $1,200 $1,500

The Movado trademark M over flat V was Registered in 1958.

MOVADO, 17J., 3 reg. chronog., date, auto wind
18k $700 $800 $1,000
s. steel $300 $350 $500

MOVADO, 17J., center sec., auto wind, c.1942
14k $150 $175 $225

MOVADO, 17J., El Primero date at 5, auto wind, c.1972
s. steel $300 $350 $500

MOVADO, 17J., center sec., auto wind, c.1948
14k $175 $195 $250

MOVADO,17J., RF#2652, rotating chapter,cal.352, c.1958
s. steel $250 $300 $450

MOVADO, 17J., "Cronoplan", Ca. 1940s
s. steel $500 $600 $800

MOVADO, 15J., aux. sec., cal.75, c.1946
s. steel $75 $95 $150

MOVADO, 17J., center sec., cal.261, c.1948
18k $195 $250 $325

Some grades are not included. Their values can be
determined by comparing with **similar** age, size, metal
content, style, grades, or models such as **time only**,
chronograph, repeater etc. listed.

MOVADO, 17J., aux. sec., cal.135, c.1960
s. steel $65 $75 $95

MOVADO, 17J., auto-wind, cal.8577, c.1957
14k $125 $150 $195

MOVADO, 17J., Tiffany & Co. on dial, center sec.,
14k $150 $175 $225

MOVADO, 15J., 2 colors of gold, tonneau, Ca. 1940
18k $300 $400 $650

The Movado trademark M over flat V was Registered in 1958.

MOVADO, 17J., "Kingmatic", center sec.
14k $125 $150 $225

MOVADO, 17J., center sec.
s. steel $75 $95 $150

MOVADO, 20J., auto-wind,
14k $150 $175 $225

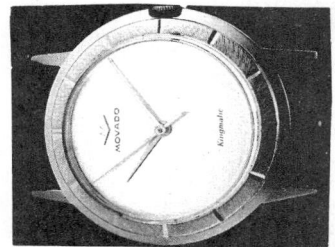

MOVADO, 28J., center sec.,"Kingmatic",
14k $150 $175 $225

In about 1895, L. A. & I. Ditesheim (before Movado) used trade
names for pocket watches such as Ralco, Tanit, Ultra, Apogee,
Record, Talma, Noblesse, Salud, Negus, Bonne, Belgravia,
Surete and Mintral.

MOVADO, 17J., aux. sec.
18k $175 $195 $275

MOVADO, 15 jewels, aux. sec.
14k C&B...............................$400 $450 $550

MOVADO, 17J., auto-w., ca. 1949
14k $175 $195 $250

MOVADO, 17 jewels, aux. sec., center lugs
14k $150 $175 $225

MOVADO, 17J., nonmagnetic, RF # 11730, Ca. 1940
s. steel $95 $125 $165

MOVADO, 17J., cal.7025, GJS, c.1964
18k $195 $250 $325

MOVADO, 15 jewels, center lugs, c. 1930
18k $250 $300 $400

MOVADO, 17J., hidden lugs, tu-tone dial, c.1960
18k $300 $350 $425

MOVADO, 17J., textured 18k dial
18k $250 $300 $400

MOVADO, 17 jewels, "Museum", date at 12 o'clock
14k C&B...............................$400 $450 $600

MOVADO, 15 jewels, fancy lugs
18k $300 $325 $400

MOVADO, 17J., wide bezel, c.1958
gold filled..................................$75 $95 $150

MOVADO, 17J., diamond bezel,
18k $175 $195 $275

MOVADO, 17J., RF#621, c.1932
gold filled..................................$75 $125 $175

MOVADO, 17J., stepped case, "Curviplan", GJS, c.1942
14k $250 $300 $400

🕐 Pricing in this Guide are fair market price for **COMPLETE**
watches which are reflected from the "**NAWCC**" National and
regional shows.

MOVADO, 17J., aux. sec., c.1940
14k $150 $195 $275

MOVADO, 17J., extended lugs, c.1945
14k $150 $175 $250

MOVADO, 17J., aux. sec., c.1945
14k $150 $175 $250

MOVADO, 17J., extended lugs, GJS, c.1940
14k $150 $175 $250

MOVADO, 17J., tu-tone case, RF#13906, Ca.1948
14k $175 $200 $275

MOVADO, 17J.,"Andy Warhol Times/5", Ca.1988
Note: Total of **5** watches (only 3 watches shown)
Quartz (250 made).... ★ ★ ★$4,000 $5,000 $7,000

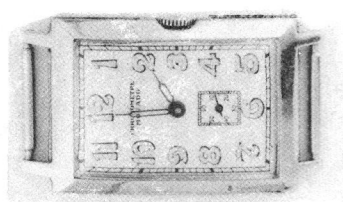

MOVADO, 15 jewels, curved, chronometre
14k $400 $450 $525

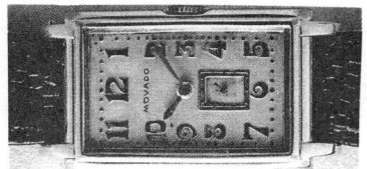

MOVADO, 17J., cal#510, ca.1941
14k $300 $350 $425

MOVADO, 17J., curviplan,
gold filled.................................$200 $250 $325

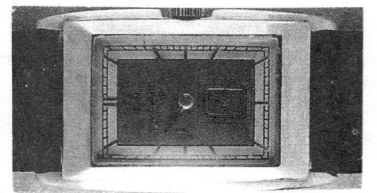

MOVADO, 17J., curviplan, ca.1941
14k $400 $450 $525

MOVADO, 17J., RF # 43872, ca.1945
14k $200 $250 $375

Wrist Watches listed in this section are priced at the collectable fair market **Trade Show** level as **complete** watches having an original gold-filled case and stainless steel back, also with original dial, leather watch band, and the entire original movement in good working order with no repairs needed.

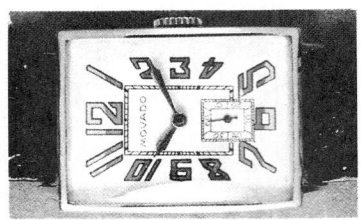

MOVADO, 15 jewels, exaggerated numbers, c. 1929
18k $400 $450 $550

MOVADO, 17 jewels
14k $95 $150 $225

MOVADO, 17 jewels, automatic, tank style
18k $300 $350 $425

MOVADO, 17 jewels, fancy lugs, c. 1947
14k $95 $150 $225

MOVADO, 17J., Ca. 1940s
14k $125 $150 $225

🕐 Pricing in this Guide are fair market price for **COMPLETE** watches which are reflected from the "**NAWCC**" National and regional shows.

MOVADO, 17 jewels
18k $300 $350 $425

MOVADO, 15 jewels, cal. 440, Ca. 1940
18k..$250 $300 $475

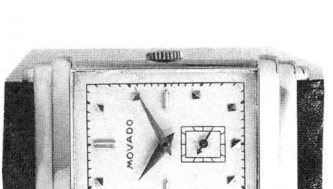

MOVADO, 17 jewels, , Ca.1948
14k $300 $350 $425
18k $400 $450 $525

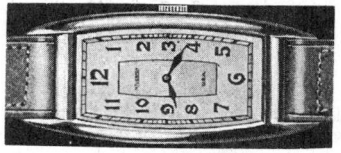

MOVADO, 17 jewels, ladies, alarm, Ca.1960
18k..$175 $195 $250

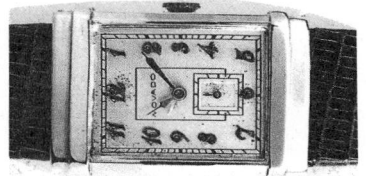

MOVADO, 17 jewels, hidden lugs, Ca.1940
14k $300 $350 $425

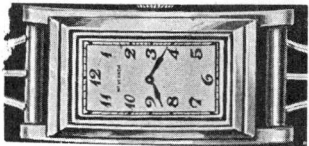

Mt. VERNON, 15 & 21 jewels, curvex style
gold plate..................................$30 $40 $55

MOVADO,17 jewels, curviplan, , GJS, Ca.1937
14k $300 $350 $425

MOVADO, 17 jewels, cal.150, Ca.1940
14k $175 $195 $250

Mt. VERNON, 15 jewels, curvex style
gold plate..................................$30 $40 $55

Mt. VERNON, 15 jewels, stepped case
s. steel.......................................$40 $50 $65

Wrist Watches listed in this section are priced at the collectable
fair market Trade Show level as **complete** watches having an
original gold-filled case and stainless steel back, also with
original dial, leather watch band, and the entire original movement in good working order with no repairs needed.

MOVADO MOVEMENT IDENTIFICATION

Caliber 35    Caliber 65    Caliber 575    Caliber25, 27-Sweep Second

Caliber 28    Caliber 575, Ermeto-Baby    Caliber 578, Ermeto Calendine    579, Calendoplan Baby

Caliber 5    Caliber 15    Caliber 50SP    Caliber 105, 107-Center Second

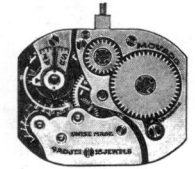

Caliber 190   Caliber 375, 377-Center Second   Caliber 440, 443-Center Second

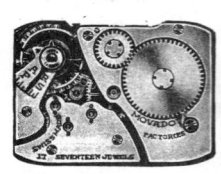

Caliber 510   Caliber 260M, 261   Caliber 150MN, 157-Sweep Second

Polyplan
(first used in1922)

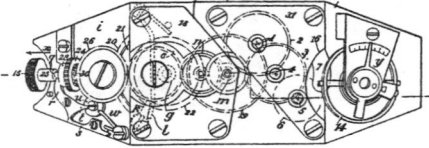

Caliber 155, Calendermeto

Caliber 470, 477-Center Second

Caliber 473, 473SC-Calendar/Moon phase

Caliber 475, 475SC-Center Second

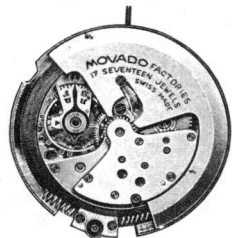

Caliber 225, 255M

Caliber 115

Caliber 118

Caliber 220, 220M

Caliber 221, 226

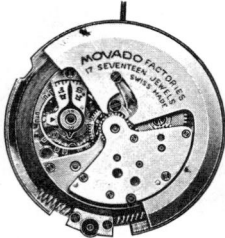

Caliber 223, 228

Caliber 224, 224A

Chronograph

Cal. 90M, 95M

12''' – 26,60 mm

U. NARDIN, 29 J., "Astrolabium," self wind, waterproof, local time, equinoctial time, months, signs of zodiac, elevation & azimuth of sun & moon, aspect in which sun & moon stand to each other. **recent**
18k $9,000 $10,000 $12,500

U. NARDIN, 17J., one button pulsations, ca.1920
18k $1,800 $2,000 $2,500

U. NARDIN, 17J., one button, Pulsations, c. 1920
18k $1,800 $2,000 $2,500

Pricing in this Guide are fair market price for **COMPLETE** watches which are reflected from the "**NAWCC**" National and regional shows.

Some grades are not included. Their values can be determined by comparing with **similar** age, size, metal content, style, grades, or models such as **time only**, chronograph, repeater etc. listed.

U. NARDIN, 17 jewels, chronog., c. 1950s
18k..$1,500 $1,600 $1,900

U. NARDIN, 17 jewels, split sec. chronog., c. 1910
silver..$3,500 $4,000 $5,500

U. NARDIN, 17 jewels, chronog., 3 reg. c. 1940s
18k..$1,800 $2,000 $2,400

U. NARDIN, 25 jewels, date
14k..$175 $195 $275

U. NARDIN, 17 jewels, auto wind, c. 1952
14k $175 $195 $275

U. NARDIN,21J.,auto-wind
18k...$250 $275 $350

U. NARDIN, 17J., center sec., chronometer, c.1950
gold filled................................$75 $95 $150

U. NARDIN, 17J., aux sec.
s. steel.......................................$95 $125 $175

U. NARDIN, 17J., center sec., auto-wind, c.1950
14k $175 $225 $275

U. NARDIN, 17J., aux. sec.
18k...$200 $225 $275

U. NARDIN, 17J., center sec., auto-wind, c.1950
18k $250 $275 $350

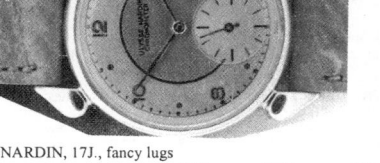

U. NARDIN, 17J., fancy lugs
18k...$250 $300 $425

⊕ A collector should expect to pay modestly higher prices at local shops

⊕ Pricing in this Guide are fair market price for **COMPLETE** watches which are reflected from the "**NAWCC**" National and regional shows.

U. NARDIN, 17J., aux. sec., carved lugs, c.1950
14k $195 $225 $350

U. NARDIN, 17J., aux. sec., chronometer, c.1950
14k $125 $150 $195

U. NARDIN, 17J., aux. sec., chronometer, c.1947
18k $195 $225 $300

U. NARDIN, 17J., aux. sec., chronometer, C.1951
14k $150 $175 $225

Wrist Watches listed in this section are priced at the collectable
fair market Trade Show level as **complete** watches having an
original gold-filled case and stainless steel back, also with
original dial, leather watch band, and the entire original movement in good working order with no repairs needed.

🕐 Some grades are not included. Their values can be
determined by comparing with **similar** age, size, metal
content, style, grades, or models such as **time only**,
chronograph, repeater etc. listed.

U. NARDIN, 17J., aux. sec., chronometer, c.1964
gold plate.................................$65 $85 $125

U. NARDIN, 17J., aux. sec., chronometer, c.1948
gold filled.................................$75 $95 $150

U. NARDIN, 17J., fancy lugs
14k...$150 $175 $225

U. NARDIN, 25J., chronometer, auto-w., date, c.1975
s. steel.....................................$125 $150 $225

U. NARDIN, 17J., fluted case, chronometer
14k $150 $175 $225

U. NARDIN, 17J., aux. sec., chronometer, c.1949
14k $125 $150 $195

U. NARDIN, 17J., aux. sec., chronometer, c.1950
18k $175 $200 $275

U. NARDIN, 17J., extended side lugs, chronometer, c.1951
14k $150 $175 $250

U. NARDIN, 17 jewels, faceted crystal & bezel
s. steel $125 $135 $175

Some grades are not included. Their values can be determined by comparing with **similar** age, size, metal content, style, grades, or models such as **time only**, chronograph, repeater etc. listed.

U. NARDIN, 17 jewels, chronometer, c. 1935
18k $275 $300 $375

U. NARDIN, 17 jewels, WW I military style
s. steel $450 $500 $600

U. NARDIN, 15 jewels, c. 1925
gold filled (w) $95 $125 $175

U. NARDIN, 17J., lady's chronometer, c.1947
14k C&B $375 $400 $500

NATIONAL, 15 jewels, day-date-month
gold filled $50 $75 $125

NATIONAL W. Co., 16 J., 1 button Chronog., red & black color enamel dial, Ca. 1925
silver $700 $800 $1,100

NEW ENGLAND W. Co., 7J., Addison, Alden, Cavour, Hale, and other models, Ca.1915, colored dial add ($25)
14k $60 $70 $95
gold filled................................$25 $30 $45

NEW HAVEN, 7 jewels, "Gem", engraved bezel
base metal $20 $25 $35

NEW HAVEN, 7 jewels, stepped case
base metal $20 $25 $35

⌚ Pricing in this Guide are fair market price for **COMPLETE** watches which are reflected from the "**NAWCC**" National and regional shows.

NEW HAVEN, 7 jewels
base metal.................................$15 $20 $30

NEW HAVEN,2 jewels, "Elf" ladies, etched case
base metal................................. $10 $15 $25

NEW HAVEN, 7 jewels, "Duchess" ladies, etched case
gold plate.................................... $5 $10 $15

NEWMARK, 17J., military chronog., c.1979
s. steel...................................... $250 $300 $400

NEW YORK STANDARD, 7 jewels, wire lugs
gold filled..................................$25 $35 $50
base metal..................................$15 $20 $30

NICE WATCH Co., 17J., one button chronog., c.1930
base metal $250 $300 $375

NICOLET W. CO., 17J., one button chronog., Ca. 1960
gold filled............................... $325 $375 $450

CHARLES NICOLET, 17J., chronog., ca. 1945
18k $300 $350 $450

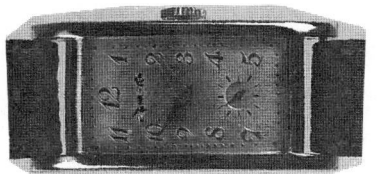

MARC NICOLET, 17J., aux. seconds
14k $95 $125 $165

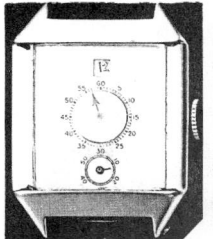

NITON, 18J., jump hr., (showing dial and movement)
(also made ebauche for P.P.&CO.)
18k(W) $3,000 $3,500 $4,500

NIVADA, 21J., center sec., c.1960
base metal................................. $30 $40 $55

NIVADA, 21J., center sec., date, auto-w, c.1965
s. steel....................................... $35 $45 $65

NIVADA, 25J., waterproof, triple date, moon ph., c. 1940
14k.. $400 $450 $550
gold filled............................... $150 $175 $225

🕑 Pricing in this Guide are fair market price for **COMPLETE**
watches which are reflected from the "**NAWCC**" National and
regional shows.

NORMANDIE, 17 jewels, compass, c. 1945
s. steel $55 $75 $125

NORMANDIE, 17J., gold train, hidden lugs, cal.4873
14k $95 $125 $175

OCTO, 17J., fluted lugs,
14k $95 $125 $175

OFAIR, 17J., chronog., cal. Valjoux 72c, c.1948
gold filled...............................$250 $300 $400
14k $450 $500 $650
18k $600 $650 $800

Wrist Watches listed in this section are priced at the collectable
fair market Trade Show level as **complete** watches having an
original gold-filled case and stainless steel back, also with
original dial, leather watch band, and the entire original movement in good working order with no repairs needed.

⊕ Some grades are not included. Their values can be
determined by comparing with **similar** age, size, metal
content, style, grades, or models such as **time only**,
chronograph, repeater etc. listed.

OGIVAL, 17 jewels, auto wind
gold filled.................................$30 $40 $60

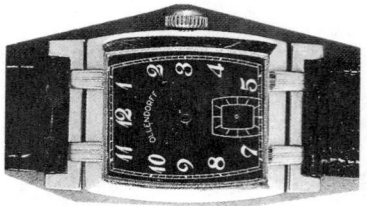

OLLENDORFF, 17 jewels, fancy lugs
14k..$125 $150 $195

OLLENDORFF, 17 jewels, movement plates made of **gold**
14k..$175 $195 $250

OLLENDORFF, 7J., direct read, stepped case, c.1930
base metal.................................$75 $95 $125

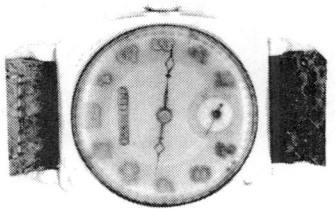

OLLENDORFF, 15J., engraved bevel,
chrome plated...........................$25 $30 $40

OLMA, 17J., **early** auto-wind, by Wyler, c.1928
s. steel $150 $175 $225

OLMA, 17J., large crab legs style lugs
gold plate $45 $55 $75

OLYMPIA, 15 jewels, double dial, c. 1938
s. steel $195 $225 $300

OMEGA, 15J., center lugs, enamel dial, Ca. 1930
18k $300 $400 $550

OMEGA, 15J., wire lugs, **enamel dial**, Ca. 1925
silver $150 $200 $275

OMEGA, 15J., wire lugs, ca. 1930s
18k..$400 $500 $650

OMEGA, 15J., wire lugs,
14k..$350 $400 $550

OMEGA, 17 jewels, center sec.
14k..$150 $175 $225

OMEGA, 17 jewels, one button chronog., c. 1935
18k..$2,500 $2,800 $3,500

⏱ Pricing in this Guide are fair market price for **COMPLETE** watches which are reflected from the "**NAWCC**" National and regional shows.

⏱ Some grades are not included. Their values can be determined by comparing with **similar** age, size, metal content, style, grades, or models such as **time only**, chronograph, repeater etc. listed.

OMEGA, 17J., 2 reg. chronog., ca. 1940s
s. steel	$400	$450	$600
14k	$700	$750	$900
18k	$1,000	$1,100	$1,400

OMEGA, 17J., "Speedmaster", chronog., c. 1970
s. steel	$500	$600	$800

OMEGA, 17J., 2 reg., chronog., c. 1958
18k	$900	$1,000	$1,200

OMEGA, 17J., "Speedmaster Pro.", chronog., c. 1969
"the first watch worn on the **moon**" on back of watch
18k C&B	$3,500	$4,000	$5,500
s. steel	$600	$700	$900

OMEGA, 17 jewels, chronog., "Seamaster," c. 1963
14k	$1,500	$1,600	$1,900
s. steel	$600	$700	$850

OMEGA, 17J., "Speedmaster Pro. Mark II", auto-w, c.1975
s. steel	$250	$300	$400

⊕ Some grades are not included. Their values can be determined by comparing with **similar** age, size, metal content, style, grades, or models such as **time only**, chronograph, repeater etc. listed.

⊕ Pricing in this Guide are fair market price for **COMPLETE** watches which are reflected from the "**NAWCC**" National and regional shows.

OMEGA, 17J., "Seamaster", chronog., cal.321, c. 1962
s. steel	$600	$700	$850
14k	$1,500	$1,600	$1,900
18k	$1,700	$1,800	$2,100

OMEGA, 22J., "Seamaster", date, 2 reg., auto-wind, c.1975
s. steel $300 $350 $500

OMEGA, 17J., "Seamaster", chronostop, auto-w., c.1965
s. steel....................................$250 $300 $400

OMEGA, 17J., Speedmaster Pro. MarkIII, auto-w, c.1978
s. steel $400 $500 $650

OMEGA, 17J., "Seamaster", chronostop., rotating bezel,
auto-w
s. steel....................................$300 $350 $500

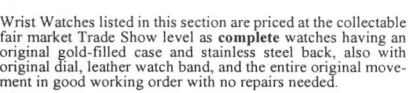

OMEGA, 17J., Speedmaster, auto-wind, chronog., c.1975
s. steel $400 $500 $650

Wrist Watches listed in this section are priced at the collectable
fair market Trade Show level as **complete** watches having an
original gold-filled case and stainless steel back, also with
original dial, leather watch band, and the entire original movement in good working order with no repairs needed.

🕐 Some grades are not included. Their values can be
determined by comparing with **similar** age, size, metal
content, style, grades, or models such as **time only**,
chronograph, repeater etc. listed.

OMEGA, 17J., "Seamaster", chronog., cal.321, c.1970
s. steel....................................$300 $400 $550

🕐 A collector should expect to pay modestly higher prices
at local shops

🕐 Pricing in this Guide are fair market price for **COMPLETE**
watches which are reflected from the "**NAWCC**" National and
regional shows.

OMEGA, 17 jewels, chronog., "Seamaster", 3 reg., auto-w
14k $600 $700 $900

OMEGA, 17 jewels, chronog., "Flightmaster", 3 reg., auto-w
18kC&B $2,800 $3,400 $4,500
s. steel $400 $550 $800

OMEGA, 17 jewels, day-date-month, moon phase
18k $1,200 $1,300 $1,600
14k $1,000 $1,100 $1,400

OMEGA, 17J., day-date-month, moon phase, c. 1940
s. steel $450 $500 $600
14k $1,000 $1,100 $1,400

OMEGA, 17J., day-date-month, moon phase, c. 1950s
14k $2,000 $2,400 $2,800
18k $2,500 $2,800 $3,500

OMEGA, 24J.,date, "Constellation", auto wind, chronometer
18k $600 $700 $900
14k $400 $500 $650
2 tone case $275 $325 $400

OMEGA, 24J., "Constellation", auto-wind, c.1960
14k $450 $550 $700
2 tone case $275 $325 $400
s. steel $225 $250 $300

OMEGA, 24J., "Constellation", auto-wind, c.1968
gold filled $225 $250 $300

OMEGA, 24J., "Constellation", auto-wind, c.1969
s. steel $175 $195 $300

OMEGA, 24 jewels, "Constellation," auto wind, date
18k .... ★ ★ ★ $1,800 $2,200 $2,800

OMEGA, 7J., "Constellation", **quartz**, cal.1342, c.1970
18k & s. s. $350 $400 $525

OMEGA, 24J., "Constellation," auto-w., date, c. 1959
18k $550 $625 $725

OMEGA, 17-24J., Chronometre, auto-w.,
14k $350 $450 $700

OMEGA, 17 jewels, "Seamaster", date, auto-w., waterproof
18k $400 $450 $525

OMEGA, electronic, "F300," c. 1950s
18k C&B $700 $750 $900

OMEGA, 24J., "Seamaster", auto-w, date, Ca. 1963
18k (rose) $500 $550 $700

OMEGA, 24J., "Seamaster", auto-wind, c.1962
14k $300 $350 $450
s. steel $150 $195 $300

OMEGA, 17 jewels, "Seamaster," auto wind
14k...$300 $350 $450

OMEGA, 24J., "Seamaster", auto-wind, cal.562, c.1962
gold filled..................................$95 $125 $175

OMEGA, 17J.,"Seamaster",chronometer, auto wind
18k..$450 $550 $700

OMEGA, 23J.,"Seamaster", auto-wind, cal.1022, c.1978
s. steel $95 $125 $175

OMEGA, 17J., "Seamaster", auto wind, c.1953
gold filled..................................$95 $125 $175

OMEGA, 17 jewels, automatic, date at 6
14k $400 $500 $700

OMEGA, 17J., "Seamaster Deluxe", auto-wind
18k..$450 $550 $700

OMEGA, 20J., "Seamaster", auto-wind, cal.501, c.1957
s. steel $150 $195 $300

OMEGA, 24J., "Constellation", auto-wind, cal.551, c.1962
2 tone case............................. $225 $250 $350
14k... $450 $550 $800

OMEGA, 17J., "Seamaster", auto-wind, cal.1570, c.1955
gold filled.............................. $100 $125 $175

OMEGA, 16-18J., gold train, center seconds, auto wind
s. steel.................................... $150 $195 $300

OMEGA, 24J., "Constellation", chronometer, auto-wind
2 tone case $225 $250 $350
18k $600 $700 $900

OMEGA, 16J., center sec., c.1940
s. steel................................... $225 $250 $300

OMEGA, 24J., "Constellation", auto-wind, cal.505, c.1958
18k $650 $750 $1,100

OMEGA, 16J., **U.S. Army**, cal., c.1948
s. steel................................... $250 $275 $350

OMEGA, 16J., center sec., c.1948
s. steel $225 $250 $300

OMEGA, 15J., Military, large, c.1930
s. steel....................................$350 $450 $600

OMEGA, 15J., Military (England), c.1946
s. steel $300 $400 $650

OMEGA, 17J., Seamaster, diamond dial, cal.563,
auto wind, Ca.1955
14K...$350 $400 $500
s. steel....................................$300 $350 $425

OMEGA, 17J., "Railmaster", center sec.
s. steel $300 $350 $450

OMEGA, 17J., 12 diamond dial, center sec.
14k(W) $350 $400 $500

OMEGA, 15-17J., 24 hour marked, Ca. 1930
s. steel $300 $350 $500

OMEGA, 17J., fancy lugs, ca.1948
14k...$300 $350 $450

OMEGA, 17J., aux. sec., cal.360, c.1950
14k..$250 $300 $400

OMEGA, 17J., aux.sec., cal.266, c.1956
s. steel $150 $195 $300

OMEGA, 17J., auto-wind, c.1949
18k..$300 $350 $500

OMEGA, 17J., aux. sec., cal.266, c.1945
14k $300 $350 $450

OMEGA, 17J., auto-wind, cal.342, c.1955
gold filled................................$95 $125 $175

OMEGA, 17J., auto-wind, c.1952
18k $350 $450 $600

OMEGA, 17J., seamaster, auto-wind
s. steel....................................$200 $250 $350

OMEGA, 17J., auto-wind, c.1949
18k $350 $450 $600

Pricing in this Guide are fair market price for **COMPLETE** watches which are reflected from the "**NAWCC**" National and regional shows.

OMEGA, 17J., aux. sec., cal.302, c.1948
gold filled..................................$75 $95 $125

OMEGA, 15J., extended lugs, c.1939
14k $325 $350 $400
gold filled................................$95 $125 $175

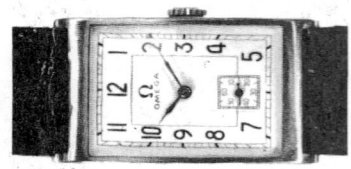

OMEGA, 15J., aux. sec., c.1937
s. steel $125 $150 $225

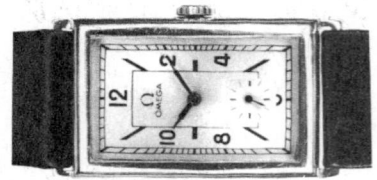

OMEGA, 15J., small lugs, c.1935
gold filled................................$95 $125 $175

OMEGA, 17J., beveled case, c.1936
s. steel $95 $125 $175

Wrist Watches listed in this section are priced at the collectable
fair market **Trade Show** level as **complete** watches having an
original gold-filled case and stainless steel back, also with
original dial, leather watch band, and the entire original movement in good working order with no repairs needed.

OMEGA, 15J., small lugs, c.1937
s. steel...................................$125 $150 $195

OMEGA, 17J., fancy lugs, ca. 1950s
14k..$150 $175 $250

OMEGA, 17J., faceted crystal,
14k(W) $125 $150 $225

OMEGA, 17J., fancy lugs, ca. 1948
14k..$150 $175 $250

OMEGA, 17J., 9 diamond dial, ca. 1955
14k(W) $125 $150 $200

OMEGA, 17 jewels, aux. sec.
14k **C&B** $600 $650 $750

OMEGA, 17J., flared & extended lugs, cal.301, c.1948
14k $300 $325 $400

OMEGA, 17J., flared & sculptured lugs, cal.302, c.1953
14k $200 $225 $300

OMEGA, 17J., flared & hidden lugs, c.1947
14k $150 $175 $250

OMEGA, 17 jewels, hidden lugs, asymmetric
14k $600 $650 $800

⊕ A collector should expect to pay modestly higher prices
at local shops

OMEGA, 17 jewels, curved center lugs, auto wind
14k...$200 $250 $325

OMEGA, 17 jewels, sculptured lugs
14k...$300 $350 $500

OMEGA, 17 jewels, c. 1948
14k...$195 $250 $325

OMEGA, 17 jewels, c. 1938
14k...$175 $195 $275

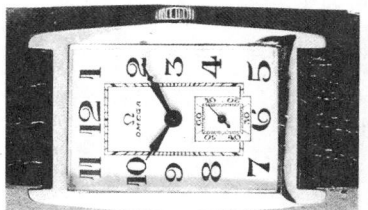

OMEGA, 15 jewels, large, c. 1935
14k...$250 $300 $350

OMEGA, 17J., wide bezel, center sec., auto-w., c.1955
14k $175 $195 $275

OMEGA, 17J., RF#347sc, cal.471, auto wind, c.1956
18k $195 $250 $325

OMEGA, 17J., wide bezel & lugs, cal.369, auto wind, c.1947
platinum ....★★$1,700 $2,000 $2,700

OMEGA, 17J., "De Ville",
18k $195 $250 $325

OMEGA, 17J., cal.620, c.1960
14k $125 $150 $225

OMEGA, 17 jewels, aux. sec.
18k...$195 $250 $325

OMEGA, 17 jewels, c. 1937
s. steel...................................$175 $195 $275

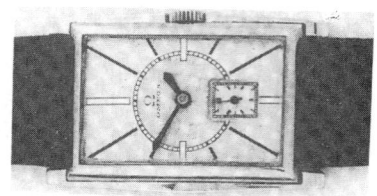

OMEGA, 17 jewels, aux.sec.,
14k...$195 $250 $350

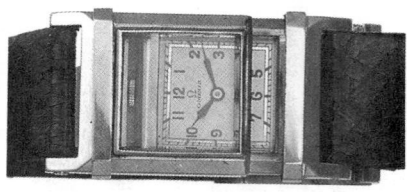

OMEGA, 15J., sliding case, winds at 12, Ca.1930s
"Marine" model
18k...$1,500 $1,800 $2,500

OMEGA, 15 jewels, hidden winding stem, c. 1930
"Marine" model, wire lugs
14k...$1,200 $1,300 $1,500
s. steel......................................$900 $1,000 $1,200

🕐 Some grades are not included. Their values can be
determined by comparing with **similar** age, size, metal
content, style, grades, or models such as **time only**,
chronograph, repeater etc. listed.

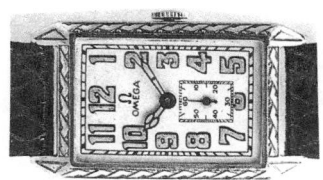

OMEGA, 15J., engraved case, c.1925
14k $275 $300 $400

OMEGA, 19J., alarm,"Memomatic", c.1975
s. steel $300 $350 $450

OMEGA, "Chrono-quartz, cal.1611, c.1975
s. steel $450 $500 $650

OMEGA, quartz, marine chronometer
s. steel $600 $700 $900

Pricing in this Guide are fair market price for **COMPLETE**
watches which are reflected from the "**NAWCC**" National and
regional shows.

OMEGA, 15J., ladies, wire lugs, c.1925
silver.......................................$50 $60 $95

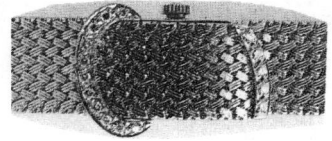

OMEGA, 17J., ladies center sec., c.1938
silver.......................................$100 $125 $175

OMEGA, 17J., ladies flip open, 16 diamonds, c.1955
14k C&B $700 $800 $1,000

OMEGA, 15J., ladies, non-magnetic, c.1945
s. steel.......................................$50 $60 $85

OMEGA, 17J., ladies, sapphire stones on lugs, c.1950
14k C&B $400 $500 $650

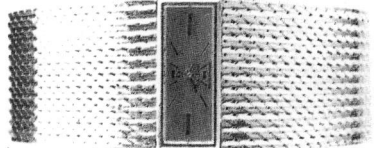

OMEGA, 17J., ladies, RF#8065, c.1965
18k C&B $500 $550 $700

OMEGA BASIC CALIBRE IDENTIFICATION

Cal. No. 100, Ca.1943

Cal. No. 210, Ca.1946

Cal. No. 220, Ca.1941

Cal. No. 230, center seconds

Cal. No. 240, Ca.1939

Cal. No. 250, center seconds

Cal. No. 260, Ca.1943

Cal. No. 280, center seconds

Cal. No. 300, Ca.1944

Cal. No. 310, center seconds

Cal. No. 330, Ca.1943

Cal. No. 360, Ca.1944

Cal. No. 440

Cal. No. 372, jumping seconds

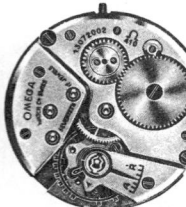

Cal. No. 410, Ca.1951

Cal. No. 420, center seconds

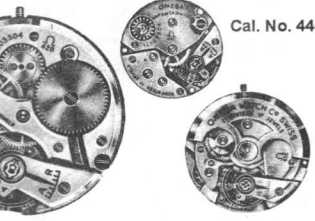

Cal. No. 455, Ca.1955

PRODUCTION TOTALS

DATE– SERIAL #	DATE– SERIAL #	DATE– SERIAL #
1895 --1,000,000	1944-10,000,000	1962-19,000,000
1902 - 2,000,000	1947-11,000,000	1963-20,000,000
1908 - 3,000,000	1950-12,000,000	1964-21,000,000
1912 - 4,000,000	1952-13,500,000	1965-22,000,000
1916 - 5,000,000	1954-14,000,000	1966-23,000,000
1923 - 6,000,000	1956-15,000,000	1967-25,000,000
1929 - 7,000,000	1958-16,000,000	1968-26,000,000
1935 - 8,000,000	1960-17,000,000	1969-28,000,000
1939- 9,000,000	1961-18,000,000	1970-29,000,000

Note: By 1980 ETA Calibers were being used by Omega.
The above list is provided for determining the APPROXIMATE age of your watch. Match serial number with date. Watches were not necessarily sold in the exact order of manufactured date.

Cal. No. 470, Ca.1955

Cal. No. 480, Ca.1955

Cal. No. 490, Ca.1956

Cal. No. 500, Ca.1956

Cal. No. 510, Ca.1956

Cal. No. 520, center seconds

Cal. No. 540, Ca.1957

Cal. No. 550, Ca.1959

Cal. No. 570, Ca.1959

Cal. No. 590, Ca.1960

Cal. No. 600, Ca.1960

Cal. No. 620, Ca.1961

Cal. No. 580, Ca. 1959

Cal. No. 660, Ca.1963

Cal. No. 670, Ca.1963

Cal. No. 690, Ca.1962

Cal. No. 700, Ca.1964

Cal. No. 711, Ca.1966

Cal. No. 730, Ca.1967

Cal. No. 980, Ca.1969

Cal. No. 1040, Ca. 1971

Cal. No. 320, chronograh

Cal. No. 321, chronograh

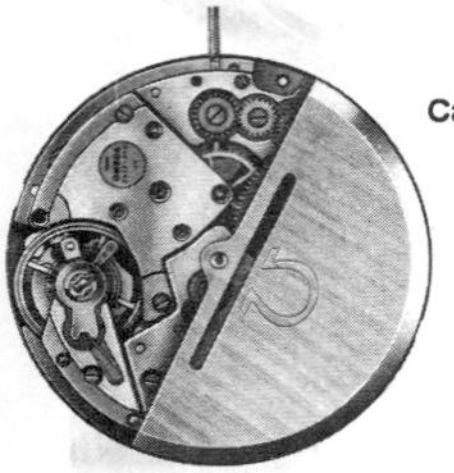

Cal. No. 1010, Ca.1973

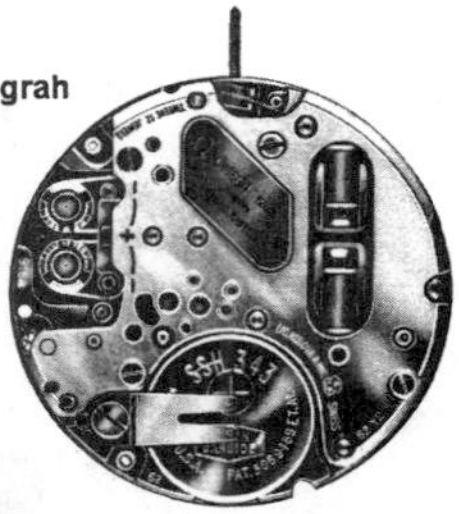

Cal. No. 1250-1260,
Ca.1970

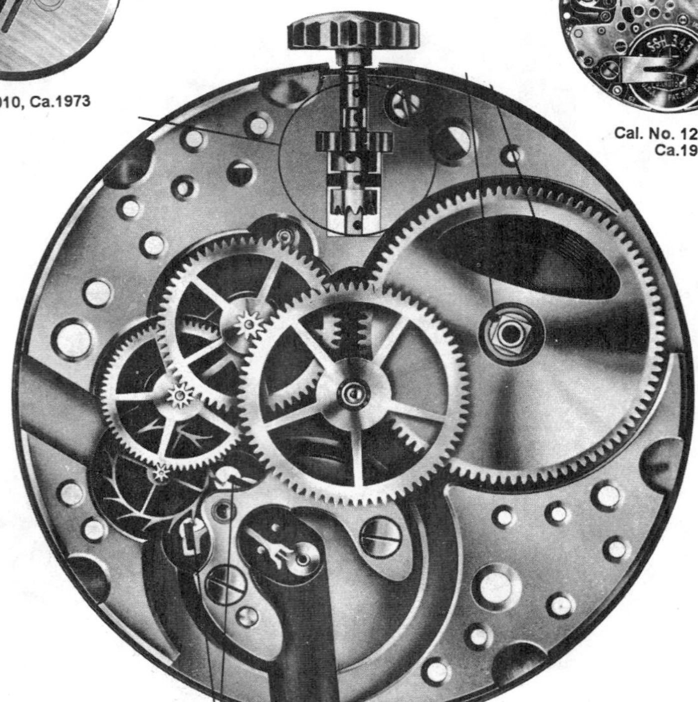

OPEL, 21 jewels, waterproof
gold filled.................................$30 $35 $50

ORATOR, 17 jewels, auto wind
s. steel $20 $30 $50

ORFINA, 17 jewels, triple date, moon phase, **bombe' lugs**
gold filled..............................$195 $250 $325

ORFINA, 17 jewels, triple date, moon phase, **carved lugs**
gold filled..............................$195 $250 $325

ORFINA, 17 jewels, day-date-month
gold filled $75 $95 $135

ORFINA, 17 jewels, date
s. steel $75 $95 $135

ORVIN, 17 jewels, day-date, c. 1945
s. steel $40 $45 $65

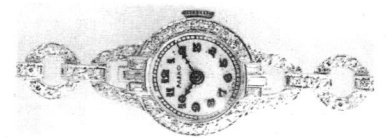

PABRO, 17J., ladies 76 diamond watch, c.1930
platinum...................................$300 $400 $550

PARKER, 17J., 2 reg. chronog.,ca.1948
s. steel $150 $175 $225

PATEK, PHILIPPE & CIE.
Swiss

Patek, Philippe & Cie. has produced some of the world's most desirable factory-made watches. Antoine Norbert de Patek began contracting and selling watches in the 1830's, later became partners with Francois Czapek and generally produced lovely decorative watches for a high class of clientele. In 1845 Adrien Philippe, inventor of the modern stem-winding system, joined the firm of Patek & Cie., and in 1851, the firm established its present name. Between Philippe's talent as a watchmaker and Patek's talent as a businessman with a taste for the impeccable, the firm rapidly established an international reputation which lasts to this day. A *classic* wrist watch the **"Calatrava"** model 96 was 1st used in 1932. The case and dial was designed at a time of transition from pocket watches to wrist watches. The coin was used as a perfect geometric shape to design a wrist watch case that has harmony and balance. Many variations from the classic model 96 have been used, but to most collectors the **classic** model 96 is known as the <u>**Calatrava**</u> model. The original 96 Calatrava model used a flat bezel, 31mm one piece case (lugs are not soldered on), manual wind, white dial, barrette-shaped hour markers, dauphine hands and aux. seconds chapter with a inside and outside circle and long 5 sec. markers. A black dial was added in 1937. The recent classic style Calatrava case is RF # 3796. To date there are many P.P. & Co. wrist watches named Calatrava.

PRODUCTION TOTALS

DATE—SERIAL #	DATE—SERIAL #	DATE—SERIAL #	DATE—SERIAL #
1840— 100	1915—175,000	1945— 850,000	1960—1,100,000
1845— 1,200	1920—190,000	1950— 860,000	1965—1,130,000
1850— 3,000	1925—200,000	1955— 870,000	1970—1,250,000
1855— 8,000	1950—700,000	1960— 880,000	1975—1,350,000
1860— 15,000	1955—725,000	1965— 890,000	1980—1,450,000
1865— 22,000	1960—750,000	1970— 895,000	1985—1,600,000
1870— 35,000	1965—775,000	1940— 900,000	1990—1,850,000
1875— 45,000	1970—795,000	1945— 915,000	
1880— 55,000		1950— 930,000	
1885— 70,000	DATE—SERIAL #	1955— 940,000	
1890— 85,000	1920— 800,000	1960— 960,000	
1895—100,000	1925— 805,000	1965— 975,000	
1900—110,000	1930— 820,000	1970— 995,000	
1905—125,000	1935— 824,000		
1910—150,000	1940— 835,000		

The above list is provided for determining the APPROXIMATE age of your watch. Match serial number with date. Watches were not necessarily sold in the exact order of manufactured date.

Patek, Philippe & Cie. REFERENCE # INDEX

" PATEK PHILIPPE" watches should be signed on the case, dial & movement to bring the prices listed in this book.
(triple signed P.P.CO.)

PATEK PHILIPPE, 29 jewels, min. repeater, c. 1920
platinum $300,000 $350,000 $450,000

PATEK PHILIPPE, 29 jewels, min. repeater, six watches finished by E. Gublin, 18k case & band, triple signed
18k C&B..........................$200,000 $225,000 $275,000

PATEK PHILIPPE, 29J., min. repeater, 30 x 34mm
18k $225,000 $275,000 $375,000

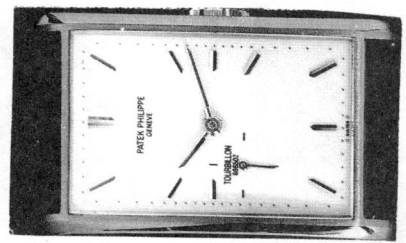

PATEK PHILIPPE, 50 sec. tourbillon, 57 hr. power reserve 5 gear train, 28 x 38mm, RF#3834
18k $185,000 $200,000 $250,000

PATEK PHILIPPE, 39J., auto-wind, min. repeater, perpetual day date month calendars, moon ph., 24 hr. ind., leap year ind., RF#3974, Ca.1989
18K..................................$200,000 $225,000 $275,000

PATEK PHILIPPE,18J., horizontal case, RF#504, 2 tone
18k $6,000 $7,000 $9,000

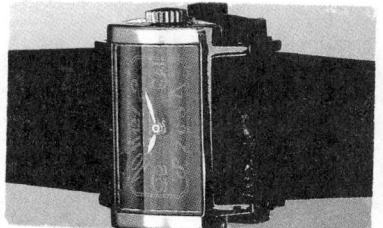

PATEK PHILIPPE,18 J., horizontal case, RF#139 &426
18k $4,000 $5,000 $7,000

" PATEK PHILIPPE" watches should be signed on the case, dial & movement to bring the prices listed in this book.
(triple signed P.P.CO.)

PATEK PHILIPPE, 29 jewels, min. repeater, RF#2524
18k $125,000 $150,000 $200,000

PATEK PHILIPPE, 18J., designed by Gilbert Albert,
RF#3412, c. 1958
18k $20,000 $22,000 $26,000

PATEK PHILIPPE, 18J., asymmetric case designed by
Gilbert Albert, RF#3413, c. 1958
18k $20,000 $22,000 $26,000

PATEK PHILIPPE,18J., fluted hooded lugs, RF#2517
18k $4,000 $5,000 $7,000

PATEK PHILIPPE, 18 J., RF#3497, diamond set case
platinum C&B...................$14,000 $16,000 $19,000

🕐 Pricing in this Guide are fair market price for **COMPLETE**
watches which are reflected from the "**NAWCC**" National and
regional shows.

PATEK PHILIPPE, 18J., RF#3424, asymmetric, c. 1960
18k $14,000 $15,000 $18,000

PATEK PHILIPPE, 18J., RF # 3424, asymmetric, diamond
set on bezel, Ca. 1960
platinum............................$18,000 $19,000 $22,000

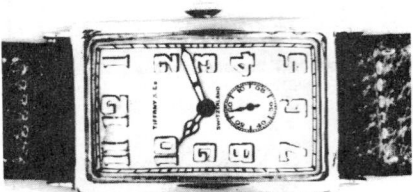

PATEK PHILIPPE, 18 J., **hinged back,** Ca. 1920s
note: **auxiliary seconds**
18k $6,500 $7,000 $8,500

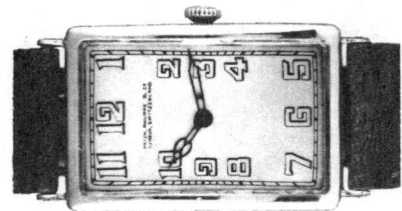

PATEK PHILIPPE, 18 J., **hinged back,** c.1920s
note: **NO auxiliary seconds**
18k $6,500 $7,000 $8,500

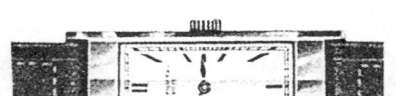

PATEK PHILIPPE, 18 jewels, RF # 137, curved, Ca. 1931
18k - 44mm $4,000 $4,200 $5,000

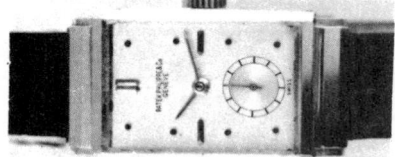

PATEK PHILIPPE, 18J., RF # 1444, Cal.# 9, c. 1940s
18k $3,000 $3,500 $4,500

PATEK PHILIPPE, 18 jewels, RF # 2461, Cal.. 9, c. 1950s
18k $3,500 $4,000 $5,000

PATEK PHILIPPE,18J., cal.990, c.1936
18K..$4,000 $4,500 $6,000

PATEK PHILIPPE,18J., RF# 409, Ca.1934
18K..$3,200 $3,600 $4,200

PATEK PHILIPPE, 18 J., RF # 433, stepped case, c. 1940s
18k $4,500 $5,000 $6,500

PATEK PHILIPPE, 18 jewels, RF # 2531, c. 1950s
18k $2,500 $3,000 $4,000

PATEK PHILIPPE, 18 jewels, RF # 1564, Cal.# 9
18k $3,000 $3,500 $4,500

PATEK PHILIPPE, 18 jewels, RF# 1560
18k $2,800 $3,000 $4,000

PATEK PHILIPPE, 18 jewels, RF # 1560, c. 1940s
18k $3,600 $4,000 $5,000

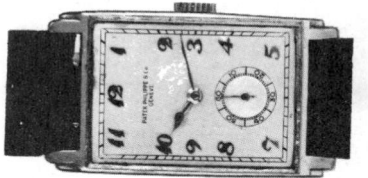

PATEK PHILIPPE, 18 jewels, RF # 1559, c. 1943
18k $3,500 $4,000 $5,000

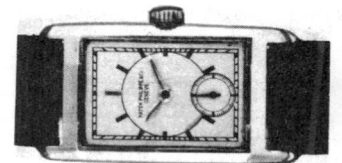

PATEK PHILIPPE, 18 jewels, RF # 404, c. 1930s
18k $2,500 $2,800 $3,500

PATEK PHILIPPE, 18J., RF # 1588, beveled crystal, c. 1945
18k $5,500 $6,000 $7,500

PATEK PHILIPPE, 18 jewels
18k $4,000 $4,500 $5,500

PATEK PHILIPPE, 18 jewels, RF # 2477, Cal.# 9, c. 1953
18k $4,500 $5,000 $6,000

PATEK PHILIPPE, 18 J., RF # 490 & 491, curved, cal. # 9
18k $7,000 $8,000 $10,000

PATEK PHILIPPE, 18J., decorated enamel case, c. 1920s
18k $9,000 $10,000 $12,000

PATEK PHILIPPE,18J., RF # 2334
18K......................$4,000 $4,500 $5,500

PATEK PHILIPPE,18J., RF # 513, extended lugs, **two tone
case,** cal. 885, c.1943
18K......................$4,500 $5,500 $7,500

PATEK PHILIPPE,18J., diamond on dial & case
18K C&B......................$3,500 $4,000 $5,000

PATEK PHILIPPE, 18 J., RF # 1486, hidden lugs, c. 1930s
18k $3,500 $4,000 $5,000

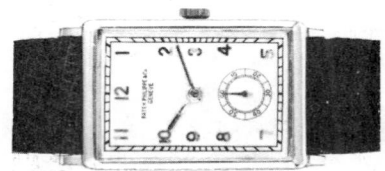

PATEK PHILIPPE, 18 jewels, RF # 1564, c. 1940s
18k $4,000 $4,500 $5,500

PATEK PHILIPPE, 18 J., RF # 1559, hinged back, c. 1920s
18k $4,500 $5,000 $6,000

PATEK PHILIPPE, 18 J., RF # 2404, applied gold numbers
18K $7,000 $7,500 $9,500

" PATEK PHILIPPE" watches should be signed on the case,
dial & movement to bring the prices listed in this book.
(**triple signed P.P.CO.**)

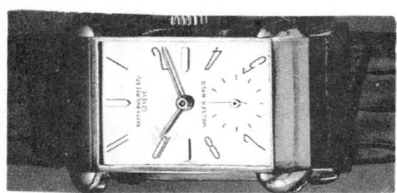

PATEK PHILIPPE, 18J., RF # 1487, Cal.#9, fancy lugs
18k $6,500 $7,500 $9,500

PATEK PHILIPPE, 18J., RF # 1402, hooded satin lugs
18k asymmetric $8,000 $9,000 $12,000

PATEK PHILIPPE, 18J., RF # 430, "Staybrite," curved case
s. steel $6,000 $7,000 $9,000

PATEK PHILIPPE, 18 J., RF # 1438, Cal.# 9, hooded lugs
18k $2,200 $2,400 $3,000

PATEK PHILIPPE, 18 jewels, RF # 513-1, curved
18k $3,500 $4,000 $5,000

PATEK PHILIPPE,18J., engraved bezel,hinged back,c.1920
18k $6,000 $6,500 $8,000

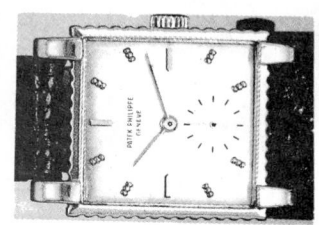

PATEK PHILIPPE, 18J., RF # 2472, ribbed case & fancy lugs
18k $3,000 $3,500 $4,500

PATEK PHILIPPE, 18 J., RF # 2518, large lugs, c. 1960s
18k $4,500 $5,000 $6,500

PATEK PHILIPPE, 18 J., RF # 1532, Ca.1940s
18k $3,500 $4,000 $5,000

PATEK PHILIPPE, 18 jewels, c. 1930s
18k $2,500 $2,800 $3,500

🕐 Pricing in this Guide are fair market price for **COMPLETE**
watches which are reflected from the "**NAWCC**" National and
regional shows.

PATEK PHILIPPE, 18J., **Ladies**, center lugs, c. 1940s
18k $2,500 $2,700 $3,200

PATEK PHILIPPE, 18 jewels, RF # 655, c. 1940s
18k $3,500 $4,000 $5,000

PATEK PHILIPPE, 18J., triple lugs, RF#2471, ca.1951
18k $16,000 $18,000 $22,000

PATEK PHILIPPE, 18 jewels, triple lugs, RF#1482
18k $9,000 $10,000 $14,000

PATEK PHILIPPE, 18 jewels, curved, c. 1940s
18k $3,500 $4,000 $5,000

PATEK PHILIPPE, 18 jewels, RF # 1570, Cal.# 9, c. 1940s
18k $4,500 $5,000 $6,000

PATEK PHILIPPE, 18 jewels, RF # 406, curved, c. 1940s
18k $4,000 $4,500 $6,000

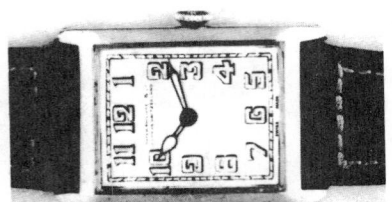

PATEK PHILIPPE, 18 jewels, hinged back, c. 1920s
18k $4,500 $5,000 $6,000

PATEK PHILIPPE, 18J., hinged back, stepped case
18k $4,000 $4,500 $5,500

PATEK PHILIPPE, 18J., RF#2520, cal. # 9, extended lugs
18k C&B..............................$7,000 $9,000 $12,000

PATEK PHILIPPE, 18J., RF # 2414, fancy lugs, ca.1949
18k $7,500 $8,500 $11,000

PATEK PHILIPPE 18J., RF# 2503, fancy lugs, ca. 1950s
18k $8,000 $9,000 $12,000

PATEK PHILIPPE 18J., RF# 1530, fancy lugs, ca. 1940s
18k $3,500 $4,000 $5,000

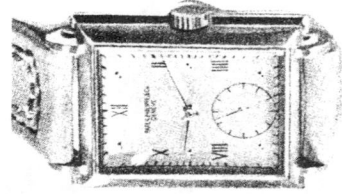

PATEK PHILIPPE 18J., RF# 1568, fancy lugs, ca. 1940s
18k $4,000 $4,500 $5,500

PATEK PHILIPPE 18J., RF# 1535, fancy lugs, ca. 1940
18k $2,500 $3,000 $4,000

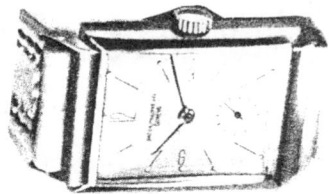

PATEK PHILIPPE 18J., RF# 1531, fancy lugs, ca. 1940s
18k $3,000 $3,500 $4,500

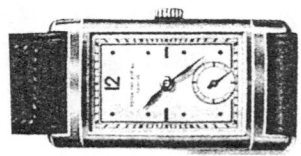

PATEK PHILIPPE 18J., RF# 422, ca. 1950s
18k $3,000 $3,500 $4,500

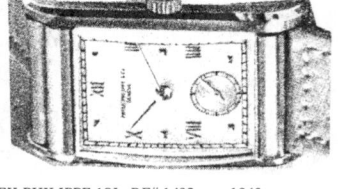

PATEK PHILIPPE 18J., RF# 1493, ca. 1940s
18k $4,000 $4,500 $5,500

PATEK PHILIPPE 18J., RF# 1442, ca. 1940s
18k $3,500 $4,000 $5,000

PATEK PHILIPPE 18J., RF# 2434, ca. 1950s
18k $3,500 $4,000 $5,000

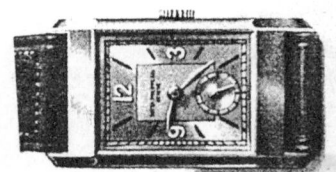

PATEK PHILIPPE 18J., RF# 420, ca. 1930s
18k $3,000 $3,500 $4,500

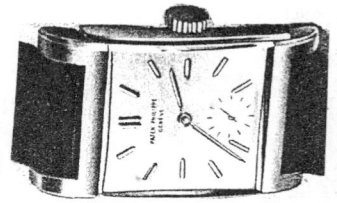

PATEK PHILIPPE 18J., RF# 2476, curved, ca. 1950s
18k $3,500 $4,000 $5,000

🕐 Pricing in this Guide are fair market price for **COMPLETE** watches which are reflected from the "**NAWCC**" National and regional shows.

PATEK PHILIPPE, 18 J., RF # 1580, Cal.# 9, concave lugs
18k $6,000 $7,000 $9,000

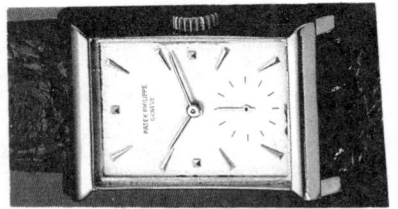

PATEK PHILIPPE, 18 jewels, RF # 2404, fancy lugs
18k $5,500 $6,500 $8,000

PATEK PHILIPPE, 18 J., Cal.#9, aux. sec., Ca.1940
18k $3,000 $3,500 $4,500

PATEK PHILIPPE, 18J., stylized hooded lugs
18k $6,000 $7,000 $9,000

PATEK PHILIPPE, 18 jewels, RF # 2066, moveable lugs
18K..................................... $6,000 $7,000 $9,000

PATEK PHILIPPE, 18 jewels, RF # 2443, Cal.# 9, c. 1940s
18k $4,000 $5,000 $6,500

PATEK PHILIPPE, 18 jewels, RF # 2403, lapidated lugs
18k $5,500 $6,500 $8,000

PATEK PHILIPPE, 18J., 2 tone, hooded & stepped lugs
18k $9,000 $10,000 $12,000

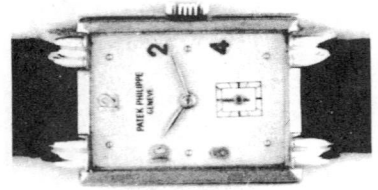

PATEK PHILIPPE, 18 jewels, fancy lugs, RF#1480
18k $5,000 $6,000 $8,000

PATEK PHILIPPE, 18 jewels, ''Reverso''
18k $20,000 $25,000 $35,000
s. steel .... ★★$25,000 $30,000 $40,000

PATEK PHILIPPE, 18J., RF # 1450, top hat style, c. 1940s
18k $5,500 $6,000 $7,000
platinum $8,000 $9,000 $12,000

PATEK PHILIPPE, 18 jewels, RF # 1450, top hat style
18k C&B..............................$6,000 $6,500 $8,000

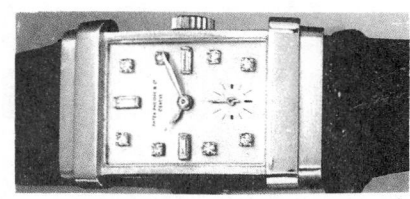

PATEK PHILIPPE, 18 J., RF # 2480, top hat, diamond dial
platinum $9,000 $10,000 $13,000

PATEK PHILIPPE, 18 jewels, M# 9, curved, tank style
18k $6,500 $7,500 $9,000

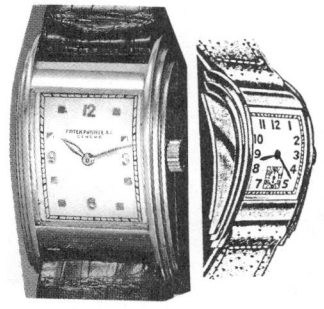

PATEK PHILIPPE, 18J., inclined & curved case, Ca.1940s
18k $16,000 $19,000 $25,000

PATEK PHILIPPE, 18 jewels, RF # 425, Adj. to 8 positions
18k $4,000 $4,500 $6,000

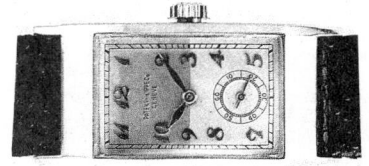

PATEK PHILIPPE, 18 jewels, RF # 425, curved, c. 1940s
18k $4,500 $5,000 $6,500

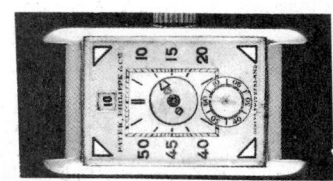

PATEK PHILIPPE, 18 J., converted to jump hr., **(recased)**
18k $2,500 $3,000 $3,500

PATEK PHILIPPE, 18 J., RF # 2468, flared case, c. 1940s
18k $8,000 $9,000 $12,000

PATEK PHILIPPE, 18 jewels, RF # 1593, Cal.# 9, c. 1950s
platinum...........................$12,000 $14,000 $20,000

PATEK PHILIPPE, 18J., RF # 2456, flared case, Ca. 1950s
18k $8,000 $9,000 $12,000

PATEK PHILIPPE, 18 J., RF # 2442, massive flared case
18k $20,000 $22,000 $26,000
platinum $30,000 $33,000 $40,000

PATEK PHILIPPE, 18J., RF#2441, Eiffel tower, c. 1945
18k $25,000 $30,000 $40,000

PATEK PHILIPPE,18J., RF#2441, Eiffel tower, c. 1945
18k $25,000 $30,000 $40,000

PATEK PHILIPPE, 18 jewels, RF # 2456, flared case
18k $5,500 $6,500 $8,000

PATEK PHILIPPE, 18J., RF # 2468, flared case, c. 1950s
18k(dial not original).........$4,500 $5,000 $6,000

PATEK PHILIPPE, 18 jewels, RF # 2554, c. 1950s
18k $7,000 $8,000 $10,000

PATEK PHILIPPE, 18J., 16 diamond bezel, ca.1960
18k C&B............................$6,000 $7,000 $9,000

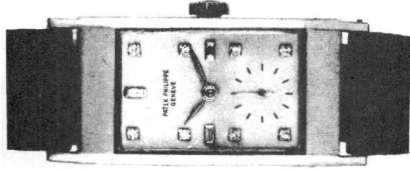

PATEK PHILIPPE, 18 J., RF # 425, diamond dial, c. 1945
18k $5,500 $6,000 $7,000

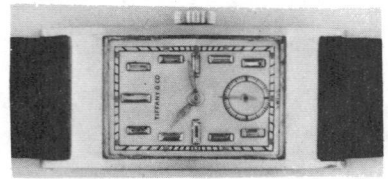

PATEK PHILIPPE, 18 jewels, RF # 425, diamond dial
platinum..............................$7,500 $8,000 $9,500

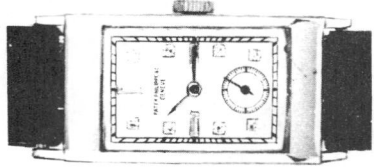

PATEK PHILIPPE, 18J., RF # 425, diamond dial, c. 1935
platinum..............................$7,500 $8,500 $9,500

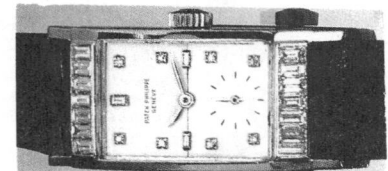

PATEK PHILIPPE, 18 J., RF # 425, diamond dial & bezel
platinum..............................$7,000 $8,000 $10,000

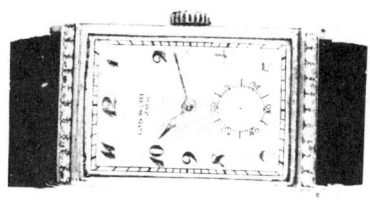

PATEK PHILIPPE, 18J., hinged back, diamond bezel
18k $6,000 $7,000 $9,000

PATEK PHILIPPE,18J., RF#2493, c.1953
18K $3,000 $3,500 $4,500

PATEK PHILIPPE, 18 jewels, Ca. 1940s
18k $4,500 $5,000 $6,000

PATEK PHILIPPE,18J., RF#1431, cal., c.1940
18K $3,000 $3,500 $4,500

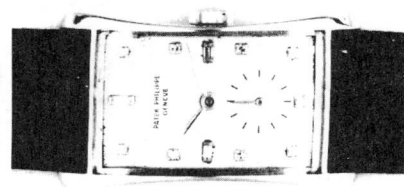

PATEK PHILIPPE, 18J., RF # 2456, diamond dial, flared
18k $8,500 $9,500 $12,000

PATEK PHILIPPE,18J., RF#2447, c.1950
18K $2,500 $3,000 $3,800

PATEK PHILIPPE, 18J, Hooded Lugs
s. steel $4,500 $5,000 $6,000

PATEK PHILIPPE,18J., carved lugs, RF#2423, c.1949
18K $4,000 $4,500 $5,500

PATEK PHILIPPE, 18J., RF# 3727, **Lapis & 54 Diamonds,**
Ca.1974
18k $6,000 $7,000 $9,000

PATEK PHILIPPE,18J., RF#2424, c.1951
18K $4,500 $5,000 $6,000

PATEK PHILIPPE,18J., RF # 2437, stepped lugs, c.1940
18K...................................$4,000 $4,500 $5,500

PATEK PHILIPPE, 18 J., RF # 1486, Ca. 1950s
18k C&B............................$3,000 $4,200 $4,800

PATEK PHILIPPE, 18J., RF # 2496, textured bezel, c. 1940s
18k $3,000 $3,500 $4,500

PATEK PHILIPPE, 18J., RF # 2491, fancy off set lugs
18k $3,000 $3,500 $4,500

PATEK PHILIPPE, 18 jewels, RF # 1567, Ca. 1940s
18k $3,500 $4,000 $5,000

PATEK PHILIPPE, 18 jewels, RF # 3405, cal. # 9, c. 1963
18k $2,000 $2,400 $3,000

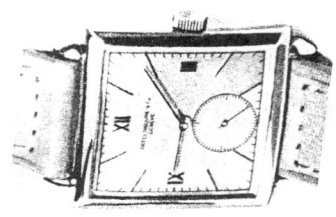

PATEK PHILIPPE, 18 jewels, RF # 1432, Ca. 1940s
18k $2,500 $2,800 $3,500

PATEK PHILIPPE, 18 jewels, RF # 3406, c. 1960s
18k $2,200 $2,400 $3,000

PATEK PHILIPPE, 18 jewels, RF # 1557, oval lugs
18k $3,500 $4,000 $5,000

PATEK PHILIPPE, 18 jewels, RF # 3555
18k $2,200 $2,400 $3,000

🕐 Pricing in this Guide are fair market price for **COMPLETE** watches which are reflected from the **"NAWCC"** National and regional shows.

PATEK PHILIPPE, 18 J., RF # 2553, Cal.# 9-90, Ca. 1955
18k $4,500 $5,000 $6,000

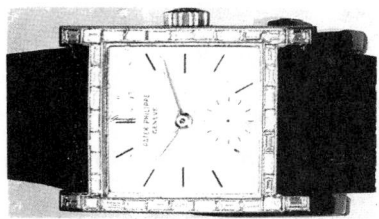

PATEK PHILIPPE, 18 J., RF # 2496, diamond bezel
platinum $8,000 $9,000 $12,000

PATEK PHILIPPE, 18 J., RF # 3519, Ca. 1967
18k(w)..................................$2,500 $2,800 $3,800

PATEK PHILIPPE,18J.,Cal.# 9, hidden dial, 18k & plat. c.1930's
"Cabriolet", remade in 2001 & list for $13,900 in 2001
18k & platinum (ca.1930's)..$22,000 $25,000 $30,000

PATEK PHILIPPE, 18 jewels, RF # 3633, Cal.# 9, c. 1980s
18k C&B.............................$3,000 $3,500 $4,500

PATEK PHILIPPE, 18 jewels, RF # 1575, Ca. 1940s
18k $2,500 $2,800 $3,400

PATEK PHILIPPE, 18 jewels, RF # 1566, Ca. 1940s
18k $3,000 $3,500 $4,500

PATEK PHILIPPE, 18 jewels, RF # 3404
18k C&B.............................$2,500 $2,800 $3,500

PATEK PHILIPPE, 18 J., RF # 3467, textured dial & bezel
18k $2,500 $2,800 $3,500

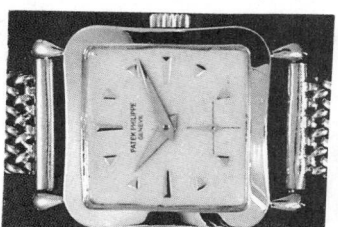

PATEK PHILIPPE, 18 jewels, RF # 2513, c. 1950s
18k $3,000 $3,500 $4,500

🕐 Some grades are not included. Their values can be
determined by comparing with **similar** age, size, metal
content, style, grades, or models such as **time only**,
chronograph, repeater etc. listed.

PATEK PHILIPPE, 18 J., RF # 2574, center sec., c. 1960s
18k C&B $4,000 $4,500 $5,500

PATEK PHILIPPE, 18 jewels, RF # 2516, Ca. 1950s
18k $2,600 $2,800 $3,200

PATEK PHILIPPE, 18 J., tank, RF#2530-1, Ca. 1959
18k C&B $4,000 $4,500 $5,500

PATEK PHILIPPE, 18 jewels, RF # 2540, Ca. 1960s
18k $3,500 $4,000 $5,000

PATEK PHILIPPE, 18J., tank, Cal.# 9, c. early 1910s
18k C&B $4,000 $4,500 $5,500

PATEK PHILIPPE, 18 J., RF # 2479, guilloche bezel
18k $4,000 $4,500 $6,000

PATEK PHILIPPE, 18 jewels, RF # 1408, Ca. 1940s
18k $2,500 $2,800 $3,300

PATEK PHILIPPE, 18 J., RF # 1574, hidden lugs, c. 1945
18k $2,800 $3,000 $3,500

PATEK PHILIPPE, 18 jewels, RF # 2486, Ca. 1950s
18k $2,500 $2,700 $3,200

PATEK PHILIPPE, 18J., RF # 556, fluted cylindrical lugs
18k $6,000 $7,000 $9,000

PATEK PHILIPPE, 18 jewels, RF # 1592, hidden lugs
18k $2,500 $2,800 $3,200

PATEK PHILIPPE, 18 J., RF # 2514-1, Ca. 1940s
18k $3,500 $4,000 $5,000

PATEK PHILIPPE, 18 J., RF # 3465, blue sapphire bezel
platinum $7,000 $8,000 $11,000

PATEK PHILIPPE, 18 jewels, RF # 1481, overhanging lugs
18k $5,500 $6,000 $7,000

PATEK PHILIPPE, 18 J., RF # 2440, fluted dropped lugs
18k $4,500 $5,000 $6,500

Wrist Watches listed in this section are priced at the collectable fair market **Trade Show** level as **complete** watches having an original gold-filled case and stainless steel back, also with original dial, leather watch band, and the entire original movement in good working order with no repairs needed.

PATEK PHILIPPE, 18 jewels, RF # 2474, Ca. 1940s
18k $3,000 $3,500 $4,500

PATEK PHILIPPE, 18 jewels, RF # 244, large bezel
18k $2,500 $2,800 $3,500

PATEK PHILIPPE, 18 jewels, RF # 2488, Ca. 1940s
18k $2,200 $2,400 $3,000

PATEK PHILIPPE, 15J.,for Baily,Banks & Biddle, ca.1920
18k $4,500 $5,000 $6,500

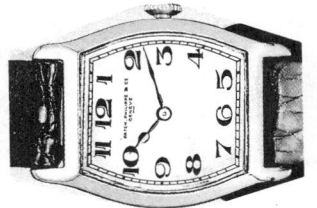

PATEK PHILIPPE, 16J., ca.1923
18k $3,000 $3,300 $4,000

PATEK PHILIPPE, 18 jewels, c. 1910
18k $3,000 $3,500 $4,500

PATEK PHILIPPE, 18 jewels, c. 1920s
18k $4,000 $4,500 $5,500

PATEK PHILIPPE, 18 jewels, c. 1920s
18k $4,000 $4,500 $6,000

PATEK PHILIPPE, 18J, **recased** & PW dial, c. 1920s
18k $1,000 $1,200 $1,500

PATEK PHILIPPE, 18 jewels, Cal.# 9, c. 1910
platinum $8,000 $9,000 $12,000

PATEK PHILIPPE, 18 jewels, c. 1930s
18k $3,300 $3,600 $4,400

PATEK PHILIPPE, 18 jewels, c. 1930s
18k $3,500 $4,000 $5,000

PATEK PHILIPPE, 18 jewels, **contract case, not signed**
18k (w) $1,200 $1,400 $1,700

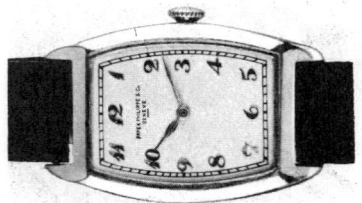

PATEK PHILIPPE, 18 jewels, Cal.# 9, c. 1925
18k $4,000 $4,500 $5,500

PATEK PHILIPPE, 18 jewels, M# 9, c. 1920s
18k $5,000 $6,000 $8,000

🕐 Pricing in this Guide are fair market price for **COMPLETE** watches which are reflected from the "**NAWCC**" National and regional shows.

PATEK PHILIPPE, 18J, jump hour, RF # 3969, Ca. 1989
18k $20,000 $22,000 $25,000

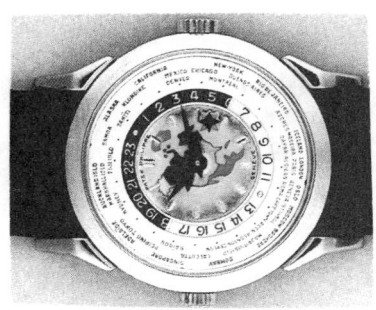

PATEK PHILIPPE, 18 jewels, RF#2523, ''World Time,''
cloisonne polychrome enamel map on dial, **41 cities**
18k .... ★ ★ ★ $350,000 $450,000 $650,000

PATEK PHILIPPE, 18 jewels
18k $2,500 $2,800 $3,500

PATEK PHILIPPE,18J.,''World Time,'' **41 cities**,   RF#1415
18k $40,000 $45,000 $55,000

PATEK PHILIPPE, 18 J., RF # 2469, made for E. Gublin
18k $4,500 $5,000 $6,000

PATEK PHILIPPE, 18 jewels, ''Chronometro Gondolo''
18k $6,000 $7,000 $9,000

PATEK PHILIPPE, 18 jewels, RF # 2481,
landscape cloisonne polychrome enamel dial
18k $80,000 $90,000 $110,000

PATEK PHILIPPE,18jewels, RF#515, world time zone,
24 hr. rotating outside chapter, **tu-tone** case and band
18K C&B $300,000 $400,000 $600,000

PATEK PHILIPPE, 18 J., RF # 2597, **2 hr. hands,**
2 time zones
18k $25,000 $30,000 $40,000

PATEK PHILIPPE, 18J., RF # 2597, **time zone**, hour hand
can be stepped forward or backward 1 hour at a time
18k $30,000 $35,000 $45,000

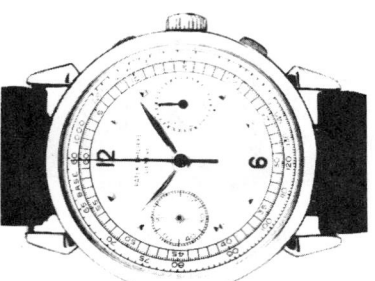

PATEK PHILIPPE,18J.,chronog., RF#1579, fancy lugs
18k $20,000 $22,000 $28,000

PATEK PHILIPPE, 18J., RF # 1436, chronog., 1940s
18k (Breguet dial)............. $25,000 $30,000 $40,000

PATEK PHILIPPE,18J., chronog., RF# 591, 2 reg., c.1943
18k (**black dial**) $30,000 $35,000 $45,000

PATEK PHILIPPE, 18J., RF#530, chronog.
18k $22,000 $24,000 $32,000

PATEK PHILIPPE,18J., RF# 130, chronog., **black dial**
18k & s. steel $28,000 $32,000 $38,000

PATEK PHILIPPE, 18J., RF # 1463, 2 reg., Ca. 1940s
18k ....,............................... $35,000 $40,000 $55,000

Ⓣ Some grades are not included. Their values can be
determined by comparing with **similar** age, size, metal
content, style, grades, or models such as **time only**,
chronograph, repeater etc. listed.

PATEK PHILIPPE, 32J., **split sec**. chronog.
18k $400,000 $450,000 $550,000

PATEK PHILIPPE, 26J., **split sec**. chronog. **one button**, for Cartier, Sq. button for Rattrapante hand, crown for start stop functions, RF#130, 8 adj., **Breguet dial**, ca.1938
18k $140,000 $160,000 $200,000

PATEK PHILIPPE,18J., RF#130,split sec. chronog.,c.1958
18k $120,000 $140,000 $180,000

PATEK PHILIPPE,18J., RF# 1506, chronog., waterproof
18k $30,000 $35,000 $50,000

PATEK PHILIPPE, 18J., chronog., pulsometer, c. 1965
18k $40,000 $45,000 $60,000

🕐 Pricing in this Guide are fair market price for **COMPLETE** watches which are reflected from the "**NAWCC**" National and regional shows.

PATEK PHILIPPE, 18J., RF#3970E, chronog,triple date moon ph., 24 hr. indicator, leap year indicator
18k $30,000 $35,000 $43,000

PATEK PHILIPPE, 23 jewels, chronog., day-date month, moon phase, made for E. Gueblin
18k C&B...........................$90,000 $110,000 $140,000

PATEK PHILIPPE, 23J., chronog., triple date, moon ph. perpetual calendar,RF# 1518, Calatrava case, Ca.1941-54
18k ....★ ★ $80,000 $90,000 $120,000

PATEK PHILIPPE, 23 J., chronog., triple date, moon ph. perpetual calendar, arabic dial, ref.2499 (1 series) square button
18K $90,000 $100,000 $120,000

" PATEK PHILIPPE" watches should be signed on the case, dial & movement to bring the prices listed in this book.
(triple signed P.P.CO.)

PATEK PHILIPPE, 23 J., chronog., triple date, moon ph. perpetual calendar, RF#2499 (2 series)
18K......................................$80,000 $90,000 $110,000

PATEK PHILIPPE, 23J., chronog., triple date, moon ph. perpetual calendar, RF#2499 (3 series)glass crystal
18k $70,000 $80,000 $100,000

PATEK PHILIPPE, 23J., chronog., triple date, moon ph. perpetual calendar, RF#2499 (3 series)only 2 in platinum
platinum $250,000 $300,000 $400,000

Wrist Watches listed in this section are priced at the collectable fair market **Trade Show** level as **complete** watches having an original gold-filled case and stainless steel back, also with original dial, leather watch band, and the entire original movement in good working order with no repairs needed.

PATEK PHILIPPE, 23J., chronog., triple date, moon ph. perpetual calendar, RF#2499 (4 series)sapphire crystal
18k $65,000 $75,000 $90,000

PATEK PHILIPPE, 37jewels, RF # 3514, date, auto wind
platinum............................$22,000 $24,000 $30,000

PATEK PHILIPPE, 18 J., RF # 3601, auto wind, date, Ca. 1970s
18k C&B............................$3,000 $3,500 $4,500

PATEK PHILIPPE,37J., Auto-wind, RF#3514/1, date, c.1967
18K C&B............................$3,000 $3,500 $4,500

PATEK PHILIPPE,37J., date, RF#3445, auto-wind, c.1961
18K...$3,500 $4,500 $6,000

PATEK PHILIPPE,18J., date, RF#3604, textured dial, c.1977
18K(w)................................$2,200 $2,400 $3,000

PATEK PHILIPPE,18J., RF # 96 or 1505 (**day, date, month, at 9-12-3**), Calatrava, manual wind, Ca.1934-38
18K................ ★ ★ ★ ★ ★$400,000 $450,000 $600,000

PATEK PHILIPPE, 18J., RF#96, Calatrava, triple date note moon phases at 12, Ca.1936
In 1996 a similar watch sold for $1.7 million US dollars
18K..................................$400,000 $450,000 $600,000
platinum $500,000 $550,000 $700,000

PATEK PHILIPPE, 37J., RF#3450, day-date-month, moon phase, waterproof, **perpetual date at 3**
18k $30,000 $35,000 $40,000

PATEK PHILIPPE, 37J,RF#3448, triple date moon ph, c.1968
platinum...........................$45,000 $50,000 $70,000
18K $27,000 $30,000 $38,000

PATEK PHILIPPE, 37J., Perpetual, triple date, moon ph. RF # 2497
18k $45,000 $50,000 $60,000

PATEK PHILIPPE,18J., triple date, moon ph., RF#2438, c.1962
18k $45,000 $50,000 $60,000

PATEK PHILIPPE, 18J, perpetual, RF# 1526
18k $50,000 $55,000 $70,000

PATEK PHILIPPE,18J., "Officer", RF#3960, c.1992
18k 2,000 made, 18k(w) 150 made, platinum 50 made
18K....................................$13,000 $15,000 $18,000
18k(w)...............................$15,000 $17,000 $20,000
platinum $25,000 $28,000 $32,000

PATEK PHILIPPE, 15J., enamel dial, c. 1910
18k $7,000 $8,000 $10,000

PATEK PHILIPPE, 18 jewels, RF#1461
18k $2,500 $2,800 $3,500

PATEK PHILIPPE, 18 jewels, RF # 1571, Ca. 1940s
18k $3,000 $3,500 $4,500

PATEK PHILIPPE, 18 jewels, RF # 1461, aux. sec.
18k $2,300 $2,700 $3,300

PATEK PHILIPPE, 18J., *Amagnetic* on dial, ca. 1960
18k $4,000 $4,500 $5,500

PATEK PHILIPPE, 18J.,RF # 448,"Calatrava", aux. sec.,
Ca. 1950s
18k $3,000 $3,300 $4,000

⊕ Pricing in this Guide are fair market price for **COMPLETE**
watches which are reflected from the "**NAWCC**" National and
regional shows.

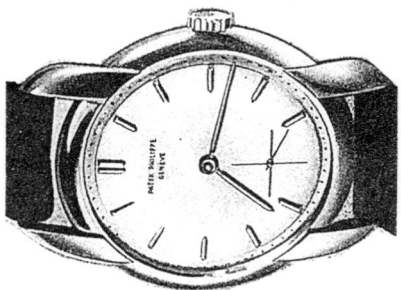

PATEK PHILIPPE, 18 jewels, RF # 2536, Ca. 1950s
18k $4,000 $4,500 $5,500

PATEK PHILIPPE, 18 jewels, RF # 2452, Ca. 1950s
18k $3,500 $4,000 $5,000

PATEK PHILIPPE, 18 jewels, RF # 2459, Ca. 1950s
18k $3,000 $3,400 $4,000

PATEK PHILIPPE, 18 jewels, RF # 1509, Ca. 1940s
18k $3,000 $3,200 $3,700

PATEK PHILIPPE, 18 jewels, RF # 2525 / 1, Ca. 1950s
18k $2,800 $3,200 $4,200

PATEK PHILIPPE, 18 jewels, RF # 2484, Ca. 1950s
18k $2,300 $2,700 $3,500

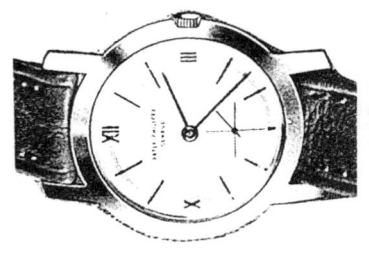

PATEK PHILIPPE, 18 jewels, RF # 2506 / 1, Ca. 1950s
18k $2,000 $2,200 $2,600

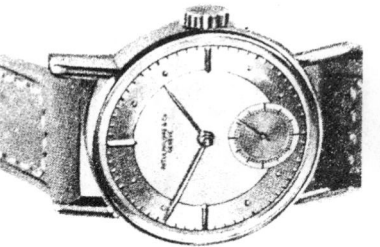

PATEK PHILIPPE, 18 jewels, RF # 534, Ca. 1940s
18k $3,000 $3,500 $4,500

🕐 Pricing in this Guide are fair market price for **COMPLETE** watches which are reflected from the "**NAWCC**" National and regional shows.

PATEK PHILIPPE, 18 jewels, RF # 2577, Ca. 1955
18k $2,500 $2,800 $3,500

PATEK PHILIPPE, 18 jewels, man's half size, c. 1920
18k $2,800 $3,200 $4,000
s. steel $2,600 $2,800 $3,300

PATEK PHILIPPE, 18 jewels, RF# 2429, Ca. 1950s
18k $3,500 $4,000 $4,800

PATEK PHILIPPE, 18 jewels, RF # 2537, aux. sec., c. 1950s
18k $2,600 $3,000 $3,800

🕐 Pricing in this Guide are fair market price for **COMPLETE** watches which are reflected from the "**NAWCC**" National and regional shows.

PATEK PHILIPPE, 30J., RF#3429, auto-wind
18k $5,000 $6,000 $8,000

PATEK PHILIPPE, 18J., auto-w, aux. sec., RF#2526, **RARE** glass enamel dial, Ca. 1957
18k auto-w ....★$10,000 $12,000 $20,000

PATEK PHILIPPE,18J., **CLASSIC Calatrava**, RF# 96
18k $3,000 $3,500 $4,200
s. steel $2,700 $3,000 $3,500
platinum..............................$7,000 $8,000 $10,000
platinum + diam. dial $7,500 $8,500 $11,000

The **above CLASSIC Calatrava** case and dial model 96 was 1st used in 1932. It was designed at a time of transition from pocket watches to wrist watches. The coin was used as a perfect geometric shape to design a wrist watch case that has harmony and balance. Many variations from the classic model 96 have been used, but to most collectors the **CLASSIC** model 96 is known as the **Calatrava** model. The original 96 Calatrava model used a flat bezel, 31mm one piece case (lugs are not soldered on), manual wind, white dial, barrette-shaped hour markers, dauphine hands and aux. seconds chapter with a inside and outside circle and long 5 sec. markers. A black dial was added in 1937.
The recent classic style Calatrava case is RF # 3796.
To date there are many Calatrava styles and models.

PATEK PHILIPPE, 18J., RF# 2500, Ca. 1950s
18k $2,200 $2,400 $2,800

PATEK PHILIPPE,18J., RF # 3420, aux. sec., Ca.1943
18K $3,000 $3,500 $4,500

PATEK PHILIPPE, 18 J., RF # 2515, Ca.1950s
18k $2,200 $2,400 $2,800

PATEK PHILIPPE,18J., RF# 1433, Ca.1940s
18K $2,000 $2,200 $2,600

PATEK PHILIPPE,30J., auto wind, RF#1516, c.1950
18K..$6,000 $7,000 $9,000

PATEK PHILIPPE,18J., aux. sec., RF#96, cal.12-20, c.1937
18K $2,800 $3,200 $3,800

PATEK PHILIPPE,18J., aux. sec., RF#2445,
18K..$2,600 $2,800 $3,300

PATEK PHILIPPE,18J., RF#1543, c.1947
18K $2,600 $2,800 $3,400

Wrist Watches listed in this section are priced at the collectable
fair market **Trade Show** level as **complete** watches having an
original gold-filled case and stainless steel back, also with
original dial, leather watch band, and the entire original movement in good working order with no repairs needed.

🕐 Some grades are not included. Their values can be
determined by comparing with **similar** age, size, metal
content, style, grades, or models such as **time only**,
chronograph, repeater etc. listed.

PATEK PHILIPPE,18J., RF# 1590, c.1951
18K.....................................$2,800 $3,000 $3,500

PATEK PHILIPPE, 18 jewels, RF # 2509, Ca. 1950s
18k $2,800 $3,200 $4,000

PATEK PHILIPPE, 18J., RF # 2494, extra long lugs, c. 1950
18k $2,400 $2,600 $3,000

PATEK PHILIPPE, 18J., RF # 2557, Ca. 1950s
18k $2,000 $2,200 $2,500

PATEK PHILIPPE, 18 jewels, RF # 570, aux. sec., Ca. 1950s
18k $2,700 $2,900 $3,500

PATEK PHILIPPE, 30J.,"Calatrava", auto wind, gold rotor
18k $6,000 $7,000 $10,000

PATEK PHILIPPE, 18 jewels, RF # 1517, aux. sec.
18k $2,300 $2,800 $3,000

PATEK PHILIPPE,18J.,"Calatrava," **RF # 96, enamel dial**,
Ca.1940s
18k .... ★ $7,000 $8,000 $11,000

PATEK PHILIPPE, 18J.,waterproof, "Calatrava," rf#2545
18k $3,500 $4,000 $5,000

PATEK PHILIPPE, 18 jewels, RF # 2406, Ca. 1950s
18k $2,500 $2,800 $3,500

PATEK PHILIPPE, 30J., RF # 2526, **enamel dial**, aux. sec.
18k C&B $11,000 $13,000 $22,000

PATEK PHILIPPE, 18J., fancy lugs, c. 1940s
18k $4,000 $4,500 $5,500

⊕ A collector should expect to pay modestly higher prices
at local shops

PATEK PHILIPPE, 18J., fancy lugs, ca. 1948
18k $6,000 $7,000 $9,000

PATEK PHILIPPE, 18 jewels, curled lugs
18k $5,000 $5,500 $7,000

PATEK PHILIPPE, 18 jewels, RF # 2549, Ca. 1950s
18k .... ★ ★$12,000 $16,000 $24,000

PATEK PHILIPPE, 18 jewels, RF # 2550, Ca. 1950s
18k $9,000 $11,000 $16,000

PATEK PHILIPPE, 18J., RF# 2533, Ca. 1950s
18k $3,500 $4,000 $5,000

PATEK PHILIPPE, 18 jewels, RF # 2482, Ca. 1950s
18k $3,000 $3,500 $4,500

PATEK PHILIPPE, 21J., RF # 3025, ''Calatrava,'' **Ca.1950s**
center sec., note **Breguet dial**
18k $4,000 $4,500 $5,500

PATEK PHILIPPE, 18 jewels, RF # 565, Ca. 1940s
18k $3,000 $3,300 $4,000

PATEK PHILIPPE, 18J., center sec., rf#2466, ca. 1949
18k $3,500 $3,800 $4,500

PATEK PHILIPPE, 18 jewels, conical lugs, center sec.
18k $4,000 $4,500 $6,000

PATEK PHILIPPE, 18J., RF# 1578, center sec., c. 1950s
18k $2,500 $2,800 $3,300

PATEK PHILIPPE, 18 jewels, RF # 2481, center sec.
18k $4,000 $4,500 $6,000

PATEK PHILIPPE, 18 jewels, RF# 1491, Ca. 1940
18k $4,000 $4,500 $5,500

PATEK PHILIPPE,18J., center sec., RF#3411, c.1960
18K $2,200 $2,400 $2,800

PATEK PHILIPPE, 18 J., RF # 2508, center sec., c. 1950s
18k $3,000 $3,500 $4,500

PATEK PHILIPPE, 18J., RF # 2457, center sec., c. 1950s
18k $2,800 $3,000 $3,800

PATEK PHILIPPE, 18 jewels, center sec., waterproof
18k $3,500 $4,000 $5,000

PATEK PHILIPPE,18J., RF#3495, cal.27sc, c.1969
18K $1,800 $2,000 $2,400

PATEK PHILIPPE, 18 jewels, RF # 2460, center sec.
18k $2,800 $3,200 $4,000

PATEK PHILIPPE, 18 jewels, RF# 2541, Ca. 1940s
18k C&B............................. $4,000 $4,500 $5,500

PATEK PHILIPPE,18J., RF# 3541, auto wind, Ca. 1966
18K...$4,000 $4,500 $5,500

PATEK PHILIPPE,18J., RF# 3410, Ca. 1971
18K C&B............................$3,500 $3,800 $4,500

PATEK PHILIPPE,18J., RF# 3558, auto wind, Ca. 1968
18K...$4,000 $4,500 $5,500

PATEK PHILIPPE,18J., RF# 3473, Ca. 1962
18K $3,000 $3,300 $3,800

PATEK PHILIPPE,18J., RF# 2451, "Calatrava", Ca. 1952
18K...$3,200 $3,600 $4,400

PATEK PHILIPPE,18J., RF# 2568-1, Ca. 1957
18K $2,300 $2,500 $3,000

PATEK PHILIPPE,18J., RF# 1595, Ca. 1949
18K(rose) $3,500 $4,000 $5,000

PATEK PHILIPPE,18J., RF# 1589, Ca. 1955
18K(rose)............................$2,700 $3,000 $3,500

PATEK PHILIPPE, 18 J., RF # 3569, auto wind, **back set**
18k $2,800 $3,200 $4,000

PATEK PHILIPPE, 18 jewels RF # 3606
18k C&B............................ $2,000 $2,400 $3,000

PATEK PHILIPPE, 18 jewels, RF # 3509
18k $2,000 $2,200 $2,600

PATEK PHILIPPE,18J., RF# 2573, c.1954
18K $2,500 $2,800 $3,500

PATEK PHILIPPE, 18 J., small "Calatrava," c. 1940s
18k $3,200 $3,600 $4,200

PATEK PHILIPPE,18J., RF#2592, c.1956
18K $2,000 $2,200 $2,600

PATEK PHILIPPE, 18 jewels, RF # 2589, Ca. 1970s
18k $2,600 $2,800 $3,200

PATEK PHILIPPE,18J., RF#3574, c.1960
s. steel $1,200 $1,400 $1,800

PATEK PHILIPPE, 18J., "Calatrava,", RF# 2588, c.1940s
18k $3,000 $3,400 $4,200

PATEK PHILIPPE, 18 J., RF # 497, unusual shape, c. 1940s
18k $6,000 $7,000 $9,000

PATEK PHILIPPE, 36J., RF # 3800, "Nautilus", gold & steel
18K.......................................$9,000 $10,000 $12,000
18k&s. steel $5,000 $5,500 $6,500
s. steel $3,400 $4,000 $4,800

PATEK PHILIPPE, **mid size, QUARTZ,** rf#3900/1, date
s. steel $3,000 $3,300 $4,000

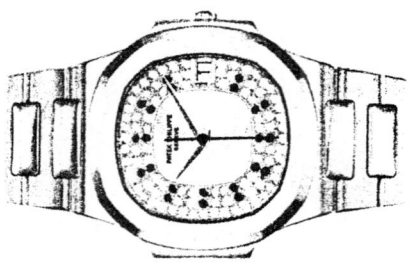

PATEK PHILIPPE, quartz, rf#3900/101, date
pave diamonds=.50ct., ruby hour markers
18k $6,000 $7,500 $10,000

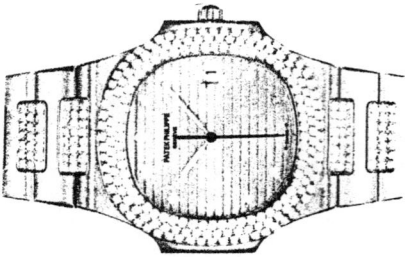

PATEK PHILIPPE, quartz, rf#3900/5, date, dia-
monds=2.27ct.
18k C&B............................$9,000 $10,000 $13,000

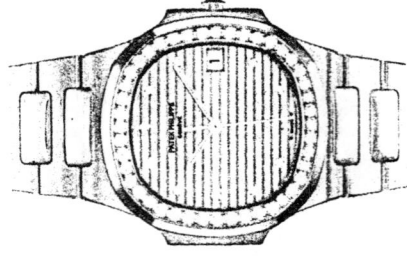

PATEK PHILIPPE, quartz, rf#3900/3, date, Carran dial
diamonds=.68ct.
platinum............................$12,000 $14,000 $17,000

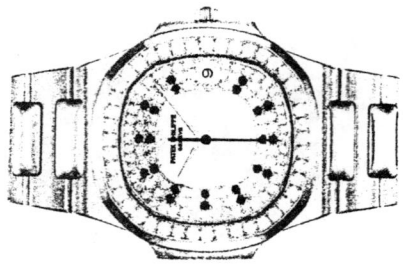

PATEK PHILIPPE, quartz, rf#3900/103, date
diamonds=.68ct, pave diamonds=.50, ruby markers
18k $7,000 $8,500 $11,000

PATEK PHILIPPE, quartz, rf#3900/105, date,
diamonds=2.27ct., pave diamonds=.50, ruby markers
18k C&B...........................$10,000 $11,000 $14,000

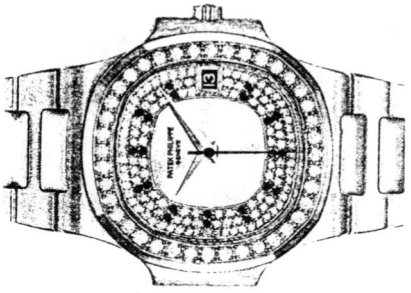

PATEK PHILIPPE, auto wind, rf#3800/103, date
diamonds=.91ct., pave diamonds=63ct., ruby markers
18kC&B...........................$17,000 $19,000 $23,000

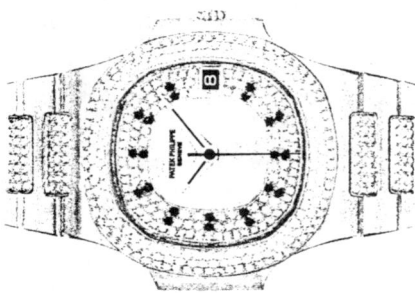

PATEK PHILIPPE, auto wind, rf#3800/105, date
diamonds=2.40ct., pave diam.=.63ct., ruby markers
18kC&B...........................$20,000 $22,000 $26,000

" PATEK PHILIPPE" watches should be signed on the case,
dial & movement to bring the prices listed in this book.
(triple signed P.P.CO.)

Some grades are not included. Their values can be
determined by comparing with **similar** age, size, metal
content, style, grades, or models such as **time only**,
chronograph, repeater etc. listed.

PATEK PHILIPPE, auto wind, rf#3800/108, date,
diamonds=7.46ct.,pave diam.=1.50ct.,sapphire markers
18k C&B...........................$30,000 $33,000 $40,000

PATEK PHILIPPE, 36J., RF # 3700, "Nautilus," large size
s. steel $5,000 $5,500 $6,500

PATEK PHILIPPE, 36 J. "Nautilus," diamond bezel
18k $12,000 $13,000 $15,000

PATEK PHILIPPE, skeleton, rf# 3885
18k $5,000 $6,000 $8,000

PATEK PHILIPPE, skeleton, rf# 3878, auto wind
18k $8,000 $9,000 $11,000

PATEK PHILIPPE, 36 J., RF # 3588, diamond dial & bezel
18k $4,000 $4,500 $5,500

PATEK PHILIPPE, skeleton, rf# 3886
18k $7,000 $8,000 $10,000

PATEK PHILIPPE, 18J., diamond dial, Contract case, c. 1952
platinum.............................. $2,500 $2,800 $3,500

PATEK PHILIPPE, skeleton, diamonds=.62ct., rf# 3885
18k $8,000 $9,000 $11,000

PATEK PHILIPPE, 18J., **diamond dial** "Calatrava"
platinum.............................. $8,000 $9,000 $11,000

PATEK PHILIPPE, skeleton, diamonds=.85ct., rf# 3884
manual wind
18k $9,000 $10,000 $12,000

PATEK PHILIPPE, 18J., "Calatrava," mid size, **dia. dial**
platinum.............................. $9,000 $10,000 $12,000

Wrist Watches listed in this section are priced at the collectable
fair market **Trade Show** level as **complete** watches having an
original gold-filled case and stainless steel back, also with
original dial, leather watch band, and the entire original movement in good working order with no repairs needed.

PATEK PHILIPPE, 18 jewels, c. 1980s
18k C&B $2,800 $3,200 $3,700

PATEK PHILIPPE, quartz, c. 1980s
18k C&B $2,500 $2,800 $3,200

PATEK PHILIPPE, 23 jewels, RF # 3738, c. 1960s
18k C&B $3,500 $4,000 $4,800

PATEK PHILIPPE, 18 jewels, RF # 3745, c. 1980s
18k C&B $2,600 $2,800 $3,300

Wrist Watches listed in this section are priced at the collectable
fair market **Trade Show** level as **complete** watches having an
original gold-filled case and stainless steel back, also with
original dial, leather watch band, and the entire original movement in good working order with no repairs needed.

🕐 Pricing in this Guide are fair market price for **COMPLETE**
watches which are reflected from the "**NAWCC**" National and
regional shows.

PATEK PHILIPPE, 18 jewels, RF # 2548, massive lugs
18k $5,500 $6,000 $7,000

PATEK PHILIPPE, 18 J., RF # 1585, concave & hooded
lugs
18k $4,500 $5,000 $6,000

PATEK PHILIPPE, 18 jewels, hooded lugs, c.1930s
18K $5,000 $5,500 $6,500

PATEK PHILIPPE, 18 jewels, mid-sized, 2 tone
note: **winds at 12**
18k (y & w) $6,000 $7,000 $9,000

🕐 Some grades are not included. Their values can be
determined by comparing with **similar** age, size, metal
content, style, grades, or models such as **time only**,
chronograph, repeater etc. listed.

PATEK PHILIPPE, 18 J., extended lugs, 2 tone, rf#497
18k (y & w) $8,000 $9,000 $12,000

PATEK PHILIPPE, 18 jewels, lady's watch
18k $1,200 $1,400 $1,800

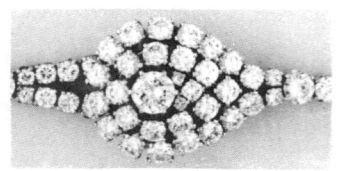

PATEK PHILIPPE,18 J., lady's, hinged lid set in diamonds
18k $7,000 $8,000 $10,000

PATEK PHILIPPE, 18 jewels, lady's watch
18k C&B.............................$2,500 $3,000 $4,000

PATEK PHILIPPE, 18 J., lady's watch, diamond bezel
platinum $3,000 $3,500 $4,500

PATEK PHILIPPE, 18 jewels, lady's watch, c. 1950s
18k $3,000 $3,500 $4,500

PATEK PHILIPPE, 18 jewels, lady's watch, c. 1940s
18k C&B $3,000 $3,500 $4,500

PATEK PHILIPPE, 18J., lady's watch, min. repeater
18k.......................................$65,000 $75,000 $95,000

PATEK PHILIPPE, 18 jewels, lady's watch, c. 1950s
18k.......................................$1,400 $1,800 $2,500

PATEK PHILIPPE, 18 jewels, lady's watch, c. 1940s
18k.......................................$1,000 $1,200 $1,500

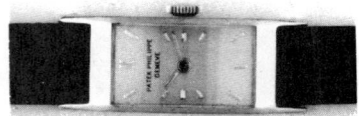

PATEK PHILIPPE, 18 jewels, lady's watch, c. 1940s
18k.......................................$1,200 $1,400 $1,700

PATEK PHILIPPE, 18 jewels, lady's watch, c. 1950s
18k.......................................$900 $1,100 $1,400

PATEK, PHILIPPE
MOVEMENT IDENTIFICATION

Caliber 6¾, no. 60
S.no. 865000-869999
(1940-1955)

Caliber 7, no. 70
S.no. 943300-949999
(1940-1960)
S.no. 940000-949999

Caliber 8, no. 80
S.no. 840000-849999
(1935-1960)

Caliber 8, no. 85
S.no. 850000-859999
(1935-1968)

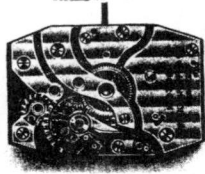

Caliber 9, no. 90
S.no. 833150-839999
S.no. 970000-979999
(1940-1950)

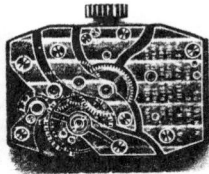

Caliber 9, no. 90a
830000-833149
(1940-1950)

Caliber 10, no. 105
S.no. 900000-909999
(1940-1945)

Caliber 10, no. 110
S.no. 910000-919999
(1940-1950)

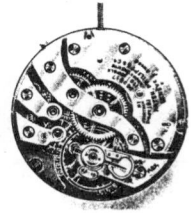

Caliber 10, no. 200
S.no. 740000-759999
(1952-1965)
S.no. 950000-959999
(1945-1955)

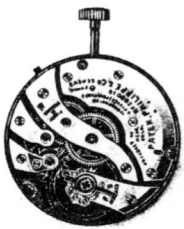

Caliber 23, no. 300
S.no. 780000-799999
(1955-1965)

Caliber 12, no. 600AT
S.no. 760000-779999
(1952-1960)

Caliber 12, no. 400
S.no. 720000-739999
(1950-1965)

Caliber 12, no. 120
826900-829999 (1935-1940)

Caliber 12, no. 120A
92000-929999 (1940-1950)
960000-969999 (1946-1952)
938000-939999 (1952-1954)

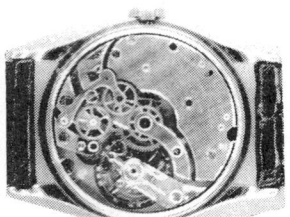

Caliber 12 , center seconds

Caliber 13, no. 130A

Caliber 13, no. 130B

Caliber 13, no. 130C

Chronograph, no. 862000-863995 (1940-1950); no. 867000-869999 (1950-1970)

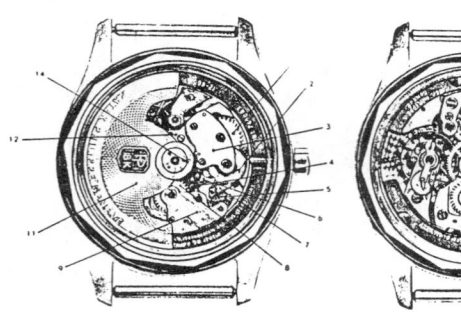

Caliber 12-600 AT, S.no. 760,000-779,999 (1960-1970)

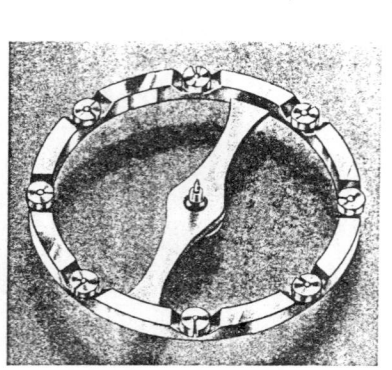

GYROMAX BALANCE WHEEL

PATRIA, 7 jewels, enamel dial, **compass**, Ca. 1920
s. steel .... ★$225 $275 $400

PATRIA, 7 jewels, enamel dial,
silver $55 $60 $95

PERFINE, 17 jewels, chronog., 2 reg.
gold filled............................... $150 $175 $225
s. steel $95 $125 $175

PERPETUAL W. CO., 15 jewels, rim wind & set,
original retail price in 1933 was $31.50
14k $800 $900 $1,100
gold filled............................... $350 $375 $450
s. steel $250 $275 $350
base metal $195 $225 $300

PERPETUAL W. CO., 15 jewels, c. 1930s
14k.. $600 $650 $800
gold filled............................... $350 $400 $550

PERPETUAL W. CO., 15J., fluted bezel, and sold for
$37.50 in 1933
base metal............................... $150 $175 $250

PERPETUAL W. CO., 15 jewels, fluted bezel
gold filled............................... $300 $325 $400

PERPETUAL W. CO., 15 J., diamond bezel, c. 1930s
platinum $550 $600 $700

PHILLIPE W. CO., 17J., RF#2501, chronog., c. 1950
s. steel...................................... $195 $250 $325

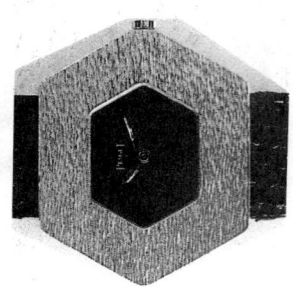

PIAGET,18J., cal.9p2 , c.1980
18k(w)....................................$500 $550 $700

PIAGET,18J., center sec., RF#1176, cal.fl 560, c.1952
18k $400 $450 $600

PIAGET,18J., center sec., c.1950
18k $450 $500 $650

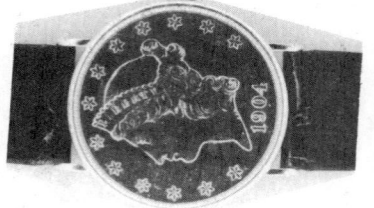

PIAGET, 18 jewels, 1904 $20 dollar gold piece, flip top
22k $900 $1,100 $1,400

🕐 Some grades are not included. Their values can be
determined by comparing with **similar** age, size, metal
content, style, grades, or models such as **time only**,
chronograph, repeater etc. listed.

PIAGET, 18 jewels, 2 movements, 2 dials,
18k..$600 $700 $850

PIAGET, 18 jewels, black dial
18k..$500 $550 $700

PIAGET, 18 jewels, center sec., auto wind
18k..$600 $700 $850

PIAGET, 18 jewels, ref. #8177, auto wind
18k..$600 $700 $850

PIAGET, 18 jewels
18k $600 $700 $900

PIAGET, 30 jewels, auto wind, gold rotor
18k $600 $700 $900

PIAGET, 18 jewels, 18k case, 14k band
18k & 14k C&B......................$800 $900 $1,100

PIAGET, 18J., for Van Cleef, center lugs, thin model
18k $600 $700 $850

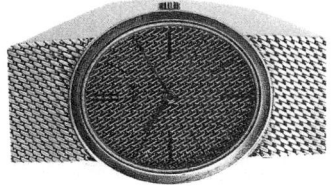

PIAGET,18J., RF#9821 , c.1975
18k C&B $800 $900 $1,100

PIAGET, 18 jewels, oval style
18k C&B $500 $600 $750

PIAGET, 18 jewels, oval style
18k...$300 $350 $500

PIAGET, 18 jewels, textured bezel
18k...$700 $750 $900

PIAGET, 18J, 2 time zones & 2 movements
18k...$800 $900 $1,200

PIAGET, 30 jewels, auto-wind, textured bezel
18k...$600 $700 $1,000

PIAGET, 18J., RF#9298, c. 1970
18k $700 $800 $950

PIAGET, 18 jewels,
18k $700 $800 $1,000

PIAGET, 18 jewels, "Emperor", RF#7131C516
18k plain dial $3,000 $3,300 $4,000
18k pave dial......................$3,500 $3,800 $4,500

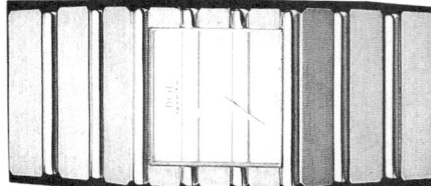

PIAGET, "Polo", RF#7131C701, quartz
18kC&B $4,000 $4,500 $5,500

PIAGET, "Polo", RF#15562C701, quartz
18k $3,000 $3,500 $4,500
NOTE: PIAGET identification # the first 3 to 5 = case de-
sign, a letter as A, B, C, =bracelet design. All models beginning with 7, 8,15 may be worn while swimming.

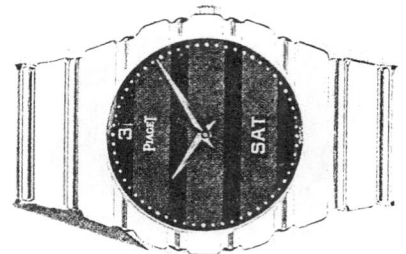

PIAGET, "Polo", RF#15562C701, quartz
18kC&B $2,500 $3,000 $4,000

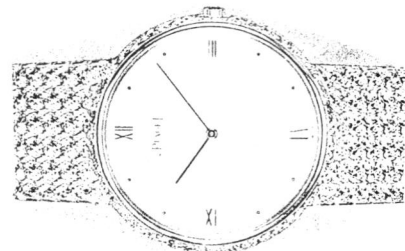

PIAGET,   RF#8065D4
18kC&B $1,500 $1,700 $2,100

PIAGET, 17 jewels, Ca. 1957
18k...$500 $550 $700

PIERCE,7J., Doctors style, Ca. 1930
base metal..................................$75 $95 $150

Wrist Watches listed in this section are priced at the collectable
fair market Trade Show **retail** level as **complete** watches having
an original gold-filled case and stainless steel back, also with
original dial, leather watch band, and the entire original movement in good working order with no repairs needed.

PIERCE, 17J., early auto wind, **"Parashock,"** Ca. 1930s waterproof, back secured by four screws.
s. steel $300 $350 $450

PIERCE, 17J., triple date, moon ph.
gold filled $250 $300 $425

PIERCE, 21 jewels, "Duofon", **Alarm**, Ca. 1955
s. steel $90 $110 $150

POBEDA, 15J., tonneau, Ca. 1930s
14k pink $195 $225 $275

PIERCE, 17 jewels, chronog. one button
s. steel $225 $250 $300

PONTIFA, 17 jewels, chronog. day-date-month, 3 reg.
14k $400 $450 $550
s. steel $250 $300 $375

PIERCE, 17 jewels, chronog., c. 1940s
s. steel $135 $175 $225
14k $350 $375 $450
18k $425 $450 $525

PORTA, 17J., antimagnetic, c.1955
gold plate $20 $30 $55

PRAESENT, 17J., triple date, moon ph., mid size, c.1948
gold filled................................$150 $175 $225

PULSAR, L.E.D. (light emitting diode), **working**, ca.1975
14k..$300 $325 $425
gold filled...............................$95 $135 $250

PROVITA, 17J., cal.1525, c.1973
18k...$150 $175 $250

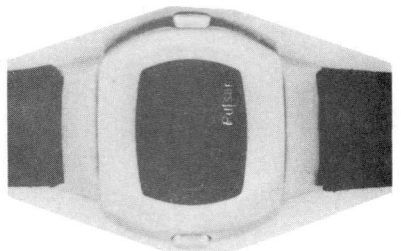

PULSAR, L.E.D. (light emitting diode), **working,**
18k..$400 $425 $550
14k..$300 $325 $425
gold filled...............................$95 $135 $250
s. steel.....................................$95 $135 $250

PRONTO, 17 jewels, triple date, auto wind, waterproof
s. steel..$75 $95 $135

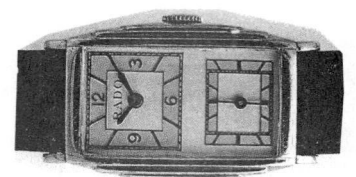

RADO, 7J., double dial, c.1938
gold filled...............................$195 $225 $275

PULSAR, L.E.D. (light emitting diode), **working**, ca.1975
18k...$400 $425 $550
14k...$300 $325 $425
gold filled................................$95 $135 $250
s. steel......................................$95 $135 $250

RADO, 17J., date, ca.1960
gold plate...............................$20 $30 $60

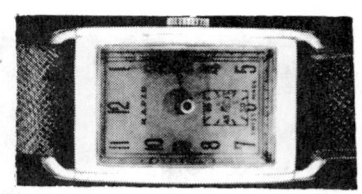

RAPID, 17J., on mvt. PATHE W. CO.
gold filled................................$35 $40 $65

RECORD, 17J., split sec. chronog., date, moon phase
18k $4,500 $5,000 $6,000

RECORD, 17 jewels, split sec. chronog.
18k $3,500 $4,000 $5,000
s. steel $2,000 $2,200 $2,800

RECORD, 17 J., triple date, moon ph., auto wind ,
2 reg. chronograph,
18k $1,200 $1,400 $1,800

RECORD, 17 jewels, triple date, moon phase, c. 1940s
18k $600 $700 $900

RECORD, 17 jewels, day-date-month, moon phase
s. steel $300 $350 $450

RECORD, 17 J., triple date, moon phase, auto wind
18k $650 $750 $950

REGINA, enamel dial, center lugs, c.1929
silver $95 $125 $165

⏀ Some grades are not included. Their values can be
determined by comparing with **similar** age, size, metal
content, style, grades, or models such as **time only**,
chronograph, repeater etc. listed.

REMBRANT, 17J., chronog., c.1942
18k $350 $400 $500
s. steel $125 $150 $195

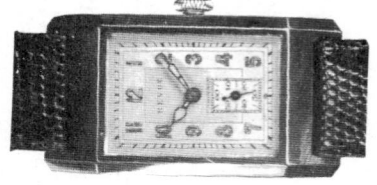

REVUE, 17J., beveled case, cal.54, c.1940
nickel... $25 $35 $55

RIMA, 17J., aux. sec.,
14k $95 $110 $150

ROAMER, 17 jewels, date, auto wind
gold filled................................. $35 $45 $75

ROAMER, 17 jewels, hidden lugs
gold filled $35 $45 $75

ROCAIL, 15J., auto-wind, c.1930s
s. steel $75 $95 $135

ROCKFORD,15J., "Winona", made in USA, S#761074
gold filled $275 $325 $475
base metal $175 $195 $275

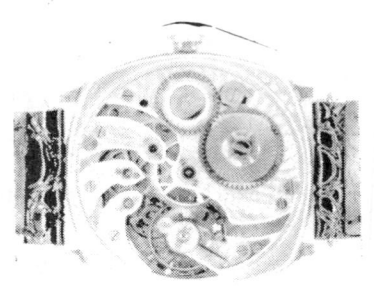

ROCKFORD, 17J., "Iroquois", gold train
gold filled $275 $325 $475

🕐 Pricing in this Guide are fair market price for **COMPLETE** watches which are reflected from the "**NAWCC**" National and regional shows.

ROLEX WATCH CO.
Swiss

Rolex was founded by Hans Wilsdorf in 1905, with his brother-in-law using the name of Wilsdorf & Davis and used movement supplier **Aegler** of Bienne, Switzerland, and bought cases from London. In *1908* the trade-mark **"Rolex"** was officially registered, and by 1919, Wilsdorf started the *"Manufacture des Montres Rolex"* and the movements were manufactured in Bienne, but finished and cased in Geneva. In 1926, they made the first real waterproof wrist watch and called it the *"Oyster"*. Rolex introduced a self-winding movement they called *"Perpetual"* in 1931. In 1945, they introduced the *"Date-Just,"* which showed the day of the month. In 1950 the *"Turn-o-graph"* was used, the forerunner of the Submariner & in 1953 the *"Submariner"* was introduced and in 1954 the *"GMT Master"* model. In 1956, a *"Day-Date"* model was released which indicates the day of the month (in numbers) and the day of the week (in letters).

IMPORTANT:

The following is a *guide* to help determine the age of your Rolex watches. However on **some** Oyster style watches Rolex added **inside** the case a Roman number (I,II,III,IV) to denote first, second, third, or fourth quarter + "53", "54", "55", "56" to denote the year of production. Example outside Oyster case # 955454 inside case IV-53 which = last quarter of 1953. Example outside Oyster case # 282621 inside case III-55 which = third quarter of 1955. Rolex went back to 100,000 in 1954 on some cases.

ROLEX ESTIMATED PRODUCTION DATES

DATE–SERIAL #	DATE–SERIAL #	DATE–SERIAL #	DATE–SERIAL #	DATE–SERIAL #	DATE–SERIAL #	DATE–SERIAL #
1925 - 25,000	1937- 99,000	1949 - 608,000	1961-1,480,000	1973-3,741,000	1985 — 8,815,000	1992 1/4-C000,001
1926 - 28,500	1938-118,000	1950 - 673,500	1962-1,557,000	1974-4,002,000	1986 — 9,292,000	1993 3/4-S000,001
1927 - 30,500	1939-136,000	1951 - 738,500	1963-1,635,000	1975-4,266,000	1987 — 9,765,000	1995 — W000,001
1928 - 33,000	1940-165,000	1952 - 804,000	1964-1,713,000	1976-4,538,000	1987 1/2-R999,999	1996 — T000,001
1929 - 35,500	1941-194,000	1953 - 950,000	1965-1,792,000	1977-5,005,000	1987 3/4-R000,001	1997 3/4-U000,001
1930 - 38,000	1942-224,000	1954 - 999,999	1966-1,870,000	1978-5,481,000	1988 — R999,999	1999 — A000,001
1931 - 40,000	1943-253,000	1955 - 200,000	1967-2,164,000	1979-5,965,000	1989 — L000,001	2000 — P000,001
1932 - 43,000	1944-285,000	1956 - 400,000	1968-2,426,000	1980-6,432,000	1990 — L999,999	2001 — K000,001
1933 - 47,000	1945-348,000	1957 - 600,000	1969-2,689,000	1981-6,910,000	1990 1/2-E000,001	
1934 - 55,000	1946-413,000	1958 - 800,000	1970-2,952,000	1982-7,385,000	1991 1/4-E999,999	
1935 - 68,000	1947-478,000	1959-1,100,000	1971-3,215,000	1983-7,860,000	1991 1/2-X000,001	
1936 - 81,000	1948-543,000	1960-1,401,000	1972-3,478,000	1984-8,338,000	1991 3/4-N000,001	

The above list is provided for determining the APPROXIMATE age of your watch. Match serial number with date. Watches were not necessarily sold in the exact order of manufactured date. The above list was furnished with the help of Jeffrey P. Hess. Jeff and James M. Dowling authored a book *"The Best of Time"* a unauthorized history of the Rolex Watch Co.

ROLEX W. CO. REFERENCE # INDEX

REF #	PAGE	REF #	PAGE	REF #	PAGE	REF #	PAGE	REF #	PAGE	REF #	PAGE
619	—1,047	1768	—1,024	3478	—1,035	4768	—1,022	6223	—1,027	6634	—1,027
678	—1,017	1803	—1,041	3492	—1,052	4891	—1,033	6234	—1,021	6694	—1,025
971	—1,024	1803	—1,042	3562	—1,015	5015	—1,038	6238	—1,021	6694	—1,032
1002	—1,028	1804	—1,041	3595	—1,034	5020	—1,032	6238	—1,022	6700-3	-1,052
1005	—1,029	1807	—1,042	3655	—1,034	5050	—1,038	6239	—1,022	6800	—1,033
1007	—1,038	1823	—1,042	3665	—1,018	5500	—1,029	6239	—1,023	6964	—1,026
1011	—1,031	1862	—1,024	3696	—1,037	5502	—1,028	6241	—1,022	7016	—1,050
1016	—1,044	1878	—1,047	3737	—1,048	5504	—1,029	6263	—1,022	7610	—1,050
1018	—1,040	1901	—1,042	3745	—1,033	5504	—1,044	6265	—1,022	7809	—1,050
1019	—1,014	2010	—1,029	3767	—1,035	5508	—1,044	6266	—1,032	7909	—1,050
1020	—1,015	2136	—1,017	3893	—1,049	5512	—1,046	6284	—1,029	7928	—1,050
1025	—1,028	2245	—1,024	3937	—1,025	5513	—1,045	6305	—1,026	8094	—1,048
1030	—1,031	2280	—1,035	3997	—1,022	6031	—1,026	6309	—1,043	8126	—1,048
1071	—1,017	2303	—1,020	4029	—1,047	6011	—1,038	6421	—1,035	8171	—1,023
1343	—1,025	2319	—1,036	4062	—1,021	6021	—1,035	6422	—1,027	8180	—1,020
1453	—1,040	2495	—1,032	4113	—1,020	6024	—1,028	6424	—1,028	8206	—1,020
1490	—1,023	2508	—1,020	4220	—1,036	6024	—1,029	6426	—1,043	8405	—1,030
1490	—1,024	2537	—1,047	4222	—1,016	6029	—1,027	6427	—1,034	8443	—1,016
1491	—1,023	2541	—1,024	4302	—1,035	6031	—1,026	6466	—1,036	8952	—1,030
1500	—1,025	2764	—1,037	4325	—1,027	6034	—1,021	6536	—1,046	9083	—1,033
1501	—1,026	2765	—1,051	4365	—1,032	6050	—1,040	6538	—1,044	9420	—1,051
1503	—1,042	2940	—1,014	4376	—1,023	6056	—1,036	6541	—1,015	9491	—1,049
1527	—1,024	2940	—1,039	4377	—1,032	6062	—1,023	6542	—1,045	9659	—1,015
1527	—1,025	2940	—1,041	4392	—1,032	6066	—1,036	6552	—1,033	9659	—1,016
1530	—1,038	3055	—1,020	4402	—1,023	6071	—1,017	6556	—1,015	9829	—1,015
1550	—1,032	3065	—1,036	4463	—1,051	6075	—1,027	6558	—1,015		
1563-3	-1,050	3116	—1,019	4467	—1,021	6082	—1,028	6564	—1,026		
1600	—1,033	3121	—1,034	4467	—1,026	6084	—1,030	6565	—1,028		
1601	—1,026	3130	—1,039	4467	—1,041	6085	—1,028	6567	—1,030		
1615	—1,025	3131	—1,037	4478	—1,031	6092	—1,031	6568	—1,030		
1625	—1,044	3133	—1,038	4486	—1,052	6094	—1,025	6581	—1,030		
1655	—1,046	3139	—1,018	4554	—1,052	6098	—1,029	6582	—1,027		
1665	—1,044	3233	—1,020	4547	—1,018	6102	—1,031	6585	—1,038		
1665	—1,045	3359	—1,019	4593	—1,052	6105	—1,026	6590	—1,031		
1666	—1,046	3361	—1,024	4647	—1,018	6151-1-1,044		6604	—1,025		
1671	—1,045	3386	—1,019	4663	—1,049	6202	—1,043	6611	—1,033		
1701	—1,052	3458	—1,039	4767	—1,021			6627	—1,033		

NOTE: See page 1,054 for more Rolex Reference numbers with **PRICES ONLY**.

DIALS FOR MINT PRICES MUST BE ALL **ORIGINAL**.

ROLEX

BIENNE

ROLEX, 15 jewels, enamel dial, ca. 1920
silver $800 $900 $1,200

ROLEX, 15 jewels, enamel dial, flip top, c. 1918
silver $900 $1,100 $1,500

Above: **Aegler, S.A. Montres**. Rolex Watch Co. used the
movement supplier **Aegler** of Bienne, Switzerland.

ROLEX, 15 jewels, enamel bezel, Ca. 1935
9K.. $1,000 $1,200 $1,500

ROLEX, 17J., RF# 2940, back is flat & tin can shaped
used a non-magnetic metal ???
non-magnetic....... ★ ★ ★ ★ $2,000 $2,200 $2,800

ROLEX, 15 jewels, enamel dial, demi- hunter style, ca. 1920
silver $1,000 $1,200 $1,600

ROLEX, 26J., **Milgauss** 1st registered in 1954, RF#1019,
Ca. 1970s
s.steel $6,000 $7,000 $9,000

ROLEX, 17J, **Milgauss** in red, oyster, perpetual, RF# 6541
Lighting bolt sec. hand, Milgauss 1st registered in 1954
s. steel $15,000 $20,000 $30,000

ROLEX, 17J., "Precision"
s. steel $350 $400 $550

ROLEX, 17 jewels,"1/4 Century Club", **BOMBE**, c. 1960s
18k $1,400 $1,600 $2,000
14k $1,200 $1,400 $1,800

ROLEX,17J., center sec., RF#9829, cal.1210
s. steel $325 $425 $525

ROLEX, 17 jewels, ''Precision,'' center sec., Roman bezel
18k $900 $1,000 $1,200

ROLEX, 17J., RF#3562 , c.1955
14k $500 $650 $850

ROLEX, 26J., **jumping** center sec., RF # 6556, cal.# 1040,
Tru-beat on dial, also RF # 6558 & RF # 1020, Ca. 1960
Note: **Jumping center sec. must be working to bring prices listed.**
s. steel .... ★ $4,000 $5,000 $7,000
14K.............................. ★ ★ $6,000 $7,000 $9,000
18K.............................. ★ ★ ★ $7,000 $8,000 $10,000

ROLEX,17J., center sec., RF#9659, c.1960
14k $500 $650 $850

🕐 A collector should expect to pay modestly higher prices
at local shops

ROLEX,17J., "Chronometer", RF# 4222, Ca.1945
18k $900 $1,000 $1,400

ROLEX, 19J., RF # 8443 , c.1965
14k $700 $800 $1,100

ROLEX, 17J., "Precision", fancy lugs,
9k $500 $600 $800

ROLEX, 17 jewels, "Precision"
18k $900 $1,000 $1,200

Wrist Watches listed in this section are priced at the collectable fair market **Trade Show** level as **complete** watches having an original gold-filled case and stainless steel back, also with original dial, leather watch band, and the entire original movement in good working order with no repairs needed.

🕐 Some grades are not included. Their values can be determined by comparing with **similar** age, size, metal content, style, grades, or models such as **time only**, chronograph, repeater etc. listed.

ROLEX, 15 jewels, enamel dial, wire lugs
9k $800 $950 $1,250

ROLEX, 15j, early waterproof,"Tropical", (case within a case)
18k $2,200 $2,500 $3,200
silver $1,400 $1,600 $2,000

ROLEX, 17 jewels, RF # 9659 , Ca 1960s
14k C&B...............................$1,200 $1,300 $1,600

ROLEX, 17 jewels, "Precision"
gold filled $300 $400 $650

ROLEX,15J., wire lugs, c.1925
silver $350 $450 $600

ROLEX, 15J., oyster, royal, 2 tone dial, c. 1930s
9k $1,200 $1,400 $1,700

ROLEX,15J.,"Aqua", RF # 2136, c.1928
s. steel $350 $450 $600

ROLEX, 15J., RF # 1071, oyster, ca. 1930
silver $800 $900 $1,100

ROLEX,15J., RF # 6071, c.1926
s. steel $500 $600 $900

ROLEX, 15 jewels, oyster, center sec., enamel dial
18k $3,400 $3,800 $4,500
14k $2,200 $2,500 $3,200
9k $1,400 $1,600 $2,000
silver $1,000 $1,200 $1,500
s. steel $600 $700 $1,000

ROLEX,15J., by OYSTER W. CO., c. 1927
s. steel $300 $400 $700

ROLEX, 17 jewels, RF # 678, oyster, enamel dial, c. 1934
18k $3,200 $3,400 $4,000
14k $2,200 $2,500 $3,000
9k $1,400 $1,600 $2,000
silver $800 $1,000 $1,500
s. steel $600 $700 $1,000

ROLEX, 15 jewels, oyster, center sec, Ca. 1930
9K $1,500 $1,700 $2,500
14K $1,800 $2,200 $3,000

DIALS FOR MINT PRICES MUST BE ALL **ORIGINAL**.

ROLEX, 17 jewels, **not** oyster case, center sec.

18k	$1,000	$1,200	$1,500
14k	$800	$1,000	$1,-300
9k	$600	$800	$1,000
s. steel	$500	$600	$750

ROLEX, 17 jewels, index bezel, **Oyster case**, c. 1928
silver $900 $1,000 $1,300

ROLEX, 18J., note dial top half & bottom, RF # 3139
Oyster case,
s. steel $1,200 $1,400 $1,800

ROLEX,17J., "Army", RF # 4647, c.1948
s. steel $1,100 $1,300 $1,700

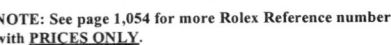

**NOTE: See page 1,054 for more Rolex Reference numbers
with PRICES ONLY.**

ROLEX, 18J., Viceroy, center sec. Oyster case, ca. 1937
s. steel $600 $700 $1,000

ROLEX,17J., "Army", RF # 4647, 2 tone dial, Oyster case,
c.1943
s. steel $550 $650 $950

ROLEX,17J., RF # 3665, enamel dial, Ca.1930
s. steel $600 $800 $1,200

ROLEX, 17 jewels, oyster, RF # 4547
s. steel $650 $700 $1,000

⏱ Pricing in this Guide are fair market price for **COMPLETE**
watches which are reflected from the "**NAWCC**" National and
regional shows.

DIALS FOR MINT PRICES MUST BE ALL **ORIGINAL**.

ROLEX, 17 jewels, oyster, metal dial, c. 1930s
18k $2,800 $3,000 $3,600
14k $2,200 $2,400 $2,800

ROLEX,17J., "Viceroy", RF # 3359, c.1943
14k & s. steel.......................$1,000 $1,200 $1,600

ROLEX,17J., "Observatory", RF # 3386, c.1940
gold filled................................$700 $800 $1,000

ROLEX, 17 jewels, oyster, extra prima "Viceroy"
18k $2,200 $2,500 $3,000

ROLEX,17J., Viceroy, RF # 3116, c.1942
14k $2,000 $2,200 $2,600

ROLEX, 26 jewels, "Viceroy", center sec.
9k $1,200 $1,500 $2,000

ROLEX, 17 jewels, oyster, cushion, 2 tone, c. 1943
14k & s. steel $1,400 $1,600 $2,000

ROLEX,17J., "Skyrocket", Ca.1944
gold filled $400 $450 $600

DIALS FOR MINT PRICES MUST BE ALL **ORIGINAL**.

🕐 Some grades are not included. Their values can be determined by comparing with **similar** age, size, metal content, style, grades, or models such as **time only**, chronograph, repeater etc. listed.

🕐 Pricing in this Guide are fair market price for **COMPLETE** watches which are reflected from the "**NAWCC**" National and regional shows.

DIALS FOR MINT PRICES MUST BE ALL **ORIGINAL**.

ROLEX,17J., 28mm, small one button chronog., RF # 2303
9k .... ★★★$15,000 $17,000 $20,000

ROLEX, 17J., one button chronog. 2 reg., curved back
18k .... ★★★$25,000 $27,000 $32,000

ROLEX,17J., Chronograph, triple date & **moon-phases**,
about **12 made**, RF# 8180 & RF# 2508, Valjoux cal. 72C,
This chronograph is being **FAKED** so beware.
18k .... ★★★★ $65,000 $70,000 $85,000

ROLEX, 17 J., chronog., center lugs, RF#3233, c. 1940s

18k	$8,000	$9,000	$11,000
14k	$5,000	$5,500	$7,000
9k	$3,000	$3,500	$4,500
s. steel	$2,500	$3,000	$4,000

🕐 Note: Rolex chronographs must have original dial, de-
duct 30% for refinished dial.

ROLEX,17J., split second chronog., RF # 4113, **15 examples**, large 43mm, Valjoux caliber 55 VBR, Ca.1943
s. steel .... ★★★★ $30,000 $35,000 $50,000

ROLEX,17J., RF # 3055 , Antimagnetique, 200 made, c.1956
18k $9,000 $10,000 $14,000

ROLEX, 17 J., chronog., 70-made, flat, tachometer, "Gabus",
RF # 8206,c.1940s
18k .... ★★★$15,000 $18,000 $25,000

ROLEX, 17 jewels, chronog., mid-sized, c. 1950s

18k	$8,000	$8,500	$10,000
14k	$7,000	$7,500	$9,000

ROLEX,17J., Valjoux cal.23, RF # 4062, c.1940
18k $6,500 $7,000 $8,500

ROLEX, 17J., chronog., triple-date, diamond style chapter,
RF # 6036, about 175 made in Y. gold , 144 made pink gold
18k $25,000 $27,000 $35,000
14k $22,000 $24,000 $30,000
s. steel $17,000 $19,000 $24,000

ROLEX, 17 jewels, chronog., 3 reg. oyster, RF # 6238
s. steel $7,000 $8,000 $11,000

ROLEX, 17J., chronog., 3 reg., RF # 6234, Valjoux 72bc
s. steel $7,000 $8,000 $11,000
14k $9,000 $10,000 $14,000

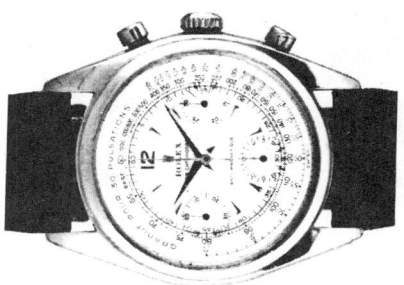

ROLEX, 17J., **pulsation**, 3 reg., RF # 6234, Ca. 1960
s. steel $8,000 $9,500 $14,000

ROLEX,17J., Antimagnetic chronog., 3 reg., RF # 6034,
about 45 made, Ca.1950s
18k .... ★ ★ ★$13,000 $14,000 $18,000

Wrist Watches listed in this section are priced at the collectable
fair market **Trade Show** level as **complete** watches having an
original gold-filled case and stainless steel back, also with
original dial, leather watch band, and the entire original movement in good working order with no repairs needed.

ROLEX,17J., triple date, RF # 4767, c.1948
Beware of **FAKES**
s. steel .... ★ ★$16,000 $18,000 $22,000

ROLEX, 17J., RF # 6238, 3 reg., c. 1950s, rect. markers
18k $9,000 $10,000 $12,000

ROLEX, 17J., RF # 4768, 3 reg., date, tear drop lugs, 1950s
18k $9,000 $10,000 $14,000
14k $8,000 $9,000 $12,000
s. steel $6,000 $7,000 $10,000

ROLEX, 17J., triple-date, 3 reg., square markers
s. steel .... ★ ★ ★ $14,000 $16,000 $20,000

ROLEX, 17J., Daytona, red outside chapter exotic dial
RF# 6241, "PAUL NEWMAN"
s. steel $10,000 $11,000 $14,000
18k & 18k oyster band $18,000 $20,000 $23,000

ROLEX,17J., exotic dial, RF#6239, Valjoux 727, c.1965
"PAUL NEWMAN", *(beware of reproduction dials)*
18k no band $14,000 $15,000 $18,000
s. steel $10,000 $11,000 $14,000

ROLEX,17J., "Daytona", RF#6263, c.1978
s. steel $8,000 $8,500 $10,000

ROLEX,17J., screw down pusher 1st used 1976, RF#6265,
s. steel $8,000 $8,500 $10,000

ROLEX, 17 jewels, RF # 3997, chronog., Ca. 1940
s . steel $2,500 $3,000 $3,800

ROLEX, 17 J., tachometer, 3 reg., RF # 6239, c.1960s

18k	$12,000	$13,000	$15,000
14k	$10,000	$11,000	$13,000
s. steel	$7,000	$8,000	$10,000

ROLEX,17J., triple-date, moon ph., RF # 8171, **1,000 made**

18k	★ ★ ★$12,000	$14,000	$18,000
14k	★ ★ ★$9,000	$10,000	$12,000
s. steel	★ ★ ★$7,000	$8,000	$10,000

Above: Watch is a ☜ **FAKE** ☞
ROLEX on dial & movement, day-date-month, moon ph.

ROLEX,17J., STARS on dial, triple date, RF # 6062, Ca.1945

18k Pink Gold	★ ★ ★ ★$25,000	$30,000	$45,000
18k	★ ★ ★ ★$24,000	$30,000	$38,000

ROLEX,17J., day-date-month, moon ph., RF # 6062,c.1945

18k	★ ★ ★$20,000	$25,000	$35,000

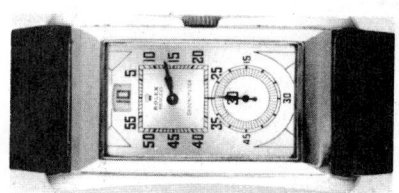

ROLEX, 15J., jumping hr., duo dial, RF # 4402 &
RF # 1491, Ca. 1930s

platinum	$14,000	$16,000	$20,000
18k	$12,000	$14,000	$17,000
14k	$10,000	$11,000	$14,000
9k	$7,000	$8,000	$11,000
silver	$6,000	$7,000	$10,000
gold filled	$4,000	$5,000	$8,000
s. steel	$5,000	$6,000	$9,000

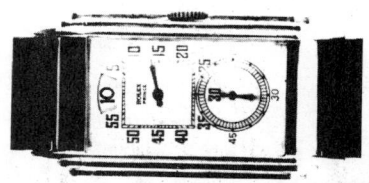

ROLEX,17J. jump hr., duo dial, stepped case, RF# 4376

18k 2 tone	$15,000	$18,000	$22,000
18k	$12,000	$13,000	$16,000
14k	$9,000	$10,000	$13,000
9k	$7,000	$8,000	$11,000
s. steel	$6,000	$7,000	$9,000

ROLEX, 17 jewels, ''Prince,'' duo dial, RF#1490

18k C&B	$5,000	$6,000	$8,000

🕐 Pricing in this Guide are fair market price for **COMPLETE**
watches which are reflected from the "**NAWCC**" National and
regional shows.

DIALS FOR MINT PRICES MUST BE ALL <u>ORIGINAL</u>.

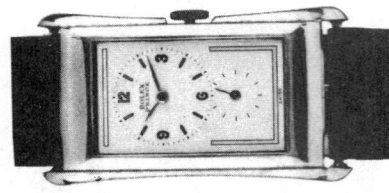

ROLEX, 17 jewels, RF # 1490, flared, duo dial, c. 1930s
9k $4,500 $5,000 $6,000

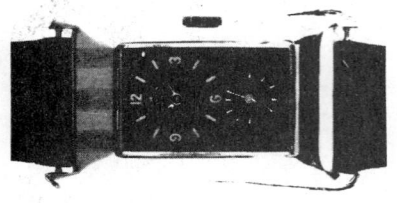

ROLEX, 17J., RF # 2245 & RF # 1768, 2 tone case,
    beware of **FAKES**
18k $18,000 $20,000 $28,000

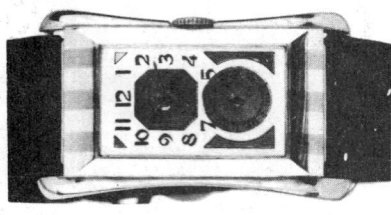

ROLEX, 17 jewels, "Prince," duo dial, stepped case

18k	$6,500	$7,500	$9,500
14k	$5,500	$6,500	$8,000
9k	$4,500	$5,000	$6,500
silver	$4,000	$4,500	$5,500
s. steel	$3,200	$3,700	$5,000
gold filled	$2,500	$2,800	$3,500

ROLEX, 17J., RF # 971, 2 tone stripes, Adj. to 6 pos.
    beware of **FAKES**

18k	$16,000	$18,000	$25,000
14k	$12,000	$13,000	$18,000
9k	$8,000	$9,000	$12,000

ROLEX, 15 jewels, RF # 971, flared, duo dial, Adj. to 6 pos.
9k $4,500 $5,000 $6,000

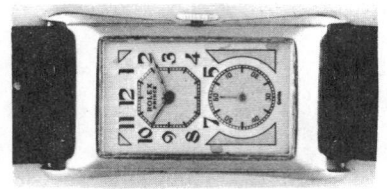

ROLEX, 15 jewels, RF # 971, "Prince," duo dial, c. 1930s
s. steel $4,000 $4,500 $6,000

ROLEX, 15 J., RF # 1862, chronometer, duo dial, c. 1930s
s. steel $3,500 $4,000 $5,000

ROLEX, 15 J., RF # 1527, "Railway," stepped case, 1930s

18k 2 tone	$8,000	$9,000	$12,000
18k	$7,000	$8,000	$10,000
14k 2 tone	$6,000	$7,000	$9,000
14k	$5,000	$6,000	$8,000
9k 2 tone	$5,000	$6,000	$8,000
9k	$4,000	$4,500	$5,500
s. steel	$4,000	$4,500	$5,500

ROLEX, 15 J., RF # 3361, "Prince," center sec., c. 1930s
18k $8,000 $10,000 $14,000

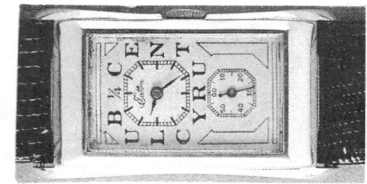

ROLEX, 15 jewels, 1/4 century club, RF # 2541
14k $4,500 $5,000 $6,000

🕐 Pricing in this Guide are fair market price for **COMPLETE**
watches which are reflected from the "**NAWCC**" National and
regional shows.

DIALS FOR MINT PRICES MUST BE ALL **ORIGINAL**.

ROLEX, 15 jewels, RF # 3937, 1/4 century club,
18k $4,500 $5,500 $7,000

ROLEX, 15 jewels, ''Prince,'' RF # 1343, c. 1935
platinum $12,000 $14,000 $20,000
18k $6,000 $7,000 $9,000
14k $5,000 $5,500 $6,500
gold filled............................$2,000 $2,500 $3,500

ROLEX, 17J., RF # 1615, ''Observatory'', c.1938
gold filled............................$1,200 $1,400 $2,000

ROLEX, 15 jewels, stepped case, RF # 1527
18k $6,500 $7,500 $9,500

ROLEX, 17J., date, mid size,
s. steel $500 $550 $700

🕐 Pricing in this Guide are fair market price for **COMPLETE**
watches which are reflected from the "**NAWCC**" National and
regional shows.

DIALS FOR MINT PRICES MUST BE ALL **ORIGINAL**.

ROLEX, 25J., RF # 6604 , date, c.1958
s. steel $600 $700 $900

ROLEX, 25J., RF # 1500 , date, c.1963
s. steel $700 $800 $950

ROLEX, 26J., RF # 6694 , date, c.1971
s. steel $400 $450 $600

ROLEX, 17J., RF # 6094 , date, Ca.1951
s. steel $500 $550 $700

ROLEX, 26J., index bezel, RF # 1501 , c.1970
s. steel $650 $750 $900

ROLEX, 17 jewels, oyster, perpetual, date, ca.1950s
14k $2,800 $3,200 $4,000

ROLEX,25J., date, **index gold bezel**, 2 tone case, RF#6305
s. steel/gold bezel $900 $1,100 $1,600

ROLEX, 25J., **"Ovettone"**, RF # 6105, auto wind, oyster,
note thin milled bezel, **Ovettone** = Big Bubble Back, Ca.1953
14k Pink......................★ ★$2,800 $3,100 $4,500
14k ....★ ★$2,500 $3,000 $4,000

ROLEX, 17J., date, RF # 6964, ca.1953
s. steel $500 $600 $800

ROLEX, 25J., oyster, perpetual, date, **"Ovettone"**,
note thin milled bezel, RF # 4467, Ca. 1950s
18k Pink......................★ ★$3,500 $4,000 $5,000
18k ....★ ★$3,000 $3,500 $4,500

ROLEX, 26J., 2 tone, date just, index bezel, RF # 1601,
Ca.1968
s. steel / gold $700 $800 $1,000
"Ovettone" = Big Bubble Back

ROLEX, 19J., **"Ovettone"**, RF # 6031, 6 positions, Ca. 1953
18k ....★ ★$3,000 $3,500 $4,500

ROLEX, 17 jewels, index bezel, RF. #4325
14k $800 $900 $1,200

ROLEX, 19-25J., RF # 6634, center sec.,gold & s. steel 2 tone case, Ca. 1952
Gold & steel...........................$600 $700 $900

ROLEX, 18J., RF # 6075, 2 tone, index bezel, Ca. 1951
s. steel & 14k $1,000 $1,100 $1,400

ROLEX, 17J., RF # 6029, index bezel, rose gold, c.1950s
18k $2,000 $2,200 $2,600

ROLEX, 17J., RF # 6223, oyster, index bezel, Ca. 1954
18k $1,000 $1,200 $1,500
14k $900 $1,000 $1,400
9k $550 $700 $1,000
gold filled..............................$400 $450 $700
s. steel $350 $400 $650

ROLEX, 17J., RF # 6582, marked bezel 2 tone, ca. 1955
gold & s. steel.......................$550 $700 $900

ROLEX, 17J., center sec., refinished dial, precision,
RF # 6422
s. steel $400 $450 $600

ROLEX, 26J., sapphire crystal, date-just, oyster perpetual
18k $2,000 $2,200 $2,600
14k $1,600 $1,800 $2,300
s. steel $600 $700 $900

ROLEX, 26J., RF # 1002, c.1965
14k $1,300 $1,400 $1,800

ROLEX, 25J., RF # 5502 , Ca. 1955
s. steel $500 $600 $800

ROLEX, 17J., RF # 6085, index bezel, Ca. 1951
14k $1,300 $1,400 $1,800

ROLEX, 16J., RF # 6082, c.1950
s. steel $450 $500 $600

ROLEX, 25J., RF # 6565 , c.1958
s. steel $700 $800 $1,000

ROLEX, 25J., RF # 1025, c.1960
14k $1,200 $1,500 $1,900

ROLEX, 25J., RF # 6024 , c.1953
s. steel $500 $600 $750

ROLEX, 17J., RF # 6424 , c.1965
s. steel $500 $600 $750

ROLEX, 17J., RF # 2010 , Ca. 1960
s. steel $400 $500 $650

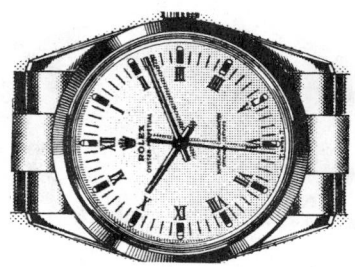

ROLEX, 26J., perpetual oyster, **recent**
s. steel $800 $900 $1,200

ROLEX, 17J., RF # 6284 , c.1955
18k $1,800 $2,000 $2,500

ROLEX, 25J.,RF # 6098 , **star dial**, c.1956
18k rose $2,800 $3,000 $3,500

ROLEX, 17J., RF # 6024 , c.1952
s. steel $500 $600 $750

ROLEX, 25J., "Air King", RF#5500, c.1962
s. steel $700 $800 $1,000

ROLEX, 26J., RF # 1005 , c.1964
14k & S.S.............................$700 $800 $1,000

ROLEX, 25J., "Air King",RF # 5504, c.1959
s. steel $500 $600 $800

A collector should expect to pay modestly higher prices
at local shops

ROLEX, 17J., RF#6084, c.1951
14k $1,400 $1,500 $1,800

ROLEX, 25J., RF#6084, textured dial, c.1953
14k $1,600 $1,800 $2,400

ROLEX, 25J., RF#6564, c.1955
s. steel $500 $600 $800

ROLEX, 25J., index bezel, RF#6581, c.1954
14k $1,600 $1,800 $2,200

⏰ Pricing in this Guide are fair market price for **COMPLETE** watches which are reflected from the "**NAWCC**" National and regional shows.

DIALS FOR MINT PRICES MUST BE ALL **ORIGINAL**.

ROLEX, 25J., RF#6568, c.1956
s. steel $500 $550 $700

ROLEX, 18J., RF#8405, c.1950
18k $900 $1,000 $1,300

ROLEX, 25J., RF # 6567, center sec., Ca. 1960
14k $800 $900 $1,200

ROLEX, 18J.,RF # 8952, center sec., Ca. 1950s
14k $900 $1,000 $1,200

NOTE: See page 1,054 for more Rolex Reference numbers with PRICES ONLY.

ROLEX,17J., RF # 4478, 9 diamonds, Ca.1948
18k $1,300 $1,500 $2,000

ROLEX, 25J., "Bomb'e"12 diamond dial, RF # 1030, c.1958
s. steel ....★★ $1,200 $1,500 $2,000

ROLEX, 17J., Linz 1877, oyster, "Bomb'e lugs", c. 1950s
18k $1,500 $1,800 $2,200

ROLEX, 26 jewels, "Bomb'e lugs", RF # 6590, c. 1950
14k $1,300 $1,500 $1,900

Note: "Bomb'e" style lug are Convexed or Bulges.

ROLEX, 25 jewels, "Bomb'e lugs", RF # 6102, c.1953
14k $1,400 $1,600 $2,000

ROLEX, 26 jewels, "Bomb'e lugs", RF # 6102, c. 1950
18k $1,400 $1,600 $2,000

ROLEX, 19 J., RF # 6092, "Bomb'e lugs", c. 1950s
18k $1,500 $1,800 $2,200
18k Pink.........................$1,700 $2,000 $2,500
14k $1,400 $1,600 $2,000
14k Pink.........................$1,500 $1,800 $2,200
9k $1,000 $1,200 $1,400
s. steel $1,500 $1,800 $2,200

ROLEX, 26J., RF # 1011, "Bomb'e lugs", Ca. 1960
14k $1,200 $1,400 $1,700
**NOTE: See page 1,054 for more Rolex Reference numbers
with <u>PRICES ONLY</u>.**

ROLEX,17J., RF # 4365, Ca.1920s
s.steel (redone dial) $400 $500 $700

ROLEX,15J., RF # 2495, "Extra-Prima", Ca.1937
9k enamel dial $600 $800 $1,100
9k $400 $500 $700

ROLEX,17J., RF # 5020, 2 tone, Ca.1943
14k & s. steel (redone dial) ...$700 $800 $900

ROLEX,17J., RF # 6694, Oyster, Date, "Honey Comb"
textured dial, Ca.1952
s. steel $700 $900 $1,200

ROLEX,15J., RF # 4377, "Oyster", refinished dial, Ca.1944
s. steel $600 $700 $900

ROLEX,17J., RF # 6266, Oyster, Date Ca.1957
s. steel $600 $700 $900

ROLEX,17J., RF # 4392, Observatory dial, Ca.1948
s. steel $800 $1,000 $1,400

ROLEX,25J., RF # 1550, rare dial(crown at 3-6-9) , Ca.1960
s. steel $1,000 $1,100 $1,400

ROLEX,17J., RF # 3745, Precision, Ca.1949
18k $1,000 $1,200 $1,600

ROLEX,26J., RF # 6627, Oyster, date, Ca.1971
18k $1,200 $1,400 $1,800

ROLEX,18J., RF # 4891, Chronometer, Ca.1957
18k $1,200 $1,400 $1,800

ROLEX,28J., RF # 6800, Oyster, date-just, Ca.1982
s. steel $1,000 $1,200 $1,500

ROLEX,25J., RF # 6611, day date, Ca.1956
Note: **First President** model
18k $3,200 $3,500 $4,000

ROLEX,26J., RF # 1600, Oyster, date-just, Ca.1987
s. steel $1,000 $1,200 $1,500

ROLEX,25J., RF # 6552, Oyster, Chronometer, Ca.1958
s. steel $600 $700 $900

ROLEX,17J., RF # 9083, Precision, Ca.1955
s. steel $300 $400 $600

ROLEX, 17 jewels, center sec., gold bezel
18k & s. steel $600 $700 $900

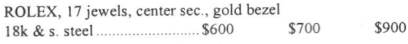

ROLEX, 17 jewels, black dial, center sec., c. 1945

18k	$2,000	$2,200	$2,600
14k	$1,200	$1,500	$1,800
9k	$1,000	$1,100	$1,400
s. steel	$500	$600	$800

ROLEX, 18J., RF # 6427, center sec. Ca. 1962
s. steel $500 $550 $650

ROLEX, 15J., RF # 3655, aux. sec. Ca. 1945
s. steel $450 $500 $650

ROLEX, 26J., bubble back, hooded lugs, rf#3595

18k	$8,000	$9,000	$12,000
14k	$6,000	$6,500	$8,000
9k	$3,500	$4,000	$5,000
s. steel & gold	$3,000	$3,300	$4,000
s. steel ★★★	$13,000	$15,000	$18,000

ROLEX, 17J., Pall Mall, manual wind, Ca. 1949
s. steel .... ★★ $1,200 $1,500 $1,700
14k $600 $700 $900

ROLEX, 17J., "Royal Observatory", RF#3121, c.1937
s. steel $500 $550 $750

ROLEX, 17J., Oyster Co., "Record", manual wind, c.1940
s. steel $300 $350 $600

⊕ Pricing in this Guide are fair market price for **COMPLETE** watches which are reflected from the "**NAWCC**" National and regional shows.

ROLEX, 17J., "Neptune", mid-size, manual wind, c.1939
gold filled................................$300 $400 $600

ROLEX, 17J., RF # 6421, Speedking, Ca.1960
s. steel $500 $600 $750

ROLEX, 17J., RF # 4302, index bezel, 2 tone, Ca. 1944
gold filled & s. steel $600 $700 $900

ROLEX, 26 jewels, bubble back, hooded lugs, 2 tone
18k & s. steel $8,000 $9,000 $12,000

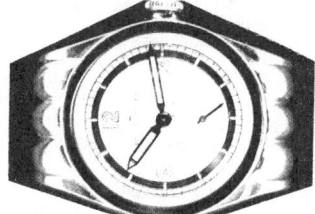

ROLEX, 26 jewels, bubble back, hooded scalloped lugs
s. steel .... ★ $8,000 $9,000 $11,000
18k & s. steel $7,000 $8,000 $10,000

ROLEX, 17J., RF # 2280, manual wind, c.1951
s. steel $500 $550 $625

ROLEX, 17J., Speedking, Oyster, RF # 6021, c.1953
index on bezel
s. steel $500 $550 $700

ROLEX, 18J., RF # 3767, mid size, Ca.1940
s. steel $600 $650 $800

ROLEX, 17J., mid size,RF # 3478, c.1940
gold filled $300 $350 $400
s. steel $400 $450 $550

🕐 Some grades are not included. Their values can be
determined by comparing with **similar** age, size, metal
content, style, grades, or models such as **time only**,
chronograph, repeater etc. listed.

ROLEX, 17J., "Speed King", RF#4220, c.1945
s. steel $500 $600 $750

ROLEX, 18J., "Royal", mid size, aux. sec.
s. steel $450 $550 $750

ROLEX, 17J., "Speed King", RF#6056, c.1952
s. steel $450 $500 $650

ROLEX, 18J., "Speed King", mid size, center sec.
s. steel $500 $600 $800

ROLEX, 17J., mid size,RF#6066, c.1951
s. steel $450 $550 $700

ROLEX, 18J., RF # 3065, B.B., hooded 2 tone yellow gold
14k Gold & steel $3,000 $3,500 $5,000

ROLEX, 17J., mid size, textured dial, RF#6466, c.1957
s. steel $500 $550 $750

ROLEX, 18J., RF # 2319, B.B., hooded 2 tone **rose gold**
14k Gold & steel $3,500 $4,000 $5,500

Wrist Watches listed in this section are priced at the collectable fair market Trade Show level as **complete** watches having an original gold-filled case and stainless steel back, also with original dial, leather watch band, and the entire original movement in good working order with no repairs needed.

🕀 Pricing in this Guide are fair market price for **COMPLETE** watches which are reflected from the "**NAWCC**" National and regional shows.

DIALS FOR MINT PRICES MUST BE ALL **ORIGINAL**.

🕀 A collector should expect to pay modestly higher prices at local shops

🕀 Some grades are not included. Their values can be determined by comparing with **similar** age, size, metal content, style, grades, or models such as **time only**, chronograph, repeater etc. listed.

ROLEX, 18J., B.B., center sec.
s. steel $1,200 $1,400 $1,800

ROLEX, 18J., RF # 2764, B.B., index bezel
18k $3,500 $4,000 $5,000

ROLEX, 18J., B.B., not 2 tone, RF # 3131
14k $2,800 $3,200 $3,800

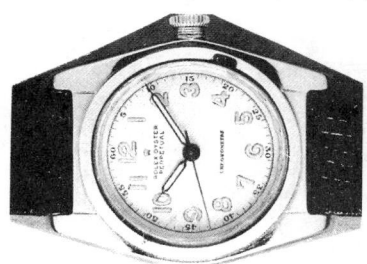

ROLEX, 18J., B.B., chronometer, RF # 3131, cal#600
14k $2,800 $3,200 $3,800
s. steel $1,200 $1,400 $1,800

ROLEX, 18J., RF # 3696, B.B., oyster perpetual, Ca. 1948
9K..$2,200 $2,400 $2,800

ROLEX, 18J., B.B., cal. # 600, aux. sec., ca. 1945
s. steel $1,200 $1,400 $1,800

ROLEX, 25J., RF # 2764, B.B., index bezel, 2 tone, c.1945
14k & s.steel. $1,400 $1,600 $2,000

🕐 Some grades are not included. Their values can be
determined by comparing with **similar** age, size, metal
content, style, grades, or models such as **time only**,
chronograph, repeater etc. listed.

ROLEX, 18J., B.B., self winding on dial
14k $3,000 $3,500 $4,500

**NOTE: See page 1,054 for more Rolex Reference numbers
with PRICES ONLY.**

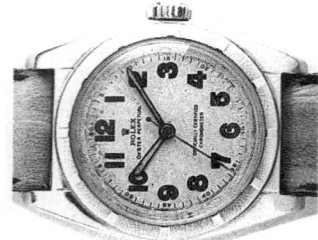

ROLEX, 17J., BB,RF # 6011, c.1948
14k $2,500 $2,800 $3,400

ROLEX, 17J., BB,RF # 3133, tu-tone, c.1940
14k & s.steel. $1,600 $1,800 $2,200

ROLEX, 18J., BB, RF # 5050, Oyster, c.1945
9k $2,000 $2,200 $2,800

ROLEX, 17J., center sec, cal.1530, c.1955
gold filled................................ $400 $500 $700

🕐 Pricing in this Guide are fair market price for **COMPLETE**
watches which are reflected from the "**NAWCC**" National and
regional shows.
DIALS FOR MINT PRICES MUST BE ALL **ORIGINAL**.

ROLEX, 25J., RF # 6585, index on bezel, c.1958
14k $900 $1,000 $1,400

ROLEX, 26J., RF # 1007, Chronometer Oyster, index on
bezel, c.1965
14k $900 $1,000 $1,400

ROLEX, 17J., RF # 5015, BB, index bezel, c.1949
s. steel $1,200 $1,400 $1,800

ROLEX, 18J., B.B., center sec. ca. 1940s
14k $2,700 $3,000 $3,500

ROLEX, 18J., RF # 3130, B.B., aux. sec., ca. 1945
14k $3,000 $3,200 $3,800

ROLEX, 26 J., bubble back, aux. sec., RF # 3458, Ca. 1940s

18k	$3,500	$4,000	$5,500
14k	$3,000	$3,200	$4,500
9k	$2,000	$2,200	$3,000
gold filled	$1,100	$1,200	$1,500
s. steel	$1,200	$1,400	$2,200

ROLEX, 26J., bubble back, index bezel, aux. sec.
14k $2,500 $2,800 $3,400

ROLEX, 26 J., bubble back, RF # 2940, c. 1940s

18k	$3,000	$3,200	$4,000
14k	$2,500	$2,800	$3,300
9k	$1,800	$2,000	$2,500
gold filled	$1,000	$1,100	$1,400
s. steel	$1,200	$1,400	$1,800

ROLEX, 19 jewels, bubble back, 2 tone
18k & s. steel $1,500 $1,700 $2,300

ROLEX, 26 J., bubble back, mercedes hands, c. 1930s

18k	$3,200	$3,500	$4,500
14k	$2,600	$2,900	$3,500
9k	$1,400	$2,100	$2,600
gold filled	$1,100	$1,200	$1,500
s. steel	$1,200	$1,400	$1,800

ROLEX, 26 jewels, bubble back, Arabic & Roman no.'s
14k $3,000 $3,500 $4,500

🕐 A collector should expect to pay modestly higher prices at local shops

🕐 Some grades are not included. Their values can be determined by comparing with **similar** age, size, metal content, style, grades, or models such as **time only**, chronograph, repeater etc. listed.

Wrist Watches listed in this section are priced at the collectable fair market Trade Show level as **complete** watches having an original gold-filled case and stainless steel back, also with original dial, leather watch band, and the entire original movement in good working order with no repairs needed.

ROLEX, 26J., bubble back, index bezel, c. 1940s
18k	$3,500	$4,000	$5,500
14k	$3,000	$3,200	$4,400
9k	$2,000	$2,200	$2,800
gold filled	$1,100	$1,200	$1,500
s. steel	$1,200	$1,400	$2,200

ROLEX, 26 jewels, bubble back, c. 1940s
14k	$2,800	$3,200	$3,800

ROLEX, 25J., RF # 6050, BB, Ca. 1949
s. steel	$1,100	$1,300	$1,600

ROLEX, 26 jewels, RF# 1018, Oyster, Chronometer, c. 1967
s. steel	$600	$700	$900

ROLEX, 26 jewels, bubble back, c. 1940s
s. steel	$1,200	$1,400	$1,800

ROLEX, 19 jewels, bubble back, center sec., rf#1453
18k	$3,200	$3,600	$4,400
14k	$2,800	$3,200	$3,800
s. steel	$1,200	$1,400	$1,800

ROLEX, 26 jewels, bubble back
18k	$3,200	$3,600	$4,400
s. steel	$1,200	$1,400	$1,800

ROLEX, 26 jewels, bubble back, c. 1945
14k	$2,800	$3,200	$3,800

NOTE: See page 1,054 for more Rolex Reference numbers with <u>PRICES ONLY</u>.

ROLEX, 26 jewels, bubble back, c. 1940s

18k	$3,700	$4,000	$4,800
14k	$2,800	$3,200	$3,600
s. steel	$1,200	$1,400	$1,800

ROLEX, 18 jewels, bubble back, RF # 2940, c. 1940s

s. steel	$1,200	$1,400	$1,800

ROLEX, 18 jewels, bubble back, c. 1942

18k	$3,700	$3,900	$4,500
14k	$2,800	$3,000	$3,500
s. steel	$1,200	$1,300	$1,600

ROLEX, 18 jewels, bubble back, original gold & s. steel band

14k & s. steel C&B	$2,600	$2,800	$3,500

ROLEX, 18 J., RF # 4467, date, <u>left hand winds at 9 o'clock</u>

s. steel	★ $1,800	$2,000	$2,500

ROLEX, 30 jewels, ''Presidential,'' 44 diamonds on dial & bezel, day-date, oyster, perpetual, RF # 1803

18k C&B (**non-Quick**)	$6,000	$6,500	$7,500

ROLEX, 26 jewels, day-date, 10 diamond dial, **non quick** hidden clasp, RF # 1803

18k C&B	$4,000	$4,500	$5,800
18k C&B (pink)	★ ★ $6,200	$6,500	$7,000
18k C&B(w)	$5,000	$5,500	$6,500

ROLEX, 26 jewels, ''Presidential,'' diamond dial, day-date, perpetual, oyster, RF # 1804, quick set

18k C&B	$6,500	$6,800	$7,500

ROLEX, 30 jewels, ''Presidential,'' (Tridor), oyster, daydate,
diamond dial, perpetual, oyster,
18k (y & w) single quick.....$6,000 $6,500 $7,500
18k (y & w) double quick ...$7,000 $7,500 $9,000

ROLEX, 26 Jewels, ''Presidential,'' day-date, Single Quick
set model RF # 1803, double quick-set RF# 1823
18kC&B double quick-set... $7,500 $8,000 $9,000
18k C&B single quick-set... $6,000 $6,300 $7,500
18k Single Quick (head) $4,000 $4,300 $4,800

ROLEX, 30J., ''Presidential,'' bark finish, RF # 1803, c.1971
18k C&B(non quick) $4,500 $5,000 $6,000

ROLEX, 26J., ''Presidential,'' day-date, perpetual, non quick,
note textured dial, **Pink gold**, RF#1803 old model
18k C & B .... ★★$5,000 $5,500 $6,500

ROLEX, 30 jewels, ''Presidential,'' day-date, perpetual, oyster, diamond bezel, bark finish, RF # 1807
18k C&B(quick set).............$7,000 $7,500 $8,500

ROLEX, quartz, RF # 1901
diamond dial & diamond bezel add $1,000-$1,200
18k $5,000 $5,500 $6,500

🕐 Pricing in this Guide are fair market price for **COMPLETE**
watches which are reflected from the "**NAWCC**" National and
regional shows.

DIALS FOR MINT PRICES MUST BE ALL **ORIGINAL**.

NOTE: See page 1,054 for more Rolex Reference numbers
with **PRICES ONLY**.

ROLEX, 26 Jewels, RF# 1503, index bezel, date, Ca. 1973
14k $2,200 $2,400 $3,000

ROLEX, 26 J., jubilee band, 10 diamond dial, date just
18k C&B quick set	$4,500	$5,000	$6,000
14k C&B non quick	$2,200	$2,500	$3,500
18K & s. steel C&B quick	$2,000	$2,200	$3,000

ROLEX, 26 jewels, date, oyster, mid-size
s. steel C&B	$450	$600	$750

ROLEX, 25J., "Turnograph", RF # 6202, Ca.1955
14k & s. steel	$2,500	$3,000	$4,000
s. steel	$2,000	$2,500	$3,500

ROLEX, 21J., RF # 6309, "Thunderbird", Ca.1965
14k gold bezel, s.steel case	$1,000	$1,100	$1,400

ROLEX, 26J., quick set, date, Oyster bracelet, c.1965
14k C&B	$2,400	$2,700	$3,200

ROLEX, 17J., RF#6426, manual wind, c.1961
s. steel	$350	$450	$650

ROLEX, 21 jewels, date just, center sec., c. 1965
18k non quick set	$2,800	$3,000	$3,500

ROLEX, 26 J., sapphire crystal, perpetual, oyster, date just
18k	$4,000	$4,500	$6,000
18k & s. steel	$1,600	$1,800	$2,200
s. steel	$900	$1,100	$1,600

ROLEX, 26J., Sea-Dweller, **Comex**, RF# 1665, date, Ca.1977
s. steel $7,000 $8,000 $10,500

ROLEX, 26J., perpetual, oyster, date, graduated bezel
14k $2,600 $2,800 $3,200
s. steel $700 $850 $1,200

ROLEX, 26 jewels, oyster, date-just, ref. #1625
18k & s. steel quick set $2,200 $2,400 $3,200
14k & s. steel C&B non Q. ..$1,200 $1,500 $1,900

ROLEX, 25J., **gold bezel**, "Explorer," RF # 5504, Ca. 1959
s. steel & gold bezel $1,200 $1,500 $2,000

ROLEX, 25 J., early Submariner, RF# 6538, Ca.1958
Note:This style watch worn by **007** Sean Connery (rf# 6538)
s. steel $2,000 $2,500 $3,500

ROLEX, 26 jewels, "Explorer," RF # 1016, perpetual, oyster
s. steel $2,800 $3,200 $4,200

ROLEX, "Submariner", RF# 5508, Ca.1958
s. steel $1,800 $2,200 $3,000

ROLEX, 17J., "**Luminor Panerai**," Italian military diving,
RF# 6151-1, Ca. **1940s**, Note: look for reproduction 1992
s. steel $3,500 $4,000 $5,000

ROLEX, 26 jewels, ''GMT-Master,'' perpetual, oyster, date ruby & diamond dial, sapphire crystal
18k $6,000 $6,500 $7,500

ROLEX, 26 J., ''Submariner,'' non quick set, RF # 5513
s. steel $1,200 $1,400 $1,800

ROLEX, 26 J., RF # 1671,''GMT-Master II,'' date sapphire crystal, quick set
18k $5,500 $6,000 $7,000
s. steel $1,700 $1,900 $2,400

ROLEX, 26 J., ''Submariner,'' perpetual, oyster, date sapphire crystal, quick set
18k C&B............................. $8,000 $8,500 $11,500
18k & s. steel C&B $3,200 $3,500 $4,500
s. steel $1,900 $2,200 $2,700

ROLEX, 26 J., ''GMT-Master'', RF # 6542, c.1957
s. steel $2,000 $2,500 $4,000

Single quick set Presidential & Jubilee use 6 screws.
Double quick set Presidential & Jubilee use 7 screws.
Presidential or Jubilee gold link $250.00
Jubilee or Oyster s. steel link $40.00
Oyster gold link $200.00
ROLEX first used **HACK** system in Ca. 1972
ROLEX first used the Quick Set feature Ca. 1977
Sapphire crystals were added in U.S.A. Ca.1989= gents $100.
steel screw-on crown=$20., gold screw-on crown=$35.

ROLEX, 26J., ''SEA-DWELLER,'' RF # 1665, 2,000 ft, date all with Fliplock Band
s. steel plastic crystal........... $1,700 $2,000 $2,800
s. steel sapphire crystal $1,800 $2,200 $2,600
s.steel (Seadweller in red letters) $3,000 $4,000 $5,500
Note: Seadweller in red letters is rare.

ROLEX factory only, mens diamond dials & bezels
Bezel 18k or platinum, W/44 full cut $3,000 $5,000
Dial W/8 brilliants & 2 baguettes for Oyster Perpetual &
DAY DATE................................... $1,000 $1,600
Dial W/ 10 brilliants for Oyster Perpetual &
DAY DATE................................... $2,000 $3,500
Dial W/ 10 brilliants for Oyster Perpetual &
DATEJUST or DATE.................. $700 $1,500

ROLEX, 21J., ''SEA-DWELLER,'' up to 4,000 ft.,
RF # 1666, date, sapphire crystal, quick set
s. steel $2,000 $2,400 $2,800

ROLEX, 26 jewels, ''Explorer II,'' RF # 1655, date
s. steel $3,500 $4,000 $5,500

ROLEX, 26 jewels, ''Submariner,'' RF # 5512, 200M
s. steel (chronometer) $1,800 $2,200 $3,000

⊕ A collector should expect to pay modestly higher prices
at local shops
Wrist Watches listed in this section are priced at the collectable
fair market Trade Show level as **complete** watches having an
original gold-filled case and stainless steel back, also with
original dial, leather watch band, and the entire original movement in good working order with no repairs needed.

ROLEX, 26J., ''Submariner'', RF # 6536,100M,c.1958
s. steel (no crown guard) ... ★★$1,800 $2,200 $3,800

ROLEX, 15J., ca. 1935
s. steel $800 $900 $1,200

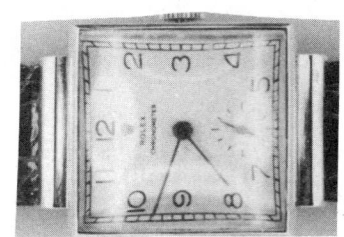

ROLEX,18J., hooded lugs
14k $1,200 $1,400 $1,800

ROLEX, 18J., stepped case, 2 tone, ca. 1940s
G & steel..............................$1,500 $1,700 $2,200

⊕ Pricing in this Guide are fair market price for **COMPLETE**
watches which are reflected from the "NAWCC" National and
regional shows.

DIALS FOR MINT PRICES MUST BE ALL **ORIGINAL**.

ROLEX, 15J., ca. 1937
s. steel $600 $700 $900

ROLEX, 18J., hidden lugs, RF # 2537,adj.6 pos. 2 tone, Ca.1940s
gold & steel $1,600 $1,800 $2,500

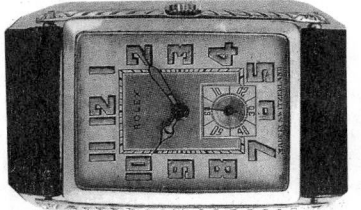

ROLEX, 15J., engraved case, c.1930
s. steel $800 $900 $1,200

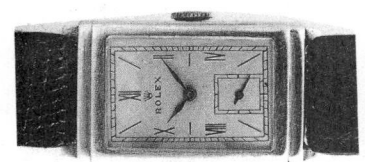

ROLEX,15J., stepped case, c.1938
18k $1,200 $1,400 $1,800

ROLEX, 15J., GJS, c.1935
9K...$1,000 $1,200 $1,500

ROLEX, 17J., 2 tone, center lug "Standard", c.1940
14k & s.s................................ $800 $1,000 $1,400

ROLEX, 18J., RF # 4029, c.1945
18k $1,600 $1,800 $2,500

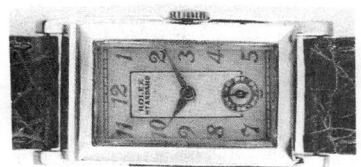

ROLEX, 17J., "Standard", c.1940 (no brass for mint)
gold filled $500 $600 $900

ROLEX, 17J., RF # 619, ROSE gold,c.1948
18k Pink $1,000 $1,200 $1,600

NOTE: See page 1,054 for more Rolex Reference numbers with <u>PRICES ONLY</u>.

ROLEX, 15J., RF # 1878, beveled case, c.1927
s. steel $700 $800 $1,200

🕐 Some grades are not included. Their values can be determined by comparing with **similar** age, size, metal content, style, grades, or models such as **time only**, chronograph, repeater etc. listed.

NOTE: See page 1,054 for more Rolex Reference numbers with <u>PRICES ONLY</u>.

ROLEX, 17J., hidden lugs,
14k $1,600 $1,900 $2,400

ROLEX, 18J., round movement, ca. 1947
18k $1,000 $1,200 $1,500

ROLEX, 17J., "31 Victories",
18k $1,400 $1,600 $2,000

ROLEX, 17 jewels, RF # 8126, "Precision", manual wind
18k $1,000 $1,200 $1,600

ROLEX, 18J., fluted bezel, RF # 3737
18k $1,400 $1,600 $2,000

ROLEX, 17 jewels, curvex style
18k C&B..............................$3,000 $3,500 $4,500

ROLEX, 18J., RF # 8094, 3 diamond dial , ca. 1940s
18kC&B.............................$1,600 $1,800 $2,500

ROLEX, 17 jewels, curved, c. 1940s
gold filled $300 $400 $600

ROLEX, 17 jewels, "Ultra Prima," gold train
18k $1,200 $1,400 $1,800

ROLEX, 18J., ca. 1940s
s. steel $500 $600 $900

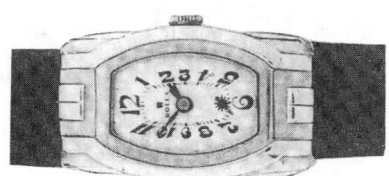

ROLEX, 17 jewels, hooded lugs, 2 tone, **ladies**
Pink & White gold..............$1,000 $1,200 $1,600

ROLEX, 17 jewels, "Standard," c. 1939
gold filled...............................$800 $900 $1,200
14k $2,200 $2,500 $3,200

ROLEX, 18J., RF# 4663, oyster, perpetual, chronometer,
24mm case, (auto wind), Ca. 1940s
18K...$2,200 $2,500 $3,000

ROLEX, 21 jewels, perpetual, oyster, c. 1945
18k $2,500 $3,000 $4,000

Wrist Watches listed in this section are priced at the collectable
fair market Trade Show level as **complete** watches having an
original gold-filled case and stainless steel back, also with
original dial, leather watch band, and the entire original movement in good working order with no repairs needed.

ROLEX, 17 jewels, "Precision," c. 1940s
18k $1,600 $1,800 $2,200
14k $1,000 $1,200 $1,700

ROLEX, 17 J. , "Precision," tank style, faceted bezel
18k $1,200 $1,500 $2,000

ROLEX, 17 jewels, extra flat, c. 1950s
18k $1,200 $1,500 $2,000

ROLEX, 17 J., RF # 9491, "Precision", Ca. 1958
18k $1,400 $1,600 $2,000

ROLEX, 17J., RF # 3893, hidden lugs, Ca. 1943
14k $900 $1,100 $1,500

ROLEX, 17J., "Victory", Tudor, mid size, Ca. 1940
s. steel $250 $300 $400

ROLEX,17J., "Tudor", auto-wind, RF # 7909, c.1955
s. steel $200 $250 $350

ROLEX, Quartz, RF # 1563-3, 2 tone, "Tudor", Ca. 1993
18k & s. steel $250 $300 $400

ROLEX, 25J., "Tudor", RF # 7016, submariner, by ETA, c.1970
s. steel $600 $700 $900

ROLEX, 17J., RF # 7928, "Tudor", ETA cal. 2438, Ca. 1968
s. steel $600 $700 $1,000

ROLEX, 25J., "Tudor", submariner, date, by ETA,
RF # 7610, Ca.1985
s. steel $700 $800 $1,000

ROLEX, "Tudor," (Prince)
s. steel $300 $350 $450

ROLEX, 25J., "Tudor", RF # 7809, auto-wind, c.1978
s. steel $200 $250 $300

ROLEX, 17J., "Tudor", auto-wind, c.1955
18k $500 $600 $750

ROLEX, "Tudor," chronog., date, RF # 9420,
Ca. 1970s
s. steel .... ★ $2,000 $2,400 $3,200

ROLEX, 17J., "Tudor", SOLAR, RF # 4463, c.1955
s. steel $225 $250 $300

ROLEX, 25J., Prince Oyster Ranger II, Ca.1973
s. steel $500 $600 $800

ROLEX, 17J., "Tudor", RF # 2765, TURTLE, Zell Bros
Gold filled..............................$175 $225 $300

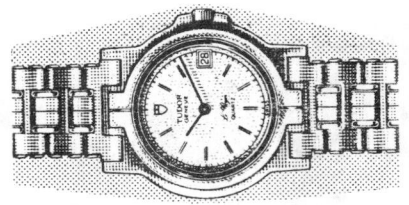

ROLEX, quartz, "Tudor," date, Ca. 1992
s. steel & gold plate................$150 $200 $275

ROLEX, "Tudor," chronog., date, 165 ft., **auto-wind**
s. steel $1,200 $1,400 $1,800
Tiger Wood's model...........$1,000 $1,200 $1,600

ROLEX, 17J., **Drivers**,Ca. 1935
gold filled $500 $600 $800

ROLEX, 18J., lady's, Ca. 1948
18k $250 $325 $450
14k $200 $250 $400

ROLEX, 17J., ladies, "Oyster",
14k $1,000 $1,200 $1,500

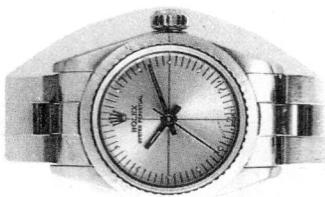

ROLEX, 29J., ladies, "Oyster", RF#67003
s. steel &14k,C&B..............$1,000 $1,100 $1,300

ROLEX, 17J., ladies, "Oyster", RF#4486, c.1957
14k & s.s.case $400 $450 $600

ROLEX, 17J., BB, ladies, "Oyster", c.1948
s. steel $600 $700 $900
s. steel & gold.........................$800 $1,100 $1,500
18k $1,800 $2,000 $2,300

ROLEX, 17J., RF # 1701, ladies, fancy lugs, Ca. 1950
14k $300 $400 $600

ROLEX, 17J., ladies, "Oyster", RF # 3492
s. steel......................................$300 $350 $500

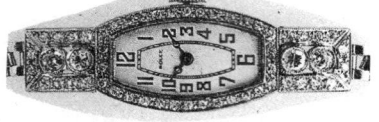

ROLEX, 17J., ladies, RF # 4593, c.1954
s. steel......................................$200 $250 $350

ROLEX, 15J., 54 diamonds, 9k band 18k(w) case, c.1930
9k & 18k $1,600 $1,800 $2,500

ROLEX, 17J.,RF # 4554, "Precision", ladies, Ca. 1955
gold filled...............................$125 $150 $200

ROLEX, 15J., lady's, curved, ca.1925
9k..$250 $300 $400

ROLEX, 15J., lady's, center lugs, ca.1925
9k enamel dial $400 $500 $650

ROLEX, 18J., lady's, ca. 1930s
18k $400 $500 $650

ROLEX, 18J., wire lugs, diamond bezel, ca. 1940s
18k(W).....................................$500 $550 $700

ROLEX, 18J., lady's,
14k $300 $350 $450

ROLEX, 18J., lady's,
14k(W) C&B $350 $450 $650

ROLEX, 18J., lady's, bubble back
18k pink $1,400 $1,600 $2,600
18k $1,200 $1,400 $2,400
s. steel & gold.........................$600 $900 $1,400

Wrist Watches listed in this section are priced at the collectable
fair market Trade Show **retail** level as **complete** watches having
an original gold-filled case and stainless steel back, also with
original dial, leather watch band, and the entire original movement in good working order with no repairs needed.

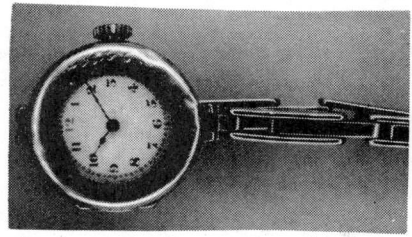

ROLEX, 15J., lady's, Ca.1925
18k band.................................$400 $450 $600

ROLEX, Oyster Perpetual Datejust, diamond dial &bezel
Sapphire Crystal, Quick Set
18k C&B $6,500 $7,000 $8,000

ROLEX, Oyster Perpetual Datejust, Plastic Crystal
18k C&B $3,500 $4,000 $5,000

ROLEX, Oyster Perpetual Datejust, Sapphire Crystal,
Quick Set
18k & s. steel $1,700 $2,100 $2,600

ROLEX, Oyster Perpetual Sapphire Crystal, no date
18k & s. steel **no** date $1,200 $1,400 $1,800

Note: The first 4 digits = RF # & the 5th digit = case Metal. -0 = stainless steel, -1 = yellow gold filled, -2 = white gold filled, -3 = S.S. & yellow gold, -4 = s.s & white gold, -5 = gold shell, -6 = platinum, -7 = 14k yellow, -8 = 18k yellow, -9 = 14k white. Bb=bubble back, band=metal, cald.= calendar, chronog.=chronograph, chronm.=chronometer, d.dial=diamond dial, Ld. = Ladies, d.just=datejust, f.diam.dial=factory diamond dial, J.band=jubilee band, mid=mid-size, Q.set=quick set, Oy.band=oyster band, 2 reg.= 2registers, sapp.=sapphire crystal, strap=leather, **Important Note:** Listed as, **band = "tight" & strap = "new leather".**

RF#-metal: Description	PRICE in $		Mint
1024-5, Shell, no date, strap	500	525	600
1024-5, Shell, no date, GF oyster	600	625	700
1401-0, Bb, Air King, Oy. band	1500	1600	1850
1406-0, SubM, sapp, no date, Oy.band	1700	1800	2000
1427-0, Explorer I, Oy.band	1700	1800	2100
1505-3, date, strap	600	650	750
1520-0, Q-set, plastic, oyster band	900	1000	1200
1523-0, Q-set, sapp., oyster band	1400	1500	1750
1523-0, Q-set, sapp., J.band	1400	1500	1750
1550-5, Shell, date, strap	500	550	650
1550-5, Shell, date, GF oyster	600	650	750
1620-0, Datejust, oyster band	1600	1700	1900
1623-0, Q-set, d.just, jubl.band	1600	1700	1800
1623-0, Q-set, d.just, Oy.band	1700	1800	1950
1623-3, Q-set, d.just, Oy.band	2100	2200	2450
1623-3, Q-set, d.just, fact.diam.dial	3100	3200	3400
1651-8, Daytona, strap	7000	7500	8000
1651-9, Daytona, strap	7200	7600	8300
1652-0, Daytona, Oy.band	5200	5400	5600
1652-3, Daytona, Oy.band	5400	5500	5800
1652-3, Daytona, f.diam.dial	5700	5800	6000
1652-8, Daytona, 18k band	9000	10000	11000
1657-0, Explorer II, Oy. band	2300	2400	2700
1660-0, Sea DW, 4000, sapp, flip band	2400	2500	2600
1662-3, YachtM, sapp, Oy.band	4000	4100	4300
1662-8, YachtM, sapp, Oy.band	10000	11000	12000
1670-0, GMT, Q.set, sapp, Oy.band	2200	2300	2500
1675-0, GMT, Oy. or J.band	1200	1300	1450
1675-3, GMT, 14k/ss Oy. or J.band	1300	1450	1600
1675-3, GMT, 18k/ss Oy.or J.band	1600	1700	1900
1675-8, GMT, sapp. 18k J.band	7500	7600	7900
1680-0, SubM, date, Oy.band	1500	1600	1750
1680-0, SubM, date, red letters, Oy.band	2300	2400	2600
1680-8, SubM, date, Oy.band	5000	5200	5500
1701-0, Quartz, band	900	1000	1150
1703-3, Quartz, band	1100	1200	1350
1824-8, Pres, dbl.Q, bark band	7500	7600	7800
2499-0, Bb, hooded lugs	11000	12000	14000
3135-0, Bb, all original	1500	1600	1800
3358-0, Viceroy, strap	700	800	1000
3372-8, SubM, all original	3900	4000	4250
3372-3, Bb, ladies	1000	1200	1450
4016-8, Cellini, fluted bezel	800	900	1100
4027-8, Cellini, manual	800	900	1100
4105-8, Cellini, 17J., manual	800	900	1100
4313-8, Queen Midas, 18k band	2800	3000	3500
4315-8, King Midas, 18k band	3800	4000	4500
4500-0, Chronog., 2 reg., strap	8400	8600	9000
5003-3, Bb, ladies, 2-tone band	2400	2500	2750
5003-7, Bb, ladies	2000	2100	2350
5011-3, Bb, strap	1500	1600	1850
5034-0, Chronog., anti-magn.	7000	7200	7600
5133-3, Bb, all original	1000	1200	1450
5508-0, SubM, no guard,	1200	1300	1500
5512-0, SubM, no guard	1000	1100	1300
6236-0, Chronog., cald., chronm.	12500	13500	15000
6262-0, Cosmograph, strap	8500	8900	9500
6431-0, Mid-size, Oy.band	700	750	850
6502-8, Non-Date, strap	2200	2300	2500
6509-1, Ladies, non-date, strap	900	1000	1150
6509-7, Ladies, non-date, J.band	1300	1400	1500
6542-0, GMT, no Guard, Oy.band	1150	1200	1300
6718-0, Ladies, non-date, oyster	1100	1200	1400
6719-0, Ladies, non-date, J.band	1100	1200	1350
6719-8, Ladies, non-date, strap	1200	1300	1500
6719-8, Ladies non-date, J.band	1700	1800	1950
6517-7, Ladies, date, J. band	2000	2100	2300

RF#-metal: Description	PRICE in $		Mint
6609-8, Thunderbird, strap	1600	1700	1900
6827-7, Date, Mid, strap	950	1000	1150
6827-7, D-just, Mid, non-Q, Oy.band	1200	1300	1450
6827-7, D-just, Mid, Q-set, Oy.band	2200	2300	2500
6827-8, Pres, mid, d.just, nonQ, Oy.band	3200	3300	3500
6827-8, Pres,mid,d.just,Q.set,sapp,J.band	4400	4500	4700
6827-8, Pres, mid, d.just, nonQ, P.band	4200	4300	4500
6827-8, Pres,mid,d.just,Q.set,sapp,P.band	4500	4600	4800
6916-0, Ladies, date, J.band	800	850	1,000
6916-3, Ladies, date, J.band	1000	1100	1250
6916-8, Ladies, date, 18k Oy. band	3200	3300	3600
6917-0, Ladies, date, Q-set, J.b.	1100	1200	1350
6917-3, Ladies, date, Q-set, J.b.	2000	2100	2300
6917-0, Ladies, D-just, non-Q, J.band	1000	1100	1250
6917-0, Ladies, D-just, Q-set, J.band	1700	1800	1950
6917-3, Ladies, D-just, non-Q, J.band	1300	1400	1550
6917-3, Ladies, D-just, Q-set, J.band	2000	2100	2350
6917-3, Ladies, D-just, Q-set, f.diam.dial	2400	2500	2800
6917-6, Ladies Pres, Plat.band	10000	11000	12500
6917-6, Ld.Pres, Plat.band, d.dial & bzl	13000	14000	16000
6917-8, Ld.Pres, D-just, non-Q, Oy.band	3500	3600	3800
6917-8, Ld.Pres, D-just, non-Q, J.band	3700	3800	4000
6917-8, Ld.Pres, D-just, non-Q, P.band	3900	4000	4200
6917-8, Ld.Pres, D-just, Q.set, J.band	4500	4600	4800
6917-8, Ld.Pres, D-just, Q.set, bark	5200	5300	5500
6917-8, Ld.Pres, D-just, Q.set, P.band	6000	6100	6300
6917-8, Ld.Pres, all above, d.dial	6500	6600	6800
6917-8, Ld.Pres, all above, d.dial/bezel	8400	8500	8700
6917-8, Ld.Pres, crown coll., d.dial/bezel	9000	9200	9500

BELOW

NOTE: NEW Sugested Retail Prices = **ABOUT** (Ca. 2000)

Air-King, rf#1400-0, 27J., Oyster, autow., s.steel
Oyster band = $2,500.00

Daytona, rf#1651-8, 31J., auto wind, screw down buttons, 18k head & leather band = $14,500.00

Daytona, rf#1652-0, 31J., auto wind, screw down buttons, s. steel, Oysterlock = $5,500.00

Daytona, rf#1652-8, 31J., auto wind, screw down buttons, 18k & 18k Oysterlock = $20,500.00

GMT II, rf#1671-0, autow., date, s. steel, Oysterlock = $3,500.00 & rf#1671-3=$6,000.00 & rf#1671-8=$17,500.00

Oyster, rf#1620-3, 31j., auto wind, date just, Oyster band=$5,000.00 with Jubilee = $5,300.00

President, rf#1823-8, 31J., autow, day date, 18k & 18k Presi-dent band = $16,000.00 & with "Pave" dial=$41,000.00

Sea-Dweller 4000, rf#1660-0, 31J., autow., date, s.steel Oyster band=$4,000.00

Submariner, rf#1661-0, 31J., autow., date, Oyster band = $3,500.00, rf#1661-3=$6,000.00, rf#1661-8=$19,000.00

BANDS & one link

Jubilee s.steel=$525 1 link=$35, s.steel&18k=$1,500 1 link=$115
Oyster s.steel=$425 1 link=$35, s.steel&18k=$1,600 1 link=$200
President 18kY=$7,300 1 link=$370, Tridor Y=$7,300

31mm 18K bezel with 44 diamonds=$5,600.00

Advertised as accurate timekeeper at a moderate price.
U = unicorn, **M** = Marcoin, **R** = Rolco.
Listed as **U., M., R.,** & 7 to 15 jewels, Ca. 1920s.

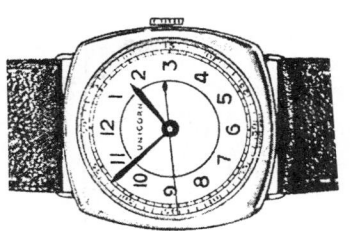

U. M. R., 7-15J., center sec. wire lugs, Ca. 1920s
base metal $300 $400 $600

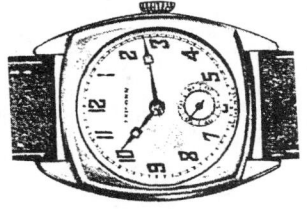

U. M. R., 7-15J., aux. sec., Ca. 1920s
s. steel $195 $250 $350
9K... $300 $350 $450

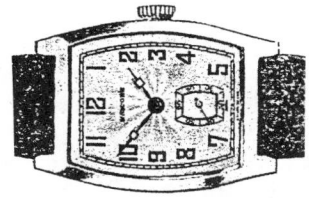

U. M. R., 7-15J., tonneau, very flat, Ca. 1920s
s. steel $300 $350 $450
9K... $400 $450 $550

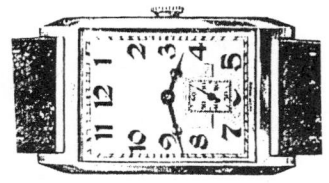

U. M. R., 7-15J., rect., aux. sec., Ca. 1920s
s. steel $450 $500 $650
9K... $400 $450 $550

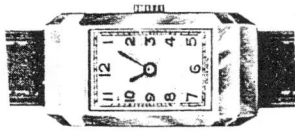

U. M. R., 7-15J., hidden lugs, Ca. 1920s
base metal $150 $195 $300

U. M. R., 7-15J., black dial, Ca. 1920s
base metal.............................. $150 $195 $300
s. steel $400 $500 $700

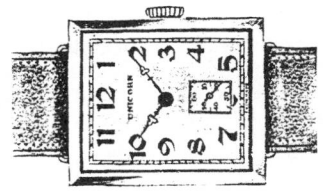

U. M. R., 7-15J., square, Ca. 1920s
s. steel $300 $350 $450
9K... $400 $450 $550

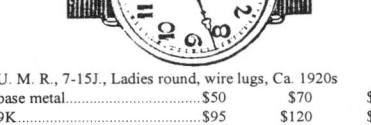

U. M. R., 7-15J., Ladies round, wire lugs, Ca. 1920s
base metal.............................. $50 $70 $100
9K... $95 $120 $150

U. M. R., 7-15J., Ladies, wire lugs, Ca. 1920s
base metal.............................. $50 $70 $95
9K... $95 $120 $150

U. M. R., 7-15J., Ladies, wire lugs, Ca. 1920s
base metal.............................. $50 $70 $95
9K... $95 $120 $150

6694

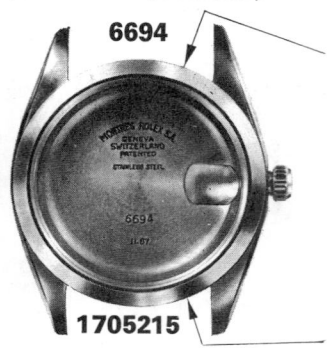

1705215

Reference number,
between the lugs

INSIDE OF BACK
Reference number
in four figures

NON-OYSTER CASE

Serial number,
six or seven figures
engraved between the lugs

On recent OYSTER models the number is engraved on the outside of the case between the lugs. Reference number of earlier models will be found engraved on the inside of the back of the case.

Reference number for NON-OYSTER models will be found engraved on the inside of the back of the case.

OUTSIDE OF BACK
Serial number
in six or seven figures

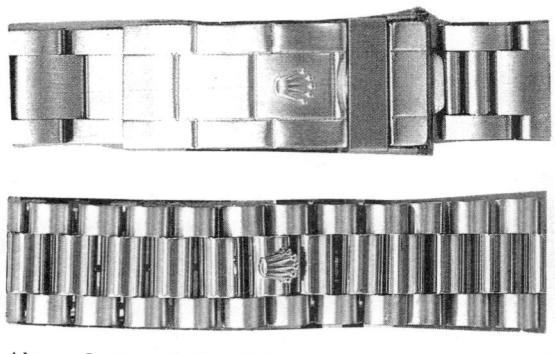

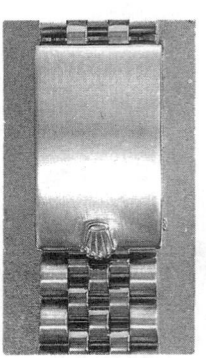

Above: Oyster style bracelet. **Below:** Presidential style band with hidden clasp. **Right:** Jubilee style bracelet.

New model Presidential bracelets use 8 screws for adjustment links.
Double quick set Presidential and Jubilee bracelets use 7 screws for adjustment links.
The older models **single quick** Presidential and Jubilee bracelets use 6 screw for adjustment links.

Note: Check Bracelet
for stretched links.

Stretched

NEW not Stretched

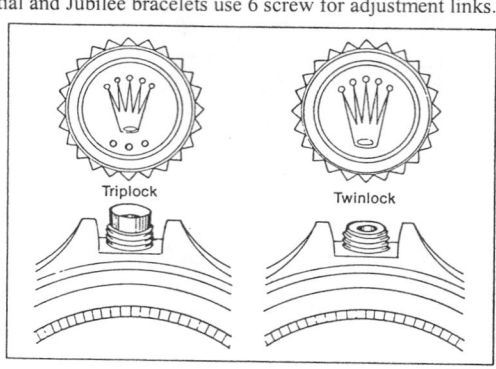

Triplock   Twinlock

ROLEX
MOVEMENT IDENTIFICATION

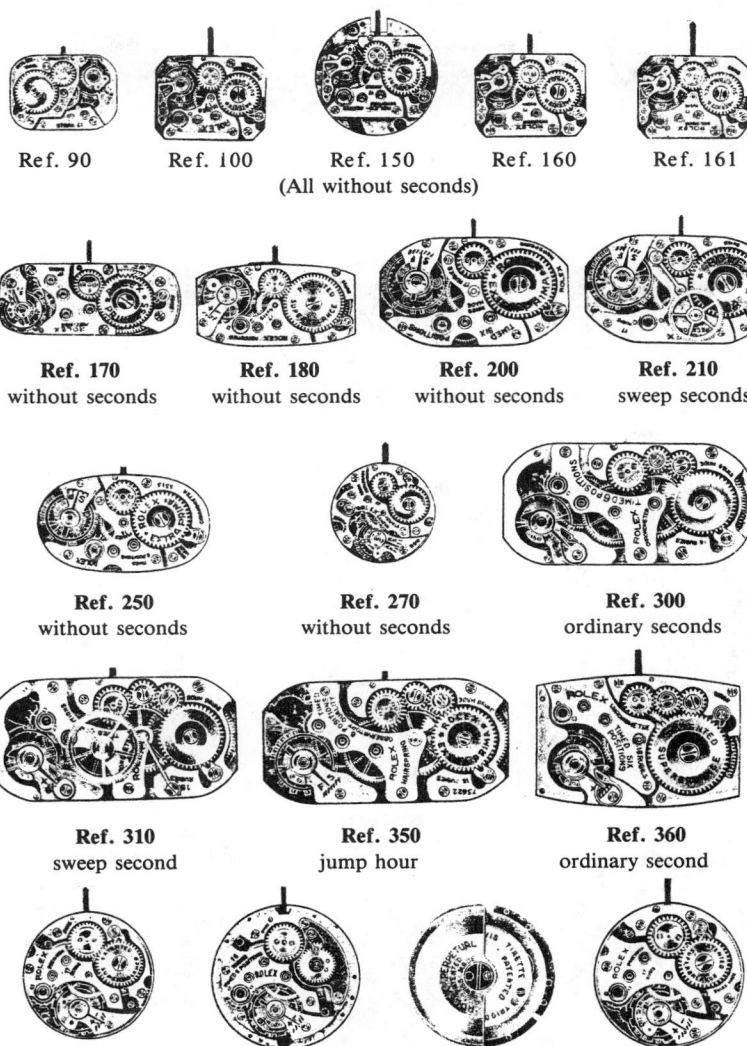

Ref. 90   Ref. 100   Ref. 150   Ref. 160   Ref. 161
(All without seconds)

Ref. 170   **Ref. 180**   **Ref. 200**   **Ref. 210**
without seconds   without seconds   without seconds   sweep seconds

Ref. 250   **Ref. 270**   **Ref. 300**
without seconds   without seconds   ordinary seconds

Ref. 310   **Ref. 350**   **Ref. 360**
sweep second   jump hour   ordinary second

Ref. 400   **Ref. 420**   **Ref. 420**   **Ref. 500**
ordinary seconds   ordinary seconds   rotor   ordinary seconds
Ca. 1941   **Ca. 1941**   **Ca. 1941**   **Ca. 1936**

Ref. 510
sweep second
Ca. 1936

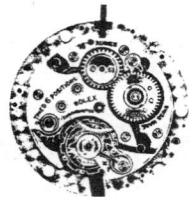
Ref. 520
sweep second
Ca. 1936

Ref. 520
rotor
Ca. 1936

Ref. 530
self wind, sweep sec.
Ca. 1936

Ref. 600   Ca. 1931
ordinary seconds

Ref. 620 Ca. 1931
ordinary seconds

Ref. 620 Ca. 1931
rotor

Ref. 630 Ca. 1931
self wind, sweep sec.

Ref. 700 Ca. 1940
ordinary seconds

Ref. 710 Ca. 1940
sweep seconds

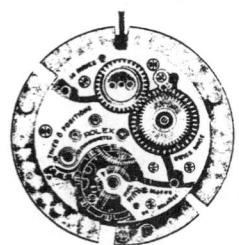
Ref. 720 Ca. 1940
ordinary seconds

Ref. 720 Ca. 1940
rotor

Ref. 730 Ca. 1945
self wind, sweep sec.

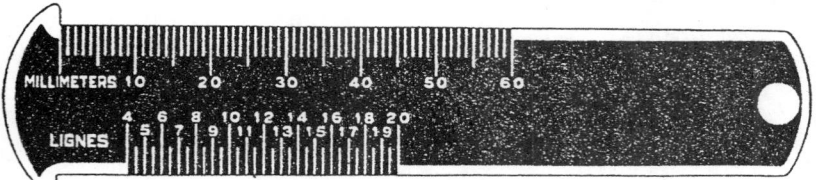

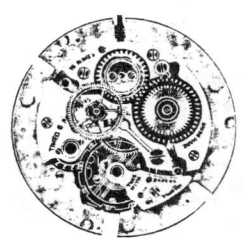

Ref. 740 **Ca. 1945**
self wind, calendar, sweep sec.

| **Ref. 850** | **Ref. 72** | **Ref. 23** |
| ordinary seconds | chronograph, 3 registers | chronograph, 2 registers |

POSITIONS OF THE WINDING CROWN FOR CALENDAR MODELS

Pos. 1

Crown fully screwed down.
In this position the Rolex Oyster is warranted pressure-proof to a depth of 330 feet/100 m.
The watch is ready to be worn.

Pos. 2

Crown unscrewed.
When the crown is free of the screw threads, the watch is in position for handwinding, if necessary.
In quartz models, this is a neutral position.

Pos. 3

Crown pulled out to the first notch.
When turning the crown from three to six o'clock, the date will change rapidly.
This position is used to correct the date when months have less than 31 days.
The timing of the watch will not be altered.

Pos. 4

Crown pulled out to the last notch.
Position for setting the correct time, the date and the day.
The watch stops and enables adjustments to be made, for Day-Date models, when the hands are turned counter-clockwise, the day of the week changes while the date remains unchanged.
Change the day before correcting the date.

ROLLS, 15J., early auto wind, by Leon Hatot, movement inside case moves back & forth to wind, c. 1920s
s. steel .... ★$225 $275 $375

ROLLS, 15 jewels, early auto wind, c. 1920s
s. steel $225 $275 $400

ROLLS, 15 jewels, "ATO," flip top
s. steel $300 $400 $800

ROLLS, 15 jewels, ladies, "ATO," flip top, by Blancpain
18k $400 $450 $550

ROTARY, 15J., aux. sec., ca.1934
9k $95 $120 $160

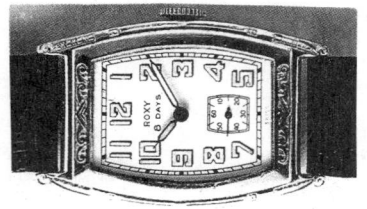

ROXY, **8 day**, engraved case, ca. 1930s
s. steel .... ★$225 $275 $400

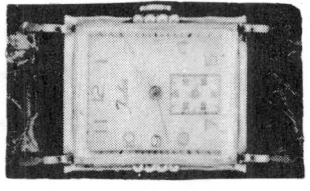

RULON, ca. 1940s
gold filled $35 $45 $65

RULON, 17J., **3 diamonds** on dial
gold plate $65 $75 $95

SCHILD, 17J., "Aqua lung", tach.chronog., ca.1972
s. steel $250 $275 $350

SCHULTZ, 17J., diamond dial, c.1930
platinum C & B $1,400 $1,600 $2,000

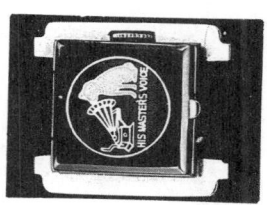

J. SCHULTZ, 17J., enamel hunter style, ca. 1949
18k $1,000 $1,200 $1,800

SEELAND, 17J., aux. sec., Ca. 1955
14k $95 $110 $145

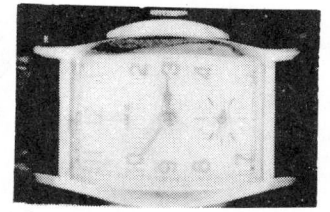

SEELAND, 7J., ca. 1950s
gold filled.................................. $35 $45 $80

SEELAND, 17J., "Quadramatic" auto-wind, c.1947
s. steel $30 $40 $75

SEELAND, 17J., manual wind, c.1947
chrome $20 $25 $40

SEIKO, 6J., wire lugs, on dial "LAUREL", ca.1925
s. steel .... ★$35 $45 $75

SEIKO, quartz, rope style bezel
14k $95 $120 $150

SEMCA, 17J., day-date-month, moon phase, c. 1950s
18k $800 $900 $1,200

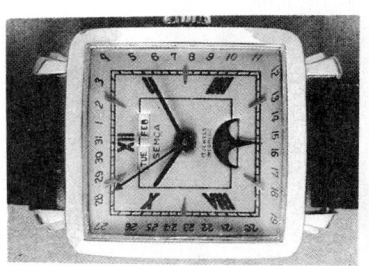

SEMCA, 17J., day-date-month, moon phase, c. 1950s
14k $500 $600 $1,000

SETH THOMAS, day date, moon phases, ca. 1949
s. steel $195 $225 $300

🕐 A collector should expect to pay modestly higher prices at local shops

🕐 Some grades are not included. Their values can be determined by comparing with **similar** age, size, metal content, style, grades, or models such as **time only**, chronograph, repeater etc. listed.

SHEFFIELD,17J., **chronog.**, by Venus, cal.189
s. steel $175 $225 $325

SIGMA,17J., textured dial,c.1940
18k $175 $195 $250

SMITH, 17J., military , Ca.1969
s. steel $95 $125 $165

SPERINA, 7 jewels, **day & date on lugs**
s. steel $65 $85 $135

🕐 Pricing in this Guide are fair market price for **COMPLETE** watches which are reflected from the "**NAWCC**" National and regional shows.

SOUTH BEND,17J., **multi-color dial**, made U.S.A.
base metal .... ★$275 $325 $450

STANDARD,17J., 24 hr. dial, world time, c.1965
s. steel $95 $125 $195

STOWA, 20-22J., Military watch, Ca. 1942
s. steel $350 $400 $500

TAVANNES, 15J., enamel dial, hunter, **flip top,** c.1915
silver $300 $350 $425

TAVANNES, 17J., chronog., c.1940
s. steel $195 $250 $350

TAVANNES, 17J., extended lugs, c.1955
gold filled................................$35 $45 $65

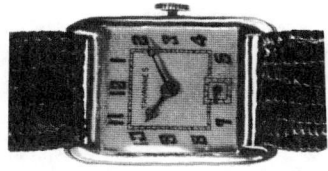

TAVANNES, 17J., aux. sec., c.1935
14k $95 $120 $150

TAVANNES, 17J., GJS, cal.365k, c.1938
14k $95 $125 $160

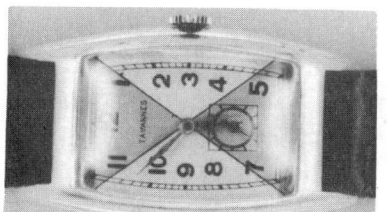

TAVANNES, 17 jewels, hour glass dial, **curved**
14k $125 $150 $195

TAVANNES, 15 jewels, "334," c. 1939
14k (w) $95 $125 $175

TAVANNES, 17 jewels, aux. sec. ca. 1940s
s. steel $35 $45 $65

TAVANNES, 17 jewels, aux. sec.
14k $95 $125 $175

TECHNOS, 17J., "Sky Diver", auto-wind, 500m., c.1970
s. steel $55 $65 $125

Wrist Watches listed in this section are priced at the collectable
fair market **Trade Show** level as **complete** watches having an
original gold-filled case and stainless steel back, also with
original dial, leather watch band, and the entire original movement in good working order with no repairs needed.

🕐 Some grades are not included. Their values can be
determined by comparing with **similar** age, size, metal
content, style, grades, or models such as **time only**,
chronograph, repeater etc. listed.

TELDA, 17J., chronog.,3 reg, date, moon ph., c.1980s
s. steel $300 $325 $400

TELDA, 17J., center sec., c.1948
gold filled.................................$35 $45 $65

NOTE: Examples of Tiffany made up watches are listed but
were not sold by Tiffany & Co.. These off-brand watches will
be listed but not priced as true Tiffany & Co. watches. EXAM-
PLES: *Kingston?, Emerson?, Banner?*, ETC. were not sold by
Tiffany. (?)

TIFFANY & CO., 15-17J., enamel dial, Ca. 1905
18k $500 $600 $800

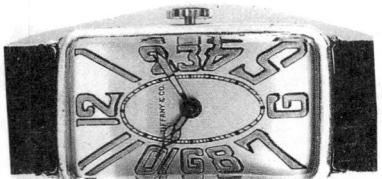

TIFFANY & CO.,17J., exaggerated numbers, Ca.1920
silver $400 $450 $600

TIFFANY & CO., 18J., by **P.P.& CO.**, exaggerated numbers, Ca. 1920s
18K $7,000 $8,000 $10,000

TIFFANY & CO., 17J., curved, mvt. by **P.P. & Co.**, c. 1910
18k $8,000 $9,000 $11,000

TIFFANY & CO.,17J., by Banner"?" , c.1926
18k $195 $225 $275

TIFFANY & CO.,17J., by Wheeler "?", c.1930
14k $95 $125 $175

TIFFANY & CO., 26 jewels, min. repeater, slide repeat,
automaton, 40mm **(conversion)**
18k $2,500 $2,800 $3,500

TIFFANY & CO., 15J., wire lugs, ca. 1928
silver $195 $225 $300

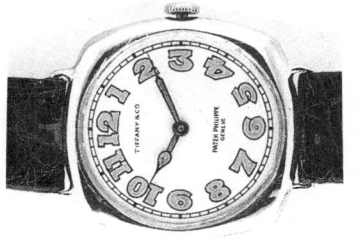

TIFFANY & CO.,17J., by **P.P. & Co.**, wire lugs, c.1915
18k (**refinished dial**)...........$3,500 $4,000 $5,000

TIFFANY & CO.,17J., by I.W.C., wire lugs, c.1918
14k $600 $650 $800

TIFFANY & CO., 15J., enamel dial, ca. 1930s
silver $450 $500 $600

TIFFANY & CO., 17J., Concord W. CO.
14k $600 $700 $900

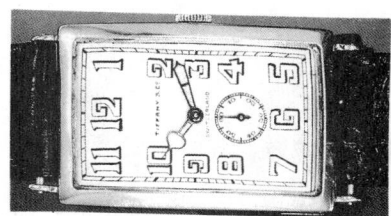

TIFFANY & CO., 18J., by **P.P.& CO.**, Ca. 1930s
platinum............................$10,000 $12,000 $14,000

TIFFANY & CO., 15 jewels, Swiss, Ca. 1926
18k $400 $450 $600

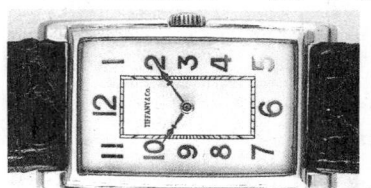

TIFFANY & CO.,17J., by Longines, c.1928
14k $195 $225 $275

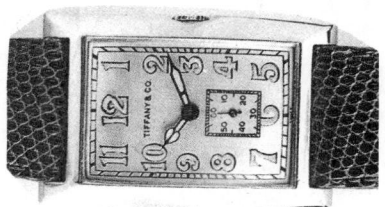

TIFFANY & CO.,17J., aux. sec., Swiss, c.1926
18k(w)....................................$400 $500 $700

TIFFANY & CO.,17J., by Fidea "?", c.1930
14k $125 $150 $195

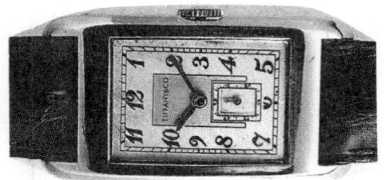

TIFFANY & CO.,17J., GJS, by Movado, c.1940
14k $275 $300 $375

TIFFANY & CO.,17J., by Kingston "?", hidden lugs, c.1943
14k $95 $125 $175

TIFFANY & CO.,17J., by Charlin W. Co. "?", GJS, c.1940
14k $95 $125 $175

TIFFANY & CO.,17J., by Hampden "?", c.1949
14k $95 $125 $175

TIFFANY & CO.,17J., by I.W.C., c.1942
14k $375 $400 $500

TIFFANY & CO.,17J., by I.W.C., hidden lugs, c.1942
14k $375 $400 $500

TIFFANY & CO., 17J., top hat, by I. W. C.
14K $700 $800 $1,000

TIFFANY & CO., 30J., auto-wind, date, Ca.1955
18K $400 $450 $600

TIFFANY & CO.,15J., one button chronog., by Goering, Cal. 69 mvt., c.1925
silver $1,000 $1,100 $1,400

TIFFANY & CO.,17J., Valjoux cal.72c., c.1948
s. steel $550 $650 $750
14k $1,200 $1,300 $1,500
18k $1,400 $1,500 $1,700

🕐 Some grades are not included. Their values can be determined by comparing with **similar** age, size, metal content, style, grades, or models such as **time only**, chronograph, repeater etc. listed.

TIFFANY & CO.,17J., by Movado, c.1947
14k $900 $1,000 $1,200

TIFFANY & CO.,17J., by Bovet"?", c.1940
18k $800 $900 $1,100

TIFFANY & CO.,17J., by Tourneau , Valjoux 72c, c.1950
s. steel $800 $900 $1,200

TIFFANY & CO., 31J., chronog., triple date, moon ph. screw-
back, note window for date at 4 & 5
18k $2,200 $2,600 $3,200

TIFFANY & CO., 17J., chronog., day-date-month
14k $1,000 $1,200 $1,500

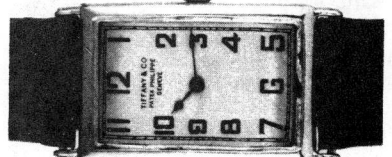

TIFFANY & CO., 21J., mvt. by **P.P. & Co.**, c. 1950
18k $3,000 $3,500 $4,500

TIFFANY & CO., 17J., curved , ca.1920s
platinum.............................. $1,200 $1,400 $1,800

TIFFANY & CO.,15J., engraved bezel, c.1919
18k $1,000 $1,100 $1,300

Wrist Watches listed in this section are priced at the collectable
fair market **Trade Show** level as **complete** watches having an
original gold-filled case and stainless steel back, also with
original dial, leather watch band, and the entire original movement in good working order with no repairs needed.

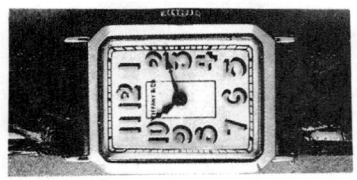

TIFFANY & CO., 15J., ca. 1920s
14k $195 $225 $300

TIFFANY & CO.,17J., by Zodiac , c.1942
14k $125 $150 $195

TIFFANY & CO.,17J., by Hampden "?", c.1945
gold filled................................$75 $85 $125
14k $125 $150 $195

TIFFANY & CO.,17J., by Glycine "?", c.1945
gold filled $75 $85 $125
14k $125 $150 $195

TIFFANY & CO.,17J., by Ollendorf "?", c.1945
14k $125 $150 $195

TIFFANY & CO.,17J., extended bezel, c.1942
14k $195 $225 $300

TIFFANY & CO.,17J., by Crawford "?", c.1947
14k $125 $150 $195

TIFFANY & CO.,17J., by Wyler "?", c.1950
gold filled $65 $85 $125

TIFFANY & CO.,17J., by Tissot, c.1948
14k $125 $150 $195

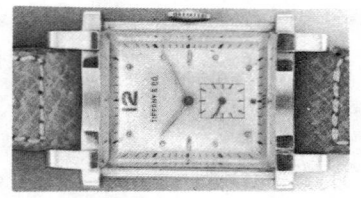

TIFFANY & CO., 17J., fancy lugs & bezel,ca.1950s
14k $195 $225 $300

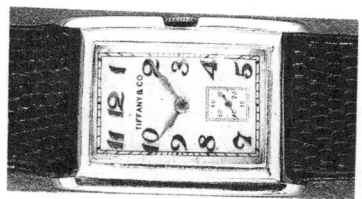

TIFFANY & CO., 17J., applied numbers, ca. 1950s
14k $175 $195 $250

TIFFANY & CO., 17J., flared & stepped, ca.1950s
14k $225 $250 $325

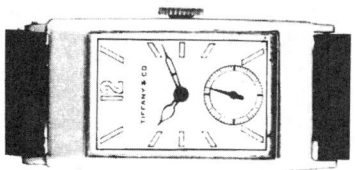

TIFFANY & CO., 17 jewels, Swiss, c. 1935
18k $350 $400 $500

TIFFANY & CO., 17 jewels, fancy bezel, c. 1942
14k $250 $300 $400

TIFFANY & CO., 17 jewels, sculptured lugs, c. 1948
14k $400 $500 $650

TIFFANY & CO.,17J., 3 diamond dial, by Lathin "?",
14k(w).................................... $175 $195 $250

TIFFANY & CO.,15J., rhinestones "?", c.1948
base metal $35 $45 $65

TIFFANY & CO., 17J., "Movado", triple date, center sec.
s. steel $300 $350 $450

TIFFANY & CO.,17J., by Movado, triple date, c.1948
gold filled $300 $350 $450
14k & s.s................................ $400 $450 $500

🕐 A collector should expect to pay modestly higher prices at local shops

TIFFANY & CO.,17J., by Tissot, triple date moon ph.,
14k $900 $1,000 $1,200

TIFFANY & CO.,17J., by Helvetia , c.1948
gold filled $95 $110 $135
14k $150 $175 $225

TIFFANY & CO., 17J., triple date, **moon ph**.
s. steel $400 $450 $600

TIFFANY & CO.,17J., "?", c.1940
gold filled $60 $70 $110

TIFFANY & CO.,17J., by Ardath "?", auto-wind, c.1950
14k $125 $150 $195

TIFFANY & CO.,17J., by Mepa "?", GJS, c.1949
gold filled $55 $65 $85
14k $95 $125 $175

TIFFANY & CO.,17J., by Nicolet, c.1955
gold filled................................. $60 $70 $125

TIFFANY & CO.,17J., by Zenith, c.1939
14k $125 $150 $195

TIFFANY & CO.,17J., c.1948
18k $300 $350 $450

TIFFANY & CO.,17J., carved lugs, c.1950
18k $250 $275 $350

TIFFANY & CO.,17J., ladies, by Longines, c.1920
18k $200 $225 $300

TIFFANY & CO.,17J., ladies, by I.W.C., c.1948
18k $95 $125 $175

TIFFANY & CO.,17J., ladies, I.W.C., c.1955
18k $125 $150 $195

TIFFANY & CO., 15J., 2 tone , ladies, ca. 1939
18k C&B................................. $300 $350 $400

TIFFANY & CO., 15J., early ladies, wire lugs ca.1925
14k $175 $195 $250

TIFFANY & CO., 17J., ladies, aux. sec., Ca.1940
gold filled $40 $45 $65

TIMECRAFT, 17 jewels, chronog., Ca. 1950
s. steel $125 $150 $185

TIMEX,**chronog.,** slide to start, stop & return to zero
base metal $45 $55 $75

TISSOT, 17 jewels, 1898 USA 20 dollar gold piece
22K.......................................$1,000 $1,200 $2,000

TISSOT,17J., military, chronog., Valjoux cal.225, c.1955
s. steel $600 $800 $1,200

TISSOT, 21 jewels, world time, 24 hr. dial, 24 cities, Ca.1950
s. steel $900 $1,100 $1,400
18k $2,000 $2,200 $2,800

TISSOT,17J., Valjoux cal.726, c.1965
18k $800 $900 $1,100
14k $700 $750 $900

TISSOT, 21J, world time, 24 hr. dial, 24 cities, mid-size
18k (1950) $2,000 $2,200 $2,800

TISSOT,17J., auto-wind,"Navigator", date, c.1972
s. steel $150 $175 $225

TISSOT, 17J., "Stadium", tachymeter, c.1960
gold plate $150 $175 $225

TISSOT, 17 jewels, chronog., 3 reg., c. 1956
s. steel $325 $350 $450

TISSOT, 17 jewels, chronog., 3 reg.
gold filled $275 $300 $400
s. steel $275 $300 $400

TISSOT, 17J., day-date-month, moon phase, ctr. sec.
18k $900 $1,000 $1,200

TISSOT, 17 jewels, chronog., 3 reg.
18k $500 $600 $800
s. steel $250 $275 $350

TISSOT, 17J., "UHF", date, auto-wind, c.1960
14k $100 $125 $200

TISSOT, Worlds first transparent plastic watch, "Idea 2001",
with model "Synthic, Astrolon & Sytal", cal.2250, Ca. 1971
plastic(working) .... ★ $300 $400 $600

TISSOT, 17 jewels, chronog., 3 reg., c. 1940s
14k $1,000 $1,100 $1,400

TISSOT, 17J., hidden lugs, c.1938
14k $125 $150 $195

TISSOT, 17 jewels, chronog., triple date, moon phase
s. steel $900 $1,000 $1,200
14k $2,300 $2,500 $2,900
18k $2,750 $3,000 $3,300

TISSOT, 15J., 1st Tissot wrist model, "Banana", Ca. 1917
18K $700 $800 $1,000

TISSOT,17J., auto wind, aux. sec., c.1951
18k $175 $195 $250

TISSOT, 15 jewels, wire lugs, aux. sec., Ca. 1915
silver $250 $275 $350

TISSOT,17J., hidden lugs, c.1950
14k $150 $175 $225

TISSOT,17J., aux. sec., c.1942
s. steel $35 $45 $75
14k $125 $150 $195
18k $175 $195 $250

TITUS, 17 jewels, chronog., 2 reg.
18k $300 $325 $400
14k $200 $225 $300
s. steel $100 $125 $200

TISSOT, 17 jewels, large lugs,
14k $125 $150 $195

TORNEX-RAYVILLE,17J., military, "SEAL", auto-wind,
water-proof, 150M or 490 ft., Ca. 1966
s. steel .... ★★$525 $575 $650

TISSOT, 17J., open shutters to reveal dial
base metal $95 $125 $175

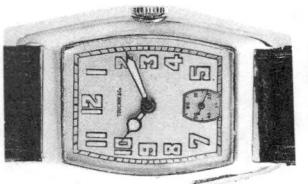

TOUCHON,17J., tonneau case, c.1928
18k(w)..................................... $195 $235 $325

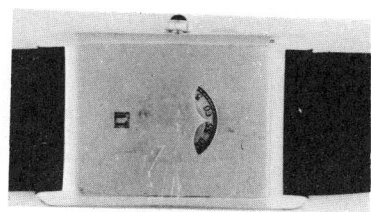

TOUCHON, 17J., jump hr., wandering min., c. 1930s
18k $2,000 $2,500 $3,000

TOURNEAU,17J., beveled lugs, c.1945
14k $125 $150 $195

TOURNEAU,17J, triple date, 3 reg., moon ph., c. 1952
s. steel $700 $750 $900

TOURIST, 17J., by MEPA, timer, c.1958
s. steel $35 $45 $65

TOURNEAU,17J.,chronog. by Valjoux cal.886, c.1965
18k $800 $900 $1,100

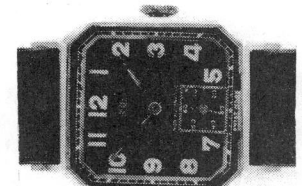

TREBEX, 15 jewels,cut corner dial, c. 1940
gold filled $45 $50 $65

TREBEX, 15 jewels, c. 1940
gold filled $35 $40 $55

TOURNEAU,17J., day date , c.1945
s. steel $175 $195 $275

🕐 Pricing in this Guide are fair market price for **COMPLETE** watches which are reflected from the "**NAWCC**" National and regional shows.

TREBEX, 15 jewels, c. 1940s
gold filled $35 $40 $55

TURLER, 15-17J., duo-dial, Ca.1930s
18k $1,000 $1,200 $1,500

UNITAS, 17 jewels, triple date, moon phase, c. 1948
s. steel $200 $250 $350

TURLER, 17 jewels, chronog., triple date, 3 reg.
18k $900 $1,000 $1,300

URANIA, 15 jewels, military style grill, c. 1915
silver $150 $195 $300

UHRENFABRIK GLASHUTTE, 17J., chronog., c. 1940s
s. steel $500 $600 $800

UNIVER, 17J., triple date , moon ph., chronog.
14k $1,200 $1,500 $2,000

ULTIMOR, 17J., chronog., cal.51, c.1945
18k $250 $300 $400

UNIVERSAL,17J.,"medico compax", c.1949
18k $900 $1,000 $1,200

Wrist Watches listed in this section are priced at the collectable
fair market **Trade Show** level as **complete** watches having an
original gold-filled case and stainless steel back, also with
original dial, leather watch band, and the entire original movement in good working order with no repairs needed.

UNIVERSAL, 17J., "uni compax", c.1942
s. steel $400 $450 $600

UNIVERSAL, 17J., tri-compax, day date moon ph.,c.1955
s. steel $1,000 $1,200 $1,800
14k $3,000 $3,500 $4,500

UNIVERSAL, 17J., chronog., triple date, moon phase
18k $1,200 $1,400 $2,000
14k $1,100 $1,300 $1,800

UNIVERSAL, 17J., chronog., aero compax, diff. meridian,
square pushers
14k $1,400 $1,600 $2,000

UNIVERSAL, 17J. chronog., tri-compax, day date moon ph.
s. steel $1,200 $1,400 $1,800

UNIVERSAL, 17 jewels, chronog., M. #281, c. 1950s
18k $1,600 $1,800 $2,200

UNIVERSAL, 17J., chronog., tri-compax, moon phase
s. steel $900 $1,100 $1,400

UNIVERSAL, 17J., chronog., aero compax, diff. meridian,
round pushers
18k $1,700 $2,000 $2,400

UNIVERSAL, 17J., chronog., compax, massive case
18k $1,800 $2,000 $2,500

UNIVERSAL, day-date-month, moon phase
18k $900 $1,200 $1,400

UNIVERSAL, 17J., chronog., dato-compax, c. 1950s
14k $1,200 $1,400 $1,800
s. steel $600 $700 $900

UNIVERSAL, 17 jewels, day-date-month
14k $600 $650 $800

UNIVERSAL,17J., compax, RF#885107, Valj.cal.72,c.1965
s. steel $600 $700 $900

UNIVERSAL,17J., "Polerouter Sub", date, auto-w., c.1960
14k $350 $400 $500
s. steel $150 $200 $300

UNIVERSAL, 17J. chronog., 10 ligne size,uni-compax
s. steel ....$ 700 $750 $900

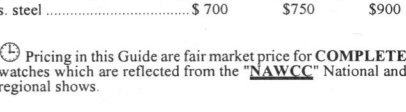 Pricing in this Guide are fair market price for **COMPLETE**
watches which are reflected from the "**NAWCC**" National and
regional shows.

UNIVERSAL,28J.,"Polerouter Sub",rotating bezel, c.1980s
s. steel $225 $250 $325

UNIVERSAL, 17 jewels, "Polerouter", auto wind, day date
18k $300 $400 $550

UNIVERSAL, 23J., auto-wind, date, c.1965
14k $95 $125 $175

UNIVERSAL, 28J., center sec., date, auto-wind, c.1958
18k $195 $250 $325

UNIVERSAL,17J., cal. 138c, date, c.1952
18k $175 $195 $250

UNIVERSAL,17J., cal.52, date, c.1965
18k $175 $195 $250

UNIVERSAL, 17 jewels, Ca. 1952
14k $195 $225 $275

UNIVERSAL,17J., Unisonic chronometer, date, c.1968
s. steel $95 $125 $175

UNIVERSAL,17J., m#264, large lugs, c.1957
gold filled $75 $95 $150

🕐 Pricing in this Guide are fair market price for **COMPLETE**
watches which are reflected from the "**NAWCC**" National and
regional shows.

UNIVERSAL,17J., cal.267g, date, center sec. c.1948
18k $195 $225 $325

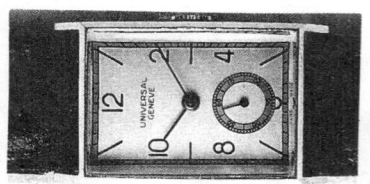

UNIVERSAL, 16J., cal#230,ca. 1940s
s. steel $95 $125 $195

UNIVERSAL, 17J., fancy lugs, Ca. 1948
14k $195 $225 $275

UNIVERSAL, 17J., fancy lugs
14k $195 $225 $275

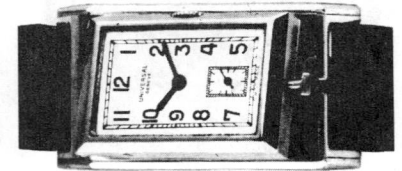

UNIVERSAL, 17 jewels, ''Cabriolet,'' reverso, c. 1930s
s. steel $2,000 $2,300 $2,800

UNIVERSAL,17J., center sec., cal.263, c.1950
18k $175 $195 $250

UNIVERSAL,17J., center sec., cal.138, c.1950
s. steel $75 $95 $150

UNIVERSAL,17J., center sec., cal.236, c.1955
18k $150 $175 $250

UNIVERSAL,17J., aux. sec., Ca.1955
s. steel $95 $125 $175

Wrist Watches listed in this section are priced at the collectable
fair market **Trade Show** level as **complete** watches having an
original gold-filled case and stainless steel back, also with
original dial, leather watch band, and the entire original movement in good working order with no repairs needed.

UNIVERSAL, 17 jewels, auto wind, c. 1955
14k $195 $225 $275
gold filled.................................$95 $110 $140

UNIVERSAL, quartz, day-date, center sec., c. 1960s
18k $175 $195 $250

UNIVERSAL, quartz, , c.1981
18k $175 $195 $250

UNIVERSAL, 17 jewels, auto wind
gold filled.................................$75 $95 $120

🕐 Some grades are not included. Their values can be determined by comparing with **similar** age, size, metal content, style, models and grades listed.

Wrist Watches listed in this section are priced at the collectable fair market Trade Show level as **complete** watches having an original gold-filled case and stainless steel back, also with original dial, leather watch band, and the entire original movement in good working order with no repairs needed.

VACHERON, 36J., skeletonized, triple date, moon phase, leap year, gold rotor
18k $12,000 $14,000 $17,000

VACHERON, 36J., diamond bezel, triple date, moon ph., leap year, gold rotor
18k C&B...........................$14,000 $16,000 $19,000

VACHERON, 17J., triple date, moon phase, c. 1947
18k $7,000 $8,000 $11,000

VACHERON, 17J., triple date, moon phase, c. 1945
18k $3,000 $3,500 $4,500

VACHERON, 17J., triple date, moon phase, c. 1950s
18k manual wind $4,000 $4,500 $5,500

VACHERON, 29 jewels, waterproof, auto-w, c. 1960s
18k $1,500 $1,800 $2,300

VACHERON,17J., triple date, fancy lugs, moon ph.,
c. 1940s
18k manual wind $4,500 $5,000 $6,000

VACHERON, 29 jewels, auto wind, c. 1960s
18k $1,200 $1,400 $1,800

VACHERON, 17J., triple date, fancy lugs, c. 1940s
18k $2,200 $2,600 $3,200

VACHERON, 17 jewels, RF # 6094, Ca. 1955
18k $1,000 $1,200 $1,500

VACHERON, 17 jewels, day-date-month, c. 1940s
18k $2,400 $2,800 $3,400

VACHERON, 29 jewels, center sec., auto wind, date
18k $1,500 $1,800 $2,300

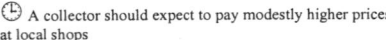 A collector should expect to pay modestly higher prices at local shops

VACHERON, 29 jewels, gold rotor, date
18k $1,500 $1,800 $2,300

VACHERON, 18J., chronog. 2 reg., ca.1942
s. steel $5,000 $5,500 $7,000

VACHERON, 33J., auto-wind 21k rotor, cal.1124 , c.1980s
18k & s.s. $900 $1,000 $1,200

VACHERON, 17 jewels, chronog., 2 reg. Ca. 1934
18k & 14k band.................$16,000 $18,000 $22,000

VACHERON,17J., enamel dial,1 button chronog.,c. 1910s
18k $25,000 $28,000 $35,000

VACHERON, 19 jewels, chronog., 2 reg., c. 1950s
18k C&B.............................$6,000 $6,500 $8,000

VACHERON, 15J., early chronog.,2 reg.,one button,
ca. 1921, large in size
18k $16,000 $18,000 $22,000

VACHERON, 17 jewels, chronog., 2 reg., c. 1945
18k $4,500 $5,000 $6,000

VACHERON, 29J., min. repeater, slide repeat, c. 1950
18k $40,000 $50,000 $70,000

VACHERON, 29J., min. slide repeater, diamond dial
platinum $75,000 $80,000 $90,000

VACHERON, 29J., min. slide repeater, ca. 1950s
18k $40,000 $50,000 $70,000

VACHERON, 18J., diamond set case, skeletonized
18k(W) $4,500 $5,000 $6,000

VACHERON, 18J., skeletonized, diamond bezel
18k $3,000 $3,500 $4,500

VACHERON, 17 jewels, skeletonized
18k $2,500 $3,000 $4,000

VACHERON, 17 jewels, skeletonized, c. 1960s
18k $2,500 $3,000 $4,000

VACHERON, 17 jewels, mystery dial with diamonds
18k C&B $1,600 $1,800 $2,200

VACHERON, 17 jewels, textured bezel
18k $800 $900 $1,100

VACHERON, 18 jewels, center sec., c. 1940s
18k $1,200 $1,400 $1,700

VACHERON, 18 jewels, center sec., Ca.1945
s.steel $600 $650 $800

VACHERON, 18J., fancy graduated bezel, c. 1950s
18k $4,000 $4,500 $5,500

VACHERON, 18 jewels, center sec.
18k C&B.............................. $1,400 $1,600 $2,000

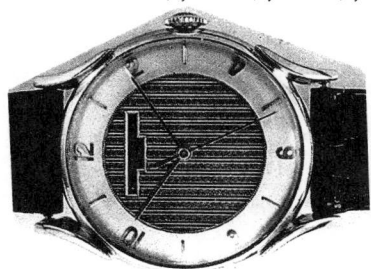

VACHERON, 18 jewels, auto wind, center sec., Ca. 1945
18k $1,600 $1,800 $2,500

VACHERON, 18 J., center sec., waterproof, c. 1950s
18k $1,700 $1,900 $2,200

VACHERON, 18 jewels, center sec., Ca. 1945
18k $900 $950 $1,100

VACHERON, 21J., auto wind, gold rotor, center sec.
18k $1,800 $2,000 $2,400

🕐 Pricing in this Guide are fair market price for **COMPLETE** watches which are reflected from the "**NAWCC**" National and regional shows.

VACHERON, 18J., center sec., ca.1940s
18k $1,200 $1,400 $1,700

VACHERON,17J., center sec., c.1940
s. steel $600 $650 $800

VACHERON, 18J., rf#6903, center sec., ca.1958
18k $800 $900 $1,100

VACHERON,17J., center sec., large lugs, c.1949
18k $1,800 $2,000 $2,400

VACHERON, 18J., center sec., ca.1953
18k $1,300 $1,800 $1,900

VACHERON,17J., center sec., c.1940
s. steel $600 $650 $800

VACHERON, 18J., textured dial center sec.
18k $1,200 $1,400 $1,700

VACHERON,17J., center sec., c.1940
18k $900 $1,000 $1,200

VACHERON, 18J., center sec.
s. steel $600 $650 $800

VACHERON, 18J., fancy large lugs, center sec., ca.1953
18k $1,600 $1,800 $2,200

VACHERON, 18J., center sec.
18k $900 $1,000 $1,200

VACHERON, 18J., rf#4730, fancy lugs, ca. 1950s
18k $1,700 $1,800 $2,300

VACHERON, 18J.,textured dial, center sec.,ca.1947
18k $2,000 $2,200 $2,600

VACHERON, 18J.,textured dial, fancy lugs
18k $1,800 $1,900 $2,400

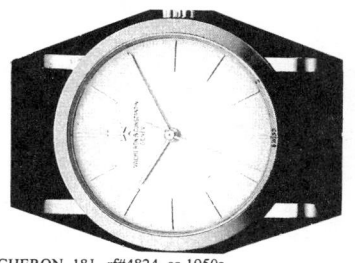
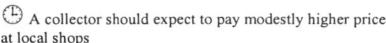

VACHERON, 18J., rf#4824, ca.1950s
18k(W)................................$1,000 $1,100 $1,300

VACHERON, 18J., center sec., ca.1944
14k $800 $900 $1,100

⊕ A collector should expect to pay modestly higher prices
at local shops

VACHERON, 18J., royal chronometer, ca.1950s
18k $1,500 $1,700 $2,000

VACHERON, 29 jewels, textured dial, c. 1948
18k $1,500 $1,700 $2,200

VACHERON, 17J., center sec.auto-w., ca.1945
18k $1,400 $1,600 $1,900

VACHERON, 29 jewels, 2 tone dial, center sec.
18k $1,500 $1,700 $2,000

VACHERON, 29J., center sec., auto wind, c. 1950s
18k $1,800 $2,000 $2,500

VACHERON, 29 jewels, center sec., center lugs,c. 1950s
18k $1,000 $1,200 $1,500

VACHERON, 29 jewels, center sec.
18k $1,000 $1,100 $1,300

VACHERON, 29 jewels, center sec., auto wind, c. 1949
18k $1,800 $2,000 $2,500

VACHERON,17J., diamond dial, fancy lugs
platinum..............................$4,500 $5,000 $6,000

VACHERON,17J., aux. sec., c.1945
18k $1,200 $1,300 $1,500

VACHERON,17J., aux. sec., RF#4073, c.1942
s. steel $700 $800 $1,000

VACHERON,17J., aux. sec., tear drop lugs, c.1945
18k $1,400 $1,600 $2,000

VACHERON,17J., aux. sec, fluted lugs, c.1950s
18k $2,200 $2,400 $2,800

🕐 Some grades are not included. Their values can be determined by comparing with **similar** age, size, metal content,
style, models and grades listed.

VACHERON, 18J.,aux. sec., fancy lugs,ca. 1944
18k $1,400 $1,500 $1,800

VACHERON, 18J., aux. sec.
18k $1,300 $1,400 $1,700

VACHERON, 18J.,fancy lugs
18k $1,300 $1,400 $1,700

VACHERON, 18J., cal#p453/3b,aux.sec.
18k $2,000 $2,200 $2,600

VACHERON, 18J., aux. sec.,
s. steel $500 $550 $700

VACHERON, 18J., aux. sec., thin model
18k(W).....................................$900 $1,000 $1,100

VACHERON, 18J., aux. sec., long lugs, ca.1942
18k $1,000 $1,100 $1,300

VACHERON, 18J., aux. sec., ca.1951
18k $1,000 $1,100 $1,300

🕐 Pricing in this Guide are fair market price for **COMPLETE**
watches which are reflected from the "**NAWCC**" National and
regional shows.

VACHERON, 18J., **winds at 12,** ca. 1928
18k $2,800 $3,000 $3,500

VACHERON, 15J., champagne dial, long lugs, ca.1935
18k $1,000 $1,100 $1,300

VACHERON, 17 jewels, aux. sec., fancy lugs
18k $1,400 $1,500 $1,800

VACHERON, 17 jewels, aux. sec., Ca. 1950
18k $1,100 $1,200 $1,400

VACHERON, 17 jewels, aux. sec., stepped lugs
18k $1,800 $2,100 $2,500

VACHERON, 17 jewels, 2 tone dial, aux. sec.
18k $1,400 $1,500 $1,800

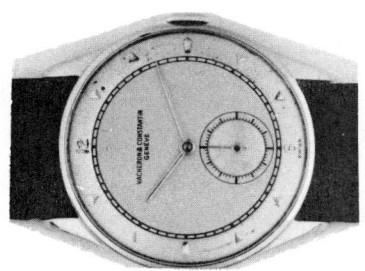

VACHERON, 17 jewels, aux. sec., c. 1940s
18k $1,400 $1,500 $1,800

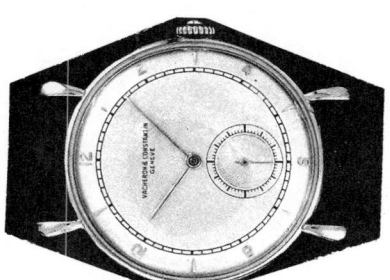

VACHERON, 17 jewels, aux. sec.
18k $1,400 $1,600 $2,000

VACHERON, 17 jewels, aux. sec., c. 1940s
18k $1,200 $1,300 $1,600

VACHERON, 17 jewels, aux. sec.
s. steel $500 $550 $700

VACHERON, 17 jewels, aux. sec., large lugs, c. 1950s
18k $1,800 $2,200 $2,800

VACHERON, 17 jewels, aux. sec.
14k C&B $1,200 $1,400 $1,700

VACHERON, 17 jewels, aux. sec.
18k $1,600 $1,800 $2,500

VACHERON, 17 jewels, aux. sec., c. 1940s
18k $1,100 $1,200 $1,500

VACHERON, 17 jewels, aux. sec.
18k $1,200 $1,400 $1,700

VACHERON, 17 jewels
18k C&B.............................$1,800 $2,000 $2,500

VACHERON, 17J., RF# 6498, Ca. 1965
18k $1,000 $1,200 $1,500

VACHERON, 17 jewels
18k $1,000 $1,100 $1,300

VACHERON, 18J., no sec. hand,
18k $800 $900 $1,100

VACHERON,17J., RF#6099, cal.1003, c.1960
18k $800 $900 $1,100

VACHERON, 17J., 20 dollar gold piece, RF # 4928
18k $2,200 $2,500 $3,000

VACHERON, 16J., hidden lugs, Ca. 1945
14k $1,200 $1,400 $1,700

Wrist Watches listed in this section are priced at the collectable fair market **Trade Show** level as **complete** watches having an original gold-filled case and stainless steel back, also with original dial, leather watch band, and the entire original movement in good working order with no repairs needed.

🕐 Some grades are not included. Their values can be determined by comparing with **similar** age, size, metal content, style, models and grades listed.

VACHERON, 16J., wire lugs, silver dial, ca.1917
14k $2,500 $3,000 $3,500

VACHERON, 18J., tonneau shaped, ca. 1930s
18k $2,500 $2,800 $3,500

VACHERON, 15J., lady's with wire lugs,ca.1920
18k(W).....................................$400 $500 $650

VACHERON, 15 jewels
18k C&B $1,600 $1,800 $2,200

VACHERON, 17 jewels , 2 tone case yellow & white
18k $1,400 $1,500 $1,700

⊕ Pricing in this Guide are fair market price for **COMPLETE**
watches which are reflected from the "**NAWCC**" National and
regional shows.

VACHERON, 36 jewels, auto wind
18k C&B.............................$1,500 $1,800 $2,200

VACHERON, 21 J., date, auto-w. ca. 1980s
s. steel $1,000 $1,100 $1,400

VACHERON, 15J., shutters with center slide to view dial, 2
tone case, ca. 1933
18k $10,000 $11,000 $14,000

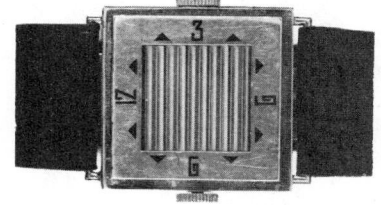

VACHERON, 17J, with shutters, crowns at 3 & 9
18k $12,000 $13,000 $16,000

⊕ Some grades are not included. Their values can be determined by comparing with **similar** age, size, metal content,
style, models and grades listed.

⊕ A collector should expect to pay modestly higher prices
at local shops

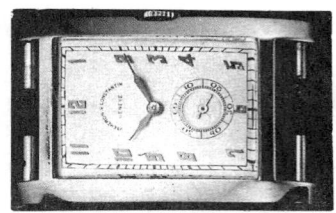

VACHERON, 18J., heavy case,ca.1930s
18k(W)..............................$2,800 $3,200 $3,800

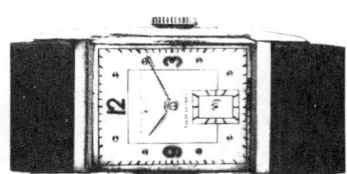

VACHERON, 18J., silver dial, ca.1941
18k $1,700 $1,800 $2,000

VACHERON, 18J., applied numbers, ca.1940
18k $1,700 $1,800 $2,000

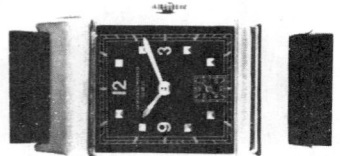

VACHERON, 18J., black dial, aux. sec.,ca.1937
18k $1,800 $1,900 $2,100

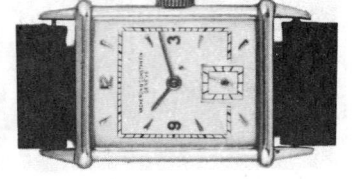

VACHERON, 18J., silver dial, ca.1942
18k $2,000 $2,200 $2,500

Wrist Watches listed in this section are priced at the collectable fair market **Trade Show** level as **complete** watches having an original gold-filled case and stainless steel back, also with original dial, leather watch band, and the entire original movement in good working order with no repairs needed.

VACHERON, 18J., hidden lugs, ca.1940s
18k $1,700 $1,800 $2,100

VACHERON, 18J., off set lugs,
18k $2,000 $2,200 $2,500

VACHERON, 18J., off set lugs,
18k $2,000 $2,200 $2,500

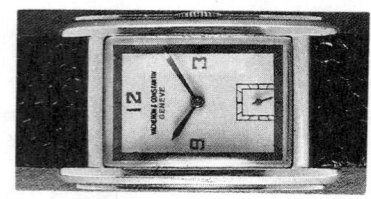

VACHERON, 18J., aux .sec.,
s. steel $1,200 $1,300 $1,600

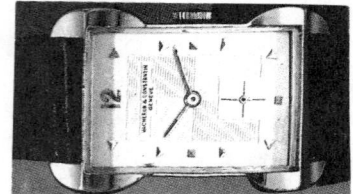

VACHERON, 18J., textured dial, large lugs, ca.1951
18k $3,800 $4,300 $5,500

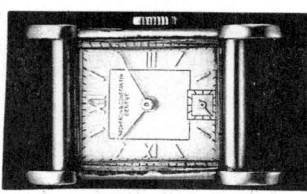

VACHERON, 18J., fancy lugs,ca.1938
18k $2,800 $2,900 $3,200

VACHERON, 17 jewels, aux. sec., c. 1945
18k $1,000 $1,100 $1,400

VACHERON, 18J., textured bezel,ca.1950s
18k $1,800 $2,200 $2,400

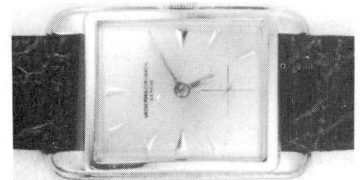

VACHERON, 17 jewels, applied gold numbers
18k $900 $1,000 $1,200

VACHERON, 18 jewels, aux. sec., c. 1950s
18k $1,500 $1,600 $1,900

VACHERON, 17 jewels, fancy lugs
18k $1,800 $1,900 $2,200

VACHERON, 18 jewels, aux. sec., c. 1940s
18k $1,500 $1,600 $1,900

VACHERON, 17 jewels, c. 1950s
18k $1,500 $1,600 $1,900

VACHERON, 17J., applied gold numbers, c. 1940s
18k $1,400 $1,500 $1,800

VACHERON, 17 jewels, fancy lugs
14k $1,200 $1,400 $1,700

⊕ A collector should expect to pay modestly higher prices
at local shops

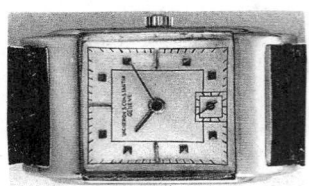

VACHERON, 17 jewels, aux. sec., Ca. 1945
18k $1,600 $1,700 $1,900

VACHERON, 17 jewels, stepped bezel, fancy lugs, Ca. 1940
18k $2,700 $2,900 $3,500

VACHERON,17J., hidden barrel shaped lugs, c.1943
14k $1,200 $1,400 $1,700

VACHERON,17J., aux. sec., c.1947
18k $1,500 $1,600 $1,900

VACHERON,17J., aux. sec., c.1942
18k $1,300 $1,400 $1,700

VACHERON,17J., RF#6249, aux. sec., c.1963
18k $1,500 $1,600 $1,800

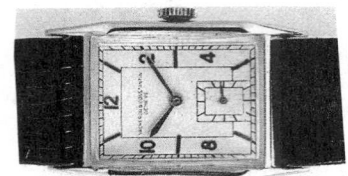

VACHERON,17J., aux. sec., c.1934
18k $1,500 $1,600 $1,800

VACHERON, 17 jewels, aux. sec., Ca. 1946
18k $1,500 $1,600 $1,800

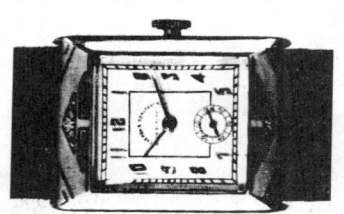

VACHERON, 17 jewels, Art Deco bezel, c. 1925
18k $4,500 $5,000 $6,000

VACHERON, 15 jewels, exaggerated numbers, Ca. 1917
18k $2,200 $2,500 $3,000

🕐 Pricing in this Guide are fair market price for **COMPLETE**
watches which are reflected from the "**NAWCC**" National and
regional shows.

VACHERON, 17 jewels, aux. sec.,
18k $2,200 $2,400 $2,800

VACHERON, 18 jewels, aux. sec.
18k C&B.............................$2,000 $2,100 $2,300

VACHERON, 15 jewels, heavy bezel, c.1925
18K C&B $2,800 $3,000 $3,500

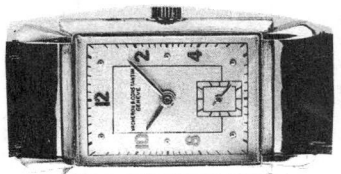

VACHERON, 17 jewels, fancy long lugs, Ca. 1940s
18k $1,600 $1,700 $2,000

VACHERON,15J., curvex,wire lugs,33mm long,ca.1923
18k $2,500 $2,700 $3,200

VACHERON, 15J., hinged back, ca. 1930
18k $2,200 $2,400 $2,800

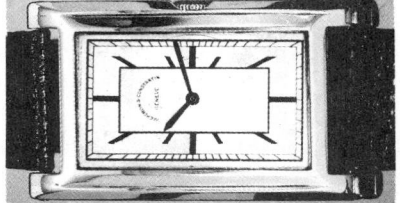

VACHERON, 18J., large 2 tone mans watch, ca.1928
18k $3,500 $4,000 $5,000

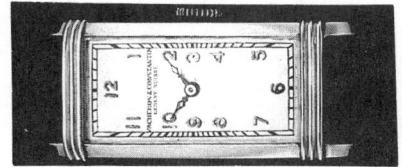

VACHERON, 18J.,long curved case, ca.1929
platinum..............................$4,000 $4,500 $5,500

VACHERON, 18J., ca. 1926
18k $1,600 $1,800 $2,200

VACHERON, 18J., ca. 1950s
18k $900 $1,000 $1,200

VACHERON, 15J., early movement, ca.1925
18k $1,300 $1,400 $1,800

VACHERON, 17 jewels, aux. sec.
14k $900 $1,000 $1,200

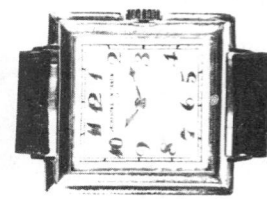

VACHERON, 15J.,2 tone case, ca. 1926
18k $1,400 $1,600 $2,000

VACHERON, 17 jewels, flat & thin model, c. 1960s
18k $800 $900 $1,200

VACHERON, 18J., tank style, ca.1960s
18k $1,200 $1,300 $1,500

VACHERON, 17 jewels
18k C&B.............................$1,500 $1,700 $2,000

VACHERON, 17 jewels, hinged back
18k $1,400 $1,500 $1,800

VACHERON, 18 jewels, stepped case & beveled lugs
18k $1,600 $1,700 $2,000

VACHERON, 15J., wire lugs, enamel dial, Ca.1920s
18k $2,000 $2,200 $2,500

VACHERON, 15 jewels, c. 1920s
18k $1,200 $1,300 $1,600

VACHERON, 17 jewels, **star dial**, hidden lugs, c. 1943s
14k $1,200 $1,400 $1,700

VACHERON, 17 jewels, flared, c. 1948
18k $3,000 $3,500 $4,500

VACHERON, 17 jewels, 68 diamond bezel
18k $2,200 $2,500 $2,800

VACHERON, 17 jewels, flared, c. 1940s
18k $3,000 $3,500 $4,500

VACHERON,17J., RF#7252, c.1962
18k $1,000 $1,200 $1,500

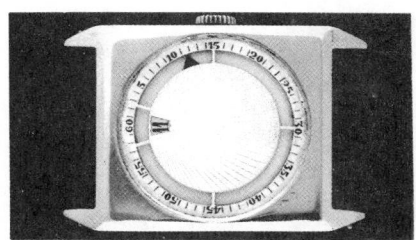

VACHERON, 17 jewels, ''Chronoscope,'' jumping hr.,
revolving ruby min. indicator, c. 1930s
18k $20,000 $22,000 $26,000

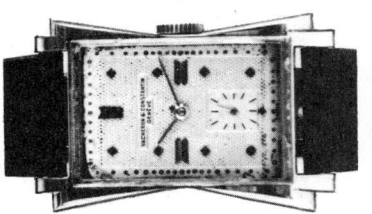

VACHERON, 17 jewels, flared, curvex, c. 1940s
18k $4,000 $4,500 $5,500

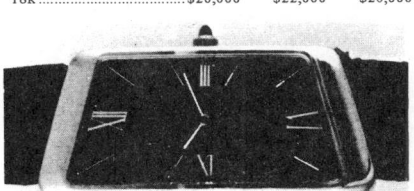

VACHERON, 20 jewels, Adj. to 5 Pos., c. 1970s
18k $2,000 $2,200 $2,500

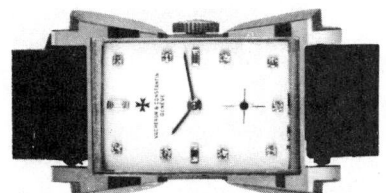

VACHERON, 17J., flared,**12 diam.dial**, aux. sec., c. 1948
platinum $5,000 $5,500 $6,500

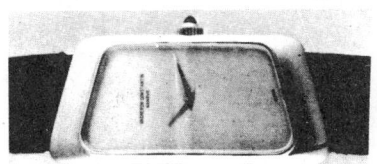

VACHERON, 22 jewels, lady's watch, c. 1970s
18k $800 $900 $1,200

⊕ Pricing in this Guide are fair market price for **COMPLETE**
watches which are reflected from the "**NAWCC**" National and
regional shows.

VACHERON, 17 jewels, aux. sec., ruby dial
18k $2,000 $2,200 $2,800

VACHERON,16J., black star & forrest, wire lugs, c.1919
18k ladies................................ $400 $450 $600

VACHERON, 21 jewels, center sec., auto wind, c. 1950s
18k $3,000 $3,300 $4,000

VACHERON, 17 jewels, heavy bezel
18k ladies............................. $1,200 $1,400 $1,700

VACHERON,17J., ladies, c.1948
18k ladies................................ $800 $900 $1,100

VACHERON, 17 jewels, aux. sec., fancy lugs, c. 1947
18k $2,500 $2,800 $3,500

VACHERON, 15 J., lady's, wire lugs, ca.1919
18k $400 $450 $600

VACHERON, 17 jewels, lady's watch, c. 1960s
18k C&B.............................$1,200 $1,400 $1,800

VACHERON, 17 jewels , swinging lugs
14k $1,200 $1,400 $1,800

Wrist Watches listed in this section are priced at the collectable
fair market **Trade Show** level as **complete** watches having an
original gold-filled case and stainless steel back, also with
original dial, leather watch band, and the entire original movement in good working order with no repairs needed.

VACHERON, 17J., cased & timed in U.S.A. by Vacheron &
Constantine , heavy 14k gold bracelet, ladies, Ca.1950s
14k heavy C&B..................$1,000 $1,100 $1,400

VAN CLEEF & ARPELS,17J., center lugs, c.1970
18k $250 $275 $375

VULCAIN,17jewels, "Grand Prix", Ca. 1940
s. steel $35 $40 $55

VERNO, 15 jewels, chased bezel
gold filled (w) $35 $45 $75

VULCAIN,17J., "Cricket Alarm", c.1965
base metal $95 $125 $195

VULCAIN, 17 jewels, digital read out
base metal $65 $75 $95

VULCAIN,17J., "Cricket", alarm, c.1948
s. steel $125 $150 $225

VULCAIN, 17 jewels, "Cricket", alarm
14k $195 $225 $275
18k $275 $325 $450

VULCAIN,17J., "Cricket Calendar", Ca. 1965
18K $275 $325 $450

🕐 A collector should expect to pay modestly higher prices
at local shops

VULCAIN, 17 jewels, "Cricket," alarm
gold filled...............................$125 $150 $225

WAKMANN,17J., "Gigandet" Valjoux cal.72, c.1955
18k $1,200 $1,300 $1,600

VULCAIN, 17 jewels, "Minstop"
s. steel $75 $85 $125

WAKMANN, 17J., chronog., 3 reg., triple date
14k $400 $500 $650

WAKMANN,17J., 24 hr. dial, c.1955
s. steel $75 $95 $135

WAKMANN,17J., chronog., 3 reg., triple date, sq.buttons
s. steel $195 $250 $350

WAKMANN, 17 jewels, chronog., 3 reg., c. 1958
s. steel $250 $300 $350

WAKMANN,17J., chronog., Valjoux cal.188, c.1960
s. steel $150 $175 $225

WAKMANN,17J., chronog., Valjoux cal.236, c.1968
s. steel $175 $195 $250

WAKMANN,17J., chronog., c.1955
18k $500 $550 $650
s. steel $175 $195 $250

WAKMANN,17J., chronog., c.1970s
s. steel $95 $150 $225

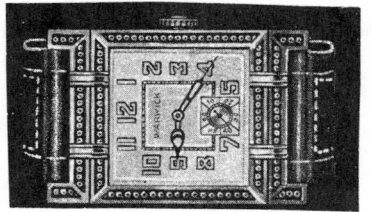

WARWICK, 6J., hinged back, 1930s
gold plate $25 $35 $55

WARWICK, 15J., 1930s
gold plate $25 $35 $55

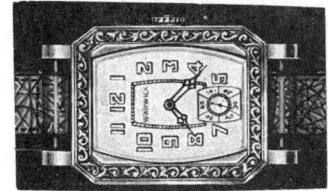

WARWICK, 15J., 1930s
gold plate $25 $35 $55

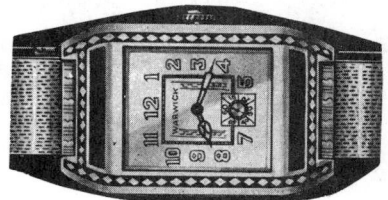

WARWICK, 6-15J., 1930s
gold plate $25 $35 $55

WARWICK, 6-15J., 1930s
gold plate $25 $35 $55

WARWICK, 6-15J., 1930s
gold plate $25 $35 $55

WARWICK, 6-15J., 1930s
gold plate $25 $35 $55

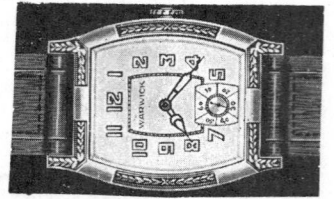

WARWICK, 15J., 1930s
gold plate $25 $35 $55

WARWICK, 15J., 1930s
base metal $25 $35 $55

WATEX, 7J., fluted case, c.1940
gold filled................................$95 $110 $150

WEISCO, 7J., aux. sec., wire lugs, c. 1928
base metal $25 $35 $55

WELDON,17J., aux. sec., large lugs c.1950s
gold filled $75 $95 $135

WELSBRO ,17J., single button chronog., c.1940
s. steel $150 $195 $275

WELTALL W. Co., floral enamel on case, cylinder escp.
wire lugs, Ca. 1910
14k $95 $125 $175

WEST END, 17J., "Keepsake", (by Longines), Ca. 1925
silver $250 $350 $500

WEST END, 17 jewels, center lugs
18k $175 $195 $250

WHITE STAR, 17J., triple date, moon phase, c. 1948
s. steel $400 $500 $650

WITTNAUER, 17 jewels, chronog., c. 1948
s. steel $250 $300 $375

WINTON, 17J., hooded lugs
14k $95 $125 $175

WITTNAUER,17J., "Professional", RF#6002, c.1955
18k $600 $650 $725
s. steel $275 $325 $400

WINTON, 16J., curvex, hinged back, c.1930s
silver $150 $175 $225

WITTNAUER,17J., chronog., waterproof, c.1958
18k $400 $450 $550
s. steel $200 $250 $325

WITTNAUER, 17 jewels, fancy lugs
14k $125 $150 $195

WITTNAUER, 17 jewels, chronog., day-date-month
s. steel $375 $450 $550

WITTNAUER,17J., chronog., by Venius, **Time Zone Bezel**,
Ca. 1955
s. steel $350 $400 $500

WITTNAUER,17J., chronog., by Valjoux, #72, cal.13w1
s. steel $255 $350 $500

WITTNAUER,7J., "Electronic", day date, c.1968
s. steel $25 $30 $50

WITTNAUER,7J., mid size , stop watch, c.1940
s. steel $125 $135 $165

WITTNAUER,17J., direct read, c.1970
s. steel $35 $45 $60

WITTNAUER, 17 J., day date, set year by button
s. steel $150 $175 $225

WITTNAUER,17J., Zircon on dial, direct read, c.1970
base metal $20 $35 $50

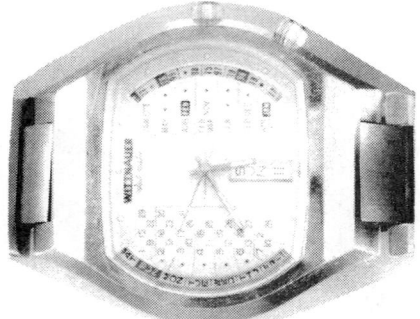

WITTNAUER,17J., perpetual calendar
base metal $70 $80 $95

WITTNAUER, 17 jewels, auto wind, sector, date
gold filled $150 $175 $250
s. steel $150 $175 $250

WITTNAUER, 17 jewels, fancy lugs, Ca. 1955
14k $95 $125 $195

WITTNAUER,17J., aux. sec., c.1958
gold filled.................................$65 $75 $95

WITTNAUER,17J., aux. sec., c.1950
14k $95 $125 $175

WITTNAUER,17J., aux. sec., GJS, c.1948
14k $95 $125 $175

WITTNAUER,17J., aux. sec., fancy lugs, c.1955
gold filled.................................$65 $75 $95

WITTNAUER, 17 jewels, curved case, c.1950
14k $95 $125 $175

WITTNAUER, 17 jewels, cal.9wn, fancy lugs, c.1954
gold filled $60 $75 $95

WITTNAUER, 17 jewels, fancy lugs, GJS
14k $95 $125 $175

WITTNAUER,17J., aux. sec., GJS, large lugs, c.1950
14k $95 $125 $175

WITTNAUER,17J., aux. sec., fancy case, c.1950
gold filled $75 $95 $135

WITTNAUER,17J., aux. sec., flared case
14k $95 $125 $175

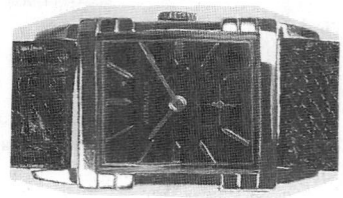

WITTNAUER,17J., aux. sec.
gold filled................................$70 $80 $110

WITTNAUER, 17 jewels, fancy lugs, c. 1950s
14k $95 $125 $175

WITTNAUER,17J., aux. sec., GJS, c. 1955
14k $95 $125 $175

WITTNAUER,17J., aux. sec., tu-tone dial, c. 1950
gold filled................................$65 $75 $95

WITTNAUER,17J., aux. sec., c. 1950
gold filled $45 $55 $75

WITTNAUER,15J., aux. sec., tonneau case, c.1945
gold plate $30 $40 $55

WITTNAUER,17J., aux. sec.
gold filled $45 $50 $75

WITTNAUER,17J., aux. sec.
14k $95 $125 $175

WITTNAUER,17J., flared case, Ca.1949
14k $95 $125 $195

🕐 Some grades are not included. Their values can be determined by comparing with **similar** age, size, metal content, style, models and grades listed.

WITTNAUER, 17J., RF#2067, c.1950
gold filled................................$55 $65 $85

WITTNAUER, 17J., auto-wind, c.1960
base metal $35 $45 $65

WITTNAUER, 17J., cal.7630, aux. sec., c.1955
14k $95 $125 $175

WITTNAUER, 17J., "Alarm", c.1960
gold filled................................$65 $75 $95

Wrist Watches listed in this section are priced at the collectable fair market Trade Show level as **complete** watches having an original gold-filled case and stainless steel back, also with original dial, leather watch band, and the entire original movement in good working order with no repairs needed.

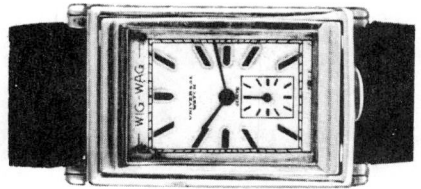

WIG WAG, 15 jewels, **early auto wind**, c. 1932
s. steel .... ★ $400 $450 $600

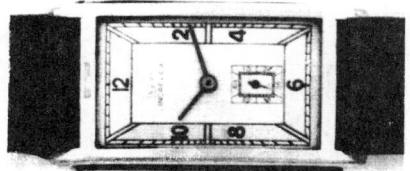

WYLER, 17 jewels, early auto wind, watch winds by using the muscular movement of the wrist, back set
gold filled .... ★ $400 $450 $600

WYLER, 17 jewels, early auto wind, back set
gold filled .... ★ $400 $450 $600

WYLER, 17 jewels, center sec., auto-wind
s. steel $55 $65 $85

WYLER, 17 jewels, aux. sec., Ca. 1955
s. steel $40 $50 $65

🕑 Some grades are not included. Their values can be determined by comparing with **similar** age, size, metal content, style, models and grades listed.

WYLER, 17 jewels
s. steel $75 $95 $135

WYLER,17J., auto-wind, c.1932
chrome $40 $50 $65

WYLER, 17 jewels, diamond dial, c. 1946
s. steel $55 $65 $95

WYLER,17J., center sec., c.1945
s. steel $45 $50 $75

WYLER,17J., day date month, c.1946
gold filled $95 $125 $175

WYLER,17J., center sec., waterproof, ca.1941
s. steel $45 $50 $75

WYLER, 17 jewels, chronog., c. 1940s
14k $250 $300 $375
s. steel $150 $175 $225

WYLER,17J., aux. sec., c.1938
s. steel $45 $50 $75

YALE, 15 jewels, calendar, c. 1939
14k $175 $195 $250
gold filled $75 $95 $125

🕐 A collector should expect to pay modestly higher prices at local shops

Wrist Watches listed in this section are priced at the collectable fair market **Trade Show** level as **complete** watches having an original gold-filled case and stainless steel back, also with original dial, leather watch band, and the entire original movement in good working order with no repairs needed.

🕐 Some grades are not included. Their values can be determined by comparing with **similar** age, size, metal content, style, models and grades listed.

🕐 Pricing in this Guide are fair market price for **COMPLETE** watches which are reflected from the "**NAWCC**" National and regional shows.

ZENITH, 23 jewels, Auto Sports, date, Ca. 1968
gold plate $65 $75 $95

ZENITH, 19 jewels, **chronometer**, 33mm, c. 1950s
gold filled $75 $95 $135

ZENITH,15J., enamel dial, wire lugs, c. 1918
silver $250 $300 $375

ZENITH, 17 jewels, chronog., Ca. 1950
18k $500 $550 $650

ZENITH,15J., signal corps on enamel dial, center lug, 1918
silver $275 $325 $400

ZENITH, 36 jewels, chronog., auto wind, c. 1969
s. steel $400 $450 $600

ZENITH,17J., Chronog., Ca. 1930
18k $1,500 $1,700 $2,200

ZENITH,17J., Chronograph 3 reg., Ca.1965
14k $800 $900 $1,100
s. steel $400 $450 $600

ZENITH, 36J., "El Primero", RF#502,auto wind, c. 1970
18k $700 $800 $1,000

ZENITH, 36 jewels, "El Primero," chronog., triple date
moon phase, auto wind, c. 1970s
18k $1,600 $1,800 $2,400

ZENITH,36J., chronog., auto-wind, triple date, moon ph.
base metal $500 $550 $700

ZENITH, 17 jewels, fancy bezel
18k $195 $225 $275

ZENITH, 17J., auto-wind, date at 5, Ca. 1959
18k $175 $195 $250

ZENTRA, 24 jewels, ladies,auto wind, c. 1958
14k $70 $85 $125

ZODIAC, 17J., chronog., 2 reg., fancy lugs, c.1948
gold filled $200 $225 $300
14k $350 $400 $500
18k $400 $450 $550

ZODIAC, 17J., chronog., auto-wind, date, c.1971
s. steel $95 $125 $175

🕐 A collector should expect to pay modestly higher prices
at local shops

ZODIAC, 17J., center sec., auto-wind, c.1959
s. steel $35 $45 $65

ZODIAC, 17J., day-date-month, moon phase, c. 1957
s. steel $300 $350 $425
14k $500 $525 $600

ZODIAC, 17 jewels, 24 hour dial
s. steel $65 $75 $95

ZODIAC, 17J., auto-wind, power reserve,
differential gearing, c. 1959
14k $175 $195 $225
gold filled $75 $95 $135
s. steel $75 $95 $135

ZODIAC, 17 jewels, ref. #8088
14k $95 $125 $175

ZODIAC, 21J., date, "Olympos", date, auto-wind,c.1965
s. steel $50 $60 $95

ZODIAC, 17J., by Valj. cal. 7733, Ca.1965
base metal $125 $150 $195

ZODIAC, 17J., center sec., Ca.1948
s. steel $55 $60 $95

ADJUSTED-Derived from Latin *ad justus,* meaning just right. Adjusted to compensate for temperature, positions,and isochronism.

ALARM WATCH-A watch that will give an audible sound at a pre-set time.

ALL or NOTHING PIECE-A repeating watch mechanism which ensures that ALL the hour & minutes are struck or sounded or nothing is heard.

ANALOGUE-A term used to denote a watch dial with hands rather than digital display.

ANNEALING-Heating and cooling a metal slowly to relieve internal stress.

ANTI-MAGNETIC-Not affected by magnetic field.

ANTIQUARIAN-Of antiques or dealing in, also the study of old and out-of-date items.

Arbor

ARBOR-The mechanical axle of a moving part; on the balance it is called the staff, on the lever it is called the arbor.

ASSAY-Analyzing a metal for its gold or silver content.

AUTOMATON-Automatic working figures moving in conjunction with the movement mechanism. Striking *Jacquemarts* or jacks which are figures (may be humans provided with hammers) striking bells to supply the sound for the hour & quarter hours. The hammers take the place of the bells clapper. *Automata* plural of **automaton.**

AUXILIARY COMPENSATION-For middle temperature errors found on marine chronometers.

AUXILIARY DIAL - Any extra dial for information.

AWI - American Watchmakers-Clockmakers Institute, 701 Enterprise Drive, Harrison, OH 45030. Tel # **(513) 367-9800**

BAGUETTE-A French term for oblong shape. A watch having it's length at least 3 times it's width. A long narrow diamond.

Balance Cock

BALANCE COCK-The bridge that holds the upper jewels and the balance and secured at one end only.

Balance Spring

BALANCE SPRING-Also called the hairspring; the spring governing the balance.

Balance Staff

BALANCE STAFF -The shaft of the balance wheel.

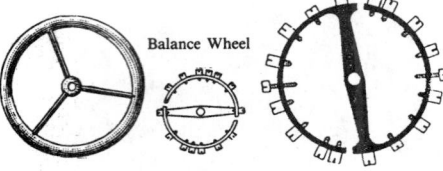
Balance Wheel

BALANCE WHEEL-A device shaped like a wheel that does for a watch what a pendulum does for a clock.

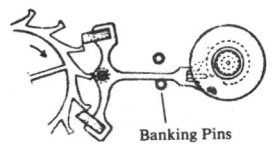

Banking Pins

BANKING PINS-The two pins which limit the angular motion of the pallet.

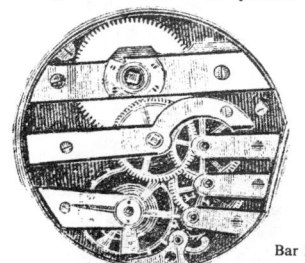

Bar Movement

BAR MOVEMENT-A type of movement employing about six bridges to hold the train. In use by 1840.

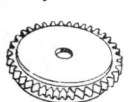

Barrel

BARREL-Drum-shaped container that houses the mainspring.

BEAT-Refers to the tick or sound of a watch; about 1/5 of a second. The sound is produced by the escape wheel striking the pallets.

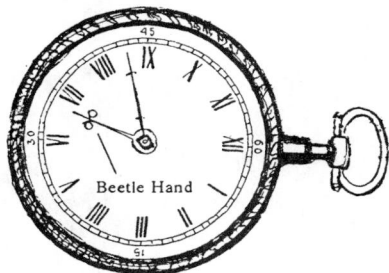

Beetle Hand

BEETLE HAND-Hour hand resembling a stag beetle; usually associated with the poker-type minute hand in 17th and 18th century watches.

BELL METAL-Four parts copper and one part tin used for metal laps to get a high polish on steel.

O S. Htg. Bezel,

BEZEL-The rim that covers the dial (face) and retains the crystal.

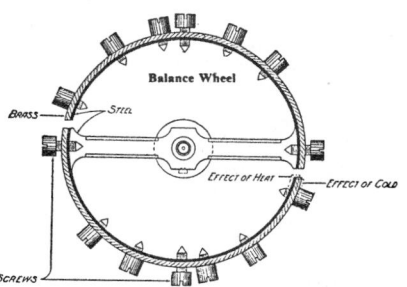

Balance Wheel

BI-METALLIC BALANCE-A balance composed of brass and steel designed to compensate for temperature changes in the hairspring.

BLIND MAN'S WATCH- A Braille watch; also known as a tact watch.

BLUING or BUING-By heating polished steel to 540 degrees, the color will change to blue.

BOMBE'- Convex on one side.

Bow

BOW-The ring that is looped at the pendant to which a chain or fob is attached

BOX CHRONOMETER-A marine or other type chronometer in gimbals so the movement remains level at sea.

BOX JOINTED CASE-A heavy hinged decorative case with a simulated joint at the top under the pendant. (BOX CASE)

BREGUET KEY-A ratcheting watch key permitting winding in only one direction.

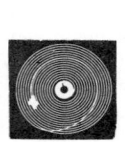 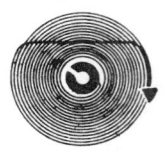

Overcoil Hairspring

BREGUET SPRING-A type of hairspring that improves time keeping also called over-coil hairspring.

BRIDGE-A metal bar which bear the pivot of wheels and is supported at both ends .(see cock.)

BUBBLE BACK-A Rolex wrist watch which were water proof (Oyster) and auto wind (Perpetual) Ca. 1930 to 1950's.

BULL'S EYE CRYSTAL-Used on old type watches; the center of the crystal was polished which achieved a bull's eye effect.

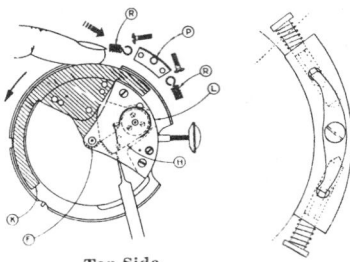

Top Side

BUFFER SPRING - Buffer spring is a stop spring for oscillating weight.

CABOCHON - An unfaceted cut stone of domed form or style. (on some crowns)

CALENDAR WATCH-A watch that shows the date, month and day.

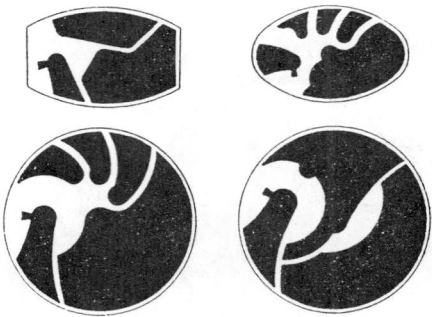

CALIBRE or CALIBER-**Size** of a watch movement also to describe the model, style or shape of a watch movement.

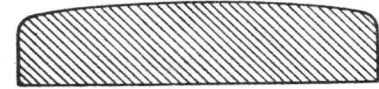

CAP JEWEL-Also called the end stone, the flat jewel on which the staff rests.

CASE SCREW-A screw with part of the head cut away.

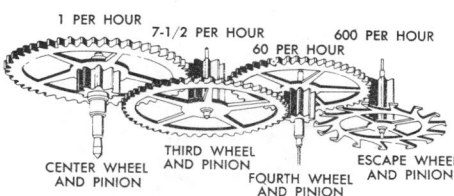

CENTER WHEEL-The second wheel; the arbor for the minute hand; this wheel makes one revolution per hour.

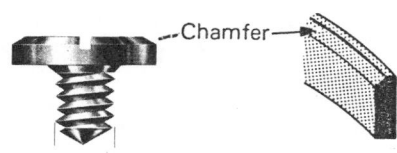

CHAIN (Fusee)-Looks like a miniature bicycle chain connecting the barrel and fusee.

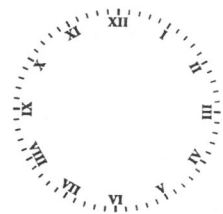

CHAMFER-Sloping or beveled. Removing a sharp edge or edges of holes.

CHAMPLEVE-An area hollowed out and filled with enamel and then baked on.

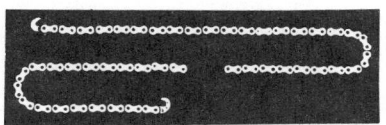

CHAPTER-The hour, minute & seconds numbers on a dial. The chapter ring is the zone or circle that confines the numbers.

CHRONOGRAPH-A movement that can be started and stopped to measure short time intervals and return to zero. A stopwatch does not keep the time of day.

CHRONOMETER ESCAPEMENT - A detent escapement used in marine chronometers.

CLICK-A pawl that ratchets and permits the winding wheel to move in one direction; a clicking sound can be heard as the watch is wound.

CLOCK WATCH-A watch that strikes the hour but not on demand.

CLOISONNE-Enamel set between strips of metal and baked onto the dial.

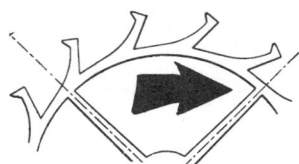

CLUB TOOTH-Some escape wheels have a special design which increases the impulse plane; located at the tip of the tooth of the escape wheel.

COARSE TRAIN-16,000 beats per hour.

COCK -The metal bar which carries the bearing for the balance's upper pivot and is supported at one end.

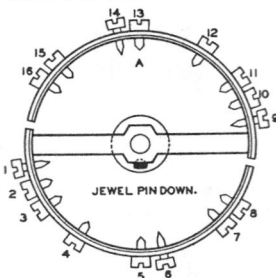

COMPENSATION BALANCE-A balance wheel designed to correct for temperature.

COMPLICATED WATCH-A watch with complicated works;other than just telling time, it may have a perpetual calendar, moon phases, up and down dial, repeater, musical chimes or alarm.

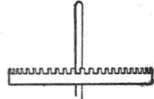

CONTRATE WHEEL-A wheel with its teeth at a right angle to plane of the wheel.

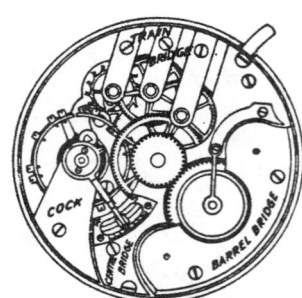

CONVERTIBLE- Movement made by Elgin & other companies; a means of converting from a hunting case to a open-face watch or vice-versa.

CRAZE(crazing)-A minute crack in the glaze of enamel watch dials.

Railroad Style

Round Style   Antique Style
CROWN-A winding button.

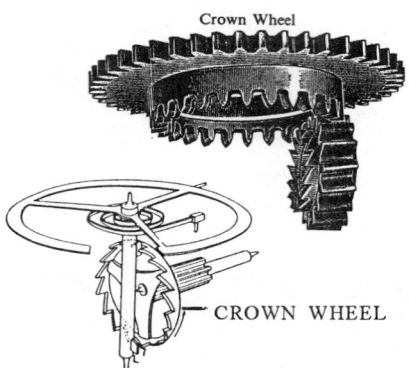

CROWN WHEEL-The escape wheel of a verge escapement; looks like a crown. Also the lower illustration shows a crown wheel used in a stem winding pocket watch.

CURB PINS-The two pins that change the rate of a watch; the two pins,in ef- fect,change the length of the hairspring.

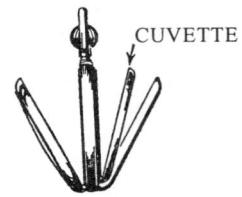

CUVETTE-The inter dust cover of a pocket watch.

CYLINDER ESCAPEMENT-A type of es- capement used on some watches.

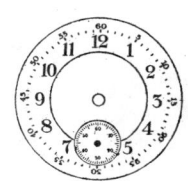

DIAL-The face of a watch. Some are made of enamel.

DAMASKEENING-The art of producing a design, pattern, or wavy appearance on a metal. American idiom or terminology used in **all** American factory ads. The European terminology was Fausse Cotes or Geneva stripes.

DISCHARGE PALLET JEWEL-The left jewel.

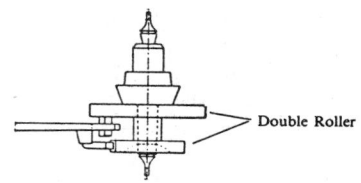

Double Roller

DOUBLE ROLLER-A watch with one impulse roller table and a safety roller, thus two rollers.

DRAW-The angular position of the pallet jewels in the pallet frame which causes those jewels to be drawn deeper into the escape wheel under pressure of the escape wheel's tooth on the locking surface.

DROP-The space between a tooth of the escape wheel and the pallet from which it has just escaped.

DUMB –REPEATER-A repeating watch with hammers that strikes a block instead of bells or gongs.

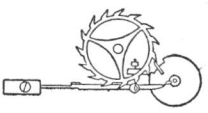

DEMI-HUNTER-A hunting case with the center designed to allow the position of the hands to be seen without opening the case.

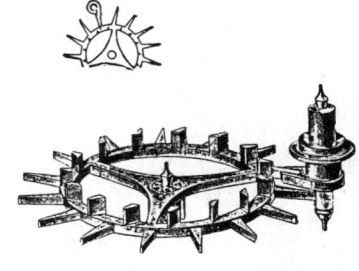

DETENT ESCAPEMENT-A detached escapement . The balance is impulsed in one direction; used on watches to provide greater accuracy. Detent a locking device.

DUPLEX ESCAPEMENT-An escape wheel with two sets of teeth, one for locking and one for impulse.

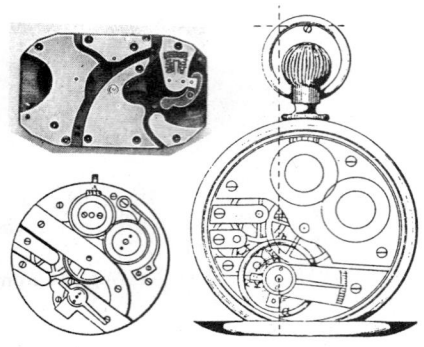

EBAUCHE(ay-boesh)-A movement not completely finished or in the rough; not detailed; a raw movement; a movement made up of two plates ,train, barrel & did not include a dial, case, or escapement.

ECCENTRIC-Not exactly circular, *Nonconcentric*. A cam with a lobe or egg shape.

ENGINE TURNING-Engraving a watch case with a repetitive design by a machine.

ELECTRONIC WATCH-Newer type watch using quartz and electronics to produce a high degree of accuracy.

ELINVAR-A hairspring composed of a special alloy of nickel, steel, chromium, manganese and tungsten that does not vary at different temperatures. Elinvar was derived from the words elasticity invariable.

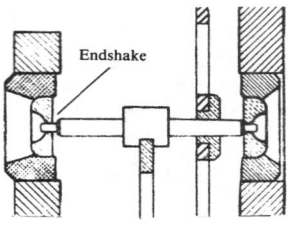

END SHAKE-The up and down play of an arbor between the plates and bridge or between the jewels.

END STONE-The jewel or cap at the end of the staff.

EPHEMEROUS TIME-The time calculated for the Earth to orbit around the sun.

ESCAPE WHEEL-The last wheel in a going train; works with the fork or lever and escapes one pulse at a time.

Fork

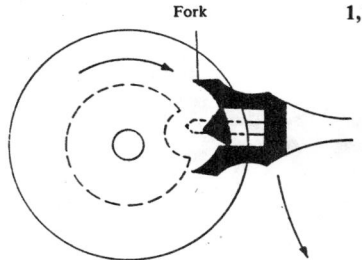

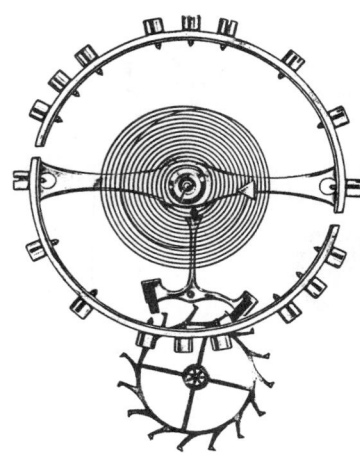

FORK-The part of the pallet lever that engages with the roller jewel.

FREE SPRUNG-A balance spring free from the influence of a regulator.

FULL PLATE -A plate (or disc) that covers the works and supports the wheels pivots. There is a top plate, a bottom plate, half, and 3/4 plate. The top plate has the balance resting on it.

ESCAPEMENT-The device in a watch by which the motion of the train is checked and the energy of the mainspring communicated to the balance. The escapement includes the escape wheel, lever, and balance complete with hairspring.

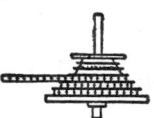

FUSEE-A spiral grooved, truncated cone used in some watches to equalize the power of the mainspring.

FARMER'S WATCH(OIGNON)-A large pocket watch with a verge escapement and a farm scene on the dial.

GRANDE SONNERIE-(Grand strike) a watch or clock that strikes the hour, 1/4 hours and minutes if minute repeater, a Petite Sonnerie strikes hour only.

FECIT-A Latin word meaning"made by ".

FIVE-MINUTE REPEATER-A watch that denotes the time every five minutes, and on the hour and half hour, by operating a push piece.

FLINQUE-Enameling over hand engraving.

FLY BACK-The hand returns back to zero on a timer.

FOB-A decorative short strap or chain.

GENEVA STOP WORK-A system used to stop the works preventing the barrel from being over wound.

GILT (or GILD)-To coat or plating with gold leaf or a gold color.

GOING BARREL-The barrel houses the mainspring; as the spring uncoils, the barrel turns, and the teeth on the outside of the barrel turn the train of gears as opposed to toothless fusee barrel.

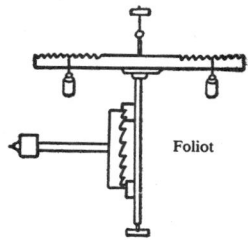

Foliot

FOLIOT-A straight-armed balance with weights on each end used for regulation; found on the earliest clocks and watches.

GOLD-FILLED-Sandwich-type metal; a layer of gold, a layer of base metal in the middle, another layer of gold-then the layers of metals are soldered to each other to form a sandwich.

GOLD JEWEL SETTINGS-In high-grade watches the jewels were mounted in gold settings.

GREAT WHEEL-The main wheel of a fusee type watch.

GUILLOCHE - A decorative pattern of cross or interlaced lines. (engraving style)

HACK-WATCH-A watch with a balance that can be stopped to allow synchronization with another timepiece.

HAIRSPRING-The spring which vibrates the balance. Above flat style hairsprings. Also called balance spring

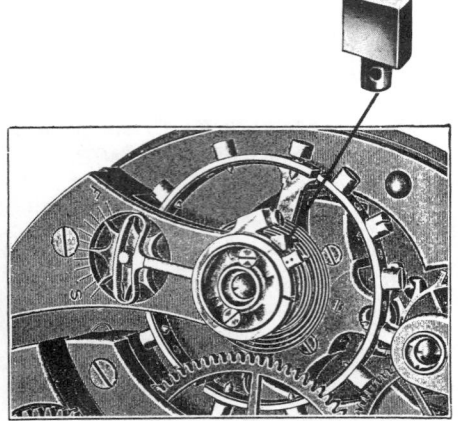

HAIRSPRING STUD-A hairspring stud is used to connect the hairsping to the balance cock.

HALLMARK-The silver or gold or platinum markings of many countries.

HEART CAM-PIECE-A heart-shaped cam which causes the hand on a chronograph to fly back to zero.

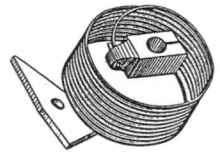

HELICAL HAIRSPRING-A cylindrical spring used in chronometers.

HOROLOGY (haw-rahl-uh-jee)-The study of time keeping.

HUNTER CASE-A pocket watch case with a covered face that must be opened to see the watch dial.

IMPULSE-The force transmitted by the escape wheel to the pallet by gliding over the angular or impulse face of the pallet jewel.

IMPULSE PIN(Ruby pin)(roller jewel)-A pin or jewel on the balance roller table which keeps the balance going.

INCABLOC-A patented shock absorbing device which permits the end stone of the balance to give when the watch is subjected to an impact or jolt. 1st. used in 1933.

INDEX-Another term for the racquet-shaped regulator which lengthens or shortens the effective length of the hairspring.

INDEPENDENT SECONDS-A seconds hand driven independently by a separate train but controlled by the time train.

ISOCHRONISM-"Isos" means equal; chronos means time-occurring at equal intervals of time. The balance and hairspring adjusted will allow the watch to run at the same rate regardless whether the watch is fully wound or almost run down.

JEWEL-A bearing made of a ruby or other type jewel; the four types of jewels include; cap jewel, hole jewel, roller jewel or ruby pin, pallet jewel or stone.

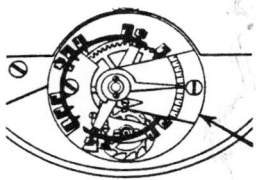

KARRUSEL-An invention of Bonniksen in 1894 which allows the entire escapement to revolve within the watch once in 52 1/2 minutes (in most karrusels), this unit is supported at one end only as opposed to the tourbillon which is supported at both ends and which most often revolves about once a minute.

KEY SET-Older watch that had to be set with a key.

LEAVES-The teeth of the pinion gears.

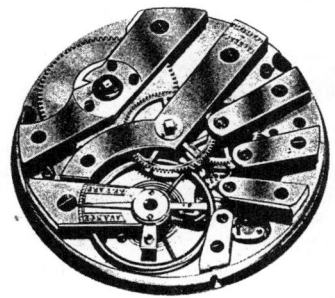

L'Epine' CALIBRE-Introduced by J.A. L'Epine about 1770. Swiss for **open face.**

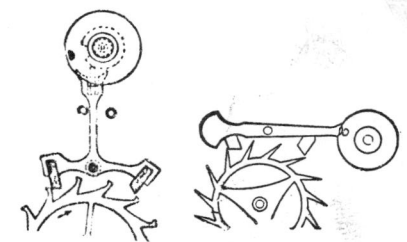

LEVER ESCAPEMENT-Invented by Thomas Mudge in 1760.

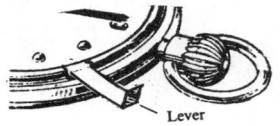

Lever

LEVER SETTING-The lever used to set some watches.

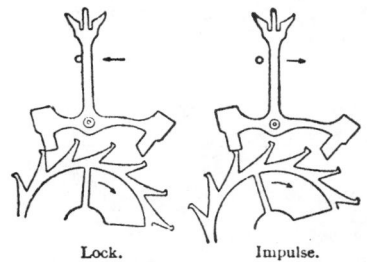

Lock.   Impulse.

LOCKING-Arresting the advance of the escape wheel during the balance's free excursion.

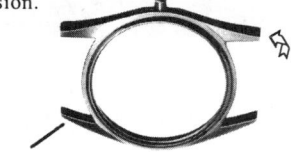

LUGS-The metal extensions of a wrist watch case which the bracelet or band are attached usually with a spring bar.

MAIN SPRING-A flat spring coiled or wound to supply power to the watch. The non-magnetic mainspring, introduced 1947.

MAIN WHEEL-The first driving wheel, part of the barrel.

MALTESE CROSS-The part of the stop works preventing the barrel from being over wound.

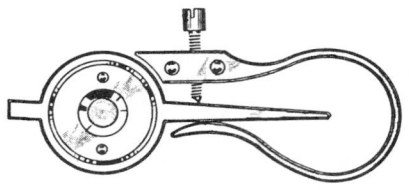

MARINE CHRONOMETER- An accurate timepiece; may have a detent escapement and set in a box with gimbals which keep it in a right position.

MEAN TIME- Also equal hours; average mean solar time; the time shown by watches.

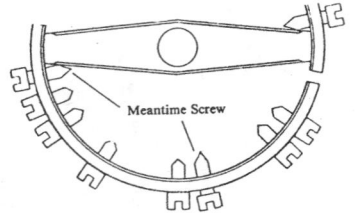

MEANTIME SCREWS-Balance screws used for timing,usually longer than other balance screws; when turned away from or toward the balance pin, they cause the balance vibrations to become faster or slower.

MICROMETRIC REGULATOR-A regulator used on railroad grade watches to adjust for gain or loss in a very precise way.

MICRO-SECOND-A millionth of a second.

MINUTE REPEATER -A watch that strikes or sounds the hours , and minutes on demand.

MOVEMENT-The works of a mechanical watch without the case or dial. (quartz watches have modules)

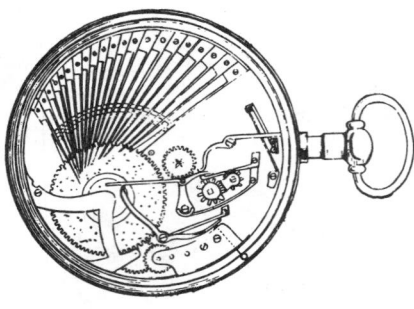

MUSICAL WATCH-A watch that plays a tune on demand or on the hour.

MULTI-GOLD-Different colors of gold-red, green, white, blue, pink, yellow and purple.

NANOSECOND-One billionth of a second.

N. A. W. C. C. - National Association of Watch and Clock Collectors 514 Poplar St. Columbia, Pa. 17512.

TEL. 1- 717- 684- 8261

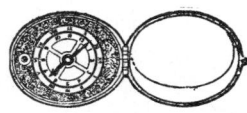

NURENBURG EGG-Nickname for a German watch that was oval-shaped.

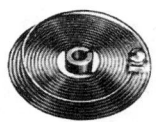

OVERCOIL-The raised up portion of the balance hairspring, not flat. Also called Breguet hairspring.

PATINA-Oxidation of any surface & change due to age. A natural staining or discoloration due to aging.

PAIR-CASE WATCH-An extra case around a watch-two cases,hence, a pair of cases. The outer case kept out the dust. The inner case could not be dustproof because it provided the access to the winding and setting keyholes in the watch case.

PALLADIUM-One of six platinum metals, used in watches in place of platinum, because it is harder, lighter and cheaper.

OIGNON-Large older (1700s) style watch in the the shape of a onion or *in the shape of a bulb.*

OIL SINK-A small well around a pivot which retains oil.

PALLET-The part of the lever that works with the escape wheel-jeweled pallet jewels, entry and exit pallets.

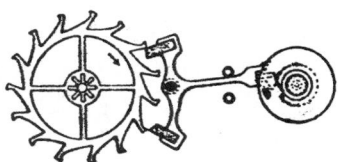

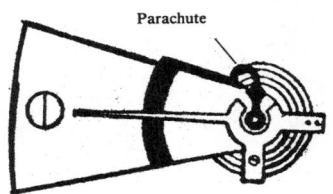

Parachute

OVERBANKED-A lever escapement error; the roller jewel passes to the wrong side of the lever notch, causing one side of the pallet to rest against the banking pin and the roller jewel to rest against the other side, thus locking the escapement and stopping the motion of the balance.

PARACHUTE-An early shock proofing system designed to fit as a spring on the end stone of balance.

PAVE'- A number of jewels or stone set close together. Paved in diamonds.

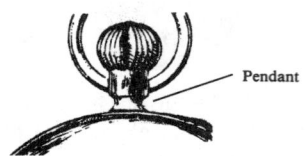

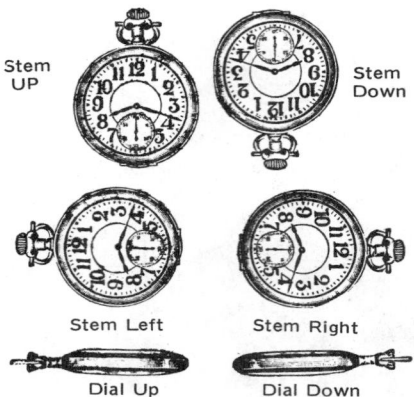

Stem UP   Stem Down

Stem Left   Stem Right

Dial Up   Dial Down

PENDANT-The neck of the watch; attached to it is the bow (swing ring) and the crown.

PILLARS-The rods that hold the plates apart. In older watches they were fancy.

PINCHBECK-A metal similar in appearance to gold. Named after the inventor. Alloy of 4 parts copper &3 parts zinc.

POSITION-As adjusted to five positions; a watch may differ in its time keeping accuracy as it lays in different positions . Due to the lack of poise, changes in the center of gravity, a watch can be adjusted to six positions: dial up, dial down, stem up, stem down, stem left, and stem right.

QUICK TRAIN-A watch with five beats or more per second or 18,000 per hour.

PINION-The larger gear is called a wheel. The small solid gear is a pinion. The pinion is made of steel in some watches.

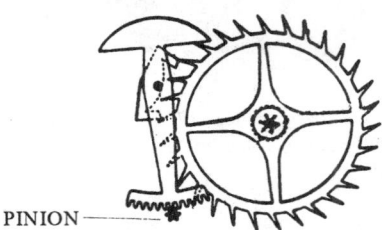

PINION

RACK & PINION LEVER ESCAPEMENT-Developed by Abbe de Huteville in 1722 and by Peter Litherhead in 1791; does not use a roller table, but a pinion.

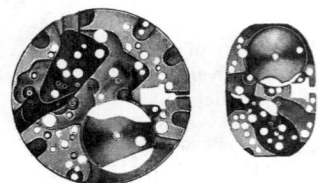

PLATE-A watch has a front and a back plate or top and bottom plate. The works are in between.

POISE-A term meaning in balance to equalize the weight around the balance.

PONTILLAGE(bull's eye crystal)-The grinding of the center of a crystal to form a concave or so called bull's eye crystal.

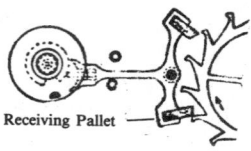

Receiving Pallet

RECEIVING PALLET-Also called left or entrance jewel, the first of two pallet jewels with which a tooth of the escape wheel comes into engagement.

REPEATER WATCH-A complicated watch that repeats the time on demand with a sounding device.

REPOUSSE'-A watch with hammered, raised decoration on the case.

RIGHT ANGLE ESCAPEMENT-Also called English escapement.

ROLLED GOLD- Thin layer of gold soldered to a base metal.

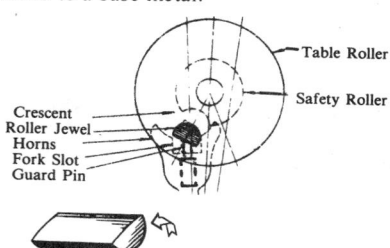

ROLLER JEWEL-The jewel mounted or seated in the roller table, which receives the impulse from the pallet fork.

ROLLER TABLE-The part of the balance in which the roller jewel is seated.

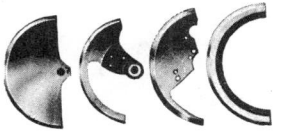

ROTOR-Oscillating weight for self-wind watches.

SAFETY PINION -A pinion in the center wheel designed to unscrew if the mainspring breaks; this protects the train from being stripped by the great force of the mainspring.

SAFETY ROLLER-The smaller of the two rollers in a double roller escapement.

SAPPHIRE CRYSTAL - Scratch resistant glass with a hardness of 9. Mineral glass has a hardness of 5.

SHAGREEN-The skin of a horse, shark, ray fish & other animal usually dyed *GREEN* or a *BLUE GREEN*. Then used as ornamental covers for older watch cases.

SIDEREAL DAY-The time of rotation of the Earth as measured from the stars. About 3 minutes 56 seconds shorter than the mean solar day.

SIDE-WINDER-A mismatched case and movement; a term used for a hunting movement that has been placed in an open face case and winds at 3 o'clock position. Open face winds at 12 o'clock.

SILVEROID-A type of case composed of alloys to simulate the appearance of silver.

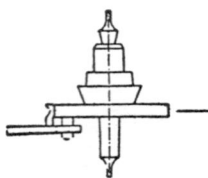

SINGLE ROLLER-The safety roller and the roller jewel are one single table.

SIZE-System used to determine the size of the movement to the case.

SKELETON WATCH-A watch made so the viewer can see the works. Plates are pierced and very decorative.

SKULL WATCH-A antique pendant watch that that is hinged at jaw to reveal a watch.

SLOW TRAIN-A watch with four beats per second or 14,000 per hour.

SNAIL-A cam shaped much like a snail. The snail determines the # of blows to be struck by a repeater.(A count wheel)

SNAILING-Ornamentation of the surface of metals by means of a circle design; also called damaskeening.

SOLAR YEAR-365 days, 5 hours, 48 minutes, 49.7 seconds.

SOUSCRIPTION- The cheapest Breguet watch which he made with high quality made in batches or group lots in advance to lower the cost.(ebauches)

SPOTTING-Decoration used on a watch movement and barrel of movements.

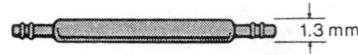

SPRING BAR-The metal keeper that attaches the band to the lugs of a wrist watch & is spring loaded.

SPRING RING-A circular tube housing a coiled type spring.

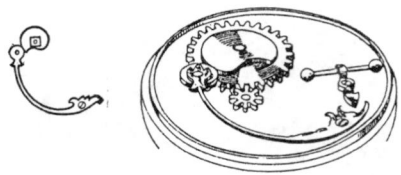

STACKFREED-Curved spring and cam to equalize the uneven force of the mainspring on 16th century German movements.

STAFF-Name for the axle of the balance.

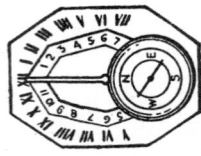

SUN DIAL-A device using a gnomon or style that cast a shadow over a graduated dial as the sun progresses, indicating solar time.

SWIVEL-A hinged spring catch with a loop of metal that may be opened to insert a watch bow.

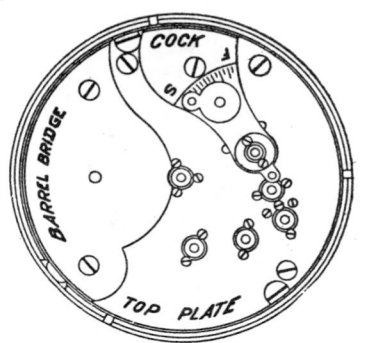

TOP PLATE-The metal plate that usually contains the name and serial #.

TORSION-A twisting force.

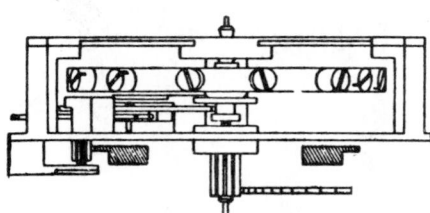

TOURBILLON-A watch that uses a escapement mounted on a platform and pivoted at both ends and revolves 360 degrees at regular intervals most often once a minute. The escape-pinion turns around the fixed fourth wheel. Design to eliminate position errors.

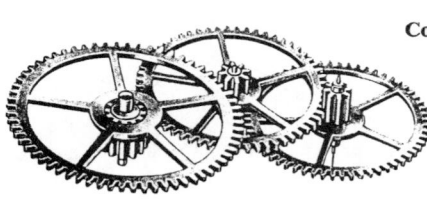

TRAIN-A series of gears that form the works of a watch. The train is used for other

functions such as chiming. The time train carries the power to the escapement.

TRANSITION WATCH - Watches sold with both key and stem-winding on same movement.

TRIPLE CASE WATCH-18th and 19th century verge escapement, fusee watches made for the Turkish market. A fourth case sometimes added is called Quadruple case.

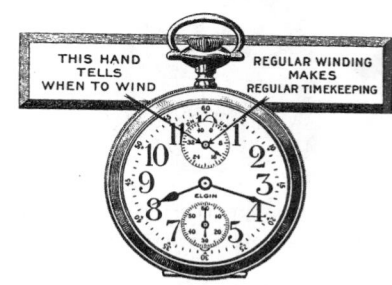

UP AND DOWN DIAL OR INDICATOR-A dial that shows how much of the mainspring is spent and how far up or down the mainspring is.

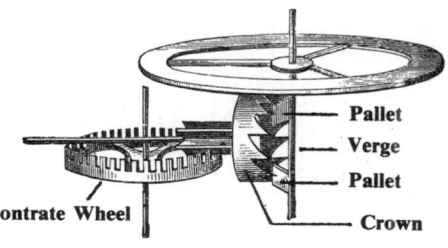

VERGE ESCAPEMENT-Early type of escapement with wheel that is shaped like a crown.

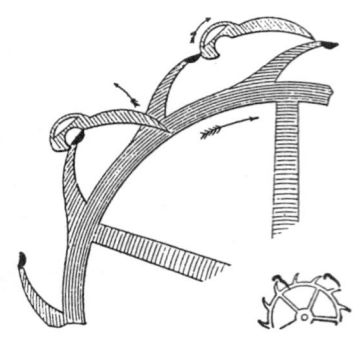

VIRGULE ESCAPEMENT-Early escapement introduced in the mid 1700s .

WATCH GLASS PROTECTOR- A snap on metal grill that covers the crystal .

WATCH PAPER-A disc of paper with the name of the watchmaker or repairman printed on it; used as a form of advertising and found in some pair-cased watches.

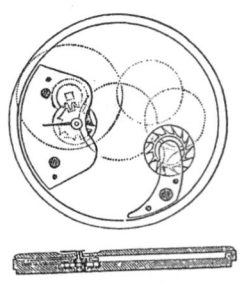

WIND INDICATOR-A watch that indicates how much of the mainspring is spent. The **illustration** shows a modified Geneva stop works. (see up and down dial)

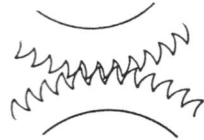

WOLF TEETH-A winding wheel's teeth so named because of their shape.

Accutron — AC-kew-tron
Agassiz — A-guh-see
Antiquarian — an-tih-KWAIR-ee-un
Art Nouveau — art new-VO
Astrolabe — AS-trow-labe
Atelier — a-teh-lee-ay
Audemars, Piguet — oh-de-MAHR, p-GAY
Automaton — aw-TAW-muh-tahn
Baguette — bah-get
Bannatyne — BAN-uh-tyne
Basse-Taille — bus-tie
Basscine — bah-seen
Basel — BAH-zuhl
Baume & Mercier — bome-MAY & mair-cyay
Beaucourt— boe-koor
Benrus — BEN-rus
Bergeon — BEAR-juhn
Berne — bairn
Berthoud — bair-TWO
Besancon— buh-sahn-son or be-sahn-SON
Bezel — BEZ-EL
Biel — beel
Bienne — bee-en
Blancpain — blahnk-PAn
Blois — blu-wah
Bombe' — boom-bay
Bovet — boe-vay
Bras en L'Air— brah on lair
Breguet et Fils — bre-gay ay fee
Breitling — BRITE-ling
Brevet — bree-VET (or) bree-VTAY
Bucherer — boo-shay-er
Cadrature — kad-drah-TUER
Calibre(er) — KAL-ih-breh or kal-ie-ber
Capt — kapt
Carillon — kah-RIL-yon
Cartier — kar-t-yay
Cartouche — kar-toosh
Champleve — shamp-leh-VAY
Chatelaine — SHAT-e-lane
Chaton — sha-tawn or sha-ton
Chopard — sho-par
Chronograph — Kronn-oh-graff
Chronometer — kroe-NOM-meh-tur
Cie — see
Cloisonne' — kloy-zoe-NAY
Cortebert — coh-teh-ber
Courvoisier — koor-voh-ahs-yeh
Corum — Kore-um
Craze — krayze (or) crazing — krayze-ing
Cuvette — kue-vet
Cyma Travannes — SEE-mah trah-VUNN
Damaskeen — dam-us-KEEN
 * damaskeen = A special terminology or American idiom
Detent — dee-TENT
Ditisheim — DEE-tis-heim
Doxa — docks-uh
Droz — droze
Dauphine — dough-feen
Ebauche — AY-boesh or e-bosh
Ebel — AY-ble (sounds like **Abel)**
Elinvar — EL-in-var
Ermeto — air-MET-oh
Escapement — es-cape-ment
Escutcheon — es-KUHCH-un
et Fils — AY feece
ETA — EE-ta
Fahys — fah-z
Fasoldt — fa-sole-dt
Favre Leuba — fahv-ruh lew-buh
Fecit — FEE-sit =(made by)
Fleur de lis — flur duh lee
Foliot — FOH-lee-oh
Fontainemelon — fone-ten-meh-loh
Francillon — fran-seel-yon
Freid — freed
Frodsham — FRAHD-shum
Fusee — few-ZEE or few-zayh
Gadroon—ga-drewn
Gallet — gah-lay
Girrard Perregaux — jir-ard per-ay-go
Glashutte — glass-huet-te
Glucydur — glu-sch-dor
Glycine — gly-seen
Grande sonnnerie — grawnd shon-uh-ree
Grenchen — GREN-chun
Gublin — goo-blin
Guinand — gwee-nahnd
Haute — AUT
Hebdomas — heb-DOM-us
Helical — HEL-ih-kul
Helvetia — hell-VEHT-sia
Henlein — HEN-line
Heuer — hoy-er (the watch Co.)

Heuer — oo-air also eu-air (French for time or hour)
Horology — haw-rahl-uh-gee
Huyghens — hi-guhnz
Illinois—ill-ih-NOY
Ingraham — ing-gram
Invar — in-VAR
Isochronism — i-SOCK-roe-nizm
Jacot— zha-koe
Jaeger — YAY-gur
Japy — zja-pee
Jaquet Droz — zha-KAY droze
Jours — djour (French for days)
Jura — yoo-rah (moutains on French & Swiss border)
Jurgensen — YUER-gen-sen
Karrusel — kare-us-sell
Kessels — kahr-rus-SEL
La Chaux de Fonds — lah show duh Fawn
A. Lange & Sohne — ah. lahn gee uhnd soehne
Landeron — lan-der-on
Lapis LAZULI — lah-pis lah-zoon-lee
Lavaliere — la-vahl-yare
Le Coultre — luh-kool-tray
Le Locle — luh LOKEl
Lemania — leh-mahn-yuh
Leonidas — lee-oh-NEE-dus
Le Phare — luh-fahr
Lepine — lay-peen
Le Roy — luh roy
Le Sentier — le san-tyay
Leschot—leh-show
Ligne — line or leen
Longines — long-djeen
Loupe—loop
Lucien Piccard (Arnex) — lew-see-en pee-kar (ar-nex)
Lyon — lee-OHn
Mathey — ma-tay
Mido — me-DOE
Mollineaux — MOLE-ih-noe
Montre — MON- tru (Swiss name for WATCH)
Moser, Henri & Cie—awn-ree mow-say eh see
Movado — moe-VAH-doe
Mozart — MOE-tsart
Nardin — nar din
Nivarox — niv-ah-rocks
Neuchatel — noo-sha-TELL
Nicole — nee-kol
Niello— nye-el-oh
Oignon — ohn-yoh
Omega — oh-me-guh
Ormolu — or-muh-loo
Otay — oh-tay
Oudin — oo-dan as in (soon)
Paillard — pay-lar
Pallet — PAL-let
Parachute — PAR-ah-shoot
Patek, Philippe — Pa-tek fee-leep
Patina—pah-teen-ah
Pave' — pah-vay
Piaget — pee-uh-jaay
Piguet — pee-gay
Pique — pee-kay
Quare — kwair
Rado — rah-doe
Remontoire— rem-on-twor
Repousse' — reh-poo-say
Rococo — roe-ko-ko
Roskopf — ROSS-cawf
Sangamo — san-guh-moe
Schaffausen — shaf-HOW-zun
Schild — sheild or shuild
Shugart — sugar with a T, or Shug-gart
Sonnerie — shon-uh-ree
Sotheby — SUTH-ee-bee
Souscription — sue-skrip-tshown
Stackfreed — stack-freed
St. Imier — sahnt imm-yay
Tavannes — ta-van
Tempus Fugit — TEM-pus FYOO-jit = (time flies)
Tissot — tee-SOh
Tobias — toe-bye-us
Tonneau — tun-noe
Touchon — too-shahn
Tourbillon — toour-bee-yohn
Vacheron & Constantin — VASH-er-on , CON-stan-teen
Valjoux — val- zhoo or val-goo
Vallee de Joux — valley duh Zhoo
Verge — vurj
Veritas — VAIR-ih-tas
Vermeil — vair-may
Vertu — ver-too
Virgule — vir-guel
Wittnauer — Wit-nower
Woerd — verd

European Terminology — U. S. A. Terminology

ACIER..Steel or Gunmetal
AIGUILLES.. Hour Hand
ALARUM ....Alarm
ANCHOR or ANCRE ....Lever Escapement
ATELIER..Small Workshop
BAGUETTE .... Long & Narrow
BALANCIER.. Balance
BOITE-DOUBLE .... Pair-case
BOMBE'..Convex or Bulges
BRAS EN L'AIR..Arms in the Air
BREVET .... Patented
CADRATURE.................Attachment (as repeater or chronograph)
CALIBRE .... Model or caliber
CHASED.. Embossing
CHATON.. Jewel Setting
CHRONOMETRE..Chronometer
CIE ....Company
COMPENSE..Compensating
CUVETTE or DOME...........................Inside Hinged Dust Cover
CUIVRE..Copper or Brass
DEPOSE ....Registered Trademark
EBAUCHE..Raw Blank Movement
EMPIERRE..Jewelled
ECHAPPEMENT A' ANCRE ....Lever escapement
FAUSSE COTES.. Damaskeening
FILS .... Sons
FLUTED ....Grooved
GENEVE STRIPES..Damaskeening
GUILLOCHE..Engine Turned
HAUTE .... High
INVENIT ET FECIT..............................Invented & Made By
JACQUE-MART .... Figures That Strike Bells
JOURS .... Days As In 8 Days
LEPINE ....Open Face
LIGNE... Size
MONTRE..Watch
MONTRE A' TACT..Watch by Touch
MARQUE DEPOSE (M.D.) ....Registered Trademark
OIGNON or TURNIP ....Large Bulbous French Watch
ORMOULU ....Gold Gilding
PARACHUTE ....Shock Resisting
PAVE .... Cover
PIQUE...Pin Work Decoration
PERPETUELLE .... Self-Winding
POLYCHROME..Color
POUSETTE ....Push Piece
REPOUSSE .... Embossing
RATTRAPANTE .... Split Seconds
REFERENCE # ....Case # & Style
REMONTOIRE ....Constant Force also Keyless Winding
RESSORT DE CROCHEMENT ....All-or-Nothing
RESSORT SPIRAL..Hairspring
ROSKOPH.. Dollar Watch
RUBIS.. Ruby Jewel
SAVONETTE.. Hunting Case
SHAGREEN ....Shark or Ray Fish Skins
SPIRAL BREGUET.............................Overcoil Hairspring
TANGENT SCREW................................. Endless Screw
TONNEAU .... Barrel Shaped
TOUT-OU-RIEN..All-or-Nothing
UHR .... Timepiece (German)

Vallee de Joux (Swiss - French cradle of watch making)

8 DAYS = 8 DIAS, 8 CIOANI, 8 JOURS, 8 TAGE

The following will explain the French days of the week abbreviations, Sunday =**DIM** (Dimanche), Monday = **LUN** (Lundi), Tuesday = **MAR** (Mardi), Wednesday = **MER** (Mercedi), Thursday = **JEU** (Jeudi), Friday = **VEN** (Vendredi), Saturday = **SAM** (Samedi).

AT THE FOREFRONT OF WATCHMAKING
ABOUT GEORGE DANIELS

George Daniels is really worth meeting as I did on May 29th, 1997, at his home on the Isle of Man. A group of us (The Time Trippers) talked with him about watches and visited with Mr. Daniels over lunch on his garden verandah. He was gracious enough to show his workshop also his stable of vintage cars and motorcycles. "Making watches came to me as naturally as music did to Mozart", observed George Daniels.

At the early age of five he had taken his father's alarm clock apart to see how it worked. By the age of 10, he was repairing watches to earn a little pocket money. He was forced to leave school and earn his keep as a factory worker, he lasted about a week, then started to work as a grocery delivery boy. Pedaling his bicycle gave him such a feeling of freedom, he swore to never work again at something he hated so much. He read every book he could lay his hands on regarding watchmaking while making living at repairing all types of timepieces and also while in uniform. By the age of 22, he purchased a basic set of tools and set up a shop to repair and restore watches. After World War II, he studied horology in Clerkenwell, London along with related subjects such as math, physics, and geometry . Over the years he worked on a large number of original Breguets giving him a insider's look and knowledge of "The Art of Breguet" which he Authored and Published into a book. He grew tired of simply restoring old master timepieces so in 1967 he designed a watch and made each component and virtually every part of each first watch himself. I would ask you to reflect on just what it takes to make, from scratch, a simple watch component, as a screw, each screw has to be turned, the thread cut, the head slit, it must be hardened, tempered and polished. How many watches has he made in well over a quarter of a century? Less than 80! In 1978 he makes a Gold-cased one-minute tourbillon with his co-axial escapement (not requiring oil). In the period 1980 to 1996 he used swiss-made wrist watches and converted them to his coaxial escapement, he used Omega, Zenith, Rolex and Patek Philippe watches. Overriding all was Georges Daniels 25 year quest for a lower friction escapement, his success and then the years long battle to gain a reluctant Swiss acceptance culminating in the Omega model. Omega introduced a limited edition of 6,000 watches featuring the co-axial escapement in 1998. They sold for about $6,600.00.

"The co-axial escapement is the first practical new watch escapement in the 250 years following the invention of the lever escapement by Thomas Mudge in the 18th century. It fulfills all the requirements of a precision watch escapment with the advantage of robust reliability and close precision rate for long term performance. In its present form the co-axial represents the culmination of 20 years of development of the watch escapement. It is intended to sustain the public affection for the mechanical watch during the 21st century". (George Daniels)

Mr. Daniels made a small number of exquisite co-axial wrist watches at his shop on the Isle of Man with the help of Roger Smith (wrist watch on the cover). These wrist watches start at $50,000.00. The Time Trippers were again at the Daniels work shop (Aug. 7th, 1999) to see Mr. Smith at work on the co-axial wrist watches. On yet a another trip to London (Apr. 5th, 2000) at the Worshipful Company of Clock Makers we saw two lucky Time Trippers receive their co-axial wrist watch from George Danials.

Three different versions of the new De Ville, Omega Co-Axial escapement are available. The standard Automatic Chronometer caliber 2500 movement and a model with a power reserve caliber 2627. Caliber 2628 has a 24-hour hand and a 24-hour scale for reading a second time zone. Each movement is a self-winding COSC-certified chronometer.

ESTIMATED PRODUCTION DATES AND SERIAL NUMBER

Am. Waltham W. Co.

Date	Serial #
1852	50
1853	400
1854	1,000
1855	2,500
1856	4,000
1857	6,000
1858	10,000
1859	15,000
1860	20,000
1861	30,000
1862	45,000
1863	65,000
1864	110,000
1865	180,000
1866	260,000
1867	330,000
1868	410,000
1869	460,000
1870	500,000
1871	540,000
1872	590,000
1873	680,000
1874	730,000
1875	810,000
1876	910,000
1877	1,000,000
1878	1,150,000
1879	1,350,000
1880	1,500,000
1881	1,670,000
1882	1,835,000
1883	2,000,000
1884	2,350,000
1885	2,650,000
1886	3,000,000
1887	3,400,000
1888	3,800,000
1889	4,200,000
1890	4,700,000
1891	5,200,000
1892	5,800,000
1893	6,300,000
1894	6,700,000
1895	7,100,000
1896	7,450,000
1897	8,100,000
1898	8,400,000
1899	9,000,000
1900	9,500,000
1901	10,200,000
1902	11,100,000
1903	12,100,000
1904	13,500,000
1905	14,300,000
1906	14,700,000
1907	15,500,000
1908	16,400,000
1909	17,600,000
1910	17,900,000
1911	18,100,000
1912	18,200,000
1913	18,900,000
1914	19,500,000
1915	20,000,000
1916	20,500,000
1917	20,900,000
1918	21,800,000
1919	22,500,000
1920	23,400,000
1921	23,900,000
1922	24,100,000
1923	24,300,000
1924	24,550,000
1925	24,800,000
1926	25,200,000
1927	26,100,000
1928	26,400,000
1929	26,900,000
1930	27,100,000
1931	27,300,000
1932	27,550,000
1933	27,750,000
1934	28,100,000
1935	28,600,000
1936	29,100,000
1937	29,400,000
1938	29,750,000
1939	30,050,000
1940	30,250,000
1941	30,750,000
1942	31,050,000
1943	31,400,000
1944	31,700,000
1945	32,100,000
1946	32,350,000
1947	32,750,000
1948	33,100,000
1949	33,500,000
1950	33,560,000
1951	33,600,000
1952	33,700,000
1953	33,800,000
1954	34,100,000
1955	34,450,000
1956	34,700,000
1957	35,000,000

AURORA W. Co.

Date	Serial #
1884	10,001
1885	60,000
1886	101,000
1887	160,000
1888	200,000
1889	215,000
1891	230,901

COLUMBUS W. Co.

Date	Serial #
1875	1,000
1876	3,000
1877	6,000
1878	9,000
1879	12,000
1880	15,000
1881	18,000
1882	21,000
1883	25,000
1884	30,000
1885	40,000
1886	53,000
1887	75,000
1888	97,000
1889	119,000
1890	141,000
1891	163,000
1892	185,000
1893	207,000
1894	229,000
1895	251,000
1896	273,000
1897	295,000
1898	317,000
1899	339,000
1900	361,000
1901	383,000

SPECIAL BLOCK OF SERIAL NOS.

Date	Serial #
1894	500,001
1896	501,500
1898	503,000
1900	504,500
1902	506,000

ELGIN WATCH Co.

Date	Serial #	
1867	10,000	
1868	25,001	Nov,20th
1869	40,001	May, 20th
1870	50,001	Aug. 24th
1871	185,001	Sep. 8th
1872	201,001	Dec. 20th
1873	325,001	
1874	400,001	Aug.28th
1875	430,000	
1876	480,000	
1877	520,000	
1878	550,000	
1879	625,001	Feb.8th
1880	750,000	
1881	900,000	
1882	1,000,000	March,9th
1883	1,250,000	
1884	1,500,000	
1885	1,855,001	May,28th
1886	2,000,000	Aug.4th
1887	2,500,000	
1888	3,000,000	June 20th
1889	3,500,000	
1890	4,000,000	Aug.16th
1891	4,449,001	Mar.26th
1892	4,600,000	
1893	5,000,000	July 1st
1894	5,500,000	
1895	6,000,000	Nov.26th
1896	6,500,000	
1897	7,000,000	Oct. 28th.
1898	7,494,001	May,14th
1899	8,000,000	Jan.18th
1900	9,000,000	Nov.14th
1901	9,300,000	
1902	9,600,000	
1903	10,000,000	May 15th
1904	11,000,000	April 4th
1905	12,000,000	Oct.6th
1906	12,500,000	
1907	13,000,000	April 4th
1908	13,500,000	
1909	14,000,000	Feb.9th
1910	15,000,000	April 2nd
1911	16,000,000	July 11th
1912	17,000,000	Nov.6th
1913	17,339,001	Apr.14th
1914	18,000,000	
1915	18,587,001	Feb.11th
1916	19,000,000	
1917	20,031,001	June,27th
1918	21,000,000	
1919	22,000,000	
1920	23,000,000	
1921	24,321,001	July,6th
1922	25,100,000	
1923	26,050,000	
1924	27,000,000	
1925	28,421,001	July,14th
1926	29,100,000	
1927	30,050,000	
1928	31,500,000	
1929	32,000,000	
1930	32,599,001	July
1931	33,000,000	
1932	33,700,000	
1933	34,558,001	July,24th
1934	35,000,000	
1935	35,650,000	
1936	36,200,000	
1937	36,978,001	July,24th
1938	37,900,000	
1939	38,200,000	
1940	39,100,000	
1941	40,200,000	
1942	41,100,000	
1943	42,200,000	
1944	42,600,000	
1945	43,200,000	
1946	44,000,000	
1947	45,000,000	
1948	46,000,000	
1949	47,000,000	
1950	48,000,000	
1951	50,000,000	
1952	52,000,000	
1953	53,500,000	
1954	54,000,000	
1955	54,500,000	
1956	55,000,000	

HAMILTON WATCH Co.

Date	Serial No.
1893	1-2,000
1894	5,000
1895	11,500
1896	16,000
1897	27,000
1898	50,000
1899	74,000
1900	104,000
1901	143,000
1902	196,000
1903	260,000
1904	340,000
1905	425,000
1906	590,000
1907	756,000
1908	921,000
1909	1,087,000
1910	1,150,500
1911	1,290,500
1912	1,331,000
1913	1,370,000
1914	1,410,500
1915	1,450,500
1916	1,517,000
1917	1,580,000
1918	1,650,000
1919	1,700,000
1920	1,790,000
1921	1,860,000
1922	1,900,000
1923	1,950,000
1924	2,000,000
1925	2,100,000
1926	2,200,000
1927	2,250,000
1928	2,300,000
1929	2,350,000
1930	2,400,000
1931	2,450,000
1932	2,500,000
1933	2,600,000
1934	2,700,000
1935	2,800,000
1936	2,900,000
1937	3,000,000
1938	3,200,000
1939	3,400,000
1940	3,600,000
1941	3,800,000
1942	4,025,000

DATE LETTERS
2B on 950B=1941-43
C on 992B=1940-59
S on 950B=1943-68
OTHER DATE LETTERS = 1930s to 1950s

HAMPDEN W. Co.

Date	Serial #
1877	59,000
1878	70,000
1879	100,000
1880	140,000
1881	180,000
1882	215,000
1883	250,000
1884	300,000
1885	350,000
1886	400,000
1887	480,000
1888	560,000
1889	640,000
1890	740,000
1891	805,500
1892	835,000
1893	865,000
1894	900,000
1895	930,000
1896	970,000
1897	1,000,000
1898	1,120,000
1899	1,255,000
1900	1,384,000
1901	1,512,000
1902	1,642,000
1903	1,768,000
1904	1,896,000
1905	2,024,000
1906	2,152,000
1907	2,280,000
1908	2,400,000
1909	2,520,000
1910	2,650,000
1911	2,700,000
1912	2,760,000
1913	2,850,000
1914	2,920,000
1915	3,000,000
1916	3,100,000
1917	3,240,000
1918	3,390,000
1919	3,500,000
1920	3,600,000
1921	3,700,000
1922	3,750,000
1923	3,800,000
1924	3,850,000
1925	3,900,000
1926	3,950,000
1927	3,980,000

E. HOWARD & Co.

Date	Serial #
1858-60)	113-1,900
1860-61)	1,901-3,000
1861)	3,001-3,100
1861)	3,101-3,250
1861)	3,401- 3,500
1861-71)	3,501-28,000
1868-83)	30,001-50,000
1869-99)	50,001-71,000
1869-90)	100,001-105,000
1880-99)	200,001-227,000
1895)	228,001-231,000
1884-99)	300,001-309,000
1895)	309,001-310,000
1890-95)	400,001-405,000
1890-99)	500,001-501,500
1896-1903)	600,001-601,500
1896-1903)	700,001-701,500

HOWARD WATCH Co. (KEYSTONE)

Date	Serial #
1902	850,000
1903	900,000
1909	980,000
1912	1,100,000
1915	1,285,000
1917	1,340,000
1921	1,400,000
1930	1,500,000

ILLINOIS WATCH Co.

Date	Serial #
1872	5,000
1873	20,000
1874	50,000
1875	75,000
1876	100,000
1877	145,000
1878	210,000
1879	250,000
1880	300,000
1881	350,000
1882	400,000
1883	450,000
1884	500,000
1885	550,000
1886	600,000
1887	700,000
1888	800,000
1889	900,000
1890	1,000,000
1891	1,040,000
1892	1,080,000
1893	1,120,000
1894	1,160,000
1895	1,220,000
1896	1,250,000
1897	1,290,000
1898	1,330,000
1899	1,370,000
1900	1,410,000
1901	1,450,000
1902	1,500,000
1903	1,650,000
1904	1,700,000
1905	1,800,000
1906	1,840,000
1907	1,900,000
1908	2,100,000
1909	2,150,000
1910	2,200,000
1911	2,300,000
1912	2,400,000
1913	2,500,000
1914	2,600,000
1915	2,700,000
1916	2,800,000
1917	3,000,000
1918	3,200,000
1919	3,400,000
1920	3,600,000
1921	3,750,000
1922	3,900,000
1923	4,000,000
1924	4,500,000
1925	4,700,000
1926	4,800,000
1927	5,000,000
(Sold to Hamilton)	
1928	5,100,000
1929	5,200,000
1931	5,400,000
1938	5,500,000
1948	5,600,000

ROCKFORD W.Co.

Date	Serial #
1874	22,200
1875	42,600
1876	63,000
1877	83,000
1878	103,000
1879	124,000
1880	144,000
1881	165,000
1882	185,000
1883	206,000
1884	226,000
1885	247,000
1886	267,000
1887	287,500
1888	308,000
1889	328,500
1890	349,000
1891	369,500
1892	390,000
1893	410,000
1894	430,000
1895	450,000
1896	470,000
1897	490,000
1898	510,000
1899	530,000
1900	550,000
1901	570,000
1902	590,000
1903	610,000
1904	630,000
1905	650,000
1906	670,000
1907	690,000
1908	734,000
1909	790,000
1910	824,000
1911	880,000
1912	936,000
1913	958,000
1914	980,000
1915	1,000,000

SOUTH BEND W. Co.

Date	Serial #
1903	380,501
1904	390,000
1905	405,000
1906	425,000
1907	460,000
1908	500,000
1909	550,000
1910	600,000
1911	660,000
1912	715,000
1913	765,000
1914	800,000
1915	720,000
1916	840,000
1917	860,000
1918	880,000
1919	905,000
1920	935,000
1921	975,000
1922	1,000,000
1923	1,035,000
1924	1,070,000
1925	1,105,000
1926	1,140,000
1927	1,275,000
1928	1,210,000
1929	1,240,000

SETH THOMAS W. Co.

Date	Serial #
1885	5,000
1886	20,000
1887	40,000
1888	80,000
1889	150,000
1890	235,000
1891	330,000
1892	420,000
1893	510,000
1894	600,000
1895	690,000
1896	780,000
1897	870,000
1898	960,000
1899	1,050,000
1900	1,140,000
1901	1,230,000
1902	1,320,000
1903	1,410,000
1904	1,500,000
1905	1,700,000
1906	1,900,000
1907	2,100,000
1908	2,300,000
1909	2,500,000
1910	2,725,000
1911	2,950,000
1912	3,175,000
1913	3,490,000
1914	3,600,000

BALL WATCH Co. (Hamilton)

Date	Serial #
1895	13,000
1897	20,500
1900	42,000
1902	170,000
1905	462,000
1910	600,000
1915	603,000
1920	610,000
1925	620,000
1930	637,000
1935	641,000
1938	647,000
1939	650,000
1940	651,000
1941	652,000
1942	654,000
(Waltham)	
1900	060,700
1905	202,000
1910	216,000
1915	250,000
1920	260,000
1925	270,000
(Illinois)	
1929	800,000
1930	801,000
1931	803,000
1932	804,000

(Elgin) 1904-1906
S # range
11,853,000-12,282,000

(E. Howard & C0.)
1893-1895
S # range
226,000-308,000

(Hampden) 1890-1892
S # range
626,750-657,960-759,720

Audemars Piguet

DATE	SERIAL #
1882	2,000
1890	4,000
1895	5,350
1900	6,500
1905	9,500
1910	13,000
1915	17,000
1920	25,000
1925	33,000
1930	40,000
1935	42,000
1940	44,000
1945	48,000
1950	55,000
1955	65,000
1960	75,000
1965	90,000
1970	115,000
1975	160,000
1980	225,000

International W.Co. (Schaffhausen)

DATE	SERIAL #
1884	6,500
1886	23,500
1888	37,500
1890	63,000
1892	87,500
1894	117,000
1896	151,500
1898	194,000
1900	231,000
1902	276,500
1904	321,000
1906	377,500
1908	435,000
1910	492,000
1912	557,000
1914	620,500
1916	657,000
1918	714,000
1920	765,000
1922	783,500
1924	807,000
1926	845,000
1928	890,500
1930	929,000
1932	938,000
1934	940,000
1936	955,500
1938	1,000,000
1940	1,019,000
1942	1,062,000
1944	1,092,000
1946	1,131,000
1948	1,177,000
1950	1,222,000
1952	1,291,000
1954	1,335,000
1956	1,399,000
1958	1,480,000
1960	1,553,000
1962	1,666,000
1964	1,778,000
1966	1,820,000
1968	1,905,000
1970	2,026,000
1972	2,218,000
1974	2,265,000
1975	2,275,000

A. Lange & Sohne

DATE	SERIAL #
1870	5,000
1875	10,000
1880	20,000
1885	25,000
1890	30,000
1895	35,000
1900	40,000
1905	50,000
1910	60,000
1915	70,000
1920	75,000
1925	80,000
1930	85,000
1935	90,000
1940	100,000

LONGINES

DATE	SERIAL #
1867	1
1870	20,000
1875	100,000
1882	250,000
1888	500,000
1893	750,000
1899	1,000,000
1901	1,250,000
1904	1,500,000
1905	1,750,000
1907	2,000,000
1909	2,250,000
1911	2,500,000
1912	2,750,000
1913	3,000,000
1915	3,250,000
1917	3,500,000
1919	3,750,000
1922	4,000,000
1925	4,250,000
1926	4,500,000
1928	4,750,000
1929	5,000,000
1934	5,250,000
1937	5,500,000
1938	5,750,000
1940	6,000,000
1945	7,000,000
1950	8,000,000
1953	9,000,000
1956	10,000,000
1959	11,000,000
1962	12,000,000
1966	13,000,000
1967	14,000,000
1969	15,000,000

OMEGA

DATE	SERIAL #
1895	1,000,000
1902	2,000,000
1908	3,000,000
1912	4,000,000
1916	5,000,000
1923	6,000,000
1929	7,000,000
1935	8,000,000
1939	9,000,000
1944	10,000,000
1947	11,000,000
1950	12,000,000
1952	13,000,000
1956	15,000,000
1958	16,000,000
1961	18,000,000
1963	20,000,000
1965	22,000,000
1967	25,000,000
1968	26,000,000
1970	29,000,000

PATEK PHILIPPE & Co.

DATE	SERIAL #
1840	100
1845	1,200
1850	3,000
1855	8,000
1860	15,000
1865	22,000
1870	35,000
1875	45,000
1880	55,000
1885	70,000
1890	85,000
1895	100,000
1900	110,000
1905	125,000
1910	150,000
1915	175,000
1920	190,000
1925	200,000
1950	700,000
1955	725,000
1960	750,000
1965	775,000
1970	795,000
1920	800,000
1925	805,000
1930	820,000
1935	824,000
1940	835,000
1945	850,000
1950	860,000
1955	870,000
1960	880,000
1965	890,000
1970	895,000
1940	900,000
1945	915,000
1950	930,000
1955	940,000
1960	960,000
1965	975,000
1970	995,000
1960	1,100,000
1965	1,130,000
1970	1,250,000
1975	1,350,000
1980	1,450,000
1985	1,600,000
1990	1,850,000

ROLEX (Case S #)

DATE	SERIAL #
1925	25,000
1926	28,500
1927	30,500
1928	33,000
1929	35,500
1930	38,000
1931	40,000
1932	43,000
1933	47,000
1934	55,000
1935	68,000
1936	81,000
1937	99,000
1938	118,000
1939	136,000
1940	165,000
1941	194,000
1942	224,000
1943	253,000
1944	285,000
1945	348,000
1946	413,000
1947	478,000
1948	543,000
1949	608,000
1950	673,500
1951	738,500
1952	804,000
1953	950,000
1954	999,999
1955	*200,000
1956	*400,000
1957	*600,000
1958	*800,000
1959	1,100,000
1960	1,401,000
1961	1,480,000
1962	1,557,000
1963	1,635,000
1964	1,713,000
1965	1,792,000
1966	1,870,000
1967	2,164,000
1968	2,426,000
1969	2,689,000
1970	2,952,000
1971	3,215,000
1972	3,478,000
1973	3,741,000
1974	4,002,000
1975	4,266,000
1976	4,538,000
1977	5,005,000
1978	5,481,000
1979	5,965,000
1980	6,432,000
1981	6,910,000
1982	7,385,000
1983	7,860,000
1984	8,338,000
1985	8,815,000
1986	9,292,000
1987	9,765,000
1987 1/2	9,999,999
1987 3/4	R000,001
1988	R999,999
1989	L000,001
1990	L999,999
1990 1/2	E000,001
1991 1/4	E999,999
1991 1/2	X000,001

VACHERON

DATE	SERIAL #
1830	30,000
1835	40,000
1840	50,000
1845	60,000
1850	75,000
1855	95,000
1860	110,000
1865	125,000
1870	140,000
1875	155,000
1880	170,000
1885	180,000
1890	190,000
1895	223,000
1900	256,000
1905	289,000
1910	322,000
1915	355,000
1920	385,000
1925	400,000
1930	410,000
1935	420,000
1940	440,000
1945	464,000
1950	488,000
1955	512,000
1960	536,000
1965	560,000
1970	585,000

The above list is provided for determining the **approximate** age of your watch. Match serial number with date. Watches were not necessarily sold in the exact order of manufactured date.

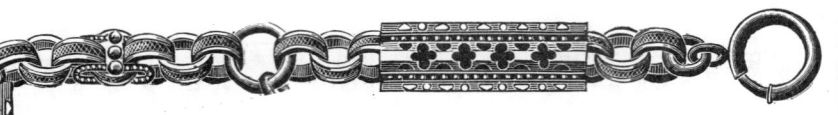

ADVERTISE IN THE GUIDE

ATTENTION DEALERS: This book will receive world-wide **BOOKSTORE** distribution, reaching thousands of people buying & selling watches. It will also be sold directly to THE WATCH COLLECTOR'S MARKET as well. We will be offering limited advertising space in our next edition. Consider advertising in the Guide, as it is an annual publication, your ad will pull all year long or longer. Unlike monthly or quarterly publications, your ad will stay active for years at a *cost savings* to YOU.

PRINTED SIZES
FULL PAGE — 7 1/2 " LONG X 4 3/4" WIDE
HALF PAGE — 3 1/2" LONG X 4 3/4" WIDE
FOURTH PAGE — 1 7/8" LONG X 4 3/4" WIDE

AD RATES ARE SET IN THE LATE SUMMER PRIOR TO EACH EDITION'S RELEASE. CONTACT US FOR AD RATES BETWEEN **(AUGUST & SEPTEMBER)**.

NOTE: Submit your ad on white paper in a version of the actual printed size. We must ask that all ads be neatly & professionally finished, *camera ready.* **FULL PAYMENT** must be sent with all ads. Your ad will be run as received.

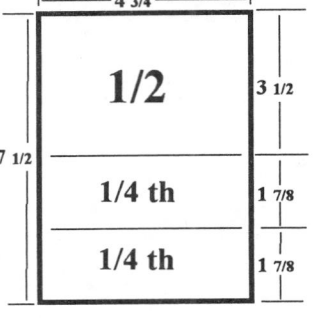

TARGET YOUR MARKET

AD DEAD LINE NEXT EDITION IS - OCTOBER 15

This "GUIDE" is the PROFESSIONAL STANDARD and used by collector's and dealer's throughout the world. Do not miss this opportunity to advertise in the guide.

SEND YOUR AD TO:
COOKSEY SHUGART PUBLICATIONS
P. O. BOX 3147
CLEVELAND, TN. 37320-3147
Office: (423) 479-4813 — Fax: (423) 479-4813

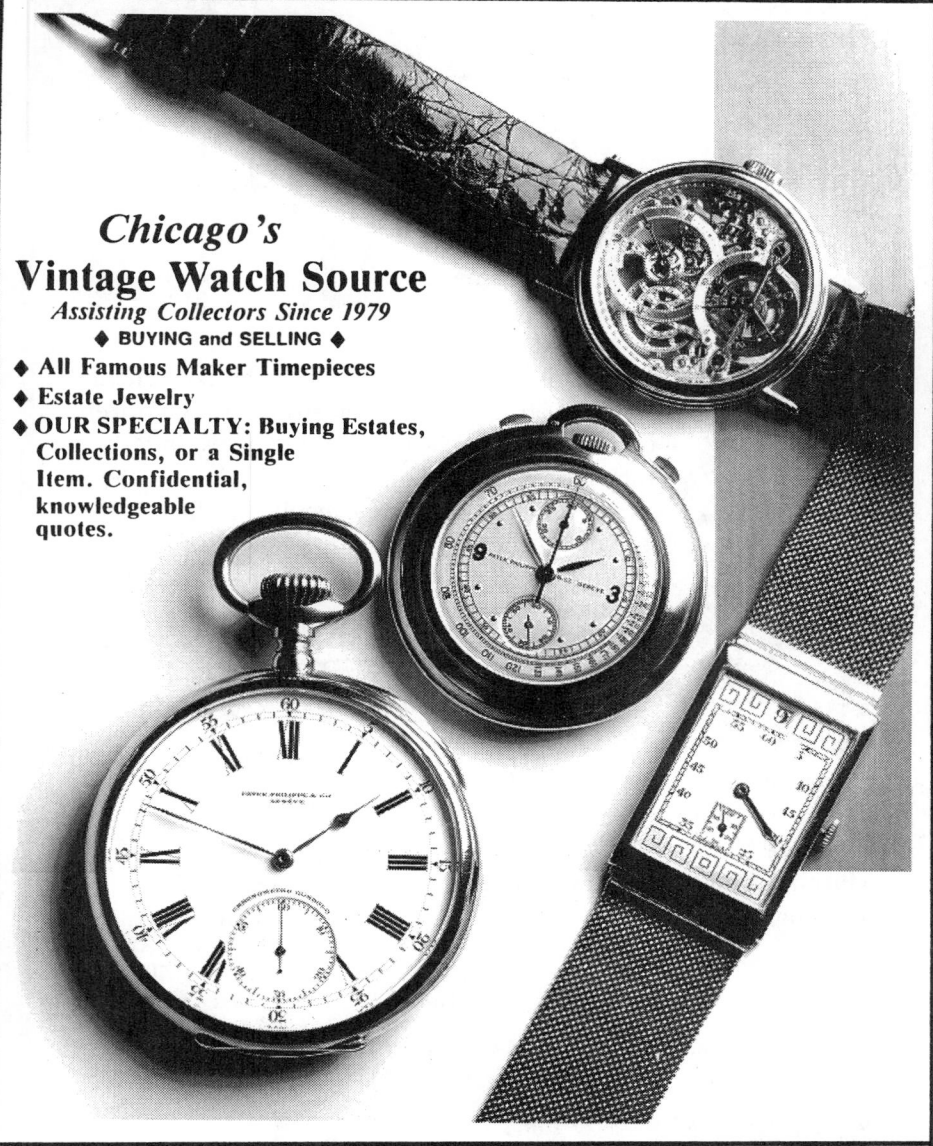

Chicago's
Vintage Watch Source
Assisting Collectors Since 1979
◆ BUYING and SELLING ◆

- ◆ **All Famous Maker Timepieces**
- ◆ **Estate Jewelry**
- ◆ **OUR SPECIALTY: Buying Estates, Collections, or a Single Item. Confidential, knowledgeable quotes.**

Old World Jewelers
OAK BROOK, ILLINOIS
630-990-0100 ● 1-800-322-3871
www.oldworldjewelers.com

It's the ultimate time share.

Join the National Association of Watch and Clock Collectors!

As a Member of the NAWCC, you'll share in these *exclusive* benefits:

- Complimentary admission to the beautifully expanded National Watch and Clock Museum — a world-class facility devoted to wonders horological.

922 Special Pocket Watch. Hamilton Watch Company, Lancaster, PA c. 1931.

  - Annual subscriptions to the NAWCC BULLETIN and THE MART, plus admission to Association "marts" nationwide.
  - Free NAWCC Library and Research Center access—on campus, via mail, or at **www.nawcc.org**
  - Local Chapter activities, Special Interest meetings, Seminars... and the camaraderie of 35,000 fellow Collectors, worldwide.

French Column Clock. Mfg. Unknown. France, c. 1830.

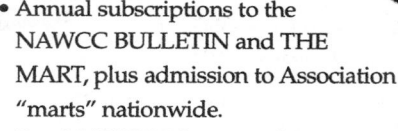
the National **ASSOCIATION OF WATCH & CLOCK Collectors, Inc.**

1-Year Membership: only $60 first year/$50 per year thereafter ($55 outside U.S.). Call 1-717-684-8261

(or mail to:) **NAWCC, Inc., 514 Poplar St., Columbia, PA 17512-2130 USA**

Name

Address

City State/Country Zip

Phone *home* ( ) *work* ( )

Fax ( ) E-mail

Sponsor **COOKSEY SHUGART** Member # **23,843**

Are you a former NAWCC member? ☐ Yes ☐ No If yes, #

Charge my ☐ MasterCard ☐ VISA ☐ Discover Card ☐ AmerX

Card # Exp. (mo/yr)

Signature of Card Holder Amt $

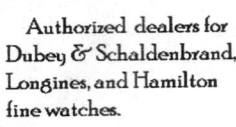

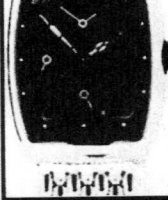

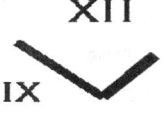

Reserve Your Place Now at the 2002 NAWCC Seminar

"Boston: Cradle of Industrial Watchmaking"

October 17-19, 2002
Ramada Rolling Green Inn & Conference Center
Andover, Massachusetts

Sponsored by: NAWCC Chapter 174 (Pocket Horology)

Join your fellow pocket watch and research enthusiasts in this very special, and long-awaited celebration of American Watchmaking. Speakers will trace the origins of the early American watchmaking industry and the key developments of its first three formative decades. Scholarly presentations and an outstanding on-site exhibit will illustrate important early American watches and machinery. Participants will tour historic Waltham, visit famous gravesites on Mt. Feake, and enjoy a special educational program at the Charles River Museum of Industry.

Speakers including:
David K. Landes, author of "Revolution in Time",
  James Arthur Lecture, topic to be announced
Michael C. Harrold, Henry Fried Award recipient,
  on Pitkins and Goddards
David Penney, past editor of *Antiquarian Horology*,
  on preceding developments in England
George Collord, on automatic watchmaking machinery at Waltham
Ron Price, on the first mass-produced American watches
Craig Risch, on the career, inventions and legacy of
  Charles van der Woerd
Philip Priestley, Gibbs Award recipient,
  Impact on British Watchmaking

Reserve your accommodations now at the special, low NAWCC rate of $105/night-double occupancy, 978-475-5400
(Shuttles available from Logan International)

Advanced seminar registrations $160, with banquet ticket $190.
For more information, contact Clint Geller, 412-521-8092
or Ron Price at: rprice@pricelessads.com

American Watchmakers-Clockmakers Institute

The American Watchmakers-Clockmakers Institute is the premier international organization dedicated to preserving and promoting the highest standards of workmanship in the horological crafts. It is the role of AWI to set the standard of excellence to be applied to the quality of instruction for both the restoration and repair practices that are taught worldwide.

Membership Benefits

- *Horological Times* magazine
- Traveling Bench Courses
- Professional Certification Program
- Continuing Education Courses
- Material Search/Movement Bank
- Henry B. Fried Lending Library
- Education, Library and Museum Charitable Trust

- Technical Support
- Referral Service
- Industry Advisory Board
- Horological Books & Videos
- AWI Affiliate & Theme Chapters
- Orville R. Hagans Museum

Name _____

Company _____

Address _____

City _____ State _____ Zip Code _____

Phone (____) _____ Fax (____) _____

E-mail _____ Web site _____

Membership Plan

❏ Regular member $ 70.00   ❏ Life membership $1000.00

❏ Student* $ 35.00

❏ Please send information on Industry Advisory Board membership

Horology School* _____ Instructor Signature* _____

Previous AWI member? ❏ Yes ❏ No   If yes, AWI membership # _____

Method of Payment

❏ Check   ❏ American Express   ❏ Discover   ❏ Mastercard   ❏ Visa

Credit Card No. _____

Expiration Date _____ Signature _____

American Watchmakers-Clockmakers Institute
701 Enterprise Drive   Harrison, OH 45030-1696
Call Toll Free 1-866-367-2924 ext. 302   Phone (513) 367-9800   Fax (513) 367-1414
E-mail: memserv@awi-net.org   Website: www.awi-net.org

POCKET WATCH COLLECTIONS WANTED

American and European Pocket Watches

If you have a single piece or an entire collection—I want to hear from you. I also keep want lists—call and let me know your needs.

Complicated Watches, Repeaters, Enamels

Also interested in collections of movements, cases, dials, parts

Special interest in early complicated unusual watches by American Waltham Watch Co. All 19 & 21 jewel 72 models. Also Waltham Watch Co. automated machinery, tools, historic documents, catalogues, advertising, etc. — for research or purchase.

GEORGE L. COLLORD III
watches, clocks, mechanical antiques
135 Marginal Way, # 262 • Portland, ME 04101

207-773-6803   FAX (207) 773-6750

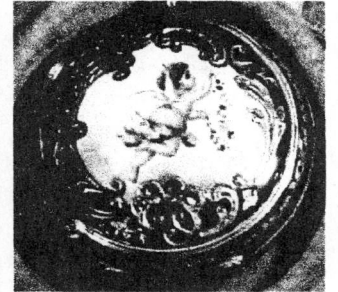
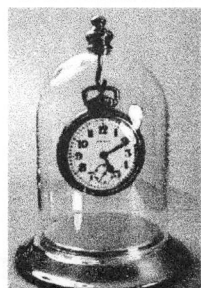

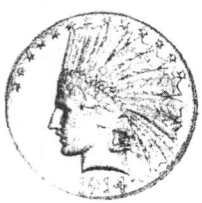

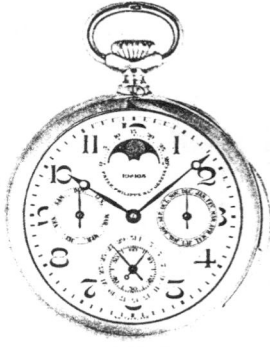

sell-a-watch.com

The *quick and simple* way to sell a watch.

Ray Vann

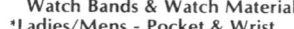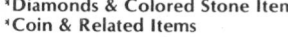
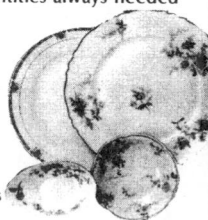

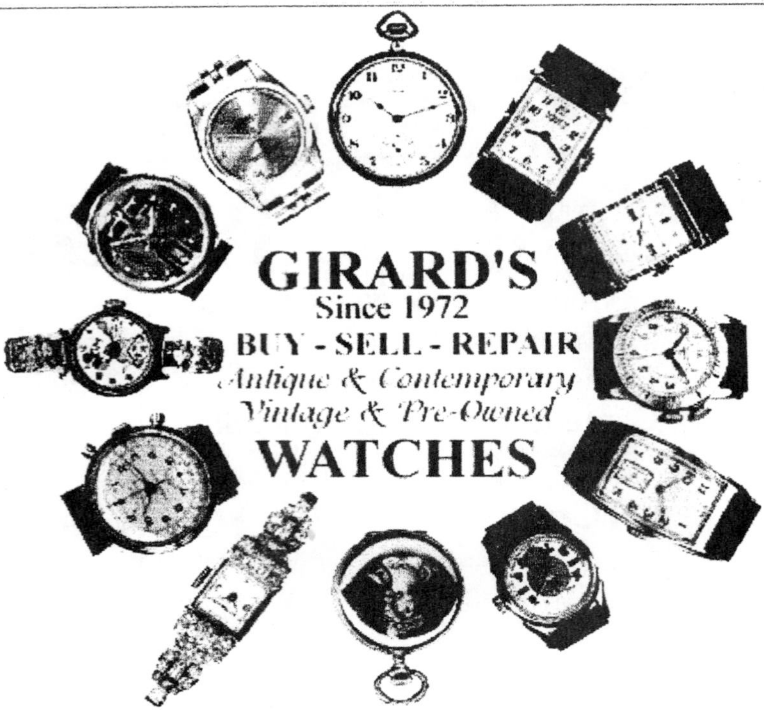

THERE'S A TERRIFIC DEMAND FOR VINTAGE WATCHES
IT'S TIME TO LET GO!
WE'RE READY TO BUY YOURS FOR THE HIGHEST PRICE
ROLEX
Jaeger
Cartier
MOVADO
OMEGA
LONGINES
Vacheron
WC
Breguet
BREITLING
PATEK PHILIPPE
Tiffany
Audemars
and many more...
FOSSNER
TIMEPIECES INC
J&P
TIMEPIECES INC
ELL US YOUR SPECIFIC NEEDS & WE CAN QUOTE PRICES & AVAILABILITY. PLEASE DO NOT ASK FOR STOCK LIST, IT CHANGES DAILY.
• NEW WATCHES AVAILABLE, AT PRICES YOU CAN PROFIT FROM! •
1057 2nd AVE. NEW YORK CITY N.Y. 10022
BRANCH OFFICES GENEVA • VIENNA • MONTE CARLO • LONDON
CALL 800-828 8004 FAX 212-935 0339
OVERSEAS ENQUIRIES PLEASE CALL 212-980 1099 or 212-249 2600
WE BUY WE SELL WE SERVICE
NOW AVAILABLE, MERCEDES HANDS FOR BUBBLE BACKS

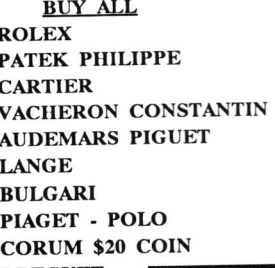